II. Genus "Mystery"
- A. Species
  1. Acclimated
     a. Social (cult, blackmail, conspiracy, etc.)
     b. Private (revenge, triangle, etc.)
  2. Neurotic
     a. Stabilized ("suspense," Gothic, Rebecca, etc.)
     b. Aggravated (HIBK, EIRF)
  3. Supernatural
     a. Ghosts (sin punished)
     b. Pagan (elemental forces)
     c. Witchcraft, orgies (always nameless)

- B. Varieties
  1. Chase (paper, necklace, girl)
  2. Napoleon of crime (Shakespeare ms;
     the Drupe Diamond; white powder bitter to taste)
  3. Mysterious East (idol's left eye; curse
     of Sing Sing Long)
  4. Domestic (poison pen; poison swig)
  5. Commercial (stolen formula, child, white slave)
  6. International (all colors; new math: 007,
     M.I.5, etc.)

A CATALOGUE OF CRIME

A CATALOGUE OF CRIME

Jacques Barzun & Wendell Hertig Taylor

1817

HARPER & ROW, PUBLISHERS

NEW YORK, EVANSTON, SAN FRANCISCO, LONDON

FIRST EDITION

STANDARD BOOK NUMBER: 06-010263-2

LIBRARY OF CONGRESS CATALOG CARD NUMBER: 75-123914

TO

POE'S PROGENY

WHO PURLOINED THE LETTER

AND

DISSEMINATED THE SPIRIT

If we err, therefore, in our liking for detective stories, we err with Plato.

—John Carter (1934)

CONTENTS

A WORD TO THE READER

In a period when crime is a leading occupation, amateur and professional, and its hourly manifestations are the dread of the humble citizen everywhere, it is a public service to refrain from uttering and publishing on subjects likely to incite to violence. Such subjects are: food, sex, government, education, business, children, women, and many others—but not crime. It is no paradox but a fact long ago understood by the Greeks that literature about crime does not so incite.

The modern forms of the same art are especially calming, because they promote the contemplation of things that are clearly impossible: crime fiction calls reason and not hatred into play; historical crime portrays strange events long past and done with. In reading the books listed in this *Catalogue,* therefore, the reader enjoys a cease-fire of the emotions.

At the same time he can discover how some of the great storytellers and their intelligent readers of the past 125 years have imagined increasingly civilized modes of law and science, "deduction" and fair play in human affairs.

The present-day reader, if he will only postpone his plans for hijacking a plane or blasting something for the general good, can with the aid of this book—albeit imperfect—turn his mind to the select literature of crime and browse at pleasure in its peaceful and nourishing pastures.

ACKNOWLEDGMENTS

The authors are full of thanks for the kind help they have received over many years from friends, librarians, and booksellers in the search for the fugitive book. Gratitude for all this informed assistance and thoughtfulness has been expressed to the helpers viva voce and by the written word. Here it is recorded as a debt incurred in the interests of the reading public as well as our own pleasure. We list, with a deep sense of obligation:

Helen King Bainbridge, of William Morrow & Co.; Alix Bartley, of Harold Mortlake & Co.; Isabel Barzun, of William Morrow & Co.; Marshall Best, of the Viking Press; Hildegard L. Borden, of the Boston Athenaeum; R. A. Brimmell, of Hastings (Sussex); Arthur Burton-Garbett, of Morden (Surrey); Sheila Bush, of Gollancz, Ltd.; Mary Louise Clifford; Frederic Dannay; Herbert Feinstein, of San Francisco State College; Michael Gilbert; Carolyn Heilbrun, of Columbia University; Allen J. Hubin; Pamela Hansford Johnson; Joan Kahn, of Harper & Row; Paul Landfried, of Orlando, Fla.; William Lichtenwanger, of the Library of Congress; Lawrence F. London, of the University of North Carolina Library; Arthur and Dolores Lovell, of Chicago, later Dallas; the late Jack McDonald, of San Francisco; Douglas Matthews, of the London Library; Bruce Montgomery; Francis M. Nevins, Jr.; Bertrand L. Smith, of Cincinnati; Francis Steegmuller; George Stevens, of J. B. Lippincott Co.; Jack Tannen, of New York; Gerrish Thurber, of the Lawrenceville School library; Oswald Train, of Philadelphia; Lionel Trilling; Paul Winterton.

For the typescript we are indebted to the skill of Violet Serwin and Virginia Brown. The intricate copy editing at the publishers' was in the capable charge of Marjorie Horvitz. The Index was made by Virginia Xanthos Faggi, with the assistance of Susan Woodcock and Nancy Milner.

HOW TO USE THIS BOOK

Each *Book* (story, play, article) is designated by a number that precedes its title. All references in the index and all cross-references in the text are to this number. Page numbers are not used for any sort of reference.

Authors are arranged in alphabetical order within each Part. The usual conventions of American alphabetizing are followed, all the Mc, Mac, and M' names being alphabetized regardless of these forms and by means of the letter following. This group as a whole precedes names beginning Ma. Joint authors and their works follow the entries on works by one author, the first named on the book by joint authors. To find the second or third authors of a joint work, consult the index.

Under the main title of any work, the *alternative title,* subtitle, series inclusion, illustrations, introduction or preface, and any other pertinent information are supplied.

As is made clear in the Introductory remarks, it seemed desirable to deal with certain books which lie outside *the designated genres,* but to which tradition (or trade) has assigned a place within. These peripheral works are listed and the entry gives them their more correct designation. A very few *Association Items* are so marked ahead of the author's name, and the reason for their insertion follows.

Publishers' names are abbreviated as convenience or familiarity dictates. See the list of abbreviations below. One or more publishers are shown when some interest attaches to the publishing history of a work.

Dates are simple or compound. The compound form *1969/1947* means that the publisher named ahead of the date first brought out the work at the earlier date and has reissued it. The form *1969; orig. 1947* means that a different publisher brought it out originally. When the dates are separated by only one year, e.g., *1970/1969,* the earlier date is almost always the date of copyright, the other the date of publication.

It should be noted that an English or American *place of publication* (as shown by the publisher's name) does not exclude the likelihood of publication in the other country. Often an English author's work appears first in this country and a few weeks or months later in his own, and vice versa. Hence an "English story" is by no means unobtainable here, or an American one abroad.

Similarly, the indication of a hard-cover publisher does not mean that one or more *paperback editions* do not exist, a new one perhaps freshly issued today, though the book first came out in 1954. But paperbacks are not to be had on demand—not even Penguins. Their lives on the rack are uncertain, and a reader who wants a book known through our listing of its first edition must keep his eyes open whenever he scans a paperback display. Alternative titles can be watched for by reading the copyright page (reverse of title page) in the paperback.

The sections headed by [*Name*] *See also:* are likewise designated by a number. The list of books following that number may include one, two, or many more titles, given in alphabetical order. When a title is looked up in the index, it may refer to such a list, which the reader must scan for the title sought.

Biographical summaries sometimes precede the series of entries by one author. These career résumés are not numbered. They are found by turning to the Part and following the alphabet, or turning to the index and finding the number coupled with B, as in: 330/B. The great dead receive no biographical treatment, and all biographies occur before the first discussion of the particular author's work. For example, a writer of novels and short stories is biographically dealt with in Part I (novels); a writer of short stories only in Part II, and so on.

Note that the *married names* of women authors who use pseudonyms or maiden names are not indexed, since the *Catalogue* is concerned with books as they come before the public. But the real names of pseudonymous authors are indexed like the rest.

Settings used in novels and short stories can be looked up in the index under the following key words: Advertising Agencies; Airplanes; Army; Art; Banks; Boating; Bohemia; Book publishers; Bookshops; Broadcasting and Filming; Camps; Caves; Churches; Circuses; Colleges and Universities; Factories; (Large) Family; Farms; Fashion Designers; Gardens; Golf Courses; Hospitals; Hotels and Restaurants; Islands; (Research) Laboratories; Law Offices; Libraries; Motoring; Mountains; Musical Events; Newspaper Offices; Parliament; Police Stations; Prisons; Railways; Schools; Seaside and Other Resorts; Ships; Sporting Events; Theaters; Villages; and Witchcraft.

In addition, a few categories of works are given index entries: Children('s books); Cases (criminal); Crimes (as basis of fiction); Genre (comments and studies); Plays (including films and broadcasts).

The *Index* unites in one continuous alphabetical list: authors, titles, and settings. Detectives are not listed or indexed and neither are topics discussed in the entries. Several of the works entered in Part III contain lists of detectives which it seemed needless to duplicate, especially as the names of recurrent detectives are well known and those of non-recurrent ones are usually of little importance. These works of reference are listed below under Miscellaneous Information.

Throughout the book, extensive *cross-reference* has been provided, to send the reader to other works by or about the same author, or to works by other authors relevant to the subject being discussed.

ABBREVIATIONS

1. *Publishers and Periodicals*

Unless otherwise noted, the publishers and publications listed below have their main office in New York City. *L* indicates London, *P* Paris; *repr.* means that the output of the firm consists chiefly of hardcover reprints; *ppb.* means *paperback,* reprints or originals.

AB	Arthur Barker (L)
Ace	Ace Books (ppb.)
Ack	Bernard Ackerman
AD	André Deutsch (L)
AL	Allen Lane
ALI	American Law Institute (Chicago)
All	Alliance Press
Alston	Alston Rivers
AM	*The American Mercury*
Amal	Amalgamated Press (L)
Amer	American Publishing Co. (Hartford, Conn.)
Amer Mag	*The American Magazine*
Amer Sch	*The American Scholar*
App	Appleton & Co., now Appleton-Century-Crofts
Arc	Arco Publishing Co.
Argus	Argus Books (Chicago)
Arkham	Arkham House (Sauk City, Wis.)
Arn	Edward Arnold (L)
Arr	J. W. Arrowsmith (L)
Ath	Atheneum Publishers
Atlantic	*The Atlantic [Monthly]*
Atomic	Atomic Books
Avon	Avon Books, ppb. div. of the Hearst Corporation
A&R	Angus & Robertson (Sydney, Australia)
A&U	Allen & Unwin (L)
A&W	*Authors & Writers' Who's Who* (L)

BA	Ben Abramson (Chicago)
Bal	Ballantine Books (ppb.)
Bant	Bantam Books (ppb.)
Barre	Barre Publishing Co. (Barre, Mass.)
BB	British Book Centre (N.Y.)
BCP	Black Cat Press (Chicago)
Bell	G. Bell & Sons (L)
Benn	Ernest Benn (L)
Berk	Berkley Books, ppb. div. of G. P. Putnam's Sons
BGUP	Bowling Green University Press (Bowling Green, Ohio)
BH	The Bodley Head, an imprint of John Lane's (L)
Blackie	Blackie and Son (Glasgow)
Blackwood	William Blackwood & Sons (L)
Blak	The Blakiston Co. (Phila.)
Bles	Geoffrey Bles (L)
Blond	Anthony Blond (L)
BM	The Bobbs-Merrill Co. (Indianapolis)
BMLA	Bulletin of the Medical Library Association (U.S.)
Bohn	H. G. Bohn (L)
Boni	A. & C. Boni, later Boni and Liveright; now the Liveright Publishing Corp.
Bonner	Robert Bonner's Sons (L)
Boris	Boriswood & Co. (L)
Bouregy	Bouregy & Curl; later Thomas Bouregy & Co.
Bowk	R. R. Bowker Co.
BP	Beaune Press (San Francisco)
BR	Blue Ribbon Books, repr. div. of Doubleday
Bram	Bramhall House
Braz	George Braziller
Brent	Brentano's
Browne	F. G. Browne (Chicago)
BSI	Baker Street Irregulars, repr. pub. name for Edgar W. Smith, q.v. (Morristown, N.J.)
BSJ	*Baker Street Journal* (var. places)
BSM	Best Seller Mystery
Burt	A. L. Burt (repr.)
Butt	T. Butterworth, now joined to Eyre and Spottiswoode
BW	Brown-Watson (L)
BWP	Brewer, Warren & Putnam
B&L	Boni & Liveright
B&T	Biblo & Tannen (repr.)
Camb	Cambridge University Press (Eng.)
Camb Rev	*Cambridge Review* (Cambridge, Eng.)
Cand	Candlelight Press (N.Y. and Copenhagen)
Cape	Jonathan Cape (L)
Card	Cardinal Books (ppb.)
Carey	Carey, Lea, & Blanchard (Phila.)
Cass	Cassell & Co. (L)
Castle	Castle Press (L)
CCC	Crime Club, Collins (L)
CCD	Crime Club, Doubleday
Cent	Century, now Appleton-Century-Crofts
Chel	Chelsea House
Chil	Chilmark Press

Chur	J. & A. Churchill (L)
Clode	Edward J. Clode
CM	Coward-McCann
Col	P. F. Collier, now Crowell-Collier-Macmillan
Coll	William Collins & Sons Co. (L)
Collingwood	Collingwood Bros. (L)
Columb	Columbine Publishing Co. (L)
Const	Constable & Co. (L)
Corgi	Corgi Books, ppb. div. of Transworld Publishers (L)
Cornell	Cornell University Press (Ithaca, N.Y.)
Cosmo	Cosmopolitan Book Corporation
Covici	Covici, Friede
Cress	Cresset Press (L)
Crit	Criterion Books, now part of Abelard-Schuman, see *Schu*
Crown	Crown Publishers
CUP	Columbia University Press
C&B	Colburn & Bentley
C&E	Carrick & Evans
C&H	Chapman & Hall (L)
C&S	Jonathan Cape & Harrison Smith
C&W	Chatto & Windus (L)
DA	Devin-Adair
Da Capo	Da Capo Press
Dakers	Andrew Dakers (L)
Daniel	C. W. Daniel (L)
DBC	Detective Book Club (Garden City, N.Y.)
Dday	Doubleday & Co., earlier: Doubleday, Page, and Doubleday, Doran
Dell	Dell Publishing Co. (ppb.)
Dent	J. M. Dent & Sons (L)
Dial	Dial Press, now a div. of Dell Publishing Co.
Didier	John Didier, éditeur (P and N.Y.)
DM	Dodd, Mead & Co.
DNB	*Dictionary of National Biography* (Eng.)
Dob	Dennis Dobson (L)
Dolph	Dolphin Books, a ppb. div. of Doubleday
Doran	George H. Doran Co.
DPS	Dramatists Play Service
Drag	Dragon Books (ppb.)
Drake	F. J. Drake & Co. (Chicago)
DS	Duell, Sloan, & Pearce
DSC	Detective Story Club (L)
Duff	Duffield & Green
Dutt	E. P. Dutton & Co.
Eldon	Eldon Press (L)
Elek	Elek Books, Bestseller Library: ppb. div. of Paul Elek Publishers (L)
EQ	Ellery Queen (as pub. or title)
EQMM	*Ellery Queen Mystery Magazine*
ESL	E & S Livingstone (Edinburgh)
Essex	Essex Press (Newark, N.J.)
Everyman	Everyman Library, a div. of Dent/Dutton
E&S	Eyre & Spottiswoode (L)

Faber	Faber & Faber (L)
Farr	Farrar & Rinehart; Farrar, Straus & Rinehart; Farrar, Straus & Cudahy; Farrar, Straus, & Giroux
Fawc	Fawcett World Library (ppb.)
Fell	Frederick Fell
Ferret	Ferret Library (repr.)
FH	Fanlight House (Ann Arbor, Mich.)
Fields	Fields, Osgood; earlier Ticknor, Reed & Fields; see Osgood (Boston)
FM	Frederick Muller (L)
Foley	Foley House
Folio	The Folio Society (L)
Font	Fontana Books, ppb. div. of William Collins & Sons Co. (L)
French	Samuel French (play pub.)
FS	Four Square (L)
FTS	Famous Trials [Series]
Furman	Lee Furman Co.
FW	Franklin Watts
F&W	Funk & Wagnalls Co.
Gallimard	Librairie Gallimard (P)
Giff	John Gifford (L)
GL	Gold Label Books (ppb.)
GM	Gold Medal Books, ppb. div. of Fawcett Publications
Goll	Victor Gollancz (L)
GR	Grant Richards (L)
Greenb	Greenberg Publisher
Griff	Charles Griffin and Co. (L)
Gross	Grossman Publishers
Grove	Grove Press
G&D	Grosset & Dunlap (repr.)
HaHa	Harrison Smith & Robert Haas
Hald	Haldeman-Julius (Girard, Kan.)
Hale	Robert Hale & Co. (L)
Hamlyn	The Hamlyn Publishing Group (Feltham, Eng.)
Hamm	Hammond, Hammond & Co. (L)
Harp	Harper & Brothers, now Harper & Row
Harrap	George G. Harrap & Co. (L)
Hart	Rupert Hart-Davis (L)
Hartn	Hartney Press
Harv	Harvill Press (L)
Hawth	Hawthorn Books, part of Prentice-Hall (Englewood Cliffs, N.J.)
HB	Harcourt, Brace & Co., later Harcourt, Brace & World; now Harcourt-Brace-Jovanovich
Hein	Heinemann Publishers (L)
Henry	Henry & Co.
Heritage	Heritage Press (repr.)
Heyw	John Heywood (L)
HH	Hamish Hamilton (L)
HIL	Hearst's International Library (repr.)
Hillm	Hillman-Curl
HJ	Herbert Jenkins (L)
HM	Houghton Mifflin Co. (Boston)
Hodge	William Hodge & Co. (Edinburgh)

Hogg	James Hogg (L)
Holt	Henry Holt & Co., now Holt, Rinehart & Winston
Horiz	Horizon Press
HR	Holt and Rinehart, now joined to Winston
HS	Harrison Smith
Hulton	Hulton Press (L)
HUP	Harvard University Press (Cambridge, Mass.)
Hurst	Hurst & Blackett, now part of Hutchinson group (L)
Hutch	Hutchinson & Co. Publishers (L)
H&C	Hollis & Carter (L)
H&S	Hodder & Stoughton (L)
H&W	Hill & Wang
IANA	International Association of Newspapers and Authors
Innes	A. D. Innes (L)
Intnl	International Printing Co. (Phila.)
Isbister	Isbister & Co. (L)
IUP	Indiana University Press (Bloomington, Ind.)
IW	Ives Washburn
Jac	Jacobsen Publishing Co. (Chicago)
Jarr	Jarrolds Publishers (L)
JD	The John Day Co., now part of Abelard-Schuman, etc.
JH	Jefferson House (repr.)
JM	John Murray Publishers (L)
Jon	Jonathan Press
Keen	W. B. Keen, Cooke, and Co. (Chicago)
Kins	H. C. Kinsey, part of G. P. Putnam's Sons
Knopf	Alfred A. Knopf
KSUP	Kent State University Press (Kent, O.)
Lane	John Lane, later also The Bodley Head, q.v. (L)
Lant	Lantern Press
Laur	T. Werner Laurie (L)
LB	Little, Brown & Co. (Boston)
LC	Library of Congress (Washington, D.C.)
LCPC	Lawyers Cooperative Publishing Co. (Rochester, N.Y.)
Lee	Lee-Collins (Toronto, Can.)
Lehm	John Lehmann (L)
LG	Longmans Green & Co. (L)
LH	London House (British Book Centre, N.Y.)
Lipp	J. B. Lippincott Co. (Phila.)
List	*The Listener* (L)
LitG	Literary Guild
Liv	Liveright Publishing Corp.
LM	Low, Marston & Co., earlier Sampson Low, q.v. (L)
LMM	*London Mystery Magazine*
Long	John Long (L)
Lounz	Gregory Lounz
Lovell	Arthur Lovell (Chicago)
Luce	Robert B. Luce (Washington, D.C.)
Lupt	Lupton
MA	Modern Age Books (ppb.)
Mac	Macaulay Co.

Macd	Macdonald & Co. (L)
Macf	Macfadden Publications
Macl	Maclehose Co. (Glasgow)
Macm	The Macmillan Co., now Crowell-Collier-Macmillan
MacV	Lincoln MacVeagh, later The Dial Press, now part of Dell Publishing Co.
Manu	Manuscript House
Marsh	Marshall Jones (Boston)
Matr	Matrix House
Maxw	H. Maxwell (Phila.)
MBG	Mystery Book Guild
McB	Robert M. McBride & Co.
McCl	McClure Co., earlier McClure and Phillips
McG	McGraw-Hill Book Co.
McK	David McKay Co.
MD	*Mystery Digest* (L)
Mel	Andrew Melrose (L)
Merc	*Mercury Mystery*
Merm	Mermaid Press (Chicago)
Messn	Julian Messner
Meth	Methuen & Co. (L)
MH	Maxwell House (ppb.)
Mill	M. S. Mill, pub. by William Morrow, q.v.
Miller	L. Miller (L)
Milne	Milne & Co. (L)
Mint	Minton, Balch & Co., now part of G. P. Putnam's Sons
MIT	Massachusetts Institute of Technology (Cambridge, Mass.)
MJ	Michael Joseph (L)
ML	Mystery League
MLN	*Modern Language Notes*
MM	Macy-Masius, now the Vanguard Press
ModL	Modern Library, a div. of Random House (repr.)
Morr	William Morrow & Co.
MRS	Murder Revisited Series (Macmillan, U.S.)
MS	McCrae Smith Co. (Phila.)
MWA	Mystery Writers of America
MY	Moffat, Yard & Co. (Boston)
M&B	Mills & Boon (L)
M&K	MacGibbon & Kee (L)
M&L	Mussey & Loring, later Barrows, Mussey
M&M	Mycroft and Moran (Sauk City, Wis.)
NAB	New Amsterdam Book Co.
NAL	New American Library of World Literature (ppb.)
Nash	J. Eveleigh Nash Co., later Nash and Grayson
Nat. Ath.	*The Nation and Athenaeum* (Eng.)
Nat. Rev.	*The National Review* (Eng.)
NBL	The National Book League (Cambridge, Eng.)
NBT	Notable British Trials [Series] (William Hodge, Edinburgh)
Nels	Thomas Nelson & Sons (L)
Newnes	George Newnes (L)
Nich	Ivor Nicholson & Watson (L)
Nisbet	James Nisbet & Co. (Welwyn, Herts)
Nort	W. W. Norton & Co.
NST	Notable Scottish Trials (William Hodge, Edinburgh)

N&G	Nash & Grayson, earlier J. Eveleigh Nash Co., q.v.
N&W	Nicholson & Watson (L)
OAF	Oliphant, Anderson, and Ferrier (Edinburgh)
Odhams	Odhams Press (L)
Osgood	James R. Osgood & Co., later Fields, Osgood (Boston)
OUP	Oxford University Press (L)
Owen	Peter Owen (L)
PA	Philip Allan (L)
Page	L. C. Page (Boston)
Pan	Pan Books (ppb., L)
Panth	Panther Books (ppb., L)
Pantheon	Pantheon Books
Payot	Payot éditeur (P)
PB	Pocket Books (ppb.)
PBC	Popular Book Club (L)
PD	Peter Davies (L)
Pears	C. Arthur Pearson (L)
Pemb	Pemberton (L)
Peng	Penguin Books (ppb., Eng.)
Penn	Wm. Penn Publishing Corp. (Phila.)
Perm	Permabooks (ppb.)
PH	Pamphlet House (Summit, N.J.)
Phil	Phillips, Sampson & Co. (Boston)
Phoen	Phoenix Press
Pilot	Pilot Press (L)
Pitm	Sir Isaac Pitman & Sons (L)
PL	Popular Library (ppb.)
Plon	Librairie Plon (P)
PMLA	*Publications of the Modern Language Association*
PMP	Pitman Medical Publishers (L)
Poly	Polybooks (ppb., L)
Pott	Clarkson N. Potter
Praeg	Frederick A. Praeger
Putn	G. P. Putnam's Sons
Pyr	Pyramid Books (ppb.)
P&C	Payson & Clarke
QBC	Quality Book Club (L)
Reg	Henry Regnery Co. (Chicago)
Rev	Revere Publishing Co.
Reyn	Reynal & Hitchcock, later Reynal & Co.; now a div. of William Morrow & Co.
RH	Random House
Rich	Rich & Cowan (L)
Rine	Rinehart & Co., later Holt, Rinehart & Winston
RM	Rand McNally & Co. (Chicago)
Rodale	Rodale Books (Berkhamsted, Eng.)
Rom Rev	*Romanic Review*
ROP	Rochester University Press (Rochester, N.Y.)
ROR	Review of Reviews
Ross	Ross Publishing Co. (Toronto)
Rout	Routledge, now Routledge & Kegan Paul (L)

Roy	Roy Publishers (orig. in Warsaw)
RP	Richards Press now part om Secker and Warburg (L)
RSMQ	*Rex Stout Mystery Quarterly*
RUP	Rutgers University Press (New Brunswick, N.J.)
SaMag	*The Saint Magazine* (L)
Samp	Sampson Low, later Low, Sampson, Marston & Co. (L)
Sat Rev	*The Saturday Review,* earlier *The Saturday Review of Literature* (N.Y.)
Schu	Schuman, now Abelard-Schuman, joined to John Day and Criterion Books
Scrib	Charles Scribner's Sons
SD	Sun Dial Press, div. of Doubleday
SE	Smith, Elder
Sears	J. H. Sears
Secker	Martin Secker, later Secker & Warburg (L)
Seltzer	Thomas Seltzer (L)
Sheed	Sheed & Ward (L)
Sher	Sheridan House
Signet	Signet Books, div. of New American Library, q.v. (ppb.)
Simpk	Simpkin, Marshall (L)
Skef	Skeffington & Son (L)
Sloane	William Sloane Associates, distrib. by Wm. Morrow
SM	St. Martin's Press (U.S. affiliate of Eng. Macmillan)
Smith	Smith & Durrell
Solar	Solar, éditeur (P)
SP	Stanley Paul & Co. (L)
Spect	*Spectator* (L)
Spenc	Spencer Blackett (L)
Stamf	Stamford House (Stamford, Conn.)
Stap	Staples Press (L)
Stev	Stevens and Sons (L)
Stokes	Frederick A. Stokes Co., later a div. of J. B. Lippincott (Phila.)
Sumac	Sumac Press (Emerson G. Wulling, La Crosse, Wis.)
SUP	Syracuse University Press (Syracuse, N.Y.)
SW	Samuel Walker (Boston)
Swain	Roland Swain Co. (Phila.)
Swan	Gerald G. Swan (L)
Sweet	Sweet & Maxwell (L)
S&B	Selwyn & Blount (L)
S&D	Stein & Day
S&M	Stone & Mack
S&S	Simon and Schuster
S&W	Martin Secker & Warburg, earlier Martin Secker (L)
TAD	*The Armchair Detective* (White Bear Lake, Minn.)
Tauch	Bernhard Tauchnitz (Leipzig)
TBC	Thriller Book Club, a div. of W. & G. Foyle (L)
Tinsley	Tinsley Bros. (L)
TLB	*Time-Life* Books
TLS	*Times Literary Supplement* (L)
Todd	Todd Publishing Group (L)
Tower	Tower Books, a div. of World Publishing Co. (Cleveland, O.)
Train	Oswald Train (repr., Phila.)
Trel	Trelawney (L)

Tri	Triangle Books, ppb. div. of Doubleday
Trident	Trident Press (ppb.)
TS	Thomas Seltzer (L)
Tudor	Tudor Books
Turns	Turnstile Press
Tuttle	Charles E. Tuttle Co. (Tokyo & Rutland, Vt.)
TVB	T. V. Boardman & Co. (L)
UB	University Books (New Hyde Park, N.Y.)
UCP	University of California Press (Berkeley, Calif.)
ULP	University of London Press (L)
UNCL	University of North Carolina Library (Chapel Hill, N.C.)
Unic	Unicorn Press, part of G. Bles (L)
Unwin	T. Fisher Unwin (L)
Vall	Vallancey Press (L)
Van	Vanguard Press
Vane	Nicholas Vane Publishers (L)
Vint	Vintage Books (ppb. div. of Alfred A. Knopf)
VP	Viking Press
VR	Van Rees Press
Walk	Walker & Co.
Warne	Frederick Warne & Co. (L)
Watt	W. J. Watt & Co.
West	John Westhouse Publishers (L)
WH	Whittlesey House, a div. of McGraw-Hill Book Co.
WHA	W. H. Allen & Co. (L)
Winch	Winchester
Wing	Allan Wingate, part of Hamlyn group (L)
Wins	John C. Winston Co. (Phila.), later Holt, Rinehart & Winston
WL	Ward, Lock & Co. (L)
WldCl	World's Classics, Oxford University Press (L)
World	World Publishing Co., (Cleveland), now joined to New American Library of World Literature, q.v.
WW	World's Work, a div. of Heinemann Publishers (L)
Wyn	A. A. Wyn
W&B	Wright & Brown (L)
W&T	Weybright and Talley
W&W	Whiting & Wheaton (L)
YUP	Yale University Press (New Haven, Conn.)
Ziff	The Ziff-Davis Publishing Co.

2. General

AA	Automobile Association (Eng.)
ARP	air-raid patrol
A&W	*Authors & Writers' Who's Who* (L)
BMu	British Museum (collection or catalogue)
BSI	Baker Street Irregulars, a society, also an imprint, q.v.

CID	Criminal Investigation Department (Scotland Yard)
C. of E.	Church of England
DNB	*Dictionary of National Biography* (Eng.)
DOA	Dead on arrival (at hospital)
DPP	Director of Public Prosecutions
ed	ed(itor)(ited)(ition)
EIRF	"Everything is rather frightening." (see Introd.)
HIBK	"Had I But Known!" (see Introd.)
H. of C.	House of Commons
JB	One of the authors of this book
JP	Justice of the Peace
K.C.	King's Counsel (title of honor, not = prosecutor)
L.A.	Los Angeles, Calif.
L.C.	Library of Congress (collection or catalogue)
MO	Modus operandi (method of the crime)
MWA	Mystery Writers of America (a society, also an imprint)
NBT	Notable British Trials (series now comprising English and Scottish series)
NET	Notable English Trials (see NBT)
NST	Notable English Trials (see NBT)
NYPL	New York Public Library
P.C.	Police constable
ppb.	paperback book, edition
Pr.	Press
Priv. ptd.	Privately printed
pub.	publish(er)(ed)(ing), publication
Q.C.	Queen's Counsel = K.C. in a queen's reign
q (qq). v.	which (or whom) see: a cross-reference
repr.	reprint(ed)
sbt.	subtitle
SF	Science fiction
SH	Sherlock Holmes
SL	The New York Society Library
SPR	Society for Psychical Research (Eng. and also U.S.)
ss	short story (ies)
tr. cr.	true crime, in actuality or in factual narrative
UCLA	University of California at Los Angeles
USC	University of Southern California
WHT	One of the authors of this book

Gems from the Literature

Something more goes to the composition of a fine murder than two block-heads to kill and be killed. . . . Design, . . . grouping, light and shade, poetry, sentiment, are now deemed indispensable to attempts of this nature.
    —Thomas De Quincey, *Murder Considered as One of the Fine Arts*

Commit a crime and it seems as if a coat of snow fell on the ground, such as reveals in the woods the track of every partridge and fox and squirrel and mole. You cannot . . . wipe out the foot-track, you cannot draw up the ladder, so as to leave no clew.
    —Emerson, "Compensation"

The drama of detection is in discovering how the victim can be killed decently and economically, within the classic unities of time and place.
    —G. K. Chesterton, *A Defence of the Dramatic Unities*

The hero of a detective novel is thinking exactly like an historian when, from indications of the most varied kinds, he constructs an imaginary picture of how a crime was committed, and by whom.
    —R. G. Collingwood, *The Idea of History*

[The reading of detective stories is] a habit . . . wasteful of time and de-grading to the intellect . . . , into which [people] have been bullied by convention. . . .
    —Edmund Wilson, *Classics and Commercials*

. . . [in detective fiction] the technique is *supairb.*
    —William Butler Yeats

. . . the art of murdering without pain . . .
    —Dr. Johnson, *The Rambler,* No. 4 (1750)

INTRODUCTORY

SOME PROPER NAMES. The conventional pronunciation of Buchan, Charteris, Cholmondely, MacLeod, Marjoribanks, Ponsonby, Urquhart, and several other names are well known or easily ascertained, but the facts about some few others depend on chance discovery or direct information from the owners. The following have been gathered in reading or in conversation with those involved and are set down here for the reader and for the record.

Peter *Death* Bredon Wimsey	= De'-ath
Dilwyn	= Dillon
Findlater	= Finlitter
Garve	= Garv'
Holmesian	= Holmee'-sian
Iams	= Eye'-amz
Le Fanu	= Leff'-noo
Le Queux	= Lekew'
Melhuish	= Mellish
Meynell	= Men'-l
Moray Dalton	= Murray
Rhondda	= Rontha
Julian *Symons*	= Simmons

DETECTIVES' NAMES. Various lists of these are given in the following books:

Boucher, Anthony	Four and Twenty Bloodhounds (No. 2365)
Hagen, Ordean	Who Done It? (No. 2954)
Haycraft, Howard	Murder for Pleasure (No. 2957)
MacGowan, Kenneth	Sleuths (No. 2642)
Murch, A. E.	The Development of the Detective Novel (No. 2988)
Osborne, Eric	Victorian Detective Fiction (No. 2998)
Thomson, H. Douglas	Masters of Mystery (No. 3047)
Queen, Ellery	The Detective Short Story (No. 3004)

MISCELLANEOUS INFORMATION

WHODUNIT. This vocable was invented by the late Wolfe Kaufman when on the staff of *Variety*, the New York newspaper written for actors, which has long had a policy of substituting new terms for existing words and locutions. Whatever the inventor's first intention, *whodunit* now refers indiscriminately to any story of crime.

DETECTION. Means "taking the roof off," i.e., uncovering what is hidden. In the Spanish literary tradition, the Devil occasionally offered one of his favorites the entertainment of looking into all the houses of a town by taking the roofs off. Detectives are consequently sons or disciples of the Devil.

THRILLER. The word is more frequently used in England than in America. English usage will sometimes contrast a thriller, which is chiefly surprise, danger, and chase, with the detective story, in which the air is not so full of bullets. But side by side with this useful distinction, *thriller* is often used by English publishers for any story of detection, crime, or mystery. For example, on the jacket of Michael Innes' *Family Affair* (1969), one reads: SOME RECENT GOLLANCZ THRILLERS, followed by the names and works of Rhona Petrie, Kenneth O'Hara, Charles Drummond, Emma Lathen, Elizabeth Fenwick, Isaac Asimov, John Bingham, S & P Wahlöö, Conrad Voss Bark, and V. C. Clinton-Baddeley. On the jacket of the Asimov detective tale: "A thriller by the famous scientist. . . ."

GUNSEL. The term is related not to *gun* but to *gosling* (German root: *Gans, gänselein*). It denotes a young homosexual killer. Howard Haycraft tells an illustrative anecdote of Dashiell Hammett's early writing days. Hammett said he was turning in a story containing two expressions, one harmless, the other shady, and he predicted that his editor would strike out the harmless one and leave the other, in the belief he was doing just the opposite. The harmless expression was *gooseberry lay*, which is thieves' slang for stealing wash from a clothesline. The editor duly struck it out. The other, left in, was *gunsel*.

G-MAN. This term, as everybody knows, means Government Man. It is said on good authority to have been first used by the gangster George Kelly, when he was caught in 1933 after his kidnapping of Charles F. Urschel: "Don't shoot, G-men, don't shoot!" (Leonard Gribble in No. 3165). Certainly by 1935 the term was current among newspapermen, criminals, and the third estate (Mathews' *Dictionary of Americanisms*).

PRIVATE EYE. The phrase is another Americanism, which probably owes its origin to the advertising slogan and symbol of the famous Pinkerton Agency—a large open eye with the motto "We Never Sleep."

"POLISH OFF" was a phrase made famous by Sweeney Todd, the mad barber of Fleet Street, in the stage version of his career by George Dibdin (1841). "I'll polish them off," says Todd as he strops his razor in high expectation.

CORPUS DELICTI. The body of the crime, not the body of the victim, though often the two are identical. For any prosecution there must be tangible evidence that a crime has been committed; this evidence establishes the *corpus delicti,* and it may do so in a case of murder without the presence of a corpse or the possibility of finding one. It is an error shared by many criminals that they cannot be charged with murder if they have made away with the corpse.

DEDUCTION. Conan Doyle popularized the mistake by asking Watson what he *deduced.* Properly speaking, a deduction merely draws out an instance from a generality: if the sum of the angles of any triangle is 180° and this before us is a triangle, we deduce that its angles will equal 180°. Far different is the leap of thought by which Sherlock Holmes *inferred* that Jabez Wilson had been in China from seeing some peculiar tattooing on his arm. As a carping critic could point out, the tattooing might have been done in London by a transplanted Chinese craftsman. Unlike a deduction, an inference is always chancy until buttressed by several other converging inferences; and even then the conclusion only acquires a higher degree of probability, not certainty. Such is the nature of circumstantial evidence. (See Thoreau on p. facing Part IV.)

BORT(Z). Means industrial diamonds, small chips or imperfectly crystallized natural stones, nonetheless of considerable market value.

CALIBERS. One would have supposed that the perpetually booming business of making firearms would long ago have standardized its measures. The fact is that the United States and Britain, on the one hand, and the Continent, on the other, follow different gauges. Besides, the U.S. and Britain use different designations. All these have become terms in the literature. They are related as follows:

U.S. (inches)	Britain (inches)	Continent (mm.)
.22	.220	5.5
.25	.250	6.5 (6.35)
.32	.320	8
.38	.360	9.3
.45	.450 (.455)	11.5

INTRODUCTORY

Plan and Purpose

The inventory that follows will, it is hoped, interest five groups of persons:

1. those who regularly read what are loosely called detective stories;
2. those who think they might like to do so;
3. historians and bibliographers of the genre;
4. booksellers who catalogue out-of-print works;
5. publishers looking for good books to reprint.

What this critical survey of some 7,500 works provides is the kind of repertory that the French call a *catalogue raisonné*—a list with reasons. Some of the reasons are negative: "Don't bother!" This injunction may save the time and money of readers who, after perusing these remarks and sampling a few entries, will know what our standards are and decide to follow them for their own pleasure.

It is open to other readers to get their enjoyment by reversing our advice and reading the works we dismiss or dislike. Our comments should serve both disciple and dissenter, for we have tried to write transparently, that is, to say what in each story seems to us entertaining, original, distinctive, or classic; or else what is clumsy, dull, imitative, or unconvincing. We indicate the setting, situation, and line of detective interest and refrain from giving away the denouement.

The noting of one or more editions with dates and form of publication is to help in identifying and securing the books; the biographical sketches are to satisfy curiosity. But all this information is for the practical reader, not the bibliophile, who would look for "points," measurements, full title pages, and the collation of variants. Within our limits we have tried to be as accurate and informative as the existing state of publishing permits. That state is chaos. Publishers' blurbs are unreliable, and the great catalogues of the British Museum and the Library of Congress are neither complete nor up to date. We often fill their gaps, but must also accept occasional incompleteness and inconsistent treatment of like cases.

At any rate, in fulfilling our main purpose we have not depended on others' statements: we have read and discussed the books we comment on; and of the works listed without comment as "see also" after our critical entries, we have taken from the shelf and examined a great many—though that listing implies, of course, no recommendation. We own in our combined collections something under half the books here reviewed. Yet we are not collectors in the strict sense. Any deliberate searches we have made over the years have been, not for first editions, but for any copy of a book which in reading or conversation we found some critic (or poet or novelist) mentioning as enjoyable. In short we are, like many others, amateurs of crime, dilettantes of detection, and we therefore side with the reviewer in the *Times Literary Supplement* who complained about the Glover-Greene bibliography of *Victorian Detective Fiction:* "We find no hint . . . that these early detective stories are worth reading. . . ." Our claim to the public's attention is that we give hints, and more than hints, about what is worth reading.

For Searchers and Browsers

Another usefulness we may claim is that we give the devotees of several genres information not easy to come by. We tell them, to begin with, about works miscast by their titles or reputations, or which for any reason have remained obscure. It is a common belief that whatever is good ultimately comes to the top unaided, by some law of reverse gravitation. This is not true, and the formal histories and usual lists of the Best Hundred do little to repair the omission. Rather, they underscore what is already famous and favor the prolific. Yet there are masterly works that lie out of the way, sleeping beauties that will awaken at the right presence.

Such, for example, are the fine performances, not followed up, by Jane Boyd, T. L. Davidson, Dermot Morrah, Edwin de Caire, Thomas Kindon, Moira Field, and Alex Atkinson. Other writers, like G. V. Galwey, who switched early to other genres, have left in the public mind little trace of their detective competence. Again, who would not pass by *A Message from Sirius,* thinking it science fiction rather than detection of the kind being sought? There are, moreover, authors appreciated chiefly on one side of the Atlantic—say Herbert Adams, Henry Wade, Leo Bruce, Marten Cumberland, Cyril Hare, George A. Birmingham, and Glyn Carr in England, and M. V. Heberden, Jack Iams, Hillary Waugh, and H. C. Branson in the United States—to say nothing of the abundant producers, wherever known, whose output contains one prize among many run-of-the-mill stories. Similarly, there are instances of the excellent tale overshadowed by the same author's inferior war-horse that reviewers and paperback publishers keep plugging.

A third use of the information here presented is to cut short the seeker's wanderings in the maze of pseudonyms, stories retitled (some more than once), and the usual misleading classifications of "mystery," "crime," "thriller," and so on given by publishers and librarians. Even

4

though not as easily sorted as apples and oranges, works of mystery do differ in the kind of entertainment they afford, and they deserve a more exact nomenclature to distinguish them. "Thriller" means different things in England and in the United States, and in England it did not always mean what it has come to mean, namely detection no less than other kinds of excitement.

As for variant titles, they can lead one to suppose that here is another work by a favorite author; or, on the contrary, that one has already read what is in fact a different work. For example, Crofts has written *Double Tragedy* and is rightly credited also with *Double Death*. These are different stories, obviously—or perhaps not obviously. But there is another *Double Death*, a collaborative effort in which Crofts also figures, and which is sometimes ascribed to him alone. This is an uncommonly bad tangle; the same sort of confusion reigns almost as a matter of course among the titles of works by Knox, Burton, Christie, and dozens of other writers.[1]

Species and Standards

In choosing from the mass of good books and shameless trash that we have read or skimmed in half a century, we have not been purists. Though we prefer the classical genre inaugurated by Poe as "tales of ratiocination," we find it easy to enjoy stories in which detection is subordinated, provided something other than mere agitation takes its place. We do not allow the trappings of the form without its substance to deceive us—or the reader. Where this palming off occurs we declare in our entry: "No detection" or "Detection feeble." To put our creed positively, we hold with the best philosophers that a detective story should be mainly occupied with detecting, and not (say) with the forgivable nervousness of a man planning to murder his wife. Crime is not detection but (usually) its opposite; mystery is not detection but (usually) its spur. Again, spying and "pursuit" are not detection though sometimes its adjuncts.

The presence of a detective is of course no guaranty that detection will occur; he may like a stage prop be "unpractical." As for "suspense," it is no genre. Blurb-writers at their wits' end are responsible for this weasel word, which is really not good enough for critics. "Story of anxiety" would be closer to the facts. Suspense belongs to every good story, and suspense is not genuine when it is created by the repetition of tricks, whether every speaker's unfinished sentences or a first-person narrator's manufactured suspicions. To sum up, detection is a game that must be played according to Doyle.

If this is true, why do we take notice of certain works written in

1. Plausible guesses will not help, whether based on the meaning of titles or the dates of publication. For example, two reference books wholly concerned with our subject erroneously aver that Knox's *Double Cross Purposes* is the same as *Settled Out of Court*—which happens to have a duplicate title and also to be a title by another writer. On page after page, one of these bibliographies lists titles by authors of detection that are anything but stories of detection, and some, indeed, that are not stories at all.

flagrant violation of these canons of reason and lacking in substitute merits? The answer is that those particular works have usurped favor in public opinion, and our *Catalogue* seemed a good place to say what they are and are not. Omission on purist grounds would, moreover, have left unanswered the question "What is that famous story (author) like?" As for stories that lie in domains cognate with detection, it was a pleasure to praise first-rate books of adventure, pursuit, espionage, or crime, from such classics as Collins' *Moonstone* and Le Fanu's *Uncle Silas* to Childers' *Riddle of the Sands,* and Buchan's *Thirty-Nine Steps,* as well as have our say about the best inventions of Le Queux and Oppenheim, Anthony Armstrong and Henry Calvin, Edward Harling and Michael Underwood.

How the Work Took Shape

The *Catalogue* shows on its face the manner and span of its composition. The reader will find here and there evidence of changed views about certain works and occasional references to the way in which a book was first come upon. The comments all together record an avocation pursued by two friends now in their sixties, who began comparing notes on literature when they were adolescents. They vividly remember the appearance, in 1923, of the first book by a new writer—Dorothy Sayers' *Whose Body?,* which, incidentally, came out in the United States earlier than in England. Since then they have looked for detection new and old in the bookshops and libraries of dozens of cities on either side of the Atlantic and have exchanged reports and opinions in a correspondence that fills many file boxes. It was about midway in the search, between 1948 and 1950, that the decision was made to form one (abstract) collection out of two, and draw up a critical inventory for private use. The idea of publishing came only latterly, from the publisher.

The area of our exploration will readily define itself for the reader. Our concern is with the literature of the English-speaking world during the period 1870–1970, with perhaps a special attention to the Golden Era (as John Strachey saw it): 1920 to 1939. We stray outside the limits either to make a critical or historical point or to draw from obscurity an interesting work and author. But as we lay no claim to completeness—it would be brash ignorance for anyone to do so—we may allow ourselves an occasional irregularity. We tell what we know, not all that is to be known, and leave large territories to our eager successors. Similarly, our judgments are influenced by our concurrent intellectual tastes, from music, science, and railroading to literature, history, and philosophy. It is in keeping with this outlook that we list a small number of Association Items, plainly marked, from which we hope our readers may derive additional information and entertainment.

It should be added that being a determined tracker in a specialized field does not compel one to be solemn about it. The goal at all times was pleasure, and it is not surprising that some of our remarks reflect our amusement in pursuing it. Humor was uppermost, certainly, when near the end of labors that professed to encompass great detection from A to Z we discovered that neither of us had ever read any work by the well-

6

known Anthony Abbot, nor yet the famous *Big Bow Mystery* by Zang-will, a pair which obviously and alphabetically deserved to open and close our endeavors.

A Tale Is Not a Novel

We might stop our preliminary remarks with this confession, if in discussing with skeptics the taste for detective stories we had not encountered a common prejudice and found its cause to lie in clichés rather than in experience. So, with no thought of changing anybody's likes and dislikes, but only the wish to strengthen the view that detection is part of literature, we must try to clear up the errors in the way.

Some readers report that the reason the genre fails to hold their interest is its "lack of reality." They mean by this: truth of character and depth of motive. For truth of circumstance and action is necessarily very strong in detective stories. But to the sophisticated reader of modern novels who has learned to despise the realism of surroundings and behavior, the presence of exact detail and plausible action and the absence of fantasy only confirm his contempt for detection. Finding that in our genre the characters tend to be stereotyped and the motives stylized, he wonders how people who also relish Flaubert, Dickens, Henry James, Tolstoy, Forster, Joyce, Lawrence, and their kind can tolerate John Rhode, Rex Stout, Ngaio Marsh, Raymond Chandler, and Agatha Christie. Even Dorothy Sayers strikes these critics as "traditional" and hence beneath notice. Is then the reading of detective stories a species of lowbrow addiction, a sign of insensitivity coupled with a mindless reaching for escape?

The fact is that from the outset detection has been written for and by highbrows. The genre has been the preserve of the intellectual and the cultivated, and not so much for relaxation in the ordinary sense as for the stimulation, in a different setting, of the same critical and imaginative powers that these persons display in their vocations. Some highly intelligent people have, of course, never felt the pleasure afforded by detective fiction, have denied its merits and even attacked it as a menace; but exceptions do not alter the generality. Historically, the theme of detection has aroused the imagination of writers from Voltaire, Beaumarchais, Balzac, Cooper, Dumas, and Poe to Dickens, Dostoevsky, Mark Twain, Henry James, Yeats, Eliot, and C. Day Lewis. Whatever it is, the detective story is not an idiot's delight.

The most general answer to objectors and demurrers is that the qualities of a genre must not be looked for in its neighbor across the way. As one of the makers of this book showed at some length elsewhere,[2] detective fiction belongs to the kind of narrative properly called *the tale*. It is a genre distinct from *the novel* as we have come to know it since Balzac. The tale does not pretend to social significance nor does it probe the depths

2. "Detection and the Literary Art," Introduction to *The Delights of Detection* (New York, 1961). Reprinted in Francis M. Nevins, Jr., ed., *The Mystery Writer's Art* (Bowling Green University Press, 1970).

of the soul. The characters it presents are not persons but types, as in the gospels: the servant, the rich man, the camel driver (now a chauffeur).

The tale, much older than the novel, appeals to curiosity, wonder, and the love of ingenuity. If it "studies" anything, it is the calculating mind rather than the spontaneous emotions, material predicaments rather than spiritual. *Candide* is a tale and a masterpiece, though without lifelike characters or depth psychology—which does not mean that it is wanting in knowledge of human character at large. *The Arabian Nights, The Decameron, Don Quixote, Gulliver, Crusoe,* the fictions of Thomas Love Peacock and the inventions of Poe, Kleist, Kafka, and Borges are tales, and they must not be judged by criteria applicable to *Père Goriot, Our Mutual Friend,* and *The Brothers Karamazov.*

Discerning readers of detection such as Yeats, T. S. Eliot, Bertrand Russell, and W. H. Auden make no such mistake; yet they can hardly be held insensitive to literature, any more than Lincoln, who, according to William Dean Howells, used to reread Poe every year.

Poe is in fact the complete authority on this question, because he not only gave all the models, but also delivered himself of definitive critical statements. It was he who first made the point (in his critique of Dickens' *Barnaby Rudge*) that the regular novel and legitimate mystery will not combine. Mystery-mongering, or the piling up of unexplained or ambiguous events, will not sustain a work of true literature. The explanations at the end are bound to be a letdown, and the foreknowledge of this weakness spoils the rereading. Even worse, in the writing the author is trapped into producing unreal effects.

To Think Is Human Too

In contrast with this trickery, Poe shifted the interest from the fumbling with mystery in the novel to the *elucidation* of mystery in a tale. What he called ratiocination supplied a genuine human concern at once operative throughout and capable of engaging interest in any number of rereadings. True, that concern is unusual in that it dwells on the workings of the mind, rather than of the emotions. But as Pascal pointed out, reason can be an emotion, too, and millions of readers of detection have proved him right. Detective Reason, moreover, works upon the stuff of life, facts material, social, and psychological, which even when reasoned about ought to interest a reader of literature. For "means, motive, and opportunity," which characterize detection, also apply to the regular novel; they simply acquire a special meaning in detection.

That special meaning is linked with the resolve of the detective author to find significance and derive understanding from physical appearances, overt acts, and uncommon aspects of familiar things. In this, too, the specialization parallels that of the novel at large. Where would *it* be without its personal remarks about the eyes, hair, teeth, hands, and tricks of speech of its characters? To see people in the round and also, it seems, to plumb their souls, we have to know about the old woman's loose lower lip and the coarse red hair on the man's knuckles. In short, in both detection and the "nobler" form, it is by evidence, often minute, that convincingness is achieved. The appeal to the eye is very strong. Pointing to signs, as William James long ago remarked, "fixes terms, but one of its uses is [also] to rouse the believing reaction and give to the ideas a more living reality. . . . [W]hen we are told a story and shown the very knife that did the murder . . . the whole thing passes from fairyland to mother earth. . . ."[3]

That the detective story is a tale by its nature, and not by trying and failing to be a novel, is further shown by its length: starting its career as a short story, it grew unwisely to the size of the "regular" novel, only to discover in our day that its proper measure was that of the novella or short novel—70,000 words.

What is also to the point is the survival of the classical detective tales. Most of the great ones are steadily reprinted and continue to compete successfully with every fresh batch of the same kind. Meanwhile, many "serious" novels hailed as masterpieces in the intervening decades, the works of psychological and social analysis that were talked about and admired and lectured upon in all sincerity, have dropped out of sight and memory.

This difference could be ascribed to the public's vulgar desire to be entertained, if it were not that tons of other entertaining matter have also disappeared. The truth is that to succeed in the writing of tales, and particularly tales of detection, the author must know *something* about human life. For the detection of crime he must command subjects often complex and not easily made clear or interesting; whereas the authors of a good many "profound" novels make up their knowledge of the soul as they go along and are shown up with the passage of time as having been merely superficial mood-catchers. And as a final contrast, writing detective fiction necessarily "selects" the storytellers whose grasp of circumstance yields a kind of lifelikeness that nothing can darken until the laws of nature change.

The successful tale of detection is, moreover, a technical feat; it unfolds in a peculiar way and moves within narrow bounds. On one side, thorough realism would make its incidents too hard to bear—or too dull. On the other side, irresponsible make-believe would insult the intelligence and again prove dull. It follows that a true appreciation of such tales must acknowledge in the good examples the presence of acute literary judgment, coupled with abundant invention and narrative power. But to admit these is to admit the genre, since every genre is to be judged only by its best examples.

The Tough and the Tender

In making such discriminations it is important to avoid another mistake. There is no warrant for the commonly held belief that the tough detective tale yields greater truth than the gentler classical form and marks a forward step toward "the real novel." The "soft" genteel story, in which the corpse is found in a library by the butler, may be a period piece, but it is in itself neither truer nor falser than the story set in the back alleys of Glasgow or Los Angeles. Butlers may be an anachronism, but so are

3. *Principles of Psychology*, 1890, II, 305.

bootleggers—and private libraries are still more numerous than private eyes. Nor is habitual vulgarity of speech "more real" than civil talk among educated people.

On these points the literary mind has been influenced, and—as it seems to us—perverted, by a famous essay written by a famous detective novelist. Raymond Chandler was one of the early masters of the tough American story that was developed in such pulp magazines as *Flynn's* and *Black Mask.* When he had risen to eminence, his definition of "The Simple Art of Murder" was taken as the burial service read over the corpse of the classical tale, and his words were reprinted over and over again.

To make his case, Chandler took A. A. Milne's *Red House Mystery* and showed how it violated the plausible in action, motive, police routine, and the expression of human feeling. Some of his points were unquestionably telling, both about Milne's work and about the tradition its critic made it stand for. But Chandler started from an untenable premise in his first sentence: "Fiction in any form has always intended to be realistic." And so he never saw the other side of the coin, which shows, not that the classical mode is more real than Chandler admits, but that real-ness is irrelevant.

This must be so, since the tough mode, including Chandler's own admirable work, is open to the same objections as the other. Consider the tough formula: a private detective, usually low in funds and repute, undertakes single-handed and often without fee the vindication of some unfortunate person—a man or woman with no other friends. The attempt pits the hero against a ruthless crime syndicate or against the whole corrupt government of the town, or both. During his search for evidence, he is threatened, slugged, drugged, shot at, kidnapped, tortured, but never downed for very long. In many of the variants of the genre, he drinks quantities of whiskey neat and proves equally ready for fighting and fornication. None of this affects his work; he is guaranteed indestructible. Others' bullets pass him by; his own—especially in the final scene of carnage—always find their mark. And despite the grueling physical pace he finds the time and the wit, without the aid of discussion or note-taking, to figure out the discrepancies that reveal the culprit and his motive.

Now if in comparing the tender and the tough conventions one is looking for "real life" in the verifiable sense, one must conclude that although the first kind of story will not bear skeptical examination, the second is— as Shakespeare says apropos of two liars—"an even more wonderful song than the other."

Nor is this all that Raymond Chandler's essay brings to mind. The tender school aims at producing a denouement having the force of necessity, as in Greek tragedy. All the facts (clues, words, motives) must converge to give the mystery one solution and one only. That by itself is a good reason for making the crime occur in a law-abiding circle, where the habits of the *dramatis personae* are by hypothesis regular and reasonable. In such a setting the violence of murder is the more striking, and stronger also the desire to manacle the offender. Murder among thugs and drug addicts is hardly unexpected, and the feeling that in this milieu anything can happen does not increase but rather lessens the interest.

Hence the artistic need for the tough writer to involve some innocent, whose ways *are* peaceable, and to put steadily in peril the detective-defender of that lump of virtue. In short, in murder à la Chandler, murder is not enough to keep us going—and neither is detection, since it is never a feature of the foreground.

Chandler as artist is so aware of these lacks that he reinforces the damsel-in-distress motive with what is nothing less than a political motive. He makes it clear in his essay that the hero of the new and improved genre is fighting society. Except for the favored victim, he alone is pure in heart, a C-green incorruptible. The rich are all crooked or "phonies," and cowards in the end. Since the police, the mayor, the whole Establishment are soon shown as a conspiracy to pervert justice and kill off troublemakers, we naturally share the detective's smothered indignation and are powerfully driven, like him, to see the right vindicated.

The tough story was born in the thirties and shows the Marxist coloring of its birth years. In Chandler's essay the critique of the classical formula seems to spring not solely from a mistaken demand for realism, but also from a hostility to the solvent way of life. That the well-to-do could be honest, "genuine," and lovable apparently was not "realistic" either. And obviously the reader was to feel morally uplifted by the solemn conclusion describing the true hero-detective:

"He must be a complete man and a common man and yet an unusual man. . . . He must be the best man in his world and a good enough man for any world. . . . He is a relatively poor man, or he would not be a detective at all. . . . He will take no man's money dishonestly and no man's insolence without a due and dispassionate revenge. He is a lonely man and his pride is that you will treat him as a proud man or be very sorry you ever saw him. The story is this man's adventure in search of a hidden truth. . . . If there were enough like him, the world would be a very safe place to live in, without becoming too dull to be worth living in."[4]

Who's the sentimental tale spinner now? After thirty years it makes no difference to our enjoyment of the great sagas by Chandler, Ross Macdonald, and others that the eternal Robin Hood should have got mixed up with Marx's angry young men and Tennyson's Galahad, and wound up in self-contradiction. What was and remains comic is that Chandler should have chosen for his California hero the name Philip Marlowe, which from first name to final *e* connotes Englishness, Elegance, and Establishment.[5]

4. *The Simple Art of Murder,* ed. J. Nelson (New York: W. W. Norton, 1968), p. 533.

5. It should interest the cultural historian that the evolution of crime fiction (meaning all the current varieties) has since 1930 accurately reflected the social mood and the catchwords of each succeeding decade. Indeed, every four or five years the tone changes and the illustrative characters and actions follow the prevailing attitude of Western man toward his world. A study of the best writers would even show that the emotions now acted out in nihilistic vandalism and violence were first voiced by the sympathetic heroes in such tales, and that the shift of moral preference from law-abiding to criminal behavior was first popularized through these new-style Byronic rebels and self-haters.

Before the heyday of the classical tradition which Chandler thought he had killed, but which, slightly modified, continues to inspire brilliant works, the tone of the detective novel was excessively melodramatic. It owed this trait to its French descent. The *roman policier*, long, improbable, and marred by courtroom rhetoric, was adapted into English by a number of gifted woman writers—Anna Katharine Green, Mrs. Belloc Lowndes, the Baroness Orczy, Mary Roberts Rinehart, Isabel Ostrander —who filled the years between 1880 and that great transformation of the 1920s of which, a decade earlier, E. C. Bentley, G. K. Chesterton, and R. Austin Freeman were the neglected pioneers.[6]

The greatest masters of the twenties and thirties were in fact mistresses. Christie, Sayers, Allingham, Marsh, and Heyer rose with the triumph of feminism and deserved the plaudits they received from both sexes. They wrote true detection; they fashioned unsurpassable models. But the formula of the nineties continued to be exploited, by other women, who wrote mostly for women's magazines. Their output, when reissued as books, must be characterized as feminine in a bad sense. This is unavoidable if warning is to be given to amateurs of the real thing. Let us repeat that many of the most brilliant, as well as solid and artful, masterpieces of detection have in our century been written by women. Hence it is not because of the authors that we dismiss certain works and writers as feminine; it is because of their *readers;* that is, their readers' insistent tastes. Books that mirror chiefly the typical aspects of women's lives are not made into detective stories by the perfunctory addition of a crime and a policeman.

What are these typical aspects? The briefest answer is: household confusion. The actual scene of the story may be a hospital or a college, but the state of mind is that of the kitchen. It is marked by interruption, change of plans, minor mishaps that pass for catastrophes, surprises, and lucky recoveries—all highly verbalized and widely communicated. All of life could no doubt be described in terms not very different; it is a matter of degree. But domestic life, by its nature and for its great purpose, remains extraordinarily discontinuous—the perpetual readjustment of small intentions. This in turn generates a characteristic tone, which one finds faithfully rendered in the "feminine" detective tale.

When to this substance is added an outside evil at work, one obtains the formula happily symbolized by Ogden Nash, and made official by Howard Haycraft, as HIBK. The letters stand for *Had I But Known,* which sums up the heroine's mind as she repeatedly ponders her failure to see the obvious traps laid for her by the villains, or as she recurrently

---

6. The year 1920 saw the appearance of Crofts' *The Cask* and Christie's *Mysterious Affair at Styles,* which publishers had been rejecting for several years. In that same year H. C. Bailey also brought out *Call Mr. Fortune.* The year before, J. S. Fletcher had won readers in high places with *The Middle Temple Murder.* Within five years Dorothy Sayers, A. A. Milne, Lynn Brock, Philip MacDonald, the Coles, Anthony Berkeley, Ronald Knox, Henry Wade, Eden Phillpotts, and R. Austin Freeman were in full spate, the earlier stories of the last named being rescued from obscurity one by one. The merit of their work severally or as a whole is not the point: between 1920 and 1925 they had established the new tone and form.

regrets not having acted with ordinary judgment and spoken out in time, for reasons never stated to herself or the reader. By taking such liberties with common sense it is possible to spin out episodes into a story—and to wear out the patience of adult minds.[7]

The latest exploitation of this vein is the story that reviewers and publishers call "story of suspense," because they find it hard to call it anything else. It is often domestic and usually rural. When all the household equipment is found oddly out of place (rice is in "Sugar") and the old dresser in the pantry begins to look "subtly sinister," we are in for "suspense." Taken out of doors, the narrator-heroine permits herself the usual vagaries of HIBK action and response—e.g., hunting for someone, alone, at night, without plan, and in a dangerous neighborhood. This folly is supposed to produce a mood of dread horror, though old Mrs. Radcliffe, at the turn of the eighteenth century, could show our damsels a trick or two.[8] In fact, since the modern psychological novel has devoted itself to exploring the abnormal and oddly alarming, no great originality was needed to raise the emotional pitch of the girlish murder story another notch and make HIBK into EIRF—Everything Is Rather Frightening.

Lest we seem arbitrary in this judgment, here is an example from a recent story by a formerly solid writer: "He had once said to her that anything could happen there, absolutely anything, and that that was what the cottage was for, that it was there simply to be a setting, a background for some strange and dramatic event. Susan had jeered at him, asking what a cottage could be for, except for people to live in. Since then a dramatic event had happened there, the murder of the girl Sandra, and who knew what else, and the thought of this, acting on Susan's horribly guilty feeling at being there at all in this secret way, made the atmosphere of the place almost more than she could bear."

Such a passage is fraudulent because it is mere verbalizing. The contrast between cottages to live in and cottages for dramatic events is puerile. When Susan challenges it, we cry, "Good for Susan!" But her brain subsides at once under the "horrible guilt" of being where she shouldn't be, in a place where a murder is supposed (never shown) to have taken place. If the atmosphere is almost more than she could bear, it is altogether more than a sensible reader can. Let her go home, and him to other books.[9]

Police Routine, Doorbell Ringing,
and Watchful Waiting

At the other extreme from the passively feminine and feebly spine-chilling is the appropriately flat-footed account of police routine. Its con-

7. Twenty years ago, critics and publishers who wished to single out serious detection would describe the specimen as "adult entertainment." Now the phrase has become the standard euphemism for high-octane pornography.

8. The term *Gothic* has lately been revived to denote stories of the sort just described. It seems a pity to confuse thereby an historic genre, in which religion and superstition played a great part, with our secular milk-and-water fantasies.

9. In this same story of vague frights and frustrated passions, it turns out that the only two attractive and sensible people in the book are the murdering desperadoes: this is a subversive attack on the fundamental decencies.

tents and pace have been subjected to many variations, but it remains a prototype, with merits and difficulties common to the class. Though police work is active, it can easily become humdrum, as the engaging Inspector West in Creasey's early tales soon proved. In the same author's Gideon stories, interdepartmental feuds and the rumblings of dyspeptic stomachs do not sufficiently enliven what is, after all, a routine. As substitute for direct emotion and dynamics, we have to content ourselves with worry about the lives and feelings of the criminal's victims (children, much too often) and the result is that in certain hands police routine unexpectedly becomes another illicit way of harrowing the reader.

To be sure, the police tale as Maurice Procter conceives it presents a great choice of characters and situations that arouse and satisfy the detective imagination. But depicting officialdom imposes obvious limits, which other writers have tried to transcend by substituting a private routine, more free-wheeling, often illegal—that of the insurance assessor, for example, or of the visiting accountant who suspects fraud.

Such an investigator can, if he deems it useful, walk naked along a canal and not be subject to demotion under Rule 42 about "Uniforms, When to Wear." He is free to make love to his female clients or quarries, and generally give the reader the impression that his is an adventurous life in a good cause. After making the rounds of gossipy women on dingy streets, being "sapped" and taken to the Boss (who dresses like a fashion plate and lives with a bored babe in a luxurious flat), he can call the case closed and return to collect his meed of glory as the Indispensable Man. Yet the reader may be pardoned for getting weary of the interviews and tailings by car and by foot which form the staple of all the ambulatory genres.

A third kind in the "routine" class is the tale of spectatorial endurance. It scarcely concerns itself with detection or mystery or crime, but with the inner life of the protagonist and the surmised emotions of those whom he watches and wears down. Simenon's stories about Maigret are of this kind. They make one think of what Proust could have done had he chosen to write a western. The cowboys' professional skill and purpose in life would be completely subordinated to their introspection, childhood memories, and emotional entanglements with particular horses.

Accordingly, anyone who says, "I can't bear detective stories, but I love Simenon" is saying that he prefers the art that is farthest from the center of detection properly so called. To make this judgment is not to deprecate the taste or depreciate the art, which is often of the highest order. But it is not detection. True, Maigret, like any other cop, wants to get his man, and he knows where to wait for him—he has had previous information. But what he contributes is the patience of a god.[10] And what his readers enjoy is his boredom, fatigue, wet feet, and hunger—all skillfully interwoven with his shrewd speculations as he looks across the road from behind the curtain in a tavern—ideal fiction for the born member of a Watch and Ward Society.

10. What a French reviewer said of him by way of characterizing the work of Boileau-Narcejac is evocative: "It is Maigret all over again; only, it rains a little less."

Quite different from Maigret's war of nerves is the cold war, which has given new life and popularity to the spy story. Its vogue is greatest, no doubt, among those who respond to mystery and adventure without qualification. But a better reason for its success is that the spy story has been taken up, after a lapse, by very skillful and highly informed writers, from Eric Ambler to John Le Carré. We think it significant that Le Carré's two detective stories before *The Spy Who Came in from the Cold* were indifferent performances. It was the swollen current of anger against institutions, against power, against authority of any kind that gave instant life to the new figure of the spy.

In his diffuse resentment and dirty deeds, his cynical manipulation of others and inventiveness in torturing and killing, the spy expresses many pent-up emotions; not, however, the sentiment of rationality. His conscious hatred of himself and others seems a continuation of the tough school of detection, in spirit at least; for although the spy is anything but a good man à la Marlowe, he typifies the same revolt. He unites in himself the feelings of all spies and conspirators regardless of cause, and embodies a common contempt for the safe and the comfortable.[11]

In the best spy stories there is more than a trace of detection: the man on whose side we are supposed to be uses physical clues to chart his course and save his skin. But the author's need to sustain secrecy is such that we have to believe in the meaning of those clues on his say-so, just as we have to believe in the miraculous gadgets brought into play. Any pleasure here comes from having dust thrown in one's eyes in an authoritative manner. And even that pleasure is often spoiled by the author's carrying too far the uncertainty as to which side the agent is really working for. The spy story is in all these ways the opposite of liberal and scientific; it is not open, coherent, and argumentative. Sleight-of-hand, carried to a brilliantly bogus extreme by Ian Fleming, is what one must relish if one is to prefer spying to detection.

As for the chase, it is most enjoyable when it is part of a larger whole. When it stands alone, credibility is strained by the mere length of the pursuit and the inevitable similarity of its incidents. And when the machinery comes to rest, our flushed and breathless pleasure is likely to be spoiled by two defects almost impossible to avoid. One is the motive for the headlong rush: drugs or diamonds, defectors or double agents, it seems too slight a cause for hounding or being hounded so relentlessly at high speeds; and the other is wrapped up in the first: after so much moving about, one can hardly stand still listening to the explanations.

11. One should perhaps add that the spy story often leans toward sadistic pornography. As a writer in the *Times Literary Supplement* once pointed out, the outré sexual fancies and modes of inflicting pain attributed by modern writers to the secret service of "worthy" governments have significance "because [they] are obviously intended for the upper reaches of crime craft. What lurks in the lower is hardly believable." (Dec. 8, 1966).

Planning for Private Welfare

The civilian counterpart of the spy adventure is the story of the man who contemplates murder on his own account. He must put together a number of physical arrangements that shall ensure a healthy absence of clues. His imagination must work like a detective's as he pictures a future state of fact and scans it for telltale signs. This operation, with its driving cause, hesitancies, and final resolve artfully laid out, can be engrossing for the reader. But in common practice most writers who begin with the killer at breakfast, plotting, spend most of their time whipping up the reader's emotions, though they call it analyzing the criminal's. They do this in order to justify his attempt, to maintain excitement, and to show their own genius. Some doubtless feel that this attention to "plumbing" brings them nearer to great literature. They think of Macbeth and Raskolnikov or, more modestly, of Stevenson's "Markheim," and believe they are doing loftier work than Rex Stout or Dorothy Sayers.

But unless one is Shakespeare or Dostoevsky or Dickens or Victor Hugo, there is no hope of moving the great heart of the world by depicting criminal anguish. How much better to use it as a mere seasoning to hard thought about practical matters! For the truth is that the less competent the planning and execution of the deed, the less interesting the tale from any point of view: if it is shallow as psychology (*ex hypothesi*) and muddled in detective imagination, it might as well not be written at all: it must be a foresight saga or it is nothing.

In the Courtroom

A certain similarity obtains between the tale of premeditated crime and the story told at the trial. Both are vulnerable to the lure of theatrics and cheap sentiment, under whose artificial heat the ratiocinative interest evaporates. This is not to say that that interest must be cold, inhuman, divorced from drama, and forgetful of the pomp of the courtroom. The point is that these powerful supports of interest must stay below what they support. The legitimately great trial stories usually retell the discovery of the events that have brought the accused into the dock and go on to vindicate him or her. Other tales diverge to other subjects: they investigate the jury (twelve life histories and peculiar minds), or else they give us "a study of the murderer," just like the criminal psychologists with their: "Wilfred Perkins had decided to get rid of his wife"; or more subtly: "Marion had really gone too far; she must go"—which sometimes creates a doubt whether Marion is the cook about to be fired. All such doubts and diversions, when they merely serve to evade difficulty, destroy pleasure and must be deplored.

The trial story, incidentally, must be scrupulously exact in every detail of court procedure—language, pace and movement of persons, attitudes of participants and spectators, including the press; otherwise, the magic is broken for the many readers who know what may and may not be, having learned it at the hands of the experts among writers of detective fiction.

The Ghost Story

Some readers take it for granted that tales of the supernatural can hold no interest for readers addicted to reasoning from clues. As Michael Gilbert once said in conversation, "the ghost story is a form of cheating." Yet the fact remains that many connoisseurs of either genre are sound readers of the other. And the explanation readily suggests itself: the modern ghost story derives its effect from the contrast between the inexplicable event and our ever more extensive knowledge of what is physically possible. Strangeness has become familiar: we get no shivers from the truly ghostly figures on the television screen because we know how mundane their production is.

The writer who raises real ghosts is therefore bound to be circumstantial in his preparation of the weird occurrence: he must produce the ungimmickable.[12] Not by shrieks and curses and bloody hands does he work on our feelings, but by a violation of physics and the implied threat to our security. The less he puts horror into his words, the more likely we are to feel it in things themselves, flatly described. Think of what M. R. James accomplishes simply with hair. In short, the scientific assumption of the regularity of nature has affected ghost-making and given it a common base with detection. That we have to accept a supernatural power at the heart of our dismay is a concession which does not spoil the pleasure of following the startling but conceivable course of events until almost the very end.

Plays and Films

The theater is not congenial to detection—or perhaps one should put it the other way around: detection is not congenial to the theater, and the reason is obvious. The audience cannot easily see what is observed or handled, nor will it tolerate disquisitions about points: all theatrical dialogue must convey feeling. So the stage is the place rather for murder, darkness, apparitions, and odd natural sounds punctuated by unnatural shrieks. The number of intellectually satisfying thrillers in play form is therefore quite small. Those noticed in Part II of this *Catalogue* are a bare handful. Other repertories (see No. 2954) give long lists, usually incomplete, of undoubted successes, but quite outside our genre.

The film could of course overcome the play's shortcomings as to observation and the handling of objects, but it suffers from an even greater need to keep action moving briskly and without ratiocination. Puzzlement, which can arouse genuine emotion on the printed page, gets lost in visual representation, and the soliloquy that might properly render mental confusion has to be heightened to frenzy if the movie-goer is to be stirred. When a film follows a great detective story faithfully, as was done in *Trent's Last Case* with Orson Welles, the result is boredom.

12. This consideration is what puts science fiction, attractive as it is, outside the boundaries of this *Catalogue*. The SF imagination is certainly interwoven with logic and reason, but it is not the imagination of the real or the logic of the actual; and whereas the ghost tale asks but one concession at the close, science fiction requires many more than one, scattered throughout.

Are there no exceptions? Well, the several versions of *The Hound of the Baskervilles* had the advantage of a flaming hound; even so, all but the version starring Basil Rathbone were failures, because the suspense, which is continuous in the book, was slack or absent whenever the dog was quietly at home eating his dinner. Other Sherlock Holmes stories that have succeeded on the screen have done so only when they were kept short and when the arresting figure of Holmes was well enacted—as by Arthur Wontner in early days. And it is possible that these old silent swifties were pleasurable only to connoisseurs.

Here and there in the *Catalogue* mention is made of good films based on stories that we discuss. It will generally be found that the novel is inferior as detection and that a farfetched transfiguration of its plot is what gives it éclat as a film—for example, Hitchcock's *The Lady Vanishes*, based on Ethel Lina White's *The Wheel Spins*.

Some Technical Terms

We have been describing, in addition to the tendencies of modern taste, the merits and faults of various kinds of tales. In the *Catalogue* itself it seemed convenient to retain the critical vocabulary that grew up between the collaborators as they discussed new books or exchanged notes about them. These terms of art might be of wider convenience if, by our readers' acceptance of at least some of them, it became possible for readers generally to abridge explanations about typical features of the literature. Such terms need not be precisely those we adopted; other critics will no doubt think of better ones. Ours, at any rate, are ordinary words that context will generally keep clear. To make doubly sure, here are further indications of their intent:

Atmosphere: unless preceded by a favorable modifier, atmosphere is a liability, being a substitute for action or for needed description of physical fact. Atmosphere is sometimes pure mood (e.g., fear), sometimes scenery or special routine (the isles of Greece, the workings of a canning factory). Unless incorporated, made functional to the story, atmosphere is filler or excess. For example, there is the perfect dose of the advertising business in Sayers' *Murder Must Advertise,* but too much about bell-ringing in *The Nine Tailors.*

Cardboard: see the next entry.

Characterization: characters, we know, are not "studied" in the detective tale as they are in the novel. Yet it is possible in the tale not only to differentiate persons, but to endow stock characters (e.g., the rural policeman) with fresh turns of mind and of phrase. Characters in Crispin, Leo Bruce, Michael Gilbert, and Christie differ radically from the puppets surrounding the detective in Rhode, Burton, and Creasey. The latter genus is henceforth to be known as *cardboard.*[13]

Cluttered: a tale in which the foreground is full of unnecessary words, persons, actions—bric-a-brac of any sort, figurative or actual. Lifelikeness can be achieved by other means than keeping up a perpetual din.

13. Warrant for this usage can claim the authority of the late Ian Fleming. In a remark quoted by the *New York Times* after his death, he referred to his creation James Bond as "that cardboard booby." (October 22, 1966)

Detection: not merely the unraveling of a mystery or the solving of a crime, but the account of the way in which this was done by rational means. Like Emerson's American Scholar, the detective is Man Thinking. A book dealer who specializes in the literature once referred in a catalogue to "fatso, fuddy-duddy Nero Wolfe." The words show how little some minds respond to the mental activity which is the mainspring of detection—even though not necessarily the mainspring of every scene in detective fiction.

Feminine: has been explained and illustrated above. Let it be added here that quite often an obsession with secondary concerns is sufficient to justify the label—e.g., preoccupation with feeding the narrator's small children, or with the young leading woman's hopeless love for a married man, when all about them are being shot, stabbed, and strangled.

Huddled: applies to those last chapters in which a flurry of earlier comings and goings is disclosed to explain the mystery. Often, a perfect mob was milling around the fatal spot within seconds of one another. The attentive reader who has been taking note of pending questions along the way is revolted by a solution more confusing and less probable than the original tangle.

Inverted Tale: one in which the crime is first shown being committed and, next, being solved with the aid of details that the clever author has adroitly slighted in his first recital. R. Austin Freeman invented the form circa 1912. Special talent is needed to succeed in it. Writers who toy with it by interlarding their detection with chapters showing the criminal at work almost always divide the interest while thinking they double it. ("Inverted tale" has long been the accepted critical term for the Freeman formula.)

Plateau: the stretch where the gathering of evidence repeats what is known without imparting forward motion. The inquest is usually a plateau, and so are the routine portions of "questioning everybody." A review of perplexities by the detective and his friend (or official superior) can be agreeable, but only if new ideas come out of it. The copy we own of one pretty fair tale has some twenty pages missing—presumably the inquest and certainly the plateau, for the gap in no way spoils the interest or intelligibility of the story.

Pseudo Detection: ranges all the way from the wanderings of the incompetent little man with a head cold to the suspicions put forth by the police that no one could possibly believe in. The crime solves itself by accident, confession, or guesswork. Detectives that do not detect have no place in a story except as foils to others that do.

"Psychology": in quotation marks means guessing the mind and motives of another with no grounds and no proof. The critic who said that Sherlock Holmes ought to be "rewritten from the psychoanalytic angle" did not know when he was well off. "Psychology," intuition, "a certain feeling" are not evidence, which is what detection seeks. "So-and-so just wouldn't do that" may be said by the family of the accused; judge and jury will not believe it, and we as readers are judge and jury.[14]

---

14. That role explains why critical readers are annoyed when the amateur detective (or a pair of them, usually young lovers) decides that the gun or some other incriminating object must be purloined from the person suspected. Clearly, it is only

Roger Ackroyd: (which gives the adjective *acroidal*) denotes the variation used by Agatha Christie in the book of that name. Her bold departure flouted the rule of playing fair with the reader, which in that period was sacrosanct, though her denouement had been anticipated by Gaston Leroux in a very different style of plot and narrative.

Rules, the: were set down once and for all by Ronald Knox in his Introduction to an anthology of short detective stories (see No. 2614). The principal rule is that no clue shall be withheld from the reader, though the meaning of the clue may, and indeed must, be. It is possible to break some of the rules and get away with it (see *Roger Ackroyd*), but it is not possible to break them all and survive—as a writer of detection.

Straightforward: a term of praise which declares a given work to be free of an all-too-frequent fault in detective fiction, namely: false excitement. Broken sentences, obscurity or misunderstanding, incessant expletives ("My God, Gethryn!") do not generate delight in the connoisseur but exasperated boredom. Certain writers of the finest talent (e.g., John Dickson Carr, Gil North, the Lockridges) occasionally fall into this error, wherefore their *straightforward* works must be singled out.

Related Genres and the Receptive Frame of Mind

Putting our thoughts and our books in order for the preparation of this *Catalogue* disclosed that we had accumulated a number of works about the history and technique of the detective story. We also owned biographies of Conan Doyle and other masters of literary and actual detection, and a good many pieces of the curious scholarship that has grown up about Sherlock Holmes and Dr. Watson. We had in addition shelves full of criminology, scientific and social; recitals of true crime, reports of trials, and sketches of the lives of advocates. Finally, there were ghost stories and studies of the supernatural. We decided to add entries on some of these books, classified by kinds. They do not profess to exhaust the literature of their subjects, but they serve as enticing and possibly useful supplements to the main body of the work.

A browser in any section of the *Catalogue* who notices the unfavorable tenor of our comments on more than a few books by the same author may wonder why we keep reading and belaboring someone we find unsatisfactory. To explain this goatlike persistence is but to say what an avocation is. The reward of the undiscourageable is that they win unexpected bonuses —the instances where one or two pieces of good work redeem a mediocre output. The user of this guide need only read our comments: we had to read the books.

In the same spirit, yet with a difference, we have not given up rereading Freeman, Crofts, Rhode, or Burton, despite their many awkwardnesses and lavish use of cardboard. They make up for these obvious faults by

---

the villain's possession of the object that proves anything; its turning up in other hands implies nothing, except perhaps a frame-up by those who produce it. The word of an engaged couple is not evidence.

the ingenuity of their situations and lethal means, and the even greater skill of their detection. Their moral and intellectual honesty is in its way as impressive as Philip Marlowe's. And from time to time their people stray into the semblance of life and show humor, with all the more effect for its not being habitual.

But though we are catholic and hopeful and patient, we do not play the wedding guest to every ancient mariner. There are whole ranges of production, including the indestructible fungus growth of HIBK, that we steer clear of. In the *Catalogue,* the notations on the authors we have learned to ignore take the form of "identifications" in a very few lines expressive of our principled intolerance.

Still, it should be clear that our most impatient remarks spring from expectations disappointed, and not from jaded taste or the affectation of those for whom only the best is good enough. On the contrary, our humble thanks go to all the talented writers who have labored to give us pleasure (and often instruction), whether or not they fully succeeded in filling with life an exacting and treacherous form. The gratitude we convey by praise implies, as is normal, our keen sense of the further favors to come from the same source.

PART I

NOVELS
OF DETECTION,
CRIME,
MYSTERY,
AND
ESPIONAGE

Gems from the Literature

"But we did not fully understand the part they had played in the tragedy."

"So far from fully," interrupted Clay, "that we began by arresting the wrong man."
— Robert Gore-Browne, *In Search of a Villain*

Bond's knees, the Achilles heel of all skiers, were beginning to ache.
— Ian Fleming, *On Her Majesty's Secret Service*

"I'm not," answered Rocco quietly. "I'm a citizen of the United States."
"The deuce you are!"
"Yes, I was born at West Orange, New Jersey, New York State."
— Arnold Bennett, *Grand Babylon Hotel*

"Sufficient at point blank range to penetrate a man's head?" Jimmy asked.
"If not to penetrate, at least to lodge in the brain," the expert replied.
— John Rhode, *Twice Dead*

If Botesdale was on the premises, he might have raised objections to the murder of his wife.
— Miles Burton, *A Will in the Way*

"There are no limits," he said, "to the destructive instincts of efficient housemaids."
— Lord Ernest Hamilton, *The Four Tragedies of Memworth*

I fancy he had the assistance of one of your more independent morons.
— Virgil Markham, *Inspector Rusby's Finale*

Charlotte Street runs north from Oxford Street, and who can blame it?
— Len Deighton, *Horse Under Water*

1   AARONS, EDWARD SIDNEY (also Paul Ayres and Edward Ronns; b. 1916), writes stories of international intrigue headed by the word *Assignment*—e.g., *Assignment Zoraya* (1960)—in which Sam Durrel undergoes vicissitudes that thrill many readers but have little to do with detection or high-grade espionage.

2   ABBOT, ANTHONY (pseud. of Fulton Oursler; also April Armstrong and Samri Frikell; 1893–1952)

About the Murder of the Clergyman's Mistress   Covici 1931
In Eng.: The Crime of the Century

A first reading in 1968 reveals a piece of work that has faded less than the once more highly esteemed efforts of Van Dine. New York Police Commissioner Thatcher Colt is credible in everything save his impeccable attire. The author, functioning as Colt's secretary, tells about an interesting case obviously modeled on the Hall-Mills affair but, unlike that, provided with a reasonably satisfactory outcome. Sensible and straightforward.

3   ABBOT. See also:

About the Murder of Geraldine Forster   Covici 1930
About the Murder of the Night-Club Lady   Covici 1931
These Are Strange Tales (episodes of true crime,
        ghosts, and autobiography)   Winston 1948

4   ADAMS, CLEVE F. (also Franklin Charles and John Spain; 1895–1950). Prolific author of low-tension, low-credibility stories on the margin of espionage, private-eye detection, and international intrigue. *The Private Eye* (1942) may be deemed representative.

5   ADAMS, HERBERT (also Jonathan Gray; b. 1874)

The Body in the Bunker   Lipp 1935

Allowing for the slow pace and ultra-respectable atmosphere of the thirties, this is a pleasant tale, with a good bit of golf, but not too much, and an entertaining clubby atmosphere. Good dodge about fingerprints used by solicitor sleuth whom the official police respect beyond the call of duty.

6   The Crime in the Dutch Garden   Lipp 1930

A period piece, but of the best kind. An early instance of the use of the phonograph, but this is not its chief interest today. Rather, it is the slow but careful characterization, the sustained atmosphere, pleasant locale, and systematic use of the brain for unraveling puzzles.

7   The Dean's Daughters   Macd 1950

The old boy can still engineer plots and murders and keep the reader going by means of unexpected twists and good dialogue, even if the characters are thin. As a method of murder, opening a trapdoor under a candidate addressing the voters is original, plausible, and satisfying. The dean's three daughters are quite unlike and the semi-amateur detective Roger Bennion has a hard time remaining a bachelor till the end.

8   Diamonds Are Trumps   Macd 1947

A Roger Bennion story that starts out full of attractive possibilities—for H.A. is a good plot-spinner—but it bogs down in what seems like repetition, owing to an overextended flashback. The detection in the latter third is not bad, though Bennion is more namby-pamby than he was to be in later books.

9   The Golf House Murder   Lipp 1933
       In Eng.: John Brand's Will

A complex but perfectly clear tale of hanky-panky with a will, which avoids the errors that usually go with this stock situation. The fact that the reader is gripped well before the murder takes place does credit to the author's skillful management of incident and command of prose. The love story is properly subordinate and even useful to the onward march.

10   The Judas Kiss   Macd 1955

This late bloom on a solid old tree is interesting for its plot and the dramatic turns of fortune, rather than for characterization. The murder is ingenious, the motives sound, and the facing of amorous and other realities not overdone. H.A.'s style has become a little too spare and rattly, but his dialogue still has wit and keeps one going. Roger Bennion also continues to detect.

11   Oddways   Lipp 1929

This belongs to the author's early phase, in which his talents were subdued to a kind of make-believe that can be very annoying. After 1930, and even more after 1950, he fused his steady sense of detective fact with freedom about character. But note here some excellent situations and well-handled scenes.

12   The Queen's Gate Mystery   Meth 1927

A very poor affair about a house to let, full of old secrets. The main "interest" is the coming together of two young things, equally silly.

13   The Strange Murder of Hatton, K.C.   Lipp 1933

A retired barrister with a young French wife is murdered just when he has cut off his elder daughter for wanting to marry an actor. His best friend, Dr. Mark Braddon, is the detective. The events are firmly handled by both

Dr. Braddon and the author, who provides some strong scenes and a smash finish. One guesses the concealed culprit around p. 100, but the story-telling is steady, sensible, and leaves no loose ends.

14   Welcome Home   Macd 1946

The Enoch Arden theme done to a turn, with a murder ultimately solved by Roger Bennion. His creator seems to make him vulnerable chiefly to lightly clad women who invade his bedroom, but he holds his own with the gruff inspectors.

15   ADAMS, H. See also:

The Araway Oath	Coll 1942	The Old Jew Mystery	Coll 1936
The Black Death	Coll 1939	One to Play	Macd 1949
Caroline Ormsby's		The Paulton Plot	Meth 1932
Crime	Meth 1929	Roger Bennion's Double	Coll 1941
The Case of the Stolen		Rogues Fall Out	Meth 1928
Bridegroom	Coll 1940	The Secret of Bogey	
The Chief Witness	Coll 1940	House	Meth 1924
The Crime Wave at Little		A Single Hair	Coll 1937
Cornford	Macd 1948	The Sleeping Draught	Macd 1951
Death off the Fairway	Coll 1936	The Sloane Square	
The Empty Bed	Meth 1928	Mystery	Meth 1925
Exit the Skeleton	Macd 1952	The Spectre in Brown	Macd 1953
The Knife	Coll 1934	The Stab in the Back	Coll 1941
A Lady So Innocent	Meth 1932	The Woman in Black	Meth 1933
Mystery and Minette	Coll 1934	A Word of Six Letters	
The 19th Hole Mystery	Coll 1939	(= Murder Without Risk)	Coll 1936

16   AIKEN, JOAN

      Beware of the Bouquet   CCD 1966

"Suspense" produced by an incessant rattle of mishaps, journeys, threats, lies, and violence—all without sanity—makes reading a chore. Note advertising and perfume-making as adjuncts.

17   AIKEN. See also:

      Hate Begins at Home   Goll 1967
      The Silence of Herondale   Goll 1965

18   AIRD, CATHERINE (pseud. of Kim Hamilton McIntosh)

      Henrietta Who?   CCD 1968

A nicely contrived tale of multiple murders, all according to plan, for depriving a young woman of her inheritance. Systematic investigation by Inspector Sloan, red herrings (but not in excess), and a modest touch of love interest. Rural scene.

Miss A., a doctor's daughter, writes clearly and simply, and with an occasional touch of wit.

19   A Most Contagious Game   CCD 1967

This attempts the unraveling of a crime over 150 years old and does that
part of the job very well, with the aid of books, parish records, and inference. But the modern murder linked with the church, priest hole, and
mysterious happenings is scamped: motive and denouement both feeble
and hard to believe.

20   The Religious Body   CCD 1966

A prentice effort marred by loss of momentum in the middle and deception
about clues. But in spite of this inexperience and an unconvincing outcome,
the life of the nunnery is very well done, and Inspector Sloan of the
Calleshire force is most attractive.

21   The Stately Home Murder   CCD 1970

Her three earlier novels all showed promise or better, and here she comes
into her own with a tale more pleasing than any of its kind found in the
past couple of years. High praise must be given an author who is able to
incorporate just the right amounts of caricature, byplay between inspector
and constable, and description of picturesque surroundings and yet hew
close to the line of systematic investigation. The plot is credible and the
clues equally well planted for the reader and for Inspector Sloan, who
emerges here as a memorable person.

        ALBRAND, MARTHA (pseud. of Heidi Huberta Loewengard
        [Freybe], b. 1911)

b. Rostock; privately educ.; began her writing career in native German,
and has won the French prize for *littérature policière*.

22   A Day in Monte Carlo   RH 1959/1958

Her fifteenth and not badly written, but desperately trite as to causes,
events, relationships, dialogue, and denouement. The first 50 pages catch
one's attention because the technique is slick, but after that the effort to
keep up suspicion and to spread it, ending with the oldest of dodges and
the hero's rescue by outside forces, makes one skip fast and reach the final
clinch as soon as may be.

23   ALBRAND. See also No. 2459 and:

        A Call from Austria   RH 1963
        Desperate Moment   RH 1951
        A Door Fell Shut   NAL 1966

24   ALDRICH, THOMAS BAILEY (1836–1907)

        The Stillwater Tragedy   HM 1880
        A Detective Novel

Not a favorable specimen of its time or of the author's fiction. A young
man who works in a factory where labor trouble is brewing is suspected of

theft, is in love with the boss's niece, has been framed, is harshly treated by the detective, and all comes out well in the end: melodramatic trash, though said to be based on a modicum of fact.

Note that Taggett, the detective, is proved wrong because he followed circumstantial evidence. This antiratiocinative attitude is strongly maintained, seven years before *A Study in Scarlet*. Possibly T.B.A. was gunning for Anna Katharine Green.

25   ALEXANDER, DAVID (b. 1907)

The Madhouse in Washington Square   Lipp 1958
A Novel of Menace

This volume lives up to its subtitle only too well. Close to unreadable.

ALINGTON, [THE VERY REV.] C(YRIL) A(RGENTINE) (also S. C. Westerham; 1872–1955)

b. Lincolnshire; educ. Marlborough and Trinity, Oxf.; first in classics; fellow of All Souls; taught at Marlborough and Eton; headmaster of Shrewsbury Sch., then Eton; chaplain to the King; dean of Durham, 1933–51. Among works of theology and popularization, see *Europe: A Personal and Political Survey* (1946). Novels other than detection: *Archdeacons Afloat* (1946) and *Archdeacons Ashore* (1947).

26   Blackmail in Blankshire   Faber 1949

Like his other extravaganzas—and using some of the same characters—this short novelette of blackmail deals with clerical and country manners and not with crime. The blackmail is but a peg on which to hang a number of mildly amusing scenes. Inspector Greenwood does no detecting of any kind.

Note, however, the witty disquisition on personal style in detectives, pp. 142-43.

27   Crime on the Kennet   CCC 1939

This is as near as the cultivated and literary Dean can get to real situations—and there is still a gap he does not bridge. But the book is entertaining nevertheless as fantasy (which includes the author's idea of American speech).

28   Gold and Gaiters   Faber 1950

Clearly, the Dean of Durham loves mystery stories, but he contrives mysteries without writing stories. His works are essays interspersed with dialogue, the present one being an amusing ramble between and about a few non-characters involved in the theft of some gold coins from a library.

Note the excellent little digression (pp. 166–68) on fictional detectives.

29   Mr. Evans   Macm 1922
A Cricketo-Detective Story

Not much detection, and perhaps too much cricket, but a good parody of "investigation" in Chapters 5 and 6, which are extremely funny.

30   ALLARDYCE, PAULA (pseud. of Ursula Torday; also Lee Blackstock and Charity Blackstock)

Witches' Sabbath   Macm 1962

Not since *Dewey Death* by "Charity Blackstock" (q.v.) has this lady written a real detective story, though she has perpetrated some *crises de nerfs* in action, which certain critics have hailed with delight. The present volume again has a damsel in distress and no detection, but it is more acceptable than her last couple because of the fair handling of witchcraft in an English village.

31   ALLEN, H(ERBERT) WARNER (b. 1881)

The Uncounted Hour   Const 1936

This unusual solo effort by E. C. Bentley's collaborator in *Trent's Own Case* (see No. 149) must be judged disappointing, despite the presence of most of the typical elements of the thirties: puckish amateur investigator with dog; financial house party at the Towers; and Lord FitzWaren gassed in his wife's bedroom. The plot unfolds with reasonable forthrightness, and some of the devices are good, but it suffers from clutter.

ALLINGHAM, MARGERY (LOUISE) [Mrs. Philip Youngman Carter] (1904–66)

She began writing as a child, being encouraged by her parents, who also were writers and domestic storytellers. Her first published tale, *White Cottage Mystery* (1927) was a newspaper serial she soon disliked and never listed among her works. Beginning in earnest in 1929, she introduced Albert Campion in *Black Dudley,* the second of the fatuous-seeming, upper-class, young, nonprofessional detectives (Peter Wimsey was ahead of him by six years). From then on, M.A. wrote one novel a year for twenty-two years, and they were her best. When she decided to take more thought and rewrite she tended to spoil her work. After her death her husband, Youngman Carter (q.v.), continued in her footsteps.

32   The Case of the Late Pig   H&S 1937

Shorter than her other novels and very short indeed for the period, but this is all to the good, since the splendid atmosphere of strangeness, ambiguity, and suspected crime should not be drawn out farther than it is. To say more about the plot would spoil it for intending readers. Let us only say: read it.

Note: Reprinted as the leading item in *Mr. Campion Criminologist* (No. 2311).

33   Dancers in Mourning   Dday 1937
       In early ppb.: Who Killed Chloe?

A splendid achievement, not only as a plot but as an exhibition of a group of characters. Though they are nearly all performers, geniuses, and egotists, they do not pall or resemble one another, and the suspense to the last page is genuine, not pulmotored. Campion falls in love, but discreetly, and this must excuse his catching on late to the ultimate fact. Only a small dose of the egregious ex-convict–valet Lugg, and tolerable at that. Very nearly her second masterpiece.

Note: We learn here that Campion was born in 1900.

34   Death of a Ghost   Dday 1934

A fairly good piece of work, based on art forgery. Campion gets bested and nearly killed in the Underground; Inspector Oates is merely complacent and complimentary.

35   The Estate of the Beckoning Lady   Dday 1955
          In Eng.: The Beckoning Lady

The B.L. is a country pub. Campion and his Amanda are made much of, especially his connection with the nobility. Corpses are numerous and Lugg is too much in view. Otherwise an undistinguished tale, despite the unusual motive having to do with the income tax.

36   The Fashion in Shrouds   Hein 1938

Margery's masterpiece. It has all the complexity that she likes and doesn't always pull off; it makes use of Campion's brains as well as his goggles; it has Inspector Oates and no Lugg; finally, it is the first of the stories set in a dressmaking establishment, where passions are understandably violent. In this one, Margery's *dramatis personae* are distinct, and the upshot is logical and satisfying.

37   The Fear Sign   Dday 1933
          In Eng.: Sweet Danger; *also* Kingdom of Death

This tale of rural hocus-pocus, convicts, etc., might as well have stayed in ms. Albert Campion is at his most idiotic throughout.

38   Flowers for the Judge   CCD 1953; orig. 1936

Mr. Campion investigates the murder of a publisher (firm of Barnabas) in his own strong room: it is one of the good Allinghams. The family relationships are well done, the suspense is steadily maintained, and the explanation of the "miracle" is acceptable, despite Margery's steadfastly bad French.

39   The Gyrth Chalice Mystery   CCD 1931
          In Eng.: Look to the Lady
          Map of Sanctuary village (Suffolk)

An early story with good scenes and relieved from murder by elegant robbery and clerical personages, but somewhat touched by the excessive lightheartedness of the period. Fortunately short, and thus worth an hour's inspection.

The English title, from *Macbeth*, II 3, 124 and 132, is also that of No. 231.

40   More Work for the Undertaker   Dday 1949

More work for the reader than any of her other books save the very early ones. The baroque mood was on her when she wrote this tale of nightwork with hearses and horses and names such as Bloplip and Palinode. Even at the end one wonders what all the bustle was about, and one only remembers the dull grossness of Lugg, with displeasure.

41   Mystery Mile   Jarr 1930

An American judge is being hounded by a mastermind of crime to whose gang he has a cryptic but dangerous clue. Taken to England by his son, the judge seeks the protection of Mr. Campion, who behaves much more eccentrically than he would do in later tales. Too much Lugg doesn't help, and Mr. C.'s final encounter with the redoubtable Simister is very weak. One good idea: S. inherited the gang from his father!

42   Pearls Before Swine   CCD 1945

The story begins with the unspeakable Lugg and Lady Carados carrying a body up narrow stairs, and it goes on in the same *voulu* style. There are bishops and talk about French vineyards, and RAF officers, and it all adds up to a clutter. Campion does not shine.

43   Police at the Funeral   CCD 1931

A story of English family life under the domination of a strong-willed great-aunt whose weak dependents do nothing but get into trouble. It is one of the early models of this now overused situation. Campion and Inspector Oates waste strength in a good deal of byplay. Lugg exists but is not seen much. The old lady and two of the middle-aged dependents are plausible—the rest nothing. There is recurrent to-do about "Albert" and "Campion" as names that Rudolph has taken instead of his own, presumably aristocratic, name.

Note as to the last point: Miss Allingham once confided to a well-known sister novelist that Campion's destiny was to inherit the British throne.

44   Traitor's Purse   CCD 1941

Campion thinks he has killed a policeman and comes out of his mental fog rather slowly. When he does, with the aid of strangers who seem to count on him, it is to save the country from politically engineered inflation preparatory to its overthrow.

Black Plumes	CCD 1940	(contains: *The Case of the*	
The Case Book of		*Late Pig,* 1937; *Dancers in*	
Mr. Campion	AM 1947	*Mourning,* 1937; *The Tiger*	
The China Governess	Dd 1962	*in the Smoke,* 1952; *On*	
Coroner's Pidgin	Hein 1945	*Christmas Day in the*	
Crime at Black Dudley	Jarr 1929	*Morning*)	C&W 1963
The Dance of the Years	MJ 1943	No Love Lost ("The Patient	
Deadly Duo ("Wanted:		at Peacock's Hall"; "Safer	
Someone Innocent,"		Than Love"). [ss]	CCD 1954
"Last Act," ss)	Hein 1950	Tether's End	Dday 1958
The Mind Readers	Morr 1965	The Tiger in the Smoke	Dday 1952
Mr. Campion and Others	Hein 1939	The White Cottage Mystery	
The Mysterious Mr.		(det. but no Campion)	Jarr 1928
Campion			

46   AMBERLEY, RICHARD

Dead on the Stone   Hale 1969

Despite the attractive setting of a printing plant, this tale suffers from
being only the bare bones of a plot, and a somewhat overelaborate one
at that. Two murders, adultery, shop friction, security risks, blackmail—
all are dumped into a situation which would have been more credible
with a few genuine persons and some breathing space between would-be
surprises. Chief Inspector Martin, the local man at Camley, where the
plant has long been a fixture, is nonetheless a competent man. Perhaps
his creator will supply him with a better milieu at his next (and third) try.

47   AMBERLEY. See also:

Incitement to Murder   Hale 1968

48   AMBLER, ERIC (b. 1909)

The Light of Day   Knopf 1963

Ambler, whose early and successful spy stories (e.g., *A Coffin for
Dimitrios*—in England, *The Mask of Dimitrios,* 1939) had freshness and
force, has by the date of this book reached 54. This dangerous age is
perhaps reflected in the present overdose of the sensational: two accu-
sations of "sodomy" (one justified), a double exposure to the two-backed
beast, and one rectal examination for contraband. The one attractive idea
is that of looting a famous Turkish shrine.

49   State of Siege   Knopf 1956
         In Eng.: The Night Comers

Indonesian current history without tears. Rather tedious communist-
anti-communist business, enlivened by fornication with a native. Hero is

pallid. Interest quickens only when he repairs machinery in order to save the building where he and the girl are being besieged. Well written, but note that though he uses the desirable "none too sure" on p. 58, he has a relapse and writes "not too good" on p. 96.

50   AMBLER. See also:

Background to Danger			Epitaph for a Spy	Knopf 1952
(= Uncommon Danger)	H&S	1937	Journey into Fear	Knopf 1940
Cause for Alarm	Knopf	1939	A Kind of Anger	Ath 1964
Dirty Story	Ath	1967		

AMES, DELANO L. (b. 1906)

We have ascertained after a long effort that Delano implies *he,* not *she,* as is supposed somewhere in the critical literature.

51   Corpse Diplomatique   H&S 1950

Jane and Dagobert Brown are a very engaging couple in this adventure in Nice, their first in foreign parts. When a gentle blackmailer is shot dead on the Promenade, Dagobert forsakes his studies of Provençal and does a lot of solid detection, the numerous suspicious residents of his hotel providing him with a fertile field. Jane tells the story, and the humor is not forced.

52   Crime Out of Mind   IW   1956

Not so hilarious as usual; indeed rather an attack on hilarity. In the Swiss Alps, a variety of odd fish and neuropaths are gathered at an inn, whose attraction is a beautiful German girl of the overripe dirndl type, full of barroom flirtatiousness. She is mercifully killed early, but her identification requires and gets a minimum of detection.

53   For Old Crime's Sake   Lipp 1959
       In Eng.: Lucky Jane

The opportunist Dagobert Brown and his wife, Jane, are a memorable pair, and the bounce and humor that distinguish the best of the tales they adorn are hard to come by; for detection-cum-humor is a perilous assignment. Here the plot (with some real detection) features Jane and Dagobert as prize winners in a contest which sends them to the small principality of Tabarca with a mixed group of other contestants. Entertaining throughout.

54   The Man with Three Chins   Meth 1965
       A Juan Llorca Mystery

Ames has given up his young pair of English people in favor of a sergeant in the Spanish Civil Guard. Humor is still ever present, and the local color is well done, but the melodrama among Spanish grandees, English expatriates, and local Gypsies is excessive. Llorca is bright but unconvincing, and the byplay with his superiors and colleagues gets tiresome.

The new titles go for threes: *Man in the Tricorn Hat, Man with Three Passports.* Very little detection is done by Llorca, who is amorous and talkative about himself, but he does latch on to the old notion of querying descent by noticing genetic characters in "recessives." This trick was used well before 1965 by E. X. Ferrars (see No. 825).

55   The Man with Three Jaguars   Reg 1961

The usual Juan Llorca episode: a great deal of local color and credible passion but no detection—and not good enough otherwise to do without it.

56   Murder Begins at Home   H&S 1949

The second Dagobert Brown adventure is laid in Palo Alto Ranch, N.M., and it is extremely poor. The humor is about U.S. "folks," whose language and motives are ridiculed, while the underlying plot involving English and U.S. soldiers in Italy during the Second World War is murky.

57   Nobody Wore Black   Rine 1950
        In Eng.: Death of a Fellow Traveller

Told by Jane Brown about the exploits of her husband, Dagobert, in tracking down the murderer of a boy who fell off a cliff. The scene is a farm in Cornwall; there are domestic animals, including two annoying children; and the marital banter is not up to the mark.

58   She Shall Have Murder   Rine 1949

Despite rather perilous balancing on the edge of forced humor, this tale of murder in London, with a solicitor's office setting, succeeds most of the time in being funny as well as serious detection. Dagobert Brown at his best.

59   AMES. See also:

A Coffin for Christopher	IW 1954	Murder, Maestro, Please	Rine 1952
Landscape with Corpse	IW 1955	No Mourning for the	
The Man in the		Matador	IW 1953
Tricorn Hat	Meth 1960	She Wouldn't Say Who	IW 1958

60   ANGUS, DOUGLAS

        Death on Jerusalem Road   RH 1963

The author is a Canadian expatriate who has written rather prolifically after his acquisition of a Ph.D. in the U.S. Unfortunately he has not the sophistication nor the art to pull off a success with the elements of rape and revenge, high and low life in Massachusetts, and adult and juvenile delinquency, which he attempts to combine. The hero is a very unconvincing young psychologist.

61   ANONYMOUS

The Notting Hill Mystery   [Serial in *Once a Week* 1862]
    Repr. in Novels of Mystery from the Victorian Age (No.
    2138)

A brilliant mosaic of letters and affidavits, gathered by the insurance investigator Henderson, about the strange deaths of Mr. and Mrs. Anderton
and the latter's sister, Madame R. The use of mesmerism and of the mutual
influence of twins is adroitly taken advantage of, and the clueing and
writing (though marked by period traits) form a superior whole.

62   ARD, WILLIAM (THOMAS) also Ben Kerr, Jonas Ward, Thomas
      Wills (b. 1922)

A Private Party   Rine 1953

A fair sample of the better-than-average tough stuff, featuring private eye
Timothy Dane in a story of waterfront crime. The lowdown on the functioning of a high-class women's gymnasium is original and entertaining.

63   ARD. See also:

      Cry Scandal   Rine 1956
      .38   Rine 1952
      The Root of His Evil   Rine 1957

64   ARLEN, MICHAEL (pseud. of Dikran Kuyumjian, 1895–1956)

Hell! Said the Duchess   Hein 1934
    A Bedtime Story

A foolish foray into parodying detection and true crime, based on the idea
of a series of Jane the Ripper murders detected in burlesque by Colonel
Wineglass. Best forgotten.

      ARMSTRONG, ANTHONY (pseud. of George Anthony Armstrong
      Willis, b. 1897)

A soldier in the regular army, then in the RAF, a playwright, a contributor to *Punch* and *The New Yorker*. His full-length crime plays include
Mile-Away Murder (1937), *Ten-Minute Alibi* (1933), *Well Caught*
(1932).

65   A Room at the Hotel Ambre   CCD 1956
        In Eng.: Spies in Amber

A spy story by the author of the classic *Ten-Minute Alibi*. The plot complications and emotional involvements are interesting as well as amusing,
particularly if one recognizes that the author is by temperament a playwright and that the scenes should be visualized as on a stage. The atmosphere of a fifth-class Paris hotel is first-rate.

36

WHT found entertaining this adventure in the Jimmy Rezaire series, of which there are at least five, most of them with the word *Trail* in the title.

67   The Trail of Fear   MS 1929

Not strictly a detective story, but a good example of a chase after dope smugglers of the type popular in the late twenties (see Rhode's *White Menace*, appropriately advertised on the dust jacket of this book). The chase goes on continuously for 275 pages, employing both motorcar and train, and it holds the attention surprisingly well. Except for some suspicious Americanisms in the railway scenes, the English landscape is admirably rendered. Equally praiseworthy, the hero is not a superman, and his strengths and weaknesses are adroitly matched.

68   The Trail of the Lotto   MS 1930
        A Jimmy Rezaire Story

This comes after *The Secret Trail:* that is all we know, though perhaps not all we need to know.

69   ARMSTRONG, ANTHONY, and SHAW, HERBERT

        Ten-Minute Alibi   Meth 1934

A version in novel form of the play of the same name. Excellent plot and neat presentation, with some character drawing. JB saw and enjoyed the play in Paris, when it was given by Edward Stirling's English Players, who toured the Continent between 1922 and 1940. (See No. 2801.)

70   ARMSTRONG, A. See also:

        He Was Found in the Road   Meth 1952
        The Poison Trail   Benn 1932
        The Strange Case of Mr. Pelham   Dday 1957
        Without Witness (with Harold Simpson; a play)   Goll 1934

71   ARMSTRONG, CHARLOTTE [Mrs. Jack Lewi] (also Jo Valentine; 1905–69)

        A Little Less than Kind   Ace 1963

A study of wayward youth in Southern California, by a writer whose abilities are genuine, even though not congenial to these assessors of the detective genre. Such voluble tales as *The Unsuspected* (1946) and *A Dram of Poison* (1956) are primarily suspense, often irritatingly so.

        ARTHUR, FRANK (pseud. of Arthur Frank Ebert, b. 1902)

London-born civil servant, A.F. seems to consider himself more a playwright than a novelist. He lists in A&W three "and other" plays but only two of his Suva novels of crime and detection. From these last it appears that Arthur is a poet who lived for some years in Fiji but left before the war.

72   Another Mystery in Suva   Hein 1956

This is a worthy sequel to the exploits of Inspector Spearpoint. The characters are well distributed, the oppressive atmosphere is not overdone, and
although the murderer is fairly evident before the end of the narrative, the
reader is still eager to find out the arrangements that permitted the deed
to take place.

73   Murder in the Tropic Night   HJ 1961

Well below the standard of the first two, despite several amusing incidents.
A Suva matron of irritable disposition and overbearing manner is
strangled and trussed upside down on a flagstaff atop a hill one hundred
miles west of Suva. Pretty much everyone in the nearby town is put under
suspicion by Inspector Spearpoint, whose work in this book falls rather
flat.

74   The Throbbing Dark   HJ 1963

Despite the absurd title, and an overuse of the word *throbbing* in the text,
this is by no means a bad tale. Spearpoint's personality has suffered, and
there is less humor than before, but the problem of how the deaths of
two plug-uglies in bachelor quarters came about is attractively presented.
Much local color and half-color and even quadroon.

75   Who Killed Netta Maull?   .   Goll 1941
      A Story of Murder in the Fiji Islands
      Map of principal streets of Fiji
      In ppb.: The Suva Harbour Mystery

A reversal of opinion occurred after a second reading in August 1957.
Inspector Spearpoint, with his abdominal exercises (see No. 1171), is a
person of stature and intelligence who does a good job of work; and the
discovery of Netta's most persistent characteristic is a first-rate surprise
nicely held back.
   Note the effect of bad literature and worse mores on the Suva setting as
depicted 28 years later in *Escale à Pago-Pago* by Gérard de Villiers (Plon
1969).

76   ASHBY, R(UBIE) C(ONSTANCE) b. 1899

      Death on Tiptoe   H&S n.d. [1931]

Certainly a story out of the ordinary—in setting, motive, and development.
In a castle in southern Wales, bought by an amiable millionaire with a
beautiful wife, her murder, the suicide of her husband's cousin, a petty
theft, and other puzzling events are unraveled by a bullying inspector and a
K.C. who is the host's oldest friend as well as an acquaintance of the inspector's. There are some well-defined characters, some needless melodrama, and a few questionable points, but on the whole it is creditable
mystery and detection besides.

77   ASHBY. See also:

He Arrived at Dusk   H&S 1933
Out Went the Taper   Macm 1934

78   ASHE, GORDON (pseud. of John Creasey, q.v.)

The Man Who Laughed at Murder   Dday 1960

This is a cock-and-bull story of three men formerly in police work who
are threatened by what appear to be a released convict and his friends.
One wife falls a victim to them, and the men are bombed every few pages
without our being told how the booby traps could be laid where they were.
In the end the murderer is unconvincing. For a better try at a similar
theme, see *To Protect the Guilty* (Walker, 1970).

79   ASHFORD, JEFFREY (pseud. of Roderic Graeme Jeffries [q.v.], b.
      1926)

The Burden of Proof   Harp 1962

The unedifying account of a young philanderer caught up in the toils of
the law because his former mistress is found dead of an overdose of abortion pills. The ensuing trial is dull, and there is no other satisfaction for
the reader.

80   Counsel for the Defense   Harp 1961

A fair account of the routine police investigation of an English bank robbery (an "inside job," though committed partly outdoors), embellished
with a highly unlikely though clever procedure by counsel for the guilty.

81   The D.I.   Harp 1961

The author turns his hand to straightforward reporting of the day-to-day
problems of a detective inspector in a medium-sized English city. The
rather too neat plot permits the solution of one crime to unravel another
involving a frame-up. Let it be added that the author has the taste to keep
his D.I.'s bed life well in the background.

82   ASIMOV, ISAAC

A Whiff of Death   Goll 1958

This brilliant expositor of science and science fiction has the right idea
about detection, and in this first try he makes an evident effort to clue, deceive, and detect. It is in fact the careful expansion of a long short story
done years ago. But the surroundings, which the author imagines as a
professor in a medical school, are occasionally out of tune for an undergraduate chemistry lab; while the ineffectual husband-professor whose conscience racks him and nearly wrecks his marriage gets to be a bore. The
tale as a whole is nonetheless worth a reading.

83   ATKINSON, ALEX (H.) (1916–1962)

Exit Charlie   Knopf 1956; orig. 1955

A first (and last) detective story by a British actor, playwright, and novelist who wrote frequently for *Punch*. The story is lively and terse; the characters are credible and attractive, yet none of this is at the expense of the
physical surroundings, which, being a provincial repertory theater, are both
picturesque and difficult to describe in short compass. The murder and its
motive are excellent, the detection reasonable, and the double red herring
satisfactory.

84   AUDEMARS, PIERRE (also Peter Hodemart)

The Crown of Night   Harp 1962

Pinaud takes on an interesting case in Haute Savoie and finally unveils a
notorious murderess who has got away with it four times. The proposed
fifth victim is a former army friend of P.'s. Good scenery and amusing
village politics. Does not drag despite foregone conclusion.

85   The Turns of Time   Harp 1961

M. Pinaud, a Parisian inspector of police who "knows something about
everything," takes on the job of guarding famous diamonds in the guise
of a shop salesman. The suspicious death of a watchmaker on the premises
provides him with numerous suspects. Not much detection but some amusing philosophy. The agreeable lore about timepieces probably comes from
the author's connection with the makers of the famous Audemars Piguet
watches.

86   AUSTIN, ANNE (b. 1895). Although her Inspector Dundee is a Yale
man solving crimes in the best society, tales such as *Murder Backstairs*
(1930) remain poorly motivated and unconvincing.

BAGBY, GEORGE (pseud. of Aaron Marc Stein; also Hampton
Stone; b. 1906)

With two exceptions noted below, it is only as Hampton Stone that this
author is tolerable to these bibliographers, for the reasons given under that
name. But it must be acknowledged that the large output of the Bagby-
Stein-Stone amalgamation commands the respect due all assiduity and self-
imposed standards.

87   The Body in the Basket   Dday 1954

Though the action takes place in Madrid and is conducted by Inspector
Schmidt, the incidents, plot, characters, and detection are all so far
superior to G.B.'s usual U.S. standard that JB found them all credible and
even delightful. The variety of scenes within the general foreignness bor-
rows a little from the atmosphere of postwar spy novels, yet it never degenerates into mere Ambling—and Inspector Schmidt has the grace, de-

spite the climate, to keep his shoes on for longer at a time than he ever manages to do on his native soil.

88   Corpse Candle   Dday 1967

Rural shenanigans in the middle of a wood, where the narrator Bagby nearly gets killed and a later murder is pulled off. Inspector Schmidt comes in late to solve a case more entertaining by its scene and characters than its plot.

BAILEY, H(ENRY) C(HRISTOPHER) (1878–1961)

Educ. Corpus Christi, Oxf., took first-class honors on the classical side, then devoted himself to the *Daily Telegraph* from 1901 to 1946. He wrote innumerable Reggie Fortune stories, half a dozen of which are small masterpieces and the rest sheer repetition and tedium. Afterward he created Joshua Clunk, but we are not amused. For the short stories, see Nos. 2334–9.

89   The Bishop's Crime   Coll 1940
        Also in No. 2336

This novel holds up very well on rereading. The suspense and the scattering of suspicion among the leading characters is admirably contrived. So is the motive and the working out of the plot, except for two elements: one, the introduction and use of the children, both tiresome; and the inexplicable step by which the criminals try to sell "the clue to the hidden treasure" before securing that treasure itself. Reggie eats a lot but does not act too infuriatingly cryptic and ejaculative.

90   Black Land, White Land   CCD 1937

In this tale of feud between new-rich and impoverished gentility in "Durshire" Reggie does a bit of deducing, and the author holds things reasonably together for a few chapters, but then futility takes over.

91   Life Sentence   CCD 1946

Although purporting to be an early exploit of Reggie Fortune's, the story shows Bailey and Fortune on their last legs: overfondness for mistreated children, cross-purposes with, and suspicion of, official police play much too large a part, Lomas is only briefly seen and Superintendent Bell not at all.

92   BAKER, RICHARD M(ERRIAM) (b. 1896)

        Death Stops the Manuscript   Scrib 1936
        Introd. by S. S. Van Dine

Only a preface by a practitioner could have got this story published in the mid-thirties. The prefacer expatiates on how fair, honest, and plain the plot-spinner is in his narrative, but the reader finds the events, characters, and motives alienating altogether. Franklin Russell is a bore; the talk veers from the stilted to the feebly colloquial; and there is no action until a short and fairly good scene at the end.

93   BAKER. See also:

Death Stops the Bells   Scrib 1938
Death Stops the Rehearsal   Scrib 1937

94   BALL, JOHN (DUDLEY)

The Cool Cottontail   Harp 1966
    *Author's ack. to various sunbathing
    associations and the Pasadena police*

A bit below the level of his first. The crime now is the murder of an inventor, but the motive and the criminal are not entirely persuasive. The engaging Tibbs moves around more but does less than in the earlier story, and the nudist setting lends only a modicum of local color.

95   In the Heat of the Night   Harp 1965

The Negro detective working under handicaps in the Southern city where he has been visiting is both likable and credible. Virgil Tibbs is said to have a topnotch reputation in his home force (Pasadena), and the author has him produce enough real observation and deduction to justify this. The crime is casual but perfectly possible; the local color is excellent and not overdone. (The movie was good, too, but quite different at many points.)

96   BALZAC, HONORÉ DE (1799–1850)

The Thirteen   Macm 1901; orig. 1833–1835
    Histoire des Treize, *trans. by Ellen Marriage*
    Pref. by G[eorge] S[aintsbury]

Balzac was inspired by the true and legendary feats of Vidocq to create a similar convict-policeman, whom he named Vautrin and to whom he attributed many secret machinations running through half a dozen novels and tales. One group of these, in the book under discussion, joined to this characteristic figure of the early nineteenth century the doings of a band of well-born men of daring, who kept up in secret and for their private advantage a war against society. Balzac thereby furnished the model of the Napoleon of crime as well as of the gentleman-criminal who preys on society out of pride—ever-flourishing types, whether called Dr. Moriarty, Raffles, Arsène Lupin, or the Four Just Men.

The one masterpiece in these linked episodes is "The Girl with the Golden Eyes," a brilliant study of lesbianism combined with predatory instincts. In the social observation that Balzac could not help interweaving with his melodramas, he anticipated the sort of milieu now being depicted for us by Hammett, Chandler, Ross Macdonald, and their followers. In addition Balzac was a keen believer in detection by physical clues. See No. 2344, Introd., and F. Roux, *Balzac jurisconsulte et criminaliste* (Paris, 1906).

Note: Saintsbury's short preface makes good points about the criminal in fiction and the taste therefor.

97   BARBETTE, JAY (pseud. of Bart Spicer, b. 1918)

Look Behind You   DM 1960

The author of *Dear Dead Days* gives us here his fourth, which is not detection but anxiety and chase, yet more plausible than most such tales, thanks to good writing. Still, not likely to be kept for rereading.

98   BARLOW, JAMES

The Burden of Proof   HH 1968

The planning of a great robbery by thugs and their dupes in gambling joints and call houses. The public is on the criminals' side and refuses help in capture. Odd without being finally interesting.

99   BARRETT, MONTE (1897?–1949)

Murder at Belle Camille   BM 1943

It rides—or skids, rather—on Southern charm and voodoo at an old plantation: amateurish and feeble.

100   BARRY, CHARLES (pseud. of Charles Bryson, b. 1877)

The Corpse on the Bridge   Dutt 1928

Although Inspector Gilmartin identifies the corpse's odd underwear as "monastic" quite early in the case, he makes little progress and admits on p. 255 that in the course of his whole career he has "never muddled a case so badly." Lay brothers and even a lay Chinaman do nothing to enliven a dull business.

101   The Detective's Holiday   Meth 1926

Inspector Gilmartin is spending his vacation at Le Levandou, where he has ingratiated himself with the natives by speaking their language and keeping out of their affairs. The murder of an English sailor draws him into a complicated business, which he solves after an inordinate amount of tramping and driving about. The French characters are comic and the English stagy, though all are "lovable." Barry, in short, is writing for children, though he doesn't know it.

102   The Witness at the Window   Dutt 1927

Not all period pieces have the power to charm. On the whole, the Coles did this better with *Poison in a Garden Suburb;* here the murder in Letch-

wyn Garden City as finally worked out by Inspector Gilmartin is sheer
tedium. The readers agree (by 1965) that they have had their Barry-full.

Association Item
103 BARSLEY, MICHAEL (b. 1919)

Orient Express   Macd 1966
The Story of the World's Most Fabulous Train
Endpaper maps; numerous photographs

The book is excellent—and not fabulous. In short compass and with great
accuracy—though no gift of style—the author gives the history of the
train from its beginning in 1883 to near the time of its demise. Description, anecdote, timetables, and all other desirable details, mechanical and
biographical, are supplied in well-organized fashion. Chapter 11 deals
competently with the works of fiction associated with the train. The map
makes clear the routes of the seven trains that once constituted *the* Orient
Express.

104 BASHFORD, [SIR] H(ENRY) H(OWARTH)

Behind the Fog   Harp 1927
Map of Helvik region

The first 125 pages present a good motorcar situation arising from the
kidnapping in London of good-looking girls. But the band of amateurs—
three men and two women—who go in pursuit of the malefactors as far as
a remote Norwegian island spend too much time traipsing, conferring,
eating, and disguising themselves improbably. The finish up north falls
flat.
    Note: The author was chief medical officer of the British Post Office.
See also No. 2345.

105 BAWDEN, NINA (pseud. of Nina Mary Kark, b. 1925)

Who Calls the Tune   Coll 1953

An unusual tale, handling its normal and abnormal psychology with excellent judgment. It is *acroidal,* latter-day style, with enjoyable Shropshire
atmosphere and a fair amount of solid police work. The *femme fatale*
who dominates the story has a wooden leg and is dead after Chapter 1,
but her influence and interest are very great.

106 BAX, ROGER (pseud. of Paul Winterton, also Andrew Garve, q.v.;
     b. 1908)

Death Beneath Jerusalem   Nels 1947/1938

The tale is a good suspense story, largely underground in both senses of
the word. The characters are a bit thinner than those the author as
Andrew Garve was to draw later, but they are workmanlike and plausible.
And the swim in the Dead Sea is a fine foreshadowing. (A very scarce
item.)

107   A Grave Case of Murder   Harp 1951

A good but not outstanding specimen of the large English family celebrating the rich old man's birthday—his one hundredth in this case. The
plotting and detection are sufficient but not memorable.

108   The Trouble with Murder   Harp 1948
       In Eng.: Blueprint for Murder

The carefully planned murder of a rich uncle, on the strength of a built-in
alibi. What goes wrong is, of course, the point of the story, plus a large
dose of Bax's favorite small-craft-on-high-seas adventure. Suspense rather
than detection and not easy to remember, despite the author's usual skill
in handling detail.

109   Two if by Sea   Harp 1949
       In Eng.: Came the Dawn

An enchanting tale, not hackneyed, despite its English title. The story is a
by-product of the author's Russian experience (see No. 964). Here the
motive power is the desire of two Englishmen to get their Russian wives
out of the ironbound country, by means of raiding by small boat. Very fine.
Clark Gable proved it so in the film *Never Let Me Go.*

110   BAX. See also:

       Disposing of Henry   Harp 1947
       Red Escapade   Skef 1940

111   BEEDING, FRANCIS (pseud. of John Leslie Palmer, 1885–1944, and
       Hilary Aidan St. George Saunders, b. 1898)

       Death Walks in Eastrepps   H&S 1931

Multiple murders in an English seaside town. Well written, though today it
seems quaint here and there. The two maps also belong to the period, but
not the surprise ending.

112   The Norwich Victims   Harp 1935

A story built on a plot that deserved livelier treatment: a scheme to fleece
trusting investors from the provinces, a school matron who wins a French
lottery prize, and some shady and some amiable characters, none of them
quite "stock." All this good stuff goes to waste for lack of firm direction.

       BELL, JOSEPHINE (pseud. of Doris Bell Collier Ball, b. 1897)

She is a physician who practiced in London until 1954 and who, before
and since, has written more than she should if she had any hope of becoming a classic. This is a pity, for she had knowledge, she can write, and
her vein of invention is not shallow. But her execution does not always
match her conception, and she neglects credibility and pace. The comments below show what extremes of good and bad she permits herself.
She has also written an earnest and valuable study, *Crime in Our Time*
(see No. 3076).

113   Curtain Call for a Corpse   Macm 1965; orig. 1939
In Eng.: Death at Half Term

The mystery is why this excellent story was allowed to lie twenty-six years unpublished in the U.S. It deals with theatricals but sets them in a school, which surely doubled the chances of going mushy and trashy. Instead, the author polishes off victim and murderer in four quick days, and leaves her critical readers only one or two regrets about small details: excellent.

114   Death at the Medical Board   LG 1944

The description on the paperback cover ". . . an original publication—not a reprint" is misleading. Dr. Bell is not writing directly for mass consumption. The tale is a wartime one and much better done than most of her recent stuff. Dr. Wintringham does a creditable job of finding out who gave the nicotine and how.

115   Death in Retirement   Macm 1956

A remarkable tale of impersonation. A nurse coming back from India in company with a woman doctor assumes a false role until discovered through her part in subsequent crimes. Quiet writing, good characterization, and some neat though not abundant detection.

116   Death of a Con Man   Lipp 1968

Dr. Colin Frost is innocently involved in the death (in hospital after an accident) of a man wanted by the police. Another doctor and a journalist help Inspector Rawlinson. Better (i.e., more active) Bell than usual lately.

117   Death on the Reserve   Macm 1966

With an attractive peninsular setting (N.W. English coast, not India!), this should have been an entertaining tale. But the characters are drab and the villains not convincingly villainous. A retired physician, Dr. Frost, is the unenergetic sleuth, impeded by his relatives on holiday. The predatory habits of gulls provide the only really serious note.

118   Double Doom   Macm 1958

This is a deplorable book, full of preposterous characters, not one of whom can be admired even for his vice. Professional detection is nil, and the amateur halfhearted; the real heroine, if any, is mentally deficient; and the three murders are uninteresting and crudely carried out.

119   Easy Prey   Macm 1959

The author's skill in handling elderly women is still evident, but this is a bumbling tale. WHT could not be brought to care which of the colorless characters had "done it" (i.e., killed an unwanted child), and was roused from his apathy only by the discovery that Dr. Bell believes carbon monoxide to be denser than air.

120   Fall Over Cliff   Macm 1956/1938
        Murder Revisited Series

A fair story in which Dr. David Wintringham plays the plausible sleuth
(a parallel to Basil Willing, but more ambulatory). The crime turns out
a disappointment, but the characterization is good and the action straightforward.

121   Fiasco in Fulham   Macm 1963
        In Eng.: A Flat Tyre in Fulham

Both flat and a fiasco: the unlikely mastermind "folds" much too easily,
and aside from the Dickensian name of one of the victims—Jeremy Ditch-
ling—the sole merit is to be found in the uncertainty in which we are left
concerning the actual involvement in vice of the elderly philanthropist. In
this one Dr. Bell is a better psychologist than mystery writer.

122   Murder in Hospital   LG 1937

A good example of its kind. The characterization is not first-rate but
locale, action, and motives are engaging.

123   No Escape   Macm 1965
        Author's Note on drug addiction and crime in England

Dr. Timothy Long, surgical registrar at a London hospital, pulls a young
woman from the Thames and becomes involved in mystery, with the help
of an attractive nurse. For Dr. Bell the book is something of a change in
the direction of briskness in dialogue and plotting, perhaps because the
subject of drug addiction and crime among the young deeply concerns
her as a physician and humanitarian (see No. 3076). The hospital setting
is admirably used, and barring a little cardboard and some unnecessary
danger to the young hero, one may call the work a success in the good
genre.

124   The Port of London Murders   LG 1938

Disliked for several good reasons by JB and for only one less by WHT. It
is, among other bad things, exceedingly long, and J. Bell lacks D. Sayers'
staying power.

125   The Seeing Eye   H&S 1963; orig. 1958

The background of art gallery and artists is not "realized" as Innes can
do it, and the detection is little more than genteel fumbling by Dr. Wintringham and his wife, during which they bring civilizing influences to bear
on one of the suspects. The actual murder plot is not striking and turns into
a huddle at the end.

126   The Summer School Mystery   Meth 1950

Music school setting. Victim appropriately found in his own kettledrum.
Despite this apt disposal, a poor tale.

Boucher's opinion that this is a well-managed tale, messy only at the end, is hard to sustain. The characters are featureless, the professional detectives less amusing than they are patently intended to be, and only the initial situation, a disbarred medico found murdered in his former home after his sudden return, is at all inviting.

128   The Wilberforce Legacy   Walk 1969

Miss Bell again indulges her liking for decrepit heroes. All the picturesque setting in "Princeton, San Fernando" (= Kingston, Jamaica) couldn't make WHT care very much about what had happened to the elderly Mr. Wilberforce.

BELL, VICARS (WALKER) (b. 1904)

Headmaster of the Little Gaddesden C. of E. School and a writer on language and church matters. Has produced at least half a dozen detective stories, three or four "straight" novels, and a play on the Nativity.

129   Death Darkens Council   Faber 1952

Told in the first person by Dr. Baynes, a lame entomologist. He interferes only moderately in the activities of the county constabulary. Village life is played up rather far, but not insufferably so. Well-designed but with an easily spotted criminal and method.

130   BELL, V. See also:

Death and the Night Watches	Faber 1955
Death Has Two Doors	Faber 1950
Death Under the Stars	Faber 1949
Death Walks by the River	Faber 1959
Two by Day and One by Night	Faber 1950

BELLAIRS, GEORGE (pseud. of Harold Blundell, b. 1902)

A graduate of the London School of Economics and a superintendent of banks in his native Lancs. He has written about forty novels of detection. He also works on hospital boards and has a penchant for good wine and food.

131   The Corpse at the Carnival   Giff 1958

Another Isle of Man story. Old Uncle Fred is killed while walking on the Parade in Douglas. It is mysterious indeed, but Inspector Littlejohn functions routinely.

132   Death Before Breakfast   Giff 1962

This and the earlier *Death in High Provence* suggest that old hand Bellairs has taken a new lease on life and learned to write more simply and with fewer irritating characters to "amuse" the reader. Inspector Littlejohn can be solid and competent, and his investigation of what appears to be a commonplace and sordid crime (dead man in a gutter) in a shabby London street is more impressive than most of Creasey's high-powered Gideon turns.

133   Death in High Provence   Giff 1957

Picked up (and paid for) by WHT during a Canadian jaunt in September 1963, this struck him as distinctly better than average Bellairs, with few of this author's unnerving attempts at humor. The French scene is done with love and knowledge.

134   Death in the Night Watches   Macm 1946

Typical Bellairs, though with less byplay than usual. In short, fairly straightforward but unmemorable.

135   Death in the Wasteland   Giff 1963

Undistinguished except for the jacket design by Edward Gorey. Otherwise a regular southern France business (Wasteland = *l'Estérel*), in which a corpse is stolen and Inspector Littlejohn is nearby to help out the French police.

136   Death on the Last Train   Macm 1949

Despite some fair technicalities about the "last train" and its stoppage in mid-country, this is a very poor story, which evolves wholly by question and answer. What is more, G.B. has adopted for this postwar affair the modern style of dwelling upon all the disgusting personal details he can find.

137   Half-Mast for the Deemster   Giff 1953

The Manx local color is well done, but the plot of blackmail and smuggling grows much too complicated before the huddled ending. All the characters except the Archdeacon, the Deemster, his widow, and Littlejohn, the detective, are stock figures whose actions are tedious. The pitched battle toward the end is good fun but solves nothing. JB further excepts the barmaid, who is quite a study.

138   BELLAIRS. See also:

The Case of the Seven Whistlers	Macm 1948
Dead March for Penelope Blow	Macm 1951
Death Treads Softly	Macm 1956
Littlejohn on Leave	Giff 1941
Murder Makes Mistakes	Macm 1958
Toll the Bell for Murder	Macm 1959

139   BELLOC, HILAIRE (1870–1953)

But Soft—We Are Observed!   Arr 1928
        Drawings of the three sleuths by G. K. Chesterton

Another attempt at foolery with serious overtones by two friends who worked to better purpose separately than together.

140   Shadowed!   Harp 1929
       With 37 drawings by G. K. Chesterton

A fantasy concocted by these two well-known friends on the vague
analogy of a story of chase and crime. Its date is half a century ahead
(1979) and it is full of references to political events conducive to satire.
The five sleuths and the self-conscious narration do not bring it up to the
level of *The Man Who Was Thursday;* the drawings are slight but
amusing.

              BENNETT, (ENOCH) ARNOLD (1867–1931)

Not a writer of detective fiction though often mentioned as such, on
the strength of an average interest in mystification and inquiry. But see
below: Nos. 2348–9.

141   Buried Alive   Brent n.d. [1908]
       A Tale of These Days

Mostly satirical about the London art world at the turn of the century,
but at the same time a good adventure story about a painter who manages
his own official death and has to face the consequences of this crime—
since it is a fraud.

142   T. Racksole and Daughter   NAB 1902
       In Eng.: Grand Babylon Hotel

Anybody who calls this work a detective story is in need of psychiatric
care. The original cause of its being so listed in dozens of histories and
book catalogues is lost, but the fact is that the tale is a long extravaganza
of the Ruritanian kind, done rather absentmindedly by a novelist who
could do much better even in the light and semicriminal genres.
    Note: Bennett wrote the book in three weeks, after being taken to tea
for the first time at the Savoy. T. Racksole is an American millionaire,
who buys a comparable hotel and finds himself and his daughter embroiled
in international intrigue.

143   BENNETT, MARGOT (b. 1903)

       The Man Who Didn't Fly   Harp 1956

Her first after a longish interlude and a promising though unsatisfactory
new try. It starts with a doubt as to the identity of the man who missed
the plane that crashed. He is detected by reference to regions of the
earth where he has or has not been, and his unmasking furthers an obvious love story. There is less detection and characterizing than in *Time to
Change Hats* ten years earlier, but a commendable stripping down of style
and detail.

144   BENNETT, See also:

       Away Went the Little Fish   Dday 1947
       Farewell Crown and Goodbye King   Walk 1961
       Someone from the Past   Dutt 1958
       Time to Change Hats   Dday 1946

145   Benson, Ben

The End of Violence   Mill 1959

The latest of a long series of tales in which the young (Mass.) state trooper Ralph Lindsey figures as a likable official sleuth. Here we have a good study of falsely imputed brutality neatly interwoven with a murder, but it is less original and certainly no more mature than the adventures of some years back. Perhaps Lindsey is to age in the manner of Dr. Priestley, at a glacier-like rate of progress.

146   Benson, E(dward) F(rederic) (1867–1940)

The Blotting Book   Dday 1908

This tale has the makings of a first-rate detective story, but it fails to materialize as such. An English solicitor and partner embezzle the funds of a nice young man who has just got engaged. Murder follows with incriminating evidence planted to convict the young man of forgery and defamation of character. The trial vindicates him by a single clue.

Bentley, E(dmund) C(lerihew) (1875–1956)

This English journalist, novelist, and poet was the regenerator of the long detective novel in English. He gave the model for the 1920 renaissance in his classic *Trent's Last Case* (1912) (in U.S.: *The Woman in Black*, 1913). Then came *Trent's Own Case*, with H. Warner Allen (1936). Meanwhile E.C.B. had published a number of short stories, all but one gathered in *Trent Intervenes* (1938). See No. 2351. *Those Days* (1940) is an excellent autobiography, and *Elephant's Work* (1950) a deplorable thriller-fantasy.

147   Elephant's Work   Knopf 1950

Not detection. As fantasy, only fair; as adventure, pretty poor, since all the bad men turn out frauds.

148   Trent's Last Case   Knopf 1930; orig. Nels 1912
      With a line sketch of the author facing title

The publishing history (Eng. ed. 1912; U.S. 1913; Knopf 1930; G&D 1939; ModL. 1941; PB 1944; many reprintings of each) and the critical consensus alike point to an undoubted classic. The book is in every way admirable, though it seems to JB a flaw and not a merit that the final twist should have three and not two turns: the motive is weakened, the surprise has been overstretched. Still, the outcome does not take away from the masterly development of the problem and the brilliant conduct of the detection.

Note that the film in which Orson Welles played Manderson was very faithful to the story—and very dull.

149   BENTLEY, E. C., and ALLEN, H. W.

Trent's Own Case   Knopf 1936

The problem is gripping and its solution good solid work. If only Bentley's generation of English writers had not strongly believed that all things mysterious and titillating must happen in France, the tale would be nearly as perfect as its predecessor.

It appears from the record that Penguin has issued this book twice.

150   BENTLEY, JOHN

The Landor Case   C&H 1937

This is one of a fairly ambitious series of Sir Richard Herrivell stories: the *Berg, Griffith, L'Estrange, Opperman,* and *Fairbairn* case(s) precede it. The present specimen is certainly one Herrivell tale, in WHT's opinion. It is the British equivalent of an S. S. Van Dine, complete with phony footnotes, persuasive reference to real persons, and a hero (Sir R.) not unlike Philo Vance. But Bentley is not of the caliber of W. H. Wright, and although his hero has a pretty enough taste in white wines, he's uncertain about his pronouns.

For the record, this story deals with a raid on a gambling establishment in London, followed by the discovery of its owner apparently dead by suicidal hanging in a locked-and-barred room.

BENTLEY, NICOLAS (CLERIHEW) (b. 1907)

b. Highgate, son of E. C. Bentley (q.v.); educ. Univ. Coll. Sch., London, Heatherley School of Art; m. daughter of Sir Patrick Hastings (q.v.). Director of A. Deutsch, Ltd., publisher. His illustrated book, *Gammon and Espionage* (1938), is parody, not adventure.

151   The Tongue-Tied Canary   DS 1949

The third book by the son of E. C. Bentley. The plot is thin, though the suspense is kept up, and the dialogue and description are not nearly so witty as in *The Floating Dutchman,* being imitation Americanese. Moreover, the hero-investigator of the Special Branch does everything to land himself in trouble that he has no real right to escape from.

152   BENTLEY, N. See also:

    The Floating Dutchman   MJ 1950
    Third-Party Risk   MJ 1948

BERCKMAN, EVELYN (DOMENICA) (b. 1900)

American-born (Phila.) author of suspense stories, Miss B. lives in London and produces at a praiseworthy—that is, moderate—rate, which permits her to give care and finish to her work, as well as allows the well of her originality to refill.

Although outside our territory, this nicely written and mercifully short exercise in the Gothic genre merits an entry for its historical skill. Miss B. has researched her mid-Victorian period thoroughly and has produced some credible characters. The mystery is that concerning the particular form which the erotic symbols in the "Folly" at Starvelings will take. Here the author does pretty well, although her ladylike heroine fails to inspect closely enough to please the exacting reader.

154   No Known Grave   DM 1958

This story is solidly based on a little-understood murder of seven years earlier. The young lawyer Kirk Halstead is his own detective, and there is good characterization and action. Scene near Albany. Powerful ending. Only a few annoying verbal mannerisms borrowed from England ("all that unmistakably") and a lack of judgment in the last few pages mar an otherwise good novel.

155   The Strange Bedfellow   DM 1956

Miss B. writes extremely well and spins a good yarn, even if her subjects are a little beyond credibility and her work slights detection. Here the inevitable young woman is an archaeologist who gets amorously involved with an attractive chap of dubious motives. The machinations take her to Germany, where she loses her illusions and nearly her life in the search for historic facts and relics.

156   BERCKMAN. See also:

Blind Girl's Buff	DM 1962	Lament for Four Brides	DM 1959
The Blind Villain	DM 1957	A Simple Case of Ill-Will	DM 1964
Do You Know This Voice?	DM 1960	Stalemate	DM 1966
The Evil of Time	DM 1954	A Thing That Happens	
The Hovering Darkness	DM 1957	to You	DM 1964
		The Voice of Air	Dday 1970

BERESFORD, J(OHN) D(AVYS) (1873–1949)

The Beresfords are a huge tribe and a house of lords all by themselves. Besides novels and short stories, JDB wrote a book about H. G. Wells in 1915.

157   An Innocent Criminal   Dutt 1931

By the author of "The Artificial Mole," a short story appearing in more than one anthology (see Nos. 2323 and 2352). The novel is remarkable for anticipating by some twenty years the currently popular suspense plot and also for a pleasing evenness of tone. Told in the first person in easygoing fashion by a young civil servant recently come into a fortune, it takes 157 pages out of a total 250 to get to the inquest on a crime committed two years before the story opens. Competent detection by two professionals is in line with the generally soft-focus presentation.

158   The Instrument of Destiny   Jac 1928
          A Detective Story

A pity! This author did several good things on the edge of detective fiction, but when he tackled the genre itself he failed. Not that his present plot and characters are not potentially good for a rousing murder mystery. But something went wrong when he planned the narrative, and especially the denouement. The culprit is probably the only one of his kind in the whole range of the literature, and correspondingly unbelievable.

159   BERESFORD, J. D. See also Nos. 2614, 3404, 3442 and (not detection):

The Decoy	Coll 1927/1936
The House in Demetrius Road	Hein 1914
The Meeting Place and Other Stories	Faber 1929
The Monkey Puzzle	Coll 1925

BERESFORD, LESLIE (GEORGE) (b. 1899)

A writer and lecturer on metallurgy at Handsworth Tech. Coll. Has also written under the pseudonym Pan, but what he has so written is not vouchsafed by our sources.

160   What's at the End?   HJ 1937

Eight people, strangers to each other, find themselves beneficiaries under the will of Colenso Hargreaves. At the Chateau de Maroc in the south of France, the ill-assorted party is gradually depleted by assorted murders, in which (*pace* Knox) the author is rash enough to involve a Chinaman. A little detecting is done by the one strong "legatee," Justin Marsh, but all goes for naught when revelations are made about the testator. A rather intriguing situation poorly handled.

161   BERESFORD, L. See also:

The Way of Deception   Odhams 1922

BERKELEY, ANTHONY (pseud. of Anthony Berkeley Cox; also Francis Iles and A. B. Cox; b. 1893)

A prolific writer and reviewer of detection (as Francis Iles), A. B. Cox belongs to the phalanx that ushered in the Golden Era. He is reticent about his career, but it has become legendary knowledge that he made his debut in humorous journalism, prepared for the bar, and lives (or lived) in St. John's Wood. He was the practical force behind the founding of the Detection Club, and on several occasions he has theorized about new departures in detective fiction. In his works he has adhered to the adventure, trial, and straight genres, adding an occasional dash of the farcical for good measure.

162   Dead Mrs. Stratton   CCD 1933
            In Eng.: Jumping Jenny

This story of murder committed on a roof during a charades party in which all the guests play the roles of famous criminals is beyond doubt the poorest Berkeley extant. It would not be worth keeping, save for a four-page introduction, "Concerning Roger Sheringham," which is a presumably authentic account of that sleuth's background and early history. Intending historians of the detective story take note.

163   Death in the House   H&S 1939

A fairly substantial tale that does not feature Roger Sheringham. It uses the workings of the House of Commons with discrimination and taste, the suspense is good, and the denouement satisfactory. What is barely tolerable is the method of introducing poison into the prime-ministerial perineum and the overlooking of its traces at the autopsy. Berkeley is more adept with poisoned chocolates.

164   Mr. Pidgeon's Island   CCD 1934
            In Eng.: Panic Party

The author's eleventh novel and a Roger Sheringham case as well. The scheme is not really satisfactory: an Oxford don becomes wealthy, entertains a party on his island, and declares, for a joke, that there is a murderer among them. The joke is that his joke is not a joke. Denouement unsatisfactory.

165   Mr. Priestley's Problem   Coll n.d. [1927]
            In U.S.: The Amateur Crime

The English have always had the wish to take their murders as farce, or with farce. And some writers such as Crispin and Delano Ames have succeeded in merging the moods. Berkeley tries it here, not for the first time, with only moderate success: too much talk in proportion to action and idea.

166   Murder in the Basement   Dday 1932

Inspector Moresby has to deal with the late-discovered body of a pregnant girl, buried in the cellar and inviting identification. The chief interest of this slow tale, apart from Roger Sheringham's firsthand account of school jealousies, is the anticipation of police routine by a good many years.

167   Piccadilly Murder   CCD 1930

Again Mr. Chitterwick mumbles and bumbles and discovers the truth of a murder committed in a hotel lounge. Clues and plot are well handled, but for us the lengthy treatment caused by the little man's ineffectuality—a pose on the author's part—robs the story of the intrinsic charm of the genre.

This is the elaboration at novel length of Berkeley's excellent short story "The Avenging Chance" (see No. 2353).

In the lengthening the plot loses much of its force: the first third of the present book is no more than chitchat, appropriate to the club that Roger Sheringham heads and that discusses crime. The members successively try their hand at Inspector Moresby's unsolved murder, and this requires the author to add twists to his original simple and strong idea. Sheringham does not shine, and the least confident member is given the star role.

169   A Puzzle in Poison   Dday 1938
       In Eng.: Not to Be Taken

Murder by arsenic of a Dorset village magnate, with suspicion falling upon his ineffectual wife. A good bit of concealment of evidence, confusion over who gave which lemonade to whom, and so on, but all in all a creditable job.

170   The Second Shot   CCD 1931; orig. 1930
       Pref. on detective fiction (see No. 2900)

This, ostensibly the seventh by B., is the one that contains a preface-dedication setting forth the intention to take the detective story into the realm of psychology and atmosphere. The result is not so impressive as the program. The first-person narrative of a sissified youth who yet manages to fool Roger Sheringham and marry an attractive girl is long-drawn-out and tires the reader by turning upon everybody, more than once, the searchlight of suspicion and "proof."

171   The Silk-Stocking Murders   Dday 1928

Multiple crimes suggested by one suspicious death. A plausible idea whose working out is only fair, considering the real-life origin of the plot. Roger Sheringham collaborates fecklessly with Inspector Moresby.

172   Top Story Murder   Dday 1931
       In Eng.: Top Storey Murder

An old woman is killed for her money on the top floor of a set of "mansions," thus providing a restricted group of suspects for Roger Sheringham. He disposes of the clues and lets Inspector Moresby use one of his better ideas to secure evidence against the criminal suspected from the start. Some entertaining dialogue.

173   Trial and Error   H&S 1965/1937
       Reissued as a Classic of Adventure and Detection

An amiable bachelor knows he has only a few months to live (aneurism, misspelled in this way, as usual) and is persuaded by his friends that he must commit murder in a good cause if he is to make the best use of his remaining days. Despite the humorous intention and execution there is some serious plotting, and suspense grows after the too leisurely start. What happens to the old boy when he confesses to what he has undoubtedly done is excellent.

174   [BERKELEY, ANTHONY] The Wychford Poisoning Case   Coll 1926
       An Essay in Criminology
       Unsigned note on detective fiction
       "By the author of The Layton Court Mystery"

Berkeley's second detective novel, designated in the first edition as "By the author of *The Layton Court Mystery."* The author's dedication to E. M. Delafield seems to promise some interesting psychology. It turns out to be fairly simple, but genuine nonetheless, and the implications of a situation suggestive of the Maybrick case are carefully and attractively drawn, despite an excess of youthful byplay between Roger Sheringham, his friend Alec Grierson, and a flapper of the Twenties named, inevitably, Sheila. Roger confesses at the end that psychology has led the trio to undervalue material fact, but the study of arsenical poisoning, the asides on the law, and the doctrine on love, boredom, and adultery are all good.

175   BERKELEY. See also:

The Layton Court Mystery   Malice Aforethought Goll/Harp 1931
   (orig. anon., 1925)   Dday 1929   *As A. B. Cox:*
Roger Sheringham and   Brenda Entertains (sketches
   the Vane Mystery   repr. from *Punch*)   HJ 1925
   (= Mystery at Lover's   *With others:*
   Cave)   Coll 1927/S&S 1927   Ask a Policeman
As Francis Iles: (see No. 2133)
As for the Woman   Dday 1939   Six Against the Yard
Before the Fact: A Murder   (= Six Against Scotland
   Story for Ladies   Goll 1932   Yard) (see No. 2845)

176   BERNARD, ROBERT (pseud. of Robert Bernard Martin)

       Death Takes a Sabbatical   Nort 1967

Boucher's review of this effort by a professor of English at Princeton is just and may be paraphrased: a good start but a poor finish. The American scholar who witnesses a murder (or was it?) on the London Underground is agreeable enough for the first third of the book but soon turns into what Boucher calls a "gothic" idiot, ignoring the police and being taken in right and left. The explication, 10,000 words long, leaves little clear except that the author is a tyro.

177   BEYNON, JANE (also Lange Lewis, q.v.; b. 1915)

       Cypress Man   BM 1944

Presumably her first book, not detection and not a success, but with many of the good characteristics that were to be defined and sharpened in the later stories. Los Angeles setting: several young people work out their destinies under the distorting influence of the psychopathic Ran Moon, would-be composer, whose progressive deterioration provides the interest, as well as a murder at the last possible moment.

178   BIGGERS, EARL DERR (1884–1933). Creator of Charlie Chan, Hawaiian detective, lovable perhaps, but not a commanding figure in the genre, whatever he may have been on the screen. See *The Celebrated Cases of Charlie Chan* (1936). For the stage version of *Seven Keys to Baldpate,* see No. 2395.

BINGHAM, JOHN (John Michael Ward Bingham, seventh baron Clanmorris, b. 1908)

The works of this newspaperman and civil servant are chiefly of criminal interest, with only a dash of detection now and then. *The Third Skin* is not even in this marginal category.

179   Inspector Morgan's Dilemma   DM 1956; orig. 1955
          In Eng.: The Paton Street Case

Chief Detective Inspector Morgan is a highly intuitive Welshman, and in this case most of his intuitions are wrong. The author plays up his detective's errors (here resulting in the unnecessary deaths of three persons) for the sake of the new realism, but the total effect is to be deplored. The actual writing is competent, the plot humdrum.

180   Murder Off the Record   DM 1957

A suspense story with little detection. Told in the first person by a bewildered and "injured" husband, it attempts to arouse interest in the insane murderer whose identity is known from the start, but it fails signally: the excitement is spurious, the Scotland Yard men are distasteful, and the Inspector Morgan of B.'s earlier work does not appear.

181   Murder Plan Six   DM 1959

JB found the plot of this fair, though marred by a little too much literary effect. WHT agrees, and liked it better than the others by this author known to him. Curiously, the minor characters, Dempster, Hartmann, and Miss de Lacer, are better done than the semi-incredible "hero," Michael Barlow.

182   My Name Is Michael Sibley   DM 1952

Told in first person, this is the story of a mess created by the hero and heroine through lying to the police about a man they knew who has been murdered. Skillful composition, style not especially attractive, type of plot dreary.

183   Night's Black Agent   DM 1961

The author appears to be attempting to outdo Garve in the variety of his plots and situations. The official police who appear are rather boorish, and the newspaperman who avenges those done in by a blackmailer is a bit flat but credible. The criminal himself, called just Green, scarcely comes to life. The victims and their families are best done, and the narrative does keep moving.

184 BINGHAM. See also:

A Case of Libel	Goll 1963
A Fragment of Fear	Goll 1965
The Tender Poisoner (= Five Roundabouts to Heaven)	Goll 1953

BIRMINGHAM, GEORGE A. (pseud. of [Canon] James Owen Hannay, 1865–1950)

Has written some sixty books of romance, travel, and unidentifiable miscellanea, all in a gently humorous vein punctuated by dramatic touches. *The Lost Lawyer,* his first true detective story, has been translated into French (*Petite Illustration,* 1933). See also: *The Island Mystery* (1918), *The Major's Candlesticks* (1929), *The Search Party* (1909). He has, moreover, written a volume of excellent true-crime recitals. *Murder Most Foul,* 1929 (see No. 3082).

185   The Hymn Tune Mystery   BM 1931

In the quiet but steady mode this is a delight. Intelligence, humor, character, and prose are in equipoise. The setting is an English cathedral church and the main figures are naturally clerics. When the organist with a penchant for the bottle is found dead in his loft, and in an uncommon posture at that, the need to avoid scandal is as great as the desire to see justice done. Inspector Smallways manages to reconcile these two interests, while displaying adequate powers—up to a certain sticky place, which fate then helps him get unstuck.

186   Wild Justice   Jac n.d./BM 1930

Not as entertaining as the preceding, but a straightforward English country house murder with Irish overtones, told in first person by the local padre. A few nice clues range from the usual muddy boots to the less usual misuse by the criminal of a language imperfectly known. One can almost forgive the author for his choice of murderer; by Irish standards the crime is justifiable homicide.

187   BLACK, LIONEL

Outbreak   S&D 1968

Dr. David Gregson, member of a London municipal board of health, helps the police to track down the contacts of a mysterious South American, who arrived by air and presumably communicated smallpox to others before being hospitalized himself. The author handles the medical aspects well, keeps the horrors reasonable, and works in a nice bit of international crime on the side. Not much detection, but full of interesting procedure. Sex mutilation in a good cause thrown in for those who want more.

188   BLACKBURN, JOHN (FENWICK) (b. 1924)

Bound to Kill   Mill 1963
   In Eng.: Blue Octavo

A bookseller-author should be able to produce one story attractively set in the world he knows best, but this plot is far from fulfilling its promise, though the writing is competent and the use it makes of photographs in a rare volume on mountain climbing is not bad. One detestable character, not the hero, is normal these days, but not the fact that the detective-bookseller goes about his work without police assistance.

189   The Broken Boy   Mill 1962

Here we have interesting characters amusingly presented and a nice English provincial city locale, but the plot is absurd. It depends upon a quite incredible cult of "wronged women," who worship their sons as well as a wooden idol from Madagascar. Terrible huddling at the end, with the attempted sacrifice of the heroine.

190   Murder at Midnight   Mill 1964
   In Eng.: The Winds of Midnight

The author's eighth is a story of amnesia and skulduggery, pursued with a considerable zest and ingenuity by a man who thinks his wife is having an affair with her employer, but who turns out to be another kind of bitch. Competent but no more.

191   A Ring of Roses   Cape 1965

The familiar Russian-and-East-German plot done in an absentminded way, very likely because what interested the author was the description of the artificially spread black plague, its consequences, and its questionably prompt control. Supposing the medical facts to be correct, they form the only gripping part of the book.

192   The Young Man from Lima   Cape 1968

His twelfth and a decline from *Blue Octavo,* which did not stand any too high. The treats set before us are "world-wide assassinations" and drugs unknown to science. Marcus and Tania Levin embark on self-appointed detection and retribution in Nuevo Leon—not our meat.

193   BLACKBURN. See also:

Bury Him Darkly	Cape 1969
Dead Man Running	Mill 1961
The Gaunt Woman	Mill 1962
Packed for Murder (= Colonel Bogus)	Mill 1964
A Sour Apple Tree	Mill 1959

194 BLACKSTOCK, CHARITY (pseud. of Ursula Torday; also Lee Blackstock and Paula Allardyce, qq.v.)

Dewey Death   Hein 1956

A mildly entertaining account of murder in the offices of the ILDA (Inter-Libraries Despatch Association), which unfortunately does not involve the Dewey decimal system in any integral manner. The striking feature is the character of the barely concealed murderer and his effect on the morale of the girl who falls for him. The author is not a bad hand at characterization, but overdoes her few tricks. Prodigious amounts of male and female weeping and frustration, and little detection.

195 BLACKSTOCK, LEE

The Woman in the Woods   CCD 1958

Suspense only: the identity of the W. in the W. is soon made clear, a goodhearted wanton, murdered by an incredible village character. The only problem is: Will the murderer get away with more murders before the boy-hero can stop him?

196 BLACKSTOCK, L. See also:

All Men Are Murderers   CCD 1958

197 BLAISDELL, ANNE (pseud. of Elizabeth Linington; also Lesley Egan, Egan O'Neill, and Dell Shannon, qq.v.; b. 1921)

Something Wrong   Goll 1968

The setting is the Wilcox Street precinct house, where Sergeant Ivor Maddox continues to be plodding and full of words and at once chased and chaste. The plot has to do with teen-agers who shoplift, take drugs, get pregnant and murdered—unrelated crimes solved by M. and his friends, whose private lives also occupy us, like the plot, needlessly.

198 BLAISDELL. See also (in U.S. as by Elizabeth Linington):

Date with Death	Harp 1966/Goll 1965
Nightmare	Harp 1961/LG 1960
No Evil Angel	Harp 1965/LG 1964

BLAKE, NICHOLAS (pseud. of Cecil Day-Lewis, b. 1904)

First a schoolmaster in Oxford, Cheltenham, and Glasgow, the present poet laureate is also an essayist and autobiographer. Blake has maintained a praiseworthy level of production in the detective genre. For a time he reviewed detective fiction in *The Spectator*. Note that the name of his detective, Strangeways, is that of a famous Manchester prison. For the author's autobiography, see No. 718.

199 The Beast Must Die   Harp 1938

The story of a father who tracks down the man who has run over his young son, and who plans and executes (with a double twist) his demise. Nigel Strangeways functions in the second half of the story, in collaboration with Inspector Blount.

200 The Corpse in the Snowman   Harp 1941
In Eng.: The Abominable Snowman

There is plenty of good work and original character and motive in this earlyish tale of Blake's, but it remains inexplicable why in the U.S. edition one of the main surprises is given away in the title. The play with Freud and sex is done in an informed and imaginative way that puts to shame all subsequent attempts. The suspense is kept up to the end, and the turn away from and back to the chief suspect is brilliantly executed.

201 Death and Daisy Bland   Dell 1960; orig. CCC and Harp 1956
Also: A Tangled Web

This is a fictional rendering of the John Williams case (1912). It yields a character study rather than a detective story. The crime is no more than an error of judgment on the part of a formerly clever crook; the detection consists in having the police listen while a "friend" of the suspected man gives him away. The central figure is the wife of the murderer. The title *A Tangled Web* alludes to Scott's line in *Marmion, VI*, 17.

202 End of Chapter   Harp 1957

A happy return to Strangeways and straight detection. The problem is to discover who in a respectable publishing firm reinstated certain important deletions in a libelous manuscript just before printing, as well as who murdered an author on the premises. Clare Massinger (Nigel's consolation since his wife's demise in the last war) plays a minor role, but in an excellent domestic scene keeps Nigel from squirting oil of vitriol into his sinuses.

203 Head of a Traveller   Harp 1949

A highly charged story of unpremeditated murder leading to the decapitation of the victim and his immersion in the Thames. Nigel Strangeways assists the attractive Inspector Blount. Not the most enjoyable Blake, but thoroughly workmanlike: he never shirks clueing and thinking.

204 Malice in Wonderland   Coll 1940
In U.S.: The Summer Camp Mystery

A book recalled by WHT as irritating in locale if amusing in Strangeways. The trouble with it is the usual one with large and busy settings: it is difficult for the author to make clear, and for the reader to keep clear, who was where doing which at what time. Still, there is good stuff in it and much amusement.

205   Minute for Murder   CCC 1947

Blake's masterpiece—an outstanding plot and high characterization. The work done by the victim's brother, the wartime office atmosphere, the motive and method, and the doorkeeper's references to the Shay-oh that is overtaking the world—all make this a memorable triumph.

206   The Morning After Death   Harp 1966

Hawthorne House at Cabot University in Massachusetts has Nigel Strangeways as guest of the Master, an Oxford contemporary. (Actually, C. Day-Lewis spent a term at Harvard giving the Charles Eliot Norton lectures on Poetry.) With great tact the author has a Professor of Classics murdered by someone not in the Humanities. Other young people are introduced, one of whom Strangeways makes love to at her insistent request. Some dozen or so slips in U.S. idiom mar an otherwise gay adventure scant on detection.

207   A Penknife in My Heart   Harp 1958

An unpromising beginning, but the tale carries one along and proves reasonably sound in construction. Its chief fault lies in the altogether despicable characters of the villains. One cares little what happens to them, though the scheme by which two men arrange to give each other alibis is good. (Blake admits others had thought of it before.)

208   The Private Wound   Harp 1968

Despite the Irish atmosphere, especially when done as well as this, one feels let down by this mystery without a detective, and not particularly exhilarated by the numerous erotic episodes. The inevitable political and religious causes are artfully touched in and made integral to the plot, but we are a long way from Strangeways. A number of interesting parallels exist between names and events in this tale and in C. Day-Lewis' autobiography, *The Buried Day* (see No. 718).

209   A Question of Proof   Harp 1935; repr. CCC 1969

For this good prep school tale Blake drew heavily upon his experiences as a master at the Summer Fields School (near Oxford) and the Cheltenham Junior School. The love affair between the up-and-coming young master and his headmaster's wife is nicely handled (both in itself and as red herring), and the motive of the actual murderer is well clued in. This is Nigel Strangeways' first case, and he does a good job. The boys, too, are genuine.

210   The Sad Variety   Harp 1964

An all-too-typical story of cold-war shenanigans surrounding the professor (here named Wragby, though he appears under a hundred names in as many novels), who holds in his head a secret the Russians want. Nigel Strangeways is detailed to guard him, and lo! the scientist has a daughter of eight, for whom he would give his life and his secret. What happens to her? You have it: she is kidnapped. Apply your own tension.

211   The Smiler with the Knife   Harp 1939

With the war as excuse, an entertaining thriller rather than a detective story. Nigel Strangeways now has an explorer-wife, Georgia, and they do a good job of ferreting out the facts of a neo-fascist dictatorship being formed in Devonshire.

212   There's Trouble Brewing   Harp 1937

Not a bad conception, but executed as if the author were tired. Perhaps a special British neurosis about pubs, drinking hours, and half-and-half bitterness accounts for the trouble. Anyhow, the perfunctoriness does not wholly blanket invention, and there are good points, though a detective story, like a poem, ought to have more than redeeming features.

213   Thou Shell of Death   Harp 1936; repr. Berk 1964

The second sally of Nigel Strangeways, in which he meets but does not woo the she-explorer Georgia Cavendish, later his wife. A story unlike his future ones, yet quite different in tone from the first: more humor, less familiarity with local ways of life, complex situation and killings. Good use of snow.

214   The Widow's Cruise   CCC 1959

His fifteenth. Strangeways and Clare Massinger take a cruise to the Greek islands on the S.S. *Menelaos.* One of two sisters is murdered, one being a beautiful flirt of mature years, the other a frumpish scholar, like their late father. Excellent characters on board; plenty of wit ("I'm laying Aphrodite"); superfluous last chapter.

215   The Worm of Death   Harp 1961

There is some detection and a good bit of interesting characterization, plus a colorful Greenwich locale and a well-drawn psychopathic killer. To keep up with the times, Blake indulges in just a bit too much soul-searching.

216   BLAKE. See also:

       The Dreadful Hollow   Harp 1953
       The Whisper in the Gloom   Harp 1954

217   BLOCHMAN, LAWRENCE G(OLDTREE) (b. 1900)

       Recipe for Homicide   Lipp 1952

The well-known free-lance writer and translator from the French provides here a not unpalatable mixture of canned soup and communism, stirred up by the medical examiner Dr. Coffee in a fairly scientific manner. For the latter's exploits in short-story form, see Nos. 2356–8.

218   See You at the Morgue   DS 1941
Note on the classification of secretions,
devised by A. S. Wiener

The most ambitious full-length work by this author, and a better job of motive and character-drawing than in any other tale of his. Detective Kilkenny weaves his way among gigolos, ex-husbands, flamboyant women with shady brothers, fur thieves, and the clues of blood and other tissues and secretions to resolve a characteristic U.S. imbroglio.

219   BODELSEN, ANDERS

       One Down   Harp 1970
       Trans. from the Danish by Carolyn Bly

Not a detective story, but a suspense yarn of fair quality, in what appears to be a satisfactory translation. The protagonist, one Vinther, is an executive in a firm whose delicate negotiations with a German auto manufacturer are likely to be upset by the fact that he is being blackmailed for covering up his accidental running down of a bicyclist. The way Vinther deals with the threats to his security makes for an interesting though rather predictable narrative, enjoyable chiefly for the contemporary Danish scene.

220   Think of a Number   Harp 1969
       Trans. from the Danish by David Hohnen

This story of crime is in the modern mode: a barrage of small details is fired at the reader to make him believe. The young author accordingly received in 1968 the Danish annual prize as author of the year. Among the details are cluelike matters, but the incidents are those of robbery, conspiracy, and blackmail, not detection. The translation is first-rate.

221   BOHLE, EDWARD

       The Man Who Disappeared   TVB 1960
Strongly disliked at sight, and subsequently found impossible to read.

222   BOILEAU, THOMAS* (b. 1906) AND NARCEJAC, PIERRE* (b. 1908)

       Who Was Claire Jallu?   AB 1965

A characteristically "French" variation on mystery and detection, the problem being: is the hero's mistress, married to an engineer who travels, the woman the hero knew in Paris and fails to recognize in Afghanistan? The solution, though highly ingenious, is somehow a letdown.
   * So printed on spine of book. For the correct first names, see Index.

     BONETT, JOHN (pseud. of John Hubert Arthur Coulson, b. 1906)
     and BONETT, EMERY (pseud. of Felicity Winifred Carter, b. 1907)

A pair, subsequently married, who began with original ideas well worked out but have fallen into the Costa Brava delusion.

223   Better Off Dead   CCD 1964
         In Eng.: Better Dead

The very poor *No Grave for a Lady* was forewarning that the fair start of this tale might not be maintained. The Costa Brava scene is well depicted, but the too numerous characters, all blackmailed by one jolly fellow, are not enough differentiated, except for the writer in the story, who acts as amateur detective and unmasks the murderer.

224   Dead Lion   CCD 1949

Though not in the strict sense detection, the thing is expertly done as to character, situation, and interrelationships—particularly that between father and stepdaughter. Well worth the connoisseur's attention.

225   Murder on the Costa Brava   Walk 1968
         In Eng.: This Side Murder

The authors, now resident in Spain, have plagiarized their earlier *Better Off Dead* to the extent that literary blackmail is again central to the plot, and a host of English visitors and expatriates peripheral. Lots of local color at a new luxury hotel and endless interrogation by the soft-spoken, "violet-eyed" Inspector Borges.

226   Not in the Script   MJ 1951
         In Eng.: A Banner for Pegasus

A gem! Beautifully plotted and set, this masterpiece is undoubtedly the best example of the motion-picture-company theme, superimposed on the city-slicker-invasion-of-peaceful-village motif. Not only is the murder adroit and deserved, and the detection competent, but the love story is charming. Long live Steeple Tottering!

227   BONETT, EMERY (see No. 223/B)

         Old Mrs. Camelot   Blak 1944
         In Eng.: High Pavement

Bought, read, disliked, and discarded. The trouble is: the situation, the people, the telling. That leaves little save the large number of suspensive dots. . . .

228   BONETT. See also:

         No Grave for a Lady   CCD 1959
         The Private Face of Murder   CCD 1966

229   BONNELL, JAMES FRANCIS, has written rather easygoing tales of detection in which a young New York attorney is the amateur. *Death over Sunday* (1940) is typical, in a Long Island setting.

230   BONNEY, JOSEPH L.

  Death by Dynamite   C&E 1940

Sometimes a writer improves as time passes. This must be the same Joseph Bonney who seven years later wrote the taut and nicely finished *Look to the Lady!* Here almost everything is laughably bad: the deaths come about not by dynamite but by guncotton or a similar explosive in a hand grenade; the explosion is brought off by leaving a note asking the victim to gargle with an unlabeled fluid in a blue flask—and so it goes. Simon Rolfe, hired to prevent the crimes, only solves them, by "psychological logic." He has his Watson (so named), and the author has his hero accoutered à la Sherlock Holmes.

231   Look to the Lady!   Lipp 1947

Despite an improbable bit of topography (a ravine 100 feet deep just off the terrace outside a very ordinary American country residence), the impression persists that this should have been a play, the theme being in fact *Hamlet*. But only four characters ponder the problem whether or not Julia—now married to Uncle Jeff—killed her former husband in such a way as to simulate suicide. A neat, compact affair.

  The title is from *Macbeth,* II, 3, 124 and 132.

232   BONNEY. See also:

  Murder Without Clues (= No Man's Hand)   C&E 1940

233   BOORE, W. H.

  Cry on the Wind   Coll 1967

The same valley and the same characters as in his first novel, with some new effects and still much interest in soul and event, but no more purposiveness. (See No. 234.)

234   The Valley and the Shadow   Hein 1963

A remarkable writer, who attempts to do a remarkable novel of crime and anti-legal retribution and who fails by excess of talent. The Welsh village and its people are wonderful, but they go on too long badgering and ridiculing the English Inspector Biggins in his search for the murderer of an old miser. The denouement by pure accident, after everybody has said a dozen times that capital punishment is bad, shows lack of judgment about structure as well as about the reader's patience. Still, a work worth writing and worth reading.

235   BOOTH, CHARLES G(ORDON) (b. 1896)

  Murder at High Tide   Morr 1930

The prolific author's third (see *Sinister House,* 1926; *Gold Bullets,* 1929; *The Cat and the Clock,* 1938) is a very long tale about the murder of a coarse and domineering tycoon on the West Coast, in which an odd lot of people become embroiled. One of the lot is an improbable agent of the Sûreté. The prose as such is not bad, but the events, motives, and dialogue are out of this world and should stay there.

236   BORDEN, MARY

The Hungry Leopard   LG 1956

What happens when an author wants to make a *mélange des genres* with genres that won't mix. The analysis of character belongs, as we said in the Introduction, to the novel. The analysis of actions, circumstances, and conventions belongs to the tale of intrigue and mystery. In attempting a sort of Jamesian international tangle and a chase for "the missing letters" at the same time, Miss B. perpetually arouses our interest—for she writes very well—and perpetually diverts and defeats it.

BOUCHER, ANTHONY (pseud. of William Anthony Parker White; also H. H. Holmes [i.e., Herman W. Mudgett], 1911–68)

The well-known critic of detective fiction, whose weekly column in the *New York Times* reflected his assiduity and information, if not always the steadiest judgment, was a Californian and an M.A. from Berkeley. He also wrote music criticism and science fiction, in the study of which he was a pioneer. He edited anthologies of SF as well as of detective fiction and was the author of seven detective novels, three of them in the top range.

237   The Case of the Crumpled Knave   S&S 1939

The detective work of Colonel Rand and Fergus O'Breen has many good points. Five suspects are provided after the murder of an elderly inventor working on a gas to counteract all war gases. The lore of playing cards and the psychology of collectors are well employed and there is a clever about-face at the end. Because of its compactness, good clues, and believability, this tale ranks as the best Boucher.

238   The Case of the Seven of Calvary   S&S 1937

The author's first good detective novel, written before his invention of yellow-sweatered detective Fergus O'Breen. WHT wrote, on finding it: "The alarming title conceals a really competent tale of the kind we like: scene laid at University of California with a fairly convincing Professor of Sanskrit doing some real armchair detection."

239   The Case of the Seven Sneezes   S&S 1942

Despite an attractive island setting, "out of touch with the mainland" (of Southern California), and the tempering of detective Fergus O'Breen's fiery personality by bringing in his sister Maureen, this tale is unsatisfactory. Give the author credit for his knowledge of pipe smokers' habits and of the Lunge paraffin test for nitrate spots on the hand that held the gun; this aside, he spreads himself thin, and his casual reference to "sulphuric acid at sixty-two degrees Baumé" suggests that he believed this to be a temperature.

240   Rocket to the Morgue   Morr 1942

The main interest of this poorly contrived and poorly told murder story is the presentation of science-fiction writers, interspersed with discussions of their craft. In an Afterword dated nine years later, Boucher points out the pioneering features of his setting and his views. In the novel itself, a homicide lieutenant and a clever religious sister collaborate to disclose faked attempts at murder to shield a real death. The L.A. lieutenant and his friends are not convincing, and the victim and plot not engaging. Boucher himself is one of the characters, so as to authenticate a double-jointed trick essential to the plot.

241   BOUCHER. See also No. 1164 and:

        The Case of the Baker Street Irregulars
          (by H. H. Holmes)   S&S 1940

242   BOWERS, DOROTHY

        The Bells at Old Bailey   H&S 1947

A pleasantly literary and leisurely tale of blackmail, induced suicide, and murder in an English village. The author plays fair with her clues and manages to present a credible picture of a Scotland Yard man working in harness with the local superintendent. Raikes, from the Yard, is thoughtful and energetic by turns. The women outnumber the men, but the tone is not feminine.

243   Deed Without a Name   CCD 1940

Chief Inspector Pardoe and his Sergeant, Salt, have to find out why a young man of blameless life should suffer three murderous attempts and then get himself killed. The collection of clues—Shakespeare quotations, birds' local names, etc.—is a bit large and a bit feminine, but the solution is workmanlike and the atmosphere good.
        The title is from *Macbeth,* IV, 1, 49.

244   Shadows Before   CCD 1940

Like the earlier *Postscript to Poison,* this is also about poisoning—arsenic for all hands—and it has grave defects side by side with solid merits. Too many interruptions and too much attention to scenery, flowers, and weather do not make us forget the excellent dialogue and suspense. Inspector Pardoe and Sergeant Salt are able men, yet at the end the explanations seem incomplete: a flawed effort.

245   BOWERS. See also:

        Fear and Miss Betony   CCD 1942
        Postscript to Poison   H&S 1939

246   BOX, EDGAR (pseud. of Gore Vidal, b. 1925)

Death Before Bedtime   Dutt 1953

The author's second, this being the tale of a senator, mostly laid in Washington, like his daughter. The memorable start is in a Pullman compartment with the hero and herself exchanging wisecracks and embraces. Told in the first person by a very witty satirist and resourceful plotter, the story suggests Crispin of the latter days, though with much more abandon and somewhat less real wit.

247   Death in the Fifth Position   Dutt 1952

This first attempt introduces Peter Sargeant, an amateur sleuth whose profession is press agentry. He falls in with a ballet company and upon the best-looking of them. But fornication, however zestfully described, does not monopolize the reader's attention. There is satire, detection, wit of an Archie Goodwinesque sort, and one extreme parody of a homosexual bruiser-type dancer, which is really funny because free from sniggering.

248   Death Likes It Hot   Dutt 1954

Below the standard of the other two. Long Island setting, with the inevitable blonde at the house party. The author writes with his usual *entrain*, but the plot is diffuse and the people dull.

249   BOYD, JANE (pseud.)

Murder in the King's Road   Har 1953

A tale written from various points of view about a crime committed in a furniture shop, presumably by the debt-ridden owner. The victim is a well-known author, once a physician, who was being blackmailed. The dozen or so participants are well sketched, including the dog—much to JB's surprise. There is excellent byplay between the two detectives, and the telling is direct and short. Toward the end a little haziness sets in about the method of the murder and the position of one or two clues, but detection is on the whole sound.

250   BRACE, TIMOTHY (pseud. of Theodore Pratt, b. 1901). Born in Minneapolis and educated at New Rochelle High School, Colgate, and Columbia university, he became a foreign correspondent for a New York newspaper and a screenwriter. Has written, without special distinction: *Murder Goes Fishing* (1936) and *Murder Goes in a Trailer* (1937).

251   BRADDON, GEORGE (pseud. of George Alexis Bankoff, b. 1903)

Judgment Deferred   Trel 1948

The author has written at least four other books whose titles suggest that they are mysteries. The present one concerns a middle-aged doctor, practicing in the West End of London, of whose early history little is known. The only detective work is the matching of the doctor's fingerprints (from his car, after it has been stolen and recovered) with those of a man wanted for many years for a brutal hammer murder. Thereafter schizophrenia takes over. Very well written.

252   BRADDON, M(ARY) E(LIZABETH) [Mrs. John Maxwell] (1837–1915)

Lady Audley's Secret   3v. Tinsley 1862

The success of this novel in the pages of the *Sixpenny Magazine* made its author's reputation, and it remains an interesting and readable book, with much mystery and more detection than is found in many a modern thriller. As a mirror of the mid-Victorian English scene it is scarcely surpassed, and the characters are far from stock, particularly the young barrister, Robert Audley, who acts as amateur detective. It is worth noting that today the original edition commands a fabulous price.

BRAMAH (SMITH), ERNEST (1878–1942)

The author of the Max Carrados and the Kai Lung stories was a secretive man with a dash of sadistic pruriency in his makeup. Two or three of the short stories and passages in the long *Bravo of London* show this trait in concentrated form. When dilute this tendency gives a peculiar humor to his detective tales.

Physiognomists will want to look up E.B.S.'s photograph in the original edition of Grant Richards' *Author-Hunting;* the second edition (or rather the reprint) has a different and unrevealing pose substituted for the face of one who looks more like a gentleman's gentleman than an author.

253   The Bravo of London   Cass 1934

A long-winded and very disappointing crime story in which Max Carrados plays a major part and yet is completely unmemorable. Everything about the book (except the good paper and print) is disaffecting—there is even a Chinaman to spite Father Knox—and the off-color bits are insufficient to hold one's interest. See Part II for the bulk of Bramah's first-class output in the detective genre.

254   BRAND, CHRISTIANNA (pseud. of Mary Christianna [Milne] Lewis, b. 1907)

Suddenly at His Residence   BH 1947

A fair example of the large-English-family tale, with the double murder logical and well concealed. The clues are sound (though sprinkled with a sparing hand), but the inspector is feeble despite an attempt to make him a character. It is easy to see that Miss B., like her sisters, was so taken with the whole family that she forgot the rest. Her dialogue, which is excellent, continues bright and breezy much too long.

255   Tour de Force   Scrib 1955

Amusing locale (small island republic off the Italian coast). Inspector Cockrill is not quite convincing and certainly not out of any drawer near the top. There are several odious characters and an inexcusable case of cousins. These, with various crude overtones, spoil what should have been an entertaining tale.

256   BRAND. See also:

Cat and Mouse	Knopf 1950	Green for Danger	Lane 1945
The Crooked Wreath	DM 1946	Heads You Lose	DM 1942
Death in High Heels	Lane 1941	London Particular	MJ 1952
Death of Jezebel	DM 1948	Welcome to Danger	Foley 1949

257   BRANSON, H(ENRY) C.

Beggar's Choice   S&S 1953

B.'s seventh and the one we read first, on publication. It opens with Bent's alighting at the far end of the train platform, to begin a case in which rumor and report take precedence over clues. There is something static and desolate, doubtless intended, in this tale, of which the gimmick occurs to the astute reader well before the end.

258   The Case of the Giant Killer   S&S 1944

In the third of his cases ex-medico John Bent is persuasive and somehow manages to gain the reader's confidence, although he really does little to control the emergence of the "killer." But Bent does clarify the issues in a nasty case of framing with threatened reprisals, and in the humid heat of the place (near Cleveland) one doesn't begrudge him his mint juleps: at least those whom Bent allows to die are wrong-uns.

259   The Fearful Passage   S&S 1945

The fourth appearance of John Bent, the singular detective who seems to do little but pacify angry people and accept their sherry or whiskey, yet who understands how they feel and act and conceal their motives; so that in the end he unravels lies and crimes. This is a tale of jealousy and magnanimity in a small town of upper New York State, where a famous historian of 50 has married a very young wife who is in love with a boy of her own age. Neat and strong.

260   I'll Eat You Last   S&S 1941

Branson's first story, introducing bearded John Bent, a medical man turned detective. In this account of the progressive elimination of heirs to a fifty-million-dollar estate, Bent drinks rather less whiskey than in the later stories, but his companions make up for this. Senator Maitland's estate is on Lake Badenoch, near a small Midwestern college town, and the crime elicits some good questioning and observing but not much action from Bent, who lets his friends die right and left.

261   The Leaden Bubble   S&S 1949

A story of double murder following the unjustified acquittal of a young killer for the murder of his wife. The second killer is the father of the dead girl, who avenges her death as well as her defamation at the hands of the trial lawyer. Bent is at his quietest and smilingest in this tale, which involves also the leading citizens of a small, semi-rural community. Still, suspense is kept up, though the denouement seems a bit sudden. The atmosphere of steady rain and glistening pavements suits the mood of night wanderings, driving to nearby towns, and steady speculation aided by brandy and Beethoven's piano works.

262   The Pricking Thumb   BH 1949

The opening finds Bent drinking bourbon in a hostelry called The English Tavern, presumably in New York, but evidently not unattractive to an English publisher. He soon goes 100 miles "out"—SW? WNW?—to a place called New Paget, where he investigates a triple murder in the nearest thing to a great ducal house the country affords. Why does one remember chiefly Bent's beard and bourbon, despite some excellent writing?
    The title alludes to *Macbeth* IV, 1, 44.

263   BRANSON. See also:

    Last Year's Blood   S&S 1947
    Salisbury Plain (a novel of the
        U.S. Civil War, not det.)   Dutt 1965

264   BREAN, HERBERT

    Hardly a Man Is Now Alive   Morr 1952

The second excursion into crime of the reporter-narrator, this time with his fiancée, so that the unraveling of theft, murder, abduction, and ghostly manifestations goes on over a bed of anxiety about the chances of the wedding taking place. The town of Concord, Mass., is a studied reproduction, not quite convincing to one who has resided there; and the mysteries are too visibly contrived to create either fear or suspense.

265   BREAN. See also:

    The Clock Strikes Thirteen   Morr 1952
    Wilder's Walk Away   Morr 1948

    BREMNER, MARJORIE (K.) (b. 1916)

American-born, educ. at Chicago and Columbia univ., a practicing psychologist and later in the U.S. Naval Reserve, came to London in 1946 and did research for the Hansard Society. Then became a free-lance journalist and reviewer for *Time and Tide* and *The Twentieth Century*.

266   Murder amid Proofs   H&S 1955

Not quite so fine a performance as the first, perhaps because of too much preoccupation with the social and amatory scene, but still an outstanding story to keep and reread.

267   Murder Most Familiar   H&S 1953

This story of family dissension and murder in an English politician's family is topnotch. The telling of it by the niece-secretary of the big shot involved is subtly done, and the motive and denouement are, for a first novel, extraordinarily adroit.

268   BRIDGES, VICTOR

        The House on the Saltings   H&S 1941
         An Adventure on the Suffolk Seaboard

Cock-and-bull pursuit; violence but no crime and no detection.

269   BRIDGES. See also:

Greensea Island	Putn 1922
Mr. Lyndon at Liberty	M&B 1950/1915
The Secret of the Creek	HM 1930
The Secret of the Saltings	Macd 1955
Trouble on the Thames	Macd 1945

270   BRINTON, HENRY (also Alex Fraser; b. 1901)

        Drug on the Market   Macm 1957/Hutch 1956

What should have been an enjoyable tale of dope smuggling in Cornwall turns by slow degrees into something unreadable. One wonders (1) how Brinton managed the good beginning, and (2) what made C. P. Snow call the author "one of the most intelligent and original . . . story writers. . . ."

271   BRINTON. See also:

An Apple a Day	W 1959
Coppers and Gold	Macm 1958

        BROCK, LYNN (pseud. of Alister McAllister; also Anthony Wharton, as playwright; b. 1877)

What with duplicate titles, dubious dates, and fictional chronology, it has taken the collaborators some forty years to straighten out Colonel Gore and his distant fair lady, Pickles.

272   Colonel Gore's Second Case   Harp 1926/Coll 1926

A tale of incredible complexity. Twenty-five pages of fine print (Gore's "notes") are provided at the end of the story, to clear up any small points, also a letter from Gore to Mrs. Melhuish, who figured prominently in the progenitor story, *The Deductions* (No. 274).

273   The Dagwort Coombe Murder   Coll 1929

On two counts it may safely be forgotten: (1) it is not a Colonel Gore tale; (2) it is stiff reading at the outset and impenetrable further on.

The first hundred pages set the stage for what might be a very good entanglement. But Colonel Gore spoils it all by being a Colonel Blimp—"surprised" at the obvious, incompetent with the unexpected, and (what is worse) remorseful in a mumbling stupid way. There is no detection. Gore gets hit on the head, not hard enough. The "Pickles" business is tolerable, and Melhuish is well drawn; the others are sticks. Evidence, in the "daring" admission of Pickles' lapse or near-lapse from premarital virtue, shows the author's interest in the "new" morality. See *The Kink* (below).

It should be added that in the present tale the locale is ingratiating; "Linwood nr. Westmouth" is Clifton nr. Bristol. The excellent maps, and the never-repeated introduction to Colonel Gore's background and that of the Melhuishes compensate in part for the offhand Colonel's imaginary deductions.

275   The Kink   Harp 1927

The author's third, and graced by short, intelligible sentences. Mrs. Melhuish occurs only in two fragments of a letter given at head and tail. The story deals skillfully with the antics of a family that has inherited strong orgiastic propensities. The goings-on are well done, without smirk or false reticence or wallowing; nor is there any prudish moralizing on Gore's part. There is in fact very little of anything on Gore's part. His job, as he says, is guessing, and he guesses always a bit late. But the story bears reading.

276   Murder at the Inn   Harp 1929
          In Eng.: The Mendip Mystery

The author's sixth, *Murder on the Bridge* being the sequel to it, as its English title, *Q.E.D.*, suggests. Although the failure of the police to win a conviction against Gretta Higgins is something of a letdown at the end, WHT thinks this is one of the best-handled Gore tales. The Colonel is methodical and attractive, and the story straightforward.

277   Murder on the Bridge   Harp 1930
          In Eng.: Q.E.D.
          A sequel to Murder at the Inn

Elaborate plot, closely tied up with the case presented in *The Deductions of Colonel Gore*. Details are kept under better control by the author than in some previous instances. The bridge is the Clifton suspension bridge.

278   The Slip-Carriage Mystery   Harp 1928

Colonel Gore's fourth case, and a disappointing reversion to the complexities of style and action which characterized his second, and which were toned down considerably in *The Kink*. The railway setting is well handled, though the very poor diagram of the railway junction and yard in the American edition looks like the work of Harper's office boy. Gore reads testimony and watches people, then waits for things to develop—namely, a bump on his head. Little, if any, detection.

279   The Stoke Silver Case   Harp 1929

After a particularly good beginning—only a few pages—this turns into an impossibly complicated, unreadable mess. Far below Brock's others, low though some of them stand.

280   BROCK. See also:

The Stoat   Coll 1940

281   BROOME, ADAM (pseud. of Godfrey Warden James, b. 1888)

The Cambridge Murders   Bles 1936

A poor tale, amateurishly written, despite six earlier efforts. A couple of African undergraduates are murdered by one of the least likely characters (shown up as demented at the very end). The promise of a tie-in with black magic—which in this case would have been a relief from the very pedestrian "detection"—is not fulfilled.

282   Crowner's Quest   Benn 1930

The collaborators tried to read this aloud and made heavy weather of it, but JB continued solo and came to like certain features of the story: the local color, which is vivid and not excessive; the characters, varied and believable; the clues and the detection, which are modest but solid; even the love story, which adds to the interest by providing the pressure of time. And the culprit is just right.

283   BROOME. See also:

The Oxford Murders   Bles 1929
The Queen's Hall Murder   Bles 1933

BROPHY, JOHN (1899–1965)

A journalist, b. Liverpool and educ. Liverpool and Durham univ.; father of the contemporary novelist Brigid Brophy. Has written, in addition to numerous novels and an interesting study of murder (No. 3095), the following works that are not fiction: *Body and Soul, The Human Face, The Mind's Eye.*

284   The Day They Robbed the Bank of England   C&W 1959

A fantasy of the year 1900, involving an American, the gold in the Bank of England, and the Cinderella theme in a mixture less potent than this author's usual product. Not detection and hardly serious crime.

285   The Front Door Key   Hein 1960

The author has written several novels whose titles suggest mystery if not detection. The present one contains a very pretty puzzle about a picture said to be by an old master. A young man solves the puzzle and marries as a result, amidst an involvement of emotions neatly contrived and unwound.

286   Turn the Key Softly   Coll 1951

An interest in keys is the first step in crime. This story starts promisingly with the release from prison of three very different women. The heroine of the lot is worth following through her development in fitful relation to the other two. A crime is committed, but there is no detection.

BROUN, DANIEL

287   Counterweight   Holt 1962

A first, by a man who has worked backstage in New York for ten years. It deals with the polishing off of an ugly-tempered stage manager by means quite properly theatrical. The dialogue and characters are good in spots. They speak an incredible lingo and have plausible quirks. One girl is especially good in her equal fervor for all men. The hero and Lieutenant Carreau are adequate, but the denouement is slipped in tamely without surprise, and indeed without enough explanation.

288   The Subject of Harry Egypt   Holt 1963

This second tale does not live up to promise, nor do technicalities about photography atone for the improbabilities of the gangster kidnaping and the coercion of the hero into participation. Much filler and weak sex.

289   BROWN, CHARLES BROCKDEN (1770–1810)

Edgar Huntley   3 v. Max 1799
    Or, The Memoirs of a Sleepwalker

This novel is notable for possibly having given a hint to Wilkie Collins for *The Moonstone:* in Brown's work the murderer commits his crime all unknowingly during the self-hypnosis called sleepwalking.
    N.B. "The Death of Cicero," a fragment, is added to eke out the third volume.

BROWN, FREDRIC (b. 1906)

This writer, born in Cincinnati and self-educated, made his name with *The Fabulous Clipjoint* (Dutt 1947) and has specialized in toughness and sex, at the last of which he is an expert, at least on paper. WHT favors *The Deep End,* and JB a story of carnival folk of which he cannot recall the title. Latterly Brown has become very mild (see No. 291).

290   The Deep End   Dutt 1952

Boucher's assessment of this work can be unreservedly agreed with. The high school hero is both "unobtrusive mass murderer" and "unusually terrifying" and the "groping detection . . . is believable and fascinating."

Brown is excellent at the management of sex as a force and not merely as a vicarious voyeur satisfaction for the reader. Smash ending; detection minimal.

291   The Five-Day Nightmare   Dutt 1962

This story has suspense enough, being based on the now frequent scheme of "If you want to see your wife alive again. . . ." But one is ready to hurl the book into the passing garbage truck when one finds out what lies behind the threat and what its business consequences are for the frightened hero, who refuses to go to the police. Here F.B. forgoes his usual sex tricks and depicts only the nicest, weakest kind of people, barring the would-be kidnaper—another proof of "scratch a tough guy to find a sentimentalist."

292   The Lenient Beast   Dutt 1956

Frank Ramos, working his police routine in Tucson, is handicapped by being a Mexican and better educated than his co-workers. This race and class problem (early example) is complicated by marital and other pressures to form a moving and entertaining story, just short of notable.

293   Mrs. Murphy's Underpants   Dutt 1963

The not specially brilliant or attractive pair of investigators, Ed and Am Hunter, who are nephew and uncle, tangle with Chicago horse-racing toughs, a child, and assorted non-characters. The humor is forced and the solution, too. The title has no bearing on the plot.

294   BROWN, F. See also:

The Bloody Moonlight	Dutt 1949	His Name Was Death	Dutt 1954
The Dead Ringer	Dutt 1948	Knock 3-1-2	Dutt 1959
Death Has Many Doors	Dutt 1951	The Late Lamented	Dutt 1959
The Fabulous Clipjoint	Dutt 1947	The Screaming Mimi	Dutt 1949

295   BROWN, WALTER C.

The Second Guess   Lipp 1929

JB's often caustic annotations indicate that he read all or most of the 304 pages of this dismal effort at a detective story. WHT could not go beyond the first chapter. All the trappings are here—a wounded man in a taxi, a mastermind, a fake burial—but absolutely nothing to hold the interest.

BROWNE, DOUGLAS G(ORDON) (b. 1884)

The son of the well-known British artist Gordon Browne, he began as a painter, then turned to writing, dividing his interest between fiction and history.

296   The Cotfold Conundrums   Meth 1933

An intricate plot, but clear and original: a woman detective novelist was writing about an unsolved murder of four years earlier, in the very village where it happened; why should she be killed and by whom? The young man commissioned to finish her book moves to Cotfold and becomes the center of intrigues and attacks of the usual kind. They would be baffling if they were more believable and if the characters had some life in them. The narrative is wordy but not such a bore as that of *The May-Week Murders*. In this case, Inspector H. H. Thew officiates but does not detect; the solution is handed in on a platter.

297　The Dead Don't Bite　　　　　　　　　　　　　　Meth 1933

This fairly short novel belongs to the author's first period, before he had created Harvey Tuke, Sir Bruton Kames, and Assistant Commissioner Wray. It is less boring than the later *May-Week Murders*, though it features the same amateur detective, Major Hemyock. The plot lacks elegance, being the tracking down of those who killed a jewel thief and secured his loot. The second world war evidently gave the author a much-needed shot in the arm.

298　Death in Perpetuity　　　　　　　　　　　　　　Macd 1950

The Wallace case fictionalized: sequel and explanation excellent. Good scenes at Brighton to conclude. See also Nos. 1055 and 1848.

299　Death in Seven Volumes　　　　　　　　　　　　Macd 1958

Douglas Browne returns to the lists with this story after giving up fiction for fact (Scotland Yard, Spilsbury) c. 1950. It is a pleasure to have Harvey Tuke and Sir Bruton Kames about again, although both show their age. The tale involves rare books in a way vital to the plot—at last, after several dismal attempts at this theme by London booksellers. Inspector Dauncey and Sergeant Hughjohn are competent, and the crippled firebrand daughter of the murdered bookseller is done to a turn.

300　Death Wears a Mask　　　　　　　Macm 1954/Hutch 1940
　　　　MRS

Certainly one of the author's best. The scene is the village of Steeple Mardyke during the blackout of an ARP practice. Harvey Tuke is visiting and has been pressed into service. A nice job of murder is fitted into the make-believe "incident." Some excellent and amusing characters in addition to the official pair.

301　The May-Week Murders　　　　　　　　　　　LG 1938/1937

The poorest in the production of the uneven Browne, so far as we know it. Aside from the Cambridge atmosphere, the story offers nothing save a ridiculous plot about the killing off of various descendants of a group which had established a trust fund; some preposterous Americans; and a featureless detective, Maurice Hemyock, whose wife tells the story.

302　Plan XVI　　　　　　　　　　　　　　　　　　CCD 1934

Browne was to do much better than this, but scarcely worse. Here he treats us to 300 pages of arch-criminality involving piracy and the deaths of thousands of innocent victims. Chief Inspector Thew's presence is insufficient to make this a detective story, or indeed anything but pretentious trash. Compare No. 1961.

303   Rustling End   Macd 1948

Unusual in plot, purpose, pace, and mode of detection. It satisfied these readers' exacting standards up to the point where they began to read separately. WHT declared himself satisfied with a slight reservation. JB felt somewhat more strongly that the final complications were excessive. Still, a very creditable performance, with Tuke at his Tukiest and no silly lovemaking. The story makes use of the Dougal case at Audley End in 1898–1901.

304   Too Many Cousins   Macm 1953; orig. 1946

The byplay between Harvey Tuke and Sir Bruton Kames is up to par, but the lengthy family tree of the Shearsbys annoyed JB, who took out his displeasure in penciling annotations to improve the author's French and the typesetter's care. Despite one flaw, mention of which would disclose the ending, WHT found this one of the best of the Tuke series, rich in incidents: related deaths, chemicals, railways, club life, etc.

305   What Beckoning Ghost?   Macd 1947

The opening suspense is good—a dinner party in a London house, where everybody seems to be fearful or hostile vis-à-vis everybody else. Then some real motives and interests are disclosed, unfortunately side by side with ghostly appearances and murder in a grilled park opposite the house. The dubious love affair does not help to sustain interest, which really goes to pieces when impersonations of dead heroes in uniform occur across the way. The dramatic close helps a little to regain esteem.

The title is from Pope's "Elegy to the Memory of an Unfortunate Lady."

306   BROWNE. See also:

The House of the Sword	Hutch	1939
The Looking-Glass Murders	Meth	1935
Sergeant Death	Macd	1955
The Stolen Boat Train	Meth	1935

Biography:
Sir Travers Humphreys   Harrap 1960

With A. S. L. Brock:
Fingerprints: Fifty Years of Scientific Crime Detection   Harrap 1953

With E. V. Tullett:
Bernard Spilsbury   Harrap 1951

307   BRUCE, JEAN (pseud. of Jean-Alexandre Brochet, 1921–63) a French writer who, in 1949, was inspired by a novel of Peter Cheyney's to take up the genre and create a secret service man whose name is DeBath,

but who is designated as OSS 117 (the numerical inspiration is Ian Fleming) and proves capable of many exploits on the international scene. They came to an end when their creator was killed driving at 100 mph. See *The Last Quarter Hour* (1955), *Trouble in Tokyo* (1958), *Double Take* and *Short Wave* (1964), *Flash Point, Soft Sell,* and *Shock Tactics* (1965), *Deep Freeze* (1966), and *Cold Spell* and *Hot Line* (1967).

BRUCE, LEO (pseud. of Rupert Croft-Cooke, b. 1903)

b. Edenbridge, Kent; educ. Tonbridge; antiquarian bookseller, soldier, intelligence officer, editor, and lecturer, as well as accomplished novelist, author of an excellent satire, *Miss Allick,* and of an autobiography in many volumes. He has also written *Thief* (1961), *Three in a Cell* (1968), and other studies of crime in real life (see No. 3121). As Leo Bruce he has devoted his talents to the writing of detection in two kinds: stories of bumbling common sense embodied in Sergeant Beef and stories of suave intellectual effort incarnated in the well-to-do schoolmaster and historian Carolus Deene. The co-authors of this book prefer Deene, but some Beef stories are attractive, too.

308   A Bone and a Hank of Hair   PD 1961

Some of Bruce's familiar apparatus begins to creak a bit here: his interrogations and peregrinations are endless; his housekeeper, Mrs. Stick, is tedious, and the Gorringers less amusing than usual. But it must be admitted that if one grants Deene the ability to synthesize from his scattered oddments of information—none kept from the reader—he deserves great credit for the effective surprise at the end.

309   A Case for Three Detectives   Stokes 1937/Bles 1936

An attempt to combine a spoof on the personalities and methods of three famous fictional detectives with a story about the less spectacular methods of Sergeant Beef. The intriguing (i.e., with servants) lady of a modest country house is found in a securely locked room with her throat slashed. Lord Simon Plimsoll (Peter Wimsey), M. Amer Picon (Poirot), and Msgr. Smith (Father Brown) appear at once and investigate. Each gives his solution of the mystery, not entirely different as to method, but accusing different persons. Sergeant Beef shows them all to be wrong. Not a bad job at all.

310   The Case with Four Clowns   Stokes 1939

Although there is a good deal of subtlety in the way the comic Sergeant Beef is handled, and although the author does his traveling-circus life extremely well, WHT could not find much detective or criminal interest in it.

311   The Case Without a Corpse   Stokes 1937

JB, who has become something of a Beef fancier, recommended this, and his collaborator found it highly enjoyable. Only by a trick can the case actually be said to lack a corpse, but the tale is well told, and Beef justifies his brawn.

312   Dead for a Ducat   PD 1956

The fourth of the Carolus Deene stories—a family affair that gravely concerns the school where C.D. teaches, for the lady who very likely polished off her unwanted son-in-law is a powerful trustee. C.D. is his usual bland and competent self. The byplay is good, the detection a trifle more advanced than in the other tales.

The title is from *Hamlet* III, 4, 23.

313   Death at Hallows' End   WHA 1965

Carolus Deene tracks down a missing solicitor, but the reader detects more fatigue than crime. There are a few good touches, but the rural toughs and the red herrings do not carry conviction. The old props (Mrs. Stick and the headmaster and wife) appear perfunctorily, and such humor as one finds comes from the pub keeper, whose habit it is to shorten long adverbs incess.

314   Death at St. Asprey's School   WHA 1967

Third in the *Death* series, which is listed separately on the author card. The school depicted in this book is grim and its members despicable—except one. Carolus Deene is borrowed from his own school, by way of his own headmaster, to detect the killer of the beastliest of the St. Asprey contingent. The relationships are intricate, and there are virtually no physical clues. The superintendent of police is as swinish and surly as the masters and the boys, and the book is thus all inspissated gloom.

315   Death in Albert Park   WHA 1964

In a dreary southeast suburb of London a series of motiveless killings occurs—two women stabbed in succession being enough to spread panic in the district. The police are at a loss, but before the third murder Deene gets interested in the shadowy figure who soon gets known as The Stabber. Deene adroitly puts his headmaster in a cleft stick—i.e., of facilitating another murder if he prevents his staff member from helping the investigation. It consists almost wholly of questioning, but the people and the talk are so good that the result is surprisingly full of suspense and variety, heightened by a keen sense of abnormal psychology—a first-rate story.

N.B., however, a dubious statement of disbelief in double personality.

316   Death of Cold   PD 1956

The murder of the mayor who was fishing from the pier is rather stretched out over a bank of red herrings not native to the local waters, but C.D.'s goings-about are good fun.

317   Death on the Black Sands   WHA 1966

Deene and the youth Priggley get into a weird tangle of events in southern Spain, where a playboy and a plug-ugly get theirs. The relationships and events are on the outré side, as befits a southern clime, but they remain pretty dull, despite Mr. Gorringer's presence and platitudes. Not the best Bruce.

318   Death on Romney Marsh   WHA 1968

The sixth in his *Death* series, and a very short affair indeed. Witty and at once satirical and nostalgic about manners, class, and stable societies. The story has drive and violence and plausibility, yet suffers a letdown at the end when Deene, in hospital for concussion, discloses what the fuss has been about.

319   Death with Blue Ribbon   WHA 1969

Carolus Deene is asked by a fancy restaurateur to cope with the demands of a "protection" gang who threaten the profitable establishment with all sorts of mishaps. This gives the author an opportunity to display his knowledge of food (he is a noted gourmet and writer on gourmetry) and gives C.D. a chance to be clever and physically active. But the preparation for the murder is long and wordy and the tale tends to continue in that vein, which only the picturesque characters make tolerable. On the whole, a halfhearted performance.

320   Die All, Die Merrily   PD 1961

Carolus Deene, the senior history master at a minor public school, is reminiscent of Gervase Fen. His Watson in this tale is a priggish youth (one Priggley), and his "methods" are attractive though not spectacular. A tape recorder is not as effectively used as might be.

321   Furious Old Women   PD 1960

Probably Bruce's wittiest and best-plotted novel to date, although *Nothing Like Blood* (q.v.) runs it close. It is happily free of the youth Priggley and of Mrs. Stick in her carping mood. A very ingenious idea creates a purposeful letdown at the end, only to produce a fine surprise in the last moments. Though the detection is perhaps a little shy on clues, the humor and wit are of a high order and suggest Crispin at his best.

322   Jack on the Gallows Tree   PD 1960

Read by both collaborators at the same time, and with *Furious Old Women* (q.v.) at hand for comparison. WHT agrees that the latter is more original in conception and execution, but he was greatly amused by scenes involving the barmaid, Miss Shapeley, in the present tale. The plot is relatively simple and direct, involving the artful use by the murderer of a dodge of long standing, to which Carolus Deene eventually tumbles.

323   Nothing like Blood   PD 1962

Carolus Deene is invited to clear up a tense situation in a genteel London boardinghouse and in so doing meets a splendid cast of characters, whose relation to the two mysterious deaths is plausible as well as gripping. Very funny byplay and conversation make this delightful from beginning to end.

324   Our Jubilee Is Death   PD 1959

At the behest of his cousin, Carolus Deene goes to a seaside town to investigate the murder of a disagreeable authoress of detective fiction. No one will tell him anything, but he manages to make up his mind about the murderer. After this person has taken a powder, Deene stages an exposition of the original crime, quite well done. But the enterprise as a whole is drab.

325   Such Is Death   LH 1963
           In Eng.: Crack of Doom

Rather all-of-a-piece and ordinary at that. Scenes and questions repeat, over and above the repetitiousness of Carolus Deene's usual "methods." As a puzzler, it is a tight little problem of who was where when, but as a plot it sags. Humor, too, is below par for Bruce. The setting, seaside at Christmas, is good.

326   BRUCE, L. See also:

Sergeant Beef Stories
     A Case for Sergeant Beef   Nich 1947
     The Case with No Conclusion   Bles 1939
     The Case with Ropes & Rings   Nich 1940
     Neck and Neck   Goll 1951

Carolus Deene Stories
     At Death's Door   HH 1955
     Cold Blood   Goll 1952
     Dead Man's Shoes   PD 1958
     Death of a Commuter   WHA 1967
     A Louse for the Hangman   PD 1962

BRUTON, ERIC (MOORE) (b. 1915)

b. London; educ. as engineer; editor, *Horological Journal, The Gemnologist,* etc. Has written the *True Book About Clocks* and an excellent *Dictionary of Clocks and Watches* (Crown 1963).

327   Death in Ten-Point Bold   HJ 1957

This is not one of the author's City of London Police stories and it suffers in consequence. The deaf and crippled clock expert Dr. Hook, who helps Inspector Reynolds of the CID investigate the death of another expert on the staff of a magazine of horology, is not impressive or pleasing, nor are the other journalists in the affair, including the narrator, who is a commercial artist. The loose weave of the plot and the mass of picturesque detail make for slack suspense and negate detection other than the casual question-and-answer kind. The addition of palmistry does not help: too bad for such a gifted author.

328   The Smithfield Slayer   TVB 1965
         A City of London Police Novel

An expertly written story, both as regards the city police routine and as regards the crime, characterization, and detection of motives and acts. It is "modern" in its stress on teen-age hardness and human antagonisms, but the touch is light. The scene is the central meat market, where the victim is bashed lightly on the head and put in the deep freeze. Nice humor in the lab man's detailed explanation of his technique to a pair of cops who want only conclusions.

329   BRUTON. See also:

The Devil's Pawn	TVB 1962	King Diamond	TVB 1961
Die, Darling, Die	TVB 1959	The Laughing Policeman	TVB 1963
The Finsbury Mob	TVB 1964	The Violent Brothers	TVB 1960
The Hold Out	TVB 1961	The Wicked Saint	TVB 1965

BUCHAN, JOHN (later Baron Tweedsmuir; 1875–1940)

b. Perth; educ. Glasgow Grammar Sch., then Brasenose, Oxf., where he won the Newdigate and a first. Next, barrister and MP, in spite of ill health and literary ambitions largely fulfilled. Died in office as Governor General of Canada.

330   Greenmantle   Nels 1956

First published in 1916, this tale of Major Richard Hannay's adventures in search of the meaning of the word *Kasredin*—which may or may not be a key to a secret which will push Turkey into the German camp—is not up to *The Thirty-Nine Steps*. The atmosphere is there, but diluted; somehow, there's nothing like a Scottish heath for gentlemanly adventuring.

331   Mr. Standfast   Doran 1919

The fourth in the Richard Hannay series, this time interweaving spying with the first world war. The war scenes are the best, together with Scotland. For the rest, romance, sentiment and villainy are rather perfunctory.

332   The Thirty-Nine Steps   H&S 1935/1915

A period piece in a genre that has multiplied without adding much to the devices here assembled. Surely the hunt of a single man by many over large and sparsely peopled tracts, preferably Scottish, has here its first modern illustration. It helps, too, that *both* the police and the evildoers are against the hero, Richard Hannay, and that on him should hang the fate of nations, though he is not represented as a superman.

333   The Three Hostages   HM 1924

A Richard Hannay story, with here and there some of the old impact but
gone soft and too long for its own good. Nevertheless, the finale among
the crags and scree of Scotland is still believable and even powerful.

334   BUCHAN, J. See also No. 2381 and:

       John McNab (not det.)   H&S 1925
       The Power-House   Doran 1916

335   BUCHAN, WILLIAM

       Helen All Alone   Morr 1961

John Buchan's second son writes well, indeed is something of a stylist,
and this tale of espionage and defection within a British embassy in a
small country behind the Iron Curtain is excellent. Helen, the young
woman called on by those higher up to save the ambassador from himself, is credible in spite of the fact that the "power" she possesses is not
made sufficiently explicit. But the buildup to the final holocaust is a very
smooth job, and there is even a little mystery along the way.

336   BUCKINGHAM, BRUCE (pseud. of Peter Lilley and Anthony
       Stansfeld; also Dane Chandos)

       Boiled Alive   MJ 1957

The scene is Tuxpan, a hot-spring resort in Mexico, where agents from
several countries do one another down for the mercury deposits in the
neighboring silver mines. The doings by day and night are melodramatic
yet tolerable, but the Mexican detective, Don Pancho, presumes a little
too much on his strange foreign ways before poetic justice overtakes the
murderer in a sort of *petite marmite*.

337   BUCKINGHAM. See also:

       Three Bad Nights   MJ 1956

338   BUDE, JOHN

       Death Makes a Prophet   Macd 1947

At this date the author's fourteenth: it is neither good nor bad. It keeps
one going by its leisurely involvement of more and more people and
motives, winding up in an intricate but clever and workable alibi scheme.
Though it is all about a queer cult, it avoids the most obvious features of
the theme and presents fairly amusing caricatures.

339   Trouble Brewing   Macd n.d. [c. 1945]

The readers mildly recommend this author's ability to present local color
and topography. Unfortunately the present tale, while reasonably competent and entertaining, does not rely on locale but confines itself to (small)

beer for the murder of a blackmailer. The method is picturesque enough, but too predictable. See also the series of *Cornish Coast, Sussex Downs, Lake District* [etc.] *Murders;* also *Death on the Riviera* (1952) and *A Twist of the Rope* (1958).

340   BUELL, JOHN

The Pyx   Crest 1960

A Montreal story of prostitution, stiff with realistic detail and untimely moralizing. Not readable.

341   BULLETT, GERALD (WILLIAM); also Sebastian Fox (1894–1958)

Judgment in Suspense   Dent 1946

The story of a headmaster, one of whose pupils is being crushed spiritually by his female guardian, the sister of a dead father who had been "wronged" by a flighty wife. This divorced wife comes to the school, bewitches the headmaster by her good manners and good sense, and he decides to find out by inquiry who was in fact wronged, for two very intriguing reasons. We are left with all the evidence neatly gathered and no proffered conclusion.

342   The Jury   Dent 1935

A murder trial presented in a fashion to put most other fictional trial scenes to shame. No detail is spared concerning the background of the jurors or their deliberations, nor of the evidence in the trial of Roderick Strood for the murder of his wife with chloral; yet the tale is neither cluttered nor too long. Its great point is that being an adulterer does not necessarily make one a murderer.

BULWER-LYTTON (SIR EDWARD GEORGE EARLE, later Baron Lytton; 1803–1873)

Anyone who thinks that the twentieth century has discovered villainy and cynicism, mental torture and the double cross, had better plunge into the rank vegetation of crime exhibited in the works of this author, who in his day was repeatedly accused of depraving the world by a false yet speciously attractive morality.

343   Eugene Aram   2 v. J. J. Harper 1832

Using the actual case (1759) of an appealing and learned man, the author exonerates him of murderous action and intent, while showing how his weakness gave the actual criminal a hold upon him. Eugene falls in love with a charming lady, but their romance is shattered by the reappearance of the murderer, and Aram pays the price of his folly.

   Note: Godwin (q.v.) suggested the idea to B.-L. after his own success with *Caleb Williams* (see No. 1002).

The Adventures of a Gentleman

The author's second and best is another tangle of seduction, hidden murder, relentless (and circumstantial) investigation, blackmail, underworld life, and ultimate vindication—all this as only the pre-Victorians had the nerve to do it and the breath to read it. If one knows how to skip judiciously, the impression that remains is favorable and powerful.

Note that the character of Thornton owes something to the actual murderer Thurtell (see No. 347), just as Varney in still another work (*Lucretia,* 1846) suggests Wainewright.

N.B. also: Bulwer's *Night and Morning* (1841) is sometimes included by booksellers among the author's crime fiction. It is actually a novel written to show that vice is as wicked as crime. To justify making social philosophy into a novel the author argues in his preface the then burning issue of art for art's sake.

345 BURGESS, ANTHONY

Tremor of Intent   Nort 1966

Advertised as, among other things, "a secret service entertainment gone mad," this affair suggests rather that earlier detective story gone mad *The Face on the Cutting-Room Floor* (No. 1422). Burgess is an English author and lecturer in linguistics, who has spent much of his life in Southeast Asia—no excuse for the present aberration.

Memo on the plot: the effort of an aging British agent to bring back from Russia a defected scientist who was his school friend. The sex business is particularly dreary and stale in its effort to be fresh and suggestive.

BURGESS, (FRANK) GELETT (1866–1951)

b. Boston; educ. Mass. Inst. of Technology; worked for Southern Pacific Railroad as mechanical draftsman for three years, then turned to belles-lettres. An early twentieth-century debunker, he created and defined the "bromide" and endowed literature with the indispensable word *blurb.* Poet of "The Purple Cow" and other masterpieces in *The Lark.*

346 Ladies in Boxes   Alliance Bk Corp. 1942

A Murder Mystery Novel

An unusual tone and outlook put forth by the first-person narrator transforms the commonplace elements of this plot into a strange yet solidly practical piece of detection. Physical clues are abundant and dramatic scenes well sprinkled throughout. That three very beautiful women should be murdered on the same day and that German espionage and British counterintelligence in the U.S. at the beginning of the second world war should form part of the explanation gives a very false impression of this unique tale. It is rational and it is detection, not spy stuff; and only a lack of right pacing keeps it from being master's work. It whets the appetite for *Two O'Clock Courage* (1934), *Master of Mysteries* (1912) being negligible.

347   BURKE, THOMAS   (1887–1945)

Murder at Elstree   LG 1936

A deft and brief retelling of the sordid murder of Mr. Weare by Thurtell
and Hunt in 1821. The form is fictional but sticks close to the facts,
including the presence and remarks of George Borrow (q.v., No. 3089)
at the execution of Thurtell.

348   BURLEY, W. J.

A Taste of Power   Goll 1966

A first novel about a coeducational grammar school, and full of good
touches. The teachers ring true, and so do the bits of chemistry. The
amateur detective, Henry Pym, fails to establish any marked personality,
despite the extravagances of taste employed to distinguish him. But his
investigation of the poison-pen letters and the murder related to them is
most satisfying.

349   Three-Toed Pussy   Goll 1968

The body of a sexually irresistible and predacious young woman of 25 is
found shot in her cottage in a small Welsh town. She had most of the
surrounding men in her power, as both partners and victims of her lust.
The discovery of her character and of her quietus is admirably done.

350   To Kill a Cat   Goll 1970

Wycliffe is now chief superintendent of the area CID (somewhere in south
Devon) and, as in *Three-Toed Pussy,* the murder is that of a beautiful
wild wench. The wayward Wycliffe is well suited to finding out which
amorous or criminal involvement led to the gentle strangulation and
vicious disfigurement of the young wife, whore, and striptease artist in
the sleazy hotel. Local people and a few London types are fairly well
done; sex is handled with evident relish; and the friction among policemen
seems not exaggerated. But the story as a whole lacks tension. JB and
WHT nonetheless agree that the *Cat* and the *Pussy* are better than the two
about Dr. Pym and his fair secretary. (The second about Dr. Pym is
Death in Willow Pattern (Goll 1969).

351   BURNHAM, DAVID

Last Act in Bermuda   Scrib 1940

A much-married but charming American actress is stabbed and mutilated
while being the guest of her oldest and most faithful male friend, and all
the other members of the house party are suspected and investigated by
Inspector Hopkins (as well as by H.'s kid sister). Local color is pleasant
and not overdone. Some fairly turbulent final scenes make up for a very
leisurely pace earlier.

BURTON, MILES (pseud. of Major Cecil John Street; also John Rhode, q.v.; 1884–1964)

It is now established by internal and ocular testimony that the prolific John Rhode and the no less prolific Miles Burton were one and the same writer. The evidence from stylistic habits was first brought out by Francis Nevins (q.v.) and clinched by reference to subject matter in *The Menace on the Downs* (No. 373). Then JB obtained direct testimony from Miles Burton's editor at Collins, now at Macmillan. Despite the identity, there are differences between the works written under the two pseudonyms. Burton's tend to be wittier and less dependent on mechanical devices, as well as more concerned with scenery and character. They are often less solid, too, the outcome being sometimes pulled out of a hat rather than demonstrated. Now that Burton and Rhode are one, the former's frequently printed birth date 1903 is obviously erroneous.

352   Accidents Do Happen   CCD 1946/1945
       In Eng.: Early Morning Murder

A series of contrived accidents is designed to save an English village from being turned into the pandemonium of a holiday camp. Desmond Merrion, the amateur, does nothing but listen to a novelist friend whom he is visiting, and Inspector Arnold does not appear, but the recital and the discovery of the motive are enjoyable despite the lack of hard thought.

353   Bones in the Brickfield   CCC 1958

A late effort, not at all to be despised. The motives and characters are as well depicted as the countryside, which B. always does well. The fall of an entire cliff adds piquancy to a series of decidedly unusual events.

354   The Cat Jumps   CCC 1946

Solidly based on village life and characters. This is probably the only tale in which the helpful amateur (here the usual Merrion) receives a legacy from the murder victim. Inspector Arnold does not dither, and the cat is well done, not overdone, and thoroughly functional in the plot, the chemistry of which—says WHT—is just possible.

355   The Chinese Puzzle   CCC 1957

This story of what amounts to Chinese gang activity in an English seaport certainly flies in the face of Father Knox's rule, but despite the pidgin English, rice, and occasional opium smoking, one can spend a soothing and enjoyable evening with it. It is one of Burton's better efforts to make Desmond Merrion effective as well as imaginative. The political background of the killings is credible and the villain reasonable enough.

356   The Clue of the Silver Brush   CCD 1936/1935
       In Eng.: The Milk-Churn Murder

The silver brush is only one of a surfeit of clues, some put into a milk can with the (headless) corpse by the murderer to *distract,* and some added later to *help,* justice. The whole thing is unsatisfactory, though Merrion stirs his stumps a bit, particularly after a second and gruesome murder right on his own hearthrug. The story ends with a remarkable chase in a railway shunting yard.

357   **Dark Is the Tunnel**   Coll 1936
        In Eng.: Death in the Tunnel

The first Burton story that the collectors ever read, and brand new at the time. Among railway stories the present tale ranks very high, as it does also among Burton's large output. The motive of revenge, the shenanigans with the airshaft, the timing, and the telling are all excellent, and the few faults characteristic of the mid-thirties in no way spoil a most rereadable affair.

358   **Death at Ash House**   CCD 1942
        In Eng.: This Undesirable Residence

A somewhat humdrum wartime tale (featuring Arnold but not Merrion, who is presumably in Intelligence), and of which the central feature is the creation of a plausible exchange of names and personalities. Threatened exposure by a relative makes a second murder necessary.

359   **Death at the Club**   CCC 1937
        In U.S.: The Clue of the Fourteen Keys

One of Burton's best in his early *Death* series. At least until the final scene, which is unconvincing, the management of people, events, clues, and interrelations among Sir Edric Conway, Inspector Arnold, and Desmond Merrion is masterly throughout. The locale is attractive, the counterplot ingenious, and the clues well chosen.

360   **Death in Shallow Water**   CCC 1948

The title should be: "Burton in Shallow Water," with inspiration at low ebb. The tale reads along well enough, but the whole business is dull. Arnold and Merrion are way below par, as well they may be in what is labeled their thirty-ninth joint endeavor.

361   **Death Leaves No Card**   CCC 1939

We have here the murder by electrocution, in a bathroom, of a man whom there is no motive to murder. Inspector Arnold solves the case without any help from Merrion, who does not appear. It is good vintage Burton, not too gadgety or too long in unwinding.

362   **The Death of Mr. Gantley**   Coll 1934/1932

One of Merrion's earliest cases—in fact his third since *High Eldersham.* Some of the props are timeworn now, but thirty years ago the will hinging on survivorship, the casual "identification" of a bearded man by quasi strangers, the fulminating gadget to provide an alibi—all were considerably fresher. Arnold functions, and the Inspector Young of *High Eldersham* is referred to.

363 Death Paints a Picture   Coll 1960

Rather better than most of the late-late Burton. No new dodges, but three murders, some smuggling, and a bit of art quite neatly tied together. Merrion sticks to his assumption of a single murderer but does little legwork to prove it.

364 Death Takes a Detour   CCC 1958

The first part of this rural tale is very engrossing, as is the size of the river, which floods ten square miles and forces various people to spend the night at unscheduled stops and to sally forth at midnight on errands undeclared. About the middle, everything begins to disintegrate: the evildoers turn out inconsequential, and the murderer and his actual deed are a great letdown.

365 Death Takes a Flat   CCC 1940
In U.S.: Vacancy with Corpse

In this excellent plot, the difficulty of fitting in all the known details, which are numerous, and the friendly antagonism between Inspector Arnold and Desmond Merrion are the main features. Psychology and atmosphere are close to nonexistent, yet a substitute interest is maintained to the very end.

366 Death Visits Downspring   Dday 1941

A wartime story in which both Inspector Arnold and Desmond Merrion function, but here Merrion, highly placed in Intelligence, gives the orders and Arnold is the subordinate. Interest surrounds a radio transmitter whose concealment is cleverer than the villain's. An alert reader should be able to guess the truth about both while enjoying murder and espionage with plenty of action.

367 The Devereux Court Mystery   CCC 1938/1935

An early Burton that suffers, in WHT's opinion, from the London setting (Merrion and Arnold operate better in the country) as much as from the author's infringement of one of the cardinal rules of the detective story. Still, the lorry business is new here and attractively done, and JB thinks extremely well of the whole affair.

368 The Disappearing Parson   CCD 1949
In Eng.: Death Takes the Living

A very poor tale in which the motive and identity of the criminal are obvious from the beginning. The only likable character is killed off on p. 46, and Arnold and Merrion's following of a clearly marked trail holds little interest.

369 Found Drowned   CCC 1956

Merrion and his wife spend a holiday at a seaside town where M. went to prep school. One of the two sons of the former school doctor is found floating off shore, and M. does a nice bit of detective work with tides and flow of the local river to show that the body "entered the water" at a town some miles upstream; but the various subplots are pedestrian and B.'s colorless characters too numerous.

370   Four-Ply Yarn   CCC 1944
       In U.S.: The Shadow on the Cliff

WHT enjoyed this account of Merrion's activities while a captain of Naval Intelligence during the second world war. Spying around an important west country port provides M. with ample opportunity to use his wits, and he does come up with two items of detection involving potatoes and fence posts. JB was not so enthralled.

371   Heir to Murder   CCC 1955/1953

Burton was to go on writing in a similar vein for seven or eight years after this but was already well past his prime. (So was Merrion's wife, apparently, for she is at the resort of Carmouth for a "cure.") Nevertheless there is some interest in the four crimes, the first achieving the death of the local medico while "reversing his car" on a pier, and all four were planned by a fairly obvious villain to secure a reversion of another kind. Superintendent Arnold not in evidence.

372   Legacy of Death   CCC 1960

Competently presented and never straying far from a convalescent home, where gossip and occasional death among the inmates provide Arnold and Merrion with a rather routine problem.

373   The Menace on the Downs   CCC 1931

This third detective tale is noteworthy for several reasons other than intrinsic merit, of which it has only a modest share. First, it contains evidence that Burton and John Rhode (q.v.) were but one man. On p. 74, the interests attributed to the character Veringham are those Rhode exhibited under his real name of Street when he wrote about the history and politics of central Europe (see his biography below). And the present tale turns on a point explicitly drawn from a life of Tomáš Masaryk. Once more the story has to do with cultist activities and it is laid in rural England. Many of the clues are best appreciated by country people, and when Inspector Arnold of the Yard comes to investigate the murders of two youths, it is only his knowledge of German and a glance into one of Veringham's books that lead him to the somewhat improbable explanation of the crimes.

374   Mr. Westerby Missing   CCD 1940

The problem of disappearance is an attractive one that is seldom treated satisfactorily. Burton did a good job of it once or twice, but not here. Despite a great deal of circumstantial matter, the pace and the characters in this tale keep it dull, the criminal being the one engaging person in the whole crew.

375   Murder at the Moorings   Coll 1932

Very Poor!

376   Murder in Absence   CCC 1954

Merrion and his wife cruise on the Mediterranean in a freighter and witness some rather well-concealed skulduggery, which M. is later able to tie in with a case that Inspector Arnold brings to his attention in London. The cruise is of more interest than the crime. Detection minimal; characterization a bit better than average for **B**.

377   Murder of a Chemist   CCC 1936

A representative early Burton. Arnold is not quite such an oaf as he subsequently became, though he does "spend an hour or two . . . jotting down a few ideas." Merrion comes in promptly and is full of ideas, some good. The "chemist" is, of course, a pharmacist, and he dies on p. 13. The detection is chiefly concerned with the alibis arising from journeys by car and train of a large party on tour, and timetables and other facilities are nicely involved. The poison is the oxalic acid so popular in the thirties.

378   Murder out of School   CCC 1951

The school hardly figures in this story of double bluff, double murder, and double investigation by the police and the secret service. Merrion plays on both sides of the last-named duplicity and helps a local as well as Inspector Arnold, both impetuous in the pursuit of red herrings. The prey turns out to be red also, but that's another matter.

379   Murder Unrecognized   CCC 1955

Intolerably padded with descriptions of hills, paths, farm implements, and sheep. No one should judge Burton by this fiasco, in which Merrion goes about with Mavis in tow, having left his "imagination" at home. But Burton readers will recognize nevertheless a good situation unrealized.

380   Not a Leg to Stand On   CCD 1945

Burton does well with his favorite country setting and country policemen. Merrion shines and Arnold is little more than grumpy throughout. The doubt as to Disappearance or Murder is skillfully protracted almost to the end without exasperating the reader. And there is, besides, the delightful extravaganza of the Golden Image, which keeps popping up without marring the credibility. The only serious flaws are that the villain is not adequately prepared for and the motive for any villain not sufficiently great to justify all the precautions.

381   The Secret of High Eldersham   Coll 1930
          Also: The Mystery of High Eldersham

This tale of witchcraft in an English village remains the classic presentation of "doings," which writers find it so tempting to combine with long-
headed detection. Desmond Merrion makes his debut here, meets his
future wife, and joins the shrewd and capable Inspector Young in the
elucidation of the mysterious happenings on an island near the river
mouth. Boating interest is served, and cases of murder and smuggling
are satisfactorily solved without benefit of any Inspector Arnold. Few
stories of this era have stood up so well.

382   Situation Vacant   CCC n.d. [1946]

Not one of the better Burtons, though there is a pair of unreformed criminals who have a certain charm, as does their cover, which is a rest home
for elderly horses in Central America. Merrion appears after 120/192
of the tale is over and does not distinguish himself. In fact he puts on a
ridiculous disguise and nearly lets himself be poisoned during his interview with his suspects. Picrotoxin, from *cocculus indicus,* is the really
active agent in this story.

383   A Village Afraid   CCC 1950

One of his very worst. The story is a mass of cardboard, incidents, and
false identities, all disclosed in the dullest manner imaginable. Arnold
and Merrion dither together.

384   Where Is Barbara Prentice?   CCC 1936
          In U.S.: The Clue of the Silver Cellar

The fur coat of a woman who has disappeared from her home in a quiet
English town is found on the buffers of a branch-line locomotive, but
there is no good evidence that she was killed or even hit by the train.
Superintendent Rowley is later aided in his investigations by Arnold
and Merrion, and the routine, though lengthy, is interesting. A not-too-
complex plot provides for a motive of theft of "plate," the guilt of the
most desirable person, and the answer to the question of the title.

385   Who Killed the Doctor?   CCD 1944
          In Eng.: Murder, M.D.

One of B.'s best-constructed tales—compact, well characterized, and full
of legitimate surprises. The denouement, in which the reader meets an
unlikely killer, is suitably prepared and comes pat without arousing disbelief.

386   A Will in the Way   CCD 1947

JB thinks better of this work than does his fellow critic. The good points
are: steady pace; much reasoning, without any patent red herrings; and
some original points and persons. The crime of killing a woman by throw-

ing her downstairs (infrequent since the days of Queen Elizabeth and Amy Robsart) marks a variation in means, and the motive is as solid as the contrived opportunity. And the will of a certified lunatic, not at large, yet sane, presents interesting problems. Also, Merrion is entertaining enough to make one wonder why he tolerates Inspector Arnold's company.

387   Written in Dust   Dday 1940
        In Eng.: Murder in the Coalhole

The body of a "school correspondent" (evidently a sort of overseer and representative of the local school board) is found, dead and gassed, in a coalhole on school premises. The story has an average plot, rather easily seen through, but is unusual among the Burton tales for its quantity of rather dry humor and its recognition of sex. Arnold and Merrion argue in more sprightly fashion than usual.

388   BURTON. See also:

Beware Your Neighbor	CCC 1951	The Man with the Tattooed Face	
The Charabanc Mystery	CCC 1934	(= Murder in Crown	
A Crime in Time	CCC 1955	Passage)	CCC 1938
Dead Stop	CCC 1943	Mr. Babbacombe Dies	CCC 1939
Death at the Crossroads	CCC 1933	The Moth-Watch Murder	CCC 1957
Death at Low Tide	CCC 1938	Murder on Duty	CCC 1952
Death in a Duffle Coat	CCC 1956	The Platinum Cat	CCC 1938
Death of Two Brothers	CCC 1941	Return from the Dead	CCC 1959
Devil's Reckoning	CCC 1948	A Smell of Smoke	CCC 1959
Fate at the Fair	CCC 1933	Something to Hide	CCC 1953
Ground for Suspicion	CCC 1950	The Three-Corpse Trick	CCC 1944
The Hardway Diamonds		The Three Crimes	CCC 1931
Mystery	CCC 1930	To Catch a Thief	CCC 1934
Heir to Lucifer	CCC 1947	Tragedy at the 13th Hole	CCC 1933
Look Alive!	CCC 1949	Unwanted Corpse	CCC 1954
		Up the Garden Path	CCC 1941

389   BUSH, CHRISTOPHER (also Michael Home, b. 1885)

        The Case of the Second Chance   Macd 1946

Though pretty late and pretty bad, this longish wartime story, complete with Superintendent George Wharton, Ludovic Travers, and an actor-manager corpse, shows that Bush has the narrative gift as well as some notion of what a detective story should contain. Did he not once long ago use as a clue the angle at which the dead man's walking stick lay in relation to the body? Here the famous team muff their first chance, land into another case, and go back for their second and successful stab at solving Manfrey's murder.

390   Dead Man Twice   CCD 1930

A work that only goes to show that, bad as Bush is in the sixties, he was even worse in some of his works of the thirties. This, one of his first half dozen, is a far cry from the middling-satisfactory *Tea-Tray Murders*.

By no means a great detective story, but WHT was pleased to find that his recollection of it as reasonably good twenty-five years ago was justified by a second reading. There is some fairly adequate characterization of the despicable headmaster, governors, and masters of an English suburban secondary school, a good twist or two to the plot, which involves oxalic-acid poisoning, and quite enough competence to qualify the author as a respectable craftsman. Travers and Superintendent Wharton are both credible, and the bit about chemical apparatus is possible, if a bit unlikely.

392   BUTLER, GWENDOLINE

Coffin in Malta   Walk 1965/1964

Fairly well-done local color, but the same surplus of girls per family that dominated *The Dull Dead* and the same humdrum detective (Winter), the expense of bringing whom from England is hardly justified by the way he waits around until the distraught criminal admits the decapitation of the retarded boy whose age is never given.

393   The Dull Dead   Walk 1962/1958

More ways of spinning a dull yarn are known to British faculty wives (Mrs. B. hails from St. Andrews) than anyone thought possible. This is pure EIRF. There are four girls in the family to whom the mix-up occurs, and the characters play on the reader's nerves, as well as each other's, à la Kelly. The official detective is a stick, and the murder lies on the fringes of a story that deals mainly with juvenile to- and fro-ing.

394   BYROM, JAMES (pseud. of James Guy Bramwell, b. 1911)

Or Be He Dead   C&W 1958

A very original tale involving the possibility of suing for libel a young author who has used a case of murder and blackmail of the 1890s as the basis of a crime story, only to find that one of those acquitted is almost certainly still alive. Well written and steadily entertaining.

395   Take Only as Directed   C&W 1959

A second effort by an author whose first proved him original. In this one we enjoy the predicament of a narrator-physician who gets involved with the police through providing a sexual alibi for a former flame, now a neurotic and asthmatic divorcée. One knows well in advance who the bogey man must be, but his unmasking is done to a turn. Not detection in the strict sense.

CAIN, JAMES M(ALLAHAN) (b. 1892)

b. Annapolis; educ. Washington Coll.; worked as reporter on Baltimore *American,* where H. L. Mencken encouraged him to write. Cain stands side by side with Hammett and Chandler as a headliner in the tough school, but competent as Cain is, he seems less original (and regional) than the other two and, lacking their style, gives the impression of having merely played exercises on a formula.

396   Double Indemnity   Knopf 1936

A novel of cynical greed which, with *The Postman Always Rings Twice*, established Cain as a familiar name. He did not produce others as notable. These two are famous for the depiction of ambitious crime but seem now less striking than they once did.

397   The Postman Always Rings Twice   Knopf 1934

This is a "powerful" account of a devouring physical passion that leads to murder, drink, death by car wreck, and execution at the state's expense. The popularity of the work continues after a third of a century and two million copies sold, but it is neither detection, nor crime in the usual sense, nor a masterpiece of fiction.

398   CAIN. See also:

The Butterfly Knopf 1947	Career in C Major	Knopf 1943
Cain x 3 (Knopf 1969), containing,	Galatea	Knopf 1953
with an Introd. by Tom Wolfe:	Love's Lovely	
The Postman Always Rings Twice,	Counterfeit	Knopf 1942
Mildred Pierce, Double Indemnity.	The Moth	Knopf 1948
(See as well a review and summary	Serenade	Knopf 1937
of Cain's work by Ross Macdonald		
in the *New York Times* for March		
2, 1969.)		

399   CAIRD, JANET

       In a Glass Darkly   Morr 1966

The small Scottish town supplies a good setting, the people are varied and arouse interest, and the impetus given by seeing murder done while the heroine is looking through a camera obscura is acceptable. But the excessive femininity and protracted wanderings, dangers, and lovelornings of the principals grow tedious before the end.

400   Murder Scholastic   CCD 1968

At a Scottish coeducational school, an elderly and selfish master is stabbed and an attractive elderly woman teacher hanged to look like suicide. Two young women and the young scholar-suitor of one of them detect and agonize in rather excessive fashion.

401   Perturbing Spirit   Dday 1967

This novel justifies its title without being Gothic, frenetic, or Fremlinesque. The scene is a small, attractive Scottish border town, and its collective problem is: just what is the black-caped Sinbad Mazaron after, as he undertakes the revival of their annual festival? The riddle is beautifully dealt with. No phony sex and a plausible ending.

The title alludes to *Hamlet* I, 5, 183.

402   CAIRD. See also:

The Loch   Dday 1969

403   CAIRNS, CICELY

Murder Goes to Press   Macm 1951

The only book by this author, described as a "journalist of wide experience," who died before the work was published. On rereading, both JB and WHT found much to admire in the characterization and evident knowledge of the journalistic world, but wondered how they had ever stomached the bickerings of the heroine-detective and her lover, much less the preposterous plot, relying far too much on French resistance.

404   CALVIN, HENRY (pseud. of Clifford Hanley)

It's Different Abroad   Harp 1963

JB calls this "a new twist in an old genre" and evidently enjoyed it. WHT presumes that the "old genre" would be "maiden in peril." He finds a group of small variations on the theme rather than any single *volte-face*, but the whole thing is artfully done. The sister and brother-in-law of the Scottish maiden who is the heroine are rather stock, and perhaps everyone escapes from peril just a bit too easily. Query also whether a Scottish virgin, having been seduced at her own urgent request on a cellar floor, cushioned only by two or three thicknesses of burlap, would ask for more of the same forty-eight hours later.

405   CALVIN. See also:

The Chosen Instrument   Hutch 1969
The DNA Business   Hutch 1967
The Italian Gadget   Hutch 1966
Miranda Must Die   Hutch 1968
A Nice Friendly Town   Hutch 1967

406   CAMPBELL, HARRIETTE

Crime in Crystal   Harp 1946

Some partial characters and a few "strong" scenes, but not believable as a whole and totally unconcerned with physical plausibility.

407   CAMPBELL, R. T. (pseud. of Ruthven Todd)

Bodies in a Bookshop   West 1946

A very disappointing little book, despite a good title and very attractive binding and printing. The byplay between the amateur detective (Professor Stubbs) and Chief Inspector Bishop is not amusing, and Stubbs' assistant, Max, falls far short of being the Archie Goodwin needed to liven up Mr. Campbell's tale. The bookishness per se is not bad; but the author, who is a good poet, is not cut out for detective fiction.

408   CANDY, EDWARD (pseud. of Barbara Alison Neville)

      Bones of Contention   Goll 1954

The author, a practicing physician, knows her art and its appurtenances—hospitals and medical journals and research. But she writes in the style of Ivy Compton-Burnett, making every character speak out his inmost thoughts in calm, detached sentences of rather stilted cast. The result is that there is no variation of pace, no excitement, and—in the end—no forceful denouement. The novelist thereby shirks her most difficult problems.

409   Which Doctor?   Rine 1953

In the University Hospital at Bantwich, the pediatric section of the Royal Academy of Medicine is holding a meeting. A boy patient sees something untoward from the balcony of his ward and is kidnapped to prevent his telling. Only some of the medicos are made distinct from the lot. The chase at the end lacks conviction, and the motive lacks circumstantiality.

410   CANDY. See also:

      A Season of Discord   Goll 1964
      Strokes of Havoc (not det.)   Goll 1966

      CANNAN, JOANNA [Mrs. J. H. Maxwell Pullein-Thompson] (b. 1898)

A delightful writer whose style and subjects attract the curious reader but who baffles him in two ways: her novels are extremely scarce, in both libraries and bookshops, and their titles do not make it easy to tell the detective fiction from the rest. The one unmistakable hint is that something called *Oxfordshire* (Hale 1952) is a guidebook.

411   All Is Discovered   Goll 1962

Again the contrast between the stupid Inspector Price (foreshadowing Dover, alas!) and his bright underlings is played up far too much. Though Price's passion for being thought "U" is amusing, it doesn't take the place of detection in this story of murder at a seaside resort. As for the solution, it is as dated as the motive.

412   And Be a Villain   Goll 1958

A physician is found dead of a broken neck in his own surgery, and his wife, sister, mother-in-law, and receptionist, plus disgruntled patients and others are suspected. The smug and snobbish Inspector Price accomplishes little, but his subordinate Macleod has points. To follow the fashion, the author has made every character and situation in this tale depressingly shabby. Even the elderly heroine, who singlehanded uncovers the murderer at her own peril, is periodically belittled for fear we should think her privileged by fate and strength of mind.

The title is from *Hamlet* I, 5, 109.

413   Body in the Beck   Goll 1952

At the outset one must admit that Detective Inspector Ronald Price is a caricature, his genteel-vulgar traits, speech, and habits deliberately overdone in order to permit a hostile kind of humor at his expense. The rest of the characters are limned more subtly and are variously engaging—from the maid at the inn who worships the hero (Oxford don and mountain climber) to the vivacious, luxurious, and amorous Lady Nollis and the irascible Dr. Muswell of St. Crispin's College. They all get involved in the murder of a blackmailer, in the midst of excellent mountaineering weather and landscape in the Lake District. The first cause and the least likely culprit are both original, and the telling has Joanna's lively literary touch.

Query: How did the convention of expressing shock or physical concussion by being sick—i.e., vomiting—ever get started in the detective novel? It is confined to the English scene but is so frequent there that it deserves a name to itself: the Emetic Moment.

414   Death at "The Dog"   Rey 1941

An excellent rural English tale. J.C. has the ability to make a group of people and their relationships vivid and dynamic. Here the method of the crime is a little shaky and the detection is largely going about and about, but Detective Inspector Guy Northeast is sensible and likable both. The setting is "Loamshire."

415   Long Shadows   Goll 1955

A short detective novel in a light vein. Two pairs of detectives function: Superintendent Price is an amusing and cliché-ridden foil for his sergeant, whose education and tastes are superior. The young American wife of a British husband and her charwoman's intelligent daughter do the unofficial detecting and get caught up in some amusing scrapes. The crime is "literary" and is done to avoid scandal.

416   Poisonous Relations   Morr 1950
           In Eng.: Murder Included; *also* They Died in the Spring
           In U.S., also: The Taste of Murder

This admirable work is certainly the most retitled story in our list. The original caption, *Murder Included,* is the best suited to the plot, which grows out of a paying-guest arrangement designed to save an old house. The horsey, no-nonsense heroine is a fine creation, and the detective work matches the other first-class elements.

417   They Rang Up the Police   Goll 1939

The motive is unusual and the character of the young Inspector Guy
Northeast marks a departure from the norm of the thirties. But perhaps
both these advantages are supplied at the cost of speed and variety in the
narrative. The all-female household pervaded by gentility and superficial
goodwill is credibly done, but at too great a length, and Northeast's
difficulties with his superiors are a trifle excessive. Still, the plot is solid
and the details show J.C.'s vigilant exactitude.

418   CANNAN. See also:

       Gin and Murder   Hamm 1959

419   CANNING, VICTOR

       Doubled in Diamonds   Hein 1966

V.C., who is but little known in the U.S., is capable of doing a very fair
English imitation of the private eye who works alone but also for the
police. Here it is diamonds and drugs, a pair of beautiful Chinese twins
(female), and a lovely English blonde that the hero, Carver, manipulates
in both senses of the term. The dialogue is witty, the action fast, and the
implausibilities well glossed over.

420   CAPES, BERNARD (EDWARD JOSEPH) (d. 1918)

       The Skeleton Key   Coll 1919; orig. 1917
         Introd. by G. K. Chesterton

Poet, romancer, historical novelist, short story writer, and author of five
tales of mystery, B.C. is praised by Chesterton for the imaginative power
of his fictions. He was also recommended to JB by the late Victor Gollancz,
but although the forepart of this tale is written with care and art, the
improbability of the mechanics, motive, and denouement rule it out of
serious consideration.

       CAPON, PAUL (b. 1912)

b. Suffolk; educ. St. George's, Harpenden; film-maker and author of some
thirty novels; translator of The French Wines by Georges Ray (Walk
1965).

421   Among Those Missing   Hein 1959

An adventure story in British Guiana, about the self-rescue of a man
wanted for murder, two women, and two other men, the only survivors of
a plane crash. It reminds one of the excellent tale Four Frightened People
by E. Arnot Robinson, neither being detection.

422   Image of Murder   TVB 1949

More easily tolerated by WHT than by JB. The entire plot—quite long-
winded—hinges on the fact that an actor uses an advertising model (male)

to substitute for him on certain occasions, and later, for purposes of his own, kills him to provide himself with a new life and identity.

423   CAPON. See also:

Brother Cain	Hein 1945
Death on a Wet Sunday	WL 1952
Malice Domestic	WL 1954
Margin of Terror	WL 1955
The Murder of Jacob Cansey	Hein 1947
No Time for Death	WL 1951

424   CARGILL, LESLIE

Death Goes by Bus   HJ 1936

As routine crime-and-detection of its period, this is not bad work. But it is overlong, and the reader becomes skeptical as more and more of the strangers on the bus are found to have dire connections, criminal or passionate. The best part of the tale is the thought and behavior of Mr. Morrison Sharpe, the chess and puzzle expert, who can think one move ahead of both crooks and police. He is quaint and eccentric in just the right way, though short of memorable.

425   Matrimony Most Murderous   Roy n.d. [1958]; orig. 1949

It is a pity that a writer with such facility should waste it on an improbable plot about amnesia, a false marriage, villains and jewels, and idiotic traps for hero and heroine. Each incident has a certain vivacity, but the chain is weak as putty.

426   CARLETON, MARJORIE (CHALMERS) (1897–1964)

The Bride Regrets   Morr 1950

A fictional account, adapted to the American scene, of the George-Joseph-Smith-Brides-in-the-Bath system. It is well done from the circumstantial and psychological points of view; it avoids harrowing, does not go on for too long, and ends happily.

427   Vanished   Morr 1955

Exceptional in its competent handling of many elements that usually produce disaster: young woman narrator, enigmatic lover, missing husband, child-niece, and grim but devoted household retainer, three murders. The reader is able to enjoy the mystery, like the characters, and feel that the whole thing works out rationally without curbing emotion—a minor triumph. Boston and rural New Hampshire scene.

428   CARMICHAEL, HARRY (pseud. of Leopold Horace Ognall, b. 1908)

Alibi   Macm 1962; orig. 1961

The detective John Piper, an insurance investigator, has figured in eighteen earlier tales, of which WHT found only *Requiem for Charles* acceptable, and a couple of others miserable. In *Alibi* plot and detective work are good enough to encourage risk-taking with other titles.

429 The Late Unlamented CCD 1961

Though hardly an inspired writer, H.C. has by now plenty of technique to keep a story of true detection going and to skate over the needed improbabilities. He can sketch characters with deftness and change their spots in keeping with events. In the story at hand his scruffy journalist, Quinn of the *Morning Post*, becomes more self-respecting and less drunk and disgusting than before, from motives of justice and of compassion close to affection for a misused girl. He is still only 33, so there's hope for him.

430 Money for Murder CCC 1955

Despite favorable comment by Julian Symons on the work of this author, this specimen presents little but sloppy writing. The railway interest in the tale is of the slightest, and the motives and actions in the crime itself are quite unconvincing.

431 Of Unsound Mind CCD 1962

Seven suicides in a row in London and vicinity lead John Piper to suspect a connection. The unpleasant Quinn helps him run to earth the common factor, which, of course, turns out to be blackmail. Not the worst Carmichael, but not the best detection, invention, or narration.

432 . . . Or Be He Dead CCD 1958

The insurance assessor John Piper and his friends, the grubby journalist Quinn and the characterless Inspector Hoyle, disentangle a kidnapping that leads to two murders and much misery for two other persons. The plot starts out well, but H.C. almost always winds up with naïve explanations. Here, by the way, the widower Piper finds his enchanting second wife.

433 Post Mortem CCC 1965

John Piper looks into a case of unhygienic death in a bath—standard fare.

434 A Slightly Bitter Taste CCC 1968

Though the unprepossessing crime reporter Quinn starts out on this adventure by getting dead drunk at a party he has crashed, interest picks up when he is taken by his female rescuer to a weekend gathering where the hostess turns up dead. The local inspector is excellently done and Quinn helps him work out the intricate but quite plausible tangle. H.C. is never brilliant, but he has become solid and moderately lively.

CARNAC, CAROL (pseud. of Edith Caroline Rivett; also E. C. R. Lorac, q.v.; 1894–1958)

435   The Affair at Helen's Court   CCD 1958

Tedious recapitulation of the details of a 27-year-old smash-and-grab raid. Improbable criminals. Julian Rivers, instead of detecting, indulges in pure guessing. The scene is a deluxe rest home.

436   Copy for Crime   CCD 1951

A dull and mechanical plot about art forgery. Inspector Julian Rivers is excessively middling, if one may so put it.

437   Death of a Lady Killer   CCC 1959

At a hotel in the resort of Bourne Regis, Brigadier Fotheringay, a rich idler, flirts with the fashionable widow Mrs. Delancie. His body is found at the foot of a cliff, and the widow has vanished. Inspector Strang goes to work but doesn't quite live up to this good beginning.

438   The Late Miss Trimming   CCD 1957/1956

A did-she-fall-or-was-she-pushed? tale, with interesting characterization and better-than-average psychological clueing-in of the right suspects. Inspector Julian Rivers this time acts with fair plausibility.

439   Murder Among Members   CCD 1955

A tale of murder on the roof of a "Parliament Hostel" in London. The story is cluttered, despite good details of a chase through Blackwall tunnel into Surrey. Miss C. is obsessed with the wonderful woman who runs the hostel.

440   Policeman at the Door   Coll 1953

The usual English family tree, not graced by much detection.

441   Upstairs and Downstairs   CCD 1950

WHT thinks this rather good: London scene, good atmosphere, demise of filing clerk in medical research center brought about by clever manipulation of automatic elevator and skylight. The author believes that victims of diabetes exhale an odor of acetylene.

442   CARNAC. See also:

       The Burning Question   Coll 1957
       The Double Turn   Coll 1956
       Impact of Evidence   Coll 1954
       Rigging the Evidence   Coll 1955

443   CARPENTER, MARGARET (b. 1893)

       Experiment Perilous   LB 1943

All the makings of a superb story—an original plot, a good set of characters, some sound motive-building, and an arrangement of the parts of the puzzle well adapted to keep up suspense to the end. But the great excess of comment and the unbelievably female responses of the male doctor-hero nullify all the other merits. The prose is fine, but what it tells us is false. Still, one can say: "Read it for the good story that lies buried here."

CARR, GLYN (pseud. of Frank Showell Styles, F.R.G.S., b. 1908)

Under his real name G.C. has written extensively on mountaineering, especially in Wales—e.g., *Modern Mountaineering* (Faber 1964)—and has led expeditions to the Arctic and the Himalayas. In addition to his numerous detective novels, he has also produced historical and sea stories, articles, juveniles, and plays. In 1961 Constable published his *Battle of Steam: Revolution in Britain*.

444   A Corpse at Camp Two   Bles 1955

The author's sixth tale, featuring as usual Abercrombie Lewker, the actor-manager who climbs. For those who take their mountains from train or plane windows the essential sameness of the technique—and landscape—may tend to blur differences among the stories. Yet they differ. Those of British locale generally fare best. The present tale, dealing with an assault on the Nepal Himalayas, is from the point of view of characterization and conciseness something of a tour de force, even though the murder occurs only in Chapter 12.

445   The Corpse in the Crevasse   Bles 1952
        Contour map of Hochkogel Glacier and surrounding peaks

This Lewker adventure, the fourth, occurs before the actor's knighthood. He is described here as much less attractive physically than he became after that honor was conferred, and it is even a wonder how the paunchy and squat Shakespearean of this book can perform the mountaineering feats he is credited with. But his "deductions" are excellent. They take place at a skiing resort thirty miles from Innsbruck, where a party of five go in search of rest, health, and sport. Another member, due later and not so popular as he might be, is overdue, then found as a c. in the c. As is true of the author's other Continental tales, this one seems more contrived than his British ones, the foreign characters being too sketchy and too picturesque at the same time, and the motives too threadbare. But the central idea is first rate.

446   Death Finds a Foothold   Bles 1961

Full of character, suspense, and apprehension. Laid in the Snowdon region, the mountaineering is wintry but intelligible. The complicating effects of army maneuvers, anonymous letters, and illicit loves are all done in masterly fashion, and there is just the right amount of Shakespeare and humor, some of this last coming from the introduction of a trio to rock climbing.

447   Death of a Weirdy   Bles 1965

A fairly good Lewker tale with a minimum of mountaineering and a group of weird English visitors to Wales, one of whom (hetero-homo) is bumped off by another (homo-homo). Despite the low company, Carr's writing continues high.

448   Death Under Snowdon   Bles 1954

The story of a would-be murderer caught in his own booby trap, the modus operandi being worked out by Abercrombie Lewker just before he is made a knight. Good Welsh scenes and dialogue; only a little mountaineering.

449   Holiday with Murder   Bles 1960

This story is laid in Majorca; there is no climbing till the very end, and that is mild. Agreeable, but not first-class Carr, except for some entertaining quotations from the "English" of a local guidebook.

450   Lewker in Norway   Bles 1963

Very different from previous tales, this one makes of Sir Ab a lone-wolf pursuer and pursued. The occasion of this semi-secret-service chase is not important when compared with the delightful accidents by fjord and crag. Some of the characters are better than others, but the whole work is an undoubted success.

451   Lewker in Tirol   Bles 1967
        Diagram of Stubai Alps

Except for the aging Lewker's recovery of nerve in a tight spot, this adventure is uninteresting and its plot unconvincing. Motives are diffuse, and not even Sir Ab's being bashed on the head contributes the genuine thrill of desire to turn the page.

452   Murder of an Owl   Bles 1956

The author's seventh, and essentially the same old stuff, this time embellished with scenes of boy scout life (plus two murders or attempted murders of scouts), and provided with the somewhat improbable collusion of a war criminal and the young man who had helped him escape to England. Snowdon locale.

453   Murder on the Matterhorn   Dutt 1953

This is now established as the first tale in which the actor-mountaineer Abercrombie Lewker figures as the detective. He has not yet been knighted. JB was put off by the Swiss-German setting and the melodramatic characters, and indeed the book suffers from "continental disease," so harmful to detection.

454   Swing Away, Climber   IW 1959

The rock climbing in Wales which furnishes the special interest does not steal the show, and Sir Abercrombie is entertaining, besides being adept at real detection. Plot and villain both unusual.

G.C. discovers new possibilities in the old witchcraft dodge. The mountaineering is minimal and certainly not technical. The quotations from Shakespeare are apt and the girls (especially the bossy one) well done, and one only regrets that Mrs. Lewker goes out of the story after being brought into it very pleasantly. To identify the tale, let it be said that one element is the hiding of masterpieces of art.

456   CARR, G. See also:

Fat Man's Agony   Bles 1969
The Ice-Axe Murders   Bles 1958

CARR, JOHN DICKSON (also Carr Dickson and Carter Dickson, qq.v.; b. 1905)

b. Uniontown, Pa.; educ. there and elsewhere in U.S.; began writing detective stories in 1930 and moved to England the following year, staying there through the war and until 1948. Worked with Adrian Conan Doyle on the life of Sir Arthur (see No. 2913) and on pastiches of Sherlock Holmes (see No. 2474) His specialty is ingenuity of means and intricacy of plot, with occasionally a strong interest in historical reconstruction. He now lives in the South (U.S.).

457   Below Suspicion   Harp 1949

A Gideon Fell story, which means an immense amount of claptrap in pointless interchanges with Patrick Butler, the barrister briefed to defend the innocent-looking girl who turns out a surprise to all. Butler is insufferably egotistical and inane, and the author plays unfair tricks with his description of several characters. Sex amateurish and repulsive at the same time.

458   The Burning Court   Harp 1937

A stunning situation to start with, which leads to steadily more complicated problems—all perfectly clear, thanks to the art of this master of plotting, who at this time still controlled his verbal exuberance in narration and did not think he had to add trivial, local suspense to the general and deeper kind produced by the story. What spoils this work for the collaborators is the parallel with a seventeenth-century she-devil, who claimed magical powers of survival and is offered to us as reincarnated in the twentieth century. To be sure, we are also given a rationally possible explanation of the events, but the odor of brimstone overcomes the factual sense and renders the story a hybrid.

459   The Case of the Constant Suicides   Harp 1941

This has been called "Carr at his best" by someone in the *Saturday Review*. The statement is true, for this tale offers a few characters and a few problems that are soberly and adroitly dealt with, instead of being enveloped in a mixture of highjinks and red herrings as the author likes to do with his good situations and brilliant solutions.

460   The Dead Man's Knock   Harp 1958

This is a mishmash of Alexandria (Va.) infidelities and neo-Leslie Fordisms, plus Fell at his most flatulent. Not for the connoisseur.

461   Death Watch   Harp 1935

The impossible Dr. Gideon Fell makes ugly noises throughout this story composed of irrelevancies and broken action and dialogue. As in Wagner, "drama" is produced by too-frequent climaxes, which are seen in retrospect to have no significance.

462   The Ghost's High Noon   Harp 1969

One of his sober and sustained efforts. It is a reconstruction of pretense and skulduggery in New Orleans before 1914, with politics, love, and murder interwoven. Too much research shown off in "period fact" and not enough attention paid to "period language," but up to nearly the end the plot is skillfully treated and the people are entertaining.

463   The Nine Wrong Answers   Harp 1952

A trick story with footnotes and much addressing of the reader to show him where he went wrong and how adroitly the author covered his tracks. There is no police work properly so called, but rather a game between reader and writer.
    Note a discussion of Sherlock Holmes matters in Chapter 21.

464   Patrick Butler for the Defence   Harp 1956

A fantasmagoria in the J.D.C. manner, with moments of real farce. Little detection, but the author's habit of irrelevance applies here to incidents rather than to the narrative. Some of the hotel scenes are good, though what P.B. does is not to be believed.

465   CARR, J. D. See also Nos. 2390–3:

*Castle Skull	Harp 1931	*It Walks by Night	Harp 1930
*The Corpse in the		*The Lost Gallows	Harp 1931
Waxworks	Harp 1932	The Man Who	
*The Four False Weapons	Harp 1937	Explained Miracles	Harp 1963
Hag's Nook	Harp 1946	Poison in Jest	Harp 1932
The House at		The Witch of the	
Satan's Elbow	Harp 1965	Low Tide	Harp 1961

    * These first five novels precede the introduction of both Dr. Fell and Sir H. Merrivale and display the talents of Henri Bencolin on a background of Paris in the twenties. Jeff Marle chronicles four of the five cases.

CARTER, (PHILIP) YOUNGMAN

b. 1904 in Herts; educ. Christ's Hospital; m. Margery Allingham (q.v.) in 1927. Reporter for *Daily Express,* later editor of *Tatler.* Collab. with his wife on her novels; completed her last one, *Cargo of Eagles,* and, using her plot for *Mr. Campion's Farthing,* produced his first solo performance (1969). A second, *Mr. Campion's Quarry,* is scheduled for 1971.

466   Mr. Campion's Farthing   Hein 1969

Margery Allingham's central idea, written out by her husband. He has wit and dialogue and descriptive skill, but the tale is a clutter. Like Dickinson's *Old English Peepshow* (No. 746), the setting is an historic house on view for tourists. The antiquities are half faked and the presiding genius, a peppery old woman, is well done, but the violent events do not bear scrutiny and the explanation is foolish.

467   CARVIC, HERON

      Miss Seeton Draws the Line   Harp 1970

The author gives us the mixture as before but it fails to charm. Although Miss Seeton continues to be a "character," her gift of detecting criminality by means of her own sketches of the subject is here played up beyond belief. The crimes in which she assists the police are child-murder and post-office robbery, and the reader's interest must lie in guessing to what extent, if at all, these are connected. The humor is not up to the standard of Carvic's first.

468   Picture Miss Seeton   Harp 1968

A first novel in a difficult genre—the serio-comic story of crime and detection. Miss S., an elderly spinster with an umbrella who teaches drawing in a girls' school, passes through dangers and assists the police in a tale of youths and drugs. She provides excellent fun and the author avoids bathos thanks to excellent prose and a good sense of English village life. Who is the Veronica suggested by the author's anagrammatic pseudonym?

469   CATALAN, HENRI, specializes in detection and mystery solved by sisters in religion who may be shy in action but are not diffident in thought or lacking in moral courage. See *Soeur Angèle and the Bell Ringer's Niece* (1957) and *Soeur Angèle and the Embarrassed Ladies* (1955).

470   CECIL, HENRY (pseud. of Henry Cecil Leon)

      No Bail for the Judge   C&H 1952

Whether one likes Cecil's specialty or not, one cannot deny it an original character, which combines ingenuity, observation of life, and knowledge of the law. Though the people often act with sudden and surprisingly powerful motives, it is the narrative briskness (as in E. M. Forster) and not the invention that gives a shock. Here a judge is tried for a murder he did not commit and his release is brought about by the cleverness of a very intelligent crook who does some first-class detection as well as high-handed persuading of witnesses. Comedy in scenes and dialogue is excellent and not out of proportion.

A characteristic extravaganza, full of serious things, such as the retrial of a convicted murderer by a judge and witnesses corralled and coerced, thanks to the escaped convict's daring and managerial ability. Excellent humor, too—the art of farce pressed into service to entertain the reader through crime and reflections about the law.

Note: This tale was made into a play by Saroyan in 1959 and a film in 1961.

472   Unlawful Occasions   Harp 1959

This work belongs to the series that does not contain the egregious Colonel Blimp, created by H.C. to make some of his points about the law. This second group consists of entertaining extravaganzas based on legal quirks and odd character traits, fused to produce excellent farce and thoughtful reflection.

473   CECIL. See also:

According to the Evidence Harp 1954	Daughters in Law	Harp 1961
Alibi for a Judge MJ 1960	Friends at Court	Harp 1956
The Asking Price Harp 1966	Natural Causes	C&H 1953
Brothers in Law MJ 1955	Portrait of a Judge & O.S.	Harp 1965

474   CHABER, M. E. (pseud. of Kendell Foster Crossen; also Bennett Barlay, Ken Crossen, Richard Foster, Christopher Monig, Clay Richards)

The Gallows Garden   Rine 1958

The insurance investigator Milo March is a former army major who has some individuality and is addicted a bit more to martinis and a bit less to wenching than some of his contemporaries. In the Republic of Santa Monica (Dominican Republic), he takes part in a thinly disguised version of the actual Galíndez murder mystery (New York, 1955). Precious little detection, and none too much suspense, but moderately entertaining set-tos with the local cops. Spanish is freely quoted.

475   Softly in the Night   Rine 1963

The author's eleventh Milo March adventure. M.M. is in California investigating suspected arson and murder. The story is fairly routine but not hopelessly so. There is some tricky faking of dental work to provide the false identification of a corpse (possible) and a supposition (impossible) on the part of the author that dental X rays of two mouths could be identical.

476   The Splintered Man   Rine 1955

One of the first by this author to feature Major Milo March. The action is typical: March is hauled out of civilian life and back into the CIA so that he can go to Berlin and track down a politically important defector. The usual cloak-and-dagger stuff is mildly believable and is given an added fillip by March's encounter with drug-induced schizophrenia. Suspense in moderation but scarcely any detection. Freely-quoted Goethe is scarcely a substitute, though it does credit to the author's taste.

477   CHALMERS, STEPHEN

The Crime in Car 13   CCD 1930

A man is murdered in a lower berth on the New York A. & M. train to Montreal, which also carries an observant newspaperman as far as Lake Clear Junction. The details are good enough, but the sophomoric talk and attitudes of the characters make this secret service tale well-nigh unreadable.

Note: The date is 1913 and President Wilson appears in the last chapter.

478   CHAMBERS, PETER (pseud. of Dennis John Andrew Phillips; also Peter Chester, b. 1924)

Murder Is for Keeps   Schu 1962

Remarkable in that it is the American hard-boiled-private-eye tale done to a turn by a Britisher, and with surprisingly few false notes. Mark Peterson is the agreeable dick, and only toward the end, where a pair of gangster brothers slobber over their respective sexual and other deficiencies, is there anything to upset the reasonably fastidious reader of the genre. There are half a dozen others by this author in his double capacity. See *The Bad Die Young* (Hale, 1967).

479   CHANCE, JOHN NEWTON (b. 1911), has written some fifty tales, many published by Robert Hale and dealing with the doings of Jonathan Blake. *Wheels in the Forest* (1935) was his first. Then came *Murder in Oils* (1935) and *Maiden Possessed* (1937). Judging by *The Fate of the Lying Jade* (1968) and reviews of some others, this author deals in perpetual peril of the most violent and least motivated kind. Only the setting varies, and the name of the wench. Other titles: *Alarm at Black Brake, Dead Men's Shoes, Death Stalks the Cobbled Square, The Double Death, The Man Behind Me, Mantrap.*

CHANDLER, RAYMOND (1885–1959)

b. Chicago, reared in England, educ. Dulwich Coll.; free lance on *Spectator* and *Westminster Gazette;* RAF in first world war; returned to U.S. (Calif.) in 1919, where successful in the oil business, only to become insolvent in the Depression. Began writing in 1933, at the age of 48, publishing stories in *Black Mask*. His locale was Southern California, his output small—seven novels and a batch of short stories, which he "cannibalized" for some of his great works. After his death, a selection of his letters was published (see No. 2918).

480   The Big Sleep   Knopf 1939

The author's first, which established him as a master of all the qualities requisite for the new tough genre made respectable by Hammett and exemplified in the short form in the magazine *Black Mask:* atmosphere, suspense, unexpected violence, sardonic dialogue, sharp-focus description, and hatred of class and of power. This story has them all and stresses the last.

481   Farewell, My Lovely   Knopf 1940

Judged his best by the author himself. It is a model of complexity kept under control, with a holocaust at the end. Its contents are the now familiar ones of political and personal corruption, double-crossing, and the woman killer.

482   The High Window   Knopf 1942

Described by Sandoe as "beyond the Hammett tradition," this early exploit of Philip Marlowe's is certainly high in the merit list. The Pasadena scene, the characterization, the tough-yet-literate style match the complex plot, involving counterfeiting and blackmail. Just how the photograph of the victim was obtained is glossed over, but all other details are clearly etched.

483   The Lady in the Lake   Knopf 1943

A young wife has been missing for a month and Marlowe is hired by the husband whom she is about to leave for another man. The exposition of situation and character is done with remarkable pace and skill, even for Chandler. The scene shifts to Little Fawn Lake, where talk between a local woman, the caretaker of the missing wife's cabin, and Marlowe produces speculation about the absent girl, her lover, and also the missing wife of the caretaker; whereupon comes the dramatic discovery of the corpse in the lake. It is *not* Marlowe's quarry. From then on this superb tale moves through a maze of puzzles and disclosures to its perfect conclusion. Marlowe makes a greater use of physical clues and ratiocination in this exploit than in any other. It is Chandler's masterpiece and true detection.

484   The Little Sister   Knopf 1949

This late exploit of Philip Marlowe's is not up to the earlier ones, though full of good *dram. pers.* Marlowe himself seems tired. The plot requires too many murders. The author does manage a nice twist at the end—a variation on the old "least-likely-person" theme—and the characters of the three Quest siblings from Manhattan, Kansas, are superbly done.

485   The Long Goodbye   HM 1954

Late in the author's output, yet showing the qualities that distinguish him. What is gone is the zest and, of course, the novelty of the genre, as a result of widespread imitation by others.

A good while after the six main works, this one is shorter, slighter, and more mechanical. Marlowe is weakening (by his own standards), since he takes on an impossible girl who is running away from a quite imaginary threat and forces her to trust him. There is some silly back-and-forth with $5,000 of traveler's checks, a double fornication without much zest, and at last a transatlantic phone call summoning Marlowe to marry his one true love.

CHARNWOOD, (GODFREY RATHBONE BENSON, 1st baron) (1864–1945)

Noted in the U.S. for his biographies of Lincoln (1916) and Theodore Roosevelt (1925), Charnwood, late in life, wrote one story of crime. He wrote only those two biographies: the sparing hand seems to have been his ideal.

487   Tracks in the Snow   Dial 1928/LG 1906

Orig. pub. as by Godfrey Benson

Told in the first person, the novel begins with the murder of the narrator's best friend, and goes on to unravel the causes with a placid, deliberate preciosity, charged with envy, revenge, and jealousy. There is little detection proper, yet the story is a unique and desirable specimen of the near-genre.

488   CHARTERIS, LESLIE (pseud. of Leslie Charles Bowyer Yin)

The Saint *versus* Scotland Yard   Burt 1930

The eighth book about the Saint, who thereafter flourished rather in the short-story form. Simon Templar and his beautiful wife live by their wits and do good on the side, in a Robin Hood–Raffles series of adventures. This volume contains three long jazzy tales, somewhat connected, but printed in different type faces: *The Inland Revenue, The Million-Pound Day,* and *The Melancholy Journal of Mr. Teal.* Not our dish.

489   CHASE, JAMES HADLEY (pseud. of René Raymond; also James L. Docherty, Raymond Marshall, and Ambrose Grant; b. 1906). Made his reputation with the grim *No Orchids for Miss Blandish* (1939) and has written many others in the same shocking shocker tone: *A Coffin from Hong Kong* (1962), *Lay Her Among the Lilies* (1950), *A Lotus for Miss Quon* (1961), *Trusted like the Fox* (1948), *You're Lonely When You're Dead* (1949), etc.

490   CHESTERTON, G. K.

The Man Who Was Thursday   Arr 1908
A Nightmare

This allegory-adventure contains no fewer than six detectives, for Chesterton liked to populate his world with the clan, but the form of the story owes more to Stevenson's *Suicide Club* than to any tale of crime and detection. It is a morality play in narrative, which depicts order and anarchy, Satan and God, the poet and the obsessive literalists at logger-heads with nature, society, and their own circumstances. It is fun and often wise, but not serious, and so paradoxical as to be a *summa* of Chestertonisms.

491 CHEYNEY, PETER (1896–1951)

   Ladies Won't Wait   DM 1951

Until 1943 this English writer turned out quantities of pseudo-American tough stories. Then he went in for spy stuff, many of his books being titled *Dark* something or other and using recurrent characters. The present one is typically thin and pointless. The Americanese of the earliest tales is carried over into this Parisian and Continental intrigue, in which the beautiful women are as false as the "intelligence" or the terror.

492 The Dark Omnibus   DM 1952; orig. 1943
     Contains: The Stars Are Dark, The Dark Street, and Sinister
     Errand
     Introd. by Anthony Boucher

Dull tales of espionage with Quayle and a variety of impossibly beautiful girls, pistols, and platitudes. Boucher's Introduction praises P.C. for adopting the "realism" of Ambler and refers slightingly to Oppenheim without remembering him accurately.

   CHILDERS, (ROBERT) ERSKINE (1870–1922)

Of Anglo-Irish descent, educ. at Haileybury and Trinity Coll., Camb.; clerk in the House of Commons from 1895 to 1910; spent holidays sail-ing in Dutch and German coastal waters; volunteered in Boer War and wrote part of its history. Then became an advocate of the Irish cause, though he served in the first world war. He joined the Republican Army of the Free State and was shot as one of the leaders in the postwar revo-lution.

493 The Riddle of the Sands   Peng 1960; orig. SE 1903
    Maps

An espionage classic antedating the first world war. Its virtues make it an undoubted masterpiece, particularly attractive to those who enjoy small-boat sailing in hazard. Dutch setting, excellent prose.

494 CHILDREN, DETECTIVE STORIES FOR. There are of course a great many stories for children that use as a main or accessory theme the pursuit of criminals or spies. Some use a domestic scene, others a historical one, still others transfer the situation to the animal world—the variations are endless, and these readers have not followed the literature, only noticed the fringes of it as children in the family or nearby required such reading.

What is remarkable is that as in the adult output, good tales have a long life—e.g., Erich Kastner's *Emil and the Detectives* (Scholastic Book Services 1966; orig. 1929); Walter R. Brooks' *Freddy the Detective* (animals); (Scholastic 1967; orig. 1932). Donald J. Sobol's *Tales of Encyclopedia Brown, Detective* (Scholastic 1967; orig. 1963) are more up to date. All three are good in their kind.

See also: Nos. 1082, 1170, 2012, 2033, and 2255, as well as Howard Haycraft, ed., *The Boy's Book of Great Detective Stories* (Harp 1938).

CHRISTIE, AGATHA (MARY CLARISSA), CBE, also MARY WESTMACOTT b. 1891)

b. Torquay, the younger daughter of F. A. Miller of New York; educ. at home. Married Colonel Archibald Christie in 1914, divorced in 1928 (one daughter). Married Max E. L. Mallowan, Professor of Archaeology at the University of London. Lives in Greenway House, Churston Ferrers, Devon, on the river Dart.

Some of her early books, such as *The Man in the Brown Suit,* are not detective stories but tales of adventure and intrigue. In some of these the bright young pair Tommy and Tuppence Beresford play at detection in a manner now intolerable. Several of Miss Christie's stories have been made into plays, with interminable success: *The Mousetrap, Witness for the Prosecution, Spider's Web, The Unexpected Guest,* etc.

495   After the Funeral   CCC 1953

Not one of Agatha's best. The scheme is obvious and worked out repetitiously. After the funeral someone says that the deceased was murdered, whereas no one had suspected it. Another murder follows, then two further attempted murders. A collection of young and old people provides suspects. Poirot finally comes in and unmasks the least likely, for a motive carefully concealed.

496   And Then There Were None   DM 1940
             In Eng.: Ten Little Niggers; *also* Ten Little Indians

A tour de force on the following trapeze: invitations go out to a group of people, all of whom have been responsible for the death of someone by negligence or intent. The island on which the party is gathered is owned by the would-be avenger of all those deaths. The events and the tension produced by the gradual polishing off of the undetected culprits are beautifully done. One improbability, well hidden, makes the whole thing plausible.

497   At Bertram's Hotel   DM 1966

This is a pleasant atmospheric tale, displaying Christie's talent for characterization by thumbnail in unimpaired condition. But the effortless drive of twenty years ago is gone. Miss Marple observes as well as ever, yet deduces little. The author's fatherly, countrified type of official detective is one Chief Inspector Davy; his bright underling is less well done. The too-good-to-be-true hotel (Brown's, actually) is superb and the plot right out of the newspapers.

498   The Big Four   DM 1927

Though a Poirot story, it is a period piece of the mastermind-of-crime variety. (See Stout's *League of Frightened Men.*) Mrs. Christie's melodrama is not done with conviction and hence does not convince.

499   Blood Will Tell   Black 1951
              Also: Mrs. McGinty's Dead

A Poirot story with Mrs. Oliver thrown in for humor; otherwise, an ingenious plot involving the discovery of one of the offspring of some scandals of twenty years earlier, so as to account for the murder of a charwoman who presumably found an incriminating photograph. Complex and well handled, as well as amusing.

500   The Body in the Library   DM 1942/1941

The author shows what she can do by taking a cliché and turning it inside out with humor and virtuosity. The body that turns up in the married colonel's library is that of a dancing hostess from a neighboring seaside hotel. The setting is St. Mary Mead, whence Miss Marple has drawn her knowledge of human evil and duplicity and applies it to the case at hand, predicting a second murder and averting a third. Superb.

501   Cards on the Table   CCC 1936

A fairly good Poirot story, in which the psychology of four bridge players is used to determine which of them is the most likely suspect in a murder committed in the card-room.

502   A Caribbean Mystery   Coll 1964

Miss Marple goes on a West Indian holiday and solves two murders, thus preventing a third. Despite the exotic setting, the characters and relationships are perfunctory, and one has the impression of reading an expanded short story rather than a full-blown tale.

503   Cat Among Pigeons   DM 1960

Three teachers die at the Meadowbrook Girls' School. Poirot is called in and does a largely intuitive job, mostly fussing.

504   The Clocks   CCC 1963

An interesting plot told in a novel manner, through an alternation of first person narrative by the young-hero-Intelligence-man and impersonal narrative about the official investigation by Inspector Hardcastle. Poirot is aged, sedentary, and bored; and Colin Lamb, who is the son of P.'s erstwhile friend Superintendent Japp, brings the pieces of the puzzle to Poirot for his entertainment and armchair solution.

A passage of some interest (pp. 122 ff.) presents Poirot's critique of certain historic crime investigators and some recent writers of detective fiction.

505   Crooked House   DM 1949

Another large family, which exists to raise the question: "Who killed the old man?" The adjunction of Levantine Leonides in quantity does not save this standard plot from tedium.

506   Dead Man's Folly   Coll 1956

A Poirot story of late birth and showing the author's weakening grip on action and dialogue. Characters are still done to a turn, though Poirot himself does not shine. The plot is complex and huddled at the end, and the principal agent (the husband) is so slightly sketched in that the reader does not credit him with the power to do what he is said to have done.

507   Death Comes as the End   DM 1944

A heavily researched story of murder in the year 2000 B.C. at Thebes on the banks of the Nile. The tale is based on letters from a farmer (the Hekanakhte Papers), discovered in A.D. 1920–21 by the Egyptian Expedition of the Metropolitan Museum of Art. A prefatory note indicates the scholarly sources of the plot and characters.

The story itself, even in the hands of the competent Agatha, shows that exotic settings adopted in toto bring on the frigid feeling of "Who cares?" Van Gulik, it is true, gets away with his Chinese judge, but one suspects he does it by being thoroughly unscholarly.

508   Death in the Air   DM 1935

Good solid Christie, with Poirot in charge from the beginning, since he is on the plane with the French woman moneylender who is done in by a poisoned dart. Methodical but not enthralling.

509   Endless Night   DM 1967

A sharp break with all her previous work: none of her usual detectives. No résumé would be fair since the impact of the book depends upon a skillfully worked-out *volte-face* involving two characters. The creator of Roger Ackroyd has done it again, in a different way, but without any pretense at detection.

510   Hercule Poirot's Christmas   Coll n.d. [1938]
              In U.S.: Murder for Christmas; *also* A Holiday for Murder

An early example of the Big English Family dominated by an eccentric old character. He and his victimized offspring are not badly done, but the discovery by Poirot of the improbable mechanics of murder and the disclosure of no fewer than three false identities among the suspects leave one gaping and dissatisfied.

511   Hickory, Dickory, Death   DM 1956

A Poirot story, and very dull. Locale, a student hostel. Thefts and a murder
occur, which P. tackles in halfhearted fashion. Substance trivial, skipping
irresistible. A typographical gem occurs on p. 6: "Not for her the state
of mind of Cortex's men upon the peak in Darien."

512   The Hollow   DM 1946

A triumph of her art, not so much of characterization—for the detective
story does not really permit true character study—but of *motive-building.*
That is where A.C. is unrivaled. She knows how to make plausible the
divergence between action and motive that maintains uncertainty until
the physical clues, the times, and other objective facts mesh with motive to
disclose the culprit. The great art is to multiply the ambiguities of feeling,
action, and gesture without falling into obvious patterns about greed,
revenge, and the like.

Here the familiar figure of the able, virile, brilliant man whom women
go for is admirably sketched and provided with three possible women
murderers and their possibly jealous men. In addition, an elderly *femme
folle* very well done—and Poirot.

513   Murder at Hazelmoor   DM 1931
In Eng.: The Sittaford Mystery

A disappointing story because so much of it is so good. The people are
entertaining, the situation is fresh and puzzling, the division of the burden
of proof between Inspector Narracott and the bright young pair is neatly
worked. JB attributes the failure to the denouement, not because of the
surprise gimmick but because of the surprise doer—a terribly weak
motive, for a character not suited to inducing belief in his act.

514   Murder at the Vicarage   DM 1930
With diagram

The interest lies in the date, which marks a turning point in Agatha's output: Henceforth Poirot and detection predominate, gradually replacing
the earlier adventure stories and the thrillers with Tommy and Tuppence.
The plot of this novel is intricate; Miss Marple is in it, and village life
plays a heavy role. But it is well constructed and holds the reader's attention on the problem of who wanted Colonel Protheroe out of the way.
The byplay between the vicar and his flirtatious wife is also an amusing
innovation.

515   Murder in Retrospect   DM 1941

A little masterpiece. Others have tried to retrace the history of an old
crime and they have failed to convince readers of the likelihood. Poirot
succeeds, while combining physical and psychological clues in an impeccable structure. Interest never flags for a minute, the liveliest concern
is felt for each of the seven characters, and the device of the least likely
person comes off once again.

516   Murder in the Calais Coach   DM 1934
       In Eng.: Murder on the Orient Express

This is the tour de force in which Agatha makes conspiracy believable
and enlivens it by a really satisfying description of the Taurus Express
(part of the Orient system; see No. 103).

517   A Murder Is Announced   Black 1950

A well-told story—her fiftieth—of blackmail and murder in an English
village. Miss Marple does the detecting, and the author plays very fair with
the reader in the laying down of a trail leading to the unmasking of a most
satisfactory least likely person.

518   Murder Is Easy   CCC 1939
       In U.S.: Easy to Kill

Unquestionably one of her triumphs. The murders are excellent, though
numerous. Miss Marple is credible and does not irritate by fussiness. The
love story is very good, and the hocus-pocus with demonology and the
Black Mass is entirely apposite.

519   The Murder of Roger Ackroyd   DM 1926
       Plan of Victim's Study (p. 89)

Presumably the clamor over the "stunt" pulled by Miss Christie in her
most famous if not best detective novel has now died down. Yet there was
no cause to complain: the narrative is straightforward and absorbing;
Poirot, drawn out of retirement and employing Dr. Sheppard as his
Hastings, is industrious and not irritating; the village scene amusing. A
Dictaphone is used effectively in a way no longer available to an author
today, but "time of death" is handled expertly, and the clues pointing to
the culprit are all there to be seen by the astute.

520   Murder on the Links   DM 1923

One of the earliest Poirot tales, and not a bad one. Poirot functions
typically, and outstrips the representative of the Sûreté; Hastings falls in
love and is to all appearances hooked at the end of the book, but his
inamorata never turns up again.

521   Murder with Mirrors   DM 1952

A school story. Miss Marple goes back, an "old girl," and unravels
"events" and a fatal accident in a gym. As is always true of such tales,
there is too much nerves, femininity, and "friendships," unrelieved by
masculine coarseness and sense.

522   The Mysterious Affair at Styles   DM 1930; orig. 1920
       A Poirot Mystery

The first book by the master, which it is hard to believe was turned down
by several publishers and then neglected for a whole year by the one that

has made a fortune out of her—200 million copies extant in all forms and languages.

Though the touch she acquired for swift motive-building and motive-breaking is not yet in evidence here, her invention of situations and clues and her skill in plotting are well developed, and the story is a marked improvement on the genre as then practiced. The murder of the elderly woman of wealth and the neighboring love affairs that provide red herrings are beautifully tangled, to be sorted out by Poirot with the aid of plentiful physical clues.

Note that Poirot (1) has a limp from wartime injury, (2) has already retired, his great period having been 1900–1904, and (3) is associated with Inspector James Japp, a small ferrety man of the Lestrade type.

523   The Mystery of the Blue Train   DM 1928

Though it comes after *Roger Ackroyd* and a few other first-rate works, this longish novel does not strike us as successful. Most of the characters are out of the prop closet, and the plot is melodramatic in a tired way. As for the train, it does not occupy the satisfying role that the Taurus Express does in the *Calais Coach*.

Memo: This Blue tale (which is not a *conte bleu*) presents the murder of a selfish American girl, daughter of a millionaire, for the possession of a string of rubies. There is double impersonation, and more oral testimony than physical clues. Poirot, retired, pontificates.

524   Ordeal by Innocence   DM 1959

A very unpleasant group of ill-assorted adopted children, finding that one of their number must have murdered their "mother," spend most of the book wondering which one did it. Detection nil, entertainment ditto. None of the usual Christie sleuths officiates.

525   An Overdose of Death   DM 1940
In Eng.: The Patriotic Murders

One of Agatha's half dozen triumphs of plotting and detection. The death of his dentist sets off Poirot's inquiry into the relationships of persons of very different kinds, united only—it would seem—by their sharing the dentist's services. The denouement that brings home the crime to the least likely person and the reason for his deed are both managed by a master hand.

526   The Pale Horse   DM 1962

An amazingly fresh piece of work, free from old saws, despite the forty-year span of authorship. Though she is now a "Ltd. Co.," Agatha can still spring a surprise on the reader, even after he has been given every chance to see it first. This story relies on Mrs. Oliver without Poirot; detection is carried out by an oldish-young scholar called Mark Easterbrook, and what he investigates is superbly organized murder compounded with black magic. A classic treatment of the paralytic suspect-cum-wheelchair is thrown in for good measure.

527   Peril at End House
DM 1932

At once melodramatic and perfunctory, this tale works the least-likely-person ploy on the audience after the criminal has worked it on Poirot. The Cornish setting doubtless inspired the author to dedicate the story to Eden Phillpotts, in gratitude for early encouragement.

528   A Pocket Full of Rye
DM 1953

Rather tired Christie. Miss Marple officiates. The murder is of a gent in an office, by poison. The scene is full of housemaids and annoying indirections by Miss Marple.

529   Poirot Loses a Client
DM 1937

The poisoning of an aunt by a niece—an everyday affair not worth the bother.

530   Le Secret de Chimneys   Librairie des Champs Élysées 1963
In U.S.: The Secret of Chimneys (DM 1925)
Trans. by Juliette Pary

A very funny cock-and-bull adventure story, half murder and detection, half Prisoner of Zenda, in which Superintendent Battle does the honors for Scotland Yard. It is translated with dash and verve and humor into very acceptable French.

531   Sparkling Cyanide
CCC 1945
In U.S.: Remembered Death

A characteristic Christie affair, though without benefit of Poirot, Colonel Race being the amateur who assists the police. Each of a large group of people is suspected in turn of having poisoned at least one (and some two) of the others. The plot is ordinary; there is even a relative from the Argentine. Only the cyanide is sparkling.

532   There Is a Tide
DM 1948

Hercule Poirot, functioning only in the latter half of this just-postwar story, does a fairly convincing though mainly intuitive job of sorting out impersonation, accident, suicide, and murder as they affect the Cloade family. After the one wealthy member is killed immediately following his marriage to a supposed widow, it is to the advantage of the others to get rid of the lady. A good example of "least likely person." A clever and unusual method of establishing an alibi by telephone is employed, yet as a whole the story is not as satisfying as it should be.

533   The Third Girl
DM 1966

Admirers of the author will not blemish their vision of her by reading this late one.

534   They Came to Baghdad   DM 1951

A standard use of the person who knows something damaging or dangerous but doesn't know that she knows it. This situation is complicated by
the unreliability—not to say pathological lying—of the chief witness
(female); altogether a mechanical and overlong affair.

535   Towards Zero   DM 1944

Agatha has always liked the combination of the big house on the cliff, the
large party composed of relatives and in-laws at odds with one another,
plus a couple of mysterious and possibly good-for-nothing male visitors.
All these give sufficient reason for fastening the murder(s) upon almost
any one of the group. The present brew is one of her best servings, en-
hanced by almost too many cleverly arranged clues, some of them laid by
the murderer to bring off a double bluff. Poirot functions only to the
extent of being wished for by Inspector Battle, who is solid and acceptable.

536   What Mrs. McGillicuddy Saw   DM 1957
         In Eng.: The 4.50 from Paddington
         Also: Murder She Said

A Miss Marple story and one of the best latter-day Christies. It owes something to Garve's *Cuckoo-Line Affair,* dealing as it does with something
seen to take place in a passing train and (naturally) misinterpreted.
    A small and curious point, in view of the original English title, is that
the U.S. version has the train leaving at 4:*54.*

537   CHRISTIE. See also Nos. 2416–30 and:

The ABC Murders	DM 1936
Appointment with Death (= Make Mine Murder)	DM 1938
The Boomerang Clue (= Why Didn't They Ask Evans?)	DM 1935
By the Pricking of My Thumbs	DM 1968
Evil Under the Sun	DM 1941
The Man in the Brown Suit	DM 1924
The Mirror Crack'd [From Side to Side]	DM 1963
The Moving Finger	DM 1942
Murder in Three Acts (= Three-Act Tragedy)	DM 1934
[The Mystery of the] Sad Cypress	DM 1940
Partners in Crime (No. 2424)	DM 1929
The Seven Dials Mystery	DM 1929
Thirteen at Dinner (= Lord Edgeware Dies)	DM 1933
The Mousetrap (= Three Blind Mice) (ss)	DM 1948

538   CLARETIE, JULES (1840–1913)

         Le Crime du Boulevard   1897

This work is listed only because it occurs in Keller's *Readers' Digest of
Books,* where the compiler reports that "the mixture of pseudo-science
and sensational detail . . . is thoroughly French." The gimmick here
seems to be the taking of a photo of the retina of the dead man's eyes,
imitated from Duboisgobey (No. 773). The rooted belief that it would

reveal the last image seen by the victim is what may have led the murderer of P.C. Gutteridge, in 1927, to shoot the dying policeman through each eye.

539   CLARK, DOUGLAS

Death After Evensong   S&D 1970

Like most of its current counterparts, this novel of murder in a distasteful English village has plenty of incident designed to be "realistic" but actually only crude. Nevertheless, the author keeps a firm hand on the plot, and his detective, Chief Inspector Masters, rises imperturbably above the nagging of his subordinates. The criminal's motive is unusual but good, and the method used to put a hole through the vicar's heart yet leave no trace of a bullet is clever, modern, and reasonable.

540   CLARKE, ROBERT

Murderers Are Silent   Hale 1969

A California setting that bodes no good to the reader, and in the event reminds him of too much that he has read before.

541   CLAYMORE, TOD (pseud. of Hugh Clevely)

Appointment in New Orleans   Cass 1950

The chief interest lies in the two women characters—TC's little daughter and the egregious witch and termagant Poppy Laleham. Both are entertaining creations. The plot is haphazard and the hero simple-minded. It is crime without detection, yet with a certain rational interest for the observer of the human scene.

542   Nest of Vipers   Cass 1948

Most of the characters have a perverse charm, but the pace seems slow and the delays uncalled for. Still, this is probably the best of those that come after Claymore's debut (see No. 544). He has power of a sort, and one would wish it concentrated in fewer words.

543   Reunion in Florida   Cass 1952

The lure in this author's stories is the well-studied relation of a father to his subadolescent daughter and to his erstwhile tennis partner, an unscrupulous and intelligent virago. It hardly matters where the story is set, or what problem is to be solved; the difficulties experienced by the hero-narrator are the center of the reader's concern.

544   This Is What Happened   S&S 1939
          In Eng.: You Remember the Case

The story that introduced Tod Claymore to the reading public, through what purports to be his own firsthand account of how he interrupted his career in tennis to help Scotland Yard solve a murder mystery in an English country house. The telling is straightforward and well spiced with humor of an agreeable kind. Characters are differentiated, the stage is set for Tod's brief marriage, and there is a fair amount of good observation and deduction.

CLEEVE, BRIAN (b. 1921)

An Irishman, he lived and studied in South Africa before returning to Dublin, where he became a Ph.D.

545   Death of a Wicked Servant   RH 1964/1963

Set in a fair-sized Irish coastal town. Inspector O'Donovan works hard and thinks a good deal without producing any very original ideas. The gentry have no morals, and the hero is a weakling. What goes on is described with the cruelty which passes current for truthfulness. Both victim and murderer are too low to be entirely satisfactory. As Irish stuff, no challenge to Dillon or Fitzgerald, who possess just as much native lore.

546   CLEMENTS, E(ILEEN) H(ELEN) (b. 1905)

      Discord in the Air   H&S 1955

The author's thirteenth and much like the earlier dozen. For JB's taste she rattles too much and doesn't supply enough substance for her wordage. In this one the "musical village" and its objection to airplane testing is a fair subject, but her hero, Woodhead-the-well-named, is tedious. Sentiment, "art," patriotism, and skulduggery are mixed with a feeble love story.

547   Let Him Die   Dutt 1940

A sound British tale of a guardian and a former love's children, without much mystery but with good atmosphere.

548   The Other Island   H&S 1956

A nicely told tale of espionage laid on two islands off the Welsh coast, one inhabited by a monkish order and the other by a marine biological station. Good characterization with rather strong clerical overtones (both R.C. and C. of E.). JB found it the least objectionable of the author's works.

549   Perhaps a Little Danger   Dutt 1942

There is always something to be said for a Scottish Highland setting. We are also given a bit of mystery, but not much detecting. The characters and writing of the first half WHT liked very much. JB disliked the book in toto.

CLINTON-BADDELEY, V(ICTOR) C(LINTON) (1900–70)

b. Devon; educ. Sherborne Sch. and Jesus Coll., Camb., from which he received an M.A. Began as actor, toured U.S. with Ben Greet Company;

returned to England, where he combined writing for radio and taking parts. Did readings of Dickens and poems of Yeats; wrote libretti of operettas; ran a recording company specializing in poetry readings; produced three works of theater history as well as the detective stories below. As an adapter, he took fictions by Stephen Leacock (q.v.) and made the plays: *Behind the Beyond* (1932) and *The Billiard-Room Mystery* (1934).

550   My Foe Outstretched Beneath the Tree   Morr 1968

A good introduction to Dr. R. V. Davie, an elderly Cambridge don, whose adventures on the fringes of the underworld (which he reaches via a chance lecture at a women's college) are both diverting and credible. Nothing very remarkable happens, but some use is made of tape recording as an adjunct to crime, and the author's knowledge of opera and of the academic life makes his pleasant prose ring true. The humor is real and unforced.

551   No Case for the Police   Morr 1970

This last (posthumous) novel by the creator of the elderly Davie shows full recovery of high talent after the weak and unsatisfactory college tale entitled *Death's Bright Dart* (1967). Here we have a delightful south Devon setting, a complex but credible hotbed of lovers (to coin a collective noun), and some unexplained deaths and deviousnesses. The Cambridge don does a superb job of collecting facts, while reconstructing for us the village of his birth as he remembers it—superb handling of past and present in one narrative.

552   Only a Matter of Time   Goll 1969

His third tale about the elderly but active Cambridge don Dr. Davie. At a music festival in southern England he gets involved in two murders and solves them quietly and shrewdly. A new point about clocks and an ingenious finish make this effort worth rereading, quite apart from the good prose and nice wit, neither overdone.

553   CLOUSTON, J(OSEPH) STORER (1870–1944)

The Lunatic at Large   Brent 1915/orig. 1900

Early in this century this gifted but lazy storyteller began to spin tales full of good ideas, insufficiently worked out, yet showing the sort of practical inventiveness suited to the writing of detection. What the Lunatic does here and in five other adventures is actually the makings of chase, espionage, and crime fiction as it is conceived today.

554   The Mystery of No. 47   MY 1912

All the elements of a serious detective story of the period—but the author is not serious. He writes extremely well (both description and dialogue), and it is a pity that while keeping to the light touch he did not give one turn of the handle toward the real or possible and away from farce.

555 CLUTTON-BROCK, A(LAN FRANCIS)

Liberty Hall   Macm 1941

A wordy but well-plotted tale of murder at Scrope House School. It does not revolve about the pupils, whom we are not aware of, but about the refugees and hangers-on of adult years, who form adulterous and other triangles. Atropine in the sherry and later suicide dispose of the unwanted. The detective is the narrator, who works with clues and psychology at low pressure.

COBB, (GEOFFREY) BELTON (b. 1892)

b. Tunbridge Wells; member of a publishing house. Contributor to *Punch* and other periodicals. Has written half a dozen books about Scotland Yard and the police, as well as upward of thirty-five detective novels.

556 Lost Without Trace   WHA 1967

Not really meant to be believed—e.g., the author seems to think that in order to imitate someone's voice, the imitator has to be a ventriloquist. Let it be lost without trace.

557 With Intent to Kill   WHA 1958

A straightforward "classic" puzzler, but superficially plotted and carelessly written—all too consonant with the author's excessive output in which poisons fill the cup to overflowing. The tenacious but rather featureless Inspector Cheviot Burmann turns up every half hour and chivvies the witness about who put oxalic acid—or was it KCN?—in the hangover "preventative." London streetwalkers are much in evidence.

558 COBB. See also Nos. 3115–6 and 2732.

COLE, G(EORGE) D(OUGLAS) H(OWARD) (1890–1959)

Economist and guild socialist, fellow of All Souls, wrote with his wife, Margaret Isabel (née Postgate, b. 1893), more than thirty detective novels and, besides work in economics and biographical essays, a *History of Socialist Thought* in three parts. (Note also *This Crooked World* [1933], a set of verses on socialism, power, and the state.)

Mrs. Cole was the editor and biographer of Beatrice Webb and wrote a history of the Fabian Society.

559 The Blatchington Tangle   Macm 1926

First read (and liked) in the late (and our early) twenties. A second reading reveals Lord Blatchington in all his nakedness as before, but shows that there is more to the book than we remembered. It is indeed a tangle, a good domestic one, with no foreigners, no London slums, no white slavery, and no dope. Wilson solves the mystery, and being no longer at the Yard connives with the B.s at *covering* things up.

Has nothing to do with the U.S. and its Brooklyn. That name is the family's. Sir Vernon B. bought Liskeard House in central London and built the Piccadilly Theater close to it. He makes a will productive of three deaths. Walter Brooklyn is unjustly suspected, but the girl believes in his innocence. It is vindicated, since he loves her and is a playwright. Despite the bright newcomer Superintendent Wilson, the unwinding is tedious and marred by the worst flubdub of the Neanderthal period of detection.

Note that it is the work of G.D.H. alone.

561   The Brothers Sackville   Macm 1937

Evidently the Coles went all out here to do a novel, and not just a detective story. The result is most tedious: long-winded description of middle-class life in the suburbs of London, and of slightly more elevated doings in Birmingham ditto. It is not worth concealing the fact that everything turns on the old dodge of having one brother play the parts of two. The inquest comes only on p. 139. Superintendent Wilson has a role much like Dr. Priestley's in John Rhode—i.e., Inspector Fairford does the work.

562   Dead Man's Watch   Coll 1931

The points of interest are the handling of confused identity and the inter-ference of a headstrong young squire with the inquiry into death, murder, and conspiracy to collect insurance. The Coles' touch of social commentary takes the form of making the blunt Cockney girl intelligent and generous and the middle-class Bittaford boy whom she loves a pathological weak-ling. There is some comedy, some detection, and a good deal of bluster.

563   Death in the Quarry   CCD 1934

A straightforward tale, free of the eccentricities which mar so many later stories by the Coles. The re-entry of Everard Blatchington is appropriately made much of, and Superintendent Wilson is less of a flat fish than usual. Detection is simple but competent, and the gradual emergence of a villain is well handled.

564   End of an Ancient Mariner   CCD 1934/1933

An attempt to write a full-length inverted tale, which the authors haven't the ingenuity or patience to clue and construct properly. Almost every scene is dully repeated while the reader and Superintendent Wilson "wonder." There is no surprise at the end, so the crime was the obvious and commonplace one from the outset. A few entertaining scenes of no importance and a good use of the phrase "mixed cargo" on the last page.

565   Greek Tragedy   Macm 1940/1939

The title is good; otherwise this more-than-twice-told tale of murder during a Mediterranean cruise is routine. Wilson is on board in mufti but soon has to pitch in and detect. The crime is committed during an excursion on shore, and the clues, characters, and detection are reminiscent of several other novels in this genre. Still, one is thankful that the Coles are at their least flighty.

566   Last Will and Testament   CCD 1936

A sequel to *Dr. Tancred Begins* and, like its forerunner, as dull as Lynn Brock at his worst.

567   The Man from the River   Coll 1928

Irritating by persistence of the misplaced light touch. "How jolly all this murdering is" makes up the first half of the book, when one ought to be getting facts. Wilson and Dr. Prendergast, his vacation companion, go in for irrelevant chitchat at the expense of cogitation. The plot is fair enough, though the characters are mostly cardboard.

To identify the business, one may cite: the firm about which rumors of bankruptcy are rife, the woman married unsuitably to "the man from the river" and suspected of intrigues with others, the busybody solicitor who repeats all he knows and creates trouble.

568   Murder at Crome House   Coll 1927

This is the Coles' masterpiece. It starts with a suspense-arousing incident, simple yet convincing: the loss (or rather the finding) in a library book of a photograph showing one man in the act of slugging another. The complications that follow from the attempt to discover the meaning, if any, of this document; the situation revealed, which involves a woman; and the final scene (desperado making away with unwelcome witness) are all splendidly pulled off. It is nice to add that the sentimental close was avoided. Throughout, the writing is terse, witty, and to the point.

569   The Murder at the Munition Works   Macm 1940

Just misses being a good tale. Freer of distractions and absurdities than most by these authors; lively treatment of labor-capital; good locus and ground plan but a bit disappointing in its murderer. His possible motive is rather too well concealed. Sound testing of alibis by Superintendent Wilson, including twice-over clearing of the same suspect.

570   Off with Her Head   Macm 1939/1938

Murderous doings at St. Simon's College, Oxford, and the part played in their unraveling by Inspector Tom Fairford of the CID. (Wilson appears only briefly.) Suspects are fairly plausible, and the Oxford atmosphere, though amusingly played up at times, is not overdone. The inspector is young and "human," and assisted in his efforts by the niece of the college Head, a young lady who is a newspaper correspondent first and a lover second.

571   The Sleeping Death   Dday 1936
            In Eng.: Scandal at School

A rather complicated school story about a poisoning. Everard Blatchington
does what casual detecting is done.

572   The Walking Corpse   G&D 1931
            In Eng.: The Great Southern Mystery

A badly cluttered tale of the dope trade carried on in England by French-
men, one of whom is murdered. A French detective on the trail of the
gang is also murdered, and the identity of the two corpses is thoroughly
confused through three-fourths of the book, much to the reader's dismay,
as well as that of Inspector Wilson.

573   COLE. See also:

The Affair at Aliquid	Coll 1933	Disgrace to the College	Coll 1937
The Berkshire Mystery	P&C 1930	Double Blackmail	Macm 1939
Big Business Murder	Coll 1935	Knife in the Dark	Macm 1941
Burglars in Bucks	Coll 1930	A Lesson in Crime and	
The Corpse in Canonicals		Other Stories	Coll 1933
(= The Corpse in the		The Missing Aunt	
Constable's Garden)			Macm 1938/Coll 1937
	Morr 1931/1930	Poison in a Garden Suburb	HB 1929
The Counterpoint		Supt. Wilson's Holiday	
Murder	Macm 1941	(ss; see No. 2432)	Coll 1928
Death in the Tankard	Vall 1943	Toper's End	Macm 1942
Death of a Millionaire	Macm 1925	Wilson and Some Others	
Death of a Star	Coll 1932	(ss; see No. 2433)	Coll 1940

574   COLES, MANNING (pseud. of Adelaide Frances Oke Manning and
Cyril Henry Coles; also Francis Gaite, 1898–1965). In 1940 this pair,
who lived in adjacent houses at East Meon, Hants, created Tommy
Hambledon as a vehicle for British Secret Service activities which Boucher
rightly describes as "good-humored implausibility." Not our meat. The
firm was launched by the success of: *Drink to Yesterday* (1940) and *A
Toast to Tomorrow* (= *Pray Silence*) (1940).

575   COLIN, AUBREY

        Hands of Death   Hamm 1963

This first novel presents the fairly usual plot of a large family at logger-
heads, a will, and three murders. There are one or two improbabilities,
and near the beginning there is some repetitious questioning. Yet at every
turn the narration has something special, distinguishing it from most other
authors' styles. The wit is woven into the substance, and the persons act
and speak all of a piece.

576   COLLINS,(WILLIAM) WILKIE (1824–89)

        The Moonstone   Cent 1903
            In the series: English Comédie Humaine
            *Orig. a serial in Dickens' All the Year Round 3 vol.; Tinsley
            1868*

Pace T. S. Eliot, this marvelous book is not "the greatest English detective story." It is a good mystery with unforgettable characters and fine melodrama, but Sergeant Cuff (copied from life) is not conspicuously a detective, and the clues, though fairly laid out from the beginning, satisfy only an antiquarian interest in ratiocination. The events that inspired the plot were those in the case of Constance Kent (1860), coupled with those of the Northumberland Street murder. (See Nos. 3094 and 3287.)

577   The Woman in White   Harp 1860

Though the striking opening of this famous story is reported to have been taken from Collins' own life—a fugitive woman in white begged for his help, received it, and was his mistress for some years—the work as a whole does not strike us as it did its first readers. With them it was a great favorite; we admit the skill in plotting, narrating, and characterization but cannot get into the mood of the lumbering adventure. *The Moonstone,* eight years later, is incomparably superior—indeed in a different class altogether.

578   COLLINS. See also Nos. 2435–6 and:

       The Moonstone, Everyman edition, for a
       remarkable Introd. by D. Sayers   Dutt and Dent 1967/1944

579   COMPTON, GUY

       Disguise for a Dead Gentleman   Long 1964

The author's fourth novel. Ben Anderson, crime writer and detective, is less interesting here than he was in *Medium for Murder,* and the school atmosphere, though entertaining, is not integral to the very slender plot and "detection."

580   Medium for Murder   Long 1963

A rather precious tale about a writer who takes lodgings with the widow of a medium in her tumble-down mansion and is nearly done in by her in an effort to prevent the discovery of the way her husband, her brother-in-law, and an old tramp died on the premises at some earlier time. Local yokels and neighbors are rung in by the enterprising hero, but the details of his thoughts and life and final "explanation" do not satisfy.

581   CONNELL, RICHARD

       Murder at Sea   Burt n.d. [1929]

This is an incredible and dreary tale, in which a python gets loose aboard a ship and looks in at portholes by way of titillating the passengers. Enough said.

       CONNINGTON, J. J. (pseud. of Alfred Walter Stewart, D.Sc.; 1880–
       1947)

A reputable British chemist and author of the well-known volumes of "Recent Advances" in various branches of chemistry. Stewart is third in the line traced out by Freeman and Crofts (qq.v.) for the scientific sleuth. As Connington he published around two dozen tales between 1927 and 1944. When at its best, his combination of the spiky Chief Constable Sir Clinton Driffield and the conventionally cautious country squire Wendover* was as satisfying and effective a pair as Thorndyke-Jervis, Priestley-Hanslet, or Merrion-Arnold. Among the first to make his detectives bicker and disagree, the author lets this suffice for characterization and devotes his mind to plotting, with science holding the middle ground, and in the foreground the details of English upper-middle-class country life in the period between the wars.

Note that the science fiction *Nordenholt's Million* (1923) preceded the detective series, and that the pleasant volume of essays *Alias J. J. Connington* (see No. 3038) formed an explanatory sequel. Stewart has also written a novel, *Almighty Gold* (Const 1926), and several "Counselor" stories of no great interest.

* Was his name (as well as outlook) consciously or unconsciously remembered from the Squire of Murewell in Mrs. Humphry Ward's best seller, *Robert Elsmere?*

582   The Boathouse Riddle   LB 1931

This excellent and typical Connington marks the return of Sir Clinton Driffield to the environs of Ambledown, possibly after lying low for a year or two following his rather highhanded activities in *Grim Vengeance.* Wendover is possibly more obtuse than formerly in following the detection of crimes which occur near and on his property, but Sir C. is first-rate, and the atmosphere of the story is beguiling.

583   The Case with Nine Solutions   LB 1929

When this was a new book both readers thought it poor: they were reading a good deal of Connington and preferred others to this seemingly cheap attempt to arouse interest by playing on the permutations of two deaths. The readers now take a juster view. The tale starts very well indeed and it ends satisfactorily. It's the plateau that offends: the anonymous missives are not convincing, and Sir C. gives the impression of doing nothing and thinking even less. But the acerb doctor is good, and the interplay of motives is sound. No Wendover. The explosion at the end is a classic of contrivance, comedy, and crime.

584   The Castleford Conundrum   H&S 1932

One of C.'s longer ones, but not without reason. Driffield is in good working order, despite a few careless contradictions. The plot requires the doing in of a foolish wealthy woman. Good detail regarding bullets and other clues. Wendover on hand.

585   Common Sense Is All You Need   H&S 1947

Four sketches of the scene and some of the clues

Despite a plethora of detectives and their hangers-on (Driffield and Wendover; Inspector Loxton; the expert Professor Dundas) and four good diagrams, this late Connington is not up to his prewar standard and shows fatigue. Good detective work based on an examination of a rope is offset by carelessness and poor judgment.

586   The Dangerfield Talisman   LB 1927/1926

This is Connington's second effort, and it comes off better than his first (see No. 587). Here we have a rather improbable house party, in the course of which a jeweled armlet worth £50,000 is stolen from its unguarded case. The detective work is done by a competent though rather colorless young engineer named Conway Westenhanger. Other guests play Watson in a fairly agreeable sequence of talk and deed. Good subsidiary puzzle, too.

587   Death at Swaythling Court   LB 1926

The author's first—as one could tell from its amateurishness. No Clinton Driffield: the little detection that is done is due to a Colonel Sanderstead, who is a sort of prefiguration of Wendover. He has the same squirish tendencies, and in the end he compounds a felony to save the county people embarrassment. The attempts at ghoulishness, false suspicion, and ingenuity are all pathetically bad.

588   The Eye in the Museum   LB 1930/Goll 1929

Standard Connington despite the absence of both Driffield and Wendover. Digitalis poisoning, clever financial skulduggery, and a good chase of motorboat by car are the components. As for the "eye" in the museum, it is a camera obscura that sees much too much for the good of either the murderer or the tale.

589   Grim Vengeance   LB 1929
          In Eng.: Nemesis at Raynham Parva

A good picture of Sir Clinton and gentry life in England between wars— at least as fiction has it. The issue is sound; the author refers to a League of Nations document for the facts and thanks Victor Gollancz for the idea; and there is *The Road to Buenos Ayres* (No. 3219) to prove it. The writing is good enough, and "Francia" is made plausible. The fact that Sir C. himself commits a crime is worth noting.

    Also noteworthy is the Meredithian echo (of *Richard Feverel*) in the English title: *Raynham Parva*.

590   The Ha-Ha Case   H&S 1934
          In U.S.: The Brandon Case

Jim Brandon's arrival at the flower-decorated platform of Ambledown station is somehow memorable apart from the substance of the plot. The situation involves a shooting party of four who follow the N-S line of a ha-ha. It is clearly presented, and Sir Clinton functions in his usual astringent style.

    The frontispiece on coated paper is delightful.

591   Jack-in-the-Box   LB 1944

A late Connington, and not a good one, despite the presence of Driffield and Wendover. The story starts with the examination of a bomb crater near a harmless village during the Blitz; there is a plethora of "scientific" methods of murder, including artificially produced "bends" (caisson disease), and there is a bit of the occult, debunked of course by Sir C.

592   A Minor Operation   LB 1937

Connington has favored brother-populated stories, preferably with one or the other a bad hat. This is certainly the best tale of the group, and in many ways a classic: nice girl disappears, corpse by the road possibly killed by the suspicious car, effective use of braille (which gives Wendover, who knows it, a chance to shine), and even the old dodge of a frame-up with forgery. But all are freshly handled by Sir Clinton, who is in his very best form.

593   Murder in the Maze   LB 1927

An early Driffield tale, again witnessing C.'s love of the fraternal angle. The villain among the three brothers is easily spotted, but the story is straightforward and full of good points.

594   Murder Will Speak   LB 1938

Like most writers with scientific knowledge, C. tends to make a tale revolve about some contemporary fad or gimmick—in this case, the ductless glands and their secretions. Wendover's absence on holiday provides Inspector Duncannon, of the P.O. Investigation Department, and Sir Clinton with a businesslike opportunity to investigate connections between anonymous letters and the murder of a lawyer. Only fair.

595   Mystery at Lynden Sands   Goll 1928

Early but not first-class Connington. Sir C. and Wendover function throughout. There is fairly good treatment of footprints in the sand, a damsel in distress, and a chase at the end in typical twenties style. The use of the card index is a good Connington touch.

596   No Past Is Dead   LB 1942

A cluttered and disappointing tale—in WHT's opinion perhaps the most unsatisfactory of C.'s output, though all those published after 1938 leave much to be desired. Sir Clinton is reasonably consecutive and analytical and works dodges about blood groups and surreptitiously obtained fingerprints, but Wendover appears only at beginning and end and is more of a stick than ever. The murderer is unconvincing, and the red herrings are too numerous and dull.

Association Item
597   Nordenholt's Million   Const 1923

This remarkable piece of science fiction was Dr. A. W. Stewart's only contribution to the genre, before he embarked on the seas of detection.

Not the least of many good things in the book is the remarkable figure of the millionaire Nordenholt himself. His scheme to save millions from the sudden "plague" caused by denitrifying bacteria is neatly thought out; we witness some strong scenes in "doomed" London (the scientific enclave which is to preserve civilization is in the Clyde valley); and of course the utilization of atomic energy saves the day, though the author's guess about the details of future science is poor.

598   The Sweepstake Murders   LB 1932

This is one of Connington's best conceptions. The joint ticket holders are an unprepossessing lot whom it is a pleasure to see gradually eliminated, leaving Wendover as one of the survivors. The use of photography is original and admirably conveyed. If anything is to be criticized it is a slight excess of plotting.

599   The Tau Cross Mystery   LB 1935
In Eng.: In Whose Dim Shadow

A rather uninteresting tale of the murder of a jealous husband, with the dubious coincidental blurring of clues by a third party. Sir Clinton and Wendover exhibit a rather strained, unfriendly relationship throughout. But as one would expect, the English provincial locale is very nicely done.

600   Tragedy at Ravensthorpe   LB 1927

A much-discussed tale of agoraphobia and a balustrade overlooking a quarry far below. The idea about the statue is undoubtedly the germ of Innes' similar device in *Hamlet, Revenge!* (see No. 1220). Here all the devices are awkwardly combined, and the book is generally unattractive. The blackouts and burglaries, the number of fugitives in tights, the double set of Leonardo plaques, the fake Americans, and Sir Clinton's ambiguous attitude leave a poor memory of the work.

601   Truth Comes Limping   LB 1938

A good title for a lame story. Nothing happens for a long time after the discovery of the murder on p. 1. Two more murders, of an improbable rural kind, temporarily enliven a narrative that soon turns wholly predictable. Sir Clinton is rude to everybody, especially the journalist Denzil, who provides the most readable passages. Wendover contributes nothing.

602   The Twenty-One Clues   LB 1941

A poor repetition of the situation in *The Case with Nine Solutions*. The twenty-one clues are in themselves ingenious and attractive, but the show gives itself away very early. The doings of Driffield, Wendover, the inevitable "young reporter," and a few yokel policemen are Connington at his weariest and wearisomest.
  WHT dissents: By no means bad. An apparent double suicide gives

Inspector Rufford a chance to collect evidence but Sir C.D. has to come back from his holiday to put the twenty-one clues in order. The plot is elaborate, but sound—there is even a rumor that it had its origin in the Hall-Mills case.

603   The Two-Ticket Puzzle   LB 1930
        In Eng.: The Two Tickets Puzzle

Sir Clinton and Wendover do not appear, but the Superintendent Ross who figured in the earlier *Eye in the Museum* handles the case well. Fair railway interest with important scenes at two stations, but the "two tickets" are merely return halves of round trips. Sayers borrowed and improved on the idea (see No. 1905). Criminal rather amusing but not well enough concealed. Good chase at the end.

604   CONNINGTON. See also:

        The Counsellor   LB 1939
        Four Defences   LB 1940
        Gold Brick Island   LB 1933

605   CONRAD, JOSEPH

        The Secret Agent   Dday 1907/1906

The earliest and best novel portraying the character and fate of a double agent. The fusion of humor, horror, psychology, social observation, philosophic reflection, and narrative art—despite a few longueurs—casts in the shade all subsequent attempts to emulate so rich a "realism."
    Note: This is the work that contains the memorable phrase "Lombroso is an ass."

606   CONRAD. See also:

        Under Western Eyes   Dday 1911

607   COOPER, JOHN C.

        The Body Was of No Account   TVB 1957

When skimmed it can look good. The problem of the body found in a sack in the river Ouse is said to be based upon an actual Scotland Yard case, no doubt the murder of Stanley Setty (q.v.) in 1949. In the fictional rendering Detective Inspector James Dale officiates.

608   CORBETT, JAMES

        Murder Minus Motive   HJ n.d. [c. 1944]

A poor tale of dirty work among highly placed medical men and home-office experts. A serum that "acts upon the brain" is the least of its surprises—everything is sacrificed to make possible a sequence of murders apparently motiveless, after which the high-principled culprit provides no game to chase.

609 CORES, LUCY (MICHAELA), b. 1914

Corpse de Ballet   DS 1944

This one has more of Skeets and Toni than the earlier tale, but it is only fair, despite the attractive theatrical setting.

610 Painted for the Kill   DS 1943

Too much upstairs-downstairs-cum-elevator in an otherwise entertaining story of murder in a beauty salon. Several good characters and amusing incidents; the two amateurs help the detective and get hurt.

611 CORRIGAN, MARK (pseud. of Norman Lee, b. 1905)

Why Do Women?   A&R 1963

Rather tame English tough stuff, featuring the author as hero—i.e., under his pseudonym. M.C. is presumed a former FBI agent who becomes trouble shooter, then actor in the English International Television Corporation. Murder and beddery with other actors, crooks, dope addicts, and plain citizens end by his coming out in one way or another on top of them all. This story is one of fourteen or more.

612 CORY, DESMOND (pseud. of John Lloyd MacCarthy; also Theo Callas)

Deadfall   Walk 1965

Since his espionage story *Undertow*, the author has done two or three others dealing with various types of excitement, and now comes a bit closer to crime with this more sophisticated tale of neatly planned jewel robberies in, of course, Spain. There is no detection; our interest is intended to be held by the psychological overtones of the delicately balanced relationships between Jeye, the thief; Moreau, the homosexual planner; and Fé, who is both Moreau's daughter and his wife. With all this, perhaps detection would be too tame.

613 Undertow   Walk 1962

British espionage agents (very "special" ones); Fedora, half Spanish, and Trout, about half male, are in Spain on some mission which is never precisely spelled out. Lots of precious conversation, a couple of "strong" scenes of bleeding in swimming pools, and a psychopathic killer who doesn't drool quite enough do not manage to carry conviction.

COURTIER, S(IDNEY) H(OBSON) (also Rui Chester)

A prolific Australian author, most of whose work features detection as well as mystery and interesting local color. The most recent novels present Inspector Haig.

614   The Glass Spear   Wyn 1950

Mysterious happenings and threats greet a young war hero returning to his
ancestral home in rural Australia. Amid the familiar big-house, big-family
doings, the detective Ambrose Mahon functions credibly, and suspense is
maintained both before and after the murder—not of course of the nice
young hero.

615   Let the Man Die   Ham 1961

A weird story of crime and retribution in an Australian provincial hospital. The CIB man, Ambrose Mahon, and his associates, as well as the
patients and nurses, are all melodramatic characters, and the action is
often incredible. Yet an air of verisimilitude is maintained and the loose
ends are neatly tied together. All in all an extraordinary though not wholly
enjoyable story, punctuated by shrewd comments on life.

616   Murder's Burning   RH 1967

Australia is clearly the place for large-scale events that are at once improbable, melodramatic, and suited to the fashioning of complex plots.
In this one, the hero-narrator investigates the facts, six years past, of the
fire that burned out Paladin Valley. His friend and correspondent, the
schoolmaster there, had died in the fire and subsequent reports did not
tally. With a good use of clues, our hero catches on to the conspiracy,
murders, passions, cattle anthrax, and other amenities, though the tale
is so nearly cluttered that he has to be told many more things at the end.

617   COURTIER. See also:

Come Back to Murder	Hamm 1964	One Cried Murder	Hamm 1956
A Corpse Won't Swing	Hamm 1964	The Ringnecker	Hamm 1965
Death in Dream Time	Hamm 1959	A Shroud for Unlac	Hamm 1958
Gently Dust the Corpse	Hamm 1960	Swing High, Sweet Murder	
Mimic a Murderer	Hamm 1964		Hamm 1962
Now Seek My Bones	Hamm 1957	Who Dies for Me?	Hamm 1962

COXE, GEORGE HARMON (b. 1901)

An American author who is presumably a journalist, something of a
photographer, and a devotee of jazz. He is a prolific producer of semi-
detective, semi-gangster stories, many of them laid in Boston and vicinity
and featuring the newspaper photographer Kent Murdock. The telling is
attractive enough, though "action clichés" (e.g., the stealing of K. M.'s
films) recur ad nauseam. In his later books, Coxe has brought in foreign
settings and new heroes.

618   The Charred Witness   Knopf 1942

Kent Murdock, press photographer, is attractively introduced into a plot
that joins private feeling and international scientific interests and leads to

a half-burnt corpse in a cottage. K.M.'s equipment gets lost again, annoyingly. Redheads abound and surround a young man named, quite appropriately, Randy. The sorting out is competent and the tricks along the way are still fresh enough to get by.

619   Dangerous Legacy   Knopf 1946

Not a K. M. story, but very like it, and not to be specially noted.

620   Eye-Witness   Knopf 1949

Poor Kent Murdock is arrested for murdering himself, when he was in fact on a friendly errand and charged (as usual) with a photographic assignment. The girls fall all over him, like the cops, but as always, sex in Coxe is discreet and Murdock is well bred and well dressed (if one may make a scabrous interplay of adjectives).

621   The Fifth Key   Knopf 1947

A complex plot to dispose of the amiable Kent Murdock by drugging him and photographing him lying next to a nude corpse—hoist with his own reflex. If this sort of thing has to be done at all, the present sample is recommended as acceptable.

622   The Groom Lay Dead   Knopf 1944

A wedding party in upstate New York, preceded by clear-cut antagonisms on an overnight train journey, provides the setting for an ingenious murder, well motivated and suitably unraveled. The accompaniment of amateur detection and burglary as well as shady cultism helps keep up suspense. Not a Kent Murdock story.

623   The Hollow Needle   Knopf 1948

Kent Murdock busies himself about a murdered tycoon, with the usual pictures taken and stolen.

624   Murder with Pictures   Knopf 1935

This is an early account of Kent Murdock's camera work: he is young and "flat-muscled," whatever that may mean. The opening is excellent: a bunch of reporters waiting for the verdict in a notorious murder case. The later gangsterisms and love passages with clean unspoiled society dames and a tedious carelessness with exposed films show which way the series will go. Still, this is well up in the readers' preference.

625   The Reluctant Heiress   Hamm 1966/1965

A Kent Murdock story with the usual trimmings, but spare and credible. The originality consists in the method of unwinding rather than in the nature of the facts. Murdock takes pictures as always, but there is no outré violence.

Not about Kent Murdock. There are three other photographers to replace him, all working for the *Express*. The murder is that of a former district attorney now in shady contact with the underworld. Too much slugging and going about to be much fun, despite the usual contrast between a sweet young thing and a "shallow beauty."

627   COXE. See also:

Double Identity	Knopf 1970
Murder in Havana	Knopf 1943
Never Bet Your Life	Hamm 1955

628   COZZENS, JAMES GOULD (b. 1903)

      The Just and the Unjust   HB 1942

This book is often listed as germane to the crime novel in one of its aspects. But although there is a protracted trial scene, the treatment and the concern are purely ethical, and the upshot has nothing to do with wrongdoing, but only with courage about life.

629   CRAIG, JONATHAN

      The Case of the Beautiful Body   GM 1967

Police routine, done with fair skill in writing, except for didactic passages that are out of character. Sex lustless and listless, "problem" quite ordinary.

630   CRANE, FRANCES (KIRKWOOD), goes in for a wacky atmosphere and has a husband-and-wife amateur detective team: Pat and Jean Abbott. *The Buttercup Case* (1959) with a New Orleans background seems preferable to *The Amber Eyes* (1962).

CREASEY, JOHN (b. 1908)

b. Southfields (Surrey); educ. Fulham elem. sch. and Sloane secondary (Chelsea); he taught himself to write. He loves travel, the United States, and people who tell him that his books make insomnia an asset. He also loves to discuss the particular works, though how he remembers them passes credulity. By 1968, J. C. had written 521 books. He contributes to numerous magazines and has been elected mayor of his adopted town. For his pseudonyms and the series thereunder begotten, see No. 2931.

631   The Figure in the Dusk   Avon 1952
        In Eng.: A Case for Inspector West

This early Creasey is very commendable. In a fairly straightforward tale— i.e., not too cluttered by children and conjugal bedwork—the handsome inspector tracks down a series of murders occurring in one family for the sake of survivorship and the money. A couple of red herrings could have been sweetened or left out, but they do not mar the plot.

632   The Gelignite Gang   Harp 1956
        In Eng.: Inspector West Makes Haste

Inspector West rounds up a murderous team of safe breakers. Standard
routine, with Roger West's ample domesticity for relief.

633   Inspector West at Bay   H&S 1952
        In U.S.: The Blind Spot

Smoothly written account of successive attempts to blind Inspector West
by members of the family of a blackmailer whom West had caused to be
sent down for ten years. Tedious because West is too much of a victim
and what little detecting is done is the work of his associates.

634   Murder on the Line   Scrib 1960

It is a pity that Creasey did not linger just a few hours (or minutes) longer
over the possibilities of British Railways as the scene of organized crime.
Inspector West is acceptable, and there is plenty of railway interest, but it
is spoiled by lack of attention to detail. Crude errors about methods of
signaling, for example, put the informed, or even moderately observant,
reader on edge.

635   The Toff Goes to Market   Walk 1967; orig. 1942

This and other Toff stories are marked by rapid, breezy, and generally
first-class narrative, devoted to stories of varying merit. The market in this
one is the London wartime black market, and the cause defended by the
rich and well-connected Toff, the Hon. Richard Rollison (Rolly), is innocence, fair play, and the war effort.

636   The Trouble at Saxby's   Harp 1959

Routine Creasey—which is not to say incompetent. The usual formula is
enlivened a bit by "Handsome" West's troubles with his new assistant
commissioner, and his efforts to finish his case before he is relieved of duty.

637   CREASEY. See also:

Early works under his own name:

        Carriers of Death   Mel 1937
        The Cinema Crimes   Pemb 1945
        Days of Danger   Mel 1937
        Death by Night   Long 1940
        First Came a Murder   Mel 1934
        Men, Maids, and Murder   Mel 1933

Inspector West tales include:

        A Battle for Inspector West   SP 1945/1934
        The Beauty Queen Killer
            (= A Beauty for Inspector West)   Harp 1954
        The Creepers (= Inspector West Cries Wolf)   Harp 1952
        Death of a Postman (= Parcels for Inspector West) Harp 1957
        Give a Man a Gun (= A Gun for Inspector West) Harp 1954
        Murder, London—Miami   TBC 1969

Also *The Valley of Fear* (Long 1943), the adoption of whose title shows no fear.

Among the Toff stories, note:

A Doll for the Toff	Walk 1963
Follow the Toff	Walk 1961
The Toff on the Farm	Walk 1958

CRISPIN, EDMUND (pseud. of Robert Bruce Montgomery, b. 1921)

Educ. at Merchant Taylors' and St. John's, Oxf., E.C. is a man of letters and a musician (organist and composer) as well as one of the masters of modern detective fiction since his 22nd year. Reserved in manner, but a charming conversationalist and as witty in life as he is in his books. His true career is in music, by which he lives as well as courts fame, writing continuities for films and requiem masses for pleasure. His preferred composer is Brahms. His first detective story (No. 644) was written in fourteen days. Like those to follow, it features an Oxford professor of English literature, Gervase Fen, who is not at all donnish. Crispin also reviews detective fiction for the *Sunday Times* (London). He lives in Devon. He will publish his first novels in some years in 1971: as Bruce Montgomery, *The White Night* (Macm); as Crispin, *The Glimpses of the Moon* (Goll).

638   Buried for Pleasure   Lipp 1949

It is in this book, mostly satirical and rural, that Gervase Fen stands for Parliament and meets Inspector Humbleby for the first time (p. 98). The murder is that of another Inspector (Bussy), an Oxford classmate of Fen's, and the poisoning of a Mrs. Lambert, an ex-prostitute turned respectable. The murders are well solved and amusement is kept up about the election, rural fornication, and the destruction of a pub by the owner's renovating mania. Still, an air of unreality hangs about the whole and Fen does not come out well.

639   Dead and Dumb   Lipp 1947
         In ppb.: Swan Song

This tale depicting an operatic cast is indefinably less successful than its companion piece, the theatrical: it has too much of Lily Christine, Fen's absurd car,* and generally the texture is looser; though, as always, Crispin can be very funny, and his people are well done.

  * Named conceivably after Michael Arlen's heroine of 1928.

640   Frequent Hearses   Goll 1950
         In U.S.: Sudden Vengeance

Humbleby and Gervase Fen badger each other pleasantly while they elucidate the murder-generating suicide of a self-centered movie actress named (à la Holmes) Gloria Scott. The descriptions of people and studios are excellent, being firsthand from Crispin's experience as a composer of film music. Fen is brilliant, and the poison is the unusual colchicine.

641 The Long Divorce DM 1951

Gervase Fen at his peak: no shenanigans and no tedious frolic with or about his car. An excellent portrait of an adolescent girl as well as of a lovable woman doctor, whose romance does not interfere with genuine detection by G.F.—a masterpiece.

642 Love Lies Bleeding Lipp 1948

This is another of Crispin's triumphs. The combination of rural life, youthful emotions, Fen's detection, and the well-worn but also well-handled idea of the lost Shakespeare manuscript is done to a turn, with no eccentricities and no exaggerations.

643 The Moving Toyshop Lipp 1946

The principal idea which gives the book its title (from *The Rape of the Lock,* line 100) is the old one of quickly camouflaging certain premises in order to prevent a witness from testifying to illicit events witnessed in a given setting. Fen is exasperating, and the events are not sufficiently credible to redeem the manner—not a representative work.

644 Obsequies at Oxford Lipp 1945
In Eng.: The Case of the Gilded Fly

One of the best early ones. It does Oxford very well, Fen is not obstreperous, and the young people in the theatricals are lively and plausible. This is not to be confused with the *opera story* by the same author entitled *Dead and Dumb* and (in England and in Penguin) *Swan Song* (see No. 639).

645 CRISPIN. See also:

Best Detective Stories (ed.)	Faber 1959
Best SF [*sic*] (ed.)	Faber 1955
Beware of the Trains (ss; see No. 2448)	Goll 1913

CROFTS, FREEMAN WILLS, F.R.S.A. (1879–1957)

b. Dublin, son of an army medical man. Educ. Methodist and Campbell Coll., Belfast; later civil engineering apprentice. Chief engineer of the Belfast and Northern Counties Railway and other lines until 1929, when he resigned to devote himself to detective fiction about Inspector French. Crofts was also an amateur organist and conductor (see No. 646). A Crime Club Collected Edition of his tales was begun in 1969.

646 The Cask Scrib 1928/Seltzer 1924/Coll n.d. [1920]
Illus. by Mackay

The story takes place around 1910–12, mostly in France, and follows the elaborate melodramatic method of the French *roman policier.* It may be significant that Crofts later called his detective inspector *French,* though the one who appears in *The Cask* is called Burnley.

The Collins edition contains the Foreword in which Crofts tells how he came to write the book, his first in the genre. Already his characteristic interests are evident: tracking down individual actions in painful detail so as to break down alibis and uncover motives. The story reflects his musical interests as well as his relentless factuality in having one of the alibis provided by a performance of Berlioz' *Les Troyens* at the Théâtre de la Monnaie in Brussels.

647   The Cheyne Mystery   Boni 1926
      In Eng.: Inspector French and the Cheyne Mystery

This early Crofts begins with the drugging of young Maxwell Cheyne at a Plymouth hotel, followed by the ransacking of his house. Part of the mystery is what the crooks Sime and Blessington are after. French goes to Belgium on the clue of a fragment of hotel bill. A fairly routine tale.

648   Cold-Blooded Murder   DM 1936
      In Eng.: Man Overboard!

A story involving trips and steamers and alibis, in the manner and in the setting of *Sir John Magill's Last Journey* (to which reference is made in the present one). But the red herring of the conviction of the semi-hero is laborious and unconvincing—as are the characters and the North Ireland brogue. What remains interesting is the discovery of "inert petrol" and the doings of the first two-thirds of the book.

649   Crime at Guildford   CCC 1935
      In U.S.: The Crime at Nornes
      Dedic. to Dr. J. Morris, for supplying the central idea

The death of the senior accountant of a firm of working jewelers while attending a business conference near Guildford is not unconnected with the looting of the firm's safe in London that same Sunday. French (only recently made chief inspector) takes quite a while to tumble to the way the tumblers were made to tumble, and even longer to the method of murder. Even so, WHT deems it better than the other Guildford tale: *The Strange Case of Dr. Earle*.

650   Dark Journey   DM 1951
      In Eng.: French Strikes Oil

An example of latter-day Crofts, which means a one-part story told with none of the Edwardian delays and flourishes, and hence characterless to the point of drabness. It reads like an office report, though it concerns the discovery of oil, a well-contrived murder, concealed marriages, and other illicit relationships. Poor fun.

651   Death of a Train   DM 1947

Crofts' factual style endues this tale of attempted sabotage of a railway shipment of radio "valves" with little charm, but the author's firsthand

144

knowledge of railway working permits him to present both the mechanism and the explanation of the derailment in a very clear manner. French performs as usual, helped by a good bit of carelessness on the part of the criminals.

652   Double Death   Harp 1932
       *Endpapers show detail of the line between
       Redchurch and Whitness*

One of our favorites. The idea is murder arising from fraud in the construction of a railway cutting, or more exactly, widening. The technical part, as usual with Crofts, is admirably done, but the human side is poor, especially the choice of criminal. The subplots are not badly managed and the suspense keeps up at least as far as the exposé.

    Note: This tale by Crofts is not to be confused with the collaborative effort, also entitled *Double Death* (No. 2134), to which Crofts was a contributor.

653   Enemy Unseen   H&S 1945

An ingenious plot, which leads one away from one's first suspicion only to return to it with an added element, and thus achieve a double-headed murder that must be unique in the literature. There are unfortunately no characters—the cardboard itself hardly deserves the name, though the wartime conditions of Home Guard life and rationing are well sketched in. The rest is mechanics and motives; to say more would disclose the secret, so ably maintained to the end.

654   Fear Comes to Chalfont   DM 1942

A poor affair indeed, bearing out the thesis that Crofts had presented the best of Inspector French by the end of the thirties. Here a woman who marries an amateur chemist not for love gets embroiled in the events following his murder. French's slow-moving investigation is not up to the "process" that provides the motive for the murder: an idea plausibly related to modern ion-exchange resins and the desalting of sea water. All the rest is dull, and the people are duller.

655   Found Floating   H&S 1937
       Endpaper Map of Journey from Glasgow to Athens

Leisurely and poor: a mysterious poisoning of all present at a family dinner is followed by the disappearance of the most disliked person during a cruise taken by the group to the Mediterranean. French is summoned by the shipping director and eventually works out the modus operandi but lets his man slip through his fingers. The best chapter is that describing the cruise ship in detail.

656   Golden Ashes   DM 1940

A routine, alibi-busting story in which the murder of an art expert and the burning down of a house containing a huge collection of old masters form the substance. It falls down badly in the matter of motive and human probabilities. In the course of the crime by the guilty too many others cooperate guilelessly with them.

657   The Groote Park Murder   Seltzer 1925

Crofts' second and one of a pair of tales on a similar plan (see No. 663). French has not yet appeared, and it falls to Inspector Ross in Scotland to investigate the consequences of a murder committed earlier in South Africa. Quite a bit of railway interest and some good Scottish topography. But the story is long for its length, and the basic plot seems a bit timeworn in these days.

658   Inspector French and the Starvel Tragedy   Coll 1927
           In U.S.: The Starvel Hollow Tragedy

A major case in French's early career, which WHT liked on first reading and in which he could still find entertainment forty years later. As one expects with this author and period, the complex plot unwinds slowly. But even though the reader guesses long before French what has been done to get away with an old miser's thousands, the process of unravelment becomes tedious only very near the final unmasking. In 1927 it must have been quite a surprise. French gets to France, as usual, and there is an unobnoxious love story neatly worked into the fabric. Scene: "Thirsby" (Thirsk) near York.

659   Inspector French's Greatest Case   Seltzer 1925

Crofts was a bit premature in making his third or fourth case of French's his greatest. It is about a jewel theft from a Hatton Garden firm, coupled with the murder of the chief clerk. There is too much impersonation, disguise, and travel to generate belief or interest.

660   A Losing Game   H&S 1941

One of the less memorable adventures of Inspector French. It requires 70 pages to compass the murder and 150 more to show French how to break what the author evidently felt was a clever alibi. Pretty routine.

661   The Loss of the *Jane Vosper*   DM 1936

A good sea story about the deliberate blowing up of a ship to effect a cargo swindle. The multiple profits from the ingenious fraud are something after French's own heart, there being innumerable arrangements to make for the crime and to be detected by French.

662   Mystery in the English Channel   Harp 1931
           In Eng.: Mystery in the Channel

A yacht is found abandoned in mid-Channel, with a couple of corpses of English businessmen aboard. French travels about a bit before he catches on to the idea that made the contradictory evidence plausible. Though concerned with motorboats and speeds, less mechanical than his average story.

663   The Pit-Prop Syndicate   Seltzer 1925

Written immediately after *Groote Park* (No. 657), to which it bears a
family resemblance. Again a crime is committed in foreign parts (France
near Bordeaux) and much of the later action is in England. But interest
derives from the fact that just what crime is concealed by the activities
of the sinister syndicate is hard to say. Two young Englishmen take turns
spying, and one falls in love with a girl whose father is a "tool." Inspector Willis manages to discover what goes on, but the whole thing
drags in its final third.

664   The Ponson Case   DM 1937; orig. 1921

One of Crofts' earliest efforts, pre-French, and featuring Inspector Tan-
ner. A well-worked-out though complicated plot requires such characteristic items of the thirties as the survivor of a marine disaster, blackmail,
and unwitting bigamy. A more original note is the baronet's plan to rid
himself of the blackmailer and how it backfired. All in all, a first-class
performance.

665   The Purple Sickle Murders   Harp 1929; orig. 1921
            In Eng.: The Box Office Murders

Despite its lurid title, one of the very best Inspector French stories. The
p. sickle plays no role except to identify one of the criminals. Young
women who sell tickets at London cinemas are enrolled in a scheme
which they suspect at their peril: when they go to the police they are
murdered. The development of the story, the kidnaping of French's
favorite among the girls, and the final chase and capture are all done
extremely well.
    N.B. In this story French eats little, except in a concealed spot.

666   The Sea Mystery   Harp 1928

This story of the brothers Pyke, first read on publication, is extremely
characteristic in its search after detail: Inspector French is one of those
men whom William James declared incapable of boredom. The motives
behind the deed are well done, the various people more distinct than was
to be the case in other tales, and the march of events and hypotheses sufficient to keep up suspense. It's a sea mystery only because it begins on
the sea: man and son fishing.

667   Silence for the Murderer   DM 1948

The latest Crofts that we know or—on present evidence—would wish to
know. Twelve slow-moving chapters introduce Dulcie Heath and Frank
Roscoe and their connivance at defrauding the patients of their Harley
Street employer. When Superintendent French is called in in Chapter 13, it
is to look into the apparent suicide of a rich elderly man whose secretary
Roscoe has recently become. When French finally ascertains the facts,
the reader has long since seen the point and could have managed it better.

JB esteems it less highly than does WHT, but even if on a second reading some of the clues seem fairly obvious and the pace more than leisurely, WHT regards it as worthy for its railway interest and its attractive treatment of Belfast, Larne, Stranraer, and Portpatrick. JB's dissatisfaction stems from the telling that permits the reader to outguess French as to the main gimmick.

669   Sudden Death   Harp 1932
       Three diagrams

This is "not good French." All the action takes place at a country house, and most of it is seen through the eyes of a young housekeeper. First the oddly behaving mistress of the house dies, then her husband. Clocks and trips to London occupy French, but somehow not with his usual gusto; the manner of telling hobbles the pace and imparts an oddly feminine tone, and the hard struggle over a gas-tap problem leaves the reader ahead of the game.

670   Tragedy in the Hollow   DM 1939
       Map of Portrush, Balliwillan, and vicinage

The tale is told in two parts, showing how the S.S. *Hellénique* becomes a floating casino and how the meeting of a travel agent and a black sheep leads to murder. French is brought in to unravel a carefully plotted elimination and alibi, which he does by studying certain photographs. The travel atmosphere is well done and not intrusive. The photographic scheme is six years later than Connington's (see No. 598), but these two are the pioneers.

671   CROFTS. See also:

Antidote to Venom	H&S 1938	dence)	DM 1941
Death on the Way	Coll 1932	Murderers Make Mistakes	
Double Tragedy (= The Affair		(ss)	H&S 1947
at Little Wokeham)	DM 1943	The Mystery of the Sleeping	
The End of Andrew		Car Express (ss)	H&S 1956
Harrison	H&S 1938	Mystery on Southampton Water	
The Futile Alibi	DM 1938	(= Crime on the Solent)	DM 1934
The Hog's Back Mystery		A New Zealand Tragedy (true	
(= The Strange Case of		crime, see No. 3287)	orig. 1936
Dr. Earle)	DM 1933	The 12.30 from Croydon	
The Hunt Ball		(= Wilful and Pre-	
Murder (ss)	Todd 1943	meditated)	H&S, DM 1939
James Tarrant, Adventurer		Young Robin Brand,	
(= Circumstantial Evi-		Detective (juvenile)	ULP 1947

672   CROSS, AMANDA (pseud.)

       In the Last Analysis   Macm 1964

A very enjoyable tale, part academic, part psychiatric, written by a woman scholar described as "teaching 18th-century literature at a large midwestern university"—a deliberately misleading clue. The two halves of her story match perfectly, and the suspense is kept up, despite an occasional drop into excess literature. There is an excellent clue based on a quotation from Lionel Trilling, and plenty of highbrow humor of good quality.

673   The James Joyce Murder   Macm 1967

The academic lady's second, and not so good as the first. The plot is not in itself bad, and the several women are done with discrimination, but the villain is unsatisfactory, and the amount of literary disquisition taxes the reader's patience. The detective, Kate Fansler, remains attractive, plausible, and witty, but she too succumbs to the author's desire to have everything on a high plane of sophistication.

674   Poetic Justice   Knopf 1970

As a tale of crime and detection this third entertainment leaves something to be desired, but as a scamper through a university English department and its fringe of genuine literary figures, it is a delight. The apt quotations from Auden, the admiring portrait of an academic sage who must be Lionel Trilling's identical twin, and the heroine's love affair with the Wimsey-like lawyer from downtown are all handled *con brio* as well as *con amore.*

675   CULLINGFORD, GUY (pseud. of Constance Lindsay-Taylor, b. 1907)

      Conjuror's Coffin   Lipp 1954

WHT liked parts of this novel; JB none of it. There are good descriptions of outdoor scenes at the coronation. But the fakery surrounding the coffin is tedious and unlikely.

676   Post Mortem   Lipp 1953

The author's second and best. It is something of a trick story in which a writer records for the reader the several unsuccessful attempts on his life. The narrative is embedded in a humorous description of a well-run old-fashioned household, maintained despite wartime austerity. The writing is elegant, the denouement unsuspected, the detection adequate though not concentrated.

677   A Touch of Drama   Hamm 1960

The wife of a young playwright disappears, which suggests to his mind that she is hiding to ruin him. Little or no detection.

678   The Whipping Boys   Hamm 1958

Excessive chitchat and home life in an English village plagued by bad teen-agers, eccentrics, and unstable relationships. The plodding sergeant (Gil North type) solves the gratuitous murder of an old-maid babysitter. Not really detection.

679   CULLINGFORD. See also:

| If Wishes Were Hearses | Lipp 1952 |
| Third Party Risk | Bles 1962 |

680   CULPAN, MAURICE

The Vasiliko Affair   CCC 1968

His fifth or sixth and he is still going strong. Making use of his excellent
musical knowledge, the author brings together a young Slavic pianist and
his drab wife, a German conductor, a married English impresario, a composer and teacher of music in a boys' school, and a plump bachelor music
critic. Two murders follow—which seems a small number—and Chief
Inspector Houghton slowly arrives at the truth despite his malicious
Superintendent Blake. The enmity between these two is the only feature
of the book that does not impress one with verisimilitude and does not add
to the admirable pace, wit, and freshness of the narrative.

681   CULPAN. See also:

Bloody Success	CCD 1969
The Minister of Injustice	Walk 1966
A Nice Place to Die	CCC 1965

CUMBERLAND, MARTEN (also R. Laugier and Kevin O'Hara; b.
1892)

b. London; educ. Cranleigh; journalist. Has written on economics and
put on plays and written straight stories, in addition to a long and even
output of detective tales.

682   Hearsed in Death   Blackett 1947
          In U.S.: Dilemma for Dax

The French commissaire, Saturnin Dax, and his Anglophile assistant,
Félix Norman, laboriously disentangle a series of plots and intrigues
that have culminated in the basement burial (after dismemberment) of
an unidentified young woman. Though there is more talk than action
and the shrewd reader is ahead of the detectives, the author's wit and
style carry him over the plateaus. M.C. knows the French, their language
and little ways, as well as general literature. Dax is more interesting than
Maigret.

683   Murmurs in the Rue Morgue   Hutch 1959

Popular in England through his Saturnin Dax stories, of which this is the
twenty-seventh, M.C. writes with skill about the French *police judiciaire,*
but makes it sound as if it performed in England rather than France. His
5-page chapters are headed with excellent literary mottoes, and the characters have great distinctness—always worth a try.

684   CUNNINGHAM, A(LBERT) B(ENJAMIN) (also Estil Dale and Garth Hale; b. 1888–1962)

The Hunter Is the Hunted   Dutt 1950

One of a dozen or so of rural tales, south of the Mason-Dixon line, in which Sheriff Jess Roden displays his knowledge of the woods, the community, and the "fundamental truths of human nature." Not especially noteworthy; dialect tiresome.

685   CUNNINGHAM. See also:

Death at "The Bottoms"	Dutt 1942
Death Haunts the Dark Lane	Dutt 1948
Who Killed Pretty Becky Low?	Dutt 1951

686   CURTIS, PETER (pseud. of Norah Robinson Lofts, b. 1904)

The Devil's Own   CCD 1960

A far-from-perfect tale of suspense—not detection—yet deserving a place here for what it skillfully avoids. A schoolteacher in a remote part of East Anglia sticks bravely to her self-imposed task of exposing a witch cult, of the detailed posturings of which she finally takes movies. She escapes through her own efforts from various traps set for her—and then help is on the way.

687   No Question of Murder   CCD 1959

Adventure of the Rebecca type, with little detection but fair character drawing and adequate suspense. Told in the first person by several narrators, including a nurse who shows up the villain, the murderer, and his accomplice.

688   CURTISS, URSULA (REILLY), b. 1923 and a product of Staples H.S. in Yonkers, is the author of a dozen magazine stories of crime— e.g., *Danger: Hospital Zone, The Deadly Climate, Hours to Kill* (= *Strangers at the Wedding*), published since 1954.

689   DALLAS, JOHN

Night of the Storm   HJ 1961

There are some powerful scenes and one or two striking characters in this Canadian tale of murder and chase after jewels, which scurries over many quarters of Toronto and Montreal, but the effort as a whole fails to convince. It is the kind of story one lays down in disgust, then picks up in boredom and finds acceptable again, only to be revolted once more.

690   DALTON, MORAY

The Body in the Road   Coll 1930

It would be a mistake to begin one's acquaintance with this author by taking up this book. It starts well and has a challenging situation, peopled with rounded characters. Who killed the pretty girl violinist on the eve of her going to the big city under impresario "protection" is a fit problem for the local young lord who was a CID inspector before inheriting the title. But his efforts, soon superseded by the unscrupulous tricks of a private eye named Norman Glide, bring down the level of quality and interest to a low point from which there is no recovery—not characteristic work.

691   The Condamine Case   LM n.d. [1947]

If the dust jacket is to be trusted, this is the author's seventeenth book, and remarkably fresh and unstereotyped if so. Indeed, here is a neglected man, for his earlier work shows him to be a conscientious workman, with a flair for the unusual, and capable of clever touches. The present volume presents Inspector Collier's capable investigation of two murders literally "staged" during the filming of a sixteenth-century witch-hunting movie in the west of England.

692   The Night of Fear   Harp 1931

This, which appears to be the author's third tale, is a classic example of the English house-party murder, but it has unusual features: D.'s star detective, Collier, plays a minor and unaccustomed part, and there is a good twist at the end, after the well-handled trial. On the evidence at hand, M.D. deserves thorough looking up.

693   DALTON. See also:

Belfrey Murder	LM 1933	The Price of Silence	Samp 1939
The Case of Alan		The Shadow on the Wall	Jarr 1926
Copeland	LM 1937	The Strange Case of	
Death in the Dark	LM 1938	Harriet Hall	Samp 1936
One by One They Dis-		The Stretton Darknesse	
appeared	Harp 1929	Mystery	Jarr 1927

DALY, ELIZABETH (b. 1878)

An American writer of considerable charm and detective merit, who burst upon the scene near the beginning of the second world war. She can write straightforward detection when she is not impeded by her own Gamadgery, that is, by an excessive interest in (a) books, (b) cats, (c) wives and children, and (d) the pseudo supernatural. By this criterion about half her output is highly commendable.

694   Any Shape or Form   Farr 1945

The murder is done in an enclosed rose garden, by means of a rifle shot. The reasons for this act and its locale are excellent and the tale stands rereading, even though a little wordy at the outset.

695   The Book of the Crime   Rine 1951

Few of the author's presentations of Henry Gamadge as littérateur and private detective have shown him in as favorable a light as this. Gamadge's dependents are touched in but not allowed to spoil a compact and direct investigation of impersonation and murder. The literary clue is legitimate and not just lucky.

696   Death and Letters   Rine 1950

This is a well-organized and appropriately atmospheric novel about a woman kept under drugs and restraint in a big Hudson River family mansion. Gamadge does a good job of work, and there are no embarrassing episodes of spiritualism or bibliomania to spoil a standard plot.

697   Evidence of Things Seen   Farr 1943

Attractive country setting in the Berkshires, where the newly married Clara awaits Gamadge's return from war work for a vacation. When the owner of their cottage is murdered on their hands it looks as though various seemingly supernatural phenomena of the week past had come to a focus. But Gamadge debunks everything very nicely, and the rather old dodge by which the strangling was done seems fresh enough.

698   Night Walk   Rine 1947

Here we have good village atmosphere setting off two apparently unrelated murders: that of an elderly male resident and that of the village librarian. Gamadge does an honest bit of detecting, destroys the "prowler" theory, and lures the real culprit to the library to provide bookish evidence against him. It is the kind of story Lockridge might like to write but doesn't.

699   Nothing Can Rescue Me   Farr 1943

WHT would place this in Daly's large group of middling stories. Gamadge is away from home and thus unfettered by Clara and pet animals, but he doesn't really do much except observe the inmates of Sylvanus Hutter's big country house, some of whom go in for automatic writing. Literary claptrap and a few amusing instances of insertions by the villain of "warnings" into a trashy text being prepared by Aunt Florence do not counteract a strong feeling of *déjà vu*.

700   Unexpected Night   Farr 1940

Pretty good Daly; it depicts hanky-panky with the corpse of a young man suffering from myocarditis, who dies conveniently for the enriching of his relatives. Conspiracy leads to two other murders, but Gamadge, who is chiefly amiable and thoughtful, finally sees through the game.

701   DALY. See also:

And Dangerous to Know	Rine 1949	The House Without the	
Arrow Pointing Nowhere	Farr 1944	Door	Hamm 1945
The Book of the Dead	Farr 1944	Murders in Volume Two	Farr 1941
The Book of the Lion	Hamm 1951	Somewhere in the House	Rine 1943
Deadly Nightshade	Farr 1942	The Wrong Way Down	Rine 1946

Death of a Millionaire   Hale 1969

The author of *Murder in Paradise* pursues his conventional way and fails to hold the demanding reader.

703   DANE, CLEMENCE (pseud. of Winifred Ashton, in collaboration with Helen Simpson, q.v.)

Re-enter Sir John   Farr 1932

Recommended by Haycraft as superior to the earlier *Enter Sir John*, but found disappointing by these readers. The crime is the arranging of some cheating at cards. Sir John Saumarez (actor-manager and amateur detective in the tale) brings the villain to book by amateurish means and sheer supposition. The style is mannered and dated. How much better is No. 1934!

DANIEL, GLYN (EDMUND) (also Dilwyn Rees; b. 1914)

Welsh archaeologist at St. John's, Camb., whose main interest is in tombs and caves. He has written a detective story under a pseudonym (see No. 1795) and the one following under his own name.

704   Welcome Death   Goll 1954

The second detective story featuring Sir Richard Cherrington as amateur sleuth. (See No. 1795.) The present tale makes pleasant enough reading, but it is one of those where there are just too many people in the same small area between 6:25 and 7:00 P.M. In short, most of the pleasure derives from the description of the South Wales setting.

705   DANIEL, ROBIN

Death by Drowning   Goll 1960

It seems that men, too, can write the nerve irritants so lavishly produced by Fremlin, Kelly, et aliae. This is an unusual tale about a bitchy wife who, through most of the book, lays plans to commit suicide in a way calculated to cause the greatest inconvenience and pain to her rather uncommunicative but faithful husband. The growth and circulation of gossip is well portrayed. No detection.

DAVEY, JOCELYN (pseud. of Chaim Raphael, b. 1908)

English economist and official in the British Treasury. The hero of his first novel, *The Undoubted Deed*, is said to be a portrait of Isaiah Berlin, who was with the author in the British embassy in Washington during the war.

706   A Killing in Hats   C&W 1965

Ambrose Usher, Oxford philosopher, linguist, and special assistant to the Foreign Office, remains a credible and appealing character, but here the setting (London this time) is cluttered. Too many highly placed characters, too many love affairs, too much talk, and too little action. Too little is made of the atmosphere of Princess Vyazensky's hat salon, and too little attention is paid to the practical details of sophisticating a lift or using a high-voltage line in homicide. Not memorable.

707   The Naked Villainy   Knopf 1958

This story is the most fantastic of those by this author, yet it holds the reader without a letdown. Monkeys, finance, politics, foreign scholars, and crazy noble dames all fit together in a pattern that Ambrose Usher finds congenial as well as a challenge to his powers. Detection is negligible, but prose is not.

708   A Touch of Stagefright   C&W 1960

The author's evident pleasure in his sojourn in America enlivens what is otherwise a humdrum mystery. Summer life on Lighthouse Island (a cross between Block and Fisher's) is nicely done, although the martinis are too numerous and too "ice-green." The problem posed by the dynamiting, Ambrose Usher solves by instinct, much telephoning, and a bit of research at the New York Public Library—not detection according to Queensberry rules.

709   The Undoubted Deed   C&W 1956

Ambrose Usher is sent to the British Embassy in Washington to look into a leakage of information. This he eventually tracks down, but on the second day of his visit, at a Guy Fawkes party given by the ambassador, he gets involved in the first of two murders. Usher, tubby, goateed, and voluble, performs several undoubted deeds (see *Moby Dick,* ch. 36), and generally talks and acts as a philosopher should. The plot is reasonably simple, but much evidence is withheld from the reader. Two *gaffes* in chemistry confirm the philosopher.

DAVIDSON, T. L.

The British Museum catalogue gives nothing but his initials, which argues obscurity. The Methuen edition of his one detective story is dated 1929 and is reported to have 247 pages. But another edition, dated 1930 and published by Newnes, is given as having only 128 pages. See below.

710   The Murder in the Laboratory   Dutt 1929

This story won second prize in the Methuen Detective Story Competition judged by Bailey, Knox, and Milne. In the opinion of JB, WHT, or any other sensible person, Mr. Davidson's work is far superior to that which won the first prize, *The Inconsistent Villains* (see No. 2036).

Murder in the Laboratory provides excellent detection in a setting of students, chemical research, and medical concern. The style is spare but the atmosphere is, as it should be, thick.

711   Davies, L(eslie) P(urnell)

A Grave Matter   CCD 1968

The author, whose earlier "mysteries" (*The Lampton Dreamers; The Reluctant Medium*) were very far out, has written here a more conventional detective story, though with more "suspense" than detection. Who were the two young children whose skeletons turned up in a remote village, and why are the villagers so reluctant to help Detective Sergeant Derwent? Neither Derwent nor his unofficial helper, John Morton, really comes alive. Disappointing.

712   The Lampton Dreamers   S&S 1967

A story of evil at work through the agency of an old doctor in a small village. "It" causes everybody to have the same dream and some people to do violent and destructive things. Well-written twaddle, much of it void of meaning. The author had written extensively for *Punch* before embarking on detection.

713   Davies. See also:

The Artificial Man	Dday 1967
The Paper Dolls	Dday 1966
The Reluctant Medium	Dday 1967

714   Davis, Dorothy Salisbury (b. 1916)

Death of an Old Sinner   Scrib 1957

Her fifth tale is about an old unscrupulous general, who for money inserts scandalous anecdotes in an old diary, wherewith to blackmail the living. This attractive idea leads to his death and this in turn to the joint pursuit of his killer by the general's housekeeper and a slim young man from the DA's office. Politics, the underworld, and other prominent features of New York life are treated in a prevailingly feminine manner.

715   Davis, D. S. See also:

The Judas Cat	Scrib 1949
Old Sinners Never Die	Scrib 1959
Where the Dark Streets Go	Scrib 1969

716   Davis, George

Crime in Threadneedle Street   CCC 1968

Mr. Davis has invented Roag's Syndicate, a collective Raffles, but more sophisticated in its knowledge of fraud and more amusing in its devising of expedients. This account of their exploits owes its delightful qualities to the high intelligence of the prose and the adroit plotting by which the Syndicate, a group of their enemies (also criminal), and Scotland Yard keep up a three-cornered fight without ever becoming inept or incredible. The high foolery here includes some magnificent scenes, such as the discombobulation of the bank computer center. Such tales require no effort at plausible characterization, since interest is monopolized by ingenuity and humor.

717   DAVIS, G. See also:

Friday Before Bank Holiday	Coll 1964
Roag's Syndicate	Coll 1960
Toledano	Coll 1962

Association Item
718   DAY-LEWIS, C(ECIL) (b. 1904)

The Buried Day   Harp 1960

For other biographical details, see Nicholas Blake. This book, which is autobiography, gives an account of the poet's mental evolution and love adventures, with passing references to his years as a schoolteacher and his work as a detective novelist (see Chapter 3). It is a curiously gripping book, and a kind of "source" for *The Private Wound* (No. 208).

719   DEAN, SPENCER (pseud. of Prentice Winchell; also Stewart Sterling; b. 1895)

Credit for a Murder   Dday 1961

The third novel about Don Cadee and his friends in the security office of Amblett's department store. These stories generally begin with a little bit of shoplifting or credit cadging and wind up with murder and chases by land and sea. The present one is good enough, but JB preferred *Price Tag for Murder* (1959), perhaps because it was his first encounter with the formula.

720   DE CAIRE, EDWIN (pseud. of Edwin Alfred Williams)

Death Among the Writers   H&S 1952

East Nettlefold is unusual in having several writers, one literary agent, and a number of beekeepers in close proximity and friendship. When the literary agent dies and one of the other writers turns out to be two persons hiding in fact and in name, the problem of the undoubted murder becomes taxing for Inspector Bootle and Sergeant Swift. Their discoveries keep the reader in steady suspense, while he is also entertained by the first-rate treatment of the literary life. Except for one curious lapse in usage and two in grammar, the writing is splendid and these specks are made up for by the highly original motive and an excellent point of differentiation between the effects of KCN and HCN. Altogether a masterpiece of the art.

721   DE CAIRE. See also:

The Umgasi Diamonds   H&S 1954

722   DEIGHTON, LEN (b. 1929), has specialized in the type of spy fiction in which the interest lies rather in the mass of realistic detail and the

sidelights on disagreeable human traits than in event or adventure—though killing, torture, and tension are present from time to time. Satire can be found, too, but rather heavy-handed, as in *The Billion-Dollar Brain*, which has many boring stretches. See also: *An Expensive Place to Die* (1967), *Funeral in Berlin* (1964), *Horse Under Water* (1963), *The Ipcress File* (1963), and the cookbook *Où est le garlic?*

723   DEKOBRA, MAURICE (pseud. of Ernest Maurice Tessier)

　　　　The Madonna of the Sleeping Cars   Laur 1927
　　　　　　La Madone des Sleepings, trans. by Neal Wainwright
　　　　　　Portrait of the author
　　　　　　Publisher's apology to Lord Howard de Walden for similarity
　　　　　　of name used in the book

This English version of a Continental best seller of 1925 is bad and fails to render its most agreeable feature—the witty dialogue and comment on contemporary life, notably the Bolshevik regime. The story itself is cock-and-bull adventure, not taken seriously even by the author. Still, it was the book that put the Orient Express on the map (see No. 103).

724   DE LA TORRE (BUENO), LILLIAN [Mrs. George S. McCue] (b. 1902)

　　　　Elizabeth Is Missing   Knopf 1945

This is the Elizabeth Canning case of the mid-eighteenth century retold in fictional form with heavy documentation. The writer is as unsatisfying in this effort as she is in her tales of Boswell and Johnson (see No. 2467). Some crude element is mixed with all the learning, or if not crude then pretentious. Her conclusion here is nonetheless right: that Elizabeth was innocent and the conspiracy against her fashioned by chance.

725   DE LA TORRE. See also Nos. 2306, 2467–8, 2774, and 3099.

726   DELVING, MICHAEL

　　　　Smiling the Boy Fell Dead   Scrib 1966

A young American bookseller visits a remote Gloucestershire village to inspect a medieval manuscript, now the possession of a hard-up lady who is sole remaining descendant of the local noble family. Murder of a ne'er-do-well on or at the foot of the lady's staircase prompts Dave Cannon to do a bit of detective work. He runs afoul of the constituted authority (Inspector Codd), who is very tolerant, all things considered. An earlier murder is uncovered and a promising love affair begun. Pleasant reading, and inviting attention to his next, *Die Like a Man* (Scrib 1970).

727   DENBIE, ROGER (pseud. of Alan Baer Green and Julian Paul Brodie)

　　　　Death on the Limited   Burt 1933

Serious and valiant attempt to tie up a murder on a fast train into a neat and convincing package. The authors lack skill in characterization, but keep times straight and get the alibi method clearly across. (According to JB, this is too high a rating for a bumbling business.)

728   DERING, JOAN

Not Proven   H&S 1966

Comments on her earlier books speak of their "strong feminine appeal." This is doubtless true, but the present book is not to be dismissed as feminine. The women in it are intelligent, courageous, and consecutive in their actions and feelings; the writing is first-rate and the plot (in the *Jane Eyre* category) is admirably put together, as is the solution of the antecedent murder. Only the very end can be caviled at as abrupt—and also the odd use of the word *rigor*.

729   DERING. See also:

Louise   IW 1957/1956
Number Two, North Steps   H&S 1965

DERLETH, AUGUST (WILLIAM); also Tally Mason; b. 1909

The sage of Sauk City (Wis.), who has written a life of Thoreau and collaborated with H. P. Lovecraft in horror stories, has also written extensively on historical subjects. In detective matters, besides the dubious Solar Pons stories, he has distinguished himself by a series of tales featuring the philosophizings and detections of Judge Peck.

730   Murder Stalks the Wakely Family   M&L 1934
       In Eng.: Death Stalks the Wakely Family

A.D. is not our dish, but there are points about the setting and the character of Judge P. that lend themselves to detective thought, and it is a pity that the author shows a provincial outlook beyond the needs of local color.

731   No Future for Luana   Scrib 1945

Strongly characterized Wisconsin scene, with Judge Peck doing the detection, aided by his secretary (male), who tells the story. The murder of a second-rate actress, member of a troupe doing the rounds of the corn-belt county seats as part of a carnival, is interestingly tied up with her girlhood in the town where the murder occurs. Good characterization and a little detection.

732   DERLETH. See also Nos. 2469–71 and:

The Man on All Fours	M&L 1934	The Seven Who Waited	Scrib 1943
Mischief in the Lane	Scrib 1944	The Sign of Fear	M&L 1935
The Narracong Riddle	Scrib 1940	Three Who Died	M&L 1935
Sentence Deferred	Scrib 1945		

733   DESMOND, HUGH

The Silent Witness   W&B 1963

A South African crime that is "32 years old" is looked into by a CID man named Forbes, who is on vacation in Capetown. The whole thing is incredible talk, talk, talk, and childish talk at that. F. does not solve the crime, and the criminal gives himself away without necessity by committing other crimes.

734   DEVINE, D(OMINIC) M.

The Devil at Your Elbow   Walk 1967; orig. 1966

A story of blackmail and murder at a smallish English university, with believable amateur detection carried out by Graham Loudon, dean of law. There is a well-justified surprise ending, which is carried off despite a certain roughness of style.

735   Doctors Also Die   DM 1962

Defects of presentation and of characterization do not discredit this clear attempt to write a detective novel. If young Dr. Turner had not been made the narrator, his garrulity and lack of incisiveness would have been less evident; as it is, he does full justice to Elizabeth Henderson, his late partner's widow and an unusual woman. Two well-motivated murders. Scottish scene, near Glasgow.

736   The Fifth Cord   Walk 1967

Knowing his academic and medical circles as he does, the author is right to stick to them, in the usual setting near Glasgow. But the story reverts to a type which is now rather dated and hard to bear: the series of related killings with interpolations of intention by the nameless murderer. Here it just gets by, because the criminal is adequately motivated and not allowed to range for too long. Other characters are well drawn, but the hero, a newspaperman prone to self-pity, irritates more than he detects.

737   His Own Appointed Day   CCC 1965

The author's familiar scene, near Glasgow, where a high school and its head and other masters play leading parts. A justly drawn picture of current Scottish juvenile delinquency, and a believable account of a young woman in peril—all of it centering in her determination to solve the challenging mystery of her brother's death.

738   My Brother's Killer   CCC 1961

A truly splendid piece of plotting and telling. The scene is the offices of a firm of solicitors in (presumably) Glasgow. The senior partner is killed and posthumously suspected of blackmail. His younger brother tells the tale and discovers the facts, with the aid of two of his office mates. The scheme and its undoing (which brings with it a change of marital status for the hero) has only one flaw—one that is generic and too often accepted as harmless in good work: the supposition, namely, that a criminal can maintain composure and infallibly say the right things and show the right attitudes when continuously present at the investigator's activities.

A messy, cluttered tale, on a distinctly lower literary level than the author's other works. The idea of a young lawyer returning to the town he had left four years earlier as the unsuccessful champion of "principle" and finding his lawyer father (lately reconciled with him and asking for help) stabbed in the offices of the local newspaper tycoon—all this has potential, but it is ill developed.

740   The Sleeping Tiger   Walk 1968

A letdown from previous work. Not only do numerous legal errors annoy the attentive reader, but the shilly-shallying of the hero is a bore. The author undoubtedly wished John Prescott to emerge slowly as a "tiger," but he behaves far too long as a house cat. P.'s trial for murder is sandwiched in among flashbacks with his ladyfriends. North of England setting this time. Here's hoping for better things in *Illegal Tender* (Walk 1970).

DEWEY, THOMAS B(LANCHARD) (also Tom Brandt and Cord Wainer; b. 1915)

b. Elkhart, Ind.; related to Admiral Dewey; has musical avocations; lives in Calif.

741   Deadline   S&S 1966

A familiar starting point—a condemned murderer awaiting execution—leads to a fresh kind of investigation by "Mac" in a hostile rural setting. Good incidents and clues, economically handled.

742   A Sad Song Singing   S&S 1963

An original idea in the private-eye genre, executed in first-rate fashion. A young singer and guitar player leaves his girl with a suitcase full of newspapers while he takes the loot it had once held to a hideout in Indiana, the girl meanwhile becoming a quarry on the run, protected by Mac, a private detective. Some good coffeehouse atmosphere and a neat and affecting ending.

743   DEWEY. See also:

As Good as Dead	Dakers 1952
The Case of the Chased and the Unchaste	RH 1959
Hue and Cry	JH 1944
Hunter at Large	S&S 1961

744   DICKENS, CHARLES

The Mystery of Edwin Drood   Heritage 1941; orig. 1870
    Ed. by Vincent Starrett
    Orig. U.S. ed. with "Some Uncollected Pieces" (Fields, Osgood 1870)

Just a century has passed since the author's sudden death left his great mystery novel only half finished. Dickens intended to rival—and if possible surpass—his friend Wilkie Collins' *Moonstone* (see No. 576). There is no doubt that Dickens was at great pains to avoid a premature disclosure of his plot and inserted not a few red herrings as well as some subtle clues pointing to a startling denouement. What this was to be has been the subject of conjecture by more than a score of critics, who are far from agreeing whether John Jasper has murdered his nephew Edwin, or whether the young man will eventually turn up safe and sound. Even the identity of the self-appointed detective-spy, Datchery, is in dispute. For some recent and persuasive "solutions," fictional and other, see Nos.: 896, 1016, 2889, 2993, 3054.

DICKINSON, PETER (b. 1927)

b. Livingston, Zambia; educ. at Eton and King's, Camb., where he read classics. Joined staff of *Punch,* of which he became assistant editor. Wrote chiefly satirical verse until his first novel (see below) was published in 1967. Now devotes his full time to writing.

| 745 | The Glass-Sided Ants' Nest | Harp 1968 |

This first novel rates pretty high on all counts: unusual scene (a New Guinea tribe brought to London by the wealthy and scholarly daughter of the missionary whom they had revered), excellent mixture of anthropology, psychology, and humor, plus the competent Superintendent Pibble of Scotland Yard. The crime (murder of an elderly chief) is just short of bizarre, its motive acceptable, and the bit of gratuitous muddle at the end is probably in the interest of verisimilitude. Sexual symbols are numerous, and the language is in keeping with that abundance.

| 746 | The Old English Peepshow | Harp 1969 |
| | *In Eng.:* A Pride of Heroes | |

The author's unquestionable power of imagination leads him into the fatal trap of *cluttering.* So much is told us about the buildings and furnishings of the Stately Home that has been turned into a tourist attraction that motives and murders sink into relative insignificance. Superintendent Pibble is less subtle than feeble, and one gets thoroughly annoyed with the whole pudder and caboodle long before the protracted denouement.

| 747 | DICKINSON. See also: | |
| | The Sinful Stones | Harp 1970 |

748	DICKSON, CARTER (pseud. of John Dickson Carr, q.v.)	
	Nine and Death Makes Ten	Morr 1940
	In Eng.: Murder in the Submarine Zone	

One of the author's most straightforward stories. Though it contains Sir Henry Merrivale, he is bearable. The action takes place on the S.S. *Edwardic* in wartime, and it consists in finding out who murdered whom for a military secret—except that the motive takes an unexpected turn. The several characters are well differentiated and suspicion fairly distributed. Shipboard life in the blackout is especially well done.

749   She Died a Lady   Morr 1943

This is another tale in which Merrivale is loud and tantrum-y but tolerable, and the narration more continuous and sane than usual. But these merits are only relative. The circus atmosphere is still present. As for the story, it is that of a beautiful woman married to a much older man and in love with a young one. Setting and situation cannot fail to attract the reader; but by the end the multiplication of farfetched clues and the twists and double twists in the evidence exceed the limit, just like the horseplay by and about Sir Henry. As for detection properly so called, it is there but obscured by the foregoing.

750   DIDELOT, (ROGER) FRANCIS (b. 1902). This French writer was hailed with some fanfare by his American publisher, but did not win much of a following in the U.S., either before the last war or since. The best of the tales, *Death of the Deputy* (Lipp 1935), was translated in the awkward way suggested by the title. It was something like a Wild West sheriff story about a French congressman. The earlier *Murder in the Bath* was even less readable. The adventurous may want to look up *Samson Clairval, contre-service secret* (Gallimard 1937) or *The Seventh Juror* (Macd 1950).

DILLON, EILIS [Mrs. Cormac O'Cuilleanain] (b. 1920)

Lecturer, novelist of Irish life, author of books for children and of three excellent detective stories by means of which—she told JB—she learned the craft of fiction. Her husband, a professor of the history of Irish literature at the Univ. of Cork, has retired, and they live in Rome.

751   Death at Crane's Court   Faber 1953

Attractively set in a country hotel near Galway, inhabited mainly by elderly buzzards, of whom the most likable is Professor Daly. The murder of a certified s.o.b. who has fallen heir to the hotel is competently investigated by Inspector Mike Kenny, with much amusing incident. One weakness of the plot is that too much is sacrificed for the sake of an unlikely murderer.

752   Death in the Quadrangle   Faber 1956

Solidly plotted murder (by nitrobenzene) of the president of a Dublin University college by one of his staff. Detection done by a retired professor, present as visiting lecturer, and his inspector friend. Denouement a trifle wobbly but not tangled. Nice writing and characterization: thoroughly enjoyable.

753   Sent to His Account   Faber 1954

A choice slice of Irish village life with a murder by implausibly administered nicotine. Though WHT thinks it lacks the dry wit and sparkle contributed by Professor Daly to the tales before and after this, JB ranks this novel as the author's best, despite the tenuous thread of ratiocination. The title alludes to *Hamlet* I, 5, 78.

754   DILNOT, GEORGE (b. 1883)

Crook's Castle   HM 1934

Better than his prewar efforts, with or without a collaborator, but still humdrum and not in a class with the U.S. tough school when it comes to depicting gangs and police routine. This fact may throw some light on the unimportance of professionalism as preparation for literature, since G.D. is—or was—a professional policeman. (See Nos. 3130–2.)

755   DIPLOMAT (pseud. of John Franklin Carter; also Jay Franklin and "Unofficial Observer," b. 1897). *Murder in the State Department* (1930) was the first in a series of murders—*in the Embassy, in the Senate, at Geneva, on the White House Lawn*—which were wildly improbable and a little witty. Not detection.

756   DIPPER, ALAN

The Paradise Formula   Morr 1970

Another tale about a "psycho drug" whose possession by the wrong people would put an end to . . . everything. Not bad from the standpoint of the chase, but the author, whose science is apparently limited to gunnery and the raising of chickens, asks us to take far too much on faith about the powers of his wonder drug: it acts instantaneously, without dangerous side effects in any dosage, to bring about complete subservience of will.

757   DISNEY, DORIS (MILES) (b. 1907). Of her more than thirty Crime Club novels, *Compound for Death* (1943) and *The Departure of Mr. Gaudette* (1964) are representative examples, competent without question, but also without distinctive appeal to mind, heart, or sense of style.

758   DISNEY, DOROTHY CAMERON, has written many suspenseful but feminine thrillers, of which *Strawstack* (1939) and *Crimson Friday* (1942) are typical.

759   DOUGLASS, DONALD MCNUTT

Many Brave Hearts   Harp 1959

Despite kind words by Rex Stout and Charlotte Armstrong, this second venture by the author of *Rebecca's Pride* does not improve on the first. It is a tale of life on shipboard—including the inevitable storm—in which the Negro policeman and narrator, Bolivar Manchenil, ponders a good deal and detects not at all. There is some plain talking and moderately amusing lechery.

An improbable tale, set on shipboard and in the Virgin Islands, introduces the Negro policeman Bolivar Manchenil, who is not much of a
detective, though he thinks about a number of things.

761   DOUGLASS. See also:

Saba's Treasure   Harp 1963

DOYLE, (ARTHUR) CONAN (1859–1930)

Despite the apparent length of four of his Sherlock Holmes stories (*A
Study in Scarlet*, 1887; *The Sign of the Four*, 1890/91; *The Hound of the
Baskervilles*, 1902; and *The Valley of Fear*, 1915), Doyle was a writer of
short detective stories. Only *The Hound* is a *whole* long story: the others
are novellas with an alien filling which, once read, may be neglected forever after, still leaving an interesting frame of true detection around the
central melodrama. Still, in deference to outward seeming, all four tales are
entered in this section. For the best text, see No. 2483.

762   The Hound of the Baskervilles   McCl 1902

The only perfect story among the four long ones, and one of the best in
the canon, irrespective of length. By a miracle of judgment, the supernatural is handled with great effect and no letdown. The plot and subplots
are thoroughly integrated and the false clues put in and removed with a
master hand. The criminal is superb, Dr. Mortimer memorable, and the
secondary figures each contribute to the total effect of brilliancy and
grandeur combined. One wishes one could be reading it for the first time.

763   The Sign of the Four   Lipp 1889
          or, The Problem of the Sholtos
          Also: The Sign of Four, *i.e., without "the" or sbt. (Spencer
          Blackett, 1890)*

The second Holmes story makes use of the Thames in an unforgettable
manner, and the detection is more active than in *A Study in Scarlet*—as
well as fraught with danger. For one thing, Watson succumbs to the charms
of Miss Morstan, and for another the two detectives are nearly disposed
of by Tonga, the Andaman Islander. It is all so well put together, and the
brothers Sholto are so well drawn—like their furnishings—that one
readily accepts the old conspiracy in India, and even the maligning of the
Andamanians.

764   A Study in Scarlet   *Beeton's Christmas Annual,* 1887

The kind of masterpiece that holds its place despite its flaws because it
came first, full-blown, and at a stroke made obsolete the accepted contemporary manner. Holmes' introduction to Watson and the reader now
has all the glamour of an historic event, and the adventures of the two in
Lauriston Gardens and at 221B Baker Street that culminate in the arrest
of Jefferson Hope and the diagnosis of his aneurysm are etched in the

memory of every connoisseur of the detective genre. With this tale the classic modern style was set.

765   The Valley of Fear   Dday 1930/1915

With the exception of *The Hound of the Baskervilles,* our favorite among the long tales of Sherlock Holmes. Chapter 1 has in its ten pages some of the best wit and humor to be found anywhere, plus the solution of a cipher, and a stunning punch ending. Nor is there any serious letdown as Holmes, Watson, and Inspector MacDonald investigate the murder of John Douglas at Birlstone Manor in Sussex. The shadow of Moriarty appears early and comes into sharper focus at the end of the story after the long—and gripping—interlude dealing with Douglas' life among the "scrowrers" of the Pennsylvania coalfields.

766   DRACHMAN, THEODORE S.

       Something for the Birds   Crown 1958
           In ppb.: Addicted to Murder

The author is an M.D. and deputy commissioner of health in Westchester County, New York, and a Columbia graduate in public health as well. He has written an overfull book, not without interest, but the tracking down of the psittacosis source alone would have been enough. WHT found himself reading more and more rapidly toward the end—a pity, for the science is sound and the people good thick cardboard.

767   DRUMMOND, CHARLES (pseud. of Kenneth Giles, q.v.)

       Death and the Leaping Ladies   Goll 1968

A visiting basketball team (female) plays in a London stadium, and its star is shot dead. Sergeant Reed, drinking steadily and unconvincingly, detects without charm or vigor.

768   Death at the Furlong Post   Walk 1968

The same tough elliptical style pursues a pair of hard-drinking policemen who uncover a jewel theft complicated by murder. It is all interviews and too much attention to the ailing stomach of the inspector.

769   The Odds on Death   Walk 1969

Another racetrack affair, with murder and horse-swapping, international style, as the motive for Sergeant Reed's delving and drinking and delaying a reasonable solution.

770   DRUMMOND, JUNE

       The Gantry Episode   Goll 1968

An imaginary town with some English characteristics is stricken with madness as a result of someone's putting LSD in the water supply. There are seven deaths, panic, and occupation pro tem by the military. Inspector David Cope, on vacation, is flown in to help his colleague Nilsen trace the author or authors of the crime, part of his difficulty being that the members of the local college of science hardly see the event as criminal. Suspense is slack and talk excessive, though J.D. is obviously an intelligent and well-informed writer. No detection.

771   DRUMMOND, J. See also:

| The Black Unicorn | Goll 1959 |
| Welcome, Proud Lady | Goll 1964 |

772   DU BOIS, THEODORA [MCCORMICK] (b. 1890). Her stories are heavily domestic, those of the past decade featuring the detective team of Anne and Jeffrey McNeill, as in *Seeing Red,* 1954. The earlier *Death Wears a White Coat* (1938) helped to make her reputation.

773   DUBOISGOBEY, FORTUNÉ (HIPPOLYTE-AUGUSTE) (1821–91), wrote innumerable sensational stories, confessedly inspired by the works of Gaboriau and affording the same unsatisfactory mixture of excellent ideas with hackneyed situations and mechanical melodrama. F.D. was introduced to the English public in the translation commissioned by Vizetelly in the 1880s. The best known is *The Crime of the Opera House* (2 vol.; 1886; orig. 1881). See also: *A Railway Tragedy* (1887); *An Omnibus Mystery* and *The Old Age of Lecoq, the Detective* (a tribute to Gaboriau; 2 vol.; 1885–86).

774   DUNCOMBE, FRANCES, is an author who knows and writes about old towns and old houses. *Death of a Spinster* (1958) is agreeable and emancipated from HIBK, yet not for those who want more than inoffensive charm.

775   DURBRIDGE, FRANCIS, is a writer of serials, TV scripts, films, plays, and stories, in some of which Paul Temple figures. But note that under the pseudonym of Paul Temple, Durbridge and Douglas Rutherford Mc-Connell have published a couple of joint efforts. The best recent solo performances by F.D. are perhaps *The Desperate People* (1966) and *The Pig-Tail Murder* (1969). They are unmistakably detection, but not notable for tension or originality. The sometimes neat details are what keep the reader going.

DÜRRENMATT, FRIEDRICH (b. 1921)

b. Canton Bern; educ. Zurich and Bern univ.; was a commercial artist; began writing in 1947. Has written the very successful play *Der Besuch der Alten Dame* and others, and three detective stories: *Der Richter und sein Henker* (1952), *Der Verdacht* (= *Suspicion* = *Traps* = *A Dangerous Game;* 1969/1953), *Das Versprechen* (= *The Pledge;* 1959/1955).

776   The Judge and His Hangman   Harp. 1955; orig.; 1952
          Trans. by Cyrus Brooks

The seriously ailing Inspector Barlach is in charge of investigating the murder of a Swiss lieutenant of police. Barlach's old-fashioned methods put him at odds with both his superiors and his assistant, but the recriminations, which might be tedious in less capable hands, are here no impediment to a very taut and tidy tale. Plenty of both factual and psychological detection, and one of the best surprise endings in recent years. WHT, who has read both the original and its translation, calls the latter excellent.

777   DWIGHT, OLIVIA

Close His Eyes   Harp 1961

A shortish story about a Midwestern university, where a famous and drunken poet has committed suicide in suspect circumstances. A young newcomer tells the story of his half-unintended, half-ineffectual poking around and speculating, which leads him to a conclusion never properly made clear to the reader. The author knows the academic world but plays rather obvious changes upon its comic side.

778   DYER, GEORGE (BELL) (b. 1903)

The Catalyst Club   Scrib 1936

The author's thesis is that modern murder can no longer be solved by an all-knowing detective; it requires the cooperation of several experts, who examine clues and criticize one another's inferences. Hence the San Francisco group of half a dozen men who tackle the strange murder of an heiress and arrive at its solution by pooling the knowledge of a chemist, a psychiatrist, an ichthyologist, and a reporter. The clues are thoroughly treated and the telling is not bad, though often overelaborated.

779   The Long Death   Scrib 1937
       A Catalyst Club Murder

This fourth case for the so-called Catalysts is closely plotted and its clues neatly jointed by the combined efforts of some—not all—of the members of the club. The occasion of the murder is theft in a laboratory, and it entails serious consequences for love and business. The people are desensitized cardboard, yet the investigation and chase generate excitement despite a surfeit of footnotes.

780   DYER. See also:

       The Five Fragments   HM 1932
       The People Ask Death   Scrib 1940
       The Three-Cornered Wound   HM 1931

781   EBERHART, MIGNON G(OOD) (b. 1899). Nurse Keate and Detective Lance O'Leary function effectively in *The Patient in Room 18* (1929), but this author's large output since then has offered little that is memorable. See, however, *The Cases of Susan Dare* (ss; 1934), *Five Passengers from Lisbon* (1946), *Run Scared* (1963), and Nos. 2694 and 2739.

782   EGAN, LESLEY (pseud. of Elizabeth Linington; also Dell Shannon, Anne Blaisdell, and Egan O'Neill; b. 1921)

Against the Evidence   Harp 1962

Miss Egan's hero-detective is a Jewish lawyer with a gentile wife—altogether an engaging couple, despite their mastiff. Jes Falkenstein quotes rather too extensively from Solomon, and puts on Bach records and then doesn't listen to them, but he does collect evidence in this case of "framed rape" involving a halfwit and a Fuller-Brush man.

ELLIN, STANLEY (b. 1916)

A New Yorker who began his life's work as a pusher for newspapers, a dairy farmer, a schoolteacher, and a steelworker. His first accepted story, "The Specialty of the House" (1945), led to his adopting the career of letters, so that we owe his output of unusual tales to the good judgment of Ellery Queen, who published his maiden effort.

783   The Eighth Circle   RH 1958

Long and admirably written exploit of a private financial investigator turned detective, but not a detective story. Murray Kirk agrees to look for evidence to get a crooked policeman off the hook, feeling that he is sure to find more evidence against the accused, and thus free the lovely, never-touched fiancée for his own attentions. Lots of talk, much of it entertaining, and in some ways a forerunner of Thorp's *The Detective,* though with less dirt and more art.

784   The House of Cards   RH 1967

A mixture of international intrigue and domestic treachery, done with skill, but not as moving as *The Key to Nicholas Street* or some of the short stories (qq.v.).

785   The Key to Nicholas Street   S&S 1952

A classic treatment of the murder of the beautiful and accomplished mistress by a member of the lover's family. There is detection in the sense that clues are found and discussed, but the solution comes by confession, and the point is not crime-solving so much as the drama of a woman's lust for respectability and her son's fixation upon her.

786   The Valentine Estate   Macd 1968

A reviewer's comparison of this book with *The Thirty-Nine Steps* (No. 332) is misleading. There is intrigue and mystery in both, but not of the same kind. Here greed is uppermost, together with love, aberration, and psychosis. Not detection.

787   ELLIN. See also Nos. 2495–7 and:

Summit: A Novel of Suspense   S&S 1948

788   ENDORE, GUY (1901–1970)

Detour at Night   S&S 1959

A fantasia on semantics as a clue to the association of ideas in the hero,
who suspects his wife (a rich woman) of a murder that puts him in a delicate position. He turns hobo to do a job of pseudo detection.

789   Methinks the Lady   DS 1945

Remarkable as much for its form and typography as for its contents. It
is the story of a trial for murder, which is interrupted by the suicide of the
judge. We are accordingly given courtroom question-and-answer, straight
prose, dialogue in play form, and a typewritten letter at the very end.
For a sensational sequence the story does pretty well, but to report enthusiasm would overstate the readers' response.

The title inverts the well-known remark of the Queen in *Hamlet*, III,
2, 240.

790   The Werewolf of Paris   Farr 1933

It is hard to see why this book was a great success in its day: it is a quasi-
historical, semi-medical, semi-magical tale of violence in France at the
time of the Commune of 1871. (There was a mad, cannibalistic Sergeant
Bertrand tried for his alleged crimes c. 1848.) The social commentary is
fitful and not profound, and some of the reported events and explanations
are hard to fit into the scheme. One suspects allegorical intentions, as in
the "fact" that werewolves are never seen, but feel themselves to be such,
and act savagely as if . . .

791   ERSKINE, MARGARET (pseud. of Margaret Wetherby Williams),
has written numerous novels starring the rather featureless Inspector
Septimus Finch—e.g., *Take a Dark Journey* (1965) and *The Case with
Three Husbands* (1967).

ESTEVEN, JOHN (pseud. of Samuel Shellabarger, 1888–1954)

Princeton professor, scholar, historical novelist, and storyteller in several
genres. Esteven is the name he reserved for his few detective tales.

792   The Door of Death   Cent 1928

A woman is strangled in her bed on Halloween. The narrator-physician is
summoned by her sister beforehand to deal with the other woman's delu-
sions. But it is Inspector Rae Norse (described as "a combination of
John Paul Jones and the composer Mozart") who undertakes to find the
murderer. The detection is circuitous by which this slight man with game-
cock courage and a tendency to dream tracks down a greedy relative
who "talks Nietzsche" and wants nothing less than the money, the woman,
and a dash of revenge against his brother. Altogether a disappointing
hodge-podge of styles and ideas.

793 Voodoo S&S 1930

Rae Norse is once again at work, as "Chief of the Metropolitan Detective Service (New York)," to protect Judge Frole from threats of death. All the judge's relatives are suspect, for many reasons. One of them deals in voodoo magic and is indeed the leader of a superstitious band. The complications of murder, Cuban and other connections, the voodoo goddess, and her enamored follower (the detective himself) lead only to a melodramatic and violent sacrifice. Not recommended.

794 EUSTIS, HELEN (b. 1916)

The Horizontal Man   Harp 1946

The first and better of the author's two novels in the genre. What makes this one noteworthy is: the quality of the prose; the atmosphere of Smith College; the characterization of several persons, drawn from well-known figures in the literary world; the touch of horror in the crime itself, and the motives leading to it.

795 EUSTIS. See also:

The Fool Killer   Dday 1954

796 EVERMAY, MARCH (pseud. of Mathilde Eiker, b. 1893)

They Talked of Poison   Macm 1938

The author easily illustrates the proposition that a domestic tale, told by a niece about her professor uncle, need not fall into the pit of HIBK. Here the Reverend Dr. Purley is found dead, and later his disaffected daughter as well. The detection carried out jointly by the official police and the elderly professor of sociology (at a university one hour from Baltimore) is leisurely but interesting.

797 EVERMAY. See also:

This Death Was Murder   Macm 1940

FAIR, A. A. (pseud. of Erle Stanley Gardner, q.v.)

E. S. G. began to write under this name some thirty years ago, when he had established himself as the author of the Perry Mason stories, the District Attorney series, and others.

In the "Fair" series, an odd partnership, between a large and tough female private detective and a small, subtle, and ingenious ex-lawyer who is man enough to make all the girls fall for him and to stand up to his partner, engages in the elucidation of plots that usually involve gambling and invariably lead to murder. The chief interest is surprise and dialogue.

798 The Count of Nine   Morr 1958

In several respects quite unlike the usual Lam-Cool problems. This one has some genuine detection besides the usual bright dialogue. But it is uncommonly short and gives the impression of ending abruptly.

799   Double or Quits   Morr 1941

One of the best A. A. Fair stories. It is witty, reasonably simple, and
brilliantly told by Donald Lam, who gets his partnership with Bertha
Cool while solving the machinations of several con men to extract money
from the widow of a wealthy doctor. The murder is plausible, and—what
is always interesting in E.S.G.'s stories—the clues that don't work out but
suggest other, deeper plotting are superbly conceived.

800   Give 'Em the Ax   Morr 1944

This tale chronicles Donald Lam's return from the South Seas after his
war service and deals with an insurance case. D.L. gets severely kissed
by the beautiful heroine and works out a lucrative scheme for Lam and
Cool after imperiling the status of the firm and his friendships with Bertha
and Elsie. A good deal of excellent dialogue but rather less pep than in
the others of the same genre.

801   Owls Don't Blink   Morr 1942

This one is chiefly laid in New Orleans and pivots on impersonation to
assist blackmail. The murders, as well as Donald's jeopardy, are done and
resolved with a free stroke of the brush—the sign of invention before it
yields to formula.

802   Spill the Jackpot   Morr 1941

The usual Reno and Las Vegas tomfoolery but done with an expert
hand and the added amusement of Bertha Cool's illness, loss of weight,
and struggle with appetite for both food and money. Donald has a nice
lovey-dovey with one of his adoring brunettes and uses his head to snag
the available thousands.

803   Top of the Heap   Morr 1952

This particular Lam's tale is a lively affair of "pressure," quasi sex,
gambling—the lot.

804   FAIR. See also:

All Grass Isn't Green		Crows Can't Count	Morr 1946
(posthumous)	Morr 1970	Cut Thin to Win	Morr 1965
Bachelors Get Lonely	Morr 1961	Fish or Cut Bait	Morr 1963
Bats Fly at Dusk	Morr 1962	Fools Die on Friday	Morr 1947
Bedrooms Have Windows	Morr 1942	Gold Comes in Bricks	Morr 1940
The Bigger They Come	Morr 1939	Traps Need Fresh Bait	Morr 1967
Cats Prowl at Night	Morr 1943	Up for Grabs	Morr 1964

805   FAIRWAY, SIDNEY

  The Long Tunnel   Dday 1936

An interesting and rather unusually written story about a professor of
bacteriology in a medical college, faced with the problem of discovering

which of his colleagues was guilty of framing him for the murder of a third—a crime for which he has been tried and found not guilty. The medical school staff is well handled and the love story extremely apt.

806   FALKNER, JOHN MEADE

The Nebuly Coat   Arn 1904

A story of church restoration, illegitimacy, and stolen peerage, which includes a murder and a covered-over painting. Long historical digressions (interesting) and fair character drawing. But disappointing close, despite the fall of the church tower.

807   FARJEON, J(OSEPH) JEFFERSON (also Anthony Swift; 1883–1955)

The 5:18 Mystery   MacV 1929

The grandson of the actor Joseph Jefferson and brother of the severally distinguished Eleanor, Herbert, and Harry has written here a pure chase story which begins very well in a railway carriage and has an excellent idea underneath it—courting a danger in order to rescue someone who has previously fallen into it. Unfortunately, the author shows little sense of character and probability, and about the time the party leaves the train the reader loses interest through losing all belief.

808   FARJEON. See also:

Death in Fancy Dress	BM 1939
Death in the Inkwell	BM 1942
Greenmask	BM 1944
The Mystery of Dead Man's Heath (Lionel North)	DM 1934
Thirteen Guests	BM n.d. [1938]

FARMER, BERNARD J(AMES) (also Owen Fox; b. 1902)

The author is a former ship's engineer with police experience. He is also a book collector and a bibliographer of the works of Winston Churchill. He evidently means to "combine his information" like the journalist in *Pickwick Papers* who wrote on Chinese Metaphysics.

809   Death of a Bookseller   Hein 1956

The flat and flat-footed style is rather lacking in art, which is all the worse that the characters all talk alike. The plot is only so-so, and the identity of the murderer a distinct letdown. This does not leave much to admire, especially since the hocus-pocus about witchcraft is badly faked and entirely irrelevant.

810   FARMER. See also:

Death at the Cascades	Hein 1953
Murder Next Year	Hein 1959

811   FARNOL, (JOHN) JEFFERY (1878–1952)

The Loring Mystery   LB 1925

This author ventured only a few times into what he thought was the territory of detection, and usually with the aid of a would-be comic character, Sergeant Jasper Shrig, of Bow Street. In this story of mixed identity, false suspicion of murder, true love, birds and flowers, and heavy doses of lower-class dialect, nothing but the remains of old-fashioned romancing is to be found and enjoyment is nil.

812   FARNOL. See also:

Friday the 13th   BM 1940
Heritage Perilous (Shrig)   McB 1947
A Matter of Business and Other Stories
   (one Shrig story: "Footprints")   Dday 1940
The Ninth Earl (Shrig)   Samp 1950

813   FARRER, KATHERINE (DOROTHY) [NEWTON] (b. 1911)

At Odds with Morning   H&S 1960

Not a detective story—nor is it easy to say just what sort of tale this is. A worldly young man, rescued from the gutter by the kind offices of the prior of a very minor order, makes use of the time his duties provide for reflection to see the wisdom of returning to his rich but frightful mother, so as to ease her last days and (perhaps) preserve his estate. A quasi miracle, an apparent "judgment," and a flood reminiscent of that in Powys' *Glastonbury Romance* help fill this small book of 190 pages.

814   The Cretan Counterfeit   Coll 1954

The author's second tale to use the talents of Richard Ringwood of the CID and his wife, Clare. It maintains the author's high standards of wit and imagination and is solidly grounded in Cretan archaeology. The several characters are distinct, interesting in themselves, and decently mysterious in their attitudes and motives until the denouement, which comes gradually as it should, and not as a kind of reversal of all we have been led to believe.

815   Gownsman's Gallows   H&S 1957

Another case for Inspector Richard Ringwood, the classical scholar turned cop, and in an Oxford setting, like his first (No. 816). Members of Pentecost College are involved from start to finish. ("Oxford murder," says the Yard: "That always means trouble.") The victim has been (1) run over and (2) carted off and burned in a haystack—all except the fully shod feet, wearing socks that are traced to an undergraduate who is alive and has an alibi. The trail leads to France (with much dialogue in not altogether correct French), and we are plunged into the sequels of the Resistance. Ringwood's action and solution are farfetched—good material spoiled.

N.B. Dog lovers will enjoy the abundant lore on bloodhounds.

A good tale of infant-snatching in Oxford, the bereaved parents being a terrifyingly intellectual young couple. Unusual plot and fair detection, plus A-1 imagination and fantasy. It has a few of the excesses and weaknesses of a first novel but makes one wish to read the next. Inspector Ringwood of Scotland Yard is the detective, and he marries at the end.

Fearing, Kenneth (Flexner) (1902–61)

b. Chicago, the son of a lawyer; educ. Univ. of Wisconsin, graduated in 1924; reporter in Chicago, millhand, then New York free-lance writer, book reviewer, and author of six volumes of poetry, as well as of novels in various genres.

817   The Big Clock   HB 1946

A truly brilliant story, laid in a large mass-communication organization where the hero works and is involved amorously with the boss's woman. Circumstances lead to her death, and he is put in the position of obvious murderer. The details by which he is caught and with the aid of which he unwinds himself are chosen and exhibited with genius. Tone and talk are sharp and often bitter—the whole business is a tour de force worthy of the highest praise.

818   Clark Gifford's Body   RH 1942

A fantasy of war and totalitarianism, which gives, via newspaper extracts, letters, and the like, an account of what happened in a mythical country when station WKBL (or something of the sort) was seized by fifth columnists. No detection.

819   The Dagger of the Mind   RH 1941

His second best. Just as *The Big Clock* must have grown out of his experience in the gears of a huge periodical outfit, so this tale must have been born of a summer at a so-called artists' colony—either Yaddo or the MacDowell Camp. At any rate, the relationships are excellently done, and so is the atmosphere, but unfortunately the locale is necessarily one in which places and times are difficult to make vivid and credible. The result is something less than right, though it is worth reading as a murder mystery.

The title is from *Macbeth*, II, 1, 38.

820   The Loneliest Girl in the World   HB 1951

Like all Fearing tales, this one has a good dose of "queerness" (asexually speaking), but here kept under rigid control and contributing to a fairly satisfactory story of the reasons why a father and son plunged from a penthouse ledge. Interesting treatment of wire recording (a major factor) and of the mental state of the daughter, who does what detecting is done.

821   FEARING. See also:

The Crozart Story	HB	1960
The Generous Heart	HB	1954
The Hospital	RH	1939

822   FENISONG, RUTH, writes stories that conform to the canons of the genre but without that special art of invention and characterization which is needed to lift one murder after another out of the rut. Her Inspector Gridley appears on a New York scene; her output is above one score. See: *The Wench Is Dead* (1953), *Miscast for Murder* (1954), *Death of the Party* (1958), *But Not Forgotten* (1960).

823   FERGUSON, [THE REV.] JOHN (ALEXANDER) (b. 1873)

The Man in the Dark   DM 1928

This rambling novel is divided into four books, two of which are narratives by the journalist Chance, who plays Watson to Francis McNab's Holmes. The reason for the crime is clear from the start, and the identity of the murderer is relatively unimportant. The interest must therefore lie in the inferences drawn by a blind man, victimized by the killer, as to where and by whom he is held captive, and in the later use by McNab of these inferences to locate the house from which the murderer plans a getaway to the Continent.

824   FERGUSON, JOHN. See also:

Death Comes to Périgord	Coll 1931
Murder on the Marsh	Lane 1930
Stealthy Terror	Lane 1933/1917

825   FERRARS, E(LIZABETH) X. (pseud. of Morna Doris Brown [Mc-Taggart], b. 1907)

Enough to Kill a Horse   CCC 1953

The eleventh story by an English writer (born in Rangoon), who seems from this one sample to have a sound enough grasp of motives and human relations and a due regard for probability and technique, but whose people and plot are so standard that reading on is a stern duty. The scheme in this longish tale rests on the mischance that two people go to a party who cannot taste the bitterness of phenylthiourea. Since there is also arsenic in the lobster patties, the wrong man gets killed and the police are puzzled. An elderly scientist who says nothing figures it all out.

826   Zero at the Bone   Walk 1968/1967

The lore of falconry does not redeem this short and would-be intense tale of passion and recklessness, written exclusively from the point of view of the anxious female participants. No detection; solution *per accidens*.

827   FIELD, MEDORA [PERKERSON] (b. 1898)

Blood on Her Shoe   Macm 1942

Unfit for rational consumption. The style is HIBK compounded with Southern femininity. See, if you must, *Who Killed Aunt Maggie* (Macm 1939).
Not to be confused with *Moira* Field (q.v.).

FIELD, MOIRA (b. 1917)

Educ. Lancashire, Heidelberg, and St. Hugh's, Oxf. Worked in London theater, married the actor Jonathan Field; then secretary to the Chinese ambassador at The Hague; later head of research at *Encyclopaedia Britannica,* London.

828   Foreign Body   Macm 1951; orig. 1950

What is remarkable about this work is the steady but unhurried pace, which gives a full chance for the intricacy of the plot to be unfolded, discussed, and made credible. There is time, too, for wit, byplay, and changing relations among the characters, as well as for a succession of lesser puzzles, which are not only created but solved. Assuming the first and only unlikelihood—that the "foreign body" would be left on the cinema manager's doorstep—all the rest follows beautifully. Inspector Flower is excellent, and so is the rest of the cast.

FIELDLING, A. (pseud. of Dorothy Feilding [*sic*], b. 1884)

As far as indirect knowledge goes, it seems the stories published under the name of A. Fielding have been wrongly attributed to Archibald E. Fielding, b. 1900. How far the confusion extends it is impossible to say.

829   The Footsteps that Stopped   Knopf 1926

S. S. Van Dine (q.v.) mentions this as one of a scant dozen of good works added to the English output of detection, which he thought, in the late twenties, was "rapidly increasing." He was a good prophet, but in this case a poor critic.

830   The Wedding Chest Mystery   Kins 1932

Inspector Pointer keeps busy throughout a long book, but accomplishes nothing significant. Two months after reading it one doesn't remember or care whose body was in the chest, much less why.

831   FIRTH, ANTHONY

Tall, Balding, Thirty-Five   Harp 1967

Not a detective story but an espionage tale of unusual cast. The author manages to make the series of scrapes through which his homosexual but not too disaffecting hero John Limbo passes sufficiently credible to be entertaining, wild though some are. The one overtly homosexual scene in the book is well done and without special pleading.

832 FISH, ROBERT L.

Isle of the Snakes   S&S 1963

The author of the distressing "Schlock Homes" pastiches in *EQMM* has here turned his hand to a more valid medium—his second tale of the Brazilian Captain José Da Silva, who is a liaison officer between the Brazilian police and Interpol in Rio. The trappings of detection are here, including an agreeable and often amusing Watson, one Wilson of the American Embassy; but the tale is actually one of pursuit, with some good local color and enough snakes (held at bay with a flame thrower) to fill the nightmares of a lifetime. The writing is first-rate. (See also No. 2501.)

833   The Shrunken Head   S&S 1963

Captain José Da Silva is reasonably competent and convincing, but his exploits would not hold one's attention so well in less striking surroundings. There is an effective crash ending in this as in the previous book, not in the sense of a criminal revealed but rather of peril escaped.

834 FISHER, DOUGLAS

What's Wrong at Pyford?   H&S 1950

Written in a queer sort of colloquial English Americanese, this story deals with rural misdoings, beginning with the mysterious killing of a prize bull. The narrator, Jeff Tellford, is a superior farmhand to whom the owner of the dairy farm assigns the task of discovering who is responsible for the crimes. The byplay, love story, and detection are below average in quality and the incidents partake of slapstick. The best thing about the book is the title.

835   FISHER. See also:

Corpse in Community   H&S 1953
Death at Pyford Hall   H&S 1952
Poison Pen at Pyford   H&S 1951

836 FITT, MARY (pseud. of Kathleen Freeman, b. 1897)

Death Finds a Target   CCD 1942

The first passable one of several Mary Fitt novels read by us. English country house complete with lake, island, and former (dispossessed) owners living in entrance lodge. Murder of moody elder son, a rifle expert, with his own "secret weapon" is well handled by Inspector Mallett and *two* doctors. The obvious suspect is acceptably managed, to the accompaniment of some young love and a good bit of fog and middle-aged philandering.

837   The Late Uncle Max

Macd 1957

The murder of an amateur archaeologist has been done more than once of recent years, and better than this; there are too many people, nearly all of them incredible or unlikable; the style is scrappy without yielding the touches that Christie manages with no effort. Inspector Mallett does not appear.

838   Mizmaze

MJ 1959

Only in her earliest novels did this author manage to keep her taste for feminine psychology subordinate to the needs of detection. Occasionally, as in *Love from Elizabeth,* which made no intellectual demands, she built up a telling atmosphere; but here the attempt is to produce a legitimate whodunit complete with country house, maze, and a detestable group of characters. Inspector Mallett is as wooden as the instrument with which the victim's skull is cracked, and Dr. Fitzbrown conducts the questioning ad nauseam. The ending is perfunctory and almost ludicrous.

839   Sweet Poison

Macd 1956

Better Fitt than usual—a rather deft mixture of poison and archaeology well managed by Inspector Mallett and his constant companion, Dr. Fitzbrown. For these characters and others also concerned in detection, see the short stories in No. 2502.

FITZGERALD, NIGEL (b. 1906)

b. Charleville, Cork; educ. Trinity Coll., Dublin; one-time pres. Irish Actors' Equity Association. Not all the near dozen of detective stories by this author feature Superintendent Duffy or Alan Russell, the actor-manager—some have one, some the other, a few both, a few neither.

840   Black Welcome

CCC 1961

Pleasant reading despite some confusion at the end. It tells the story of a young Irishman's return to an abandoned love after he has gone off with another girl. No detection.

841   The Candles Are All Out

CCC 1960

A tale of murder in an Irish mansion isolated by flood. The theatrical Alan Russell has been toned down and is less full of himself than heretofore. There is, in fact, no stage stuff and a good confrontation scene at the end. The plot is simple, and the reader has a fair chance to deduce for himself.

842   Echo Answers Murder

Macm 1965/Coll 1963

Orig.: The Day of the Adder

A young couple, not well matched, go back from London to Ireland following the death of the man's mother. She was the Squiress of the place and successfully married off her son to put an end to an unsuitable local affair. The woman in that earlier affair is strangled the night of the hero's arrival. Inspector Duffy does a quick and not very interesting job of spotting a local murderer, but there are one or two excellent farcical scenes.

843   The House Is Falling   CCC 1955

Like *The Rosy Pastor*, well told and nicely set. The writer, who knows his Ireland, has a knack of drawing attractive places and bringing their independent life into likely connection with his plot. Though complex, the tangle here is plausible and the treatment of character and motive satisfactory. Good dialogue, as before, and the ending not huddled. Yet the same fault remains in another form: the mechanics of the killing are by far too elaborate for anyone to have compassed.

844   Imagine a Man   Coll 1956

The worst concoction ever put together by our Irish friend. It begins in Ireland, like the others, but badly—there is protracted uncertainty, of the wrong kind, about who is who and what corpse is which. Soon the scene shifts to an improbable Italian hotel, where the hero switches his affections, while people continue to be bopped on the head, hanged, and suspected. Inspector Duffy is long awaited and does little after he arrives.

845   Midsummer Malice   CCC 1953

Inspector Duffy is not a bad detective, the setting is scenically agreeable, and one or two of the eccentrics are all right, but the plot and the main people in this first novel are a bore. The actor pair talk too much and to no purpose, and the murders are in fact not ever clearly assigned to mania or to premeditation. As for calling all the horrors committed by the murderer "malice," that's like calling a world war "an affray."

846   The Rosy Pastor   Coll 1954

A considerable improvement over this author's first. Laid in Ireland, in a well-treated geographical setting that plays a part in the tale. The characters are distinct, interesting, and articulate. Only toward the end does the recital of who did what while seeming to do something else become so thick as to disengage the reader from his belief.

847   The Student Body   CCC 1958

Not really detection. The story tells of extralegal action by a group of Dublin students who want to exact private justice for a political crime. They kidnap a stranger outside a pub; the man is killed while the students are elsewhere; the tale consists in finding out how this could have been done. Despite some flaws, the book is not without drive.

848   Suffer a Witch   CCC 1958

The merits of the tale are two: the excellent idea of having a girl of fifteen persuade herself that she is a witch, and the absence of the actor-manager Alan Russell. Superintendent Duffy does a fair amount of thinking, but the real hero of the story is one Benedict Carey, a writer of detective stories, who see things first, including the desirability of Sally Marsh. The start is slow, and the author waits a bit long to pull things together.

849   This Won't Hurt You   Macm 1960

The introduction of phenol into a patient's jaw by a dentist is fatal. The criminal is, of course, *not* the dentist—poor fellow—and it is sad to say that the identity and discovery of the doer involve too much scurrying and masquerading and being seen here or there. Yet good detection and characterization fill about four-fifths of the book. The last chapter, as usual, is huddled and hard to take.

850   FITZSIMMONS, CORTLAND (b. 1893)

The Bainbridge Mystery   McB 1930

In the collaborators' long experience, the perfect stimulus to alternating boredom and hilarity. The detective is slow-witted Arthur Martinson, handicapped by "Mary." Crime and detection equally difficult to discover or remember. Plot and style endlessly circular.

851   FITZSIMMONS. See also:

The Girl in the Cage   Stokes 1939
        (in collaboration with the master magician
John Mulholland, d. 1970)

852   FLAGG, JOHN (pseud. of John Gearon)

Murder in Monaco   Miller 1959

A "swift" and talented specimen of the drinking-and-wenching genre. The artistic fornication in the beach cabin has good dialogue to go with the moonlit thighs and other appurtenances.

FLEMING, IAN (1908–1964)

Educ. at Eton, Sandhurst, and Univs. of Munich and Geneva. Corresp. for Reuters and the *Sunday Times,* loosely attached to British secret service, wrote about a dozen stories that fed the fantasy of readers and film viewers about deceit, sex, gadgets, and the modern style of killing (the kind that hurts me more than it does you). The author was a restless, melancholy man and superior to his own fictions. He latterly lived in Jamaica. The titles of his books have acquired a kind of proverbial quality: *Live and Let Die, From Russia With Love, Goldfinger, Diamonds Are Forever*—modern readers having, as to this last one, forgotten Anita Loos' original remark.

853   Live and Let Die   Macm 1955

James Bond, English secret agent, has numerous incredible adventures in the U.S.A., while on the trail of (or rather while being trailed by) a monstrous Negro gangster. Noteworthy for its amusing ineptitude and for the scenes in Jamaica where the final depth charge goes off.

854   On Her Majesty's Secret Service   NAL 1963

The story in which Bond gets married and loses his bride in the shortest time on record for anyone not George Joseph Smith (see No. 3279). It has skiing, explosions, Corsicans, big hotels—everything.
     Note: The title was first used by an anonymous writer in 1878.

855   FLEMING, JOAN (MARGARET), has since 1950 steadily produced tales that show competence and keep up with current styles, but no special flavor or detective interest attaches to them. One may list: *The Man Who Looked Back* (1951); *Maiden's Prayer* (1957); *Malice Matrimonial* (1959); *The Man From Nowhere* (1961); *Death of a Sardine* (1963) and *The Chill and the Kill* (1964).

        FLETCHER, J(OSEPH) S(MITH) (1863–1935)

Antiquarian, journalist, and author of more than a hundred volumes, Fletcher wrote with a fatal ease. His many detective novels are filled with atmosphere rather than detection and the settings of some are memorable. Fletcher's real merit lies in his having made the reading of detective fiction acceptable.

856   The Copper Box   Doran 1923

This story is a little unusual for Fletcher in that it is laid over the border, in Scotland, and is relatively short. It uses the old scheme of the valuable object that unscrupulous people try to get under transparently false pretenses. The theft, identification, and recovery of the box are not so much tedious as uninspired, and the romance is not able to lift the level of interest.
     One other defect is the all-too-common one of names so alike that the reader gets confused and irritated. Here we have: Parslewe, Pebling, Pawley, and Palkeney—unbelievable!

857   The Herapath Property   WL 1920

A fairly early and good Fletcher. The tale has a London setting, a sure-enough murder, and no foreign adventuress.

858   The Middle Temple Murder   Knopf 1919/1918

JB and WHT read this soon after original publication and retained pleasant memories of it. Rereading it over thirty years later, both found it dull, *pace* Woodrow Wilson, whose public approval helped the author and the genre.

859   The Orange-Yellow Diamond   Knopf 1921

Tedious in the extreme; indeed, one notch below *Scarhaven Keep*. In the latter there is some attractive North of England coastal scenery, in the former we don't leave London; both degenerate into meaningless chases, ill supervised by the official police. Neither comes close to *The Middle Temple Murder,* mediocre though that is.

860   The Secret of Secrets   Clode 1929

One of his amiable rambles through mysteries he himself hardly believes in. The honeymooners on the ship from Ostend to Dover set a pretty scene, but the upshot is mild and just inside the edge of readability.

861   FLETCHER, J. S. See also Nos. 2504–7 and:

The Borough Treasurer	Knopf 1921	Murder in the Pallant	Knopf 1928
The Box Hill Murder	Knopf 1929	Murder in the Squire's	
The Dressing-Room		Pew	Knopf 1932
Murder	Knopf 1921	Paradise Court	CCD 1929
The Ebony Box (ss)	Knopf 1930	The Rayner-Slade	
The Great Brighton		Amalgamation	Knopf 1922
Mystery	Knopf 1926	Scarhaven Keep	Knopf 1922
The King *versus*		The Secret of the	
Wargrave	Knopf 1924	Barbican (ss)	Doran 1925
The Markenmore		The Strange Case of Mr.	
Mystery	Knopf 1923	Henry Marchmont	Knopf 1927
Memorials of a Yorkshire		The Wrist Mark	Knopf 1928
Parish (not det.)	Lane 1917	The Yorkshire Moorland	
Murder in Four		Murders	Knopf 1930
Degrees (ss)	Knopf 1931		

862   FLETCHER, LUCILLE, is a competent writer of suspense novels somewhat in the Leslie Ford tradition but often with a marine atmosphere, as in *The Strange Blue Yawl* (1964). Still better wrought is *Blindfold* (1960), in which a physician uses all his senses except sight to locate the place of concealment of a kidnapped scientist. See also *And Presumed Dead* (1963), *The Girl in Cabin 54* (1968), and *Sorry, Wrong Number* (1948).

863   FLYNN, BRIAN

        Conspiracy at Angel   Long n.d. [1947]

Straight tripe and savorless. It is doubtful, on the evidence, if any of the thirty-two others by this author would be different.

864   FOLEY, RAE (pseud. of Elinore Denniston; also Allan Dennis, b. 1900)

        Where Is Mary Bostwick?   DM 1958

A disappointing affair, which contains a good many unrealized possibilities, beginning with the hero-detective, about whom the author has written some of her previous eleven stories. Hiram Potter is a sort of American Mr. Campion, elegant, well-to-do, mild yet "penetrating." The trouble is that the only detecting he does is to see through people's rather feeble false pretenses. Otherwise, no wit, not much character, little eye for places, and at the end a "surprise" that is surprising only because so unlikely and unwelcome.

FOOTNER, (WILLIAM) HULBERT (1879–1944)

Canadian by birth, wrote first about the Northwest of his native land; then actor and playwright and later serious novelist in the stoic-sardonic vein (mid-1930s). In between and to the end of his laborious life, wrote thrillers and short stories of detection. His investigators were successively: the young B. Enderby; the amateur who resembles Mr. Pickwick, Amos Lee Mappin; and the dazzling beauty Mme. Rosika Storey.

In the road company of Gillette's *Sherlock Holmes* (q.v.), Footner doubled in two or three parts.

865   Orchids to Murder   Harp 1945
       Obituary note on the author by Christopher Morley

Posthumously published, this story puts the author among those whose production exceeds one score. We see again the detective work of the middle-aged Amos Lee Mappin, whose skill lies chiefly in facing possible suspects with the inferences he has drawn from clues, times, and motives. The prose is undistinguished and the narrative somehow perfunctory. C.M.'s biographical note is excellent, but it presents a man different from his image in the book.

866   FOOTNER. See also:

       The Folded Paper Mystery (= Mystery of the
         Folded Paper)   H&S n.d. [1946]
       The House with the Blue Door   Harp 1942
       Murder Runs in the Family   Harp 1934
       The Murder That Had Everything   Harp 1939
       Unneutral Murder   Harp 1944

FORD, LESLIE (pseud. of Mrs. Zenith Jones [Brown], b. 1898)

The wife of Dr. Ford K. Brown of St. John's College, Annapolis, has been a prolific contributor to the lists of detective fiction for over forty years. A visit to Oxford sparked the production of half a dozen "Mr. Pinkerton" tales, published under the pseudonym of David Frome. For us the hen-pecked Pinkerton, always in Inspector Bull's way, and perpetually awash with a cold, is the epitome of the tedious nondetecting detective.

As Leslie Ford, the author has written a long series of suspense stories that betray their origin as magazine serials, but they are put together with competence and grace. Colonel Primrose and Mrs. Latham are a good pair, and if they are not found in Washington, they could have been. Manners and mystery prevail, detection is usually nil, but explanations are rational.

867   By the Watchman's Clock   Rine 1932

Remembered (correctly) from the days of its first appearance, as "a very pleasant Annapolis tale with a college setting," but deserving also of a few other adjectives on the negative side. Toward the end feminine fear and foolish silence are excessive. The final twist is legitimate and deftly handled, but detection loses force by being distributed among several persons; yet as a whole the work is good entertainment.

868   FORD, L. See also:

As David Frome:

The Black Envelope (= Mr. P. Again)	Farr 1937
The Body in Bedford Square	LG 1935
The Eel Pie Murders	Farr 1937
The Hammersmith Murders	Dday 1930
Homicide House (= Mr. P. Returns)	Rine 1950
In at the Death	LG 1930
The Man from Scotland Yard	Farr 1932
Mr. Pinkerton Finds a Body	Farr 1934
Mr. Pinkerton Goes to Scotland Yard	Farr 1934
Mr. Pinkerton Has a Clue	Farr 1936
Scotland Yard Can Wait (see No. 911)	Farr 1933

As Leslie Ford:

All for the Love of a Lady	Scrib 1944
The Bahamas Murder Case	Scrib 1952
Burn Forever	Farr 1935
The Clue of the Judas Tree	Farr 1933
Date with Death	Scrib 1949
The Devil's Stronghold	Scrib 1948
False to Any Man	Scrib 1939
The Girl from the Mimosa Club	Scrib 1957
Ill-Met by Moonlight	Farr 1937
Invitation to Murder	Scrib 1954
Murder in Maryland	Tri 1942
Murder Is the Payoff	Scrib 1951
Murder with Southern Hospitality	Scrib 1942
The Philadelphia Murder Story	Scrib 1945
Siren in the Night	Scrib 1943
The Sound of Footsteps	Dday 1933
The Strangled Witness	Farr 1934
Three Bright Pebbles	Farr 1938
Trial by Ambush (Baltimore scene)	Scrib 1962
Washington Whispers Murder	Scrib 1953
The Woman in Black	Scrib 1947

FORD, PAUL LEICESTER (1865–1902)

A born scholar, whose father owned a remarkable Library of Americana, and thus facilitated his son's early production of historical writings and editions. Then Ford turned to fiction and wrote two popular novels still worth reading as period pieces—*The Honorable Peter Stirling* and *Janice Meredith*. (See also the next item.) This brilliant career was cut short by murder at the hands of a disinherited brother.

869   The Great K. & A. Train Robbery   IANA 1901; orig. Lipp 1896

In a couple of hundred small pages the author tells in the first person the story of a faked train robbery committed with intent to thwart intended financial takeover of the Kansas & Arizona. Scene: Flagstaff; added interest: the narrator's love story (he is railway superintendent and she a member of the private-car party). But the tale drags badly in its latter half, and Francis Lynde kept things going much better in *The Taming of Red Butte Western* (Scrib 1910).

FORESTER, C(ECIL) S(COTT) (1899–1966)

b. Cairo, Egypt; educ. Dulwich and Grey's Hosp., London. Gave up medicine on success of his first novel (see No. 870), which soon reached stage and screen. Succeeding fiction and historical studies made his reputation secure as a novelist of the revolutionary and Napoleonic periods. A leading authority on the puppet theater.

870   Payment Deferred   LB 1942; orig. 1926

An excellent title for this stark story of crime (murder for gain) committed in full view of the reader, and of the remorseless fate which pursues the criminal and his family. No mystery, but the good writing keeps one going. A classic of its unusual kind. Lower-class English South London scene.

For a play based on the novel, see No. 2395; a film ensued, starring Charles Laughton.

871   Plain Murder   Lane 1930

The author's second crime novel, so similar in general plan to his first that it may provide the reason for his switching to the more salubrious air of the Captain Hornblower tales. The scene is an advertising office in London: two murders are committed and one more attempted but foiled by a repentant accessory of the first. People and details as in *Payment Deferred*—lower-middle-class English family life; death of an innocent by motorcycle accident; no detection. But a well-turned piece.

872   FORSYTE, CHARLES

Double Death   Cass 1965

A new author who deserves following up, both in future and for his first two: *Diving Death* and *Diplomatic Death*. The present work is full of good touches, and though a spy story it has enough detection and speculation to make JB class it as a very pleasant hybrid. The London scene is excellently used.

873   FRANCIS, BASIL

Death at the Bank   Const 1938

The author, who has also written the aptly titled *Slender Margin*, knows his banking firsthand. This one is a slightly amateurish but entertaining tale in which the chief flaw is the multiplicity of injured people, all potential murderers.

FRANCIS, DICK (b. 1920)

b. Tenby, Wales, educ. local schools till age of 15, then groom in father's hunting stable and ultimately champion steeplechase jockey, incl. four years as jockey for the Queen Mother. Retired 1957 and soon became noted writer of crime stories, as well as racing correspondent for the *Sunday Express*.

874   Blood Sport   Harp 1967

One of the best plotted of his adventures, this one takes the hero to the American Rockies to recover stolen stallions which are being used in fraudulent stud work. The hero's self-torture here is over a lost love, but it is a bit more bearable than usual. The other characters are excellent and the events and stratagems full of invention and suspense. Master's work without question.

Note for masochists: two well-plotted tales flanking this one (*Nerve*, 1964, and *Forfeit*, 1968) abundantly show the infliction of pain here deprecated.

875   Dead Cert   Harp 1962

This English tale of horse racing shows how one should write to create suspense. An unusual smash climax features taxi drivers gone criminal—a natural enough transition. The master criminal is not well concealed, but the hero's detecting in Brighton and vicinity is entertaining, and the tough stuff reasonably convincing.

876   Flying Finish   Harp 1966

One of his good ones—that is, with the sadism kept to a minimum. The combination of horse knowledge and aviation is excellent, the love story credible, and the hero—though, as usual, a depressed character—emerges triumphant and strong more plausibly than in earlier tales.

877   Odds Against   Harp 1965

The ex-jockey writes and plots well, but he has a penchant for turning on the screws intolerably hard. One tires of his hero's abasement and sufferings, knowing as one does that all will end in moral and physical triumph. Here the financial crimes of the villain and the rescue of a racecourse provide the skeleton for a long-drawn-out struggle against odds. Both hero and heroine are maimed and subjected to humiliation. Radnor Associates, Investigators, do not detect much.

878   FRANKAU, PAMELA (also Eliot Naylor; b. 1908)

        Appointment with Death   Dutt 1940
            In Eng.: A Democrat Dies

The daughter of Gilbert Frankau dedicates to him this solidly worked-out tale of politics and murder without detection. The murder is, in fact, deceptive, and the cabinet minister involved in the Phoenix movement of national renovation tells all in the end. Attractive characters among the younger set in the foreground, good writing and good entertainment.

879   FRASER, JAMES

The Evergreen Death   HB 1968

Young Inspector Bill Aveyard is well drawn, and it is a pity that his first case should be so cluttered with improbable motivations and multiple philanderings as to make the whole affair implausible. The strangling of a young girl in a teen-age hangout is possible, the accompanying mutilation unlikely as described, the actual circumstances pure fantasy. Despite all this, clear narration and some good characters. English village scene.

880   FREELING, NICOLAS (also F. R. E. Nicolas; b. 1927)

Double Barrel   Harp 1965

Inspector Van der Valk and his semiattractive wife, Arlette, go to a dismal, rapidly expanding industrial town in N.E. Holland to ferret out a writer of anonymous letters. Not bad—a sort of cross between Maigret and Douglas Browne. In addition to the poison-pen stuff there are some ill-enunciated political overtones at the end.

881   The Dresden Green   Harp 1967

This spy story by our friend pleases neither of his readers. Its main point seems to be: "What wickedness it was to bomb Dresden!" The point is conceded especially readily by JB, who lived there for one enchanted spring many years ago. But the novelist's plot, his chiefly disagreeable characters, and (above all) his alternative endings put this work in the class of gratuitous harrowers.

882   The King of the Rainy Country   Harp 1966

All the usual tricks that disclose Van der Valk's superiority through his little mundane reflections, often hostile to others. In time this novel will seem dated because it plays up to the reader by flattering his ungenerous motives. The plot is unmemorable, though spiced with violence, plus skiing, chasing about in cars, accessible young women, grumpy or in-quisitive hotelkeepers, et al.
The title is from Baudelaire's "Spleen," l. 1.

883   Love in Amsterdam   Goll 1962

The author's first, based in part on his experience of being unjustly accused of theft and jailed. But here the hero is accused of murdering his former mistress. In both cases, it is the discovery of a kind and just policeman that is important. The author shows and succeeds in the desire to capture something of the postwar European world. He has been influenced by Simenon and Graham Greene, but explicitly disowns their formulas.

The title refers to the cut-and-dried forms of officialdom, and detective (now Commissaire) Van der Valk spends as much time deriding these as he does detecting the criminal. The killing of a rather useless inn-keeper—by a horse or by a man?—involves three households whose varied snobbery and misdoings afford a plethora of suspects. The bulb-raising country between Haarlem and Leiden supplies pleasant local color. Though long and wordy, a genuine story of detection.

885   FREELING. See also Nos. 2514–5 and:

Criminal Conversation	Harp 1966
The Kitchen (autobiog.)	Harp 1970
Tsing Boom	Harp 1970
Valparaiso (adven., not det.)	Harp 1959

886   FREEMAN, MARTIN JOSEPH (b. 1899)

The Murder of a Midget   Eldon 1934

We list this book only because of its possible confusion with the work of R. Austin Freeman. A quick glance at the first pages would quickly dis-close the error. The present tale is of dope-running via a three-ring circus; the murder is investigated by Judo Marriott, a girl reporter from the Austin, Tex., *Times*. The midget is named Sarza Bonheur. The language is Southwest U.S. colloquial and childish besides.

FREEMAN, R(ICHARD) AUSTIN (1862–1943)

b. Soho, London; his father a tailor in modest circumstances. Deter-mination took him through his medical training at the Middlesex Hospital, and lack of funds made him assistant colonial surgeon in the then pes-tilential Gold Coast. He contracted malaria (i.e., blackwater fever) and after four or five years in the colonial service he never left England again. His conception of a straightforward scientific investigator of crime dates from c. 1905, and two years later John Thorndyke made his bow in *The Red Thumb Mark*, brought out by an obscure publisher (Collingwood), perhaps at Freeman's own expense. Some of the Thorndyke tales, such as *The Mystery of 31, New Inn,* were written earlier, but the unpopular novella length Freeman used made it hard to find a publisher. Freeman made a name for himself only after publishing the "inverted tales" that appeared as *The Singing Bone* in 1912. Besides collaborating with Dr. J. J. Pitcairn in the "Ashdown" tales (q.v.) and writing a little light fic-tion under his own name, Freeman brought out works of travel and social criticism and reviewed for *The Eugenics Review*. In an Introduction to Freeman's *Social Decay and Regeneration,* Havelock Ellis called its author "a man of penetrating observation, of independent judgment, capable of outspoken criticism when required. . . ." Probably no detec-tive in English fiction has commanded more serious intellectual respect than Dr. John Evelyn Thorndyke. His resemblance in appearance and manner to that impressive expert Sir Bernard Spilsbury is very striking, but, as Freeman explained, Thorndyke had no living model and he made his appearance several years before Spilsbury became a public figure.

For long and short studies of Freeman, see No. 2937.

887   As a Thief in the Night   DM 1928

An original situation, especially in the works by this author, who tends to run to formula in his conception of life and character. Here a man of enough attraction to be the hero stands in a peculiar relation to three women: one dead, one a murderess, and one—perhaps—his subsequent wife. The ingenious murder is by arsenic, and the detection by Thorndyke *cum* Polton plays a minor role.

888   The Cat's Eye   DM 1927
       Pref. by the author on a coincidence with factual crime

An early Thorndyke: Jervis is in New York, and Anstey replaces him, A. being a lawyer and no medicus, and highly susceptible to feminine charm. The plot itself is interesting, though it contains many twists that Freeman uses in other tales: X rays, identification of a bone mascot as Australian because it is a vertebra of a porcupine anteater, identification of a corpse via an old fracture, etc. But the cabs are autos.

889   The D'Arblay Mystery   DM 1926

A good Thorndyke story, in one continuous part. Dr. Stephen Gray tells it, a complex affair but not unbearably so. Polton plays an important role. Much detail re waxwork and its manufacture. Internal evidence of composition much earlier than date of publication.

890   Dr. Thorndyke Intervenes   DM 1933

This tells of the spurious claim to a title and estate, based on the rumor that a certain English nobleman lived a double life as a publican, in which capacity he had issue. Exhumation, etc. Humdrum Thorndyke without subplot.

891   Dr. Thorndyke's Discovery   DM 1932
       In Eng.: When Rogues Fall Out

In this story poor Inspector Badger meets his end inside a tunnel. Thorndyke is a bit slow about tying together the elements gathered from three separate sets of events, but the pace is good, and on the whole the plot ranks as one of the best tripartite Freeman stories.

892   Felo de Se?   H&S 1929
       In U.S.: Death at the Inn

The book is dedicated to Freeman's brother, Robert, and is full of interest. It concerns the activities and fate of one John Gillum, a gambler of unusual cast, who is presented in the first third of the book. Dr. Jervis' account of Thorndyke's activities follows. They form, perhaps, the most impressive collecting and combining of minute evidences to bring about

discovery and proof that the Freeman corpus offers to the connoisseur—
and they are dramatic as well.

893   For the Defense: Dr. Thorndyke   DM 1934

A man falsely accused of murder tries to escape by assuming an identity
which he then cannot shake off. Thorndyke does a cool and ingenious
job of solving both his predicaments.

894   Mr. Polton Explains   DM 1940

The Introduction and Polton's autobiography take up half the book, the
better half. The case of Moxon, deceased, is a fairly obvious one of fire-
raising to secure an inheritance, and Polton's accurate description of the
"mottled" (i.e., fluoridated) teeth of a young scoundrel met early in P.'s
career quite gives away the feeble deception attempted by the chap who
turns the tables on his enemy. Nonetheless entertaining.

895   Mr. Pottermack's Oversight   DM 1930

This is the tale of the suburban garden with the sundial, where Mr. Pottermack pursues his study of British *mollusca* while being blackmailed. The
sequential photographing of the footprints with Polton's telephoto camera
and the usual mummy are all vintage Freeman, as is Thorndyke's humane
confrontation scene at the end.

896   The Mystery of Angelina Frood   H&S 1924

The plot incorporates, in the most literal sense, a fatal flaw, which dooms
it from the start. Thorndyke has some good remarks on establishing
identity and on secondary sex characteristics, and he also debunks the
belief in the "corrosive action" of quicklime on corpses. But if the hero,
Dr. Strangeways, is in love with Mrs. F., and yet never recognizes her in
her disguise, one of two things follows: (1) he was captivated by the
factitious dark eyebrows, and then the love story evaporates, or (2) he is
blind, would never qualify as a physician, and all the acute anatomical
observations at the beginning are superfluous.
    Note the pastiche of Dickens' *Edwin Drood* announced by the title and
locale. Note also that in this book Freeman writes with unusual vivacity.
Excited?

897   The Mystery of 31, New Inn   DM 1930; orig. 1913
           Pref. by the author

In this memorable tale Thorndyke has Jervis locate a house, to which the
latter is driven in a blacked-out cab, by the construction of a track chart
based upon time, compass bearings, and horses' hoofbeats per minute. The
preface explains and justifies the method used.

898   The Penrose Mystery   H&S 1936

A fairly late Thorndyke story, easygoing and pleasant in the telling, with
no flashbacks or prologues. Penrose, a pedantic and affected amateur of

curios, is murdered and his body put in a barrow (archaeological variety). The disappearance is brought to T.'s attention by Brodribb; Jervis acts as T.'s assistant.

899   The Red Thumb Mark   Nort 1967/DM 1924/H&S 1911/
                                                              Collingwood 1907
              Introd. by James Nelson
              Also: The Debut of Dr. Thorndyke*

This classic deserved reprinting after sixty years, for it introduced not only Thorndyke but genuine science into detective literature—Holmes was a dabbler in comparison. At this early date Thorndyke is more jocular than he was later, and he is twice threatened by violence. Moreover, he theorizes with the consciousness of being a pioneer as he unmasks a villain whom we shall meet again, like Jervis and Polton.
   Note: The Introduction is negligible and contains two blunders.

* Though first to be published, this tale was written after No. 897.

900   The Silent Witness   DM 1929/H&S 1914
              Also: A Silent Witness

An early example of the body that is discovered and then vanishes when help comes. Told in the first person by Dr. Jardine, whose life is attempted for what he unsuspectingly knows, who weaves his own romance out of murder and other machinations and who is loved and guarded by the villain's wife. She dies in saving him, and all ends well, after an orgy of complexity in which Thorndyke, Polton, and Jervis work like beavers.

901   The Stoneware Monkey   DM 1939
              Illus. with a photograph of the monkey

Very nearly a masterpiece: the plot and the accessories are all done with great skill, and the detection also. But Freeman can rarely make more than one of his characters sound genuine (here it is the villain), and he always reaches a plateau where overdeliberateness in stock-taking chills the desire to keep going. All the same, not to be missed by any devotee of R.A.F., especially because of its rare humor.

902   The Unconscious Witness   DM 1942

An intricate affair in which the criminal kills his wife in order to impersonate her and kill another person. The evidence of handwriting, ringed hair, etc., finally enables Thorndyke to bring him to book. The larger part of the tale is told consecutively by the author in the third person; the rest is by Jervis, so as to bring in Thorndyke and the hearing at the probate court. Not the best Freeman.
   Query: Why the reported alternative title of *The Jacob Street Mystery* for this tale rather than for *The Stoneware Monkey,* which occupies more space at that address?

903   The Uttermost Farthing   **Wins 1914**
       A Savant's Vendetta

Certainly a story of crime, with a bit of detection at the beginning and a great deal of circumstantiality throughout. It is remarkable how Freeman manages to give variety to a series of episodes fundamentally alike and to make us accept the melodramatic conception of the whole.
    The title is from Matthew 5:26.

904   The Vanishing Man   DM 1929/1912; orig. 1911
       Later: The Eye of Osiris: A Detective Romance

The earliest of all the tales that deal with the disappearance of a man (here the archaeologist John Bellingham) and his reappearance thoroughly transformed by one means or another to conceal his murder. Thorndyke spots the fraud by the then new and impressive means of X rays.

905   FREEMAN. See also Nos. 2516–23 and 2944 and:

A Certain Dr. Thorn-
   dyke   DM 1928/H&S 1927
Dr. Thorndyke's Cases
   (= John Thorndyke's
   Cases)   DM 1931/C&W 1909
Dr. Thorndyke's Crime
   File   DM 1941
   Contains: The Eye of Osiris, 5A
   King's Bench Walk, Mr. Potter-
   mack's Oversight, and The Mystery
   of Angelina Frood, *plus:* "Meet Dr.

Thorndyke" (by R. A. F., but un-
signed) and "The Art of the Detec-
tive Story" (see No. 2944)
Helen Vardon's Con-
   fession   H&S 1922
Pontifex, Son and Thorn-
   dyke   DM 1931
The Shadow of the Wolf
   (Thorndyke)   DM 1925
The Unwilling Adventurer H&S 1913

906   FREEMAN-HILTON, THOMAS

     The Sayle Case   TBC n.d. [1940]

Though the story starts uncertainly and shows inexperience in writing, it soon improves on both counts and turns into a fair sample of its period, with impersonation, murder, collusion, and detection well distributed over a span of moderate length.

      FREMLIN, CELIA (MARGARET) (b. 1914)

Educ. Berkhamsted and Somerville, Oxf.; her married name is Goller.

907   The Trouble Makers   **Goll 1963**

Although the author uses the popular "method," which consists of rubbing her characters' sensibilities raw, she does so as a legitimate part of her plot. First-class writing makes believable all one is told about the quarrels of the couples, and the extramarital psychology is also sound, though it scarcely promotes the detective interest.

908   Uncle Paul   **Lipp 1960**

The denouement redeems this story of expectancy and housekeeping in a caravan. Uncle Paul, long in prison for bigamy, keeps the seaside family guessing, as the fluent author does the reader who likes his anxiety pure.

More children, housekeeping, and anxiety on the part of two women, one who remembers a tragic wedding of sixty years before, in the same house, the other the bride-to-be, who has been engaged for half a dozen years and wonders whether the event will come off—"sus-pants"?

910   FROEST, FRANK

The Grell Mystery   Coll 1929/Nash 1913

Late Superintendent of the CID in charge of foreign crooks, the author dedicates his book to George Dilnot (q.v.), and thanks him for suggesting the writing of the story and helping with its composition. The tale is one of murder solved by professionals, and indeed it may well be the first police-routine adventure. The writing is anything but sophisticated, but the now familiar steps, the experts, the equipment, and the attitudes are all present and clearly laid out. The plot is period melodrama and the characters puppets. Still, the machinery makes up for the lack of lifelikeness, which includes a neglect of the Judges' Rules and a good deal of unnecessary wrestling and handcuffing. Superintendent Heldon Foyle has only historical interest now, though he makes the point that "he rarely wore a dressing gown and never played the violin."

911   FROME, DAVID (pseud. of Mrs. Zenith Brown, i.e. Leslie Ford, q.v.)

Scotland Yard Can Wait   HR 1933

A fair example of the juggling sort of plot, which would go to pieces on p. 30 if our hero did the sensible thing and went to the police. For the rest, tolerable, but Chief Inspector Lord would earn more credit for detection did we not know beforehand (and better than he) the events he reconstructs. See also titles listed under David Frome in No. 868.

912   FULLER, ROY (BROADBENT) (b. 1912)

Fantasy and Fugue   Macm 1956

Even the reader sympathetic to a poet-turned-detective-novelist finds little in extenuation of a tedious tale of amnesia and parricide, seasoned with pathologically large doses of vomiting and purging. The homosexuality is melodramatic, and there is little wit or humor. Harry Sinton, the hero, does, however, triumph over the powers of darkness.

913   The Second Curtain   Macm 1956

George Garner, a novelist of repulsive bodily habits, weak character, and easily flustered presence, becomes casually involved in a pair of murders caused by Big Business. The said Garner mooches around, pays a few visits, and has a few incoherent thoughts, at the end of which he is beaten up by The Interests, and the story ends.

914   With My Little Eye   Macm 1957/1948
       Murder Revisited Series

This story sheds light on the author's progress. The teen-aged sleuth who
officiates is an offshoot of Fuller's children's stories, and his dedicatory
verses to Julian Symons are the best thing in the book. The plot is by
turns fantastic and unoriginal, and the adolescent narrator is a fraud
compared to one done by, say, Salinger.

915   FULLER, TIMOTHY (b. 1914)

       Harvard Has a Homicide   LB 1936

The author's first and, in the year of publication, fame-begetting. But on
rereading it both judges found it altogether flat and disappointing. Not
even the Yard (Cambridge, not Scotland) affords any pleasure.

916   Reunion with Murder   LB 1941

Fuller's best effort, in the same year as the unsatisfactory *Three Thirds of
a Ghost*. In it Jupiter Jones is credible, active, and successful. The story
begins in the good old Herbert Adams manner, with a corpse on a golf
course, and the disclosure of the relationships as well as the denouement
are done economically and attractively.
    The author, interrupted by the war after *This Is Murder, Mr. Jones*
(LB/1943), wrote only one more tale, of fair quality, *Keep Cool, Mr.
Jones* (LB 1950).

917   FUTRELLE, JACQUES (1875–1912). The Canadian journalist who
lost his life at 36 in the *Titanic* had a fluent pen and a good smattering of
scientific information. He created Professor S. F. X. Van Dusen, "The
Thinking Machine," and in several short stories about him succeeded in
giving entertainment, detection, and a touch of character well above the
average set by the imitators of Conan Doyle. But Futrelle lacked the power
to construct or characterize and too often neglected plausibility. His long
stories are therefore unreadable. *The Chase of the Golden Plate* (1906)
revolts the reader's imagination and sense of truth in every part—dialogue,
motive, and chase. *The Thinking Machine on the Case* (1908) is a novel
of looting and shooting, diamonds and suspicion, all equally absurd. For
the best Futrelle, see Nos. 2526–9.

918   GABORIAU, EMILE (1833–73)

       File No. 113   Scrib 1904/Osgood 1875; orig. 1867
       Le Dossier No. 113

The French *roman policier* is a taste that the present readers never
acquired. Even when one of the pair was in France as a child, a native
knowing no English, he was drawn to Conan Doyle and to what was in
fact the critique and parody of the French crime story, namely, *Arsène
Lupin*. Hence no encomiums here for the present book, hastily skimmed
forty-five years ago, or its companion works: *M. Lecoq, La veuve Lerouge,*

Le Mystère d'Orcival, etc., which have been translated into a kind of English but are hard to come by.

For the record, *File No. 113* is about a bank robbery, a frame-up, multiple disguises and impersonations, illegitimacy, and coerced consent to marriage—all resolved into justice and bliss at the end. Devotees may want to go on to the sequel: *Young Ernest: File No. 114,* and will certainly want to hear G.'s admirers praise him in Nos. 2920 and 3174.

919   GADDA, CARLO EMILIO (b. 1893)

That Awful Mess on Via Merulana   Braz 1965
Quer Pasticciaccio brutto di via Merulana (*1946*),
    trans. (and Introd.) by William Weaver

A good example of what happens when a serious novelist takes up crime and detection in ignorance of the genre. The crime is there, but the detection gets lost in the pursuit of human confusion and misunderstanding. This great work of modern Italian literature gives us a holdup, then a brutal murder, but neither is solved while we get realism, satire, and a picture of Rome under Mussolini c. 1927. Detective Incra Vallo's name is not even constant throughout the book.

920   GAINES, ROBERT (b. 1912)

Against the Public Interest   Walk 1959

A disappointment compared to the quite original *Invisible Evil.* This is but the usual MI5–007–Special-Branch kind of stuff, with the now intolerable counterpoint of hatred and envy among English civil servants. The one touch of novelty is the love pursuit carried on wholly by the young woman against spirited resistance by her older man.

921   The Invisible Evil   Walk 1963

A well-written tale in which Irish "patriots" conspire to place a bomb inside a dispatch box taken into the House, where the Prime Minister is winding up debate on a scheme for the reunification of Ireland. A spy story rather than a detective tale, but original in plot and tone. For one thing, the bomb does go off, and the P.M. benefits.

922   GAIR, MALCOLM
Snow Job   CCD 1962

The fourth detective novel by this author. Mark Raeburn is an English private investigator who manufactures burglar alarms on the side. The present tale finds him retained by an incredibly foolish and wealthy young American, to find out who killed a maiden aunt at a Swiss ski resort. Much to- and fro-ing between Zurich and London, an illicit denouement— altogether a tasteless dish.

923   GALE, JOHN (pseud. of Richard Gaze, b. 1917)

Death for Short   Macm 1962
     In Eng.: The Short Reaction

Better things were to be expected from a director of research in a large industrial company when he turned his attention from international intrigue to industrial organic chemistry. The present tale badly messes up a potentially amusing situation: euphoria turned into aphrodisia by an unscrupulous bunch who command the services of the inventor of the original drug. Action and characterization incompetent.

924   Spare Time for Murder   Macm 1961

Anthony Somers, who gets innocently involved in the doings of a sinister "consulting research organization" (they are making an atomic bomb for the Egyptians with stolen plutonium), is credible, and he works with the police rather than in spite of them. His adventures are short, moderately sexy, and well explained at the end.

925   GALLIE, MENNA

The Small Mine   Harp 1962

More nearly akin than her first to the crime-anxiety genre for which it tries to qualify. But the Welsh atmosphere, well done though it is, tends to pall. Miss Gallie is guilty of several revolting similes and likes to have too many people whose features she describes in ugly terms. One good point: the young hero-lecher gets blown up halfway through the tale.

926   Strike for a Kingdom   Harp 1959

Not a detective story but a perceptive tale of the Welsh coal mines.

927   GALWAY, ROBERT CONNINGTON

Assignment in Malta   Hale 1966

Listed mainly to differentiate him by spelling and first names from the preferable Galwey below. Malta is an interesting setting, which deserves more extended treatment by a more original writer: the present story is predictably average.

GALWEY, G(EOFFREY) V(ALENTINE) (b. 1912)

b. Madras; educ. Merchant Tailors' and Hertford Coll., Oxf.; career in advertising. Director of Lovell and Rupert Curtis.

928   Full Fathom Five   H&S 1951

A long and listless hundred pages of sordid hand-to-mouth existence by some half-dozen shady characters introduce the activities of Chief Inspector Bourne in this third and last of the author's detective stories. Bourne has just retired and married the widow whom he used to visit. Her daughter has also married, and all four are going on a pleasure trip on the Inspector's barge. The two groups of people—shady and ex-police—converge accidentally through finding a child of the chief crook, now dead. The narrative continues "realistic" and meandering, to end up in a story of dope and mother love: most disappointing, no detection and not even good solid crime.

929   The Lift and the Drop   BH 1948

This is the author's second detective novel featuring Chief Inspector ("Daddy") Bourne. It is a somewhat complicated tale of a lift that dropped in the London offices of *The Voice,* Lord Swale's publishing complex. Political overtones are important, but expertly handled, and so is the detection.

930   Murder on Leave   Lane 1946

Inspector Bourne is a likable Scot who has an odd relation to two women, mother and daughter, while pursuing a rather complicated puzzle which he works out with ingenuity and knowledge of human affairs. A most engaging story.

931   GARDINER, STEPHEN

       Death Is an Artist   IW 1959

An account of English artists and their hangers-on, annoyingly but not abominably written. The fundamental point of the plot became all too clear about a quarter of the way through, after which it is difficult to go on to the big "surprise" on p. 172.

       GARDNER, ERLE STANLEY (also A. A. Fair, Charles M. Green,
       Carleton Kendrake, and Charles J. Kenny; 1889–1970)

b. Malden, Mass.; educ. Palo Alto H.S.; member of various institutes and academies of law and police science. Began career in California as trial lawyer, became writer in 1933.

   His output consists of three kinds of crime stories: the legal, showing off the arts of Perry Mason and his henchmen, including Della Street; the private eye, exemplified in twofold fashion in Donald Lam and Bertha Cool (see the works of A. A. Fair, above); the general mystery, ranging from the "D.A." stories, some of them very ingenious in detection, to the Chinese gangland stuff of his early days.

   G.'s interest in justice also led him to write and to lecture on scientific police work, and his love of travel has produced books about Mexico, lost mines, and desert exploration.

932   The Case of the Angry Mourner   Morr 1951

Off Perry Mason's beaten track both geographically and constructively. There is genuine detection in this vacation-camp murder, and the culprit is kept well hidden while various suspects lie not too outrageously: an excellent detective story.

933   The Case of the Crooked Candle   Morr 1944

Of the Perry Mason cases we know, this is the closest to a true detective
story. The details of the boat grounded at low tide with a corpse in the
cabin are superbly handled, and the rest of the story—motives and
characters—is both believable and reasonably straightforward. The
courtroom scene, likewise, is full of good points; there is a final adventure
and smashup; and only at the very end does the author indulge his love of
clutter through double twists. Even so, it is an absolutely first-rate job.

934   The Case of the Curious Bride   Morr 1934

A good Perry Mason except for one great flaw, which the author would
scarcely be guilty of today: he tampers with the evidence, by having a
friend move into an apartment and testify to the state of the doorbells.
Actually, Mason has changed the bells. One is left with the uncomfortable
idea that maybe the murder did not take place as Mason reconstructs it.

935   The Case of the Demure Defendant   Morr 1956

JB read this close on the heels of the *Curious Bride*, written twenty-two
years earlier. The comparison is interesting, for although the two cases
have similarities, each is perfectly distinct in its legal subtleties, and both
show a flaw in the telling. In the D. D. case, Gardner does what he now
seems to prefer: having shown the reader how the tables are going to be
turned, he huddles the explanation in court. What has seemed clever when
first hinted at now becomes not quite credible. A few more pages and the
whole thing would have carried conviction.

936   The Case of the Green-Eyed Sister   Morr 1953

A latish Perry Mason, but one of the tightest knit and richest in gimmicks
and characters. P.M.'s fiddling with tape recorders is excellent, and
the dialogues in and out of court show what can be done with backchat
to create drama.

937   The Case of the Negligent Nymph   Morr 1950

The lively tale of the girl who swam naked to the island to steal some
letters. Query: Why not write some of her own? But the modern generation
is lazy!

938   The Case of the Perjured Parrot   Morr 1939

This early Perry Mason is uncommonly full of detection, and the games
played in it with parrots do not detract from plausibility. Denouement not
huddled—all in all, a model in his special genre.

939   The Case of the Restless Redhead   Morr 1954
          Foreword by the author

In recent years, ESG's forewords have served as dedications to friends,
usually medical jurists and police officers, whose work the author briefly

explains and justifies. The story that follows here is good, typical Perry Mason, with some nice evidence of substitution of weapons in a shooting case in which the redhead is the defendant.

940   The Case of the Vagabond Virgin   Morr 1948

Despite the fact that compelling evidence of virginity is not offered, the lady vagabond is well done, and the plot is better-than-average Gardner; indeed, it is surprisingly good when one considers the deluge that had already gone over the dam by 1948.

941   The Case of the Velvet Claws   Morr 1933

The mainspring of this first of the Perry Mason tales is a blackmail sheet. A woman tries to get Mason to buy its silence. Her husband is murdered, she is suspected, then Perry as well. The working out is a bit messy and the end is huddled as was not true again until the very late P.M. stories.

942   The D.A. Breaks an Egg   Morr 1949

Doug Selby, aided by the reporter Sylvia Martin, undoes the machinations of the ruthless lawyer A. B. Carr, who has the knack of combining his cases—using his hold on one client to make him or her serve as false witness in the prosecution of another. There are some pretty bits of skulduggery, shrewd guessing, and also improbability in this well-told item in the D.A. series.

943   The D.A. Draws a Circle   Morr 1939

The D.A. series is usually a little less imaginative than the one about Perry Mason, but this sample of Doug Selby's work is really distinguished, as is the creation of the unscrupulous but smooth lawyer-villain A. B. Carr. The hostile byplay with the police chief is also well done—one can read this book and dispense with all the other D.A.s.

944   GARDNER, E. S. See also:

The Case of the		The Case of the	
Counterfeit Eye	Morr 1933	Sun Bather's Diary	Morr 1955
The Case of the		This Is Murder	Morr 1935
Dangerous Dowager	Morr 1937		
The Case of the		*As Carleton Kendrake:*	
Fiery Fingers*	Morr 1951	The Clew of the	
		Forgotten Murder	Morr 1935

* Contains a foreword on finding clues.

945   GARDNER, JOHN

A Complete State of Death   VP 1968

The author has written three or four earlier novels. His hero, Inspector Derek Torrey (Italian extraction, American-trained, now in British CID), suffers from repressions and complexes without number, being a Catholic who feels guilty in his simulated intercourse with his more insistent girl friend, etc., etc. While all this is going on, Torrey manages to track down an American gangster operating in England, but is depressed when he finds that three banks in Stratford-on-Avon are robbed simultaneously in spite of him. Avoid.

946   GARVE, ANDREW (pseud. of Paul Winterton; also Roger Bax and Paul Somers, qq.v.; b. 1908)

The Ascent of D-13   Harp 1968

Garve has done it again and set his adventure story (not detection) in an unusual spot: the mountains on the Turkish-Armenian border. The story is well told, as always, and in its brief span has quite a few thrills and a fair dose of love interest.

947   The Ashes of Loda   Harp 1964

As entertaining a piece of suspense (not anxiety) as one could wish. Garve is up to his usual standard of colorful and uncommon atmosphere, this time present-day Russia from a newspaper correspondent's point of view. He deftly manages his love interest so that the adventures of his titled hero seem both justified and plausible. The winter chase, on foot, by car, and by train, to Odessa, is superb. Not a detective story.

948   Boomerang   CCC 1969
        In U.S., Subt.: An Australian Escapade

From time to time, this ingenious plotter has a yearning to defeat morals and justice by a great swindle (see Nos. 962 and 963). He fulfills his wish again in this tale, whose action occurs mainly in Australia. It is all worked up from books and beautifully done—graphic and exciting—but as one knows that truth and right will prevail over the attractive villains, it seems in retrospect much effort for little yield. (Serialized with success in the New York *Daily News*.)

949   By-Line for Murder   Harp 1951
        In Eng.: A Press of Suspects

As the titles suggest, a story of homicide in a newspaper setting. For some reason—too great a familiarity with the surroundings?—this is not one of Garve's best. He has confided that his "domestic" plots greatly outsell his political or professional ones, and he argues that the public does not like to think so much as to feel. But it may be that fanciful dangers to mother, child, and lover arouse in G. a greater power to animate the work.

950   The Cuckoo-Line Affair   Harp 1953

Like all Garve's tales, this is carried off with dash, and its implausibilities are cunningly hidden. The main idea is fruity, and the characters, scenery, boating, and suspense could hardly be improved upon. The denouement is strong and lacks only a bit of explanation about the engineering of the murder, the death of the villain being premature. It makes up for these defects by being a truer detective story than some of his later ones.

951   Death and the Sky Above   Harp 1953

A stirring chase, told from the point of view of the fugitive, who has escaped from prison so that he can prove his innocence of the murder of his ex-wife. His new girl helps him up to and beyond the high moment (or low point) of his self-immersion in a swamp. No detection.

952   The End of the Track   Harp 1955

A forest warden is blackmailed for a noncriminal act that would reflect on his beloved daughter. He yields after much anguish. One blackmailer polishes off his partner and our hero thinks he himself has dealt with the second, as he meant to. Neither suspense nor detection nor good red herring.

953   The Far Sands   Harp 1960

Here we have female twins (identical), and ravishing beauties both. Carol marries the narrator, while Fay marries a man with a secret. When the latter is murdered the problem is: did Fay do it (it looks like it), or is her twin's "feeling" that Fay is guiltless worth anything? Good storytelling, though a bit contrived.

954   Fontego's Folly   Harp 1950
          In ppb.: No Mask for Murder

Murder during a fiesta in a British colony. The facts are completely known to the reader as to motive, method, and murderer. The interest lies in the local color, good characterization, and political intrigue about a leprosarium. The description of lechery is outstanding. No detection.

955   Frame-Up   Harp 1964

A slender affair, but something of a detective story. The mystery of who killed the second-rate artist John Lumsden is well handled by Chief Inspector Grant, who has to pick between a psychologically likely candidate with an apparently complete alibi and another almost too obvious suspect. A gimmick—or rather gadget—is what everything turns on, but it is not well concealed from the reader.

956   The Galloway Case   Harp 1958

The plot is potentially good: a young newspaperman endeavors to clear the father of his girl friend, said father having been actually convicted on a charge of murdering an inept writer who accused him of stealing the plot of a story which became a great success. The loving pair succeed, not too easily, nor until they have undergone an appalling ordeal.

957　The Golden Deed　　　　　　　　　　　　　　Harp 1960

The members of a nice English family, obligated by the "golden deed" of
a ne'er-do-well, take him to their bosom and are shortly implicated in
what appears to be crime but is actually a put-up job by the real criminal
and his associates. Slender and on the verge of anxious-making.

958　A Hero for Leanda　　　　　　　　　　　　Harp 1959

A most ingenious piece of scheming and adventure. A political exile wants
to arouse rebellion in his own country (presumably Cyprus). The hero,
an experienced solo navigator of small boats, is hired to transport the old
man. The heroine is a political partisan of the exile, but the latter's callous
and self-seeking behavior alienates her. The denouement wrought by the
hero deserves her joy and embraces.

959　Hide and Go Seek　　　　　　　　　　　　Harp 1966
　　　　　In Eng.: Murderer's Fen

Seduction and attempted murder end with relief for all but the villain,
after some professional detective work. Slight and episodic and less than
engrossing.

960　A Hole in the Ground　　　　　　　　　　Harp 1959

A half loony M.P. with communist sympathies plans to blow up an atomic
plant from a cave below it, which he goes in and out of by virtue of his
hobby (tell that to your speluncle!). All ends well, with the widow in the
arms of t'other side. No detection.

961　The House of Soldiers　　　　　　　　　　Harp 1961

The author continues to show great versatility in his settings, but we get
less and less detection. The source of pleasure here is local color and
action—the terrorizing of an archaeologist and his family by Irish rebels
plotting against Dublin. Query: How should such a story be classified?

962　The Long Short Cut　　　　　　　　　　　Harp 1968

Short and slick. Garve's excellent storytelling carries the reader along, but
at the end one feels as if dropped into an air pocket. The elaborate plan of
the charming pair of adventurers to sneak a wanted man out of England
almost deserves to succeed, but Inspector Kirby notes one small detail,
and that's that.

　　　Note: This book is on record as the first set in type by computer
(April 1968).

963　The Megstone Plot　　　　　　　　　　　　Harp 1957

Has all the appurtenances of a detective story, but doesn't quite belong.
Well told, it describes a clever get-rich-quick scheme and how it fell
through. One is left with the pangs of unsatisfied hunger. The film, *A
Touch of Larceny,* was enjoyable without reservations.

In U.S.: Murder Through the Looking Glass

A masterpiece: the atmosphere, the bureaucracy, the adventures—amorous and political—that keep this tale going are done with a sure hand and with evident zest. The author likes it almost the best of his stories (March 1967) and cannot understand our placing it next to *No Tears for Hilda,* which he regards as prentice work.

965   The Narrow Search   Harp 1957

Pleasant but pointless: a young mother and her male friend try to discover her child, kidnapped and hidden by her psychotic husband. The chase leads along the inland waterways of England and makes for good reading, but in retrospect the plot seems less and less plausible.

966   No Tears for Hilda   Harp 1950

The first book by this author that we read, though not his first. Yet there is about *Hilda* a freshness suggestive of a new voice. It is, moreover, a solid work, which can be reread at intervals with the greatest pleasure. The detection is adroitly divided, or doubled (as one may want to look at it), so that the business of being on both sides of the hunt does not produce the usual disintegration of suspense. The hero and heroine are likable, and so is the murderer. Garve writes with economy and color— another rare combination.

967   Prisoner's Friend   Harp 1962

There is not much mystery here, but it makes pleasant reading without any special interest of situation or character. One knows, of course, that the young veterinarian hero will get his discharged prisoner "off," but he works to do it.

968   The Riddle of Samson   Harp 1955
In ppb.: The Man on the Cliff

On first reading (aloud) this did not please the collaborators. But reread solo it proved solid and interesting. The anguish of the hero, who certainly looks as if he had committed a murder, and the love affair intertwined *damit* are both neat and strong, the hallmark of Garve's best work.

969   The Sea Monks   Harp 1963

An attractive presentation of the routine of lighthouse-keeping, suddenly broken into by four young thugs (one female), the "king" of whom already has (or ought to have) a murder on his conscience. The quite absorbing recital of how the surviving keepers finally gain the upper hand is not entirely free of moralizing, but it is convincing, though devoid of mystery or detection.

970   A Very Quiet Place   Harp 1967
      Endpaper map of locale

A shortish novel about a girl photographer who snaps a holdup in progress,
is threatened by the criminals, and thereupon is used as a decoy. Doings
at the deserted millhouse are in G.'s best vein, though in retrospect the
story is seen for what it is—a slim episode.

971   GASK, ARTHUR

      Marauders by Night   HJ 1951

If this tale is representative of an output numbering thirty titles, then the
connoisseur had better keep away. Excitement is sought by piling implausibilities on top of one another, including a feeble parody of Poirot,
Lupin, and Holmes. The official detective, Gilbert Larose, who apparently
runs through a long series, is futility personified.

972   GAULT, WILLIAM CAMPBELL (also Bill Gault)

      The Day of the Ram   RH 1956

Though fairly stereotyped, the doings of Brock ("the Rock") Callahan,
a former professional football player now turned private eye, are told
with directness and force. Drinking and the expected Californication are
kept within bounds, and the hero does not get himself beaten up unnecessarily. Not advisable for a steady diet, however, for one gets tired of
Armenian gamblers, floozies, society degenerates, and especially of the
temperamental little interior decorator with whom the Rock flirts,
quarrels, and sleeps.

973   Sweet Wild Wench   Crest 1959

This is a "Crest Original Novel of Suspense," and there are presumably
others by this author featuring private eye Joe Puma. One is glad to say
that many others have done this sort of thing much worse. Puma's
detection is modest but real; red herrings in the form of police enmity,
etc., are subordinate, and sexual activity is constrained within human
limits.

974   GAULT. See also:

Blood on the Boards	Dutt 1953	End of a Call Girl	Crest 1958
The Bloody Bokhara	Dutt 1952	Murder in the Raw	Dutt 1955
Death out of Focus	RH 1959	Run, Killer, Run	Dutt 1954

975   GEROULD, GORDON HALL (1877–1953)

      A Midsummer Mystery   App 1925

In this smoothly written tale of Washington in the summer, the author, a
genial professor of Victorian literature, tries valiantly to be a man of
the world and almost succeeds. His young men are rather too much alike,
his blackmailed senator is, of course, innocent, and in the end *tout*

s'explique. But Gerould knew his Washington and must be given whatever credit accrues to one who anticipated Leslie Ford (q.v.) by a decade.

976   GIELGUD, VAL (HENRY) (b. 1900)

    And Died So?   Coll 1961

The bashing of a disagreeable operator named Heseltine brings on the village scene Inspector Gregory Pellew—a local, not a Yard man—and he enlists the aid of his friend Viscount Clymping, a bohemian Lord who is visiting his mother, Lady Hannington, in the vicinage. Mother and son form a variant of Sayers' Peter Wimsey and the Duchess of Denver, but are not nearly so much fun. The story lacks drive, despite a perfectly good plot, and the dialogue, meant to be racy, is just facetious. The author was to do better later on, but not with this team of sleuths, who appeared twice before (*To Bed at Noon; Gallows' Foot*) and who became overtly professional in *Prinvest—London* (1965).

The title quotation is from *Julius Caesar* IV, 3, 174.

977   Cat   RH 1956

A good writer and restless in his choice of subjects. In this tale we are soon shown a murderer who confesses to the crime: he killed the attractive young woman whose body we discover at the outset. But, says he, it was done for good reasons. The book is the reasons, and they are good; not so, from the detective point of view, the book.

978   A Necessary End   CCC 1969

Of the many shipboard stories this ranks near the top, with those of Bruce Hamilton and Simon Nash (qq.v.). The exposition is long, but not too long, given the lively character histories; and the detection—barring a bit of unnecessary banter—is first-class (as the ship is not). In addition: amusing sidelights on the U.S. by an observant Londoner.

979   Through a Glass Darkly   Scrib 1963
    In Eng.: The Goggle Box Affair

A well-written and generally entertaining tale of murder suspected but suicide proved, affecting a TV executive who did intelligence work on the side and whose "world was made to collapse" by the moderately clever method of playing him edited tapes when he was depressed after an unsuccessful spy hunt.

The (hackneyed) title is from Corinthians, 13:12.

980   GIELGUD. See also:

Conduct of a Member	Coll 1967	The High Jump	
Confident Morning	Coll 1943	(= Ride for a Fall)	Coll 1953
Fall of a Sparrow	Coll 1947	Prinvest—London	Coll 1965
Gallows' Foot	Coll 1958	Special Delivery	Coll 1950
		To Bed at Noon	Coll 1960

981   GILBERT, ANTHONY (pseud. of Lucy Beatrice Malleson, b. 1899) is one who writes from the point of view of harrowed womankind about damsels, children, and others in peril, stretching out the villainy beyond credence. Her knight-errant is a coarse and shady lawyer, Arthur Crook, who gets his way rather too easily when the author finally decides to turn the tide in favor of righteousness and a happy ending. See *Looking-Glass Murder* (1966), *Out for the Kill* (1960), *A Question of Murder* (1955).

GILBERT, MICHAEL (FRANCIS) (b. 1912)

Both father and mother were writers. His uncle, Maurice Gwyer, who was Lord Chief Justice of India, influenced him to study law at London University. In the second world war was a gunner, visited Canada, was taken prisoner by the Germans in Africa, and thus "did time" in Tunis and Italy. Is now a solicitor in London, in which capacity he advised Raymond Chandler and drew up his will. Besides his large output of detection, he has written *Dr. Crippen* in Odhams Trials series (1952), a work on the Tichborne Claimant (No. 3157), and several plays (see Nos. 2533–7). He is moreover the editor of the Classics of Adventure and Detection for Hodder and Stoughton.

982   After the Fine Weather   Harp 1963

This is essentially suspense: a young English girl, visiting her brother, who is vice-consul in a South Austrian city, witnesses an assassination and causes the local politicos great annoyance by testifying against the "wrong" man. She is eventually got out of the city to safety, in a somewhat mushy conclusion.

983   Be Shot for Sixpence   Harp 1956

A tale of international intrigue on the model of Symons' *Broken Penny*, but less well plotted emotionally. The hero is made disagreeable and even despicable; the beautiful blonde with whom the hero sleeps turns out as convention requires; and the other characters are so distorted in their "strong" features as to become flatly uninteresting.

As for action, the fundamental idea is that not only is all fair in war and espionage, but this cruelty must obtain among fellow agents, to keep one "fit." The author also believes that a diesel-electric locomotive needs a "conductor rail."

984   Blood and Judgment   Harp 1959

M.G.'s first effort at "police routine" and very well done. His hero is Sergeant Petrella, who has appeared in several short stories in *EQMM* (see No. 2535). Here he unravels the murder of a woman, wife of a convict, on the bank of an isolated London reservoir, while also tracing a vanished employee of the Metropolitan Water Board. The politics within the CID interrupt his search, and he and a friend do some night skin diving on their own, with the happiest results.

The title is a phrase from *Hamlet* III, 2, 74.

985   Close Quarters   Walk 1963/H&S 1947
       Map of the grounds

One of the good stories of murder in godly surroundings, it was the
author's first attempt at detection, written while he was a schoolmaster at
Salisbury. He now considers the tale cluttered, but the plan showing who
was where in the close of Melchester Cathedral on the critical evening
makes clear the theories of the official and unofficial detectives: Chief
Inspector Hazelrigg and the dean's nephew.

986   Death Has Deep Roots   Harp 1952
       In Eng.: The Trial of Victoria Lamartine

There have been many mystery tales based upon the activities of the
French Resistance; few have been good, and fewer stand up to current rereading. This is one of the very best. Approximately alternate
chapters deal with scenes at the trial of a young woman accused of the
murder of the putative father of her (deceased) child; in between we have
the activities of agents employed by her solicitors to uncover the facts.
Scene of the crime is a small London hotel. Counsel on both sides are
excellently portrayed. A gripping tale: one of the author's triumphs.

987   Death in Captivity   H&S 1952
       In U.S.: The Danger Within

A superb, though harrowing, story of murder in a prisoner-of-war camp
in northern Italy toward the end of the last world war. The skill with
which suspense is kept up during a series of trivial incidents related to
oppression and plans of escape is equaled only by the management of a
large number of characters, Italian and English. It seems clear that autobiographical matter has been woven in.

988   The Doors Open   H&S 1953/1949

This author's least satisfactory work. The usually competent Inspector
Hazelrigg stays on the sidelines while a pair of male amateurs (too reminiscent of the bright young things of the thirties) look into possible crookedness in a large insurance firm, thus inviting the usual sequence of non-
fatal retaliations.

989   The Etruscan Net   H&S 1969
       In U.S.: The Family Tomb

A very smooth and entertaining tale of adventure and intrigue in Florence
shortly after the great flood. Art objects form the center of the crookedness, and the social and political entanglements are done with a sure hand,
together with a few persuasive characters. The suspense is light.

990   Sky High   H&S 1955
       In U.S.: The Country-House Burglar

An original affair, well worth rereading. The choir, musical chapter titles,
and quotations from Elizabethan plays do not weigh down the tale, of

which the atmosphere and persons are unusual yet not at all outré. And it is detection.

991   Smallbone Deceased   Harp 1950

Two splendid murders on the premises of a London solicitor. The motives are good, and one must call excellent the detection by Inspector Hazelrigg and an amateur assistant, who enjoys parainsomnia. As a bonus we are given a method of mortgaging property already fully mortgaged, and a pleasant bit of fooling about the Ascheim-Zondek test and its antecedents. All in all, Gilbert's masterwork.

992   GILBERT, M. See also:

The Crack in the Teacup	Harp 1966
Fear to Tread	H&S 1953
Overdrive (= The Dust and the Heat)	Harp 1967
They Never Looked Inside (= He Didn't Mind Danger)	H&S 1947

993   GILES, KENNETH (also CHARLES DRUMMOND and EDMUND MC-GIRR, qq.v.)

Death Among the Stars   Goll 1968

His sixth and rapidly worsening. What we have here is a cheap newspaper office, whose astrologer is murdered on his desk. Spy links develop as Sergeant Honeybody and Inspector Harry James crawl from pub to pub and we endure trivialities about the Inspector's false teeth, foolish wife, and outsize dog. The life is lower-middle-class English aping the U.S. gangster culture. Not till p. 114 do we hear anything about the twine with which murder was done. Sophomoric. But see below, No. 996.

994   Death and Mr. Prettyman   Walk 1967

A great disappointment after his first. This one falls into patterns much too well known and not redeemed by the artful use of slang and cant.

995   Death Cracks a Bottle   Walk 1969

Death in a dumbwaiter is always picturesque; it becomes poetic justice when it overtakes a universally hated man, head of a wine-importing firm, and the victim has been dispatched with the aid of an oversize bottle of vermouth. Inspector James and Sergeant Honeybody are the only killjoys in this story, by reason of their unnaturally intrusive personal affairs, which obscure their detective skill. So much talent spoiled by a false notion of what is "real" and "amusing."

996   Some Beasts No More   Walk 1965

In his first detective novel the author manipulates his complex plot well and comes out with no loose ends. Such pits for the unwary as multiple murders, fiends incarnate, and the detective falling in love with a suspect are skirted with skill. Sergeant James is credible and likable. Scene: a small English town near Manchester.

997 GILES. See also:

The Big Greed	Goll 1966
Death in Diamonds	Goll 1967
Murder Pluperfect	Walker 1970
A Provenance of Death	Goll 1966

998 GILL, JOSEPHINE (ECKERT)

Dead of Summer   CCD 1959

Avowedly one of the damsel-in-distress type, but not intolerable and graced by a modicum of interesting Albany local color. The damsel in question is not particularly foolish, but not sufficiently well characterized. The rich man is likewise cardboard thin.

999 GILLETTE, WILLIAM (HOOKER) (1855–1937)

The Astounding Crime on Torrington Road   Harp 1927

A period piece, and what one would expect from one who was so at home in the "Stepney Gas Chamber" (see No. 2487). Not a detective story but an overelaborate and very gradual revelation of the way a mechanical genius used one of his inventions to counterfeit murder. Useful bits of lore about travel between New York and Boston in the twenties.

1000 GODWIN, JOHN

Requiem for a Rat   HJ 1963

Mr. Godwin is a superb writer, who tells of murder and other misdoing in Sydney, Australia, with speed, wit, and dash. It is true that the detection is not minute and the policeman, Fowler, not attractive, but the hero-journalist is good and his girl excellent. So are the subplots, motives, and most of the physical details.

1001 GODWIN, J. See also (both true crime):

Killers in Paradise	Hart 1966
Killers Unknown (No. 3160)	HJ 1960

1002 GODWIN, WILLIAM

The Adventures of Caleb Williams   1794

Certainly a story of crime and investigation, the latter carried out by the secretary of the suspected man, himself a recluse. There is much psychology (some of it shrewd and anticipatory of a later day), considerable drama (including blackmail frame-up, low life, and trial scene), but the whole is ill organized and verbose. An interesting motive to detection is Caleb's religious fervor. In its day the book was popular and furnished the plot of a successful play.

1003 GOLDSMITH, GENE

Murder on His Mind   Mill 1947

Dr. Dan Damon, psychiatrist, defends a mixed-up young playboy in the suspected murder of the young man's own psychiatrist. New York scene and straightforward telling. As for the characters, the cardboard is at least clean-cut.

1004 GOODCHILD, GEORGE (also Alan Dare, Wallace Q. Reid, and Jesse Templeton; b. 1888)

Inspector McLean's Holiday   Pan 1951
    Rev. by the author from McLean
    Takes a Holiday (H&S 1942)

Perhaps worth listing as a sample of the work done by this prolific Britisher. Good topography (Cornwall) and plenty of shooting at the end, but nothing to engage the mind or the heart. More interesting were the author's collaborations with Bechhofer Roberts in the fictional rendering of true crime. See No. 3248.

1005 GOODIS, DAVID (1917–1967)

Of Missing Persons   Morr 1950

Help given by a Los Angeles police officer and acknowledged in the dedication does not keep this first effort from being standard sentiment about the hard life of the cop in charge of the Missing Persons Bureau: the clients are ungrateful, the higher-ups are unjust, the work is burdensome, your wife leaves you, etc. In the end all comes right, but it is to be hoped that the later stories show more real grit—e.g., *Night Squad* (1961) and *Somebody's Done For* (1967). See also the earlier *Nightfall* (1948).

1006 GORDON, NEIL (pseud. of A[RCHIBALD] G[ORDON] MACDONELL, 1895–1941

The Silent Murders   LG 1929

We have here an early and impressive specimen of police routine, full of legitimate excitement and complete with friction between superior and subordinate on the force. The variety and surprise in the incidents maintains a high pitch of suspense and the detection is as solid as the explanation, which dawns on the reader just a few seconds before it does on the Scottish Inspector Dewar. When it comes, it constitutes what is probably a first instance of its use: altogether a book to be cherished for its worth and its wit.

1007 GORDON, N. See also No. 1299 and:

The Big Ben Alibi   Lane 1930
Murder in Earl's Court   Lane 1931
The Professor's Poison   LG 1928
The Shakespeare Murders   AB 1933

Death on Delivery   Coll 1929
    In U.S.: By Way of Confession

Mass murder of various wealthy and prominent people, mostly adherents
of the sect "New Search," which has been organized for the purpose of
removing them for pay. Lucien Clay is not so funny as he was in *In
Search of a Villain,* and the mad scientist who is head of the bogus cult
is crazy in more ways than one.

1009   In Search of a Villain   Dday 1928

This is the famous tale distinguished by the phrase "so far from fully"
(see Gems from the Literature) and originally read by the collaborators
c. 1930. It sets forth a tangle of amateur and professional criminals, a
plausible and not stupid Inspector Heppel, and the erratic but witty painter-
detective Lucien Clay, who makes the classic remark just quoted, after
the mystery of the means of murder has been solved.

1010   GORE-BROWNE. See also:

The Crater	Coll 1925
An Imperfect Lover	Coll 1929
Murder of an M.P.	Coll 1927

1011   GORELL, LORD (Ronald Gorell Barnes, 3rd baron) (b. 1884)

The Devouring Fire   JM 1949/1928

This cheap reprint, the sixth in twenty years, attests the vitality of this
novel, which is jejune in many ways yet retains something of the deliberate intelligence of the twenties. The characters are goody-goody or villainous without admixture, but the plot is credible and the clues abundant
and respectfully handled—up to the point where the intolerable trick
ending begins.

1012   Earl's End   WL 1951

Supposedly "set in the House of Lords," this ineffectual story takes place
rather in nightclubs and flats, where a collection of stupid young people
mess about with a stolid superintendent who is not badly done; but the
plot is childish.

1013   In the Night   LG 1917

A period piece which, whatever its faults of omission, has almost none
of commission. It is one of the few written after *Trent's Last Case* and
before the dawn of the "golden era" of the late twenties-mid-thirties
which can still afford pleasure.
    JB dissents from what he considers an overcharitable estimate.

1014   GORELL. See also:

    D.E.Q.   JM 1922
    Murder at Manor House   WL 1954
    Murder at Mavering   JM 1943

1015   GRAAF, PETER

    The Sapphire Conference   IW 1959

First of the then newly launched "Chantecler" series of detective novels
and, for such mass production, fair enough. Joe Dust, an American private
eye now living in London, is taken by his friend Superintendent Hebden
to a conference at Iron Head College, Minster University. Academic ri-
valries are aired and a nuclear big wheel disappears. The plot is sound,
and the method of the murder and its concealment, as well as the not-
too-numerous red herrings, well handled. This success makes one want to
look up the author's earlier *Give the Devil His Due* (= *Dust and the
Curious Boy*), Morrow, 1957.

1016   GRAEME, BRUCE (pseud. of Graham Montague Jeffries; also Peter
    Bourne and David Graeme; b. 1900)
    Epilogue   Lipp 1934

By making his Inspector and Sergeant go back in time to 1857—dream,
hallucination, time-reversal: take your choice from the outset—the author
supplies an ingenious reconstruction of the case of Edwin Drood that
Dickens left unfinished. The contrast in times gives opportunity for excellent humor, and the serious outcome is carefully built up; but in order
to do both at once, characterization suffers a bit—which may be excused
when Dickens is in the background.

1017   The Undetective   LH 1963

A detective-story writer decides to make money by producing tales under
another name which will give the lowdown on police methods, revealed
to him by his brother-in-law. When the police run into a difficult case
of murder, the new pseudonymous author becomes suspect and a main
target of police wrath. Adroitly written—for the author has had long
practice after producing some sixty books in three series—and the dramatic twist at the end must rank as a notable feat in the acroidal style.

    Note: the opening pages contain a clear, detailed account of the eco-
nomics of writing and publishing detective fiction.

1018   GRAFTON, C(ORNELIUS) W(ARREN) (b. 1909)

    Beyond a Reasonable Doubt   Farr 1940

A very ingenious tale of murder left in doubt, followed by the putative
culprit's defense of himself in court: a new twist to the inversion of ordinary detection, for it is full of clues and inferences from them—a brilliant and gripping narrative.

A nice example of the moderately hard-boiled school. The operative, Gilmore Henry, is atypical in being small, not a private eye but a lawyer, and more given to thinking than to screwing. The scene is Kentucky and south Ohio; the crimes hinge upon earlier depravity and bastardy. If it were not that the plot is allowed to become unnecessarily complex, the tale would rate as grade A of its kind.

1020   The Rope Began to Hang the Butcher   Farr 1944

Longer and less believable than the previous one, of which we are now told that the action took place only one month earlier. In this later adventure Gil Henry is very slow to uncover a rather transparent substitution plot; then the end is huddled after an excess of delay and only the legal tricks are any fun.

1021   GRAHAM, WHIDDEN

Crimson Hairs   Grove 1969
   An Erotic Mystery Story

An attempt was bound to be made that would capture two publics at once among those who scan paperback shelves. The subtitle tells what these publics are. Unfortunately, though the pornography in this work is graphic and comprehensive as to combinations and permutations, the mystery is lost sight of after a promising beginning; and when, after all beds and bodies have been raked for clues, the potent young detective springs the answer, it is a fraud—or rather, the mystery is. For the author, by playing an unfair trick with the word *hair,* conceals what the police and the reader would have latched on to at once. Let it be added that the writing is competent, though not so delicate and harmoniously proportioned as the female nude, seen from the back, on the cover.

1022   GRAY, DULCIE

Died in the Red   Macd 1968

Murder in a woman's hairdressing establishment. Inspector Cardiff stomps about and solves. Undistinguished and the tenth in a row.

1023   GRAY, JONATHAN* (pseud. of Jack Taylor)

Untimely Slain   Hutch [1947?]

An excellent Oxford college setting and an interesting murder make the first 50 pages of this story by a University of Rochester economist (M.A. Oxon.) a joy. The following letdown into espionage and Nazi infiltration in Poland are disappointing. The rank blood-and-guts of Part II contrast strongly with the competent detection of Part I.

   * The same pseudonym was used earlier by Herbert Adams (q.v.).

In private life she was Mrs. Charles Rohlfs. Eminently successful in representing the tempo and the mores of New York and Washington society in the period 1875–1900, she was less skillful in merging fact with the melodrama necessary for the Victorian detective novel. Thus even her best work is now dated, and her best detective, Mr. Gryce, is memorable chiefly for the excesses which he avoids. Still, one must respect the careful workmanship which persisted for forty years and the imagination which bodied forth so many good situations. Another point: though full of women, her tales avoid the "Had I But Known" tedium of her successors.

1024 The Circular Study   McCl 1900

This is one of the author's most complex plots, and surely one of the last to be unraveled in the presence of (certainly not by) Mr. Gryce, described here as an octogenarian. A family feud follows the seduction of a ward. The circular study which is the scene of homicide is in a New York mansion, completely equipped with electric colored lights, a talking starling, and Amelia Butterworth, who is Gryce's able helper. But midnight meetings in graveyards are also frequent.

1025 The Filigree Ball   BM 1903

Forsaking her usual New York scene, the author deals with Washington society at a time when the Civil War was within memory and the invasion of Cuba a current reality, taking young men (and witnesses) out of circulation. The nameless young detective, who does a fair job of seeking clues, could have been molded by a sterner hand into a memorable sleuth. As for the lethal ball above the half-upholstered settee, it is to be taken in a Pickwickian sense, or, shall we say, credited only by a very Green intelligence. But the psychology is sound, and the lengthy coroner's inquiry (90 pages) is a masterly job.

1026 Hand and Ring   DM 1926; orig. 1901

A long book, but making allowance for the leisurely pace of its era, as well as for a heroine named Imogene, interesting to the end. The eternal triangle is still isosceles and pillars of society vulnerable. Mr. Gryce comes in only in the last quarter to lend assistance to his young aide, who is trying to find out who killed the widow Clemmens in her own house and dropped a diamond ring on the floor. Physical clues are expertly treated.

1027 The Leavenworth Case   Putn 1878
      Plan of bedroom and library

The first by this author, and a solid achievement. Mr. Gryce of the New York police makes his appearance on p. 5 and picks his surefooted way among the numerous clues (planted and genuine) in the mansion of the late Mr. L., shot in his library with his own pistol. Suspense is well maintained as to which of the two beautiful nieces did it; and a good diagram, solid work on trajectories, and clever deductions from writing paper all help to set a substantial tone, despite a fair dose of love story.

1028   A Strange Disappearance   Putn 1881/1879

A wealthy New Yorker is saved from bandits by the daughter of their leader; the gang attempts to abduct the young woman; but Mr. Gryce and an unnamed assistant track them down, with apparently little need of detection. The town of Putney (scene of some of the action) is misplaced in "northern Vermont."

1029   The Woman in the Alcove   BM 1906

Told by Miss Van Arsdale, who saves and marries the man suspected of murdering for the sake of a diamond. Anna K.'s masterly melodrama and use of superstition provide pleasure for anyone who can put himself back into the mood of the period.

1030   GREEN. See also No. 2541 and:

The Amethyst Box	BM 1905	The House in the Mist	BM 1905
Behind Closed Doors	Putn 1888	The House of the	
The Chief Legatee	DM 1916	Whispering Pines	Putn 1910
Cynthia Wakeham's		Initials Only	DM 1911
Money	Putn 1892	Lost Man's Lane	Putn 1898
The Dark Hollow	DM 1914	Marked "Personal"	Putn 1893
A Difficult Problem		A Matter of Millions	Bonner 1891
(ss; see No. 2541)	Lupton 1900	The Mill Mystery	Putn 1896
The Doctor, His Wife		The Mystery of the	
and the Clock (ss)	Putn 1895	Hasty Arrow	DM 1917
The Forsaken Inn	Bonner 1890	7 to 12: A Detective Story	Putn 1887
The Golden Slipper		The Step on the Stair	DM 1923
(stories of Violet Strange,		That Affair Next Door	Putn 1897
detective)	Putn 1915	X Y Z: A Detective Story	Putn 1883

1031   GREENE, GRAHAM (b. 1904)

A Gun for Sale   Hein 1936
An Entertainment

A hired gunman (English underprivileged youth) murders a socialist minister on the Continent and almost plunges Europe into war. Inspector Mather trails him, but M.'s own fiancée gets drawn into the chase and almost succeeds in humanizing the murderer. Several deft slaps at the Anglican Church and a few subtle boosts for the R.C. Suspense only.

GREGG, CECIL FREEMAN (b. 1898)

Produced, between 1930 and 1960, at least forty detective novels, mostly featuring Inspector Higgins.

1032   Murder on the Bus   Dial 1930

This relatively early case of Inspector Cuthbert Higgins' sheds a somewhat more favorable light on the author than do his many later novels.

Though long and slow, this tale is still readable. It is a London omnibus, of course.

1033 Tragedy at Wembley   Dial 1936

A long, slow tale of robbery and murder, in which the portly inspector does nothing to speak of.

1034 GRIBBLE, LEONARD REGINALD (also Leo Grex, Louis Grey, Landon Grant, Dexter Muir, and Sterry Browning; b. 1908), has been an extremely prolific writer of detective fiction, as well as of studies of crime and detection. Poor characterization, as well as a distressing lack of style, make for heavy going. For the detective novels, most of which feature Inspector (later Superintendent) Anthony Slade, see: *Atomic Murder* (1947); *The Case of the Malverne Diamonds* (1936); *Hangman's Moon* (1950); *Inspector Slade Investigates* (ss) (1952); *The Inverted Crime* (1954); and *Wantons Die Hard* (1961).
See also Nos. 3164–6.

GRIERSON, EDWARD (b. 1914)

Educ. St. Paul's and Exeter Coll. Oxf. Read for the bar, then turned to writing, including history (*The Fatal Inheritance: Philip II of Spain and the Netherlands,* 1969); served in Egypt, promoted to lt. col.; is deputy chairman of the Northumberland Quarter Sessions.

1035 A Crime of One's Own   C&W 1967

As poor a story as can be written by a good man in a bad vein. The young owner of a provincial bookstore who imagines spies from trifling events linked with his circulating library and the mess of girls and shadowy men mooching in the shop leave the reader uninterested till the young man's trial for murder on skimpy evidence. Then the course of discovery is too fantastic to take seriously.

1036 The Massingham Affair   Dday 1962

A well-constructed and well-told tale of the way a lawyer and a clergyman labor for eight years to uncover the truth of a mystery enveloping the events of an evening in 1891, when burglars broke into a lonely rectory in northern England, following which two men were sentenced to life imprisonment on insufficient evidence. In the Victorian style, just short of perfect reconstruction.

1037 Reputation for a Song   C&W 1952

Not strictly a detective story, though it contains much which in other books is palmed off as detection—e.g., endless questioning. The author, whose second tale this is, writes with charm and power. The virago woman who is pilloried here is exceedingly well done, and so is the husband torn away from his natural moorings in placidity and fairness by her diabolical prodding.
  Note: The author clearly implies that the jury system and the rules

for controlling witnesses produce injustice. But a point not cleared up is why the daughter does not testify for her father.

1038   The Second Man   Knopf 1956

An excellent story about a woman lawyer who has difficulties getting accepted by an officeful of male colleagues but who turns out to be the capable hunter-down of the mysterious man in a case involving murder. She is having a nice love affair at the same time, and the book is altogether perfect.

1039   GRIERSON, E. See also:

Shall Perish by the Sword   C&W 1941

1040   GRIERSON, FRANCIS DURHAM (b. 1888), is little known to present-day readers, but remembered by older ones for *The Limping Man* (1926), which had merit.

1041   GRIFFITHS, [MAJOR] ARTHUR GEORGE FREDERICK (1838–1908)

The Rome Express   Milne 1897

A tolerable period piece: amusing and not-too-unfair presentation of French officialdom at work on a sleeping-car murder, while a British general protects the rights of a lady suspect in distress. The plot brings in a defaulting banker, a venal policeman, and a change of identity; much interrogation, not much detection, but plenty of Paris as it was.

1042   GRIFFITHS. See also No. 2543 and:

The Passenger from Calais   Dday 1906
The Wrong Road   Blackwood 1888

1043   GRUBER, FRANK (also Stephen Acre, Charles K. Boston, and John K. Vedder; b. 1904), is the author of *Simon Lash, Private Detective* (Farr. 1941), a run-of-the-mill thriller in which the bad man's identity is in doubt and murder is condoned (though not unexpiated) for the sake of a girl. Other books in series (*Limping Goose, Laughing Fox, Hungry Dog*) have appeared since the forties, while in another group (*French Key, Greek Affair*, etc.) a book salesman named Johnny Fletcher does his peering and pursuing with his friend Sam Cragg.

1044   GUINNESS, K(ATHERINE) D(ORIS)

Fisherman's End   Macd 1958

An attractive tale by a young lady from Dublin. But the pleasant atmosphere of the posh guesthouse in County Kerry and the well-restrained fishing background are pointless when we learn that the detestable Sir Joseph Garston was not killed as desired by several people with good motives and poor alibis, but took off on another line.

1045   GUNN, VICTOR

Dead Men's Bells   Coll 1956

Despite the improbability of the device used for hearing at a distance,
not a bad tale at all, considering the author's huge output. Straightforward and a real detective story besides, with Inspector Cromwell in
charge.

1046   Murder at the Motel   Coll 1964

The problem is: how did a small redheaded man, stark naked and killed
by the ingestion of alcohol and carbon tetrachloride, come to be in an
empty cabin behind the big motel in Suffolk? The mystery is compounded
when a lovely girl, just engaged to the motel owner's son, is also found
murdered by strangulation in her own cottage nearby. Chief Inspector
Cromwell, assisted by Sergeant Lister, do a good job of rounding up suspects and clues to reach the unexpected solution. But the telling and the
dialogue are matter-of-fact and the detectives' byplay mechanical.

1047   GUNN. See also:

        Death on Bodwin Moor   Coll 1960
        The Road to Murder   Coll 1949
        Sweet Smelling Death   Coll 1961
        The Treble Chance Murder   Coll 1963

1048   HADDOW, DENNIS

Hanged by a Thread   Hutch 1947

Dozens of detective novels have been written with plots similar to this,
and most of them are as good or better. There is nothing memorable
about Detective Inspector Greve and his doting sergeant; the houseful of
shady suspects, all with motives for doing in the host, are mostly lay
figures, and the mechanism for firing the gun is absurd. The one nice bit
comes when the butler (an old lag), moved by admiration, returns the
inspector's watch, which he'd lifted.

1049   HAGGARD, [SIR] H(ENRY) RIDER (1856–1925)

Mr. Meeson's Will   Harp 1888

An interesting story-extravaganza about love and inheritance, of which
the important feature is the description of a publishing house that employs
2,000 people to edit and sell and cheat the authors. The heroine is one
of these. She revolts and by chance is shipwrecked with the head of the
firm and others, and it so happens that he has to make his will by tattooing
nine words on her back. The nephew-heir is in love with her, and the
rest of the book deals—very amusingly—with the legal aspects (hearings,
etc.) for probating and filing that will. The sex element in exposing her
back for inspection, etc., is very modern and risqué.

HAGGARD, WILLIAM (pseud. of Richard Henry Michael Clayton, b. 1907)

b. Croydon; educ. Lancing Coll. and Christ Church, Oxf.; joined Indian Civil Service, became a judge, served in second world war, then became an official of the Board of Trade and Controller of Enemy Property in 1957. Began writing the next year.

1050   The Arena   IW 1961

In reply to JB's sending a (second) copy of this to WHT, the latter said that he "found neither the private bankers nor the hero's diabetes able to entertain. . . ." JB agrees.

1051   The High Wire   Cass 1963

The best Haggard: a good-natured and somewhat slow engineer gets enrolled against his will in spy activities. He acquits himself with credit, especially at the end, in Switzerland, where he comes to grips with his enemy in a funicular car that has been purposely stalled. He acquires a wife, also a spy, who has been using her sexual talents as lure and payment.

1052   Slow Burner   LB 1958

This must be an early, if not the first, Haggard. It starts very well indeed, and some scenes (including a memorable meal offered by the middle-aged hero to his female chauffeur) are done with loving care. But the tale soon bogs down and becomes a slower burner even than the new source of atomic power whose epsilon rays finally reach one of the villains. The author likes to dabble in fictional science and does it adequately.

1053   The Unquiet Sleep   IW 1962

A mediocre tale in which a tranquilizer developed by an ethical British firm develops unpredictable properties varying from batch to batch and is habit-forming for some users. While the problem is under investigation, the underworld (mainly Cypriots) horn in and make a killing, unseating a minister but eventually failing of their objective because the "hot stuff" cannot be made predictably. Little if any detection. Political repercussions well handled.

1054   HAGGARD, W. See also:

    Closed Circuit   IW 1960
    The Teleman Touch   LB 1958
    Venetian Blind   Cass 1959

1055   HALL, ANGUS

    Qualtrough   HJ 1968

Still another fictional reconstruction of the Wallace case. It is freely but dully handled and cannot compare with either Rhode or Browne (qq.v.).

1056 HALL, CYRIL

    Leave to Presume Death   BH 1947

A musician (not credible) disappears, and his wife goes partly out of her mind, while her men friends hover around and speculate on what has happened. There is a sinister force, embodied in a man named Axel Flint, and we are to suppose that some allegory is intended: to wit, that the artist must lead a painful life of devotion to his art; if a wife interferes, the forces of art take the artist away by means of cypresses and ruined temples. Overwritten and underthought. It would be no surprise if the author mistakenly reminded himself of Henry James.

1057 HALL, GEOFFREY HOLIDAY

    The Watcher at the Door   S&S 1954

Reasonably credible spy stuff, Viennese, centered in Casey Homes, his wife, and their friend Al. Characters engaging, Vienna grim rather than attractive, little rough stuff, and too much Turkish-bath and street-corner snooping. The innocent American is a bore and so is the pseudo psychology about F-f-f-fear.

    The author has also written *The End Is Known* (1949), to us unknown.

      HALLIDAY, BRETT (pseud. of Davis Dresser; also Asa Baker, Don Davis, and Hal Debrett; b. 1904)

Since 1938 this author has written a large number of tales featuring Mike Shayne, a red-haired private detective in Miami; his secretary, Lucy Hamilton; police chiefs Peter Painter and Will Gentry, and newspaperman Timothy Rourke. The plots are complicated but often adroitly worked out, action is swift and rough, liquor flows like water (for Shayne nearly always brandy), and sex is somewhat surprisingly underplayed. Shayne gets away with murder, but he does have an occasional brain wave and perform some legitimate detecting.

1058 Counterfeit Wife   Ziff 1947

A kidnapping serves as a means of passing counterfeit money. The scheme backfires when a go-between decamps with the funds, but all is satisfactorily accounted for at the end, after a murder or two and a suicide. Here and elsewhere Shayne asks us to believe too much—e.g., that after he has driven the car through a garage door to make his escape, the headlights will still turn on. Such liberties detract from the effect produced by Shayne's other good dodges.

1059 HALLIDAY, B. See also:

    Die Like a Dog   Long 1961
    Marked for Murder   Long 1945

1060　HALLIDAY, DOROTHY [MRS. DOROTHY HALLIDAY DUNNETT]

　　　　Dolly and the Singing Bird　　　　　　　　　Cass 1968

A woman singer who narrates in the first person accepts an Edinburgh
Festival date in order to meet one Kenneth Holmes, whom she finds dead.
The complications are possible, but no more.

1061　HALLIDAY, MICHAEL (pseud. of John Creasey, q.v.)

　　　　Hate to Kill　　　　　　　　　　　　　　　　H&S 1962

The tale starts with an excellent situation: a girl waits in a lonely cottage
for her lover-to-be and gets involved with a stranger who comes to see
said lover and appears to have sinister intentions, though not toward the
girl. Mystery increases as the stranger flees from the police following
the discovery that he has ostensibly murdered his wife. The cottage girl
defends him, and she herself becomes a victim. It is here that improbability sets in, and the huddled end ruins the whole.

　　　　HAMILTON, (ARTHUR DOUGLAS) BRUCE (b. 1900)

Educ. Westminster and Univ. Coll., London, a history master and a principal in Barbados, as well as president of its Arts Council (1958–59),
playwright, and author of historical and political works.

1062　Dead Reckoning　　　　　　　　　　　　　　S&S 1937
　　　　　In Eng.: Middle Class Murder

An egotistical little dentist in a Sussex town sets about ridding himself
of a wife grown hateful through an accident which has maimed and
aged her. His plans are good, but not quite good enough, and the last
third of the book is a gripping account of the progressively desperate
measures he takes to avoid consequences. Good to the finish, but not detection.

1063　The Hanging Judge　　　　　　　　　　　　　Harp 1948
　　　　　In Eng.: Let Him Have Judgment

Again, not exactly detection, but a good plot pivoting on a murder committed by the criminal under a misapprehension. The plausibility is well
maintained. Unfortunately, on a second reading, the exposition seems
overlong.

1064　To Be Hanged　　　　　　　　　　　　　　　Faber 1930

This is a well-engineered affair in which a girl full of repressed physical
passion hates her father for keeping her from men. A young journalist
and a solicitor friend try to save an unjustly convicted lover of the girl.
Characterization not bad, even if everybody talks the same rational English. The factual details and the atmosphere of sex are excellently done.

1065   Too Much of Water   Cress 1958

A superb sea mystery. A passage to Barbados with a medley of odd characters aboard yields the inevitable three or four murders resulting from
their predatory interrelations. The prose is excellent. There is much
about music to delight these two readers, and just the sort of humor they
relish.
The title is from *Hamlet* IV, 7, 186.

1066   HAMILTON, B. See also:

The Brighton Murder Trial, Rex v.		Pro: An English Tragedy	Cress 1946
Rhodes (a novel, of which B. H.		So Sad, So Fresh	Cress 1952
is named *ed.*)	Boris 1937	Spring Term	Meth 1933
Hue and Cry	H&S 1931	Traitor's Way	Cress/BM 1939

HAMILTON, DONALD (b. 1916)

After *Date with Darkness* the author felt compelled to create a tough
private eye, one Matt Helm, who now fills rather predictable paperbacks
and movies with spy stuff, shootings, and dames.

1067   Date with Darkness   Rine 1947

Of its kind—counterspy work in the U.S. just after the second world
war—this is an outstanding example. Its good points are many, first and
foremost an entirely credible young navy lieutenant, almost ready for
discharge after several years' service away from the salt water which he
loves, and equally ready for some plausible heroics. His relationship to
the *femme fatale* and his rejection of her are good, and the denouement,
in which the astute young sailor leaves his captors to sink or swim in the
darkness, is a masterstroke.

1068   The Steel Mirror   Rine 1948

The story of a young widow, who under Gestapo grilling gave away her
husband and his associates. Now neurotic, she is picked up by a young
chemist, who is thereupon suspect as a spy. They travel about in a car,
seeking vindication; they kill, chase, and third-degree various people,
while keeping up between themselves an overlong misunderstanding.

1069   HAMILTON, D. See also:

Murder Twice Told (containing *Deadfall*	
and *The Black Cross*)	Rine 1947
The Night Walker (= Mask for Danger)	Dell 1954

HAMILTON, LORD ERNEST (WILLIAM) (b. 1858)

Sixth son of the duke of Abercorn, capt. of Hussars, author of many
novels (not det.) before 1928, when he published the masterpiece listed
below.

A detective story which is the exception to Father Knox's strictures on Chinamen (see No. 2614): here those nationals are integral yet unobtrusive and perfectly credible. The author has also dared to include what in other hands might prove very risky—multiple murder, an architectural mantrap, and a bad man from Edmonton—all this with a charming love story and other engaging features and persons. The result is engrossing, perhaps because Lord H. writes with inside knowledge of such people as the successive Lords Fenfield. On this account one overlooks one or two errors in law and police routine.

1071   HAMILTON, IAN

The Creeping Vicar   Lipp 1967
A Pete Heysen Thriller

It tells of a marauder who collects his revenue at night by disguising himself and peeping at his victims at a late hour. Having narrowed the circle of suspects for reasons of his own, the Sydney broadcaster Heysen imitates the "Vicar," is strongly suspected by the police of being the criminal, and finds corpse after corpse until he finally unmasks the killer. Undistinguished in idea, but adroit in execution.

1072   The Persecutor   Lipp 1965

Another, earlier "Pete Heysen Thriller." The story, laid in Sydney, shows why a disc jockey—the hero—uses the radio and his own wits to persecute a weak and low character, who is vaguely accused of sex perversion. The idea is to get at the truth of a murder for which his girl's brother has been convicted. The pace is good till near the end, when it goes Fitzgerald-like (the famous contraction) and no one can figure out who did what or why.

1073   HAMILTON, (ANTHONY WALTER) PATRICK (b. 1904), is best known for *Hangover Square* (1942), which deals with a schizophrenic criminal in Earl's Court—not detection or true crime but horror and psychology. Other tales of a kindred sort present the same figure, Ernest Ralph Gorse. See also *The Midnight Bell* (1930), *Unknown Assailant* (1955), and *Angel Street* (also *Gas Light,* see No. 2395).

HAMMETT, DASHIELL (also Peter Collinson) (1894–1961)

D.H. was for some years a Pinkerton detective. He has acknowledged deriving his style from Ernest Hemingway's, and he has been associated at least by rumor with communist partisanship. See the long autobiographical reminiscences of Lillian Hellman about Hammett in a reprint of earlier versions of his famous tales: *The Big Knockover* (RH, 1966). He made his debut in long fiction in 1929 with *Red Harvest* and *The Dain Curse.* His most popular creation, Sam Spade, first appeared in *The Maltese Falcon* (1930) and made his reputation. Nick Charles appeared four years later in *The Thin Man* and was universalized in a movie of that name with William Powell and Myrna Loy. For H's short stories, see Nos. 2545–2551.

Note that Hammett's detectives are sedate non-killers with little or no penchant for fast women and hard liquor; Hammett provided only a tone and style of detection, not the garish decorations that came later.

1074   The Dain Curse   Knopf 1929

The violence is a little too frequent, arbitrary, and contrived.

1075   The Maltese Falcon   Knopf 1930

The "daring" in this classic was to present a homosexual as villain, to make the hero repeatedly stupid, and to associate (for all time) the beautiful girl with treachery, cruelty, and crime.

1076   Red Harvest   Knopf 1929
         In serial: The Cleansing of Personville

In many respects D.H.'s best book. The violence is not overdone, nor are the motives and characters outré. The writing is terse without being galvanic in effect, and the cynicism is of just the right intensity and no more. Besides, it is the first of the "rotten town" novels that have since flooded the market. (The events are said to bear some resemblance to Anaconda Copper activities in Montana.)

1077   The Thin Man   Knopf 1934

Nick Charles, a San Francisco detective, is the narrator. He and his amusing wife, Nora (on a visit to New York), take time out from drinking and dancing to solve the problem of what happened to an inventor whose disappearance coincided with the murder of his mistress-secretary. There is the right amount of underworld, and in lieu of the usual tough stuff we are treated to an adolescent (son of the disappeared-and-deceased), who battens on the more lurid aspects of toxicology and pathology. A fine period piece.

HARE, CYRIL (pseud. of Alfred Alexander Gordon Clark, 1900–58)

b. Mickleham; educ. Rugby and New College, Oxf., where he took a first in history. His practice at the bar was chiefly in the criminal courts, and in 1942 he joined the staff of the Director of Public Prosecutions. Later he became a county court judge, trying only civil cases and writing fiction while traveling his circuit. His favorite among his books was *Tragedy at Law*.

1078   Death Is No Sportsman   Faber 1947/1938
         Map

Although WHT is not much of a fisherman, he considers this tale to be second only to *When the Wind Blows*. The crime is thought-provoking, and Inspector Mallett is steady and satisfying. JB dislikes the story, not because of the fish, but because of the long windup and fumbling detection.

1079   An English Murder   LB 1951

Smoothly written, but perhaps unduly short and not very substantial, as well as lacking in variety. There is one highly amusing out-of-doors scene in winter, which would be a high spot in any tale, but the claim implied in the title that the kind of murder done tells much about contemporary England is not borne out.

1080   He Should Have Died Hereafter   Faber 1958
       In U.S.: Untimely Death

This is the one which starts with Pettigrew and his wife, Eleanor, on vacation and rather bickering (as well as picnicking) and the discovery of a dead body on the moor. Hanky-panky with a pony, the date of death, insurance, etc. A tired effort.
    The title makes use of *Macbeth,* V, 6, 17.

1081   Suicide Excepted   Macm 1954/1940
       MRS

As a tale, it is about one-third good, two-thirds fumbling. The middle portion, of actual detection by three amateurs, is full of good ideas. The final double twist spoils this in retrospect, though the characterization of the hero-villain and his two coadjutors is fine work. Hare maintains (or establishes) here his liking for unpleasant scenes among relatives. No Pettigrew in the case. Inspector Mallett is a lay figure.

1082   Tenant for Death   Faber 1938

From all appearances, Hare's first, and a very engaging debut it is. No Pettigrew, only Inspector Mallett, who unravels a complex plot for murder, to the accompaniment of sound yet uncommon philosophizing by the author.
    The title on the author page, *The Magic Bottle,* is a tale for children.

1083   That Yew Tree's Shade   Faber 1954
       In U.S.: Death Walks the Woods

It is hard to say why this particular Hare won't run. Pettigrew and his wife, Eleanor, are there, bantering as acidly as usual, the murder of Mrs. Pinks is well engineered and has a good motive, but somehow the drive is lacking and one loses momentum with every page, soon foreseeing the end and not caring about it.

1084   Tragedy at Law   Faber 1942

Long and complex but extremely entertaining, especially for its view of life on the circuit. The surprise ending is well managed and no letdown. But the story cannot rank with the others *as detection.*

1085   When the Wind Blows   Faber 1949
         In U.S.: The Wind Blows Death

The best, unquestionably, of all the Hare stories, and a masterpiece by
any standards. It is the one about the amateur orchestra and the Prague
Symphony. Full of observation, wit, and richly decorated characters, and
unflagging in its keeping up of suspense.

1086   With a Bare Bodkin   Faber 1952/1946

In this tale the second world war catches up with Pettigrew. An amusing
account of civil servants, files, and murder at a remote station housing the
Ministry of Pin Control, somewhere in the north of England. It is not
quite the success that one expects from its other virtues: Inspector Mallett
is competent but no more, so that Pettigrew's cynicism and his romance
supply the chief pleasure. See also Nos. 2555–8 for the author's short
stories.

1087   HARLING, ROBERT

         The Endless Colonnade   C&W 1958

An adventure story in Palladian Italy that combines in one engrossing tale
a sightseeing tour, a double love affair, and the tragedy of a young traitor
physicist. It is done with passion, wit, and inventiveness perfectly blended.
The only flaw is a repeated mistake about the colors of friars' habits.

1088   The Enormous Shadow   C&W 1955

In some ways the best spy story of the modern period, for it treats the two
men who are caught up in the business as compassionately as the characters we are supposed to side with. The writing is terse and vivid without
side effects, the love story unexceptionable, and the ending full of action
on the Thames—altogether first-rate.

1089   The Hollow Sunday   C&W 1967

Again, politics and scandal about the M.P.'s wife, slowly but aptly investigated by the hero-narrator.

1090   The Paper Palace   C&W 1951/Harp 1951

Another first-person narrative about the newspaper and political worlds
(the author has been a reporter and an art critic), the action oscillating
between London and the Balkans. The problem is to find out what a dead
man did and why. Ingenious and well told.

1091   HARRINGTON, JOSEPH

         Blind Spot   Lipp 1966

The author, a former newspaperman, gives in this second tale another
difficult assignment to Lieutenant F. X. Kerrigan; and although there is a
good deal of similarity with *The Last Known Address* (pursuit of a very
cold trail, etc.), the present book stands on its own feet. The author uses

direct quotation from court records, introduces a good bit of psychology, and comes out with a strong plot about an attractive young woman accused of the murder of her lover in his own apartment. The New York scene may be relied upon—it is good.

1092 The Last Known Address   Lipp 1965

A delightful novel. It belongs to the procedural school, but in an original way; it holds the reader's attention with its portrayal of a man-and-woman police team tracking down a missing witness and "interacting" in human fashion without bickering or nursing internal ailments. The pair occur again in *The Last Doorbell* (Lipp. 1969), whose title indicates the continuation of the ambulatory method.

1093 HARRISON, RICHARD (MOTTE) (also Peter Motte; b. 1901)

    Murder-on-Sea   Jarr 1949

This tale is one in the series that presents Chief Inspector William Bastion as detective. The setting is Cutlin's Holiday Camp, where a pretty girl who fancies herself as a future movie starlet winds up a corpse in the sea. The writing is competent on a low level and the motives, clues, and detection are in keeping with the ordinariness of the whole affair. The camp is of no particular interest, except that it is said to serve 3,000 campers, with a staff of 700.

1094 HARRISON. See also Nos. 3175–6 and:

    Aftermath of Murder   Jarr 1942
    Black Widow   Jarr 1946
    The Dog It Was   Jarr 1940

1095 HART, FRANCES NOYES

    The Bellamy Trial   Dday 1927

Through the eyes of a pair of journalists—pretty, susceptible female and hard-bitten male—the author presents minutely all the events of the eight-day trial of Susan Ives and Stephen Bellamy, for the murder of the latter's wife. It remains a classic, still engrossing, and providing plenty of interesting evidence to take the place of detection. The character-drawing and narration are superior, and the reader's attention is kept on the defendants and witnesses rather than on the "reactions" of the jury—which is the modern mode.

1096 Hide in the Dark   Dday 1929

Though admired by Harrison Ross Steeves (q.v.), not in a class with her masterpiece. Far too ambulatory and feminine.

1097 HARVESTER, SIMON (pseud. of Henry Gibbs)

    Silk Road   Walk 1963

Not the first of the adventures of Dorian Silk and not a bad tale by any means, though hardly a detective story. The Afghan scene is well done, says a woman writer on Afghanistan to whom WHT lent the book, and there is a telling tableau in which the strongly hinted-at treachery of one of Silk's comrades in espionage is brought just close enough to the surface without breaking out.

1098   HARVESTER. See also:

The Bamboo Screen   Jarr 1955

1099   HASTINGS, MACDONALD (b. 1909)

Cork in Bottle   Knopf 1954
    Map of Stagg Hall Estate, East Anglia

If one likes Cork, this may pass, but the emotions and the traipsing around strain patience and credulity.

1100   Cork on Location   Walk 1967
    In Eng.: Cork on the Telly

Aside from a few amusing insights into British television practice, this story about Montague Cork's efforts to recover a million pounds' worth of jewels insured by his firm has little to recommend it. The author uses too much cardboard and enjoys too much muddling about in snowdrifts. As for the jewels, one knows from p. 18 where they will eventually be found.

1101   Cork on the Water   RH 1951

Rereading this earliest Cork fifteen years after publication, WHT found it full of good things; the stuffy but engaging Cork himself being not the least. The elderly insurance director on the trail of a murderer in Scotland is suitably handled, and the fishing atmosphere not overdone.

1102   HASTINGS. See also:

Cork and the Serpent   MJ 1955
Cork in the Doghouse   Knopf 1958

HAWTHORNE, JULIAN (1846–1934)

Son of Nathaniel Hawthorne, educ. U.S. and abroad, reared in England, but returned to make a name for himself as a writer of popular melodramatic novels, beginning with *Bressant* in 1873. Side by side with these he produced half a dozen novels of crime and detection about Inspector Byrnes and some short stories, besides editing the valuable Lock and Key Library (No. 2568).

1103   Section 558; Or, The Fatal Letter   Cass 1888
    From the Diary of Inspector Byrnes

Straight thin cardboard from p. 1, without even the pretense at representing a policeman or his diary. The case is poison-pen stuff followed by murder and interspersed with high sentiment and the then common distrust of "finance." When the pitiable plot is untied, the praise given to the

Inspector for his shrewd efforts (i.e., posting men to watch mailboxes) reads like irony. Other volumes in this series look no different on quick inspection.

1104   HAWTHORNE. See also, from Inspector Byrnes' diary:

An American Penman	Cass 1887
Another's Crime	Cass 1888
The Great Bank Robbery	Cass 1887
A Tragic Mystery	Cass 1887

1105   HAWTON, HECTOR (b. 1901)

Murder by Mathematics   WL 1948

The story is not, of course, about murder *by* mathematics; it is a murder loosely connected with the mathematics department of a college (English and poorly defined). The character of Sir Clifford is made repellent from the start as that of an egotist without self-knowledge—or plausibility. He is involved with women, and moreover has managed to steal a colleague's formula, nothing less than the solution to Fermat's theorem! A few good passages about other characters do not redeem this fourth novel, whose ending is huddled.

1106   HAWTON. See also:

Murder at H.Q.	WL 1945
Murder Most Foul	WL 1946
Unnatural Causes	WL 1947

HEAD, MATTHEW (pseud. of John [Edwin] Canaday, b. 1907)

As art critic for the *New York Times,* Canaday has written *The Mainstream of Modern Art* (1959) and *Embattled Critic* (1962). As Matthew Head he has written several detective stories, the best being set in Africa and presenting the collaboration of Dr. Mary Finney, an African medical missionary, with her friend Emily Collins, and the young narrator, Hooper Tolliver.

1107   The Accomplice   S&S 1947

A story set in Paris and mostly about love and trust, though the challenge to these arises out of conspiracy and crime. Not up to the "African" standard.

1108   Another Man's Life   S&S 1953

The confession by a double murderer of the causes and consequences of his acts. Not a success in this difficult and overattempted genre.

1109   The Cabinda Affair   S&S 1949

The reader is caught by the attractive scene—a small Portuguese enclave at the mouth of the Congo River—and by an interesting family situation. But the story is flawed by the manner of its telling: Tolliver recites the facts as he remembers them while Dr. Finney drives him around Brazzaville in her old jalopy. As for the investigation of the trouble following a broken "mahogany contract" and several broken souls, it seems too much compressed. The character of Mary Finney comes off best in what is not a perfect whole.

1110   The Congo Venus   S&S 1950

The best of the Mary Finney tales. The heavy dose of Brazzaville is not excessive, any more than the byplay between the two women missionaries and Hoop Tolliver, who plays Watson. The humor is first-class, like the ending; and the killing of an old flame and covering up by someone else makes a good puzzle. As usual with Head, a picturesque confession helps.

1111   The Devil in the Bush   S&S 1945

Told in the first person by Hooper Taliaferro [*sic*], the maiden appearance of that inquisitive young man under the original spelling of his name. Scene: the Congo, where Dr. Finney and Mary Collins turn up and solve a murder in the middle of a native revolt. The motive is commonplace but the tricks are excellent, and so are the characters.

1112   Murder at the Flea Club   S&S 1955

Found entertaining by JB, who is glad, for once, not to be in Brazzaville and its girls with or without bras. The atmosphere of Paris is authentic, the characters are plausible despite their bibulousness, and the crime is simple and solid, like the detection. One might argue that the title is unattractive and even unfunctional.

1113   The Smell of Money   S&S 1943

Not in Africa, not featuring Hoop Tolliver and the lady missionaries, but an attempt to do a gathering of pseudo artists who sponge on an extremely rich old lady near San Francisco. The slow buildup, given by the young painter and curator Bill Echlen, is not much more convincing than the murder and its unreasoned unraveling, while the steady drone of snappy talk about this large complex of neurotics makes it hard to finish the book or care about its outcome.

HEARD, H(ENRY) F(ITZGERALD) (also Gerald Heard; b. 1889)

b. London; educ. Cambridge; science commentator for the BBC; lecturer at several American universities; author of numerous books about contemporary culture, religion, sex, and morality, as well as one or two historical summaries of the modern period. See especially *These Hurrying Years: 1900–1933* (C&W 1934).

1114   A Taste for Murder   Van 1941
          Orig.: A Taste for Honey

A curio, with sufficient special interest to outweigh the annoying mannerisms of Sydney Silchester (the narrator), who, one hopes, does not derive from the author's ideal of himself. The science is shaky but amusing: "Mr. Mycroft" is an unconvincing latter-day Holmes.

1115 HEARD. See also:

The Great Fog (ss), No. 3418	Van 1944
Murder by Reflection	Van 1942
The Notched Hairpin	Van 1949
Reply Paid	Van 1942

HEBERDEN, M(ARY) V(IOLET); also Charles L. Leonard; b. 1906

A very capable woman writer whose routine work deals with Desmond Shannon, another Irish private eye with a censorious middle-aged secretary and an unquenchable idealism that makes him take up hopeless cases. But M.V.'s occasional books unencumbered by Shannon are superior stuff.

1116 Engaged to Murder   CCD 1949

Many stories tell of murder at a dinner party, but this example is very nearly unflawed. The Buenos Aires scene is discreetly done and most enticing, the seven prime suspects are credibly such, and the investigation conducted by private eye Rick Vanning, with the help rather than the hindrance of the local police, is systematic and sober. The characters are Anglo-Argentines, Americans, and French expatriates. Add to the merits a satisfactory showdown and unmasking at the end.

1117 They Can't All Be Guilty   Dday 1947

A well-knit and characteristic Desmond Shannon story, in which he takes on all the crooked politicians and bankers in town to save a boy framed for a murder. If it has to be done at all, let it be done this way.

1118 To What Dread End?   Hale 1952
        In U.S.: The Doctor Was a Lady

Though it may seem to some surprisingly slow in getting under way, this tale, laid in England during the last world war, is a splendid example of anxiety without harrowing. Not much detection, but enough to be reread with renewed admiration and pleasure.

1119 HEBERDEN. See also Nos. 1367–8 and:

The Case of the		Murder of a Stuffed Shirt	CCD 1944
Eight Brothers	CCD 1948	Murder Unlimited	CCD 1953
Murder Cancels All Debts	CCD 1946	Subscription to Murder	CCD 1940
Murder Follows		That's the Spirit	CCD 1950
Desmond Shannon	CCD 1942	Vicious Pattern	CCD 1945

1120 HECKSTALL-SMITH, ANTHONY (b. 1904)

The Man With Yellow Shoes   Wing 1957

British intelligence work in the Near East: picturesque and above average in style, but much like others in plot.

1121   Murder on the Brain   Roy 1958

Nicely written but undistinguished. The crime is the shooting of a lewd
comedian on the stage of a British summer theater (or rather, music hall)
by the ancient method of loading a stage pistol with live ammunition and
letting someone else do the job. Inspector Hyde is over-tall, something of a
gourmet, and uninteresting. Detection practically nil.

1122   HECKSTALL-SMITH. See also:

    Crime Without Punishment (criminology)   Wing 1955
    Where There Are Vultures   Roy 1958

1123   HELY, ELIZABETH (pseud. of Elizabeth Hely [Mrs. William
    Anthony] Younger, b. 1913)

    Dominant Third   Hein 1959
      In U.S.: I'll Be Judge, I'll Be Jury

A honeymoon couple in Paris is shattered by the murder of the bride. The
technique of narration and unraveling is original but unsuited to detection,
a main interest being the depicting of lower-middle-class life in Paris.

1124   The Long Shot   Hein 1963

This time Austria is the locale, and the adventure is virtually a Gothic
melodrama played out among people who are heartless and cruel. As
usual, good telling but little intellectual interest.

1125   A Mark of Displeasure   Scrib 1960

Although the identity of the murderer is known from the beginning, the
author achieves the nearly impossible feat of making the exploits of a
visiting French detective (one Cirret) plausible, sensible, and moderately
exciting. The Music Festival is brought in for good reasons, and the local
color is excellent. The theme, however, verges on the *allzuweibliches.*

    N.B. *Blue Moon in Portugal* (1958), written with her husband (=
William Mole, q.v.), is a travel book, not detection.

1126   HENDERSON, DONALD (LANDELS) (b. 1905)

    Mr. Bowling Buys a Newspaper   RH 1944

Raymond Chandler liked the realism of this tale, so different from the
works of A. A. Milne and Agatha Christie. Today the realism seems a
bit thin, and what remains of interest is the reason why Mr. B. is so often
intent on buying a newspaper. The reason is that he makes news, secretly,
but would prefer his acts to go unpublicized. Entertaining if the repetition
of the formula does not get on your nerves.

1127   A Voice Like Velvet   RH 1946

By day Ernest Bisham announces for the BBC. On his nights off he is a
cat burglar, blithe and careless. Good about the BBC.

1128   HERBERT, [SIR] A(LAN) P(ATRICK) (b. 1890)

   The House by the River   Knopf 1921

A story of deception and murder, but in no sense a detective or crime
story. The killing comes in the last few pages and is the working out of an
artist's odyssey in life and love, not a departure planned by anybody.
Worth reading for what it is, and unique in the author's output for the
avoidance of gaiety and humor.

1129   HEXT, HARRINGTON (pseud. of Eden Phillpotts, q.v.)

   The Thing at Their Heels   Macm 1923

Unorthodox in form but powerful in effect. Seldom has Phillpotts used his
knowledge of the countryside and his feeling for passionate characters
more artfully to produce a series of murders that are clearly described and
assiduously investigated—though without result till the very end, when all
the talk about socialism and religion finds its due place as part of the plot
and the solution is given without diminishing the stature of Inspector
Midwinter. The elimination of the Templer family then appears inevitable though unjust. A masterpiece in a rare variety of the species.

1130   Who Killed Cock Robin?   Macm 1924
       In Eng: Who Killed Diana?

The author's concern with moral strength and weakness and his power to
create dramatic scenes are evident in all his works. Not so his judgment
about details. The crime in this novel occupies only the last 100 pages out
of 350, and the detection is but a part of the part; so one is left with many
questions about the sinister murder plot, its execution and reconstruction
by the colorless Nicol Hart, private investigator and friend of the accused.
Other participants are well-drawn, and the tale repays reading, once. But
this writer is at his best in more rural, less fashionable settings than this.

1131   HEXT. See also:

   The Monster   Macm 1925
   Number 87   Macm 1922

   HEYER, GEORGETTE [Mrs. George Ronald Rougier] (b. 1902)

The republishing of her detective *corpus* in the mid-fifties—that is, some
twenty years after their first appearance—attests to the sterling merits of
this inadequately prized writer. She ranks with Sayers, Allingham, and
Marsh, possessing the sure touch of the first and avoiding the occasional
bathos of the other two.

1132   Behold Here's Poison   Hein 1936

One of the early large-English-family stories and also one of the early uses
of nicotine as a dispatcher. The chief interest lies in the mutual suspicion,
the side aberrancies, and the determined lying of some seven people. The

nephew Randall is one of Georgette's favorite "snake" types, who turn out decent once the motive for the foulness is made clear. Inspector Hannasyde is present and passable. Not the very best Heyer.

1133   A Blunt Instrument   Dday 1938

The author's masterpiece when one is reading it, for there is another contender for the title (see No. 1134). This is the tale that opens with P. C. Glass looking over the dead body. He quotes Scripture with the frequency and appositeness of Betteredge quoting Robinson Crusoe in *The Moonstone*. Characters excellent and plot superb. Inspector Hannasyde's detection is worth every bit of one's professional attention.

1134   Death in the Stocks   Hein 1952/1935
In U.S.: Merely Murder

Equal to *A Blunt Instrument,* and therefore a masterpiece also. The plot is neat, the circumstances picturesque, and the brother and sister who protect each other while making others miserable around them by effrontery and sarcasm are the perfection of tightrope-walking over dangerous excess. Hannasyde is not a brilliant detective, but he commands respect and does not merely go round in circles.

1135   Detection Unlimited   Hein 1953

The second after her return to detection and a trifle too unlimited: the story is mostly gossip in the county set, entertaining enough when you add the byplay between Inspectors Hemingway and Harbottle, but not the kind of thing we expect from G. H. in top form. The ten people who hated the victim are never really worth suspecting, even the culprit, and both mechanics and detection lack the serious touch amid the chatter.

1136   Duplicate Death   Hein 1951

According to the publishers, this book marks G. H.'s return to detection after a ten-year lapse covering the war years. The result is by no means dazzling. The characterization is good only in spots, and the terror and suspense are a little long-drawn-out. Chief Inspector Hemingway, never a genius, remains a pleasant companion to crime.

1137   Envious Casca   Hein 1941

The large family of rough-tongued gentry with a few outsiders brought in for a Christmas party follows a predictable pattern in which G.H.'s humor and good observation occur only fitfully, side by side with bad boners. It is a locked-room murder, solved by Inspector Hemingway, since Hannasyde is now superintendent and therefore sedentary. Hemingway is steadily rude to his sergeant, but he does latch on to the essential fact. Incidentally, Miss H.'s French is usually good, but in this book she consistently misspells *ouistiti,* the "little monkey" implement for locking and unlocking doors from the wrong side.

1138   Footsteps in the Dark   LG 1936/1932

A less than successful attempt to combine banter with spookery and to
ring the changes on the old dodge of covering up criminal activities in a
ruined priory by ghostly happenings that should scare away the new
tenants. Only at the end does G. H. show that she has a born detective
mind, by thinking of clues even after they don't matter.

1139   No Wind of Blame   CCD 1939

Possibly not to be enjoyed on a first reading. On a second, it will be found
to contain excellent humor and the memorable characters of Ermyntrude
Carter and her daughter Vicky. Not principally a tale of detection, it
nevertheless belongs in the canon of her tales of mystery.

1140   Penhallow   Hein 1942

A long story about a family of terrorizing and oversexed males, embroiled
with one or two victimized females, halfwits, illegitimate boot boys, and
others. Very British, rural, and somewhat artificially "tense." Its resemblance to several other tales of English family life dominated by some old
man or woman does not endear it to these readers, though here technique
is equal to all improbabilities.

1141   They Found Him Dead   CCD 1937

Another large-English-family affair. Silas Kane is found dead, and a whole
raft of suspects is tossed about for the reader's entertainment. By p. 200
discussion goes on about the possibility that old Kane died by accident.
The witty byplay which often enlivens her tales is curiously absent, so that
this specimen stands in the middle range of her accomplishment. As
always, the writing is excellent and the detection abundant.

1142   The Unfinished Clue   LG 1934

An old boy is shot at his desk, on which there is a pad bearing a half-
written message. As usual, excellent clues, good writing, and solid
suspense—all in spite of rather conventional characters.

1143   Why Shoot a Butler?   LG 1933

In many ways typical of the golden age of detection: the amateur investigator Frank Amberley, who is also a fast driver; the slow village constable;
the sulky girl discovered in incriminating circumstances; the girl's dog—
all are given the full treatment. And the title is not the least clever bit in
the story.

1144   HICHENS, ROBERT (SMYTHE) (1864–1950)

       The Paradine Case   Benn 1932

By the author of the famous *Green Carnation* (1894), which is a fictional
parody of aestheticism—"the arsenic flower of an exquisite life"—the

present tale is a well-plotted and well-written novel of a KC's failure to save a woman who has murdered her blind hero-husband. She makes use of her charms to embroil everybody, because she is passionately in love with another soldier and considers anyone a means to her purpose. Some detection, long harangues, yet the 450 large and closely printed pages are worth reading—once.

1145 HIGHSMITH, (MARY) PATRICIA (also Claire Morgan; b. 1921)

The Talented Mr. Ripley   CM 1955

Not a detective story, but a well-told tale of psychology and suspense, which displays an unusual grasp of the doings and feelings of a couple of ambivalent males on the loose in Italy—one of them commissioned by the father of the other to get him to come home to the U.S. The book is good, but the moving picture *Purple Noon,* made from it in Italy, is even finer.

1146 HIGHSMITH. See also:

Strangers on a Train   Harp 1949

1147 HILLERMAN, TONY

The Blessing Way   Harp 1970

An interesting departure about settings: the first Indian (Navajo) reservation (but see No. 2617). The characters and superstitions that entangle whites, Navajos, and cultural hybrids are attractive and they sound authentic. But if the author is to exploit this wild region as Upfield did the Australian aboriginal scene, he will have to devise less routine plots. Here the self-pitying hero with hackneyed marital troubles, the perfunctory romance, and the unbelievable feats of survival and retaliation by people badly wounded and hemorrhaging make the reader impatient. So does the excess of fact and repetition in the first part, before the story proper begins.

1148 HILTON, JAMES (also Glen Trevor; 1900–54)

Was It Murder?   Harp 1935
    Orig.: Murder at School (*by Glen Trevor*)

Sound and satisfying. Colin Revell is thoroughly believable as the semi-unwilling (old boy) private detective at Oakington School; the school atmosphere is expertly rendered; the identity of the murderer comes as a lively surprise; and the motives stand up to scrutiny.

1149 HILTON, JOHN BUXTON

Death of an Alderman   Walk 1968

English north country tale about the life of a murdered "pillar of society." Detective Superintendent Kenworthy is made interesting enough, but his detection consists chiefly in prying into the secrets of love, life, and finance, with the aid of one of the town's female teen-agers. The ending is nicely turned and timed, but the tale as a whole is not for rereading.

1150 HIRSCHBERG, CORNELIUS

Florentine Finish   Harp 1963

The author is a jewelry salesman, and this is his first detective story. Interesting and presumably authentic background of the New York diamond trade, with a reasonably clear plot involving the placing of stolen goods in the stock of reputable merchants when honest diamonds are flying about. There is a not wholly believable heroine and some rather artless Western background to provide motive for the five murders. JB liked it better than did WHT.

1151 HITCHENS, BERT [HUBERT] and DOLORES (BIRK OLSEN) (also Dolan Birkley and Noel Burke; b. 1907)

End of the Line   Dday 1957

Good railroad atmosphere, as in the earlier *F.O.B. Murder,* but not much more. Again a pair of railroad detectives work out the case and their own relationship simultaneously. The former story featured theft of baggage and went haywire at the end; this one reinvestigates a tunnel wreck of six years' standing, also in Southern California. The plot is weak, though fairly well set forth.

1152 HOBSON, FRANCIS

Death on a Back Bench   Harp 1959

Written by a political newspaper reporter who knows his London and Palace of Westminster, this is an attempt to combine suspense with farce in the Delano Ames fashion. Nuclear secrets (for once not stolen for treason) and murder in the House of Commons are handled efficiently but without real tension. Farce should not be a random seasoning. Here it makes one feel that the bright young couple are never really running any risk.

1153 HOBSON, HANK (actually Harry Hobson; also Hank Janson; b. 1908)

Death Makes a Claim   Cass 1958

Another English version of the U.S. private-eye genre. It is all blondes, coshing, murders in TV studios, impossible homosexuals, and "magnates." The rushing about and wenching are unintentional parody. The problem itself is not bad: which of the expensive voices insured by Radiovision House has faked loss of same and has also brought about the real ailment in the others? Motive is never clear, and the tapped tapes and "sophisticated" throat lozenges and final murder could have been better packaged.

1154 HOBSON, H. See also:

The Gallant Affair   Cass 1957

1155 HOBSON, POLLY

Murder Won't Out   HJ 1964

An English village scene, fitted out with a reasonably unprepossessing
Inspector and a good least-likely criminal detected by her habits, but not
really brought to book. Mediocre.

1156 HOCKING, ANNE ([Mrs.] Mona Naomi Anne Messer)

Death Disturbs Mr. Jefferson   CCD 1950

An English story about the poisoning of a subtle criminal with a passion for
collecting rare glass. Inspector Austen of the CID goes through the usual
careful and convincing paces. The criminal, at first obvious, recedes, and
then comes back into first place. Characterization good and style more
mature than in earlier tales.

1157 A Victim Must Be Found   CCD 1959

Blackmail again, unconvincing, and written up in a tone sickeningly coy.
Superintendent Austen and his assistants do nothing of interest.

1158 HOCKING, MARY, writes about Miss Milverton and other heroines in
situations of anguish and danger. See *Death Leaves a Shining Mark*
(1943) and *Poison Is a Bitter Brew* (1942).

HODGKIN, M(ARION DE KAY) R(OUS)

Daughter of Dr. Peyton Rous, well-known New York physician and Nobel
Prize winner. Married Alan Hodgkin, British physiologist, in 1944 (Nobel
Prize, 1965), now living in Cambridge; four children, three detective
stories, one of them unwritten!

1159 Dead Indeed   Macm 1956

Written with the same felicity and wit as her first story, but less satisfactory in plot and outcome. Still, not to be overlooked among stories that
use a publishing house for locale. What makes this tale a little oppressive
is the presence of too many women, though this surplus is plausible in the
"juvenile" trade. But their antics and refusals to hear, or to tell or to
understand, bring the plot within inches of HIBK. Fortunately, the author
has a good head and things are worked out in reasonable fashion.

1160 Student Body   Scrib 1949

A coed college story ("Caradoc College" being a composite of various
real and imaginary Midwest, Pennsylvania, and near-South colleges).
Though very well written, the tale suffers from a complex plot that the
official police are never given a fair chance to unravel, and the amateur
detection multiples clues out of proportion to the work done with

them. Still, there are interesting characters, a nice case of academic fraud, two murders, and an amusing branch-line railroad with a preposterous 300-foot-high trestle.

1161   HOLDEN, GENEVIEVE (pseud. of Genevieve Long Pou, b. 1919)

Deadlier Than the Male   CCD 1961

Here is more evidence tending to show that it is possible for an author of detective fiction to outgrow his or her earlier deficiencies. Miss H. has written at least three other tales featuring the deep South and miscellaneous private eyes, examination of which disclosed nothing palatable. The present work differs markedly. Hank Ferrell, the private detective, is a plausible ex-cop; the chase of a lady who does in one rich husband after another is reasonable; and it is enlivened by the discovery that she is hot on Ferrell's trail.

1162   HOLDING, ELISABETH SANXAY (1899–1955). James Sandoe neatly summed up her work as: ". . . half-understood horrors viewed in a nightmare of uncertainties." There is usually a large dose of family wrangling, too. See *The Innocent Mrs. Duff* (1946). *The Obstinate Murderer* (1938) is perhaps less trying.

1163   HOLMES, GORDON, is the pseud. of Louis Tracy (q.v.), as well as of Tracy and M. P. Shiels (q.v.), under which joint name were published *By Force of Circumstance* (1909) and *The House of Silence* (1931), both negligible.

1164   HOLMES, H. H. (pseud. of Anthony Boucher, q.v.)

Nine Times Nine   DS 1940

This early story introduces several of the characters that we find again in *Rocket to the Morgue,* and in the same unsatisfactory way. Apart from elements extraneous to the plot (e.g., good theorizing references to Sherlock Holmes), the story is messy, and the motives weak and hard to credit. Domesticity and calf love take up space and leave Lieutenant Marshall little chance to shine. It is Sister Ursula who does the work of explaining a locked-room murder arising out of a Los Angeles "cult." Why the author borrowed the name of a murderous American maniac of the nineties is hard to fathom.

1165   HOLT, GAVIN (pseud. of Charles Rodda, b. 1891). Among numerous rather undistinguished novels, *The Theme Is Murder* (1939) stands out for its attempt to provide a musical (mainly operatic) background.

1166   HOLT, HENRY

The Midnight Mail   Dday 1931

A tale of Scotland Yard detection purporting to deal with a crime committed in a train. Actually, the train plays no significant role, and the story is absurd.

1167 HOLT, VICTORIA (pseud. of Eleanor Burford Hibbert), is a writer of feminine fantasy and adventure—garden-club Gothic, e.g., *Mistress of Mellyn* (1960).

1168 HOMES, GEOFFREY (pseud. of Daniel Mainwaring, b. 1902). His dozen works of adventure span the decade beginning in 1936. See *The Doctor Died at Dusk* (1936) and *Then There Were Three* (1945; orig. 1938).

1169 HOPKINS, KENNETH (b. 1914)

Dead Against My Principles   Macd 1960

A semicomic tale, not particularly well written, about corpse substitution on the Isle of Wight. A deep-freeze unit and blackmail are involved, as well as three very old people—an old maid and two bachelors—who act as a triune detective. They are to be shunned.

1170 HORLER, SYDNEY (also Peter Cavendish and Martin Heritage; 1888–1954). The creator of Tiger Standish attempted to follow in the Buchan tradition, but what he wrote was essentially for juveniles.

       Association Item
1171 HORNIBROOK, F. A.

The Culture of the Abdomen   Hein 1924
       Illus.

In Frank Arthur's tales of Suva (qq.v.), this "programme of exercise for the abdominal muscles which will enable them to function efficiently" ruled the mind (and muscles) of Inspector Spearpoint. It is no doubt an admirable book, ludicrous as may be its solemn injunctions ("Tensing and Retracting; Pumping") and its satirical use by the ingenious writer of detective fiction.

1172 HOUGH, S(TANLEY) B(ENNETT) (also Rex Gordon and Bennett Stanley)

The Tender Killer   Walk 1959
       Orig.: The Bronze Perseus

A remarkably adroit telling of the story of a man convicted of rape on a false accusation by a woman, whom he seeks out after his release. He then commits a robbery, marries the woman, and kills her, not out of revenge but pity—only to find himself confronted by a perceptive sergeant of police, who destroys all his rationalizations and punishes him by letting him continue believing that he will be pursued. Not detection, but crime psychology as it ought to be done. It makes one eager to look up *Dear Daughter Dead* (Walk 1966).

1173 HOUSEHOLD, GEOFFREY (b.1900). *Rogue Male* (1939) and *A Rough Shoot* (1951) are good examples of this author's not unsuccessful patterning after Buchan.

1174 HUBBARD, P(HILIP) M(AITLAND)

Flush as May   Maxw 1963

Considerable art, a well-controlled wit, and a fresh approach characterize
this tale of murder in a remote Wiltshire village. A credible pair of Oxford
undergraduates (m. and f.) unearth the "secret of the village," which includes, and to some extent justifies, the murderer. For WHT, a delightful
evening's reading. JB prefers by far P.M.H.'s skits in *Punch*.

1175   High Tide   Ath 1970

The author has forsaken his former whimsical style and has produced a
straight suspense yarn with few characters and great continuity. The hero,
Curtis, has just completed a term of four years in jail for killing a man
whose car had killed Curtis' dog. The mystery is: What did the last
mumbled words of the dying man mean, especially in relation to the fact
that Curtis is being kept under close and unfriendly scrutiny as he proceeds by car and boat along the Devon coast? Told by the hero, who
supplies several love episodes and some good exploring of tidal waters to
hold the reader's attention.

1176   Picture of Millie   MJ 1964

WHT continues to approve even this flawed effort. An ambiguous and
never fully documented detective (he is on holiday), a repetitive style,
and a questionable matter of law-and-morals inherent in the "trick ending" did not keep him from enjoying a couple of the characters and the
well-done sea- and landscapes. JB disliked it all.

1177   HUGHES, DOROTHY B(ELLE) (FLANAGAN) (b. 1904)

The Expendable Man   RH 1963

In the attractive setting of Phoenix (Ariz.) and nearby Scottsdale, a young
Negro intern from L.A., Dr. Hugh Densmore, has to fight to get evidence
that will keep him from being convicted of the murder of a hitchhiker
(white teen-age female), whom he had picked up en route to his cousin's
wedding. Good suspense and worthy handling of the race relations, made
a bit less heartbreaking than usual because of the standing and financial
means of the hero's relatives.

1178   HUGHES. See also:

        The Davidian Report   DS 1952
        In a Lonely Place   DS 1947
        The So-Blue Marble   DS 1940

1179   HULL, HELEN

        A Tapping on the Wall   DM 1960
             The College Faculty Prize Mystery

Uncommonly moving and compact account of a few weeks in the life of a
wife-ridden professor of English, who is roused from his usual torpor by

injustice done to a young woman graduate student through gossip in his department. The university setting is excellent (albeit a mixture of a large metropolitan with a much smaller institution), and the touch of parapsychology is not distasteful. There is a death but no detection or real mystery.

HULL, RICHARD (pseud. of Richard Henry Sampson, b. 1896)

b. London; educ. Rugby; a chartered accountant by training. Famous after writing *The Murder of My Aunt** and others in the tour-de-force class. His ingenious plots are marred for us by a streak of cruelty beyond the needs of modernism in crime.

* Not to be confused with *Death of My Aunt,* by Hull's contemporary C. H. B. Kitchin (b. 1895).

1180   Excellent Intentions   Faber 1938

There is no turn of the screw in this one—unless one takes the victim to be too nasty to believe in—and the underlying idea is good: a lovable spinster polishes off her employer, from conscientious motives and without horror; the trial judge perceives what has happened and takes steps to mitigate her ultimate fate. Beautifully told; a bit of reverse detection.

1181   Keep It Quiet   Faber 1935

This is one of the novels in which Hull displays his penchant for moral or psychological torture. The basic idea is this: a club secretary of weak character fails to satisfy any faction in the club, because he dithers and fumbles. The accident of a death on the premises enables one member to blackmail the secretary into doing many things the blackmailer desires, including persecuting other members. It *could* be called detection, of a sort.

1182   My Own Murderer   Faber 1940

To JB the most gripping and best written of the Hull novels he has read. Not a detective story, but one of conspiracy to substitute an innocent man for the murderer of another by first enlisting the help of the substitute in the concealment of the crime. It may be tripe, but the last 20 pages keep one on the edge of one's chair.

1183   HULL. See also:

Beyond Reasonable		Murder Isn't Easy	Faber 1936
Doubt	Messn 1941	The Murder of	
And Death Came Too	Coll 1939	My Aunt	Mint 1934/1935
The Ghost It Was	Faber 1936	The Murderers of Monty	Faber 1937
Last First	Coll 1947	The Unfortunate	
Left-Handed Death	Coll 1948	Murderer	Messn 1942

1184   HUME, DAVID (pseud. of John Victor Turner; also Nicholas Brady, 1900–45); was a prolific producer of the mid- and late thirties in the chase-and-peril genre. Usually the stories start with crime (a good solid burglary) or lead to it (a clever conspiracy), and the attractive innocents

are caught along the way. For a painless dip into the stream of uncon-
sciousness, try *Call In the Yard* (1955), which contains *The Secret of the
Strong Room, Call In the Yard,* and *Murder Trap.*

1185   HUME, FERGUS W(RIGHT) (1859–1932)

    The Mystery of a Hansom Cab   Hansom Cab Pub. Co. 1887
        *A Startling and Realistic Story of Melbourne Social Life:
        75th Thousand*

That this melodramatic and badly written tale of secret marriage and
threatened respectability was a bestseller earlier in the year that marked
the first appearance of Sherlock Holmes is a measure of what Doyle did
for the genre. In Hume the hero-lover-detective does little or nothing but
mouth clichés, and confession ends the paper-thin suspicion of the
innocent.

1186   HUNT, KYLE (pseud. of John Creasey, q.v.)

    Cruel as a Cat   Macm 1968

This and three other "psychological suspense thrillers" by Creasey feature
the psychiatrist-detective Dr. Emmanuel Cellini. It is to be hoped that the
others in the series present their hero in a more favorable light than does
this first tale. The problem is: who strangled Jim Clayton's cousin Gloria,
and for what purpose has the catlike Midge Benison offered Jim a hiding
place in her attic? Dr. Cellini takes tea with the lady who owns the now
subdivided house and puts her twice in peril of her life before he
accumulates enough evidence to inculpate the obvious villain. Alas, poor
Creasey.
    Note: The English editions of the Dr. Cellini novels appear under the
by-line of Michael Halliday.

1187   HUNT. See also:

    Cunning as a Fox   Macm 1965
    Sly as a Serpent   Macm 1967
    Wicked as the Devil   Macm 1966

1188   HUNTER, ALAN (JAMES HERBERT) (b. 1922)

    Gently by the Shore   Rine 1956

This is much better than the first (*Gently Does It*), though it is all done
by question-and-answer, with a good deal of coincidence to help. The
pseudo-American backchat among the officers is a little trying, but the
finish (collapse of a cliff with a house on top) is grandly managed.

1189   Gently Floating   Cass 1963

Superintendent Gently has a nice outing on the Broads while tracking
down that one of a number of detestable people who might have caused a
depressed fracture in the skull of a local boat builder. Good touches about

yachts and sailing, but predominantly sordid in tone. The author's insistence on a maximum of non-punctuation and his choice of criminal tempt one to characterize the work as "Gently at low tide."

1190   Gently in the Sun   Cass 1959

Dull goings-on at a watering place, where a girl's body is found on the beach, then an old skeleton, finally the ancient history that accounts for an old sea dog's fierce isolation. Except for wearing loud toggery, Gently does nothing but run well behind the developments.

1191   Gently Where the Roads Go   Cass 1962

Gently, according to an English reviewer, is "our native rival to Simenon." He may be; in this book there is certainly a parallel to Maigret's chief merits—dourness and watchful waiting. Gently is partly vamped by a woman who is the lover of a man masquerading as a truck driver. The story is told in fragments—from the press, a policeman's notebooks, and sharp little dialogues. More "literary" than the rest.

1192   Landed Gently   Roy 1960

The creator of Gently appears to be one of those rare authors whose work improves (even though gently) as they write more and more. WHT found this tale of the murder of a young American officer (a gay Lothario) while the guest of the local lord (whose nearest neighbor is the chief constable) quite entertaining. Inspector Gently still sucks peppermints but is quite sensible in his role of adviser to the local constabulary. Some fair character drawing, too. (JB dislikes the tale in toto.)

1193   HUNTER. See also:

Gently Does It	Rine 1955
Gently Down the Stream	Cass 1957
Gently Through the Mill	Cass 1958
Gently with the Painters	Cass 1960

1194   HUTCHINSON, HORACE GORDON (also Horatio Gordon; 1859–1932?)

The Fate of Osmund Brett   Hutch n.d. [1924]

A rather slow-moving tale of considerable charm, with plenty of well-conceived detail involving trains, and a credible detective—all in a London-and-suburban atmosphere. The author was an authority on golf, angling, and other sports, but his half-dozen tales of crime all avoid such frivolities.

1195   The Mystery of the Summer House   Doran 1919
Plan of roads and sketches of summer house and footprints

Perfectly fine work for two-thirds of the way—a good situation, entertaining people, good writing, and a good sense of English gentry-country life. Then for some reason we reach a plateau and never get off it. The detective, though an original, gets to fumble badly and the final twist is also muffed.

1196 HUTCHINSON. See also:

The Crime and the Confessor	Murray 1928
The Foreign Secretary Who Vanished	Hutch [1927]
The Twins Murder Case	Murray [1930]
Murder in Monk's Wood	Hutch [1926]

HUXLEY, ELSPETH (JOSCELINE) (GRANT) (b. 1907)

A cousin by marriage of Aldous and Julian; born in Kenya; her husband a tea expert. She has traveled in Australia, New Zealand, Ceylon, and several parts of Africa, plus the U.S. She writes ably about social and colonial problems and the education of young children.

1197 The African Poison Murders   Harp 1939
          In Eng.: Death of an Aryan

The suspense, "night life," and love affair involving the agreeable detective Vachell are superbly done. A local Nazi bund is used with discretion and does not derail the story into espionage: it is pure detection. The "happenings" are gory and puzzling enough, though the identity of the murderer is a letdown and somewhat overexplained.

1198 The Merry Hippo   C&W 1963

After too long an absence from the mystery lists, this competent author returns with another that affords as much pleasure as any in her output.
    The vice-chairman of an English commission sent to Africa to frame a new constitution for the protectorate of Hapana is murdered with a poisoned sandwich. Such detecting as is done is carried out by Alexander Burton, D. Litt., another member of the commission. The Merry Hippo is the guesthouse where the rather ill-assorted group are put up. Entertaining local color and clever take-offs on colonial sensibilities and committee procedure.

1199 Murder on Safari   Harp 1938

The author's second book, begun on board ship while returning from Africa. The safari, organized for the benefit of Lord and Lady Baradale and their hangers-on, offers a rich opportunity to satirize the iniquities of such organized offensives against unoffending animals, while the theft of Lady B.'s jewels gives Superintendent Vachell another chance to uphold the honor of the Chania Police. Lots of intrigue, risky attempts on Vachell's part to set mantraps, and some clever detection by the use of movies. The old dodge of least likely person is fairly well brought to life, and the book as a whole is first-class.

1200   HUXLEY. See also:

Murder at Government House   Meth 1937

1201   HYLAND, (HENRY) STANLEY (b. 1914)

Green Grow the Tresses—O!   Goll 1965

Much touted by literary critics beginning with J. B. Priestley and including the regular detective-story reviewers, this author may well have
written a good first book about the House of Commons in *Who Goes
Hang?* But if it is like his second, it is not for us. Half of his space goes
to descriptions of belching, bellowing, oily sweat, double chins, and perpetual bad temper, knocking over furniture, malicious pleasure in others'
hurts, screams of "anger and outrage" (a favorite phrase), bullying by a
chief inspector, and stupidity by all and sundry. In the interstices a
murder story is cryptically told and slowly elucidated. Despite everybody's
shouting and "jumping three inches into the air," there are no characters
and no detection, but a barrelful of red herrings.

1202   IAMS, JACK (orig. Samuel H.) (b. 1910)

The Body Missed the Boat   Morr 1947

If not precisely a detective story, this is more fun than five or six of the
usual kind rolled together. Scene: the American consulate at Brazzaville,
French Equatorial Africa. The narrator, Freddy Benson (acting consul),
runs Archie Goodwin extremely close. The tale consists in the elucidation
of the murder of Mallory, U.S. consul, and his temporary encasement in
a gorilla's cage. The sexy French typist and the sweet English girl journalist
are as entertaining as the hero and his friends.

1203   Death Draws the Line   Morr 1949

One of the author's happiest concoctions. The scene is one of those
modern factories where reading matter is put together, in this case a
syndicated cartoon strip. Good murder, high tension, fair ratiocination.

1204   Girl Meets Body   Morr 1947

Not the best Iams. The New Jersey shore is less attractive than Equatorial
Africa and so are the inhabitants. Plot and character being obvious, the
fun seems laid on, and it falls flat, like the horrors.

1205   Into Thin Air   Morr 1952

A story of spying and violence centering in the Voice of America offices in
New York City, coupled with a rather routine love affair, which nonetheless permits Iams to indulge his talent for witty dialogue between young
men and girls. The Voice procedures are well done, and so is New York
life in bars and apartments and newspaper offices; but the Russian strong-
arm stuff is a little hard to take.

1206   A Shot of Murder   Morr 1950

Lightly written, like all the author's semi-detective stories, this one concerns a Midwestern reporter's adventures in Communist Poland. The byplay is mildly amusing, but the plot is a continual strain on credibility.

1207   What Rhymes with Murder?   Morr 1950

Good dialogue and a rapidly twisting intrigue with several strands to it
do not save this tale from being commonplace in effect. That result is
something of a mystery in itself, for the underlying ideas are well suited
to the author's unquestionable humor and sense of fact.

1208   IAMS. See also:

       Do Not Murder Before Xmas   Morr 1949

1209   ILES, FRANCIS (pseud. of Anthony Berkeley [q.v.] Cox)

       As for the Woman   Dday 1939

Dedicated to E. M. Delafield, which raises one's hopes, this story is not
detection or mystery but uncertainty in the loves of a young man and an
older married woman. Berkeley-Cox's liking for what he calls psychology
is to the fore.

1210   Before the Fact   Goll 1932
       A Murder Story for Ladies

The only detection here is incidental to the foolish heroine's gradual
realization through 250 pages that the man she married is a complete
rotter. Anthony Boucher, Boris Karloff, and Louis Untermeyer judged this
a "great mystery." The author's grasp of reality may be judged from his
employment of ". . . a certain alkali . . . in daily use everywhere . . .
an exceedingly powerful poison . . . far too common to be put on the
poison list."

       INNES, MICHAEL (pseud. of John Innes Mackintosh Stewart, b.
       1906)

b. Edinburgh; educ. Oriel, Oxf. Professor of English at Univ. of Adelaide
till 1945. Tutor at Christ Church, Oxf., since 1948. Has written on character and motive in Shakespeare and contributes to *The New Statesman, The
London Magazine,* and *The Review of English Studies.* Began his career
in detective fiction in 1936 with *Seven Suspects* and achieved fame with
Hamlet, Revenge! The next few were too wild for these readers (see *The
Spider Strikes,* 1939), but about 1950 Innes sobered down and produced
a good proportion of first-rate stories. He has also written a dozen novels
without detection and an excellent little book on Kipling.

1211   Appleby at Allington   Goll 1968
       In U.S.: Death by Water

This village tale, cum squire and garden fête, displays M.I.'s strong talents
at their best. The amount of ironic social criticism and deft character-

ization of scenes and people would serve another author for six books, and yet this one gives no sense of being stuffed to choke the reader into admiring. The murders, too, though mechanically dubious, are spaciously handled, and the difficulty of using Appleby, retired and a mere guest, is brilliantly got around. Appleby's wife, Judith, plays an agreeable obbligato to John's speculations and all ends as it should.

1212   The Bloody Wood   Goll 1966

Innes is very slow about getting going in this story of intrigue and murder for money-and-house by one of three possible heirs. The use of a tape recorder is clumsy and belated, the characters are made out to be more complex and interesting than they actually are, and the author is on one of his Henry James grammatical binges. Not recommended.

The title is an allusion to Frazer's *Golden Bough.*

1213   The Case of the Journeying Boy   DM 1949

A failing attempt to be funny in the manner of Edmund Crispin. The wild plot is full of improbabilities one is willing to swallow, but the long-winded analyses of feeling and action are intolerable almost from the start.

1214   A Change of Heir   DM 1966

In somewhat lighter vein than usual, and in the absence of Sir John Appleby, Innes manages to be quite entertaining in this straightforward tale of a fraudulent heir to large estates.

1215   The Crabtree Affair   DM 1962

Well knit—more so, perhaps, than others of Innes' recent output. The attractive locale is an abandoned canal, complete with tunnel, and a credible minor country house dating only from 1786. Sir John Appleby and his wife are on holiday and do a good job (she really helps) of exposing the murderer, who is just well-enough concealed. There is only one corpse, and Sir John's detection is simple but honest.

1216   Dead Man's Shoes   DM 1946

This begins in a railway train compartment and has to do with the discovery by an attractive girl of a slain merchant. The hero, not very bright, is enlisted by the girl to help her get over the shock and surprise. Ultimately Appleby gets into it, and a rather too elaborate plot develops, with disappointment for the young man and rising incredulity for the reader. Though not Innes at his best, it avoids his extremest faults.

1217   Death at the President's Lodging   Goll 1936
        In U.S.: Seven Suspects

On rereading, both JB and WHT found their earlier reservations fully justified. Much of the Oxford scene and conversation is empty and pretentious, and there is far too much running about the quadrangles at night on the part of senior dons. Appleby, though personally agreeable, is served up an eyewitness to the highly improbable shenanigans, for the elucidation of which he then takes credit.

1218   Death on a Quiet Day   DM 1958

This affair starts attractively with a student "reading party" and presents some interesting characters, but it soon turns into a fantastic chase, at the end of which Appleby only partly restores order.

1219   A Family Affair   Goll 1969

This story of art frauds, which brings on the Falstaffian figure of Hildebert Braunkopf and engages the interest of Sir John Appleby (retired), is told in the author's most straightforward prose, with plenty of good comedy, besides the occasional dialect of aged peers and Viennese art dealers. How the frauds turn sinister and how Appleby's undergraduate son gets involved make up the rest of an entertaining and murderless tale.

Note: The book was announced as being the first of several featuring young Appleby. No objection to the young, but why Bobby, with its nursery connotation and poor sound pattern with Appleby?

1220   Hamlet, Revenge!   Goll 1937

This early Innes with the magnificent title captivated the imagination of these readers early in their critical career, for the situation, the setting, and the narrative are of high quality, but the solution proved a letdown. It was a great stroke to have the aristocratic damsel pose in the nude (and the moonlight) as garden statuary (though see the earlier No. 600); but other events and details lack reality, and indeed, after this one, Innes went into culpable fantasy.

1221   Hare Sitting Up   DM 1959

After a good start at Oxford, marked by Innes' best academic wit, the story settles down into a tale of spywork, impersonation, and blackmail, which a catastrophic ending does not redeem from mediocrity.

1222   The Long Farewell   DM 1958

Though it seems a fantasy at the beginning, the problem is ingenious and its treatment sustained. The two wives of one dead man are excellent and the good characterization offsets a heavy dose of Jamesian idiom. Note that Innes uses what might be called the intermediate form, not a novel, not a long short story, which has the advantage of making unnecessary the former shoal of red herrings.

1223   The Man from the Sea   DM 1955

A departure for Innes and a good one: the opening situation a Scottish beach at night, the classic chase and escape from the heather to Kensington, and the interplay of motives, deception, and devices—all centering in an inversion of the defector theme—produce a taut and tingling narrative that avoids excesses save perhaps at the very end.

1224   Money from Holme   Goll 1964

By no means a detective story—no Appleby and little suspense—but an amusing though longish account of an artistic fraud carried out under the direction of one Cheel, one of the lowest of art critics ever to reach the fictional page. Here Innes writes with his best skill and uncommon directness. The Hildebert Braunkopf of earlier tales is amusing as before, and so is the political history of the new republic of Wamba.

1225   A Night of Errors   DM 1947

Bloody confusion at Sherris Hall is witnessed by Appleby, who sorts it out more by luck than cunning. There are too many references to "abominable maniacs" and "devouring monsters," about whom Appleby keeps "wondering."

1226   Old Hall, New Hall   Goll 1956

Though the contents are at first glance enticing—a university setting, improbable but amusing professors, and some semblance of plot (for once no Appleby)—this tale of murder by dropping weights on reclining dons is a bad jumble of old and young, prosiness and wit, action and irrelevance.

1227   One-Man Show   DM 1952
In Eng.: A Private View

It begins with a stunning description of a lecture by Mervyn Twist, the art critic, to a group of people in the gallery where the show opening takes place. The account of the facial expressions of the listeners is a marvel, and the ensuing events live up to this flourish of virtuosity. Paintings are stolen from the duke of Horton's mansion (where the murder of *Hamlet, Revenge!* occurred). The object of the chase, the murder, and the missing girl are all well conceived and cleverly combined, and at the end the character of the duke and the melee in which he takes part are excellently done: Innes' undoubted masterpiece.

1228   Silence Observed   DM 1961

Good Innes, but a little crowded with events and double bluffs for the length of the tale. Forgery—of poems and paintings—leads to murders, kidnapping, and a smash finish between a police cutter and a motorboat. Appleby shows his stuff.

1229   There Came Both Mist and Snow   Peng 1958/Goll 1940
In U.S.: A Comedy of Terrors

Told in the first person by a man returning to his family in the country for Christmas. They go in for pistol shooting as a sport and a cousin is shot. Everybody suspects everybody else till Appleby figures out how all can be guiltless. Coleridge is quoted as a clue, and the author rightly terms the story "Much Ado About Nothing."

1230 INNES. See also:

The Daffodil Affair	DM 1942	Operation Pax	Goll 1951
The Dromio Family	DM 1946	Picture of Guilt	Goll 1969
The New Sonia Wayward		The Secret Vanguard	DM 1941
(= The Case of; The		The Weight of the Evi-	
Last of S.W.)	Goll 1960	dence	DM 1943

IRISH, WILLIAM (pseud. of Cornell Woolrich; also George Hopley; 1903–68)

b. New York, son of a civil engineer with whom he traveled widely as a youth. For two years this amiable and prolific writer was a class-mate and friend of JB's in Columbia College, where the two shared English classes, and where Woolrich wrote his first published book, *Cover Charge* (1925). W. I.'s stories show invention and narrative skill, but little wit or variety in characterization. The interest resides in suspense and gimmick.

1231 Deadline at Dawn   Lipp 1960/1944
      In: The Best of William Irish

Slick and steady, but the plot is standard fraud, blackmail, and murder among entirely uninteresting people. Hero and heroine are treated sentimentally, and the only genuine or vigorous emotion is the underlying hatred and contempt for the big city.

1232 Phantom Lady   Lipp 1960/1942
      In: The Best of William Irish

An elaborate and skillful run-around that includes detection and maintains suspense. But in order to enjoy it in retrospect one must forget the longish explanation; for it fails to convince, lacking any but the most simplistic psychology.

1233 IRISH. See also Nos. 2289, 2590, and 2864–9.

JACOBS, T(HOMAS) C(URTIS) H(ICKS) (pseud. of Jacques Pendower; also Tom Curtis, Penn Dowers, Lex Pender, Marilyn Penders, and Anne Penn; b. 1899)

Soldier in the first world war, then a civil servant and writer of more than sixty novels by 1961. Of these, *Target for Terror* (Hale 1961) and *Documents of Murder* (Mac 1933) are secret-service tales. *The Grensen Murder Case* (1943) appears to have been a magazine serial, later turned into a radio drama.

1234 Broken Alibi   Roy 1957

Long sought-after, this story turns out to be a fictional solution of the un-solved Brighton trunk murder case of 1934. The job is well done, though it could have been concluded without bringing in a French adventuress, a semicomic Sûreté inspector, and that dreary recourse of English writers at their wits' end, the South of France.

1235 JAMES, BRÈNI

Night of the Kill   S&S 1961

This tale provides exceptionally good characterization, local color (down-at-heel San Francisco), and true-to-life talk on the part of several characters. The plot as a whole is not up to the standard set by most of the writing, and the counterfeiting business is not convincing. But Gun Matson is a first-rate cop, whose sympathy is not mawkish.

1236 JAMES, B. See also:

The Shake-Up   S&S 1964

1237 JAMES, HENRY

The Other House   Macm 1896

Anybody who wants murder and mystery—to say nothing of suspense—served up in perfect equipoise by a master hand had better read this novel, unjustly neglected by the critics but appreciated by these readers long before the centenary outburst of 1943. One unusual feature of this tale is that the murder is of a child; another is that the work was written as a serial for an English magazine. Not detection in the traditional sense, but surely in the Jamesian.

JAMES, P. D.

b. Oxf., 1920; educ. Cambridge Girls' H.S. Married to a doctor who died in 1944, Mrs. James became a hospital administrator. Her writing is so far a hobby.

1238   Cover Her Face   Scrib 1966; orig. 1962

Her first detective story, immediately pleasing and impressive. The pace is deliberate, the characterization of the members of an English county family very well done, and the central character of Sally Jupp—a servant girl with imagination and a love of power—most unusual but convincing. Inspector Dalgleish is perhaps too quietly competent in his disclosure of Sally's killer—and, despite the title, the girl isn't a Duchess of Malfi.

1239   A Mind to Murder   Faber 1963

This is her second, and excellent it is. Adam Dalgleish, a saturnine widower, publishes poetry and works for Scotland Yard. He is called to investigate a death in a psychiatric clinic, whose administrative officer (female) is found stabbed. The characters are admirably done, including Dalgleish and his ladylove. The author is equally good with porters, nurses, doctors, patients, and lovers, which is saying much.

1240   Unnatural Causes   Scrib 1967

Something of a letdown. The country-house setting and the characterization of the unfortunate criminal are excellently handled, and the powerful
ending under rushing waters is both credible and mysterious, but the
method of murder as well as its cause is farfetched. Dalgleish has had a
tiff with his lover and lets her go out of his life in a psychologically odd
instance of inaction. What next?

1241   JAPRISOT, SÉBASTIEN

The 10:30 from Marseilles   CCD 1963
Compartiment de tueurs, *trans. by Frances Price*

A young woman of easy virtue is found DOA of the *Phocéen* in the
Gare de Lyon on an early October morning. The inspector in charge,
Grazzioni, and his lieutenant, Jean-Loup Gabert, do a good job of tracking
down the other occupants of the six-berth compartment. Much realism
insisted on. Too much byplay between very young boy and older girl.
The movie was faithful and entertaining.

1242   JAPRISOT. See also:

The Lady in the Car With Glasses and a Gun   S&S 1967
A Trap for Cinderella (trans. by Helen Weaver)   S&S 1964

1243   JAY, CHARLOTTE (pseud. of Geraldine Mary Jay, b. 1919)

Beat Not the Bones   Harp 1953

Deals with skulduggery in Malaya; not a true detective story. Fair atmosphere and suspense; not much liked by JB who tires easily of nervous girls.

1244   The Brink of Silence   Harp 1956

New Guinea and vicinity, much native atmosphere, and some art in the
storytelling; no detection.

1245   The Fugitive Eye   Harp 1954

A suspense story pure and simple. A blind man the hero; no detection;
organization poor.

1246   The Yellow Turban   Harp 1955

Little or no detection, but better than any of the preceding. The locale is
Pakistan, and the narrator is interesting even though passive. The man
referred to in the title wears what is actually a saffron-colored turban.
The few digressions are short and worth having, and the "mysterious
East" is not overdone. A good hour's entertainment, for it's very short.

1247   JAY, SIMON (pseud. of Colin James Alexander)

Death of a Skin Diver   CCD 1964

Presumably the author's first, and commendable. New Zealand scene
(Auckland and vicinity) is attractive, and the hero, Dr. Much, is good as

man and pathologist. The Watson is an entertaining lawyer, and the friendly detective sergeant, one St. Giles, is plausible. The plot might have been simplified to advantage, but clues are fair and generous, and the science and psychology stand up to scrutiny.

1248   JEFFRIES, RODERIC (also Jeffrey Ashford and Roderic Graeme; son of G. M. Jeffries; see No. 1017)

Evidence of the Accused   Maxw 1963

Something of a tour de force. Instead of the eternal triangle we have a foursome: one woman and three men. After hubby and his best friend have each made a false confession of murder and after each has been found not guilty at his trial, not much remains but an acroidal solution. The detective superintendent, Pope, is a sound character and the English scene redolent of dogs and brussels sprouts. Well worth reading.

1249   A Traitor's Crime   CCC 1968

A duly tense account of a policeman's leaking news of raids to the crooks and of the framing of another policeman to protect the traitor. On top of this, a struggle between father and daughter over marrying the man who is framed, the father being chief constable. The trial scenes are, as usual with this author, very good; and the dialogue, when it is not tough, serves to make the book a restrained tearjerker.

1250   JENKINS, CECIL

Message from Sirius   DM 1961

Not the science fiction that one might expect from the title, but a regular detective story, embellished with social comment and personal self-searching by the detective, part of it pretentious, the rest not. Situation better than detection, though clue hunting is well to the fore. Scene: a London nightclub, with assorted politicos, professors, journalists—and police.
    Note: The author is lecturer in French at Exeter University, and his book won the Collins Crime Novel Competition jointly with *The Smartest Grave* by R. J. White (q.v.).

1251   JEPSON, EDGAR (ALFRED), 1863–1938, wrote a good many novels of adventure, sprinkled with a little mystery and somewhat less detection, all in the free-and-easy fashion that preceded the rules of art. For good examples, see *The Loudwater Mystery* (1920) and *The Murder in Romney Marsh* (1929). In the former, the plot is solid enough, but the solution is pulled out of the air rather than out of anybody's wits. Jepson also introduced Arsène Lupin to the U.S., in an odd collaboration-adaptation-translation involving Maurice Leblanc (1909).

1252   JEPSON, SELWYN (b. 1899) followed in his father's footsteps, bringing to the genre rather more thrills and stronger motives for revenge, love, etc. *I Met Murder* (1930) was indicative at the outset. A better-known effort, *Keep Murder Quiet* (1941), is a reworking of the *Hamlet* theme, which has been compared to Philip MacDonald's "great story,

Warrant for X." (q.v.). A pleasant account of Jepson's friendship with Max Beerbohm is given in David Cecil's *Max* (1964), pp. 437–40.

JESSE, F(RYNIWYD) TENNYSON [MRS. HAROLD MARSH HARWOOD] (1889[?]–1958)

Daughter of a clergyman and great-niece of Tennyson; began to study painting but turned self-supporting journalist at 20; reviewed for *T.L.S.*, visited U.S., worked for Ministry of Information in first world war; married and collaborated with husband on numerous plays; declared that her "chief passion was murder"; traveled and lived in many countries.

1253   A Pin to See the Peepshow   Dday 1934

The first three parts of the novel deal with the life and loves of the heroine, Julia; only in Book Four do we get the murder of Julia's stodgy and jealous husband. The ensuing trial confirms the earlier suspicion that the work is a fictional account of the Thompson-Bywaters case (1922), despite the usual disclaimer at the front that all the characters are imaginary. The title refers to the children's entertainment at which Julia first met her lover-to-be.

1254   JESSE. See also Nos. 2597–8 and 3196–8.

1255   JESSUP, RICHARD

Cry Passion   Dell 1956

The second and sexy-plus wife of a Georgia tycoon is murdered, naked, after an all-afternoon session with one of her numerous boyfriends. Detective Lieutenant Chester Wierlock nearly cooks his own goose by trying to keep an innocent youth from being framed for the killing. He finally succeeds in locating a key witness (known to the reader since p. 17), by applying the computer technique to mass interviews. JB is impressed by the uncommon plot and some "strong scenes." WHT found it cheap, vulgar, a prototype of slick-magazine writing, with only a bit of "plumbing" to ease the pain.

JOHNSON, E(MIL) RICHARD (b. 1929)

"The fact is, I am a convict. I do my writing from the Minnesota State Prison [at Stillwater], where I have been an inmate since 1964." So wrote Johnson in his second letter to Joan Kahn, mystery fiction editor at Harper, who had suggested revisions in the author's first, unsolicited script.

Stillwater seems to favor writers. It was there that Frank Elli wrote *The Riot* (1967). All this literary work seems not to arouse hostility in the other convicts, and the authorities are glad to bend regulations, so as to allow free time for composition. If the news gets around, they will be receiving applications for admission.

Mr. Johnson is serving a forty-year sentence for a holdup killing, which was also a third offense. He declares that he has no grudge against society and no wish to exonerate himself. He is now extremely well-to-do, thanks to royalties and movie rights.

1256   Silver Street   Harp 1968

The author's first, and a hard-hitting tale of pimping and murder in a
region specified only as "the Strip" of a large American city. The reader
may safely assume that Mr. Johnson knows whereof he writes—i.e., from
inside. There is some but not much detection about Willie, found stabbed
in a Silver Street gutter. The author keeps his compulsive killer credible,
and sheds no false tears when Inspector Lonto discovers the facts about
his one true love. Terse and readable, though scarcely a guide to good
conduct.

1257   JOHNSON. See also:

        Cage Five Is Going to Break   Harp 1970
        The Inside Man   Harp 1969
        Mongo's Back in Town   Harp 1968

JOHNSON, W. BOLINGBROKE (pseud. of Morris Bishop, b. 1893)

The distinguished scholar and critic, biographer of Pascal and noted limeri-
cist, has provided a tantalizing sketch of the life of his alter ego Johnson:
born at Rabbit Hash Landing, Ky., educ. South Dakota Wesleyan, Ph.D.
Teachers College, Columbia Univ.; then asst. editor of *The Boot and
Shoe Recorder* and *The American Mussulman,* Librarian at Okmulgee
A. and M. (Amer. Dairy Goat Assoc.). Pub. two privately printed works
and a novel, *The Jelly-Like Mass.*

1258   The Widening Stain   Knopf 1941

An academic double murder in a library, solved by the semi-young librarian heroine. The relationships are well drawn, but there are few
physical clues and not enough sound work on the space-and-time question. What makes the book delightful is the witty narration, dialogue,
and interspersed limericks.

1259   JONES, ARTHUR E.

        It Makes You Think   Long 1958

An English adaptation of the American private-eye tale by a man who
has written two others before this. Occasional flashes of originality but
no real detection.

1260   KANE, FRANK (also Frank Boyd; 1912–68)

        Poisons Unknown   IW 1953

An undistinguished item in a long series. Johnny Liddell is featureless,
the New Orleans scene is not made particularly attractive (double-crossing
looks much the same anywhere), and the plot is complex without being
interesting. The "poisons" introduced into the orgy-inducing potion provided for the patrons of a phony religious cult are not completely unknown, but more or less surmised to include hashish and yohimbine. The
planner is uncovered through everyone else's being killed off.

1261   KANTOR, McKINLAY

Signal Thirty-Two   RH 1950

There can be little doubt that actual police routine is more like the substance of this book than it is like the streamlined stuff we get in plotted stories that go under that generic term. The repetition, inconsequence, brutality, and language of the gutter that are generously dished out here hang upon a slender thread of interest in the professional development of a rookie, his friendships, and his love pursuit. The dedication to the police of the 23rd Precinct in New York suggests indebtedness for facts as well as atmosphere. The capsule biographies of dozens of figures in the book, the occasionally strange use of words, and the sheer power to keep going through 340 closely packed pages make this work unique and valuable, not as detection but as a documentary.

1262   KATHRENS, (W. H.) VAUGHAN

The Lady Makes News   Mel 1952

Murder in the Manchester offices of a large newspaper chain gives an opportunity for private investigation by the man whose free-lance articles exposing a gambling racket seem to have precipitated the crime. Harry Marston, that fearless journalist, tells the story in a breezy, sexy, modified-U.S. style. Despite a fair use of Berlioz' *Symphonie Fantastique* to parallel the fictional events, the tale is not elegant detection, but thriller stuff with the usual sluggings, sex bouts, escapes, and mistaken identities, ending with exactly the same smash finish as *Death in Ten-Point Bold* (No. 327).

1263   KATHRENS. See also:

Violent End   Mel 1953

1264   KAUFFMANN, LANE

Waldo   Lipp 1960

A novel about murder by the author of *The Perfectionist,* a one-time popular first novel of psychology and manners. Knowing the author, WHT found the present one good reading if judiciously skimmed. The meddling of an elderly amateur of crime in a perfectly justifiable murder contains more shopworn philosophy than detection.

1265   KEATING, H. R. F.

Inspector Ghote's Good Crusade   Dutt 1966

The little Indian Inspector, a somewhat downtrodden figure, has to match his wits against an interesting group of suspects at a Foundation for the Care of Juvenile Vagrants. The head has been poisoned with arsenic, and Ghote does a good job of finding how it was administered, when, and by whom, despite run-ins with the supercilious woman physician of the foundation and with a goodly number of the amusing vagrants. The motive for the crime is credible, which does not always happen.

JB dislikes Ghote and all his works.

1266   The Perfect Murder   Dutt 1965

With this volume the author broke away from the fanciful style and began to give accounts of the ill-treated but conscientious detective—Inspector Ganesh Ghote of the Bombay CID. The "murder" is "perfect" only because Perfect is the name of the intended victim. Plenty of interesting local color and almost as much humor as various English papers and critics claim to have found.

1267   A Rush on the Ultimate   Goll 1961

This author's earlier works were often praised for oddity and "humor" rather than for skill in plotting and detection. In this sample the main activity is a croquet tournament—parts of it very amusing—in the course of which the host gets up early to practice and is hit on his bald dome with a mallet. Detection nil.

1268   Zen There Was Murder   Goll 1960

Surprising in view of the title is the fact that this book gives us less fantasy and more detection than any other book by H.R.F.K. The scene is a large house in which Zen doctrines are being taught to the usual bunch of miscellaneous converts. Objects disappear, people conceal their true or previous relationships, murder is committed by the least likely person (for extraneous motives) and under great pressure of time. The Japanese sage convinces, and one or two of the other people are good also.

1269   KEATING. See also:

   Death and the Visiting Fireman   Goll 1959
   Inspector Ghote Plays a Joker   CCC 1969

1270   KEELER, HARRY STEPHEN (1890–1967) was a writer for the popular magazines, whose plots defy analysis and credibility. Typical titles are: *Find the Clock* (1927), *The Green Jade Hand* (1930), and *The Box from Japan* (1932).

1271   KEENE, DAY

   So Dead My Lovely   Pyr 1959

Both JB and WHT found this cleverly plotted and highly sexed thriller one of the best of its kind. It moves at a good clip and has some genuine human feeling and an outstandingly good smash finish.

1272   KEINZLEY, FRANCES

   A Time to Prey   WHA 1969

An original variation on the theme of mutual suspicion among seven people who are brought together at an isolated spot. This time it is a mountain lodge near Auckland and the seven are presumably being blackmailed by an unknown. Two others, a girl and a young man, are caught up in the violent doings that ensue, and the young man works out the solution amid a good deal of sadism and one or two large improbabilities. Some scenes are extremely well done, others quite clumsy.

1273 KEIRSTEAD, B(URTON) S(EELEY) (b. 1907) and CAMPBELL, D(ONALD) FREDERICK (b. 1906)

The Brownsville Murders   Macm 1933

Read at the time of publication and remembered for its attractive locale (Fredericton, N.B., and upriver). On rereading, WHT felt let down, but the book is still enjoyable, if only for the fact that it is the one tolerable work that contains a disappearing corpse, quickly found again. As expected, the authors indulge in a few harmless pokes at the "culture" of the U.S.

KEITH, DAVID (pseud. of Francis Steegmuller; also Byron Steel; b. 1906)

Educ. Columbia Coll., Columbia Univ.; wrote his first book as an undergraduate—a fictional account of Ben Jonson; became critic, novelist, and scholar in the study of Flaubert and modern French literature. His wife is the novelist Shirley Hazzard.

1274   The Blue Harpsichord   DM 1949
In ppb. as by Francis Steegmuller

This accomplished writer tried something new—the marriage of the frothy (but deep) psychological novel à la Aldous Huxley with crime and the need to vindicate the innocent. The offspring is entertainment but neither detection, mystery, nor social satire. The reader cannot believe in a murder that isn't shown or an alibi that is worked at in bouts of talk about art scholarship, divorce, and internal meditation on the self. If the author took himself seriously, the verdict would be "cock-and-bull"; as he doesn't, it's "chicken-and-calf."

1275   A Matter of Accent   DM 1943

Best out of three, it is a straightforward story that starts in a picture gallery, revolves around Short Wave House (for war propaganda), and winds up with contraband ships, strong-arm violence, and a hairbreadth denouement.

1276   A Matter of Iodine   DM 1940

Even after a quarter century one readily understands how this book won a Red Badge Prize. The crippled young American, Ted Weaver, sent by his brothers to look into "a matter of iodine" (i.e., shipments from France of inferior quality), is unusual and tells his story well. The machinations are credible, pointing, of course, to a foreign power, and in the excitement the young hero overcomes some of his reluctance to face the life he had avoided since his wife's death. There are other sexual overtones and one satirical episode, also sexual, which may be a trifle too subtle to carry their weight.

1277 KELLAND, CLARENCE BUDINGTON (1881–1964). Though one or the other of us used to glance at this writer's work in the *Saturday Evening Post* during the twenties, we soon became content to let *Death Keep[s] a Secret* (1953).

1278 KELLY, MARY (b. 1927)

A Cold Coming   S&W 1956

The author's first story and not so good as the second, flawed as that is. Here the detective Nightingale and his singer wife are lovey-dovey instead of fighting, but the events as a whole are improbable and dull. Two Edinburgh University students get mixed up in a shady scheme run from a nunnery; they are kidnapped, one has a bad attack of nerves, from which Mrs. N., with her husband's approval, helps to rescue him by measures close to those of *Tea and Sympathy*. Meanwhile, girls, an erring doctor, and a poet driven mad by mistreatment confuse the issue till the young hero's classmate is shot dead behind Covent Garden by N.'s fault. Poverty versus wealth are also played on—quite a catchall.

1279 Dead Man's Riddle   S&W 1957

Setting: the University of Edinburgh. The opening scene—a traditional college rag—is a splendid cloak for murder. Then we move to the dealings of the London inspector with the local man and with his own wife, who is an opera singer. It takes pages for the two policemen to appreciate each other, and this routine is repeated for the married pair. On the whole, an entertaining narrative, characters credible, and atmosphere sustained. But the denouement won't do—fake British toughness and international intrigue.

1280 Due to a Death   MJ 1962

A tedious essay in self-torture. The hero detective is a middle-aged man whom the young married heroine pines for, while she is under suspicion of killing a young girl. At the end, in an effort to be gruesome *à la moderne*, there is abortion and the handling of its components. The detective leaves and misery and futility reign, to the author's delight. Is the title not a solecism to boot?

1281 The March to the Gallows   Rine 1965/1964

Told in the first person by a young woman librarian (ill and neurotic, of course), who encounters various undefined and unlikely perils as she scours the lower sections of London for her stolen handbag. The title comes from the fact that the heroine's nephew, aged 11, spends all his spare time playing the Berlioz *Symphonie Fantastique,* fourth movement. No detection.

1282 The Spoilt Kill   MJ 1961

An interesting situation: a private investigator is brought in to trace the source of a leakage of designs for china in an old and tradition-ridden family business in Stoke. The plunge in medias res is neatly geared to the flashback of necessary history. But all goes for naught because the author insists on laying bare each nerve of each character and playing a sinfonietta thereon. A double pity, for two or three of these characters are worth knowing.

1283 KELSEY, VERA

    Whisper Murder!   Coll 1946

Picked up in the hope that it might turn out to be a classic in murder by carbon monoxide, a poison which, in the words of the author, "would rise. More than that, it would penetrate. . . ." Unfortunately it proves to be a trashy tale of arson, in which two hotels are burned down in twenty-below weather. The plot is hideously complicated and the people absurd.

KEMELMAN, HARRY

Educ. Boston Univ. and Harvard, taught until 1942, when he entered government service as wage administrator for the Port of Boston, then set up as free-lance consultant in wage problems and began to write fiction. Won *EQMM* special prize with "The Nine-Mile Walk" (q.v.) in 1946.

1284 Friday, the Rabbi Slept Late   Crown 1964

Styled by the author an "unorthodox mystery." Its chief virtue is its introduction of a scholarly young rabbi, David Small, into the family of amateur detectives who have hitherto been strangers to Small's type of learning. The collaboration between Small and the local Chief Lanigan (naturally Roman Catholic) provides more ecumenical impetus than detectival. New England suburban scene.

1285 KEMELMAN. See also:

    Saturday, the Rabbi Went Hungry   Crown 1966

1286 KENDRICK, BAYNARD (HARDWICK) (b. 1894)

    The Odor of Violets   LB 1941

This is the outstanding feat of the author's blind detective, Captain Duncan Maclain. Though praised by some good judges, he is not so convincing as Bramah's Max Carrados (q.v.). In earlier exploits, e.g., *The Last Express* (1937), when Maclain was not yet blind, he was not an impressive figure, so that he owes his memorability almost wholly to his handicap. But see *Blind Man's Buff* (1943) and Nos. 2605–6.

The 154 closely printed pages devoted to Captain Duncan Maclain's trapping of a female psychopath in the Tennessee mountains are more than enough, despite a few original if rather far-fetched clues and a powerful though long-drawn-out confrontation scene at the end. Not much mystery, either, since the author makes no secret of Marcia Fillmore's propensities.

> KENNEDY, MILWARD (pseud. of Milward Rodon Kennedy Burge; also Evelyn Elder and Joseph Cabot) (b. 1884)

Educ. Winchester and Oxford. Civil servant and journalist; one-time reviewer of detective fiction.

1288   Bull's Eye   Kins 1933

The tale which preceded *Corpse in Cold Storage* and introduced Sir George Bull as a private professional detective. His dubious (though astute) behavior in society is not so amusing as the author intended, and the complications fail of their satirical effect. Not the best Kennedy, by far.

1289   Corpse in Cold Storage   Kins 1934

A disappointment. Too much space is given to the "reactions" of the parties to one another's remarks in the absence of action that would justify such analysis. Even the murder, on an island development, is told at second hand by various people, not including the police. Such detection as there is is done by Sir George and Lady Bull, a pair of genuine gentry who are also genuine spongers and not above blackmail. In short, conception fair, execution poor.

1290   The Corpse on the Mat   Goll 1929

Though amusingly written, this effort is a bit confused and hard to swallow. It presupposes two mirror-image apartment houses side by side and communicating on certain floors. The author's favorite device recurs: a character who is equivocal in thought and behavior turns out worthy of respect for his intelligence if not for his morals.

1291   Death in a Deck Chair   CCD 1931
          Introd. by the author

Solid British detection inspired by the wish to "write a detective story as it really happens." Only toward the end do things get a bit out of hand, with a silly and unnecessary bit of impersonation. Another blemish is the supersmooth Inspector H. H. Huskisson, who luxuriates at Prince's Bay while his CID colleagues in London do all the work. Does this "really happen"?

1292   Death to the Rescue   Goll 1931

An interesting and unusual tale, dedicated to Anthony Berkeley, but resembling nothing in Kennedy's, Berkeley's, or anyone else's output. The narrator is of necessity unpleasant, but convincingly so, and the startling denouement is one which might well occur.

1293   Escape to Quebec   Goll 1946

An extremely good bit of spy nonsense against a background of Canadian lakes, rivers, and islands, all of it free of torture and showing that the low key of an earlier day, even minus sex, holds up very well.

1294   Half-Mast Murder   CCD 1930

At this stage, Kennedy did not yet know how to impart any excitement to detection, whether by action or ratiocination. It thus takes effort to push oneself through the incidents of a murder in a summerhouse, the flag above being found at half mast. The motive remains obscure to the end.

1295   The Murderer of Sleep   Kins 1933

M.K.'s masterpiece. It has a good river, on which the plot is well floated. The people in the village that gives its name to the story, as well as those in the big house at which a party is being given, are equally endearing, and the denouement is satisfactory. Much humor of the right kind, and nowhere outré, as it tends to be in the author's other tales.

The title alludes to *Macbeth*, II, 2, 37.

1296   Poison in the Parish   Goll 1935

A virulent one-page dedication to an unnamed "friend"* is followed by a "Prologue or Epilogue" and the story begins, told in the first person by a middle-aged bachelor whom the chief constable enlists to do a little sleuthing "in the parish." A well-to-do-spinster has died and is then exhumed and found full of arsenic. Superintendent Cole of the CID consults that narrator about local facts and gossip. It is very much a rural tale of small events and jealousies, lightly managed and neither stodgy nor dramatic. The discussions are adequate, and the whole fulfills the plan (with a final surprise) announced in the dedication—"to suspect pleasant and charming people of murder."

* To ———, Esq.

Dear Friend,

I take it that, considering our friendship in no way impaired by the candour of your uninvited criticism, you see no reason why I should not so address you? Very well.

Though you are no book-reader (as, believe me, I should have known without your boasting of it), I dedicate this book to you. In your omniscient superiority, you have pointed out that in all my books, of which you have read so few, the characters are unpleasant: here is an attempt at something different.

[One more paragraph about the unlikelihood of pleasant people committing murder. Then comes the conclusion]:

If you are found with your throat cut, no one will suspect your wife or the bishop, but all will account it suicide.

Most humbly yours,
Milward Kennedy

1297   Sic Transit Gloria   Goll 1937/1936
       Dedicatory Pref. to Victor Gollancz

M.K. here expresses the desire to break the stereotypes of the detective
story and keep the genre alive. But the effort to depict "a few days in
the life of a man whose friend dies" does not accomplish much that was
new in 1936. Against a background of inconsequential policemen and
with the aid of a few good clues, the hero does track down the man who
poisoned Gloria.

1298   KENNEDY. See also:

Corpse Guard Parade	Goll 1929	The Top Boot	Hale 1950
I'll Be Judge, I'll Be Jury	Goll 1937	Two's Company	Goll 1952
It Began in New York	Goll 1943	Who Was Old Willy?	Hutch 1940
The Man Who Rang			
the Bell	CCD 1929		

1299   KENNEDY, ROBERT MILWARD [and MACDONELL, A(RCHIBALD)
       (GORDON)]

       The Bleston Mystery   CCD 1929

A cock-and-bull story of deception and chase, with a least-likely-person
ending. Not worth attention. But see A.G.M.'s solo work, No. 1006–7.

1300   KENYON, MICHAEL

       May You Die in Ireland   CCC 1965

A bad first try showing the antics of the American Professor Foley, who
scampers, impeded by too hairy tweeds, all through Cork and southern
Ireland while pursued by villains never properly identified or motivated.

1301   KEVERNE, RICHARD (pseud. of Clifford James Wheeler Hosken, b.
1882). Highly appreciated by many readers, this writer of mixed mystery
and adventure fails to hold our attention for reasons hard to define and in
no way detracting from his competence. See *The Fleet Hall Inheritance*
(1931) and *The Man in the Red Hat* (1930).

1302   KINDON, THOMAS

       Murder in the Moor   Dutt 1929
       Endpaper map of Dukesmoor

Liked on its first appearance because of its atmosphere and the then
unusual detective—an engaging and able but not omniscient or faultless
creature. The principal interest lies in the eccentricity of Peregrine Smith,
his ingenious inferences from the contours of the moor, and the character
drawing all around. The denouement is slightly burlesque, but acceptable.
    Note: The author apparently waited thirty years before writing another
book, not detection: *Black Béret* (Roy 1959).

KING, C(HARLES) DALY; also Robert Courtney (1895–1963)

Educ. Yale; served in first world war; briefly in business, then dedicated to the scientific study of psychology and to writing, for which purposes he took a Ph.D. at Yale with an electromagnetic study of sleep. With two colleagues published *Integrative Psychology* (1931), and alone *The Psychology of Consciousness* (1932). His last work, *States of Human Consciousness,* and one other were posthumous.

1303   Arrogant Alibi   App 1939
           Three floor plans

Excellent from start to finish. Not much wit, but written in a true style, with knowledge of people's ways and practical facts. Scene laid in Hartford, Conn., at the time of a great flood (March 20, 1936).* The Egyptian business does not interfere.

* JB was there.

1304   Obelists at Sea   Knopf 1933

A mixture of aims: to plan an ingenious murder, to satirize four types of psychology, and to use the atmosphere and limitations of a murder at sea. The writing is stilted and the story slow-moving. Motives are mechanical, people hardly differentiated in manner, and the denouement seems pulled out of a hat, just like the descriptive names of the chief characters. An inferior, though original, tale.

1305   Obelists Fly High   HS 1935

The third in the "Obelists" series and better than the one on board ship (see above). The double twist in this one is legitimate, though the additional surprises of the Prologue (which comes last, not first) are unnecessary and unconvincing. Good flying drama and interesting "psychology" to help out the adventure. Perhaps unique in having one plan, two timetables, and an Index of Clues.

1306   KING, C. D. See also Nos. 2608–9:

          Bermuda Burial   Coll 1930
          The Careless Corpse   Coll 1937
          Obelists en Route   Coll 1934

1307   KING, RUFUS (b. 1893). His French-Canadian Lieutenant Valcour (of the New York police) is intelligent and imaginative in *Murder by the Clock* (1966/1929) though the wordage is excessive and dated.

KITCHIN, C(LIFFORD) H(ENRY) B(ENN) (b. 1895)

b. Harrogate; educ. Clifton and Exeter Coll., Oxf. Novelist and writer on general subjects, who has produced detection sparingly but with care.

1308   Death of My Aunt   HB 1930
The classic model of the first-person story in which the narrator must do the detecting in order to remove suspicion from himself. The other sus-

pect, husband of the murdered woman, is an equally credible character, which makes the running even, and the clues, the ratiocination, and the interplay of feeling among the members of the large family are as effective as the terse, bare prose and the headlong drive of the narrative: no loose ends, no foolish supers.

Note: The author is not to be confused with Frederick Harcourt Kitchin (= Bennet Copplestone, q.v.).

1309 KITCHIN. See also:

The Cornish Fox	S&W 1949
Crime at Christmas	HB 1935
Death of His Uncle	Con 1939

1310 KLINGER, HENRY

Lust for Murder   Trident 1966

The Israeli detective Shomri Shomar first appeared in three tales (see below) presenting him during an extended visit to New York. Here he is on his native sands and, when not too busy attending to the needs of an American movie star involved in the filming of *The Tower of Babel*, he does a fair job of investigating two murders loosely linked with "the pornographic love-coins of Sheba." WHT's verdict is: Just passable, largely because of a good disquisition on the modern use of fingerprints.

1311 KLINGER. See also:

The Three Cases of Shomri Shomar   Trident 1968
(contains:
  Wanton for Murder, 1961; *Murder Off Broadway*, 1962;
  The Essence of Murder, 1963)

1312 KNIGHT, KATHLEEN MOORE (also Alan Amos). Prolific producer of feminine stories, many featuring the featureless Margot Blair. See *The Clue of the Poor Man's Shilling* (1936) and *Design in Diamonds: A Margot Blair Mystery* (1944).

1313 KNOX, BILL (b. 1928)

The Ghost Car   CCD 1966

The author of *The Grey Sentinels, The Killing Game, The Scavengers*, as well as six other tales of suspense-cum-detection not easy to remember. The present one is another of the same type: north Scottish scene, industrial background (testing of the revolutionary Hydrostat Drive car, for which the Russians are panting). Not so the reader of the grisly scenes— the victim's last moments in the 250° F. enameling oven and the well-timed bit of car-aiming that sends the villain to flaming death on a Highland road. Colin Thane is the unremarkable detective from Glasgow.

1314 The Scavengers   CCD 1964

One more item in the current crop of British rough-and-tough tales, and the best we know by this author. Scene: the fishing waters off western Scotland (Ayr harbor and vicinity); subject: the death of a professor of marine biology during a skin-diving expedition to gather specimens. Needless to say, the professor had accidentally come upon evidence of a sinister plot. Scientifically pretty sound and quite suspenseful.

1315   The Taste of Proof   Dday 1965

As the title suggests, the author has taken advantage of Scotland's largest export industry to secure a colorful background for this rather humdrum story. Though the whisky liqueur (not liqueur whisky) business is below true gangster level, the three protagonists form a pretty den of thieves.

KNOX, [MSGR.] RONALD A(RBUTHNOTT) (1888–1957)

Educ. Eton and Balliol, son of bishop of Manchester, brother of "Evoe" of *Punch,* classical scholar, fellow and tutor of Trinity, Oxf. Accomplished theologian, essayist, versifier, Bible translator, and founder of the modern Sherlock Holmes scholarship (see No. 3358), Monsignor Knox was not a born storyteller, but he managed to put together half a dozen detective stories that can be read with varying pleasure for reasons literary and detectival. See also Nos. 2614, 2780, and 2967.

1316   Double-Cross Purposes   H&S 1937

Knox's last detective novel turns on a complex and unrealistic problem involving a young man of good family and his rather shady "colonial" helper, who together plan to hunt for Prince Charlie's treasure on an island in a Scottish river. Thereupon comes the justification for the title, the trickery being observed by Miles Bredon and his wife, representing the insurance interest. At the end of a long book we are asked to marvel at the way in which both Bredon and the swindlers dealt easily and quickly with the problem of interpreting a chart that had been subjected to elaborate optical transposition. More talk than action. (A scarce item, usually misrepresented as being an alternative title of No. 1318).

1317   The Footsteps at the Lock   Meth 1950; orig. 1928
          Map

Not one of our favorite Knoxes: the telling is insufficiently visual and exact. Two ill-assorted cousins canoeing on the upper Thames provide Knox with an opportunity to indulge in double and triple bluff. There is trick photography, too.

1318   Settled out of Court   Dutt 1934
          In Eng.: The Body in the Silo
          Diagrams

One of Knox's neater tales, despite his introduction of a meddling monkey. Title page shows the picture of a silo, and there is a good drawing of the environs of Lastbury Hall. The discovery of two bodies, one at the beginning, one at the end, affords satisfaction of the right kind when coupled with a good turning of the tables on the criminal through a device that might just work (poetic license).

1319 Still Dead   H&S 1934
        Map of estate as endpapers; timetable on page before Contents

A story difficult to keep separate from *Settled Out of Court*. Here we are
told about the fate of Colin Reiver of the Reivers of Dorn, in Scotland,
who kills a child with his car when driving drunk, is acquitted but goes off
to salve his conscience, presumably on a cruise, and is then found dead.
Miles Bredon, investigator for the Indescribable Life Assurance Co., investigates with his wife, Angela, and their son, Francis. Good byplay (as
always) between Miles and Angela and some fair detection: the work is
among Knox's best.

1320   The Three Taps   S&S 1927

Nothing menacing about the three taps—they are only three cocks or
valves distributed along a typical English system of flexible gas piping to
light a hotel room. By turning one and not another it is possible to
asphyxiate oneself without extra charge. A likable gent in a large way of
business and with money to leave is the victim of this heptarchic arrangement, and since the R.C. Church comes into the considerations of the
detective, the enigma has some urgency. The end is a letdown. The good
part is Bredon's wit.

1321   The Viaduct Murder   S&S 1926
            Map and timetable

The separate scenes have great charm and so have the chief characters,
but the presence of a secret passage and the incredibility of what is done
with it are strong detractions from the will to assent. First in order of
publication, it is not first in quality.

1322   KRASNER, WILLIAM (b. 1917)

         The Gambler   Harp 1946

Not a detective story, but a first-rate tale of meanness and crime in dingy
streets. W.K.'s best work.

1323   North of Welfare   Harp 1956

Tries to be more definitely detectival. The figure of Captain Burge is
interesting, the locale still sordid, and the crime too bloody, but what
spoils the tale is the windup with the Christlike figure of the hero.

1324   Stag Party   Harp 1956

Dull, long-drawn-out, and moralizing. Burge is still at it: he interrupts his
holiday to investigate the death of a girl who fell, drunk, from the fire-
escape exit on the second story of a hotel, during a binge-cum-women of
conventioning insurance men. Only a modicum of detection enlivened
by sidelights on immorality in the Ozarks, and depressed by too much
friction between Burge and his assistant.

KUTTNER, HENRY (also Will Garth, Lewis Padgett, and Jack Vance; 1914–58)

b. Los Angeles; became a miscellaneous writer in 1939, married one of his enthusiastic readers, with whom he followed classes in English and psychology at the University of Southern California, continuing to write stories of crime and detection until his death.

1325 Murder of a Wife   Perm 1958
        Published posthumously

This second psychoanalytic tale is superior to *Murder of a Mistress* (1957), which features the same doctor-detective, Michael Gray. He discovers the fears that make the heroine lie, and thereby unmasks the murderer of several people. The relations of the psychologist to the police, to the girl, and to the reader are done with great judgment, and suspense is maintained without melodrama. A pity the author did not live to write more, for he was fully aware of the demands of physical objects, time, and space.

1326 KUTTNER. See also:

The Brass Ring (by Lewis Padgett)   DS 1946
The Day He Died (by Lewis Padgett)   DS 1947
Man Drowning   Harp 1952

KYD, THOMAS (pseud. of Alfred B[ennett] Harbage, b. 1901)

1327 Blood Is a Beggar   Lipp 1946

The Shakespeare scholar, till lately professor at Harvard, wrote this excellent tale as his first foray in detective territory and it is beyond cavil. The university lecturer who is shot during a projection in a darkened classroom; the plain, sensible policeman; the delightful but dangerous girl; the abundant wit and well-sprinkled clues make this a memorable performance.

Note: The French translation, *Dette de Sang* (Lyon, n.d.), has some unintentionally comic passages arising from ignorance of the Philadelphia scene.

1328 Blood on the Bosom Devine   Lipp 1948

After a dip in quality in his second work (*Blood of Vintage*, 1947), T. K. recovered his equal mastery of humor and detection. The second was amusing in its satire of gentlemen farmers on the Main Line, but the murder was too complex for unravelment proper. In the present one, Detective Sam Phelan is as good as ever, and although the scene of the crime is a musty old theater, it justifies itself over and over again. The psychology of the criminal is noteworthy, and Phelan's interview with the absentminded old Professor Surtees is incomparable.

1329 Cover His Face   Lipp 1949

The not entirely impossible adventures of Dr. Weldon, of Allegheny University, while in England on the track of some Johnson letters. Not the best Kyd, but full of Crispinesque entertainment, with crime rather tucked in out of sight.

1330   LACY, ED (pseud. of Leonard Zinberg, 1912–68), wrote some two dozen stories on the tough and sexy side, one of which—*Room to Swing* (1957)—received a prize.

1331   LAING, ALEXANDER

> The Cadaver of Gideon Wyck   Macm 1960/1934
> *Abridgment by the author for MRS*

A quarter century has not made this piece less meretricious. There is little suspense, no good dirt, and no detection. Of interest only as a period piece, with its footnotes by "Ed." and its pretense of being a manuscript written by a medical student.

1332   LAIT, ROBERT

> A Chance to Kill   Macm 1968

To those who like uncertainty and general misery, this story will give every satisfaction in the most accomplished way. An unlikely premise starts things going: that the police must watch day and night a released homicidal maniac to prevent his murdering again. Detective Constable Ricks is assigned the task by Superintendent Bront, who is a tartar. Ricks' wife is a complaining and sex-ridden Irish girl. The released convict is an obsequious and strangely furtive man, who combines odd actions with a show of having had his fangs drawn. All this is enough to generate anxiety, provide scruffy details for twenty books, and make one grateful to the author for terminating the torture with a good strong antisocial twist of the rope.

1333   LAMB, LYNTON

> Death of a Dissenter   Goll 1969
> *Map of Fleury Feverel*

A famous illustrator and author of nonfiction ventures on his first detective story and follows rather well-worn paths in so doing. Chief Superintendent Quill and Inspector Glover detect in a mythical village, which is an object of comedy (and nostalgia) because it retains its old decent ways. The village dialect is excessive and hard to read, the quaint characters are tedious, and the events inflated. There is too much cricket, an improbable quarrel between the rector and the baronet, and when all is said and done the murder of the old eccentric turns out a fraud.

1334   LANDON, CHRISTOPHER (GUY) (b. 1911)

> Dead Men Rise Up Never   Hein 1963

Certainly a story of murder and detection, and on a well-established pattern, but the telling and the devices of discovery are original enough to make it an affair *sui generis* and of high quality. The semi-likable villain is a triumph, and the successive settings—school, London, Ireland, and Spain—help give momentum to a relentless narrative.

The title is from Swinburne's "Garden of Proserpine," st. 11.

1335   Hornets' Nest   Hein 1956

A bank robber talks to a dying man after a train accident and changes identity with him. He eludes justice but is drawn into a labyrinth of international intrigue, which leads him to the Arctic North Cape of Norway. The characterization is inadequate, and the great final scene uniting villain and villainess in an underwater cave does not quite come off.

1336   The Mirror Room   Hein 1960

Good writing, as usual, but an essentially tedious story of identical twin brothers, one of whom is suspected of selling secrets to a foreign power. The other then seeks him out in East Berlin while being himself suspected of impersonation. The ending is weak despite rat-infested bomb sites, and a happy twist of rescue by the heroine does nothing to strengthen it.

1337   Stone Cold Dead in the Market   Pan 1955

Excellent local color about the incredible but actual customs of the London Stock Exchange; fair byplay between detective and whorehouse mistress of attractive appearance; poor characterization of others, including the victim; yet the whole has an air and can stand rereading.

1338   Unseen Enemy   CCD 1957

A chase-and-adventure story to recover a kidnapped child. Harry Kent, investigator, his wife, Joan, and their eccentric friend Josh go to the Loire country on this crusade. They are entertaining and plausible, and suspense never turns into deliberate harrowing. The one bad point is that the villain is named Jacques.

1339   LANDON. See also:

Ice-Cold in Alex   Hein 1957

1340   LANG, ANDREW (1844–1912)

The Disentanglers   LG 1903

Found amusing by JB; heartily disliked by WHT. The book shows the growing influence of Sherlock Holmes on modes of fictional thought, and depicts other novelties of the time, such as the charm of the automobile and the Emancipated Woman. What is disentangled by the flirtatious group of young people is the mismanaged lives of their friends and acquaintances. In its mild way a tour de force.

1341 LANGLEY, LEE (pseud. of Sarah Langley)

Dead Center   CCD 1968

The author adds one more to the scant list of sports detective stories. But
it is only a passable job. The basketball trimmings are minor, the "star"
despicable, and the plot cluttered. The method of killing is original and
the detective, Lieutenant Chris Jensen, is engaging and competent.

1342 Osiris Died in Autumn   CCD 1964

Presumably a first novel, which can boast good features. The characters,
especially a middle-aged female associate professor, who is also an
aviatrix, and a young police lieutenant tackling his first homicide, are
well portrayed, while the author's evident love of these people is kept under
control. The actual motive for the killing of a professor of geology is weak
when it need not have been.

LANHAM, EDWIN (b. 1904)

b. in Texas; educ. Williams Coll., studied painting in Paris, then became
a journalist. Has for some years been a free-lance writer, living in Connecticut. His half dozen detective stories between 1946 and 1957 reflected
chiefly the environment of newspapermen and politicians with which the
author was most familiar.

1343 Death of a Corinthian   HB 1953

A well-constructed tale of multiple murder among the members of the
yachting set on Long Island Sound. The author has effected a nice balance
between marine and criminal interest and one hardly knows why the
result is not more striking. Perhaps everything is too smooth. The nice
young lawyer who tells the tale and nearly gets killed solving the mystery
does little to mitigate the blandness.

1344 LATHEN, EMMA (pseud. of Mary J. Latis and Martha Hennissart)

Accounting for Murder   Macm 1964

The top one of the first three by this interesting pair of New England
businesswomen. Here the picture of low life and inventory fraud in high
banking circles holds the reader breathless despite all technicalities—or
rather, because of their expert handling. John Putnam Thatcher, V.P., is as
urbane and perceptive as ever and, thanks to the appearance of a daughter,
Laura, even more likable and worthy of belief.

1345 Banking on Death   Macm 1961

This first work is a tale of businesslike detection carried out almost in
spite of himself by the senior vice-president of a large New York trust
company. Blizzards in Buffalo, the atmosphere of modern airports, and,
of course, the unflappable Thatcher himself are adroitly built into a story
whose method, motive, and character are all first-class.

1346 Come to Dust   S&S 1968

The best among the most recent exploits of John Putnam Thatcher, who
tangles here with the traditions of an Ivy League college as he tries to
find out who stole a $50,000 bearer bond intended for the college coffers,
and to ascertain what has happened to a model husband and alumnus,
presumably the thief. Larceny leads to murder, and Thatcher has a hard
time pursuing his quest, trammeled as he is by the commencement
traditions of Brunswick College. The Lathen humor is well to the fore.

1347 Death Shall Overcome   Macm 1966

The use made here of the civil rights movement, with its attendant sing-
ins and sit-ins, is masterly, and one can forgive the authors' playing down
of mystery and detection in favor of social comment and superb characterization.

1348 Murder Against the Grain   Macm 1967

The ladies' power to depict dramatic scenes that are also comic remains
high, but the fascination that this virtuosity has for *them* makes them
neglect clarity of plot and detective concern. Details needed early on are
withheld till p. 105, and even then are not thoroughly gone into. The
international wheat trade and the U-5 Russia imbroglio are well done.

1349 Murder Makes the Wheels Go 'Round   Macm 1966

The automotive industry, as typified by "Michigan Motors," provides a
field day for the Lathen amalgamation. The story is one of their best
for pace, humor, and all-around competence. John Putnam Thatcher survives translation to Detroit and does a fine job of identifying the murderer,
who takes advantage of the public delivery of a bulletproof car ("Super-
Plantagenet") for Crown Prince Bulbul to stash his own private victim
in it. A tour de force.

1350 Murder to Go   S&S 1969

There are now enough Lathen books to permit the observation that they
fall into at least three classes: good, better, and best. WHT would place in
the first group those novels in which social and political commentary steals
the show: *Murder Against the Grain, When in Greece.* The "best"—e.g.,
*Accounting for Murder, Come to Dust, Murder Makes the Wheels Go
'Round*—effect a superb combination of plot, character, and humor.
Murder to Go probably belongs in the as yet undistinguished middle. John
Putnam Thatcher does a bit of traipsing about between Trenton and the
Eastern Shore, and unmasks the sponsor of a mass-poisoner, but what
stays in the mind is the name and nationwide organization of Chicken
Tonight, Inc.
     In the classification suggested above, the 1970 consignment, *Pick Up
Sticks,* belongs to group 2: Better.

1351　A Place for Murder　　　　　　　　　　　　　　Macm 1963

This time John P. Thatcher oscillates between New York and northwest
Connecticut (there is a bit of tedium here) and eventually solves a double
murder involving people who think so much of capital that they are easily
bamboozled. Perhaps too many gentleman farmers, dog-lovers, and
kennelists, but good motivation; method a trifle unlikely.

1352　A Stitch in Time　　　　　　　　　　　　　　Macm 1968

It was too much to expect that these ladies would continue indefinitely to
produce masterpieces. Here the variations on the formula of John Putnam
Thatcher's shrewdness versus skulduggery in big business is not up to par.
The hospital is hardly portrayed from a medical standpoint, and the get-
rich-quick scheme is not clever enough. Even Thatcher is tired, and leaves
the work to his juniors, without supplying humor as formerly.

1353　When in Greece　　　　　　　　　　　　　　　S&S 1968

There is no reason why the development of a hydroelectric project in
Greece should not be a suitable background for Sloan Guaranty Trust
activities, nor why revolution and counterrevolution by colonels and
leftists should not impede the progress of the negotiations. But this tale
is a travelogue and little else. Such detection as Thatcher does is in the
facial expression of the Greeks he deals with in an effort to find his lost
field representative. The later kidnapping in "broad daylight" (its breadth
is enormous in Athens) and the revenge taken by "Mr. Thatchos" both
seem outré and not especially entertaining.

1354　LATIMER, JONATHAN (b. 1906)

　　　　Headed for a Hearse　　　　　　　　　　　Dday 1935

A routine story about framing a husband for the murder of his wife, the
object being to get the wife and the money both.

1355　LEA, G. F. PERCIVALE

　　　　A Detective Unawares　　　　　　　　　　Hurst [1928]

Internal evidence suggests 1920 as the approximate date of this story
about a young painter and his gentle patron. What makes it unreadable
is the goody-goodyness of the characters and the time spent on their
making one another physically comfortable and at ease in their minds
while a murder and disappearance have to be explained.

1356　LEASOR, JAMES

　　　　Passport to Oblivion　　　　　　　　　　Lipp 1965

The reporter-author's first novel of crime and spying moves along very
fast, juggling the usual elements of the genre with some distinction of
style, if not of thought. The scene takes in Persia, Canada, and London.

The attempted assassination of the shah in Teheran, with a seething mob and a helicopter rescue of the hero (by his enemies), is rich. There are in the story two nymphomaniacs, one a masochist, and much about American vintage cars. (The author reports on the jacket that he owns three Jaguars, a Cord, and three other irreplaceables.)

1357   Spylight   Lipp 1966

Laid in Pakistan, the story recounts a Red Chinese attempt to blackmail an Indian prince by ruining his son's eyesight at a distance by means of a laser beam. Dr. Jason Love, a college friend of the prince's, helps him out. There are harassing encounters, torture, sexual perversions, and pure sentiment about a Cord car.

LEBLANC, MAURICE (1864–1925)

A highly successful purveyor of light literature in serial, novel, and play form, M.L. gave a new twist to the French *roman policier* by shortening it and substituting the Robin Hood–Raffles theme for the previous crime-reporter-seeking-justice. Brother of the great actress and singer who was Maeterlinck's companion, Maurice goes in for *coups de théâtre* and imparts to his dialogue a pseudo sophistication that has been widely imitated. See Maurice Dekobra, No. 723.

1358   The Crystal Stopper   Mac 1913

JB skimmed through this old book and found that it was not at all the one he thought, but an absolutely inferior sample of the author's work. In this one, Arsène Lupin is baffled at every turn by a bestial *député* who commits murder and blackmail with ease and relish. A.L. does not even get the beautiful widow whom he desires: she despises him. It all goes to show that Leblanc's true genre was the short story (see No. 2621) or the play, usually written with the aid of an actor: Firmin Gémier performed much the same function for Leblanc as Gillette for Conan Doyle (see No. 2487).

1359   Sherlock Holmes *versus* Arsène Lupin
       The Case of the Golden Blonde   Atomic 1946
       Adapted into English by J.B.

The first thing to get clear is that "J.B." is not JB but an anonymous workman in the vineyard. A number of Lupin stories seem to have been drawn on for this production, in which Holmes is successful, but whose quality may be judged by this extract: "Sherlock Holmes appeared to be the sort of man you see every day. About fifty years old, he looked like a clerk who passed his life keeping his books. Just an honest citizen of London, but his eyes, terribly sharp eyes, were quick and penetrating!" (p. 41)

N.B. The original battle between the two heroes was entitled *The Fair Haired Lady,* repr. as *Arsène Lupin* vs. *Holmlock Shears* (GR 1909), this formula being the title of a long short story as well: she is the golden blonde.

LE CARRÉ, JOHN (pseud. of David John Moore Cornwell, b. 1931)

Taught at Eton; then a member of British foreign service as consular officer in Bonn, Hamburg, etc.

1360 Call for the Dead   Walk 1962

WHT cares less for George Smiley here than he did in the second tale (No. 1361). He is a sort of modified Mr. Pinkerton without the cold in the head, but acting even more sluggishly. The story is one of espionage, unusual if only because all the spying is done at second hand. The telephone-call clue which gives the book its title turns out to be piffle, and the twist at the end no great surprise. A few good characters are the reader's sole reward.

1361 A Murder of Quality   Walk 1963

One comes to the end of this neatly written tale with a feeling of dissatisfaction. Carne School is something of a travesty, although a picturesque one. Clever things are said about various people, but one rarely sees them. The boys might almost not exist, despite the use of one or two as props. As for George Smiley ("bland and deadly" according to the blurb), he is really quite ordinary. The author manages a fairly good double twist, but the actual ending is only pop goes the weasel.

1362 The Spy Who Came In from the Cold   Goll 1963

A runaway best seller of 1964. During its run JB wrote in an essay on the spy genre: "The point of *The Spy* is that he wants to quit but is impelled to go on by professional routine. . . . He does not believe in what he is doing; he is anything but a hero; he is a good deal of a masochist. And being a spy in the field, a potential martyr to an unfelt cause, he entitles himself to certain low pleasures—despising his associates; having, skill apart, a poor opinion of himself; sinking morally and physically into degradation almost beyond control; falling in love listlessly like a convalescent; and, after being betrayed in action by headquarters for double-cross purposes, making a sacrificial end. Death, we are to think, is the only 'coming in from the cold' there is." No detection.

1363 LEE, GYPSY ROSE (orig. Rose Louise Hovick, 1914–70)

The G-String Murders   S&S 1941
In ppb.: The Strip-Tease Murders

Anyone keen about sex in fiction will admire this workmanlike job for its account of a performing group, its use of technicalities—if that's the word—about stripping, and its handling of the clues by a likable lieutenant. In short this is one of a handful of books about backstage murder that are tolerable. It is not made worse by being told in the first person, or by a bit of sentimental lovey-dovey between the narratrix and one of the cast of the characters. WHT dislikes the entire business, partly because the stage is to him a rarely satisfactory setting for detection. Perhaps he should be the one to look up *Mother Finds a Body* (S&S 1942).

1364 LE FANU, J(OSEPH) SHERIDAN

Uncle Silas   Cress 1947; orig. 1864
Introd. by Elizabeth Bowen

This neglected masterpiece starts and ends with murder, but its interest consists wholly in the gradual discovery of Uncle Silas' true character. The slow pace, the descriptions of domestic and outdoor life, the interplay of quite genuine persons, and the singular nature and position of the girl-narrator make this a tour de force of "modern Gothic." Its literary virtues quite outshine Collins' in *The Woman in White* (No. 577). See also *Carmilla* in No. 2138.

1365 LEMARCHAND, ELIZABETH

Alibi for a Corpse   TBC 1970; orig. 1969

There is in this story a relentless sticking to the point which is impressive. Once the body is discovered in the boot (trunk) of the car in the dump, nothing is allowed to get in the way of tracking down the leads pointing to several persons. Motives, times, opportunities, and probabilities are expertly balanced, yet there is room for character, scenery, and a little wit—all integrated by a steady mind and will. This, the author's third, makes one want to catch up and read *Death of an Old Girl* and *The Affacombe Affair*.

1366 LENEHAN, J. C.

The Tunnel Mystery   ML 1931

The murder, in a train, of a London jeweler carrying a necklace. The crime is done in the Highpen Tunnel, by shooting through a hole in the partition between the compartments. The beginning of the investigation is fairly good, but the story degenerates fast into excessive complications and improbable identities.

1367 LEONARD, CHARLES L. (pseud. of M. V. Heberden, q.v.)

The Fourth Funeral   CCD 1948

Another excellent story about American and English expatriates, this time in Belém (Brazil). The local color and police, the close-knit and unhappy relations of the foreign group, and the singular motive for three murders and two additional attempts are all superbly done. It is also evident that the author loves and admires heroic women doctors (see No. 1118), while not diminishing the merit of the detective hero Kilgerrin.

1368. LEONARD. See also:

The Fanatic of Fez	CCD	1943
Search for a Scientist	CCD	1947
The Secret of the Spa	CCD	1946
The Stolen Squadron	CCD	1940
Treachery in Trieste	CCD	1951

1369 LE QUEUX, WILLIAM (TUFNELL) (1864–1927)

The Mystery of a Motor Car   H&S 1905

A period piece marked by the usual longueurs and occasionally stiff dialogue, but fundamentally a sound novel of detection. The plot has plausible international overtones, the suspense is kept up to the end, and the characters have vivacity side by side with mystery, malice, and other desirable traits. The author produced scores of novels in the mixed detective-adventure genre (see *The Mysterious Mr. Miller*, 1906, and *The Tickencote Treasure*, 1903), and one eccentric study of true crime (see No. 3212).

1370 LEROUX, GASTON (1868–1927)

The Mystery of the Yellow Room   Brent 1908

Undoubtedly a date in the gimmickry of the genre, but unreadable today. Tone and incident are fatal to credibility, and the dragging out of motive and verbiage destroys suspense. The young reporter Rouletabille thinks, but discloses nothing till the end. Readers fortified against these evils may want to go on to *The Perfume of the Lady in Black* (1909) and *The Phantom of the Opera* (1910).

LEVIN, IRA (b. 1929)

b. N.Y.C.; educ. Horace Mann Sch., Drake Univ., Iowa, and N.Y.U.; playwright by preference.

1371 A Kiss Before Dying   S&S 1953

A coldblooded introvert with an eye to a fortune in copper loves up and murders two of the three daughters of the metallic magnate (in Midwestern college settings) but doesn't quite make it with the third, who has had the benefits of a Columbia education, plus the help of another blond young man who wishes not to be mistaken for the murderer. Redeemed to some extent by a really tremendous scene in which the evil youth gets his quietus. Rather long for its length. Detection minimal.

LEWIS, LANGE (pseud. of Jane Lewis Beynon, b. 1915)

Daughter of the marine painter and cartoonist Arthur Lewis; B.A. from U.S.C., which she used as a setting for her first two detective stories. She lives in Los Angeles and has also written other kinds of books, including the novel *Cypress Man*, published under her own name in 1944. She is interested in Beethoven and, one gathers, in marriage and the family.

1372 The Birthday Murder   BM 1945

This neat novel about love and life in L.A. gives Inspector Richard Tuck ample opportunity to demonstrate his powers; there is no lost motion and no verbiage. The author's sense of character is displayed, too: the book is full of women sharply differentiated. The plot is a classic example of sodium fluoride poisoning, with a good twist at the end. Almost perfect in its playlike purity and delightful prose.

1373   Juliet Dies Twice   BM 1943

Theatricals at a university in Los Angeles, presumably U.S.C., with Lieutenant Tuck in charge and a psychology student (girl) in attendance. The crime is plausible and the young people suitably young in thought and action. The interweaving of Shakespeare and psychology is restrained and effective, and one may say that this second work is as good as No. 1376 and promises even better things.

1374   Meat for Murder   BM 1943

Something of a tour de force. Excellent as to plot and character, though not so attractive in setting and motive as her preferred works.

1375   The Passionate Victims   BM 1952

In this, her fifth (and last) detective novel, Lange Lewis is less successful in developing her complicated plot than was the case in earlier, less ambitious tales. The story is dominated by a woman who holds the clue to a long-past murder and finally acts upon the knowledge. Inspector Tuck is less active here, and the details of the case not so original as usual with L.L.

1376   LEWIS, L. See also:

Murder Among Friends   BM 1942

1377   LEWIS, MATTHEW GREGORY (1775–1818)

The Monk   1795

Written at nineteen and published a year later, this famous piece of gore-wallowing was a best seller and earned the approval of so good a critic as Sir Walter Scott. Its mysteries seem to us feeble or cheap and the temptations that lead the hero, the Abbot Ambrosio of Madrid, to his downfall may appear ineffectual claptrap to our saturated minds, but they testify alike to the permanent lust for sex and terror which books must give if life cannot. The murder has at least a sound motive, and the Devil and the Inquisition are equally believable.

1378   LIMNELIUS, GEORGE (pseud. of Lewis George Robinson; also George Braha, b. 1886)

The Manuscript Murder   CCD 1934

The present effort is a disappointment after the first. Detection starts on p. 210, when Major Weston Pryme first appears. By that time it is hard to care what is about to "transpire."

1379   The Medbury Fort Murder   Dday 1929

An unusual setting and plot for a murder linked with adultery, military jealousy, blackmail, and the interplay of divergent characters. All are well drawn, but the soldier-hero and his hardheaded lady love are beautifully done. The detection is solid, and only a bit of hesitation toward the end keeps this from a place in the first rank.

1380 LININGTON, ELIZABETH (also Lesley Egan, Egan O'Neill, Anne Blaisdell, and Dell Shannon; b. 1921)

Date with Death   Harp 1966

Another *langweilig* tale about Sergeant Maddox of the L.A.P.D. All the girls fall for him and *he can't think why.* He goes and sleeps with them discreetly in the intervals of driving around L.A. in search of those guilty, first, of a series of practical jokes, then of the murder of an engaged couple who at the time were canoodling outside the girl's house. Dreary looking up of possible suspects, interlarded with the doings of a subversive organization. The same pensive phrases are repeated ad nauseam— a book to be exiled from the premises.

1381 Greenmask!   Harp 1964

There is merit in the attempted parallel of crime committed with crime written up in books, but the style and characterization are too weak to sustain an idea that would have required a Dorothy Sayers to pull off.

1382 LITTLE, CONSTANCE and GWENYTH (together: Conyth Little), were among the first to show how to destroy rationality by a judicious application of nerve irritants, as in *The Black Dream* (CCD 1952) about a boardinghouse murder.

1383 LIVINGSTON, KENNETH (pseud. of Kenneth Livingston Stewart, b. 1894)

The Cloze Papers   Rich 1936

Unfortunately to be judged not worthwhile, since it is a loose-jointed novel *not* featuring Cedric Dodd, whose *Cases* we admire with a tempered enthusiasm (see No. 2624). The present story is but a dull rehearsal of malice domestic.

LOCKRIDGE, RICHARD (ORSON) (b. 1898), and FRANCES (LOUISE DAVIS);* also, jointly, Francis Richards, q.v.

This husband-and-wife team used to write three sorts of tales: (1) about Captain Heimrich, who studies Putnam County felonies; (2) Mr. and Mrs. North and their insupportable cats, often in New York City and Florida, and (3) unseried stories of suspense.

* Mr. Lockridge's first wife, deceased.

1384 Accent on Murder   Lipp 1958

A Captain Heimrich story of a killing in rural Westchester Co., in which the study of American regional accents by the elderly Professor Brinkley plays a part in the unmasking of the criminal. Some of the atmosphere (old ladies and such) is thickly laid on, yet this is far from unacceptable Lockridge.

1385   Catch as Catch Can   Lipp 1957

Very entertaining indeed. No cats, no Norths; instead, some good intrigue in New York, New Canaan, and vicinity, competent narrative and fair action. Geoffrey Bowen, of the DA's office, New York County, is the unassuming protagonist in what does not pretend to be a detective story.

1386   The Distant Clue   Lipp 1963

A representative example of their better work. The murder of the "last of the Putnam County Lenoxes" and of the local librarian (male), who was assisting Lenox in his researches into "family," is cleared up by Captain Heimrich with but little intrusion from his wife, son, and dog. Detection includes the counting of toes with the aid of binoculars—guess why!

1387   First Come, First Kill   Lipp 1962

More free of mannerisms than most of the L. output, but very obvious in plot. Capt. Heimrich, his wife Susan, and their Westchester life are fairly palatable. But the little asides, the precious stream-of-consciousness, and the "now, Mr. Jones; now, Mrs. Jones" are still present in excess.

1388   Murder and Blueberry Pie   Lipp 1959

The report in two words is: im-possible.

1389   Murder Roundabout   Lipp 1966

This second solo effort by R.L. is marked by the author's usual capacity for a bright remark or an encapsuled situation. But the crime—murder of a wife by a hard-up husband facing divorce—is routine, and the red herrings too many and too fat.

1390   Think of Death   Lipp 1947

Great unity of time and place makes this the best Lockridge known to us. The lawyer-detective Martin Brooks, ex-OSS, uses most of the book to meditate on his past and present relations with his former wife, now widow of the corpse. But despite the evident lack of action (what there is goes on within and around a country house), the tale is close-knit and absorbing. Motive and execution of the crime are reasonably convincing, and suspense quietly sustained.

   Note: Reread in 1958, the plot holds up very well, but the narrative seems frequently pretentious—pseudo psychology and "depth" about life in general. Atmosphere is steady discouragement—all the characters, cop included, are "drained." The word itself recurs obsessively. Means and motive, though, remain good, and the detection, too.

1391   With Option to Die   Lipp 1967

When alone, Richard L. writes more simply and idiomatically. In this
Heimrich story of race violence in Westchester County, the former
Captain, now Inspector Heimrich, says, "Now, Mrs. So-and-so" only a
few times, and he does detect a variety of crimes mixed with rightist
intimidation.

1392   LOCKRIDGE, R. and ESTABROOKS, G. H.

       Death in the Mind   World 1945

This affair purposes to center our interest on hypnotism and scientific
passion. Why Lockridge needed help to perpetrate this semi-demi kind of
tale is not clear.

1393   LOFTS, NORAH (ETHEL ROBINSON LOFTS JORISCH; also Peter
Curtis; b. 1904), has been prolific since 1938 as historical novelist and
mystery spinner, but not precisely as a writer of detective fiction. See
Dead March in Three Keys (1940) and Nos. 686–7.

1394   LONDON, (JOHN GRIFFITH) "JACK" (1876–1916)

       Assassination Bureau, Ltd.   AD 1964
          Completed by Robert L. Fish
          Not previously published

This affair is remarkable for having collaborators at head and tail: the
plot was sold to Jack London by Sinclair Lewis and London's notes for
the latter third were written up by Mr. Fish. In between, the call of the
wild kept Jack busy working out the consequences of this scheme: the
head of a Murder, Inc., agrees to kill an unknown, who turns out to be himself. How does he escape his own well-trained assistants? Rationality
becomes a scarce commodity and the indispensable love story is perfunctory, but there is good intellectual comedy and some rather heavy-
handed socialist-moralist propaganda.
     Note: The ending outlined by J.L. in the 4-page appendix differs from
that provided by R.L.F.

       LONGMATE, NORMAN (RICHARD) (b.1925)

A newspaperman, Oxford graduate, and socialist pamphleteer; lives in
Surrey, and is keen on vocational education. Why are his books so hard to
get, new or secondhand, here or abroad?

1395   Death in Office   Hale 1961

Up to standard, warranting further hopes for something as good as *A
Head for Death*. Longmate handles the murder of a personnel officer in
the London headquarters of a big metallurgical syndicate with competence
and humor. There are decent clues, a touch of sex, and plenty of work
done by Inspector Bradbury and his Sergeant Chris. The jargon of the
personnel office is as amusing as it should be.

1396   A Head for Death   Cass 1958

A first and agreeably amateurish story of the doing-in of a highly unpopular headmaster at an English public school. Good glimpses of school
life offset some infelicities of expression and execution, and the atmosphere is genuine. Superintendent Bradbury and his sergeant (an "old
boy") are well beyond cardboard.
   The title suggests a line in Wagner's *Tristan*.

1397   Strip Death Naked   Cass 1959

Someone is apparently taking pictures of important and respectable people
in the nude and sending the prints to their superior officers—in government, schools, hospitals, and the church. No attempt is made to blackmail
the men and women victims, some of whom are brave and bright enough
to apply to Scotland Yard. There Superintendent Bradbury hands the
investigation to Sergeant Christopher Raymond, Oxford-trained, and also
experienced as a detective. The plot develops with plausibility, spiced
with excellent fun about the Sergeant's disinclination to disrobe, and such
apposite touches as naming the owner of the nudist camp Roger Madrigal.
When murder happens, Bradbury is there to take over the job, and he does
a solid piece of work, interspersed with discussions of facts and suspects
with the Sergeant. A workmanlike and often witty tale, just short of
brilliant, and notable for an original twist about HCN in the teapot.

1398   Vote for Death   Cass 1960

The disappointed readers found this performance distressingly poor,
especially as regards the basic police work of the official investigators.
Some amusing details of a provincial election, but Bradbury and Sergeant
Chris are in a fog.

1399   LONGMATE. See also:

Death Won't Wash   Cass 1957

1400   LORAC, E. C. R. (pseud. of Edith Caroline Rivett; also Carol Carnac, q.v., 1894–1958)

Bats in the Belfry   Mac 1937

An early Lorac and a disappointment. The first half of the story is
cluttered by the attempt to blacken most of the characters and provide too
many motives, meanwhile giving away the too-good-to-be-true murderer.
Inspector Macdonald deals with the mess, which has only a neat twist
about passports to redeem it.

1401   Fire in the Thatch   MH 1946

We have here a good bit of Devon red mud and muck, not to mention
a conservative farming colonel, and Inspector Macdonald's tracking down
of the character who tried to make arson-murder look like accident is
quite satisfactory. British petrol rationing is integral to the tale, and the
only flaw is the somewhat elaborate traipsing about necessary for the alibi.

1402　I Could Murder Her　　　　　　　　　　　　CCD 1951
　　　　In Eng.: Murder of a Martinet

A well-told and deftly characterized story of hates among in-laws in a
London town house, after the second world war. Chief Inspector Macdonald is quiet and humane, but doesn't do much detecting. Rather, he stands
an overdose of listening to witnesses. Better points are: the use of insulin
as a poison and a topnotch charwoman.

1403　The Last Escape　　　　　　　　　　　　　　　Dday 1959

Rory Macshane manages a clever escape from prison on Dartmoor and
heads north. Inspector Macdonald, meanwhile, is called in to investigate
the case of a man's body found walled up in a neglected manor house in
the north of England, and some 100 pages of very leisurely and highly
rural investigation follow. Mild stuff.

1404　Murder by Matchlight　　　　　　　　　　　　MH 1946

One of the two first-quality performances by this author. The situation in
the park is good. Inspector Macdonald is solid and credible. There is
detection and a variety of suspects and only some circus characters spoil
an otherwise congenial tale.

1405　Murder in St. John's Wood　　　　　　　　　　Mac 1934
　　　　Pref. dated 1933

WHT had always preached the excellence of this tale. When finally read
by JB, it proved acceptable and somewhat more. It is the story of a
financier hated by his family and friends, who is done away with in his
own summerhouse. Young Inspector Macdonald does a fair job; his great
art is to be always "equable."

1406　People Will Talk　　　　　　　　　　　　　　CCD 1958

Even more unfocused and "soft" than usual, this tells of the mysterious
disappearance of two elderly people, recently wed. Poor detection by
Superintendent Kempson, rather better by a couple of youngsters in Italy,
where the subsequent crime takes place.

1407　Lorac. See also Nos. 435–42 and:

　　　　Accident by Design　　　　　　　　　　　　CCC 1950
　　　　And Then Put Out the Light　　　　　　　　CCD 1950
　　　　The Greenwell Mystery　　　　　　　　　　　Mac 1934
　　　　Part for a Poisoner (= Place for a Poisoner)　CCC 1948
　　　　A Screen for Murder　　　　　　　　　　　　CCC 1948

1408　Loraine, Philip (pseud. of Robin Estridge)

　　　　And to My Beloved Husband　　　　　　　　Mill 1950
　　　　　In Eng.: White Lie the Dead

This first work is a savage disparagement of British justice as ground out
by a cruel inspector of police named Keen and the other gears of the

judicial mill. The plot is the old one of suicide rigged to look like murder for private ends. The people are credible and occasionally interesting. P.L. gets his points across quickly—the book is rather shorter than average.

1409   The Break in the Circle   Mill 1951

Perceptive and graced as usual with good prose, this story is adventure pure and simple; some "mystery" winding up in communist sabotage.

1410   Day of the Arrow   Mill 1964
         In ppb.: Thirteen

Good suspense amid elegant surroundings, a nice blend of sex, witchcraft, and French landed proprietors, and a more or less incredible ending, which it is a pleasure to believe in for the last half hour of the reading. Not detection, but a successful pulling off of the scheme attempted by Bellairs in *Death in High Provence.*

1411   Nightmare in Dublin   Mill 1952
         In Eng.: The Dublin Nightmare

A suspense story of which the familiar components are: plausible scoundrel with fascist-communist leanings, false identification of his corpse (a convenient murder having provided a substitute), concealed wireless transmitter calling all hands to sabotage, and a fine, upstanding young professional photographer to suspect, act as sitting duck, and console the lovely jilted girl. But these elements have rarely been put together so lucidly and attractively. Dublin atmosphere authentic.

1412   LORAINE. See also:

         The Angel of Death   Mill 1961
         The Dead Men of Sestos   Goll 1968
         A Mafia Kiss   Goll 1969

1413   LOVESEY, PETER

         Wobble to Death   Macm 1970
           Winner of the Panther-Macmillan First Crime
           Novel Competition

The vogue for historical settings and reconstructions is in full swing and worth encouraging, for it taps new sources of interest, as in this first novel, which draws on a fad of the 1870s and '80s, the Six-Day Pedestrian Race, known as a Wobble. With purely imaginary participants—athletes, trainers, managers, newspapermen and women, and crowds—Mr. Lovesey has recreated the right atmosphere without any attempt at period language, but also without any violation of it. The prime murder takes place soon and subtly, and the work of detection is properly interwoven with sound characterization, class prejudices, and love affairs. Sergeant Cribb and Constable Thackeray do a first-rate job as further violence and fraud bespangle the grueling, dirty, and dreary race in Agricultural Hall. A new writer to watch.

LOWNDES, [MRS.] (MARIE-ADELAIDE) BELLOC [Mrs. Frederic Sawrey Lowndes] (1868–1947)

The great-great-granddaughter of Joseph Priestley, protegée of Robert Browning, sister of Hilaire Belloc wrote some two dozen full-length, thickly plotted novels, which harked back in form if not in tone to the standards of an earlier day. She had hardly any education beyond two years at a convent, but her work is generally well-organized and stoutly put together, like that of her elder contemporary Anna Katharine Green, and her rhetoric is by no means oppressive. She had a genuine interest in literature, edited in English the letters and journals of the Goncourts, and kept up an informed interest in true crime.

1414   The End of Her Honeymoon   Meth 1904

Another working of the vanishing-room theme, well conceived though a trifle over-circumstantial: we believe sooner than the author thinks we will.

1415   Lizzie Borden   Hutch 1941
          A Study in Conjecture

Mrs. L. accepts Pearson's account without a qualm and concerns herself with motive exclusively: what turned the intelligent and quiet girl into a double murderess? The answer is: passionate love. This is fictionally represented with a good deal of skill in both invention and telling, but the events after the trial and the analysis of the case by Radin (q.v.) make one skeptical. Prologue and Epilogue in this novel are factual and critical résumés.

1416   The Lodger   Dell 1964; Meth 1950; LG 1940;
          Orig. a short story, see No. 2341   Scrib 1913/1911

The publishing history of this fictional treatment of the murders by Jack the Ripper establishes it as a classic, not of detection, but of crime, social description, and at least plausible psychology.

1417   LOWNDES. See also Nos. 2316, 2779 and:

The Terriford Mystery	Dday 1926; orig. 1913
The Uttermost Farthing	Newnes 1908
What Really Happened	Tauch 1926
When No Man Pursueth	Hein 1910

1418   LUSTGARTEN, EDGAR (MARCUS) (b. 1907)

One More Unfortunate   Bant 1949/Scrib 1947
   In Eng.: A Case to Answer

The reader familiar with this author's work may take the title as denoting one more of his capable studies of crime. It is in fact a novel of the courtroom, where the trial of a young man for the murder of a Soho prostitute moves to its inexorable finish with memorable speechmaking by both counsel, but especially by the defense. E.L.'s experience of famous cases and the fallibility of justice enables him to produce an ending at once grim and surprising.

The title is from Thomas Hood's poem, "The Bridge of Sighs."

1419 LUSTGARTEN. See:

Game for Three Losers   Scrib 1952

McBAIN, ED (pseud. of Evan Hunter, b. 1926)

He has written many stories, short and long, about the detectives of the 87th Precinct station of a large city suspiciously like New York, but explicitly stated not to be. The teamwork is carried on by a group comprising Steve Carella, Cotton Hawes, and Meyer Meyer.

1420 Lady Killer   S&S 1958

For the detectives of the 87th Precinct of the city of Isola, the problem is to find, in twelve hours and among eight million inhabitants, the man who has announced his intention to kill "The Lady." How they do it in 11 hours, 59 minutes is enlivened by a scene or two in La Via de Putas, in a Turkish bath, and similar Edens. There is, besides, enough extraneous matter and trouble to suggest life in the round, while the diverse ethnic origins and characters of the cops create additional tension. The whole cannot but be admired, even when police routine is not one's favorite genre.

1421 McBAIN. See also:

The Con Man	S&S 1957	Killer's Wedge	S&S 1959
Cop Hater	S&S 1956	The Mugger	S&S 1956
Killer's Choice	S&S 1957	The Pusher	S&S 1956
Killer's Payoff	S&S 1958		

1422 McCABE, CAMERON (pseud. of Ernest Wilhelm Julius Borneman)

The Face on the Cutting-Room Floor   Goll 1936

A good layout spoiled by the determination to be literary, i.e., symbolic and deep. The murder of the movie director in his own office, his character, and his associates are well done, but soon the dialogue defies reason without achieving poetry or profundity.

McCLOY, HELEN (WORRELL CLARKSON) [Mrs. Davis Dresser] (b. 1904)

Educ. Friends' School, N.Y.C.; then journalism in Paris and London, some of it in the *Morning Post* under the name of H. C. McCloy. Began writing mystery novels in 1938, not all given over to detection.

1423 Alias Basil Willing   RH 1951

A good tale of "murder for sale" under guise of psychiatric dinner parties. Basil Willing, the psychologist-detective, is now married to Gisela von

Hohenems, whom he saved in the no less interesting circumstances of *Through a Glass, Darkly.*

1424   Before I Die   DM 1963

A young married woman catches her wayward husband, Bob, in the arms of his stenographer, Kyra. The latter maneuvers Bob into a situation where he is suspected of murdering her husband. Bob's alibi is worthless but the good little wife goes to work to save him. Little or no detection; no Basil Willing.

1425   Cue for Murder   Morr 1942

An early one and very good it is. The intricate clueing and cueing of this story of actors in New York City is justly noted by Boucher, who ignores the slight technical inaccuracies about diabetes and its chemical symptoms. Basil Willing stands in peril of his life at the end when he confronts his quarry in an unusual and unhealthful spot, but "the dog it was that died."

1426   The Deadly Truth   Morr 1941

Basil Willing is courting Gisela von Hohenems (leaving her at 4 A.M.) and spending the summer in a hut on a large Long Island estate. Thrice-married Claudia Bethune administers a stolen "truth drug" to her house-party guests and is strangled with her own necklace. B.W. does fair detection of the plausible murderer, working in a test of real versus fake deafness. Good finale.

1427   The Goblin Market   Morr 1943

Basil Willing follows the path of all detectives in wartime: he goes in for Intelligence. Here we are in Latin America. Beautiful foreigners, ship signaling, cable faking are exhibited, all within the limits of credibility. Willing is made out an expert at street fighting, and there is a fine scene at the close in a taxi from Union Station, Washington, D.C.

The title alludes to the poem by Christina Rossetti.

1428   Mr. Splitfoot   Goll 1969

A Basil Willing tale in a New England setting. At Christmas, B.W. and his wife are snowed in as enforced guests at a house party where a poltergeist planned as a joke turns real and lethal. Unmemorable in comparison with the eminent psychologist's earlier adventures.

1429   The One That Got Away   Morr 1945

Laid in Scotland, with the usual trimmings (scree, dree, and the like), but unconvincing despite its accuracy. We meet a disappearing boy of 14, an ex-German POW, and an American naval lieutenant who brings in Basil Willing around p. 150. Much psychology about the boy, and some very bad French attributed to the murdered tutor. Denouement strains everything.

Not a Basil Willing story. A young woman lured to or stranded in the Adirondacks is surrounded by doubtful characters. There is need of a very elaborate cipher, which is neatly solved. Despite a great deal of helter-skelter, the tale has the quality that made *The Goblin Market* enjoyable.

1431   The Slayer and the Slain   RH 1957

Not a detective story, but a psychological novel, depending for its suspense upon the gradual recognition by the hero of his relation to a set of "multiple personalities." Though liberally documented with near-quotes from the psychology texts, not entirely convincing.

1432   Through a Glass, Darkly   RH 1949

It comes as no surprise that H. McC. should have based an early novel on the *Doppelgänger,* with very satisfying results. The girls'-school atmosphere is ably conveyed, and Basil Willing, back from six years in Japan, lives up to his name in assisting his Gisela in unraveling the death-dealing plot. (For an early version in short form, see No. 2458.)
   The title is from 1 Corinthians, 13:12.

1433   Two-Thirds of a Ghost   RH 1956

Basil Willing, now resident in suburban Connecticut, functions smoothly but not very impressively in this tale of authors, critics, and publishers. There are too many murders, and the details lack reality—to say nothing of the artificial main idea.

1434   McCLOY. See also Nos. 2367, 2458, 2500, 2631–5, and:

Dance of Death		The Man in the Moonlight Morr	1940
(= Design For Dying)	Morr 1938	She Walks Alone	RH 1948
Do Not Disturb	Morr 1943	The Unfinished Crime	RH 1954
The Long Body	RH 1955	Who's Calling?	Morr 1942

MacCLURE, VICTOR (also Peter Craig; b. 1887)

b. Scotland, went to sea, then to Univ. of Glasgow. Resumed sailing till an injury turned his talents to painting and architecture. Studied at Beaux-Arts, took up journalism and scene-painting simultaneously, later joining the Granville-Barker Company and designing sets for plays by Masefield and Shaw. Wounded at Gallipoli, he took up writing after serving in military intelligence and finding that other occupations were denied him by his multiple injuries.

   His output includes science fiction and some novels of adventure, plus books on general topics. *A Certain Woman* deals with Mary Magdalen. *The Golden Snail* (1925) is a fantasy ramble through London with fictional episodes and verses. Other works treat of elocution, Scottish cookery, and world affairs. For true crime, see No. 3225.

1435   The Clue of the Dead Goldfish   Harr 1936/1933
        Map on title page

Detective Inspector Archie Burford's third case, and, despite a sufficiently
interesting situation, a dull book. The plot is threadbare, the criminal far
too easily spotted, and the clueing perfunctory. The dead goldfish has
practically nothing to do with the tale, and that is its best feature.

1436   The Counterfeit Murders   Harr 1933/1932

Archie Burford's introduction to the Russian lady Mme Radaskova, who
later becomes his wife. Flimsy and flighty.

1437   The Crying Pig Murder   Harr 1933

Competent but not topflight. It is evident early on that the distinguished
Sir Aylmer Considine is too good to be true. That the Crying Pig is a pub
neither helps nor hinders. The plot is adroit and the detection adequate
in the hands of Edward Blayne, solicitor.

1438   Death Behind the Door   HM 1933

MacClure's best and simplest. In the attractive country-house setting, Inspector Archie Burford is likable and competent. There is an original
and plausible modus operandi, as well as good characters. Here, too, the
theme (later so overdone) of police officials at cross-purposes is developed
in a natural and non-irritating fashion.

1439   Death on the Set   Lipp 1935

Probably second in merit to the preceding. In this one the characters and
actions are clear and potent until nearly the very end, when by a trifling
error the author discloses prematurely the agent and the motive of the
murder. The atmosphere of a film studio in England is ably done and,
above all, there is not too much *va-et-vient*. Recommended to all those who
think the thirties out of date.

1440   The Diva's Emeralds   Harr 1937

This wretched piece of sentimentality and unbelievable *peripeteia* was
fortunately a cheap purchase, because it is fit only for discard.

1441   MacClure. See also:

        Hi-Spy Kick the Can: An Archie Burford Detective Story   Harr 1936

        McCutcheon, Hugh (Davie Martin) (b. 1909)

b. Glasgow; educ. Greenock Academy, Paisley Gram. Sch., and Univ. of
Glasgow.

1442   And the Moon Was Full   CCD 1967
        In Eng.: Killer's Moon

One of the frequent British tales of solicitors, their offices, and their
secretaries. The present author is no portraitist, but he draws Aberdeen

and vicinity very well. The young solicitor who has just been awarded a "Not proven" verdict at his trial for the murder of his partner sticks it out in his small town and tracks down the killer, being assisted therein by a girl journalist.

1443   Murder at "The Angel"   Dutt 1952
            In Eng.: The Angel of Light

A tolerable tale about a private investigator named Anthony Howard, who like so many recent heroes is obsessed with his dead wife. Despite his boring guilt and the author's uneven sense of probability, a promising start.

1444   McCUTCHEON. See also:

Comes the Blind Fury	Long	1959
Cover Her Face	Rich	1955
None Shall Sleep Tonight	Dutt	1953
To Dusty Death	Long	1960
Yet She Must Die	CCD	1962

MacDONALD, JOHN D(ANN) (b. 1916)

After attending the Harvard Business School, turned to writing and particularly to the tough genre. Many of his novels feature hard-boiled do-gooder Travis McGee. Most of his score of thrillers are written direct for paperback publication, usually a "Gold Medal Original."

1445   Dead Low Tide   GM 1953

One of his best stories of sex and violence in Florida. The murder occurs early and is therefore an object of detection to a greater extent than is usual with him. The emotions of the hero suspected of murdering his boss in order to possess the boss's wife and business are sufficiently intense to make that old plot seem fresh and acceptable.

1446   The Deep Blue Good-by   GM 1964

McGee is scarcely the private eye so brilliantly incarnated by Ross Macdonald's Lew Archer—he is more the private avenger. But in this tale, at least, one is willing to substitute good psychology and some real suspense off the Florida coast for Lew Archer's intricate dealings with the zombies of Southern California.

1447   A Key to the Suite   GM 1962

The story of Floyd, a nice guy at a convention of "AMG," with subsidiaries, phony salesmen, dirty slobs, and their kind. To discredit and hamper the nice guy, a classy doll is set to seduce him and then give him away in front of the others. It partly works, she partly falls for him, giving him and herself much satisfaction. But by a set of mischances two deaths occur, one a murder. Disgusted, Floyd then teams up with a sweet sad whore and goes home tarnished and rather unhappy. Excellent convention satire and "superior" sex.

1448   Murder in the Wind   Dell 1956

A "powerful" story about a tornado in progress, during which murder gets committed. Complete with truck drivers en route, adultery ad lib, and some good tough writing, but no detection.

1449   Nightmare in Pink   GM 1964

Travis McGee, whose moral and social creed in the tradition of Chandler's Marlowe is given on p. 21, leaves his beach bum's paradise in Florida to solve in New York City the murder of the man who was to marry Travis' war buddy's sister. The suspense is expertly done as usual, the sex is explicit but poeticized, the evil of riches and cities is virtually out of the Bible, and the hanky-panky of the sanatorium, though outré, is scientifically sound.

1450   The Quick Red Fox   GM 1964

A Travis McGee story that allows him to philosophize in an antisocial way about the evil world, because it brings him in contact with a ruthless female movie star, assorted playboys and their victims, and a thoroughly good and attractive woman, who leaves him from sheer goodness. McGee's object has been to secure or suppress damaging photos of the movie star. He succeeds thanks to good reasoning and a strong use of brass.

MacDonald, Philip (also Oliver Fleming, Anthony Lawless, and Martin Porlock, q.v.)

One of the phalanx that broke out in the thirties. His one-syllable titles and books in the classic genre made a great stir in those palmy days, especially *The Rasp*. MacDonald subsequently went to Hollywood, whose atmosphere influenced his later work in the direction of complexity and melodrama, so much so that his Colonel Gethryn—never very long on consecutive reasoning—gave up explanation in favor of solutions by fiat.

1451   The Crime Conductor   Burt 1931

Gethryn's wife being away, he can make her do the work by writing her long reports of "the case." This last is theatrical in both senses of the word, and what is deplorable, it is full of good clues treated in a fantastically loose and garrulous manner.

1452   The Link   CCC 1930

Undoubtedly the best Gethryn novel. True, the central idea is visible to the astute reader well before it is disclosed by G.'s efforts, but those efforts are authentic. Useless talk and comings and goings are at a minimum, thanks to the attractive physician-veterinary, who is busy and cannot be everywhere and to whom Gethryn must therefore confide his secrets tersely and rationally. Today, the American local color makes one smile—imagine the word *racketeer* being thought strange!—but it is legitimate period stuff.

WHT dissents from the favorable estimate.

1453   The List of Adrian Messenger   CCD 1959

This is something of a comeback for MacDonald, considering the length and sustained effect of the tale. It develops in England, though its somewhat implausible running down of the villain is in California. A list of ten names, when discovered, suggests men murdered, presumably by a Napoleon of Crime, in ways calculated to look like accident: how to connect them up? MacDonald manages a new wrinkle in the old cloak-cum-dagger. Gethryn, too, is less odious and obvious than usual with him.

1454   The Noose   CCC 1930

The third of the Gethryn tales and the first book to be published under the label "Crime Club" (Collins). In this largely unsatisfactory effort Gethryn sets himself the task of securing evidence within five days which will save a condemned man from hanging for a crime six months old. G.'s wife, Lucia, and his long black car are more in evidence than any detection, and the chief constable of the county plays an unsuitable role.

1455   The Polferry Riddle   Burt 1931

This is easily one of the worst Gethryn stories; full of activity, yet nothing happens, and patience balks.

1456   The Rasp   Dday 1925

The first of the Anthony Gethryn affairs. G. is one of the toplofty gentlemen detectives, whose creation leans heavily on Bentley's Philip Trent without matching his stature. The story is the conventional body-in-the-study, with a fair amount of obvious detection. The marks left by the rasp are much too silly to be believed and the killer's fakery is plain from the start. Despite all this, it has several times been declared "a classic" and "epochmaking" by students of the genre.

1457   Warrant for X   CCC 1938
         In Eng.: The Nursemaid Who Disappeared

A good idea: a forgotten shopping list as slender clue, but too much chasing about and too many Napoleons of crime. Average for MacDonald, with his bad trick of telling by not letting the teller finish any sentence and his perpetual "My God, Gethryn!" At times this exactly expresses the reader's feelings.

1458   The White Crow   Coll 1928
         A Story of Crime

This tale seems to be his second, eighteen months after *The Rasp* (q.v.). Its style apes H. C. Bailey's—staccato, self-interrupted, exclamatory. In the Office of the President and Controller (also marked "Enquiries Here"), Sir Albert Lines-Bower sits at his desk in his underwear, his jugular cut. His blond stenographer, who talks inaccurate American, is suspected, then let go. Other red herrings and violent actions are also unconvincing, as is the mixture of heavy irony and jolly schoolrag attitude. Gethryn's harangue at the end is fatuous, but the scene is good drama and it inspired imitation in Michael Gilbert's play *A Clean Kill* (q.v.).

1459   X. v. Rex   Coll 1933
        First publ. as by Martin Porlock

Not a Gethryn story, but a series of killings of police constables out of a grievance against that inexhaustible body of men. Neither detection nor good reading.

1460   MacDonald, P. See also No. 2638 and:

Death on My Left	CCD 1933	Mystery in Kensington Gore	
Guest in the House	CCD 1955	(by M. Porlock)	Coll 1960/1932
Mystery at Friar's Pardon		Mystery of the	
(by M. Porlock;		Dead Police	CCD 1933
see No. 1732)	CCD 1932	Persons Unknown	CCD 1931
		Rope to Spare	CCD 1932

MacDonald, Ross (formerly John Ross Macdonald; pseud. of Kenneth Millar, b. 1915)

b. near San Francisco, the Canadian-educ. husband of Margaret Millar (who, says one blurb, "lives quietly" with him in California and also writes mysteries) has produced a number of excellent detective novels of the neo-tough variety, with Lew Archer as private-eye hero. The California scene is often better (because less outré) than Chandler's and the psychology and social observation are more original and penetrating.

1461   The Doomsters   Knopf 1958

The bloody consequences of acts by an unscrupulous doctor who wenches, gives drugs, and commits murders to hoist himself up the social ladder. Well-done in its genre, but after 100 pages it is predictably devoid of detection or surprise.

1462   The Drowning Pool   Knopf 1950

Admirers of the later Ross Macdonald will detect in this early book the capacities subsequently so well exploited. Lew Archer started as he continued: tough and straight; clever and informed, but not omniscient; full of love and hostility toward Southern California. This story, of a woman who has made a bad marriage to a mother-dominated husband of ambivalent sexual character, has a bit too much violence, but the character-drawing shows a sure hand, and the tangle is so capably manipulated that it does not annoy. Detection modern, not classical.

1463   The Far Side of the Dollar   Knopf 1965/1964

A remarkably complex plot, which nevertheless stays perfectly clear in this able spinner's hands and develops a series of gripping relationships, notably that of the young to their parents and other elders and to well-to-do existence. On this point the book is more informative and intelligent than many essays by experts. The mystery and murders are secondary to the emotional tangle and past misbehavior which Lew Archer unravels.

1464   The Ferguson Affair   Knopf 1960

This just fails to click—the young lawyer hero Bill Gunnerson seems a poor substitute for Lew Archer, and there are too many characters, too much plotting, and not enough story. Macdonald as usual tells his tale competently, but it lacks force.

1465   The Galton Case   Knopf 1959

One of the best Lew Archer stories. It combines private-eye work with excellent characterizing, and adds the engrossing problem of a man missing for twenty years, plus well-done Canadian scenes to balance the usual Los Angeles surroundings.

1466   The Ivory Grin   Knopf 1952
          In ppb.: Marked for Murder

An amazing job: few plots so complex hold together to the end, and a tale so full of killings should make one disbelieve, yet it is sound and believable from A to Z.

1467   The Moving Target   Knopf 1949

The mixed tawdriness and glamor of L.A., which the author was to exploit for twenty years, is here in full view. Archer is solid and reliable, a safe man to be with in a tight place, or to use as a shoulder by a distressed damsel. But the tough characters who frequent the bars and arrange the kidnapping of a semi-degenerate millionaire now seem less fresh than they did when first unpacked.

1468   MACDONALD, R. See also:

          Black Money   Knopf 1966
          The Instant Enemy   Knopf 1968
          The Way Some People Die   Knopf 1951
          The Zebra-Striped Hearse   Knopf 1962

1469   MACDUFF, DAVID (b. 1905)

          Murder Strikes Three   MA 1937

A lonely try about an imaginary college in the vicinity of Delaware Water Gap, where improbable hell-raising by a pair of young instructors winds up in detection. The murdered man is an unlikely professor of archaeology. High-speed navigation on the upper Delaware, hijacking, drugs, a girl, and unprepared underground passages furnish out the rest of this mixed-up effort.

1470   McGERR, PAT(RICIA)

Catch Me if You Can   CCD 1948

A variation on the problem of *Pick Your Victim* (No. 1474): A woman who has assisted her sick husband into the hereafter is faced with four persons, one a woman, any of whom may be the detective set on her trail. A splendid idea executed with surprising amateurishness.

1471   Fatal in My Fashion   CCD 1954

Paris *haute couture,* with the usual trimmings. Not so bad as *Save the Witness* but not so good as earlier and later ones (see No. 1475).

1472   Follow as the Night   CCD 1950

The dedication tells us that Miss McG. has three sisters. The book is well written, but the plot is a little too melodramatic for credence: A man invites four women to dine, that he may dispose of the one he has his eye on. Detection slight.

1473   Murder Is Absurd   Goll 1967

A summer troupe puts on a new play of the absurd by the son and stepson of famous actors, which discloses an old murder: the *Hamlet* theme refurbished; no detection.
   Note: Greatly admired by Edmund Crispin.

1474   Pick Your Victim   CCD 1946

A masterpiece, unique in conception: not "whodunit?" but "whodunin?" That is, the unraveling, for high money stakes, and from scraps of newspaper, of a murder done in Washington, D.C., those panting for a solution being U.S. soldiers marooned in an army base thousands of miles away. The figure of the woman temperance leader and the others in Washington political life are limned in masterly fashion. Pat McGerr could hardly hope to equal this performance but see the ingenious narrative treatment of a similar theme in *The Seven Deadly Sisters* (1947).

1475   McGERR. See also:

Death in a Million		The Missing Years	CCD 1953
Living Rooms	CCD 1951	Save the Witness	CCD 1949
Die Laughing	CCC 1952	The Seven Deadly Sisters	CCD 1947
Is There a Traitor in the		Stranger With My Face	Luce 1968
House?	CCD 1964	Your Loving Victim	CCC 1951

1476   McGIRR, EDMUND (pseud. of Kenneth Giles, q.v.)

An Entry of Death   Walk 1969

The author, we are told, now has experience in publishing, and has settled down to write the kind of mystery he himself would like to publish. This first is a dismal augury of things to come. In a jerry-built Welsh castle, near an unrealistically odious seaside town, a wealthy American has been shot, possibly by his young wife. Piron, the detective acting for an American insurance company, is not a bad fellow, but any system in his actions is snafued by an impossible crew of locals. Welsh myth and Arthurian legend not being enough to make his prose interesting, the author has recourse to a reckless overdose of vulgarity.

McGIVERN, WILLIAM P(ETER)

A Hammett follower who has published numerous tales of corruption in city government and police forces. The books are strong on procedure, conventional as to morals, and lacking in detection. In the latest stories, from 1960 on, the scene has shifted from the big city to Morocco or Spain.

1477   The Big Heat   DM 1953

The suicide of a corrupt police clerk gives homicide sergeant Dave Bannion of the Philadelphia police an opportunity to exercise his imagination, and the death of Bannion's wife (incidental to gangster protest over his investigations) spurs him on. The hero has more luck than intelligence and the bad boys are rather too easily smoked out, but the picture of dogged persistence shows much skill.

1478   Very Cold for May   DM 1950

In the present tale of triple murder for a scandalous diary, the texture is thin, the tone commonplace, and the detection, though genuine, too mechanical to excite the speculative nerve.

1479   McGIVERN. See also:

But Death Runs Faster	DM 1945	Margin of Terror	DM 1953
The Caper of the		Night Extra	DM 1957
Golden Bulls	DM 1966	Rogue Cop	DM 1954
A Choice of Assassins	DM 1963	The Seven File	DM 1956
The Crooked Frame	DM 1952	Seven Lies South	DM 1960
The Darkest Hour	DM 1955		

McGUIRE, (DOMINIC) PAUL (b. 1905)

b. and educ. south Australia; has had a distinguished career as diplomat and author of works on Australia and world politics, and has also written some popular works on Australian theater, inns, etc., as well as some poetry. Was Australian minister to Italy (1954–58) and ambassador (1958–59). Delegate to U.N. General Assembly, 1953.

1480   The Black Rose Murder   Bren 1932

A slow story of Jewish pawnbrokers and jewel dealers transplanted into
English village life, out of some quixotic interest that leads to a mixed
marriage. The author has an ax to grind, as in one or two of his others.
The inwoven love is tedious, detection feeble.

1481   Death Tolls the Bell   CM 1933
         In Eng.: Death Fugue

The book starts badly with 35 pages of chatty philosophy and willful
strangeness, but a real situation soon develops. Crime and detection follow
and are seriously sustained, as is the atmosphere. What prevents a full
recovery of tone is the author's persistence in forwarding his religious
point of view, apparently High Church Anglican.

1482   Enter Three Witches   Morr 1940
         In Eng.: The Spanish Steps

A sensitively written story full of humor and Roman atmosphere, with two
or three fairly live characters—so live, in fact, that no corpse turns up
until nearly the end of the book. The hero is a newspaper correspondent,
and there is little detection, though some entertaining snooping about
house-and-grounds after dark.

1483   A Funeral in Eden   Morr 1938
         In Eng.: Burial Service

A masterpiece. The murder of an intruder into the tropic island "empire"
of Kaitai, ruled over by George Buchanan (the "sultan") and his competent woman physician, Alicia Murray, is dealt with in a steadily brilliant
and enchanting manner. Adventure, atmosphere, character, and detection
are rarely so well blended.

1484   Murder at High Noon   Dday 1935
         In Eng.: Daylight Murder

The financial specialist of a London daily is made away with and his body
concealed in a hayrick (= stack). The story is told in the first person by
Blight, a reporter on the same paper. Stylistically not McGuire at his
best, nor does one relish the rather routine detection, sprinkled with humor
that is dated.

1485   Murder in Haste   Skeff 1934

A fair sample of McG.'s good middle manner. It deals with the killing
of an innocent witness to an illegal operation who is disposed of by an
ingenious trap requiring a sophisticated bus. A very pretty problem is left
for Chief Inspector Cummings and Superintendent Watchet. The relation
of these two, by the way, is a good early example of subdued hostility.

The murdered man is introduced at once, and it arrests our attention that his name should be Swann and his death take place in France. But the main action of the tale goes on in London, told in the first person by a male screen star. It is thriller adventure more than detection, but written with sparkle, 1930 style, and a certain amount of reasoning and method in the shenanigans. The CID inspector and his sergeant are fairly good types, and by reading quickly one can maintain a degree of belief in the nonsense, which (by the way) involves the Modstone Agency the author is so fond of.

1487   Three Dead Men   Bren 1932

The present tale has what we both find trying—a nervous, incompetent "Mr. Pinkerton" type of hero. Endless jerky sentences do not advance matters, and when this fault is combined with an improbable romance and a hastily explained melodramatic denouement, the novel as a whole is hard to bear. Note that one of the characters is connected with the Modstone Inquiry Agency, which figured largely and dully in *The Black Rose Murder*.

WHT is not nearly so adverse in his judgment.

1488   Threepence to Marble Arch   Skeff 1936

One of three brothers who are of divergent political views and modes of life ostensibly falls out of his office window while writing a journalistic blast against his capitalist brother. The brothers' young cousin, a girl, arrives on the scene with an escort, who is a novelist and who knows Inspector Wittler, in charge of the case. The talk goes round and round at first, but by p. 110 detection begins in earnest. Unhappily, the author's penchant for bright repartee tends to swamp the story as it unwinds in predictable fashion. There is, however, one excellent forgery, and incidental as it is to the plot, it offers a parallel motive to the one used in *Gaudy Night* (No. 1900).

1489   McGuire. See also:

Born to Be Hanged	Skeff 1935	Murder in Bostall	Skeff 1931
Cry Aloud for Murder	Hein 1937	Prologue to the Gallows	Skeff 1936
Murder by the Law (= The		There Sits Death	Skeff 1933
Tower Mystery)	Skeff 1932	W. 1	Hein 1937

MacInnes, Helen [Mrs. Gilbert Highet] (b. 1907)

Not a writer of detective stories. She does tales of espionage and propaganda with taste and knowledge of attractive places abroad and an old-world sense of who is likable and who detestable.

1490   Assignment: Suspense   HB 1961

This omnibus volume contains *Above Suspicion* (her first; 1941),

Horizon (1945), and *Assignment in Brittany* (1942). In the first and the last there is much to admire about the twists of espionage in Germany before the second world war and in war-torn France. The violence is controlled and perhaps the only flaw is an excess of smoothness in the way things work out. An attractive husband-and-wife team functions in *Above Suspicion;* and the Brittany tale profits from its well-drawn solo hero, Martin Hearne, scholar, parachutist, and lover.

1491   The Double Image   HB 1966
      Sketch map of Greece and the islands

Mild excitement of a well-known kind surrounds Americans and French people in Greece, the places and situations being rather less conspicuous than the persons and their relationships.

1492   Pray for a Brave Heart   HB 1955

The fine quotation from Juvenal that is used in the title comes at the close of a story about young Americans embroiled in cloak-and-dagger stuff in Switzerland. Some feminine small talk holds back an otherwise clean-cut plot. The bad men haven't their heart in the job.

      McIntyre, John T(homas) (also Kerry O'Neil; 1871–1951)

This author acquired a certain reputation as a practitioner of the realistic novel before the first world war (see *Shot Towers* and *A Young Man's Fancy*). As a writer of detective fiction he is not precisely a realist, but rather an imitator of Doyle and Arthur Morrison, whom he resembles in his dual literary role, but scarcely approaches in quality.

1493   Ashton-Kirk, Investigator   Penn 1910
      Introd. by the author
      Illus. by Ralph L. Boyer

The first Ashton-Kirk story, the second being announced in the Introduction as *Ashton-Kirk and the Scarlet Scapular.* The period demanded the filling of 336 pages with a complicated plot involving a numismatist bayoneted in his shop (by a Frenchman from Bayonne) so that the stolen plans might be recovered, etc. Amidst all this Ashton-Kirk makes a few Holmesian deductions from a candle end and the punched-out bit of a railroad ticket. The detective's allusions to Poe, Marryat, and Ibsen establish his literary judgment, but his knowledge of the German language must be classed as imperfect.

1494   The Museum Murder   CCD 1929

This story is written with strange inconsequence—some telling phrases and good dialogue mixed with wrong idiom and sentences that cannot be construed. Yet the central idea is not bad: the theft of a picture from a museum as part of an elaborate revenge involving fakery, blackmail, and moral turpitude. The business leads to murder, and this in turn to its unraveling by a fat young man and gourmet named Duddington Pell Chalmers.

Note that D.P.C. foreshadows Nero Wolfe, feebly but truly, for he, too, works by interviewing people en masse.

1495   MACKAIL, DENIS (GEORGE) (b. 1892)

The Majestic Mystery   HM 1924

The author usually goes in for romance and light fooling. Here he avoids romance but combines fooling with a murder, which turns out quite ambiguous and is in fact never brought home to its perpetrators. The shy journalists and the theatrical people sometimes grow a bit tiresome, but the hotel headwaiter and some good scenes redeem what is no doubt a murder story but not detection.

1496   McKIMMEY, JAMES

Run if You're Guilty   Lipp 1963

The author has written nine other novels, says the blurb, but there is no evidence that any of these were detection. The present effort is a suspense yarn pure and very simple. Miscellaneous shooting by a psycho in a cabin motel in northern California might divert a near-adult for an hour or so.

1497   MacKINNON, ALAN

Appointment in Iraq   CCD 1960

Very poor stuff; much running around, and no real suspense. The author is hardly ever convincing outside the Scottish scene he knows and does so well.

1498   Cormorant's Isle   CCD 1962

Something of a comeback, after three disappointing tales. A Turkish lad is kidnapped from his camp in Scotland, and the young man who was acting as camp leader at the time is led an exciting chase all over Britain in pursuit of the boy and his own reputation. Everything is laid on: attractive Norwegian blonde, a castle on a Highland isle, and good rough stuff— i.e., kept within sensible limits. The blonde surrenders only on the last page.

1499   House of Darkness   CCD 1947

His best. The Scottish castle where persons are unlawfully detained, the nitwitted actress with golden hair whom the hero seduces on the train, two other interesting women who severally help him, and a variation on the theme of the high-placed culprit make this a perfect compendium. The chase on the scree of the Oban hills is in the great tradition—Scott, Stevenson, and Buchan topped off.

1500   Map of Mistrust   Coll 1948

Third in order of merit. Postwar spy work is carried on by Anthony Carne, an academic historian and former M-I man. He finds an improbable red-headed young girl doctor whom he marries (presumably), but although he solves the puzzle and one of the murders, the second, remains touched with an ambiguity that the author probably intended.

1501   Money on the Black   Dday 1946
         In Eng.: Nine Days' Murder

Next to the best tale by this author, this one plays with black-market operations in wartime London. The opening is the murder in a fur ware-house of the night watchman, whose cat is named Franklin Roosevelt. What follows is just believable, and what more can one ask?

1502   Murder, Repeat Murder   CCC 1952

Probably MacKinnon's only attempt to write a thriller without benefit of fugitives and with professional detection. The plot is complicated and made to appear more so than it is. The title is no excuse for too many murders, but the central idea of having a film company produce its version of an unsolved London boardinghouse murder is good, though rather thrown away. Official detectives acceptable.

1503   Report from Argyll   CCD 1964

This latest return of MacKinnon to the Scottish scene has little save topography to recommend it. Action is not lacking: the London news-paperman Don Kendrick tracks, prowls, and is knocked out on numerous occasions by adversaries who may be friends in disguise. What the chase is all about never becomes clear, though the author manages to ring in Russian agents, anti-communists from the Middle East, and a not im-possible she, who takes part in an undressing contest with the hero in a canoe.

1504   Summons from Baghdad   CCC 1958
         In Eng.: Red-Winged Angel

On the whole weak, though the "second-sight" portion at the beginning is beautifully done. The international intrigue and murdering in the Near East leaves one listless, despite the vivid background, well sketched in.

1505   McLaren, Moray

         The Pursuit   Jarr 1959

An easygoing account of the adventures of a young Scottish lawyer in London when he is seeking evidence to support the appeal of a wrongly convicted man. Mild entertainment.

1506   McLean, Allan Campbell (b. 1922)

         The Carpet-Slipper Murder   IW 1957/1956

This poorly titled tale is the author's first, but a commendable job. Told in the first person by Inspector MacLeod, it takes one through a group of British suspects in a village-manor setup with artistic overtones, and reveals the killer of the masquerading artist. No striking clues, intrigue, or sex, though all are there.

1507   Death on All Hallows   IW 1958

Here the Hebridean atmosphere (Skye) is underdone as to topography and overdone as to people, which takes the edge off a good plot—the murder of a tycoon who wants to desecrate the place with Happy Holiday camps. Plenty of action, and a good try at a surprise ending with the least likely person. Detective Inspector Neil MacLeod is the narrator.

MacLeod, Angus (b. 1906)

b. Wester Ross, Scot.; educ. Edinburgh Coll. of Art; art master in several schools in England. Full-time writer since 1952.

1508   Blessed Above Women   Dob 1965

A well-knit tale about Inspector Gilroy, who unriddles the murder of two men at a Scottish fishing hotel. The story is gripping and masterly in incident and character, but it ends abruptly and in a flawed manner when, in the last twenty-five pages, we are told the strange life histories of two people we thought we knew à fond.

1509   The Dam   Roy 1968

Not a detective story at all, nor really one of crime, though there is plenty of guilt. The author has given himself over to the character-drawing which he does so well. In the space of a few hours on an extremely hot summer day in a little Scottish town we are introduced to a dozen or so persons of extremely variable virtue, the worst of whom get their just deserts when the dam has had its fill.

1510   The Tough and the Tender   Roy 1960

The murder of the "factor" Boswell in a tight little Scottish community gives Inspector Gillandrew a chance to use his belief in the correlation of temperament and physical type for the elucidation of crime. But the pleasure afforded by the tale, as in others by MacLeod, comes much less from detection than from character-drawing. The Scots are, by definition, characters.

1511   MacLeod. See also:

        The Body's Guest (semi-supernatural)   Roy 1958
        The Eighth Seal   Roy 1962

1512   McMullen, Mary

        Death of Miss X   CCC 1952

Another advertising agency supplies the premises for the murder of an unknown—female, young, and naked—in the board room. We see the unraveling through the eyes of a new employee of the firm, Eve Fitzsimmons, who occasionally verges on HIBK. Yet other scenes are excellent and strength of plotting and characterization cannot be denied—a mixed-up first effort, probably written earlier than 1952.

1513 McShane, Mark

Untimely Ripped   CCD 1963/Coll 1932

A tiresome attempt to fix a series of murders of semi-retired prostitutes (with evidential slicings and gore) upon a self-styled evangelist. The latter's mouthings and droolings are not badly done, but the growing evidence of the insanity of Detective James Matric is so clear that his exposure as the criminal comes as no shock. Matric's middle name is Caesar, an early clue to his style of birth, and this irregularity, plus a prostitute mother, were what started him off wrong!

The title is from *Macbeth,* V, 8, 16.

1514 MacTyre, Paul. *Bar Sinister* (1964) and several others by the same hand are thrillers, sex-ridden and cluttered. Detective interest negligible.

1515 MacVeigh, Sue (pseud. of Elizabeth [Custer] Nearing, b. 1898). Wrote *Murder Under Construction* (1939) and several other railroad mysteries. Being married to a construction engineer, she narrates the doings of her detective Andy MacVeigh from the point of view of a wife. Scene: New York State; quality: fair. See *Streamlined Murder* (1940) and *The Grand Central Murder* (1939).

MacVicar, Angus (b. 1908)

b. Duror, Argyll: educ. Glasgow Univ.; this author had written more than 60 books by 1965, half of them mystery or suspense. Some of them make room for legitimate detection. Recently he has featured Inspector Samuel McLintock and, needless to say, Scottish settings.

1516 The Grey Shepherds   Long 1964

A girl is killed near the Druid stone where archaeologists have been digging. Meanwhile, Shamus MacDonald, a free-lance journalist, is asked by British TV to investigate the plans of a suspected gang, which assignment takes him to various places, including Baldorno, Scotland, whence everything clicks together into a familiar pattern of spy stuff, without novelty of manner or matter. (The Grey Shepherds are stones, not men.)

1517 Murder at the Open   Long 1965

A better-than-average tale of murder on the golf course at St. Andrews. Professor Adrian Campbell of Glasgow assists the police.

1518 MacVicar. See also:

The Canisbay Conspiracy	Long 1966
Crime's Masquerader	SP 1938
The Dancing Horse	Long 1961

Flowering Death   SP 1937
The Hammers of Fingal   Long 1963

1519 MAGILL, MARCUS (pseud. of Brian Hill) is not adequately known to us, but seems better than most of the practitioners of the thirties. In addition to *Who Shall Hang?* (1929) and *Mystery of the East Wind* (1930), he has written: *Death in the Box, I Like a Good Murder,* and *Murder Out of Tune.* Detective in some tales: Dwight Manfred; scene usually New York.

1520 MAINWARING, MARION

Murder in Pastiche   Macm 1954
   Nine Detectives All at Sea

On board the S.S. *Florabunda,* Poireau, Nappleby, Jerry Pason, Trajan Beare, Spike Bludgeon, Mallory King, Lord Simon Quinsey, Miss Fan Silver, and Broderick Tourneur cooperate to solve the murder of a despicable man. As Max Beerbohm showed by flawless examples, it takes much penetration and wit, plus a full command of the literary art, to produce a successful parody. This one is only mildly amusing.

1521 MANER, WILLIAM

Die of a Rose   CCD 1970

A deplorable book. A football star is stabbed in a classroom at a poorly characterized Virginia college, and the efforts of young Professor Harley to elucidate the crime by the "pure Baconian method" of putting each ascertained fact on a separate 5 x 7 card would have failed at the hands of the Lord Chancellor himself. Sex, drugs, student violence, and gambling do not adorn the tale, but make it the more tedious.

The title is from Pope's *Essay on Man,* l. 200.

1522 MANN, LEONARD (b. 1895)

A Murder in Sydney   Dday 1937

A successful attempt at making a novel out of life in Sydney during the Depression, when art and business, socialism and youthful uncertainty get entangled with the usual course of love and jealousy, and lead to murder. The various tones and traits are mingled and distinguished with great skill, and though the extended police inquiry does not uncover anything the reader does not already know, it develops character and maintains suspense.

1523 MANSFIELD, PAUL

Final Exposure   Macm 1958

An amateurish piece of prose, but till near the end not a bad tale. A Caribbean household is shown in a clear light, and two camera artists from New York City are excellently done. A wild party in semi-darkness yields confusion and killing. What is bad is (*a*) the part played by the camera and (*b*) the person we are asked to believe committed the crime.

1524   MARDER, IRVING

The Paris Bit   CCC 1967

A lively, witty, sexy bit about murders in Paris, investigated by one Max
Moritz, newspaperman on *The Trombone*. With the tough wisecracking
and fornication goes some bitter but intelligent criticism of modern life
in general and Gaullist France in particular.

1525   MARKHAM, ROBERT (pseud. of Kingsley Amis, q.v.)

Dr. Sun   Harp 1968

This pastiche of a James Bond adventure is as expertly done as one would
expect from an accomplished novelist and critic, but the fire of temporary
belief is lacking and the book is only amusing and only in spots; which
shows that on every plane of performance some form of conviction is
needed before even puppets move agreeably.

1526   MARKHAM, VIRGIL (b. 1899)

The Black Door   Knopf 1930
   *The Mystery of the Fate of Sir Anthony Veryan's Heirs in
   Kestrel's Eyrie Castle Near the Coast of Wales, Now Set
   Down, etc., etc.*
   Folding map of Ramsey Is. and coastline; three floor plans

The subtitle suggests a recital of true crime. The book is fiction, of the
kind that uses a Gothic setting to pile up impossible mysteries and compass the extermination of an eccentric family. The reader frequently feels
impatient with the persons and events, or with what the author chooses to
say about them. But in fairness it must be conceded that *his* belief in the
story and his command of words manage to carry the thing off. Not nearly
so good, though, as the next item.

1527   Inspector Rusby's Finale   Farr 1933

The enticing and perfectly phrased first page is not belied by the succeeding pages, which tell of the Inspector's careful and reasonable and also
passionate inquiries, for like Philip Trent he is in love with the most
likely suspect in a strange and "causeless" murder. The denouement,
which takes in a hoax, a family scandal, and a private insane asylum, is a
bit hard to swallow, but the author manages it with virtuosity and the
reader has all the pleasure.
   V.M.'s narrative powers encourage the reader to seek out *Death in the
Dusk* (1928) and *The Devil Drives* (1933), both elusive items.

1528   MARLOWE, PIERS. The author has written *Demon in the Blood,
Loaded Dice, The Double Thirteen,* and *The Dead Don't Scare.* The
fifth—*The Men in Her Death* (1964)—is about the death of a famous
cocotte and blackmailer. Superintendent Frank Drury and Inspector Bill
Hazard work at it in fairly routine fashion. Relationships wildly tangled
at the end.

1529 MARQUAND, JOHN P(HILLIPS) (also John Phillips; 1893–1960). Whoever wants run-of-the-mill adventure vaguely reminiscent of other *Saturday Evening Post* fiction will look up *Mr. Moto's Three Aces* (1956), which contains typical tales about Mr. Moto dating from the thirties, before the author became a semi-serious novelist.

1530 MARRIC, J. J. (pseud. of John Creasey, q.v.)

Gideon's Fire   Harp 1961

The seventh in the Gideon series of police procedural novels inaugurated by Creasey in 1955. For those who like a detective story, this is not really satisfying, despite a fairly rich tapestry of crime (rape, mistress-murder, burglary) which is the backdrop to Commander George Gideon's war against a crackpot who hopes to burn down enough London slums to encourage the demolition of the rest. Competently written, with a fair amount of the hero's home life to fill up the transitions from one crime to another, but essentially a report, not a novel.

1531 Gideon's Night   Harp 1957

Later exposure to more of Commander Gideon's exploits has made WHT realize their substantial merits in matters of CID procedure and as reflectors of the London scene. But this one, dealing with the search for a sexual prowler, remains his least favorite.

1532 Gideon's River   Harp 1968

Unquestionably the best of the Gideon series. Earlier efforts at interweaving several pending investigations with the lives of the police force and his own left Gideon looking more distracted than capable and the reader more badgered than entertained. In this tale, balance of elements and tightness of plot are remarkable. From the diamond smuggling which starts the ball rolling to the kidnappings and murders, the fête on the river (Thames, of course), and the checkmate planned by Gideon, everything fits with precision and naturalness. Form and contents seem one, and only the carping would complain that it doesn't leave enough to be desired.

1533 Gideon's Vote   Harp 1964

Within its limits—that is, detection on the basis of "information received" and a plentiful supply of manpower—a very fair job. Gideon handles a complex situation involving the "influencing" of a general election with great skill, and the suspense is maintained by Marric's usual means— interweaving several current minor crimes under investigation—though the whole is more instructive than detective.

1534 MARRIC. See also:

The Gideon Omnibus   H&S 1964
(contains *Gideon's Day, Night,* and *Week*)

MARSH, [DAME] (EDITH) NGAIO, [orig. N'gaio] O.B.E. (b. 1899)

b. Christchurch, N.Z.; educ. St. Margaret's and Canterbury Univ. Coll. School of Art, Christchurch, N.Z. Has exhibited her talent for the theater as producer and lecturer, both in England and at home; lives in Christchurch; has written a book on New Zealand (Coll 1942) and an autobiography, *Black Beech and Honey Dew* (LB 1965).

1535   Clutch of Constables   LB 1969
Endpaper map of the journey on the Thames

An adroitly designed tale in which Alleyn in two places and his wife alone on a short Thames cruise dovetail information leading to the capture of a picturesque gang. Motives, murders, and suspense quite freshly invented and depicted.

1536   Colour Scheme   LB 1943

This tale recounts espionage in the N.E. of "New Zillund" (as the natives call it), and it treats scenery and people in N.M.'s most loving fashion. The incompetent family and the temperamental actor are both here, but not objectionable, thanks to a sharp-eyed and humorous young hero and to the author's relish for satire. Roderick Alleyn appears two-thirds of the way through.

1537   Dead Water   LB 1963

Disappointing, in view of the excellent opportunities afforded by the novel setting—a "healing spring" in the west of England, with all the animosity aroused by the new owner's decision to decommercialize it. The usual team of Alleyn and Fox functions efficiently, but there is a decided lack of the light touch. Even the frustrated spinster and her diary are not made much of. Those guilty of murder are fairly obvious.

1538   Death at the Bar   Coll 1940

A seaside public house gathers a picturesque group of characters. Death by poisoned dart is not quite what it seems at the outset, and the murderer's plan, though psychologically tricky, is physically quite practical. The book's outstanding contribution to the genre is its management of the problem: How to keep the reader from suspecting the most obvious suspect.

1539   Death in Ecstasy   Bles 1936

One of the early treatments (and a good one) of The House of the Sacred Flame, the "cult" for weak-minded creatures that is so useful to writers of detective stories. Alleyn and Fox perform extremely well and the fun along the way is first-class.

1540   Death of a Fool   LB 1956

A tedious story of ancient village mummery used to conceal modern murder. The atmosphere is good, but the strain to make details clear in pitch darkness weakens the impetus, and the work of Alleyn is more contemplative and aphorismic than the situation calls for.

1541 Death of a Peer   LB 1940

Note and mark well: this is the intolerable tale of the impoverished New Zealand family (now in London) who are liars in unison from a desire to protect one another when the head of the family, Lord Wutherwood, is dispatched with a skewer in the eye during a lift journey down from their flat.

1542 Died in the Wool   LB 1945

An unusual tale, with detection by Alleyn under great handicaps. The pace is slow and the tactics mainly psychological. Only at the end is an old-fashioned trap set for the murderer, who is reasonably surprising, in view of the extremely small group of possible suspects. A grim tale, without the author's quondam wit.

1543 Enter a Murderer   Furman 1935

A classic case of the murder in full view, with all clues and actions fairly presented in the tersest, most lucid way. First-rate satire of actors serves in place of gush, and this presentment of Roderick Alleyn makes him more truly a man than anywhere else in the canon.

1544 False Scent   LB 1959

A theatrical tale, but wholly unobjectionable. The fading first lady throws tantrums and exerts tyranny and gets done in by spraying herself with what she believes is scent. The family relationships are prime, as are scenes and eccentricities. Alleyn and Fox recessive but not dull.

1545 Final Curtain   LB 1947

An excellent early Marsh, of the sort that relies on the large family. Alleyn's wife, Troy, paints the portrait of the old patriarch who is about to marry the young chorus girl—results predictable. Arsenic plays the role of a blind for thallium acetate. Character and dialogue in the author's best style. Alleyn and marital problems handled with a discreet subtlety soon to be forgotten in the rush to explicit sexuality by inferior writers.

1546 Hand in Glove   LB 1962

Another who was everybody's choice for murderee. He is found in a ditch, under a heavy sewer pipe. Among the weird characters is one named Pyke Period; the scene is Little Codling. A full set of "young people," one of whom Alleyn declares to be a stinker, which suggests Ngaio's own blasé feelings about detection. Indeed, Alleyn and Fox do practically nothing except speak sharply once or twice. The narrative is smooth and occasionally witty.

1547 Killer Dolphin   LB 1966

Here an old theater is the killer, by reason of what happens in it to the likable group of young people who restore the place and act a successful piece in it. But the mystery is forced and the outcome dull.

1548 A Man Lay Dead   Bles 1934

Ngaio Marsh's first book; and though a bit dated, an auspicious beginning. It is overlaid with country-house amenities and Russian brotherhoods, and the dodge—or rather sweep—of the little man who simultaneously fells his victim and saves time on his alibi is something to marvel at rather than to duplicate.

1549 Night at the Vulcan   LB 1951
         In ppb.: Opening Night

The Vulcan is a theater in London. The stage often brings out the worst in Ngaio. The crime is committed at the dressing table. Almost the whole cast deserves to perish in the same way.

1550 Overture to Death   Bles 1936

Ngaio Marsh's best work. Alleyn and Fox unmask the person who arranged a pistol in an upright piano so that with the first use of the soft pedal in Rachmaninoff's sempiternal prelude the lady performer is extinguished. Excellent detection amid village scenes, with a splendid contrast between the local squire and family and the vicar with his lovelorn flock. The treatment of female jealousy is superb.

1551 Scales of Justice   CCC 1952

Alleyn alert and witty, other characters stock but lively, plot and detection excellently sustained, atmosphere enjoyable, and side comments ingenious. The drawback comes at the end, when the implausible culprit is revealed. The setting is rural England, including: a large fish in a trout stream, a local family of proud bearing, and a gentle man whose integrity leads to his death.

1552 Singing in the Shrouds   LB 1958

A better-than-average try at the old business of spotting a murderer at sea. Inspector Alleyn (the pronunciation of his name comes in for thorough treatment) is somewhat hampered by the necessity of keeping the murderer's presence a secret from the eight other passengers; so that— what is rare at sea—a plateau appears about the middle of the journey.

1553 Spinsters in Jeopardy   LB 1953

Alleyn, wife, and cub in the south of France engage in moderately entertaining cloak-and-dagger stuff, culminating in the very amusing but infamous ceremonies based on the "Book of Ra." These are described by the author as "unbridled Phallicism." With so much visceral excitement, what is being detected remains obscure.

1554   A Wreath for Rivera   LB 1949
           In U.S.: Swing, Brother, Swing

The scene is London, and the presence of a peculiarly irritating crowd of jazz artists and a most eccentric peer do not engender tedium or annoyance. The details of the crime (murder of a piano-accordionist) are well wrapped up and tied in with the personalities of the story. Some detection by Alleyn, but his great revelation is that his wife is pregnant.

1555   MARSH. See also No. 2651 and:

    Artists in Crime   Bles 1938
    Death and the Dancing Footman   LB   1941
    Death in a White Tie   Bles 1938
    Vintage Murder   Bles 1937

1556   MARSH, NGAIO, and [DR.] JELLETT, HENRY

           The Nursing Home Murder   Sher 1941

There is only one murder, although the paperback cover gives a plural, no doubt to increase the appeal. Home Secretary Sir Derek O'Callighan unexpectedly dies on the operating table. Alleyn makes his steady way among the plethora of syringes, nurses, assistants, anesthetist, and surgeon, finally bringing the crime home to one whose motives were ethical if distorted. More accurate than most hospital stories, and beautifully put together.

1557   MARTIN, A(RCHIBALD) E(DWARD) (b. 1885). This Australian comedian, film actor, prizefighter, etc., writes breezy stories without special merits or differentiation among themselves. See *The Bridal Bed Murders* (1953), *The Curious Crime* (1952), and *The Outsiders* (1945).

1558   MARTIN, STUART

           The Fifteen Cells   Burt 1928

A tour de force, of which JB thinks more highly than does WHT. A criminal, planning to save a friend from execution, forces the governor of a prison to acquiesce (seemingly) in his plan. The governor, held at pistol point, does a Scheherazade about fourteen criminals who fill as many cells. These subjects are well chosen and the governor is very good. No detection.

1559   MARTIN, S. See also:

    Capital Punishment (a novel)   Hutch 1931
    The Mystery of Clough Mills   Harp 1930/Macd 1920
    The Trial of Scotland Yard   Hutch 1930

1560   MASEFIELD, JOHN (1878–1967)

Dead Ned   Macm 1938
The Autobiography of a Corpse

The poet laureate of England wrote this paradoxical affair without much conviction, despite a complicated plot to make appearances lie. The next year he produced an even more unconvincing *Live and Kicking Ned.* Best forgotten and forgiven.

MASON, A(LFRED) E(DWARD) (WOODLEY) (1865–1948)

b. London; educ. Dulwich and Oxf.; one-time actor; successful playwright of *The Witness for the Defence.* M.P. for one term; civilian head of British Naval Intelligence during first world war. A novelist in several genres, who created Hanaud, a French Sûreté agent, to serve him in several long stories and one short one. They are now somewhat dated but far from unreadable. In Mason's other incarnation, read *The Four Feathers,* a best seller of the year 1902, and the undetective imbroglio *The Dean's Elbow* (1931). For essay and short stories, see No. 2977 and 2652–3. *The Winding Stair* (1923) is a story of ambition, not detection.

1561   At the Villa Rose   H&S 1910

A story about Hanaud and his friend Ricardo, who work together to defend the reputation of a young Englishwoman accused of murder when the rich woman she lived with as companion is found dead and robbed. The germ of the story is an actual crime in France. The scene is the Riviera, gambling is involved and portrayed, the characters are cardboard, and the least likely suspect is unmasked. As usual Hanaud waits until after the denouement to explain "how he knew." Skill in plotting and telling do not make up for period faults.

1562   The House of the Arrow   Doran 1924

It is difficult to do justice to this milepost in detective fiction. Not counting the author's own apologia in the omnibus volume *Inspector Hanaud Investigates* (H&S 1931), there are lengthy discussions of Mason's work by H. Douglas Thomson, Haycraft, and Sutherland Scott (qq.v.) to support his claims. The question is, how satisfying are Mason's productions for the modern reader of detection? The answer is that romance, melodrama, good characterization, and by no means negligible humor cannot compensate for Hanaud's failure to play fair with his Watson. This does permit Hanaud a surprise at the end: after he has the criminal handcuffed he explains every detail. But much fun is lost, for there is no *developing* concern. Poirot may well have learned from Hanaud how to hold back, and from his mistakes how not to overdo it.

1563   The House in Lordship Lane   DM 1946

The fourth Hanaud novel, with the crime in Brittany this time, and benefiting from the change to a northern climate: less circuitousness in the telling and a little fairer play with the reader.

1564   No Other Tiger   Doran 1927

Not a Hanaud story, but mystery and deception rather better done than
in the detective tales that lack detection. French locale again and fierce
women as well.

1565   The Prisoner in the Opal   Dday 1928

Probably the most pretentious and cluttered adventure of Hanaud and
his friend Ricardo. The title is a reference to Ricardo's vision of the
world "as a vast opal inside which I stood." That simple-minded and conventional wine-taster was oppressed and confused by the complications
which surrounded him in the château country of the Gironde, where everything short of "the worst" happens to the fair Diana Tasborough, whom
he is sworn to protect. Murder and Black Mass are incidental and Hanaud
does not shine.

1566   They Wouldn't Be Chessmen   CCD 1935

Another Hanaud-and-Ricardo tale, starting with a theft and going on to
murder, houseboats, a tidal wave, and much mixing of motives and identities. Hanaud is rather fatuous and also playful with the English language.
The scene is Trouville and vicinage. Young women abound, one of them
(as usual) a ruthless vixen.

1567   MASON, (FRANCIS) VAN WYCK (also Geoffrey Coffin and Ward
Weaver, b. 1897), may be read in *Captain North's Three Biggest Cases*
(1932), which contains: *The Vesper Service Murders, The Branded Spy
Murders,* and *The Yellow Arrow Murders.* These show their nature in
their titles—early days in espionage.

MASTERMAN, [SIR] J(OHN) C(ECIL) (b. 1891)

b. Surrey; educ. Royal Naval Colleges at Osborne and Dartmouth,
Worcester Coll., Oxf.; Fellow of Christ Church since 1913; interned in
Germany while studying there in 1914. Has also written *Fate Cannot
Harm Me* and a play on Marshal Ney. Vice-chancellor of the Univ. of
Oxford, 1957–58.

1568   The Case of the Four Friends   H&S 1956

His second detective novel, after a long interval. It is an attempt to relate
a case of preventive detection, executed by Ernst Brendel, the scholar
who twenty years before solved *An Oxford Tragedy.* This new affair is
closely woven and well told, despite the narrator's interrupting it periodically to discuss the problem with his friends. The motives and actions are
both plausible and tense, and JB rates the book higher than did the critics.
WHT sides with the critics.

1569   An Oxford Tragedy   Goll 1933

A first-rate story, which unlike other attempts to "do" Oxford or Cambridge projects the genuine atmosphere, establishes plausible characters,

and furnishes detection, logic, and discussion of "method" in admirably simple and attractive English. The plot is an early example of murder gone wrong; the detective is Ernst Brendel, an Austrian professor of law, who is visiting for the week and whose peculiarities are just marked enough to make him interesting without clownishness. The narrator is ticked off by his own comments as just the sort who would watch and do little—a masterpiece.

Association Item
1570 MASTERMAN, J. C.

To Teach the Senators Wisdom   H&S 1952
    An Oxford Guide Book
    Illus.

A most entertaining and instructive tour through Oxford, cast in semi-fictional form by the author of *An Oxford Tragedy* (q.v.), who at the time of writing was provost of Worcester College and later vice-chancellor of the University. No comparable work exists for Cambridge, but then many more fictional murders occur in Oxford than in Cambridge: it is the *genius loci*.
    The title comes from *Psalms* 105, 22.

1571 MASTERMAN, WALTER S.

The Wrong Letter   Dutt 1926
    Introd. by G. K. Chesterton

Chesterton's 4 pages are superb; but, as he allows us to guess, the story, despite a good opening scene and some attractive clues, does not live up to promise. This might have been due to inexperience, but later work shows a comparable kind of looseness, indicative of poor pot-boiling.

1572 MASTERMAN, W. See also:

The Wrong Verdict   Dutt 1938

1573 MASTERSON, WHIT, is one of the pseudonyms of Bill Miller and Bob Wade, who also write as Dale Wilmer and Wade Miller (all b. 1920). They write prolifically in the easy-thriller category, the products under different names showing no different traits. See *Dead Fall* by Dale Wilmer (No. 2248), *Killer's Choice* by Wade Miller (1949), *Play Like You're Dead* by Whit Masterson (1967).

1574 MASUR, HAROLD Q. (b. 1912)

The Last Gamble   S&S 1958

Masur writes fairly good private-eye tales about Scott Jordan, who loves records and is nice to women. Since S.J. doesn't spend all his time in bed with them, he has enough brains left to do a competent job. This story is about a substitution of persons designed to snag a fortune. Jordan bestirs himself amid credible complications. Only, he drives all night to Chicago from a spot less than 100 miles away.

1575   Make a Killing   RH 1964

Scott Jordan gets involved in the intricate corporation finances of the movie industry. Murder, quite ordinary, and subdued melodrama keep up the interest without satisfying the mind. Characters unmemorable except for one of the girl clerks.

1576   MASUR. See also:

Bury Me Deep   S&S 1947
The Legacy Lenders   RH 1967

1577   MATHER, BERKELEY

The Achilles Affair   Scrib 1959

Colorful cloak-and-dagger stuff on the Grecian-Yugoslav border during the second world war, and afterward in Cyprus. The characterization is fair and the writing passable. But the puzzle of the last fifty pages—who is to be trusted and who not—is insufficient to hold the reader. For the rest, the Australian author, who has served in the British army, knows whereof he writes.

1578   MATTHEWS, BRANDER (1852–1929)

The Last Meeting   Scrib 1885
Floor plan on p. 121

In a company of young artists and lady patronesses, a member of the Full Score Club, who is engaged to be married, suddenly disappears. He is known to have had a quarrel with a ruthless Greek. A disfigured body is found in New York Bay. Inquiries (but not real detection) take place and all ends well. The tone is light, the telling swift and punctuated with good touches. One of them is the ingenious "living death" organized by The Brotherhood of the Sea.

1579   MAUGHAM, ROBIN (Robert Cecil Romer, Viscount Maugham, b. 1916)

The Link   McG 1969
A Victorian Mystery

This expeditious novel by Somerset M.'s nephew and biographer is an attempt to explain the Tichborne case (see No. 3157) by recreating its imagined antecedents and suggesting a resolution of the contradictory elements. Everything in the tale is plausible, including the healthy doses of sex and the emotional relations of the English family of Steed and their wandering offspring, legitimate and other. The ending is adroitly touching and inconclusive.

1580   MAUGHAM, W(ILLIAM) SOMERSET (1874–1965)

Ashenden; or, The British Agent   Dday 1956; orig. 1928
      Pref. on fiction and espionage

Loosely linked episodes in the career of the hero, who gives his name to
the book and who stands for the author himself: Maugham was in intelligence during the first world war and got as far as Russia in 1917. But he
makes clear that the work is fiction and very far from history. What is
new here is the flat dull tone that later writers so successfully exploited as
an effective set-off for violent and unexpected events. Conrad, Maugham,
and Le Carré (qq.v.) mark the line of this development.

1581   MEADE, DOROTHY COLE

Death over Her Shoulder   Scrib 1939

Reading attempted and given up before the end of Chapter 1. The author
is another incarnation of the HIBK heresy, and not to be confused with
dear old Mrs. Lillie Thomas Meade (see Nos. 2660–1).

1582   MELVILLE, ALAN (pseud. of William Melville Caverhill, b. 1910)

Death of Anton   Skeff 1936

Before turning popular playwright, this author wrote half a dozen novels,
of which the present detective one seems to have been the last. Its setting
is a traveling circus, in which Anton is the lion-tamer (or more exactly,
tiger-tamer) and a dapper little man named Minto is the amateur detective who looks into the murder (with dope-running on the side), as an
adjunct to attending his sister's wedding. A bit cluttered and perfunctory
at the same time.

1583   MESSENGER, ELIZABETH (MARGERY ESSON) (b. 1908)

Dive Deep for Death   Hale 1959

Suspense in New Zealand, with topographical interest (speleology) com-
pensating for the lack of formal detection. Straightforward narrative by
an English physician who has abandoned his profession after losing his
wife under painful circumstances. His rehabilitation "down under" fills
a short but competent book.

1584   The Wrong Day to Die   Hale 1961

Not up to scratch and close to HIBK. Characters null and plot mechanical.
Still, qualities in the earlier book may recur in: *Light on Murder* (1960),
Material Witness (1959), and *Murder Stalks the Bay* (1958).

MEYNELL, LAURENCE (WALTER) (also Valerie Baxter, Robert
Eton, Geoffrey Ludlow, A. Stephen Tring; b. 1899)

b. Wolverhampton; educ. St. Edmund's Coll., Wareham; soldier, schoolmaster, and estate agent before becoming a writer and editor of *Time and
Tide* (to 1960).

1585   Death of a Philanderer   CCC 1968

The central idea and characters of this beautifully plotted tale are most
attractive, and so is the denouement. Seldom have a headmistress and a
free-lance writer been done with so convincing a mixture of convention
and originality. Steady suspense keeps one going till the necessary murder
near the end and its clearing up without detective effort. As a result the
tale is hard to classify. It celebrates neither crime nor detection and it is
not adventure; but it is first-rate and as such makes one overlook several
small inaccuracies of language, quotation, and the like.

1586   The Mystery at Newton Ferry   Lipp 1930

Reading this author suggests that he may have learned as he went along.
This early work is largely tripe, illiterate here and there, but with an
occasional nice bit. The plot concerns the too-usual delightful brother
and sister living in a country house, who are actually the brains of a gang
of crooks set on getting away with Treasury "plates." Lots of running
about in cars, but no detection.

1587   "On the Night of the 18th . . ."   Harp 1936

Six years later the product is quite enjoyable: the murder of a miser-cum-
lecher in an English village is investigated by Inspector Kingsley Hylton,
whose long, thin cigars are more conspicuous than his detective ability.
And the criminal is a frost. But despite these serious flaws, the story
moves along, exhibits good local color, and includes scenes reminiscent of
Lady Chatterley.

1588   Saturday Out   Walk 1962; orig. 1956

The first three-quarters of the book are good fun, but it deteriorates soon
after. Not only is the "devilishness" unconvincing to the reader because
the author doesn't feel it, but the style of writing changes and becomes
fragmented and cheap.

1589   Sleep of the Unjust   CCC 1963

A free-lance writer between jobs undertakes to catalogue the 15,000 books
of a newspaper baron. When the latter's mistress appears and turns out to
be the *femme fatale* in the life of the cataloguer's dead friend, drama and
death ensue. Though the murder occurs very late in the game and is confessed, not detected, the plot is neat, well-told, and forceful. The social and
personal attitudes of the narrator are a bit tiresome, but not enough to
spoil the tale or the obligato sex.

1590   Virgin Luck   Coll 1963

The cottage murder of a bookmaker's clerk is enticingly discussed for one
chapter by two rural policemen, then dropped for the next twelve chapters,
in which we read the adventures with life and men of a young woman of
19 who is emancipating herself from a narrow background and learning

ethics and lovemaking. We know the murderer at the end, but he is not booked. Agreeably written. No detection.

1591   MILES, STELLA

     Saddled with Murder   HJ 1954

A horsey tale which succeeds despite the depressing presence of a sterile stallion. The detection is negligible but not the author's sense of words, as shown by her description of the personality of a photographer (whose plates and prints are under discussion) as "almost entirely negative."

1592   MILLAR, MARGARET (STURM) [MRS. KENNETH MILLAR] (b. 1915)

The wife of Ross Macdonald (Kenneth Millar) has transcended the limits of the HIBK tale of terror in her several sophisticated psychological novels (see *Wall of Eyes*, 1943; *The Iron Gates*, 1945; *The Beast in View*, 1955). In all these the workings of a terrified mind are studied, and detection of causes is secondary, though present. In *An Air That Kills* (originally: *The Soft Talkers*, 1957), some wit and satire have been added.

1593   MILLS, HUGH (TRAVERS), also Hugh Travers, q.v.

     In Pursuit of Evil   Lipp 1967

Unusual, yet not easy to cherish and remember. One Franz Keppel tells how he meddled with other people's business in Lugano and vicinity, so that he could think of himself as a detective working with the police. His official connection is nil and official toleration is slight. The blackmail (for the commoner sexual reasons) is not particularly adroit.

    One might not expect detection from an author whose other work, *Prudence and the Pill,* has been acclaimed as "a rejuvenation of the bedroom farce," he does not supply it here, but see Nos. 2062–3.

       MILLS, OSMINGTON (pseud. of Vivian Collin Brooks, b. 1922)

b. Liverpool; educ. City of London Coll. and London School of Printing. Journalist in Isle of Wight, then with *Yorkshire Evening Press,* BBC, etc. Lives in Clifton, York.

1594   At One Fell Swoop   Bles 1963

A complicated and slow-paced story of murder linked with youthful revolt from a strict puritanical sect in northern England and snagged by jurisdictional police disputes. Too many pages, people, details, visits, and red herrings. Superintendent Baker is credible but dull as he investigates the murder of a colleague.

1595   Dusty Death   Bles 1965

The explanation and concomitants of the murder of a charwoman are reasonable and well organized, though the diversions provided by two groups of young people are not worked in quite close enough to the main concern. Inspector Irving and the amusing P.C. Shirley investigate, and the net product is thoroughly enjoyable.

The title is from *Macbeth*, V, 5, 23.

1596   Traitor Betrayed   Bles 1964

Colorful in setting and situation, and marred by only a few flaws and one or two dull stretches, this is an original treatment of the scientist-turned-traitor theme. It is admirably set in a country hotel during a meeting of the British Association, and there are at least six first-rate characters, men and women, whose dramatic connections make good reading, Sir Noel being the best. Superintendent Baker is a bit dim as usual.

1597   MILLS, O. See also:

The Case of the		No Match for the Law	Bles 1957
Flying Fifteen	Bles 1962/1956	Sundry Fell Designs	Bles 1968
Enemies of the Bride	Bles 1966	Trial by Ordeal	Bles 1961
Headlines Make Murder	Bles 1962	Unlucky Break	Bles 1956
Misguided Missile	Bles 1957		

MILNE, A(LAN) A(LEXANDER) (1882–1956)

The writer of light verse and sketches for *Punch,* the creator of Christopher Robin and Winnie the Pooh, the playwright of *The Ivory Gate* and *Mr. Pym Passes By* was interested enough in the detective genre to contribute to it one classical novel, two short stories, and one play. His dicta on the genre and his later attempts to practice it do not equal his main successes.

1598   Four Days' Wonder   Meth 1933

Starts with a corpse but is 99 percent whimsy. The "body" turns out "accident." There is some good dialogue and neat satire of authors, but the young people are embarrassingly young.

1599   The Red House Mystery   Dutton 1928; orig. 1922
       Introd. by the author

Pace all the critics born and reared in the tough world, this fantasy remains a delightful, if contrived, masterpiece. Dialogue, clues, night life, and characters hold the willing reader—and the book is still in print.

1600   MILNE. See also Nos. 2662–4.

MITCHELL, GLADYS (MAUDE WINIFRED) (also Stephen Hockaby; b. 1901)

Producer of thrillers overcharged with fantasy which feature Mrs. Bradley, consulting psychiatrist to the Home Office. It is hard not to resent the author's plausible beginnings and preposterously (often semi-supernatural) continuations. Mrs. B. (the heroine) is now a Dame of the British Empire and lives in great luxury.

1601   Spotted Hemlock   MJ 1958

For a change, a straightforward and amusing tale in which Dame Beatrice Bradley takes apart a complex but not impossible scramble of identities involving students at two neighboring agricultural colleges. There is murder, but of which girl remains a problem for over 100 pages. During that time the details of pig farming help to keep the reader entertained. This tale is so direct and competent that one is moved to wonder why the others differ so unprofitably.

1602   Watson's Choice   MJ 1955

Guided and sustained by her plan to post-shadow Holmes and Watson, Mrs. Mitchell outdoes herself and produces a memorable plot, straightforward prose, and no nonsense. A honey of a book.

1603   MITCHELL, G. See also:

       Twelve Horses and the Hangman's Noose   MJ 1956

1604   MITCHELL, LEBBEUS (HORATIO) (b. 1879)

       The Parachute Murder   Mac 1933

The author's only venture in this form. Perhaps the parachute did not open. Unique as to locale and ominous as to first name.

1605   MOFFATT, JAMES (1870–1944), was a respectable scholar and publicist, who ventured only once to write a mystery. *A Tangled Web* (1929) answers all too accurately to its label and discourages belief in both character and event.

1606   MOFFETT, CLEVELAND (1863–1926)

       The Seine Mystery   DM 1925

Alan Esterbrooke, a journalist in Paris, comes upon the facts of a strange embroilment of persons, in which a reckless artist is accused of murdering a man who is said to be still alive. The plotter presumably used a conveniently drowned man to effect his disappearance from wife and society. The detective Brousse is not incompetent, but he lacks access to the facts, and the ending is artfully inconclusive.

1607   Through the Wall   App 1909
         Illus.

Why this old-fashioned melodrama should be cited again and again as a little *chef d'oeuvre* is hard to guess. The detective Paul Coquenil, who works with Papa Tignol of the regular force, uses very primitive methods for his time and place, and the courtroom stuff is both ridiculous and unoriginal.

1608   MOFFETT, CLEVELAND, and HERFORD, OLIVER (1863–1935)

　　　The Bishop's Purse   App 1913
　　　　Illus.

A novel of imbroglio, impersonation, theft, and suspicion. The scene is
England, but most of the characters are American. There is mild clueing
and detecting, but the story is in no way arresting—or as funny as was
doubtless intended.

　　　MOLE, WILLIAM (pseud. of William Anthony Younger, 1917–62)

b. Scotland; educ. Canford and Christ Church, Oxf.; poet (three volumes
published); wrote five novels, of which three are crime stories.

1609   Goodbye Is Not Worthwhile   E&S 1956
　　　　Frontispiece map of Barbados

This second case solved by the young wine merchant Alistair Casson
Duker (called Casson), is the closest of the three to the classic form, which
it fulfills with great skill and much adventitious interest. The motive is
original and the two murders are not linked in the usual way. Casson's
work is first-rate, as are all the relationships—those involving C. no less
than the resident and visiting "Bajans" (= Barbadians). No doubt the
ending is overelaborate, but one can stand it after so much entertainment.
　　　Note: This may be the only book of the genre in which *crime passion-
nel* is correctly spelled.

1610   The Hammersmith Maggot   E&S 1955
　　　　In U.S.: Small Venom

The amateur Casson Duker is led to investigate the tactics of the elusive
Perry, and his shadowing of that strange creature holds one entranced for
rather more than half the book. The pace then slows a bit and the ending
is a trifle forced. Nonetheless an original tale, which (incidentally) won
the approval of Queen Elizabeth.

1611   Skin Trap   E&S 1957
　　　　In U.S.: You Pay for Pity

Casson Duker's third appearance. The crime here is seen by the reader
from both sides; its motive is peculiar and the characterization is, as one
might expect, engrossing. But it is not detection in any sense.

1612   MONIG, CHRISTOPHER (pseud. of Kendell Foster Crossen; also
　　　　M. E. Chaber, q.v., and Clay Richards; b. 1910)

　　　Once Upon a Crime   Dutt 1959

A so-so story of the usual tough private eye who lays every dame, but in
this one he is himself laid in South Africa, which lends a touch or two of
novelty. The crimes and the death of the heroine (the hero being careless

and very much to blame) are not of much interest, but the figure of the amiable con man is extremely well done and supplies the one morsel of satisfactoriness.

1613   MONIG. See also:

Abracadaver   Dutt 1958

1614   MONTEILHET, HUBERT

The Praying Mantises   S&S 1962
        Grand Prix de la littérature policière;
        Inner Sanctum Award

This is a reworking of Laclos's great novel, *Les Liaisons Dangereuses,* neatly done: a Russian woman insures her husband and uses a younger man who loves her to murder said husband, plus his own young new wife, who has been especially chosen for seducing the husband. Tape recorder, diary, and thirst for revenge are used to trap the conspirators and prepare their self-destruction. Excellent up to this point, the tale plummets into bathos with a bad sermon by a Jesuit Father.

1615   Return from the Ashes   S&S 1963
        Trans. by Richard Howard

An ingenious tale of double-bluff impersonation, that is, of pretending to pretend to be someone that one might possibly be. Of course, only the confusions and terrors of the Nazi era and its concentration camps permit this plot to be plausible, and it ends with a suitable surprise calamity. The translation leaves something to be desired.

1616   MOORE, H(ARRY) F. S.

Little is known about this writer, whose works are not generally found on any kind of shelf. Still, the following can and should be said: *Death at 7:10* has to do with poisoning on a train. Boucher reports that the investigation "makes dull reading" because "it is methodical." Yet, he adds, the final scene is "exciting and satisfactory." Since we might like the investigation and even the final scene, we intend to pursue the search for the book. Other titles: *Murder Goes Rolling Along* (1942), with an army locale, and *Shed a Bitter Tear* (1944).

        MORLAND, NIGEL (also Mary Dane, John Donavan, Norman
        Forrest, Roger Garnett, and Neal Shepherd; b. 1905)

b. London; publicity director of Ivor Nicholson and Watson, co-founder with John Creasey of the Crime Writers' Association. Prolific author in many genres, he is said to be well past his 200th book. His early *Clue of the Bricklayer's Aunt* (1937) owes details to the Seddon Case and he has since dabbled in criminology, notably in his *Outline of Scientific Criminology* (No. 3242) and *An Outline of Sexual Criminology* (1966).

1617   The Moon Murders   Cass 1955

Edgar Wallace gave N.M. the idea of his heroine, the hard-bitten, glitter-eyed Mrs. (Palmyra) Pym, who is employed by the War Office but is seconded to Scotland Yard on special occasions. This first occasion seems to these readers inadequate and incoherent, though the lady emerges unmistakable and is clearly out for blood in adventures to come. The author is greatly to be preferred in his rare incarnation as Neal Shepherd. See No. 1927.

1618   MORELAND. See also Nos. 2668–9 and:

The Careless Hangman	Farr 1942
The Corpse on the Flying Trapeze	Cass 1941
Murder at Radio City (= A Knife	
for the Killer)	Farr 1939
A Rope for the Hanging	Cass 1938

1619   MORLEY, CHRISTOPHER (DARLINGTON) (1890–1957)

The Haunted Bookshop   Faber 1951

Like other writings by this author, this tale is marked by fantasy, a bit on the sentimental side. The bookshop's contents are delightful and its frequenters try to be. But there is a plot—in the double sense—and the premises suffer violence at the end, in the interests of spying and other sinister activities. When the dust settles down, the hero characteristically remarks: "Thanks to that set of Trollope, I think I'm all right."

1620   MORLEY, F. V.

Death in Dwelly Lane   Harp 1952

A clever idea—that of having Professor Moriarty's nephew come back to England after having served time for his misdemeanors in Chicago, and of presenting his gradual lapse from the pursuit of pure mathematics into criminal ways—is soon spoiled by precious verbosity and allusiveness. Too bad.

MORRAH, DERMOT (MICHAEL MACGREGOR) (b. 1896)

Educ. Winchester and Oxf.; Fellow of All Souls, and Arundel Herald Extraordinary, after being an editor of *The Times,* whose history he has written, together with other scholarly and popular works. See *The Work of the Queen* (1958) and *To Be a King* (1968), both important essays on British culture. But, alas, only one detective story.

1621   The Mummy Case Mystery   Harp 1933
          In Eng.: The Mummy Case

Designed and executed for those who relish academic settings, wit, and deft characterization, with a plausible plot to house them all. This first-rate tale is moreover typical of the best writing done in the thirties. The young investigators are just bright and chatty enough, and their activities are at once serious and this side of pure farce—a triumph.

1622 MORRIS, R. A. V.

The Lyttelton Case   Coll n.d. [1922]

An early specimen of the well-written, slow, carefully plotted puzzle. Chief Inspector James Candlish takes it at the pace he was brought up on. Nearly everything is cardboard, and inexperience makes for needless repetition, but as the game then went, this is an acceptable tale of murder, impersonation, and abduction, with entertaining asides about the contemporary scene.

MORRISON, ARTHUR (1863–1945)

b. Kent; modest educ.; clerk in the civil service till 1890, when he took up free-lance journalism. The publication of *Tales of Mean Streets* (1894) and *A Child of the Jago* (1896) established him as a naturalistic story-teller with a peculiar gift of rendering the atmosphere of slum London. He belongs to the tradition begun by Dickens, pursued by Gissing, and followed—after Morrison—by Thomas Burke. While producing such works, Morrison took up the popular line of imitating Doyle's Sherlock Holmes tales (see Nos. 2670–4).

1623 The Green Diamond   Page 1904
         Also: The Green Eye of Goona

Sometimes found listed as a Martin Hewitt (long) detective story, it is nothing of the kind, but a regular chase having as its object the jeweled eye of an Indian idol. It ends in murder, but without need of detection, since the act is done in front of witnesses, from frustrated rage. A poor affair altogether, not because of its kind (early example), but because the author doesn't believe it himself.

1624 The Hole in the Wall   E&S 1947/orig. 1902
         Pref. by V. S. Pritchett

Not detection or mystery, though murder occurs. It is a study of slum life and the influence of a ghastly environment on character—the whole made dramatic by a child's bewilderment and fear. The period, incidentally, is not contemporary but mid-nineteenth century.

1625 MORRISSEY, J. L.

Off with His Head   Giff n.d. [1947]

A curious mixture of arrant nonsense with pretty fair plotting and detection. The number of beheaded Chinamen and hidden passages revolt the intellect, yet some of the surprises and some of the police work show that the author had a germ of talent for the genre. Not for the impatient connoisseur.

1626 MOYES, PATRICIA

Dead Men Don't Ski   Rine 1960

The author's first, and a successful attempt to write detection in the classic
pattern. The setting in the Dolomites and the well-directed group of
English and Italian characters are attractive, nor is the skiing overdone.
There are two timetables, the close inspection of one of which permits
one to anticipate the solution of one of the crimes. Inspector Henry Tibbett (small and unprepossessing) and his wife work together but do not
notice one serious inconsistency in the testimony, which might have led
to a better ending than the author's.

1627 Death and the Dutch Uncle   CCC 1968

International stuff with violence visited upon Tibbett and his wife in Holland. It is a tedious tale, even though the Chief Inspector emerges more
sharply characterized than elsewhere in the series.

1628 Death on the Agenda   Rine 1962

Such interest as this affords lies in its colorful account of contemporary
Geneva, where the colorless Tibbett is attending an international conference on dope-running—or rather, its detection and prevention. The plot
is complicated and the lapses from fidelity on the part of both Henry
and his wife are not done with conviction. The modernized version of the
old phonograph dodge adds little to a tale well below Miss M.'s first two.

1629 Down Among the Dead Men   Rine 1961

A pleasant English affair featuring sailing off the Norfolk coast. Again
the Scotland Yard man is on holiday with his wife, and there is an assorted and somewhat trying crowd of amorous and criminally inclined
yachtsmen for him to choose from. The plot is capably managed, but—
what sport or hobby next?

1630 Johnny Under Ground   Rine 1965

WHT cared less for this than did JB, but admits that it stands close to
the author's best. Tibbett is less mousy than usual, and the implicating of
his wife, Emmy, in the action less gratuitous. The story deals with events
that occurred at an air force fighter station during the war, when Emmy
was WAAF and in love with a pilot grounded because of injuries suffered in action. Twenty years later a reunion of the survivors and the
proposal to write a life of the dead hero stir up another kind of enemy
action.

1631 Murder à la Mode   Rine 1963

Except for the vivid picture of dress designing in modern London, this is
a disappointing brouhaha about Paris *toiles*. Tibbett's niece fails to enliven the proceedings, though her involvement does provide a second

motive for his flaccid powers to exert themselves. No humor, though opportunity for it is plentiful.

1632   Murder Fantastical   Rine 1967

The Manciple family is a sizable collection of oddballs in the normal British way, yet special enough to hold our attention, for the author cultivates them with love and care. Two deaths occur, which Chief Inspector Tibbett (his wife tagging along) quickly solves, though his disclosures are slow to come. Query: Was the spy stuff necessary?

1633   MOYES. See also:

    Falling Star   Rine 1964
    Many Deadly Returns   Holt 1970

1634   MUIR, (CHARLES) AUGUSTUS (also Austin Moore; b. 1892)

    The Shadow on the Left   Burt 1928

Impossible nonsense in Scotland. When that setting is so well used by several competent writers, why bother with this one?

1635   MUNRO, HUGH

    Who Told Clutha?   IW 1958

Clutha is a private detective employed by a Glasgow shipyard and the story is a fair example of the British hard-boiled school. The investigation of the killing of a workman is highly seasoned with love interest and gangsters.

1636   MURRAY, MAX (1901–56)

    The Neat Little Corpse   Farr 1950
       Orig. The Corpse in the Sea

A story of sunken treasure off the island of Jamaica. Like the author's other *Corpse* stories, this one has good points; but the decoration by means of witchcraft and love is not sufficiently artful and credible.

1637   The Right Honorable Corpse   MJ 1952

This is reported to be the Australian author's last book. A good locale and considerable versatility of prose and plotting keep the thing going despite weak motives and mechanics. One gets a little tired of the pianist–secret-agent hero, who goes out of his way to make everyone hate him for his "cynicism." Yet there is enough in the tale to inspire a wish to see the earlier works.

1638   MURRAY. See also:

    The Doctor and the Corpse   MJ 1953
    The Voice of the Corpse   MJ 1947

1639 NASH, ANNE (b. 1890), is a California author of stories whose titles are good but deceptive: *Cabbages and Crime* (1945), *Death by Design* (1944), *Said with Flowers* (1943), *Unhappy Rendezvous* (1946) entice the literate; but if the last is typical, her people are juvenile and solutions unconvincing.

1640 NASH, SIMON (pseud. of Raymond Chapman) (b. 1924)

Dead of a Counterplot   Bles 1962

In North London College, where the capable but lazy senior lecturer in English, Adam Ludlow, holds forth, a girl visiting her young man is found dead in the latter's room. Inspector Montero and his sergeant, Jack Springer, promptly turn up. This is the beginning of the working friendship between Ludlow and Montero, Ludlow wanting to spare his brightest student waste of time as a suspect in the hands of the police.

Ludlow owes a good deal to Crispin's don, Gervase Fen (both have cantankerous cars and characters), but his questioning and reflecting, interspersed with pleasant pedantry and apt quotations, are all his own. Nor are the official police behindhand: their reasonings are fully as good as Ludlow's and it is the author's special skill to dovetail results in a way creditable to both sides. The author's knowledge is from inside: Lecturer at the London School of Economics, Warden of Passfield Hall, etc.

1641 Dead Woman's Ditch   Bles 1964

Inferior to the other tales in which Adam Ludlow performs. Plot rural and scrappy, quite undistinguished.

1642 Death over Deep Water   Bles 1963

A Mediterranean cruise on which Adam Ludlow, reader in English Literature at the University of London, is present and enjoying himself (despite a habitually sardonic view of existence) produces two corpses under quite natural circumstances. Everything is sharply presented, including the incompetent ship's doctor, the scenes ashore, and the passengers. A couple of technical details—e.g., the poison and its medium—could be improved on by these readers, but otherwise all is beautifully visualized and dealt with. Topnotch.

1643 Killed by Scandal   Bles 1962

The second tale featuring Adam Ludlow and Inspector Montero–cum–Sergeant Springer. It is to be rated A-1, and particularly meritorious in view of its (private) theatrical scene. Terse, witty, occasionally very funny, it is also straightforward and quietly logical.

1644 Unhallowed Murder   Bles 1966

A first-rate affair in a London church setting. The vicar is murdered, satanism is suspected, but reason prevails at the hands of Inspector Montero and his eccentric friend and counselor, Adam Ludlow. The "valuable books" involved in the crime are well handled—that is, by someone who knows books.

1645 NELSON, HUGH LAWRENCE (b. 1907)

The Title Is Murder   Rine 1947

A rather over-feminized story of murder in a San Francisco bookshop, with the common crowd of multiple suspects, cross-purposes, and unlikely motives, plus a few pet animals.

1646 NEVILLE, MARGOT (pseud. of Margot Goyder, b. 1903, and Neville [Goyder] Joske, b. 1893)

Drop Dead   Bles 1962

Laid in Australia, written with something too much of female softness, but not disagreeable; composition choppy, characters and love relations perfunctory. Withal suspense is maintained and the pair of official detectives, Grogan and Manning, are good.

1647 NEVILLE. See also:

Come Thick Night	Bles 1951	The Hateful Voyage	Bles 1956
Confession of Murder	Bles 1960	Murder Beyond the Pale	Bles 1961
The Flame of Murder	Bles 1958	Murder of Olympia	Bles 1958

1648 NEWMAN, BERNARD (CHARLES) (also Don Betteridge; 1897–1968). English writer of spy stories linked to current events: *Moscow Murder, Death to the Fifth Column, The Spy in the Brown Derby.* An early tale, *Death of a Harlot* (1936), seems a trifle less machine-made. His 128th book, *The Dangerous Age* (1967), has humor and adventure, with a smidgen of detection, but no crime.

1649 NICHOLAS, ROBERT

The White Shroud   CCC 1961

Long awaited (because praised by a good judge), this story turns out to be the work of a writer not gifted with much invention, wit, narrative ability, or sense of the probable. A chemistry lecturer is done to death at a small red-brick university shrouded in snow, and a meticulous investigation of the seething passions unleashed is carried out by one Inspector Stone. No loose ends is the best that can be said. WHT rates it higher.

1650 NICHOLS, (JOHN) BEVERLEY (b. 1899)

Death to Slow Music   Dutt 1956
    Pref. by the author

Brief and pointless remarks introduce the third of the murder stories by this writer. All three are recommended by Somerset Maugham, but—caveat emptor. The detective, one Horatio Green, is short, plump, old, and inarticulate. True, he winds up with some reasoning, but he does nothing of the sort before the final chapter, and the questions he raises and then runs away from are peculiarly irritating.

1651   The Rich Die Hard   Dutt 1958

All the objections to *Death to Slow Music* apply equally to the present tale. It's too bad, because the stylistic level is high, and the author has the gift of characterization. The plot (English country house) discloses the murder of a mistress by a wife who couldn't bear a child to her disgustingly rich husband.

1652   NICHOLS. See also:

The Moonflower Murder (= The Moonflower)   Dutt 1955
Murder by Request   Dutt 1960

1653   NIELSEN, HELEN (also Kris Giles; b. 1918)

The Crime Is Murder   Morr 1956

Not a detective story, but the working out of a good natural situation: the music festival held annually in a small north Michigan city is the center of activities that puzzle the writer Lisa Bancroft and end in death. As a newcomer, what is Lisa to think and to do? A crashing end with real thunder.

1654   NOLAN, JEANNETTE (COVERT) (b. 1896)

Sudden Squall   IW 1955

The author's third book, featuring the woman detective Lace White, whose age is uncertain but evidently in the middle range, and whose detective ability is also decidedly middling. Kentucky locale. Good use of a typing (not typewriter) clue.
   JB takes a gloomier view of the proceedings.

1655   NORTH, GIL (pseud. of Geoffrey Horne, b. 1916)

More Deaths for Sergeant Cluff   C&H 1963

An odd kind of police-routine story, in which Sergeant Cluff (Caleb), known to all the inhabitants of his small and primitive English village, is both criticized and trusted by them in the discovery of crime. The tale is told in an elliptical manner which often violates prose and taxes the ingenuity of the reader to find out what has just been done or said. Yet this style gives a new tone to routine, and in this tale the motive is also fresh.

1656   Sergeant Cluff and the Price of Pity   C&H 1965

This storyteller and broadcaster pulls a clever stunt in concealing under scrambled dialogue, often repetitious, the bare bones of a melodramatic plot. An affectation of profundity about the woes of mankind gives

Sergeant Cluff the appearance of a wise man, but in fact everything comes out because of the author's say-so: there are no clues and no detection. This particular tale is trickier and more cluttered than its predecessors.

1657 NORTH. See also No. 2682 and:

The Methods of Sergeant Cluff	C&H 1961
Sergeant Cluff Goes Fishing	C&H 1962

OFFORD, LENORE GLEN (b. 1905)

A respectable member of the retreaded HIBK school, with several substantial works to her credit. Mrs. Offord reviews detective fiction in Portland, Ore., writes good light verse, and shows a nice wit in all she does.

1658 Walking Shadow   S&S 1959

Todd McKinnon, a mystery writer, solves the problem of who has been sabotaging the Ashland (Oregon) Shakespeare Festival—a question of which way the eternal triangle pointed. There's the usual hanky-panky about a theater, some fairly good business of confused identity, but most of McKinnon's "detection" consists in waiting for police reports.

1659 OFFORD. See also:

Cloth of Silver	Scrib 1939	The Nine Dark Hours	DS 1941
Clues to Burn	DS 1941	Skeleton Key	DS 1943
The Glass Mask	DS 1944	The Smiling Tiger	DS 1949
Murder on Russian Hill	Scrib 1938		

1660 O'HARA, KENNETH

The Bird-Cage   Goll 1968

Deliberate nerve-racking with fanciful sadism. Pseudo detection takes place amid a great deal of misbehavior, personation, improbable switches of mood and relationship, the whole narrated in a precious idiom. The two young doctor friends who come to a bad end are beyond belief, and so is the witch that compasses their doom. Cluttered fore and aft.

1661 Sleeping Dogs Lying   Macm 1962; orig. 1960

An English tale of murder and espionage which starts well and ends poorly. Two-thirds of the way through, one no longer cares who has done for whom. The trappings are nuclear, refugeean, and feminist.

1662 OLESKER, HARRY

Exit Dying   RH 1959

An amusing tale by the author of the highly touted best seller *Now Will You Try for Murder?* All the fun here lies in the early part of the first-person account by the stage-struck young woman from Wyoming who comes to New York. The plot manages to be at once trite and complicated, and what detection goes on is managed through a downpour of Gibsons.

1663   OLESKER. See also:

Impact   RH 1961
Now Will You Try for Murder?   S&S 1958

1664   OLSEN, D. B. (pseud. of Dolores [Birk] Hitchens; also Noel Burke and Dolan Birkley; b. 1907)

The Clue in the Clay   Phoen 1938

Presumably the author's first novel. Despite an overelaborate plot, the murder of a sculptress in her San Francisco studio has points. Inspector Mayhew lets it drag too long, and insists on the now-dated re-enactment of the crime, but the author has tried her hand at honest detection. JB thinks the estimate too generous.

1665   OLSEN. See also No. 1151 and:

Bring the Bride a Shroud   CCD 1945

1666   O'NEILL, DESMOND

Life Has No Price   Goll 1959

Tough adventure, American type, in Ireland, with girls and vocabulary to match. Chase and smash finish quite good. Third in a series.

ONIONS, OLIVER (later George Oliver by deed poll) (1873–1961)

b. Bradford; went to London to study art and was employed as a draftsman; then turned to writing and produced several novels and many stories before the first world war. Not until after the second did he receive general acclaim, with the publication of *The Story of Ragged Robyn* (1945) an historical novel.

1667   In Accordance with the Evidence   Nisbet 1915

Not detection, but a minor classic of crime. The background, planning, and execution are told in the first person, which unfolds the sufficient motive. The London scene, centering in a business college and its students in the early 1900s, is full of life. So much so, that the author wrote two sequels, each interesting for different reasons and forming the massive work *Whom God Hath Sundered* (Doran 1926).

1668   ONIONS. See also No. 3451 and:

A Case in Camera (not det. but crime)   Macm 1921
Ghosts in Daylight (ss)   C&H 1924
Whom God Hath Sundered (rev. into
    one novel of No. 1667 and its sequels,
    The Debit Account and *The Storie of Louie*)   Doran 1926

OPPENHEIM, E(DWARD) PHILLIPS; also Anthony Partridge (1866–
1946)

b. Leicester, son of a leather merchant; began to write at 15, under encouragement from schoolteacher, but had to put in a few years "in leather,"
chiefly as firm representative in Paris, where connections with the entertainment trade led him to observe the antics of those on the fringes of
politics and high society. His first story appeared when he was 20. He
married an American girl before he was 30 and lived in Norfolk, overlooking the North Sea. There he spun his plots, dictating and having only a
general idea of their outcome. During the war of 1914 he worked at the
Ministry of Information with Arnold Bennett, John Buchan, Hugh Walpole, and a host of others, who were nearly annihilated together by a
bombing in the autumn of 1918. In later years he spent his winters on the
Riviera and came to Hollywood to make a movie or two, much to his
discomfort. His novels and short stories are numerous and appeal to diverse tastes. In addition to the unquestionable classics below (Allen Dulles
in 1969 put *The Great Impersonation* at the top of all spy novels for
virtuosity) see Nos. 2685–8.

1669   The Evil Shepherd   LB 1922

The story—as only the old magician could do it—of a lawyer well-satis-
fied with his ability to save men from the gallows, and who finds that he
has thereby condemned an attractive woman to misery at the hands of a
sadistic husband. He falls in love with her and ultimately unravels a
series of crimes, including one he thinks she has committed. Altogether a
triumph in the mode of high make-believe.

1670   The Great Impersonation   LB 1920

Still readable and credible after half a century, this story is as it were
the counterpart on dry land to Childers' *Riddle of the Sands* (q.v.) The
disgraced English aristocrat who retrieves his honor by tangling with
Prussian Intelligence in East Africa is a genuine character, well rooted
in reality, tradition, and current history.

1671   The Illustrious Prince   LB 1910
         Illus.

An excellent sample of the politico-misterioso genre of international intrigue, love relations, and high-toned behavior before 1914, and still believable in that perspective, thanks to Opp's straightforwardness and skill.

1672   A Maker of History   LB 1906

Those who think the mid-twentieth-century spy story is a new birth, full
of genius and relevance, had better read this and see how the tricks have
remained the same while the current history employed has diminished in
sparkle and explicitness. To be sure, the old manners and restraints no
longer hold, but it is easy in the modern versions to degrade behavior

while coasting on the traditional plots and incidents. A splendid opening, by the way, with railroads in action.

OSTRANDER, ISABEL (EGENTON) (also Robert Orr Chipperfield, David Fox, and Douglas Grant; 1885–1924)

Query: Did overwork cause this lady to die so young? She deserves credit not only for hard work and versatility, but for pointing the way to something popular, though dubious, by naming a story *Suspense* (1918) and by making one of her chapter headings read: "If I Had Only Known!"—ch. 9 of *The Second Bullet* by Robert Orr Chipperfield (1919).

1673   The Twenty-Six Clues   Watt n.d. [1919]

Although very dated in its use of situations and devices long since overworked, clearly a competent piece. We have two murders in a private museum of crime, the inevitable compromising letters, the rivalry between the scientific detective Terhune and his police force opposite, McCarty. Detection mostly by leg work; the twenty-six "clues" are simply the letters of the alphabet, rather nicely worked in.

1674   OSTRANDER. See also:

As Isabel Ostrander:
    The Clue in the Air   Skeff 1917
    The Heritage of Cain   Watt 1916
    How Many Cards?   Skeff 1920
As Robert Orr Chipperfield:
    The Man in the Jury Box   McBride 1921
    The Second Bullet   Skeff 1919
    Unseen Hands   McBride 1920
As David Fox:
    The Doom Dealer   Hurst 1923
    The Handwriting on the Wall   Hurst 1924
    The Man Who Convicted Himself   Hurst 1920

1675   OTTOLENGUI, RODRIGUES (1861?–1937)

    An Artist in Crime   Putn 1893

Carolyn Wells has something good to say (see No. 3057) about this author's earlier tale, *A Conflict of Evidence* (1893), which is hard to find. The present story is neither a total success nor a total disappointment. It suffers from the period plush—stilted dialogue, excessive incident, and melodramatic disclosures. But there is no fudging of facts or forgetting of previous puzzles: it all works out.

For another example of the transplanted Gaborismus, see also the sequel: *Final Proof; or, The Value of Evidence* (Putn 1898).

OZAKI, MILTON K. (also Robert O. Saber)

Reared in Kenosha, Wisc., a graduate of Ripon College, newspaperman, artist, and writer, is now a Chicago tax accountant who also owns the

Monsieur Mettoine beauty salon. In *The Cuckoo Clock* he uses his own apartment and shop as the locale for his story.

1676   The Case of the Deadly Kiss   GM 1957

Of this, JB has remarked: "A certain zip informs this improbable tale. Sex done with gusto and speed. Drama of last scene good. Motive forced and 'rivalry' false." WHT must regretfully dissent and disallow what he deems a triumph of mediocrity.

1677   The Cuckoo Clock   Ziff 1946

Trails off, after a promising start, into a series of interviews. The three cooperating detectives are a poor imitation of the real thing. This author's forte is not on this level, but on the lower one of tough and sexy stuff.

1678   PAGE, MARCO (pseud. of Harry Kurnitz, 1908–68)

       Fast Company   DM 1938/1937

This semi-tough story of Joel Glass, bookseller turned detective, is entertaining, even though not worthy of Alexander Woollcott's absolute praise: ". . . one of the best . . ." What it shows is zest and promise of applied intelligence.

1679   Reclining Figure   RH 1952

A well-constructed tale of art forgery, bohemianism, misplaced wealth, and straightforward detection. This third one is neither so diffuse as *Fast Company* nor so hilariously good as *The Shadowy Third*.

1680   The Shadowy Third   DM 1946
              Also: Suspects All

Though he won the Red Badge prize of $1,000 with his first, Page does far better in this, his second. The orchestra is done with great gusto and knowledge, and the props (including the Strad) serve the plot admirably. David Calder, the hero-insurance-agent–detective, has a nice love affair and gets pushed around a bit, but he is witty, clever, and not too knowing. Lieutenant Flummer (marvelous name!) in the usual role of opposition is in good form, and so is the collection of villains.

1681   PAGE. See also:

       Invasion of Privacy   RH 1955

1682   PAIN, BARRY (ERIC ODELL) (1864–1928)

       The Death of Maurice   Skeff 1920

The author was clearly out to write a "real novel" and he succeeds in fusing solid characters with a plausible killing and intelligent pursuit of clues. His commentary on human affairs is always his own and his narrative brevity is refreshing and new. It anticipates Henry Cecil (q.v.) by thirty years, and only the lack of models at this early date keeps this from being a topnotch specimen of the genre; even so, it is well worth reading. For some interesting short stories from the same hand, see Nos. 2696–2700.

1683   PALMER, STUART (HUNTER) (also Jay Stuart; 1905–68). Born in Baraboo, Wisc., and educated at the Chicago Art Institute and University of Wisconsin, this writer did better in the ghost-short-story form than in the long detective tale, because he cared only for plot. The spinster school-teacher Hildegarde Withers is not a good caricature even in the pages of *EQMM*, and she does not hold up in a full-length affair such as *The Green Ace* (1950). *A Study of Murder* (1960) is not fiction.

1684   PATRICK, Q. (pseud., at first, of Richard Wilson Webb and Martha [Patsy] Mott Kelly [Mrs. Stephen Wilson]; later of R. W. Webb alone; then of R. W. Webb and Hugh Callingham Wheeler, b. 1913; also Jonathan Stagge and Patrick Quentin)

Cottage Sinister   Swain 1931
        With Martha Mott Kelly

A confused and melodramatic tale of murder (four women are dispatched with poison "floated" on lumps of sugar) for the sake of money and privacy. The telling is half roguish. Inspector ("Archdeacon") Inge does very little but guess wrong. Two romances clutter the narrative.

1685   Murder at Cambridge   Farr 1933
        Glossary of Eng. college terms

Apparently the next after *Cottage Sinister* and, if so, a great improvement. The young American at All Saints' College, close to King's, does a fair job of establishing himself and his love affair while detecting and chitchatting with friends. The murders, though, seem too numerous and not called for after the first, nor is the killer plausible; still, it is an agreeable period piece.

1686   PATRICK. See also:

As Patrick, using Detective Timothy Trent of the N.Y. Homicide Squad:

Death and the Maiden	S&S 1939	Murder in One Scene	S&S 1948
Death for Dear Clara	S&S 1937	White Carnations	S&S 1944
Footlights and Murder	S&S 1947	Who Killed the Mermaid?	S&S 1949
The Grindle Nightmare	Hartn 1935		

As Quentin:

Green-Eyed Monster	RH 1960	A Puzzle for Wantons (and	
The Man with Two Wives	S&S 1955	other *Puzzle for* titles: *Fools,*	
My Son, the Murderer	S&S 1954	*Fiends, Puppets,* etc.)	S&S 1936–47
		Run to Death	S&S 1948
		Shadow of Guilt	RH 1959

In the short story "Girl Overboard" (in *Four and Twenty Blood-hounds*), Patrick has adapted the murder of the Gibson girl by the ship's officer James Camb (see No. 2365).

PAUL, ELLIOT (HAROLD) (also Brett Rutledge; 1891–1958)

War correspondent settled in Montparnasse, known for *The Life and Death of a Spanish Town* and some critical writings, invented Homer Evans as his American-Parisian detective and put him to work in several picaresque tales. Paul has also written *The Last Time I Saw Paris* (1942), autobiographical and full of pleasant reminiscence, including an account of the Berlioz *Requiem*.

1687 Hugger-Mugger in the Louvre   RH 1940

The aim of the book is to amuse with semi-satirical, semi-affectionate scenes of ordinary Paris life. The theft of a painting and the murders that ensue are not taken seriously by the author, who is always ready to digress. He makes fun of his characters (such as they are), of scholarship, business, the U.S.A., and detection itself. There is no denying his humorous bent, but the effect is rather faint and spotty. Homer Evans and his gun-toting girl, Miriam, do not excite much more affection than the other local types.

1688 PAUL. See also:

Fracas in the Foothills	RH 1940
Mayhem in B-Flat	RH 1940
Murder on the Left Bank	RH 1951
The Mysterious Mickey Finn	MA 1939

1689 PAYN, JAMES (1830–98)

Found Dead   Tauch 1869

An old-fashioned melodrama in novel form, transparent from the start and not worth perusal. What it shows is that a successful writer of romances cannot turn to the murder and mystery genre without special talents. A worse discredit: Payn was the editor of *The Cornhill* who could not see his way to publishing Doyle's *Study in Scarlet*.

1690 Lost Sir Massingberd   C&W 1896
       A Romance of Real Life

This is a better specimen than *Found Dead*. Its chief interest lies in the depiction of a Bow Street runner in the last ten chapters. The melo-dramatic tone persists, but the story is readable and one scents the salutary influence of Dickens.

1691 PAYNE, LAURENCE (b. 1919)

The Nose on My Face   Macm 1961
       In ppb. The First Body

Despite the publisher's claim that this novel introduces two "new per-sonalities," Sam Birkett is only mildly amusing and his sergeant featureless. As for the plot, it is a conventional mixture of the nice girl who takes to drugs, the phony TV star, and the chase after ill-defined objectives. The least likely murderer here is pitiable.

1692 PAYNE. See also:

Too Small for His Shoes   Macm 1963

PENTECOST, HUGH (pseud. of Judson Pentecost Philips, b. 1903)

Since winning first prize in Dodd Mead's mystery competition in 1939 with his excellent novel *Cancelled in Red,* this author has written prolifically in both the long and short forms and under both his names.

1693   Hide Her from Every Eye   DM 1966

John Jericho, red-bearded painter and champion of lost causes, fights to expose collusion among a group of men trying to frame a woman alcoholic. The mystery of how Marcia Potter's eight-year-old son died— if not by drowning, as alleged—is only part of Jericho's problem, which includes a genuine murder as well. Told by Jericho's Watson, Arthur Hallam; pleasant New England scene; detection minimal; ending somewhat forced.

1694   Sniper   DM 1965

Based to a large extent on the actual shooting of a headmaster at a famous New England preparatory school some years ago. The author has done a good job of characterizing the members of the Pelham family, one of whom is guilty of two murders by the end of the story. John Jericho, commissioned to do a portrait of the dead headmaster, is a better psychologist than he is a detective, but his stature as man and artist comes through very well. The author also performs the difficult task of making the late headmaster sound like a commanding figure.

1695   PENTECOST. See also Nos. 1711–2, and:

The Assassins	DM 1955	Lieutenant Pascal's Tastes in	
The Brass Chills	DM 1943	Homicides (ss; Nos.	
Cancelled in Red	DM 1939	2708–12)	DM 1954
Choice of Violence	DM 1961	Shadow of Madness	DM 1950
The Creeping Hours	DM 1966	The Shape of Fear	DM 1964
The Evil That Men Do	DM 1966	The 24th Horse	DM 1940
The Fourteenth Trump	DM 1942	Where the Snow Was Red	DM 1949
I'll Sing at Your Funeral	DM 1942		

PERDUE, VIRGINIA (1900?–45)

Wrote only five stories, in which horror vied with the rational curiosity of the detective mind, but in all of them were signs of a potentially fine or great contributor to the classic genre.

1696   Alarum and Excursion   CCD 1944

He Fell Down Dead (1943) made the author's reputation and this excellent suspense story maintained it. No detection, save what is done by a man of 63, an immigrant to the U.S. who succeeded and was blown up at his own factory by those who were on the trail of his new fuel. Many books are said to be difficult to put down before finishing; this is one. Excellent characterization, including a wife with a split personality; a respectably sober plot, despite the war; and a real smash ending as well.

1697 PERDUE. See also:

The Case of the Foster Father	CCD 1942
The Case of the Grieving Monkey	CCD 1940
The Singing Clock	CCD 1941

1698 PERTWEE, ROLAND (1885–1963)

Interference   HM 1927

Many things try to come between Dr. (Sir) John Marley and his wife Faith, including a previous husband from Australia, a female blackmailer, and Sir John's own effort to get rid of these annoyances. Needless to say, love triumphs over all. Quite good melodrama, which made it one of the best murder plays of the twenties, A. E. Matthews starring. Some clueing but little detection.

1699 PERUTZ, LEO (1884–1957)

The Master of the Day of Judgment   Coll 1963/Boni ppb. 1930
    Introd. by Dr. Fritz Wittels
    Trans. by Hedwig Singer

The introducer and others call this short novel by a once locally well known Czech novelist a detective story. If this claim is to be admitted, it must be with the qualification that Central European ways interfere a good deal with ratiocination. The plot is straightforward enough: three inexplicable suicides suggest a sinister influence at work, which would mean indirect murder. The hero-narrator takes various detective-like steps to uncover the hidden cause, but these steps are feeble and inconclusive and his own position as suspect is only made clear by the author at the cost of absurdities; e.g., this nobleman-captain-huntsman who has commanded regiments in action stammers like a nervous girl and even faints and then defends himself sternly and tersely, like a soldier. The other characters are somewhat dim, and the final twist, which turns the hint of a supernatural solution into a psychological one, leaves many threads untied.

Note: The translation is first-rate. A second novel done into English, *From Nine to Nine* (VP 1926), is not mystery or detection; it *ends* with a murder, after interludes of passion and deceit in old Vienna.

1700 PETERS, ELLIS (pseud. of Edith Pargeter, q.v., b. 1913)

Death and the Joyful Woman   CCD 1961

Both JB and WHT liked this very much and wish that the author had enjoyed equal success in her later presentations of the adolescent detective Dominic Felse. Here the 16-year-old boy is depicted with much skill, both in relation to his family (his father, George Felse, is the professional on the case) and to the heiress Kitty Norris, whom Dominic worships. The motives that made someone kill a rich brewer with a bottle turn out to be sound, there are not too many suspects, and the operations of the detectives—both professional and amateur—are sensible and straight-forward. It is Dominic who appropriately sets up the stunning final scene.

1701   Flight of a Witch   CCD 1965

A frost, alas! The same detective who appeared in *Death and the Joyful Woman* works here with the aid of his schoolboy son and others, to unravel the murder of a jeweler in nearby Birmingham. But too many persons are supers, and motives are never made clear enough, especially in the marital relationships.

1702   Funeral of Figaro   CCC 1962

Mozart one can take in large quantities, though L. A. G. Strong knows better how to work him in. But the murderer of the richly deserving Figaro who is "protected" from police and reader by the cover-up of all the rest of the cast—no, thank you!

1703   The Grass Widow's Tale   CCC 1968

Mrs. Felse, the policeman's wife, turns 41 and feels lonely, her son being and acting grown up and her husband being away on a case in London. So she goes to the local pub and winds up in serious trouble, not on account of drink taken.

1704   Who Lies Here   Morr 1965
        In Eng.: A Nice Derangement of Epitaphs

E.P. is hipped on the subject of adolescent feelings and she sacrifices everything to their depiction. Her detective Felse does nothing but look after the young, then says to the people who have unraveled the crime that he knew the facts all along. One part of this plot is first-rate: the ancient scheme of the pirate and his wife, which miscarried and led to the modern murder.

    The English title is a literal application of Mrs. Malaprop's phrasing in Sheridan's *Rivals*.

1705   PETERS, E. See also:

Black Is the Colour of My True Love's Heart	CCC 1967
Death Mask	CCD 1960
The House of Green Turf	CCC 1969
The Piper on the Mountains	Morr 1966
The Will and the Deed (= Where There's a Will)	Coll 1960

1706   PETERS, GEOFFREY (pseud. of Peter Trippe)

        The Mark of a Buoy   WL 1968

This author apparently writes routine stories about the Sydney police, rather than good stories of police routine in Sydney. *Mark of a B(u)oy* is well-named; it is about drug smuggling by ship via Sydney harbor, and it is essentially a boy's book about the doings of Chief Inspector Trevor Nichols and his pal Sergeant Tom Burton. Their lovely young wives, parents-in-law, and scuba equipment play their prearranged parts and evoke no particular interest.

1707   The Twist of a Stick   WL 1966

Though praised by the critics quoted on the jacket, this story of the Australian outback is kid stuff. The murder is uninvolving and the outcome of detection and love affairs predictable. The only matters of interest are the language and the scenery.

1708   PETERS, G. See also:

    The Claw of a Cat   WL 1965
    The Eye of a Serpent   WL 1967
    The Whirl of a Bird   WL 1968

1709   PETRIE, RHONA

    Death in Deakins Wood   DM 1964/1963

A fair tale of arson and murder in an English county town. Inspector MacLurg, not featured in her later tales, does the needful.

1710   PETRIE. See also:

    Murder by Precedent   Dday 1964
    Running Deep   Dday 1965

1711   PHILIPS, JUDSON (PENTECOST) (also Hugh Pentecost, q.v.; b. 1903)

    Nightmare at Dawn   DM 1970

In 1964 the author introduced Peter Styles as journalist-detective in *The Laughter Trap*. This is the seventh in the series, a rather poor mystery-suspense yarn which relies heavily for its interest upon contemporary black-white antagonisms, just as Styles, who is not much of a detective, relies on the help of young women. One sees his artificial right leg more clearly than his face or character. The New England private-school scene, with a Special Summer Project for black students, provides ample opportunity for violence.

1712   PHILIPS. See also:

    The Black Glass City   DM 1964
    Thursday's Folly   DM 1967

PHILLPOTTS, EDEN (1862–1960)

b. Mt. Aboo, India; sent to Devon as a youth; studied acting, then started writing while working for an insurance company. Primarily a regional novelist (Devon) in the tradition of George Eliot and Thomas Hardy,

Phillpotts was drawn to the murder-mystery genre by his very knowledge of rural passions and his rationalist religion. Though not the strongest spinner of detective plots, he has done a few stories that stand out for the combination of virtues he can muster—and his encouragement to Agatha Christie in early days is a tribute to his critical capacity about the genre. For one of his best novels other than detection, read *The Three Brothers* (1909), and for perceptive sketches of old-fashioned boyhood, the first two volumes of *The Human Boy*.

1713   The Anniversary Murder   Dutt 1936
            In Eng.: Physician Heal Thyself

Not an "Ackroyd" though it is the first-person account, made public posthumously, of the part played by a young doctor in the unexplained murders of a youth and his father just one year apart. The Dorset coast scene brings out the best in Phillpotts, and he is equally good at characterizing his narrator. The CID is twice "baffled" and the final explanation of the first shooting is weak. Otherwise this is a fair specimen of what P. can do.

1714   The Captain's Curio   Macm 1933

The colorless Detective Inspector Midwinter goes to a Devon village to solve the murder of an old gent found stabbed in his bedroom twenty minutes after his physician has finished "osculating the heart" [*sic*]. The motive might have been made interesting by its mixture of politics, science, and philanthropy; but the method is absurd; which leaves P. exerting most of his strength on local color.

1715   A Clue from the Stars   Macm 1932

Really too bad. The trick used to explain the absence of traces around the dead man's body (in the middle of a large field) is outrageous enough to have kept this pair of readers from going back to Phillpotts for twenty years. Which shows how risky a sound judgment about X is when applied to X prime.

1716   "Found Drowned"   Macm 1931

A delightful and atypical story, in the author's best vein. It is not a powerful or intricately clued tale of murder, but there is plenty of ratiocination and suspense. The relation between the retired surgeon and the country inspector—close friends—is as attractive as the humor and the characterization. A single murder, a private investigator, a rare but genuine poison masked by hanky-panky, a case of identity, and some politico-sociological ax-grinding give this tale a memorable coloring.

1717   The Grey Room   Macm 1931

A good deal shorter than most of this author's attempts in the classic genre. The country-house setting has charm and the secret of the Grey Room on whose fine Italian bed a series of blameless characters die is well kept. Its keeping is, of course, possible only because the modus operandi is so improbable. The author would have done better to omit much of the ill-assimilated "scientific" hearsay with which he tries to rationalize the final explanation.

1718   Jig-Saw   Macm 1926
          In Eng.: The Marylebone Miser

The detection in this long and slow-moving tale is done by Detective Inspector Joseph Ambrose, assisted by the retired John Ringrose, who occurs in other tales. The death by stabbing of an elderly miser in a locked-and-barred room is so great a challenge to the two investigators that they "accept it" and concentrate on two less miraculous murders that follow. Ringrose eventually brings these home to a rather unlikely killer and gets an inkling of the way the first killing was managed. The method is unconvincing on paper and virtually impossible in practice.

1719   The Jury   Macm 1927

Whether Lady Heron murdered her husband is the question before the jury at the Redchester assizes, and to answer it they reconsider the evidence given at the trial, mostly circumstantial. Something about juries is a spur to talent in English novelists—see Postgate and Bullett—and Phillpotts is sustained by the form thus given to his tale. Religion, metaphysics, and village life are beautifully blended, and characters and relationships benefit from his humor and grasp of simple minds, so that even if the ending is a bit forced, this story without detection remains one of his best tales of crime.

1720   Monkshood   Meth 1939

This late bloom on the tree is long-drawn-out but not rambling. Perhaps it should be taken like a Bruckner symphony, on its own terms, which are not those of the modern detective novel. Four mysterious deaths, three by aconite poisoning, plus a final shooting, take place in a Devon village, and baffle the official police. The solution, almost exclusively by means of psychological clues, is arrived at by an elderly forensic scientist, who takes four evenings to explain it to his friend.

1721   The Red Redmaynes   Macm 1922

This is a classic detective novel that has never received due recognition. It holds attention throughout its great length, which can be defended as necessitated by the systematic extermination of the brothers. The first detective is baffled and an American, one Peter Ganns, who takes snuff and is occasionally oracular, is called in. He is a memorable man, just like the one female Redmayne. Action takes place on Dartmoor, in Cornwall, and in Italy. Having regard to the date, WHT rates this only one cut below *Trent's Last Case.*

1722   They Were Seven   Macm 1945

Seven repellent cousins band together to do in their elderly uncle. The plot miscarries yet he dies. The Scotland Yard detective (an attempt at a "real life" type) is ineffectual. Suspicion bloweth where it listeth but the plot does not come out. The text affords odd hints of rewriting from an earlier version.

1723 A Voice from the Dark   Macm 1925

More suspense than detection, but entertaining. John Ringrose, just retired from the CID, discovers the problem while on vacation on the Dorset downs, later pursuing investigations in Italy. Who killed a father and his son so as to "succeed" is little in doubt; just how it was done is more of a mystery. Fewer improbabilities than usual in P., who even manages a credible source for the ghostly voice.

1724 PHILLPOTTS. See also Nos. 1129–31, 2716, and:

A Close Call	Hutch 1936	Mr. Digweed and	Hutch 1933
A Deed Without a Name	Macm 1942	Mr. Lumb (det.)	Macm 1934
Lycanthrope: The Mystery		Peacock House &	
of Sir William Wolf		Other Mysteries	
(fiction)	Macm 1938	(See No. 2717)	Macm 1927
Miser's Money	Macm 1920	The Ring Fence	Hutch 1928

1725 PICKERING, HARRY

Himself Again   Goll 1966

Spy stuff in Vienna, smoothly done and showing some inventiveness in the political part.

PIM, SHEILA

An Irish girl with horticultural interests who has four detective novels and some others to her credit. Her style has simplicity and easily conveys the atmosphere of her birthplace.

1726 A Hive of Suspects   H&S 1952

Competent handling of mineralogy, an abandoned mine, and bees, plus some very human policemen and the inescapable traveling theatrical troupe. See above for other qualities.

1727 PIM. See also:

A Brush with Death	H&S 1950
Common or Garden Crime	H&S 1945
Creeping Venom	H&S 1947

1728 PIPER, H. BEAM (1904–67?). Originally a railroad policeman and a self-made expert on guns, he became a miscellaneous writer specializing with success in science fiction. In his one attempt at the crime genre, the implausible Colonel Jefferson Davis Rand, a gun fancier, solves the *Murder in the Gun Room* (1953) after much delving in technicalities.

1729   POATE, ERNEST M.

Behind Locked Doors   Chel 1923

The hero and narrator is a young intern at Bellevue in horse-drawn-ambulance days. The detective, Dr. Bentiron, attired in a green bathrobe, sprawls and smokes in a mechanical easy chair but is less convincing than Holmes. All in all, a not contemptible period piece representing the transition from A. K. Green to whatever is the American equivalent of Thorndyke.

1730   POATE. See also:

Dr. Bentiron, Detective   Chel 1930
Pledged to the Dead   Chel 1925
The Trouble at Pinelands   Chel 1923

1731   PONSON DU TERRAIL, PIERRE ALEXIS, VICOMTE DE (1829–71)

Les exploits de Rocambole   1859

The most prolific of French *feuilleton* writers began this "elastic series"—as someone aptly called it—with the three volumes entitled as shown above. There followed a play, then the *Resurrection of R.* in 5 vols., *The Last Word of R.*, and finally *The Truth About R.* (1867). All these adventures have a police flavoring, but they begin with the hero as the twelve-year-old helper of a villain, and they do not serve detection even in a French sense. They ensured the success of the newspapers that published the install-ments: circulation soared to 100,000 copies and more.

1732   PORLOCK, MARTIN (pseud. of Philip MacDonald, q.v.)

Mystery at Friar's Pardon   Coll n.d. [1931]

The MacDonald lack of consecutiveness and the abundance of conver-sational filler cannot be hidden even under a pseudonym sanctified by Coleridge and Conan Doyle.

1733   PORTER, JOYCE

Dover Goes to Pott   Cape 1968

The formula by which Chief Inspector Dover was created is simple enough: combine the opposites of all pre-existing detectives—the opposite of ability, charm, education, good manners, candor, and a conscience. The result is a "comic" monster that soon palls; the laughter reported by some critics is of the embarrassed kind with which an audience greets a misfire when it wants to spare the author. Miss Porter has great gifts of narrative and dialogue and her plots are ingenious; hence she has no need to concentrate on depicting, with increasing improbability, an object of disgust and contempt. She should move away from Dover to, say, Folkestone.

1734   Dover One   Scrib 1964

In addition to the disagreeables in this tale, which include the Inspector who gives his name to the book, there is the additional pang that one must in the end call the story well plotted and laced with detection. A servant girl who moves among the ill-assorted lodgers of a country estate (late "hall") is murdered, dismembered, and disposed of. How and why are Dover's problems.

1735   Dover Two   Cape 1965

Miss P. keeps the reader going by depicting the gross, incompetent, and bad-tempered Chief Inspector Dover, who takes advantage of his amiable and more intelligent Sergeant MacGregor as he fumbles around and finally solves an otherwise well-constructed and well-unraveled case about the shooting of a spinster. The fun is supposed to come from the sardonic outlook of the author upon human frailty.

1736   PORTER. See also:

Dover Three   Scrib 1966

POSTGATE, RAYMOND (WILLIAM) (b. 1896)

b. Cambridge, Eng., educ. Liverpool Coll. and St. John's, Oxf. Sub-ed. on *Daily Herald,* then asst. ed. *Lansbury's Weekly;* worked on *Encyc. Britannica,* 14th ed. He shared the socialist views of G. D. H. Cole, who married his sister. The two men collab. on a *Hist. of the British Common People;* Postgate revised Wells' *Outline of History,* wrote lives of Wilkes and Lansbury and books about 1848, as well as guides for gourmets and wine bibbers. His output of detective fiction is small and his contribution to the discussion of crime consists of No. 3260.

1737   The Ledger Is Kept   MJ 1953

In a British atomic plant a civil servant with a shrewish sister is up to skulduggery. The detective is slow and sympathetic, and there is a well-managed love story of an uncommon kind. The final impression is: worth reading but top-heavy.

1738   Somebody at the Door   MJ 1943

This tale of the murder by a wife of her detestable husband suffers from two defects—one sees through it long before the police, and one is bored by the long individual biographies, the technique adopted here being that of *The Bridge of San Luis Rey.*

1739   Verdict of Twelve   CCD 1967/1940

His first and a complete success. It comes five years after Bullett's *The Jury* (see No. 342), but it does as well—and differently—what that valuable work accomplished: i.e., to show in fiction how the diversity of twelve minds takes evidence. Here only five or six matter in the trial of a woman accused of poisoning her nephew, but they are splendid, and the twist at the end is fair and gratifying. What is less so is the quotation from Karl Marx, which argues a determinism belied by the story.

1740　POTTER, JEREMY

The Dance of Death　　　　　　　　　　　Const 1968

His fourth is an extravaganza that does not spur the mind or the risibles. The elderly art collector who presumably killed the young woman and who is at work on a great study of Thomas Rowlandson is no more credible than his shrewish wife or his scholarly activity.

1741　Death in Office　　　　　　　　　　　Const 1965

Sayers started it all with *Murder Must Advertise* and only a very exceptional office murder can now stand out from so many. This one is pleasant and no more. For the record, the story is told by a young woman secretary, the same who, after 178 pages of the usual bickerings among staff, interoffice politics, and the like, notices a discrepancy in a document which in turn discloses the murderer. The murderee is editor of the London *Trumpet* and his doings ring true.

1742　Hazard Chase　　　　　　　　　　　Const 1964

This odd title should revive the memory of royal tennis antedating the lawn game. The mystery—murder and theft of a manuscript history of the game—is good, and so is the author's knowledge, wit, and narrative style. Where he falls down is in character-drawing and economical dialogue; the tale is too long.

1743　POTTER. See also:

Foul Play　　　　　　　　　　　　　　Const 1966

1744　POTTS, JEAN (b. 1910)

The Footsteps on the Stairs　　　　　　　Scrib 1966

Extremely tedious: for nearly 200 pages the seven characters remaining after the murder of the only interesting one—a woman interior decorator—suspect each other for a variety of reasons, mostly marital. No official detective appears, there is little analysis, and practically no action. The only discovery made by Martin Shipley, an ineffective amateur, is a psychological one affecting only himself, this on the last page of the book.

1745　Go, Lovely Rose　　　　　　　　　　Scrib 1954

We came to this detective author's first novel after having sampled her later output, which is disappointing. Here the plot is good, the characterization fair, but the telling is cluttered and long-drawn-out. The central character is the dead woman, Rose Henshaw, a despicable housekeeper assisted down the cellar stairs by a push which terminates her numerous illegal activities. Females at cross-purposes, a featureless private detective, the furniture itself, "crouched and ready to spring at some prearranged signal," do little to elucidate a mystery that eventually solves itself. It seems clear that the central idea comes from the Peasenhall mystery, whose victim was Rose Harsent. See Nos. 2223 and 2473.

The title is from Edmund Waller's poem of the same name.

1746   The Little Lie   Goll 1969

Psychological suspense: a madwoman's growing edifice of lies and its eventual crash—a crashing bore. New England setting.

1747   POWELL, P(ERCIVAL) H(ENRY)

Murder Premeditated   Roy 1958

Who would not be attracted by a dish containing the matriarch in the decaying mansion, the lonely local medico who is visited rather unconventionally by granddaughter Flora, and the redoubled poisonings? Yet good writing does not save this story from mediocrity.

1748   POWELL, RICHARD (PITTS) (b. 1908?)

False Colors   S&S 1955

A story of the Philadelphia art world, a bit on the jazzy side, but undistinguished.

1749   POWELL, R. See also:

Shoot if You Must   S&S 1946

1750   PRATHER, RICHARD S(COTT) (also David Knight and Douglas Ring; b. 1921)

Strip for Murder   GM 1955

Shell Scott, L.A. private eye, is husky and white-haired. All that he wanted at the nudist camp was the bare facts, and he considered himself disguised when stripped among the inmates. The puerility is not relieved by the use of a handful of small balloons filled with natural gas to lift and hold the detective's 250 pounds over the edge of a cliff while he recovers the incriminating bullet.

1751   PRATHER. See also:

Kill Me Tomorrow   PB 1969

1752   PRIESTLEY, J. B., and BULLETT, GERALD (q.v.)

I'll Tell You Everything   Macm 1933

Despite a compelling beginning in an English railway carriage, this tale of romantic intrigue has no further charms to carry one along, and many drawbacks to make one discouraged. The Royal Seal of Euravia is not enough of a lure; it only reminds one that Stevenson (and even Anthony Hope) did this sort of thing much, much better.

PROCTER, MAURICE (b. 1906)

b. Lancashire; spent nineteen years in the police (mostly in Manchester, which is the Granchester of his police-routine tales); published his first book in 1946 and has written about one a year. He writes four and a half hours a day, likes music, and plays patience.

1753   A Body to Spare   Hutch 1962

Inspector Martineau directs a far-flung operation against a group of thugs who have involved a couple of innocent men in their large payroll theft. Murders pile up, a nice romance is interwoven, and Dixie Costello appears toward the end as the suave profiteer of others' cruder crimes—altogether a neat affair, but not outstanding.

1754   The Graveyard Rolls   Harp 1964

Standard police routine, yet variegated by interesting side issues. Though one suspects organized crime in the background, the people in the foreground show a normal diversity, and their loves, schemes, secrecies, and untimely ends suggest a real place. There is no doubt the author knows his big town and can reproduce its atmosphere. The title refers to a parked Rolls-Royce.

1755   Hideaway   Harp 1968

For some readers the exploits of Inspector Martineau of the Granchester CID reached their peak in the tenth or twelfth volume of the series. This tale may confirm their estimate. An attempt to besmirch Martineau is soon over, and then the usual mixture of Dixie Costello, jail-breaking, and hijacking is presented. JB thinks better of it, even after reading two others quite recently.

1756   Man in Ambush   Harp 1958

Despite a bit of ill-advised questioning which interrupts the climax, the story is excellent. The crime is the murder of a police officer, Gutteridge-fashion. Inspector Martineau, JB notes, listens to records and likes the Boston Symphony version of the *Symphonie Fantastique*. (This judgment comes shortly before his house burns down.)

1757   The Midnight Plumber   Harp 1957

A competent tale of the rounding up of a gang of burglars in the English midlands. Nothing out of the ordinary.

1758   The Pennycross Murders   Harp 1951
         In Eng.: The Chief Inspector's Statement

In a rural setting, presumably Yorkshire, two attacks on little girls have occurred, one a year in the past and the other recent. The Yard takes a hand, with the usual trailings at night, false clues, and a love affair between the young inspector and a local girl of Hardyesque beauty and character. Unusual enough to reread, when it is likely to prove more striking than at first.

1759   The Pub Crawler   Harp 1956

A superb combination of drab police duties with a story of some complexity of feeling. The sordid is not laid on; the hero's introspection is original as well as plausible; the boardinghouse keeper, mother of the criminal, approaches great characterization.

1760   The Ripper   Harp 1956
         In Eng.: I Will Speak Daggers

The author's best, both dramatically and as a tale of detection. The marital relationships are excellently done, the murder and attempted murders are plausible and well-clued, and the catastrophe is as original as it is powerful. So far, his masterwork.

The English title is from *Hamlet,* III, 2, 421.

1761   Rogue Running   Harp 1966

Not so good as the previous ones and yet not quite routine or flat. Martineau and his boys are perhaps the best of the police groups in fiction.

1762   Spearhead Death   Hutch 1960

The setting here is Hatton Garden, London, not Manchester. The diamond trade and the resident blacks provide M.P. with good opportunities for local color and specialized knowledge. The two official detectives are very good—not so the white heroine; and one is sorry to see the attractive culprit found out.

1763   Two Men in Twenty   Harp 1964

Inspector Martineau is getting on in years, and Granchester is very familiar, but the opportunity to spend more time with the criminals and less with the "force" is welcome. Safe-blowing is the hobby this time, and the gang numbers some charming fellows.

1764   PROCTER. See also:

        Hell Is a City (= Somewhere in This City)   Harp 1954
        Hurry the Darkness   Harp 1950
        No Proud Chivalry   LG 1947
        Three at the Angel   Harp 1957

1765   PROPPER, MILTON M(ORRIS) (b. 1906)

        The Boudoir Murder   Harp 1931

One of the overlong tales typical of the late twenties and early thirties. The Philadelphia scene (including nearby Swarthmore) is well handled, and the old Broad Street Station is heavily featured. The crime is murder and police detective Tommy Rankin is the investigator. Good motor chase at the end.

PUNSHON, E(RNEST) R(OBERTSON) (b. 1872)

Writer of innumerable romantic thrillers and some detective stories, active in the field since before 1910. It would take much determination to comb through the output on the chance of discovering any solid work. Sampling has proved discouraging.

1766   The Dusky Hour   Goll 1937

The exploits of Sergeant Bobby Owen are in keeping with his adolescent name and are to be avoided by all serious readers of the genre. The story tells of share-pushing, impersonation, cliffs, quarries, and young people.

1767   Information Received   Benn 1933

Completely vacuous and forgettable.

1768   Night's Cloak   Goll 1944

One of Bobby Owen's most recent adventures and more of a conventional detective story than those above, but thoroughly unsatisfactory.

1769   PUNSHON. See also:

The Mystery of Lady Isobel	Hurst 1947/1907
The Solitary House	WL 1919
The Spin of the Coin	Hurst 1947/1908

QUEEN, ELLERY (pseud. of Frederic Dannay and Manfred B[ennington] Lee; also Barnaby Ross, Daniel Nathan, and Ellery Queen, Jr.; b. 1905)

Both cousins b. Brooklyn in the same year; their first pseudonym is also the name of their hero-detective. The hero's father, Inspector Richard Queen, and other regulars, male and female, serve as foils to E.Q., who unravels complicated murders, usually of more than average length. The ingenuity is often great, less often practical. The prose tends toward the jocular, and sometimes, as in J. D. Carr, the trimmings spoil the narrative for those unaccustomed to this special brand of U.S. make-believe. Their influence on the short story through their world-enveloping magazine and through their research on the bibliography, collecting, and criticism of the genre has been both great and beneficial. See Nos. 2492–4.

1770   And on the Eighth Day   RH 1964

A marked departure from the complex and mundane mysteries previously favored by the ingenious authors. In this new-style tale, E.Q. blunders into the desert retreat of a religious-utopian community unknown to the rest of the world. Motives, characters, and practical arrangements are all unfamiliar, yet Ellery detects and solves a more than uncommon violation of the exotic norm.

1771   The Dutch Shoe Mystery   Sto 1931

An exploit of Ellery and his father's, earlier than the similar *Roman Hat Mystery*, though published later. The title refers to the Dutch Memorial Hospital (N.Y.) where the two murders occur. "Shoe" refers to the two clues, one quite legitimate, the other questionable; for would not a person suddenly faced with the problem of a broken shoelace (to be repaired as quickly as possible) have taken a quicker way out of his predicament? Nevertheless, in spite of great length and unnecessary imitation of Van Dine, a well-reasoned solution of an intriguing problem.

1772   The House of Brass   Goll 1968

Inspector Richard Queen has just returned from his honeymoon with his pleasant middle-aged second wife, formerly a nurse, when she receives an invitation (loaded with cash) to visit an old eccentric near Tarrytown, N.Y. Five other people (all told seven, counting spouses) have been gathered in order to enable the old man to choose his heirs—all prospects being offspring of persons who helped him at bad times in his career. The expected (or unexpected) happens and after too many ups and downs Ellery arrives to "help his Dad" straighten things out.

1773   Inspector Queen's Own Case   S&S 1956
Sbt.: November Song

A good, straightforward account of how the retired Inspector Queen, aided by Nurse Sherwood and a good bit of illicit badge-flashing, solves the mystery of the murder of an adopted infant. Ellery is safely abroad, and the late-middle-age love affair is beautifully handled. There is more than one murder, more leg work than deduction, but a good twist at the end.

1774   The Roman Hat Mystery   Sto 1929

A landmark rather than a cornerstone, perhaps, being the first of a dozen mysteries by these authors, each subtitled "A Problem in Deduction." Inspector Richard Queen and his son Ellery tackle a puzzling murder with immense thoroughness and almost fatiguing pertinacity. Though the egregious bonhomie of the Queens and Ellery's pseudo bookishness occasionally irritate, the neatness of the plot involving a missing hat in a theater murder cannot be denied. But the police procedure is not what it would be now, and the criminal's luck in carrying out his complex plan strains the believables.

1775   The Spanish Cape Mystery   Lipp 1935

"Spanish Cape" must not be interpreted in the light of "Roman Hat." The Cape is a geographical feature, on which a kidnapping and a murder take place, just as Ellery Queen arrives for a little fishing. Much is made of the nudity of the corpse, corresponding to that of the murderer, who came out of the sea. A fair example of the chat and comment that enliven the Queen cases for some and make them a trifle too rich for others.

1776   QUEEN. See also Nos. 2734–51, 3004–8, and:

The American Gun Mystery	Sto	1933	The Egyptian		
The Bizarre Murders (contains			Cross Mystery	Sto	1932
The Chinese Orange, The			The Four of Hearts	Sto	1938
Siamese Twin, and *The*			The French		
Spanish Cape mysteries)	Lipp	1962	Powder Mystery	Sto	1930
The Black Dog Mystery	Sto	1941	The Greek Coffin Mystery	Sto	1932
The Chinese			Halfway House	Sto	1936
Orange Mystery	Sto	1934	The Siamese Twin Mystery	Sto	1933
The Door Between	Sto	1937	Ten Days' Wonder	LB	1948

1777   QUENTIN, PATRICK (pseud. of Q. Patrick, q.v.), has written a series of stories all headed *Puzzle for: Pilgrims, Fiends, Fools, Puppets, Players,* and *Wantons* (1936–47). They feature Peter Duluth and are run-of-the-mill thrillers.

1778   RABE, PETER. This author has written a dozen stories about Daniel Port, who is the regular tough, cynical, hard-drinking, and long-wenching hero. His efforts to wipe out his enemies on a mass scale follow accepted patterns. See *Bring Me Another Corpse* (1959).

1779   RADCLIFFE, ANN (WARD) [Mrs. William Radcliffe] (1764–1823)

The Mysteries of Udolpho   1966; orig. 1794
   Oxford English Novels
   Ed. with Introd. by Bonamy Dobree

Laid in Italy in the seventeenth century, the story relates what happens to an aunt-dominated niece, in a castle characterized by witchcraft and murder threats, sliding panels and long tunnels. An English pair of lovers undergo these rigors in a plot that defies synopsis. Horrors and abduction abound as in our contemporary offprints of this classic model, and it is fair to say that for verisimilitude there is not much to choose between Mrs. Radcliffe and her descendants. Note that in its day *Udolpho* was universally praised for dignity of conception, magnificence of landscape, excellence of characterization, and power to keep the reader shivering. Note further that all the supernatural doings are in the end explained rationally.

1780   RADCLIFFE. See also:

The Italian or, the Confessional of the
Black Penitents (ed. Frederick Garber)   OUP 1968; orig. 1797

1781   RANDOLPH, MARION (pseud. of Marie [Freid] Rodell, b. 1912). Most competent as editor and theorist, but rather too soft and discursive as plot-spinner: see *Grim Grow the Lilacs* (Holt 1941), which Macmillan reprinted in Murder Revisited Series (1955).

1782   RAVEN, SIMON (Arthur Noel) (b. 1927)

Brother Cain   S&S 1960

Partly autobiographical, partly imaginative on a high level, this story of
international intrigue is melodramatic and intellectual at the same time.
The author (educated at Charterhouse and King's, Cambridge) is a
remarkable essayist and social critic, whose works are worth attention. In
this one, a cashiered English officer takes up a strange offer that leads
him into shady doings and his ultimate undoing.

1783   RAVEN. See also:

Close of Play (not det.)   Blond 1962
The Feathers of Death   Blond 1959

1784   RAWLINS, E(USTACE) (pseud. of [Dr.] Eustace Robert Barton; also
Robert Eustace, b. 1854), preferred collaboration to solo flights. See
Nos. 1910 and 2780. With Clifford Halifax and L. T. Meade (qq.v.) he
worked on *The Sorceress of the Strand* (1922). The inference seems to be
that he provided ideas that others worked out.

RAWSON, CLAYTON (also Stuart Towne; 1906–1971)

b. Elyria, O.; educ. Ohio State Univ. and Chicago Art Inst. Became
mystery fiction editor of Ziff-Davis Co., then of Inner Sanctum Mysteries
at Simon & Schuster.

1785   Death from a Top Hat   Putn 1938

Having as detective the Great Merlini, magician and showman, permits
some startling effects, but takes away from credibility, even though one
does not doubt that magicians, acrobats, and spellbinders can achieve the
improbable. But to argue in that way is to miss the point of detective
fiction. The magic trick is perhaps more palatable in the short form (see
Nos. 2365 and 2367). For the author's views on detection see No. 3010.

1786   RAWSON. See also:

The Footprints on the Ceiling   Putn 1939
The Headless Lady   Putn 1940

Association Item
1787   READE, (WILLIAM) WINWOOD (1838–75)

The Martyrdom of Man   The Truth Seeker Co.,
                                                    17th ed., n.d. [c. 1935];
                                                    orig. Trübner 1872

Sherlock Holmes in *The Sign of the Four* called this book "one of the
most remarkable ever penned," and indeed it has still a great impetus and
sincerity which, if the thesis of anti-clericalism and freethinking did not
imbue it with a time-worn tediousness, would ensure engrossed attention.
The spiritual and material "history of mankind" is sketched here in broad

and telling strokes—an anticipation of Wells' *Outline of History* by half a century and in the midst of the great warfare between science and theology. W.W. himself is an endearing figure.

1788 REED, [SIR] EDWARD J(AMES), M.P. (1830–1906)

Fort Minster, M.P.   Simpk 1885
A Westminster Mystery
Arrowsmith's Bristol Library, No. 4

The tale is written as if by an official of the House of Commons who saw from a distance a murderous assault on a member, one John Fort Minster. The assassin vanishes: the hour is three in the morning. The date is 1882, and the possible occasion of the crime is the passion generated by the Irish Question. Though by our standards excessively explicit about motives and clues, the narrative moves along with speed and the prose is not too mouth-filling. An Irish M.P. is arrested, and the book is devoted to his vindication by a friend of the narrator's, the barrister Goodchild Strange, who finds the actual culprit. A period piece of rare quality for its day; an interesting contrast with No. 2239, as regards the customs of the House; and a true detective story—even to the usual misspelling of *bête noire*.

1789 REES, ARTHUR J(OHN) (1872–1942)

Mystery at Peak House   DM 1933

A somewhat cluttered tale of murder linked with scientific research and African exploration. There are (in England) tunnels, pygmies, and a denouement *à la rue Morgue*. Not in his best vein.

1790 The Shrieking Pit   Lane 1919

A first-rate novel of the length and pace customary at the time of its writing, but distinguished from its fellows by an absolutely steady forward march through a variety of clues and contradictions. The Anglo-American detective David Colwyn is not omniscient or colonially offensive, but natural in his moods and his relations with three police officials. As for the principals in the murder story, they are credible and worthy of study. One or two details could be carped at, including the title, which suggests unconvincing horror, whereas it betokens only a neat use of superstition. The Norfolk scene is extremely well done.

Note: The author's dedicatory verses to his sisters in Australia are awkward here and there, but very moving and a genuine poem.

1791 Tragedy at Twelvetrees   DM 1931

Inspector Luckraft of Scotland Yard looks into the murder of a woman in a home-based moving-picture studio. Her solicitor tells the tale after her doctor finds her, the two men being brothers-in-law. For complicated reasons a French Sûreté officer, M. Roche, gets into the act and predicts that only chance will give the clue—and so it turns out: the murder was accidental and all the dirty linen (a large trousseau) has been washed in vain. "Chance is the best detective." Veto.

1792 REES, A. J. See also:

The River Mystery   DM 1932
The Unquenchable Flame   DM 1926

1793 REES, ARTHUR J., and WATSON, JOHN (REAY) (b. 1872)

The Mystery of the Downs   Lane (NY) 1918

A good period piece for those who relish length and complexity and do not mind seeing things a bit ahead of the fictional unravelers.

1794 REES and WATSON. See also:

The Hampstead Mystery   Lane 1916

1795 REES, DILWYN (pseud. of Glyn E[dmund] Daniel, b. 1914)

The Cambridge Murders   Goll 1945
    Map of the college

The author, a Fellow of St. John's College, has done his damnedest to provide a full-blown Cambridge tale, complete with a detective who doubles as master—or rather, vice-president—and enough local color to render residence and a BA unnecessary. The result is solid and amusing but overblown. (See also No. 704.)

REILLY, HELEN (ABBY KIERAN) (also Kieran Abbey; 1881–1962)

The sister of John Kieran, journalist and radio star, and wife of Paul Reilly, avoided in her work most of the mannerisms of the HIBK school and wrote several straightforward procedural stories featuring Inspector McKee and later Inspector Todhunter. Her early work may be sampled in *Dead for a Ducat* (1939).

1796 Compartment K   RH 1955

The author's 28th story still features Inspector McKee and his assistant Todhunter, and it is good to report that a train trip from Montreal to Field, B.C., plays an important part in it. But two or three ill-assorted crimes, too many former lovers covering up for each other, and little or no detection make the whole thing seem in retrospect rather a plug for British Columbia resorts.

1797 Follow Me   RH 1960

A sophisticated chase from New York to New Mexico, in a legitimate search for needed evidence.

1798 RENDALL, RUTH, is a fairly conservative practitioner of detection. Several of her stories feature Chief Inspector Wexford—e.g., *A New Lease of Death* (1967), in a Sussex setting. *Wolf to the Slaughter* (1968) is a good piece of suspense with some detection, marred only by an elliptical beginning and an overdose of atmosphere.

1799 REVELL, LOUISA. The detective efforts of Miss Julia Tyler in *The Bus Station Murders* (1947) or *The Kindest Use a Knife* (1953) will not hold the masculine mind when it is fully awake.

>   RHODE, JOHN (pseud. of Cecil John Charles Street; (also Miles Burton, q.v. and F.O.O.; 1884–1964)

Long as is the list of books to Major Street's credit, it would be a mistake to class him with those whose abundance comes from practicing small variations on a single formula. John Rhode was steadily inventive in his special department, which is situation and practical detail. His gift of characterization was slight, but not wholly absent, and in his best work his storytelling is both adroit and straightforward.

He had, moreover, intellectual interests outside the scientific ones used in his stories. Those interests led him to publish such books as *Hungary and Democracy* (1923) and *Thomas Masaryk* (1930) and to translate Daniel Halévy's *Vauban* (1925). In the domain of true crime, he produced an excellent book on *Constance Kent* (1928), and his study of the Wallace case yielded what is perhaps the best fictional rendering of that supreme enigma (see No. 1848).

1800 The Affair of the Substitute Doctor   DM 1951
>   *In Eng.:* Dr. Goodwood's Locum

As the U.S. title foolishly makes plain, this case is one of impersonation, which in turn provides the criminal opportunity. Much active participation by Dr. Priestley makes this late book unusual; he is even present at the final confrontation in Inspector Waghorn's office and tells the cringing criminal exactly what he did.

1801 Blackthorn House   Bles 1949

Even though Priestley leaves his easy chair and goes to a provincial town to interview a man on Superintendent Waghorn's behalf, this tale is routine Rhode and beyond belief dull. The scheme is the usual one of connecting three separate crimes—systematic car theft, arson, and murder. There is painstaking research but no real detection and absolutely no suspense.

1802 The Bloody Tower   Coll 1938
>   *In U.S.:* Tower of Evil

The estate of an impoverished rural clan includes a tower that may conceal a hidden treasure. A cipher exists and is solved by an interloper, who contrives the two murders. Pretty dreary stuff.

1803 Body Unidentified   DM 1938
>   *In Eng.:* Proceed with Caution

A disappointing example of the kind of story Rhode produced after the advent of Jimmy Waghorn. Here Inspector Hanslet is still active and has *his* diamond robbery, while Jimmy investigates a murder (corpse dumped in a county council tar boiler). Priestley holds the stage for about one-third of the book and contributes some missing links.

1804   The Claverton Affair   DM 1933
            In Eng.: The Claverton Mystery

A fine example of good early Priestley. The puzzle is sound, the atmosphere menacing in a splendidly gloomy way, and the treatment of spiritualistic seances above reproach. Add an unusual method of murder and the advantage of finding Dr. Priestley on p. 1, and you have a book to hang onto.

1805   The Davidson Case   Bles 1949; orig. 1929
            In U.S.: Murder at Bratton Grange

Inspector Hanslet is puzzled and calls on Dr. Priestley to do his thinking for him. That helpful friend and man of science (*not* a physician but a physicist) uncovers the scheme by which Sir Guy Davidson polishes off his cousin who was letting the old firm go to rack and ruin from a highly cultivated penchant for drink and women. A good ending, which almost makes attractive the idea of settling things by "taking a pellet."

1806   Dead Men at the Folly   DM 1932

A moderately entertaining pre-Waghorn tale in which Hanslet and the still active Priestley help the police in S.W. England to unearth the connection between two murders and a series of country-house burglaries. Plenty of moving about by road and rail.

1807   Death at Breakfast   DM 1936

This follows soon after the Threlfall case (see No. 1825), to which a couple of references are made. Jimmy Waghorn is still unmarried; Dr. Oldland's first name is revealed to be Mortimer, and Priestley is in very good form. However, the plot is rather routine Rhode: nicotine poisoning, blackmail, and a helpful inconsistency in the form of the apparent murder of the blackmailee.

1808   Death at the Dance   DM 1952

In themselves the robberies, murders, motives, and modes of concealment are ingenious and original, but the telling is a-weary. Priestley and his usual coterie do their usual uninspired arguing. One wonders whether Dr. P.'s continuous somnolence represents the author's writing mood. Note by the way that the dance is not a private affair indoors, but a village festival in broad daylight.

1809   Death at the Helm   DM 1941

Though there are in this tale the usual sticks who get killed and the four-some at Priestley's laconic dinners, two characters are well done—the masterful K.C. whose wife gets poisoned with her lover on a cabin cruiser and a brother-in-law who was a fellow professional of the lover. The clues are abundant and well handled, and the countryside rambles attractive and justified.

1810   Death in Harley Street   DM 1946

Surely the best of the lot. Here Priestley works from the word *go* to unravel a scheme of revenge so contrived that the avenger remains outside the law. A diabolically clever use of suggestion, coupled with sound science, compasses the crime.

1811   Death in Wellington Road   DM 1952

A good opening in Cornwall with a man found dying in a bedroom full of gas. Situation and suspense are pleasingly above average, but unfortunately the red herring brought in to make us absolve the real murderer is set out with a deplorable lack of conviction. The story picks up again with the discovery of the motive and it ends appropriately.

1812   Death of an Artist   DM 1956
            In Eng.: An Artist Dies

Competent, matter-of-fact presentation of the murder of a young artist in a picturesque (i.e., artist-ridden) English town, and of Waghorn's leisurely tracking down of the killer, aided by the passage of time and a fair amount of gossip and luck.

1813   Death on the Boat Train   DM 1940
            In Eng.: Death in the Boat Train

An elderly millionaire in disguise dies after arrival at Waterloo, from an injection into his backside. The complications of plot and relationship are well conceived, but Rhode spoils them by listless narrative. So it cannot be Jimmy Waghorn's blushfully recent marriage to his Diana that makes this story bearable, but the somewhat extended conversations with Dr. Priestley, who even goes to Southampton to see whether it is possible to get on a boat train without having been a passenger all the way from Guernsey.

1814   Death Pays a Dividend   DM 1939

Hanslet and Waghorn do little (except that the latter finds a wife in the course of the story) and it is up to Dr. Priestley to make all clear, which he does without stirring from his study. Unusual among the Rhode tales for its sexual innuendos—was it to spur Jimmy Waghorn to either proposal or proposition?

1815   Death Takes a Partner   DM 1958

This does not fall quite so limp as *Murder at Derivale,* also 1958, but it is pretty humdrum. Local color is largely lacking, and the only amusement comes from the naïve way in which "research" is treated as an absolute occupation, like tinsmithing or hair-cutting.

1816   Dr. Priestley Lays a Trap   DM 1933

This novel depicts Priestley's truly classic performance at the murder committed under cover of the All-Britain Motor Rally. The plot and its motive are first-class, and the suspense is as well managed as any in Rhode. It belongs with *Death in Harley Street, The Claverton Affair,* and *Hendon's First Case.*

1817   Dr. Priestley's Quest   Bles 1948; orig. 1926

One of the earliest Priestley tales, it is told in the first person by his secretary, Harold Merefield, and is not far from the peak stories in Rhode's output. The amount of clueing, inference, adventure, and drama is great, and the characterization has richness of detail as well. Priestley and Merefield are in excellent form whether they ratiocinate or explore dene holes together.

1818   The Double Florin   Bles 1924

Presumably the author's second effort. His first was *A.S.F.* (see No. 1856); this one has to do with L.I.D.O., another capital organization, which enlists the services of a young English aristocrat in need of funds to do some detecting and spying. The enemy is Bolshevism and what ensues is fairly standard adventure: i.e., more setbacks than success, yet all right in the end. "The Double Florin" (originally a coin struck in honor of Queen Victoria's jubilee) is the name of a pub in Bermondsey and also a token of identification, for the coin was still current in the twenties. Despite a general strike, murder, and romance, pretty tame stuff. It shows the influence of Major Street's serious reading rather than of John Rhode's ingenuity in plotting.

1819   The Ellerby Case   Bles 1927

Again told in the first person by Harold Merefield. The illicit sale of a (homemade) drug leads to murder. Much activity by both Priestley and M., the former letting himself be nearly caught in three separate mantraps. On p. 113 a note left by Priestley for Harold is signed "J.P." What, then, of the first name Lancelot, which, however improbable, must be the truth, since we are told so in both earlier and later tales?

1820   The Elm-Tree Murder   DM 1939

Read when it first came out, it struck both collaborators as very bad. They were not used to Waghorn's steady ineffectuality. On a rereading, this account of a contrived accident shows a considerable amount of variety in incident, character, and suspense—and one lets Waghorn wag.

1821   The Fatal Pool   DM 1961

The dullest conceivable Rhode, despite three consultations with Priestley, who speaks oracularly and pointlessly. Well-nigh unreadable.

1822   The Fourth Bomb   CCC 1942

J.R. wrote three books about wartime England under enemy action. This
is the poorest, even though it has an excellent idea to work on and (as
usual) a plot carefully put together. But the characters are worse than
nonexistent. Waghorn and his wife chatter to no purpose, and when
Priestley goes to the scene of the crime he simply pulls the solution out
of a hat.

1823   Grave Matters   DM 1955
          In Eng.: The Domestic Agency

Humdrum Waghorn—an employment agency is not what it seems, and
the reader sees through it sooner than the police.

1824   The Hanging Woman   DM 1931

An early Rhode, in which plotting and character are solid. Priestley intervenes reasonably early and stirs his stumps in pursuit of clues. Near the
end of Priestley's long visit to a fellow scientist, the other man "suggests
retirement." Needless to say, Priestley overlooks this and merely goes
to bed.

1825   Hendon's First Case   DM 1935

This tale introduces Jimmy Waghorn, a Cambridge man who has gone
through the new Police College and thus finds himself in conflict with
Inspector Hanslet, but is supported by Priestley. At this stage in his life
Waghorn had a little gumption, though it is still P. who solves the crime:
the murder of a chemist and assorted sabotage on and around his
premises. One of Rhode's best.

1826   The House on Tollard Ridge   DM 1929

On rereading in 1957, both critics found it not up to their favorable recollections, based on the mechanics (radio and such) and a rather charming love story. Query: Has the book aged faster than the readers, or the
reverse?

1827   In Face of the Verdict   CCC 1936

The two murders linked with natural death are ingeniously contrived for
the purpose of securing a large estate. Telepathy also comes in aptly, and
so does Priestley, in Chapter 1, p. 1.

1828   The Last Suspect   DM 1950

The son of a wealthy brewer is found dead in his ditched car, with the
money collected from pubs missing. Usual family antipathies cause Inspector Waghorn endless trouble, and even Priestley is misled. There is
an abundance of devices, ingenious as usual, and fruitful for detection.

1829   Licensed for Murder   DM 1959

The pace is slow, but the country pub and its surroundings give Rhode
a chance to do what he does best—places and activities rather than people.
Ingenious plot, but more than the usual apathy by Priestley and his lay
figures.

1830   Murder at Derivale   DM 1958

Pedestrian Rhode, with very little Priestley and too much running about
by Jimmy Waghorn. Only a bit of interest attaching to tramp steamers
and port activity saves this tale from worthlessness.

1831   Murder at Lilac Cottage   DM 1940

The essential business is to find out why one of the squire's underlings
was murdered for no perceptible reason. Priestley takes a fairly active
part, but it is Merefield who gets a load of buckshot fired at his retreating
rear—a day to remember.

1832   Murder at the Motor Show   DM 1936
       In Eng.: Mystery at Olympia

The victim is killed by having a large motor part—gear box or differ-
ential—rammed into his kidney in a crowd. No doubt possible, but somehow not very striking in a detective story. Still, the tale is one of Rhode's
most tight-knit jobs; one looks elsewhere for drama.

1833   The Murders in Praed Street   DM 1928

A very early specimen, coming soon after *The Ellerby Case,* to which it
refers. Though Priestley does nothing but blunder around and get himself
nearly gassed, the story serves to remind us that in the beginning Rhode
had in mind a truly athletic and ambulatory detective. Priestley must
have been converted to Zen soon after.

1834   The Mysterious Suspect   DM 1953
       In Eng.: By Registered Post

A tired effort dealing with the poisoning of an elderly businessman and
the mechanically inept faking of a suicide by the fall guy. What distinguishes the book is the flat statement on p. 59 that Harold Merefield
is Dr. Priestley's son-in-law—twenty-eight years after the young man's
engagement to "April," of whom nothing is ever heard again.

1835   Night Exercise   DM 1942
       In U.S.: Dead of the Night

Dr. Priestley does not appear, nor does Waghorn. Most of the book is
devoted to the joint exercise of the Home Guard and the Civil Defense,
in the course of which a well-disliked officer disappears. Not much detection, but splendid action and more characterization than in other
Rhode—altogether an enjoyable story.

1836   Nothing but the Truth   Bles 1947
        In U.S.: Experiment in Crime

Rhode now goes at his plots like a contractor: the deliberate laying out
of equipment on ground carefully surveyed generates a powerful tediousness. Here a dislikable businessman is found as a corpse in an AA box.
Waghorn unfolds false theories to Priestley, who merely says they are all
conjecture. Little thinking done by anybody.

1837   Open Verdict   DM 1957

The scene is rural—a group of villages in the midst of farmland, about
which Rhode waxes lyrical. Waghorn spends all his time gossiping pleasantly with local inhabitants, who give him answers in long, well-organized, and perfectly worded paragraphs. The plot is complex, especially
in its antecedents, though the unraveling of the murder is oversimple.

1838   The Paddington Mystery   Bles 1925

Not a bona fide detective story, but a spate of information concerning
Priestley's early years and those of his secretary-to-be, Harold Merefield.
Harold's fall from grace, life of sin, and partial estrangement from P.'s
daughter April (soon lost without trace) are all rectified in the course
of investigating the frame-up perpetrated upon the innocent Harold.

1839   The Paper Bag   Bles 1948

Quite standard late Rhode. Waghorn rather an ass; Priestley functioning
from time to time. He is able, without leaving his chair, to recognize
"Doryl" as a drug and not a girl's name.

1840   Peril at Cranbury Hall   DM 1930

Good early Priestley, with amusing references to the coolness between
Dr. P. and Inspector Hanslet caused by the failure of the Crown case
against Sir Guy Davidson to come off (see *The Davidson Case*). Harold
Merefield acts as legman in Hanslet's stead, and miscellaneous features
include a good cipher and its solution and two elegant mantraps.

1841   Pinehurst   DM 1930
        In U.S.: Dr. Priestley Investigates

Apparently the fifth tale in which Priestley appears. He stays in the thick
of things from start to finish. The business is the murder of a retired hi-
jacker from Prohibition days, and the locale is the "Lenhaven" which
figures in Tollard Ridge. Vintage Rhode.

1842   Poison for One   DM 1934

How to stop an old lecher from marrying a nice girl? Rhode solves
that perennial problem, but someone (Sayers?) questions whether the
murder trick proposed here would work, and WHT withholds his approval until he has tried it on his collaborator under the heading of ap-

plied toxicology. Dr. Priestley lectures at length in his final explanation, and JB is convinced ahead of the experiment.

1843   Robbery with Violence   DM 1957

In this a plan is developed for robbing a bank—a most ingenious plan, which might well work. A man who has tumbled to the system gets murdered. Very little Priestley; too many charwomen.

1844   The Robthorne Mystery   DM 1934

Not valued equally by WHT and JB, who cannot believe in the villain's character as described. The situation, however, is excellent: fear driving a man to kill the man who, he knows, is preparing to kill him. An interesting legal question is raised but not pushed to its conclusion: given a man on trial for the murder of X who at the trial gives full evidence of being X himself, thereby showing that the *corpus delicti* is Y: could X be tried again for the murder of Y, the same *corpus delicti,* having once stood in the dock?

1845   The Secret Meeting   DM 1951

In this one the culprit winds up at Priestley's house and it is the Professor who pops the question "Would you care to tell us why you resorted to murder?" The person asked explains why to everybody's satisfaction. Guess what happens next.

1846   The Secret of the Lake House   DM 1946
          In Eng.: The Lake House

One of the last cases in which Dr. Priestley gets about and does things. Here he demonstrates at first hand how the peculiar circumstances in which a wealthy eccentric is found dead in his alchemical hobby shop tie in with the possibilities of suicide, murder, or the one made to look like the other. The writing and characterization are above par for Rhode, and he adds a bonus of dry wit and satire. The ideas are original, artfully combined, and carefully, but not too carefully, explained.

1847   Shadow of a Crime   DM 1945
          In Eng.: Bricklayer's Arms

A dull tale, although the ingredients are not bad. A motorcyclist's death is contrived as he drives under a railway underpass with the setting sun in his eyes. But the red herrings are obvious and neither Dr. Priestley nor Jimmy Waghorn particularly shines.

   Under its U.S. title, not to be confused with Hall Caine's novel (1885), not detection.

1848   The Telephone Call   Bles 1948
          In U.S.: Shadow of an Alibi

A first-rate reconstruction of the Wallace case. When Rhode has a start on a situation—i.e., does not have to clothe it himself with human detail

—he does an excellent job. And his mastery of physical fact is here admirably applied, leading to a very plausible outcome. *Hors concours,* gold medal.

1849   Three Cousins Die   DM 1960

Routine stuff; the murderer confesses in detail, after Priestley asks Waghorn to find out what the man was wheeling in the pram.

1850   Too Many Suspects   DM 1945
          In Eng.: Vegetable Duck

The setting in a London flat is admirable, and Jimmy Waghorn starts off well, but Hanslet's revelation that the husband of the murdered woman had probably committed an earlier crime blinds him to other possibilities. Postprandial sessions with Priestley do no good. Parts of the plot are reminiscent of the Wallace case, which is twice referred to (pp. 55 and 73).

1851   Tragedy at the Unicorn   DM 1928

This tells of the death at an inn in a small yachting port of a despicable elderly man, perhaps at the hands of one of a jolly group of young men and women of which Harold Merefield forms part. When his close friend is suspected, Harold gets his employer to come in and solve the problem: Priestley is active and sociable, and unmasks the villain in short order.

1852   Tragedy on the Line   DM 1931

The railway interest is modest, and the criminal is obvious. Rhode is also a bit weak on the Canadian background, which is brought in somewhat in the manner of *A Study in Scarlet.* Here we have perhaps the only recorded instance of P.'s kissing another member of the human race, albeit a dying one.

1853   Twice Dead   DM 1960

A cranky baronet announces his own death to see what his relatives will do; then he makes a will and is promptly bumped off by an ingenious method. The genuine surprise is that the doctor and coroner do the postmortem in less than ten minutes in the very room where the old boy died. Priestley and his mates do very little, and for once Waghorn spots the criminal.

1854   The Two Graphs   Bles 1950
          In U.S.: Double Identities

This must stand as one of the few good examples of the classic tale of confused identities between a pair of brothers, not twins. Extremely well handled, and though late Priestley it is full of merit.

1855 The Vanishing Diary   DM 1961

There are two sides to every question—and to every family. Each party
possesses a key to the padlocks that secure a box said to contain the
intimate diaries of the Empress Eugénie. The younger, literary members
do one another in so as to secure this valuable material. In spite of this
rivalry, dull in the extreme.

1856 The White Menace   Bles 1924
    In Eng.: A. S. F.: The Story of a Great Conspiracy

A non-Priestley story of the drug traffic. Better written than most of the
similar examples of the twenties, and thus something of a period piece to
be cherished.

1857 RHODE. See also Nos. 2780, 352 ff., and:

The Alarm	Bles 1925	The Harvest Murder	DM 1937
The Corpse in the Car	DM 1935	Invisible Weapons	DM 1938
Dead on the Track	DM 1943	The Links in the Chain	DM 1948
Death in the Hop-fields	Coll 1937	Men Die at Cyprus Lodge	Coll 1943
Death Invades the Meeting	DM 1944	Murders at Greycombe	
Death of an Author	Bles 1947	Farm (= Fire at Grey-	
Death on the Board (= Death		combe Farm	Coll 1932
Sits on the Board)	DM 1937	Shot at Dawn	Coll 1934
Death on Sunday	Coll 1939	Signal for Death	DM 1941
Delayed Payment (= Death		Up the Garden Path (= The	
of a Godmother)	Bles 1955	Fatal Garden)	Bles 1949/DM 1949
Family Affairs	Bles 1950	The Venner Crime	Odhams 1933

1858 RHODE, JOHN, and DICKSON, CARTER (q.v.)

    Fatal Descent   DM 1939
        In Eng.: Drop to His Death

This is the original and classic elevator story, in which the murder is adroitly
committed in absentia. The atmosphere is important to the plot and to
the reader's enjoyment, and the gadgetry as convincing as the internal
politics of the big publishing concern.

1859 RICE, CRAIG (pseud. of Georgiana Ann Randolph [Mrs. Lawrence
Lipton]; also Daphne Sanders and Michael Venning; 1908–57) generally
goes in for ill-advised humor and an excess of home life. But there is invention and charm in those of her stories, short and long, that present the
efforts of the lawyer John J. Malone to see justice done against odds. See
Trial by Fury (1941); *The Lucky Stiff* (1945), *The Fourth Postman*
(1948), *My Kingdom for a Hearse* (1957). For capsule true crime recitals, see *Forty-Five Murderers* (1952).

1860 RICHARDS, FRANCIS (pseud. of Richard and Frances Lockridge,
    qq.v.)

    Practise to Deceive   MBG 1957

This exclusively European pseudonym covers a middle-period Heimrich
tale, in which H. and Susan Faye are courting. Heimrich solves the mys-

tery of the death of a prospective wealthy client of Susan's by destroying the alibi that a raging river affords.

1861   RIDDELL, JOHN (pseud. of Corey Ford, q.v.)

The John Riddell Murder Case   Scrib 1930
A Philo Vance Parody

A period piece. Corey Ford was a good humorist in the American (Missouri) tradition, and the preciosity of Philo Vance certainly deserved Riddell-ing. But the book-length scale is not well adapted to parodying what is ridiculous to start with. Even with a stronger victim to take off, Fielding stopped early in *Joseph Andrews*. (See also Nos. 2510 and 3147.)

RINEHART, MARY ROBERTS (1876–1958)

A native of Pittsburgh and the wife of the physician Dr. Stanley Rinehart, this writer bridges the gap between Anna Katharine Green and Leslie Ford. More sophisticated and less long-winded than the former, she avoided the superficiality of the latter in her Washington phase. Except for Nurse Pinkerton, no single detective appears in more than one of M.R.R.'s twenty long novels, and the detection, though conscientious, is often smothered in domestic detail. (The Tish stories are not detection and rely on feminine appeal.)

But the best of her novels survive the present thronging competition: in the 1960s, the publishing firm of which she was a director (now Holt, Rinehart & Winston) kept in print fifteen of her works in four large omnibus volumes, and in 1970 the newsstands sport eighteen single novels overlapping the preceding collections.

1862   The Door   Farr 1930

As good an example as any of the way this author developed a domestic mystery at great length by having a maiden lady of impeccable social standing relate complex and mysterious events. Three murders are plausibly linked with a spurious will, and the killer's identity is neatly revealed in the next-to-last line of the last page. The "door," though introduced late, furnishes a clever clue.

1863   The Man in Lower Ten   BM 1909

Her masterpiece in the genre she affected. Told breezily in the first person by a lawyer nearing middle age, this story would now be called overclued and melodramatic—but think of the early R. A. Freeman, who is her contemporary. The Washington Flier is wrecked, just after a murder has been committed as a result of a tangle of forgery and blackmail. The mystery is genuine, as well as hard on the nice people: the narrator is the murder suspect, and his girl nearly marries a scoundrel.

1864   RINEHART. See also:

The After House   HM 1914
The Album   Farr 1933
The Case of Jennie Brice   Doran 1913

| The Circular Staircase | BM 1908 |
| The Red Lamp | Doran 1925 |

The omnibus groupings are entitled:

Miss Pinkerton: Adventures of a Nurse Detective	Rine 1959
The Frightened Wife and Other Murder Stories	Rine 1953
The Mary Roberts Rinehart Crime Book	Rine 1960
Mary Roberts Rinehart's Mystery Book	Rine 1961

For her stage success, "The Bat," see No. 2395.

1865 ROBBINS, CLIFTON (b. 1890)

Death on the Highway   Benn 1933

The cigar-smoking detective Clay Harrison is not badly drawn, but is more impressive as a man than as an investigator. The gang opposing him (based near Toulon and headed by a formidable elderly English-woman) is close to ludicrous. Dated beyond recall.

1866 Methylated Murder   Butt 1935

This is in the mood and time of Temple-Ellis (q.v.). Called a "new Clay Harrison adventure," it chronicles the exploits of an infallible, gentle-manly super-sleuth who thinks hard, quotes Sherlock Holmes, and praises his antagonist for profound scheming. The criminality is puerile, but there are a few good ideas. "Methylated spirits," by the way, account for the ferocity of an otherwise mild giant of retarded intelligence.

1867 ROBBINS. See also:

| Dusty Death | App 1932 |
| The Man Without a Face | Benn 1932 |

1868 ROBERTS, MARY-CARTER

Little Brother Fate   Farr 1957

The one-time book editor of the *Washington Star* has combined murder with social criticism and abnormal psychology. The form, tone, and de-tail are those of a novel of character, not a tale of crime or detection. Indeed, the point of the story is that a ruthless drive toward "position" carries disaster in its train and that killing is but one form of sin. It may be wondered why the work has been reprinted by Penguin in the green covers of its mystery series.

1869 ROBERTSON, HELEN (pseud. of Helen Jean Mary Edmiston, b. 1913)

Swan Song   CCD 1960
     In Eng.: The Chinese Goose

Here is proof that originality is never impossible. The great swannery that gives the book its title, the small rural community on the Thames estuary, the tidal mere on the grounds of the ruined castle kept up by one vain man, the unusual situation of the 18-year-old heroine from London, the murder by strange means before her arrival and the one she half witnesses in the dark, the relations of Inspector Dynes, who is on vacation at the house of his Sergeant Benwick, with the local forces— all these freshly conceived elements fit together without constraint to form a quietly gripping narrative with no excess and no letup in interest and variety. The motive of the crime is also new and the solution comes, bit by bit, out of action as well as out of the reasoning of four intelligent persons, including the likable Dynes and Benwick.

1870   ROBERTSON. See also:

The Crystal Gazers	Dday 1958
The Winged Witnesses	Macd 1955

ROBINSON, ROBERT (HENRY) (b. 1929)

Educ. Exeter Coll., Oxf., after studying under L. A. G. Strong (q.v.) at Raynes Park Grammar School. Film critic for the *Sunday Telegraph*, and once upon a time columnist for all three Sunday papers simultaneously, he combines writing with being chairman of BBC 3, and has written an autobiography called *Inside Robert Robinson*.

1871   Landscape with Dead Dons   Rine 1956

An Oxford ("Warlock College") tale, somewhat in the manner of Innes, but less embellished. Crispin praised it, but would have done a better job. Enjoyable with reservations.

1872   ROBINSON, TIMOTHY (b. 1934)

When Scholars Fall   Hutch 1961
   New Authors Series

A first novel by another well-informed Oxonian. Four undergraduates of divergent but similarly amusing types undertake to solve the mystery of who killed the hated historical don. They muddle about in a very gentlemanly manner until a second person is killed. The third killing they predict and prevent. Tidied up a bit, this would be excellent.

1873   ROGERS, SAMUEL (GREENE ARNOLD) (b. 1894)

You Leave Me Cold!   Harp 1946

A fair plot, laid in university surroundings, exhibiting medical students and professors, and based on an unusual motive. All is present to produce a first-class affair of detection, including the author's determination to detect. But for a reason hard to spot, the whole thing fails to move. Characters and narrative are above average, and so is the style, but oomph is missing.

1874   ROGERS. See also:

Don't Look Behind You!	Harp 1944 (repr. Lancer 1966)
You'll Be Sorry!	Harp 1945

1875 ROHDE, WILLIAM L. In *Murder on the Line* (1961/1951) the railroad detective Mohawk Daniels is appealing as he works out sources of sabotage on a small New England line. The RR atmosphere is genuine. Not to be confused with the works of Robert H. Rohde.

1876 ROHMER, SAX (pseud. of Arthur Sarsfield Ward[e], 1883–1959), b. in Ireland, was obsessed with the East, visited Egypt, took up painting, entered journalism, then created the insidious Dr. Fu Manchu under that now famous phrase in 1913. The Doctor's adventures may entertain once, partly because of well-contrived suspense, partly because of one's enjoyment of one's own folly in believing what one is told, for ex. the presence on Wimbledon Common of a menagerie of lethal creatures kept by this sinister Chinese. The battered hero, Nayland Smith, is rescued several times by the Dr.'s byutchus daughter, until the tales begin to show a mellowing malefactor, who ends by using his powers for the League of Nations. See *The Hand of Fu Manchu* (1917); *The Daughter of Fu Manchu* (1931).

Meanwhile, this indefatigable writer started a bigger thing than he knew when he wrote *Dope: A Story of Chinatown and the Drug Traffic* (1919). He also tried other genres—for example, *The Dream Detective* (1920), which tells nine episodes in the life of the antiquarian dealer Morris Klaw, who solves baffling problems in equally mysterious ways, to an accompaniment of portentous utterances and flat narration.

1877 ROLLS, ANTHONY (pseud. of C[olwyn] E[dward] Vulliamy, q.v., b. 1886)

Clerical Error   LB 1932
   In Eng.: The Vicar's Experiments

Unsatisfactory despite the author's cleverness and extensive vocabulary. The first 30 pages or so are good, and the U.S. title is excellent, but there the willing suspension of disbelief comes to a stop.

1878 ROLLS. See also Nos. 2142–3 and:

Scarweather   Bles 1934

1879 ROOF, KATHARINE M(ETCALF)

Murder on the Salem Road   HM 1931

An historical novel in which murder is incidental and conducive only to romance in the feminine mood. The time is the early nineteenth century in Massachusetts and the hero is a Frenchman who cuts window shades (perhaps also lampshades) for a living and calls himself an artist.

1880 ROSS, BARNABY (pseud. of Frederic Dannay and Manfred Lee, otherwise "Ellery Queen," q.v.)

The Tragedy of X   VP 1932

A good example of what these versatile authors can do when untrammeled by the relationships of Queen and his retinue. The retired actor Drury Lane does a good, deliberate job of identifying the man who placed a cork bristling with nicotine-dipped needles in the victim's overcoat pocket. The Weehawken ferry and the West Shore RR are featured and two more murders occur before the elderly Shakespearean gets it sorted out. But his explanation is cogent and complete.

1881   The Tragedy of Y   VP 1932

Somewhat in the style of Van Dine's *Greene Murder Case* of four years earlier, the author fills an old New York mansion with a detestable tribe and has the actor Drury Lane help the police in the mysterious poisonings that ensue. Overlong by modern standards (344 pages), the novel has sections of compelling ratiocination by the hero. Others are blemished, by inexpert chemistry, but the (sub rosa) syphilis is well handled.

1882   Ross. See also:

  Drury Lane's Last Case   VP 1933
  The Scroll of Lysis   S&S 1962
  The Tragedy of Z   VP 1933

  ROSTEN, LEO (CALVIN) (b. 1908)

b. Lodz, Poland; educ. Univ. of Chicago and London School of Economics. Famous as Leonard Q. Ross for his "Hyman Kaplan" sketches in *The New Yorker*.

1883   A Most Private Intrigue   Ath 1967

The writing shows practiced ease and virtuoso wit, but this venture in adventure, despite a few inventions more fantastic than original, does not stand out from the mass of similar Russo-Turkish-CIA tales—which does not mean that the book is not a good evening's entertainment.

  ROTH, HOLLY [Mrs. Joseph Franta] (also K. G. Ballard and P. J. Merrill; 1916–64)

b. Chicago; educ. in U.S. and Europe; one-time model and magazine editor, then writer for the periodical press, and finally author of stories of detection and espionage, till her own mysterious death off a small sailing vessel in the Mediterranean.

1884   Button, Button   HB 1966

Her last book, finished by a friendly editor after her death. This ultimate tale by a gifted writer sounds a little mechanical, though it uses good ideas, such as the expiry of a patent application and a new style of frame-up. An Oklahoma insurance agent does the detecting in New York summer heat and shows how the bomb was put on the plane. An unnecessarily near-death finish.

1885   The Content Assignment   S&S 1954
          In ppb.: The Girl Who Vanished

An excellent spy and counterspy story, the legwork being done by an English journalist who fell in love with an American girl agent while in

Berlin. He comes to the United States to find her when she disappears. Witty and full of good description.

1886   The Crimson in the Purple   S&S 1956

The fourth of her novels and not in the top class. That is often true when actors and playwrights and "dramatic" atmosphere are mixed with murder on or off stage. Here the trouble is compounded with the rather stale devices of the family dynasty and the old mansion. Told in the first person by the young (male) playwright, the plot includes blackmail, counter-blackmail, fraud practiced on an invalid, and generally more confusion than detection.

1887   Shadow of a Lady   S&S 1957

A good tale that combines detection, the trial of an innocent man, a chase, and a pair of excellent character studies, all in a very small compass. There is only one weak chapter, that in which the concussion victim comes to. Otherwise, first-class.

1888   The Sleeper   S&S 1955

As elegantly written as the others—she knows her Fowler—but is here inclined to digress, so that the total effect is slighter than it need have been.

1889   Too Many Doctors   RH 1962
        In Eng.: Operation Doctors

Her brand of suspense is attractive (as she was herself), because it is nicely spaced and not a steady dose of anxious irrationalism. We have a ship at sea with an amnesia case (female) and two doctors; on land, three physicians dead, including the former doctor of this same ship. Detection by Inspector Medford follows, but when he rounds on a likable character, also detecting, it rather spoils the fun.

1890   ROTH. See also:

As K. G. Ballard:
    Bar Sinister   CCD 1960
    The Coast of Fear   CCD 1958
    The Gauge of Deception   CCD 1963
As P. J. Merrill:
    The Mask of Glass   Van 1954
    The Slender Thread   HB 1959

1891   ROUECHÉ, BERTON (b. 1911), is a staff writer on *The New Yorker*, who is named here only because his books have been listed as fiction in booksellers' catalogues. His *Annals of Medical Detection*—(in U.S.: *Eleven Blue Men and Other Narratives of Medical Detection* (1968/ 1947)—belong to the history of medicine, as do three other works. When he writes fiction it is of the advanced kind published in *Evergreen Review*.

1892　Ruegg, [Judge] A(lfred) H(enry) (b. 1854)

Flash   Daniel 1928
　　　A Moorland Mystery

Flash is a place in Staffordshire, and the tale is not a mystery in the
modern sense, but a mixture of legendary ghostliness with a love story,
set among the county folk and their dependents. The events occur in
the early part of the nineteenth century; there is a colliery accident,
an ambiguous butler, the investigation of forgery, sorrow, and a sentimental ending in a snowstorm.

1893　Russell, E. S.

She Should Have Cried on Monday   CCD 1968

In a New England countryside, a selfish woman who was going to sell
land regardless of its probable misuse is strangled. The wrong man is
suspected, but his extrication leaves one with a lackluster eye.

1894　Russell, W(illiam) Clark (1844–1911)

The Copsford Mystery; or, Is He the Man?   NAB 1896
　　　Anon. Introd. about the author and
　　　pencil sketch by the latter
　　　Illus.

The famous author of sea stories that Conan Doyle praised through Dr.
Watson is not in his element in land-based adventure. Robbery and disappearance, suspected murder and discovered imposture are told in formal sentences and stilted dialogue all the way to the inevitable confession.
There are clues but no work upon them.

1895　Rutherford, Douglas (pseud. of James Douglas Rutherford Mc-
Connell, b. 1915), writes thrillers without detection. In *Comes the Blind
Fury* (1950) we learn how Paddy Regan avenges the shooting of his
partner in a "special agency." The setting is Paris nightclubs. Other
books use Brittany, Torquay, and Tunis. See *Meet a Body* (1951), *Murder Is Incidental* (1961), *The Black Leather Murders* (1966).

1896　Saltus, Edgar (Evertson) (1855–1921)

The Paliser Case   Boni 1919

The brilliant first chapter—almost a match for the opening of *Trent's
Last Case*—does not lead to a detective story, alas!, but to a romance in
which murder, false arrest, and denouement take place without the help
of reasoning. It is the title and the first sentence, which speaks of murder,
that have caused the book to be listed by booksellers under detective
fiction.

1897　Sanders, Bruce

To Catch a Spy   HJ 1958

The tenth routine repetition of familiar intrigue, with exactly the amount
of inventiveness suggested by the title.

Novels / 373

SAYERS, DOROTHY L(EIGH) [Mrs. (Oswald) Atherton Fleming]
(also Johanna Leigh; 1893–1957)

Trained as a scholar, began career as detective novelist in 1923 with
Whose Body?, concluded thirteen years later with *Busman's Honeymoon*,
after which she devoted herself to religious (Anglican) propaganda
through plays, translations, essays, and lectures. Numerous introductions
and articles—some gathered in *Unpopular Opinions* (see No. 3373)—
deal in masterly fashion with the history and nature of the detective genre;
other essays with true crime. (See Nos. 3019–21 and 3280.)

1898   Busman's Honeymoon   HB 1937

Not near the top of her form, but remarkable as a treatment of the newly
wedded and bedded pair of eccentrics, Peter Wimsey and Harriet Vane,
with Bunter in the offing and three local characters, chiefly comic. Peter's
mother—dowager duchess of Denver—Peter's sister, John Donne, a case
of vintage port, and the handling of "corroded sut" provide plenty of
garnishing for an indifferent murder, even if we weren't also given an
idea of Lord Peter's sexual tastes and powers under trying circumstances.

1899   Clouds of Witnesses   Dial 1928
         In Eng.: Clouds of Witness

Like *Suspicious Characters,* this is likely to be more highly esteemed on
a second reading. It is the story of the duke of Denver's extramarital
adventure. His younger brother's brilliant exculpation of the duke gives
rise to the famous remark, uttered in the House of Lords: "Gentlemen,
the barometer is falling." Read it to find the context.
   The allusion is to Heb. 12:1.

1900   Gaudy Night   Goll 1936/1935

Stories laid in educational institutions for women suffer from one fault:
the combination of gossip and "outrages." These last are not what the
newspaper reader understands by that term but merely vandalism and
attempts to frighten. In detective fiction, where murder is standard fare,
"outrages" are comparatively weak—the report being nothing like the unnerving actuality. This flaw aside, *Gaudy Night* is a remarkable achievement. Harriet Vane and the grown-up nephew of Lord Peter help give
variety, and the college scene justifies good intellectual talk. The motive
is magnificently orated on by the culprit, a scene that in itself is a unique
bit of work. And though the don-esses are sometimes hard to keep apart,
the architecture is very good.
   Note a reference to C. P. Snow's *The Search,* and sound views on
counterpoint versus harmony.

1901   Have His Carcase   Goll 1932

A great achievement, despite some critics' carping. The people, the motive, the cipher, and the detection are all topnotch. Here, too, is the first
(and definitive) use of hemophilia as a misleading fact. And surely the
son, the mother, and her self-deluded gigolo are definitive types.

374

1902   Murder Must Advertise   Goll 1933/21st ptg. 1953

A superb example of Sayers' ability to set a group of people going. The advertising agency is inimitable, and hence better than the De Momerie crowd that goes with it. The murder is ingenious and Wimsey is just right, but one flaw mars the criminal scheme: would the postman, after a few weeks, continue to deliver letters that the tobacconist declined to accept?

1903   The Nine Tailors   **HB 1934**
         Maps

For many reasons, no great favorite of these readers, despite Dorothy's swotting up of bell-ringing and the two good maps. The cause of death, however, is original, and the rescue scene in the church amid the flood shows the hand of the master.

1904   Strong Poison   **HB 1938/Goll 1930**

JB puts this highest among the masterpieces. It has the strongest possible element of suspense—curiosity *and* the feeling one shares with Wimsey for Harriet Vane. The clues, the enigma, the free-love question, and the order of telling could not be improved upon. As for the somber opening, with the judge's comments on how to make an omelet, it is sheer genius.

1905   Suspicious Characters   **HB 1931**
         In Eng.: **The Five Red Herrings**

A work that grows on rereading and remains in the mind as one of the richest, most colorful of her group studies. The Scottish setting, the artists in the colony, the train-ticket puzzle, and the final chase place this triumph among the four or five chefs d'oeuvre from her hand.

1906   Unnatural Death   Goll 1936; orig. 1927
         In U.S.: **The Dawson Pedigree**
         Six-page preface by P. A. Delagardie, Lord P.'s uncle,
         rectifying the facts about the life of Lord Peter.

The tale is perhaps a little forced in conception and remote in tone. That is the trouble with all the great masters—they accustom us to such dazzling performances that when they give us what would seem wonderful coming from other hands, we sniff and act choosy. The mode of compassing death has been carped at, but no one could do anything but rejoice at Miss Climpson and her subterfuges.

1907   The Unpleasantness at the Bellona Club   **HB 1928**

By all odds the dullest Sayers: nothing about it is interesting after the grotesque but effective opening, and some of the sentiments are embarrassing.

1908   Whose Body?   Boni 1923

A stunning first novel that disclosed the advent of a new star in the firmament, and one of the first magnitude. The episode of the bum in the bathtub, the character (and the name) of Sir Julian Freke, the detection, and the possibilities in Peter Wimsey are so many signs of genius about to erupt. Peter alone suffers from fatuousness overdone, a period fault that Sayers soon blotted out.

1909 SAYERS. See also: Nos. 2775–82 and 3019–21.

1910 SAYERS, DOROTHY and EUSTACE, ROBERT (see No. 1784)

The Documents in the Case   Goll 1949; orig. 1930

A highly diverting account, largely in letter form, of a case of poisoning by synthetic muscarine alkaloid made to look like mushroom poisoning. Evidence of optical activity and what it means beautifully handled, although the authors are said to have made a mistake in their choice of the particular mushroom to which the "accidental" death should be attributed. Characters outstanding.

1911 SCERBANENCO, GIORGIO

Duca and the Milan Murders   Cass 1970

The story of Duca Lamberti's exploits was awarded the French *Grand Prix* for the genre, which prepares one for a book to be read in a Continental frame of mind. The Italian physician who is unfrocked for practicing euthanasia and assists the police in the expectation that he will be rehabilitated goes after a gang of vicious criminals, at first by questions aimed at establishing a doctor-patient relation. But when this Hippocratic method fails he resorts to actions akin to his opponents'. In so doing he finds how and why three couples have drowned in one canal and what the conspiracy is all about. The translation is good and the toughness interesting in its differences from Anglo-American models. As for the doctor-detective, he probably deserved being struck off the register.

1912 SCHERF, MARGARET (b. 1908). Beginning in 1940 with *The Corpse Grows a Beard* (bad physiology!), this writer has specialized in the fusion of crime, detection and farce—an English monopoly, one might think, if one did not add Miss S.'s twenty to the tales by Iams and Box (qq.v.). Her work deserves the epithet "charming" often bestowed upon it, but it must be added that the density of detection in her extravaganzas is low. *The Curious Custard Pie* (1950) is typical: the Reverend Martin Buell and his dog Bascomb join to make fun of Farrington, Montana, its churches, merchants, and old ladies. But when he goes to a Peace Society summer camp and, to offset the vegetarian diet, bakes a pie, it fells the consumers and two perish. Though he uncovers the hand that interfered, his detection is at a pace that would give confidence to any criminal with a good car. Equal in merit—and in faults—may be mentioned: *The Banker's Bones* (1968), *The Cautious Overshoes* (1956), *The Corpse in the Flannel Nightgown* (1965), *Glass on the Stairs* (1954), *Judicial Body* (1957), *Never Turn Your Back* (1959), and *The Owl in the Cellar* (1945).

1913 SCHOLEY, JEAN

    The Dead Past   Macm 1962/1961

This first mystery by an unknown Englishwoman is more enjoyable than
most of what comes nowadays from well-known hands. The setting is a
town on the coast of Tanganyika; the crime is the murder of a ne'er-
do-well with whose past some of the government-post group are unfortunately concerned. Cut off from official police support by the rains,
District Commissioner Geoffrey Hallden does a good job of clue-hunting
and meditating and finally gets his man.

      SCOTT, SUTHERLAND

British physician and author, best known for his poorly composed but
useful *Blood in Their Ink,* which discusses "The March of the Modern
Mystery Novel" (see No. 3023). Scott is the inditer of Dr. Septimus
Dodds and Inspector Verity, whose doings are described in at least a
dozen indifferent novels.

1914 Escape to Murder   SP 1946

His sixth or seventh work, which shows him as a male practitioner of the
HIBK school. Badly written, full of needless murders and unexamined
clues, winding up in an unbelievable least-suspected denouement, the
story is told in the first person by the Hon. Alex Stacey, an old fool
who is a partner in an agency run by Septimus Dodds, M.D. This M.D.,
in turn, does not know, on intercepting the message "A-Z positive,"
whether this reminds him of something he read in *The Lancet* or in *The
Pharmaceutical Record!*

1915 SCOTT. See also:

      Doctor Dodds' Experiment   SP 1956
      The Mass Radiography Murders   SP 1947
      Tincture of Murder   SP 1951

1916 SEELEY, MABEL (HODNEFIELD) (b. 1903). HIBK may be found
at its best (i.e., worst) in *The Listening House* (1938) or *The Chuckling
Fingers* (1941).

1917 SELLARS, ELEANORE KELLY, was a prizewinner with *Murder à
la Mode* (1941), a work not readable at this late date. Witness the heroine in that work who after being "poisoned with potassium cyanide" lies
in hospital telling her girl friends that it is a most unpleasant experience.
(No other work listed by this author.)

1918 SEMYONOV, JULIAN (SEMYONOVICH); also sp. SEMENOV

    Petrovka 38   S&D 1966/1965

This is a police-routine story Russian style. A gang murders a policeman
in order to get his gun, with which to commit holdups. The investigating

permits the familiar vignette of every character's private worry and inner life. We get the wives and sweethearts of the cops, who are moved by the same idealism and cynicism as the U.S. and English sort. But the kind of sordidness we are treated to differs from ours.

1919 SHAFFER, ANTHONY (JOSHUA) and PETER (twins) (Eng. pseud.: Peter Anthony; b. 1926)

How Doth the Little Crocodile?   Macm 1957; orig. 1952

Mr. Fathom is elderly, bearded, and too much like a Carr-Dickson sleuth, but not wholly a caricature. His forthrightness has its points in the present murder case. Previously messed up by the police, who brought about a false arrest, it ends conventionally in something else than murder.

The title is from *Alice in Wonderland*, ch. 2, in which the author parodies Isaac Watts' "How doth the little busy bee" (Divine Songs, XX).

1920 SHANNON, DELL (pseud. of Elizabeth Linington, q.v.)

Coffin Corner   Morr 1966

Not for those who like police routine tough and breathless. Here Lieutenant Mendoza and his sergeants come out genteel, as are the feeble attempts at vulgar talk and vulgar crime by others. L.A. setting. None of the events or people credible or engaging.

1921 SHARP, DAVID

The Code-Letter Mystery   HM 1932

A preposterous English story which is of interest only because of the hero-detective, Sheridan Orford. Though he asks more questions than he answers, he has an entertaining side, and JB is amused by the intentional cock-and-bull development of a chase across Europe. The reader tolerates far less original complications in current stuff, because it is dressed up in vogue language. Sharp's is terse and clear and humorous as well.

1922 I, the Criminal   Benn 1932

This is an extravaganza about Professor Fielding, whose quiet lust for an old book leads him into the heart of organized crime. Sheridan Orford, the dilettante detective, investigates his friend's doings and at the end helps him round up the gang. Detection incidental.

1923 SHARP. See also:

My Particular Murderer   HM 1931
When No Man Pursueth   Benn 1930

1924 SHEARING, JOSEPH (pseud. of [Mrs.] Gabrielle Margaret Long [Campbell]; also Marjorie Bowen, Robert Paye, George Preedy, and John Winch, 1886–1952), was pre-eminent in the short story of real-life horror (see No. 2601) and the fictional retelling of real crime. See *The Golden Violet* (1941); *Mignonette* (1949); *Moss Rose* (1935); *So Evil My Love* (1947).

1925   SHEPHERD, ERIC

      Murder in a Nunnery   S&W 1940

Somewhat Chestertonish and *not* in a nunnery, but in a convent school, this tale holds the interest partly by the unusualness of the setting, partly by the skill with which the author fashions the young-girl suspects and especially the mother superior. The detective does not amount to much, and the motive is outré. The tale is short and its sententiousness only occasional.

1926   SHEPHERD, E. See also:

      More Murder in a Nunnery   S&W 1954

1927   SHEPHERD, NEAL (pseud. of Nigel Morland, q.v.)

      Death Walks Softly   Const 1938

Some excellent clues and motives adorn this tale of passion, ambition, industrial spying, and revenge which disrupt the firm of industrial chemists Paralder and Hyde (not a bad punning name). The detection is brisk and clear, and the culprit, a double murderer, remains attractive. It's a pity that Chief Inspector Michael Tandy has to be called Napper, but he and Sergeant Holland are agreeably distinguishable from other similar pairs, and the remaining characters have the same gift of individuality— a good job fore and aft.

      SHERWOOD, JOHN (HERMAN MULSO) (b. 1913)

BBC scriptwriter who by the mid-sixties had published at least eight novels of suspense or detection.

1928   The Half Hunter   Goll 1961

Both Allingham and Maurice Richardson have praised this work for its freshness, youth, gaiety, and so on. It rather seems workmanlike than especially lively. The boy hero's detective introspections are slow and sometimes annoying; and the intended smash ending is merely silly. There are, it is true, one or two new twists, and the sidelights on British teen-agers are illuminating.

1929   SHERWOOD. See also:

      Ambush for Anatol   Dday 1952
      Dr. Bruderstein Vanishes   Dday 1949
      Undiplomatic Exit   Dday 1963
      Vote Against Poison   H&S 1956

1930 SIMENON, GEORGES (-JOSEPH-CHRISTIAN) (also: George Sim, Christian Brulls, etc.; b. 1912)

The Man Who Watched the Trains Go By   Reyn 1946
Trans. by Stuart Gilbert

This is generally conceded to be the author's best "straight" novel, i.e., without Inspector Maigret. It is an absorbing account of the progressive mental decay of Kees Popinga (a Dutch ship chandler of Groningen), after the embezzlement and flight of his employer enables Kees to leave his stodgy home and go to Paris to fondle miscellaneous women. His killings and capture, once his money are gone, are routine.

1931 SIMENON. See also Nos. 2792–3 and 2940 and some forty titles beginning *Maigret: Abroad, Afraid, Goes Home, Goes to School,* etc. (1940–69). For a general view of these works (in their way as sentimental as Raymond Chandler's), see Introductory.

1932 SIMMS, WILLIAM GILMORE (1806–70)

The Story of a Criminal   Martin Faber 1837; orig. 1833

A tale, notable for its early date, of pathological crime and the later standard situation of Dreiser's *An American Tragedy:* seduction, pregnancy, and murder, done to enable the desperate evildoer to marry the heiress. A good twist is given by the involvement of the friend to whom the murderer confesses, and who has to turn detective in his own defense.

1933 SIMONS, ROGER (pseud. of Ivar and Margaret Punnett)

Bullet for a Beast   Roy 1964

Trashy, though aiming at better things. The colorless Inspector Wace ferrets out a dull collection of "nameless orgies" following the shooting of a loose young woman in a London street. Unconvincing murderer.

1934 SIMPSON, HELEN (DEGUERRY) [Mrs. D. J. Browne] (1897–1940; also, with Winifred Ashton, Clemence Dane, q.v.)

The Prime Minister Is Dead   Dday 1931

Not strictly detection, but a remarkable and witty story of politics, murder, English life, and character. To say more would disclose the original theme—but watch that tennis game and say whether suspense as now understood comes within miles of the quality generated there.

1935 SIMPSON. See also Nos. 703, 3287, and:

Acquittal   Knopf 1925

1936 SINCLAIR, FIONA

Dead of a Physician   Bles 1961
In U.S.: But the Patient Died

One of the best stories of murder in hospital. The author (wife of a physician) has procedure down pat and keeps her characters clearly distinguished. Perhaps too many people on the staff have good reasons for killing the senior administrator, but the actual culprit is cleanly spotted. Superintendent Grainger is credible and likable.

1937   Meddle with the Mafia   Bles 1963

This lady's melancholy, classical-scholar detective is a widower, Superintendent Paul Grainger. In Sicily he half falls in love with an attractive touristess and she with him and both get involved in a not quite believable mess engineered partly by the Mafia and partly by a German doctor who runs a sinister *Klinik*. In short, a curate's egg.

1938   SINCLAIR. See also:

Scandalize My Name   Bles 1960
Three Slips to a Noose   Bles 1964

SJOWALL, MAJ, and WAHLÖÖ, PER

Wife and husband team. She is a poet and crime reporter; he is a novelist; together they edit a Swedish literary magazine and write about the Stockholm policeman Martin Beck.

1939   Roseanna   Goll 1968

Trans. by Lois Rotà

A police-routine story about Martin Beck, a Swedish first detective inspector in Stockholm. He is called to a case on the coast—the murder and rape of an unknown young woman, who turns out to be a tourist from Nebraska on her vacation. We see mostly M.B.'s unhappy marriage and hear a lot about his dyspepsia, headaches, insomnia, and hostile private thoughts. The tone and tenor, copied from English and U.S. models, have struck American reviewers unfamiliar with the genre as new and important for social criticism.

1940   SJOWAL and WAHLÖÖ. See also:

The Man Who Went Up in Smoke   Pantheon 1969
The Murder on the Thirty-first Floor   MJ 1964

SMITH (ALEXANDER) CLARK (b. 1919)

b. Glasgow; educ. Queen's Park Secondary School; chief accountant of Mullard Ltd.; has written a textbook on internal auditing.

1941   The Case of Torches   Hamm 1957

The author's third could be called absolutely better than the two earlier Mahoun tales, were it not that the upsurge of "industrial crime" tends to blot from the memory the successive details. The human interest in this one is notable, and the chase of one naked killer by another along a riverbank *is* rememberable.

1942   The Deadly Reaper   Hamm 1956

Mild British version of American tough stuff. The plot is commonplace, but Nicky Mahoun (accountant-detective) almost emerges as a live creature. Little drinking and not enough sex to satisfy a cub scout.

1943   The Speaking Eye   Hamm 1955

Detection by a chartered accountant who is also a chartered libertine. The setting is a factory near Glasgow and the scenery is accurate, but the language and attitudes are entirely American. ("So what?" "Okay.") The superimposed love story is quite unbelievable, doubtless purposely so.

SMITH, GODFREY (b. 1926)

b. London; educ. Eggars Grammar School and Worcester Coll., Oxf., after service in RAF; assistant to Lord Kemsley, then news editor of *Sunday Times;* author of "Atticus" columns; now assistant editor of *Daily Express,* author of novels of contemporary manners: *The Friends* (1957); *The Business of Loving* (1961).

1944   The Flaw in the Crystal   Putn 1954

Not detection, but subtle suspense and Oxonian wit in a Holmes-Watson relation of intrigue. A fine novel, even if a little precious here and there. A ruthless condensation of it appears in Faber's *Best Secret Service Stories,* II (1967).

1945   SMITH, H(ERBERT) MAYNARD (b. 1869)

Inspector Frost in the City   CCD 1930

Between 1929 and 1941 this writer produced half a dozen Inspector Frost stories, all of them negligible as detection and tedious as mere adventure. The short chapters in which the Scotland Yard inspector, his godson, and his subordinates report confused identities, flights from pursuit, or plain failure add up to cock and bull that cannot be remembered even while one reads.

1946   SMITH, SHELLEY (pseud. of Nancy [Hermione] Bodington, b. 1912)

An Afternoon to Kill   Harp 1953

A Victorian episode of adultery and murder is told in the first person by an old woman living in the desert to a young Englishman stranded by airplane failure. But things are seldom what they seem, and the surprise ending is excellent. Not a detective story. The author's more conventional tales are not up to this level of taste and skill.

1947   SMITH, S. See also:

The Cellar at No. 5	Harp 1954	The Lord Have Mercy	Harp 1957
Come and Be Killed	Harp 1946	The Man with a	
The Crooked Man	Harp 1952	Calico Face	Harp 1950
He Died of Murder	Harp 1948	The Woman in the Sea	Harp 1948

1948   SMITH, THORNE (1892–1934)

Did She Fall?   Cosmo 1930

This once-famous writer of collegiate stories of sex, who came on the
scene prematurely and left it the same way, here tried his hand at crime
and detection and failed: the heartless slut who is killed by a push over a
cliff is no more credible than the young idiots in her entourage or the
would-be detective Scott Munson. Not a scrap of character, realism, or
believable dialogue in 300 pages—which argues something about the
nature of the author's vogue in another genre.

1949   SMITH, WILLARD K.

Bowery Murder   CCC 1930

The chief distinction of this long tale about a murdered girl found in a
cellar is that it is told through newspaper extracts. This device had
already been used by Poe in *Marie Roget,* but sparingly. In a novel of the
length favored in the twenties, the monotonous style and form add to the
length and become unbearable.

1950   SMITHIES, RICHARD H. R.

Death Gets an A   Horiz 1965
        Orig.: An Academic Question

Implausible university doings made worse by a surplus of irrelevancies in
narration and dialogue.

1951   Death Takes a Gamble   Horiz 1966
        Orig.: Disposing Mind

A complicated "family" story, full of lawyers and trusts, and neither as
amusing nor as terrifying as the author would like it to be.

1952   SMITHIES. See also:

Shoplifter   Horiz 1968

1953   SNOW, C(HARLES) P(ERCY), [LORD] (b. 1905)

Death Under Sail   Hein 1932
        Sketch of wherry Siren *and map of Northern Broads*

Told in the first person by a middle-aged civil servant who is fellow guest
in a yachting party of young people, this story of murder aboard a small
boat provides infinitely more entertainment than the layout suggests. The

detective, Finbow, is really bright; the preposterous professional, D. S. Aloysius Birrell, is truly funny; the crime well-motivated, and the complexities nicely unraveled. A delightful tour de force.

1954 SOMERS, PAUL (pseud. of Paul Winterton; also Andrew Garve; qq.v.)

Beginner's Luck   Harp 1958

Not noticeably different in narrative or complication from the latter-day Garve stories of predicament. The first-person hero is a cub reporter who is assigned a trivial inquiry, finds a body, then a bright girl reporter, and finally the ruthless murderer, who captures them. The horrors are a bit overlong and end a bit abruptly.

The Somers pseudonym was soon abandoned, but note that *The Broken Jigsaw* (1961), originally by Somers, came out in paperback as by Garve. The others are: *Operation Piracy* (1961) and *The Shivering Mountain* (1959).

1955 SPILLANE, MICKEY (pseud. of Frank Morrison Spillane, b. 1918)

Kiss Me Deadly   Dutt 1952

The author's great popularity rests on the ease with which he mixes familiar elements—sex, sentiment, violence—without giving them any particular force or flavor. His numerous stories have the speed of a shallow stream and are almost indistinguishable. One good point: the sex is usually tender and friendly, not sadistic or hostile, and it offsets the smashing of skulls. No detection.

1956 STANNERS, H(AROLD) H. (b. 1894)

The Crowning Murder   E&S 1938

The title of this pleasant novel refers to the celebrations observed in Britain on Coronation Day, especially in the evening. In the absence of most of his servants on this festival occasion, Sir Jabez manages to get himself killed in a quarry immediately adjoining his grounds. But was he killed, or did he fall? A quite well-drawn and tolerable American professor (of law) is a guest and contributes handsomely to a clearing up of the case. Good characterization and clues point toward the unlikely criminal. Despite the period length, first-rate.

STARRETT (CHARLES) VINCENT (EMERSON) (b. 1886)

Long a Chicago journalist and an acknowledged master of the Sherlock Holmes literature. See Part V.

1957 Murder on "B" Deck   CCD 1929

Starrett has rendered great services to the lover of detection, though not principally as a writer in the genre. This tale is a fair sample of his novel-length work. Walter Ghost, an amateur of everything, is the sleuth on board the *Latakia;* his novelist Watson is rather too inept; and the

384

"method," simple in the extreme, consists in hoping that answers to two cablegrams will solve the riddle before Cherbourg. They do.

1958 STARRETT. See also Nos. 2794–5, 3033–4, 3380–3, and:

Dead Man Inside	CCD 1931
The End of Mr. Garment	CCD 1932
The Great Hotel Murder (= Recipe for Murder)	CCD 1935
Murder in Peking (= The Laughing Buddha)	Lant 1946

1959 STEEVES, HARRISON ROSS (b. 1881)

Good Night, Sheriff   RH 1941

This novel by the one-time head of the English Department in Columbia College and an authority on the English novel can claim the merit of elegance and consecutiveness, as well as the working out of two fairly remarkable characters, the heroine and her old nurse. What mars a fair show is the relative neglect of practical matters—relative only, because there are physical clues of a sort, though the main one is hard to believe. Distinguished writing.

1960 STEIN, AARON MARC (also George Bagby and Hampton Stone, qq.v.; b. 1906)

Days of Misfortune   Coll 1963

This writer, a Princeton graduate, is a highly variable variable. In the Mexican scene of this tale, he piles up the surprises and the crimes without losing his hold on credibility, and his narrative and side observations are to be praised, like the archaeology that unites the detective efforts of Tim Mulligan and Elsie May Hunt.

1961 STEPHENSON, H(UMPHREY) M(EIGH) (b. 1882)

Death on the Deep   CCD 1931

This book is a perfect illustration of the maxim that, in storytelling, style and judgment are all. Compare this tale of large-scale piracy and ruthless murder with Browne's *Plan XVI* (No. 302) and you discover virtually identical plots; but Browne gives us nonsense unbelievable and Stephenson the same nonsense believable. For one thing, S. adds the fillip of detective curiosity, differentiates his villains, understands motives, and writes with great force. To whet the appetite still further, let it be said that the story turns on the successful highjacking and looting of an ocean liner, followed by mutual extermination among the criminals. The mastermind is for once shown as having a mind. One is encouraged to look up *Missing Partner* (Hutch 1932).

1962 STERLING, STEWART (pseud. of Prentice Winchell; also: Jay de Bekker, Dev Collans, and Spencer Dean, q.v.; b. 1895). In this incarnation, the ready spinner of tales concentrates on Gil Vine, Chief of Security at the Plaza Royale Hotel in New York. Something untoward is always happening in the topmost high-priced suites. In *The Body in the Bed*

(1959), for instance, a "dedicated compatriot" who tried to rid the world of a South American ex-dictator is killed. Vine handles the complications adroitly, just as adroitly as the author works in a monkey, or deals with the anxieties of a fire chief faced with arson. See: *Five Alarm Fire* (1942), *Too Hot to Handle* (1961), and *Where There's Smoke* (1946).

1963 STERLING, THOMAS (L.) (b. 1921)

The Evil of the Day   S&S 1955
In ppb.: Murder in Venice

A brilliant modernization of Ben Jonson's *Volpone* in novel form. This tale, which satisfies JB more than WHT, unquestionably illustrates a rare type—the detective story made out of a fiction well known in another form and not originally designed for ratiocination. See the reworkings of *Hamlet, passim.*

1964 The House Without a Door   S&S 1950

The author transforms a fairly standard tale of murder and blackmail by the expedient of throwing into the plot a woman who has been a recluse for thirty years but is still active and intelligent. The telling is perhaps a bit long, but the characters and events are uncommonly full of suspense.

1965 The Silent Siren   S&S 1958

Crime and cocotterie vaguely historical and, as usual, very well done, but less moving than the other two, for unanalyzable reasons.

1966 STERLING, T. See also:

Strangers and Afraid   S&S 1952

STEVENSON, BURTON E(GBERT) (1872–1962)

Librarian and compiler of reference works (*Home Book of Quotations,* etc.); wrote half a dozen or more mystery stories in the elaborate form and magisterial tone still current just before the *coup d'état* by E. C. Bentley.

1967 The Mystery of the Boule Cabinet   DM 1912

The reprint in the Ferret Library (1929) shows updating in its references to Prohibition and ships not in service before 1920, but the work survives by qualities it possessed from the time of first issue. The old-fashioned elements are more noticeable in the beginning than in the middle, when the momentum masks the melodrama. Plot too complex to summarize.

1968 STEVENSON, B. E. See also:

Affairs of State	Holt 1906
The Gloved Hand	DM 1912
The Holladay Case	Holt 1903
The Marathon Mystery	Holt 1904
The Red Carnation (= Death Wears a Carnation)	DM 1939

1969 STEVENSON, ROBERT LOUIS (BALFOUR) (1850–94), and OSBOURNE, LLOYD (1868–1947)

The Wrecker   Cass 1892
Epilogue: To Will H. Low (see No. 3036)

One of Stevenson's modern and realistic tales of adventure, which happens—unlike those often listed as such—to contain murder and detection. The story adds the uncommon elements of piracy and student life in Paris to the more usual treasure hunt in the manner of Hammond Innes. The sailors and the hero, Jim Pinkerton, are done with Stevenson's usual seeing eye and economy of words.

1970 STEVENSON, R. L. See also Nos. 2797–9 and 3036.

1971 STEWART, MARY (b. 1916). No detection and scarcely any mystery, but much Gothic malaise—often due to the bad baronet in the big house. See *Nine Coaches Waiting* (1958).

1972 STOKER, BRAM (orig. Abraham) (1847–1912), was born in Dublin and educated first at home because of a sickly constitution, but grew to be a champion footballer at the University of Dublin in his twenties. Civil servant, then dramatic critic, barrister, and finally Henry Irving's manager-secretary for twenty-seven years. He wrote for the *Daily Telegraph,* received many academic honors, and achieved fame with the classic tale of vampirism, *Dracula* (1897). It is perhaps the only mystery where length is felt as both an excess and a necessity. He also wrote *Dracula's Guest and Other Weird Stories* (1914), *The Mystery of the Sea* (1905), and *Famous Impostors* (1910), the last-named a disappointing work despite the evident research on which it is based. See also No. 2466.

1973 STONE, HAMPTON (pseud. of Aaron Marc Stein, q.v.)

The Murder That Wouldn't Stay Solved   S&S 1951
Convincing Manhattan background and fair DA's assistant make memorable this account of the murder of a middle-aged man by a younger ditto in circumstances difficult to handle (hotel-room homosexuality). The puzzle itself is less interesting than its treatment.

1974 The Strangler Who Couldn't Let Go   CCD 1956
This is the author's fifty-fifth book, written in the best of his three incarnations, though not all the Mac and Gibby stories are palatable: beware, for instance, of *The Man Who Had Too Much to Lose* (1955). The one under review deals with a Long Island family who hold together like a caste against the outside world, but are forced to let it in when trouble comes. The investigators are not cops or private eyes but members of the New York County DA's office.

STOUT, REX (TODHUNTER) (b. 1886)

b. in Indiana; educated ubiquitously; widely traveled and experienced in a great assortment of trades and professions; gourmet and horticulturist, defender of copyright, and master moderator of meetings. Began writing in late 1920s. Several of his early detective novels are without recurring characters, a few feature Tecumseh Fox as hero-detective, and some a woman operative, Doll Bonner. The rest depict the doings of Nero Wolfe and Archie Goodwin, by now classic figures in the folklore of crime and detection.

1975 And Be a Villain   VP 1948

A first-rate sample of the authors' art, this tale brings us face to face with the radio advertising of a beverage which the lady who promotes it cannot abide. Hence hanky-panky with the bottle of substitute liquid and resulting doubt as to whom the dose was intended for. Archie is spectacular in word and deed.

The title is from *Hamlet*, I, 5, 109.

1976 Bad for Business   Farr 1940

A Tecumseh Fox story, in which all the elements of the later Wolfe tales are as it were held in solution: the attitude toward people and the use of reason, the holding of conferences, the description of places and characters, and the pace of story telling (though here we have a bit of a plateau). Fox helps a girl (assistant to the operative Doll Bonner) exculpate herself when her uncle is murdered. He was a disagreeable character whose business was being ruined by sabotage and whose employees and relatives had no cause to love him. A good job.

1977 Before Midnight   VP 1955

Nero has to save the TV agency from losing $9 million offered to prize contestants, by finding out who killed the supervisor so as to steal the right answers. It is brisk and clever enough, but not one in which Archie shines with special luster.

1978 The Broken Vase   VP 1941
A Tecumseh Fox Mystery

Rare coins, a Wan Li vase, and a Stradivarius violin which is eventually doused with varnish do not help make this tale dramatic or amusing. A sponger on his wife takes up collecting so he can cadge money and carry on with girls. This leads to murders, which T.F. detects in hit-and-miss fashion.

1979 Champagne for One   VP 1958

Archie and Nero shine, once again, on the question: Who slipped the cyanide into the glass of the girl attending the unwed mothers' annual party at the house of their benefactress? Two small queries: would the dead philanthropist write the odd letter of gift that provides no better control of large funds than someone's probity? And how was the poison actually administered? One can't buy ready-mixed KCN.

1980 Death of a Doxy   VP 1966

First-rate Stout done at the age of eighty. The tightness of the plot, the
wit, and the people are done with sureness and speed, so that the book,
though short, gives one the sense of having lived through a long stretch
of tense expectation. New roles, too, for Orrie Cather, Cramer, and
Wolfe in relation to a murder which they are not asked to investigate.
Wolfe gets his $50,000 fee, which one hopes he splits with the author.

1981 Death of a Dude   VP 1969

No doubt, after many interrogations in his familiar habitat, Nero Wolfe
felt the need of fresh air.* Montana provides it in plenty, and Wolfe
"reacts" enough but not too much to the luxurious rigors of Lily Rowan's
ranch. The great man delivers himself of several well-turned homilies, but
the detection (suffering from the disadvantage of Archie's being in jail)
is confined to questions by telegram. The answers confirm the reader's
hopes.

   * There is some doubt about the exact number—hence location—of Nero's house
on West 35th (See No. 2891).

1982 The Doorbell Rang   VP 1965

The plot is transparent and the detection is fairly simple, but one or two
of the dodges practiced here by Wolfe are new (for him). The scene in
which the New York head of the FBI is "rated" in Wolfe's office and
told he can't have a set of credentials belonging to one of his own men is
rich. The anti-"bugging" scheme is also amusing.

1983 Fer-de-Lance   Farr 1934

The first and longest of the Nero Wolfe stories, in which all the familiar
characters and their habits get established. The murder is done by means
of a golf club—the implement, not the membership—and it entangles a
college president, a baby, some Italian nondescripts, and much philosophizing by Wolfe and futilizing by the police.

1984 The Final Deduction   VP 1961

Archie not at his best and not amusing, though we do get information
about his mother, and Wolfe has some fair repartee. The kidnapping and
ransoming, for once, dully treated. JB enters an amendment to the effect
that Nero is ingenious in getting his fee, Archie subtle as well as useful,
and Inspector Cramer able to work off his anger outside the house.

1985 Gambit   VP 1962

There is more detection in this story than in any other of the mulling-and-
quizzing sort; here we really see N.W.'s thoughts whirring. Moreover,
Archie is in excellent form, and although a chess tournament is a feature,
the game itself is not. The great scene is that in which Nero reads and
burns the pages of Webster's Dictionary, Third Edition.

1986 How like a God   Van 1947; orig. 1929

One of the author's five "straight" novels, preceding the creation of Nero and Archie. It is not a detective story but a psychological suspense novel of considerable power, despite some awkwardness of construction. Interludes A through Q slowly and painfully transport the killer from the ground-floor hall up the stairs and into the room where he rids himself of his incubus.

The title is from *Hamlet*, II, 2, 319.

1987 If Death Ever Slept   VP 1957

Though Archie Goodwin is here in top form, not much else can be said for this dose of the mixture as before. Archie is put in as secretary to a rich operator whose business secrets are being stolen. Wolfe neither foresees nor prevents a couple of murders. His activities are limited to three lengthy interviews, at the last of which the killer is unmasked by the use of evidence supplied largely by Inspector Cramer.

1988 In the Best Families   VP 1950

Not good, despite the fact that N.W. loses 117 pounds in a few months and leaves home under his own steam. The mastermind Zeck is unconvincing, like most of his breed, Archie is not up to snuff, and there are too many Doberman pinschers. The snarl of one of these is the only good clue.

1989 The League of Frightened Men   Farr 1935

Archie gets some rough handling and even cries in this longish and complicated story of threatened and actual violence embracing two and a half dozen men of various occupations and characters, who in the past have injured a youth whose revenge they now fear.

1990 Might as Well Be Dead   VP 1956

The problem is to find a missing young man from Omaha and save him from being framed on a murder charge when he does turn up in the dock. The plot is full of incident and variety, but there are no special high spots or scintillating words.

1991 The Mother Hunt   VP 1963

Nero and Archie make one of their flights from home, and the grand confrontation scene is staged at their refuge. Nero is competent but not remarkably so in finding out who did the two murders and the giving birth.

1992 Plot It Yourself   VP 1959

A plagiarism racket brings Nero and Archie into conflict with each other and with crime. Excellent repartee on all hands and strong suspense. The murderer's confession alone is below the surrounding perfection.

1993   The Red Box   Farr 1937

Stout rarely has Nero Wolfe lured away from home on a case, but in this
one Archie does it with orchids. Poisoning at a fashion show is the crime
that Wolfe's method of exhaustive interrogation mixed with bluff is in-
voked to solve. Archie is thinner and less amusing here than elsewhere,
but we learn more about Wolfe from himself.

1994   Red Threads   Farr 1939

An example of non-Wolfe work, but with Inspector Cramer rather
Wolfishly in charge. It is far better than *The Hand in the Glove* and not
nearly so good as *Bad for Business,* while sharing important elements
with each—e.g., a straining for the fantastic and the wildly feminine and
a marked ability for handling crowds, institutions, and businesses. But the
killing and detecting against a background of hand-weaving and American
Indian attitudes are negligible.

1995   A Right to Die   VP 1964

Archie bestirs himself in Louisville and Evansville on the trail of a
murderer whose identity is suggested to Nero by the abnormal frequency
of a certain diphthong. How timely all this is is shown by the fact that
Wolfe's client is a Negro whose son is about to marry a white girl, and
by the nature of Wolfe's light reading: *Science, the Glorious Entertainment.*

1996   The Second Confession   VP 1949

This, which is vintage Stout, has the memorable scenes of Archie's stay
at a posh country house and putting all the owners and their in-laws at
their ease. Absolutely top notch, which means: in a class with *And Be a
Villain, Some Buried Caesar,* and *Too Many Cooks.*

1997   The Silent Speaker   VP 1946

A novella about the murder of a dedicated Washington civil servant
(price regulator) and of one of his aides. The least likely suspect is well
hidden, Wolfe does some thinking, and Archie is Archie. Not too much
wrangling with the police, and in truth one of R.S.'s best in the semi-
demi form.

1998   Some Buried Caesar   Farr 1939

The story of the prize bull, to be highly esteemed by all Stout partisans.
Nero and Archie in top form despite rural surroundings.

1999   Too Many Clients   VP 1960

Good treatment of the love-nest theme, integral as well as central, which
implies good characterization. Several new touches prevent the reader from
taking Wolfe as a cliché. The sole reservation to be made is that the villain
is not well enough concealed, perhaps because he is so well cast.

2000   Too Many Cooks   Farr 1938

The masterpiece among three or four by Stout that deserve the name. In
addition, it is the most amusing, thanks to such incidents as Nero's being
shot in yellow pajamas, the altercation over *saucisse minuit,* and the
triangle of Archie, the young lawyer, and the beautiful girl. Locale: White
Sulphur Springs.

2001   Too Many Women   VP 1947

Archie is the center of a seraglio of designing creatures, who want to
bribe or seduce him as he helps Nero discover who killed a stockbroker
in a Wall Street firm that employs five hundred women. Longer than the
later tales, this one has a great many lively turns and a good surprise
ending.

2002   Where There's a Will   Farr 1940

Endless talk over how to keep a kept woman from inheriting millions
which only she thinks have been left her, and then—after deceased is
shown to have been murdered—more talk about who did it. Wolfe spots
the criminal by looking closely at six small photographs (poorly reproduced in the book) and applying his knowledge of floriculture.

2003   STOUT. See also:

Alphabet Hicks (= The		Murder by the Book	VP 1951
Sound of Murder)	Farr 1941	Over My Dead Body	
The Black Mountain	VP 1954	(Wolfe)	Farr 1940
Double for Death		The Rubber Band	
(Tecumseh Fox)	Farr 1939	(= To Kill Again)	Farr 1936
The Hand in the Glove			
(= Crime on Her Hands)			
(Doll Bonner)	Farr 1937		

2004   STRAHAN, KAY (CLEAVER) (b. 1888), does the usual variations on
Had I But Known. See *The Desert Lake Mystery* (1936) and six earlier
works.

2005   STRANGE, JOHN STEPHEN (pseud. of Mrs. Dorothy [Stockbridge]
Tillet, b. 1896), has written approximately thirty mystery and detective
tales since 1928. *The Clue of the Second Murderer* (1929) is discursive
but agreeable. See also: *All Men Are Liars* (= *Come to Judgment*)
(1948); *The Man Who Killed Fortescue* (1928).

STRONG, L(EONARD) A(LFRED) G(EORGE) (1896–1958)

b. Devonshire of Irish and west country parentage; educ. Brighton Coll.
and Wadham, Oxf.; began as schoolteacher at Raynes Park Grammar
School (see No. 1871/B); poet and writer of broadcast plays and TV
scripts since 1930; on the staff of the Central School of Speech Training
and Dramatic Art (see No. 2007); a director of Methuen & Co. Literary
work includes a study of James Joyce, a book on road transport, *The*

Rolling Road (1956), an autobiography, *Green Memory* (1960), and a life of Thomas More, *The Minstrel Boy* (1937). His poems were collected as *The Body's Imperfections* (1957). Of his stories and novels other than detective fiction, the best liked is *Dewer Rides*.

2006   All Fall Down   CCC 1944

In his investigation of the murder of an elderly bibliophile in a Devonshire village, Chief Inspector Ellis McKay, who is also a composer, is accompanied and assisted by his bookseller friend Gilkison. The story develops along psychological lines, without much action, but there is a second murder and McKay bestirs himself. He is a well-marked character, and it is here that he first meets another of his kind, Inspector Bradstreet.

2007   Murder Plays an Ugly Scene   Dday 1945
          In Eng.: Othello's Occupation

High entertainment: wit, character, plot, and detection all of first quality; the modus operandi only a trifle elaborate. The use of the gramophone is intelligent and not stale.

2008   Slocombe Dies   CCC 1942

This first effort at a crime novel begins with the dramatic discovery of a corpse on the road, two quarreling girls, and a sullen young man. The discoverers are a pair of friends, vacationing in the west of England village where this scene is the climax of a conflict of passions, which the rest of the book unfolds with great skill and a rich variety of detail. The story purports to be the result of one of the friends' investigations, he being a writer of detective stories; but we are given only the story and none of the detection.

2009   Treason in the Egg   CCC 1958

A further "police diversion" with McKay and Bradstreet, this time at a house where art and social affairs form the subject of lecture and discussion courses. Refugee Germans, suspected spies, neurotics, love-sick young things mix to create confusion around a matter-of-fact murder. Much that is agreeable, but the atmosphere becomes wearing and the book is not Strong's finest.

2010   Which I Never   Macm 1952; orig. 1950
          A Police Diversion

From internal evidence, the third of the McKay-Bradstreet tales. In a freer style than previous ones, it starts off with the (seldom used) activities of a firm of vanity publishers, the disappearance of sundry maidens, and the echoes of wartime espionage. The setting is rural Devon, where Bradstreet is stationed, and where McKay is soon enlisted for his musical powers. The story takes unexpected turns, and despite the lack of hard detection and the possible excess of banter by McKay, the book incites to reading at one sitting.
    The title is the local sergeant's favorite asseveration.

2011 STRONG. See also Nos. 2821–6.

2012 STYLES, SHOWELL (also Glyn Carr, q.v.)

Journey with a Secret   Goll 1968

By using boys and girls aged 14 and 15, and setting them on a camping
holiday in the Wales he knows so well, the author produces a juvenile
that avoids most of the defects of the genre. No doubt, the skill and
judgment of these pubescents are a little exaggerated, but their grasp of
police and spy matters is plausible, considering what the essence of those
matters is. And at no point is the language highfalutin or condescending.
Four previous books, presumably of the same type, are listed on the
author page.

2013 SUE, EUGENE (1804–57)

Les Mystères de Paris   10 v. in 6. 1842–43

An admirer of Mrs. Radcliffe and Balzac, Sue followed the latter's
example in drawing from the real Vidocq (q.v.) a fictional hero who helps
the unfortunate and battles criminals high and low. In the course of these
chivalric doings, the prince of Gerolstein becomes a quasi detective who
investigates some of Paris' darkest mysteries. Sue earned high praise from
the reigning critic Sainte-Beuve, and he formed a varied following of
French and English imitators. His principal innovation was in acclimating
the readers of the respectable *Journal des Débats*, where his work
appeared as a serial, to the niceties of criminal slang.

2014 SUE. See also:

The Female Bluebeard   Wins 1844

2015 SWINNERTON, FRANK

On the Shady Side   Hutch 1970

The experienced reader rejoices that an old and accomplished hand
has tackled the special genre of detection which consists in discovering,
post mortem, what an enigmatic or self-concealing personality was really
like. The attempts and failures at this game have been numerous (e.g.,
No. 2034). Here, the conception, situation, detection, and solution are
perfect. The two brothers are done with incomparable talent, and all
those involved fit without apparent effort. Every word of the 225 pages is
telling, though F.S. has a curious notion of what is meant in the U.S. by
"in the doghouse." The ultimate triumph is that, with a minimum of
material clues and a maximum of psychological, the whole work has the
solidity of true ratiocination, heightened by the kind of suspense that
comes not from fret but from the noble wish to understand.

2016 SYKES, W(ILLIAM) STANLEY (b. 1894)

The Harness of Death   Lane 1932

The second and last tale by this frugal author opens with a strong scene
and goes on to a somewhat melodramatic conspiracy but the narrator's

command of language makes it plausible. The handling of clues, questions, and red herrings is firm enough to make continuously interesting what is after all an inverted tale of novel length: throughout we see the murderer acting and plotting and the detectives Ridley and Drury catching up with him. The second murder, which involves the use of actual herrings— fresh, not red—is genuine drama and so is the denouement. Altogether a second effort worthy of the first.

N.B. The author makes in passing an interesting point about the Moat Murder, which is that the culprit Dougal was caught thanks to an illegal act by Chief Inspector Scott.

2017   The Man Who Was Dead   DM 1931
     In Eng.: The Missing Money-Lender

Written with wit, despite the tiresome British deriding of Jews about money matters. Full of interesting clues, well followed up. The great weakness of the plot is its transparency (guessable c. p. 50), but the author keeps one going even after he discloses the main trick, and Inspector Drury does a neat job with "optical activity."

SYMONS, JULIAN (GUSTAVE) (b. 1912)

Brother and biographer of A. J. A. Symons, who wrote *The Quest for Corvo.* J.S. reviews detective fiction for the *Sunday Times* and has also edited *A Pictorial History of Crime* (see Nos. 2828–33 and 3298–9).

2018   The Belting Inheritance   Harp 1965

A boy's relationship with his two uncles who reared him is complicated by the unexpected appearance of a third uncle, supposed dead, and therefore possibly an impostor. Scenes in Folkestone and Paris vary the locale. Smoothly told, but not equal to the strain implicit in the situation.

2019   Bland Beginning   Harp 1949
     Dedicatory verses to the author's infant daughter
     Postscript on the Wise forgeries

Symons himself introduces the events by means of a conversation in the London Library between himself and his friend Detective Inspector Bland. After this agreeable start we turn the page to an entry in the *DNB,* followed by a family history, a will, and numerous fragments of verse from the works of one of the characters. Serious crime begins with forgery of a special sort. The testing of paper and ink is scamped in favor of psychology, good of its kind, and Bland discovers all in a rather long retrospect. Solid stuff, even though a trifle labored.

2020   Bogue's Fortune   Harp 1956
     In Eng.: The Paper Chase

A great disappointment after *The Narrowing Circle.* S. tries his hand at a neo-Innes tale of a progressive school with idealistic headmaster and inebriate wife, nymphomaniac matron, and murdered master, and manages to flub everything but the matron. English gangsters and hidden papers bring no help; indeed, cock-and-bull, mostly b.

2021   The Broken Penny   Harp 1953

The Thirty-first of February was more of a detective story than this, though not a favorable specimen of the genre. The present tale is of spying abroad, communists and fascists at home, and perpetual bewilderment as to who is who. It shows the writer as better able to build up emotional and sexual scenes than to plot. The villains are too easily detected and discomfited, and first and last the hero is an idiot.

2022   The Color of Murder   Harp 1957

A lengthy confession extracted by a psychologist is served up with interludes, followed by trial scenes in which the hero-victim seems no more palatable than before.

2023   The End of Solomon Grundy   Harp 1964

Not detection, hardly mystery, but suspense modern style, that is, by way of symbolism, introspection, and a general sense of the wrongness of things.

2024   The Immaterial Murder Case   Goll 1948/1945

The attractive substitution of a corpse for one member of a statuary group, a good full-page timetable, and detailed alibi-checking by Detective Inspector Bland do not suffice to redeem this story from the inferior role of a fantasy-parody. Quite likable in that guise.

2025   The Man Who Killed Himself   Harp 1967

Not a detective story, nor even a mystery, since the author lets the reader know early on who meditates the murder and why the amorous proprietor of Matrimonial Assistance, Ltd., is a bigamist. The interest derives from deterioration of character and sexual drive once the ill-executed murder is done. Excellent writing, spiced with gratuitous eroticism.

2026   The Narrowing Circle   Harp 1954

Symons has become more obscure with the passage of time, yet this tale may be his best to date. Of the numerous stories of murder in large publishing firms, this must be rated among the most plausible and entertaining.

2027   The Pipe Dream   Harp 1959
          In Eng.: The Gigantic Shadow

A well-constructed affair, in which an ex-convict turned TV "investigator" gets his comeuppance. This good beginning then turns conventional, except for Inspector Crambo, a novel type, but not convincing.

2028   The Plain Man   Harp 1962
          In Eng.: The Killing of Francie Lake

Again we have a publishing firm, but such an unusual combine, with such a remarkable head (Ocky Gaye, ex-member of Parliament) that it is unlike any other in fiction or fact. There is a murder, and it is solved by one of the firm's editors. Symons' technical ignorance (he develops photographic negatives, etc.) is but a minor blemish.

Note: Plain Man Enterprises is the name of the magazine empire.

2029   The Progress of a Crime   Harp 1960

High-pressure defense on a murder charge of two young hooligans who brought about the death of a man they disliked on Guy Fawkes night. Not much detection.

2030   The Thirty-first of February   Harp 1951

Detection occurs, but is swamped in personal problems and unpleasant physical characteristics—i.e., an attempt to do what others were doing, without the stomach for it, and therefore overdone.

2031   SYMONS. See also Nos. 2828–33, 3298–9, and:

    Murder! Murder!   CCC 1961
    Pattern of Murder   TVB 1962

2032   TACK, ALFRED (b. 1906)

    The Big Kidnap   Long 1969

With this one, A.T. is on his fourteenth and it is evident that he has made great strides in narrative skill, characterization and dialogue. He has developed a kind of business repartee all his own, and his businessmen and business details are all good. Sex is laid on, but with taste. The plot to kidnap a defector and return him for trial by his peers (?) is excellently managed, though the denouement meant to be a surprise cannot help being a letdown.

2033   Murder Takes Over   Long 1966

The author's tenth murder story. If this writer were not a man of limited education, whose main work is the production of handbooks on salesmanship, he might have made a good story out of the ideas consigned to these excessively commercial pages. The dialogue occasionally takes a witty turn and the hero is attractive and not at all "stock." But the rest is boys' stuff.

2034   TATE, SYLVIA

    Never by Chance   Harp 1947

Few situations are better than that of the person faced, by another's death or disappearance, with the task of finding who the departed really was. This novel sets this type of problem quite dramatically and keeps up suspense for a bit, but eventually swamps interest by a plethora of introspection and comment, and winds up in a dubious use of the supernatural.

2035   TAYLOR, PHOEBE ATWOOD (also Alice Tilton; b. 1909). In her Cape Cod novels featuring the homespun detective Asey Mayo, she has contributed much humor and some good plots, as in *The Cape Cod Mystery* (1931), *Spring Harrowing* (1939), and some twenty others. As Alice Tilton she writes about the more scholarly Leonidas Witherall, who looks like Shakespeare. Several of his exploits of the forties have recently been reprinted: *Dead Ernest* (1966/1944), *The Hollow Chest* (1967/1941).

TEMPLE-ELLIS, N. A. (pseud. of Neville Aldridge Holdaway, b. 1894)

Outside fiction, the author's career seems to boil down to the feat of having once "given a lecture on Marxism with three other people" (1934).

2036   The Inconsistent Villains   Meth 1930/1929
        Two maps

Awarded first prize in Methuen's Detective Story Competition, the judges being Bailey, Knox, and Milne. Second prize went to Davidson's *Laboratory Murder* (see No. 710). Amid incredible and irreproducible complexities of plot, Arbuthnot (the Holmes) and Sir Edmund King (the Watson) are often amusing. There is nothing else to be said.

2037   The Man Who Was There   Meth 1930

A long and complicated mystery, attractively based in the Isle of Wight and provided with the same protagonists as before, Montrose Arbuthnot and Edmund King. They give us a few shrewd observations in the midst of fair situations; they lie in wait, and confer, but all is set at naught by the plot, which finally totters and crashes of its own weight.

2038   Murder in the Ruins   Dial 1936

Features Arbuthnot only (Sir Edmund King is stated to be "circumnavigating the globe in quest of health"). A consecutive but long-winded narrative presents arson and murder in an English country house. The reader will care little about the mix-up in identities or the last-ditch attempt to produce a least likely murderer, but the sanity and continuity of this work contrast favorably with the author's previous plotting.

2039   TEMPLE-ELLIS. See also:

        A Case in Hand   H&S 1933
        The Cauldron Bubbles   Meth 1930
        Death of a Decent Fellow   H&S 1941

        TEY, JOSEPHINE (pseud. of Elizabeth MacKintosh; also Gordon Daviot; 1896–1952)

b. and educ. Inverness; taught physical training; began by writing plays, historical novels, and biography. John Gielgud achieved his first success in one of her plays. Her first venture in detective fiction (1929) was under the Daviot pseudonym; then in 1936 she began to use her great-great-grandmother's name, Josephine Tey. She died a few weeks before the U.S. appearance of *The Daughter of Time*.

2040   Come and Kill Me   Macm 1950
        In Eng.: Brat Farrar

JB and WHT entirely disagree about this book. JB detests it and would
rather reread *The Man in the Queue*, which is going some. But he finds it
hard to say why this portrait of a degenerating character annoys him so
much, when his collaborator, known for his sensibility and taste, rather
admires the novel.

2041   The Daughter of Time   Macm 1952/1951

As in *The Franchise Affair*, the author goes back to history for her plot;
this time it is the reputation of Richard III that is to be looked into and,
if possible, cleared. Grant, the detective, is in bed in hospital, but has
amiable legmen (and women) bring him the materials. It is agreeably
written and holds up to the standards of J.T.'s best works, though it necessarily suffers from lack of action.

2042   The Franchise Affair   Macm 1948

The eighteenth-century cases on which this modern tale is built are those
of Elizabeth Canning's unexplained absence from home (See No. 724)
and of the ferocious Mrs. Brownrigg, who deservedly hanged for her mistreatment of servants. In J.T.'s handling the real victim is the family
(mother and daughter), suspected of being Brownriggs because of a
"Canning." They suffer legal and popular assault in consequence, but the
denouement implies an adverse interpretation of Elizabeth Canning's disappearance. The purposely half-hearted love affair and excellent characterization throughout form a superb piece of work, full of action and
suspense; but it is detection only in a roundabout sense.

2043   The Man in the Queue   Macm 1953/1929
        Orig. as by Gordon Daviot

Inspector Grant's first case, the author's first story—and a dismal one. The
murder is not credible and the detection is nonexistent, though the idea
of stabbing somebody in one of those law-abiding English queues that
form of their own accord, like crystals around a twig, is fine. It deserved
treatment by the author at a more experienced stage of her career.

2044   Miss Pym Disposes   PD 1946

Events in a girl's physical-education college, Leys, culminate toward the
end of the story in a dubious incident resulting in death. A great deal of
flutter and "darlings" and no detection. Instead, cocoa and coyness,
though a few characterizations come through.

2045   A Shilling for Candles   Macm 1958/1936
        Murder Revisited Series

A splendid work, despite its somewhat baroque ending. Inspector Grant
emerges as a character, not just a typical Scot, and the sympathy shown

for *all* the *dramatis personae,* which is this author's hallmark, is beautifully displayed in these pages, inspired (it is said) by an actual crime.

2046   The Singing Sands   Macm 1953

Published posthumously, which may account for certain defects that the author might have altered in proof. The plot seems overwrought and the chief characters occasionally fall out of drawing. But other features come out of Miss Tey's best vein, and the work belongs in the middle range between bad and superb.

2047   To Love and Be Wise   PD 1950

Attractive because of its setting and the arty-acty characters in it. Grant does some nice going about and thinking, though little down-to-earth detection. It should also be noted that even though history records many instances of transvestism going undetected, that fact becomes less and less plausible in fiction by reason of modern dress and free habits.

The title is a phrase reversed from *Troilus,* III, 2, 163.

2048   THAYER, LEE (Mrs. Emma Redington [Lee] Thayer) (b. 1874), produced pleasant, prewar period pieces—over sixty titles—often with a New York scene, and typified by *Dead Storage* (1935), in which amateur Peter Clancy assists Captain Kerrigan. See also: *Doctor S.O.S.* (1925), *Dark of the Moon* (1936), and *Accessory After the Fact* (1943).

2049   THOMAS, ALAN (ERNEST WENTWORTH)

The Death of Laurence Vining   Meth 1924

Recommended to JB by the late Victor Gollancz, the tale itself does not seem to either of these readers to have anything else to recommend it.

THOMSON, [SIR] BASIL (HOME) (1861–1939)

Son of the Abp of York; educ. Eton and Oxf.; called to the bar, then in civil service and at 29 Prime Minister of Tonga, the Polynesian "Friendly Isles." Returned to head Dartmoor and Wormwood Scrubbs; finally CID in 1913 and wartime chief of espionage the next year. Began writing on criminology, turning to detective fiction in 1925. He completed his autobiography in 1937 and dealt with actual crime in *The Criminal* (1925), see No. 3302.

2050   The Case of the Dead Diplomat   CCD 1935
       In Eng.: Richardson Goes Abroad

The poorest of the Richardson cases; most of the action is in Paris and consists of difficulties with language, misplaced suspicion, and feeble clues feebly handled. Anglo-French non-cooperation is the only element that is strong—and all about a lottery ticket.

2051   The Dartmoor Enigma   CCD 1936
          In Eng.: Richardson Solves a Dartmoor Mystery

Solid and unimaginative but competent. A fair amount of journeying
about by Scotland Yard officers, coupled with adroit keeping up of uncertainty as to the guilt of an obviously suspicious party right to the end—
the sort of tale that a less diffuse J. S. Fletcher might have written a
decade after his own *floruit.*

2052   P.C. Richardson's First Case   CCD 1933

This tale, like its companion piece, *Richardson's Second Case* (1934), is
somewhat plodding, but not without London charm—and historical
interest. For what it amounts to is early police routine *minus* the contrived
bickering, stomach ulcers, and pub-crawling with which later writers have
masked poverty of invention and the dullness of repetitious questioning.

2053   When Thieves Fall Out   CCD 1937
          In Eng.: A Murder Arranged

Not a bad plot to cover up stealing and receiving, but awkwardly told,
because Richardson has become chief constable and simply "files reports."
Hardly any characterization or atmosphere. Said to be based on a true
crime, not readily perceptible which.

2054   THOMSON. See also:

The Case of Naomi Clynes (= Detective-
    Inspector Richardson, C.I.D.)   Dday 1934
Death in the Bathroom (= Who Killed Stella Pomeroy?)   Dday 1936
The French Milliner   SD   1937
The Metal Flask   Meth 1929
My Experiences at Scotland Yard   Dday 1923
The Story of Scotland Yard   Dday 1936

2055   THORP, RODERICK

The Detective   Dial 1966

This effort to present everything in the relationship of deceased, accused, detective, in-laws, and assistants of all parties concerned was
doomed to artistic failure from the start—though it has proved a popular
success, and a fair movie has been cut out of the underbrush. The pathological details that certain readers might find gratifying are buried in a
mass of other matter which also obscures the gist of the book: in the
imaginary city of Manitou, Captain Joe Leland investigates suicide and
murder arising out of sexual irregularity. Tapes and psychiatry come into
it, as well as interminable questioning, and confession ends it all.

2056   TOMS, BERNARD

The Strange Affair   Const 1966

The author's second novel (it is not clear whether his first is also about
police work) is an account of the pressures encountered in the force by a

young man of good character and little experience. PC Strange tangles with various corrupt persons and groups and comes out last, with unmerited punishment. Little or no detection.

2057   TORR, DOMINIC

Diplomatic Cover   HB 1966

A young American attached to the U.S. embassy in Paris is also attached to a Negro (male) sculptor, passionate scenes with whom are described in poetic language, the young diplomat being all the while married to a beautiful girl. A Russian spy and his aide (brutally treated) are looking for U.S. military information: it is the predictable working out of a standard plot, and later works (*A Mission of Mercy*, 1969; *The Treason Line*, 1969) do not warrant a longer scrutiny.

2058   TRACY, LOUIS (also Gordon Holmes; 1863–1928), wrote many tales featuring Inspector Furneaux which are adventure mysteries rather than detective stories—e.g., *The Manning Burke Murder* (1930). As Gordon Holmes, he published *A Mysterious Disappearance* in 1905 and later collaborated with M. P. Shiel (q.v.) under the same pseudonym. For later work, see *Number Seventeen* (1919) and *The Lastingham Murder* (1929).

2059   TRAIN, ARTHUR (CHENEY) (1875–1945), was the creator of the shrewd old Yankee lawyer Ephraim Tutt, whose fictional autobiography Train published in 1943. Train was a practicing lawyer, district attorney, and voluminous writer in several genres. His folksy stories of Mr. Tutt in the *Saturday Evening Post* won him renown, and they were so sound in law—a foretaste of Perry Mason—that collections of them were assigned in law-school courses. For a long police-routine tale, see *Manhattan Murder* (1936) and for true crime, 3306–8 as well as 2838.

2060   TRAVER, ROBERT (pseud. of John [Donaldson] Voelker, b. 1903)

Anatomy of a Murder   SM 1958

Another massive attempt to show that juries and justice are independent variables. The story is written by a retired Michigan Supreme Court judge, whose style is not above reproach, though he is capable of wit and even elegance. The facts are painstakingly detailed, but the man and woman who help the former district attorney are no more credible than "Mary," the heroine dragged in toward the end. One physiological clue in the testimony about the alleged rape is unintentionally obscure.

2061   TRAVER. See also No. 3309.

2062   TRAVERS, HUGH (pseud. of Hugh Travers Mills)

A Case for Madame Aubry   Harp 1967
         Alt. title: Mme Aubry and the Police

The announcement of a "first book of a proposed series" about a lady detective aroused misgivings, but Mme Aubry justifies her existence. Her acceptance by the Sûreté one must grant if the tale is to get off the ground, and from there the plot develops plausibly. It is a minor triumph to have got away with two nearly simultaneous murders on the same premises, without a common murderer or a common motive. Food, wine, and sex kept in their place within the framework of routine.

2063   Madame Aubry Dines with Death   Harp 1967

Mme Aubry remains charming and cultivated—in fact, she might now be said to be tilled, since a good part of the book is devoted to her bed life—but however agreeable this fun may be, it is not detection in any sense. The over-rich American wife and photographer's cyanide add nothing new.

2064   TREAT, LAWRENCE (acquired name of Lawrence Arthur Goldstone, b. 1903), writes stories with an alphabetical tag—*D as in Dead* (1941), *H as in Hangman* (1942), *O as in Omen* (1943), etc. The short story form (see Nos. 2839–40) seems better adapted to his talents, which tend toward detection but keep it fairly mechanical.

TRENCH, JOHN (b. 1920)

b. Newick, Sussex; educ. Wellington College and Woolwich Military Academy. Served in Kenya, Somaliland, Western Desert, Tunisia, and Europe. Invalided in 1946.

2065   Beyond the Atlas   Macm 1963

Not a detective story like the author's earlier efforts, but suspense involving a British diplomat and his girl friend, ambushed on holiday near Addis Ababa.

2066   Dishonoured Bones   Macm 1955

The author's second novel featuring the amateur archaeologist Martin Cotterell, whose honorably acquired aluminum hand is more notable than any feats of detection he accomplishes in this or the first of his cases. Rereading does not alleviate a complicated plot productive of murder (to avoid recognition and taxes). The characters are almost all steadily detestable and incoherent, which shows again that not all those in the irritant school are women.

2067   What Rough Beast   Macm 1957

An unpleasant farrago of juvenile delinquency and imputed immorality among Anglicans, in a highly unconvincing cathedral town, with trifling detection by venal police and the one-handed Martin Cotterell. The quality of the writing is high, especially in the opening scenes, but prose is not enough.

The title is from Yeats' "Second Coming" and refers to the chimera.

2068 TRENCH. See also:

Docken Dead   Macm 1954

2069 TROLLOPE, ANTHONY

The Eustace Diamonds   C&H 1876

The great novelist, who said he did not like stories in which it was important to remember what had happened on the Tuesday, has written here a
tale of intrigue and malfeasance that includes two burglaries, two trials,
and much legal action—all about a necklace "valued at more than
£10,000." No detection but some mystery, swift action, and plenty of
characters.

TROY, SIMON (pseud. of Thurman Warriner, q.v.)

The author has written upward of a dozen detective tales, many of them
featuring the easygoing Inspector Smith and playing down detection in
favor of suspense, local color (Cornwall, Channel Islands), and psychology.

2070 Cease upon the Midnight   Goll 1964

An obvious challenge to the reader and to Inspector Smith, who is still
bound down to the island of Guernsey, yet a not wholly satisfying story
when one slips out from under the spell and reflects on people and motives—the loves and the wives and the illnesses and reticences: all betray
a searching for effect that they shouldn't. Still, the work is so much better than the average run of stories that complaints should be muted.

2071 The Road to Rhuine   DM 1952
        In Eng.: Half-Way to Murder

The fact that it is to be pronounced Re-ween doesn't make it any better:
though it can be read through, because the author is an old hand at narrative. The tale is merely a variation on the theme of Evil in Our Midst.
The villain, known from the start, the victimized wife and children, the
angry villagers—all are fundamentally trite. Detection fitful.

2072 Second Cousin Removed   Macm 1961

The interest comes from tension rather than mystery, and there is something close to murder. But the hypocritical, canting husband and the old
family friend who finally takes a hand (as well as other things) are excellent. The investigation is by an unusual elderly Welsh police inspector,
who finds out rather than detects.

2073 Swift to Its Close   Goll 1969

His very best so far—indeed very nearly a masterpiece. The setting is
Wales and the characters are connected in one way or another with a
music festival (not jazz, not Eistedfodd). By genuine detection, Inspector

Smith defends his likable friend, the founder and composer, whose behavior and love story are equally delightful.

2074   Waiting for Oliver   Macm 1963/1962

The present yarn omits Inspector Smith and is a suspense tale pure and simple. If the author had managed to make Oliver a bit more lifelike, the rating would be very high. As it is, the attraction and antagonism between the two former schoolmates is neatly shown and the action is good. Guernsey scene.

2075   TROY. See also Nos. 2176–80 and:

> No More a-Roving   Macm 1965
> Sup with the Devil   Macm 1967
> Tonight and Tomorrow   Goll 1962/1957

2076   TRUSS, (LESLIE) SELDON (also George Selmark; b. 1892)

   Footsteps Behind Them   H&S 1937

The lieutenant of Scots Guards in the first world war is a prolific writer, pushing the half-century mark in his output, nearly all of it aiming at detective interest. The present business begins admirably, with the escape of a convict from Dartmoor. A friend is in wait for him, and they reach the town from which the resentful, misjudged man originally came. We are led to think that he is going back for revenge, and when in his vicinage half a dozen people die it is hard to resist the inference. But things get less and less plausible or clear, and the interest peters out.

2077   Never Fight a Lady   CCD 1950

Not badly written, yet a little odd in its wobbling between the satirical and the serious tone. The heroine is the alert daughter of an ineffectual assistant commissioner at Scotland Yard, and she rescues her fiancé, son of a big businessman, who has been kidnapped as well as framed in order to force his father into a dangerous deal. The businessman's woman secretary is a splendid portrait of cool and affectionate efficiency.

2078   TRUSS. See also:

> Always Ask a Policeman   Dday 1952
> Foreign Bodies   H&S 1938
> The Hunterstone Outrage   ML 1931
> The Living Alibi   CM 1929
> Put Out the Light   H&S 1954
> Technique for Treachery   CCD 1963

2079   TURNER, WILLIAM PRICE

   Bound to Die   Walk 1967

A first novel by a young man of Scottish parentage, who has been Fellow in Poetry at the University of Leeds and has had plays broadcast.

His story starts well but finishes poorly. The murder by strangling and (non-sexual) torture of a girl who has fallen for a redheaded ex-journalist involves him in suspicion and ultimately gets him seduced by the girl's mother, an unusual and well-drawn character. But all this good work is wasted when it turns out that killing and killer have little if anything to do with what we know.

> TWAIN, MARK (pseud. of Samuel Langhorne Clemens; also Solon Lycurgus, Hi Slocum, Ab Originee, Sieur Louis de Conte and other pseudonyms; 1835–1910)

This great writer circled around the detective plots that were popular in his time, and he toyed with both comic and serious versions and variations, no doubt feeling that the plush-covered melodramas that then stood for the genre were laughable and yet contained a core of genuine life-stuff. But he never managed to simplify or energize the idea of the detective tale, long or short. He only made sallies into its territory, as can be best shown by the contrasts indicated below.

One ought to add that "The Facts Concerning the Recent Carnival of Crime in Connecticut" is humor about morals, not crime or detection; and that "The Man Who Corrupted Hadleyburg," though it holds some mystery, is again an expression of Mark Twain's somewhat Nietzschean outlook in later years. Both pieces are in *Selected Shorter Writings of Mark Twain,* ed. Walter Blair (HM 1962). (See also No. 2841.)

2080   A Double-Barrelled Detective Story   1902

This is the western tale of injustice, revenge, and serio-comic detection that is most often reprinted, usually with healthy cuts (see No. 2741). Being neither one thing nor the other, it disappoints alike the admirers of the master, the fanciers of western life, and the devotees of detection.

2081   A Murder, a Mystery, and a Marriage   Manu 1945

This rather silly tale of intrigue was written in 1876 and never printed in the author's lifetime. It was first issued in an unauthorized edition of sixteen copies in 1945 and was the occasion of a lawsuit, *Chamberlain v. Feldman.*

2082   Simon Wheeler, Detective   NYPL 1963
       Introd. by Franklin R. Rogers
       Portraits and facsimiles

A posthumous satire of detective fiction, regrettably not good detection and not funny.

2083   The Tragedy of Pudd'nhead Wilson   Amer 1894
       And the Comedy of Those Extraordinary Twins

Interesting as anything of Mark Twain's is, and a sign of his early notice and use of fingerprinting, but not mainly or even partly a detective novel.

2084 TYRE, NEDRA

Hall of Death   S&S 1960
    In ppb.: Reformatory Girls

The mystery is suicide (dimly sketched) at a girls' reformatory, with a
poorly characterized young woman narrator and a clumsily managed
murder. The identity of the culprit is never in doubt and the suspense
trivial.

2085 TYRE. See also:

Death of an Intruder   Knopf 1953
Journey to Nowhere   Knopf 1954
Mouse in Eternity   Knopf 1952

2086 TYRER, WALTER

Such Friends Are Dangerous   Stap 1954

A tour de force of a non-repeatable kind. We are shown the physical and
mental tribulations of a suburban housewife, who sees her lumpish husband being lost to the village siren. Another woman, the wife's free-
living and free-thinking friend, Vera Sylvaine, has an influence over her
that leads to the final disaster and the astonishing denouement. Inspector Frodsham functions conventionally, most of the investigating
being done by an engaging small-town journalist. A prize piece.

2087 Trunk Crime No. 3   Columb 1939

An amateurish and melodramatic attempt to account for a trunk crime.
The plot is engineered by a nurse who knows how to lie, blackmail,
and organize; and doubtless in other hands the plot would hold interest
and suspense. But nothing here gives any hint of the skillful writing
found in *Such Friends Are Dangerous.*

2088 TYRER. See also:

The Case Against Dr. Ripon   Amal 1948
The Motor Coach Mystery   Amal 1948
The Mystery of the Woman Overboard   Amal 1948

UNDERWOOD, MICHAEL (pseud. of John Michael Evelyn, b. 1916)

b. Worthing; educ. Charterhouse and Christ Church, Oxf.; barrister in
government service since 1946, now Director of Public Prosecutions.

2089 The Anxious Conspirators   Macd 1965

A new line, in which our author displays more sophistication and wit
than before. The plot spins around the importation of forged travelers'
checks into England, the capture of the distributors, and a murder—all
this seen through the eyes of the familiar Inspector Manton, and even
more through those of a young lawyer befriended by M. Short but good,
though scarcely detection.

2090   The Crime of Colin Wise   CCD 1964

Underwood under par. From the moment when the greedy novice in
crime dismembers the corpse in the bath of the flat to which he has lured
his victim, detection and conviction are only too evidently in the offing,
and the case drags as Inspector Manton accumulates the evidence. Query:
were some of the details inspired by the murder of Stanley Setty in 1949?
See No. 3284.

2091   False Witness   Walk 1957

This (probably) maiden effort is dedicated to Christianna Brand but remains otherwise undistinguished. A young barrister who is in love with
the local magnate's daughter, herself just engaged to the other suspect,
gets embroiled in theft and murder. The rural English setting is vague and
unskillfully used. Another girl, two court officials, and the local head of
police achieve no more than a wooden existence.

2092   Lawful Pursuit   CCD 1958

This tries with little success to infuse some exotic flavor (Algerian scenes
and bodies in tubs of acid) into a good scheme of disappearing plaintiffs
and the cause of their absence. Mechanics and trappings inadequate to
the conception.

2093   The Man Who Killed Too Soon   Macd 1968

In the author's new vein, which reduces the trial scene to a few pages
(though keeping for this the surprise twist) and which spreads itself on
crime rings, damsels in jeopardy, and the qualms and hesitations of the
lawyer hero. Trips to Japan and a tentative love affair enliven the discovery of a not altogether plausible conspiracy.

2094   Murder Made Absolute   IW 1957

A clean-cut debut—the dispatching of a queen's counsel in the courtroom
during the hearing of a case. The tracking down of the killer from among
the rather limited group of well-motivated suspects is neatly handled by
Detective Superintendent Manton, with the aid of adequate clues and
sufficient characterization.

2095 Murder on Trial   IW 1958

This author's second, only a shade less admirable than the first. A man is
decoyed and killed on Hampstead Heath (always a good terrain), the
deed being a mere preparation for a second murder, this time in public.
Inspector Simon Manton risks no hernia of the mind in his efforts to find
the culprit, but neither is he futile.

2096   The Shadow Game   Macd 1969

If we have to have an endless stream of spy stories set in curtained-off
countries, let them be of this quality and tone. Without torture, improbable

rescues, and outré settings, suspense is maintained throughout a long bus ride from Munich to Istanbul. The hero is a London barrister who has agreed to serve as witness in an intelligence ploy, just once, as an amateur. Naturally, things go wrong, he has not been told enough, and he meets real danger. But the utmost likelihood reigns in his thoughts and feelings and in his eventual escape. The telling is deft and witty, and the pair of hippies whom he encounters at the right moment are superbly done—altogether a master's handiwork.

2097   The Silent Liars   Macm 1970

A middling performance: the opening in court is the best part, and the young "hero" in the dock is well portrayed as the modern youth who never takes thought for the morrow and is unscrupulous about girls. All the rest, though well enough plotted, is done in cardboard.

This book furnishes in addition a fit occasion to say something about dust jackets for the genre: they are well below average in thought and execution. In this one, what is meant to represent gold ingots and blood accurately resembles chocolate bars awash in strawberry sauce.

2098   The Unprofessional Spy   CCD 1964

A young barrister goes to East Berlin as an inconspicuous counterintelligence officer, qualified solely by his earlier knowledge of the city and love for a girl now suspected in England of being a Russian spy. The chase, acrobatics, and tear-jerking situations are competently done.

2099   UNDERWOOD. See also:

The Arm of the Law	Hamm 1959
Cause of Death	Hamm 1960
Death by Misadventure	Hamm 1960
Death on Remand	Hamm 1956
Girl Found Dead	Macd 1963

UPFIELD, ARTHUR W(ILLIAM) (1888–1964)

b. England; shipped by father to Australia after refusing to become a real estate surveyor. Worked down under as cowhand and sheepherder till 1914, when he enlisted. Fought at Gallipoli, in Egypt, and in France. Returned to Australia, prospected for gold, and worked as fur trapper. He had meanwhile written four novels he knew to be unpublishable and now determined to make a success of writing for magazines. A chance meeting gave him the model for "Bony," who first appeared in *The Barrakee Mystery* (1929) and set the course of his later production.

2100   Bony and the Black Virgin   Hein 1959

A rather "poetic" treatment of the bush and the relations of aborigines and whites. Bony solves the murder of two wastrel whites, tracking down the white hero and his black virgin love. A great drought in which cattle, sheep, and dogs die covers the first half of the book and supplies its mood.

2101   Death of a Lake   Hein 1954

Another complete success, for the author and for Bony. The drought
scene, the motive, the characters, the concealment of Bony's role till near
the end, and the dramatic use of rabbits, birds, and kangaroos in the final
extermination are all first-class.

2102   The Devil's Steps   A&R 1965; orig. 1946

Bony is on the outskirts of Melbourne, not in his outback wilds, when
he is seconded to the Intelligence Branch to investigate a German general
masquerading as an American tourist. But this is not a chase story; it is
good solid detection of murder and robbery done on domestic premises—
an attractive mountain chalet—and Bony shines in his handling of abundant physical clues. Worth rereading; close to a masterpiece in the pure
genre.

2103   Man of Two Tribes   Hein 1956

More interesting for its topography and anthropology than for its detection, which is minimal. Bony finds five murderers and a murderess captive in a cave or giant pothole somewhere in western Australia, their
predicament having been arranged by a "fellowship" of the vigilante kind.

2104   Mr. Jelly's Business   A&R 1964/1937
In U.S.: Murder Down Under

The mood is leisurely, the plot slow-paced but steady, and the moralizing
distinctly prewar. And yet the tale holds up very well, being the expression
of a full conception of place and persons. Bony is especially well studied,
in all his relations; and of the double mystery (murder and periodic
disappearance), the obvious one is as good as the more hidden.

2105   The New Shoe   Dday 1951

A prime example of Bony's work. The murder in the lighthouse in Victoria is slowly traced home to its perpetrator, while characters and incidents develop and dovetail. The scene is memorable and even the dog
is attractive and functional. A second reading confirms the opinion that
the work is unsurpassed in the author's output.

2106   Sinister Stones   Dday 1954
In Eng.: The Cake in the Hatbox

Upfield uses his double advantage—the Australian outback affords scope
for "Zadig work," that is, human and animal tracking by Bony or the
natives; and the conditions of life chosen for the tale necessarily elude
the American reader's criticism of plausibility. This is another excellent
piece of the kind.

2107   The Will of the Tribe   Hein 1962

Shows the author sustaining his powers till nearly the end. The local
color (northwest Australia, 500 miles south of Darwin) is attractive and

matched by the personalities of family and stockmen at the Brentner homestead. Bony does a good job of elucidating the reasons behind the depositing of the body of a mysterious stranger in a meteor crater nearby; political overtones are credible and a man-woman chase involving two ex-aborigines livens things up in fine style.

2108   Winds of Evil   A&R 1937

Hardly to be recommended as more than good-average-Upfield. Perhaps we are given more evidence pointing to the identity of the non-sexual, practically sleepwalking strangler than is usual with Upfield, but the sandstorms pall after the first few chapters.

2109   UPFIELD. See also:

An Author Bites the Dust	Dday 1948
The Barrakee Mystery (= The Lure of the Bush)	Hutch 1929
The Bone Is Pointed	A&R 1938
Death of a Swagman	Dday 1945
Murder Must Wait	CCD 1953
Venom House	Dday 1952
Wings Above the Claypan	CCD 1943

2110   URQUHART, MACGREGOR

The Grey Man   TVB 1965
A Case for Inspector Smarles

The Grey Man is a bestial apparition in the Highlands near Cairngorm. It is blamed for scaring women and old men and killing a philandering lassie. Much of the story goes toward uncovering the sordid bargains, gripes, and sex vagaries of a bunch of unprepossessing but consistent characters. The two detectives, Scottish and Cockney, are naturally at loggerheads, and the solution drags, though the detection is rational and steady. What is not so is the prose, which consists of broken phrases written like stage directions, an appalling device.

2111   USHER, JACK

Brothers and Sisters Have I None   Mill 1958

Praised in a blurb by Erle Stanley Gardner, this is a familiar plot based on the idea that the wealthy and powerful can do whatever they like to oppress the rest of society. They hush up the facts and hire others to kill whoever exposes the truth. Writing substandard, suspense missing, sex laid on.

2112   VANCE, ETHEL (pseud. of Grace Zaring Stone, b. 1896). The great-granddaughter of Robert Owen, she began a career as a musician, turned with success to novel writing, and was so moved by the events in central Europe just before the second world war that she produced a sensational thriller full of anti-Nazi feeling and anguishing adventure: *Escape* (1939). She followed it up in 1942 with *Reprisal*.

2113 VANCE, LOUIS JOSEPH (1879–1933), wrote adventure stories of the Raffles and "Saint" type and of a uniformly tabloid level. His trademark character is the Lone Wolf, who appears in half a dozen or more books. *Detective* (1932) is not what Poe would acknowledge as a legitimate offspring, but love, misunderstanding, and heroics in the middle of the first world war.

2114 VANDAM, ALBERT D(RESDEN) (1843–1903)

The Mystery of the Patrician Club   Lipp 1893

A period piece to be sampled rather than read. The author was a journalist who perpetrated a very successful historical hoax in two volumes, *An Englishman in Paris,* [1885]. He also wrote an acceptable *Masterpieces of Crime* (1892). This detective tale is another matter. Its plot is not bad, but the telling and, even more, the imagined emotions are hard to take. Why the detective is not told by the villain and his family to go climb a tree is a mystery in itself.

2115 VANDERCOOK, JOHN W(OMACK) (b. 1902)

Murder in New Guinea   Macm 1959

Unlike the earlier *Murder(s) in: Trinidad, Fiji,* and *Haiti,* which were poor but could be read, this is unendurable after the first 50 pages or so. It is, moreover, full of outrageous mistakes concerning radioactivity, uranium ore being the basis of the feebly organized skulduggery.

VAN DINE, S. S. (pseud. of Willard Huntington Wright, 1888–1939)

It is hard to believe that V.D. once topped the market in detection—at least in the U.S.—and was popular with intellectuals and groundlings alike. But even then, the phony footnotes, the phony English accent of Philo Vance, and the general apathy of the detective system in all these books were apparent to the collaborators. Wright rode on his brass and swank, plus his reputation as the blaster of the *Encyclopaedia Britannica* in *Misinforming a Nation.* As aesthete and critic he has, however, a place in America's artistic coming of age. (See No. 2936.)

2116 The Benson Murder Case   Scrib 1926

The first and best, partly because V.D. had the real-life model of the Joseph Elwell murder (1920) to hold his fancy in check.

2117 The Canary Murder Case   Scrib 1928

The "Canary" is a singer and the evil deed requires a gramophone. How many before and after this have been used? *The Dutch Garden* by Adams is only a trifle later and it is better done (see No. 6). Here Philo Vance saunters in his usual irritating way, but the footnotes are not excessive and the Régie cigarettes (a gift from Régie Fortune?) are not too much in evidence.

2118   The Greene Murder Case   Scrib 1928

An overblown and overfootnoted tale recording the exploits of P.V. He
solves a series of murders in an old New York mansion, ostensibly by
tumbling to the fact that the murderer's method was plagiarized from
Gross's *Handbuch für Untersuchungsrichter,* but actually by waiting until
the criminal has disposed of most of the family.

2119   The Scarab Murder Case   Scrib 1930

The collaborators can remember reading this one in monthly installments
in *The American Magazine,* even while they were disgusted by the author's
bland insults to the reader's intelligence—e.g., the heavy Egyptian statue
in the gallery, upended on a piece of pencil and conveniently toppling
on the designed victim. By that date they were fed up with the whole
bag of tricks, which successive settings did not rejuvenate.

2120   The Winter Murder Case   Scrib 1939

This is W. H. Wright's last work, left in an only semi-expanded outline
form at the time of his death. Philo Vance is still the detective but the
pseudo-scholarly footnotes are not in evidence nor is the pearl-handled
telephone. In fact, this short book is pleasant reading; add your own nostalgia if you wish.

2121   VAN DINE. See also:

The Bishop Murder Case	Scrib 1929	The Gracie Allen	
The Casino Murder Case	Scrib 1934	Murder Case	Scrib 1938
The Dragon Murder Case	Scrib 1933	The Kidnap Murder Case	Scrib 1936
The Garden Murder Case	Scrib 1938		

VAN GULIK, ROBERT (HANS) (1910–67)

b. Zutphen; educ. Leyden and Utrecht (Ph.D., 1935); married a Chinese, served the Netherlands as diplomat in Far East and U.S., doing
scholarly work in sinology that led, after retirement, first to the translating
of an eighteenth-century Chinese detective story and then to the writing
of the Judge Dee stories, set in a much earlier time.

2122   The Chinese Bell Murders   Harp 1959
       Illus. by the author

The legendary magistrate and detective of the seventh century of our
era, Judge Dee, himself the subject of Chinese detective tales during the
seventeenth and eighteenth centuries, made his American debut in this
book. The local color of the provincial city of Poo-yang, where the three
interwoven crimes are perpetrated, is agreeable, but the telling is pompous
and amateurish.

   Note the postscript by the author giving data on the administration of
justice in the early Chinese empire.

2123   The Chinese Gold Murders   Harp 1961

Much better than the first. What this one offers is a version of the modern
Hollywood type of tale, fitted to the manners of China in the seventh

century. Judge Dee is lively, and so are the gangsters, harlots, and others whom the Judge outwits by disguise, deception, and detection.

2124 The Chinese Lake Murders   Harp 1962
        Illus. by the author

The murder of Almond Blossom on the Flower Boat, while Judge Dee is being entertained, is preceded by a confusing chapter of pseudo-supernatural tenor. The rest is a good gangster story: lowlifes and blondes translated into Chinese. Only the Judge and his three loyal goons are original and freshly entertaining.

2125 The Chinese Nail Murders   MJ 1961
        Preface and Postscript
        Sketch map of Pei-chow
        Illus. by the author

Not essentially different, but one of the author's best reconstructions of ancient Chinese crime and detection. Two valuable postscripts make clear, among other matter, that the proper sequence of Judge Dee's adventures is Gold-Lake-Bell-Maze-Nail and that this tale concludes the series of Judge Dee mysteries, though they cover only the first half of his career.

2126 The Emperor's Pearl   Hein 1963
        Illus. by the author

Whether the reader or the writer is the first to tire of a formula may be argued with the aid of any given example such as this story. The fact remains that the characters, events, and tricks now seem played out.

2127 Murder in Canton   Hein 1966
        Illus. by the author

A new locale for Judge Dee's activities and a new style, which seems closer to that of the first good tales than to the middle period of straight theft, wenching, and gangsterism. Here the unraveling of the political intrigue and love affairs is as subtle as the plot is complex, and modernity and antiquity are well blended. The illustrations, alike in all the stories, add little.

2128 The Phantom of the Temple   Scrib 1966

It is regrettable that this late-comer to detection should have died suddenly and at a relatively early age, but this next-to-last product of his pen suggests that the quite original formula he popularized is played out. The concealment of robbery by faked supernatural doings is old hat, and the events that Judge Dee unravels here are too cluttered to be either attractive or puzzling.

2129 VAN GULIK. See also:

        The Chinese Maze Murders   Lounz 1957
        The Lacquer Screen   Lounz 1963

| The Red Pavilion | Lounz 1961 |
| The Willow Pattern | Scrib 1965 |

2130 Van Siller (full name: Hilda Van Siller)

The Biltmore Call   WL 1967

The story is sufficiently full of sharp turns and suspense, and it is adroitly told, barring a few naïvetés. But something is lacking here as in others by this author—perhaps a belief in the reality of her hero-detective, Allan Stewart, who is a peg for a self-developing situation rather than a thinking investigator. He does see beyond appearances and is visited by ideas, but he does not work so much as "wonder." The plot here is intricate and lacks a good motive.

2131   A Complete Stranger   WL 1966/1965

Excellently plotted and told with a fine economy, but altogether lacking in charm and in characters, too—except from the old stockpile. Still, the setting (fashionable New York State inn) and the details and motives are quite fresh, despite a touch of boy scout sentiment. The hero (amateur sleuth-detective-story writer, Allan Stewart) is bright but emotionally a stick. He does find out why a stranger seeking to buy a house should have been lured there to his death.

2132   Van Siller. See also:

The Curtain Between	WL 1947	Paul's Apartment	WL 1948
Echo of a Bomb	WL 1943	Somber Memory	WL 1949
Good-Night, Ladies	WL 1943	Under a Cloud	WL 1944
The Lonely Breeze	WL 1965	The Widower	WL 1959
One Alone	WL 1946		

Various Hands

The notion of a team of distinguished writers collaborating on a novel was popular in Edwardian times. Henry James himself took part in one such venture, born, like the others of its kind, out of the publisher's hope of multiplying the sales by adding the great names. The scheme would seem ill-suited to serious work, which includes the serious business of making a detective plot credible and consistent. But such is the technical mastery of the leading performers in our genre that on two or three occasions out of half a dozen, they succeeded in producing excellent collective tales, as shown below.

2133   Ask a Policeman   Morr 1933
By John Rhode, Helen Simpson, Gladys Mitchell, Dorothy Sayers, Anthony Berkeley, and Milward Kennedy
Floor plan of the study

Rhode sets forth the problem of "Death at Hursley Lodge," the shooting of a newspaper tycoon in his study. The other authors are then each given a chance to solve the problem through the medium of another writer's fictional detective. Simpson does Mrs. Bradley, Mitchell does Sir John Saumarez, Sayers does Roger Sheringham, Berkeley does Lord Peter Wimsey. In conclusion, Milward Kennedy makes order out of the divergent views of the several detectives and manages a reasonable solution. The upshot is a really beautiful job of mystifying and serious parody. The solution *per accidens* is a purposeful letdown, which in no way spoils the tale.

Note: The floor plan, on which much depends, is small and poorly reproduced, which unfairly puts the reader at a disadvantage.

2134   Double Death   Goll 1939
    Supervised and with a Preface and Prologue by John Chancellor;* suggested and edited by James W. Drawbell and William Lees
    Maps by Crofts and Sayers

The contributors, besides J.C. above, are: Dorothy Sayers, F. W. Crofts, Valentine Williams, F. Tennyson Jesse, Anthony Armstrong, and David Hume (qq.v.). The Preface makes a point of the difficulties encountered in weaving a coherent tale and in bringing the authors to heel. Notes by the authors are appended to each chapter, a feature they did not expect to see reproduced, but which the "supervisor" and Victor Gollancz, the publisher, insisted on.

Sayers opens with the classic situation of an older woman suspecting her niece-companion, her nephew, her doctor, et al. of poisoning her. In an excellent railway-station scene, a "neutral" nurse from London arrives and is poisoned in situ. Suspects innumerable. Then Crofts introduces Inspector Billingham, in a characteristically Croftsian state of hunger. He is nonetheless sent off to Creepe [*sic*] to investigate. Naturally he goes after alibis and finds that none are much good. But Crofts' prose is terse and to the point.

Next Valentine Williams turns the tale into ordinary melodrama-mystery, winding up with a protracted death scene of the invalid woman, surrounded by three young people, all interested in legacies. (V.W.'s notes are excellent.) We switch to domesticity below stairs as Miss Jesse takes up the thread, fomenting suspicion all around, and introducing the murdered nurse's niece. Billingham interrogates and nothing happens. Again, F.T.J.'s notes outshine her chapter.

Armstrong's notes come next, preceding his chapter and making one excellent point, obvious and heretofore culpably overlooked. A.A. then goes on to do a fine chapter, distributing suspicion better than Miss J., and adding further notes to help his successor interpret his hints. But David Hume goes off on his own to provide a surprise ending, with a general comment and no notes.

*Pseudonym of Charles de Balzac-Rideaux (b. 1900).

2135   The Floating Admiral   CCD 1932
    G. K. Chesterton, Victor Whitechurch, G. D. H. and M. Cole, Henry Wade, Agatha Christie, John Rhode, Milward Kennedy, Dorothy Sayers, Ronald Knox, F. W. Crofts, Edgar Jepson, Clemence Dane, and Anthony Berkeley
    Map, Introd., and Appendices

These members of the (London) Detection Club collaborate with skill in a piece of detection rather more tight-knit than one had a right to expect. There is enough to amuse and to stimulate detection; and the Introduction by Dorothy Sayers and supplements by critics and solvers give an insight into the writers' thoughts and modes of work.

2136   The President's Mystery Story   Farr 1935

Propounded by Franklin D. Roosevelt and solved by Rupert Hughes, S. H. Adams, A. Abbot, Rita Weiman, S. S. Van Dine, and John Erskine, with a Preface by Fulton Oursler (Anthony Abbot, q.v.), it is a continuous tale never very intense or believable.

2137   VICKERS, ROY (also David Durham, Sefton Kyle, and John Spence; b. 1899), educated at Charterhouse and Brasenose; journalist and free lance, has cultivated the short-story length, including the inverted form, in his tales of the *Department of Dead Ends* (see No. 2848 as well as *The Best Detective Stories of Roy Vickers,* 1965). He has also edited *Novel Magazine* and done court reporting. In the long form, see *Murder in Two Flats* (1952), *Murder of a Snob* (1951), and *Whispering Death* (1940).

VICTORIAN AGE
2138   Novels of Mystery from the Victorian Age   DS 1945
       Maurice Richardson, ed.

Contains: Collins, *The Woman in White;* the anonymous *Notting Hill Mystery;* LeFanu, *Carmilla;* Stevenson, *Dr. Jekyll and Mr. Hyde.* (For comments, see the first two of those titles, as well as No. 3014.

2139   VIVIAN, FRANCIS (pseud. of Ernest Ashley, b. 1906)

       Darkling Death   HJ 1956

The author has written a dozen and a half novels in which Detective Superintendent Knollis appears; this is one of the later ones and below average strength. Knollis is acceptable, but pseudo-literary and philosophic tosh prevents any account of the inquest being given until p. 144 of an 189-page book.

2140   The Singing Masons   H&S 1950

The situation is rural, the goings-on are complicated, and only one or two of the characters sound plausible. The murder (for reasons easily forgotten) is well-meant but it boomerangs and intolerable pressure develops from false accusation, etc., etc. The agriculture is doubtless as accurate as it is attractive.
       The title is from *Henry V,* I, 2, 181.

2141   VOLTAIRE (pseud. of François Marie Arouet, 1694–1778)

       Zadig ou La Destinée   1748

       First Eng. ed. by John Brindley (1749)

Is this a short or a long? No need to decide: its importance and that of its author require its presence at this point. It is in the third chapter of this tale that the hero after which it is named takes up the study of nature to console himself for his marital troubles and uses the observation of natural facts to infer events he has not seen. However implausible and "agrarian" his method, he is the first systematic detective in modern literature, and that priority itself adds to his troubles in the story until his royal vindication.

Note: For the distant origins of this primitive sort of detection, see Nos. 2566, pp. 24–5, where Arab, Hebrew, and Greek sources are cited and where the Three Princes of Serendip (Ceylon) also have a share.

VULLIAMY, C(OLWYN) E(DWARD) (also Anthony Rolls, q.v.; b. 1886), has written brilliant works of satire and historical criticism (e.g., *Doctor Philligo*, 1944), besides extravaganzas such as *Clerical Error* (= *The Vicar's Experiments*), 1932 (see No. 1877). In his quasi detection, extravagance also colors the scene and excludes the work from the serious genre without quite qualifying as good farce.

2142   Tea at the Abbey   MJ 1961

Scientists at the University of Mansterbridge are pursuing experiments to effect changes of personality with the aid of drugs. A young woman student, who is engaged to one of the assistant experimenters, is stabbed to death. There are plenty of red herrings as well as of detectives, but little or no real detection. Chief Superintendent James Plascoed is described one way and acts another, and all his efforts are but pseudo investigation. The court scene at which an innocent man is tried and freed is well done, but for the rest we have only occasional humor as our reward for reading. In contrast with these mysteries *manqué,* the author's straight satires are the perfection of pointedness.

2143   VULLIAMY. See also:

    The Body in the Boudoir   MJ 1956
    Cakes for Your Birthday   MJ 1959
    Don Among the Dead Men   MJ 1952

WADE, HENRY (pseud. of Sir Henry Lancelot Aubrey Fletcher, 6th baronet, b. 1887)

Educ. at Eton and New College, Oxf.; joined Grenadier Guards and served in the first war (DSO and Croix de Guerre); later JP, High Sheriff, and Lord Lt. of Bucks; author of *A History of the Footguards to 1856.* Chose his mother's maiden name as pseudonym when he began writing detective stories. For his short works, see Nos. 2849–50.

Though insufficiently known in the U.S., Wade is one of the great figures of the classical period. He has been not only productive but also varied in genre. His plots, characters, situations, and means rank with the best, while his prose has elegance and force.

Wade shows the police work he knows at first hand, adds sentimental touches, but is full of practical detail and genuine detection. A young constable is shot in cold blood by one of a pair of burglars. The young detective's childhood friend, who is also a detective, is angered by the suspension of capital punishment, and starts sleuthing to avenge his friend but is accused of another murder. Certain details suggest the Gutteridge case of 1927.

2145   Bury Him Darkly   Const 1936
Plans of Bond Street shop and North London

This is surely one of the early police-routine stories (after Froest, q.v.), and done with fine attention to a great variety of details. Inspector Poole has done good work before and it is referred to in this affair, which starts as a jewel robbery on Bond Street, goes on to the killing of a police officer, and ends with a reprimand for Poole and much grief for friends he has made in the course of his investigations. The handling of suspense, characters, and topography make this one of Wade's notable departures from the formula of the thirties.

The medical examiner, Dr. Blathermore, is also memorable for his name, which it is but fair to say he does nothing to justify.

2146   Constable Guard Thyself   Const 1934
A Detective Story
Plan of police station

Each of this writer's stories seems to be conceived as a challenge to himself; he likes to tackle new difficulties. The obstacle here is that the Chief Constable of Brodshire is killed in his office at police headquarters, and Inspector Poole of Scotland Yard soon comes to suspect one or more of the police officers whom he has been called on to assist. The various possibilities of collusion, graft, disgrace, revenge, suicide, and blackmail are juggled with great virtuosity, and although at a first reading one might dismiss the story as a mere puzzle of clues and identities, the practiced eye will find much social comment and characterization.

2147   Diplomat's Folly   Macm 1952

A young man, put out of civilian stride by his commando training, settles down to a job which involves doing dirty work—or at least rough-stuff—for money. He double-crosses and kills, for plausible reasons but without our sympathy. No detection.

2148   The Duke of York's Steps   Const 1929

The title refers to the flight of steps in London leading from Waterloo Place to the Mall and St. James's Park, down which Sir Garth Fratten and a financier friend were passing when the former met his death as the result of a missile projected in an unusual manner by an unknown assassin. In many ways this is a classic of the golden age. The pace is steady, if leisurely, the suspects numerous, the financial sleight-of-hand very credible, Inspector Poole engaging and competent. At the end the author provides a sound motive, a workable method, and a fair enough double identity.

2149   The Dying Alderman   BW 1930

Reread in 1967, this story of forty years ago holds up extremely well. There is narrative economy, the right kind of antagonism between police officers, sufficient characterization, unbroken suspense, subdued wit, local color, and a first-rate plot with a fine twist at the end.

2150   A Dying Fall   Macm 1953

A beautifully plotted and superbly told affair, shorter than most of Wade's. The horsey background is just full enough to convince without boring. The only weakness is that there are two independent murders, though the character-drawing will stand it. Clues and incidents original, as is also the climax in the last line.

2151   Gold Was Our Grave   Macm 1954
        Plan of murder scene as frontispiece

A brisk account of the lives of two rascally stockbrokers, whose rotten core comes into view after these bad apples have served a jail term. The financial malfeasance is clearly presented, Poole being once again the detective.

2152   The Hanging Captain   Const 1932

One of Wade's triumphs, in a class with *No Friendly Drop*. The murder of the syphilitic elder son is credibly and creditably brought home to the one who at first seemed a very unlikely suspect. The local constabulary make good with a little assistance from Detective Inspector Lott of Scotland Yard, a cocky young sidekick of Wade's usual Poole. Admirably detailed treatment of clues.

2153   Heir Presumptive   Const 1935

Douglas Browne (No. 304) was better able to bring life and humor to this theme, which is that of cousinly extermination for inheritance. There is no conspiracy, so that the one whose knowledge of the difference between "tail male" and "general entail" is imperfect obligingly serves his rival. The deeper of the two villains then goes to work on the survivors: not as murky as it sounds.

2154   The High Sheriff   Const 1937

A classic story of an army officer turned lord of the manor, who is blackmailed by a former companion. The blackmailer dies, but it turns out that the actual witness of the "shameful event" which led to blackmail is still alive. A tale several times told in the literature but never so well as here. The Brackenshire hunt and the associated doggy and horsey life are tellingly portrayed.

2155   The Litmore Snatch
Const 1957

Leisurely, competent, but lacking in drive or verve. Quite aside from the undistinguished crime, there is little to appeal to a lover of detection. He knows that the suspect can't be guilty, and isn't particularly interested in the way the obvious criminal is brought to book.

2156   Lonely Magdalen
Folding map
Const 1940

Probably the most ambitious of Wade's books. Inspector Poole takes over the flagging investigation of the murder of a prostitute found strangled on Hampstead Heath, and his systematic checking of alibis plus long flashback of family history swells the book to treatise length. Good detection and realistic treatment of police work. The large dose of routine human interest is what seems excessive.

2157   The Missing Partners
Const 1928

Rereading and comparing with others by Wade in the same years puts this story at a disadvantage. Large doses of love interest, rum-running, and disagreeable characters (including Inspector Dodd, who functions in this pre-Poole era) are not counterbalanced by the Liverpool shipping scene, some good railway detail, and the author's fair success in pinning the crime onto the least likely person.

2158   Mist on the Saltings
Map of the Saltings as frontispiece
Const 1933

This ambitious attempt at a novel of character, combined with crime and detection, must be judged a failure, despite some excellent scenes and solid detective work. The setting, too, is expertly interwoven with the events and the clues; but the elaboration of the marital tangle, on one side, and of the disagreement among the police, on the other, has a perpetually retarding effect which kills suspense. In spite of all, one is left feeling that Wade knows what he is about.

2159   New Graves at Great Norne
Const 1947

The theme is that of a misjudged (and missing) man determined to wreak vengeance on a whole group of people. Splendid local color, but little detection and that—such as it is—done by Inspector Myrtle rather than by Poole (now retired or promoted). The characters, the village, the murders, and the climax at the bridge—all first-rate.
   WHT thinks it weak and negligible.

2160   No Friendly Drop   Const 1931

The first appearance of Inspector Poole, with Lady Grayle, her butler, and his method of making tea, combine to make this story linger in the mind. Poole is the first of the educated upstarts in the force, but his politics are radical, and his cunning rests on a humorous view of life.
    The title is from *Romeo and Juliet*, V, 3, 163.

2161   Released for Death   Const 1938

A dull tale of vengeance by an ex-convict—the only interesting bits being interviews with wardens.

2162   Too Soon to Die   Const 1954

Other tales have been based on the provision (in the U.K.) that five years elapse between making a gift to an heir and the gift's escaping death duties. It is an invitation to fraud, and here it leads to murder. But since we start with the plotters, the detecting is wearisome. Not everybody can, like Freeman, handle the inverted genre, and it is a question whether it will stand the long haul, no matter who attempts it.

2163   The Verdict of You All   Const 1926

The perennial tale of the attractive young man who is engaged to the boss's daughter: is he good or bad? Geoffrey Hastings is charged with the murder of Smethurst, his fiancée Emily's papa. There is in the offing a badly used mistress to complicate the problem. The detection embraces clues and timetables in the classic way, but modern analysis might have blown the gaff by showing that the saliva on the dead man's cigar was not of his blood group.

2164   WAINWRIGHT, JOHN

Death in a Sleeping City   CCC 1965

The Mafia sends a pair of executioners to a town in the north of England, where Chief Superintendent Lewis has the task of heading them off. The writing is in the penny-dreadful style, wielded by a man who is himself a police officer, and who dedicates the work to his wife because "she understands." Little encouragement to look up *The Crystallized Carbon Pig* (1966), *The Darkening Glass* (1968), or *The Take-Over Men* (1969).

2165   WAKEFIELD, JOHN

Death the Sure Physician   DM 1966/1965

The author is head of a research unit at a British hospital and writes straightforwardly and with truth of such an institution in a city resembling Manchester. When a nurse is murdered, Inspector Speight is worth watching; the touchiness of the various staff members on being interviewed is deftly done; and the way a likely suspect is built up, then dropped, prepares an adequate solution. The reversal of the Shakespearean phrase for the title is a happy touch, the source being the *Cymbeline*, V, 4, 4.

2166 WALLACE, (RICHARD HORATIO) EDGAR (1875–1932). The famous and prolific author of *The Four Just Men* (1905) has never appealed to the collaborators, chiefly by reason of his subjects and his style, though they admit that they have not sampled him extensively. "J. G. Reeder" is the kind of semi-hero that they find tiresome in conception and manner. *The Ringer* (1926) seems more a trick than a tale. *The Clue of the Twisted Candle* (1916) undoubtedly has importance when one considers its date. But by and large Wallace's incredible output gives only thrills without substance—which soon means no thrills. It is only fair to add that Wallace keeps his devotees and they include good judges—witness the reissue of *The Northing Tramp,* in Classics of Adventure and Detection (1968), edited with an introduction by Michael Gilbert, who uses the 1965 version of the book, *The Tramp,* but restores the original title of 1926.

WALLING, R(OBERT) A(LFRED) J(OHN) (1869–1949)

b. England and became journalist and writer of books about the same time, concluding newspaper career as editor of *The Western Independent* of Plymouth (Eng.). Edited the diaries of John Bright and published some thirty detective stories, the last of which (*The Corpse with the Missing Watch*) appeared in the U.S. the week after his death.

2167   The Corpse with the Grimy Glove   Morr 1938

This author came too soon to the easy belief that a clutter of misunderstandings and wrong leads suffice to create suspense. In this story, which presents Philip Tolefree as the supersleuth whose guesses are as good as evidence, the dullness comes from the excess of false starts. No characters and no sparkle in the dialogue.

2168   The Fatal Five Minutes   H&S 1932

In this first appearance, Philip Tolefree, who detects, is a private investigator with an insurance business as cover, and the narrator is a ship's underwriter named Farrar. They seal their friendship at "Midwood," where an old friend of Farrar's gets bumped off just after he has called Tolefree for help in an undisclosed "difficult matter." Characterization throughout is nil, and the chief incidents are stereotyped "night work." In keeping with the period custom, the final scene is protracted by means of false implications, but it achieves a tension not found elsewhere in the tale, which critics have overrated.

2169   That Dinner at Bardolph's   Morr 1928
          In Eng.: Dinner Party at Bardolph's

In this early effort the suspense is well contrived and the sinister character of the host who is later murdered is quite credible. One is even ready to believe in the mutual suspicion of the friends (also relatives) who look into the affair, but their mania for transporting themselves hither and yon and the pretexts they invent in place of ratiocination end by discouraging the reader.

2170 WALLIS, RUTH (OTIS) SAWTELL (b. 1895)

Cold Bed in the Clay   DM 1947

The author won the Red Badge Prize for detection with *Too Many Bones* in 1943, but would not win much praise or gratitude for this one. The prose is mannered, the university commencement and its participants are implausible, and the piffling tale never gets properly going.

2171 WALPOLE, HORACE (1717–97)

The Castle of Otranto *in* Three Gothic Novels
Penguin 1968; orig.   1764

The progenitor of all Gothicists* wrote only this one tale—as good a piece of trumpery as was ever penned. The principle is that of supernatural powers interfering in the lives of men to disclose and punish their crimes. The first mystery is the death of Conrad, son of the prince of Otranto, felled by a gigantic helmet in his own courtyard and on the eve of his marriage. Politics, portents, paintings that make meaningful signs to the company, and hairbreadth escapes from threatened marriage and persecution keep the reader wondering what marvelous impossibility will come next. Walpole had the sense (absent in his imitators) to keep the story short.

  * This fact is the reason for including the work in this section, instead of later, among tales of the supernatural. (See Voltaire.)

2172 WARD, COLIN

House Party Murder   Morr 1934

The author made his American debut with this book, which is a crudely plotted tale with more complication than characterization. The name Garstang (that of the dashing young man who is finally unmasked) is the most memorable feature of the work.

2173 WARMAN, ERIK (b. 1904)

Relative to Murder   Harrap 1940

A weak blend of local color, cynicism, and bright talk concerning an English country murder—that of a much-hated enfant terrible who caught a tramp snooping. The surprise ending is no better than the rest and is slow to come.

2174 WARREN, VERNON

Brandon in New York   BW 1958

A fair specimen of the dozen or more devoted to Brandon, a predictable private eye done in the consecrated clichés. Some unintended amusement comes from the description of the New York scene.

2175 WARREN. See also:

Brandon Returns   Giff 1954
Brandon Takes Over   Giff 1953

Bullets for Brandon   Giff 1955
No Bouquets for Brandon   Giff 1955

2176 WARRINER, THURMAN (also Simon Troy, q.v.)

Death's Bright Angel   H&S 1956

The fifth book in which Mr. Ambo and Archdeacon Toft appear, with
Mr. Scotter doing the leg work and providing the earthiness. It starts well
but soon degenerates. The plot is this: heartless legatees try to hasten the
demise of a young man who has presumably received a fatal dose of radia-
tion during research in America and has come back to England to inherit
and die. The problem of his survival is (alas) cluttered with irrelevancies,
love included—as it need not be.

2177 Death's Dateless Night   H&S 1952

The third case of Mr. Ambo and company. Persecution by magic in an
old and unbelievable French castle. Beautiful girl married to old man.
Tedious, narcissistic.
   The title is from Shakespeare's sonnet 30.

2178 Ducats in Her Coffin   H&S 1951
        The Second Case of Mr. Ambo, Scotter, and the Archdeacon
        Map of Urmsbury church and access lanes

The opening finds Mr. Ambo, nearly 70, accosted in a bookshop by a
respectable girl of 17, who says she is in fear of her life and needs help
and advice. He gives what he can, including lunch and tea. The next day
he reads of her sister's body being found in the girls' home town. The
survivor, Patricia, had told Mr. Ambo she was sure her (older) sister
had been murdered. A call on John Scotter, inquiry agent, starts the investigation rolling. The tone is a trifle facetious and the background given
in talk seems especially excessive after the younger sister has disappeared
and is in danger. Inspector Forbes, also inactive, is unconvincing, and so
is the secret, the unbalanced Shearstone family, and the complicated denouement.
   The title is from *The Merchant of Venice*, III, 1, 94.

2179 Method in His Murder   Macm 1950

An "old world" setting and a respectable crime keep one amused through
the first two-thirds of this tale, but the rest goes rapidly downhill. One
very funny scene redeems the last part, but the unnaturally long finale
(40 pages) is spoiled by the revelation of a subplot hitherto unsuspected
by all.

2180 WARRINER. See also Nos. 2070–5 and:

The Doors of Sleep   H&S 1955

WATSON, COLIN (b. 1920)

b. Croydon; educ. Whitgift. Editorial writer for the Kemsley Press, uneven as a writer of detection, but often hilarious and worth following at

all costs. His latest work, *Snobbery with Violence,* is announced by E&S for 1971. It is said to be an attack on the writers of detection in the Twenties and Thirties (especially Agatha Christie and Dorothy Sayers) for their lack of responsible views on economic and social problems.

2181   Bump in the Night   E&S 1960

Inspector Purbright solves the crime, which consists in blowing up several hideous monuments in a small English town. The author cruelly describes the local worthies—all shopkeepers, newspapermen (his pet hate), and policemen. But they are not puppets, the wit is varied, and the incidents original. Detection fitful.

2182   Charity Begins at Home   Putn 1968

In this story again, the author tries to make every remark and comment witty, and thereby obscures the important elements in his plot and characters. The interweaving of murder for revenge with charitable canvassing is diabolically clever, but the desire to make every person contemptible leaves the reader indifferent to all. Even Inspector Purbright (a symbol in his name?) turns dull by comparison with so much turpitude.

2183   Coffin, Scarcely Used   E&S 1958

An excellently told tale of a syndicate of professional men in a small English town, who get polished off as the result of their crooked proceedings. The clever system of genteel prostitution and other details of their lives give opportunities for humor and suspense both. A first-rate job, Purbright doing his full share of work.

2184   Hopjoy Was Here   E&S 1962

After two very amusing tales of diversified interest, Watson let himself go all out for humor and ceased to bother about the crime save for its trappings, which of course are bizarre. Inspector Purbright has really no chance. The crime is the doing-in of a gay Lothario in a tub of H_2SO_4, but the reader has been anesthetized and does not care.

2185   Lonelyheart 4122   Putn 1967

The humor which swamped this author's third book is here kept under control, though it remains pervasive—and delightful. Inspector Purbright investigates the possibilities of crime inherent in the matrimonial bureau Handclasp House, and a very neat touch of the biter bit brings an amusing tale to a sound conclusion.

WAUGH, HILLARY (BALDWIN) (also H. Baldwin Taylor and Harry Walker; b. 1920)

b. New Haven; educ. Yale; ed. *Branford Review;* began writing detection after second world war. His work deserves more praise than it has received, no doubt because he has declined working to formula while not being graced with a distinctive tone.

2186   The Con Game Goll 1968

A police-routine story with a difference. The group of young-to-middle-aged residents of Stockford, Conn., among whom theft, adultery, and murder take place are put before us in clear detail ahead of and during Chief Fellows' systematic search for the criminals. The police work with clues while the suspects entangle themselves in lies and broils. Meanwhile the chief's ratiocinating is first-rate, as well as unimpeded by any friction with his helpers or any upheavals of his digestive tract: bravo!

2187   The Late Mrs. D. CCD 1962

An original twist on the "suspicious death" theme, notable also for abundance of clues well handled, and for a series of good situations hung upon the personality of a fat doctor whom all the women adore without reason. Brief and well written, by an author whose ideas repay attention.

2188   The Missing Man Goll 1964

The interest lies in a skillful and relentless search for the man who murdered a girl on a beach near a Connecticut lake. There are no clues to begin with; they are found, because imagined, somewhat in the manner of "The Nine-Mile Walk" (see No. 2604). The policemen are attractive and credible, and some of the other people are characters, too. The locale plays little part. The missing man, though, is a marvel, possibly strengthened by the story's roots in a real crime: the Yarmouth Beach Case of 1901.

2189   30 Manhattan East Goll 1968
A Case for Homicide North

Monica Glazzard, a virulent and well-hated columnist, is found dead in her luxurious bed, a presumable suicide. Medical examination shows that she has been quietly strangled, and since she is surrounded by dubious characters, the field is wide open. Lieutenant Frank Sessions, a gay dog who does one improbable thing, forges ahead through a mass of lies, clues, and alibis, and finds the culprit in what proves to be a first-rate surprise ending. The police routine is superbly done, that is, in no way overdone, and there is plenty of good dialogue, social commentary, and hard thought. Only one query: Do cops invariably refer to "the perpetrator"?

2190   WAUGH. See also:

Death and Circumstance	Dday 1963	Prisoner's Plea	Goll 1964
Jigsaw (= Sleep Long,		Road Block	Dday 1960
My Love)	Goll 1960	Run When I Say "Go"	Goll 1969
Last Seen Wearing	Dday 1952		

2191   WAYE, CECIL

The Prime Minister's Pencil Kins 1933

Early use of atomic energy for homicidal purposes. Narrative slow; characterization poor but attempted; British politics vague. Yet a word of praise is due the lucidity and reasonableness of several early discussions of the data. Not a success but a good try.

2192   WEBB, RUBIN (pseud. of Robert G. Weaver and S. Leonard Rubinstein)

  The Grave Maker's House   Harp 1964

Not detection, but suspense-in-sordidness. A brute in a Pennsylvania Dutch town terrifies everybody, including his young son, and presumably kills the boy's protector. That death sets the schoolteacher investigating until he and his pregnant wife are in danger, and so it goes—no reason for the chain to stop. Writing undistinguished.

2193   WEBSTER, HENRY KITCHELL (1875–1932)

  Who Is the Next?   BM 1931

Though it starts slowly, this story works up to a series of tense moments, all logically connected with an unusual situation. A double murder, private-plane piloting, a neat impersonation, and a delicate courtship are adroitly combined by a writer who knows how to use the language. He numbers this work among eight "romances"—not novels—and of the eight *The Sealed Trunk* and *The Man With the Scarred Hand* also sound as if they might (like this one) deal with crime and detection.

  WEES, FRANCES SHELLEY [JOHNSON] (b. 1902)

This Canadian author has been producing since 1930 and has about twenty stories of mild detection to her credit. She tries over and over again to create a competent amateur detective—doctor or lawyer—but always coquettes with him so as to damage his performance and the progress of the story. The Canadian scene is often well done.

2194   The Mystery of the Creeping Man   Burt 1931

Both this and *The Maestro Murders* (the author's second and first books respectively) will alienate the critical. A tangle of young love, cluttered plots, and a dehydrated scene reduce these works to the bare bones of *he said* and *she said;* e.g., the university and the city found in each of these tales are triumphs of anonymity. If one goes on to *This Necessary Murder* (HJ 1957) and is willing to tolerate the "Oh my goodness!" style, the failure to act that marks the handsome stalwart men who appeal to the lady author will show that they were not conceived for detective fiction. Let it be added that any of her stories that include Dr. Jonathan Merrill are likely to be superior to these.

2195   WEES. See also:

Faceless Enemy	Dday 1966
The Keys of My Prison	Dday 1956
My Lord, I Am Not Guilty	Dday 1954
Where Is Jenny Now?	Dday 1958

WELCOME, JOHN (pseud. of John N(eedham) H(uggard) Brennan, b. 1914)

b. Wexford, Ireland; educ. Sedbergh and Oxf.; began writing sporting tales, then adventure, while becoming also an indefatigable anthologist for Faber and Faber. In the first category of works, see *Red Coats Galloping* and *Mr. Merston's Hounds*. In the last, consult the *Best* series: *Gambling, Motoring, Hunting, Secret Service, Legal Stories*. He has also written *Fred Archer: His Life and Times*.

2196   Beware of Midnight   Knopf 1961

The present chase owes its interest to the hero's being an ex-convict (framed) and to the change of scene from rural Ireland via the Cotswolds to Spain, for once not over-glamorized. Good use of black magic, again subdued. The author loves fast and expensive cars, but one may doubt that from inside the boot of a well-built Aston Martin one could see the lights of a following car.

2197   Hell Is Where You Find It   Faber 1968
       A Richard Graham Adventure

R.G. is an ex- (horse-) racing man, who occasionally works at intelligence for an improbable cynic and department head, Sir William Bellamy. At the beginning of this tale, the narrator hero is badly in debt and much in request for his services as a spy. He soon finds that an old enemy has engineered the financial and other disasters that beset him and his friends, mostly in France. There is a beautiful girl drug addict whose allegiance seems to shift, and the usual sluggings and druggings and alternating victories. The final one comes a bit easily, but the whole make-believe moves fast. South-of-France ending.

2198   Run for Cover   Faber 1958

The author's first in the thriller genre and a bit cluttered with Lugers. The ambivalent villain, Rupert Rawle, doesn't quite come up to his excellent name; but Saint-Tropez and environs are vividly done and the use of sex is both subtle and (so to speak) functional.

2199   Stop at Nothing   Knopf 1960

Much like *Run for Cover:* a dissatisfied hero full of pills and self-pity over his former racing days; a couple of thugs and some ambivalent villains—all on the Côte d'Azur. One or two good fast-driving scenes and some pretty comparisons between what it takes to fly a plane and to drive a fast car are not enough to lift the spirits.

2200   Wanted for Killing   Faber 1965

The mixture as before, expertly done, but getting too predictable. The place is Corsica now, and J.W. knows how to make it attractive. The motive for blackmail and murder is freshly devised and the use of the

Foreign Legion is plausible. At the end, Richard Graham, who tells the story, decides to become a regular secret service man, not a free lance. *On s'assagit avec l'âge.*

WELLS, CAROLYN [Mrs. Hadwin Houghton] (also Rowland Wright; 1870?–1942)

b. Rahway, N.J.; educ. at home. Began writing jingles and children's books and editing anthologies, but never read detection till c. 1910, after hearing one of A. K. Green's novels read aloud. The vogue of the genre owes much to this gentle American lady (born hard of hearing), who wrote indefatigably (170 books, 75 of them mysteries), edited anthologies, and produced the first theoretical treatise on the form (see No. 3057). She often had ingenious ideas for stories, but her executive powers were slight—or swamped by a bad convention she did not resist or outgrow. To her credit be it said that although she wrote mostly magazine fiction—and feminine at that—she did not succumb to HIBK. Her husband was the son of the Boston publisher.

2201 The Mystery of the Sycamore   Lipp 1921

The worst cock-and-bull story ever put together by a rational being. The things said and done in this pseudo-political tale would not only not get published today, but would get the author committed by her loving friends and relatives. There is nothing worse than fantasy which does not know itself to be such—and this is it.

2202 The Omnibus Fleming Stone   Burt 1923

This obese volume contains *Vicky Van, Spooky Hollow, The Mystery of the Sycamore,* and *Curved Blades.* When Vicky Van does not fling herself into surmise and pursuit, Fleming Stone goes about reassuringly amid a dovecote of fluttered pigeons, male and female, making use of clues and characters competently enough to sustain his pretensions as a detective. It is the setting and the talk that are bad.

2203 Vicky Van   Burt 1916

The author was not a stupid woman, but in almost all her novels of crime she supplies the reader with very little he can get a grip on: the situations are silly, the characters unbelievable, and the detection so at odds with the foolishness as to seem intrusive when it appears. One good observation in the present book is that a woman leading a double life would make her appearance vary in either incarnation, while many of her belongings—cosmetics and the like—would be the same.

2204 Wells, C. See also Nos. 2854–7, 3057, and:

The Broken O	Lipp 1933
The Clue	Lipp 1909
The Diamond Pin	Lipp 1919
Feathers Left Around	Lipp 1922
The Room with Tassels	Doran 1918

2205 WELLS, SUSAN (pseud. of Doris Siegel)

Murder Is Not Enough   S&S 1939
   With diagrams

Assorted murders are committed on board one of a couple of yachts
anchored in Catalina harbor, but after the first 50 pages one no longer
worries about which of the three improbable red-haired girls had or had
not . . .

2206 WELLS, TOBIAS, is the pseud. of DeLoris Stanton Forbes, b. 1923,
who has written, alone or with Helen Rydell as Forbes Rydell, some two
dozen tales of crime aimed at horror and terror rather than mystery or
detection. A fair sample with a Boston scene is *Dead by the Light of the
Moon* (1967). For work done as Stanton Forbes, see *A Business of
Bodies* (1966).

2207 WENTWORTH, PATRICIA (pseud. of Dora Amy Dillon [Mrs. G. O.
        Turnbull]; also Delta; d. 1961)

This competent and productive exponent of the damsel-in-distress school
has written nearly eighty suspense stories, many of them featuring Miss
Silver as the gentle nurse-detective, others the equally woolly Inspector
Lamb.

Miss Silver Comes to Stay   Lipp 1949

This example of her art is not so anodyne as the bulk of her work but
it is clearly aimed at the tired and somewhat distrait reader: language and
gesture and event are girlish and trivial. For similar specimens, see: *The
Alington Inheritance* (1958), *The Fingerprint* (1956), *Pilgrim's Rest*
(1946), and *The Silent Pool* (1953), all published by Lippincott.

2208 WESTBROOK, PERRY (DICKIE) (b. 1916)

The Sting of Death   Arc 1955

At the Hammersmith Institute of Apitherapy the bees are not intrusive or
the plot opaque, but the routine of the incredible institute lends no verisimilitude to the conspiracy hatched by the greedy quack of 94. What
charmed WHT was the excellent humor and the good scenery between
Rutland and Whitehall. But are they enough to make one overlook the
universally childish behavior?

2209 WESTMACOTT, MARY (pseud. of Agatha Christie, q.v.)

A Daughter's a Daughter   Hein 1952

Not a detective story, but one of love discovered late in life. Under this
same name, A.C. has written six novels, from *Giant's Bread* (1930) to
The Burden (1956).

2210   WEYMOUTH, ANTHONY (b. 1887)

The Doctors Are Doubtful   AB 1935

This is the second appearance of Inspector Treadgold, who looks into poisoning by radium, by carbon monoxide, and by "incompatible" drugs. The physicians who cross the stage are acceptable figures, but it is to be hoped that the author's first, *Frozen Death* (1934), proceeded more simply.

2211   WEYMOUTH. See also:

Inspector Treadgold Investigates   Rich 1941

2212   WHALEY, F(RANCIS) J(OHN) (b. 1897)

Reduction of Staff   Skeff 1936

This attractive tale with its excellent title is a school story playing up the masters and playing down the boys. The two murders are sensibly accounted for, and the apparent alibi of the otherwise obvious suspect rather cleverly managed. Excellent clueing and writing.

2213   Swift Solution   Hale n.d. [1939]
         Map of countryside

A poor thing, all the more disappointing after the first. The villages portrayed do little to mitigate the tedium of the very un-swift solution to the problem: who killed the doctor's wife? The trickery of the answer adds to the general dissatisfaction, for it takes a Christie to do an Ackroyd.

2214   Trouble in College   Skeff 1936

A second, not so good as the first. St. Chad's College, Cambridge, is well done, and so are the several dons, including the dapper Dean of College, who wears a monocle and does the detecting. But the young men seem a bit young in thought and speech, though their doings are genuine college stuff. What is disappointing is the meandering, over-worded narrative and also the denouement, which is a give-away solution rather than the result of detective action.

2215   WHALEY. See also:

Challenge to Murder	Skeff 1937	The Mystery of	
Death at Datchets	Hale 1941	Number Five	Hale 1940
Enter a Spy	Hale 1941	Southern Electric Murder	Skeff 1938
		This Path Is Dangerous	Hale 1938

2216   WHEATLEY, DENNIS

Murder off Miami   Hutch 1936
         In U.S.: File on Bolitho Blane

As the American title suggests, this book attempts to give the ultimate in realism by adopting the form of routine reports, with photographs and physical clues, supplied by the detective in the field to his chief at the desk. The final section is sealed (or was when first published), so that the reader can solve the mystery, as the field man fails to do. The chief's comments in the sealed pages show how the experienced interpreter succeeds, but the astute reader will note an omission in the reports which is both unlikely and crucial. Otherwise a story of no great originality.

2217 WHEATLEY. See also:

File on Robert Prentice   Greenb 1937

Note: *The Man Who Killed the King* and *The Rising Storm* are fictional accounts of the French Revolution; *Sword of Fate, Black Baroness,* and *Scarlet Impostor* (1940–44) are about France and Germany in Nazi times.

2218 WHITE, ETHEL LINA, wrote a dozen indifferent loose-weave tales of adventure before the public at large became aware of her as the author of *The Wheel Spins* (1936), from which Alfred Hitchcock made the superb film *The Lady Vanishes.*

2219 WHITE, LIONEL

The House Next Door   Dutt 1956

In suburbia (it is commonly thought) the houses are all alike. Hence when a man comes home drunk and finds a corpse on what he thinks his hearth, he does not report it to the police but starts "dealing" with it. Meanwhile the reader is shown a planned robbery and murder, and it takes a deal of bad prose to connect the two halves of this poor imbroglio.

2220 Obsession   Dutt 1962

Perhaps some of the twenty-one other tales by this author do not involve drunkenness. Here alcohol helps a killing by a moll for whom the first-person narrator develops a consuming passion. After hiding from the police in Aiken and Las Vegas, he throttles her in "the moment of consummation." Bung ho!

2221 WHITE, L. See also:

The Night of the Rape   Dutt 1967

WHITE, R(EGINALD) J(AMES)

Lecturer in history at Univ. of Cambridge; won a joint award for his first detective story in a competition judged by Christie, Day Lewis, and Symons. All the competitors were university dons. R.J.W. seems to be specializing in the fictional treatment of true crime, very freely handled.

2222 The Smartest Grave   Harp 1961

Dedicated to the memory of F. Tennyson Jesse—another practitioner of fiction made from real life. The basis of this tale is the Moat House Farm murder of 1901. Atmosphere, delicate humor, and character study are evidently the chief aims; suspense and detection coming in poor seconds. But the writing is of high quality, admirably suited to the leisurely pace intended. (See also No. 303.)

Note that the motto-title comes from Sir Thomas Browne: "Though earth hath engrossed the name, yet water hath proved the smartest grave" (*Urn Burial,* Ch. I, par. 3).

2223   The Women of Peasenhall   Harp 1970

This second essay is based on the murder in 1902 of Rose Harsent, a pregnant housemaid, and the ensuing trial of William Gardiner. The author is free in his use of language and adaptation of manners and character to make his story read to us like a contemporary affair. Most enjoyable. (See also Nos. 2473 and 3068.)

WHITECHURCH, VICTOR L(ORENZO) (1868–1933)

This amiable Anglican clergyman, after a lifetime of writing pleasant clerical romances akin to George Birmingham's (q.v.), devoted his last half-dozen years to as many detective novels, which, according to him, he wrote without plan or premeditation. The verdict must be that he was the greatest improviser in the genre—all but one of his stories have distinctive merit. Perhaps the canon had been prepared for his task by his early interest in railways and his writings in the short form (see Nos. 2860–1).

Of his fiction other than detective, the following may be recommended: *A Canon in Residence* (1904), *A Downland Corner* (1913), *Concerning Himself* (1909), and *Mute Witnesses* (1933).

2224   The Crime at Diana's Pool   Unwin 1927

A good job of murder at a lawn fête, despite the sin of keeping certain evidence from the reader, as Haycraft has duly noted. A likable vicar is the unassuming detective aiding the professional. Some South American stuff, but smoothly worked in. The love interest, too, though typical of the twenties, is unobjectionable.

2225   Murder at the College   Coll 1932

The author must have wearied of the form—and what a pity!—for he was equipped to do a college story as well as anybody, and he had the experience of five years' work and five good tales. But his Exbridge is nonexistent, the puzzle childish, and the detection nil.

2226   Murder at the Pageant   CCC 1930

The strongest-knit of all the Whitechurch tales. The setting is excellent, the people all credible (albeit not especially original), and the detection and action steady from end to end.

2227   The Robbery at Rudwick House   Duff 1929

Whitechurch here combines his knowledge of clerical life and his capacity for soft-focus humor. The criminality quotient is low—who cares about stolen snuffboxes?—but it makes excellent reading. The big problem is whether Alexander Washington Lakenham is Archdeacon Lakenham's American nephew or an impostor.

2228 Shot on the Downs   Unwin 1927
        Author's Foreword on Method

The development of this tale, we are informed, observes the limitations laid down for *The Crime at Diana's Pool* (i.e., no foreknowledge of the criminal, no false alarms, no thrills). The result is a small masterpiece. It begins charmingly, and the trail which leads us to the one who did fire the famous shot is full of topographical and other interest.

2229 The Templeton Case   Clode 1924

Most promising for a first essay in a difficult genre, and attractive for its marine setting. The motives at work are mild and canonical, but their acceptability shows that when a story is written by a person whose mind, style, and literary ambition are in balance, the absolute degree of force or suspense is no measure of effectiveness. (That may be what is meant by *art*.)

2230 WHITFIELD, RAOUL (also Ramon Decolta)

        Green Ice   Knopf 1930

A well-to-do young man, who has served two years in Sing Sing for manslaughter, because he took the rap for his drunken girl friend's driving mistake, comes out determined to fight the big crooks who exploit little crooks. Naturally, he gets caught up in a counterplot designed partly to neutralize his effort and partly to achieve something else. He tells his tribulations in the first person and the result is so-so. A certain drive carries the improbable story forward; an excess of repetition and slang discourages reading. It is early and not fully matured tough stuff, though the language, scene, and attitudes are studied.

2231 WHITFIELD. See also:

        Death in a Bowl   Knopf 1931
        The Virgin Kills   Knopf 1932

2232 WHITNEY, ALEC

        Every Man Has His Price   WHA 1968
        A Novel of Industrial Espionage

The author of this unusual tale is multi-competent. He not only knows drug manufacturing and the chemistry that goes with it, but he has the art of making the significant details clear and even gripping. In addition, he has an eye for human traits and he uses his knowledge to good effect in making his people act as if from within. Finally, he has a sense of drama and suspense. The only question one could raise against this first-class piece of detection is that it idealizes not people, but the gadgets used: they work perhaps a little too perfectly. Still, the wry ending and the superb tag line atone for everything.

Note that the title of the book, a saying commonly attributed to Robert Walpole, garbles what he said. The Prime Minister was pointing to a particular group when he remarked, "Everyone of these men has his price."

Note further that the book is copyright not in the author's or publisher's name, but in that of Rhetoric, Ltd.

2233 WHYTE-MELVILLE, G(EORGE) J(OHN) (1821–78)

M or N   Longmans n.d. [1900]
Similia similibus curantur
Illus.

Although it is of modest length and contains a good scene burlesquing the theater of melodrama characteristic of its age, this story of crime and counterplot, revenge and planned abduction, love misunderstandings and separated sisters of like appearance proceeds and winds up in melodramatic fashion, with an accidental killing and a helpful insanity to leave everybody happy. Not recommended on any count.

2234 WICKWARE, FRANCIS SILL

Dangerous Ground   Dday 1945

Not a detective story, this solo effort recounts the trial of Serena Wilson for the murder of her paranoiac and detestable husband, with flashbacks to establish the presumption that the husband had killed himself vindictively. The defendant's psychiatrist lover puts a severe dent in his Hippocratic oath to secure evidence leading to the establishment of her innocence.

2235 WIEGAND, WILLIAM

At Last, Mr. Tolliver   Rine 1950

This novel, winner of the Mary Roberts Rinehart Prize for 1950, is an ambitious attempt to build former gang-doctor Tolliver into a hero-detective with a yen for service to humanity. A few nervous thrills in lieu of detection.

2236 WILCOX, COLLIN

The Lonely Hunter   RH 1969

Narrated in the first person by Detective Sergeant Frank Hastings, this account of multiple murder among the hippies of Haight-Ashbury has little to recommend it to the reader of detection. As a concise "trip" through our newest underworld it will serve, and suspense is kept up by the ex-alcoholic detective's hunt for his own daughter among the free-lovers of San Francisco—the whole not badly written.

2237 WILCOX. See also:

The Black Door   DM 1967

2238 WILDE, PERCIVAL (1887–1953). Two of his books have acquired a certain reputation—*Rogues in Clover* (1929) and *Tinsley's Bones* (1942). The short stories, either humorous or specialized in card-sharping episodes (see Part II), show the same breeziness and indifference to detail that has always put off these readers.

2239 WILKINSON, ELLEN (CICELY) (b. 1891)

The Division Bell Mystery   Harrap 1932

The drab title conceals a first-rate story, rightly praised in its day by Dorothy Sayers. Not only is Miss W. equipped by her work as parliamentary reporter to give a lively and picturesque account of life in and around the House of Commons, but she uses her knowledge of politics and persons to generate a great deal of drama and sketch some passionate encounters, political and private. The crime itself is less interesting than its detection, which is done by young Robert West, private parliamentary secretary to the Home Secretary, and more officially by Inspector Blackitt. All in all, a neglected landmark of the genre.

Note one defect: The author does not make clear how small the particular H. of C. dining room (Harcourt Room) actually is. One has to see it to understand some of the events that take place there.

2240 WILLIAMS, BEN AMES (1889–1953)

Death on Scurvy Street   Dutt 1929
      In Eng.: The Bellmer Mystery

A mixture of amateurish and competent writing, with definable characters emerging. The young reporter through whom we see the action is hardly believable—or a reporter—but the victim and his associates are well done, as is Inspector Tope. A curious, not a regular, period piece.

2241 WILLIAMS, BRAD (b. 1918)

Make a Killing   Mill 1961

The main setting is a "beat" retreat in Los Angeles, complete with lingo and arguments for escape from the square world, and this is made so good in itself and so integral to the murder and the love story (with a bit of California history added) that the reader is entertained and the demands of detection are satisfied. B.W. writes simply and with natural terseness —even though he thinks that a hassock is something worn by monks.

2242 WILLIAMS, BRAD. See also:

A Borderline Case   Mill 1960
Death Lies in Waiting   HJ 1961
Due Process (history of a crusade against
      capital punishment)   Goll 1961

2243 WILLIAMS, CHARLES* (b. 1909)

Don't Just Stand There   Cass 1967
      In U.S.: The Wrong Venus

Very funny in spite of improbability: a chap at loose ends makes up to a

* Different from the English author of religious thrillers (1886–1945).

girl on a plane after she hears the 300 Swiss watches he is smuggling into London begin to tick. Their partnership goes on to ghost-writing a sexy novel for a best-seller woman who is off on a binge, and winds up with a kidnapping in France, a tangle with the police, and a love feast in Rhodes—expertly done and told.

2244   The Sailcloth Shroud   VP 1960

There is much to admire in this clean-cut tale of suspense (and a little detection) involving a yachtsman innocently caught up in the doings of the underworld because he hired a wrong-un as deckhand. Without the intense moral overtones of J. D. MacDonald, the author nevertheless makes his hero, Stuart Rogers, emerge as a man, and he avoids multiplying incidents of violence past the point of disbelief.

2245   WILLIAMS, (GEORGE) VALENTINE (1883–1946). His numerous mysteries, such as *The Eye in Attendance* (1927) and *The Portcullis Room* (1934), have little detection, but *Death Answers the Bell* (1932) is better. He also wrote a study of the genre: "Gaboriau: Father of the Detective Novel": see No. 3058.

2246   WILLOCK, COLIN (DENNISTOUN) (b. 1919)

       Death in Covert   Hein 1961; orig. 1934

The author is an ardent fisherman and wildfowler, who manages to make attractive the blowing up of an odious fellow during a neo-Regency Rakes midnight steeplechase. Not great work, but it holds the attention.

2247   WILLOCK. See also:
       Death at Flight   Hein 1956
       Death at the Strike   Hein 1957

2248   WILMER, DALE (pseud. of Bill Miller, b. 1920)

       Dead Fall   Bouregy n.d. [1954]

A story of spying and murder in a California airplane plant. Not much detection, but a good account of hate-and-love between hero security officer and his boss, who is the heroine.

2249   WILSON, COLIN (b. 1931), is the brilliant essayist who won fame with his cultural analysis *The Outsider* (1955). He writes novels that explore the psychology of sex and crime—e.g., *Ritual in the Dark* (1959), and *The Glass Cage*, (1967) but that are quite remote from murder mystery or detection. As for Wilson's concern with true crime, see No. 3322.

2250   WILSON, P(HILIP) W(HITWELL) (1875–1956)

       Black Tarn   Farr 1945

An "historical," but not true-crime, story of detection. The year is 1909; an impoverished earl, with a castle on an island near the narrator's own place in Westmoreland, dies suddenly and the body is slipped into his private lake, like his ancestors'. The reporter Gus Trevining, Sir Julian Morthoe, assorted Scotland Yard men, and Gus's arch and tiresome bride, Ruth, slowly unwind an ingenious plot that deserved a less self-conscious treatment. Surely the worst of Wilson's three.

2251   Bride's Castle   Farr 1944

An odd kind of overwriting and antiquarian interest conceals from the reader as he goes along the absurdity of the mystery in the Earl's Italian Room, where his daughter and son-in-law, just married, are to take up residence. The machinery, human and inanimate, creaks; but somehow the characters impose themselves, and so does the reconstruction of the year 1893. Sir Julian Morthoe, the antiquarian detective, does some lucky jumping to conclusion.

2252   The Old Mill   Rine 1946

A reconstruction of the mood and attitudes of 1912 to set off two mysterious deaths in the rural surroundings of an old mill in Westmoreland. There is genuine detection and an ingenious (but not practicable) method of killing. The characters hold one's interest, except for the narrator's irritatingly coy wife. The prose is distinctive and at times odd. Reference is made to other local mysteries—see above.

2253   WINCHELL, PRENTICE (also Jay de Bekker, Dev Collans, Spencer Dean, and Stewart Sterling; b. 1895), writes glib and entertaining stories of fraud and shoplifting linked with murder (as Spencer Dean), and of murder committed in or out of the life of a deluxe hotel in New York (as Stewart Sterling). For titles, see under those pseudonyms. The rest of his output is equally slick and run-of-the-mill.

2254   WINSLOW, HORATIO (GATES) (b. 1882), and QUIRK, LESLIE W. (b. 1882)

Into Thin Air   CCD 1929

This dated American confection tries to make suspense out of séances leading to murder—a project that can, in the hands of a skillful narrator, succeed. In this attempt the *dramatis personae* are all out of the old property room and no spark of interest is struck off their startled or facetious dialogue. A university setting is referred to but not used—an entirely negligible book.

2255   WINTERFELD, HENRY

Detectives and Togas   Const 1957
      Illus. by Charlotte Kleinert

Written by a classical scholar, one hopes, and based on an actual inscription at Pompeii, this story of burglary and politics in first-century Rome is about young boys and done in the manner appropriate to them. For adults interested in Roman crime, Cicero is preferable (see No. 3113).

Inquest on an Ally   Cress 1948

A political interpretation of the Soviet Union after the war, based on the
author's leaders in the London press shortly after his return from being
a special correspondent in Moscow. The unfavorable response to his clear-
eyed vision of fact at a time when sentiment still prevailed in western
minds contributed to P.W.'s giving up journalism for fiction. In three of
his stories—one written fifteen years later—his firsthand knowledge of
Russia lends a unique coloring to the adventures. See Nos. 109, 947,
and 964.

2257   WISE, ARTHUR (also John McArthur)

The Death's Head   Cass 1962

This author's works and pseudonyms are difficult to trace, but Wise is his
name, though not his condition. The investigator Sanderson is an amorist
and a sorehead, who in this case looks into industrial (research) leakage,
succeeding largely by unpleasantness and persistence. Some good scenes,
but sameness of character pattern in all such stories matches sameness of
plot and yields the least common denominator of fun.

2258   WITHERS, E. L. (pseud. of George William Potter, b. 1930)

Diminishing Returns   Rine 1960

The title is a neat pun that expresses what happens to a group of six who
are killed off one by one. Some are well drawn, but their motives stay
obscure. The old hedonist and retired lawyer and the angry young lieutenant seem engaged in futile talk until the somewhat artificial surprise
resolution. The author, moreover, thinks arsenic acts immediately after
ingestion.

2259   WITHERS. See also:

The Birthday	CCD 1962
Heir Apparent	CCD 1961
The House on the Beach	Rine 1957
Royal Blood (true crime, to reach the throne)	Dday 1964
The Salazar Grant	Rine 1957

WITTING, CLIFFORD (b. 1907)

A Rotarian and a Traveler, who has edited a book of travels in China, and
who since 1937 has written a group of detective stories featuring Inspector
Charlton. In other tales the detective is Peter Bradfield, who was Charlton's
sergeant, and in more recent books, professional and amateur detectives
vary from story to story. Witting started feebly, improved to a point of
high competence, and has since shown a marked capacity for character
and situation, with uneven success in keeping up the detective interest.

2260   A Bullet for Rhino   H&S n.d. [1950]
        Inspector Charlton's Ninth Case

One tale of murder and detection in which the official detective and hero
does little or nothing toward elucidating the crime and yet retains our
respect. Inspector Charlton is charming and makes an excellent observer
on the sidelines. The setting (school—old boys' celebration) is perfect, the
characters diversified and picturesque, the villain wisely subdued, the
whole business written with complete mastery of all the requisite arts.

2261   The Case of the Michaelmas Goose   H&S 1938

Witting has elected to use a three-part presentation, the middle half showing the commission of the crime. This scheme spoils most of the fun. Inspector Charlton falls in love, but otherwise does little of note except to
diagnose correctly the injuries of a man (and of his watch) found at the
foot of a tower.

2262   Catt out of the Bag   H&S n.d. [1939]

Plot and characterization are sound, though Rutherford (Witting's
amateur detective and former proprietor of *Voslivres*) seems still a bit
soft around the edges. Another weakness is the hauling in of a second
amateur, Cloud-Gledhill, who also doubles as suspect. The tale is perhaps
too elaborate for its cargo.

2263   Dead on Time   H&S 1948
        Floor plan

Pleasant Witting but far from gripping. The crime is another pub killing,
the motive rather loosely moored, and the foiled perpetrators pretty
obvious from their first appearance.

2264   Let X Be the Murderer   H&S 1947
        A Novel of Detection

A fair example of Witting's middle period. Inspector Charlton solves a
case of inheritance and murder, but was too slow to prevent the crime.
Superb treatment of an elderly man whose sanity is constantly in doubt
and credibly kept in this tantalizing condition. The surprise ending comes
off well.

2265   Measure for Murder   H&S 1945
        Illus.

A most interesting variation in form, by means of interposed dialogue and
a kind of inverted technique based on a fictional diary that constitutes
Part I. In Part II, sorry as we are to lose the attractive narrator, we are
engrossed by Inspector Charlton's intense and rapid detection. He is
aided by Sergeant Martin (Bradfield is still in the ranks) and the turn at
the end into a new channel does not spoil the pleasure of consorting with a
dozen well-drawn characters and undergoing the rigors of their theatricals

in a cramped space. The work, until further notice, is Witting's master-piece.

Note: Scene is Lulverton, still in Southshire, but biggish town, not rural.

2266   Midsummer Murder   H&S n.d. [1937]

A well-wrought affair, which is fun to read, but which ends badly from lack of a good motive. Detective Inspector Charlton and Sergeant Martin are pleasant companions to the reader and to each other.

Note that it is the author's second work and far beyond anything one could have expected from his first, No. 2268.

2267   Mischief in the Offing   H&S 1958
        Epigraph from "The Adventure of the Copper Beeches"

A superb opening chapter by this master hand is followed by a series of incidents, puzzling in themselves, but rather overlaid by local color—the backward village and its quaint types. Inspector Clam is competent enough and the clues are fairly solid, but there is a lack of continuity in the telling of his efforts which lessens suspense. The reason why a pair of unlikely sailors and smugglers act as they do is obscured by an excess of picturesque vignettes with talk to match. A pity, for the start was excellent and the underlying idea not bad.

N.B. *Mischief* is the name of a boat.

2268   Murder in Blue   Scrib 1937

Downshire is a good place and the crime is provided with all manner of good properties, but the whole is deplorably handled. The murder of a police constable deserves a recital other than meandering and precious, and requires a sense of practicality here totally lacking.

2269   Murder in Whispers   H&S 1964

A case of identity: Is it his amiable bro-in-law or a chance-met crook who takes the house while the owner is abroad? Discovery and retribution well worked out, but too much local color. What detection occurs is done by the local police; the introduction of Peter Bradfield toward the end is gratuitous.

2270   Silence After Dinner   H&S 1953

No Inspector Charlton. Chinese doings. Bad.

2271   Subject—Murder   H&S 1945

A wartime effort perhaps too long on reminiscence and too short on detection, but memorable for the picture of an army camp and its tensions. Peter Bradfield emerges as a strong and likable person. Charlton functions as usual, and the victim is as appropriate as his name, q.v. by reading the book.

2272 There Was a Crooked Man   H&S 1960

Notable for variety of incidents and skill of plotting, as well as for the allusiveness and wit of the prose. Inspector Bradfield does some thorough detecting with clues numerous and freshly thought up. Rural Downshire is as attractive as ever.

2273 Villainous Saltpetre   H&S 1962

An excellent prologue with a surprise ending leads only to murky doings that show a playwright recluse in an island castle, hidden passages, fall over cliff, and characters inordinately like other characters in other novels.

The title is from Guy Humphries McMaster's *Carmen Bellicosum,* st. 3.

2274 WITTING. See also:

The Case of the Busy Bees	H&S 1952
Driven to Kill	H&S 1961

2275 WOOD, SALLY (CALKINS) (b. 1897), wrote *Murder of a Novelist* in 1946, a fussy and wordy story of murder in a Middlebury garden. It is disengaging from the start and does not entice one to look up *Death in Lord Byron's Room* (1948).

2276 WOODS, KATHERINE

Murder in a Walled Town   HM 1934
  The Private Memoirs of Wayne Armitage
  Floor plan of the inn at Neyronnes

The attractive title leads one to read of murder in a small and ancient town of central France, where Americans are stranded by the fall in the value of the dollar. But the author's lack of the most rudimentary fictional power makes this longish novel unreadable.

2277 WOODS, SARA (pseud. of Sara Hutton [Bowen-Judd])

Bloody Instructions   Harp 1962

One more detective story set in a solicitor's office, where the elderly partner gets stabbed at the end of an afternoon of interviews with clients. The cast is lifelike, and the writing is firm, but the author has a habit of playing down her climaxes—e.g., the big trial scene is allowed to fade away; nor are we ever given a clear account of how the crime was committed. The legal atmosphere saves the tale.

The title is from *Macbeth* I, 7, 9.

2278 The Case Is Altered   Harp 1967

The lady sticks pretty closely to her old last: Tony Maitland, with his stiff shoulder, pretty wife, and baronet uncle, is perhaps more mature here than before, but the plot is not particularly convincing. A French girl who is being forced into a loveless marriage would in real life scarcely generate the passions which lead to murder and a tremendous motor chase across London. Some exposure, but no detection.

2279   Error of the Moon   CCC 1963

Secret missile research on a lonely moor provides a chance for wrong-doing, which Antony Maitland, barrister, and his uncle Sir Nicholas Harding, Q.C., investigate together. This formula still works well here, the setting and the killings and the issues—some domestic—being well within the author's scope. She often seems nervously tempted to use excessive detail, and she huddles the ending, but she offers a palatable brew.

2280   Let's Choose Executors   Harp 1966

Something is wrong here at head and tail; only the middle is solid: the trial of a young woman accused of having poisoned her puritanical godmother for an unexpected inheritance. What spoils a good plot is the excess of petty feelings in Antony Maitland, the barrister, and the complicated and unconvincing explanations at the end. Judge and prosecutor change their spots.

The title is from *Richard II,* III, 2, 148.

2281   Past Praying For   Harp 1968

Starts off well: the relations between young Maitland, wife, and uncle are not so nagging, to them and to the reader, as they usually are. The legal business, too, is original, enabling Camilla Barnard to be twice on trial for murder. But things go badly to pieces at the end, when Maitland sells out in unbelievable fashion to a badly drawn Napoleon of crime.

2282   The Third Encounter   Harp 1963

The uncle-nephew relation between the lawyers of two generations is now a bit shopworn and so is the raking up of treachery among former members of the French Resistance. Furthermore, the hero leads too much of a charmed life.

2283   WOODS. See also:

Knives Have Edges   CCC 1968
Malice Domestic   Cass 1963

2284   WOODTHORPE, R(ALPH) C(ARTER) (b. 1886)

Death in a Little Town   CCD 1935

Not up to this author's best. The village setting and characters are poor-grade Christie, the detective is given little chance to shine, and the plot works itself out without help from the author. Cattiness prevails and provides some amusing conversation at a tea party.

Hard to classify: the author is no amateur but his aim here is diffuse and he seems to have no control over his story. The "humor" grows and grows at the expense of credibility and sense.

2286   The Public School Murder   N&W 1932

Is it true to say that, like beer, all school stories are good, but some are better than others? One's only regret about this tale (a small regret) is that Woodthorpe's pleasure in gossip and in his own invention of it are a bit too pronounced for perfect art. Still, the plot and persons are excellently contrived, and even if the business with the rifle is protracted, the story is fun throughout and the double twist satisfying.

2287   Rope for a Convict   CCD 1940

An engaging story that shows movie people "on the Moor": a beauty, a director, and a matinee idol entangled with an escaped convict who turns out unexpectedly. It is plausible and lively throughout. The most remarkable feature of the work is a twelve-year-old boy, who is at once credible and a pleasure to have around. Though the murder is incidental, there is detection, emotional concern, and narrative suspense.

2288   WOODTHORPE. See also:

Dagger in Fleet Street	Nich 1934
Death Wears a Purple Shirt	Dday 1934
The Shadow on the Downs	Dday 1935

2289   WOOLRICH, CORNELL (GEORGE) [HOPLEY-] (also George Hopley and William Irish; 1904–68) was born in New York City, the son of a civil engineer with whom he traveled widely as a solitary child and youth. Educated at Columbia College (JB's classmate for two years), he wrote there his first book, *Cover Charge,* in 1925. His style of writing and type of invention were close to those current in *Black Mask.* In all his later tales, his characteristic mood is that of intolerably tense fear or desire for revenge. He creates suspense without effort, especially in dingy surroundings, and the mechanics of his crimes are ingenious, like the surprise endings. But apart from breathless apprehension, the outcome is all that matters; which puts his work outside the range of ratiocinative literature. See, besides Nos. 1231/B-32: *Nightmare* (1938), *The Bride Wore Black* (1940), *Violence* (1958), and *The Doom Stone* (1961), as well as Part II, Nos. 2590 and 2864–9.

2290   WORSLEY-GOUGH, BARBARA (KATHLEEN) (b. 1903). The well-known author of *Cooking Ahead* (1957)* has published several novels and a book on London fashions since 1850. Her one venture in detection is *Alibi Innings* (1954), of special rather than general interest. Her half dozen other novels are "straight," including *The Sly Hyena* (1951), which has plenty of excellent malice and misdoing but does not qualify as mysterious.

* Not to be confused with the earlier *Cook It Ahead,* by Elinor J. Marvel (1951).

2291 WRIGHT, S(YDNEY) FOWLER (also Sydney Fowler; b. 1874), wrote some forty stories of adventure and mystery, marked by loose plotting and writing and inexistent characters. The earliest tales were the least slapdash—e.g., *The Case of Anne Bickerton* (also *Rex vs. Anne B.; The King Against Anne B.*) (1930), and *The Bell Street Murders* (1931).

2292 WYLIE, PHILIP (GORDON) (b. 1902). Has a dozen or so tales of crime-cum-detection (a modi-cum) to his credit, but they belong to the magazine world for which they were intended and do not compare with the author's satirical novels, in which his seriousness and literary gifts can rightly be appreciated. See in the mystery genre: *The Murder Invisible* (1932), *The Smuggled Atom Bomb* (1965), *The Spy Who Spoke Porpoise* (1969).

WYNNE, ANTHONY (pseud. of Robert McNair Wilson, b. 1882)

Thirty or more detective novels do not make an old master when they yield so little to bolster the often attractive titles: *Sinners Go Secretly, The Yellow Crystal, The Blue Vesuvius, Emergency Exit,* and so on. Their atmosphere is always solid and reassuring, as is the manner and often the oracular style of the snuff-taking Dr. Eustace Hailey, doctor-psychologist, but the working out is altogether too free of emotional force or mental activity.

2293   Death of a Banker   Lipp 1934

WHT feels honor-bound to comment on two good things in the present book, bad though most of it is. The author does work out a possible if not plausible explanation of the method by which a horseman was apparently stabbed to death in the middle of a paddock, the assailant unseen by fourteen onlookers. He also has Dr. Hailey meditate to excellent effect on the passing of the railway age, while the doctor's train pauses in York station.

2294   Death of a Golfer   Lipp 1937

A tale of false confessions, vague photography, and air guns made out of golf clubs. The thing is not serious though the telling is solemn.

2295   WYNNE. See also No. 2778 and:

    Death of a Shadow   Hutch 1952
    Door Nails Never Die   Lipp 1939

2296   XANTIPPE (pseud.)

    Death Catches Up with Mr. Kluck   CCD 1935

The author is obviously at home in the world of broadcasting; she was in fact the originator and writer of the earliest Sherlock Holmes program. Her first long story recounts, with satirical intent, the murder of a sponsor during "his" hour. It is the radio engineer, Benjamin Franklin Butts, who solves the case after a good deal of confusion, low humor, and technicalities. A good period piece about radio.

2297 YATES, DORNFORD (pseud. of [Major] Cecil William Mercer, 1885–1960). Born in England, educated at Harrow and University College, Oxford, he became a barrister; served in both wars; wrote thirty-four books; died in southern Rhodesia, having used his pseudonym in private life as well as in his books. Insofar as these were "mystery," they belonged to the perfunctory type on which critical attention cannot linger without unfairness to itself and the author. On its own level, *She Fell Among Thieves* (1935) has been praised for its dramatic qualities.

2298 YATES, MARGARET EVELYN [Taylor] (1877–1952), and BRAMLETTE, PAULA

The Widow's Walk   Dutt 1945

This collaboration by two unqualified amateurs is notable only as being an attempt to do a murder on Nantucket. This desirable event occurs on p. 105, but the previous dollops of local color do not justify so lengthy an exordium.

2299 YORK, ANDREW (pseud. of Christopher Robin Nicole, b. 1930)

The Co-Ordinator   Lipp 1967

The story of an English spy-assassin, for whom all the beauties fall and who, naturally, hates his job. Good taut dialogue and impossible feats of strength by hero. Much cruelty, disloyalty, duplicity, and some rather long-winded political background.

2300 YORK, JEREMY (pseud. of John Creasey, q.v.)

Come Here and Die   Scrib 1957
    In Eng.: Death of a Stranger (*by Michael Halliday*)

When reviewers can call this excellent in any respect, then anything goes. The story is a farrago about an American cousin (male) calling on an English girl whose family has deserted her for the weekend. He spends the night at her house after confessing he has covered up for a murder at his hotel, thinking his patron and benefactor had done it. More unbelievable incidents follow thick and fast, police nonplussed, reader noncaring.

2301 YOUNG, EDWARD (PRESTON)

The Fifth Passenger   Harp 1963

First-rate in the arts of suspense and pursuit. The traitor is believable and not either vilified or sentimentalized, and his solicitor friend who plays a thankless role of hanger-on in a Devon port town is well drawn and likable. The friend's seduction by a woman police officer in the course of duty is an absolutely top-notch sequence. Good local color and interesting matter re submarines.

2302　Young, Eric Brett (also Eric Leacroft)

The Murder at Fleet　　　　　　　　　　　Lipp 1928

A story that could have been first-rate if the author had devoted as much effort to choosing physical probabilities and giving physical descriptions as he has to producing dialogue and probing psychology. The motive of the murder is well engineered: a psychiatrist goads a paralyzed soldier, who is his brother-in-law, into expressing his suppressed emotions, doing this by way of cure. The doctor falls victim to his own success, while his secret purpose produces mystery and perplexity. There is a surfeit of detectives and too much vehiculation, but as a first effort it showed promise.

2303　Young, E. B. See also:

Dancing Beggars　　　　　　　　　　　　Lipp 1929

2304　Zangwill, Israel (1864–1926)

The Big Bow Mystery　　　　　　　Henry 1892/1891

Period piece though it is, this neat locked-and-barred-room puzzle retains much freshness and charm. It is brief (180 pages), humorous, and plays strictly fair with the reader. The victim of throat-slashing is a young, idealistic labor leader; the chief suspect an older ditto. How the retired Inspector Grodman solves the twin mysteries of access and escape is worth a couple of hours of any reader's time to find out.

Note: The story has been reprinted separately a number of times (1895 ff.); was included with other tales by the author in *The Grey Wig* (1903); was joined with Doyle's *Sign of the Four* to make a volume in the S. S. Van Dine Detective Library (1929), and has been anthologized *passim*.

PART II

SHORT STORIES,

COLLECTIONS,

ANTHOLOGIES,

MAGAZINES,

PARODIES,

AND PLAYS

Gems from the Literature

He shut his eyes in a supreme effort toward intensive thought.
    —Brian Flynn, *Conspiracy at Angel*

"The effect, according to the program, was antiphonal, but I liked it."
    —Delano Ames, *The Man with Three Chins*

His slender fingers dropped a slice of lemon into his cup with the deliberate motion of science.
    —R. T. M. Scott, "Bombay Duck"

From a quivering wretch she had become now a self-confident neurasthenic.
    —Arthur B. Reeve, "The Coke Fiend"

Gethryn then picked up a telephone that was not listed anywhere.
    —Philip MacDonald, *Warrant for X*

Very grey and very steady eyes which nearly met under thin eyebrows.
    —Quentin Reynolds, "The Man Who Dreamed Too Much"

. . . prone on his back . . .
    —Ross Macdonald, *The Way Some People Die*

2305   ADAMS, SAMUEL HOPKINS (1871–1958)

    Average Jones   BM   1911
      Illus.

Eleven short stories including the classic pair: The One Best Bet and The Man Who Spoke Latin, and all containing excellent snatches of the American scene before the first world war. The two just named are marked by true drama besides, and moderate detection.

2306   "A.L.C.C.," ed.   Hulton   1952

    Mystery
    Thirty-Six Tales from the London Mystery Magazine, *1949–1952*
    Foreword by the editor
    Illus.

An excellent representation of the magazine's early span of existence. Work by: Daniel Pettiward, Negley Farson, Christopher Morley, Algernon Blackwood, Kathleen Freeman, Geoffrey Grigson, Mary Fitt, Joan Fleming, and Sagittarius. Banesh Hoffmann takes part in a series of three articles on telepathy, and Lillian de la Torre contributes a good historical essay on George Barnwell. The volume deserves reprinting in paperback.

    ALLEN, (CHARLES) GRANT (BLAIRFINDIE) (also Cecil Power and J. Arbuthnot Wilson; 1848–99)

b. nr. Kingston, Ont.; educ. Edwards' Sch., Birmingham, and Merton Coll.; named Professor of Mental and Moral Philosophy in Negro Coll., Jamaica; ret. to Eng. 1876 and published works on evolution, the physiology of aesthetics, and over two dozen works of fiction, including *The Woman Who Did* (1895), which brought him notoriety and was much imitated in its treatment of sex.

2307   Hilda Wade   Putn   1900
    A Woman with Tenacity of Purpose
    With 98 illus. by Gordon Browne

This book is repeatedly put forward by booksellers and even bibliographers as a set of detective short stories. It is not even tolerable adventure or medical incident. Its only merit—quite adventitious—is that Conan Doyle wrote the last chapter on the indications of his dying friend and neighbor. More plausible specimens might be found in the stories on the rogue theme collected in: *An African Millionaire* (1897) and *Ivan Greet's Masterpiece, etc.* (1893).

2308   ALLINGHAM, MARGERY

    The Case Book of Mr. Campion   AM   1947
    Introd. by Ellery Queen

The seven stories range in time of publication from 1938 to 1946. They are: The Crimson Letter / Safe as Houses / The Case of the Question

Mark / The Definite Article / The Magic Hat / The Meaning of the Act / A Matter of Form.

Note that in the original collection (No. 2310) Crimson Letter was entitled The Case of the Longer View, and Magic Hat was The Case of the Hat Trick.

Note further that these last two plus The Case of the Question Mark were originally collected in *Mr. Campion and Others* (Hein 1939).

2309 Deadly Duo   Dday 1949
        In Eng.: Take Two at Bedtime

These two longish tales of malice domestic are a good deal alike. Pleasant reading of the Rebecca type, beamed explicitly at the feminine readers of glossy magazines. No Campion. The tales, each told in the first person by the heroine, are: Wanted: Someone Innocent and Last Act.

2310 Mr. Campion and Others   Hein 1939

A fair collection of short Campion stories. They usually show an idea, even if some are sketchily worked out. No Lugg to speak of, but perhaps too many young society girls who get into trouble and fawn upon Campion to enlist his aid, without any thought on their part or his of paying him in kind or any other way.

The contents of this volume form a bibliographical tangle with two others (Nos. 2308 and 2311). The present one has these cases: White Elephant / Borderline / Widow / Old Man in the Window / Name on the Wrapper / Hat Trick / Question Mark / Frenchman's Gloves / Longer View. (But see No. 2308 for alternative titles of two of these cases.)   .

Finally, the present volume contains five tales not about Campion: The Perfect Butler / It Didn't Work Out / Publicity / They Never Get Caught / The Mistress in the House.

2311 Mr. Campion: Criminologist   Macf 1963; orig. Dday 1937/1936

Contains the following Cases of: the Late Pig (a novella; see No. 32) / the White Elephant / the Man with the Sack / the Borderline / the Widow / the Pro and the Con / the Old Man in the Window.

The next four after *The Late Pig* are excellent work; the last two inferior. The use of summary head notes to each story adds nothing to one's faith in Mr. Campion.

2312 "Mr. Campion's Lucky Day"   *EQMM* Apr 1947

Too short a short for much interest to develop in Campion's detection, though one or two points are well observed.

2313 "One Morning They'll Hang Him"   *EQMM* Aug 1950

One of Margery's triumphs: just the right length, beautifully told, and with more characterization and clueing than one would suppose it possible to cram into 12 pages. Campion *thinks* from beginning to end and therefore knows how to prevent a miscarriage of justice.

2314   AMBLER, ERIC

"The Case of the Landlady's Brother"   *EQMM* Feb 1949

A crime story in which Dr. Czissar lectures the CID man as he tells him
the facts of an ordinary triangle murder. The telling is compact and attractive and inconclusive on purpose.

2315   ANDERSON, FREDERICK IRVING

"Murder in Triplicate"   *EQMM* Dec 1946

An old-style story of detection by means of information received plus
special knowledge, neatly put together and equipped with a strong windup.

2316   ANONYMOUS, ed.

The Best Detective Stories of the Year 1929   Faber 1930
     Introd. by the editor

The Introduction is a brief apologia for the short detective story. It says
much for the standards of that (golden) age that there should be so little
poor stuff in this collection of nineteen tales. In addition to half a dozen
famous authors, others less well known make valuable contributions.
Among these Vincent Cornier's The Flying Hat is outstanding. The table
of contents:

Mrs. Belloc Lowndes	A Labor of Hercules
Anthony Berkeley	The Avenging Chance
G. K. Chesterton	The Purple Jewel
Agatha Christie	S.O.S.
Vincent Cornier	The Flying Hat
Marten Cumberland	Mate in Three Moves
Ralph Durand	Artful Jane
Arlton Eadie	Written in the Waters
G. A. England	Ping-Pong
J. S. Fletcher	The Button and the Banknote
Maurice Leblanc	Arresting Arsene Lupin
E. Phillips Oppenheim	The Great Bear
Stephen Phillips	A Man with Big Hands
H. M. Richardson	The Man Who Made Rings
Grenville Robbins	The Broadcast Murder
Will Scott	Clues
H. deVere Stacpoole	The Ten Franc Counter
Valentine (=A. T. Pechey)	An Exploit of the Adjusters

2317   Best Mystery Stories   Faber 1933

The editor (or perhaps it was merely a printer's devil who functioned in
that capacity) is to be congratulated on the wide variety of tales culled
from various British periodicals. Though a mixed bag, the twenty-five
tales include several that feature true detection, such as the two by
Douglas Newton with detective Paul Toft. W. A. Darlington, H. de Vere

Stacpoole, and David Evans also contribute to the genre, and among the eighteen other authors only one (Christie) is a frequenter of anthologies.

2318   "The Blue Wash Mystery"   *EQMM* Jan 1951

A mystery indeed: what happened when the family came back to find that the painters had been in and changed the color of the walls? Very short, rather ancient (1889), and attributable to the right author by anyone who owns the *Wide Awake Pleasure Book* of that date.

2319   A Century of Detective Stories   Hutch n.d. [1935]
       Introd. by G. K. Chesterton

Forty-five stories by forty-four strong practitioners of the twenties and thirties, almost all worth reading. Poe is represented by The Purloined Letter and The Gold Bug. The uncommon tales to be noticed are: G. D. H. and M. Cole, A Lesson in Crime / Christopher Bush, The Hampstead Murder / Antony Marsden, Heredity (not det.) / W. F. Harvey, The Lake (superb).

The Introduction by Chesterton is the best and briefest apologia for the short form to be found anywhere. It is in fact found in two places in this book—at the front, where it belongs, and then (perhaps because it is only two pages long) a piece of it occurs again at the bottom of p. 256.

Note also that Abel Crew, by Mrs. Henry Wood, author of *East Lynne,* is a fine piece of rural narrative, though entirely null as crime or detection.

2320   Crime and Detection   OUP 1930
       World's Classics, Second Series

Far inferior to E. M. Wrong's first series, this group of eleven tales (without Introduction) relies on well-known titles for any appeal it may have had. That must have been small, for the book has not been kept in print. The contents:

Hawthorne	Mr. Higginbotham's Catastrophe
Poe	The Mystery of Marie Roget
Doyle	The Bruce-Partington Plans
Phillpotts	Prince Charlie's Dirk
W. W. Jacobs	A Tiger's Skin
Freeman	The Man with the Nailed Shoes
H. Steevens	The Leak
Sapper	The Hidden Witness
Sayers	A Matter of Taste
Chesterton	The Five Swords
N. Olde	Black and White

Note that the Sayers is one of her poorest efforts, and not detection; also that the Chesterton (which is fair) is attributed to *The Man Who Knew Too Much,* but it does not appear in the Harper edition of that work.

2321   Evening Standard Detective Book   Goll 1951
       Second Series

Thirty-two stories, mostly short and many good, first published in the
London *Evening Standard*. Included are:

Adrian Alington	Sealed Letter
	Not So Deep as a Well
Josephine Bell	The Packet-Boat Murder
Nicolas Bentley	Double Exposure
Leo Bruce	Murder in Miniature (Sgt. Beef)
Victor Canning	A Matter of Time
Michael Carreck	Death Warrant
Edmund Crispin	Humbleby Agonistes (G. Fen)
Edmund Crispin & Geoffrey Bush	Baker Dies (G. Fen; clever)
Freeman Wills Crofts	The Suitcase (French)
Lord Dunsany	A Tale of Revenge
J. Jefferson Farjeon	Sgt. Dobbin Works It Out
Peter Fraser	An Interesting Development
Anthony Gilbert	What Would You Have Done?
Michael Gilbert	The Indifferent Shot
Cyril Hare	I Never Forget a Face
	As the Inspector Said . . .
Richard Hull	Mrs. Brierly Supplies the Evidence
Michael Innes	A Dog's Life ⎱ (both Appleby
	The Furies ⎰ and good)
Selwyn Jepson	Letter of the Law
Milward Kennedy	The Accident (very neat)
Tom Lake	A Most Reliable Witness
E. C. R. Lorac	A Bit of Wire-Pulling (good)
Gladys Mitchell	The Jar of Ginger ⎱ (both above
	Manor Park ⎰ par for G.M.)
Stephen Pollak	Split-Second Salvage
E. R. Punshon	Where There's a Coffin There's
	a Way (Insp. B. Owen)
Michael Rogers	The Nine of Diamonds
Julian Symons	The Desk ⎱ (F. Quarles
	The Case of S.W.2 ⎰ in both)
Alan Thomas	Force of Habit

2322 **Fifty Famous Detectives of Fiction**   Odhams n.d. [1938]
     Illus.

A landmark in anthology-making, this huge volume raked the literature
for representative tales and achieved comprehensiveness at the cost of
cubical shape and 696 pages of print. The authors include: Allingham,
Bailey, Bentley, Berkeley, Bramah, Bush, Carr, Chesterton, Christie,
Crofts, Doyle, Fletcher, Frome, Daly King, Knox, Leblanc, Lowndes,
Oppenheim, Post, Rhode, Sayers, Thomson, Wallace, Wynne, and several
others.

2323 My Best Detective Story   Faber 1931

Twenty-two detective stories, selected by their authors, and containing
several good ones not easily found elsewhere (e.g., the Beresford, the
Crofts, the Knox). In the order of printing they are:

"Sapper"	The Horror at Staveley Grange
Dorothy Sayers	The Inspiration of Mr. Budd
E. Phillips Oppenheim	The Thirteenth Card
Father R. Knox	Solved by Inspection
Ian Hay	Petit-Jean
R. Austin Freeman	A Mystery of the Sand Hills
G. K. Chesterton	The Queer Feet
H. deVere Stacpoole	The Chinese Girl
H. C. Bailey	The Violet Farm
H. A. Vachell	My Double
J. J. Bell	The Message on the Sun-Dial
J. D. Beresford	The Artificial Mole
Bertram Atkey	George H. Jay and the Lady from Moolgamboolloo
Mrs. Belloc Lowndes	Popeau Intervenes
Thomas Burke	The Hands of Mr. Ottermole
Agatha Christie	Philomel Cottage
Freeman Wills Crofts	The Greuze
John Ferguson	The White Line
J. S. Fletcher	The Convict and the Clerics
Gilbert Frankau	Misogyny at Mougins
Ernest Bramah	The Tragedy at Brookbend Cottage
G. R. Malloch	Murder Without Motive

2324 My Best Mystery Story   Faber 1939
A Collection of Stories Chosen by Their Own Authors

The well-versed reader's opinion will be likely to quarrel with some of the choices, which are as follows:

P. Cheyney	Portrait of a "G" Man
Agatha Christie	Dead Man's Mirror
J. J. Connington	The Thinking Machine
Freeman Wills Crofts	Mr. Pemberton's Commission
J. Jefferson Farjeon	The Room in the Tower
Arthur Gask	The Destroyer
Bruce Graeme	The Empty House
Cecil Freeman Gregg	Second Sight
Leonard R. Gribble	The Case of Jacob Heylyn
Philip MacDonald	Ten O'clock
Laurence W. Meynell	The Cleverest Clue
Arthur Mills	It Happened in China
Nigel Morland	Double Lover
Ellery Queen	The Adventure of the One-Penny Black
John Rhode	The Vanishing Diamond
Edmund Snell	The Head of Taui-Passu
Roy Vickers	The Parrot's Beak
E. Charles Vivian	Locked In
Ethel Lina White	An Unlocked Window

The Christie contribution is long, but not a novel. MacDonald's Ten O'Clock would be excellent if at the end the horror were not spoiled by protracted hysterical writing. The Connington and the Crofts are both poor samples of their authors' work; yet the collection as a whole is fair enough.

2325 ANVIL, CHRISTOPHER

"The Problem Solver and the Burned Letter"   *EQMM* Apr 1967

The singular professional "heuristician," Richard Verner, smacks of the omniscient detective of former days, but though he explains that his label means problem-solver, he confines himself to single clues that are diagnostic in simplified situations, whereby he leaves police and suspects open-mouthed. This story (with an original clue in it) ends: " 'Heuristician,' Verner smiled. . . ." To which the reply that suggests itself is: "Heuranother."

2326 "The Problem Solver and the Hostage"   *EQMM* Feb 1966

Richard Verner, the "heuristician," uses working hypotheses, true or not, to reach his goals. Here is his second problem: how to keep a shooting type of burglar from killing the little girl he has taken as hostage when he found himself cornered. The solution is worthy of the dilemma and of the author.

2327 ARLEN, MICHAEL

"Fool-Proof"   *EQMM* Apr 1947; orig. 1923

An excellent story in which the official detectives are led up the garden path by a skillful amateur in a case of some complexity and originality, set in Cannes and involving child murder. Unfortunately, a first-rate tale is spoiled by a needlessly long explanation, with a double motive where one would have served.

2328 ARMSTRONG, CHARLOTTE

"The Splintered Monday"   *EQMM* Mar 1966

A moving and delicately told story about the character of truth as it relates to a crime, but not detection and not fundamentally about crime.

2329 ASHDOWN, CLIFFORD (pseud. of R. Austin Freeman, q.v., and Dr. John James Pitcairn)   Train 1968; orig. 1902
The Adventures of Romney Pringle

In their salad days the two authors were friends, united by scientific training and literary ambitions. They wrote these tales together for *Cassell's Magazine* and managed to get this half dozen published in book form. The plots run true to type in presenting an ingenious fellow who swindles the crooked and well-to-do in order to help the poor and victimized, but there is enough dash in the prose and enough common sense in the tricks to deserve the modern reader's attention. Freeman was surely the partner who scattered excellent clues and inferences throughout the adventures.

2330 The Further Adventures of Romney Pringle   Train 1969
Introd. by August Derleth
Memoir by Norman Donaldson

The six stories making up this collection have never previously appeared in book form; they came out in *Cassell's Magazine* beginning in 1903.

Slender as they are, they evoke the early years of the century, with much emphasis upon cycling, at which R.P. is expert. Donaldson's 8-page essay, "Clifford Ashdown: A Retrospect," is excellent, and makes one eager to see his forthcoming biography of Freeman. Here he gives credit to Pitcairn for tiding his friend over a bad moment by helping him to a prison medical post.

2331   ASHTON, EDWARD G.

"Cameron's Cave"   *EQMM* Dec 1950

A highland setting with all the accessories of superstition gives "my uncle Hamish" the opportunity to solve a murder, by a combination of motive and observed clues. Simple but good.

2332   ASQUITH, CYNTHIA

The Black Cap   Hutch n.d. [1929]
New Stories of Murder and Mystery

The first "story" is a playlet, Barrie's effective enigma Shall We Join the Ladies?, not before published. The other thirteen tales are all by good writers and favorable samples of their work, though they are not exactly of a kind as to effect: "murder and mystery" covers a lot of ground. The group contains:

L. P. Hartley	The Killing-Bottle
Mrs. Belloc Lowndes	An Unrecorded Instance
Barry Pain	A Considerable Murder
Hugh Walpole	The Taru
Arthur Machen	The Islington Mystery
Edgar Wallace	Circumstantial Evidence
W. B. Maxwell	The Prince
Oliver Onions	The Smile of Karen
D. H. Lawrence	The Lovely Lady
Shane Leslie	The Hospital Nurse
Elizabeth Bowen	Telling
W. Somerset Maugham	Footprints in the Jungle
Lady Cynthia Asquith	The Lovely Voice

2333   AUMONIER, STACY

Miss Bracegirdle and Others   Hutch n.d. [1923]

Not a collection of detective short stories (though often listed as such in catalogues) but a group of tales among which three fleetingly relate to crime: Miss Bracegirdle Does Her Duty / The Accident of Crime / The Brown Wallet. Expert storytelling and some philosophy, but no concentration on crime or tracking it down.

2334   BAILEY, H. C.

A Clue for Mr. Fortune   Stamf 1946; orig. 1936

Six short stories, all but three found in one or another of our anthologies. The three additional ones are: The Torn Stocking / The Swimming Pool / The Dead Leaves. The last of these is the best.

2335 "A Matter of Speculation"   *EQMM* Feb 1961

The creator of Reggie Fortune here introduces his "lady detective," the Hon. Victoria Pumphrey, in her first case. A slender but amusing story of confused identities and inheritance. Victoria is a convincing and urbane runner-up for Miss Marple.

2336 Meet Mr. Fortune   CCD 1942
      A Reggie Fortune Omnibus

Contains, in addition to a 4-page biographical sketch of Reggie Fortune by the author, who knew him well, the following, of which The Greek Play is a masterpiece:

The Bishop's Crime (full-length   The Wistful Goddess
  novel; see No. 89)   The Little Finger
The Broken Toad   The Holy Well
The Yellow Slugs   The Yellow Cloth
The Hole in the Parchment   The Point of the Knife
The Gypsy Moth   The Yellow Diamonds
The Greek Play   The Brown Paper

2337 Mr. Fortune Here   CCD 1940

The last volume of Mr. Fortune tales in the series of over a dozen issued between 1920 and 1940. One or two of the nine tales have been extensively anthologized (marked * below), others reflect too clearly the author's concern for mistreated children to the disadvantage of the story (marked cc), while one or two others are good enough to be looked up (†).

†The Brown Paper   The Primrose Petals (cc)
*The Bottle Party   The Spider's Web
†The Fight for the Crown   The Gilded Girls
*The Blue Paint   The Bird in the Cellar (cc)
The Point of the Knife

2338 Mr. Fortune Objects   Dday 1935

This volume contains: The Broken Toad / The Angel's Eye / The Little Finger / The Three Bears / The Long Dinner / The Yellow Slugs.
     All are good Bailey, the first, second, and fifth being among his best. The Angel's Eye has a twist at the end (planting evidence against the criminal so as to make prosecution impossible) unmatched in any other tale known to these readers. In most of these stories Reggie is amusing and sapient throughout, not foolish as he sometimes came to be.

2339 Mr. Fortune's Practice   Meth 1923

Seven excellent stories, forming the second volume of Reggie Fortune's exploits (*Call Mr. Fortune* appeared three years earlier), and including the fine Unknown Murderer, in which Fortune nearly meets his end. He is also courting Joan Amber and marries her; his mannerisms—later so irritating—are here pleasantly characteristic, real wit inspiring the back-chat with Lomas.

Contents:

I. The Ascot Tragedy
II. The President of San Jacinto
III. The Young Doctor
IV. The Magic Stone

V. The Snowball Burglary
VI. The Leading Lady
VII. The Unknown Murderer

2340 BALDWIN, WILLIAM

"The Last Man Aboard" *EQMM* Feb 1964

Perhaps worth noting because of its neat use of the railway scene (slightly transformed New Canaan branch of the former N.Y.N.H. & H.R.R.), combined with a motive for murder credible to railway buffs. The detection is competent and relies on tried-and-true methods. The author's first story.

2341 BARNARD, ALLAN

The Harlot Killer DM 1953
The story of Jack the Ripper in fact and fiction
Introd. by the editor

Thirteen accounts, which take in the best-known: Burke, The Hands of Mr. Ottermole / Sansom, The Intruder / Lowndes, The Lodger / Pearson, Jack the Ripper / Bloch, Yours truly: Jack the Ripper; and then: the Spanish Sherlock Holmes pastiche found by A. Boucher, Jack el Destripador; a fine sequence of newspaper reports from the London *Times* (1888), and half a dozen more short fictions.

2342 BARR, ROBERT (also Luke Sharp; 1850–1912)

b. Glasgow; educ. Toronto; journalist in Detroit and London; collaborator of Jerome K. Jerome and Stephen Crane.

The Triumphs of Eugene Valmont Hurst 1906

Only one story—and not of detection at that—makes this collection interesting: The Absent-Minded Coterie. A tale of elegant swindling, achieved by simple yet well-jointed means, this little masterpiece outstrips all the author's other efforts and has deservedly been reprinted over and over again.

2343 BARR, STEPHEN

"The Unique Guinea" *EQMM* Oct 1959

The familiar setup: a unique coin is passed around the table; it disappears; the hero refuses to be searched. The solution is pretty good, but there was no need to make two historical boners, one about the Walpole administration and one about Greuze.

2344 BARZUN, JACQUES, ed.

The Delights of Detection Crit 1961
Introd. by the editor

A grouping of seven classic, seven modern, and three historic tales of detection, unmixed with specimens of other genres. Useful as an indication of the variety within the one line pursued and as the nearest repository of the early detective skits by Beaumarchais, William Leggett, and Alexandre Dumas (qq.v.).

2345 BASHFORD, [SIR] HENRY

"The Man on Ben Na Garve"
In: E. C. Bentley, ed., The Second Century of
Detective Stories (No. 2350)

Sir Henry has written a good short tale of dinner-table conversation in which the duty to inform the police of suspected crime is discussed. As an example of responsibility avoided but later met, a guest tells of his experiences while bird-watching in Scotland. The point is brought home to the assembled company by a neat twist at the end.

2346 BEACH, STEWART, ed.

This Week's Stories of Mystery and Suspense   RH 1957
Introd. by Alfred Hitchcock

Thirty short shorts—all 7 or 8 pages—preceded by an essay on how to write mystery stories (by the editor) and a glossary of writers' terms covering only one page. It is all quickie come, quickie go.

2347 BEAUMARCHAIS, PIERRE AUGUSTIN CARON DE (1732–99)

"Cloak Without Dagger"   1776
Trans. by Jacques Barzun of Gaîté faite à Londres
In No. 2344

Beaumarchais was a passionate admirer of Voltaire's, and it is from the famous chapter in *Zadig* (q.v.) that he drew his inspiration for this skit of pure detection. Its historic importance is that it is the first attempt to make detection contemporary and matter-of-fact, rather than legendary and miraculous. (See also No. 2622.)

2348 BENNETT, ARNOLD

The Loot of Cities   Alston 1905
*Being the Adventures of a Millionaire in
Search of Joy: a Fantasia*

The six episodes in this semi-continuous tale present Cecil Thorold as the adroit and rich young man who does good and thwarts crime by illicit if not illegal methods. It is Bennett's contribution to the Raffles literature (see also Ashdown, Nos. 2329–30), but is well above it in style and observation of life, and superior also to the longer and uneven *Grand Babylon Hotel* (No. 142).

2349 The Night Visitor and Other Stories   Dday 1931

This varied collection contains Murder, a good tale of semiaccidental murder that unfolds in a direct yet unusual fashion and takes into account the detectives' calculations and the actuality of clues. Some irony about detection and the clichés about murder add to the merit of this noteworthy piece.

Strange Affair in a Hotei has some criminal features, but is a rather silly story.

2350 BENTLEY, E. C., ed.

The Second Century of Detective Stories   Hutch n.d. [1938]
    Introd. by the editor

The author of *Trent's Last Case* (q.v.) has done a remarkable job in sticking to real detection for his omnibus, but the biographical notes on the thirty authors are tantalizingly poor; one doubts that Bentley wrote them. Many good and inaccessible tales more than compensate for this lack. The items are drawn from Livingston's *Dodd Cases*, the Coles' *Superintendent Wilson's Holiday*, Wade's *Here Comes the Copper*, Bramah's *Eyes of Max Carrados* (qq.v.).

Also: Knox's tale The Motive and H. Russell Wakefield's The Inevitable Flaw. One of F. Tennyson Jesse's rare Solange Stories is included, and samples from Bailey, Bell, Chesterton, Gribble, Keverne, Leacock, Oppenheim, Phillpotts, Wallace, plus well-known tales by Conan Doyle, Bramah, Bentley, Freeman, and Sayers.

2351 BENTLEY

Trent's Case Book   Knopf 1953
    Introd. by Ben Ray Redman

This omnibus adds to the author's two classic novels the collection *Trent Intervenes*, made up of twelve short stories:

The Genuine Tabard	The Old-Fashioned Apache
The Sweet Shot	Trent and the Bad Dog
The Clever Cockatoo	The Public Benefactor
The Vanishing Lawyer	The Little Mystery
The Inoffensive Captain	The Unknown Peer
Trent and the Fool-Proof Lift	The Ordinary Hairpins

All are ingenious and contain much more than "the one gimmick" that most short-story writers exploit beyond its worth. The first three are little classics, The Inoffensive Captain is funny, and The Little Mystery is charming.

Note that the tale about a man who circumvents his shrewish wife by a secret will clued in his rock garden is not among these twelve. It is The Ministering Angel, in *Famous Stories of Code and Cipher* (see No. 2360).

2352 BERESFORD, J. D.

The Meeting Place and Other Stories   Faber 1929

Contains The Artificial Mole and The Clever Mr. Fall, the only near-detective stories in the collection. One or two others touch on the fringes of mystery, but without professional or even qualified amateur detection—

e.g., The Last Tenants. Most of the tales are pleasantly romantic stories, with a fair dose of love interest.

2353   BERKELEY, ANTHONY

"The Avenging Chance"   EQMM Apr. 1950; orig. 1929
    Also in Nos. 2361 and 2780

This long short story is the author's masterpiece: not a word, move, clue, or comment is out of place, and nothing omitted that should be there. The situation, moreover, is classical, like the beautifully justified runaround. How good it all is may easily be seen by comparing the tale with its longer version, *The Poisoned Chocolates Case* (see No. 168). Filler reduces tension and with tension relaxed, pleasure goes.

2354   BLACK MASK (magazine) ran from 1920 to 1950, part of a string of pulp magazines collectively called Popular Publications and owned by their founders, Henry Steeger, Sr., and Harold Stanford Goldsmith (q.v.).

Those magazines, but principally *Black Mask,* developed the talents of Dashiell Hammett, Raymond Chandler, Erle Stanley Gardner, Edna Ferber, and their contemporaries of the thirties, though older writers, such as the Baroness Orczy, C. S. Forester, and T. S. Eliot, were also among the contributors. The tough American crime tale was the chief new product of *Black Mask.* After it had ceased publication, a *Black Mask* section was added to *EQMM,* inaugurated in May 1953 with Hammett's Gatewood Caper (see No. 2547) and Woolrich's Dormant Account.

Note that the title *The Black Mask* was first used by E. W. Hornung for a group of Raffles stories (GR 1901).

2355   BLACKWOOD, ALGERNON

"First Hate"
    In: No. 3390

A splendid story of crime and impunity; setting: the western woods of Victoria, B.C. All this writer's other tales treat of the supernatural, so far as these readers have been able to ascertain.

2356   BLOCHMAN, LAWRENCE G.

Clues for Dr. Coffee   Lipp 1964
    Introd. by Dr. Milton Helpern

This second series of shorts about Dr. Coffee is written with the same competence in science and ineptitude in art which characterized the first set. The plots are reasonably varied but the people are cardboard.

2357   Diagnosis Homicide   Lipp 1950
    Introd. by Thomas A. Gonzalez, M.D.
    Pref. by the author

Eight short stories, with remarks on the coroner's inquest versus the medical examiner. The tales appeal to the popular-mechanics strain in the reader and their science is sound enough, but they must be classed (on their level) with the modern genre of nonfiction fiction.

2358   "The Man Who Lost His Taste"   *EQMM* July 1958

An interesting short tale of murder in the world of professional tea-tasters, with the pathologist Dr. Coffee contributing good observation as well as technical know-how to the police case.

2359   BOILEAU, PIERRE

"Triangle"   *EQMM* Dec 1948
Trans. by Anthony Boucher

A tale of double bluff in the commission of murder for gain. Brisk and startling, though the elements are banal.

2360   BOND, RAYMOND T., ed.

Famous Stories of Code and Cipher   Rine 1947
Introd. by the editor

The editor not only distinguishes between codes and ciphers, but gives numerous illustrations of the latter plus information about the deciphering of Japanese codes in the second world war. The stories number sixteen, and are mainly familiar items by the following authors: Freeman, Post, Bentley, M. R. James, Boucher, Poe, Doyle, Barker, O. Henry, Christie, Webster, Sayers, O'Higgins, Allingham, Alfred Noyes, and De la Torre.

The notable ones are those by Bentley, Webster, M. R. James, Poe, and O. Henry—the latter's Calloway's Code being both original and amusing.

2361   Handbook for Poisoners   Rine 1951
A Collection of Famous Poison Stories,
with an Introd. on poisons

The editor's remarks consist of 75 pages of miscellaneous information about poisons and poisoning, from Socrates to Crippen. The section on snake venom and other animal poisons is better than the rest. A final group of notes on twenty common poisons (actually only nineteen) is poorly selected but reasonably accurate on most items.

The twelve tales include:

Dorothy Sayers	Suspicion
Anthony Wynne	The Cyprian Bees
E. C. Bentley	The Clever Cockatoo
Anthony Berkeley	The Avenging Chance
Miriam Allen deFord	The Oleander
Rudyard Kipling	Reingelder and the German Flag
Phyllis Bottome	The Liqueur Glass
Irvin S. Cobb	An Occurrence up a Side Street
Agatha Christie	Accident
R. Austin Freeman	Rex *v.* Burnaby
Nathaniel Hawthorne	Rappaccini's Daughter
G. K. Chesterton	The Quick One

2362   BONNAMY, FRANCIS (pseud. of Audrey [Mrs. Jay] Walz)

"The Loaded House"   *EQMM* Dec 1950

A short story about the stylish college professor Peter Utley Shane, in which he finds a murderer (with the help of three other people) in a complex plot that brings in antique pistols and furniture, the town of Alexandria, and a few tricks by cops and robbers, both. Slick telling.

2363   BOUCHER, ANTHONY, ed.

Best Detective Stories of the Year   Dutt 1963
   18th Annual Collection
   Introd. by the editor

Sixteen short stories of crime and (some) detection, of which only four are drawn from *EQMM*. Boucher's choice is very uneven: good items by Garve and one or two others, including a tale by Crispin from *Beware of the Trains,* but mostly unreadable. An appendix provides (for 1962) lists of anthologies, critical works, awards, and necrologies. Boucher may have done the preliminary biographical notes on the authors represented.

2364   BOUCHER

"Crime Must Have a Stop"   *EQMM* Feb 1951

A longish story about Nick Noble, the retired, drunken detective who thinks with the aid of too much sherry. Here he does very little and the unwinding is rather psychological than logical.

   For the author's other detective (Fergus O'Breen) in short form, see "The Last Hand" (poker on a train), *EQMM,* Aug. 1958.

2365   BOUCHER, ed.

Four and Twenty Bloodhounds   S&S 1950
   Introd. by the editor
   Biographies of detectives by their creators

The stated emphasis is on the detective short story written by Americans —indeed by members of MWA. There are twenty-five stories and a few more "biographies" than stories. What A.B. chose was:

Verne Chute	Never Trust the Obvious
Joseph Commings	Death by Black Magic
W. T. Brannon	The Perfect Secretary
J. D. Carr	The Wrong Problem
Ken Crossen	Too Late for Murder
Matthew Head	Three Stories of Flesh (Dr. Mary Finney)
Lillian de la Torre	The Disappearing Servant Wench
Harold Q. Masur	Widow in Waiting
Frank Kane	Slay upon Delivery
Jerome & Harold Prince	The Finger Man
James M. Fox	Start from Scratch
Clayton Rawson	The Clue of the Tattooed Man

Robert Arthur	The Fuzzy Things
D. B. Olsen	The Big Money
Anthony Boucher	Screwball Division
Lawrence G. Blochman	The Zarapore Beat
Stewart Sterling	Never Come Mourning
August Derleth	The Adventure of the Purloined Periapt
Ellery Queen	The Ides of Michael Magoon
Brett Halliday	Michael Shayne as I Know Him (an anecdote rather than a story)
Fredric Brown	Mr. Smith Kicks the Bucket
George Harmon Coxe	Death Certificate
Q. Patrick	Girl Overboard
Kelley Roos	Two over Par
Stuart Palmer	The Riddle of the Tired Bullet

2366 BOUCHER, ed.

Great American Detective Stories   World 1945
    Introd. by the editor

In this collection the best stories are these:

C. Woolrich	I Won't Take a Minute
R. Chandler	No Crime in the Mountains
D. Hammett	Too Many Have Lived
A. K. Green	The Second Bullet
M. D. Post	The Hidden Law
A. Boucher	Black Murder
E. Queen	The Adventure of the African Traveler
J. Futrelle	The Stolen Rubens
T. S. Stribling	A Passage to Benares
W. MacHarg	Too Many Enemies
Poe	Thou Art the Man

Five others, less distinguished, extend the variety still further. The Introduction gives a good account of the changes of fashion in the history of the detective short story.

2367 BOUCHER, ed.

The Quintessence of Queen   RH 1962
    Best Prize Stories from 12 years of EQMM
    Introd. by the editor

Thirty-one tales of varying merit, some obviously selected for their authors' names, as is too often true of anthologies. Notable and hard to find elsewhere are the Blake, Borges, and Davidson. The full list is as follows:

William Faulkner	An Error in Chemistry
Q. Patrick	Love Comes to Miss Lucy
Roy Vickers	The House-in-Your-Hand Murder
Helen McCloy	The Other Side of the Curtain
Clayton Rawson	From Another World
Stanley Ellin	The Specialty of the House
Jorge Luis Borges	The Garden of Forking Paths

Nicholas Blake	A Study in White
Leslie Charteris	The Arrow of God
Miriam A. de Ford	Beyond the Sea of Death
John Dickson Carr	The Gentleman from Paris
Philip MacDonald	Love Lies Bleeding
A. H. Z. Carr	The Trial of John Nobody
Wilbur Daniel Steele	The Lady-Killer
Charlotte Armstrong	The Enemy
Hugh Pentecost	The Contradictory Case
Oliver La Farge	Woman Hunt No Good
Veronica P. Johns	Homecoming
Edgar Pangborn	The Singing Stick
John W. Vandercook	The Challenge
Eleazar Lipsky	The Quality of Mercy
Zenna Henderson	You Know What, Teacher?
Margery Allingham	Tall Story
James Yaffe	Mom in the Spring
Vinnie Williams	Dodie and the Boogerman
David Alexander	The Man Who Went to Taltavul's
Thomas Flanagan	The Customs of the Country
Mark Van Doren	Only on Rainy Nights
Avram Davidson	The Necessity of His Condition
B. J. R. Stolper	Lilith, Stay Away from the Door
Ellery Queen	The Gettysburg Bugle

2368   BRAMAH, ERNEST

  The Eyes of Max Carrados   Doran 1924; orig. 1923
        Introd. by the author

Contains:

The Virginiola Fraud	The Ghost at Massingham Mansions
The Disappearance of Marie Severe	The Missing Actress Sensation
The Secret of Dunstan's Tower	The Ingenious Mr. Spinola
The Mystery of the Poisoned Dish	The Kingsmouth Spy Case
of Mushrooms	The Eastern Mystery

Except for Dunstan (fair) and Massingham (superb), this lot is in
general inferior to the first volume of tales. The introduction is a great
piece, dealing in part with the blind and their power to develop their
senses when sight is absent. Bramah refers to James Wilson's *Biography
of the Blind* (1820) in support of his creation of Carrados.

2369   Max Carrados   Meth n.d. [1914]

Contains:

The Coin of Dionysius	The Last Exploit of Harry the Actor
The Knight's Cross Signal Problem	The Tilling Shaw Mystery
The Tragedy at Brookbend Cottage	The Comedy at Fountain Cottage
The Clever Mrs. Straithwaite	The Game Played in the Dark

Nearly all are first-rate. The characterization of the blind Carrados
and of his relation to his friend Carlyle is subtle, humorous, shifting, and
superior to most of the subsequent attempts at friction in fiction. More-

over, the feats of the blind man are made thoroughly plausible. If one has
to choose a masterpiece in Bramah's work, Brookbend is it.

2370   Max Carrados Mysteries   H&S 1927

Never seen in this country till Penguin reissued it in 1964, a first edition
has attained the exorbitant price of $965. The book is worth having, but
not as much so perhaps as the two earlier collections. The first four tales
in the following table are better than the remainder:

The Secret of Headlam Height	The Ingenious Mind of
The Mystery of the Vanished	Mr. Rigby Lacksome
Petition Crown	The Crime at the House on
The Holloway Flat Tragedy	Culver Street
The Curious Circumstances of the	The Strange Case of Cyril Bycourt
Two Left Shoes	The Missing Witness Sensation

2371   Short Stories of Today and Yesterday   Harrap n.d. [1929]
     Pref. Note by F.H.P. (unidentified)

The volume contains three Carrados tales: The Secret of Headlam
Height / The Curious Circumstances of the Two Left Shoes / The Missing Witness Sensation. For comments, see No. 2370.

2372   The Specimen Case   Doran 1925
     Pref. by the author

One Carrados story not found elsewhere: The Bunch of Violets, and
twenty other tales, not detection. The one story is not outstanding; the
preface has general interest.

2373   BRAND, CHRISTIANNA

     "The Gemminy Crickets Case"   *EQMM* Aug 1968

Better-than-average treatment of the sealed-room problem by this author,
who still dedicates herself to detection rather than nerves. The elderly
solicitor could well have been murdered in his bolted, fourth-floor office by
the method employed.

2374   "Poison in the Cup"   *EQMM* Feb 1969

A good tale of murder committed before the reader's eyes, with the cocky
Inspector Cockrill providing a clever last-minute but eminently fair
solution.

2375   "Twist for Twist"   *EQMM* May 1967

Inspector Cockrill is better than ever in this compact tale of poisoning at
a wedding breakfast. Modus operandi well thought out.

2376   What Dread Hand   MJ 1968

These fifteen short stories of murder, detection, and horror span the
thirty years preceding and including the publication date. All are accomplished, though not equally credible or satisfying. Perhaps the most

elaborate and the best detection is Murder Game, and the best twist of fate in planned murder is Hic Jacet. The others are:

The Hornets' Nest	The Death of Don Juan
Aren't Our Police Wonderful!	Double Cross
The Merry-Go-Round	The Sins of the Fathers
Blood Brothers	After the Event
Dear Mr. Editor	Death of a Ghost
The Rose	The Kite
Akin to Love	

N.B. The author regrettably implies that Bertillon introduced finger-printing. (The title is, of course, from Blake's "Tiger.")

2377 BREBNER, PERCY JAMES

Christopher Quarles, Detective and College Professor   Dutt 1914

A group of period pieces barely one cut above *Malcolm Sage* (No. 2594). Rudimentary and rather short shorts, they make one wonder why those who imitated Sherlock Holmes did not improve upon him rather than re-gress to a transparent simplicity. The incidents are not bad but character and motive are null.

2378 The Master Detective   Dutt 1916
       Being Further Investigations of Christopher Quarles

Of some historical interest, like the previous set, but not on that account readable.

2379 BROWN, FREDRIC

Mostly Murder   Dutt 1953

Eighteen stories, on the short side, detailing violence and horror rather than detection. All are competent and nearly all ingenious.

2380 BROWN, ROBERT CARLTON

The Remarkable Adventures of Christopher Poe   Browne 1913
       Illus.

Another epigone of Sherlock Holmes, this time a banker who goes by the name of Hardy but is really C.P., engages in impossible activities to foil and convict bank robbers, for the most part. He uses disguises—but what can he do about his "violet eyes"?—and takes risks with the law and with the underworld. There are clues, some of them pretty fair, but unreality prevails and the verdict must be: well below Morrison and even Jenkins (qq.v.).

The best thing in the book is the look on the face of "Constance" in the colored frontispiece.

2381 BUCHAN, JOHN

The Runagates Club   H&S 1929

Fifteen acquaintances and friends united by experience in the first world war form a club that devotes part of its time to storytelling about notable experiences. The twelve tales, including one by Sir Richard Hannay, are of horror, espionage, or the supernatural, not detection.

2382   BULL, R. C.

Great Tales of Mystery   H&W 1960
Illus. by Edward Pegram

One more classic tale would have put a dozen in this good but uninspired collection, which consists of: The Purloined Letter / The Biter Bit / The Adventure of the Sussex Vampire / The Absent-Minded Coterie / The Lenton Croft Robberies / The Queer Feet / The Blue Sequin / The Tragedy at Brookbend Cottage / The Level Crossing / The Treasure Hunt —all of which see. The Appalling Politician (Leslie Charteris) is the only original contribution to anthology-making.

2383   BURKE, THOMAS

The Bloomsbury Wonder   Mandrake 1929
Also in Dark Nights (HJ) 1944

In this well-known masterpiece of crime, impressionism and realism are combined to leave in the memory a sense of terror about the recesses of the human mind. The lightning-like murder of a whole family by a motive-less man who is never caught is explained on Dostoevskian grounds; there is no detection.

2384   BYRNE, (BRIAN OSWALD) DONN (1889–1928)

The Hound of Ireland and Other Stories   Samp 1934

Of these eight tales, The Bronze Box is an unusual piece of supernatural-ism, being holy. It is in fact a piece of Biblical history translated to Brook-lyn and interwoven with a poor love story. Also unfortunate is the jocose style common to Byrne, Sabatini, and other writers of the thirties who thought they were followers of Kipling. In the same tone but of realistic substance is the sentimental crime story Fiddler's Green. The others are trifles of no interest.

2385   CAMP, WADSWORTH

The Communicating Door   Dday 1923

Seven tales, written between 1913 and 1923. The title story has a bit more atmosphere than the rest and a cleaner separation of the author's fog from that necessitated by the semi-supernatural doings in an old house in northern New York State. Three other stories feature one Garth, a color-less American version of Martin Hewitt, whose acts are not memorable and whose ideas—if any—are not recorded.

2386   CANNING, VICTOR

"To Whoever Finds This"   *EQMM* Mar 1966

The exposure of a singular racket by means of one small clue, told in a very short short.

2387 ČAPEK, KAREL (1890–1938)

"The Disappearance of an Actor"
  In: The Second Mercury Story Book (No. 3445)

Semi-detection, with good novelistic touches of central European origin.

2388 Tales from Two Pockets   Faber 1932

Episodes rather than stories, crime rather than detection. Any literary flavor that one might expect from this accomplished Czech playwright and novelist has somehow disappeared in the translation.
  Note: *The Makropoulos Secret* (1925) is not mystery, but science fantasy about the prolongation of life.

2389 CARR, A. Z. H.

"The Man Who Understood Women"   *EQMM* Jan 1960

A piece of armchair deduction that impresses the reader and the narrator's three friends—till the twist at the end, which shows the price of being fooled. A brilliant piece of inference, from outward seeming, even though the author feels compelled to destroy his own handiwork. Compare Beaumarchais (No. 2347).

2390 CARR, JOHN DICKSON

"The Incautious Burglar"   *EQMM* Nov 1956
  Orig.: "The Guest in the House" (1947)

Dr. Gideon Fell is very easy to take in this compact tale of many twists, all of them surprising yet credible. Country-house scene, in which the attempted theft of paintings appears to end with murder of the burglar.

2391 The Man Who Explained Miracles   HH 1964

A novelette and six tales, as follows:

1. Sir Henry Merrivale in All in a Maze (novelette)
2. From *The Department of Queer Complaints* (q.v.): Wm. Wilson's Racket and The Empty Flat
3. Dr. Gideon Fell in The Incautious Burglar and Invisible Hands.
4. Two secret service tales: Strictly Diplomatic and The Black Cabinet

2392 "The One Real Horror"   *EQMM* Aug 1966
  Orig.: "New Murders for Old" (*1940*)

Sir Charles Hargreaves, police commissioner, tells an absorbing yarn about a young man who reads of his own suicide. Despite a few loose ends, a gripping narrative.

2393 The Third Bullet and Other Stories   Harp 1954

Seven tales, originally published between 1942 and 1954, of which the title story is much the longest. It is ingenious but told without vim. The gem of a rather lackluster collection is the dramatic House in Goblin

Wood. The book lacks a table of contents but is made up of: The Third
Bullet (Col. Marquis) / The Clue of the Red Wig (Insp. Bell) / The
House in Goblin Wood (Sir H. Merrivale) / The Wrong Problem (Dr.
Fell) / The Proverbial Murder (Dr. Fell) / The Locked Room (Dr.
Fell) / The Gentleman From Paris (dated 1849).

2394 CARTER, YOUNGMAN

"The Most Wanted Man in the World"   *EQMM* Nov 1962

Not a bad tale about a chase after a man who acquires a tube containing
a lethal virus, accidentally included among his routine pain-killers. But it
suggests that the Carter-Allingham combine has lost its better half by the
death of Mrs. C.

2395 CARTMELL, VAN H., and CERF, BENNETT

Famous Plays of Crime and Detection   Blak 1946
Foreword by the editors
Introd. by John Chapman

The stage is a poor place for ratiocination, no matter how many armchairs
are provided. For this truth we should be prepared, and willing to accept
in exchange the more active thrill of pistol shots, eerie noises, and villains
gnashing their teeth—perhaps the last two are in fact one. At any rate,
one can recall but a handful of genuinely detective offerings in the Anglo-
American theater of the last half-century. They have been listed in this
book under their authors, with or without comment.

As for the anthology under review, it is excellent for its avowed purpose of reprinting great thriller successes, but it includes only two works
that come close to the main idea of mystery-detection, those by Gillette
and Mary Roberts Rinehart. The full list is as follows:

William Gillette	Sherlock Holmes (see No. 2487)
Bayard Veiller	Within the Law
George M. Cohan	Seven Keys to Baldpate
Elmer Rice	On Trial
Roi C. Megrue	Under Cover
Bayard Veiller	The Thirteenth Chair
John Willard	The Cat and the Canary
Mary Roberts Rinehart &	
Avery Hopwood	The Bat
Philip Dunning &	
George Abbott	Broadway
Jeffrey Dell	Payment Deferred (see No. 870)
Edward Chodorov	Kind Lady (adapted from The Silver Mask, by Hugh Walpole, a story in *All Souls' Night* (1933)
Emlyn Williams	Night Must Fall
Patrick Hamilton	Angel Street

The introduction by the one-time drama critic of the *New York World*
is longer but less to the purpose than the editors' terse preface.

2396 CECIL, HENRY

Full Circle   C&H 1948

Sixteen short stories, four or five about murder and other crimes, which
are linked by the enveloping story of a professor of law who is hustled
into an insane asylum for telling stories instead of giving lectures. The
author has a great narrative gift, knows his law, and is at once ingenious
and wise in the ways of the world.

2397 CENEDELLA, ROBERT

"The Novelist and the Critic"   *EQMM* May 1966

A satirical tale in which murder is made to serve as a book review. Ipso
facto, not serious detection, but good fun for seven short pages.

2398 CHANDLER, RAYMOND

Five Murderers   Avon 1944

Five stories written for *Black Mask* from 1933 to 1936 and brought together in paperback once more; the best and the worst of Chandler are
found here side by side: Blackmailers Don't Shoot / Spanish Blood / Guns
at Cyrano's / Goldfish / Nevada Gas. The last two give signs of the later
characteristic style.

2399 Killer in the Rain   HM 1964
        Introd. by Philip Durham

The introducer gives an excellent account of these stories and how they
were cannibalized by the author for his long novels. Apart from three
that reappeared in anthologies, these eight from *Black Mask* were virtually
unknown until collected in this volume. They are:

Killer in the Rain   Mandarin's Jade
The Man Who Liked Dogs   Bay City Blues
The Curtain   The Lady in the Lake
Try the Girl   No Crime in the Mountains

2400 Pick-up on Noon Street   PB 1952; orig. HM 1950

Four stories from *The Simple Art of Murder* (see No. 2402), forming
with that paperback the original HM volume of 1950. (But see No. 2398.)
In this group we have: Pick-up on Noon Street / Nevada Gas / Guns at
Cyrano's / Smart-Aleck Kill. The first three are the best.

2401 Red Wind   World 1946

Contains: Red Wind / Blackmailers Don't Shoot / I'll Be Waiting / Goldfish / Guns at Cyrano's.

2402 The Simple Art of Murder   PB 1952; orig. HM 1950
        Introd. by the author

Four stories and the famous essay which gives its title to the collection.
The stories are: Pearls Are a Nuisance / Spanish Blood / The King in

Yellow / I'll Be Waiting. Note the later and larger collection under the same title, No. 2403, and also Nos. 2398 and 2400–1.

2403   The Simple Art of Murder   Nort 1968
            Editor's Introd. by James Nelson
            Introd. by the author

A collection of the twelve short stories that Chandler wished to keep, the others having been used up in the novels. This dozen comprises:

Finger Man	Pearls Are a Nuisance
Smart-Aleck Kill	I'll Be Waiting
Guns at Cyrano's	Red Wind
Pick-up on Noon Street	Nevada Gas
Goldfish	Spanish Blood
The King in Yellow	Trouble Is My Business

"The Simple Art of Murder," also included, is an essay originally published in *The Atlantic Monthly* in 1944. See the Introductory to this *Catalogue*.

2404   CHEKHOV, ANTON

            "The Safety Match"   *EQMM* July 1965

This minor classic, set in the Russia of 1885, bears up quite well, with both clues and humor to its credit.

2405   CHESTERTON, G. K.

            The Father Brown Omnibus   DM n.d. [1951]
                Foreword by R. T. Bond

Fifty Father Brown stories—all of them except one—are included in this reprint of the five volumes collected by the author:

The Innocence of Father Brown	1911
The Wisdom of Father Brown	1914
The Incredulity of Father Brown	1926
The Secret of Father Brown	1927
The Scandal of Father Brown	1935

For the one uncollected story, see No. 2412.
For a readers' choice of the ten best Father Brown tales, the following may be listed:

The Absence of Mr. Glass	The Mirror of the Magistrate
The Chief Mourner of Marne	The Queer Feet
The Insoluble Problem	The Sins of Prince Saradine
The Invisible Man	The Vanishing of Vaudrey
The Miracle of Moon Crescent	The Worst Crime in the World

2406   Four Faultless Felons   Cass 1936

The quartet in the title are not so religious or whimsical that anti-Chestertonians need take alarm. But the incidents are loosely tied together and contain less detection than the best exploits of Father Brown or Horne Fisher. Notice especially: The Man with the Green Umbrella, in a good Egyptian ("Polybian") setting.

2407　The Man Who Knew Too Much　　　　　　　　Harp 1922
　　　　Said to have "illustrations by W. Hatherell, R.I.,"
　　　　but no list is given and the only one in the book is the
　　　　frontispiece, illustrating The Bottomless Well

Eight tales about Horne Fisher, plus the longer and somber Trees of Pride. In the Fisher series, The Bottomless Well is a masterpiece and The Hole in the Wall close to it. The rest may irritate as only G.K.C. could, but in those stories his moralizing is sound and connected with the plot itself. The regrettable anti-Semitic remarks are a serious flaw, though in character for the speaker at least.

　　The remaining titles are: The Face in the Target / The Vanishing Prince / The Soul of the Schoolboy / The Fad of the Fisherman / The Temple of Silence / The Vengeance of the Statue.

2408　The Paradoxes of Mr. Pond　　　　　　　　DM 1937

Amusing adventures made out of verbal, moral, and accidental contradictions—no crime, even in the stories that refer to the subject, and no detection, except in the discovery of character by the unfolding of the narration itself.

2409　The Poet and the Lunatics　　　　　　　　DM 1929
　　　　Episodes in the Life of Gabriel Gale

Characteristic and entertaining Chestertonian tales, not intended to be detection. Even the story with "Crime" in the title is a spiritual adventure, not a crime. Mr. Pond also occurs.

2410　Tales of the Longbow　　　　　　　　　　DM 1925

Eight tales, not of detection, but of deliberate improbability. In the hands of G.K. this means humor and a moral point, and since he is a practitioner of *the* genre, his improbabilities are full of practical detail such as might furnish food for thought in a piece of detection.

2411　"The Tower of Treason"　　　　　EQMM Dec 1950; orig. 1920

A hermit, a Cambridge graduate, a girl, and treachery in Transylvania provide the elements of a longish short story of melodramatic cast. Not Chesterton in highest form, but worth reading.

2412　"The Vampire of the Village"
　　　　In: Ellery Queen, ed., Twentieth-Century Detective Stories
　　　　(World 1948) (No. 2751)

The one Father Brown detective story to have escaped book publication elsewhere, though the tale appeared in private editions earlier. (See also No. 2405.)

2413 CHILD, CHARLES B.

"Death Was a Wedding Guest"   *EQMM* May 1961

Inspector Chafik solves a murder which prevents a wedding in Baghdad.
A bit more attention to clues than is usual with this author provides a
better balance with his local color. Pretty good psychology, too.

2414 "A Lesson in Firearms"   *EQMM* Dec 1965

This tale of Baghdad in which Inspector Chafik rescues a lost child and
solves a native murder is fairly representative of a long series. The Inspector depends heavily upon his "index-card memory," and his detection
consists largely in recognizing the description of an assailant. The local
color will attract some readers.

2415 CHOLMONDELEY, MARY (also Pax; ?–1925)

The Danvers Jewels and Sir Charles Danvers   Harp 1890

A good pair of long shorts, full of mystery, well worked out, but with only
tangential detective detail.
    M.C. is also the author of *The Hand on the Latch* (DM 1909; orig.
1903 ff.), the title story in a small collection. The oddity of that title story
is that its plot exactly follows that of Anna Katharine Green's Midnight
in Beauchamp Row (1895). (See No. 2542.)

2416 CHRISTIE, AGATHA

Double Sin   Dell 1964 / PB 1962 / DM 1961

Eight short stories of widely varying date, all but two featuring either
Hercule Poirot or Miss Marple. Included are: Double Sin (Poirot) /
Wasps' Nest (Poirot) / The Theft of the Royal Ruby (Poirot) / The
Dressmaker's Doll (no det.; supernatural) / Greenshaw's Folly (Miss
Marple) / The Double Clue (Poirot) / The Last Seance (no det.; super-
natural) / Sanctuary (Miss Marple). Hastings appears in the two
"Doubles," which are very early Christie—1925–29.

2417 The Labours of Hercules   Peng 1953; orig. DM & Coll 1947

The linking of these twelve short stories is a tour de force, the scheme
being to parallel the twelve mythological labors of Hercules with a variety
of situations in modern life. The excellent poet Robert Graves, who abomi-
nates A.C., has not in his *Greek Myths* made better analogies between
real life and ancient legends. The plots are full of double twists and skillful telling, but Poirot's detection is of the question-and-answer kind, which
ultimately wearies. The best tale is The Lernean Hydra, about a doctor,
his wife, and a nurse.

2418 The Listerdale Mystery and Other Stories   Coll n.d. [1934]

A dozen tales of roughly equal length. Most are light in content and
meant to amuse, the powerful Philomel Cottage being an exception.
Poirot figures in none of them. In the last, Swan Song, music (in the

form of *Tosca*) plays a large part and makes this tale evidently unique in Christie's output. The other titles are:

The Girl in the Train	A Fruitful Sunday
Sing a Song of Sixpence	Mr. Eastwood's Adventure
The Manhood of Edward Robinson	The Golden Ball
Accident	The Rajah's Emerald
Jane in Search of a Job	

2419   The Mousetrap   DM 1949
      Also: Three Blind Mice and Other Stories

Nine stories (1925–48), including the excellent Poirot tale (Third-Floor Flat) in which two young men, of whom one is a murderer, use the coal lift to enter a flat of which their young hostess has mislaid the key. The story that gave its title to the original collection is a poor variation of the pattern "Here we are, cut off from help, and a killer is among us." The last of the nine, The Love Detectives, is a mediocre example of her Harley Quin formula. The other stories in it are: Strange Jest / Tape-Measure Murder / The Case of the Perfect Maid / The Case of the Caretaker / The Adventure of Johnny Waverley / Four and Twenty Blackbirds.

Is it fair to see in the title of the book, tale, and play an allusion to "The Mousetrap" play within the play in *Hamlet,* act III? Of course, the plot is obvious and has been previously used for plays and tales with perhaps no thought of Shakespeare.

2420   Mr. Parker Pyne, Detective   DM 1934
      In Eng.: Parker Pyne Investigates

A collection of twelve stories, half on the London scene and half in the Near East, featuring the ministrations of Parker Pyne. In at least two of the tales P.P. states categorically, "I am not a detective." Well, the bald ex-civil servant with thirty-five years' experience of compiling statistics who now acts as adviser to the "unhappy" actually does do quite a bit of detection (cf. The House at Shiraz, and several others). On rereading, the collection holds up very well.

2421   Murder in the Mews and Other Stories   Peng 1961; orig. Coll 1937
      In U.S.: Dead Man's Mirror*

The best collection of her short stories, though it contains only four: the title story, an excellent inversion of murder made to look like suicide; The Incredible Theft, a variant on the state paper and the shady woman at the politician's house; Dead Man's Mirror, a good murder in the library, with the least likely person the criminal; and Triangle at Rhodes, not a detective story but also a drama with the usual relationships upside down. All four find Poirot functioning in top form.

   * Except for the story Triangle at Rhodes.

2422   The Mysterious Mr. Quin   DM 1930
      In ppb.: The Passing of Mr. Quin

Twelve short stories of semi-real, semi-symbolic invention, in which Mr. Harley Quin appears as the agent of discovery and justice, helping the bumbling, inquisitive Mr. Satterthwaite to unravel the murders and other mysteries that abound in high and mixed society. Though short and similar in atmosphere, these pieces show the master hand.

2423   "The Mystery of the Spanish Shawl"   *EQMM* Apr 1947

As slick a piece of storytelling as A.C. ever did, but this time all spoofing, humor, make-believe, and virtuosity. That she can be funny without guffaws is part of the reason why she can be serious without implausibility: art is seeming but also seamless.

2424   Partners in Crime   Pan 1962; orig. Coll 1929

The only tolerable book about Tommy and Tuppence Beresford, because it is a spoof. It consists of ten short-story-parodies of other detectives, which are also ingenious tales in themselves, though not meant to be taken straight. The takeoff on Father Brown and the one on the Old Man in the Corner are gems, and they show as much as anything in Beerbohm what a literary mind actually is.

2425   The Regatta Mystery and Other Stories   Dell 1964; orig. DM 1933
       In ppb. also: Poirot and the Regatta Mystery (1943)

Eight tales of detection and one (equally good) of semi-supernatural drama. Here is the excellent Yellow Iris, a small and incomplete version of A.C.'s novel *Remembered Death*, which is also *Sparkling Cyanide*. The other stories show Agatha's ability to sketch in a very few words characters that, although conventional, exist as such and do not have to be accepted by the reader on the strength of abstract propositions.

The other titles are: The Mystery of the Baghdad Chest / How Does Your Garden Grow? / Problem at Pollensa Bay / Miss Marple Tells a Story / The Dream / In a Glass Darkly / Problem at Sea.

2426   Thirteen for Luck   DM 1961

This baker's dozen gives samples of a baker's half dozen of the author's detectives: Poirot, Miss Marple, Mr. Harley Quin, Parker Pyne, Tommy and Tuppence, and Inspector Evans. The tales are familiar ones from the previous collections, the only one not listed in these readers' entries being The Market Basing Mystery from *The Under Dog* (DM 1951).

2427   "The Time Hercule Poirot Failed"   *EQMM* Nov 1962
       Orig.: "The Chocolate Box" (1925)

Poirot tells his friend of an early case involving poisoned chocolates in which he was mistaken about the identity of the murderer, but validates his little gray cells by showing what were the clues that he should have followed.

2428   The Tuesday Club Murders   Dell 1963; orig. DM 1933
       In Eng.: The Thirteen Problems

The U.S. title is a misnomer, for the club membership deals with only the first six of the ten short stories celebrating Miss Marple's gifts of ratiocination. The remainder exhibit a different group of people, still with Miss M., who live at St. Mary Mead and occur again in *The Body in the Library* (q.v.). The most ingenious of the present ten are Motive v. Opportunity / The Affair at the Bungalow / and the title story.

2429 Witness for the Prosecution   Dell 1958; orig. DM 1924–1948

A collection of short stories, including the excellent one used for the title. Others are the equally famous Philomel Cottage / Accident / The Second Gong / S.O.S. / The Red Signal / The Fourth Man / Where There's a Will / The Mysterious Blue Jar. Poirot appears in a few.

In The Witness for the Prosecution, later a play, a woman saves her lover by impersonating a relentless woman scorned and testifying against him: not detection.

2430 CHRISTIE, AGATHA, has also written seven original plays and has adapted or permitted the adaptation for the stage of twelve of her novels and short stories. The Mousetrap (1952), based on Three Blind Mice from the collection of that name (see No. 2419), has been played in London ever since, the longest continuous run of any play in England. For further details, see the Appendix to No. 3009.

2431 COLE, G. D. H. and M.

Mrs. Warrender's Profession   Macm 1939

Mrs. W. first figures in *A Lesson in Crime,* which the collaborators have never bothered to look up, because her appearance here in five longish tales does not recommend her. The idea throughout is that this mature lady, who is the mother of a Scotland Yard detective, sees more and does better than her somewhat fussy, short-tempered son in the detection of crimes. She "understands people" and he is insensitive or blind. The humor arising from all this palls on p. 1. It is a poor aftermath of the prewar (1914) vindication of women—hence perhaps the title suggestive of Shaw's play.

2432 Superintendent Wilson's Holiday   Coll 1934; orig. 1928

The tale in the collection of eight which gives the book its name is not the first but the second. The first story, In a Telephone Cabinet, is one involving a broken light bulb, an owl in the ivy, and an interesting gadget. The other stories are: The International Socialist / The Disappearance of Philip Mansfield / The Robbery at Bowden / The Oxford Mystery / The Camden Town Fire / The Missing Baronet. All contain good detection, though often spare in the telling. The Oxford Mystery and In a Telephone Cabinet are the fullest and best.

2433 Wilson and Some Others   CCC 1940

This volume groups seven Wilson short stories and six others—some pure crime, others crime and detection; all quite short and unmemorable.

Superintendent Henry Wilson is so entirely featureless that he makes

Inspector French look like an eccentric by comparison. But Wilson knows his business and the tales would be good reading if the authors had put a little drive and suspense into them. They prefer to go in for mild satire about English life, and accordingly the only tale here with any power to it is Murder in Church, which is original in means and atmosphere as well.

N.B. Several of these tales and those in No. 2432 were originally published in Polybooks, Vallancey Press, London.

2434   COLE. See also:

Death of a Bride	Vall 1945
Superintendent Wilson's Cases	Coll 1933
Wilson Calling	Vall 1944

2435   COLLINS, WILKIE

After Dark   2 v.   SE 1856

Three of these six tales, originally published in Dickens' *Household Words,* contain crime and some detection. They are: A Terribly Strange Bed and The Stolen Letter (vol. 1) and The Lady of Glenwith Grange (vol. 2). The first two owe much to Poe; all three are told with characteristic fullness of detail and the whole set is organized with the aid of prologues related to the imaginary narrators. Thus the three above are, in order: The Traveller's Tale, the Lawyer's, and the Angler's. See also: Mr. Lepel and the Housekeeper and Mr. Policeman and the Cook, in *Little Novels* (C&W 1887).

2436   "The Biter Bit"
          In: The Queen of Hearts (*1859*)

His most anthologized short piece, somewhat lumbering in its humor, which is used to show that detection takes brains and arrogance gets a deserved slapping down.

2437   CONKLIN, GROFF, and FABRICANT, NOAH, eds.

Great Detective Stories About Doctors   Col 1965
          Introd. by the editors

The seventeen tales include: Doyle, The Blanched Soldier / Wynne, The Cyprian Bees / Arnold Bennett, extract from *Grand Babylon Hotel* (see No. 142) / G. Kersh, The Eye / Rufus King, The Seven Good Hunters / Francis Leo Golden, The Testimony of Dr. Farnsworth.

The two-page Introduction is negligible.

2438   COOKE, DAVID C., is the editor of an annual series, *Best Detective Stories of the Year 19——*, which began in 1946. The stories, drawn almost exclusively from current magazines, are rarely pure detection and only occasionally first-class in any genre. This is not the editor's fault, but a function of magazine publishing.

2439   COPPARD, A(LFRED) E(DGAR) (1878–1957)

"A Broadsheet Ballad"   *EQMM* Feb 1949

The psychology of crime and the reasons for justice miscarrying as those
subjects should be treated in the short story: master's work, without violence or detection.

2440   COPPARD. See also:

Collected Tales   Knopf 1948

2441   COPPLESTONE, BENNET (pseud. of Frederick Harcourt Kitchin,
       1867–1932)

The Diversions of Dawson   Dutt 1924

The four Books into which this volume is divided are: I. Mr. Cholmondeley Jones; II. Ned Grimes, Deck-Hand; III. The Prime Minister;
IV. The Butler. All present Chief Inspector Dawson in various disguises
and on both sides of the law. In the first and longest adventure he is
assisted by his journalist friend Bennet. The humor of The Butler has made
it better known than the others, but each has some merit, though not in
detection: the book is quite *sui generis.*

2442   The Lost Naval Papers   Dutt 1917

Inspector William Dawson made his first appearance in this series of
loosely connected tales in which he is involved in various problems of
naval intelligence. Dawson is held up as a master of disguise, but less
dated is his versatility in bamboozling enemy agents. Not much detection
but pleasant enough reading. The adventures are presented by one "Mr.
Copplestone," who is not quite a Watson to the Inspector.

2443   CORNIER, VINCENT

"The Smell That Killed"   *EQMM* Dec 1946; orig. 1935

A long, rather rambling short story about lethal research, which is
brought to the attention of the amateur detective Barnabas Hildreth by
the peculiar changes found in a casual corpse. The science, a trifle farfetched, would be acceptable if the tale were not overdecorated with
Gypsies, heron's quills, balloonettes [*sic*], and verbal hocus-pocus. But see
No. 2316.

2444   CORYELL, JOHN (?) et al. (?)

Nick Carter, Detective   Macm 1964/1963
       The Adventures of Fiction's Most Celebrated Detective
       Introd. by Robert Clurman

The creation of Nick Carter in 1886 makes him an exact contemporary of
Sherlock Holmes, for Doyle's work was delayed by the publisher—*absit
omen!* But although the exploits of each continue to be printed and read,
a world of ideas separates them. Not only are N.C.'s adventures told in

sentence-paragraphs, abysmally simple-minded, stilted, and unconcerned with plausibility; but the incidents and motive power of the typical Carter episode are precisely those of the modern U.S. tough crime novel: we go in circles. If the worst-drawn characters in detective fiction are cardboard —i.e., faintly flexible—those in the Carter adventures are plywood. The hero himself is uninteresting, even in his feats of strength. What is interesting is that he started out in a relation to the old detective Seth Carter in what may be called the Ellery Queen position—the protégé brighter than his older progenitor. The huge output of tales employed the talents of about a dozen hacks. The Reverend Samuel Spalding is said to have written over 100 episodes between 1910 and 1916.

Besides the title episode, we have in this collection: The Counterfeiter's Gold Tooth / Nick Carter's Mysterious Case / Nick Carter's Beautiful Decoy / Nick Carter's Enemy / and Nick Carter and the Professor.

The short Introduction is excellent.

2445   COXE, GEORGE HARMON

"There's Still Tomorrow"   *EQMM* Oct 1959

A simple and not very thrilling affair about a girl bashed in a man's bathroom. Alan Marsh, who steps into the tangle, solves it intelligently and quickly: it would make a good opening for a regular Coxe novel.

2446   CRAWFURD, OSWALD, CMG

The Revelations of Inspector Morgan   C&H 1910

In this rarity the four tales represent a transition from Martin Hewitt's humdrum adaptation of Holmes' methods to the more efficient police represented by Inspector French. There are numerous felicities of speech and description characteristic of the period 1900–10—the status of the English telephone, for example, in the last story; and dated though the plots are, each affords actual detection. Inspector Morgan recounts his adventures to a rather shadowy Watson.

2447   CRISPIN, EDMUND, ed.

Best Detective Stories   Faber 1959
     Introd. by the editor

Ten tales, of which six are good, three poor, and one other (by Crispin and G. Bush) is excellent as a surprise story rather than as crime or detective fiction. The Introduction is topnotch critical writing. The first is the rather long Dead Man's Shoes (q.v.) by Innes.

Then come:

H. C. Bailey	The Burnt Tout
J. D. Carr	The Gentleman from Paris
Roy Vickers	The Rubber Trumpet
Ellery Queen	The Dauphin's Doll
Anthony Gilbert	You Can't Hang Twice
Harry Kemelman	The Nine-Mile Walk
Rex Stout	The Dog in the Daytime

Charlotte Armstrong   The Enemy
E. Crispin
and G. Bush   Who Killed Baker?

2448 CRISPIN

Beware of the Trains   Goll 1953

A collection of sixteen shorts originally published in newspapers, which Crispin has had the honorable urge to rework and upholster. The first fifteen contain many excellent tales, in which Humbleby and Fen play off each other to great effect and the reader's pleasure. The sixteenth, a longer story of adolescent complicity in crime, is good for its local color and psychology, but the geography is difficult and the emotions fail to resolve themselves, at least for JB.

2449 "Gladstone's Candlestick"   *EQMM* Aug 1957

A minor but clever effort of Gervase Fen's. Alleged theft of a valuable candlestick by one of his pupils is disproved by finding evidence of a new kind of fraud.

2450 "Merry-Go-Round"   *EQMM* Nov 1953

A delightful Humbleby-Fen short short (3 pages) about a forgery done to render ridiculous a disagreeable police inspector—ingenious and witty and full of nice historical touches.

2451 CROFTS, FREEMAN WILLS

Many a Slip   H&S 1955

These twenty-one short short stories are no more than sketches—virtually notes for stories to be written. As such they are unsatisfactory, though two or three have good railway situations.

2452 "Mr. Sefton, Murderer"   Poly 1944

The story of a crime planned in order to avoid discovery as an embezzler. The mechanics are interesting, and it *is* an inverted tale: Inspector French goes over the culprit's traces and finds the one flaw. Unfortunately, the people and the talk are wood and sawdust.

2453 The Mystery of the Sleeping Car Express   H&S 1956

Ten stories, of which those marked (F) feature Inspector French. The first was Crofts' first published work.

The Mystery of the
  Sleeping Car Express
Mr. Pemberton's Commission
The Greuze
The Level Crossing
East Wind (F; a train story)

The Parcel
The Motive Shows the Man
The Affair at Saltoner Priory (F)
The Landing Ticket (F)
The Raincoat (F)

2454 CROMIE, ROBERT, and WILSON, T. S.

The Romance of Poisons   Jarr 1903
  Being Weird Episodes from Life
  Ghoulish red-and-black picture on cover

Twelve tales, unsophisticated by modern standards, and certainly fiction.
Surgeon Colonel John Hedford, late of the Indian Medical Services,
exudes quiet competence although his detection is modest and often late
in the day. Yet he is not all cardboard. The problems are mainly toxicological, with a virus here and there to hint of the better life ahead.

2455 CULLINGFORD, GUY

"The Incurable Complaint"   *EQMM* May 1969

A nice treatment of the eternal triangle with a clever twist suggesting
suspected poisoning—but of whom and by whom?

2456 CUPPY, WILL, ed.

The World's Great Mystery Stories   Tower 1943
  Introd. by the editor

A good collection (though its date of publication ensures its physical disappearance by the crumbling of its bad paper) which includes more unusual tales than is common in anthologies: e.g.: Doyle, The Fiend of the
Cooperage / Edith Wharton, Miss Mary Pask / Arthur Machen, The
Cosy Room / F. Scott Fitzgerald, A Short Trip Home / H. G. Wells,
The Door in the Wall / Stephen Leacock, Who Do You Think Did It?
    The Introduction is breezy and knowledgeable, but shrugs off differ-
ences of genre cavalierly and with a touch of literary demagogy.

2457 CUTLIP, JACQUELINE

"The Trouble of Murder"   *EQMM* Apr 1967

Nearly a detective story of the inverted genre, thanks to good plotting
and subtle suggestion: U.S. setting (mountain country in the Bible belt).

2458 DALY, MAUREEN [Mrs. William P. McGivern], ed.

My Favorite Mystery Story   DM 1966

These fifteen are notable for the inclusion of a strong historical tale by
Maurice Procter (West Riding to Maryland), a short spoof by Michael
Innes (Appleby's First Case), a character study pivoting on crime by
Susan Glaspell (A Jury of Her Peers), and a fair sample of Karel Čapek's
fiction (An Attempt at Murder).
    None of these are strictly detection. The rest include familiar titles:

Agatha Christie	Double Sin
Helen McCloy	In a Glass Darkly (short version)
William P. McGivern	The Sound of Murder
Conan Doyle	The Adventure of the Priory School

484

Howard Browne	So Dark for April
Donald A. Yates	Inspector's Lunch
Ellery Queen	Trojan Horse
R. M. Gordon	The Murder of George Washington
Marjorie Vetter	A Night in the Old House
Thomas Walsh	Sentence of Death
Maureen Daly	The Gold-Digger Happening

2459   Danger: Great Stories of Mystery and Suspense from
         The Saturday Evening Post   Goll 1968

Though it includes Poe's Black Cat, the best are two modern American efforts by Richard Stern: Set Up for Murder and Motive for Murder, both of the crime-and-police variety, yet so crammed with action and suspense that they transcend their kind. Faulkner's Hand Upon the Waters is dreary stuff and Robert Standish's The Mystery of the Master Safe-Cracker is ingenious. As for Geoffrey Household's Run from the Hangman, it starts well but huddles at the end. The others are: Martha Albrand, Reunion with Terror / Agatha Christie, The Dream / Philip Wylie, Dead Man in the Water / William Wood, One of the Dead / Shirley Jackson, The Possibility of Evil / Gerald Kersh, The Woman Who Wouldn't Stay Dead.

2460   DARDIS, MARTIN

         "Letter Writing as a Fine Art"   *EQMM* Feb 1957

A tightly written and most effective story about a first offender's revenge, written for the "Black Mask" section of *EQMM*. The title plays on that of De Quincey's famous essay and rightly suggests murder—no detection.

2461   DAVIDSON, AVRAM

         "The Affair at Lahore Cantonment"   *EQMM* June 1961

A prose amplification, brilliantly done, of Kipling's "Ballad of Danny Deever"—Indian setting and triple treachery for love. A clever tale, which reminds one of Doyle's Crooked Man story that Holmes unravels. But the present one is original all the same—unless the Bible is at the back of both.

2462   "The Importance of Trifles"   *EQMM* Jan 1969

A good historical reconstruction of official detection in New York City in the 1840s. The story is not especially attractive or subtle in clues and characters, but it is procedural and forms a pendant to Poe's ratiocination in Marie Roget.

2463   DAVIS, DOROTHY SALISBURY

         "Born Killer"   *EQMM* Nov 1953

A psychological tale about a misunderstood farm boy, somewhat precious in the telling and uncertain in direction, but with "strong" moments. The author does better in the longer form.

2464　DAVIS, DOROTHY SALISBURY, ed.

A Choice of Murders　　　　　　　　　　　　　Scrib 1958
　　　The eleventh annual Mystery Writers of America anthology
　　　Introd. by the editor

A few clever pieces by Stanley Ellin, M. Gilbert, and Garve; for the rest, average magazine fiction, unfocused on detection or even on crime, and perhaps to be described as Excitement.

2465　DAVIS, RICHARD HARDING

In the Fog　　　　　　　Harp 1901; incl. in *Ranson's Folly*
　　　Illus.　　　　　　(Scrib 1910), but not in Eng. ed. of that work.

This classic novella deserves a place of honor in any collection, even if it does not exactly correspond to the detective genre. Rather, it goes with R.L.S.'s spoof on adventure stories in *The New Arabian Nights Entertainment*. But Davis has a style and zest all his own, and the double twist at the end is as good as the wonderful atmosphere at the beginning. (See No. 2795 for a reprinting.)

2466　DEANE, HAMILTON, and BALDERSTONE, JOHN L.

Dracula　　　　　　　　　　　　　　French 1933/1927
　　　The Vampire Play in Three Acts

It was the presence of Bela Lugosi, the Hungarian actor, which made this play based on Bram Stoker's classic a far-flung success in the thirties. The script itself is rather flat and little more than a pointless collection of words to fill in the gap between shocks. Indeed, in this printing, the lively part is the 20-page appendix, "Notes on Production," which detail makeup, tricks, flights of bats, and color schemes: amusement and thrills combined.

2467　DE LA TORRE, LILLIAN (Lillian de la Torre Bueno [Mrs. G. S. McCue], b. 1902)

Dr. Sam Johnson, Detector　　　　　　　　　Knopf 1946
　　　Author's Note to the Reader

The first collection of nine tales "as from the pen of James Boswell," in which the Great Cham detects imposture, murder, and the rest. It is all done with great accuracy and feeling for the language of the period (1763–84), but this very care gets in the way of narrative movement, and the ingenuity of the episodes evokes admiration rather than enjoyment.

2468　DE LA TORRE. See also No. 724 and:

The Detections of Sam Johnson　　　　　　　Dday 1960

2469　DERLETH, AUGUST

In re Sherlock Holmes:
The Adventures of Solar Pons　　　　　　　M&M 1945
　　　Introd. by Vincent Starrett

The misunderstanding of Sherlock Holmes is apparent on every page of these attempts at pastiche, and perhaps sufficiently revealed in the name chosen for Holmes' would-be alter ego. Language, manners, and circumstance should fit, even when ridicule is intended, which this collection has no thought of.

2470　The Memoirs of Solar Pons　　　　　　　　M&M 1951

A second and a better try. Two or three of the tales have a portion of authentic Baker Street atmosphere, which the author means to suggest rather than to duplicate. But in several instances—e.g., the railway doings in The Adventure of the Lost Locomotive—the author's lack of familiarity with English ways and terminology is painful.

2471　DERLETH. See also:

　　　The Case Book of Solar Pons　　　　　　　Arkham 1966/1965

2472　DICKENS, CHARLES

　　　"Hunted Down"　　　　　　　　　C&H n.d.; orig. 1859
　　　　In: The Works of Charles Dickens, *Gadshill Ed., vol. 25*
　　　　Introd. by Andrew Lang
　　　　Illus.

The passion that Dickens and his friend Collins shared about old crimes and the new police led them to write between them a large number of tales which, fifty years later, would have been acknowledged and recognizable detective stories. (See Nos. 2435 and 3129.) Hunted Down, written for the *New York Ledger* at a high price, is a tale of detection in the sense that the hero, who has seen a lovely young woman poisoned by her uncle for her insurance money, vows to avenge her. He resigns from his post in the Inestimable Life Assurance Co. (splendid name) and embarks on a misleading life to lure the uncle—the well-named Slinkton—to his undoing as the murderer of the damsel and would-be slayer of our hero. Slinkton's suavity is superb—he owes something to the actual poisoner Wainewright, q.v.—but like most foiled criminals he tries his own recipe in vain.

2473　DICKSON, CARTER

　　　The Department of Queer Complaints　　　　　Morr 1940

Seven stories about Colonel March and four others, of which one, New Murders for Old, belongs to the supernatural. The seven March tales are all splendid feats of ingenuity and straightforward narrative, showing that the author's genius really lies in the short form, free of eccentric detectives. The first of the seven, The New Invisible Man, has excellent humor added; Hot Money is a little masterpiece of suspense; and of the rest, The Other Hangman is a fine bit of U.S. rural life and crime; Persons or Things Unknown is highly ingenious and beautifully told; and Blind Man's Hood uses the probable solution to the puzzle in the actual death of Rose

Harsent in the Peasenhall case (see Nos. 2223 and 3218).

Other titles in this collection are: The Footprint in the Sky / The Crime in Nobody's Room / Death in the Dressing-Room / The Silver Curtain / Error at Daybreak.

2474   DOYLE, ADRIAN CONAN, and CARR, JOHN DICKSON (q.v.)

The New Exploits of Sherlock Holmes   RH 1954
Pref. by the publishers

It is a pity to have to include among the Doyle entries this volume of inadequate imitations by his son and his son's collaborator. They can only be called by devout Holmesians "bad blood in the art"—the allusion will be clear to all connoisseurs. The trouble is not that the detective ideas lack ingenuity—trust J.D.C. for invention—but the atmosphere of 1890–1914 is largely missed or else unconsciously burlesqued, and the effect is that of daubing good stonework with weak whitewash. These pseudo adventures are called: The Adventure of the: Seven Clocks / Gold Hunter / Highgate Miracle / Wax Gamblers / Black Baronet / Sealed Room.

By Adrian Conan Doyle alone are these additional six: The Adventure of: Foulkes Rath / the Abbas Ruby / the Dark Angels / the Two Women / the Deptford Horror / the Red Widow.

2475   DOYLE, ARTHUR CONAN

The Adventures of Sherlock Holmes   Harp 1892
Illus.

The first set of twelve, almost all gems. Though popular taste has long since fastened on spectacular ones, such as The Speckled Band and A Scandal in Bohemia, the really choice ones are the quieter: The Man with the Twisted Lip, The Noble Bachelor, and The Beryl Coronet. A gratifying overlap of taste occurs between connoisseur and plain man about The Red-Headed League. Meanwhile Christopher Morley points out that The Blue Carbuncle is the best Christmas story ever written (see No. 3342). The truth is, it is impossible not to admire each of the twelve.

2476   The Case-Book of Sherlock Holmes   JM 1927

By universal consent these twelve stories are deemed inferior to every previous collection. The reason is not in their conception, which is often splendid, but in their execution, which is slovenly. Doyle was tired of Sherlock Holmes, he had picked up a great deal of American slang, and the effort to recreate the Victorian or Edwardian scene was beyond his strength.

Still, there are fragments of dialogue and of description in these tales that equal or surpass anything done earlier, and some of Holmes' most frequently quoted *mots* come from these decried adventures. The three best are Thor Bridge, The Three Garridebs, and Shoscombe Old Place, even though the middle one is but a (second) variant of The Red-Headed League. The worst are the Mazarin Stone and The Veiled Lodger.

Note that two out of twelve are told by Holmes and one by a novelist-narrator who is neither Holmes nor Watson. Apart from the cherishable bits, the only appealing thing about the *Case-Book* is that its stories appeared during the young manhood of WHT and JB, not only in *The Strand* but in the magazine supplement of the old *New York World*.

2477　The Complete Sherlock Holmes　　　　　　Dday 1930 ff.
　　　Memorial Edition, 2 v.
　　　Foreword, "In Memoriam," by Christopher Morley

The first substantial gathering of the sixty stories, but marred by such defects as bad paper, discontinuous pagination, typographical blunders, and the duplication of passages. For a reliable edition, see below, No. 2483.

2478　His Last Bow　　　　　　　　　　　　　　Doran 1917
　　　Some Reminiscences of Sherlock Holmes

There is no doubt that the very even and high quality of the three earlier collections of Holmes adventures is not maintained here: the advent of the first world war in the final tale, His Last Bow, is perhaps symbolic of the end of a world of gaslight and order in which Holmes and Watson could function so predictably. But just as a ragbag has a way of yielding delightful scraps, this collection offers elements of the bizarre largely missing in earlier tales. In The Adventure of the Cardboard Box horror is mixed with passion; The Dying Detective pretty well reached the summit of the histrionic; in The Bruce-Partington Plans (those of a submarine), the railroad clues put the tale in a class by itself. Nos. VI and VII below also have much to be said for them:

    I. The Adventure of Wisteria Lodge
    II. The Adventure of the Cardboard Box
   III. The Adventure of the Red Circle
   IV. The Adventure of the Bruce-Partington Plans
    V. The Adventure of the Dying Detective
   VI. The Disappearance of Lady Frances Carfax
   VII. The Adventure of the Devil's Foot
  VIII. His Last Bow

2479　The Memoirs of Sherlock Holmes　　　　　McCl 1894

Eleven stories, intended by their author to terminate the career of his remarkable detective with The Final Problem, in which Holmes and Moriarty confront each other on a narrow Alpine ledge by the Reichenbach Falls. A bronze tablet now marks the spot, but Doyle was forced by an irate public to bring Holmes back. All but three tales (The Yellow Face / The Stock-Broker's Clerk / The Crooked Man) are topnotch, many having scenes that must be called inspired. Silver Blaze (horse-racing) has the famous "curious incident of the dog in the night-time" and Holmes is at his most masterly; The Reigate Puzzle contains one of the most dramatic exposures of villainy; The Greek Interpreter introduces Sherlock's brother Mycroft.

 Not all the adventures occur during Holmes and Watson's joint tenancy of 221B Baker Street: in three of them Holmes comes to Watson's surgery to bespeak his help and companionship.

2480   The Return of Sherlock Holmes   McCl 1905

Both in fertility of imagination and in felicity of phrase most of these thirteen stories which pacified a public outraged by Holmes' "death" set a high level. Only three are weak: The Adventure of the Dancing Men, with its foolish cipher and Holmes' failure to save his client; The Adventure of the Golden Pince-Nez, and The Adventure of the Missing Three-Quarter, in the last two of which Holmes does little but use an obvious method of finding a concealed person. Most of the others have memorable scenes which it would be a disservice to recount. These readers rate The Adventure of the Six Napoleons near the top, and give very honorable mention to those featuring the Priory School, Black Peter, the Second Stain, and the Abbey Grange.

The stories in this volume are all Adventures, respectively of:

2481   Round the Fire Stories   Dday 1909; orig. 1908
       Pref. by the author

If most well-read followers of the genre were asked: "In what book by Doyle, not about S.H., can you find four tales of detection and four more that are close to the same species?" few would be able to name this book. Yet it does contain such stories and nine others of crime or horror without detection. As one reads The Man with the Watches / The Lost Special / The Jew's Breastplate / The Black Doctor, and the rest, one marvels again at Doyle's natural gift of storytelling and one relishes his ingrained habit of giving clues, even when they serve narrative and are not to be used for ratiocination. These stories are worth reading even around a radiator.

The Lost Special and The Man with the Watches, peripheral to the Holmes canon, do not mention S.H., and are not fully satisfying, but belong to the same order of inspiration. (Repr. by Edgar W. Smith in *Letters from Baker Street*, No. 3378). See also No. 2485.

2482   Round the Red Lamp   App 1894
       Being Facts and Fancies of Medical Life

A collection of short stories, several of which are as "powerful" and as neatly turned as any in the Holmes canon. Not mystery or detection, though **Vincent** Starrett has pointed out that one of them, Behind the Times, should be classed with the early Holmes stories, thanks to a remark about "Mrs. Hudson . . . my housekeeper." Excellent fiction.

2483   Sherlock Holmes   3 v.   Heritage 1950
         Introd. by Vincent Starrett
         Illus.

This edition of the complete Sherlock Holmes tales (long stories included) is the only one that offers a carefully edited and corrected text. This scholarly task was performed by the incomparable Edgar W. Smith (q.v.), who also chose the superb and historically representative illustrations. For the fifty-six short tales, this edition is obligatory, else the duplications and interpolations will confuse.

Volume 1: *A Study in Scarlet, The Sign of the Four, The Adventures of S.H., The Memoirs of S.H.*

Volume 2: *The Return of Sherlock Holmes, The Hound of the Baskervilles.*

Volume 3: *His Last Bow, The Valley of Fear, The Case-Book of S.H.*

2484   The Speckled Band: A Play   Unpub.

A sensational play, written by the author of the tale that bears the same title, and produced with success in London for some six months, after which it had a long life as a surefire melodrama for English stock companies, including Edward Sterling's (q.v.).

Note the modern dramatization of the same story under the same title in No. 3350.

2485   Strange Studies from Life   Cand 1963
         Illus. by Sidney Paget
         Ed. limited to 300 copies

Doyle had planned to furnish *The Strand* magazine twelve retellings of actual crime. He produced three (March, April, May 1901), here reproduced with an Introduction by Peter Ruber and supplemented with a note on Sidney Paget and an interview with Doyle as trainer of commandos in the Boer War.

The tales are: The Holocaust of Manor Place, The Love Affair of George Vincent Parker, The Debatable Case of Mrs. Emsley—all reworkings by Doyle of cases "from the actual history of crime," each c. 1860.

2486   DOYLE, ARTHUR C. See also:

Sherlock Holmes: Selected Stories (ed. with introd. by
   S. C. Roberts. World's Classics)   OUP 1967/1951
Sherlock Holmes's Greatest Cases (ed. with introd. by
   Howard Haycraft; large-type ed.)   FW 1967

2487   DOYLE, ARTHUR CONAN, and GILLETTE, WILLIAM

Sherlock Holmes   French 1922; orig. 1899
      A Drama in 4 Acts; Rev. ed. 1922

At first called "a melodrama" and given its premiere at the Garrick Theater in New York on November 6, 1899, with Gillette in the title role. He played it again in New York in 1929 and it was still a success. Full of good scenes, but not completely Holmesian: he is endangered by obvious things and he succumbs to the girl Alice, on the strength of "her ability to observe"!

2488   DULLES, ALLEN WELSH (1893–1969), ed.

Great Spy Stories from Fiction   Harp 1969
A Giniger Book

The OSS agent in Switzerland, later head of the CIA, had given in *The Craft of Intelligence* (1963) an account of his own part in the spying diplomacy of the second world war before he turned anthologist of fictional and actual narratives of espionage. (See No. 3137.)

The present collection and its critical introductions and headnotes show an admirable balance between the professional and the literary judgment. The page about "The Bruce-Partington Plans," a Sherlock Holmes story, is a piece of perfect criticism in both kinds, and good prose besides. The stories are grouped in eleven sections according to the chief technical feature of each spy adventure, plus two classed as spoofs. The 32 authors include the expected famous names, from Conrad and Mark Twain to Oppenheim and Kipling, and in addition: Rebecca West, Nabokov, Duff Cooper, Lawrence Durrell, Arthur Koestler, Compton MacKenzie, Maugham, Graham Greene, and Virgil. The rest are the steady purveyors of modern spy stuff—Fleming, Cheyney, et al.—but every one of the selections is choice and exhibits a different facet of the ugly profession.

2489   DUMAS, ALEXANDRE (1802–70)

"The King's Private Eye"   Michel-Lévy 1869; orig. 1848
Trans. by Jacques Barzun in No. 2344

This extract from Chapter 4 of *The Vicomte de Bragelonne* is the first European detective episode of the nineteenth century. Doubtless inspired by Voltaire (and possibly the lore of Cuvier's zoological "reconstructions"), this feat of inference is impressive and convincing, but lacks the contemporaneity which made the skit by Beaumarchais (q.v.) an advance on *Zadig* (q.v.).

Dumas' interest in crime produced an eight-volume series of *Celebrated Crimes* (Col 1910), semi-fictionalized history.

2490   DUNSANY, LORD (EDWARD JOHN MORETON DRAX PLUNKETT, 18th baron) (b. 1878)

The Little Tales of Smethers and Other Stories   Jarr 1952;
orig. 1934

Contains the famous Two Bottles of Relish and other narrations by the simple-minded relish salesman named Smethers. He tells the exploits of his friend Linley, who unravels crimes. The detection is slight but the cases are interesting. The remaining tales are fantasy.

Note: Two Bottles of Relish first appeared in another collection by the author entitled *Powers of Darkness,* and may owe something to the murder of Elise Boehmer by Albert Pel.

2491   ELKIN, SAMUEL

"Survival of the Fittest"   *EQMM* Jan 1960

A very neat plot by a fortune hunter to marry the heiress of two sisters by arousing each of them to kill the other. He dies and Lieutenant Rogers has to find out the counterplot that saved their lives and lost the schemer's.

2492   ELLERY QUEEN's anthology(ies) are paperbound collections of fifteen to twenty items totaling 300 pages or more. The first issue (Vol. 1) came out in 1960; two more annual issues appeared, but beginning with 1963 the publication appeared twice yearly. Thus Vol. 4 is 1963, Vol. 5 is 1963 Midyear. . . . Vol. 19 is 1970 Midyear. (See also No. 2747.)
    Each thick volume usually contains a couple of short novels and a few novelettes besides the dozen or so of short stories, none of them drawn from earlier EQ anthologies, but some from *EQMM.* For a sample, see next entry.

2493   ELLERY QUEEN

Anthology Vol. 19   Mar 1970

A particularly good number, which includes a typical Rex Stout Nero Wolfe: The Zero Clue; a good historical reconstruction: Hover Through the Fog, by Hugh Pentecost; an amusing Wodehouse: Jeeves and the Stolen Venus; and two neat tricks: John F. Suter, The Impossible Theft and Stephen Barr, Hat Trick. The remainder is solid work by Michael Gilbert, the Lockridges, Holly Roth, Cornell Woolrich, Patricia Highsmith, Ben Hecht, Lawrence Blochman, Erle Stanley Gardner, Victor Canning, William March, Bryce Walton, Whit Masterson, and Ellery Queen.

2494   ELLERY QUEEN MYSTERY MAGAZINE, the only long-lasting enterprise of its kind, began publication in the autumn of 1941, later becoming a monthly. It prints or reprints short stories and novelettes in a wide range of genres, from detection and crime to horror and the supernatural. Its authors new and old belong to the elite of the several species and are carefully edited. The introductory remarks to many of the stories contain valuable biographical and bibliographical information. Since 1960 the magazine has issued annual paperbound anthologies (see No. 2492).

2495   ELLIN, STANLEY

"Broker's Special"   *EQMM* Jan 1956

A grim tale of crime and retribution. Railway interest not solely because of the rather easily anticipated final scene.

2496 Mystery Stories   S&S 1956
      In ppb.: Quiet Horror
      Pref. by Ellery Queen

Ten stories only partly described by the general title. Some are horror, some pure crime, none detection. They consist of:

The Specialty of the House	The Best of Everything
The Cat's Paw	The Betrayers
Death on Christmas Eve	The House Party
The Orderly World of Mr. Appleby	Broker's Special
Fool's Mate	The Moment of Decision

2497   "You Can't Be a Little Girl All Your Life"   *EQMM* May 1958

Another of this author's very "strong" and psychologically sound tales, this time about a young woman who, against tremendous odds, refuses to let herself be made a dupe. Not detection.

2498   ELLIS, H. F.

     "Hartfield and Homicide"   *Punch* Dec 14, 1955

An excellent parody by the distinguished essayist, based on the plausible idea that Jane Austen would, in a later day, have been a leading writer of detective fiction. Here we are given a sample of her work in that vein, the interrogation of Emma by Inspector Elliott.

2499   FAULKNER, WILLIAM

     Knight's Gambit   RH 1949

One can be a great admirer of Faulkner (as these readers are) without caring much for the short stories in which he plays at uncovering crime. The two most frequently "used against him" as detective stories are An Error of Chemistry and Hand Upon the Waters, and if these are his best, then the rest must be deemed unconscionably dull.

2500   FERRARS, ELIZABETH, ed.

     Planned Departures   H&S 1958
      Introd. by the Editor

This collection is a Crime Writers Association Anthology. In Miss F.'s short Introduction the reader is challenged to identify the genre to which each of the dozen tales belongs. They are:

Bell	The Sea Decides
Boucher	Like Count Palmieri
Creasey	The Chief Witness
Cullingford	Kill and Cure
Ferrars	Drawn into Error
M. Gilbert	The Oyster Catcher
Hare	The Magnifying Glass
McCloy	The Singing Diamonds
Queen	The Gettysburg Bugle

L. A. G. Strong	The Bird Watcher
Symons	Eight Minutes to Kill
Vickers	Murder in the Cowshed

An uneven assemblage, and nearly all turn on small stunts or gimmicks.

2501 FISH, ROBERT L.

"Double Entry"   *EQMM* Jan 1969

A hard-bitten short tale of the undoing of a professional killer. Spare telling, no detection.

2502 FITT, MARY

The Man Who Shot Birds   Macd 1954
And Other Tales of Mystery and Detection

The *London Mystery Magazine* first published most of these twelve stories about the elderly Mr. Pitt and his Siamese cat, Georgina. Five or six are excellent bits of crime and detection; others are just oddities. Throughout, the cat contributes hints or judgments by giving signs of anxiety or disapproval, rather improbably, for the Siamese breed is usually quite self-centered. The setting is rural and Miss Fitt shows herself a good nature writer and observer.

2503 FLAUBERT, GUSTAVE

Bibliomania   Rodale 1954; orig. 1837
A Tale
Illus. by Arthur Wragg; trans. not named
Endpaper: facsimile page of orig. ms.

Undoubtedly the most recherché item in our collection, for several reasons: the author was not quite 15 when he wrote it; he became a very great writer; and it is surely the shortest fictional treatment of actual crime on record.

The story is that of the contemporary Spanish monk Don Vincente, whose obsession about books led him to murder the owner of a unique fifteenth-century volume, and whose only penitent feeling came when he learned that the volume was not the only copy. The monk was executed in 1836.

Andrew Lang gives a somewhat different version of the facts (see No. 3208).

2504 FLETCHER, J. S.

Behind the Monocle   Dday 1930

Twenty-one short stories of adventure and often of deception, which are agreeable reading if one switches off one's critical sense. J.S.F. can make suspense out of a thread of milkweed and he is always good at English scenes, buildings, lanes, and fields, which are often enough to carry the reader along for a half hour. But mark the twenty-first story, A Little

Tyrant of the Fields, for a successful attempt at characterization and drama—a perfect gem, despite the happy ending.

2505 "Bickmore Deals with the Duchess"   *EQMM* Nov 1951

A well-told tale of diamond-cut-diamond, about a necklace that is not what it seems. In the author's best manner, which turns a trifle into a source of pleasure.

2506 The Case of the Artificial Eye   Hillm 1939

A collection of nine short stories, the first giving its title to the set. The private detective Paul Campenhaye is featured, though he is featureless. He describes himself in a press notice as "famous," but the claim seems to the reader hallucination or megalomania. The stories contain numerous simple clues, but the reasoning is of kindergarten strength. At that, C. endears himself by failing, which must mean that J.S.F. is a great artist.

2507 The Secret of the Barbican and Other Stories   Doran 1925

Fifteen short stories, all of a sameness. In most, the usual Fletcherisms: ancient boroughs, highly respected but defalcating treasurers, slow-witted and ankylosed policemen abetted by keen young men from London. All this has a kind of charm, but it can be endured only for the sake of the 1900 atmosphere.

2508 FLORA, FLETCHER

"The Scrap of Knowledge"   *EQMM* May 1968

A long short in the classic pattern with Lieutenant Marcus facing the problem of how the dying man tried to identify his murderer. Interesting despite the dependence upon a gimmick at the very end.

2509 FOOTNER, HULBERT

The Casual Murderer   Lipp 1937

Six tales embodying the investigations of the beautiful Madame Storey and Inspector Ramsey: too casual to withstand the critical attention they invite.

2510 FORD, COREY (1902–69)

"One on the House"   *EQMM* Dec 1946

A short short surprise affair (less than 2 pages), based on a good old escape dodge for the man caught *in flagrante delicto*. Neatly told.

2511 FRANKAU, GILBERT (b. 1884)

Concerning Peter Jackson and Others   Hutch [1931]

A loose collection of feeble fictions in the short form, nowhere near his standard in the later collection, but containing a Kyra Sokratesco story: Who Killed Castelvetro?

For average-strength spy stories, see *The Lonely Man* (1932) and *Secret Services* (1934).

2512   Experiments in Crime   Dutt 1937

Presumably the author refers to his own "experiments," for in the nine tales of crime out of these fourteen he never makes use of the same detective twice. There is a certain unity of style and some plausible villains, though not much detection. Only one tale (Tragedy at St. Tropez) features the promising Roumanian detective, Kyra Sokratesco, of whom one would be glad to have more. The tales are:

Executions at Cape Remittance	Auto-da-Fé in the Estérels
Blackmail in St. John's Wood	Robbery at the Castle
Murder at the Magnificent	Tragedy at St. Tropez
Forgery from the Fantastic	Cardsharps in the Cellar
Moral Outrage in Marseilles	plus five "other stories."

2513   "Who Killed Castelvetro?"
           In: Concerning Peter Jackson and Others. See No. 2511.
           2511.

Not so good as the other "Kyra" tale in No. 2512, but worth reading and analyzing just the same. Often anthologized.

2514   FREELING, NICOLAS

           "Van der Valk and the Four Mice"   *EQMM* Nov 1969

As Chief Inspector of the Juvenile Brigade of Amsterdam, Van der Valk tangles with four of the young toughs of that city. Interesting, if truly representative of Dutch conditions. One feels that in New York or L.A. the Inspector would have had his hands more full than in this Dutch crisis.

2515   FREELING. See also: Van der Valk: the High School Riot (*EQMM* Mar 1970).

2516   FREEMAN, R. AUSTIN

           Dr. Thorndyke's Case Book   H&S 1923
               In U.S.: The Blue Scarab

Thorndyke functioning in a variety of predicaments with his little green case full of equipment, his medico-legal knowledge, and his Spilsbury-like imperturbability. The best tales—if one must make a choice—are Nos. III and VII of the list that follows:

I. The Blue Scarab	V. A Fisher of Men
II. The Case of the White Foot-Prints	VI. The Stolen Ingots
III. The New Jersey Sphinx	VII. The Funeral Pyre
IV. The Touchstone	

2517   Dr. Thorndyke's Cases   DM 1931; orig. 1909
           In Eng.: John Thorndyke's Cases

Remarkably finished tales for a time when scientific detection was a word rather than a fact. The most interesting are Nos. I, III, IV, VII, and VIII.

I. The Man with the Nailed Shoes	V. The Moabite Cipher
II. The Stranger's Latchkey	VI. The Mandarin's Pearl
III. The Anthropologist at Large	VII. The Aluminium Dagger
IV. The Blue Sequin	VIII. A Message from the Deep Sea

2518   The Great Portrait Mystery   H&S 1918

Seven short stories, of which the title tale is the longest. It starts off best, with a good puzzle and crime engendered on copying day in the National Gallery (London). But it peters out in unlikely complications and even more unlikely solutions. Dr. Thorndyke takes part only in the third and the fifth stories, and it is (regrettably) someone else who makes the remark: "There is something about a really methodical procedure that inspires confidence." Note also that except for Conan Doyle (*Hound of the Baskervilles*), no other investigator makes reference to the cranial index, so popular in the 1890s. The titles of the remaining tales, none especially worthy of notice, are: The Bronze Parrot / The Missing Mortgagee / Powder Blue and Hawthorn / Percival Bland's Proxy / The Attorney's Conscience / The Luck of Barnabas Mudge.

2519   The Magic Casket   DM 1927

More of the same sort, but all Thorndyke; the choice this time bearing on Nos. II, IV, VIII, and IX of the following:

I. The Magic Casket	VI. Pandora's Box
II. The Contents of a Mare's Nest	VII. The Trail of Behemoth
III. The Stalking Horse	VIII. The Pathologist to the Rescue
IV. The Naturalist at Law	IX. Gleanings from the Wreckage
V. Mr. Ponting's Alibi	

2520   The Puzzle Lock   DM 1926

Here No. VII seems the most ingenious of the series:

I. The Puzzle Lock	VI. Rex v. Burnaby
II. The Green Check Jacket	VII. A Mystery of the Sand-Hills
III. The Seal of Nebuchadnezzar	VIII. The Apparition of Burling Court
IV. Phyllis Annesley's Peril	IX. The Mysterious Visitor
V. A Sower of Pestilence	

2521   The Singing Bone   Nort 1965; orig. 1912
            In ppb.: The Adventures of Dr. Thorndyke
            Pref. by the author
            Introd. by Vincent Starrett

The recent hard-cover edition is a reprint of the classic collection that introduced the "inverted tale." (See Introductory of this *Catalogue*.) Starrett's Introduction is general and not remarkable. Note that of the five tales, only the first four are in the inverted form and of these four, one, A Case of Premeditation, presents a successful and sympathetic murderer. The full table of contents follows:

The Case of Oscar Brodski
  I. The Mechanism of Crime
  II. The Mechanism of Detection
A Case of Premeditation
  I. The Elimination of Mr. Pratt
  II. Rival Sleuth-Hounds
The Echo of a Mutiny
  I. Death on the Girdler
  II. "The Singing Bone"

A Wastrel's Romance
  I. The Spinster's Guest
  II. Munera Pulveris
The Old Lag
  I. The Changed Immutable
  II. The Ship of the Desert

2522   The Surprising Experiences of Mr. Shuttlebury Cobb   H&S n.d.
                                                                   [1927]

Six adventures of the solicitor's clerk S. Cobb, who stands on the fringes
of the criminal world. They are strung on a common thread, somewhat in
the style of Stevenson, and are moderately entertaining. (A rare item.)

2523   FREEMAN. See also "Clifford Ashdown" (Nos. 2329 and 2330)
and The Dr. Thorndyke Omnibus (DM 1932), which contains the thirty-
eight ss in the collections called: *Dr. Thorndyke's Cases, The Blue Scarab,
The Singing Bone, The Magic Casket,* and *The Puzzle Lock,* plus a satisfactory but unsigned ten-page essay on R. Austin Freeman, which quotes
from his correspondence. (The English edition has only 37 cases.)

2524   FROME, DAVID

    "The Policeman's Cape"
       In: The Third Mystery Book (Farr 1941)

A Mr. Pinkerton story, very much like the long ones in spirit and style.
Mr. P. is less annoying because there is less of him in a few pages than in
many.

2525   FURMAN, A. L.

    Third Mystery Companion   GL 1945

A distinctly low-grade sort of anthology, but the best of a series of four.
The stories are humdrum. Even the contribution by Margery Allingham
(The Old Man in the Window) is not among her choicest. Besides the
Allingham and Chandler's perennial article, "The Simple Art of Murder,"
the contents offer:

Louis Paul	The Calling Card of Mr. Engle
A. V. Elston	The Unloaded Gun
Mindret Lord	The Experts
E. S. Holding	The Kiskadee Bird
John Collier	Wet Saturday
Will Payne	One Chance in a Million
Richard Sale	Death Had a Pencil
Cornell Woolrich	The Phantom of the Subway
Sax Rohmer	The Mark of Maat
Philip Ketchum	The Third Ladder
Leslie T. White	Hangin' Crazy Benny

Frank Owen	The Long Still Streets of Evening
Stuart Palmer	The Riddle of the Blueblood Murder
Thomas Grant Springer	Ways That Are Dark
Howard Bloomfield	The Case on Turkey Point
William Brandon	The Witness
Vincent Starrett	Murder at the Opera (= Bloody Crescendo)

2526 FUTRELLE, JACQUES

"The Case of the Mysterious Weapon"   EQMM Oct 1950

One of this author's four last stories, saved because left behind in London when he sailed to his death on the *Titanic*. The device used by the murderer to kill three people is a slender—one might say a highly attenuated—one, and its workability is open to doubt, but we are treated to more detail than usual about the remarkable detective, Professor Augustus S. F. X. Van Dusen, whose science (if not his technology) is impeccable.

2527   The Diamond Master   BM 1909
      Also contains: The Haunted Bell, *a Professor Van Dusen story*

The Diamond Master is a tale of success in forcing natural diamonds off the market by the threat of large-scale synthesis based on Henri Moissan's work. Though one has to laugh at some of the remarks about diamonds ("there is some theory that they are pure carbon, crystallized"), the technical explanation in the last chapter is solid stuff.

   The Haunted Bell (88 pages) is a bit of claptrap featuring "The Thinking Machine," his journalist assistant, Hutchinson Hatch, a murder, and a Japanese gong.

2528   "The Leak"   EQMM Feb 1949

The first reprinting by the vigilant Queen of an uncollected story which is a fair specimen of Professor A. S. F. X. Van Dusen's work, with a bit of period gadgetry and some resounding affirmations of logic: good fun in the course of finding out who gave away the confidential stock-market information. Old S.F.X.V.D. utters one paragraph worth framing and hanging over other writers' desks.

2529   The Thinking Machine   DM 1907
      Also: The Problem of Cell 13 (*1917*)
      Being a True and Complete Statement of Several Intricate Mysteries which came under the Observation of Professor Augustus S. F. X. Van Dusen, PH.D. [sic], L.L.D., F.R.S., M.D., etc.
      Four Illus. by the Kinneys

The first collection of seven tales originally published in the Hearst papers. It contains the famous Problem of Cell 13 and presents other good or amusing points, set in the usual period melodrama and written with dash at the expense of grammar. Futrelle's professor owes much to Sherlock

Holmes, yet he displays features not in Holmes and which turn up in Rhode's Dr. Priestley. The volume contains:

The Problem of Cell 13	The Flaming Phantom
The Scarlet Thread	The Ralston Bank Burglary
The Man Who Lost	The Mystery of a Studio
The Great Auto Mystery	

The first is the best; the others have points—and unintended humor, especially The Great Auto Mystery.

See also Nos. 917, 2526, and 2528.

2530   GARDNER, ERLE STANLEY

"The Clue of the Hungry Horse"   *EQMM* Mar 1966

A slow tale in which a slow sheriff comes out with the right answer in a rural murder. Pleasant reading, but the complications are not up to the author's usual level of originality and interest.

2531   GASKELL, [MRS.] ELIZABETH

"Disappearances"
        In: Cranford and Other Tales, *ed. A. W. Ward,* Works, *vol. 2*
        (*JM 1920*)

This small group of four episodes was prompted by the author's reading of Dickens' four articles about the new Metropolitan Police in *Household Words* (No. 3128), to which Mrs. G. herself was a regular contributor and which printed this essay in June 1851. They are part recollections of legendary events in and around Knutsford (Cranford), and the editor of the volume gives an account of such basis in fact as they had.

2532   "The Squire's Story"
        In: Works, *vol. 2* (*JM 1920*)

The full-fledged reconstruction of an eighteenth-century imposture, criminal and tragic, based like several of her other writings on tales picked up in the vicinage of Knutsford, Ireland. There is a version of the same events in De Quincey's *Autobiography.* Mrs. G.'s treatment is compact, moving and masterly.

2533   GILBERT, MICHAEL

A Clean Kill   Const 1960
        A Murder Mystery in Three Acts

And a clean job, too. The marital triangle which inspires to murder is set forth without frills, though temperaments are well marked. The detective does no very brilliant feat of detection, but everything moves to its appointed conclusion, in a surprise ending which the playwright privately credits to the inspiration of a similar scene in Philip MacDonald's *White Crow* (No. 1458). In that novel it is indeed the only bit worth lifting.

The play was reprinted in Trewin, J. C., ed., *Plays of the Year 1959–60.*

The adventures of Mr. Calder and Mr. Behrens (and the Persian deer-hound Rasselas) in the service of counterintelligence. There is clueing and detecting and danger and driving around, and (as one would expect) the storytelling is first-rate. But the genre seems to us more liable to repetition of effects than crime and detection. The best stories here include the longest, The Spoilers, and The Headmaster, *not* a school story.

2535   "The Second Skin"   *EQMM* Sept 1958
       Also: "The Oyster Catcher"

The "scientific" examination of a raincoat comes in for humorous de-bunking, which makes this tale the skeptical antithesis of all Thorndyke's work in Freeman. Sergeant Petrella gets his man by independent means, the whole neatly told (see Nos. 2344 and 984).

2536   "Stay of Execution"   *EQMM* Sept 1964

Harry Gordon is convicted of the murder of an actress, but his friends, both legal and extra-legal, pull strings, nearly all unusual and interesting, to place the guilt elsewhere. Forty-two pages of mounting suspense inter-woven with good investigation.

2537   "Tea Shop Assassin"   *EQMM* July 1958

Few tales as short as this (4 pages) succeed so well in hoodwinking the reader and yet leave him feeling satisfied rather than cheated. Super-intendent Hazelrigg is more than competent as he expounds in a teashop to a crime reporter who knows that there is a killer in the room with them.

2538   GILBERT. See also: The Shot in Question (play)   Const 1963

2539   GOODCHILD, GEORGE

       Call McLean   H&S 1937

Eighteen short stories exhibiting Inspector McLean and bearing no separate titles. Several describe unusual situations, but the group as a whole is spoiled by the evident haste and carelessness with which they were turned out.

2540   GORDON, MILDRED (NIXON) and GORDON
       (= The Gordons)

       "The Terror Racket"   *EQMM* Aug 1967

Competent and adorned with a good train episode. Described by E.Q. as the "inexorable pursuit of a faceless killer."

2541   GREEN, ANNA KATHARINE

       A Difficult Problem   Lupt 1900; orig. 1895

The first by this author to be read by WHT, c. 1915. The six stories are quite varied. Psychological detection pervades the title story; The Staircase at the Heart's Delight is Mr. Gryce's own account of his first case; Midnight in Beauchamp Row is able to stir a trace of apprehension and terror fifty years after first reading, though it is but a short thriller.

Note the identity of plot of the last-named with Mary Cholmondely's The Hand on the Latch (No. 2415), published some fourteen years later.

Contains: A Difficult Problem / The Gray Man / The Bronze Hand / Midnight in Beauchamp Row / The Staircase at the Heart's Delight / The Hermit of ——— Street.

2542   GREENE, [SIR] HUGH, ed.

The Rivals of Sherlock Holmes   Pantheon 1970
    Introd. by the editor
    Map of London c. 1898
    Directory of Detectives

The brother of Graham Greene has culled from his large library of Edwardian detection thirteen tales that he considers evidence for entitling this book as he does. To students of the genre, the claim seems untenable. The authors presented here have long been known, except perhaps Guy Boothby and William Hope Hodgson, and their works do not belong in the same class as the Sherlock Holmes stories, for one reason or another. Leaving aside style, narrative skill, and maturity of mind (which together is a good deal), the verdict must be that some are mere imitations of Holmes, others are Raffles-type adventure, one (Hodgson) is a ghost story, and the best (Bramah and Freeman) are new departures, to be developed later in better specimens than these. The contents are: Max Pemberton, The Ripening Rubies / Arthur Morrison, The Case of Laker, Absconded / Guy Boothby, The Duchess of Wiltshire's Diamonds / Arthur Morrison, The Affair of the Avalanche Bicycle and Tyre Co. / Clifford Ashdown, The Assyrian Rejuvenator / L. T. Meade and Robert Eustace, Madame Sara / Clifford Ashdown, The Submarine Boat / Wm Le Queux, The Secret of the Fox Hunter / Baroness Orczy, The Mysterious Death on the Underground Railway / R. Austin Freeman, The Moabite Cipher / Baroness Orczy, The Woman in the Big Hat / Wm Hope Hodgson, The Horse of the Invisible / Ernest Bramah, The Game Played in the Dark.

The reader will find listed in this *Catalogue* other works by all these authors except Boothby.

2543   GRIFFITHS, [MAJOR] ARTHUR

Criminals I Have Known   C&H 1895

Sixty-two anecdotes, evidently fictional, and told with the naïveté that does not equal art. Some are humorous, others serious and mysterious. The vein of invention is far from poor, but the explanations tend to be huddled and implausible. Is the prolific Major the inventor of the short short? See, for example, Detected by a Dog.

2544   HAMILTON, LORD FREDERIC (SPENCER) (b. 1856). Fourth son of the duke of Abercorn; diplomat and novelist; editor of the *Pall Mall*

Magazine (1893–1900). He concerns us tangentially as the author of boys' stories of espionage and detection about P. J. Davenant, himself a youth of pre-college age. Pleasant and mild tales: *The Holiday Adventures of Mr. P. J. Davenant* (with his photograph as frontispiece), Eveleigh Nash (1915); *Further Adventures of*, etc. (1915); *The Education of*, etc. (1916); and *The Beginnings of, etc.* (1917).

HAMMETT, DASHIELL

He began by writing short stories in the approved *Black Mask* manner, but found his genius in the full form. Various overlapping collections contain his output of shorts. They are hard to get hold of, and the few listed below sample the several grades of performance along the author's way to mastery. (See No. 1074/B.)

2545   The Adventures of Sam Spade and
        Other Stories   Tower 1945; orig. 1944

Three Sam Spade adventures and four miscellaneous tales. Spade is the hero of Too Many Have Lived / They Can Only Hang You Once / A Man Called Spade, in the second of which he is at his best. (See No. 2551.)

2546   "The Assistant Murderer"   *RSMQ* Aug 1945; orig. 1926

An early novelette by the only begetter of the tough detective and his situation. It is clear that the unlovely characteristics of the "new man" in detection are what generates confidence—traits that changed when the imitators took up the line. Alec Rush is ugly and bearlike and an "unfrocked" cop, but he radiates competence and kindness and he proves he has both when he unravels a tangle of crookedness, murder, false marriage, and unlimited sentimentality. It is good by virtue of narrative power but terrible nonsense on reflection.

Note that the prose is prim and at times even genteel—not what we have come to expect from the tough guys.

2547   The Big Knockover   RH 1967
        Selected Stories and Short Novels
        Introd. by Lillian Hellman

Ten short stories and novellas, preceded by the illuminating reminiscences of a lifelong friend. The stories, though unrevised for book publication, show the author's unmistakable genius and fertility. The titles are:

The Gutting of Couffignal	Dead Yellow Women
Fly Paper	Corkscrew
The Scorched Face	Tulip
This King Business	The Big Knockover
The Gatewood Caper	$106,000 Blood Money

2548   Hammett Homicides   Dell 1946
        Prefatory Letter by Ellery Queen

Six stories: four about the Continental Op, one about Chief of Police Anderson, and one about Guy Thorp. All are laid in San Francisco and all exploit the customary toughness of the *Black Mask*erade. This volume, incidentally, is one of a series edited by Ellery Queen (see starred titles in No. 2551) and published by Dell, 1944–47.

2549   "House Dick"   *EQMM* Apr 1947; orig. 1923

The style is Early Pulp and quite bad. No one would detect the promise of later art in this crude, lumbering, and bloody tale of revenge and mistaken identity that pivots on one small and obvious numerical gimmick.

2550   "A Man Named Thin"   *EQMM* Mar 1961

Probably written in the mid-twenties and acquired by EQ in 1946. Preceding *The Maltese Falcon,* no doubt, since the not-so-hard-boiled detective is a young poet. More than a curio—the master's hand shows.

2551   HAMMETT. See also:

A Man Called Spade*	Dell 1944	A Man Named Thin	*Merc* 1962
The Continental Op*	BSM 1943	The Return of the	
The Creeping Siamese	Jon 1950	Continental Op*	Jon 1945
Dead Yellow Women*	Jon 1947	Woman in the Dark	Jon 1952

2552   HAMMOND, WILLIAM A., and LANZA, CLARA [his daughter]

     Tales of Eccentric Life   App 1886

Ten chapters constituting nine tales of mystery, quite incredible, but nonetheless in the Poe-Bierce-Fitzjames-O'Brien tradition. Strong medical flavor.

2553   HANSHEW, THOMAS W. (also Charlotte May Kingsley; 1857–1914)

     Cleek, the Man of Forty Faces   Cass 1910

In the innumerable tales about Cleek may be seen as in a mirror the vogue of Raffles, Arsène Lupin, Colonel Clay, The Grey Seal, and other daring heroes who did evil cleverly and for incomprehensible motives, except that the evil was really all to the good. Cleek got away from his pursuers thanks to the extreme mobility of his features (his mother had played with a plastic toy during his gestation), which enabled him to look instantly like somebody else. This talent saved him untold amounts in false beards, spirit gum, and the like. His enemies couldn't tell a hawk from a Hanshew, but it must have been hard on Cleek's ladylove that when he turned from crime to law enforcement (as all noble natures wind up doing) he was just as much on the run.

2554   HANSHEW. See also:

     Cleek, the Master Detective   Dday 1918

    With his wife, Mary Hanshew, another half dozen titles on the pattern of The Riddle of: . . . the Frozen Flames, the Mysterious Light, etc.

2555   HARE, CYRIL

[His] Best Detective Stories   Faber 1959
Introd. by Michael Gilbert

Three types of tales are represented here—legal, murder, and other crimes. They are not of equal merit, and many of them are very short stunts pivoting on very small points. But the telling is always adept and urbane, and the collection is a fit memorial to a master prematurely lost to the high genre.

2556   "Margin of Safety"   *EQMM* Feb 1951

A crime story with a biter-bit twist at the end, well told, but short and inconsequential compared to the author's best work.

2557   "The 24-Carat Heel"   *EQMM* Jan 1956

A nice short tale of an American miscreant in England who gives himself away during a call from the police by his careless use of Americanisms. How could this be?

2558   "The Unluckiest Murderer"   *EQMM* May 1957

A club-room story of the type Hare does so well. Not in the collection edited by Michael Gilbert (No. 2555).

2559   HARRISON, ERNEST

"English Lesson"   *EQMM* Oct 1959

Actually not an English lesson but one in the small conventions of life on this continent compared with the U.K.—a neat little trick to catch a faker.

2560   HARRISON, MICHAEL

"The Assassination of Sir Ponsonby Brown"   *EQMM* Sept 1968

The problem faced by "Dupin" as resuscitated by the author) was not: Who killed Sir Ponsonby? but rather: Who was able to get the news of his whereabouts to his killers within a very few minutes of obtaining this information? Dupin's solution of the problem is a nice bit of ratiocination, and the criminal *might* have succeeded.

2561   "The Clew of the Single Word"   *EQMM* Oct 1969

Another clever imitation of Poe's stories about Dupin, this time forcing the Chevalier to spot the use of a single word (innocent enough in itself) to convey information from a spy to his associates.

2562   "The Facts in the Case of the Missing Diplomat"

EQMM Apr 1968

An ingenious account by Dupin's reincarnation of how it was possible for a secretary of the American legation in Paris to vanish into thin air. More credible than most such attempts.

2563 "The Fires in the Rue St. Honoré" *EQMM* Nov 1967

The "new" Dupin works out an ingenious scheme (foolproof enough for most readers) by which it was possible to set fires at predetermined times without leaving traces of the usual arsonical apparatus.

2564 "The Man in the Blue Spectacles" *EQMM* May 1966

The third of the Dupin pastiches and a superb job. M.H. knows history, is full of interesting detail, and has the Poe period style down pat.

2565 HARTLEY, L. P.

"The Island" *In:* The Mercury Story Book (No. 3444)

A crime story of great intensity, though based on a simple and indeed commonplace situation. The suggestion of a power greater than that of the ordinary will is produced without any hint of the supernatural and none of the common verbal tricks.

2566 HAWORTH, PETER, ed.

Classic Crimes in History and Fiction App 1927
In Eng.: Before Scotland Yard
Introd. by the editor

The senior lecturer in English at the University of Bristol has collected nineteen disparate items, ranging from Herodotus and the history of Susanna in the Apocrypha to episodes from Defoe, Voltaire, De Quincey, and Dickens. The introduction is short and superficial. The volume is convenient for the extracts from medieval sources and the Elizabethans, which show conclusively that nothing like believable detection is to be found before Voltaire (in *Zadig,* excerpted here; see also No. 2141). Likewise there is an extract from Mrs. Gaskell's crime tale The Squire's Story (see No. 2532) and three of Dickens' sketches of the "new police" (No. 3128).

2567 HAWTHORNE, JULIAN, ed.

Library of the World's Best Mystery and
Detective Stories 6 v. ROR 1908

Arranged by country of origin, this series comprises a very miscellaneous lot of 101 pieces, some hardly fiction, some fiction but dull, some good and by now insistently well known. But being early, this enterprise helped develop the taste by which it may now be criticized. (See the next item.)

2568 The Lock and Key Library 10 v. ROR 1909–15
Classic Mystery and Detective Stories of All Nations

The ten volumes cover: North Europe; Mediterranean; German; Classic French; Modern French; French Novels; Old Time English; Modern English; American; Real Life.
The Modern English volume (No. 8)—perhaps the best of the set—con-

tains stories by Kipling (4), Doyle (3), Egerton Castle, S. J. Weyman, R. L. Stevenson, and Wilkie Collins (1 each), as well as five by anonymous authors, some of whose works are not negligible. The Stevenson tale is the powerful novelette The Pavilion on the Links, not mystery or detection but adventure, though this set of volumes tends more toward detection than the earlier set (No. 2567) and also includes the supernatural.

HAYCRAFT, HOWARD (b. 1905)

b. Minn., educ. at state Univ., and joined its press on his graduation. In 1929 went to N.Y.C. to work for H. W. Wilson Co., pub. of reference books, and became its president after collaborating on many of its volumes, notably *Authors Today and Yesterday* (several edns). Meantime estab. himself as leading U.S. authority on detective fiction and as a formidable anthologist and omnibuster.

2569   HAYCRAFT, HOWARD, ed.

Fourteen Great Detective Stories   ModL 1949
    Introd. by the editor

A revision of the volume edited by Starrett in 1928 (No. 2795). The new editor has written a somewhat neutral introduction, dwelling on the newer material. He notes the rise of the story of suspense as a device for varying the classic formula—not "who?" and "how?" but "why?" The stories are:

Poe	The Purloined Letter
Doyle	The Red-Headed League
Futrelle	The Problem of Cell 13
Freeman	The Case of Oscar Brodski
Chesterton	The Blue Cross
M. D. Post	The Age of Miracles
Bentley	The Little Mystery
Christie	The Third-Floor Flat
Bailey	The Yellow Slugs
Sayers	The Bone of Contention
Queen	The Adventure of the African Traveler
Stout	Instead of Evidence
Carter Dickson	The House in Goblin Wood
Woolrich	The Dancing Detective

2570   HECHT, BEN

    "Miracle of the Fifteen Murderers"   *EQMM* Sept 1962; orig. 1943

Once every three months the fifteen doctors making up the X Club met to drink together and confess their mistaken diagnoses; upon admission a new member had to confess to such a "murder." But young Dr. Warner finds a way to shake them down and saves a life in the process. Very clever indeed.

2571   "Rehearsal for Murder"   *EQMM* Jan 1955
    Orig.: "Guilty!" (*1951*)

A somewhat mechanical affair based on a good idea: the "detection" of hidden purposes in a mother-ridden man, who is then persuaded that he has killed his wife. With other details a trifle baroque, this effects a cure without bloodshed.

2572 HELLMAN, LILLIAN

>The Children's Hour   DPS 1953; orig. 1934
> *Review-Preface by Harry Gilroy:* "The Bigger the Lie"
> *Illus.*

This was the play that made its author's reputation when she was 26 years old and had never had a stage success. It was produced in late 1934 and ran for 691 performances.

The theme was supplied by William Roughead in his book *Bad Companions* (1930), which told of a scandal of the year 1809, when a schoolgirl at Edinburgh maliciously slandered two of her teachers by saying they had an inordinate affection for each other. When dramatized by L. H., the story was deemed powerful but unplayable. Leading actresses refused the adult roles. The play was put on nevertheless, controversy helped its popularity, and it was revived in 1952. Today, it would probably inspire a no-clothes production. But it is the excellent prose and sound psychology that constitute its strength. (Roughead's piece is also in No. 2774.)

2573 HELÚ, ANTONIO

>"Professional Debut"   *EQMM* Dec 1946
> *Trans. by Anthony Boucher*

A new idea in the interpretation of small mysteries visible to those present, in this case a pair of policemen in a Mexican city who are taking the ingenious Máximo Roldán to the police station. His ratiocination wins him freedom and them protection—perhaps.

2574 HEYER, GEORGETTE

>Pistols for Two   Dutt 1964

Too bad, but all eleven of these stories are of Regency times; some dueling but no detection, charm but no great fictional force.

2575 HITCHCOCK, ALFRED, ed.

>The Fireside Book of Suspense   S&S 1947
> *Introd.:* "The Quality of Suspense," *by the editor*
> *Biog. notes about each author*

Twenty-seven tales of widely varying merit, though most are by well-known authors. The noteworthiest pieces are:

Perceval Gibbon	The Second-Class Passenger
Graham Greene	The News in English
Carl Stephenson	Leiningen *versus* the Ants
William Outerson	Fire in the Galley Stove (fictional solution of the *Mary Celeste;* see No. 3091)

Ralph Straus	The Room on the Fourth Floor (still another retelling of the woman who vanishes, together with her room, in a respectable hotel)
A. D. Divine	Flood on the Goodwins (a variant of *Date with Darkness* and *A Hero for Leanda,* qq.v.)
Ralph Milne Farley	The House of Ecstasy
William Irish	After-Dinner Story (also in No. 2590)
Hanson Baldwin	RMS Titanic (facts scarcely fictionalized, with Jacques Futrelle [q.v.] miscalled a French novelist)
Lord Dunsany	Two Bottles of Relish (see No. 2490)
Ex-Private X*	Smee
W. W. Jacobs	His Brother's Keeper (see also No. 2591)
Albert Payson Terhune	The Blue Paper (a near duplicate of Cleveland Moffett's The Mysterious Card, but without the sequel; see No. 2666)

* Pseudonym of Alfred McLelland Burrage.

2576 HITCHCOCK. See also:

Stories for Late at Night	RH 1961
Stories Not for the Nervous	RH 1965

2577 HOCH, EDWARD D.

"The Seventh Assassin" *EQMM* Mar 1970

A very short tale that combines the typical Oriental "suspense by repetition" with modern details of contrivance. Instant entertainment from the hand of a versatile writer.

2578 "The Spy Who Came out of the Night" *EQMM* Apr 1967

The seventh story in which Rand works as a counterspy, this time in Switzerland. The tale is dead serious and entails killings and moves that will end in more killings. The ingenuity of the espionage writer ends—as it does here—in a grisly parody of itself, because there is no control by plausibility and possibility: anybody can impersonate, imitate, duplicate, implicate, and deceive. The denouement thereby becomes long-winded and dull.

2579 "The Spy Who Took the Long Route" *EQMM* Mar 1966

Rand, of the Department of Concealed Communications, is an American intelligence officer who works both abroad and at home. His adventures are the usual stuff and this is a chunk of it. See three more in *EQMM* for May and Oct. 1970 and Jan. 1971.

"Grounds for Divorce"   *EQMM* Mar 1966

A good, strong, very short story, in which the single clue is original and enormously effective and the difficulty of using it at all is adroitly handled with the aid of superb characterization.

HORNUNG, E(RNEST) W(ILLIAM) (1866–1921)

b. Middlesbrough, Yorks.; educ. Uppingham; in poor health as a youth, went to Australia till his 20th year. On return to Eng. became newspaperman and succeeded with a first novel (1890). Married Conan Doyle's sister Constance in 1893; gave much time to cricket; enlisted, aged 48, in first world war, saw service in France though a sufferer from asthma, and narrowly escaped being taken prisoner in 1918.

2581 Raffles   Coll 1955
      Orig.: The Amateur Cracksman (*1898*) *repr. with* The Black
      Mask (*1901*)
      Introd. by M. R. Ridley
      Biog. sketch by G.F.M.

These sixteen tales, which form the basis of the hero's reputation, recount his burglarious adventures with his friend, accomplice, and narrator, "Bunny." What Haycraft has called "the necessary obverse of the detective story" is exhibited with a good deal of charm and narrative skill, though the prose sometimes falls into bathos. The episodes capture the late Victorian atmosphere of [the] Albany, Mount Street, and Richmond, and owe some of their devices to Doyle and Sherlock Holmes. Note that the haze of moral feeling brings Bunny to prison and Raffles to a hero's death in the South African War.

N.B. the evolution in the meaning of "Black Mask" from the eighteenth century through the nineteenth to the twentieth.

2582 HORNUNG. See also:

      Mr. Justice Raffles   Scrib 1909
      A Thief in the Night   C&W 1905

It is worth noting that Barry Perowne (q.v.) obtained the right to produce Raffles tales after the death of the originator and was responsible for: *The Return of Raffles* (1933), *She Married Raffles* (1936), and *Raffles and the Key Man* (1940).

2583 HUXLEY, ALDOUS

      "The Gioconda Smile"   *EQMM* Sept 1950; orig. 1922

Murder, not detection, but done with all the art necessary to make us believe in a commonplace plot. The hero-victim is destroyed by his equally commonplace philandering, which his disparate women take seriously. A classic rendering of the situation. No detection.

2584 HYNE, C(HARLES) J(OHN) (CUTLIFFE) W(RIGHT)

Mr. Horrocks, Purser   Meth 1902

The creator of Captain Kettle and other seafaring types, who was also an amateur chemist intent on the manufacture of artificial diamonds as far back as 1886, includes half a dozen stories of crime and (a little) detection in this entertaining period medley.

2585 INNES, MICHAEL

Appleby Talks Again   DM 1957

Eighteen short stories, the first, A Matter of Goblins, being the longest (45 pages). All are told with skill and are fairly down-to-earth in the matter of clues. Several fill only 4 or 5 pages and turn on stunts. Tape-recording comes in a couple of times, also Daltonism and various gadgets. Thanks to amusing characterizations, the volume entertains without pretending to be substantial.

2586 "Death as a Game"   EQMM Nov 1965

Not what its title suggests—that is, not a fancy-free kind of murder tale. Rather, it is complementary to E. S. Gardner's study in the same area (see No. 2945) but with more attention to the reading and writing of detective fiction. Many interesting reminiscences, including some of Sayers and Knox.

2587 "Death in the Sun"   EQMM Mar 1966

A short short in which Appleby, vacationing in Cornwall, finds an ostensible suicide, goes haywire in his fancy reasoning, but comes down to earth just in time.

2588 "The Heritage Portrait"   EQMM Nov 1956

Good use by this author (who is at his best when his tales center upon the world of art) of a shocking incident at a portrait unveiling to veil a killer's real motive. Fine chase at the end, but Inspector Appleby doesn't do much detecting.

2589 "The Mysterious Affair at Elsinore"   Goll 1950
         In: Three Tales of Hamlet, *by Rayner Heppenstall and
         Michael Innes*
         Pref. by Mr. Heppenstall

The "tales" here collected are texts of radio programs, two being playlets. Innes' contribution is A New Investigation, in the form of a talk. It was broadcast by the BBC in June 1949 and must have been prime entertainment, as it still is today in the reading. What it offers is the solution to the baffling deaths in *Hamlet* of eight important people. Brilliantly written and solidly reasoned, it accounts for the ghost no less than for motive, means, and opportunity.

The two playlets have good points, too, but are dramatic excursions, not investigations.

2590 IRISH, WILLAM   Lipp 1960
        The Best of William Irish

Half a dozen short stories born of W.I.'s peculiar genius for creating sensation out of the commonplace. Good narrative without verbal or intellectual distinction. Includes: After Dinner Story / The Night Reveals / An Apple a Day / Marihuana / Rear Window / Murder Story. That last is a plot within a plot with an O. Henry twist to conclude.
        See also Nos. 2680 and 2864–9.

2591 JACOBS, W. W.

        Sea Whispers   Scrib 1926
          Illus. by Bert Thomas

Among twelve predominantly humorous tales by this master of the short form are two stories of murder and expiation: His Brother's Keeper and The Interruption. Both skirt the supernatural but end with all surprises rationally accounted for. No detection—just the workings of conscience.

2592 JAMES, HENRY

        "In the Cage" *In:* The Complete Tales of Henry James,
          ed. L. Edel, vol. 10   Lipp 1964; orig. 1898

Certainly a mystery, and without solution, though nothing supernatural occurs or is hinted at. The messages from and about the Captain and the Lady suggest rather a most natural but secret intrigue, beautifully developed and sustained, thanks to the intelligence of the telegraphic observer and the genius of the author.

2593 JAMES, P. D.

        "Moment of Power"   *EQMM* July 1968

The first short story by this outstanding detective novelist. Unusual in all ways and strong stuff in at least two: the power held by a man able to give evidence which would exonerate a convicted murderer, and the power packed in the surprise ending. The later Murder, 1986 (*EQMM,* Oct. 1970) is really SF, not detection.

2594 JENKINS, HERBERT (GEORGE) (1876–1923)

        Malcolm Sage, Detective   Doran 1921

In setting and intention these stories are a feeble copy of Sherlock Holmes, marred by dull and hence irritating eccentricities. Some of the plots are not bad, but the telling is unrelievedly flat, and the assumptions about motive far below the quality achieved about the means.
        One hopes the author did better in his biography of George Borrow.

2595 The Stiffsons and Other Stories   HJ 1928

Contains a Malcolm Sage story not elsewhere in book form.

2596 JEPSON, EDGAR

     Garthoyle Gardens   Hutch 1913
          In U.S.: Gardens at 19

Lord Rupert Garthoyle flits through episodic adventures, of which some
are criminal and would-be mysterious, but they suffer from the lighthearted tone of the period.

2597 JESSE, F. TENNYSON

     "Lord of the Moment"   EQMM Feb 1951

A story of crime discovered not by detection but by "psychology"—flimsy
and elaborate at the same time. Miss Jesse writes well, but rather overdoes
the ponderings of tentative adulterers and their friends.

2598 Solange Stories   Hein 1931
          Introd. by the author

Miss J. first discourses capably about the ways of presenting detective
tales and makes a clear distinction between tales of crime and those of
detection. Her five stories of the French girl Solange Fontaine (whose
father is a police scientist) are agreeably written and show a good bit of
humor, but are spoiled by Solange's dependence upon "a certain feeling"
which tells her that some people are evil. A little use is made of scientific
tests and there are both English and French settings.

2599 JOHNSON, OWEN

     Murder in Any Degree   Cent 1913
          Illus.

Of the nine short stories in the book, only the famous One Hundred in
the Dark and the title story are to be classed as crime or detection. The
first of the pair is a tour de force that one can reread with ever-renewed
pleasure: character, setting, and situation are so beautifully matched. The
other is satisfactory but undistinguished.

2600 KAHN, JOAN, ed.

     The Edge of the Chair   Harp 1967
          Introd. by the editor

A suspense anthology of 34 items, drawn unequally from the realms of
fiction (21) and fact (13). As the editor says, there is suspense in all good
fiction and much fact. This is borne out by the present collection, which,
in addition to the stories by authors of the caliber of Bierce, Ellin,
Faulkner, Pinter, and Pushkin, is also to be esteemed for the several accounts of true crime. Outstanding among these is F. Tennyson Jesse's

penetrating yet sympathetic account of the Rattenbury-Stoner case. In the excellent biographical notes which conclude the volume one runs across such interesting facts as the identity of Mary Fitt and the circumstances of Jack London's death.

2601   Hanging by a Thread   HM 1969

Miss Kahn has performed the difficult feat of producing a worthy successor to her first anthology (No. 2600). The thirty-seven new items (twenty-seven stories and ten accounts of true crime or adventure) are imaginatively selected: Charlotte Armstrong's The Splintered Monday and Stephen Crane's The Blue Hotel, and the two classics, Bulwer-Lytton's The Haunted and the Haunters and Marjorie Bowen's Cambric Tea. It is also good to have readily available Russel Crouse's account of the Rothstein murder, William Roughead's Sandyford Mystery (Glasgow 1862), and James Thurber's pulling together of the messy Hall-Mills case.

2602   KANE, HENRY

         Report for a Corpse   S&S 1948

Told in the first person, the six stories are detection-by-discrepancy at its most primitive—e.g., in the title story a woman speaks of destroying a private detective's report, when in fact his report had been made orally. All the girls are luscious and criminal. The narrative tries for wit and fails; it is tough on grammar as well as in other ways.

2603   Trinity in Violence   ГVB 1955

Three short stories about the private eye Peter Chambers—routine business in the usual mood of self-pity and self-congratulation. Prose and plots off the assembly line.

2604   KEMELMAN, HARRY

         The Nine Mile Walk   Putn 1967
         The Nicky Welt Stories
         Introd. by the author

Created in 1947, Professor Welt is in his semi-arrogant way more fun to read about than the author's other detective, the modest and virtuous Rabbi Small. Welt's great feat, told in the title story, is a masterpiece of ratiocination. The professor's other exploits are:

The Straw Man (1950)   The Whistling Tea Kettle (= The
The Ten O'Clock Scholar (1952)   Adelphi Bowl) (1963)
End Play (1950)   The Bread and Butter Case (= A
Time and Time Again (= The Man   Winter's Tale) (1962)
   with Two Watches) (1962)   The Man on the Ladder (1967)

The fourth and the next-to-last are very good. In the others the author has a slippery grip on plausibility, inference, and style; the university arrangements are odd; and sometimes the data will not sustain the plot. Even in the superb title story, the time and the distance walked do not jibe—a point easily remediable. Still, K. gave reality to that feat much-talked-of but rarely seen, armchair detection.

2605 KENDRICK, BAYNARD

"A Clue from Bing Crosby"   *EQMM* Jan 1963

The blind detective Duncan Maclain needs no eyes but only good ears and a keen imagination to figure out where the kidnapped six-year-old is being hidden. A Bing Crosby record provides "color," but the clue is quite independent of it.

2606 "5 − 4 = Murderer"   *EQA, vol. 8* (1965)

Captain Maclain is a long way from New York in this tale of graft in a state police force, but he gives a good account of himself by eliminating the four suspects who couldn't have committed a murder in his presence.

2607 KERSH, GERALD (d. 1969), was a prolific author of short stories in which the main interest is verbal flourish and the caricature of character by exaggeration. Numerous such tales appeared in *EQMM*. His earlier efforts at more sober narratives lack distinction and drive. See *Clock Without Hands* (1949), which contains the title story, together with Flight to the World's End and Fairy Gold.

2608 KING, C. DALY

The Curious Mr. Tarrant   CCC 1935

All that anybody seems to know of this collection of eight "episodes" is that Dorothy Sayers thought well of the author. She reprinted The Nail and the Requiem in No. 2780,* never published in the U.S. The other episodes are: The Codex' Curse / The Tangible Illusion / Torment IV / The Headless Horrors / The Vanishing Harp / The Man with Three Eyes / The Final Bargain.

Mr. Trevis Tarrant, who is defined as "interested in the bizarre," is not remarkable in any way. He is merely another of the insightful imperturbables who followed Sherlock Holmes and astonished the simple minds of their hangers-on and erstwhile readers. The narrator of his exploits is one Jerry Phelan, a young athlete, wholly featureless. The episodes are essentially simple tricks, upholstered in scholarly or technical detail and giving only the illusion of seriousness. It is a case of too much matter and very little art. (One might except the inspiration by which a sleazy psychiatrist is named Dr. Backenforth.)

The best tale is Torment IV (the name of a boat), written as a modern parallel, with solution, of the *Mary Celeste* (see Nos. 3091 and 3142). The Final Bargain is quasi-supernatural, pseudo-Egyptian nonsense, not convincingly done. For anthology reprintings of Torment IV and Codex' Curse, see No. 2774.

* The Episode of the Nail and the Requiem raises a musical question after we read that "it is the Requiem of Palestrina." P. did not write *a* Requiem as Berlioz, Verdi, and Fauré did. Among the hundreds of his masses, the *Missa pro defunctis* is to provide a service for the dead, but it is hardly a Requiem, since the *Introit* and *Dies Irae* are not set.

2609   "The Episode of the Sinister Inventor"   *EQMM* Dec 1946

An affair in the life of Trevis Tarrant that comes after The Nail and the
Requiem (see No. 2608) and deals with the death of a woman inventor
at the hands of a male rival. The details are purposely comical and Tarrant gives a pastiche of Holmes' ways while using his slogans. But for this
effect a good deal of ingenuity, both sound and misplaced, is frittered
away. Not worthy of the author of *Arrogant Alibi* (q.v.).

2610   KING, RUFUS

       "The Gods, to Avenge . . ."   *EQMM* June 1963

A fairly well-turned tale on the old theme of one sister dominated by the
other and what ensues. Detective Stuff Driscoll officiates in Halcyon, Fla.,
and uses botanical and zoological evidence to convict the culprit.

2611   "Miami Papers Please Copy"   *EQMM* Oct 1956

For once, what is intended to amuse really does, and this highly improbable tale of the attempted kidnapping of the redoubtable Miss Violet
Fitzhutt with the aid of a motor cruiser can be highly recommended. No
detection, nor is any needed.

2612   KNOWLTON, DON

       "The Coconut Trial"   *EQMM* Feb 1966

A trick-ending story that uses a well-known historical mystery to work up
a rather neat legal defense for a trivial crime in a land which takes a
harsh view of misdemeanor—five minutes' amusement, readily forgotten.

2613   "The Curious Quints"   *EQMM* Aug 1962

The members of a club—all professors—who meet to stave off dry rot by
discussing and solving problems, find themselves faced with the murder
of one of their members. Professor Atwater (English) does an excellent
job of working things out with psychological and linguistic clues.

2614   KNOX, RONALD, and HARRINGTON, H.

       The Best English Detective Stories: Liv 1929
       First Series [of 1928]
             Introd. by R. A. Knox

Valuable if only for *the* Introduction, supreme among all prefatory essays
on the genre: it is here that Knox laid down the ten commandments that
the self-respecting practitioner must obey. The stories do not all live
up to the ideal—the world was young and the choice limited by inadequate supply. Still, a good few deserve their place and would earn it
again in any new anthology. They are:

J. D. Beresford	The Artificial Mole
K. R. G. Browne	Through the Window
Marten Cumberland	The Diary of Death
J. S. Fletcher	Mr. Leggatt Leaves His Card
Arthur Hougham	The Night of the Garter

Denis Mackail	An Artist in Crime
E. Phillips Oppenheim	Blackman's Wood
Gladys St. John-Loe	The Langdon Case

plus two familiar pieces by Agatha Christie and the Baroness Orczy.

2615 KYD, THOMAS

"Cottage for August"   *EQMM* Aug 1957

Suspense-horror rather than detection, but a tidy piece of its kind. Gruesome experiences on Cape Cod are related by Professor Hinman to a group of his colleagues.

2616 "High Court"   *EQMM* Oct 1953

Breezily told, but a good airtight and intelligent story of detection done in a transatlantic plane, right after the murder has been committed there. The detective, a statistician named Andrew One, uses in fact no statistics but common inference.

2617 LA FARGE, OLIVER (1901–1963)

"Woman Hunt No Good"   *EQMM* Nov 1951

A poorish tale, except for its setting in American Indian country, a region that the author knew well, like the Indians themselves, to whose welfare he devoted so much of his life. (See also No. 1147.)

2618 LANG, ALLEN KIM

"Murder in a Nudist Camp"   *EQMM* Apr 1966

Though the unusual setting accounts for some of the merit of this story, Professor Amos Cooney (president of the Spice Pond "Swimming Club") shows skill in disentangling the identities of a murderer and a peeping Tom. During the visit of the police, "formal dress" (i.e., swmming trunks) is adopted.

2619 LARDNER, RING(GOLD WILMER) (1885–1933)

"Haircut"   *RSMQ* Aug 1945; orig. 1926

A superb murder story—without detection—told in authentic dialect, the kind of speech that only Mark Twain, Lardner, and Damon Runyon succeeded in making the vehicle of emotion and literature. The tale is to be found in *The Love Nest and Other Stories* (Scrib 1926).

2620 LEACOCK, STEPHEN (BUTLER) (1869–1944)

"Maddened by Mystery; or, The Defective Detective"
   In: Nonsense Novels   Lane 1917

A rather crude parody of the omniscient and perpetually disguised detective. The date excuses the choice of details. Leacock does much better in his essays on the genre (see Nos. 2969–70).

2621 LEBLANC, MAURICE

The Confessions of Arsene Lupin   H&S 1967; orig. 1912
Orig.: Les confidences d'Arsène Lupin, *trans. by*
Joachim Neugroschel

Reprinted in Michael Gilbert's series of *Classics,* with an introduction
by the editor, who makes out a case for this volume as giving the quintes-
sential Lupin. The ten adventures contain a bit of clueing and thinking,
but the surprise endings are the main attraction—at least they were to
the young boy who read the book in the original tongue shortly after its
first appearance.

2622 LEGGETT, WILLIAM

"The Rifle"   [1828]
In: Mary Russell Mitford, ed., Stories of American Life (C&B,
1830). *Orig. pub. in* The Atlantic Souvenir Annual (1828);
and next in Tales and Sketches by a Country Schoolmaster
(*Harp 1829*)

The earliest tale of murder proved by ballistics, unearthed by Vincent
Starrett, who published his discovery in June 1948. Reprinted (with cuts)
in *The Delights of Detection* (No. 2344).

2623 LE QUEUX, WILLIAM

The Crimes Club   n.d. [c. 1925]

Like so many disappointing finds, this book is neatly printed on good
paper, but the twelve stories by a passed master at the narrative art are
childish beyond belief—well-nigh unreadable.

2624 LIVINGSTON, KENNETH

The Dodd Cases   CCD 1933

Seven short stories featuring Cedric Dodd, M.D., an amateur investigator
in the Holmes tradition. The chief shortcoming of the stories besides their
small number and hence narrow range is that the pace is too relaxed.
Compression would enhance drama. But as the one novel by the author
showed, his power and inspiration, though genuine, were of the slightest.
For a representative sample, see No. 2344.

2625 LONDON MYSTERY MAGAZINE, THE. A quarterly published in both
London and New York, 1949 ff. It prints articles, reviews, and verse as
well as stories of crime, detection, and the supernatural. The editors and
authors are English, and the level is perhaps a bit below that of *EQMM,*
the reason being the absence of reprinted stories by the masters of the
several genres.

2626 LYNDE, FRANCIS (1856–1930)

    Scientific Sprague   Scrib 1912
    Illus. by E. Roscoe Shrader

Calvin Sprague is a government chemist sent West to test soils, but he stops off in the RR town of Brewster to see his old classmate Maxwell, and solves a tidy little problem of who is causing trouble (arranging wrecks, undermining morale) on the 500-mile "Short Line." The six tales are varied, the science sound, the railroad detail perfect. For any reader who is interested in the prewar West, these tales would be hard to beat; for anyone who combines a taste for detection with a passion for railroads, they are unequaled.

2627 LYNDON, BARRE

    The Amazing Dr. Clitterhouse   French 1936

Another crime play of the thirties, when the genre greatly flourished. Ingenious clues lead to the undoing of the attractive hero, but he has taken the precaution of making himself conviction-proof by an amusing trick. Here the running of a gang of robbers by an intelligent physician has research as its purpose. The doings are excellent and the suspense very great—until the inevitable capture and final twist that allows us to foresee an appropriately light sentence for Dr. C., despite his being a thief on the large scale and a murderer.

2628 McBAIN, ED

    "Eighty Million Eyes"   *EQMM* May 1966

The men in the 87th Precinct do a good, deliberate job of tracking down an absent murderer, whose victim perished (for good reasons) in front of a TV camera. A bit laborious at the end and somewhat purposely obtuse in the middle—therefore lifelike?

2629 "The Empty Hours"   *EQMM* May 1967

A good sample of this author's procedural tales, here concerned with the murder by strangulation of a "poor" girl, who nevertheless had $60,000 to her account. The boys of the 87th Precinct unravel a complex but credible situation.

2630 "Nightshade"   *EQMM* Aug 1970

The 87th has to cope with the up-to-date in crime, naturally, and in this tense affair every sort of sophisticated urban outrage is threatened or takes place. One of the shortest and best by an author who must be given credit for making a hero out of a whole precinct squad.

2631 McCLOY, HELEN

    "Better Off Dead"   Dell No. 34; n.d.; orig. *Amer Mag* 1949

This brief story requires only 64 pulp pages to show the master hand. Although Basil Willing does not appear, the reader is ably shown the attempts to do away with a young man returning to his native town (Philadelphia suburb, south and on the river) after a fifteen-year absence. The ashes that Stephen Longworth rakes up are neither dead nor negligible, and suspense is well maintained through several plausible attacks. In typical McCloy fashion, a fine piece of furniture looms large.

2632 "The Black Disk" *EQMM* Apr 1961
     Orig.: "The Nameless Clue" (1941)

These readers generally prefer the McCloy tales that feature the psychologist Basil Willing, but this novelette proves the author capable of handling rough stuff, too. The "disk" (highly compressed paper) is the sole clue to the murder of a second-rate actress. Alec Norton, a reporter, is the amateur detective.

2633 "The Silent Informer" *EQMM* July 1958

Basil Willing adroitly figures out how a lady pianist was murdered in a Cape Cod village hall, using not only his professional knowledge but also his familiarity with electrical circuitry.

2634 McCLOY. See also:

The Singing Diamonds and Other Stories DM 1965

2635 McCLOY, HELEN, and HALLIDAY, BRETT, eds.

Murder, Murder, Murder Hillm 1961
     Pref. by Baynard Kendrick

These tales and playlets gathered on behalf of the Mystery Writers of America are for the most part routine stuff by authors of the second rank, and the book is so economically put together that it forgoes a table of contents.

2636 McDONALD, JACK and MARY

"The Apartment Hunter" *EQMM* Feb 1957

An attractively told anecdote—nothing more. But the single clue that Satan interprets for the murderer who has just arrived in his territory is a good one, and the tale is well rounded for its 4¼ pages.

2637 MacDONALD, JOHN D.

"The Homesick Buick" *EQMM* Sept 1950

The author's first appearance in this magazine, as winner of a third prize in the usual contest. The story has special merit as a study of small-town life; it is full of good touches of character, among them some of the well-hidden clues. For a reprinting, see No. 2344.

2638 MacDONALD, PHILIP, has not equaled in the short form his few but solid successes (qq.v.) in the long. Three collections, of which the first is best, may nonetheless be listed for the curious: *Something to Hide* (1952), *Death and Chicanery* (1962), and *The Man out of the Rain* (1955).

2639   "Two Exploits of Harry the Hat"   *EQMM* Feb 1949

These miniature affairs of crime are of no great importance in themselves, but they are the occasion for a valuable page of criticism by the editor (preceding the stories), in which he reports and accepts the author's observation that a short short will not allow the telling of a detective story but will accommodate a story of crime, even an idea fit for a novel.

2640   MACDONALD, ROSS

"Murder Is a Public Matter"   *EQMM* Oct 1959

Lew Archer in a novelette that rather cramps his style—or else it is the restricted world of studio and museum, quite artificially limited for the purposes of this story, that will not let him do his best. The characters are stiff, the murders excessive, and the cause of all the misery inadequate.

2641   McGIVERN, WILLIAM P.

"The Last Word"   *EQMM* Feb 1963
   Orig.: "The Sound of Murder" (*1952*)

A neat little package wrapping up a murder on the Orient Express in its palmy days. Thanks to his knowledge of human relationships, Adam James, foreign correspondent, spots the killer.

2642   MACGOWAN, KENNETH, ed.

Sleuths   HB 1931
   Twenty-three Great Detectives of Fiction
   and Their Best Stories
   Introd. by the editor, and chronological bibliography

The choice of authors, detectives, and stories is praiseworthy, and well argued by the editor in his opening remarks. The Carrados tale, The Holloway Flat Tragedy (see No. 2370), is a good example of a rare but interesting story that deserves more frequent anthologizing. The editor also shows good sense in selecting The Unknown Murderer from Bailey's variable outpourings. The contents are:

E. A. Poe	The Murders in the Rue Morgue
A. C. Doyle	Silver Blaze
A. Morrison	The Case of the Dixon Torpedo
Robert Barr	The Absent-Minded Coterie
Jacques Futrelle	The Missing Necklace
Baroness Orczy	The Dublin Mystery
A. B. Reeve	The Seismograph Adventure
Melville D. Post	The Treasure Hunter
R. A. Freeman	The Puzzle Lock
G. K. Chesterton	The Queer Feet
Gelett Burgess	Missing John Hudson
E. C. Bentley	The Inoffensive Captain

E. Bramah	The Holloway Flat Tragedy
B. Copplestone	The Butler
H. C. Bailey	The Unknown Murderer
A. Christie	The Disappearance of Mr. Davenheim
Octavius Roy Cohen	Homespun Silk
G. D. H. & M. Cole	The International Socialist
Dorothy L. Sayers	The Entertaining Episode of the Article in Question
Anthony Wynne	The Dancing Girl
Edgar Wallace	The Treasure Hunt
Harvey J. O'Higgins	The Fogull Murder
T. S. Stribling	The Prints of Hantoun

2643 McKENNA, STEPHEN

"Blackmail"   *EQMM* Mar 1950

Absolutely topnotch in conception and execution. This is the way to philosophize about blackmail and carry it out, to frame a situation—and a man. Detection is not in it, but crime in the grand manner.

2644 MACLAREN-ROSS, J.

"Maigret at Oxford"   *Punch* Dec 3, 1954

Good critique through parody.

2645 McNEAR, ROBERT

"Anatomy of Body Disposal"   *EQMM* Sept 1970

A series of sharp twists, all legitimate, brings forth a happy blend of literary effort and practical murder, this last coming apart at the right moment and in the most natural way. No detection, although, as the title suggests, it is all *about* detection.

2646 McSPADDEN, JOSEPH WALKER, ed., put together in all-too-early days three thin volumes called *Famous Detective Stories* (1920), *Famous Ghost Stories* (1919), and *Famous Mystery Stories* (1922). The last is the best collection, devoted to horror, not mystery. The others reprint the old war-horses, together with feeble pieces by dated authors. The one good touch in the book of detective stories is the editor's thanks to Anna Katharine Green and Arthur B. Reeve for "personal assistance."

2647 MACHEN, ARTHUR (1863–1947)

The Three Impostors   Knopf 1923
   Introd. by the author

Contains The Three Impostors and The Red Hand. The major work consists of thirteen loosely connected episodes in which the young Londoners Dyson and Phillipps (a scientific-literary pair) encounter the fringes of the Unknown via the Stevensonian method of listening to very tall but entrancing tales told by mysterious strangers in cigar divans. One of these,

The Novel of the Black Seal, may be found in the first *Omnibus of Crime* (see No. 2778). All are worth reading. The Red Hand is much shorter, confines itself to a single murder, and Dyson and Phillipps investigate rather than just listen.

2648   MANSFIELD, KATHERINE

"Poison"   *EQMM* Dec 1950; orig. 1924

A very short short, but full, like all K.M.'s work. Not crime or detection, but suspicion—indeed, a foreshadowing of Agatha Christie's Philomel Cottage, though infinitely richer in mood and character.

2649   MARRIC, J. J.

"Gideon: The Hooligans"   *EQMM* Mar 1970

In this short and almost unfictionalized account of a delinquent, his distraught mother, and Gideon, it is interesting to see that the author is as foolishly sentimental in his vision of the facts as his colleague Nicolas Freeling (see No. 2514). They mistake their subject, it would seem, in both fiction and reality, and those pseudo stories show it.

2650   "Gideon's War"   *EQMM* May 1968
       Orig.: "Crooks' Harvest" (*1962*)

The procedures of Commander Gideon and his CID forces sometimes grow tedious when stretched out, but in this short novelette about a summit meeting in London the interest is admirably sustained.

2651   MARSH, NGAIO

"Death on the Air"   *EQA,* vol. 16 (1969); orig. 1939

The author's first detective novelette: a Christmas story featuring Inspector Roderick Alleyn, and only fair. It is not distinguished by plot or individuality, and the use of the radio is labored and questionable. It all goes to show that one talent does not imply another.

2652   MASON, A. E. W.
       Dilemmas   H&S 1934

Twelve short stories, plus two "war notes," by this experienced teller of tales. Two or three are outright detection, and all involve mystery and suspense. The contents comprise:

The Strange Case of Joan Winter-bourne	The Law of Flight
	The Key
The Wounded God	Tasmanian Jim's Specialty
The Chronometer	The Italian
Sixteen Bells	Magic
The Reverend Bernard Simmons, B.D.	The Duchess and Lady Torrent
A Flaw in the Organization	

The two War Notes are about Mata Hari and the cruise of the *Virgen del Socorro.*

2653   The Four Corners of the World   H&S 1917

Contains (among fourteen all told) the only Hanaud-Ricardo short story, The Affair at the Semiramis Hotel. It is unique in showing Ricardo at home in Grosvenor Square and receiving Hanaud as his guest. Murder for jewels, singers at the opera, and rather long-winded speculations about motive and odd personal traits make up this rather tedious novella. The other dozen deal variously with crime and contain a little detection.

2654   MASUR, HAROLD Q., ed.

Dolls Are Murder   Rev 1956
   An MWA Anthology

Eight stories (some going back as far as 1939 for first publication) by: Brett Halliday, John D. MacDonald, Raymond Chandler, Ellery Queen, George Harmon Coxe, Bruno Fischer, Georges Simenon, and Rex Stout. All are competent; the MacDonald is the best; the Rex Stout (very short) is not about Nero Wolfe.

2655   MATHER, FRANK JEWETT, JR.

The Collectors   Holt 1935; orig. 1912

Nine delightful tales of the unscrupulous and near-criminal in the world of art-collecting, by the late eminent Princeton professor and critic.

2656   MATTHEWS, BRANDER

Tales of Fantasy and Fact   Harp 1896

Six tales of mystery and fantasy by a man who, though all his life a professor of literature at Columbia, gets his storytelling done with dispatch and a certain grace. One of these stories (The Twinkling of an Eye) got a prize as detective fiction, but except as an anticipation of modern bank protection, it is weak. The better ones are: The Kinetoscope of Time, The Dream-Gown of the Japanese Ambassador, and The Rival Ghosts (which uses characters from *The Last Meeting,* No. 1578.

2657   MAUGHAM, W. SOMERSET

"Footprints in the Jungle"   Dday 1934
   In: East and West: Collected Short Stories (vol. I)

Major Gaze, head of the Malayan police, tells of a murder that he never solved and that he almost condones. The couple depicted (and the daughter) are typical Maugham characters—"gray," not black and white in morals and manners. The irony is plain to the meanest understanding.

MAUPASSANT, GUY DE (1850–93), was greatly interested in crime and punishment, but properly speaking he wrote no detective stories. When murder for revenge or greed occurs in one of his many short short stories, it is usually in connection with love, jealousy, or secret adultery. Francis Steegmuller has pointed out that many tales attributed to M. are spurious. Apart from the genuine ones singled out below, one semi-humorous sketch is sometimes reprinted as a tale about crime (see No. 2659).

2658   Complete Short Stories   Dday 1946; orig. 1903
     Ten volumes in one
     Trans. by M. Walter Dunne

A Piece of String (Vol. 1; a brilliant example of the power of suggestion)
A Mistake (Vol. 4; suspected crime in progress that turns out something quite different)
Room No. 11 (Vol. 4; adultery, accidental death)
Ghosts (Vol. 5; more criminal trickery than supernatural; *not* by Maupassant)
The Ill-Omened Groom (Vol. 6; detection in bed to get a wig off; *not* by Maupassant)
An Artifice (Vol. 6; doctor helps woman get dead lover out and away)
The Traveler's Story (Vol. 6; ghostly)
Beside a Dead Man (Vol. 7; Poe's Valdemar again)
The Spasm (Vol. 8; theft from a dead body of prematurely buried girl who reawakens)
The Victim (Vol. 9; brutal drunken murder of wife)
The Englishman (Vol. 9; supernatural murder feud and revenge)
The Assassin (Vol. 10; murder from jealousy)

The translation of all these is deplorable. Any subtlety in the originals, any quality in description or dialogue, is extinguished in pure Ollendorffian. Other collections are either incomplete or not much better, or overstuffed with forgeries. But see: *Selected Tales of Guy de Maupassant*, ed. Saxe Commins; illus. (RH 1950).

2659   "The Expense of Justice"   *EQA, vol. 16* (1969); orig. 1888

This skit about the man condemned to death in a small and poor principality which cannot afford to dispatch him, and which thereby makes him a state pensioner, has sometimes been attributed (as here) to Leo Tolstoy. It is in fact a passing anecdote in Maupassant's little travel book *Sur l'eau,* first published in the year given above and reprinted (in French) by Ollendorff in 1907 (pp. 229–35).

2660   MEADE, L(ILLIE) T(HOMAS) (pseud. of Elizabeth Thomasina (Meade) Smith, 1854–1914), was a determined writer of short stories in collaboration with Drs. Clifford Halifax and Robert Eustace (qq.v.). See especially: *The Sorceress of the Strand* (1903), *Micah Faraday* (1910), *A Master of Mysteries* (1898), and *The Sanctuary Club* (1900). The tales themselves vary from Raffles-like crime to mysterious adventure, but some of the contemporary interest in Sherlock Holmes and his use of clues rubbed off on this as on other popular writers of the day.

2661   MEADE, L. T., and HALIFAX, [DR.] CLIFFORD (pseud. of Edgar Beaumont)

Stories from the Diary of a Doctor   Lipp 1895
    Illus.

Twelve semi-scientific stories emphasizing hypnotism, Spencerian psychology, and the new ideas of the day. Despite occasional implausibility, readers with a sense of period will find their interest sustained, especially if they have a taste for well-managed English locale. A second series, published in England only, came out in 1896.

2662   MILNE, A. A.

    The Fourth Wall   French 1929
    A Detective Story in Three Acts
    In U.S.: The Perfect Alibi

This neat plot constitutes as great a contribution to the dramatic form of our genre as does *The Red House Mystery* to the novelistic. For it is almost the only play in which the audience is permitted to see the murder in detail and then to hear the reasoning by which it is unmasked. All this takes place without lessening suspense and concern; though it must be conceded to those who dislike Milne that in both works the chitchat of the young people is dated and somewhat irritating. All the more merit is to be ascribed to the idea and handling that can overcome this defect.

    N.B. *The Perfect Alibi* was reprinted in Milne's *Four Plays* (Putn 1932).

2663   "Once A Murderer . . ."   EQMM Nov 1963
    Orig.: "The Wine Glass" (*1946*)

A clever story with a couple of surprises at the end; so well told that one must excuse a few liberties taken with the rules. The moral is: the one who sends the poisoned wine should be deemed the most likely person, not the least. Told by Superintendent Mortimer.

2664   A Table Near the Band   Dutt 1950

The accomplished craftsman includes in this set two stories of murder and detection. Portrait of Lydia is a good alibi tale, in which a girl makes a fool of a solicitor in the interests of crime. Murder at Eleven, although slight, is what its title proposes, and it is compact and satisfying. Both deserve exhumation from the oblivion into which they have sunk, despite the reprinting of the second in *EQMM* for Mar. 1954.

2665   MITCHELL, S(ILAS) WEIR (1829–1914)

    "A Dilemma"   EQMM Dec 1948

A good short trick story about a rich legacy which lies forever beyond the legatee's reach. (From Mitchell's *Little Stories,* 1903.) The situation begins with the same elements as Doyle's Norwood Builder. Incidentally, Mitchell combined prolific storytelling with a physician's practice (in Philadelphia) and the hobbies of verse-writing and book-collecting.

2666   MOFFETT, CLEVELAND, is famous for his telling—was his the first setting down?—the tale of the man who asks friends and strangers to read a message in a tongue he does not understand and who finds them refusing and turning from him in horror. The Mysterious Card first appeared in 1896 and has been incessantly anthologized since. Its sequel, The Mysterious Card Unveiled, is worthy of its forepart. Both in *The Black Cat,* Feb. and Aug. 1896. For C.M.'s other works, see Nos. 1606–8.

2667   MONTANYE, C. S.

"Not for a Chorus Girl"   *EQMM* Mar 1950; orig. 1934

A brief account of the way to swindle a jeweler—and get caught. The scheme was actually tried in New York, with longer success than is permitted by the righteous author of this tale.

2668   MORLAND, NIGEL

"All in the Night's Work"   *EQMM* June 1961

A short short of London police routine that hinges on one point to be conclusive, but builds on a series of clues to get to that clincher.

2669   "Introducing V.I. Pybus"   *EQMM* Dec 1963

The author reports that he thought this story of a minor civil servant who doubles as detective might be "too leisured and too English for *EQMM.*" WHT found it most agreeable without being particularly original. At least its 11 pages are devoted almost exclusively to real detection.

2670   MORRISON, ARTHUR

The Chronicles of Martin Hewitt   Page 1908; orig. 1895

Pretty tired plotting and lackluster writing. The collection contains: The Ivy Cottage Mystery / The Nicobar Bullion Case / The Holford Will Case / The Case of the Missing Hand / The Case of Laker, Absconded / The Case of the Lost Foreigner.

2671   The Dorrington Deed Box   WL 1897

Half a dozen tales, unconventional for Morrison, and for his time as well. All revolve about the unscrupulous Dorrington, who is a consulting detective when it suits him, and otherwise a swindler and outright criminal. M.'s effort at six types of ambiguity doesn't really come off, but he deserves a pass for trying.

2672   Martin Hewitt, Investigator   WL 1895/1894
         Illus. by Sidney Paget

Notable as being the first collection of M.H. tales and the nearest approximation to the Sherlock Holmes adventures—though a long way behind. The presence of Paget as illustrator for both authors shows something of the mood in which Hewitt was received and ought to be taken. His best performances are here, in The Stanway Cameo Mystery and The Lenton Croft Robberies. The five others are much less entertaining.

Being some further chronicles of Martin Hewitt

Feebler and feebler efforts to keep the reader tense about routine crimes—
or at least hackneyed plots. Some of the stories are linked by the activities
of a master criminal. The contents are: The Affair of Samuel's
Diamonds / The Case of Mr. Jacob Mason / The Case of the Lever Key /
The Case of the Burnt Barn / The Case of the Admiralty Code / The Case
of Channel Marsh.

2674   MORRISON. See also:

The Adventures of Martin Hewitt   WL 1896

2675   MOSKOWITZ, SAM (also Sam Martin), ed.

The Man Who Called Himself Poe   Goll 1970

This volume tries to do for the imitations of Poe what Ellery Queen did
for those of Sherlock Holmes. There are a dozen pieces by Robert Bloch,
Lovecraft and Derleth, Julian Hawthorne, Vincent Starrett, Douglass
Shirley, R. H. Barlow, and others; there are six poems and a biographical
essay by the late Thomas Ollive Mabbott, the great authority on Poe. But
the mass makes no coherent or critical impression—and one is shocked to
find that the most skillful resuscitator of Poe and Dupin, Michael
Harrison, is not represented. (See Nos. 2560–4.)

Association Item
2676   MÜNSTER, SEBASTIAN (1489–1552)

Comosgraphei, oder Beschreibung aller Länder stetten
                        Da Capo Press 1969; orig. Basel 1550/1544

The chief best seller of the sixteenth century, an early example of team
research—said to have employed 120 men—and the main source of contemporary scientific knowledge about geography, ethnology, and general
history, this book is the central item in Dorothy Sayers' short story The
Learned Adventure of the Dragon's Head (see No. 2777).

2677   NASH, OGDEN

"They Don't Read De Quincey
in Philly or Cincy"   *EQMM* May 1966; orig. 1965
    A Poem

The Quincey-essence of bath water as understood by George Joseph Smith,
or 22 lines in praise of the domestic tub.

2678   NESBIT, E(DITH) [Mrs. Hubert Bland] (1858–1924)

Something Wrong   Innes 1893

The Judgment: a Broadmoor Biography is a tale of crime, not detection;
of social psychology, not action; in effect, a period piece of the New
Thought epoch of emancipation from prejudice and class consciousness.

2679   NESBIT. See also:

In Homespun   Lane 1896

2680   NEVINS, FRANCIS M., JR., ed.

Dark City, Dark Men   Harp 1971
        Stories by Cornell Woolrich
        Introds. by the editor and by Donald Yates; bibliog.

The essays by the editor and Donald Yates give particulars of Wool-
rich's life and last years and a collaborative effort supplies a bibliography.
The stories, twenty-two in number, include a posthumous manuscript,
Life Is Weird Sometimes, and these characteristic successes:

Graves for the Living	Three Kills for One
The Red Tide	The Screaming Laugh
I Wouldn't Be in Your Shoes	The Death of Me
The Corpse Next Door	One and a Half Murders
Mind Over Murder	Dead on Her Feet
You'll Never See Me Again	One Night in Barcelona
Dusk to Dawn	The Penny-a-Worder
Murder at the Automat	The Number's Up
Death in the Air	Too Nice a Day to Die
Murder in the Middle of New York	For the Rest of Her Life
Mamie 'n' Me	

The time span is 1935 to 1968.

2681   NEW ERA, was published between 1914 and the midsummer of
1968 by inmates of the Federal penitentiary at Leavenworth, Kansas. It
contains fiction, essays, and autobiography, entirely written and edited by
men of experience as criminals and prisoners; so the work belongs in this
section as well as under true crime. Its contributions are valuable in both
departments of the literature. The merit of the contents has varied widely,
as might be expected, and was never of professional quality. Yet the dis-
continuance of the publication—for reasons of economy—is a loss to
readers and writers alike.

[As this work goes to press, news comes of the revival of *New Era;* an
unnumbered issue of 76 pp., dated Fall 1970, is out (Dec).]

2682   NORTH, GIL

Sergeant Cluff and the Madmen   C&H 1964

The present volume is made up of two longish shorts—The Blindness of
Sergeant Cluff and Sergeant Cluff Laughs Last. The theme is as before:
other people are obsessed, maddened by some defect in themselves. The
Sergeant is "unorthodox, compassionate, and essentially human, fighting a
battle against himself as well as against crime." The author, it is clear, is
trying to adapt Simenon to English small-town life and to a narrow though
"compassionate" morality. Cluff is gruff and noncommittal, but his assistant, Detective Barker, goes through the most "sensitive," agonizing introspection over everybody he meets. Mood kills him in a way not to be

530

believed. While all this is given at length, the dialogue is purposely incomprehensible, so that it takes three pages to discover whether a murdered body that has just been found is also recognized or not.

2683   O'FARRELL, WILLIAM (also William Grew; b. 1904)

"Exhibit A" *EQMM* Jan 1955

A brief crime story that combines fantasy with surprise by means of a first-class gimmick, the modern camera.

2684   O'HIGGINS, HARVEY (JERROLD) (1876–1929), was a productive author who used the vogue of the Pinkerton Agency to provide opportunities for the youth Barney Cook to show what he could do in the detective line. The details are not at all contemptible, but the people and the emotions are difficult to believe in. See *The Adventures of Detective Barney* (Cent 1915), Nos. 2360 and 2642, as well as No. 3258. For another kind of tale, using modern psychology, see *Detective Duff Unravels It* (Liv 1929).

2685   OPPENHEIM, E(DWARD) PHILLIPS (also Anthony Partridge; 1866–1946)

Curious Happenings to the Rooke Legatees   H&S 1937

Ten linked episodes involving the varied lot of recipients who share in the fortune of the late Desmond Rooke, a rich man murdered on Sark. Some of the tales depict crime, others sentiment, adventure, or secret charity. Stevenson's *New Arabian Nights* suggest themselves as model, and one or two of these imitations approach the original in quality of style and invention. Not detective stories.

2686   The Ex-Detective   LB 1933

A series of uneven but amusing short stories. Malcolm Gossett "goes private" after having been on the force, and acts as general uncle to the distressed. Not detection, though there are clues and they are used.

2687   Nicholas Goade, Detective   LB 1929

Disappointing as to detection, but full compensation in Goad's escapades while on vacation in Devonshire. Related with great ease and fine literary effect.

2688   OPPENHEIM. See also:

General Besserley's Puzzle Box	H&S 1939
The Hon. Algernon Knox, Detective	H&S 1920
Inspector Dickens Retires	H&S 1931
Many Mysteries	Rich 1933
The Mysteries of the Riviera	Cass 1916

ORCZY, BARONESS EMMUSKA [Mrs. Montagu Barstow] (1865–1947)

Educ. in England from her sixteenth year; hoped to be a painter; her first literary work (c. 1900) was detective fiction for magazines. The Scarlet Pimpernel series began four years later. She created an unassuming, but not fumbling, detective in The Old Man in the Corner, who sympathizes with the criminal and does nothing to hinder his escape. Later, she created Skin o' My Tooth, the progenitor of Josiah Clunk, Arthur Crook, and all other unscrupulous lawyer heroes.

2689   The Case of Miss Elliott   Unwin 1905
         Cover picture in four colors of The Old Man knotting string
         and talking to the girl interviewer
         Illus.

The twelve tales follow the single pattern of being baffling mysteries that The Old Man in the Corner unravels by dint of sheer assertiveness coupled with a single unexpected suggestion—e.g., a murder done by two accomplices "solves" the contradictions in witnesses' reports and suspect's alibi. Entertaining situations well told keep the reader from noticing the paucity of reasoning. But he may be thankful for the absence of melodrama and stilted prose. The titles are:

The Case of Miss Elliott	The Tremarn Case
Tragedy in Dartmoor Terrace	The Fate of the *Artemis*
Who Stole the Black Diamonds?	The Disappearance of Count Collini
The Murder of Miss Pebmarsh	The Ayrsham Mystery
The Lisson Grove Mystery	The Affair at the Novelty Theatre
The Mystery of Cigarette	The Tragedy of Barnsdale Manor

   N.B.: Cigarette is a horse whose circumstances remind one strongly of Silver Blaze (q.v.).

2690   The Man in Grey   Doran 1918

Nine semi-historical tales about a secret agent of Napoleon's time. The suspense is good despite the old-fashioned narrative style, and the situations are different from each other and from what one might expect the Baroness would have chosen from the record.

2691   The Man in the Corner   DM 1909; orig. Pears 1902
         Also: The Old Man in the Corner
         Cover drawing of the title character, rejuvenated
         Illus. by H. M. Brock

The thirty-six chapters serve to present about half that number of cases, unraveled (to and for his own satisfaction) by the Man in the Corner as he makes knots in string while talking to a young lady journalist. She— Miss Burton—rather cleverly breaks him of this habit in the final chapter. Good detection with action indirect but often effective.

2692   Skin o' My Tooth   CCD 1928
         His Memoirs by his Confidential Clerk

The unscrupulous lawyer who goes by the repellent nickname in the title is Patrick Mulligan, a resourceful unraveler of mysteries and defender of

The Innocent. He is an early specimen of a type frequently exemplified since, always with the same deceptive characteristics of grossness, ruthlessness, and self-confidence. The dozen tales given here show the author's gift for situation and exposition, though the style is more flat-footed than in the stories about The Old Man in the Corner, and some of the clues are very much dated for adventures written in the twenties. The best are: The Case of Major Gibson / Overwhelming Evidence / The Case of Mrs. Norris / The Murton-Braby Murder.

Note the convention followed by Bramah, Sayers, Doyle, and others that the final problem in the series must put the detective in peril of his life.

2693   Unravelled Knots   Doran 1923

The Old Man in the Corner and his mannerisms dominate this collection of thirteen stories told in a belated ninetyish manner. The plots and the clues are not ill-conceived—far from it—but the excess of windup destroys a good deal of the fun.

2694   OWEN, FRANK, ed.

Murder for the Millions   Fell 1946
   A Harvest of Horror and Homicide

This fat book, rather pretentiously touted by its editor, reprints thirty-seven stories, most of them by first-rate authors, but not all first-rate stories. The best are: Dashiell Hammett, Two Sharp Knives / Freeman Wills Crofts, The Vertical Line / Damon Runyon, What, No Butler? / William Irish, The Orphan Diamond / Vincent Starrett, Too Many Sleuths.

Others by Nicholas Blake, George Harmon Coxe, Ellery Queen, Hugh Pentecost, C. S. Forester, Mignon G. Eberhart, Elisabeth Sanxay Holding, James M. Cain, Gelett Burgess, Cornell Woolrich, and Nelson Bond are in various ways less satisfying than one would hope and expect.

2695   PACKARD, FRANK L(UCIUS) (1877–1942), wrote, among thirty other thrillers, *The Adventures* and *The Further Adventures of Jimmy Dale* (1917 and 1919). They are Robin Hoodish improbabilities done with some gusto, but not adult reading. For samples of the mad-silly doings of "The Gray Seal," see No. 2387, vol. V, 62–111.

2696   PAIN, BARRY

Here and Hereafter   Meth 1911

In this collection by a writer who is often original and true despite his failure to make the best of his material, there are two stories of interest to connoisseurs of our genres: Post Mortem is a crime story of considerable power, and The Unfinished Game is a piece of supernaturalism that just misses the bull's-eye. Perhaps it is intended to make one pensive rather than horrified.

2697 The Memoirs of Constantine Dix   Laur 1930; orig. 1905
       Section II of More Stories
       Introd. by J. H. Bowden

A series of adventures suggestive of *Raffles,* but done with greater literary art and an ironic turn of mind. Dix is a sermonizing crook of the Robin Hood sort; he specializes in friendly burglary and confidence tricks, but with a detective attention to detail.

2698 One Kind and Another   Stokes n.d. [1914]

A representative group of sketches and stories by this witty and prolific writer, now unjustly neglected. It contains the four stories "Detection Without Crime," of which E. M. Wrong reprinted two in his anthology (see No. 2875). They are: On Green Paper / The Face of the Corpse / The Lady of the Pillar Box / In the Marmalade. All but the third are good. The foursome are presented as "From the Notebook of the Late Horace Fish," a retired gentleman of insatiable curiosity.

2699 The Problem Club   Coll 1919

Not detection but ingenuity: the club members are supposed to perform socially difficult or embarrassing feats within a given time and thus earn the purse provided by the membership—or else be ejected from the club. Twelve very entertaining sketches. They are:

The Giraffe Problem	The Shakespearean Problem
The Kiss Problem	The Impersonation Problem
The Free Meal Problem	The Alibi Problem
The Win-and-Lose Problem	The Threepenny Problem
The Handkerchief Problem	The Q-Loan Problem
The Identity Problem	The Pig-Keeper's Problem

2700 PAIN. See also:

       Short Stories of Today and Yesterday: Barry Pain   Harrap 1928

2701 PALMER, STUART

       "Where Angels Fear to Tread"   *EQMM* Feb 1951

The joint efforts of the maiden schoolteacher Miss Hildegarde Withers and Inspector Oscar Piper are often too farcical to be funny, but once in a while—as in this story of a niece's disappearance—there are good clues and good detection.

       PARGETER, EDITH (MARY) (also Ellis Peters, q.v.; b. 1913)

A native of Shropshire; educ. at Coalbrooke Grammar School, writes fiction for ladies' magazines and does translations from the Czech. Her longer stories (as Ellis Peters) reach a higher level than her shorter works. See below.

2702 The Assize of the Dying   Dday 1958

In addition to the tale of 104 pages which gives the title to the book, there is Aunt Helen, running to 78 pages. The first holds the reader's interest despite its being based on the shaky business of a condemned man's "curse." The shorter tale is a more stock affair about a pseudo-invalid wife who is determined to kill rather than let go.

2703   PARRY, HENRY T.

"An Academic Crime"   *EQMM* Feb 1969

A good academic tale, told by one professor about the squabbles and subsequent criminal activity of his colleagues—diversion of funds from one department to another being the "justification" for murder. The narrator's detection is simple but adequate, his action minimal, as befits his calling.

2704   "A Place of Sacrifice"   *EQMM* Mar 1966

Murder by omission—a rare occurrence—and done in a classical setting at that. The culprit is an amiable man who thinks about justice and sacrifice and knows that he will carry a burden for the rest of his life. No detection, no prosecution, only execution.

2705   PATRICK, Q.

"Who Killed the Mermaid?"   *EQMM* Feb 1951

A quick job of detection on a train, by means of a magazine and a facial peculiarity, at the hands of the clever Lieutenant Trant. The author is also clever in the way he describes the persons concerned, each by his necktie, which is how the mermaid comes into the story—figure it out.

2706   PEMBERTON, [SIR] MAX (1863–1950)

Jewel Mysteries I Have Known   WL n.d. [1894]
   From a Dealer's Note Book
   Illus.

The one-time editor of *Cassell's Magazine* was evidently a jewel-fancier and an adventurous traveler, for he weaves his ten stories around unusual gems and exotic situations. His narrative gift and creation of incidents are equaled by his witty ninetyish dialogue, and the collection is worth its total weight in carats.

2707   PENTECOST, HUGH

"Jericho and the Dying Clue"   *EQMM* Oct 1965

The painter John Jericho solves a tidy problem concerning the death of a senator with presidential aspirations, and continues to justify his reputation as a sound moralist. Very compact (9 pages) and solid.

2708   Lieutenant Pascal's Tastes in Homicides   DM 1954
   Pref. by the author about Lt. P.

A group of three, of which the last is the most lively and humanized. The Murder Machine has the useful setting of a quarry being blasted, but makes poor use of it; Eager Victim has a good plot linked with journalism but unwinds it too slowly; and Murder in the Dark shines by its attractive characters, engaged in complicated but custom-bound dealings in diamonds. Here the excitement is steady and unforced, and the solution apt.

2709 "The Man with Half a Face"   *EQMM* Dec 1958

The title refers to a damaged ex-movie actor who sees justice done in the case of Jane Wardman, a schoolteacher who is the victim of baseless slander. John Beaumont (clearly a predecessor of paladin Jericho) does a bit of sound detection and the ending is as satisfying as the telling.

2710 "The Masked Crusader"   *EQMM* Nov 1969

The novelette length is well suited to the Hotel Beaumont scene, where the resident manager, Pierre Chambrun, is almost as much of a detective as his public relations director, who tells the story. The title is that of a projected TV series, whose hero is a guest of the hotel. But can a character come out of the script and commit murder?

2711 "Murder de Luxe"   *EQMM* Oct 1963

The story that introduced Pierre Chambrun and the Hotel Beaumont to the reading public. The murder of a private detective on the premises is too much of a contretemps for Chambrun to stomach, and he helps to identify the killer. Later stories in the series improved on this original.

2712 "Pierre Chambrun and the Black Days"   *EQMM* Nov 1968

A slender but convincing tale of how the formidable manager of the Hotel Beaumont deals with the disappearance of a chic young woman from his New York luxury stopping place. In all these Chambrun stories, the routine about breakfast, deference, telephones, and bar etiquette is more entertaining than the detection, which is slim.

2713 PEROWNE, BARRY

        "Up the Garden Path"   *EQMM* Feb 1949

A first-rate story of murder for the old triangular motive, reinforced with money. But when you come to the violent climax that should mean a second murder, you find a quite different view of the facts thrust at you, with a possible doubt as to present or future reality.

For this author's Raffles tales, see No. 2582.

2714 PETRIE, RHONA

        "What We're All Hooked On"   *EQMM* Sept 1968

A gripping tale of a young woman taken over, when she leaves prison, by a former associate who has plans for the two of them. First-rate storytelling.

2715 PETTIWARD, DANIEL

"The Weir"   *LMM* Summer 1954

A splendid tale of detection, original in setting and plot, and deceptively casual in the pursuit of clues and inference. There is only one red herring and it is a good one. The couple who think and find the facts are excellent—where are there more works of this kind by Mr. Pettiward? This one is reprinted in No. 2344; see also No. 2306.

2716 PHILLPOTTS, EDEN

My Adventure in the Flying Scotsman   Hogg 1888
A Romance of the London and Northwestern Railway Shares

A short tale, possibly written as an advertisement of the railway, and the author's first published book. It depicts the stealing, by an unscrupulous half brother, of the fortune in shares rightly due to the other half bro, a weak man, who tells the tale. The villain and his victim tussle in the train, but the villain gets his in the yards at Carlisle, as per schedule. Not detection, but make-believe fun.

2717 Peacock House and Other Mysteries   Macm 1927

Of these fifteen tales the best (and best-known) are: Three Dead Men / The Iron Pineapple / My First Murder. All deserve their fame, and the rest are not to be sneezed at. E.P. is a born storyteller, especially in his Devon-dialect pieces. Worth anybody's attention, but not detection in the active voice.

POE, EDGAR ALLAN (1809–49)

One salutes the Father of the Genre, rereads him at regular intervals, and desists from gratuitous comment about what is above all praise. His four model masterworks are: The Murders in the Rue Morgue / The Purloined Letter / The Mystery of Marie Rogêt / and The Gold Bug.

Note, however, a modern heresy according to which The Gold Bug is denied a place among stories of detection. On the face of it, the tale is nothing but detection, originating in crime. Certainly the story contains more detective work than The Purloined Letter, and it contains also the archetypal solution of a cipher.

2718 Tales of Mystery and Imagination   Everyman 1966/1908
Introd. by Padraic Colum

The forty-six stories, admirably introduced, but in a less than perfect text. By the loose standard of today, many more than the famous four tales would pass as "crime and detection"—e.g., The Oblong Box, The Cask of Amontillado, and others.

Bibliographical note: The copy of the 1845 edition of the *Tales,* published by Duyckinck, which was annotated by Poe himself and which used to belong to the library of the Century Association in New York (see No. 2928) is now part of the library of the University of Texas in Austin.

The text of The Purloined Letter in that volume, about which there has been controversy, is a subject of discussion in Nos. 2957 and 2895.

2719   PORGES, ARTHUR

"The Scientist and the Bagful of Water"   *EQMM* Nov 1965

The first of a variable but interesting series featuring Cyriack Skinner Grey, the "first wheelchair detective," who, with the aid of his son (IQ 180) and a 20-inch slide rule, is able to set Lieutenant Trask on the right track every time. The science is generally very sound and one must applaud the author's competence and originality.

2720   PORGES. See also:

"The Scientist and the Vanished Weapon"   *EQMM* Mar 1966

2721   PORTER, JOYCE

"Dover Pulls a Rabbit"   *EQMM* Feb 1969

In her first novelette about the oafish Inspector Dover, the author manages to make him as repellent as he ever was in longer yarns. But here one does not have to wait so long for Dover's one clever flash, and the tale is worth reading for the sake of the method (involving, characteristically, a toilet seat) by which he spots the murderer.

2722   POST, MELVILLE DAVISSON (1871–1930)

The Bradmoor Murder   Sears 1929
     Alt. title: The Garden in Asia
     Including the Remarkable Deductions of Sir Henry Marquis of Scotland Yard

Seven tales which give the impression of being good plots resolved too quickly, as by sleight of hand. They are: The Bradmoor Murder / The Blackmailer / The Cuneiform Inscription / The Hole in the Glass / The Phantom Woman / The Stolen Treasure / The Garden in Asia.

2723   "Dead Man's Gloves"   *EQMM* Jan 1963
     Orig.: "The Age of Miracles" (*1918*)

Uncle Abner, in Jeffersonian Virginia, does a nice job of exposing a murderer by the simple expedient of insisting that the corpse not be buried with gloves on.

2724   "The Instrument of Darkness"   *EQMM* June 1960
     Orig.: "The Adopted Daughter" (*1918*)

How one brother killed another with a pistol shot after losing a slave girl in a chess game, but left one trace, is neatly explained by Uncle Abner. We are treated to interesting information about dueling besides.

2725   The Mystery at the Blue Villa   App 1919

Seventeen stories which it would be a pleasure to praise and describe. Unfortunately, this author's capacity for creating situations is not matched by a sense of unfolding and rational solution, so that a ratiocinative reader feels aroused, hustled, and cheated. It is only fair to add that many good judges deem these works excellent. In this collection the tales are not told as detective stories, though following clues does occur. Rather, they are adventure, mystery, and romance. As always, Post knows how to arouse and keep up suspense, and his somewhat melodramatic prose does not prevent his striking off some splendid phrases to describe character or sensation. He does repeat his plots occasionally, and even his thoughts within one tale, but he carries it all off by sheer belief in what he is saying. The outstanding pieces are: The New Administration (a "Virginia-type" narrative) / The Laughter of Allah / The Wage-Earners / Lord Winton's Adventure / The Sunburned Lady / and (save for the denouement) The Baron Starkheim. And the other eleven all have points of interest, some of them of detective interest.

2726   "Naboth's Vineyard"   EQMM Aug 1950; orig. 1918

An Uncle Abner story, melodramatic in tone and plot, and not among the most convincing or ingenious in the series about this quasi-Biblical, quasi-political character.

2727   The Silent Witness   Farr 1930/1929
Foreword by the author

These thirteen tales are tied together by locale, leading characters, and the idea set forth in the Foreword, which is that man cannot contrive a set of appearances that will fit deceptively into the real order of events. There is always a "silent witness" in the form of a fact that will not jibe with the rest; and that fact is enough to sustain the moral law and bring about justice to the wronged parties.

All the tales show how Colonel Braxton, sometimes aided by Dabney Mason, redresses wrongs committed chiefly from greed in the western counties of (old) Virginia. The scene is rural but clues are abundant, despite the author's trust in the single "witness." The five best are: The Survivor / The Heir at Law / The Mark on the Window / The Vanished Man / The White Patch.

2728   The Sleuth of St. James's Square   App 1920

These sixteen stories are not all about Sir Henry Marquis, the sleuth of the title, who is at once head of the CID at Scotland Yard and directing secret service operations in Asia. Three of the tales belong to the Virginia series (i.e., West Virginia along the Ohio in pre-partition days) and exhibit that quasi-Biblical atmosphere and strong moralism which are Post's sign manual and which often produce situations, scenery, and reversals akin to Chesterton's in the Father Brown stories. In the present volume the best are: The Thing on the Hearth / The Reward / The Cambered

Foot / The Wrong Sign / The Fortune Teller / The Hole in the Mahogany Panel / The Spread Rails (excellent detection, by a woman, of deliberate train-wrecking).

2729   The Strange Schemes of Randolph Mason   Putn 1896
           Introd. by the author

M.D.P. begins by presenting an interesting argument in favor of the tale which shall explore the possibility of baffling not the detector of crime but the punishing power of the law. His central character, Randolph Mason, is a lawyer of great acumen, but "without moral sense." In the seven tales that follow, the New York scene of the 1880s and 1890s alternates with that of rural or small-town West Virginia. In each case Mason provides a mechanism by which a desperate man can recoup serious financial loss without actually putting himself within the power of the law, though in each case again he is brought to trial. If Mason were a bit more down to earth the tales would be little masterpieces. As it is they are novel and worth looking up if only for their foreshadowing of a later and more famous Mason (see Nos. 932–44).

2730   Uncle Abner, Master of Mysteries   App 1918

Uncle Abner is a variant of Randolph Mason, the difference being that Abner is a man of complete integrity and indeed Biblical power to bring about justice. His cases are dramatic, but they fall just short of greatness through the same air of legerdemain that affects all the stories by Post. Their origin in actual cases perhaps made him embroider too much.

2731   POST. See also:

           Randolph Mason, Corrector of Destinies   Putn 1923; orig. Clode 1908

2732   POSTGATE, RAYMOND, ed.

           Detective Stories of Today   Faber 1940

Twenty stories, all of literary worth, but only eight are stories of detection. Among those that are not is the excellent tale by Belton Cobb, Mr. Flexman's Boast. The rest include a good many not readily accessible elsewhere, so that the contents deserve listing in full:

M. Allingham	It Didn't Work Out
F. Beeding	Me Ne Frego
E. C. Bentley	The Sweet Shot
A. Berkeley	The Wrong Jar
Belton Cobb	Mr. Flexman's Boast (a real gem!)
G. D. H. & M. Cole	In a Telephone Cabinet
F. W. Crofts	The Hunt Ball
Winifred Duke	A Thousand Pounds
E. Ferrars	After Death the Deluge
Mary Fitt	The Box of Coins
R. A. Freeman	The Case of Oscar Brodski
M. Kennedy	End of a Judge
R. Keverne	The Night Call

Mrs. Belloc Lowndes	Quietly . . . Comfortably
Gladys Mitchell	Daisy Bell (Mrs. Bradley cut down to size in a rare but good short tale)
E. R. Punshon	The Double Six Domino
R. Ellis Roberts	The Narrow Way
D. L. Sayers	The Inspiration of Mr. Budd
Ethel Lina White	The Gilded Pupil
D. Winser	The Boat Race Murder

2733 PROCTER, MAURICE

"The Million-Dollar Mystery"   *EQMM* Jan 1960

There is apparently such a thing as honest illicit dealing in diamonds, and like all honesty, it invites crookedness by others. An international pair of detectives work here to unmask the supercrooks, in a story not especially of detective interest.

2734 QUEEN, ELLERY

The Adventures of Ellery Queen   Stokes 1934
Problems in Deduction

Eleven tales, full of ingenious gimmicks and adorned with excellent titles, each being The Adventure of . . . in the best Holmesian style. The outstanding ones are: The One-Penny Black / The Invisible Lover / The Glass-Domed Clock. The problems are engaging and hold the eye; the solutions hinge on one point, well-concealed and generally to be accepted as practicable. The characters are necessarily sketchy and the motives conventional—the pleasure is in seeing the riddle solved.

For additional tales, see *The New Adventures . . .* (1940), *The Further Adventures . . .* (1946), *The Case Book . . .* (1945), *Calendar of Crime* (1952), and the entries below.

2735 Challenge to the Reader   Stokes 1938
Introd.: "Challenge," by the editor

A group of twenty-five tales in which the names of the detectives have been switched and the reader is expected to infer the right performer from the circumstances and the manner of their elucidation. The authors subjected to this sleuth transplant are: Conan Doyle, Chesterton, H. C. Bailey, Agatha Christie, M. Leblanc, R. A. Freeman, Melville Davisson Post, Edgar Wallace, Bramah, Orczy, Futrelle, Anthony Wynne, The Coles, Octavius Roy Cohen, Stribling, Hammett, Reeve, and Arthur Morrison.

2736 "Cold Money"   *EQMM* Jan 1956

A good example of the brief puzzler which these authors do so well. When ex-convict Mullane died of a heart attack in his hotel room he had $62,000 stashed away, but it wasn't there for Inspector Queen and Sergeant Velie to find. Ellery notes one conspicuous absence from the bathroom and names the thief.

2737 "The Death of Don Juan" EQMM Aug 1964

Both Boucher and WHT find this one of the best of E.Q.'s exploits—here a tidy job of finding the murderer of a theatrical star playing at the Wrightsville theater. Well-clued; Ellery's detection is both smart and sound.

2738 (*As editor*)

Ellery Queen's Minimysteries World 1969

Here are seventy very short tales of crime, mystery, and detection, many by famous authors but in too many cases having brevity as their chief merit. From the editor's fun-and-games "mintroduction" to Boucher's The Ultimate Clue, which is no more than a play on words, the emphasis is on cleverness. The twenty-one items of actual detection are by Allingham, Ambler, Blochman, Arthur Clarke, Coxe, Crispin, C. P. Donnel, Garve, M. Gilbert, Hecht, O. Henry, Innes, the Lockridges, A. Porges, Queen, Quentin, Craig Rice, M. Sharp, Simenon, Stout, and Symons. Most of the better ones are available elsewhere.

2739 The Female of the Species LB 1943
      The Great Women Detectives and Criminals
      Introd. by the editor

The stories lead, through good sampling, to important collections by their respective authors. But as a whole the "literature" here represented is disappointing. Since many if not most of the great writers of detective fiction since 1920 have been women, there is no reason why women detectives should not shine. It is perhaps the effort to make them appear "woman-like" in standard ways that detracts from their impressiveness, especially when taken in bulk. The stories are:

Detectives
M. Eberhart	Susan Dare in "Spider"
Stuart Palmer	Hildegarde Withers in "Green Ice"
Paul Gallico	Sally Holmes Lane in "Solo Job"
Hulbert Footner	Mme. Storey in "The King of the Gigolos"
Vincent Starrett	Sally Cardiff in "Murder at the Opera"
H. H. Holmes	Sister Ursula in "Coffin Corner"
Agatha Christie	Miss Marple in "Village Murder"
F. Tennyson Jesse	Solange Fontaine in "Lot's Wife"
Baroness Orczy	Lady Molly in "The Man in the Inverness Cape"
Fergus Hume	Hagar Stanley in "The Florentine Dante"
Stacey Aumonier	Miss Bracegirdle in "Miss B. Does Her Duty"
Gilbert Frankau	Kyra Sokratesco in "Tragedy at St. Tropez"

Criminals
John Kendrick Bangs	"Mrs. A. J. Van Raffles"
Roy Vickers	"Fidelity Dove"
Edgar Wallace	"Four Square Jane"

plus six others of lesser note.

Note: The Vincent Starrett tale is the same as The Bloody Crescendo (1934), and H. H. Holmes is Anthony Boucher, q.v.

Ellery demonstrates "instant detection" by solving the problem of which of three stepchildren had committed stepatricide with the aid of a poisoned antibiotic capsule. Simple but neat.

2741   (*As editor*)

The Misadventures of Sherlock Holmes   LB 1944
   Frontispiece by F. D. Steele
   Introd. and other apparatus by the editor

Of all the specialized anthologies owed to the researches of the editor, this one is perhaps the most valuable and scholarly. Besides the thirty-three tales and skits here reprinted, we are given a useful introduction, a one-page biography of Sherlock Holmes by Kenneth MacGowan, a full bibliography of fifty-eight authors of Holmes parodies, some head notes, and an index. The work deserves reissue in paperback.

The stories run as follows:

Stephen Leacock	Maddened by Mystery; or, The Defective Detective (1911)
	*An Irreducible Detective Story (1916)

By Devotees and Others

Zero (Allan Ramsay)	The Adventure of the Table Foot (1894)
R. K. Munkittrick	The Sign of the "400" (1894)
Oswald Crawfurd	Our Mr. Smith (1907)
Jules Castier	The Footprints on the Ceiling (1920)
A. E. P.	The End of Sherlock Holmes (1927)
August Derleth	The Adventure of the Norcross Riddle (1928)
*William Q. Fuller	The Mary Queen of Scots Jewel (1929)
*Hugh Kingsmill	The Ruby of Khitmandu (1932)
Rachel Ferguson	His Last Scrape: or, Holmes, Sweet Holmes! (1932)
*Frederic Door Steele	The Adventure of the Murdered Art Editor (1933)
F. A. Kummer and Basil Mitchell	The Canterbury Cathedral Murder (1933)
Logan Clendening	The Case of the Missing Patriarchs (1934)

By Detective Story Writers

*Robert Barr	The Great Pegram Mystery (1892)
Maurice Leblanc	Holmlock Shears Arrives Too Late (1907)
*Carolyn Wells	The Adventure of the Clothes-Line (1915)
Vincent Starrett	The Unique Hamlet (1920)
Anthony Berkeley	Holmes and the Dasher (1925)
*Agatha Christie	The Case of the Missing Lady (1929)
Anthony Boucher	The Adventure of the Illustrious Impostor (1942)
Ellery Queen	The Disappearance of Mr. James Phillimore (1943)
*Stuart Palmer	The Adventure of the Remarkable Worm (1943)

By Famous Literary Figures

Sir James Barrie	The Adventure of the Two Collaborators (1893)
Mark Twain	A Double-Barrelled Detective Story (1902)
Bret Harte	The Stolen Cigar Case (1902)
O. Henry	The Adventures of Shamrock Jolnes (1911)

By Humorists

R. C. Lehmann	The Umbrosa Burglary (1893)
John Kendrick Bangs	The Stranger Unravels a Mystery (1897)
	*Shylock Homes: His Posthumous Memoirs (1903)
Richard Mallett	The Case of the Diabolical Plot (1935)
S. C. Roberts	Christmas Eve (1936)
Manly Wade Wellman	The Man Who Was Not Dead (1941)

* Those so marked are the best for plot or humor, combined with the essence of parody, which is fidelity in wit. It might be added that this valuable work had to be withdrawn after publication, under the pressure of a threatened suit for damages by the late Adrian Conan Doyle. This overzealous heir would not even allow booksellers to use short quotations from his father's works in catalogues listing copies of early Sherlock Holmes collections.

2742   "The Needle's Eye"   *EQMM* Sept 1965

Deals with Ericsson's Island and Captain Kidd's buried treasure—a refreshing change from Ellery's usual haunts. Murder comes in, too, and here Ellery adorns his investigation with identification of a rare seventeenth-century wallpaper before explaining how the murderer—hit by a bullet—still displayed no wound.

2743   "No Parking"   *EQMM* Sept 1965
       Also in Q.E.D. (*No. 2746*)
       Orig.: "Terror in a Penthouse" (This Week *Mar. 18, 1956*)

This is a classic of "instant detection": three men are in love with an actress who can't make up her mind which to choose. She is found shot dead in her penthouse on a rainy night. Ellery happens to be going into the building after difficulty in finding a parking space and he sees a figure in a trench coat leaving the place—that is all. But he solves the case and nabs the culprit in short order. Beautifully told and plotted.

2744   (*As editor*)

101 Years' Entertainment: 1841–1941   LB 1941

An historical anthology that begins with Poe and ends a little over a century later; of necessity a group of oft-anthologized stories, fifty in number. Notable novelties are: M. P. Shiel, The S.S.: Viola Brothers Shore, The MacKenzie Case; and Pearl Buck, Ransom.

2745   Poetic Justice   NAL 1967

The indefatigable and imaginative anthologist who likes to think in categories has hit upon the famous poets from Chaucer to Dylan Thomas as sources for his twenty-three stories of crime and mystery. Detection is there, too, but less prominently. Some of the poets who had an eye and a pen for the genre include: Scott, Byron, Longfellow, Whitman, Hardy, Yeats, Mark Van Doren, Robert Graves, Conrad Aiken, Edna St. Vincent Millay, and Ogden Nash. Some of the episodes are of course very short. All are prose. A Signet paperback edition appeared in 1970.

2746   Q.E.D.   Goll 1968
       Queen's Experiments in Detection

Sixteen stories that originally appeared in *EQMM, This Week, Argosy,
Cavalier, Signature,* and *MD* between 1949 and 1966. The collection
opens with a novelette, Mum Is the Word, and includes that splendid tale
of instant detection, No Parking (q.v.). Then come:

Object Lesson	Half a Clue
No Place to Live	Eve of the Wedding
Miracles Do Happen	The Last Man to Die
The Lonely Bride	Pay-Off
Mystery at the Library of Congress	The Little Spy
Dead Ringer	The President Regrets
The Broken T	Abraham Lincoln's Clue

2747   (*As editor*)

       The Queen's Awards   LB 1946
           Later: EQ Mystery Annuals *and* EQ Anthologies (*qq. v.*)
           Introd. and notes by the editor

The first volume to draw on *EQMM* for its contents, and particularly
on the winners of the annual contests, begun in 1945. Among the sixteen
stories one finds: T. S. Stribling, Count Jalacki Goes Fishing / Michael
Innes, Lesson in Anatomy / and Kenneth Millar, Find the Woman.

    A second volume (LB 1947) includes, with a new introduction: Carter
Dickson, The House in Goblin Wood / Q. Patrick, Love Comes to Miss
Lucy / Michael Innes, Tragedy of a Handkerchief / T. S. Stribling, The
Mystery of the 81st Kilometer Stone / Edmund Crispin, Deadlock / Jack
Finney, The Widow's Walk / Harry Kemelman, The Nine-Mile Walk /
and eleven others, plus prefatory notes to each story.

    Ten more volumes of *Awards* appeared up to 1954. Then the editors
changed the form to *EQ Mystery Annuals,* alternating with *Anthologies,*
which were at first also annual and are now semi-annual, in paperback.
See Nos. 2492–3.

2748   Queen's Bureau of Investigation   LB 1949

Eighteen tales, classified among several departments: blackmail, rare-book,
murder, embezzlement, suicide, magic, etc. They all hinge on one point,
which E.Q.'s imagination or systematic thought fastens upon to unmask
the culprit. They are necessarily all quite short—10–12 pages long.

2749   (*As editor*)

       Rogue's Gallery   LB 1945
           The Great Criminals of Modern Fiction

Thirty-two stories by good authors from O. Henry onward depict the
fictional doings of murderers, confidence men, thieves, crooked lawyers,
and other skaters on thin ice.

    A Foreword, four Betweenwords, and an Afterword provide informative
and rather "literary" chitchat. There are also extensive bibliographical
notes before each story.

2750   Sporting Blood LB 1942

The Great Sports Detective Stories
Introd. by Grantland Rice

The idea is self-explanatory: stories of crime and (occasional) detection in which the setting or the participants is or are sporting. This includes gambling. The stories are fair.
Contains:

A. C. Doyle	Silver Blaze
E. C. Bentley	The Sweet Shot (golf)
G. K. Chesterton	The Fad of the Fisherman
E. Queen	Man Bites Dog (baseball)
A. Morrison	The Loss of Sammy Crockett (track)
F. A. M. Webster	The Double Problem
E. Queen	Trojan Horse (football)
D. Hammett	His Brother's Keeper (prizefighting)
Stuart Palmer	Tomorrow's Murder (polo)
David Winser	The Boat Race Murder
Theodore Bentley	Morning Swim
E. W. Hornung	A Schoolmaster Abroad (Dr. Dollar: tobogganing)
Rufus King	The Seven Good Hunters
L. Charteris	The Mugs' Game (poker)
George A. England	Ping-Pong
A. Christie	A Chess Problem (Poirot)
R. W. Chambers	The Purple Emperor
E. Queen	The One-Penny Black
E. Bramah	The Vanished [Petition] Crown
Dorothy L. Sayers	The Dragon's Head (book-collecting)

2751   Twentieth Century Detective Stories World 1948
Illus. by Seymour Nydorf
Suppt.: Queen's Quorum and Checklist

Fourteen stories out of the common, though some have been, or were previously, anthologized. The unusual items are: T. S. Stribling, The Shadow / E. C. Bentley, Greedy Night (a parody of Peter Wimsey) / C. S. Forester, Some Kinds of Bad Luck / Anthony Boucher, The Stripper / Roy Vickers, The Man Who Murdered in Public / Leonard Thompson, Squeeze Play.

The Queen's Quorum is a list of 100 important books of short stories in the genre, with comments and bibliographic notes. Several of these are detective fiction only by stretching definitions; but the notes are all useful.

For further collections and comments by the same hands, see *The Literature of Crime* (1950), *Murder by Experts* (1947), and the *Presidents' Edition E. Q. Anthology* (1965).

2752   QUENTIN, PATRICK

"The 'Laughing Man' Murders" *EQMM* Aug 1963

In this competent novelette Inspector Martin Field investigates a series of murders in San Francisco, whose solution comes uncomfortably close

546

to home. The reader has a fair chance to guess the surprising but logical culprit.

2753   The Ordeal of Mrs. Snow   RH 1962

Short stories depicting small crime and low cunning in a manner nowise distinguished; sexual overtones not particularly titillating; no detection and much adolescence.

RAMPO, EDOGAWA (pseud. of Hirai Taro, b. 1894)

Educ. Waseda Univ. (Tokyo); put by father, who was merchant and lawyer, in various clerical jobs that proved distasteful. Unemployed in 1923 and happening to read a western story of mystery, H.T. tried his hand and found success through the pages of the only Japanese mystery mag. After thirty years of successful production he is deemed by his compatriots equal if not superior to Poe, whose name he cannibalized into the form shown above: in Japanese it is pronounced Edoga-aram-po. As to the native estimate of his merits, see below.

2754   Japanese Tales of Mystery and Imagination   Tuttle 1956
           Trans., with a pref. by James B. Harris

Only the outside of this little volume is attractive. The ten tales are strong on imagination but weak on mystery (except that of why they were published). Detection nil—the method employed by the detective of disguising himself as an overstuffed chair scarcely recommends itself. The translator's preface contains some information on the history and present status of the d.s. in Japan.

2755   RAY, CYRIL, ed.

           Best Murder Stories   Faber 1965
               Introd. by the editor

Of the fifteen pieces here gathered, only four or five warrant the greater permanence of book publication. They are: John Collier, The Touch of Nutmeg Makes It / Roald Dahl, The Way up to Heaven / Aldous Huxley, The Gioconda Smile / Poe, The Cask of Amontillado. The rest do include tales by Sayers, Kipling, Stevenson, Stanley Ellin, Ray Bradbury, Somerset Maugham, Elizabeth Bowen, William Sansom, and H. G. Wells—all deservedly reputed authors, but they have done better than these samples of their work. (The Maugham Before the Party errs by being too long; the Stevenson Body-Snatcher by turning suddenly into a ghost story.)

   The Introduction, including a mistake about D. Sayers, is not reassuring about first principles.

REDMAN, BEN RAY (also Jeremy Lord; 1896–1961)

b. Brooklyn; educ. Pawling, N.Y., schools and Columbia Univ.; author, editor, and translator. In *The Bannerman Case* (1936) and *Sixty-Nine Diamonds* (1940), social observation and criticism predominate over mystery or detection, which are more often found in this writer's short stories. On the genre itself see his Introd. to Bentley's *Trent Intervenes* (No. 2351).

2756   "The Perfect Crime"
          In: Thwing's Best 100, vol. V (No. 2837)

A brilliant tour de force, being a story within a story, which provides the motive and "justifies" the means. This writer never wrote a better piece and it makes one regret that he wrote so few.

2757   "The Tougher They Come"   *EQMM* Jan 1955

A story labeled *Black Mask* Department, but neither very tough nor very interesting. Somewhat wandering dialogue leads to finding out the earlier profession of a man who has collected insurance for his wife's death, and the discovery shows how he contrived that familiar exchange of values.

2758   REES, ARTHUR J.

          "The Finger of Death"
          In: Thwing, vol. IX (No. 2837)

Extracted (condensed) from *The Unquenchable Flame* (DM 1926), and worth reading in either form.

2759   "The Missing Passenger's Trunk"
          In: Thwing, vol. IX (No. 2837)

A neat tale for its day. It no longer provokes surprise, but it still holds attention.

2760   REEVE, ARTHUR B(enjamin), 1880–1936

          The Dream Doctor   VR 1913

A pioneering use of "soul analysis" (psychoanalysis) in conjunction with the usual scientific analysis of material clues, carried on here by Craig Kennedy. Elsewhere, Reeve uses a woman doctor to the same end (see No. 2762), and with less creaking of the crude machinery than in these thirty episodes. The plots are often good, the dialogue and motivation wooden.

2761   The Silent Bullet   Harp 1910
          The Craig Kennedy Stories, vol. I

Twelve short stories featuring the scientific method of crime detection pursued by Craig Kennedy. A good bit of sound stuff amidst the dross. In narrative and character-drawing Reeve is several degrees below his contemporary and counterpart, R. Austin Freeman, which means that Reeve can be read only for his scientific imaginings and "modern" outlook—e.g., applying Freud to detection twenty years before the general public had heard of psychoanalysis.

2762   "The Veiled Prophetess"
            In: Thwing, vol. V (No. 2837)

Taken from the author's *Constance Dunlap* (1913), this story makes a
remarkable use of Freudian analysis at a time when it was neither well-
known nor respectable. The "detection" is of course not physical but
psychological, and the situation and sentiments belong to the period, but
it and the other tales in the original volume form an impressive series.

2763   RENDALL, VERNON (HORACE) (b. 1869)

        The London Nights of Belsize   Lane 1917

Sketches that offer a mixture of detection in small things and "Arabian
Nights" adventure of the R.L.S. variety. Chapter 8 is Belsize as Commentator: Sherlock Holmes—a destructive analysis of one of the weaker
tales. (See No. 3369.)

2764   REYNOLDS, QUENTIN

        "Never Trust a Murderer"   *EQMM* Feb 1949; orig. 1946

After an apt reference to the Elwell case (1920), the story takes up a
racing situation mixed with burglary and murder that end up in posthumous revenge with a double twist.

2765   RHODE, JOHN, ed.
        Detection Medley   Hutch n.d. [1939]
            In U.S., abridged: Line-Up (*1940*)
            In ppb., Line Up = The Avon Book of Detective and Crime
            Stories (*1942*)
            Foreword by the editor; Introd. by A. A. Milne

The original volume is so rich in substance and variety that even shorn
of 17 items for U.S. publication it is still a desirable collection. The notable
pieces are, besides the two prefaces: The Sweet Shot and The Genuine
Tabard, by E. C. Bentley / Persons or Things Unknown, by J. D. Carr /
The Best Detective Story, by Chesterton / The Hiding Place and The
Crime in Nobody's Room, by Carter Dickson / A Criminologist's Bookshelf, by J. J. Connington / The Art of the Detective Story, by R. A. Freeman / Are Murders Meant? and Murderers in Fiction, by Milward Kennedy / The Live Wire, by E. C. R. Lorac / and The Perfect Close, by
Hugh Walpole.
    The remainder consists of pairs of stories by: Agatha Christie, Dorothy
Sayers, Henry Wade, Anthony Gilbert, E. R. Punshon, Lord Gorell, and
Margery Allingham, and a scattering of singletons. The whole deserves
reprinting.

2766   RICE, CRAIG, and PALMER, STUART

        "Once Upon a Train"   *EQMM* Oct 1950

This once-startling collaboration which puts bibulous John J. Malone
(lawyer) and Hildegarde Withers (schoolteacher) together on a Chicago–

New York train has little more than novelty to recommend it. The poorly matched detectives do solve the problem of who stabbed the undressed man in Malone's compartment, but chance reveals the hiding place of the stolen money, and the railway atmosphere is unconvincing (e.g., the train, running via the N.Y. Central through Toledo, starts from the Illinois Central Station). There is a little humor.

2767 RICHARDSON, MAURICE, ed.

Best Mystery Stories   Faber 1968

As one might expect, the well-known critic knows what he is about and tells us how he chose the seventeen tales of "mystery" as he defines it. And yet by no means all these seventeen tales answer to the definition. The first three are Hindu, Buddhist, and Old Testament pieces. Then we have Collins' Terribly Strange Bed (q.v.) / Doyle's Greek Interpreter / two Dr. Czissar anecdotes by Eric Ambler / Sayers' Cave of Ali Baba / and the parody Bond Strikes Camp by Cyril Connolly (q.v.).

The rest represent the work of Julian Symons, Patricia Highsmith, Michael Gilbert, Celia Fremlin, Robin Maugham, Dafna Dan, Eric Parr, and the editor, whose "Horroratario" in verse is a good review of the literature of the macabre, but would have been funnier if rhymed.

2768 ROTH, HOLLY

"The Girl Who Saw Too Much"   EQMM May 1970; 1956

Not a complex plot, but enough uncertainty and enough contrast in characters and circumstances to make a memorable novelette.

2769 "The Six Mistakes"   EQA, vol. 16 (1969)

A gripping tale in which the fantastic becomes compelling and true as the reporter Blake tracks down the current activities of a former "boy prodigy," now turned—what?

2770 RUNYON, DAMON (1888–1946), wrote many excellent short stories in which much went on that was on the wrong side of the law. His characters live in the area where show business, gambling, fashion, and felony meet. But in devoting himself to that milieu, he discussed crime only incidentally—except in the one splendid murder tale What, No Butler? (see No. 2694).

One should add that D.R.'s works provided the substance for the American classic Guys and Dolls, as well as for a play and film, A Slight Case of Murder. Trials and Other Tribulations (1947) retells six actual crimes. For other works, see The Best of Damon Runyon, ed. E. C. Bentley (1938), who adds a remarkable introduction, and A Treasury of D.R., ed. Clark Kinnaird (1958), which contains articles and poems as well as stories.

2771 RUSSELL, BERTRAND

"The Corsican Ordeal of Miss X"   *EQMM* Apr 1966; orig. 1953

Those fortunate enough to have known Lord Russell will easily recognize in these 18 pages the command of language, the imagination, the love of freedom which made his company memorable. But such qualities are more apt to produce Stevensonian adventure than the deductions of Doyle. Such is the case here, but accept it for the fantasy it is.

2772 RUSSELL, RAY

"The Man Who Spoke in Rhyme"   *EQMM* Nov 1969

In the author's own words, a baroque tale; certainly one of crime and horror if not detection. In the style of a letter purporting to have been written from Venice in 1876 and relating a tale of blood and lust dating back another century.

2773 SAINT MYSTERY MAGAZINE, THE

Vol. 1, No. 1 appeared Spring 1953 as a quarterly with the name *The Saint Detective Magazine*. Later became a monthly under the editorship of Hans Stefan Santesson, later still under Leslie Charteris. New title adopted November 1958. Last issue in October 1967.

2774 SANDOE, JAMES, ed.

Murder Plain and Fanciful   Sher 1948
    With Some Milder Malefactions
    Foreword by the editor
    Various plans and sketches

This virtually perfect anthology seems never to have been reprinted, which is a disgrace as well as a deprivation to the reading public. What the public would find is a collection of twenty-eight tales and reports, divided into three sections—true crime, fiction based on fact, and pure fiction. The first and last categories are particularly rich and unusual. From the contents below one readily singles out the items by Clarke, Eisenschiml, Hotson, Roughead, Boucher, Bramah, Davis, Kennedy, and Walsh as topping the list.

And for good measure the editor supplies a stunning Foreword and a *critical* inventory of novels and plays based on true crime. The contents:

1. Murder:	Plain
Robert Blake	The Law Takes Its Toll
Thomas Burke	The Obsequies of Mr. Williams
Sir Edward Clarke	The Pimlico Mystery
Samuel Herbert Dougal	A Murderer's Confession
Otto Eisenschiml	The Orpet-Lambert Case—1916
Janet Flanner	Murder Among the Lovebirds
Felix Frankfurter	The Case of Sacco and Vanzetti
J. Leslie Hotson	Tracking Down a Murderer
F. Tennyson Jesse	The Rattenbury and Stoner Case

Raymond Postgate	The Respectable Mr. Thompson
William Roughead	Closed Doors; or, The Great Drumsheugh Case
Henry David Thoreau	Hannah Dustin

2. Murder:	Fancy from Fact
Miriam Allen DeFord	Homecoming
Lillian de la Torre	Goodby, Miss Lizzie Borden
Melville Davisson Post	The Man in the Green Hat

3. Murder:	Fanciful (with some lesser crimes)
Pierre Audemars	Hercule and Jou-Jou
Ludwig Bemelmans	The Murderer of the Splendide
Anthony Boucher	Elsewhen
Ernest Bramah	The Clever Mrs. Straithwaite
Freeman Wills Crofts	The Parcel
Norbert Davis	Kansas City Flash
Walter Greenwood	The Practised Hand
Milward Kennedy	End of a Judge
C. Daly King	The Episode of the Codex' Curse
Edith R. Mirrielees	Professor Boynton Rereads History
Coley Newman	Melancholy Baby
Thomas Walsh	Break-Up
Iolo A. Williams	Their Masterpiece

2775 SAYERS, DOROTHY L.

Hangman's Holiday   Goll 1933

This group contains four Peter Wimsey tales, six Montague Egg, and two others. Of the Wimsey foursome—The Image in the Mirror / The Incredible Elopement of Lord P.W. / The Queen's Square / The Necklace of Pearls—all but the last are very good. The Montague Egg half dozen are superior to the other set in No. 2776; and the remaining pair— The Man Who Knew How / The Fountain Plays—are a couple of stunts about crime neatly told though not exactly original.

2776   In the Teeth of the Evidence   Goll 1939

A collection containing two Peter Wimsey stories, five Montague Egg stories, and ten others. Some are very fine, but not the P.W. ones, which are: In the Teeth of the Evidence and Absolutely Elsewhere. The Montague Egg stories are: A Shot at Goal / Dirt Cheap / Bitter Almonds / False Weight / The Professor's Manuscript. The remaining titles are:

The Milk Bottles	The Inspiration of Mr. Budd
Dilemma	Blood Sacrifice
An Arrow o'er the House	Suspicion
Scrawns	The Leopard Lady
Nebuchadnezzar	The Cyprian Cat

2777   Lord Peter Views the Body   Goll 1929

This is her prime collection, under one of the best titles ever devised for a book of detective short stories. They are not all equally fine, but so many are—even the melodramatic one at the end—that it would be hard to find a rival entry in a competition for variety, balance, picturesqueness, and sheer ability to handle detective ideas, let alone invent them.

2778   (*As editor*)

>   The Omnibus of Crime   P&C 1929; orig. 1928
>   *Introd. by the editor*

A cornerstone volume, in which the editor opens with a 47-page account of the development of the detective story under the significant headings: Early History; Poe; Intellectual vs. Sensational; The pre-Doyle Period; S.H. and His Influence; The Scientific Detective; The Modern Fair-Play Method (with details of *Trent's Last Case*); Artistic Status; Love Interest; The Most Unlikely Person; Unexpected Means; and Tales of Mystery and Horror.

About half the book is given over to pure detection, including both primitives and sophisticates: Mrs. Henry Wood, Poe, Doyle, Bramah, F. A. M. Webster, B. Roberts, Bentley, Phillpotts, R. Barr, Meade and Eustace, Wynne, F. B. Austin, R. Allen, P. Wilde, Whitechurch, Chesterton, H. C. Bailey, Basil Thomson, Huxley, Lowndes, E. W. Hornung.

Stories of the Supernatural make up the remainder.

2779   The Second Omnibus of Crime   CM 1932
>   *The World's Great Crime Stories*
>   *Introd. by the editor*

The tales in Part I, Detection and Mystery run as follows:

F. Britten Austin	The Fourth Degree (a good psychological tale)
Robert Barr	Lord Chizelrigg's Missing Fortune (Eugene Valmont)
E. C. Bentley	The Ordinary Hair-Pins (Philip Trent & Norway)
A. Berkeley	The Avenging Chance (the author's masterpiece)
Ernest Bramah	Who Killed Charlie Wimpole? (Max Carrados & mushroom poisoning)
Agatha Christie	The Adventure of the Clapham Cook (Poirot in the days of Hastings)
W. Wilkie Collins	The Biter Bit (Mid-Victorian parody)
F. W. Crofts	The Mystery of the Sleeping-Car Express (the author's first; good, but not det.)
J. S. Fletcher	Blind Gap Moor (from *The Secret of the Barbican;* short and good)
Milward Kennedy	Death in the Kitchen (not quite 4 pages; stunt ending)
Mrs. Belloc Lowndes	An Unrecorded Instance
Baroness Orczy	The Regent's Park Murder
John Rhode	The Elusive Bullet (for the only other ss by Rhode see No. 2324. In this one Dr. Priestley gets kissed.)
Dorothy L. Sayers	The Cave of Ali Baba (from *Lord Peter Views the Body,* q.v.)
J. C. Squire	The Alibi (old-school-tie-relationships but a fair tale nonetheless)
Sir Basil Thomson	The Vanishing of Mrs. Fraser (from *Mr. Pepper, Investigator;* rather poor)
Henry Wade	Duello (good tale featuring Inspector Poole)

Victor Whitechurch   How the Captain Tracked a German Spy (from *Captain Koravitch*, q.v.; dull stuff now)

Percival Wilde   The Pillar of Fire (from *Rogues in Clover*, 1929, a very scarce work about the rascals Bill & Tony)

For the thirty items of Mystery and Horror, see No. 3459.

The editor's 16-page introduction grows in merit as the years pass (see No. 3020), and so does her choice of stories with which to live up to her professions.

2780   Tales of Detection   Everyman 1936
       Introd. by the editor

Nineteen stories, of which ten or eleven have been frequently reproduced, before or since this collection. Those hard to find and very much worth reading are: Edgar Jepson & Robert Eustace, The Tea-Leaf / Thomas Burke, The Hands of Mr. Ottermole / Ronald Knox, Solved by Inspection / John Rhode, The Elusive Bullet / Milward Kennedy, Superfluous Murder / C. Daly King, The Episode of the Nail and the Requiem.

The Introduction is, as usual with D.L.S., a work of rare insight and judgment.

2781   The Third Omnibus of Crime   CM 1935/1934
       Introd. by the editor

The proportion between the two headings in this third *Omnibus* is 21 Detective and Mystery to 31 Mystery and Horror. Of course, most of those in the second group have nothing to do with crime, whether detected or not. The Introduction is short and adds little to either our knowledge or the author's just reputation for literary originality.

Note: The first, second, and third *Omnibus of Crime* have also appeared as *The Great Stories of Detection, Mystery, and Horror*, in groups of two, three, five, and six volumes under various imprints (1929–61).

2782   SAYERS, DOROTHY, and BYRNE, MARY ST. C.

       Busman's Honeymoon
       A Detective Comedy in Three Acts
       In: Famous Plays of 1937   Goll 1937

A very actable version of the somewhat extended novel, plus an Author's Note on what the difference amounts to.

2783   SCOTT, R. T. M.

       Aurelius Smith, Detective   Dutt [1927]

Twelve short stories of very uneven merit, featuring the rather elderly Aurelius Smith, who sometimes manages a trick or two worthy of Holmes. There are amusing sidelights on the New York of 1925. In The Crushed Pearl and Underground, the same ability is shown as in Bombay Duck, not in this collection. (See No. 2837.)

2784   SEABORNE, E. A., ed.

The Detective in Fiction   Bell 1954; orig. 1931
    A Posse of Eight
    Bell's English Language and Literature Series
    Introd. by the editor

The eight are familiar: Poe, Doyle, Chesterton, Orczy, Bramah, and
M. D. Post stories, supplemented by an early Christie—The Jewel Robbery
at the "Grand Metropolitan"—and Leacock's parody in *Nonsense Novels*
(No. 2620). The Introduction is discursive and entertaining but not
original or altogether accurate.

2785   SHARMAN, MIRIAM

"Battle of Wits"   *EQMM* June 1967

The dozen pages of this story live up to its challenging title, and the
reader is kept on edge as the "battle" ebbs and flows between a headmaster
and a parent who wishes to avenge his son—a suicide after expulsion
from school.

2786   SHARP, MARGERY

"The Perfect Model"   *EQMM* Feb 1957

An English tale in which too many of the participants are groggy or
sleepy or stupid, so as to make possible a crime they witness but don't
quite latch on to. Why do writers think readers are so easily fobbed off?

2787   SHAW, JOSEPH T., ed.
    Pref. by the editor on the special genre

The Hard-Boiled Omnibus   S&S 1946

Twelve stories from *Black Mask,* dating from 1929 to 1936 and including
good ones by Hammett, Chandler, and Raoul Whitfield.

2788   SHIBATA, TETSUO, ed.

The Confession and Two Other Stories   Kenkyusha (Tokyo) 1966
    Introd. and Notes in Japanese by the editor

Three stories reprinted as readings for Japanese students: Henry Cecil,
The Confession / Dorothy Sayers, The Inspiration of Mr. Budd / Michael
Gilbert, The Coulman Handicap. The choice is as fine as the stories, all
of them being unusual in theme and beautifully told. What better way
for students to enjoy learning English?

2789   SHIEL, M(ATTHEW) P(HIPPS) (1865–1947)

The Best Short Stories   Goll 1948
    Ed. by John Gawsworth

Published posthumously, this volume contains three stories displaying the
wisdom and deductions of Prince Zaleski: The Race of Orven / The Stone

of the Edmundsbury Monks / The S.S. Each mixes the amusing and the annoying, and smothers detection under verbiage and incense.

2790   "The Return of Prince Zaleski"   *EQMM* Jan 1955; orig. 1945

The fourth and last short story about the Prince who plays at being arm-chair detective, written fifty years after the first three, which date back to 1895. Half a century has not improved the rational powers of the Prince, but the fantasy is still strong and amusingly unbelievable. It is not clear whether this printed text follows the author's original or has been altered by John Gawsworth. But the prefatory note by E.Q. on the loss and recovery of the typescript yields even more suspense. It also implies a providence eager to spare Shiel's reputation but foiled in the event.

2791   SHULMAN, MAX

   "The Baffling Case of the Cigarette Lighter"   *MD* July 1957

A good short spoof on the spy story—messages, torture, dames, and head-waiters, all present and running true to form.

2792   SIMENON, GEORGES

   "Inspector Maigret Deduces"   *EQMM* Nov 1966

It is a pleasure to have Maigret confronted with five suspects (the other occupant of the railway compartment being the victim) and the job of deciding who stuck a needle into the heart of the rich Berlin banker, traveling with only a few marks in his wallet. A brief tale but tidy.

2793   "Inspector Maigret Thinks"   *EQMM* June 1967

Although Maigret's ratiocination is not more impressive here than in many other tales, the setting of this one, on Seine barges, makes interesting reading. Two murders, by hanging, are competently dealt with by Maigret after he has learned to "think bargee."

2794   STARRETT, VINCENT

   The Blue Door   CCD 1930

Ten short stories, of which only the two Jimmy Lavender tales are of classic cut and strictly detective interest. Another, Too Many Sleuths, is a fictional rendering of the Oscar Slater case with a solution that violates the historical facts. The rest include humor, suspense, international intrigue, etc. V.S. is a good plotter, but his narrative and dialogue are crude.

2795   (*As editor*)

   Fourteen Great Detective Stories   ModL 1928

The fourteen are all classics (except perhaps Balmer and MacHarg's Private Bank Puzzle) and therefore widely anthologized, ubiquitous. The authors are Poe, Doyle, Chesterton, Arthur Morrison, Freeman, Bramah,

Richard Harding Davis, M. D. Post, Robert Barr, Baroness Orczy, Jacques Futrelle, S. H. Adams, and Owen Johnson.

2796   STERN, JAMES

"The Cloud"
In: The Second Mercury Story Book (No. 3445)

A good murder tale, without detection.

2797   STEVENSON, ROBERT LOUIS

"Markheim"
In: Novels and Tales, vol. 7   Scrib 1896/1887

A prototype of the tale of compulsive murder. The devices for raising the tension and delaying the consummation have not changed, nor has the prose aged as much as some might suppose. The moralizing alone gives its date. This tale has served as a model for those writers whose intention is to delineate the mind of the murderer Before, During, and After, and who cannot be bothered to read Dickens or Dostoevsky. A brilliant story, closer to reality than *Dr. Jekyll and Mr. Hyde,* and in a class with Thrawn Janet.

2798   New Arabian Nights Entertainment   Scrib 1925; orig. 1882

A prophetic series of interlinked tales that combine the light cynicism of the nineties with sophisticated adventure and suspense, based on the then new contact between elegance and the underworld. Being ahead of their time, these stories are said to have "insured" the failure of the magazine *London.* But their influence proved lasting. The opening story certainly gave Dorothy Sayers the model of The Cave of Ali Baba in *Lord Peter Views the Body* and had its influence on Chesterton *passim.* The whole set forms a little classic, but detection is slight and incidental.

2799   "Was It Murder?"
In: Dorothy Sayers, ed. Tales of Detection (*No. 2780*)

An early short short about a murder apparently well plotted and which comes off, yet leaves hanging the question in the title.

2800   STEWART, J. I. M. (pseud. of Michael Innes, q.v.)

The Man Who Wrote Detective Stories and Other Stories
Nort 1959

The principal tale—perhaps it deserves the name of novelette—is entertaining though slender in plot. It deals with odd ways of plagiarizing and one senses that it was inspired by a visit to Venice, where the action takes place. The three other tales, each of 25 to 35 pages, are more typical Innes, though not in any sense mystery or detection. In one or two the Jamesian affectation which has characterized some of the Innes books is strongly marked, and fantasy (nuclear-atomic) informs the last one.

2801 STIRLING, (W.) EDWARD

>   Something to Declare   FM 1942
>   *Illus.*

An autobiographical yet unassuming account of The English Players, who
between 1922 and 1939 entertained audiences of the Continent by producing a broad repertory of English plays, including several in the mystery
genre, notably: *The Ten-Minute Alibi, The Speckled Band, The Ringer,
The Ghost Train, Payment Deferred, The Silent Witness,* and *The Thirteenth Chair.* JB can testify from a good number of performances seen at
various capitals between 1929 and 1937 that this unusual repertory company deserved the success which only the outbreak of war interrupted.

2802 STONG, PHIL(IP DUFFIELD) (1899–1957), ed.

>   Twenty-five Modern Stories of Mystery and Imagination BR 1942
>   *Alt. title:* Other Worlds

The novelist of village and farm as well as historian of the state of Iowa
was perhaps not the best judge of what was implied by the title chosen for
this collection. It is not merely a descriptive phrase open to anyone's use;
it is Poe's phrase, sanctified by genius and time. The moderns here chosen
suffer by having to stand comparison.

2803 STOUT, REX

>   And Four to Go   VP 1958

In this quadrille, the customary holidays play a role—in Christmas Party,
Nero Wolfe serves as Santa Claus; in Easter Parade, Archie, cameras, and
orchids are concerned; at the Fourth of July Picnic of the Restaurant
Workers of America, whom Nero Wolfe is to address, he discovers a man
stabbed, makes his speech and solves the case, though *not away from
home.* In Murder Is No Joke, it is the season of killing in a dressmaking
establishment—a good tight knot about a woman's throat and a good tight
plot with original clues. (Reprinted in No. 2344.)

2804 Black Orchids   Farr 1942
>   *A Nero Wolfe Double Mystery*

Two 100-page tales, which first appeared in *The American Magazine* as
Death Wears an Orchid and Invitation to Murder (= Cordially Invited to
Meet Death). In the first, Wolfe and Archie are in fine form, and murder
at a flower show provides a suitable background for Wolfe's talents and
predatory instincts. Archie himself innocently pulls the trigger. The
second story is less satisfactory, involving as it does a highly debatable
move by the murderer to disarm suspicion. Besides, too many animals.

Note that in the Avon reprint of Invitation to Murder (1946) a Poe
story has been added: Some Words with a Mummy.

2805 "Booby Trap"   Dell 1944

An army officer who has tumbled to suspicious circumstances in the presumably accidental death of a captain of Military Intelligence is himself blown up by a booby trap. Nero Wolfe does a neat job of selecting the culprit by arranging a booby trap of his own. The final scene, in which Wolfe plays God, is unique: no beer, no audience except Archie (a major of three weeks' standing), and the murderer in a car in Van Cortlandt Park.

2806 Not Quite Dead Enough   Dell 1944

This edition, earlier than the hard-cover (Farr 1944), contains the 70-page title story and the slightly longer Booby Trap (No. 2805). Neither is to be missed by anyone with an interest in the Wolfe-Goodwin saga. In this one Archie has to incriminate himself to get Wolfe to abandon physical training and get back to ratiocination and both help win the war. Full of amusing characters and with more action and fewer words than is sometimes true of the longer tales.

2807 "Poison à la Carte"   *EQMM* Apr 1967; orig. 1960

A fairly good Nero Wolfe affair, enlivened by the presence of twelve beautiful girls who serve food and drink at a select dinner which Nero and Archie also attend. How the poison got to one of the guests and whether he was the intended one is elucidated by Wolfe's usual methods.

2808 Three Doors to Death   VP 1949
      Foreword by Archie Goodwin

In the forties Nero Wolfe novelettes used to appear first in *The American Magazine* (now defunct), then in hard covers, and almost immediately in paperback, where he still leads a lively existence. The present grouping takes in Man Alive / Omit Flowers / Door to Death. Archie's Foreword is a Forewarning that Nero Wolfe solves crime for money, even though in two of these cases he fails to get paid—"which might develop into a nuisance." All three cases are worth any reasonable amount of money.

2809 Three Men Out   VP 1954

This "threesome" brings together: Invitation to Murder (= Cordially Invited to Meet Death) / The Zero Clue (see No. 2813) / This Won't Kill You. The first two present good situations and expert reasoning; the third is a baseball story (= The World Series Murder), which ought to benefit from the double sport of playing and killing, but doesn't.

2810 Three Witnesses   VP 1956

This is unquestionably the best of the Nero Wolfe "threesomes," containing as it does the little masterpiece called The Next Witness, about a telephone-answering service / When a Man Murders . . . , a first-rate Enoch Arden tale / and Die Like a Dog, in which a dog and a raincoat mixed up figure prominently and skillfully. Archie is tops in all, and in the first we not only enjoy Wolfe subpoenaed and in a courtroom, but subsequently driving around and doing genuine detection on the hoof.

2811 Trio for Blunt Instruments   VP 1964/1963

The collection consists of Kill Now, Pay Later / Murder Is Corny / Blood
Will Tell. Of these the first is a compendium of all the author's merits—
a fast tale of double murder, drama, conflict with officialdom, banter about
love, and a violent ending on Wolfe's premises, where the vulnerable
heroine is a refugee. The second has agricultural elements that do not go
well with the quasi-sexual drama; and the third is a premeditated crime
rather simply untwisted. Archie is good throughout.

2812 Trouble in Triplicate   VP 1949

A particularly good bunch of early shorts: Before I Die / Help Wanted:
Male / Instead of Evidence. All three start with victims or potential victims—of murder chiefly, but also of blackmail. The plots and their unraveling by Wolfe and Archie are superior examples of art, with plenty of
drama, humor, and exact reasoning.

2813 "The Zero Clue"   EQMM Apr 1963
        Orig.: "Scared to Death" (1953)

A novella in the classic Wolfe-Goodwin pattern, perhaps a short-story idea
unduly blown up. But the characters are unusually interesting, and Wolfe's
reversal of his adverse opinion of the murdered man (a "probability
wizard") is based on a clever interpretation of a clever clue.

2814 STOUT. See also:

        Curtains for Three   VP 1951
        Homicide Trinity   VP 1961
        Three at Wolfe's Door   VP 1961
        Three for the Chair   VP 1957
        Triple Jeopardy   VP 1952

2815 STRIBLING, T(HOMAS) S(IGISMUND) (1881–1965)

2816 Clues of the Caribbees   Hein 1930
        Being Certain Criminal Investigations
           of Henry Poggioli, Ph.D.
        Illus.

A group of five longish short stories featuring the Italian-American psychologist from Ohio State University and his only partly successful efforts
to unravel sundry mysteries encountered in his travels through the West
Indies. The variety of local color lends a certain charm to these examples
of that very rare and perhaps dubious genre, the humorous detective story.
The contents are: The Refugees / The Governor of Cap Haitien / The
Prints of Hantoun / Cricket / A Passage to Benares. The third and the
last are perhaps the most enduring.

        "A Daylight Adventure"   EQA, vol. 5 (1963)

The psychologist-detective Poggioli stops for lunch in a small Tennessee
town and takes time out to make a superb speech in defense of a woman

accused of murdering her husband. Good entertainment and sound psychology; little detection.

2817   "Judge Lynch"   *EQMM* Sept 1950; orig. 1934

A strong melodramatic story of family violence over the liquor laws—not detection, but a criticism of American justice.

2818   "The Mystery of the Choir Boy"   *EQMM* Jan 1951

A Poggioli story, but psychological mystery arising out of juvenile obsession rather than crime or detection properly so called.

2819   "Poggioli and the Fugitive"   *Samag* Dec 1954

Dr. Henry Poggioli does a nice job of relating a headless corpse found in tropical waters to larger issues of international crime. But his best detecting serves to identify the body, and understand the circumstances of the beheading.

2820   "The Telephone Fisherman"   *EQMM* Jan 1955

Poggioli detects in a spirit of irony about himself. The Tennessee setting affords opportunity for satire at the expense of the locals, to match Dr. P.'s self-debunking.

2821   STRONG, L. A. G.

"The Birdwatcher"   *EQA, vol. 14* (1968)

Minor but readable detection by Inspector Ellis McKay as he and Sergeant Bradstreet work on a narcotics case in a quiet English coastal town. The characters are too few to permit much mystification, but the tale is nonetheless enjoyable.

2822   Odd Man In   Pitm 1938
         Illus. by Phoebe Lefroy

Five stories of the odd and the criminal, titled as follows: The Job in the City / The Case of the Corpse in Barbel Court / The Case of the Corner Shop / The Case of the Red Cliff / The Case of the Soho Restaurant.
   The character of young Peter Black, quite engaging and just above average in all respects but his instinct for the unusual, runs through the series, of which the best undoubtedly are the first and the last two.

2823   "Trial and Error"   Meth 1939
         Methuen's One-Act Plays

The editor of the series is the author as well. The play, which is very short indeed, retells in trial form what purports to be a case of attempted suicide; it turns out something else. The little skit is entertaining and full of good detail. Only the end lacks punch and falls into sentimentality.

Seventeen short stories, many of considerable merit. Two or three are school stories—in all the characterization is first-rate and some of the situations original, but no detection.

2825   "You Can't Love Two Women"   *EQA, vol. 11* (1966)

Expert treatment of the classical situation with a most unusual twist at the end. No detection is attempted—or necessary.

2826   STRONG. See also:

"The Clue That Wasn't There"   *EQMM* Nov 1953

2827   SWINNERTON, FRANK

"Ms. in a Safe"   *EQMM* Oct 1953

A fine tale, sparely told, of murder for literary purposes, which is always good for a fresh run in the hands of a craftsman. There is no detection, but a good strong kick in the last paragraph.

2828   SYMONS, JULIAN

"The Crimson Coach Murders"   *EQMM* Apr 1967; orig. 1960
In Eng.: "The Summer Holiday Murders"

An ordinary setting and group of characters witness murder for gain, and an amateur (writer of detective fiction) takes a hand. Clues and red herrings show some originality, but a sense of the unreal—and the sound of worn machinery—pervade the whole.

2829   Francis Quarles Investigates   Panther 1965; orig. 1960 ff.

Uneven in length and quality, but all about the portly Quarles, who detects some one discrepancy (e.g., the *e* in whis*k*ey as an Irishism), which becomes diagnostic in a murder, kidnapping, or other case. Little to rejoice or wonder at in these starved modern plots.

2830   "Love Affair"   *EQMM* Nov 1969

Short and sweet, with an unusual triangle, a motorcar being No. 3. Although Don had always been more aggressive than his wife, Moira, it is she who finally resolves their problem in an unusual way. Crime without detection.

2831   Murder! Murder!   Coll 1961

Advertised as "21 Outstanding Stories from the Casebook of Francis Quarles," these sketches by the actually amiable Symons, who pretends to sophisticated fierceness, are on the whole rather dull.

2832 "A Pearl Among Women" *EQMM* Jan 1968

Francis Quarles, private investigator, is a specialist in "instant detection," and in this short tale of a theft of pearls he doesn't even leave his chair. An amusing trifle.

2833 "The Santa Claus Club" *EQMM* Jan 1967

At a meeting of the Santa Claus Club, Francis Quarles does a fair job of "instant detection" by spotting the one man present at the select dinner able to substitute napkins in the manner required for murder.

2834 THOMSON, BASIL

Mr. Pepper Investigator Castle 1925

A very odd book. Apparently its first intention is to make fun of the omniscient private detective à la Sherlock Holmes. The man Pepper is an American, full of conceit yet not pompous, and able to wriggle out of situations in which his boasting and his predictions are shown up. He bamboozles an assistant who is the narrator into doing his leg work for him, and some of the fifteen tales are genuine bits of good detective fiction. The rest are spoofs. One should add that the humor varies from fair to nil.

2835 THOMSON, H. DOUGLAS, ed.

The Great Book of Thrillers Odhams n.d.
    Introd. by the editor
    Illus.

Seventeen mysteries, twelve detective stories, and twenty-one tales of the supernatural fill this mammoth but well-considered anthology. The contributors are nearly all famous; the stories are by no means their equally well-known anthology pieces. Go to this volume for these (among others):

Val Gielgud	Hot Water
L. P. Hartley	The Island
E. Phillips Oppenheim	The Café of Terror
Hugh Walpole	The Tarn
G. D. H. & M. Cole	A Lesson in Crime
Eden Phillpotts	Peacock House
Daniel Defoe	The Ghost of Dorothy Dingley
Sheridan Le Fanu	Madam Crowl's Ghost
John Galt	The Black Fury
James Hogg	Mary Burnett
H. G. Wells	The Red Room

2836 The Mystery Book Odhams 1934
    Introd. by the editor
    Illus.

A volume of 1,079 pages, with but remarkably little poor material. The three sections are devoted to Mystery and Adventure (fifteen tales),

Crime and Detection with another fifteen, and finally, twenty Stories of the Supernatural. Though it is an excellent bedside volume for the general reader, the expert in detection will find too many well-known items by Bailey, Bramah, the Coles, Crofts, Doyle, and Sayers. To compensate are good tales by A. J. Alan, My Adventure at Chislehurst / J. Storer Clouston, The Envelope / Michael Kent, Another Shot in the Locker.

Moreover, we find here James' Turn of the Screw, and notable pieces by Stevenson, Hawthorne, and Chekhov.

2837 THWING, EUGENE, ed.

The World's Best One Hundred Detective
Stories 10 v.   F&W 1929
    Introd. by the editor

The editor's boast that this is an international collection is legitimate and so—or nearly so—is the title of the collection; that is, if one bears in mind the literature available forty years ago. It may prove useful to single out a few stories hard to find elsewhere:

Vol. I	Richard Connell	The Sting of the Wasp
	Sidney Gowing	The Poacher
Vol. II	Edwin Baird	The Mystery of the Locked Door
	Ben Ames Williams	The Cigaret
Vol. III	Herman Landon	The Pigeon on the Sill
	Bertram Atkey	The Unpunctual Painting
	John Ferguson	The White Line
Vol. IV	Hulbert Footner	The Murder at Fernhurst
	Frederic F. Van DeWater	The Great Wet Way
Vol. V	R. T. M. Scott	Bombay Duck
	Ben Ray Redman	The Perfect Crime
Vol. VI	Vincent Starrett	The Eleventh Juror
	Henry South Williams	The Subconscious Witness
Vol. VII	Edmund Snell	Farrar Fits In
	William B. Maxwell	Suspicion
Vol. VIII	Arthur Somers Roche	The Club of One-Eyed Men
	H. deVere Stacpoole	The Story of O Toyo
Vol. IX	Frederic Arnold Kunmer	Pig's Feet
	Arthur J. Rees	The Missing Passenger's Trunk

Almost all the eighty-one others will be found in more than one anthology or in famous authors' collections of their own stories.

2838 TRAIN, ARTHUR

Mr. Tutt at His Best   Scrib 1961
    A Collection of His Most Famous Cases
    Ed. Harold R. Medina
    Introd. by the editor

Sixteen stories chosen from the famous series that began to appear in the *Saturday Evening Post* in 1919. Ephraim Tutt is a forerunner of Perry Mason, a shrewd lawyer whose efforts extricate the innocent from the toils of the designing. He works in New York City and also in his native Pottsville, N.Y., where his antagonist is one Hezekiah Mason. Some of the tales bring in clueing and inference, but they are chiefly legal, as Judge Medina's excellent introduction makes clear.

2839 TREAT, LAWRENCE

"'A' as in 'Alibi'" *EQMM* Feb 1966

Another tale about Lieutenant Decker, whose life is meant to wring our hearts, but who gets the point just as failure stares him in the face—this time the flaw in a clock alibi, somewhat accidentally disclosed.

2840 "The Heart of the Case" *EQMM* Mar 1970

The Forensic Club—judge, inspector, narrator—hold a postmortem on a case, which turns out unusual as to motive, though plain enough in execution and delayed solution.

2841 TWAIN, MARK

The Stolen White Elephant, etc. Osgood 1882

The title story is a parody piece of detection ridiculing the efforts of Inspector Blunt. It occurs also in a collection entitled *Tom Sawyer Detective and Other Stories* (1924/1878). Here too the leading tale is disappointing. For a brief account of M.T.'s efforts in detection short and long, see No. 2081/B.

2842 UZZELL, THOMAS H.

Short Story Hits: 1933 HB 1934

A collection of stories for classroom use. From cheap and fair to good magazine stuff, they are all by less than first-rate authors, and supplied with comments and analysis by the editor. Only two are about crime (tough school) and not otherwise distinguished: William Corcoran, Manhattan Midnight / McKinlay Kantor, Something like Salmon.

2843 VAN DINE, S. S., ed.

The World's Great Detective Stories BR 1931; orig. 1927
A Chronological Anthology
Pref. by the editor

This overpraised volume contains a number of indifferent Continental stories, side by side with classic and original U.S. and English detection. The Introduction is fair; it should be better since S.S.V.D. writes here not like the creator of Philo Vance but rather like the art critic Willard Huntington Wright. The chief items of interest are: Anna Katharine Green, The Doctor, His Wife, and the Clock / Melville Davisson Post, The Straw Man / Eden Phillpotts, Three Dead Men / H. C. Bailey, The Little House / Maurice Leblanc, Footprints in the Snow.

2844 VAN GULIK, ROBERT

New Year's Eve in Lan-Fang   Beirut 1958
    A Judge Dee Story (Limited Edition)

A short tale, written *pour l'occasion.*

2845 VARIOUS HANDS

Six Against the Yard   S&B n.d. [1935]
    In U.S.: Six Against Scotland Yard
    Anon. Introd.

In each of six longish stories by Allingham, A. Berkeley, Crofts, Knox,
Sayers, and Russell Thorndike, the author hopes he has depicted a "perfect
murder." Following each tale, Ex-Superintendent Cornish, CID, shows
where the author went astray in supposing his criminal to be safe. The
plots are about what one would expect from their authors. Sayers is the
neatest and the most "psychological," but her hero in Blood Sacrifice
actually commits no crime and so is outside the pale.
    The unsigned introduction oddly refers to "the instigator of this unique
volume."

2846 VICKERS, ROY, ed.

Best Police Stories   Faber 1966
    Introd. by the editor

An indifferent collection, valuable chiefly for two of the accounts of true
crime, one by J. D. Casswell, Q.C., of the Hulten and Jones case, in which
he defended the foolish and immature girl; the other by Julian Symons,
of the Otterburn Case (Evelyn Foster), which he himself looked into on
the spot. Then follow a fair Maurice Procter / a Sergeant Petrella tale by
Michael Gilbert / a poor Allingham in which Campion sits and listens /
an extract from L. Gribble's *Feats of Detection* (No. 3165) / Christianna
Brand's Aren't Our Police Wonderful? / and Burke's Hands of Mr.
Ottermole. Finally: The Chief Witness, by John Creasey / Miss Paisley's
Cat, by Roy Vickers / My Brother Down There, by Steve Frazee, intolerable in length and mood / Sentence of Death, by Thomas Walsh /
and All in the Night's Work, by Nigel Morland.

2847 "The Dacey Affair"   EQMM Feb 1957; orig. 1939

A genuine detective story in form, but the actions and complications strike
the reader as cluttered because so few outsiders and external circumstances
are brought in to suggest a lifelike haphazardness—compare any Sherlock Holmes tale. It is the Vickers sort of inbred intricacy that has given a
bad name to the detective tale.

2848 The Department of Dead Ends   Faber 1949
    Introd. by Ellery Queen

Not nearly so successful as Freeman in the inverted genre of short tale.
Despite elaborate efforts to give variety there is a sameness about these
murders solved by single discrepancy, and the technique should rather be

called scrambled than inverted. The best part in each incident is the author's social commentary on money, class, or profession.

2849 WADE, HENRY

Here Comes the Copper   Const 1938

Thirteen cases from the records of an ordinary police constable—John Bragg—whose motto is "Notice and Remember." A most engaging set of stories in Wade's easiest manner. Their titles are:

These Artists!	Toll of the Road
The Seagull	November Night
The Ham Sandwich	The Little Sportsman
Summer Meeting	Lodgers
Anti-Tank	One Good Turn
A Puff of Smoke	Smash and Grab
Steam Coal	

2850 Policeman's Lot   Const 1933
      Stories of Detection

In addition to the much anthologized Duello / The Missing Under-graduate / The Sub-Branch, there are four other Inspector Poole tales: Wind in the East / The Real Thing / The Baronet's Finger / The Three Keys. None of these is outstanding. In addition, the book contains six non-Poole tales, dealing largely with the sporting world, and turning on small points of luck or cunning. There is a bit of humor in Jealous Gun—a thing rather rare in Wade.

2851 WALSH, THOMAS

"Before the Act"   *EQMM* Oct 1953

A good plot that combines some detection and much heartbreak in an atmosphere of tense expectation.

2852 WEBSTER, F. A. M.

Old Ebbie, Detective Up-to-Date   Warne 1930

Twelve cases strongly derivative from Sherlock Holmes and amateurishly told. Old Ebbie is one Ebenezer Entwistle, a Pimlico "chemist" who cures his Watson-to-be of malaria. His chemistry consists in the knowl-edge that cooking salt is sodium chloride (two references to this!); his "up-to-date-ness" is reflected in his garb, which includes a shabby morn-ing coat, rabbit-skin waistcoat, and Gladstone collar. But when the under-pinnings of Sherlock and Watson are removed, what remains is pitifully weak. Old Ebbie's one solid achievement is the code story found in No. 2360.

2853 WELCOME, JOHN, ed.

Best Secret Service Stories   Faber 1965
      Introd. by the editor

The editor once before brought together a group of Secret Service stories (Faber, 1960) as well as five other collections of tales dealing with:

crime, motoring, gambling, law, and hunting (Faber). His own detective
novels (qq.v.) lean heavily on some of the above pursuits, especially
motoring. The introduction to the present collection deals largely with Ian
Fleming and John Le Carré, and is followed by eleven tales of espionage
including items by Maugham, Allingham, Fleming, Wheatley, Wallace,
Doyle, Sapper, Haggard, Alan Williams, M. Gilbert, and William Le
Queux.

2854   WELLS, CAROLYN (d. 1942), ed.

　　　　American Detective Stories   OUP 1927

Poe	The Gold Bug
Brander Matthews	The Twinkling of an Eye
Melville Davisson Post	The Corpus Delicti
Mary E. Wilkins Freeman	The Long Arm
Anna Katharine Green	The Ruby and the Caldron
Gelett Burgess	The Denton Boudoir Mystery
Bret Harte	The Stolen Cigar Case (parody)

2855   American Mystery Stories   OUP 1927
　　　　　Introd. by the editor

Miss Wells distinguishes between detective stories, ghost stories, and
mystery tales without ghosts, hence best called "riddles." Her selection of
fourteen pieces by American authors includes several well-known tales by
Poe and Hawthorne, Fitz James O'Brien's What Was It?, F. Marion Craw-
ford's The Upper Berth, two tales each by Cleveland Moffett and Madeline
Yale Wynne, and a few other items, undistinguished save for Bierce's
Occurrence at Owl Creek Bridge and Dreiser's The Lost Phoebe. Note
these unusual ones: Anonymous, Horror / M. Y. Wynne, The Little
Room and Sequel / C. P. Gilman, The Yellow Wallpaper / H. P. Spofford,
Circumstance.

2856   Best American Mystery Stories   Boni 1932
　　　　　Introd. by the editor

Twenty stories of mystery and detection, all but one published in 1930.
The intention was to match the yearly issue of *Best English Detective
Stories* (No. 2614) but the project was short-lived. Authors include: Ben
Ames Williams, A. S. Roche, Hammett, Burgess, C. B. Kelland, L. G.
Blochman, and others, but the tales are mostly disappointing. Faraday
Keene's The Little Dry Sticks is one of the best. A. V. Elston's Drawing
Room B is not a bad railroad tale.

2857   WELLS. See also:

　　　　All for Fun: Brainteasers   1935
　　　　The Best American Mystery Stories of the Year [1930–1931]
　　　　　　(a very large collection)   JD 1932

2858   WELLS, H(ERBERT) G(EORGE) also Reginald Bliss (1866–1946)

　　　　"The Hammerpond Park Burglary"
　　　　　　　In: The Stolen Bacillus and Other Incidents   Meth 1895

A story of criminal activity with strongly social and moral implications. The tale also appears to be an attempt to bring back naturalistic detail into descriptions of felony, after the gallant nonsense of Raffles and his peers.

2859   The Short Stories of H. G. Wells   Benn 1927

The contents of five collections plus five more stories make a total of sixty-three stories. They range from science fiction to the supernatural and from slapstick humor to contemporary satire, taking in a couple of crime and adventure situations on the way.

The principal crime stories in various moods, none of them detection, are:

A Deal in Ostriches   The Stolen Bacillus
Through a Window   The Reconciliation
The Hammerpond Park Burglary   Mr. Ledbetter's Vacation
The Treasure in the Forest   Mr. Brisher's Treasure
The Cone
    For the ghost stories, see No. 3474.

2860   WHITECHURCH, VICTOR L.

       The Adventures of Captain Ivan Koravitch   Blackwood 1925

Three tales from this elusive volume were first printed in *The Railway Magazine,* vol. 1 (1897): The Slip-Coach Mystery (p. 30) / The Escape of Koravitch (p. 148) / Frustrated on the Frontier (p. 225). To these may be added that reprinted by Dorothy Sayers in *The Second Omnibus of Crime* (No. 2779): How the Captain Tracked a German Spy. Mildly entertaining spy stuff, with a fair amount of railway interest in the first three.

2861   Thrilling Stories of the Railway   Pears 1912
           Six diagrams of railway tracks

This very rare volume contains fifteen short stories, not all detection or crime, though the nine that are "from the private notebook of Thorpe Hazell," the railway detective, do deal with crime or attempted crime. Unfortunately, the author saw fit to make his detective a figure of fun, while the feats attributed to him are not all feasible. For a fair sample of the probable-improbable, see No. 2778. The contents are as follows:

Peter Crane's Cigars   How the Bishop Kept His Appoint-
The Tragedy on the London & Mid-   ment
  Northern   The Adventure of the Pilot Engine
The Affair of the Corridor Express The Stolen Necklace
Sir Gilbert Murrell's Picture (see No. The Mystery of the Boat Express
  2778)   How the Express Was Saved
How the Bank Was Saved   A Case of Signalling
The Affair of the German Dispatch- Winning the Race
  Box   The Strikers
                                   The Ruse That Succeeded

2862   WHITFIELD, RAOUL

"The Rainbow Murders"   *EQMM* Feb 1949; orig. 1937

One of the founders of the hard-boiled school, R.W. attributed his stories about Jo Gar in *Black Mask* to one Ramon Decolta. His creation, Jo Gar, is a Filipino in search of ten diamonds that have been stolen from a jeweler in Manila. The machine-gun prose matches the ready hail of bullets, but the now familiar incidents of the tough genre lead to inconclusive results, so that five other adventures are needed to bring success to the small-sized Island detective. For the modern reader, of period interest only.

2863   WILDE, PERCIVAL

P. Moran, Operative   RH 1947

A collection of seven stories originally published in *EQMM* about the Acme International School of Detection. Supposedly comic and written in letter form, some of the tales actually contain detection and plot, but in insufficient amounts and of indifferent quality.

2864   WOOLRICH, CORNELL

"All at Once, No Alice"   *EQMM* Nov 1951

Another treatment—and a good one up to nearly the end—of the theme of Disbelief: the young married man leaves his wife at a hotel, she is spirited away, and no one pays attention to his requests for a search—or almost no one. Unfortunately, the adventure ends with a bit too much talk.

2865   "Cab, Mister?"   *EQMM* Sept 1950; orig. 1937

A typical Woolrich story—tough in language, violent in action, and sentimental throughout. Good plotting and steady clueing, but no ratiocination, and after reading, no reverberation.

2866   "Hot Water"   *EQMM* June 1961

An improbable but amusing tale of (pseudo) impersonation and (fake) kidnapping at Agua Caliente, where anything ought to be able to happen. Told by one of C.W.'s engaging illiterates—no detection.

2867   "It Only Takes a Minute to Die"   *EQMM* July 1966

A strong story of one man murdering another in a hotel, with a bit of sound detection at the end to ensure that justice is done.

2868   "One Drop of Blood"   *EQMM* Apr 1962

A good modern example of the inverted detective story. We learn why and how the murder was committed (actually without premeditation and hence a risky business), and are forced to admire the murderer's bold challenge to the detective that the latter produce proof. Eventually he does, very cleverly.

2869   "The Talking Eyes"   *EQMM* Apr 1967

A perfect example of what C. W. could do: take the situation of an entirely paralyzed old woman who overhears murder being plotted and is determined—for the best reason—to stop it. The author makes an ample novelette out of this, the texture being made of ordinary objects and the suspense extraordinary.

2870   WOOLRICH. See also: Nos. 2680 and 2873.

2871   WRIGHT, LEE, ed.

      The Pocket Book of Great Detectives   PB 1941
         Introd. by Alfred Hitchcock

An episode from the Book of Daniel is the only one out of seventeen items that may not be familiar to the connoisseur. The other detectives at work are: Dupin, Father Brown, Max Carrados, Reggie Fortune, Inspector French, Dr. Hailey, Martin Hewitt, Sherlock Holmes, Poirot, Ellery Queen, J. G. Reeder, Roger Sheringham, Dr. Thorndyke, Philip Trent, Professor Van Dusen, and Lord Peter Wimsey. The stories chosen are good representative choices. Note The Cyprian Bees (Hailey) and East Wind (French) as not easy to find in reprints.

2872   The Pocket Book of Mystery Stories   PB 1941
         Introd. by William Lyon Phelps

A dozen and a half substantial tales, more given to the strange and horrifying than to crime and detection. The introducer from Yale spends half a page on the value of paperbacks and the other half on the reasons for preferring murder to sex and straight novels. The striking items included are:

Robert Hichens	How Love Came to Professor Guildea
Edward Lucas White	Lukundoo
Ronald Knox	The Motive
Eden Phillpotts	Prince Charlie's Dirk
Eugene Manlove Rhodes	The Fool's Heart
Max Beerbohm	A. V. Laider
Saki (H. H. Munro)	The Open Window
G. B. Stern	Gemini
Walter de la Mare	Seaton's Aunt

   Leonard Gribble's The Case of Jacob Heylyn is a genuine detective story, neat and compact.

2873   The Pocket Mystery Reader   PB 1942
         Introd. by the editor

The choice is by a woman justly renowned as editor of detective fiction associated with various publishing houses. It includes articles, poems, and puzzles as well as tales of crime and horror. Among the noteworthy are: E. S. Gardner, The House of Three Candles / Evelyn Waugh, The Man Who Liked Dickens / Cornell Woolrich, Cocaine / Saki (H. H. Munro), The Hounds of Fate.

The poems are excellent but their connection with mystery or detection is nil. The articles receive mention under their authors' listing in this *Catalogue,* except for: Elliot Paul, Whodunit / P. G. Wodehouse, About These Mystery Stories / Edmund Pearson, The Perfect Murder / and Howard Haycraft, Dictators, Democrats, and Detectives.

2874   Wicked Women   PB 1960
      Foreword by the editor

Twelve rather short tales by the well-known and the obscure; the well-known being: Allingham, Christie, E. Queen, Q. Patrick, M. R. James, Dorothy Sayers, Kenneth Millar, and Edgar Wallace. The theme is the deadliness of the female, though in most instances the crime itself does not seem beyond the reach of the weaker sex, man. Note the otherwise inaccessible: Robert Arthur, Weapon, Motive, Method / Emily Neff, Partner in Crime / Wilbur Daniel Steele, The Lady Killer / Joan Vatsek, The Balcony.

2875   WRONG, E(DWARD) M., ed.

      Crime and Detection   OUP 1926
      World's Classics Series
      Introd. by the editor

The difference between Wright and Wrong in the matter of detective anthologies is not invidious but it is perceptible: Wrong classified his contents with great exactness and he wrote a 20-page introduction which is a "cornerstone" contribution to the studies of the detective genre. The choice of tales also could hardly be improved upon:

Crime and Detection
Poe	The Murders in the Rue Morgue
Poe	The Purloined Letter
Doyle	The Adventure of the Red-Headed League
A. Morrison	The Stanway Cameo Mystery
R. A. Freeman	The Case of Oscar Brodski
R. A. Freeman	The New Jersey Sphinx
E. Bramah	The Tragedy at Brookbend Cottage
G. K. Chesterton	The Invisible Man
H. C. Bailey	The Business Minister

Crime Without Detection
E. W. Hornung	A Costume Piece

Detection Without Crime
Barry Pain	On Green Paper
Barry Pain	The Face of the Corpse

Note the anonymous attempt at a sequel collection, No. 2320.

2876   WYLIE, PHILIP

      "Not Easy to Kill"   *EQMM* Oct 1965
      Orig.: "The Trial of Mark Adams" (*1935*)

A ship's doctor doubles as detective in this novelette about the murder of a millionaire, made to appear suicide, and he does some fair detection despite the indestructibility of the victim.

2877   X. L. (pseud. of Julian Osgood Field)

   Aut Diabolus, Aut Nihil   Meth 1895

These five long short stories dedicated to Walter Besant belong to the genre
of mystery-suspense that was invented by Balzac, perfected by d'Aurevilly
and Wilkie Collins, and disseminated by many followers in the nineties.
Every writer, Wilde and Stevenson included, wrote one or more of these
sinister adventures.

   The present set is a favorable lot—none is superb and none beneath
notice. The collection was fairly widely read, since it ran into a second
edition, and the tales first appeared in good magazines.

2878   YAFFE, JAMES

   "Mom Sings an Aria"   *EQMM* Oct 1966

Representative of this author's very amusing tales, in which the homicide
lieutenant gets good advice from his mother concerning his puzzling cases.
Mom's homely wisdom is real and here she makes use of her love of opera
to elucidate a murder at the Met. A fine example of rocking-chair detection.

2879   YOUNG, ALAN K.

   "Ponsonby and the Shakespeare Sonnet"   *EQMM* Oct 1969

The literary detection of forgery is always good for a short story, and since
few writers have attempted it, the field is still wide open. Here the idea
has merit, but it contains a fatal limitation, namely, that anyone capable
of spotting the telltale word would do so on first reading. Others would
miss it altogether. Therefore Professor P.'s mulling and pondering is
annoying and not suspenseful, especially if the reader sees the joker
right off.

2880   YOUNG, HOWARD IRVING

   Not Herbert   French 1926

A "Comedy of the Night in Three Acts" and remembered as delightful
by JB who saw and reviewed it in 1926. The plot is crime rather than detection, but the idea hinges on the pleasure derived by a bored young
bourgeois from organizing robberies and hobnobbing with free-and-easy
types. Not detection.

2881   ZANGWILL, ISRAEL

   "Cheating the Gallows"   *EQA, vol. 13* (1967)

A year after his exploration of the locked-and-barred-room problem in
The Big Bow Mystery, this author made another contribution to basic
situations with this tale, any résumé of which would spoil the reader's
pleasure. It remains deft and satisfying after 77 years.

PART III

STUDIES

AND HISTORIES

OF THE GENRE,

LIVES

OF WRITERS,

AND THE LITERATURE

OF

EDWIN DROOD

Gems from the Literature

"Those chaps are certainly hard to please. If you plunge straight into murder they say the story starts well but tails off. If you keep the fireworks until the end they say it's a slow beginning. If it starts well and finishes well they say it sags in the middle. Difficult."

"Why not keep the tension up all the way through?"

"Then it's melodramatic."

—Andrew Garve, *The Cuckoo-Line Affair*

It is to me a distressing thought that in nine-tenths of the detective stories of the world murderers are continually effecting an egress when they might just as easily go out.

—A. A. Milne, "Introducing Crime"

We are immediately on the tiptoe of suspense. Sigsbee Manderson is dead; the great financier is dead. Sigsbee *is* such a good name for the murdered man. It is also an additional motive to murder.

—H. Douglas Thomson, "Trent's Last Case"

If that Ming vase is on the mantel because it looks well, and because it's fun to have a bit of Ming about when the bullets start flying, well and good; but if the motive for the murder turns on the difference between Ming and Sung, then you will do well to get it absolutely right.

—Michael Gilbert, "Technicalese"

Personally, I think the gramophone should be given a rest.

—Dorothy Sayers, "The State of the Genre"

Detective story: one in which a detective or detectives solve the crime.

—Ordean A. Hagen, Glossary

Often the very writers who can invent the best detective puzzles are those who invent the most intolerable detective heroes. Think of all . . . those Scotland Yard policemen who are married to lady artists! (I must confess to a weakness for Mr. Day Lewis's Nigel Strangeways, because some of his habits were taken from mine.)

—W. H. Auden, "Detective Fiction"

The detective's friend acts in the dual capacity of very average reader and of Greek chorus; he comments freely on what he does not understand.

—E. M. Wrong, "Crime and Detection"

2882 ALINGTON, C. A.

[A discussion of detectives]
In: Gold and Gaiters (*No. 28*), *pp. 166–68*

The following are ticked off, in support of the contention that detective stories confirm an English prejudice in favor of the amateur: Inspector French, Lord Peter Wimsey, Mr. Campion, Sherlock Holmes, Roderick Alleyn, Appleby, Ludovic Travers, Desmond Merrion, Inspector Arnold, Reggie Fortune, Bobby Owen, and Miss Marple.

2883 AMIS, KINGSLEY

The James Bond Dossier   Cape 1965

The standard argument for the view that the Ian Fleming tales are "just as complex and . . . have just as much in them as more ambitious kinds of fiction." Apart from this thesis, Mr. Amis tries to correct a carload of misconceptions about what James Bond really is and does, and to repel attacks on the stories by imputing rather low motives to the attackers. After that the essay becomes a close reading of the text for a list of Bond's attributes and actions and their cultural implications. The book started as a 5,000-word article: it might now be returned to that scope, taking the evidence for granted. The best chapter is about style.

See also No. 2894 for a different interpretation of the secret agent as a culture hero.

2884 ANON.

Saint Mystery Magazine   Apr 1961

"No one can point to any particular genre as exemplifying the sort of story known as the detective story, mystery, or crime story." The writer goes on to glory in this "fact," the statement of which sufficiently defines his rank among would-be critics. He can be excused only as one forced to make a principle out of an error, so as to cover the uneven supply of good material for such magazines as his.

2885 ANON., ed.

For Bond Lovers Only   Dell 1965
Introd. by the editor
Illus.

Authors are assembled to sing the praises of James Bond in all his manifestations. The opening essay is an interview with Ian Fleming; Donald McLachlan discusses Fleming as a colleague in Naval Intelligence; Simenon and Fleming swap views on the Thriller Business; J. Bernard Hutton talks with our author about spies; Raymond Chandler gives an estimate of Fleming's work; and Allen Dulles winds up with a recollection and judgment of Fleming as an agent. Other pages deal with less profound matters.

2886   ARMCHAIR DETECTIVE, THE, ed. and pub. by Allen J. Hubin (3656 Midland Ave., White Bear Lake, Minn., 55110), is a quarterly that first appeared in October 1967 and that devotes its substantial bulk to the bibliography and criticism of detective fiction, the biography of its authors, and its other manifestations on stage and screen. There are departments for correspondence, queries, and the exchange of books. The highly capable editor is a scientist, lawyer, and scholar who also reviews detection in the *New York Times*.

2887   AUDEN, W(YSTAN) H(UGH) (b. 1907)

"The Guilty Vicarage"   *Harper's* May 1948
Notes on the Detective Story, by an Addict

A splendid defense of the pure detective story, from the standpoint of a logician and classical scholar, treated under the subheadings: Definition, Why Murder, The Milieu, The Victim, The Murderer, The Suspects, The Detective, Sherlock Holmes, Inspector French, Father Brown, The Reader.

2888   AYLMER, FELIX

The Drood Case   Hart 1964

An attractive volume, which includes a synopsis of the novel, as well as Dickens' rarely reprinted notes on the first twenty-three chapters. F. A., who has been concerned with the Drood case since 1914, examines the statements by Dickens' contemporaries (particularly that of John Forster, Dickens' biographer), who claimed to have learned from the author himself that Edwin Drood had died at his uncle's hand. Aylmer finds reasons to discount these and spins a fairly persuasive completion of the novel, as well as a highly detailed and less convincing Egyptian background for the protagonists.

2889   BAKER, RICHARD M.

The Drood Murder Case   UCP 1951

The author is a teacher of French who published three detective novels between 1936 and 1938 (see Nos. 92–93). S. S. Van Dine's encouragement is perhaps reflected in his choice of title for the present set of five studies. Mr. Baker writes well and his identification of "Mr. Datchery" as the elderly lawyer Grewgious is persuasive. Almost equally so is his pinning of the murder of Edwin upon his uncle Jasper, though for reasons much more circumstantial than those usually adduced. Another study deals interestingly with the genesis of the novel as revealed in Dickens' letters and notes.

2890   BALDICK, ROBERT, ed.

Pages from the Goncourt Journal   OUP 1962

Only one entry has relevance to our subject, but it is a perceptive and important statement. Discussing Poe on July 16, 1856, the Goncourts assert that he ushers in the scientific and analytic literature of the twentieth century, in which "things play a more important part than people; love gives way to deductions; and the basis of the novel is transferred from the heart to the head."

BARING-GOULD, WILLIAM S(TUART) (1913–67)

b. Minneapolis, the son of the British consul general there, and descendant of a family distinguished in scholarship and literature. Educ. Univ. of Minn., B.A. in 1935. Journalist, biographer of Sherlock Holmes and Nero Wolfe, author of *The Lure of the Limerick: An Uninhibited History* (1968), and annotator of the Holmes canon entire. (See Nos. 3328–9.)

2891   Nero Wolfe of West Thirty-Fifth Street   VP 1969
       The Life and Times of America's Largest Detective

A pleasantly discursive gathering of facts about N.W. from the novels of his creator, Rex Stout, and by plausible extension a critical and biographical treatment of the writer. Section 27, on Nero's philosophy and made up of aphorisms, is especially indicative and amusing.

Note that the title does not give N.W.'s full address. In the sources it varies from the 600s to the 900s—somebody is bound to fall into the North River, preferably Inspector Cramer; and that may be the reason for the discrepancies.

2892   BARZUN, JACQUES

       "The Book, the Bibliographer, and the
       Absence of Mind"   *Amer Sch* Winter 1969

A review of *Who Done It,* by Ordean Hagen (No. 2954), who attempted with little success to provide a complete bibliography of the detection-mystery-suspense genre. The reviewer shows the extensive lacunae and serious errors that make the book unreliable—a false friend to amateur and connoisseur alike.

2893   "A Briefbag of Felonies"   *Amer Sch* Autumn 1962

The contention here is that formulas wear out fastest when they are slickest, and that originality comes, not from turning a striking cliché inside out, but from seeing a familiar situation with an unfamiliar eye.

2894   "Meditations on the Literature of Spying"   *Amer Sch* Spring 1965

Suggests that the spy is the representative figure of our age (as against the soldier, the statesman, the divine). For an extract, see entry on Le Carré (No. 1362).

2895   "A Note on the Inadequacy of Poe as a Proofreader
       and of His Editors as French Scholars"   *Rom Rev* Feb 1970

A very short elucidation of the mystery of La Bougive, who occurs in "The Purloined Letter," with passing comments on detective fiction.

2896   "A Tribute to Rex Stout on His 80th Birthday"   VP Dec 1, 1965

A light but serious treatment of the characters of Nero Wolfe and Archie Goodwin as seen from the perspective of American literature and society, together with a brief discussion of the seminar method inaugurated by Wolfe for the detection of crime.

2897   "The World's Second Detective"   *EQMM* Nov 1956

On the basis of a solo flight in deduction by Pierre-Augustin-Caron de Beaumarchais in 1776, the author makes out a case for him as the worthy predecessor of Dupin and the disciple of Voltaire's Zadig.

2898   BARZUN. See also Nos. 2927 and 2992 and:

"Bright Facts and Pleasurable Fears"	*Harper's* Aug 1947
"Not 'Whodunit' but 'How'?"	*Sat Rev* Nov 4, 1944
"From *Phèdre* to Sherlock Holmes," in	
The Energies of Art	Vint 1962
"The Detective Story," in *Party of Twenty*	
(Clifton Fadiman, ed.)	S&S 1963
"Suspense Suspended"	*Amer Sch* Autumn 1958

2899   BENTLEY, E. C.

Those Days   Const 1940
       Portrait of the author

An agreeable autobiography by the author of *Trent's Last Case,* to which Chapter 9 is devoted. Bentley writes with simplicity and forthrightness, shows a few quirks and prejudices combined with a fairly wide view of human affairs and literature, too. The facts about *T. L. C.* and interesting remarks about Chesterton give a good notion of what detective fiction was like, and how regarded, before the great novel shift of 1920.

2900   BERKELEY, ANTHONY

Preface-Dedication of *The Second Shot*   Dday 1930

Berkeley questions the future of the detective story and gives it as his opinion that it is toward the development of character and atmosphere ". . . that the best of the new detective-writing energies are being directed." He allows that "the puzzle element will no doubt remain, but it will become a puzzle of character rather than a puzzle of time, place, motive, and opportunity." Freeman's *Singing Bone* and Mason's *At the Villa Rose* are cited as examples of tales which hold the reader's interest long after the criminal's identity is known. But see entry No. 170, which touches on Berkeley's neglect of his own doctrine.

2901   BIOGRAPHIES. Those of most writers of detective stories are hard to find in reference books, owing to the legitimate desire to protect pseudonyms. (It would appear that about one-third of all writers in this genre elect this form of anonymity.) Yet a number of anthologies give condensed accounts of their contributors' careers, and this fact is usually recorded in our comments on the work. Hence looking up an author's name in the Index to this *Catalogue* may lead to a source containing his *vita*.

Note especially A. L. Furman's several *Mystery Companions*, in which the sketches about contributors are often autobiographical.

2902　Boileau-Narcejac*

　　　Le roman policier　　　　　　　　　　　　　　　Payot 1964

These two practitioners of the genre should have had better judgment or a wider range of reading to guide them through the modern period. To list E. C. Bentley as an American also-ran and to single out Ellery Queen and Roy Vickers as far superior to all their contemporaries is indefensible. The book is fair for the earlier period and tosses out some good aperçus.
　* This is the form used on the title page. See Index to this *Catalogue* for their separate names.

2903　Bond, Raymond T., ed.

　　　Introductory Essay on Poisons and Poisonings
　　　　　　In: Handbook for Poisoners　　　　　　　Rine 1951

The 75-page preface makes this a very special kind of anthology—one to be consulted by the mystery-writer who wishes to embark upon a course both toxic and lethal. In addition to adequate discussion of a dozen or so famous historical poisonings, we are given succinct accounts of the action of snake venom, stingrays, spiders, bees, and scorpions, as well as of various vegetable poisons and some of the commoner industrial mineral poisons.

2904　The Bookman

　　　The Christmas Number　　　　　　　　　　　H&S 1929
　　　　　Illus. by Dulac of poems by Poe

Although the theme of the special issue is "The Mysterious in Literature," the articles preponderantly interpret the subject as meaning the supernatural. The Introduction by Ellis Roberts is called "The Other Side of the Moon." It is followed by:

G. K. Chesterton	Magic and Fantasy in Fiction
Alfred Noyes	The Supernatural in Poetry
M. R. James	Some Remarks on Ghost Stories (excellent on Walter Scott and ballads as the earliest ghost tales)
Algernon Blackwood	Dreams and Fairies
Edgar Wallace	Mystery Stories Today and Yesterday
Various Hands	The Mysterious in Real Life (13 writers) including:
	J. D. Beresford, W. W. Jacobs, H. de V. Stacpoole, J. S. Fletcher, Edgar Jepson, F. Britten Austin, and John Ferguson.

This elusive magazine supplement is on the whole disappointing; bibliographers misrepresent it; but the M. R. James essay should be reprinted.

2905 BOOKSELLERS' CATALOGUES are a rich source of history and criticism about detective fiction as about other forms of literature and scholarship. Some booksellers specialize, wholly or in part, in the genres here inventoried. Some of the persons and firms that have been longest and most expertly in the field include:

Aardvarks (Orlando, Florida)
Acres of Books (Cincinnati, Ohio; also Trenton, N.J., unrelated firms)
Biblo and Tannen (New York)
R. A. Brimmell (Hastings, Sussex)
Arthur Lovell (Mrs.) (Dallas, Texas)
Harold Mortlake (London)
Bertram Rota (Bodley House, London)
Schulte's Bookstore (New York)
Strand Bookstore (New York)
Oswald Train (Phila.)

Specially famous catalogue issued on the subject are:

Aardvarks' first:	"Blood, Guts, Tea, and Crumpets," Sept. 1961; the latest is Oct 1970.
Brimmell and Charles:	Detective Fiction: a Century of Crime (1967); Brimmell Catalogues since 1958.
John Carter:	Detective Fiction Scrib 1934
Charles Rare Books (Hildenborough, Kent—no longer in business):	A Second Catalogue of Detective Fiction, No. 55, n.d.
William Hodge & Co. (Edinburgh):	Notable British Trials and War Crimes Trials (1954).
House of El Dieff (orig. Jamaica, N.Y., now N.Y.C.):	Detective Fiction (E. A. Poe, Mark Twain, Crofts, Doyle, and others), 1954; a second issue appeared in Jan. 1955. Its three sections are: (1) 80 items, trials and other true crime from Conan Doyle's library; (2) 81 items, non-S.H., written by Doyle; (3) 33 S.H. items by Doyle, plus 53 association items, chiefly Sherlockiana. Also listed are 477 books from the library of Vincent Starrett, as well as the dates of magazine appearances of the S.H. tales in both Gt. Britain and the U.S.
Arthur and Dolores Lovell (then in Chicago):	Library of Mr. George Merryweather (perhaps the bank director of "The Red-Headed League"?), Autumn 1949. The latest is dated Dallas, 1970.
Harold Mortlake:	The Strand Magazine (Sherlock Holmes and other works of Conan Doyle) Cat. 133, n.d.

Oswald Train's earlier catalogues (1963) combined detection with SF; now (No. 28, 1970), the lists are almost exclusively of detective fiction.

2906   BOUCHER, ANTHONY

    "There Was No Mystery in What the
    Crime Editor Was After"   *EQMM* June 1961

A short essay on the detective short story and the role of Ellery Queen in acclimating it to the United States—a good piece of testimony, coupled with valuable references to other magazines specializing in the genre, including pulps.

2907   BOUCHER. See also Nos. 2365–6, Introds.

2908   BREAN, HERBERT, ed.

    The Mystery Writer's Handbook   Harp 1956
        Pref. by the editor

The editor overdoes humility when he opens his preface with the words: "This is to say the least a curious book." Intelligent readers will be much more curious than the book, which is chock full of good things about the art and craft and factual stuff of mystery writing. The handy and lucid volume was sponsored by the Mystery Writers of America, but their English colleagues were also laid under contribution. The outstanding essays are:

Michael Gilbert	Technicalese
Lawrence Treat	The Real-Life Policeman
Edward D. Radin	Police Procedure in Homicide Investigation
Barbara Frost	How to Make It Authentic
Various Hands	When I Write
Sidney Porcelain	Credibility and Vividness
Anthony Gilbert	The British or the American Story
Howard Haycraft & Ellery Queen	Source Books and Bibliography

Note also a long extract from a letter by Dorothy Sayers on *The Nine Tailors,* pp. 64–5.

2909   BROWNE, NELSON

    Sheridan Le Fanu   AB 1951
        English Novelists Series

This small volume tells very economically and with sympathy the life of a remarkable Irish writer, whose character was almost as strange as some of the plots he invented. Le Fanu had a rich fantasy and a genius for making it seem plausible. One needs to adjust to his deliberate pace, but once that is done, what a wizard!

2910   CAILLOIS, ROGER (b. 1913)

    Le roman policier   SUR 1941

Ou comment l'intelligence se retire du monde pour se consacrer à ses jeux, et comment la société introduit ses problèmes dans ceux-ci
Edns. des Lettres Françaises, Buenos Aires

The authority on aesthetics and one of the first theorists of "games" as a sociological interpretation of life carries out his thesis in this solid study of the detective genre. Doctrine does not spoil his critical sense and the work belongs on the connoisseur's shelf.

2911   CAIN, JAMES M.

Preface to *Three of a Kind*   Knopf 1944

The preface, dated 1942, is a full essay dealing with the author's efforts, failures, and final conquest over style, which he thinks central to story-telling in any genre. He takes up objections to his work advanced by Edmund Wilson and Clifton Fadiman, and asserts that he writes as he hears American spoken. He used to give his stories frequent and sudden twists in order to avoid monotony; now he thinks he has written the last of his "intense" novels. Of the group which he introduces he has come to prefer *The Embezzler* to *Double Indemnity* and *Career in C Major*.

2912   CARR, JOHN DICKSON

"The Grandest Game in the World"   *EQMM* Mar 1963

In an essay written in 1946, the author states the principles on which detective novels should be written, and defends his choice of the ten best: Doyle, *The Valley of Fear;* Leroux, *The Mystery of the Yellow Room;* Mason, *At the Villa Rose;* Christie, *Death on the Nile;* Queen, *The Lamp of God;* Berkeley, *The Poisoned Chocolates Case;* Van Dine, *The Greene Murder Case;* P. MacDonald, *Murder Gone Mad;* Stout, *The League of Frightened Men;* Sayers, *The Nine Tailors.*
In 1963, Carr would change a few titles, no authors.

2913   The Life of Sir Arthur Conan Doyle   Harp 1949

A splendid biography, at once sympathetic and detached, skillful and thorough, as well as strong on the natural gifts Doyle possessed for detective investigation and its transfusion into fictional plots. Consult for important facts in the Edalji and Oscar Slater cases (Nos. 3068 and 3277).

2914   The UNC Detective Collection*
          In: The Bookmark, *Friends of the UNCL (Sept 1968)*
          Introds. by Mary S. Cameron and C. Hugh Holman

Descriptive of an important group of modern works spanning the first two-thirds of this century, with remarks by J.D.C. on the origins and developments of the genre and anecdotes about Chesterton and the founding of the Detection Club. The oath is reproduced in full.
Note that Carr began reviewing detective fiction for *EQMM* in Jan 1969.
*University of North Carolina.

2915 CARTER, JOHN (compiler)
Detective Fiction
A Collection [*really a Catalogue*] *of First & Early Editions*
(*Scrib n.d.* [*1934*])
Introd. by the compiler

The first serious catalogue of detective fiction (388 items). It is well done, though the opinions enunciated in the Introduction and elsewhere often seem odd to later judgment. There is an index of authors and one of detectives.

2916 CARTER, JOHN

"Detective Fiction"
In: New Paths in Book-Collecting, *ed. John Carter*
Const 1934

An epochmaking essay for book collectors and a sound bit of description, criticism, and scholarship for students of the genre. J.C. knows what a detective story is, and the examples he uses to persuade collectors to consider detection literature are well-chosen and argued for. The essay is reproduced in No. 2955 and see above No. 2915.

2917 CHANDLER, FRANK WADLEIGH (1873–1947)

The Literature of Roguery   2 v., HM 1907

This exhaustive and entertaining work is based on the author's Columbia University dissertation of 1899, *Romances of Roguery: Spain.* The definition of roguery is occasional crime—or if professional, then crime that stops short of villainy. In literature the rogue-hero dates from the later Renaissance and begins his career in Spain. The modern reader will be most interested in Chapter 12 of Vol. II, which discusses the nineties, including Raffles, but not Arnold Bennett, Clifford Ashdown, Maurice Leblanc, or other reincarnators of Gil Blas.

2918 CHANDLER, RAYMOND

Raymond Chandler Speaking   HH 1962
Ed. Dorothy Gardiner and Kathrine Sorley Walker

Selections from Chandler's letters, plus aphorisms, partial essays, fragments of fiction, and one parody tale. In the letters, the author takes a much broader and juster view of the genre than in "The Simple Art of Murder," though cynicism frequently breaks in. An indispensable source book for the student and the amateur, and good reading besides.

2919 "The Simple Art of Murder"
In: The Simple Art of Murder   Nort 1968

Originally published in the *Atlantic Monthly,* December, 1944; later reprintings embody revisions. A quotation and some critical views on the essay appear in the introduction to this *Catalogue.*
To these may be added Chandler's remark: "I doubt that Hammett

had any deliberate artistic aims whatever; he was trying to make a living by writing something he had first-hand information about." This surmise is to strengthen Chandler's great point about realism, first-hand knowledge, and no nonsense about art. The best comment on it is a quotation from a letter Hammett wrote to Mrs. Blanche Knopf on March 20, 1928: "I am one of the few . . . people moderately literate who take the detective story seriously. . . . Some day somebody's going to make 'literature' of it." (Ms., University of Texas Library).

2920   CHESTERTON, CECIL (1879–1918)

"Art and the Detective"   *Temple Bar,* 10 Oct 1906

G. K.'s younger brother argues against the arty habit of dismissing whole departments of literature as intrinsically bad and maintains that Gaboriau's *Crime d'Orcival* is better as detective fiction than many a well-known sonnet as poetry. Mystery is obviously a legitimate literary effect, but he insists that both the object of wonder and its explanation should be good, which is a hard requirement. Especially, he wants all the circumstances to be accounted for, which is what Descartes wanted in his *Méthode.*

As to works extant, C.C. is a bit down on SH, good on Poe, Morrison, and Collins, and he offers encouragement to Miss Florence Warden* and Anna Katharine Green. What confirms his competence is that he can tell the difference between Collins' lifelikeness, Gaboriau's ingenuity, and Poe's imagination. To a man of the nineties, Dupin and the "Purloined Letter" constitute superior manifestations of mind.

*Author of *The Mystery of Dudley Horne* and *No. 3, the Square.*

2921   CHESTERTON, G. K.

Autobiography   Hutch 1936

An interesting and important work, of which the eighth chapter deals with the author's beginnings in Fleet Street and general literature. Mention is made of *The Man Who Was Thursday* and *The Napoleon of Notting Hill,* with comments that throw light on G.K.'s mind; but there are no references to the Father Brown stories or the lifelong concern with detective fiction. E. C. Bentley occurs again and again from schooldays onward, but it is the clerihew* and *Biography for Beginners* that monopolizes the literary concern, not *Trent's Last Case.*

* For those who may not recall what the term means, it may be said that the clerihew, named after E. C(lerihew) Bentley, is the modern equivalent of the 2-vol. "Life and Times." Its form is vivid and it concentrates on one point, as in:

> It had to be concealed
> From E. M. Delafield
> That what made her sell
> Was confusion with E. M. Dell.

or again:

> Cecil B. De Mille,
> Much against his will,
> Was persuaded to leave Moses
> Out of the Wars of the Roses.

2922   "A Defence of Detective Stories"
        In: The Defendant (*Dent 1914; orig. 1901*)

The first of G.K.C.'s several essays on the genre, republished from the
London *Spectator,* it starts by recording the popularity of what it defends
and goes on to show that good detective fiction exists, "a perfectly legitimate form of art." It is curious and a little sad to see that the points that
had to be made at the turn of the century still have to be made seventy
years later. The reader will note that in this first collection of his essays,
Chesterton's style is not fully formed, but there is typical phrasing,
notably the remark about the detective standing "somewhat fatuously
fearless amid the knives and fists of a thieves' kitchen."

2923   "The Domesticity of Detectives"
        In: The Uses of Diversity (*Meth 1920*)

A discussion of the artistic difference between French and English crime
fiction and of fiction generally. The point of detective rigor is well made
and eight years before Knox (see No. 2614) this critic disallows the
"Chinese"—i.e., Oriental and occult—elements in the literature.

2924   Introduction to Capes' *The Skeleton Key* (No. 420)   Coll 1919

A particularly poetic account of the detective genre, with some telling
phrases and a good paradox, but chiefly about the character and talents
of the author of this particular tale.

2925   Preface to Walter S. Masterman's *The Wrong Letter*   Dutt 1926

An excellent summary in 4 pages of what affords pleasure and displeasure in the genre. The last page and a half consists of great negatives
that supplement Knox's decalogue. Deserves reprinting: *Armchair Detective* please note.

2926   CHESTERTON. See also:

      "About Shockers," in *As I Was Saying*   DM 1936
      (A stand against psychologizing and in favor of murder
      among the law-abiding.)

      "The Innocence of the Criminal,"
      in *Fancies versus Fads*   DM 1923

      "On Detective Novels," in *Generally Speaking*
      (Technique should concern the critics and theorists,
      and G.K.C. prefers the short-story form.)

2927   CHIMERA. Special Issue on Detective Fiction   Summer 1947
        Ed. Barbara Howes

The issue is interesting as an early critical venture by the highest of highbrows into the literature they distrusted and despised, but it is not marked
by much originality of opinion or feeling. JB in his contribution was de-

pressed by the recent crop of detective stories properly so called and regrettably declared the genre moribund. Perhaps the best essays were Hector Hoppin's and Ruthven Todd's. Authors and titles were:

J. F. Montesino	Imperfect Myths
Patrick Quentin	Who'd Do It?
Donat O'Donnell	Graham Greene
G. Robert Stange	The Detective Story Mystery
Hector Hoppin	Notes on Primitive Modes of Detection (fine use of the Oscar Slater case)
Ruthven Todd	A Trinity of 'Tecs: from Where to Where? (good on D. Hammett)
Jacques Barzun	Requiescat
Roger Caillois	Order and License (an extract from No. 2910).

A few months later the Columbia University Press made a survey (27 questions with subheads) and published the results in *The Pleasures of Publishing* (Apr. 5, 1948). It turned out that Dorothy Sayers was the favorite among the critics, librarians, authors, editors, publishers, and other readers, and they reported a consumption of tales at the rate of 4.8 a month.

2928   COLLECTIONS OF DETECTIVE FICTION

The largest and best arranged is at the University of Texas at Austin. It consists of a nucleus of 5010 volumes of short stories, originally the property of Ellery Queen. To it have been added 1285 volumes (not all ss), and 2136 items from Erle Stanley Gardner, chiefly his works. There are in addition manuscripts by Doyle, Mark Twain, and other masters.

A second large collection is at the University of North Carolina in Chapel Hill, N.C. It numbers approximately 4900 volumes, has been catalogued, and forms the subject of No. 2914.

The collection made by Graham Greene and Dorothy Glover is wholly of early works; it has been catalogued. See No. 2998.

Rumors of huge private collections are frequent and difficult to verify. California is reputed rich in the literature as in other resources. The late Paul Elmer More, a resident of Princeton, was said to own several thousand volumes, classified as A, B, and C according to quality. No one seems to know when this library was removed or dispersed.

The able critic of the *New York Times* and editor of *TAD,* Mr. Allen J. Hubin (q.v.) owns a large collection to which he is continually adding.

The JB-WHT collection numbers approximately 3000 volumes. It includes a few rarities and oddities, but is not otherwise notable.

Many English and American public libraries are discarding detective fiction in large quantities as the books fall apart and space for new books becomes as overcrowded as the planet. It is consequently probable that a good many books listed in these pages or elsewhere no longer exist on any shelf of easy access.

Fortunately, the Library of Congress and the British Museum continue to gather in new titles as incidentals to the process of copyrighting. Since those libraries do not circulate books and such books are rarely sought by researchers, one most often finds there pristine, unopened copies— mint condition.

2929 COLUM, PÁDRAIC

Introduction to Poe's *Tales of Mystery and
Imagination*   Everyman 1966

Terse but definitive statement of Poe's understanding and execution of
"the tale." Pádraic Colum's high worth as a critic has not yet been recognized, but this sample of his work should establish it for any other critical mind.

2930 CONNOLLY, CYRIL

"Bond Strikes Camp"
In: Previous Convictions   HH 1963

A masterly parody of the standard Bond episode, remarkable for its plot
no less than for its narrative and dialogue. The piece is a demonstration of
the way in which pastiche can be a high form of criticism.

2931 CREASEY, JOHN

"John Creasey—Fact or Fiction?"   *TAD* Oct 1968

A candid commentary in the third person by this prolific author, in which
he describes his start and his methods. With the assistance of R. E. Briney
he provides a 17-page bibliography of his works under his many pen
names. Here is a summary of their findings:

CREASEY, JOHN   His 521 titles (up to 1968):

By-Line	Series	No. of Titles
John Creasey	Roger West	38
	Dr. Palfrey	28
	Department Z	28
	The Toff	54
	Misc. incl. juvenile	62
	Nonfiction	12
Gordon Ashe	Patrick Dawlish	35
	The Crime Haters	9
	Misc.	3
M. E. Cooke	Paperback originals	11
	Paperback romances	14
Henry St. John Cooper	Romances	6
Norman Deane	Bruce Murdoch	6
	The Liberator	3
	Misc.	12
Elise Fecamps	Paperback romances	3
Robert Caine Frazer	Mark Kilby	6
Patrick Gill	Sports paperbacks	4
Michael Halliday	The Fane Brothers	4
	Dr. Emmanuel Cellini	6
	Misc. thrillers	40
Charles Hogarth (with Ian Bowen)	Mystery	1
Brian Hope	Suspense Novels	4
Colin Hughes	Mystery paperback	1
Kyle Hunt	Mystery paperback	1

Abel Mann	Mystery paperback	1
Peter Manton	Mysteries	12
	Juveniles	2
J. J. Marric	Commander Gideon	15
James Marsden	Sports paperback	1
Richard Martin	Mysteries	2
	Novel	1
Rodney Mattheson	Mystery paperbacks	2
Anthony Morton	The Baron (John Mannering)	41
	Misc.	2
Ken Ranger	Westerns	2
Tex Riley	Westerns	14
William K. Reilly	Westerns	13
Jimmy Wilde	Autobiography (ghost-written)	1
Jeremy York	Superintendent Folly	6
	Misc.	15

2932 CRISPIN, EDMUND

Introduction to *Best Detective Stories*   Faber 1961

One of the summit practitioners reaffirms in brief compass the overwhelming reasons for *structure* in detection, and the strong arguments against substitutes for contrivance. He goes at Julian Symons' heresies with gusto, and he shows where the aesthetic pleasure lies in reading the species of the genus he desiderates.

2933 DAVIS, DAVID B.

Homicide in American Fiction: 1798–1860   Cornell 1957

A dissertation, of course, but lucid and informative if not inspired. It is amazing how much blood flowed on the printed page and between the lines of our early fiction, always accompanied by passion and articulate purpose—a far cry from the sullen and almost inadvertent knifings we relish today, and sometimes undergo in our own persons.

2934 DEL BUONO, ORESTE, and ECO, UMBERTO

The Bond Affair   Macd 1966
     Trans. by R. A. Downie

Eight essays, highly sophisticated and jargon-laden, about the meaning, psychological, social, sexual, economical, historical, historical-pastoral, tragical-historical, etc., etc.—in short, what an inspired critic once called the wild bull of the pompous.

2935 DISHER, M. WILLSON

Melodrama: Plots That Thrilled   Macm 1954
     Illus.

In this compendious and capable survey, Chapters 21, 25, and 27 deal with plays based on the kind of subjects sampled in this *Catalogue*. The illustrations are excellent, and the comments, though not profound, are adequate.

"The Writer in America: The Strange Case of S. S. Van Dine"
In: Literatur und Sprache der Vereinigten Staaten (*Winter-Universitätsverlag, Heidelberg, 1969*)

A splendid essay on the career and merits of Willard Huntington Wright, including the genesis of "S. S. Van Dine" and the relation of his fiction to the embattled and embittered critic W.H.W.

2937 DONALDSON, NORMAN

"R. Austin Freeman"   *TAD* Jan 1968

A sympathetic account of Freeman's career, including comments on many of his stories, and followed by a complete checklist of his works, with dates of English and U.S. publication. For N.D.'s full-length study of Freeman, see *In search of Dr. Thorndyke* (BGUP, 1971).

2938 DONOVAN, FRANK P.

"Mystery Rides the Rails"   *TAD* July 1968, Oct 1968
                                               Jan 1969, Apr 1969

This essay in four parts supplies an intelligent commentary upon and bibliography of the American and English novels and short stories that involve railroads. The author does a good job of distinguishing railroad stories from those that merely touch the rails in passing.

2939 DOYLE, A. CONAN

Memories and Adventures   LB 1924
   Illus.

An endearing account of a varied and active life by a man who belongs to the small company of writers–men-of-action. Chapter 8 is the one that deals with his literary beginnings, between 1885 and 1890. It gives a somewhat different impression from that in *My First Book* (No. 3343), and it records unexpected influence from Henry James; it indicates that *A Study in Scarlet* was probably finished by the end of 1885, though not published till Christmas 1887; and it modestly takes credit for the *Strand*'s innovation of monthly stories about the same characters (Holmes and Watson) to replace the long serial story.

Again, the decisive turn from medicine to writing occurred in London, not Portsmouth, as several interpreters have believed. Finally, the doubts about materialism—characteristic of the nineties—which landed Doyle in the morass of spiritualism, were present early in his life and thought, not the result of anguish during the first world war, as alleged.

Chapter 21 records Doyle's brilliant detection in the Edalji case and his heroic effort to vindicate Oscar Slater (see No. 2913). On pp. 97–100 the Barrie parody is reproduced for the first time (see No. 2741), and we learn nearby that in Spanish South America a *Sherlockholmito* is a clever inference suggestive of great "powers."

2940   DUBOURG, MAURICE

"Maigret and Co.: The Detectives of the
Simenon Agency"   *TAD* Jan 1971
    Trans. by Francis M. Nevins, Jr.
    Orig. in Mystère-Magazine, *No. 203*

A thorough review of Simenon's work in the genre, before and after the
creation of Maigret, noting the shifts in character and the inconsistencies
of the heroes' fictional histories.

2941   ELIOT, T(HOMAS) S(TEARNS) (1888–1965)

Introduction to Wilkie Collins' *Moonstone*
    World's Classics   OUP 1966/1928

A demonstration, if needed, of what an uneven critic Eliot was. Much of
this very brief essay is about Dickens, not Collins, and the repeated
assertion that *The Moonstone* is the first, longest, and best of modern
English detective novels fails, for lack of evidence, on at least two counts.
When it comes to details, Eliot is weak or impercipient (e.g., Collins and
character-drawing) and he leaves no impression of thoroughness and
judicial competence, though the judicial is his stance. Compare the
definitive essay by Dorothy Sayers (No. 3021).

2942   ELLIS, H. F.

"No Murders at Andermatt?"   *Punch* Nov 23, 1955

A parody-ramble through the minds and acts of leading detectives
(Gethryn to Brown, Poirot to Thorndyke). It is evident from the title and
subsequent disbelief in the suitability of the Alps for good murders that
the veteran humorist does not know (or admire?) the works of Glyn Carr
(q.v.).

2943   FOSCA, FRANÇOIS (pseud. of Georges de Traz, b. 1881)

Histoire et technique du roman
policier   Edns. de la Nouvelle Revue Critique P. 1937

In this work the distinguished art historian has produced the best study of
the genre for its time and place. His scope is large and his judgments are
sound, that is, unimpeded by Continental ideas of drama and mystery.
For later writers, see Nos. 2902, 2910, 2957 and 2988.

2944   FREEMAN, R. AUSTIN

"The Art of the Detective Story"
    In: Dr. Thorndyke's Crime File (*No. 905*)
    (*Together with the author's account of the genesis of
    Thorndyke*)

Freeman tells us that the success of Sherlock Holmes in the early years
of this century suggested to him the possibility of a different kind of hero,

whose talents would spring from medico-legal knowledge, and whose principles would rest upon the identifiability of persons and actions through laboratory scrutiny. Freeman was inspired to this by his work in prescribing eyeglasses. He acknowledges the disadvantages of such a hero in the eyes of a public ignorant of science; at the same time he vindicates Thorndyke's good looks as a protest against the physical monsters palmed off by his fellow writers as great detectives. (Thorndyke was not copied from life, but his assistant Polton was.)

The author adds that *31 New Inn* was written before *The Red Thumb Mark* (qq.v.) and he makes a puzzling reference to *4* King's Bench Walk.

2945   GARDNER, ERLE STANLEY

"Getting Away with Murder"   *EQMM* Nov 1965

The creator of Perry Mason recalls the early days of the hard-boiled school, with many suggestive comments on the relation of an author to his characters.

2946   GARDNER. See also: "Mysteries in Our Modern World," an oft-reproduced jacket blurb, in which detective fiction is put in competition with tranquilizers and barbiturates—not the author's best effort.

2947   GILBERT, MICHAEL, ed.

Crime in Good Company   Const 1959

Gathered for the Crime Writers' Association, this group of essays discusses (1) crime itself, (2) the general practitioners of murder fiction, and (3) the specialists—writers of films, short stories, etc.

The authors include: Eric Ambler, Jacques Barzun, Josephine Bell, Raymond Chandler, Stanley Ellin, Michael Gilbert, Cyril Hare, Maurice Procter, Julian Symons, L. A. G. Strong, and a few others.

2948   GILBERT

Introductions to *Best Detective Stories of Cyril Hare* (No. 2555) and *Crime in Good Company* (No. 2947)

Both these essays show M.G.'s grasp of essentials, clarity of expression, and wit integral to prose.

Note: Michael Gilbert now selects and edits Classics of Detection and Adventure for H&S. He supplies biographical introductions and critical remarks on the works.

2949   GIRVAN, WAVENEY, ed.

Eden Phillpotts   Hutch 1953
    An Assessment and a Tribute
    Illus.; endpapers of Dartmoor Forest

Eight essays, including an Introduction by the editor, and a chapter on P.'s detective fiction (see No. 3017). Reginald Pound is particularly good on the friendship and collaboration with Arnold Bennett.

2950   GOLDSMITH, HAROLD (SANFORD) (1903–69)

Editor and co-founder of Popular Publications, which included *Black Mask, Dime Detective, G-8,* and *Argosy,* and which gave a start to such writers as Erle Stanley Gardner, Dashiell Hammett, and Raymond Chandler. His collaborator in these ventures was Henry Steeger, Sr. Other contributors to his pages were: T. S. Eliot, Baroness Orczy, C. S. Forester, and Harold Lamb.

2951   GRAVES, ROBERT (b. 1895)

"After a Century, Will Anyone Care
Whodunit?"   *N.Y. Times Book Rev.* Aug 25, 1957

The usual attack on the genre, on the assumption that the tales ought to be novels. The authors "do not believe in their outrageous charades." Hammett and Simenon are excused, because they occasionally "climb into the pages of their books." Why there has to be petulance and prophecies of extinction on the part of those who dislike tales has yet to be explained. (See also No. 3060.)

2952   GRAVES, ROBERT and HODGE, ALAN

The Long Weekend   Macm 1941
   A Social History of Great Britain: 1918–1939

"Low-brow reading was now dominated by the detective novel." No more erroneous statement was ever set down in a work professing to be a history. Detective novels, as the merest inspection would reveal, were written and read by patent highbrows. The period referred to is "The Days of the Loch Ness Monster," i.e., 1930–35. Low-brow reading, then as now, was: love romances, westerns, and tales of the Horatio Alger cast. The "historians" above disclose their prejudice on top of their ignorance by making an exception to their dislike in favor of Dashiell Hammett and realism. Hammett, they discover, is a first-rate writer, qualified by years of experience as a Pinkerton operative. All other authors lack professional knowledge of their subject matter (like Lewis Carroll and Shakespeare) and had no right to write.

2953   GRIBBIN, LENORE S. [MRS.]

Who's Whodunit   UNCL 1968
   Library Studies Number 5

An indispensable work of reference, whose author plays the role of Ariadne in conducting the searcher through the maze of pseudonyms used by practitioners of the genre. She lists with very few errors or omissions the 1,100 pen names used by 3,218 writers; and others keep turning up. (The University of North Carolina has a large and interesting special collection of detective and crime fiction; see No. 2914.)

2954   HAGEN, ORDEAN A.

Who Done It?   Bowk 1969
   A Guide to Detective, Mystery, and Suspense Fiction

One of the handsomest reference books ever printed. The misfortune is that the contents were assembled by one confessedly ignorant of the subject matter and not otherwise gifted as a compiler. A summary of his short-comings will be found in No. 2892, and their detail began to form a regular department in *The Armchair Detective* in the issue for October 1969.

2955 HAYCRAFT, HOWARD, ed.

The Art of the Mystery Story   S&S 1946
    Foreword by the editor

This massive volume of nearly 550 pages brings together fifty-three essays on various aspects of detective and mystery fiction. Many are otherwise inaccessible, and some were written especially for this book, which Grosset & Dunlap, as its paperback publishers, ought not to let remain out of print. The major divisions of the work and the contents of each are as follows:

1. *Mystery Matures: The Higher Criticism*
   A Defence of Detective Stories   G. K. Chesterton (orig. 1901)
   The Art of the Detective Story   R. Austin Freeman (1924)
   Crime and Detection   E. M. Wrong (1926)
   The Great Detective Stories   Willard Huntington Wright (1927)
   The Omnibus of Crime, Dorothy L. Sayers (1928; Introd. to the *First Omnibus,* which, good though it is, is surpassed by the Introduction to the *Second Omnibus.* See No. 3020)
   The Professor and the Detective   Marjorie Nicolson (*Atlantic* Apr 1929)
   From *Masters of Mystery*   H. Douglas Thomson (1931)
   From *The Private Life of Sherlock Holmes*   Vincent Starrett (1933)
   From *Murder for Pleasure*   Howard Haycraft
       (the chapter on Poe, from H.'s book of 1941)
   Only a Detective Story   Joseph Wood Krutch (*Nation* Nov 25, 1944)
2. *The Rules of the Game*
   Twenty Rules for Writing Detective
       Stories   S. S. Van Dine (*American* Sept 1928)
   A Detective Story Decalogue   Ronald A. Knox
       (from Introd. to *Best Detective Stories of 1928*)
   The Detection Club Oath (the London Detection Club was founded by Anthony Berkeley in 1928)
3. *Care and Feeding of the Whodunit*
   The Case of the Early Beginning   Erle Stanley Gardner
       (historical; written for this vol.)
   Gaudy Night   Dorothy L. Sayers
       (an essay on the problems encountered by the author in her own work; orig. in *Titles to Fame,* ed. Denys K. Roberts, London 1937)
   The Simple Art of Murder   Raymond Chandler
       (orig. 1944; rev. for this vol.)
   Murder Makes Merry   Craig Rice
       (discussion of humor in the d.s.; written for this vol.)
   Trojan Horse Opera   Anthony Boucher (development of the spy novel)
   Dagger of the Mind   James Sandoe
       (the psychological thriller; *Poetry* June 1946; orig. a lecture)
   Clues   Marie F. Rodell (a chapter from her book *Mystery Fiction,* 1943)
   The Locked-Room Lecture   John Dickson Carr

(delivered by Dr. Fell in a chapter reprinted from *The Three Coffins,* 1935)

Command Performance   Lee Wright
(an editor's account of how the reader's taste influences the character of the d.s.; written for this vol.)

Mystery Midwife: The Crime Editor's Job   Isabelle Taylor
(ed. of Doubleday's Crime Club; written for this vol.)

Hollywoodunit   Richard Mealand
(emergence of mystery films from earlier emphasis on horror)

There's Murder in the Air   Ken Crossen
(stresses the backward state of murder fiction in broadcasts as compared to the bookstall)

4. *The Lighter Side of Crime*

Watson Was a Woman   Rex Stout
(a travesty on Holmesian scholarship; orig. 1941)

Don't Guess, Let Me Tell You   Ogden Nash
(a poem satirizing the HIBK school, to which Nash was the first to attach this label; orig. in *The Face Is Familiar,* 1940)

The Pink Murder Case   S. S. Veendam
(a parody of the Philo Vance cases by Christopher Ward; *Sat. Rev.* Nov. 2, 1929)

Murder at $2.50 a Crime   Stephen Leacock (1937)

Everything Under Control   Richard Armour
(a short poem, inspired by fascist control of mystery novels; *Sat. Rev.* Oct 18, 1941)

The Whistling Corpse   Ben Hecht
(another parody on the HIBK school; *EQMM* Sept 1945)

Oh, England! Full of Sin   Robert J. Casey
(an amusing study of the *mores* of the British school of mystery writers; *Scribner's* Apr 1937)

Murders and Motives   E. V. Lucas (a trifle; orig. 1927)

Murder on Parnassus   Pierre Véry
(amusing projection of the place of detection in the studies of a French *lycée* in 2935; orig. 1933)

5. *Critics' Corner*

Among minor contributions by Isaac Anderson, the pseudonymous "Judge Lynch" (= William Weber), and Will Cuppy, there are interesting contemporary reviews of Collins' *The Moonstone,* Doyle's *The Sign of Four,* Bentley's *Trent's Last Case,* and Van Dine's *The Benson Murder Case* (only the last is signed: a damning indictment by Dashiell Hammett). Other substantial essays are:

The Ethics of the Mystery Novel   Anthony Boucher (orig. 1944)

Who Cares Who Killed Roger Ackroyd?   Edmund Wilson
(*New Yorker* Jan 20, 1945)

The Detective Story—Why?   Nicholas Blake

Leaves from the Editors' Notebook   Ellery Queen

6. *Detective Fiction vs. Real Life*

From the Memoirs of a Private Detective   Dashiell Hammett
(his eight years' experiences with the Pinkertons; *Smart Set* Mar 1923)

Inquest on Detective Stories   R. Philmore
(looks into the plausibility of fictional murder methods; *Discovery* Apr and Sept 1938)

The Lawyer Looks at Detective Fiction   John Barker Waite
(good strictures; *Bookman* Aug 1929)

The Crux of a Murder: Disposal of the Body   F. Sherwood Taylor
(*Spectator* Apr 9, 1937)

7. *Putting Crime on the Shelf*
  Collecting Detective Fiction   John Carter (see No. 2916)
  The Detective Short Story: The First Hundred Years   Ellery Queen
  (1946 rev. of Introd. to *101 Years Entertainment: The Great Detective
  Stories*, 1941)
  Readers' Guide to Crime   James Sandoe
  Haycraft's prefatory note is almost as long as Sandoe's list, but both are
  worth reading, however much one may disagree.
8. *Watchman, What of the Night?*
  A Sober Word on the Detective Story, by Harrison R. Steeves (*Harper's*
  Apr 1941), is the outstanding item in this section but there are other, minor
  contributions by Philip Van Doren Stern, and by the editor himself.

2956   HAYCRAFT

    "Evolution of the Whodunit in the Years of
    World War II"   *N.Y. Times Book Rev.* Aug 12, 1945

An excellent survey of the British and American output, with all the
author's scholarly care and knowledge of cognate matters, biographical
facts, and apposite anecdotes.

2957   Murder for Pleasure   App 1941
        The Life and Times of the Detective Story
        Illus.

An extremely thorough and sensible treatment of its subject. It lacks
Douglas Thomson's wit and eccentricity, but has the virtues of a reference
work, including a broad-bosomed tolerance that admits to honorable
mention writers of painful mediocrity. A list of detectives and their
creators is supplied.
    Note that in the reprint by Biblo & Tannen (1968) the text is word for
word the same and the enlargement consists in 5 pages of notes by
Haycraft on the additions to the so-called Cornerstone Library of detective
fiction (i.e., some titles published between 1941 and 1951) and the
Haycraft-Queen Definitive Library of Detective-Crime-Mystery Fiction,
1748–1948 (No. 2959). The author is at work on a comprehensive
revision of the whole volume (1970).

2958   "The Pleasures of Reading Mystery Stories"   1940 ff.

A blurb regularly used on the jackets of books issued by the Dollar
Mystery Guild; but though a blurb, it is a truthful historical and critical
statement of the case, in five short paragraphs.

2959   HAYCRAFT, HOWARD, and QUEEN, ELLERY

    "The Haycraft-Queen Definitive Library of
    Detective Fiction"   *EQMM* Oct 1951

Until reprinted in No. 2957, 2d ed., the only appearance of this interesting
list, which spans the period from 1748 to 1948. It is possible to quarrel
with the inclusion of certain items under the rubric Detective Fiction, but
not with the quality of the works chosen, whatever their correct classifi-

cation may be *sub specie aeternitatis*. See also "Queen's Quorum" in No. 2751.

2960   HEILBRUN, CAROLYN (G.) [MRS. JAMES]

"Sayers, Lord Peter, and God"   *Amer Sch* Spring 1968

A spirited defense of Sayers' detective fiction against the anti-snob snobs of the world of letters, and at the same time a reappraisal of the author and her stories as artistic and cultural documents, by the gifted critic and biographer of the Garnett family.

2961   HELLMAN, LILLIAN

Introduction to Dashiell Hammett's *The Big Knockover* (No. 2547)   RH 1967

An extraordinarily fine essay about Dashiell Hammett by one who knew him intimately and who, as a fellow writer, can assess his work, mind, and heart with retrospective justness and critical poise.

2962   HOLMES, SHERLOCK (pseud.)

"The Mystery of Edwin Drood"   *Longman's* Sept 1905

"Holmes" takes up the events proposed by Charles Dickens for the completion of his novel, these being given to Holmes by Andrew Lang in the character of Dr. Watson. S.H. demolishes the hypotheses of Walters and Procter and will not have it that Datchery is Miss Landless in disguise. Rather, Drood is to return as Datchery. The Holmes touches are few and poor, but one remark is to the point: "I knew that Sherlock disliked Mr. Lang, who had pointed out that my revered friend knows nothing about the Andaman Islanders or Thucydides."

2963   HUBIN, ALLEN J.

Additions, Corrections, and Alterations to Ordean Hagen's *Who Done It?* (No. 2954)   *TAD* Oct 1969 ff.

The editor of *TAD* established this very necessary if regrettable "department" at the suggestion of William F. Nolan, who, with others, sent in the first lists of errata. The three parts published thus far total thirty-eight pages and are to be continued.

2964   INNES, MICHAEL

Introduction to *The Mystery of Edwin Drood*   Lehm 1950
Chiltern Library
With orig. illus. by Luke Fildes

The accomplished scholar and writer of detective fiction gives a masterly analysis of the evidence for and against the several possibilities suggested by Dickens' fragment as to: what happened, what would happen, and who is who (including male impersonation by females). External evidence from contemporary reports and the Fildes illustrations is also brought in, and though no positive conclusion is advanced, two important ideas are left with the reader. One, that the data are too meager to support and exclude rival hypotheses; the other, that Dickens' novel must not be supposed to carry more mystery and detection than the novel of his time was used to doing—i.e., it is not an early modern detective story. M.I.'s own technique of composition is clearly disclosed by his comments on both the facts and others' speculations.

2965 JOHNSTON, CHARLES

> Preface to *Oriental Tales*
>   *In: Julian Hawthorne, ed., Library of . . . Mystery, etc.*, No. 2567, vol. VI.

The one-time Indian civil servant and member of the Royal Asiatic Society makes out a case for finding the origin of Sherlock Holmes and other modern detectives in the traditional tales of the ancient Near East, especially the Arabic. Assent is a question of the degree of generality or abstraction one is willing to accept as establishing kinship: Robinson Crusoe was sharp about footprints. These readers do not accept the regress to antiquity—or to the Orient.

2966 KEDDIE, JAMES, JR.

> "Freeman Wills Crofts"   *TAD* Apr 1969

The author was a correspondent of F.W.C.'s and writes an admiring but temperate account of Crofts' work, with a portrait of his subject and an interesting autobiographical letter. The bibliography lists several items not published in the U.S. and, in the case of the short stories, each is listed separately and attributed to the proper collection.

2967 KNOX, RONALD A.

> Introduction to Chesterton's Selected Father Brown Stories
>   *World's Classics* (OUP 1966/1955)

A superb critical essay, which not only does full justice to Chesterton's great creation, but also sets forth the characteristics of the secular form that Chesterton—in Knox's word—"overflowed." The piece is a model of acute judgment and English prose. See also No. 2955.

2968 KRUTCH, JOSEPH WOOD (1893–1970)

> "Only a Detective Story"   *Nation* Nov 25, 1944

The critic of literature and drama, biographer of Dr. Johnson, and desert naturalist pitches into the prejudice that holds detective fiction to be subliterary and intellectually degraded. He shows the extent to which the genre exhibits the genuine traits of literature and makes clear the fallacy whereby certain books are thought to be read with high motives and others with low. A gem of an essay. (Reprinted in No. 2955).

2969   LEACOCK, STEPHEN

      "Twenty Cents' Worth of Murder"
        In: Too Much College   DM 1940

Brief instructions to writers of detective stories. They are asked to omit features grown too common, such as: fingerprints, the chase, and the smash finish. Very amusing, especially the critique of an unnamed author who is quite obviously J. S. Fletcher.

2970   LEACOCK. See also:

Frenzied Fiction (Lane 1918)	"My Revelations as a Spy"
	"Personal Adventures in the Spirit World"
Nonsense Novels (Lane 1911)	"Maddened by Mystery; or The Defective Detective" (repr. in No. 2741. See also No. 2620)
Further Foolishness (Lane 1916)	"An Irreducible Detective Story"
Short Circuits (DM 1928)	"The Criminal by Proxy"
	"The Great Detective"
	"A Guide to the Underworld"
	"Inference as an Art"
Last Leaves (DM 1945)	"Living with Murder"

      LEGMAN, G(ERSHON), orig. George Alexander Legman; b. 1917

b. Scranton, Pa., early devoted to scholarship and polemics; edited *Neurotica* with J. I. Landesman (1948–51), the earliest of the U.S. mags. devoted to the sexual revolution; pub. books on folklore, the Knights Templar, and the psychology of the dirty story; collected and edited *The Limerick,* the most comprehensive collection. Lives in southern France in a Templars' cloisters.

2971   Love and Death   Breaking Point (N.Y.) 1949
        A Study in Censorship

A study of the sadistic genre, at once sardonic and serious, with a good deal of the element it deplores, but remarkable for the volcanic force of its prose and the psychological penetration of its animus.

2972   LUBBOCK, SAMUEL GURNEY

      A Memoir of Montague Rhodes James   Cambr 1939
        Bibliography on the writings by A. F. Scholfield
        Illus.

A "purely personal sketch" of "Monty," done with tact and charm and no syrup. The friendships with Arthur and E. F. Benson, the early eminence as a scholar (noted by Lord Acton), the love of cycling and the French countryside—all are told in few words. We learn that the ghost stories (see No. 3427) were first meant for reading to friends, the occasions beginning in 1893. Publication soon followed, and continued.

2973 MacDonald, Philip [Comments on the length of fictional forms]
EQMM Feb 1949

An extremely perceptive essay, untitled, that throws back into the melting pot for later recasting all the usual notions about the sort of idea suitable for the long, medium, and short tale of detection.

2974 Macdonald, Ross

"Cain x 3" *N.Y. Times Book Rev.* Mar 2, 1969

A highly technical study of a fellow craftsman, published as a front-page review of a new omnibus volume. See Nos. 396–8 and 2911.

2975 Mackenzie, Compton

"The Man Behind Sherlock Holmes"
In: On Moral Courage QBC 1962

A short essay but a good one, which shows what is perfectly obvious but hidden from superficial critics, to wit, that Conan Doyle, the supposed patriotic, sentimental, "average" middle-class Englishman was a fearless and persistent dissenter, dedicated to justice in the teeth of all oppositions, and unmoved by criticism and ridicule when pursuing his independent course.

2976 Marshall, Margaret

"Alkali Dust in Your Eyes" *Amer Sch* Autumn 1968

A spirited onslaught against *A Study in Scarlet* for its lack of verisimilitude in geography, language, religion, and behavior in the interpolated Utah episode, by a native who is also an experienced literary critic. Doyle himself said that he was "not nervous about details."

2977 Mason, A. E. W.

"Detective Novels" *Nat. Ath.* Feb. 7, 1925

In this somewhat self-regarding piece, Mason is at pains to refute two ideas: that detective fiction is easy to write, and that crime in real life is more "probable" in its details than crime in "sensational" fiction. He argues from the factual basis of his own works, cites the help he has had from a physician for *The House of the Arrow,* and claims that the true detective is he who finds the "secret history" that Boswell refers to in speaking of Johnson and Chesterfield. Mason also opines that great detective novels live by virtue of their detectives—"Dupin, Lecoq, Sherlock Holmes, Father Brown."

2978 Mathews, Brander

"Poe and the Detective Story"
In: Inquiries and Opinions Scrib 1908/1907

An important essay first published in 1904, which dispels numerous confusions and notably that between mystery and detection. B.M. gives Poe credit for turning the interest from mere mystery-mongering, of which the effect is bound to be disappointment, to the intellectual concern with discovery, which makes the explanation a climax instead of a letdown, while also creating a new human interest.

The author, in criticizing Collins and others, makes use of the phrase "fair play [with the reader]": it marks a date.

2979 MAUGHAM, W. SOMERSET

Preface to *Ashenden; or, The British Agent*   Dday 1941

The author discusses fiction at large, then espionage in its relation to realism in fiction. A clear and important set of principles. (See Nos. 1580 and 3137.)

2980 "The Decline and Fall of the Detective Story"
             In: The Vagrant Mood   Dday 1953/1952

The title of this extended and thoughtful piece is somewhat misleading. Rather than a prediction or postmortem, it is a careful study, by a craftsman, of the chief points to consider in judging the genre, the faults often found in it, and the altered meaning of detection in the Hammett-Chandler school. This last style, Maugham thinks, has been quickly ruined by excessive imitation. In the earlier style, he deprecates the piling up of corpses in one book, is against humorous detectives, farfetched means of killing, and the love interest. Indeed, he would exclude passion and sex as plausible motives, his experience telling him that if these are not buttressed by money or fear of exposure they do not lead to murder: a doubtful point in the light of true crime recorded; see Part IV of this *Catalogue*.

2981 MESSAC, RÉGIS

Le "detective novel" et l'influence de la
pensée scientifique   H. Champion (P) 1929

A monumental dissertation which does not miss a trick. If, after reading it, anyone disbelieves in the influence of scientific habits of thought (or thought clichés?) on fiction at large and detection in particular, he ought to start reading again on p. 1. But note that the discussion stops with Sherlock Holmes and the nineties: no attention paid to the English renaissance of the twentieth century.

2982 MILNE, A. A.

By Way of Introduction   C&W 1929

A collection of the author's prefatory writings. Two essays relate to the genre: "Dr. Watson Speaks Out" and "Crime." Both are in A.A.M.'s usual casual charming vein, which makes it desirable to take them in small doses, for the amenity hides or sweetens out of recognition some excellent points.

2983 MOONEY, JOAN M.

Best-Selling American Detective Fiction   *TAD* Jan 1970 ff.

This Ph.D. thesis in nine chapters, submitted to the graduate faculty of
the University of Minnesota, runs to some 100,000 words. Because the
author treats detective fiction as a reflection of society, and stresses the
factors that make certain writers most popular, the writers dealt with
are not necessarily those esteemed by critics. A serious and scholarly work,
with extensive bibliography.

2984 MORAND, PAUL

Préface à *Lord Peter devant le cadavre*   Nels (P) 1934
   [*Short stories by D. Sayers (see No. 2777)*]

It is always entertaining to read the Continentals (and especially the
French) on English and American contemporary literature. Paul Morand
was a clever man, a good novelist, a traveller and a diplomat, and he
knew English. But read this "appreciation" and see the next study.

2985 "Réflexions sur le roman détective"   *Revue de Paris* Apr 1, 1934

That the French novelist was at home in the English literature of the
genre is shown by his abundant references to the works of Dorothy Sayers,
Philip MacDonald, Agatha Christie, and others, some of whom he trans-
lates in order to quote. He rightly views the rise of detective fiction as
linked with that of science and technology after 1850. But he ends with
the curious suggestion that the modern detective has the role of "shaming
the great" in the name of science as Bossuet did in the seventeenth century in the name of religion.

2986 MORLAND, NIGEL

How to Write Detective Novels   A&U 1936

Seventy-four pages of somewhat self-evident advice. It could be followed
to the letter and not produce an acceptable work.

2987 MUNDELL, E. H., JR.

A Checklist of Detective Short Stories   KSUP (to be pub.)

The author has worked many years seeking and examining short story
collections in the following categories:
   Author Collections: 810 titles
   Anthologies: 265 titles
   Experiences (real life): 115 titles
   Spy and secret service: 50 titles
   Problems: 20 titles
He has printed two tentative lists and reports some 100 titles still to be
got hold of and looked at (March 1970).

2988   MURCH, A. E.

The Development of the Detective Novel   Owen 1958
  Illus.

Mrs. Murch has written a solid, well-documented study of the origins of
the detective novel from its earliest days. She is excellent on Collins and
Dickens, good on Poe and Doyle. Unfortunately, the period since Freeman is compressed into one relatively short chapter which can scarcely do
justice to the subject. She omits, for example, any mention of Burton,
Connington, or Wade. There are two bibliographies and an index with
some odd variations from accepted nomenclature.

2989   NARCEJAC, THOMAS (b. 1908)

The Art of Simenon   Rout 1952
  Le cas Simenon, *trans. by Cynthia Rowland*

The difference between the original title in French and its translated form
is noticeable in the text, which is not a glorification of S., but a cool
assessment of his merits and defects by one of a team of writers who
are but part disciples of the mass-murderer of literary detection.

2990   NARCEJAC. See also:

Esthétique du roman policier   Payot 1947

2991   NEVINS, FRANCIS M., JR.

"Cornell Woolrich"   *TAD* Oct 1968; Jan & Apr 1969

A detailed account of the life and work of this talented writer, followed,
in *TAD* July 1969, by a complete Woolrich bibliography, in the preparation of which Nevins had the assistance of Harold Knott and William
Thailing.

2992   (*As editor*)

The Mystery Writer's Art   BGUP 1971
  Introd. by the editor

The first collection of essays on the subject since Howard Haycraft assembled No. 2955. The new one is divided into sections: Appreciations,
Taxonomy, Speculation and Critique, which mark only approximately the
difference between successive groups of 12, 5, and 4 essays.
   The first section includes pieces on Poe, Sax Rohmer, Freeman, Wade,
Hammett, "Drury Lane," "Cool and Lam," and six mystery movies. Section 2 deals with *Black Mask,* locked rooms, the "game" from the writer's
point of view (by J. D. Carr), and winds up with JB's "Detection and the
Literary Art." Finally, there are articles on the detective as a nineteenth-
century metaphor, the writer as detective hero (Ross Macdonald) and
detective fiction as an historical source (William D. Aydelotte). The last
essay, "The Shape of Crimes to Come," will doubtless inspire readers to
act out their fantasies.

2993 NICOLL, W. ROBERTSON

The Problem of Edwin Drood H&S n.d. [1912]
Frontispiece reprod. of Edwin Drood *wrapper*

An early, discursive, and not very critical study of the problems posed by
the unfinished novel. W.R.N. leans heavily on John Forster's recollections,
reprints a long statement supporting Forster and written by Dickens'
younger daughter, and rather inclines to Cuming Walters' notion that
Datchery was none other than Helena Landless in disguise. He wisely
rejects the illustrations of the Drood "Original Wrapper" as evidence. (See
Nos. 2888–9, 2962, 2964 and 3054.)

2994 NICOLSON, HAROLD [later SIR]

"Marginal Comment" *Spect* Mar 23, 1951

The cultivated biographer, diarist, and diplomat first declares his pleasure
in the anodyne of detection, then takes a sideswipe at Ellery Queen's
"appalling volubility," and settles down to an encomium of Simenon,
devoting the rest of his article to the soothing effect of Maigret's largely
stationary ruminations.

2995 NICOLSON, MARJORIE

"The Professor and the Detective" *Atlantic* Apr 1929

A fine essay, semi-novelistic in manner, which disposes of the objections
based on "blood-lust," "unreality," and "low literacy." It goes on to exhibit the refinements and virtues of the genre, discusses its reading public,
and shows why the method is sufficient justification for the madness. By
a surprising miscalculation, however, the author asserts that the writing of
good detection is man's business, not woman's.

2996 NORDON, PIERRE

Conan Doyle: A Biography Rine 1967

Head of the English Department at the University of Nantes and a
thorough scholar, P.N. documents in detail the reception of Doyle's works
and does justice to his historical novels, as well as to the strange religious
career and great moral courage of the creator of Sherlock Holmes. The
biographer's prose is unfortunately marred by jargon.

2997 OFFORD, LENORE GLEN

"Memoirs of a Mystery Critic" *EQMM* Apr 1967

An excellent résumé in verse of what the jaded reviewer is likely to find
in his weekly or monthly fare, but cheerfulness insists on breaking in at
the end.

2998 OSBORNE, ERIC, bibliog.

Victorian Detective Fiction BH 1966
Pref. by Graham Greene
Introd. by John Carter

A catalogue of the collection made by Dorothy Glover and Graham Greene. An appendix gives the publishing history of Fergus Hume's *The Mystery of a Hansom Cab,* and there are indexes of detectives and illustrators as well as of the 471 listed items. In the bibliography itself there are some surprising omissions, such as G. R. Sims' *Dorcas Dene* and Melville Davisson Post's *Strange Schemes of Randolph Mason,* both pre-1900. No critical comments about the books listed, but see the author's article in *The Bookman* for Feb. 1932.

2999   OVERTON, GRANT (MARTIN) (1887–1930)

> "The Art of Melville Davisson Post" *and*
> "A Great Impersonation" (*E. P. Oppenheim*)
>   *In:* Cargoes for Crusoes   App, Doran, LB 1924

If it took no fewer than three publishers to bring out these conscientious and still informative essays, that unwonted act of cooperation was worth the effort. G.O. ranges over the fiction and memoirs of the previous quarter century and in so doing provides solid studies of E. Phillips Oppenheim and Melville Davisson Post (qq.v.). To each he assigns a special artistic merit, and he adds useful bibliographies and biographical sources. In other pieces he touches on Doyle, Bennett, and other lights with whom our own pages have been concerned. A full index will guide the seeker.

3000   PEARSON, HESKETH

> Conan Doyle: His Life and Art   Meth 1943

A rapid run-through of the adventures of a man who looked stolid, lacked literary genius of the accepted kind, and was in many ways insensitive, but managed to establish a pair of characters and broach a great many subjects still lively in other hands. H.P. is only fair about S.H.'s *raison d'être.*

3001   POE, EDGAR ALLAN
>   [Dickens and Mystery in the Novel] *Apropos of* Barnaby Rudge
>   *In:* The Works of E. A. Poe, *ed. Stoddard, vol. 6, pp. 545 ff.*

For the Founder all rules are suspended, and this entry consists in direct quotation:

The impression here skillfully conveyed is that the ghost seen is that of Reuben Haredale; and the mind of the not-too-accurate reader is at once averted from the true state of the case—from the murderer, Rudge. . . . The author, who, cognizant of his plot, writes with this cognizance continually operating upon him, and thus *writes to himself* in spite of himself, does not, of course, feel that much of what is effective to his own informed perception must necessarily be lost upon his uninformed readers; and he himself is never in condition, as regards on his own work, to bring the matter to test. . . .

If the mystery leak out, against the author's will, his purposes are immediately at odds and ends.

The particulars . . . being withheld, the strength of the narrator is put forth . . . to *whet curiosity* in respect to these particulars. . . . But from this

intention he unwittingly passes into the error of *exaggerating anticipation*. . . .
[And] it is a condition of the human fancy that the promises of [exaggerated mystery, horror, etc.] are not redeemable.

3002   "Letter to Philip P. Cooke," Aug 9, 1846
       In: The Letters of E. A. Poe,
       ed. John Ward Ostrom, vol. 2, p. 328   HUP 1948

Quotation suffices:

You are right about the hair-splitting of my French friend [Dupin]: that is all done for effect. These tales of ratiocination owe most of their popularity to being something in a new key. I do not mean to say they are not ingenious— but people think them more ingenious than they are—on account of their method and *air* of method. In the Murders in the Rue Morgue, for instance, where is the ingenuity in unravelling a web which you yourself have woven for the express purpose of unravelling? The reader is made to confound the ingenuity of the supposititious Dupin with that of the writer of the story.

3003   POND, [MAJOR] JAMES BURTON (1838–1903)

       Eccentricities of Genius   C&W 1901
       *Memories of famous men and women of the
       platform and stage
       91 portraits*

The Major's claim to fame is not as a soldier but as a lecture manager. The short chapter on Conan Doyle tells us that he came to the United States in 1894 and gave forty readings from October to December. In that latter month, according to a pleasant spoof, Doyle was greeted in Boston by the Cabmen's Literary Guild, one of whose members deduced Doyle's identity and itinerary from Buffalo mud in the instep of his shoe, the twisted lapels of his coat grabbed by New York reporters, and so on.

3004   QUEEN, ELLERY

       The Detective Short Story   B&T 1969; orig. LB 1942
       *A Bibliography
       New Introd. by the author*

An indispensable guide to this highly fugitive literature, which the author has long been collecting and collating. A few inclusions of non-detection do not spoil scholarliness since they are correctly labeled and permit valuable *obiter dicta*.

3005   In the Queens' Parlor   S&S 1957
       And other leaves from the Editor's notebook

Listed by the author as one of three "critical works," it consists of fifty "leaves," entertaining and informative. Few are longer than two or three pages, enough to discuss the naming of detectives as well as of detective stories, authors' and critics' favorite tales, and even more esoteric minutiae.

3006 "Letter to the Reader"
  In: Hammett Homicides   Dell 1946

Important for three reasons: the introducer gives much information in little space about Hammett's early stories and their relation to the later works; he quotes from André Gide's *Imaginary Interviews* a paragraph about Hammett; and he quotes from a letter by Hammett himself about scientific detection and circumstantial evidence.

3007 "Meet Sam Spade"
  Pref. to: A Man Called Spade   Dell 1944

A short but analytic introduction to Hammett's characteristics, at a time when the *Black Mask* style was still new and did not seem so natural as it does now.

3008 A Poll of Twelve* on the
  Best Dozen Detective Stories   *EQMM* Mar 1950

The choice among 83 [short] stories named was:

Thomas Burke	The Hands of Mr. Ottermole
Edgar Allan Poe	The Purloined Letter
Conan Doyle	The Red-Headed League
Anthony Berkeley	The Avenging Chance
Robert Barr	The Absent-Minded Coterie
Jacques Futrelle	The Problem of Cell 13
G. K. Chesterton	The Oracle of the Dog
Melville Davisson Post	Naboth's Vineyard
Aldous Huxley	The Gioconda Smile
H. C. Bailey	The Yellow Slugs
E. C. Bentley	The Genuine Tabard
Dorothy Sayers	Suspicion

These stories are all first-rate, like their authors, but it will be noticed that only seven out of the twelve are true detective stories. Other issues of the magazine contain similar polls of other groups of connoisseurs.

  * Actually thirteen, if Queen is resolved into his component parts.

3009 RAMSEY, G. C.

  Agatha Christie, Mistress of Mystery   DM 1967
    Introd. by the author
    Illus.

A deserved tribute to a great producer, not very critical but with some good features. The author's opening essay ("The Mystery Story as a Form") is perfunctory, but he supplies the following useful information about his heroine: A.C. was born in 1890, not 1891; her attack of amnesia in 1926 was real, not feigned as a publicity stunt. In six appendices Mr. Ramsey provides a complete alphabetical list of Christie titles, full-length novels summarized, and lists of plays, films, and titles not published in America as well as those not published in England.

3010   RAWSON, CLAYTON

> [Remarks on Detective Fiction]
> *In:* Death from a Top Hat *Chap. 1*   Putn 1938
> *Double-page frontispiece photos of the model of
>   an apartment, showing layout, furniture and corpse*

Two pages of small print, interrupted by comments, state the conviction that the detective story is played out. This is "proved" by an enumeration of plots, characters, situations, and detectives. Though sometimes cited as important, this little essay is not particularly original or engaging.

3011   REYNOLDS, AIDAN, and CHARLTON, WILLIAM

> Arthur Machen *A Biography*   RP 1963

The heartbreaking story of a great but forever insolvent writer who, in the nineties, gave a new direction to the tale of horror and the supernatural, replacing the old props and devices with fresh ones, which others quickly exploited. His originality and his little masterpieces are acknowledged by his sympathetic biographers equally with his penurious life and weaknesses of character.

3012   RHODES, HENRY T. F.

> "The Detective in Fiction and in Fact"
>   *In:* The Tracks of Crime   Turns 1952

The opening chapter of this uneven book plays with its subject without sticking to it, including within its confines a Sherlock Holmes story, a pair of true crimes, and some fairly obvious observations. For opinions on the remainder of the book, see No. 3272.

3013   RICHARDS, (THOMAS FRANKLIN) GRANT (1872–1948)

> Author Hunting   Unic 1960; orig. 1934
>   *Illus.*

The autobiography of a farsighted publisher, who brought out Shaw's plays when there was no assurance of their success in any form. The relevance of the book to this *Catalogue* lies in the reminiscences about Alec Waugh and Ernest Bramah (q.v.), and the portraits (different in successive printings of the book) of the last-named elusive personage.

3014   RICHARDSON, MAURICE

> Introduction to *Novels of Mystery from
>   the Victorian Age*   Pilot 1945

The well-known reviewer of detective fiction for various English journals gives a scholarly yet elegant account of the works he has chosen for this anthology (No. 2138) and much of interest about their authors (when known). He is especially good on Wilkie Collins and Stevenson.

3015   ROBERTS, [SIR] SYDNEY CASTLE

> Introduction to
> *Sherlock Holmes: Selected Stories*   OUP 1950

The former master of Pembroke College, Camb., deals in witty fashion with the biography and bibliography of his subject, which he has abundantly written about elsewhere. For those not interested in the details of S.H.'s "life," the early publishing history of the Holmes stories forms the main attraction of this essay.

3016 RODELL, MARIE F.

    Mystery Fiction   DS 1943
        Rev. ed.: Heritage House 1952 (Professional Writers' Library)

An uneven set of suggestions for the intending writer, some being excellent and the rest commonplace. No new insights into the form or history of the genre, but much good sense about Author and Audience, Techniques, Starting Points, Plotting and Writing, and the Economics of Publishing. Compare Nos. 2908 and 3057.

3017 ROWLAND, JOHN

    "Phillpotts's Detective Fiction"
        In: Girvan, Waveney, ed. Eden Phillpotts:
        An Assessment and a Tribute   Hutch 1953
        Illus.

This short but fair account of E.P.'s contribution to the genre stresses the willingness of serious writers to attempt the detective form and gives examples of novelistic power in the writing of tales.

    The Selective Bibliography lists thirteen of E.P.'s detective novels, but inadvertently omits *The Jury* from the category.

3018 SANDOE, JAMES

    The Hard-Boiled Dick   Lovell 1952
    A Personal Checklist

The distinguished professor of bibliography and English literature at the University of Colorado is well-known for his reviews of detective fiction in the now defunct *New York Herald Tribune,* as well as for the compilation of expert opinions (including his own), which under the title "Readers' Guide to Crime" forms an important chapter of Haycraft's *Art of the Mystery Story* (No. 2955). In the present pamphlet we have from J.S.'s pen another genuine piece of critical reporting, this time on the native American tradition. By his evidence, it would seem that few writers can produce more than one good example of the tough genre. The three dozen or so of such authors are here sharply characterized and several works by each listed; Hammett gets an especially full treatment. The whole is a model of incisive criticism.

3019 SAYERS, DOROTHY L.

    "Aristotle on Detective Fiction"
        In: Unpopular Opinions   HB 1947

A lecture delivered at Oxford on March 5, 1935, to show that Aristotle's *Poetics* foretells the creation of the detective genre. His appetite for the

gruesome and his love of Discoveries alike predispose him to be a connoisseur. Serious critical are made beneath the banter.

3020   Introduction to *The Second Omnibus of Crime*   Dday 1932

This 16-page essay must rank as one of the very best discussions of the
genre ever penned. Every page is crammed with shrewd observations on
how the detective story grew in popularity, and why; how it is written;
the proper place of characterization and "psychology"; the relative merits
and requirements of the short story and the novel. Miss S. is particularly
good in her discussion of the fictional detective, and her delicate hint
that she is "put off" by Tommy and Tuppence (see No. 2424) should
endear her even if she had said no more.

3021   Introduction to Wilkie Collins' *Moonstone*   Everyman 1967/1944

A definitive statement on this great work and on Collins' output as a
whole. D.S. is not merely a scholar who has got up all the facts, she is a
judge and a practitioner as well; so that all features of the subject are
reviewed, in amazingly brief compass and impeccable prose.

3022   SCARBOROUGH, DOROTHY

    The Supernatural in Modern English Fiction   Putn 1917

The Columbia University scholar undertook the first study of this subject
as a doctoral dissertation and managed to encompass it in a book of
reasonable size despite the vast amount of matter to cover. The Gothic
Romance is the obvious beginning, after which comes the influence of
Poe, Hawthorne, Hoffmann, Balzac, and other nineteenth-century masters,
winding up with Kipling, Henry James, and Conan Doyle. Then the
author analyzes the modern ghost, the diabolical, supernatural, and science-fiction genres, and concludes that the long English tradition of
supernatural make-believe has now branched out into innumerable chan-
nels. It is a pity that the study ends before the flowering of Russell Wakefield and M. R. James, yet the index provides a rich catalogue of authors
and works that one still considers modern and even contemporary.

3023   SCOTT, SUTHERLAND

    Blood in Their Ink   SP 1953

This treatise by a British physician and author of detection (see No.
1914/B) is poorly written but nevertheless valuable for its fairly comprehensive description and discussion of modern mystery novels. Scott is
better at listing than he is at criticism, and his praise is too indiscriminate,
but in few other places can one find any information concerning the plot
and locale of certain obscure detective novels. Dr. Scott has the modesty
to refrain from a description of his own works, but eleven are listed, most
of which feature his investigators, Dr. Septimus Dodds and Inspector
Verity. (See Nos. 1914–5.)

3024   SCOTT, [SIR] WALTER (1771–1832)

"Mrs. Ann Radcliffe"
   In: The Lives of the Novelists   Everyman 1959; orig. 1821

The superb essay on Mrs. R. is perhaps the best in this remarkable set which Scott wrote as prefaces to an unfinished *Novelist's Library*. He is critical of her prentice work, makes proper reservations about aspects of her supernatural machinery when it turns out natural, but gives her full credit for the quality and arrangement of her effects, taking up in passing and with finality two or three points which show the master critic: a genre that gives pleasure and shows the application of art is not to be sneered at for neglecting other merits and techniques that afford a different pleasure. Again, critics should remember how much easier it is to "devise a complicated chain of interest, than to disentangle it with perfect felicity." And last, he gives a flick of the whip to HIBK: "Her heroines voluntarily expose themselves to situations which in nature a lonely female would certainly have avoided."
   See also, in the same volume: "Horace Walpole."

3025   SEABORNE, E. A.

Introduction, headnotes, and questions in
   The Detective in Fiction   Bell 1954

For the eight stories chosen, see No. 2784. The introduction and comments by the headmaster of the Bablake School (Coventry) are competent history and criticism, though visibly lacking in sharp focus. The pedagogical intention may have rendered his expression ingratiating but the result should be called mild rather than feeble.

3026   SHEPPERSON, ARCHIBALD BOLLING

The Novel in Motley   HUP 1936
   Illus.

Although professing to treat of the English burlesque or parody novels down to 1900, this agreeably written work of scholarship also gives a great deal of information about the targets of the parodies, and notably the Gothic novel and other types of mystery tales. The appended checklist (with descriptions) of the parodies published from 1830 to 1900 is most useful.

3027   SHIBUK, CHARLES

"Cyril Hare"   *TAD* Oct 1969

A brief but informative essay on one of the best and (in the U.S.) most neglected British detective authors. Shibuk discusses the novels and short stories intelligently and tells us also how Alfred Alexander Gordon Clark, J. came to choose his pseudonym.

3028   A Preliminary Checklist of the Detective
Novel and Its Variants   Pub. by author, Bronx, 1966

Together with a Supplement praised in the Oct. 1967 *TAD*, this list was not continued beyond the very beginnings of whatever Preliminary may mean. A few interesting items are given here their full citation and date.

3029   SHIBUK, CHARLES, and LACHMAN, MARVIN

"Dramatizations of the Great Literary Detectives
and Criminals"   *TAD* var. d. (see below)

The four Parts, dealing successively with Radio, Television, Theater, and Film, are of very unequal length—the last being naturally the most extensive—but all are tabulated in four columns, under Author, Name of Show, Character, and Actors. These invaluable and laborious compendia appeared in *TAD* as follows:

Part I: Radio   Jan 1968
Part II: Television   Apr 1968
Part III: Theater (with a brief essay by Mr. Lachman, & giving also name of theater, date of opening, & length of run) July 1968
Part IV: Film

     Sect. 1 (Abbot–Hughes)   Oct 1968
     Sect. 2 (Jacques–Wiley)   Apr 1969

See also some miscellaneous observations on detective films by Charles Shibuk in the Jan 1969 issue of *TAD*.

3030   SIMENON, GEORGES

"An Interview on the Art of Fiction"   MIT *Humanities Pub.*
With Carvel Collins   No. 23, 1956

Artist's guff about "creation," in no way distinctive about either this author or his chosen genre.

3031   SIMENON (subject)

Special Number of *Adam International Review*   ROP 1969
Illus.

Half a dozen essays and shorter estimates of the writer by notables in general and in detective literature; including Agatha Christie, J. B. Priestley, C. Day Lewis, Storm Jameson, C. P. Snow, Henry Miller, and Pamela Hansford Johnson. In addition, letters from André Gide to Simenon.

3032   SIMENON. See also: *Magazine Littéraire* no. 20 (Aug 1968), which includes articles on Arsène Lupin, Agatha Christie, Simenon, and the tough genre, French and American. In addition, a kind of lexicon of the pulp tradition, consisting of short comments on many of its followers, mostly American.

3033 STARRETT, VINCENT

[On William Leggett's "The Rifle"]
In: Chicago Sunday Tribune Books
"Books Alive" column   June 20, 1948

A remarkable find in early Americana and prophetic ballistics, admirably handled by this veteran critic of the genre. For a reprinting of Leggett's story, with cuts, see No. 2344.

3034 "From Poe to Poirot"
In: Books Alive   RH 1940

Leisurely and rich in aperçus, this long essay-review of the life of detective fiction is good in itself and a corrective to many misconceptions still current as to who did what and how.

Note that the author has also paid his respects to the cognate works of Bierce, but in other writings: *Ambrose Bierce* (Kennikat Press, 1969; orig. 1920) and *Ambrose Bierce, Bibliography* (Centaur Bookshop, Chicago, 1929).

3035 STEEVES, HARRISON R.

"A Sober Word on the Detective Story"   *Harper's* Apr 1941

An outstanding performance in both sobriety and sense, which quietly modulates from skepticism about the literary qualities of detective fiction to a demand for those qualities and then to an affirmation that certain authors supply them. (Reprinted in No. 2955.)

3036 STEVENSON, ROBERT LOUIS, and OSBOURNE, LLOYD

"Epilogue: To Will H. Low"
In: Novels and Tales, *vol. 10*   Scrib 1896/1891

Manifestly this short disquisition on detective tales, appended to *The Wrecker,* is Stevenson's critical view of the attraction and difficulties of the genre. He discusses the genesis of his novel and the qualities of mystery stories, but expresses regret that in the pure form the "mind of the reader is always bent on picking up clews" and in being so satisfied misses "life." Therefore he and his collaborator have tried to supply interest of both kinds, which he hopes are in balance. Finally, he credits the later works of Dickens with making mystery into literature.

3037 STEVENSON, W(ILLIAM) B(RUCE)

Detective Fiction   NBL 1958
Introd. by the author

One of the third series of Reader's Guides. Except for being up-to-date, this shows little advance over the author's earlier effort (1949). The selection of "representative" novels by the various authors is poor, and the comments upon them often naïve. Still, the list is fairly complete (e.g., Dillon, Ellin, Fitzgerald are included) and it discloses pseudonyms as well as information on what was in print in 1958.

3038   STEWART, A. W.

Alias J. J. Connington   App 1947
Pref. by the author

Twelve essays by the distinguished chemist covering a variety of subjects, from ether-drinking to the nature of evidence, from Sherlock Holmes to Gilles de Rais. They show erudition, critical powers, and more humor than he allowed to come through in his stories. (See Nos. 582–604.)

3039   STINNETT, CASKIE

"Rex Stout, Nero Wolfe, and
The Big Fish"   *Her-Trib* Oct 10, 1965

A chatty but lengthy article apropos of the publication of *The Doorbell Rang* (No. 1982), but covering many aspects of its author's career, tastes, and method of composition.

3040   STONE, EDWARD

"Caleb Williams and *Martin Faber:*
a Contrast   *MLN* Nov 1947

The scholar (then at Duke University) defends the first novel by William Gilmore Simms (q.v.) from the conventional charge of being an imitation of Godwin's *Caleb Williams* (q.v.). The character of Martin is original at least in being evil through and through, from earliest youth, the author being concerned to probe into the reasons for his worthlessness, which a recent case had brought vividly before him as a psychological problem.

3041   STOUT, REX

"Reading and Writing Detective Stories"   [var. book jackets] 1952

Three paragraphs of autobiography and confession which assess the difference between reading and writing stories, on the one hand, and watching and playing baseball, on the other. The upshot is that at home, in the evening, "I would swear that reading them is more fun than writing them."

3042   STRACHEY, (EVELYN) JOHN (ST. LOE) (1901–63)

"The Golden Age of English Detection"   *Sat Rev* Jan 7, 1939

Another brilliant prediction of the imminent decline of the detective story —unless . . . unless the new white hopes of the genre, Nicholas Blake, Margery Allingham, and Michael Innes, developed as they should. They did.

3043   SYMONS, JULIAN

"The Detective Story in Britain"
In: Writers and Their Work *No. 145*   LG 1962

Thirty pages suffice the accomplished author for his review of the genre from Poe to the crime novel, which he hails with delight. His sense of the changes in form is accurate, though his prediction of its falling apart seems a little premature. Other judgments peppery, and choice of quotations excellent, as is the bibliography *in the main:* like so many others, it lists as detection and mystery what is manifestly something else.

3044　TAYLOR, ROBERT LEWIS

　　　"Two Authors in an Attic"　　　*New Yorker* Sept 8 and 15, 1951

A profile of John Dickson Carr, chock-full of details literary and personal, sympathetic and indeed awe-struck at the spectacle of the author's precocity and wide scope. We learn with satisfaction of Carr's impatience with the plots and pretenses of films that profess to afford the delights of crime and detection.

3045　THOMAS, GILBERT

　　　How to Enjoy Detective Fiction　　　　　　　Rockcliff 1947

Imagine being willing to write on such a subject! These 99 pages are pretty feeble, and they do not fulfill their contract, but they are worth citing for a few names of authors and books not known in the U.S.

3046　THOMSON, H(ENRY) DOUGLAS

　　　Introduction to:
　　　The Great Book of Thrillers　　　　　Odhams n.d. [c. 1937]

Witty and brief and to be noted for its indications of the feelings and pastimes of the period—e.g., "the Murder Game–that last infirmity of Mayfair minds."

3047　Masters of Mystery　　　　　　Folcroft 1970/Coll 1931
　　　A Study of the Detective Story

No one can write with the same irony and wit—and yet be as serious about the genre—as this remarkable student and anthologist. His treatise is delightful and fundamental: its judgments have stood up well and his epigrams have engraved themselves in the memory of "those that know."

3048　TIMES LITERARY SUPPLEMENT, THE (London)
　　　"Detective Fiction," *Special number*　　　　Feb 25, 1955

Valuable but uneven, as might be expected. The articles, all unsigned, range from the classic genre to chase, suspense, horror, and true crime. There is a discussion of publishing; an attempt at history, "The Silver Age" being now (1950); and a critical estimate of "five writers in one—Agatha Christie."
　　Note: The ads are as interesting as the text.

3049　VAN DINE, S. S.

　　　Introduction to *The Philo Vance Omnibus*　　　Scrib 1936

Contains "20 rules for writing detective stories." They are not nearly so concise or so fundamental as Knox's (see No. 2614), but in their day they helped.

3050 VARIOUS HANDS

The Cleverest Murder in Fact or Fiction   *Strand* Dec 1926–
    Illus.   Jan 1927

Eight answers form a symposium of notables discussing the impossible question posed by the title.

Association Item
3051 VARIOUS HANDS

My First Book   Lipp 1894
    Introd. by Jerome K. Jerome
    Illus. with port. of authors

Twenty-two authors tell how they first managed to get published (or to finish their first ms.). Often hope is born in infancy or at school. The important names are: W. Besant, James Payn, W. Clark Russell, Grant Allen, Hall Caine, Kipling, Conan Doyle, M. E. Braddon, Rider Haggard, I. Zangwill, Marie Corelli (she is all indignation about reviewers), J.K.J., Bret Harte, Q., and R.L.S. Note that Doyle's account here differs from that in his memoirs, No. 2939.

3052 WAITE, J. B.

"If Judges Wrote Detective Stories"   *Scribner's* Apr 1934

The start of a controversy along familiar lines: the necessary scruples and formalities of the law are ill-observed in fiction and the novelist's notion of evidence is often feeble.

3053 WALSH, JOHN

Poe the Detective   RUP 1968
    The Curious Circumstances behind
    "The Mystery of Marie Roget"

The author, a newspaperman turned scholar, studied the facts of the murder (in 1841) of Mary Cecilia Rogers, facts upon which Poe based his story. Then the research turned to the devices and changes in Poe's tale, by which its author kept abreast of developments during the serializing of his fiction and made it appear that his reconstruction had been right all along. J.W. has done a good piece of historical and literary detection— but why did Rutgers have to print it like blank verse? See an earlier study of the case by Wimsatt (No. 3323).

3054 WALTERS, J. CUMING

The Complete Edwin Drood   C&H 1912

An early study of the famous unfinished novel. The author's most original contribution is his identification of "Mr. Datchery" (the mysterious detective-spy who first appears in Chapter 18 of the novel) as Helena Landless in disguise. For a refutation in criticism, see R. M. Baker, *The Drood Murder Case* (No. 2889), and for a treatment of the idea in fiction, see No. 896.

3055 WARD, A. C.

The Nineteen Twenties   Meth 1930
Literature and Ideas in the Post-War Decade

In this excellent summary, the second section of Chapter 9 is devoted to detective fiction. The author is clearly not a professional consumer, but he writes with discrimination and assurance—the same assurance that led him to take up the subject in a many-sided survey of culture, and to turn prescriptive in the eight rules he lays down for the genre.

3056 WAUGH, EVELYN

Monsignor Ronald Knox   LB 1959

A sympathetic and well-documented biography by a fellow author and fellow Catholic. It judges the Knox detective tales fairly, but discusses the priority of Frank Sidgwick as initiator of the Sherlock Holmes literature without (*a*) referring to the work of Maurice, and (*b*) distinguishing between the flimsiness of these early squibs and the elaborate essay by Knox, which Knox himself came to abominate. (See No. 3358.)

3057 WELLS, CAROLYN

The Technique of the Mystery Story   1929/1913
Rev. ed.: Home Correspondence School,
Springfield, Mass.
Introd. by J. Berg Esenwein

This is the pioneer work on the genre, originally intended to engender or encourage accomplished producers. Contrary to what one might expect from acquaintance with C.W.'s own work, this manual shows her as extremely tough-minded and superbly critical. The book is not so well-arranged as the serried ranks of chapters make one hope for, but the topics, the extracts, the historical remarks, and the critical thumbnail sketches of authors and their detectives are all solid stuff. Here are the chapter headings, all with four to six subheadings:

I. The Eternal Curious	XII. The Rationale of Ratiocination
II. The Literature of Mystery	XIII. Close Observation
III. Readers and Writers	XIV. Other Detectives of Fiction
IV. The Moderns	XV. Portraits
V. The History of Mystery	XVI. Devious Devices
VI. Ghost Stories	XVII. Footprints and Fingerprints
VII. Riddle Stories	XVIII. More Devices
VIII. Detective Stories	XIX. False Devices
IX. The Detective	XX. Murder in General
X. Deduction	XXI. Persons in the Story
XI. Applied Principles	XXII. The Handling of the Crime

3058   WILLIAMS, (GEORGE) VALENTINE (b. 1883)

"Gaboriau: Father of the Detective Novel"   *Nat Rev* Dec 1923

A compendious life sketch of the indefatigable producer who died of overwork at 39, having written twenty-one novels in thirteen years (fourteen of them in the last seven years of his life), and established several types of detective, as well as buried excellent clues and detection in an inherited mass of melodrama. We are told that G. called his work *romans judiciaires*, isolated one series of five as "Processes of reasoning in judicial affairs," and was at work on "The Foreman of the Jury" when he died in 1873.

3059   WILLIAMS. See also: Notes on plot construction in *Double Death* (No. 2134).

3060   WILSON, EDMUND

A Literary Chronicle: 1920–1950   Farr 1950

Contains his three attacks on the genre (see "Gems" facing the introduction to this *Catalogue*): "Why Do People Read Detective Stories?" "Who Cares Who Killed Roger Ackroyd?" "Mr. Holmes, They Were the Footprints of a Gigantic Hound!" (There is something to be deduced from this conjunction of titles.)

3061   WÖLCKEN, FRITZ

Der Literarische Mord   Nest (Nürnberg) 1953
    Eine Untersuchung über die englische und
    amerikanische Detektivliteratur
    Bibliog.

An able treatment of English and American detective fiction from Poe to Hammett and Chandler, giving full and typically German-academic attention to categories, ethical and artistic. The author's knowledge of English developments since Dorothy Sayers is skimpy compared to what precedes.

PART IV

TRUE CRIME:

TRIALS,

NARRATIVES

OF CASES,

CRIMINOLOGY

AND POLICE SCIENCE,

ESPIONAGE,

AND CRYPTOGRAPHY

Gems from the Literature

Some circumstantial evidence is very strong, as when you find a trout in the milk.
    —Thoreau, *Journal,* November 11, 1854

Now in walking, the only object is to advance in the direction in which we desire to go.
    —Hans Gross, *Criminal Investigation*

. . . evil deeds in every field—regicide, parricide, fratricide, homicide, or simple strangulation.
    —Frank Owen, *Murder for the Millions*

Then there was Maria Greywolf, a half-breed Sioux Indian. She stabbed and castrated her lover in an empty carriage of the B.M.T. railway in New York, and honestly believed that she was attending a revivalist meeting at the time.
    —John Blackburn, *Murder at Midnight*

The windows were intact but the doors had been blown off their hinges. "This made it obvious," his report explained, "that something quite unusual must have occurred."
    —E. B. Block, *The Wizard of Berkeley*

I cannot understand why people read detective novels when they can have "Notable British Trials."
    —Compton Mackenzie

Death is, of course, an excellent reason for not calling a witness.
    —Lord Maugham, "The Problem of Proof"

Today's Moonrays go underground, prevent surface knowledge, favor detectives, snooping wives, and scientific research.
    —Cullen Moore, *New Orleans Times-Picayune,* November 18, 1968

3062   ABBOTT, WILBUR CORTEZ

"Colonel Thomas Blood: Crown Stealer"   HUP 1935
In: Conflicts with Oblivion

The distinguished professor of history at Harvard retraces in this long essay the incredible career of the seventeenth-century adventurer and double agent, who tried to steal the jewels from the Tower, killed a good many of his enemies, won over Charles II in a private interview, and survived to be his secret-service chief—a kind of Vidocq before his time.

3063   ABRAHAMSEN, DAVID

The Psychology of Crime   CUP 1960

A sober and thorough treatment of what occurs and what is known, with a minimum of superadded views. The suggestion is made that criminals be handled in three categories—the legally insane, the abnormal but not insane, and those without apparent pathology; the aim being fairness and the depopulating of prisons.

3064   ADAM, H(ARGRAVE) L.

Oriental Crime   Laur n.d. [1908]
Illus.

The author, whose earlier book *The Story of Crime* had a considerable success, here turns his attention eastward with the intention of producing a companion volume. Judging from the somnolent effect produced by this thick, unwieldy, and unyielding volume, his first work on prison life is not an immediate "must." In the present book, the description of convict life in the Andaman Islands is one of the better sections, though it must be looked for in the Part headed "Transportation." See also the author's *Woman and Crime* (Laurie 1914).

3065   ADAM, ed.

Trial of Dr. Lamson   2d ed. Hodge 1951/1912
NBT (orig. NET)
Illus.

Dr. Lamson made away with his young brother-in-law, for his money. The trial took place in March 1882. Excellent appendices containing press reports of the crime and Dr. Lamson's own description of his experiences with morphine and aconitine, to which he was addicted. For some reason, Dr. Lamson remains a figure more pathetic than abhorrent.

3066   ALDINGTON, RICHARD (1892–1962)

Frauds   Hein 1957

The Introduction surveys the brilliant race of impostors and their feats. Of the next seven chapters, the best two retrace the doings of Thomas Griffiths Wainewright, the poisoner, and Arthur Orton, the Tichborne Claimant; and perhaps the second is the finest essay in the whole, as well as the shortest clear account of the case. The Wise forgeries and the lesser swindles of George Psalmanazar, "Dr." Graham (of the "Celestial Bed"), and Maundy Gregory, the seller of peerages, add their touch of humor and imagination to the central store garnered by Mr. Aldington.

3067   ALTICK, RICHARD D.

Victorian Studies in Scarlet   Nort 1970
Illus.

A deft introduction to the great trials of the nineteenth century, preceded by a scholarly, lively discussion of the emotional and social reasons for the Victorians' addiction to the spectacle of murder. Chapter 5, on "Murder and the Literary Life," is the complete answer to all the ignorant or doctrinaire objections.

The cases retold and illuminated by comparisons and comments are: J. B. Rush, Palmer, Smethurst, Pritchard, Madeleine Smith, Jessie M'Lachlan, Franz Müller, Wainewright, Kate Webster, Charles Peace, Adelaide Bartlett, Mrs. Maybrick, Cream, George Chapman, and Dougal. Passing references are made to Constance Kent and Charles Bravo and sound remarks offered on the novels engendered by all this bloodshed.

3068   ANONYMOUS, ed.

Great Unsolved Crimes   Hutch n.d. [1938]
Illus.

A remarkable work, in which all forty-two contributors are admirable. Each recital is done in seven to nine pages and even if we allow for the literary mastery of those chosen to write (see below), the editing remains a feat. Lucidity and force and accuracy and fullness of detail characterize nearly every one of the small chapters. The whole is a model of what such a book should be and what the English can do without fuss. Whoever made up the list chose the best writers of detective fiction (Sayers, Wade, Strong, Berkeley, Bullett, Crofts, Freeman, Fletcher, M. Kennedy, Margaret Cole, Bechhofer Roberts, et al.) and gave them—or let them have—the cases best suited to their talents. If one had leave to take but one book of this kind to a desert island, this would be the one.

The cases discussed are: Green Bicycle, Crippen, Crowborough, Warsop, Charles Bravo, Fish Pond Woods, Dr. Smethurst, Madeleine Smith, Peasenhall, Blackheath, Clapham Common, Maybrick, Vera Page, Wallace, Madame X, Reading, Ardlamont, Battersea, Camden Town, Willie Starchfield, Jack the Ripper, Gorse Hall, Yarmouth Beach, Otterburn, Le Touquet, Rouse, Dr. Knowles, Sydney Street, Campden, M. Prince, Thompson-Bywaters, Dr. Lamson, Merstham Tunnel, Christina Gilmour, Jessie McPherson, The Stauntons, Edalji, John Watson Laurie, Oscar Slater, Adolf Beck, Brixton Taxi, and Brighton Trunk No. 1.

3069   ANONYMOUS

Mysteries of Crime   Walk 1869
As Shown in Remarkable Capital Trials
Illus.

This work by "A Member of the Massachusetts Bar"* presents twenty-nine trials for murder, mostly in New England, a few in England and the Continent, and all dating from the first half of the nineteenth century. The first, longest, and most interesting is that of Professor John Webster of Harvard for the murder of Dr. George Parkman. Also of great interest are the assassination of Thomas D'Arcy McGee, M.P., at Ottawa in 1868, and several other cases whose locus and cast of characters evoke no recognition today. Throughout there is more detection and deduction (i.e., inference) than one would expect, and greater freedom of expression in sexual matters.

* His identity has eluded persistent search. There is a possibility that he was Peleg Whitman Chandler (1816–89), who published a review of the D'Hauteville case in 1841.

3070 BALCHIN, NIGEL (MARTIN) (1908–70)

The Anatomy of Villainy   Coll 1950

It would be good to have from so competent a novelist as Balchin an anatomy of villainy. This collection of skits is certainly not such a treatise. It professes to take types, from Judas the Traitor to Rasputin the Court Favorite (note the disparity of the labels), but it shilly-shallies in the concluding chapter and leaves villainy nowhere. Among the cases, it is offensive to find Richard III, Robespierre, D. D. Home, and the Marquis de Sade mixed together and put on the same plane as Titus Oates, Guy Fawkes, and Rasputin.

3071 BARZUN, JACQUES

Review of *Criminal Law,* by R. C. Donnelly, Joseph Goldstein, and R. D. Schwartz
In: Yale Law Journal   Nov 1963

A critique of the sociological attitude toward the law which this textbook puts forward by means of extracts from many kinds of sources other than legal—e.g., newspapers, local polls, etc.

3072 BECCARIA, [COUNT] CESARE (1738–94)

"On Crimes and Punishments"   BM 1963; orig. 1764
The Library of Liberal Arts

Most people who refer to this famous and influential work think of a massive treatise written by a learned legal mind. The fact is that it is a pamphlet of less than 100 pages, composed under prodding and with the help of friends by a young man who had improvised a harangue on the central thought while in that same circle of friends. Indeed it was the brevity and eloquence of the essay that made it accessible to all Europe at a time when penal reform was much discussed. Letting the punishment fit the crime was B.'s one idea, which he relates to all sorts of current abuses, from dueling to torture. In its historical parts the essay is inaccurate and unjust. As propaganda, it was an appeal to central power (the enlightened monarchs) to put an end to aristocratic tyrannies. Its effect was to help destroy both kings and nobles and bring on the sovereignty of the people.

3073   BEDFORD, SYBILLE (b. 1911)

The Faces of Justice   S&S 1961

The able reporter who wrote *The Trial of Dr. Adams* traveled to Austria, Germany, Switzerland, and France to gather impressions of lower-court procedures, which she then compares with English practice. She favors simplicity, business suits, and the advisory attitude in place of the legal or legalistic. Shrewd observations, not adequately linked with comprehensive views.

3074   The Trial of Dr. Adams   S&S 1959

Dr. John Bodkin Adams was charged with the murder of his patient Mrs. Morell and was tried in London in March 1957, before Justice Sir Patrick Devlin. The trial lasted seventeen days—the longest in the history of English justice. Dr. Adams was acquitted, though he later had to face charges of malpractice and was eventually struck off the Medical Register. An American reader is shocked by the freedom with which a respectable British physician of twenty years ago dosed his patients with morphine, heroin, and other dangerous narcotics. The surprise enables one to overlook the rather coy way in which Mrs. Bedford reports the trial.

3075   BEELEY, ARTHUR L.

"Fact and Fiction in Criminology"   *Scient Mthly* Jan 1952

A brief but thorough survey of the (short) history of criminology and a discussion of ten popular fallacies about crime, followed by a critique of existing methods and a plea for the application and extension of tested knowledge.

3076   BELL, JOSEPHINE

Crime in Our Time   Vane 1962

Despite an impulse to compassion which sometimes turns sentimental, Dr. Bell gives a clear-eyed account of modern crime and criminals and upholds the notion that forgiving everything means encouraging everything. Her writing here is terse and consecutive, but she says or implies a few things contrary to fact, such as ascribing fingerprinting to Bertillon.

3077   BEMIS, GEORGE (1816–78)

Report of the Case of John W. Webster . . . indicted for the murder of George Parkman . . . before the Supreme Court of Massachusetts   C. C. Little & J. Brown 1850

Prepared by one of the counsel and still the best, because fullest and clearest, account of this celebrated affair, to which one returns from academic interest and other motives. But see also No. 3297.

3078   BENNETT, JESSE LEE, ed.

    The Arts of Cheating, Swindling and Murder   Arn 1925
      Introd. and Notes by the editor
      Illus.

A delightful little book that contains Bulwer-Lytton, "Maxims on the Popular Art of Cheating" (1840); Douglas Jerrold, "The Handbook of Swindling" (1839); and De Quincey's two essays "Murder Considered as One of the Fine Arts" (1827 and 1839).
    The editor's contributions are apt and useful.

3079   BIRKENHEAD [1ST EARL OF] (Frederick Edwin Smith, 1872–1930). The meteoric statesman, solicitor general, lord chancellor, law reformer, and father of Lady Eleanor Furneaux Smith (q.v.) was particularly proud of his literary works. He wrote essays on fourteen English judges (1926), discussed his own life together with literature and the law (2 v., 1927), and boasted of nine *editions* of *Famous Trials of History* (1926) being called for in the first six months. He means printings, of course, and one surmises that the demand was due to his reputation rather than the merit of the work. The choice of cases is commonplace and the treatment choppy, at times indeed incoherent, suggesting dictation ill-revised. The same must be said of *More Famous Trials* (1928), bringing the total of cases to forty-three. Among them the unusual and better ones are: Bacon, Marie-Antoinette, Cobbett, and Joan of Arc.

3080   BIRKETT, SIR NORMAN (later Lord), ed.

    The Newgate Calendar   Folio 1951
      Selected, with an Introd. and Contemporary Engravings

A splendid group of reports from contemporary broadsides, spanning the years 1700–80. Notable cases are those of Captain Kidd, Richard Thornhill, Jack Ketch, Jonathan Wild, Dick Turpin, Elizabeth Canning, Eugene Aram, Earl Ferrers, Elizabeth Brownrigg, and the Reverend William Dodd.

3081   Six Great Advocates   Peng 1961

The careers of Marshall Hall, Patrick Hastings, Edward Clarke, Rufus Isaacs, Charles Russell, and Thomas Erskine are retold, with (of course) sketches of some of their cases. Satisfactory and sapient but not full.

3082   BIRMINGHAM, GEORGE A.

    Murder Most Foul!   C&W 1929

This "Gallery of Famous Criminals" covers twenty-three cases in exemplary fashion. Despite the title of the book and the chapter headings, the author imports no false drama or easy moralizing into his recitals, which are ample, clear, and exact. Particularly noteworthy are: Mary Blandy, Katharine Ogilvy, Adelaide Bartlett, Spencer Cowper, Eugene Aram, Franz Müller, J. A. Dickman, Dr. Lamson, and Steinie Morrison.

3083 BISHOP, JIM

The Murder Trial of Judge Peel   S&S 1962

Municipal Judge Joseph Peel went on trial in March 1961 for the murder, five years earlier, of Circuit Court Judge C. E. Chillingworth. The alleged victim and his wife had disappeared and no trace of their bodies was ever found. It took the Florida state attorney seventeen days to bring things home to Peel and two other defendants who had helped protect his interests in the moonshine racket. Justice was only partly triumphant. The case is messy as well as sordid, and the narrative is not of a high order either.

3084 BLEAKLEY, HORACE

The Trial of Henry Fauntleroy   NBT (Toronto) 1924

The expert and lucid retelling of the activities of a famous forger who concentrated on banks.

3085 BLOCK, EUGENE B.

Great Train Robberies of the West   CM 1959

This fluent but conventional writer devotes twenty chapters to the subject stated in the title of his book. All the great holdups are here in outline, but the lack of sufficiently vivid background and biography tends to reduce these epics of the frontier to a deplorable routine. Start here, perhaps, but seek out richer reportings elsewhere.

3086   The Wizard of Berkeley   CM 1958

A journalistic and sometimes ludicrous account of the work of Edward Oscar Heinrich, scientific criminologist at Berkeley, Calif. The story opens with an interesting railway holdup and goes on to a variety of other crimes solved by the scientific acumen and patience of "the wizard." His self-confidence is occasionally naïve—and may have been dangerous.

3087 BOCCA, GEOFFREY

The Life and Death of Sir Harry Oakes   Dday 1959

This *cause célèbre* is retold with only moderate competence about the crime and the trial, but considerable feeling and narrative power in the biographical part, which is the larger. The unsolved murder deserves a treatment concentrating on evidence and willing to indulge in speculative reasoning.

BOLITHO, WILLIAM (full name: William Bolitho Ryall; 1891–1930)

b. Cape Town; began as newsboy and laborer, served in first world war; then corresp. for Manchester *Guardian* and N.Y. *World*. Wrote, among other works: *Italy Under Mussolini, Leviathan, Cancer of Empire, Camera Obscura,* and *Twelve Against the Gods.*

3088   Murder for Profit   TLB 1954; orig. 1926
          Pref. by the editors
          Introd. by Fredric Wertham

Five cases (Burke, Landru, Troppmann, Haarman, and G. J. Smith) retold and analyzed with psychological penetration and artistic skill. A
classic unjustly neglected on its first appearance and even since its reprinting. Dr. Wertham's introduction, on the social meaning of murder, is,
like his other writings, worth the closest attention. See Nos. 3316–7.

3089   BORROW, GEORGE (1803–1881)

          Celebrated Trials and Remarkable Cases of Criminal
          Jurisprudence . . . to 1825   2 v.   P&C 1928; orig. 1825
          Introd. by Edward Hale Bierstadt

The celebrated classic by the celebrated writer, attractively reprinted and
very well edited. The trials are all English, except for Louis XVI and his
Queen.

3090   BOSWELL, CHARLES, and THOMPSON, LEWIS

          Practitioners of Murder   Coll 1962

Ten medical men are the "practitioners" that the authors have in view in
recounting the untimely end of a much larger number of victims. The
facts are well enough marshaled, but the effort to jazz up the atmosphere
for the benefit of the first serial readers often spoils what should be sober
narrative.

          Association Item
3091   BRADFORD, GERSHOM (b. 1878?)

          The Secret of Mary Celeste and Other Sea Fare   Barre 1966
          Four diagrams and two illus. by H. D. White

Those who know their Conan Doyle by heart will recognize the *Mary
Celeste* as the ship that was found in the Atlantic on December 4, 1872,
still sailing but totally abandoned, for no ascertainable reason. Conan
Doyle was caught by this sea mystery and wrote the first fiction based on
it ("J. Habakkuk Jephson's Statement," 1884). Nautical experts and
weather men have dealt with the riddle on numerous occasions. In this
volume, the leading essay supports the waterspout hypothesis that Fay
(q.v.) dismisses as untenable in view of the time and the evidence of the
ship's condition. The present author is a sailor and one-time employee of
the hydrographic service; his prose shows the airs and graces of the un-
literary, but he manages to be clear, and the four diagrams of the *M.C.*
are excellent aids to reconstruction. An adroit last paragraph likens the
ship's secret to a crime. (See also Nos. 3142 and 3344.)

3092   BRAND, CHRISTIANNA

          Heaven Knows Who   MJ 1960
          Illus.

Following in the footsteps of William Roughead, who edited the trial of Jessie M'Lachlan (Glasgow 1862) for *Notable British Trials,* Miss Brand has provided a few new details of this spectacular case. She has also provided a sympathetic understanding of the two young women—the accused and her alleged victim—and of the elderly and detestable James Fleming, whose precise activities at the scene of the crime were never made clear, even after M'Lachlan's sentence had been commuted to life imprisonment. A bloody, fascinating, unsolved affair.

3093   BRIDGES, YSEULT (b. 1888)

How Charles Bravo Died   Jarr 1956
   Illus. and endpaper plan

A perennially enticing case of murder and pre- and post-marital sexual adventures in the nineteenth century. Miss Bridges produces a crystal-clear account, complete with plausible explanations based on clues and characters.

Note: It is a pity she takes the wrong view of the Wallace Case (see Nos. 3095, 3162 and 3280).

3094   The Tragedy at Roadhill House   Rine 1955/1954

The retelling of the murder by Constance Kent of her younger brother, on June 30, 1860. As good as her treatment of Charles Bravo, on both the human side and the police work. But it does not make Rhode (q.v.) superfluous, nor Collins' *Moonstone* less gripping.

3095   BROPHY, JOHN

The Meaning of Murder   W&W 1966

The author's not inconsiderable contributions to both fiction and non-fiction came to an end with this flawed but interesting book, which he did not live to see in print. The reader who does not know his Sayers, Rhode, Radin, Lustgarten, Tennyson Jesse, *et al.* on various cases must tread carefully. Nevertheless, one finds highly interesting treatments of motive and purpose in murder apropos of Charles Peace, Neill Cream, Mrs. Maybrick, Madeleine de Brinvilliers, the Rouse Murder and the epics of Lizzie Borden and George Joseph Smith, plus able commentary on punishment, executions, and crime detection. Note especially the chapters on "Intellectual Murder" (Loeb and Leopold), and "Monsters" (Crippen, Neville Heath, and others). The Wallace case is brilliantly dealt with—the perfect antidote to Miss Bridges.

3096   BROWNE, DOUGLAS G.

The Rise of Scotland Yard   Harrap 1956
   A History of the Metropolitan Police
   Illus.

A detailed, chronological, and rather dull account of the growth of Scotland Yard and its predecessors. The organization of the force and the characteristics of the various commissioners are well presented, but the author is less happy when he retells celebrated cases in which the Yard figured.

3097 BROWNE, DOUGLAS G., and BROCK, ALAN

Fingerprints   Dutt 1954
Fifty Years of Scientific Crime Detection
Foreword by Chief Supt. Fred Cherrill

A history studded with cases and narrated with an enthusiasm for scientific method which makes acceptable a mass of technicalities. The former head of the Fingerprinting Department at Scotland Yard is not a writer of elegant prose, but he attains eloquence in objecting to Milton's remark about "printless feet." (Milton should have known better, having lived for years at Scotland Yard.)

3098 BROWNE, DOUGLAS G., and TULLETT, E. V.

The Scalpel of Scotland Yard   Dutt 1952
The Life of Sir Bernard Spilsbury
Pref. by W. Bentley Purchase, C.B.E., M.C.
Illus.

The definitive biography of the Home Office analyst who was not but might well have been the model for Freeman's Dr. Thorndyke. The Man and the Scientist were equally admirable until the very last (see No. 3289) and the concluding events are heart-rending. The incidents in the life as a whole form a running commentary on our age, even in this less than artistic treatment of many great cases.

3099 BULLOCK, HUMPHRY

"Laurels for a Baronet"   *LMM* Summer 1954

About the trial and execution in 1781 of Captain John Donellan, whose habit was to distill laurel water, but who may not have had a hand in the death of Sir Theodosius Boughton. This is a study in toxicology, favorable to Donellan; but see "The Stroke of Thirteen," by Lillian de la Torre (*EQMM,* Oct 1953), which takes a contrary view.

3100 BURKE, THOMAS

"Did Bierce Die, Or—?"
In: Essays of Today and Yesterday (Harrap 1928)

One of the eleven essays, reminiscent and speculative, by the naturalistic novelist who wrote long and short stories of crime. (See Nos. 347 and 2383.) His interest in Bierce grew out of kindred feelings about fiction. An incomplete Bibliography of the author is appended. For another account of Bierce's death, see No. 3389.

3101 BURNEY, CHRISTOPHER

Solitary Confinement   2d ed.   Macm 1961/1952

A remarkable book and in some ways the most remarkable in this entire
Catalogue. It records eighteen months' life in a French prison as a captive
of the Gestapo during the second world war. The observation and recall
are not more amazing than the writing and the compression of thought.
Implications for criminology (especially discussions of capital punishment)
and for sociology and education occur on every page. It is enough to
mention that the prisoner's transfer to Buchenwald toward the end of his
ordeal struck him as disagreeable because of the threat of sociability.

3102 BURNS, WALTER NOBLE

The Saga of Billy the Kid   Dday 1926/1925

This history of the most precocious bandit of the Southwest—he killed
his first man at 12 and died at 21—is virtually a classic, for it made
known to a postwar generation what New Mexico was like before law
and order. The incidents of cattle-stealing and shooting surrounding the
Kid's career show how a "culture" brings out its geniuses, for it is evident
that Billy (born William H. Bonney in New York City in 1859) was not
an ordinary being: his modesty and good manners, his ruthlessness and
tactical art, as well as his moral forgetfulness, suggest the Uncommon
Man. He has lived in legend and this book is a fit memorial.

3103 BYRNES, THOMAS

1886 Professional Criminals of America   Chel 1969; orig. 1886
    Introds. by Arthur M. Schlesinger, Jr., and S. J. Perelman
    Illus.

A reprinting of the massive chronicle of crime (with biographical sketches
of some 400 criminals and photographs of more than half) which was
compiled by Inspector Byrnes when he was Chief of Detectives in New
York City (1880–95). The author limits himself pretty much to pick-
pockets, swindlers, burglars, and bank robbers, crimes against the person
being largely omitted, although a few murder cases of the early nineteenth century are described, emphasis being upon horror rather than
detection.

    It is a cumbersome, disappointing book, in which the whiskered and
bowlered criminals seem too much alike. But Schlesinger's introduction
is excellent. He gives a compact account of crime in America after the
Civil War, depicts the New York police system of that era, makes it clear
that the escalation of crime in the eighties was not to be explained by the
rising tide of immigration, and tells the story of Byrnes' downfall after the
Lexow Report on police corruption in 1895, and the appointment of
Theodore Roosevelt as president of the Police Board. Perelman is amusing,
as expected, but one may doubt whether his recommendation of the book
to ". . . the detective story writer in quest of plots" has merit.

    See also Julian Hawthorne's "Diaries" of T.B. (Nos. 1103–4)

3104 CAMINADA, JEROME

Twenty-four Years of Detective Life   Heyw 1895

Twenty-five episodes involving a variety of lesser crime, retold in a stilted prose which only emphasizes their commonplaceness. One sometimes wonders whether many of these cases were not in fact imaginary—or borrowed from a general fund.

3105 CARR, JOHN DICKSON

The Murder of Sir Edmund Godfrey   Harp 1936

The author's masterpiece in true-crime reconstruction. Research and narrative are first-class; and the device, borrowed from his fictional art, of summarizing evidence in such a way as to raise questions is wholly free of sensationalism. As for the series of possible solutions and his choice of the most likely, they round out a book which is a classic in the best sense—i.e., rereadable indefinitely.

3106 CECIL, HENRY

Brief to Counsel   Harp 1958
Pref. by Lord Devlin (q.v.)
Illus.

The barrister and novelist (see No. 470–3) sets down in simple but technically explicit terms what an intending barrister should and should not do from the moment of choosing the profession to that of winning or losing the case. A delight to read for anyone in any profession or in none.

3107 CEILLIER, RÉMI

La Cryptographie   Presses Univ. de France 1945
Series: Que sais-je?
Bibliog.

It is a remarkable feat of condensation to present the history and technique of the subject in 134 pages. Classification and lucid examples enable the author to start the reader thinking intelligently from the beginning.

Association Item
3108 CHADWICK, JOHN

The Decipherment of Linear B   2d ed., Camb 1967
Port. of Michael Ventris, maps, and diagrams

The "breaking" of Cretan writing (Linear B) by the young British architect Michael Ventris is a detective story full of excitement, suspense, and of course ratiocination. The personal tragedies and characters linked with the feat make this an appropriate work to insert in this book at this place.

3109 CHEATHAM, ELLIOTT (EVANS)

A Lawyer When Needed   CUP 1963

In these chapters a legal philosopher deals with the predicaments, individual and social, in which the law is the savior—to those who are poor, eccentric, hated, victimized, abused, or oppressed, and who may also be caught up in situations, accidental or contrived, where crimes are charged against them and they need stout defense. For all these purposes, he argues, we need more and better defenders.

3110 CHERRILL, FRED

Cherrill of the Yard   PBC 1955
  Illus.

The title should be "Cherrill by the Yard": the late chief superintendent of the Fingerprint Bureau, New Scotland Yard, is long-winded and generally dull. On the credit side are some good comments on William Herschel and Francis Galton, a fair though sketchy outline of the methods of cataloguing prints, and several photographs in which bowlers are much in evidence.

3111 CHESTER, SAMUEL BEACH

Anomalies of the English Law   LB 1912

A discursive work by a barrister who was apparently a geographer and a U.S. military man as well. If one follows his wanderings, one picks up some curious points about death and burial, the right of property in surnames, executions, marriage and divorce, and the Criminal Appeal Act of 1907.

3112 CHRISTIE, TREVOR L.

Etched in Arsenic   Lipp 1968

A well-organized presentment of the trial and conviction of Florence Maybrick on the charge of having murdered her husband (1899), and of the efforts of Lord Chief Justice Russell and others to secure commutation of her sentence and, later, her release from prison. That this famous case represents an extraordinary miscarriage of justice is likely; certainly Judge Stephen, who presided at the trial with failing powers, was guilty of gross impropriety in his charge to the jury. The mystery remains.
  See also Nos. 3238 and 3243.

3113 CICERO, MARCUS TULLIUS (106–43 B.C.)

Murder at Larinum   Camb 1959

This convenient and well-edited little book gives the narrative portions of Cicero's courtroom speech *Pro Cluentio,* with an introduction in English for those to whom Latin is all Greek. The tale is a real Raymond Chandler: Statius Albius Oppianicus, suspected of having poisoned his first wife, forged a will and murdered its ostensible maker, squandered two fortunes and planned to recoup them by marrying or eliminating (or both) the members of three neighboring and respectable families at Larinum, on the Gulf of Venice. All this good work occupied the decade 82–72 B.C. Poison, hired assassins, death upon death, trials of henchmen, and a fifth marriage finally brought Oppianicus face to face with the able survivor of this aggression, Aulus Cluentius Habitus, Cicero's client and the hero of the thriller. To learn the denouement, read Cicero.

For a good English version, see *Pro Cluentio,* trans. by H. Grose Hodge, Loeb Classical Library (HUP 1966/1927).

3114   CLARK, GEOFFREY, ed.

Trial of James Camb   Hodge 1949
The Porthole Murder
    NBT; Introd. by the editor
    Illus.

The subtitle sums up the salient fact in this celebrated case of murder on the high seas. Before Mr. Justice Hilbery at Winchester in March 1948, it required only four days to establish to the jury's satisfaction that steward James Camb was in fact responsible for the death of Eileen Gibson by pushing her through the porthole of her cabin on the S.S. *Durban Castle* into "shark-infested waters." Just what preceded this act is for the interested reader to determine.

For a fictional treatment, see No. 2365.

3115   COBB, BELTON

The First Detectives   Faber 1957

A lucid account of the founding in 1829 of the London Metropolitan Police, under Commissioner Charles Rowan (an army man) and his lawyer colleague Richard Mayne. A number of murder investigations undertaken by the new force are described in detail, and the skillful blend of contemporary attitudes with individual portraits makes this book an outstanding performance on a subject that can easily be dull.

3116   Murdered on Duty   WHA 1961
    A Chronicle of the Killing of Policemen
    Illus.

The range is limited to Great Britain between 1829, when the Metropolitan Police came into being, and 1960. Such accounts must by their very nature be much of a sameness, but the author makes them interesting by pointing up the changing social scene. From the approximately 100 cases available, eleven are discussed in detail, including the Houndsditch "Anarchist Club" murder of three policemen in 1910, the atrocious shooting of P.C. Gutteridge in 1927 by a pair of ex-convicts who had stolen a car, and—with one of the best chases in police annals—the murder of Chief Inspector Simmons by armed burglars in 1885.

The author has also been concerned with miscarriages of justice. See *Trials and Errors* (WHA 1962).

3117 COLLINS, WILKIE

"The Poisoned Meal"
In: Household Words (*Sept 18, Sept 25, Oct 2, 1858*)
Sbt.: In Five Chapters

A retelling, with full details and sharp analysis, of the facts in a French *cause célèbre* of the eighteenth century. Collins ascertains the culprit to his own and the reader's satisfaction.

3118 CONNINGTON, J. J.

"A Criminologist's Bookshelf"
In No. 3038

The practiced author of fictional detection does not mean *criminologist* in the ordinary sense; he means "writer of crime stories who wants to get his facts reasonably straight." For this purpose he gives a good short list of indispensable reference works which includes: Hans Gross, A. S. Osborn, Locard, and Yardley (qq.v.), in addition to:

A. J. Quirke	Forged, Anonymous and Suspected Documents
Major Burrard	Identification of Firearms and Forensic Ballistics
C. A. Mitchell	The Scientific Detective and the Expert Witness
Justice Wills	Essay on Circumstantial Evidence
Sir Howard Vincent	Police Code and Police Law

3119 CRITCHLEY, MACDONALD

The Black Hole and Other Essays   Pitm 1964
Illus.

The first essay of this interesting collection (all medical studies and biographies) attempts to determine from the records the cause of the high mortality that resulted from one night's imprisonment in the so-called Black Hole of Calcutta, actually a small guardhouse. The incarceration was undoubtedly a crime against humanity and the laws of war, but it was never rationally investigated between 1756 and the date of this essay.

3120 CROFT-COOKE, RUPERT

Smiling Damned Villain   S&W 1959
The True Story of Paul Lund, Confessed Criminal

A crook with redeeming candor is interviewed in Tangiers by the distinguished novelist and detective-story writer. The subject's brag and bounce are more evident than his ingenuity.
    The title is from *Hamlet* I, 5, 106.

3121 Three in a Cell   E&S 1968

Like *Thief,* a story of the criminal character and the influence upon it of prison life.

3122   CROUSE, RUSSEL (1893–1966)

Murder Won't Out   Dday 1932
    Foreword by Alexander Woollcott
    Illus.

Twelve unsolved killings, from 1799 (Elma Sands) to 1931 (Starr Faith-
full), and including Poe's Mary Cecilia Rogers (1841), excellently retold
by the late playwright.

3123   DEACON, RICHARD

A History of the British Secret Service   FM 1969
    Illus.

A compact history from the days of Walsingham, Sir Henry Wotton, and
Defoe to Sir Basil Thomson, A. E. W. Mason, Zaharoff, Sir Paul Dukes,
and Ian Fleming. A bit on the spare side, but easy to read and neither
pedantic nor sensational.

3124   DE MILLE, AGNES

Lizzie Borden: A Dance of Death   LB 1968
    Illus.

The famous dancer tells the story of the genesis and realization of her
ballet *Fall River Legend,* first presented by the Ballet Theatre in 1948.
She devotes at least a third of her book to an account of her researches into
the Borden case, in which she was assisted by Joseph Welch, a lawyer.
Together they visited Fall River and talked with many of those who remembered the Bordens. It is safe to say that no other writer has presented
as clear a picture of the Borden house and household of 1892. Miss
De M.'s solution of the mystery follows Pearson rather than Radin.

3125   DENNING, LORD

Report to the Prime Minister   H.M. Stationery Office 1963

The judge's elegant historical account of the Profumo case. The erotic
activities of Miss Christine Keeler and the proxenetic ones of her friend
Dr. Ward are related without moralizing or pruriency. They justify the
attitude taken by John Sparrow in rebuking the British public and press
for creating a scandal harmful to government and entertaining only to the
masses. See Sparrow's circumstantial review of six books (plus this *Report*)
on the Profumo affair, under the title "The Press, Politics, and Private
Life," in *Controversial Essays* (Chil 1966).

3126   DE QUINCEY, THOMAS

"Murder Considered as One of the Fine Arts"
    In: English Mail Coach, etc. (*Everyman 1912 ff.; orig.*
    Blackwood's 1827, 1839)

The magnificent two-part essay which proves the author's dictum that
there is a natural affinity between murder and mirth, and that literature,

whether discursive or dramatic (i.e., this essay or Shakespeare's *Macbeth*), should somehow exhibit the combination in due measure.

Note that the author's narrative of the Williams murder is now generally appended as a P.S. to the other parts. See Everyman ed., 1912 ff.

3127   DEVLIN, (LORD) PATRICK

The Criminal Prosecution in England   YUP 1958

This distinguished judge and gifted writer used the Sherrill Lectures to set forth a critical yet admiring view of prosecution in England. It is a corrective to the popular notion that "science should decide" both the facts of the case and treatment of the criminal.

3128   DICKENS, CHARLES

"The Detective Police"
"On Duty with Inspector Field"
"Three Detective Anecdotes"
        In: Household Words (*July 13, July 27, Aug 10, Sept 14, 1850*)

These articles mark an important date in the public awareness and acceptance of the Detective Police, whose activities were first regarded as sneaking and "un-English." In those early days of Scotland Yard, the detectives who succeeded the Bow Street Runners were still men of small education—and small, too, was the entire force: the two inspectors and five sergeants whom Dickens invited for an interview in his office constituted the whole excepting one man. Though these men did their work in plain clothes, they were uniformed constables and appeared as such in court. For a good while beyond this time, an official detective could be hired by a private person to investigate a crime or the suspicion of one.

For these essays see the volume *Reprinted Pieces* in Dickens' collected works and also No. 2566.

3129   "Some Recollections of Mortality"
        In: The Uncommercial Traveller (*1860 ff.*)

Begun to fill the pages of his own paper *All the Year Round,* the largely autobiographical essays collected under the book title above include as chapter 19 the record of Dickens' visit to the Paris Morgue—he and the crowd hoping for a murdered body—and his service on an English coroner's jury over a case of infanticide. The narrative is in C.D.'s maturest style, morbid grotesque—black humor.

3130   DILNOT, GEORGE

Great Detectives and Their Methods   HM 1928
        Illus.

The General Editor of the Famous Trials Series (18 vols., Bles, 1928–31) has given us here an anecdotal saunter through the period 1870–1920, which affords a good view of the passage from early detection à la

Dickens to Spilsbury and science. Most of the cases are English and French, but Pinkerton and other American detectives are competently referred to. One of the most interesting chapters is about the legendary Frank Froest (q.v.), even though the author's other characterization of great figures is rudimentary.

3131 The Trial of the Detectives   Bles 1928
      Famous Trials Series

The affair recorded in this volume is that of four Scotland Yard men who, in the late 1870s, connived at the fraudulent practices of a pair of interesting gambler-crooks. The exposition is clear and deliberate, with perhaps a little too much repetition for the modern taste. The story supports the novelist's belief that a murder is better than any fraud, however ingenious.

3132 DILNOT

    See also No. 754 and:

Great Detectives and Their Methods	Bles 1927
Man Hunters: Great Detectives and Their Achievements	Hale 1937
New Scotland Yard	Nels 1938
The Story of Scotland Yard rev. Centenary ed.,	Bles 1929/1926

3133 DODGE, FRED

    Under Cover for Wells Fargo   HM 1969
      The Unvarnished Recollections of F.D., Carolyn Lake, ed. Illus.

No one interested in train robberies and the lawlessness of the Far West should miss this "lived document" by the man who, with the Earp brothers, helped pacify Arizona, Oklahoma, and part of Texas. The memorable town of Tombstone is central to the narrative, and the diary and memories about it are given in terse—sometimes illiterate—English, but the *style* is always perfect.

    See also: F. Waters, *The Earp Brothers of Tombstone* (N. Spearman, 1962).

3134 DRESSLER, DAVID, ed.

    Readings in Criminology and Penology   CUP 1964

The former head of the New York State Parole division and a professor of sociology at the University of California (Long Beach) has put together a massive volume of 700 pages which covers the types of offenders and the methods of crime control and prevention. We start with Durkheim and end with an explanation of the failure to prevent juvenile delinquency. The prevailing, but not uniform, attitude is scholarly and liberal; that is, the attention to fact is disciplined and sincere and the presupposition is that social and medical measures can reduce, prevent, or modify criminal behavior.

    There is a splendid essay by Monrad G. Paulsen, "The Exclusionary

Rule Is Necessary," which introduces legal thought into a mass of sociological and psychiatric doctrine. Also a series of documents, from the U.S. Constitution on Civil Liberties to the M'Naghten rules and departures therefrom in cases involving the unsound mind. On the whole, the work fairly represents the division of opinion existing today about crime and the law and the groping toward a synthesis of normal and abnormal psychology in dealing with it. Robert K. Merton's chapter on "The Doctrine of 'Socially Derived Sin' " is a fine example of intelligence at work on the clichés and bringing new light.

3135   DUKES, SIR PAUL, KBE (1889–1967)

      Secret Agent ST 25   Cass 1949
      Orig.: The Story of ST 25 (*1938*)

The full account of the author's intelligence work in Russia during and after the first world war. Parts were previously published in *Red Dusk and the Morrow* (1927). In Russia first as a student of music, P.D. accidentally fell into espionage and he writes about it with skill and vigor. His adventures are of the usual unbelievable yet genuine kind, and in Russia—outdoing the fictional Cleek (see No. 2553)—he was known as "The Man of a Thousand Faces." His life after the war was in journalism.

3136   DUKES. See also:

      An Epic of the Gestapo   Cass 1940
      Come Hammer, Come Sickle   Cass 1947

3137   DULLES, ALLEN, ed.

      Great True Spy Stories   Harp 1968
      A Giniger Book

There is a distinct literary talent for making anthologies as there is for writing novels or compiling textbooks. Offhand one would not assume that the diplomat and secret agent who closed his career as head of Central Intelligence in the U.S. would also have mastered the anthologist's art. He has, and this volume together with No. 2488 are there to prove it.

    The extracts from memoirs and histories span the last two centuries—from Casanova and George Washington to "the Red Orchestra" and the latest defectors. The organization of the 39 pieces in ten sections is critically sound, and the judicious Preface and headnotes are written with much more vivacity than the editor's account of his own exploits in No. 3138.

3138   DULLES

      The Craft of Intelligence   Harp 1963

3139   ELLIS, J. C.

      Blackmailers & Co.   S&B 1928

The portion on blackmailers is so-so, but the last two sections—"Four Unsolved Murder Mysteries and an Attempt to Solve Them" and "Six Almost

Perfect Crimes"—contain excellent ratiocination. See also the theft of the Gainsborough "Duchess of Devonshire," pp. 120 ff., and "The Train Robbery of 1855," pp. 145 ff.

3140   ENDORE, GUY, wrote three pamphlets in the cause of justice: *The Crime at Scottsboro* (1937); *Sleepy Lagoon Mystery* (1944); *Justice for Salcido* (1948). It is hard to judge their effectiveness when so much else went into the elucidation of those cases. The pleas here are full of passion, which does not obscure the issues, but leaves some of the facts in doubt.

3141   FARRER, J. A.

Literary Forgeries   LG 1907
    Introd. by Andrew Lang

Excellent up to its time—the best was yet to come. (See No. 3066.)

3142   FAY, CHARLES EDEY

The Greatest Sea Mystery   Florida Ptg Co.,
                                                  Lake Worth, Fla. 1950

The story of the *Mary Celeste,* reprinted from articles by the author, who has also devoted a book to this baffling case publicized by Conan Doyle. Fay demonstrates to his satisfaction that the waterspout hypothesis is untenable. (But see No. 3091 and also 3344.) What is clear is that Mary Celeste should have married Edwin Drood.

3143   FEIFER, GEORGE

Justice in Moscow   S&S 1964

A scholarly and agreeably written firsthand account of Soviet law and practice in the people's courts. Chapter 13 deals with murder as it is tried in the Moscow City Court. The reporter's sense of immediacy is well balanced by the scholar's knowledge of jurisprudence—and literature.

3144   FELIX, CHRISTOPHER (pseud.)

A Short Course in the Secret War   Dutt 1963

A professional (U.S. agent) sets forth the theory and practice of intelligence work. Lucid, critical, and enthusiastic about his art, he also gives as its rationale the deterrent effect of the secret war on open war.

3145   FINGER, CHARLES J., ed.

A Book of Strange Murders   Hald 1925
    Little Blue Book No. 819

Ten (or rather nine, as will appear) cases told briefly but in good homey style, with strong pacifist and libertarian propaganda interwoven. The tenth case of murder is colonialism, in seventeenth-century America and nineteenth-century Australia. The other cases are: Overbury, Marie

Schneider, Gabrielle Bompard, Bellingham, John Williams, Eugene Aram, Catherine Hayes, Wild Goose Lodge, and "Sir William Courtenay."

3146   FISHER, JACOB

The Art of Detection   RUP 1948
      A later reissue has a Preface by Erle Stanley Gardner

A semi-literate but not at all inept work about the practical details of going about ringing doorbells and extracting information from willing, over-eager, and mendacious witnesses; after which the detective matches words with facts. The salient piece of wisdom is: in a strange house, always sit on the wooden chair; the upholstered furniture may be full of bugs.

3147   FORD, COREY (1902–69)

A Peculiar Service   LB 1965
      Endpaper map of lower Manhattan

An excellent account, based on original research, of espionage in and around New York during the American Revolutionary War. Major André, Benedict Arnold, Lafayette, Washington, and Nathan Hale are among the principals in the story, which occasionally breaks out into (authenticated) dialogue. The author was moved to research and writing by an ancestral connection with the events and by service in the OSS during the second world war.

3148   FRANK, MARTIN M.

Diary of a D.A.   Rine 1959

The author relates the doings of his chief, the Bronx County District Attorney, Charles McLaughlin. The result is a splendid book, which tells of city crime and city justice in the United States. Without hardening the heart, the recital of facts removes illusions and dispels sentimentality about criminals and their chances of reform.

3149   FRIEDMANN, WILLIAM F. and ELIZABETH S.

The Shakespearean Ciphers Examined   Camb 1957

The definitive demonstration by two experts of the nullity of all "mes-sages" found in Shakespeare's text. In the course of their work the reader learns the history of the Shakespeare superstitions as well as the principles of cryptology. The incredible folly of intelligent, learned, and well-to-do people who insist on being the first or only ones to reveal a great secret is sad but important to remember. Beautifully written, researched, and organized.

3150   FURNEAUX, RUPERT

Famous Criminal Cases   5 v., Roy 1955–59
      Illus.

Altogether fifty-four cases briefly summarized. They cover the classic collection, add a few, but do not compare for analytic or literary skill with the narratives elsewhere discussed. At best, this set of books is a beginner's course.

3151   The Medical Murderer   Elek 1957
            Illus.

Though badly written, this volume has value for its concise accounts of murders committed by twenty-two physicians and two nurses. Drs. Palmer, Lamson, Cream, Pritchard, Crippen, and Sheppard are here, as well as numerous Continentals, such as the notorious Dr. Pétiot of France, who scored sixty-three victims. In few if any of the cases is the technique rational: take a good look at your family physician.

3152   GALTON, [SIR] FRANCIS

            Fingerprints   Da Capo 1965; orig. 1892
            Introd. by Dr. Harold Cummins
            Illus.; fingerprints of the author

Historical, descriptive, and classificatory, this is the work that established the practice of fingerprinting on a scientific basis and led to its world-wide diffusion. Galton writes with great skill and makes useful asides and comparisons.

3153   GARDNER, ERLE STANLEY (q.v.), introduced most of his later Perry Mason stories with short essays on the work in criminology or police science of various persons to whom, as friends, he was dedicating the particular tale. Often these short biographical essays contain valuable information about current practice in crime detection and prevention in the United States.

3154   Cops on Campus and Crime on the Streets   Morr 1970

Virtually posthumous, this serious attempt to remind the American people that law-breaking is not a negotiable affair expresses the author's sense of justice and right reason, but is not a notably effective argument. The fault is not lack of knowledge, sympathy, or logic, but inadequate rhetoric and failure to pursue a topic to its conclusion. Nonetheless, the book contains useful information and insights.

3155   The Court of Last Resort   rev. ed. Card 1954/Slo 1952

The prolific and prosperous author of scores of detective and crime stories had for years before his death given time, thought, and money to rescuing the unjustly convicted. This book tells their story and that of their volunteer defenders, who often obtained justice. The critical will be surprised to find how poorly written and badly organized this account is. The recital of cases is frequently not clear, from lack of order and method, and the prose is awkward and heavy. This matters less in itself than as an indication of the difference between writing exposition and writing fiction.
    On real-life detection, read pp. 256–62 of the revised edition.

3156   GAVIN, CLARK

Famous Libel and Slander Cases of History   Col 1962
Orig.: Foul, False, and Infamous (*Schu, 1950*)

Seven cases indifferently told, but worth looking up for the Whistler-Ruskin trial and another version of the card-cheating affair in the presence of the Prince of Wales, later King Edward VII. (See also No. 3314.)

3157   GILBERT, MICHAEL

The Claimant   Const 1957

A history of the Tichborne case by a lawyer who, being also a novelist (q.v.), is deeply interested in the characters of this unbelievable drama. But although M.G. gives less space than his predecessors to the two trials, he treats them from an original point of view and after much independent research into contemporary publications and sentiments.

3158   GLAISTER, JOHN (1856–1932)

Medical Jurisprudence and Toxicology   ESL 1945
8th ed.
Illus.

Scotland has always held a leading place in the subjects treated in this textbook. The present work is in fact a family concern: the first six editions (1902–38) were published by J.G., Sr.; the sixth being edited by J.G., Jr. (b. 1892), since when the text has appeared under the latter's name. As a source, it ranks with the best.

3159   GLAISTER, JOHN, and BRASH, JAMES COUPER

Medico-Legal Aspects of the Ruxton Case   ESL 1937
Illus.

The expounders of forensic medicine at Glasgow write with great expertise and some dry wit about a crime of no inherent complexity that nevertheless required elaborate indirect proof to secure a conviction. Buck Ruxton was a Parsee doctor named originally Hakim, who disposed of his common-law wife and the nursemaid of their three children by dismembering the bodies and transporting the remains to a secluded ravine in Scotland. It was the mutilations designed to prevent identification that actually clinched the identity of the two women. Sir Sydney Smith also took part in the reconstruction of the bodies. See No. 3289.

3160   GODWIN, JOHN

Killers Unknown   HJ 1960

Of these thirteen unsolved cases, two are well known from other treatments—Mrs. Luard (see No. 3068) and Rosemarie (No. 3205). The rest, though possibly remembered from newspaper accounts, have not received much analytic attention. They are the murders of: Anastasia in a New York barbershop (1957); Officer Lundy in Chicago (1932); Shirley Hughes in Melbourne (1953); Father Dakme in Bridgeport, Conn. (1924); the child Georgina Moore (Yalding, 1882); King Ananda of Siam (1946); William Desmond Taylor (Hollywood, 1922); Wilma Montesi, near Rome (1953); James Smith (of the Shark arm case, Sydney, 1936); George Puchert (Frankfurt, 1959); and Serge Rubinstein (New York, 1955). The accounts are a bit on the short side, six of them having been written for the London *Evening News*. But they are lucid and intelligent in conjecture.

See also: *Killers in Paradise* (HJ 1962).

3161   GOLDSTEIN, ABRAHAM S.

The Insanity Defense   YUP 1967

The professor of law at Yale and one time fellow of the Cambridge Institute of Criminology under Radzinowicz (q.v.) summarizes in these brief pages the legal history and the modern critique of what the English now call "diminished responsibility" in crimes of violence. The conclusions offered are tentative and expectant rather than committed to solutions or prophetic of future wisdom.

3162   GOODMAN, JONATHAN

The Killing of Julia Wallace   Harrap 1969
   Foreword by Edgar Lustgarten
   Illus.

Doubtless the murder of Mrs. Wallace has provoked more conjecture than any other case of the present century. James Agate said: "Either the murderer was Wallace or it wasn't. If it wasn't, then here at last is the perfect murder." Mr. Goodman has lavished great care upon his retelling of this Liverpool affair of 1931 when, in the absence of her husband (called away on a fruitless errand devised either by himself or by another), Julia Wallace was brutally bashed to death in her own parlor. Gross incompetence on the part of the police and the medical examiner permitted the bringing to court of a case against William Wallace which only a jury with its mind made up could accept.

The trial before Mr. Justice Wright is well presented in four chapters, and Roland Oliver, counsel for the defense, emerges as a superior talent. Found guilty—after a charge from the judge which practically demanded the reverse finding—Wallace appealed and was freed by a tribunal whose head (Lord Chief Justice Viscount Hewart) was a firm believer in the impeccability of the English jury system.

Mr. Goodman concludes by examining some of the inconsistencies in the Crown case, and refers guardedly to one or two people whose "antecedents and actions on the night of the murder should have been investigated." What really happened remains a mystery. But see Nos. 1848, 3095, and 3280, which include fictional solutions.

3163 GOULD, [LIEUTENANT COMMANDER] RUPERT T.

Oddities   PA 1928
  A Book of Unexplained Facts

Most of these nine cases are attested occurrences that present scientific puzzles or contradictions, and the first two partake of the criminal and detective interest. "The Devil's Hoof-Marks" in Devon defy imagination as they defied investigation. Holmes should have hurried to Paddington. Again, "The Vault at Barbados," in which coffins waltz around, has not been satisfactorily explained. Neither of them is an old wives' tale. The author is a scientist and skeptic with an outstanding gift for exposition and analysis, though rather heavy-handed in his literary allusions.

3164 GRIBBLE, LEONARD

Adventures in Murder   Roy 1955
  [Murder] Undertaken by Notorious Killers in Love
  Illus.

We really do not know whether the killers were in love, or even whether they killed for love, but the nineteen short recitals tell us the essential facts in the lives of unhappy pairs caught in marital or other bonds that they sought to break by murdering. Most of the cases are the familiar ones and the retelling is adequate but no more.

3165 Famous Feats of Detection and Deduction   Dday 1934

This author's titles betray a desire to stretch the appeal beyond what the contents afford. In these eleven cases (four French or Belgian, three English, and four American), the "feats" are often ordinary police work, solid and successful. The best performances are: Goron's in the Bompard case; Berrett / Gutteridge; Heinrich / Schwartz. In addition, the Messiter case at Southampton in 1929 is fresh and interesting.

3166 Murders Most Strange   Long 1959
  Short pref. by the author

The fourteen cases were chosen because of the supposed "strangeness" of the circumstances or characters, which yields a very mixed bag. A few (the multiple murderer Dr. Pétiot, Loeb-Leopold, and James Camb, the porthole man) are well known and better treated elsewhere. Many of the cases are minor—if murder can ever be such—in the sense of not providing much intellectual interest. Nor is there any distinction in the writing, in comparison with Tennyson Jesse, Lustgarten, or Radin.

3167 GROSS, GERALD, ed.

Masterpieces of Murder   LB 1963
  An Edmund Pearson True Crime Reader
  Introd. by Miriam Allen de Ford

It is good to have these twenty or more essays by the late Edmund Pearson (1880–1937) brought together in an accessible volume. From the various *Studies in Murder* and later works the editor has made a selection which includes some of Pearson's most felicitous general reflections on the deadly art, as well as his treatments of the cases of Cream, Crippen, G. J. Smith, Parkman-Webster, and Major Armstrong, among others. Two final chapters present the Pearson-Radin controversy regarding Lizzie Borden (See No. 3263).

GROSS, HANNS (1847–1915)

The Professor of Criminology at the University of Prague is to be credited with helping to give pleasure to millions of readers as well as with helping to convict criminals, both achievements indirect, through the medium of his studies and the books that record them. For it is to them that detectives and writers of detection alike have gone in this century for the technical data relevant to their cases, real and imaginary. Other experts in forensic medicine have of course contributed ideas to the pool of interesting facts held in narrative solution by the masters of the fictional genre, but it is fair to say that Gross has replaced Taylor (q.v.) and outstripped Dixon Mann. Gross's chief works are:

> *Criminal Psychology,* ed. and trans. by Horace M. Kallen, 4th ed. Introd. Joseph Jastrow (1911; orig. 1898). A Manual for judges, practitioners, and students.
> *Criminal Investigation* [as by *Hans,* not Hanns, Gross], ed. and trans. by J. & J. C. Adam (1906); by Norman Kendel (1934); by Ronald Martin Howe (1950/1949), and by Richard Leofric Jackson (5th ed.; 1962).

3168   Criminal Investigation   Sweet 1962
> *A Practical Textbook for Magistrates, Police Officers and Lawyers, Adapted from* System der Kriminalistik *by J. and J. C. Adam; 5th ed. by Richard Leofric Jackson (Asst. Commissioner, CID Scotland Yard)*
> *Illus.*

Readers of this book will readily perceive its influence on contemporary culture, of which the literature and the commonplaces of detection are familiar parts. Such readers may even recognize the factual basis of well-known tales, such as the Case of A.M., which inspired Doyle's "Problem of Thor Bridge" and similar plots by others.

An earlier English editor of the treatise substituted a chapter on "Road Accidents" for the original one on "Steam-boiler explosions," and took out the picturesque chapter on "Wandering Tribes and Superstitions." (It may soon have to be reinstated.) The latest editor has kept the initial arrangement thus modified, but has transferred certain sections to new places, for logic and convenience. The thoughtful reader of detective fiction will note in Chapter 5 the extent to which Freeman's Thorndyke (see Nos. 887/B and 2944) anticipated or paralleled the methods advocated by Gross and his editors, even to the makeup of the "[green] research suitcase" (illus. pp. 76–77).

Note that Gross gives relatively few instances from life compared with his English and Continental colleagues.

3169 GUTTMACHER, MANFRED S.

The Mind of the Murderer   Farr 1960

The author, who is a medical man and psychiatrist, divides murderers into twelve categories, of which only one contains the "normal" killer. He goes on to argue for impartial expert testimony as a means of making these distinctions, which the ordinary jury is scarcely able to arrive at unaided.

3170 HALE, LESLIE

Hanged in Error   Peng 1961

Eleven cases, of which six proved fatal. The accounts are terse and the bearing of the collection obvious.

3171 HAMER, ALVIN C., ed.

Detroit Murders   DS 1948
    Regional Murder Series, ed. Marie F. Rodell, vol. VIII
    Pref. by A.C.H.

Nine true crimes retold by several hands in good style. Interesting sidelights on police methods and psychiatric futility, as well as picturesque characters and events. See also: the Cleveland, Denver, New Orleans, and San Francisco murders (No. 3194).

3172 HAMILTON, PETER

"Industrial Secrets and Crime"
    In: Journal of the Royal Society of Arts (*Feb 1970*)

A cool and circumstantial account of the extensive spying, bribing, and stealing which now form part of industrial operations, and of the methods of detection and prevention thereto applicable. For a brilliant story based on these conditions, see No. 2232.

3173 HAMMETT, DASHIELL

"From the Memoirs of a Private Detective"
    In: The Smart Set (*Mar 1923*); *repr. in No. 2955*

Twenty-nine numbered paragraphs filling three pages and embodying now the writer's experience, now his cynicism. The experience is related flatly, as befits matter of fact; only in the cynicism is there any humor. All in all, very little of this reminiscing about the years with Pinkerton (not mentioned) would suggest the stuff of hard-boiled fiction—or any other. Two of H.'s remarks make the difference clear—one that leaving fingerprints at the scene of the crime is usually safe, since few are sharp enough for identification; the other, that whereas in fiction clues are always scarce, in real life they are overabundant.

3174 HARDY, A(LFRED) (E.) GATHORNE, later Lord Cranbrook (1814–1906)

"The Examination of Prisoners: Emile Gaboriau" *Nat. Rev.* July 1884

This legal light recommends reading Gaboriau as an introduction to French criminal practice and for the "infinite pleasure" the novels afford. Bismarck and Disraeli are cited as enjoying them, too. A.G.H. is properly critical of Gaboriau for his long retrospects explaining the crime and feels that only the detection is lifelike. He stresses the fact that Lecoq's master, Père Tabaret, was an amateur, and he discusses *The Widow Lerouge, File 113,* and *The Orcival Crime,* arguing for better English legislation on the admissibility of evidence, a better staff for the DPP, and the instituting of a quasi-French examination of suspects.

3175   HARRISON, RICHARD

       Criminal Calendar   Jarr 1951

Short accounts of real crimes by an English reporter and fiction writer. About half are familiar stuff, but the author gives special attention to clues. A 40-page Glossary gives short definitions of laws and facts governing the concomitants of crime—everything from Accomplices and Bloodstains to Transport and ultra-violet light. Not technical but sensible.

3176   Criminal Calendar II   Jarr 1952

The fate of sequels is well known, though occasionally averted. Not so here. All but one of the cases are too short to engage the mind. The long one, "The Case of the Safes," formless as its retelling is, arouses interest by the odd details and actions in the pursuit of a gang that had keys to many P.O. and business safes. "The Case of Mrs. Weatherall" is also remarkable for its probable explanation, which is the unknown man's act of homicide in self-defense against his partner's violence during sexual climax.

3177   HASSARD, ALBERT R.

       Not Guilty and Other Trials   Lee 1926

The author, who is a BCL and has also written *Famous Canadian Trials,* has followed up his earlier effort with accounts of ten more criminal cases of Canadian origin, dating from the early nineteenth to the early twentieth century. There is some horror and a little detection, but most of the wonder for today's reader lies in the author's uncanny choice of the wrong or pretentious word and the inept cliché.

3178   HASTINGS, SIR PATRICK

       Cases in Court   Hein 1949

The suave autobiography of a latter-day-style advocate. His life was not all murder, but slander, fraud, breach of promise, and blackmail; and then the case of the blazing car, that of Mrs. Barney, of Vaquier, and others. For exemplary "fornification" one can recommend the case of the three sisters and the septuagenarian. Subtle narrative and good English throughout.

3179   HECHT, BEN

Gaily, Gaily   Signet (Dday) 1963
   Illus. from the film

The first six chapters out of nine deal with the author's recollections as a crime reporter in Chicago before the first world war. He gives vivid but very short accounts of a number of murders and murderers, with the aid of diaries he kept at the time. How accurate this rewriting is does not appear from casual reading, but the book is entertaining.

3180   HENDERSON, WILLIAM

Clues; or, Leaves from a
Chief Constable's Notebook   2d ed. OAF 1889

The chief constable of Leeds and later of Edinburgh tells with rather hazy detail and a good deal of complacency the stories of some of his triumphs as detective inspector in the seventies and eighties. More interest attaches to the manners of the time than to the crimes or their detection. Such books as this, incidentally, were numerous in the latter part of the nineteenth century—and not all were authentic.

3181   HEPPENSTALL, RAINER

French Crime in the Romantic Age   HH 1970

The widely read author of *A Little Pattern of French Crime* (during *la belle époque,* 1969) goes back in the present book to the period when crime as a theme began to attract the highest literary talent, and for reasons other than the merely picturesque. Stendhal, Hugo, Balzac, and other French masters are brought into this entrancing and consecutive discussion of the cases of Praslin, Lacenaire, Fieschi, Hélène Jegado, and the men involved in the affair of Lyons Mail (see No. 3249).

3182   HOLMES, PAUL

The Sheppard Murder Case   McK 1961
   Pref. by Erle Stanley Gardner

A sharp and breezy report on the deplorable handling, by the newspapers and the authorities, of the trial of Dr. Samuel H. Sheppard. The facts remain puzzling, but there is no doubt that the accused did not receive a fair trial. He was retried and released in 1967, married a second and a third time, and died in 1970.

3183   HOPKINS, R. THURSTON

Famous Bank Forgeries, Robberies, and Swindles   SP 1936
   Photographs

No book could hope to exhaust this topic, so full of instances on both sides of the appealing enterprise. But the fifteen chapters of this work cover a good bit of ground rapidly, though without much distinction of style.

3184   HOUTS, MARSHALL

Where Death Delights   CM 1967
The Story of Dr. Milton Helpern and Forensic Medicine
Illus.

That Dr. Helpern, Chief Medical Examiner of the City of New York, knows more about violent death than anyone else in the world was once affirmed by the *New York Times,* and any reader who samples this crowded, ill-organized book will be likely to agree. He will not derive much pleasure, but his imagination may be stimulated by the frequent allusions to the work of the Warren Commission. Dr. Helpern was not consulted after President Kennedy's assassination; one wonders why.

3185   HUMPHREYS, CHRISTMAS

The Great Pearl Robbery of 1913   Hein 1929
Foreword by Justice Travers Humphreys
Illus.

A true plot, full of ingenuity and suspense, mixed with high comedy and a series of attested but incredible facts. Well told by a barrister who is the son of the famous judge who has written the Foreword.

3186   "How the Modern Detective Gets His Man"   *List* Apr 27, 1950

A broadcast on the Home Service of the BBC by the distinguished advocate, son of the distinguished judge, on the techniques of scientific detection, apropos of the issuing of the fourth edition of Hanns Gross (q.v.), (ed. Ronald Howe). The talk in fact is a plug for buying the book "with 80 illustrations," but it is in itself informative and entertaining for the man in the street who is simultaneously listening to the Home Service.

3187   HUMPHREYS, TRAVERS

Criminal Days   H&S 1946
Illus.

An urbane autobiography, composed largely of recollections of criminal defenses and prosecutions. Note especially the reflections on Crippen and Seddon, on a miscarriage of justice, and on the cases of Sir Roger Casement and Horatio Bottomley.

3188   HYDE, H. MONTGOMERY

Trial of Roger Casement   rev. ed. Peng 1964/ Hodge 1960
Illus.

The trial and execution of Casement for treason, after a distinguished career in the British Civil Service, form one of the most heart-rending episodes of twentieth-century history, and one's sense of a grievous misclassification of Casement's undoubted deed is made worse by the recrimination over the diaries, an extract from which is added to the revised edition of this workmanlike report.

3189   The Trials of Oscar Wilde   Hodge 1948
       Foreword by Sir Travers Humphreys, PC
       NBT
       Illus.

The editor's 92-page Introduction is excellent and goes far to establish
the mood and sensibilities of that far-off 1895 when the unfortunate Oscar
appeared three times in court, first as plaintiff in the trial of *Reg.* v.
Queensberry. Wilde had had the sporting Marquess arrested on a charge
of criminal libel, but soon found the tables turned, first in *Reg.* v. *Wilde
and Taylor,* on April 26, and later (after release on bail May 7) on May
20 in his separate trial on the same charges as those preferred earlier,
namely numerous counts of having committed ". . . acts of gross in-
decency with another male person . . . against the form of the statute
in such case made and provided and against the peace of our said Lady
the Queen her Crown and dignity."
    This is a magnificent volume, in which the reader will find many things
to repay his attention, from the judge's comment that 16 shillings for
"chicken and salad for two" at the Savoy is very high, to the evidence
of Wilde's misplaced courage in staying in England to face his tor-
mentors when he could easily have fled.

3190   United in Crime   Roy 1955

An M.P. and miscellaneous historian, Hyde does not give the impression
of a strong or exact mind. He writes agreeably enough (and sometimes
sloppily) of the cases fought by Sir Travers Humphreys, Patrick Hastings,
and Lord Simon, as well as of numerous aspects of the criminal law in
England (see "The Case Against Flogging"). His short chapters appeared
first in several London newspapers.
    The title is a quotation from Voltaire.

3191   IRVING, H(ENRY) (B(RODRIBB) (1870–1919)

       A Book of Remarkable Criminals   Doran 1918 ·

Ten peculiarly repulsive murderers, grouped by kind, form the subject of
these analyses. The author was the son of the great actor and himself began
on the stage. He is good on detail, for he is abundant in knowledge, and
he philosophizes swiftly and well. Note in particular his treatment of
Dr. Parkman and H. H. Holmes.

3192   Studies of French Criminals of the
       Nineteenth Century   Hein 1901

These sixteen cases range from murder for lust and theft to assassination
and private murder for antisocial and philosophic reasons. They are ably
told and commented on, with full references to trial transcripts and many
quotations from letters, reported dialogue, and other documents. The culprits' names are: Lacenaire; Troppmann; Barré and Lebiez; the Abbés
Auriol, Boudes, and Bruneau; Campi; Pranzini; Prado; Mme Weiss; Albert

Pel; Euphrasie Mercier; Ravachol; Vaillant; Emile Henry; and Henri Charles.

3193 JACKSON, JOSEPH HENRY, ed.

The Portable Murder Book   VP 1945
Introd. by the editor

Ranging over the U.S., the British Isles, and Continental Europe, these eighteen cases of murder are discussed by as many different critics, some famous and nearly all highly competent. Highlights are: The Man Who Was Too Clever (Frederick Small of Massachusetts) by Edmund Pearson / Belle of Indiana (Belle Gunness) by Stewart Holbrook / The Master of the Murder Castle (H. H. Holmes of Chicago) by John B. Martin / Poison in the Pantry (Dr. Pritchard) by William Roughead / Constance Kent by John Rhode / The Murder of Julia Wallace by Dorothy Sayers / The Philanthropy of Fritz Haarman by William Bolitho.

3194 JACKSON, JOSEPH HENRY, and OFFORD, LENORE GLEN

The Girl in the Belfry   GM 1957
Gold Medal Series of Classic Murder Trials

As if made up to catch the twentieth-century taste, this true crime of 1895 "presents" a beautiful nude girl in a church belfry and a villain (or fiend) in the shape of a Sunday-school superintendent. Excellent retelling by these colleagues on the *San Francisco Chronicle,* whose interest in crime and in the region is matched by literary competence.

3195 JENKINS, ROY

Victorian Scandal   Chil 1965

Of perhaps greater interest to JB than to WHT, this is nonetheless an engrossing account by a recent Chancellor of the Exchequer of the decline and fall from power of Sir Charles Dilke when on the point of succeeding Gladstone in 1885. D. was named co-respondent in the divorce proceedings instituted by Donald Crawford against his wife. Evidence given in the two subsequent hearings leads one to believe that Dilke—although found guilty—was actually innocent of the particular charges preferred. It is also likely that he was guilty of similar offenses otherwise, though not necessarily of "trio sex" as testified to in the present case.

3196 JESSE, F. TENNYSON

Murder and Its Motives   rev. ed. Harrap 1958/1924

The 51-page introduction surveys the field thoroughly if not compactly, and is followed by well-chosen case studies: Murder for Gain (Palmer), for Revenge (Constance Kent), for Elimination (the Quérangals), for Jealousy (Mrs. Pearcey), for Lust of Killing (Neill Cream), and from Political Conviction (Orsini). The author shows her mastery throughout this pioneer work. She incidentally coined the word *murderee* and the idea of unconscious cooperation that goes with it.

3197   Trial of Madeleine Smith   rev. ed. Hodge 1927
          NBT; orig. ed. by Duncan Smith (1905)
          Illus.

The fearsome damsel who got rid of her lover, presumably with well-seasoned cocoa, is the interesting feature of the case. Her outspoken letters in the Appendix show that sex was not invented by advertisers in the twentieth century. Miss Jesse has made fluent and modern the solid work of her predecessor.

3198   Jesse, ed.

          The Trials of Timothy John Evans and
          John Reginald Halliday Christie   Hodge 1957
          NBT
          Illus.

Whether Evans was a principal or only an accessory in the murder of his wife and little daughter in a squalid London flat in 1949 cannot be said to have been established, although he was executed for the crimes. The discovery, four years later, that his co-tenant Christie was a multiple murderer (self-confessed) threw grave doubt on what Evans had actually done, and was an important factor in the then current campaign for the abolition of capital punishment in Britain. Yet to this day, judging from letters to the press, many English people think that Evans was guilty of at least one killing.

3199   Joyce, James Avery

          Capital Punishment   Nels 1961

A strong plea for abolishing the death penalty. Much of the argument rests on the practices now in force, rather than on ultimate principles, though a deceptive appearance of philosophy is given by relating life and death to the threat of nuclear weapons and the aims of the United Nations.

3200   Justice at Work   rev. ed. Pan 1957/C&H 1952

A well-composed account of "The Human Side of the Law," concentrating of course on English law and treating it historically and actually in all its divisions, from murder to motoring offenses and from the handicaps of the poor to the salaries of judges. At times the author reveals himself as something of a brute, which is not incompatible with opposing capital punishment and the law as now administered.

3201   Kennedy, Ludovic

          Ten Rillington Place   S&S 1961

The facts of the ghastly Evans-Christie massacre at the address given above. The author is careful and reasonably calm and complete, but although one does not suspect any factual inadequacy, there remains a sense of insufficiency on the social and moral plane. It is only fair to add that this may be due to the nature of the case and not to the work of the author.

3202   KILGALLEN, DOROTHY [Mrs. Richard Kollmar]

Murder One   RH 1967

The well-known crime reporter who died in 1965 did not complete as she wished her account of the Sheppard case, which is one of the half dozen here treated in a perceptive though breezy fashion. The others are: the wife-killing by Dr. Finch and Carol Tregoff; the lover-killing by Greta Peltz; the killing of Harry Wright for which Eva Coo was executed, perhaps unjustly; the murder of Ada Appelgate by Mary Creighton and Everett Appelgate; and the Sheppard case. The accounts are full, well organized, and stuffed with extracts from the trial records.

3203   KNOTT, GEORGE H., ed.

Trial of William Palmer   Hodge 1952/1912
   NBT
   Rev. ed. by Eric R. Watson
   Illus.

One of the greatest of English trials, in which the ill-developed toxicology of the day had to expose a villain who "prepared" his victim with antimony and finished him off with strychnine. Palmer, a physician long dedicated to horse-racing, had by 1855 found it a losing game; it led to forgery and eventually to the murder of John Parsons Cook, his racing associate. The trial, before Lord Chief Justice Campbell in May 1856, required twelve days. Palmer was executed on June 14.

3204   KORGANOFF, ALEXANDRE

Le Mystère de Scapa Flow   B. Arthaud 1969

This latest book on the sea mystery that rivals the *Mary Celeste* for inexplicability and variety of solutions takes no dogmatic view, but inclines toward the opinion that the second British vessel hit in Scapa Flow when the *Royal Oak* was sunk by a German submarine raider on October 13, 1939, was *The Iron Duke*. Yet the official British statement, reiterated in August 1969, asserts that no "second vessel" was there or was hit, though eyewitnesses saw it, as well as the column of water that marked the impact of the torpedo. Despite his use of fictional devices here and there, the author gives abundant proofs of competence and objectivity, which preceding writers on this mystery rarely do.

   See also Günther Prien, *I Sank the Royal Oak* (1954) and Malcolm Brown and Patricia Mechan, *Scapa Flow* (Peng 1968).

3205   KUBY, ERICH

Rosemarie   Knopf 1960
   Trans. from the German by R. C. P. Muller

Though disliked by WHT, this book is nevertheless a valuable account of high-class prostitution ending in murder in postwar Germany. The psychological explanations are sound, and the mixture of big industry, fornication, spying, gangsterism, and fashionable life is extremely well described by a man with both moral and philosophical principles.

Note that Rosemarie Nitribitt's slayer was acquitted in 1960.

3206 KUNSTLER, WILLIAM M.

The Minister and the Choir Singer   Morr 1964
    Illus.

Writing forty years after the event, the author has done a reasonably good job of presenting the known facts of the Hall-Mills murder of September 1922. But the case remains as unsatisfactory now as it was during the four years when it was dragging through the New Jersey courts, to end with the acquittal of the three defendants. The author's own solution of the mystery is both plausible and logical, even if a bit startling.

For a fictional treatment, see No. 2.

3207 LANG, ANDREW

Historical Mysteries   SE 1901
    Portrait of Elizabeth Canning

Fourteen splendid essays on famous or obscure affairs, ranging from The Queen's Necklace and Elizabeth Canning's disappearance to the identity of The Chevalier d'Eon and the incredible conspiracy of the Gowries. Lang writes a bit more spiritedly than is common today, and that is all to the good.

3208 The Library   2d ed. Macm 1892/1881
    Chapter on Book Illustration, by Austin Dobson

Contains an account of the murder committed by the monk Don Vincente in 1836 for possession of a book. Flaubert as a youth made it the subject of a tale (see No. 2503). Lang's account, p. 54 ff., differs somewhat from Flaubert's, but the discrepancy may lie in the original sources, rather than in novelist's license.

3209 LANG, GORDON

Mr. Justice Avory   HJ 1935

A halfway satisfactory book about the severe but just man who is probably the model of D. Sayers' judge in *Strong Poison* ("a beast but a just beast."). The author of this pseudo biography is an M.P. like Montgomery Hyde, and like him writes naïve reflections in poor English, but his narrative is good. Of chief interest are his summaries of the following cases: Jabez Balfour, Adolf Beck (with a full reproduction of Avory's examination during the subsequent inquiry), the London Detectives (see No. 3131), Field and Gray, Allaway, Patrick Mahon, Vaquier, Browne and Kennedy, Edward Hopwood, "Stella Maris," Alien Property Fraud,

Clarence Hatry, and Lord Alfred Douglas' libel of Winston Churchill. There is also a good account of Assizes and the judge's gowns.

3210   LANGFORD, GERALD

The Murder of Stanford White   BM 1962
   Illus.

As a murder case, not interesting, despite the prominence of the persons involved. Harry Thaw's shooting of White on June 25, 1906, in the old Madison Square roof garden, was in the presence of many witnesses, and the question disputed in both of the first two trials was that of Thaw's sanity. Sentenced to Matteawan after the second trial, Thaw eventually escaped and even regained his legal freedom, but his recorded actions in later years will leave few readers in doubt of his mental imbalance. One thing not in doubt is that Thaw's young wife, Evelyn (whom White had "ruined" before her marriage), was an extremely beautiful, if devious, girl.

3211   LAURENCE, JOHN

A History of Capital Punishment   Samp [c. 1935]

Not an argument for or against, but an historical review of methods and attitudes since Roman times, with special attention to English facts, by the author of four books on true crime. He writes with a pleasing subacidity and an evident knowledge of sources.

3212   LE QUEUX, WILLIAM

Landru: His Secret Love Affairs   SP 1922
   Frontispiece photo of the author helping the French police

The double-barreled title tells what the book is about; detection is hardly the word for the way in which these tedious and murderous wooings came to light. And as a narrative of true crime, the sequence lacks impetus and form.

3213   LINCOLN, VICTORIA

A Private Disgrace   Putn 1967
   Lizzie Borden by Daylight
   Three plans of Borden house and yard

The author claims "forgotten evidence" but praises Pearson and omits Radin; her recital, somewhat garrulous, uses twisty sentences in which she asserts proprietary claims to New England: "I was born an insider. My family had lived in Bristol County for 300 years marrying neighbors," etc. She condescends to Lizzie's "little world," and displays her own knowledge of medicine and psychology—e.g., that migraine and epilepsy are related by "a genetic bond." She pictures Lizzie as living in fantasy and maintains that she killed her stepmother from hate, and then her father to hide the deed.

3214 LITTNER, NER

"A Psychiatrist Looks at Television Violence"
   In: Northwestern University Television Symposium (*Spring 1969*)

A good exposition of the arguments pro and con in the debate whether TV violence leads to actual violence. The author makes useful distinctions and sets forth very ably the "trigger hypothesis" about viewing violence, but he neglects the influence of visual repetition on the sensibility and the effect on the unimaginative of demonstrating all the tricks of the torturer's trade.

3215 LOCARD, EDMOND

   Manuel de technique policière   Payot 1939
   3rd ed. rev.
   Illus.

This work is a short course introductory to the author's seven-volume treatise on the same subject (see below). He was for years head of the police laboratory at Lyon, a great researcher and writer, and the counterpart of Hanns Gross (q.v.). He divides his subject into twelve parts, of which the principal are: Fingerprints, Other Clues and Traces, Written Documents, Secret Writing, Counterfeiting, Firearms and Other Weapons, Drugs, Identifying Recidivists, Identifying Animals, Using Experts. There are no case histories.

The writing and organization of topics are superbly clear. The illustrations, incidentally, show how absurd it is for a fictional detective to wrap up the knife or glass in his handkerchief and expect it to retain fingermarks.

3216 LOCARD. See also:

   Policiers de roman et policiers de laboratoire   Payot 1924
   L'enquête criminelle et les méthodes scientifiques   Flammarion 1920
   Contes apaches   2 v., Ed. Lugdunum (Lyon) 1933
   La Criminalistique   Desvigne (Lyon) 1937
   La malle sanglante de Millery   Gallimard 1935
   Traité de criminalistique   7 v., Desvigne (Lyon) 1931–39

3217 LOCKHART, R. H. BRUCE

   British Agent   Putn 1933/1932

Reminiscences of espionage in Bolshevik Russia, fit to put beside Paul Dukes' (q.v.). The events form a thriller whose mood and contents show that nothing much was new in the comparable incidents of the cold war twenty-five years later: exchanges, threats, hairbreadth escapes, and the same incoherent and immature diplomacy.

3218 LOGAN, GUY B. H.

Guilty or Not Guilty?   Duff 1929
    Illus.

The author has elected to tell the stories of "Celebrated Crimes" of which
he feels that ". . . the secret still eludes us." Most are little-known,
though a couple are famous. Included are:

1. The murder of Mary Ashford (Warwickshire 1817)
2. The murder of Mrs. Candler (Yarmouth 1844)
3. The assumed murder of Rose Harsent (Suffolk 1902)
4. The acquittal of Edmund Pook in the murder of Jane Clousen (Kent 1879)
5. The murder of John Nesbit in a railway compartment (nr. Newcastle 1910)
6. The motiveless murder of George Storrs (Gorse Hall, Cheshire 1909)
7. The case of Willie Starchfield (North London train, 1914)
8. The murder of Mrs. Reville (Slough 1881)
9. The murder of Jessie M'Pherson (Glasgow 1862 at Sandyford Place, in
   which the old but not venerable James Fleming was a confused witness)
10. The murder of William Bradbury and his son (Moorcock Inn, Yorkshire
    1832)
11. The disappearance of Urban Stanger (London 1881)
12. Miscellaneous mysterious Murders of Women
13. The Gutteridge Case (Essex 1927)
14. The murderers Voirbo, Mullins, and Maynard

Of these only Nos. 3, 6, 9, and 13 are adequately treated elsewhere. Mr.
Logan writes well, sketches in essential background, and avoids the sameness that afflicts most omnibus volumes of this type.
    For fictional accounts of No. 3, see Nos. 2223 and 2473.

3219 LONDRES, ALBERT (d. 1932)

The Road to Buenos Ayres   BR 1931; orig. Const 1928
    Trans. by Eric Sutton
    Introd. by Theodore Dreiser

An extraordinary mixture of fictional realism and quiet social comment,
which makes the traffic in women all the more hideous for expressing no
indignation. The mood of the complying victim, which goes with so many
modern crimes, is admirably rendered by the author, who continued to
specialize in social history. This work influenced Connington (see No.
589) and perhaps Armstrong as well (No. 69).

3220 LOOMIS, STANLEY

A Crime of Passion   Lipp 1967
    Two plans of indoor premises

A detailed and well-researched account of the murder in 1847 of Fanny,
Duchesse de Praslin, by her husband; a performance so clumsy that the
first policeman to view the scene said at once that it was not the work of
a professional and surely "the act of a gentleman." The many open
questions are commendably dealt with in the spirit of detection, which

includes an examination of the objects still kept at the *Archives Nationales* in Paris. The social and artistic commentary is conscientious rather than perceptive, but the main story is well told and worth the modern reader's attention.

3221 LUSTGARTEN, EDGAR

Defender's Triumph   Wing 1951

Detailed accounts of four murder trials in which the plaintiff was acquitted as the result of expert advocacy.

Edward Clarke defends Adelaide Bartlett (1886; poisoning by chloroform; interesting comparison with the Maybrick case)
Marshall Hall defends Robert Wood (1907; Camden Town murder of a prostitute)
Patrick Hastings defends Elvira Barney (1932; Mayfair society murder)
Norman Birkett defends Tony Mancini (1933; the first of the Brighton Trunk Murders)

3222 The Murder and the Trial   Scrib 1958
      Introd. by Anthony Boucher

The seventeen criminal cases here assembled form about half of Lustgarten's essays in the true-crime genre. They are of uneven length and merit; a few were originally BBC broadcasts. The best of the longer essays cover the cases of Edith Thompson and Frederick Bywaters (1922); William Wallace (1931); Norman Thorne (1924; with Spilsbury featured as prosecution witness); Robert Wood (1907; the Camden Town Case); and perhaps most thorough of all, the trial of Adelaide Bartlett in 1886 on the charge of killing her ailing husband with chloroform. She was acquitted for a good reason that has left the unanswered question: how does one force chloroform down a patient's throat?

3223 Prisoner at the Bar   AD 1952

A series of BBC talks-with-dialogue on six cases, including William Wallace, Seddon, and Steinie Morrison. A *leetle* primitive, owing to the intended audience, which was the Light and Home programs, not the Third. None of the verdicts here are "in dispute."
   For a fuller treatment of some of these cases by the same expert, see No. 3224.

3224 Verdict in Dispute   Scrib 1949

A British pro at the game retells the uncertainties attending the trials of Florence Maybrick (1889), Steinie Morrison (1911), Norman Thorne (1925), Edith Thompson (1922), William Wallace (1931), and Lizzie Borden (1892). An appendix discusses the adroit questioning of the maid Bridget by Governor Robinson in the Borden case (see No. 3315). The author evidently thinks this part of any trial decisive.

3225 MacClure, Victor

She Stands Accused   Harrap 1935
    Dedic. to Rafael Sabatini
    Introd. and Illus. by the author

Seven cases: Jean Livingston (Kincaid), who murdered her husband in
1600, with some words about Mary Norwood (1765); the Countess of
Essex and Anne Turner (1610); Sarah Malcolm, the murder of Mrs.
Duncomb et al. (1733); Sophie Dawes, Baronne de Feuchères, putative
murderer of the Prince de Condé (1830); Hélène Jegado, poisoner (1851);
Mmes Boursier and Lacoste (1823 and 1844).

The Malcolm-Duncomb affair is presented most interestingly as a piece
of detection.

3226 MacGregor, Geddes

The Tichborne Impostor   Lipp 1957
    Illus.

The unbelievable element in this piece of English history is the belief of
thousands of people in the impostor and the length of the trials, which
ended his claims but not the faith of his followers. This brilliant and concise reconstruction of the consecutive actions (1867 to 1874) gives a clear
sense of the relative weight assigned by the Victorians to legal and to
scientific evidence of identity. Several interesting points are the result of
fresh research.

The author is an authority on religious thought and it may be that the
drama of greed, stupidity, and lying shown in this case reminded him of
much that is recorded in the scriptures of all nations.

3227 MacLaurin, C(harles) (b. 1872)

Post Mortem   Cape 1923
    Essays Historical and Medical
    Illus.

The lecturer in surgery at the University of Sydney treats in a detective
spirit such figures as Anne Boleyn, Joan of Arc, Marat, Don John of
Austria, and Napoleon. An excellent collection, which went through five
impressions in one year. By request he wrote *Mere Mortals* (Cape 1925)
and the two volumes were joined as *De Mortuis* (1930).

3228 Maeckel, O. V.

The Dunkelgraf Mystery   Hutch n.d. [1928?]
    With the collaboration of Mrs. Aubrey LeBlond
    Illus.

An historical enigma about a mysterious pair, man and woman, of whom
the man was certainly Dutch and the woman probably of royal birth.
They retired together from the normal world and achieved nearly total
seclusion between 1807 and 1845. The unknown motive seems to have

been political, that is, to protect the "princess" from reprisals. Equally unknown are the personal relations of the two before and during this retreat. The authors do a great deal in a detective way with the scant sources, and the writing is agreeably terse.

3229 MANN, J(OHN) DIXON

Forensic Medicine and Toxicology   6th ed. Griff 1922; orig 1893
    6th ed. rev. by William A. Brend

This is the useful and respectable work that many writers of crime fiction relied upon for inspiration and clever clueing in the Early Golden Age—say up to 1929. After that the more formidable (because Germanic) authority of Hanns Gross (q.v.) superseded D.M., while all along the authors born and bred north of Hadrian's wall stuck patriotically to John Glaister (q.v.). Only R. Austin Freeman and J. J. Connington, it seems, remembered old Taylor (q.v.).

3230 MANNING, EMMERSON W.

Practical Instruction for Detectives   Drake 1921
    A Complete Course in Secret Service Study

Unintentionally amusing and useless as instruction. It has been kept by the collaborators for its inspired remark about the gun "whose calibre should be gone into."

3231 MARJORIBANKS, EDWARD, M. P.

The Life of Sir Edward Marshall Hall   Goll 1929
    Introd. by Lord Birkhenhead

A biography of the first order about a legendary defender of candidates for the rope. The cases—most of them among the best known of this century —are retold in great detail and Marshall Hall's detective genius fully shown. The biographer committed suicide from overwork four years after publishing the book.

3232 MARTIENSEN, ANTHONY

Crime and the Police   S&W 1953
    Pref. by R. M. Howe
    Illus.

A good supplement to Harold Scott's *Scotland Yard* (q.v.) in that it covers the whole of Britain and discusses variations in police strength, attitude, and methods. Agreeably written and all quite clear except for a singular reference to "the marmoreal of a woman's breast."

3233 MASON, A. E. W.

"Mata Hari," in Dilemmas   H&S 1934

See No. 2652 for a full entry on the volume. The note at the end is on the supposed leading female spy of the first world war.

3234   MASTERS, R. E. L., and LEA, EDUARD

Sex Crimes in History   Matr 1966; orig. 1963
   Orig.: Perverse Crimes in History
   Appendix: Historical Survey of Sexual Savagery in the East,
   by Allen Edwardes
   Introd. by John Holland Cassity, M.D.

Discussions of sadism, vampirism, necrophilia, and other pastimes, laced
with references to well-known criminal practitioners and with miscellaneous information about ancient Rome, the East, and the literary use of
perversion from de Sade onward. Not altogether scholarly or satisfying,
but serious in intention and fully illustrative of its libertarian thesis. The
range is roughly Gille de Rais to Jack the Ripper.

3235   MAUGHAM, [VISCOUNT] FREDERIC HERBERT

   "The Problem of Judicial Proof"   Holdworth Club, Univ. of
                                        Birmingham March 3, 1939

The Presidential Address by the Lord Chancellor excludes questions of
logic and philosophy and deals with the practical meaning of its title: "the
law does not insist on certainty in a strict sense, but is content with what
may be termed, perhaps not very accurately, a moral certainty" (p. 3).
He stresses the importance only recently attached to the *corpus delicti*
—proof of the fact that the crime alleged has been committed. (He refers
to the Campden mystery; see No. 3068.) The idea of a fair trial does not
go back much farther than to the sixteenth century, and that of the
admissibility of evidence to the seventeenth. About the competency of
witnesses, the point is made that since the Criminal Evidence Act of 1898,
not only may the accused testify in his own behalf, but his or her spouse
may also be called if the defendant wishes.

3236   The Tichborne Case   H&S 1936
   Illus.

The classic study, embracing all the varied elements—psychological, social, legal, and circumstantial—of this extraordinary case of imposture
and popular gullibility. Admirably composed and pellucid.

3237   MAXWELL, SIR HERBERT

   Inter Alia   Macl 1924
   A Scottish Calendar of Crime and Other Historical Essays

The friend of Andrew Lang discusses crime and punishment in Scotland
in the sixteenth and seventeenth centuries and goes on to "The Casket Letters"—an aspect of the story of Mary Stuart. The Gowrie conspiracy and
other famous murders and mysteries are taken up with judgment and
knowledge and set forth in a quiet conversational style.

My Fifteen Lost Years   F&W 1905
Mrs. Maybrick's Own Story
Illus.

The author was tried in 1889 for the murder of her husband by arsenic
and was found guilty. The trial, in Liverpool under Justice Fitz-James
Stephen, was marred by conflicting evidence and gross misdirection of
the jury. The verdict immediately called forth some 5,000 petitions for
the prisoner's reprieve, with upwards of half a million signers. As a consequence Mrs. Maybrick's sentence was commuted to life imprisonment,
and although almost constant efforts were made to have her case reviewed
she was not released until 1904.

Mrs. Maybrick writes clearly and without excessive emotion. The
best parts of the book are those dealing with prison life for women in late
Victorian England. Grim though the recital is, Mrs. M. recognizes such
attempts at humanization as were then being made.

3239 MELVILLE, LEWIS, ed.

Trial of the Duchess of Kingston   Hodge 1927
NBT
Illus.

Elisabeth Chudleigh (1720?–88) was a remarkable woman, an opportunist of the first order, who, while Maid of Honor to the consort of
the Prince of Wales, not only married Augustus John Hervey (later Earl
of Bristol) and had a son by him, but also contracted marriage in 1769
with the Duke of Kingston. Notwithstanding a flamboyant career in England and on the Continent, the lady was brought to book in 1776 and
tried for bigamy. She was found guilty but discharged after she had
claimed "benefit of peerage." She cut a wide swath in Russia and elsewhere
for the next twelve years. The trial itself is not of much interest today.

3240 MINOT, GEORGE E.

Murder Will Out   Marsh 1928
Pref. by Philip Hale

Originally published in the *Boston Herald*, these twenty-nine cases make
good reading, though they are short and do not pretend to philosophize
or even to discuss law and evidence. They include: Dr. Buchanan,
H. H. Holmes, Leo Frank, and a good selection of the less rehashed New
England affairs. The Preface by the well-known music critic justly praises
the narrator for the direct style in which he straightens out the tangled
web of life.

3241 MOORE, DAN TYLER, and WALLER, MARTHA

Cloak and Cipher   Harrap 1965; orig. 1962

A miscellaneous and discursive work about cryptography and the murders
or mysteries linked with its use. The chapters, rarely more than 8 pages

long, skip about the historical scene to garner anecdotes or plunge into the how-to of decipherment. Entertaining only for the most casual reader; the work is written in pretty poor Americanese.

3242   MORLAND, NIGEL

   An Outline of Scientific Criminology   Cass 1950
      Illus.

Short and very elementary. The photographs rather naïvely show the study of documents by various means but all the samples are in the same childish handwriting. The main headings are: Fingerprints, Identification, Ballistics, Medical Jurisprudence, Forensic Chemistry, Documentary Evidence, Cryptography, and The Use of Microscope and Camera. Few or no case histories; good bibliographies.

3243   This Friendless Lady   FM 1957
      Illus.

A competent account of the Maybrick poisoning case, with good illustrations and an amazing list of the medicine and other bottles (numbering about 200) found by the police when the Maybrick house was searched. Evidently life in Liverpool in 1889 was a liverish business.

3244   NEW ERA. See No. 2681 for this periodical, produced by the inmates of Leavenworth Federal Penitentiary. It contains confessions and discussions of crime, as well as fiction, and is being reissued after a two-year lapse. The first number of the new series is dated Autumn 1970.

3245   NOTABLE BRITISH TRIALS

A series originally composed of Notable Scottish and Notable English Trials, most titles published in the period 1900 to 1920 by William Hodge of Edinburgh. By now the joint series numbers almost 100 titles. Some have been revised, but generally the current volumes are photo-offset reproductions on thinner paper. Not to be confused with Famous Criminal Trials or Old Bailey Trials series, the volumes under review are based on the trial record, contemporary newspaper reports, legal, medical, and historical data. The literary quality is uniformly high. The range is from Mary Queen of Scots (1586) to the present.

3246   O'DONNELL, ELLIOTT

   Great Thames Mysteries   S&B 1929/1928

The narrator of *Fatal Kisses* (e.g., "The Beautiful Nuzzly") and other historical calamities has brought together in lucid fashion a large number of crimes and other unexplained occurrences related to The River and its tributaries near London. Good though not elegant reading, it successfully straddles the unexplained and the inexplicable. Names, places, and persons are picturesque without effort on the author's part (e.g., Mrs. Overy, the prostitute), and some of the facts are of general import. It has been forgotten, for example, that during the years of Jack the Ripper's activities, another craftsman was at work close by who dismembered four women, also presumable prostitutes. But perhaps it was a stylistic variation and not another operator.

3247   Strange Disappearances   DM 1928

Thirteen historical mysteries, including a good short retelling of the Dunkelgraf enigma (q.v.) under the title of "Mysteries of Eishausen." The other dozen are equally out of the common, and among them those of greatest interest are the cases of: Mlle de Béthune, Benjamin Bathurst, Martin Guerre, Jean Petit, the Rev. Benjamin Speke, and Urban Napoleon Stanger.

3248   OLD BAILEY TRIAL SERIES,   Jarr 1944 ff.
       C(ARL) E(RIC) BECHHOFER ROBERTS, gen. ed.
       Illus.

These attractive volumes are all too few and hard to find. The editor was a barrister and a journalist, who specialized also in Russian affairs. With George Goodchild (q.v.), he wrote an excellent fictional account of the Jessie M'Lachlan case (The Sandyford Mystery) under the title of *The Dear Old Gentleman* (MRS 1954; orig. 1930). A good example of his competence may be seen in No. 3270, which is the kind of uncommon affair preferred for this series and not likely to be taken up by NBT. Note especially: *Mrs. Duncan, Jones and Hulten,* and *William Joyce.*

   The series should not be confused with Bernard O'Donnell's history, *The Old Bailey and Its Trials* (1950).

3249   OMAN, [SIR] CHARLES (WILLIAM CHADWICK) (1860–1946)

       The Lyons Mail   Meth 1945

The master historian of the Peninsular War has reconstructed the tangled affair named in the title, which occurred in France in 1796. It remains one of the great mysteries of recent centuries, specially notable for coincidences of names, looks, and events, as well as for the muddleheadedness of the police and magistrature in dealing with the determined ruffians who robbed and killed with almost total impunity.

3250   OSBORN, ALBERT S(HERMAN)

       The Problem of Proof   2d ed.   Essex 1926; orig. 1922
       Introd. by John Henry Wigmore

JB and WHT differ markedly in their estimates of this, the former finding it long-winded and full of commonplaces. But WHT, reading the chapters in the order directed by the author (for the general reader), was much impressed by some of them—e.g., that on "Advocacy," which surely deserves to be read by every young lawyer. And something must be said for an author who points out that circumstantial evidence is not a series of "links" (with one weakest) but a cable of many strands. If further evidence of high caliber be needed, Osborn (in Chapter 26) recommends the reading of detective stories, and his Bibliography includes Dewey, Doyle, Freeman, William James, Jevons, and Tyndall.

3251   Questioned Documents   2d ed.   LCPC 1940

       Introd. by John Henry Wigmore
       Illus.

The outstanding treatise on the subject for the first half of the twentieth century. In 26 chapters the author presents in detail the methods used in the examination of every kind of questioned document, including the then newfangled typescript. Osborn is good on pens and inks; one wonders what he would have made of the ballpoint. Recent advances in microscopy and photography have added to his work, but have invalidated little of it. See No. 3313 for the more modern aspects.

3252   PASLEY, FRED D.

       Not Guilty!   Putn 1933
       The Story of Samuel S. Leibowitz

A breezy recital of some fifteen defenses by this famous and indomitable lawyer, later a judge. Little mystery and a great deal of courtroom drama.

3253   PAULSEN, MONRAD G.

       The Problem of Sentencing   ALI 1962

A succinct account (122 pages) of the procedure, the problems, and the facts (statistical and other) relevant to the logic of sentencing. Social and psychological effects are touched on but not discussed at length.

3254   PAULSEN, MONRAD G., and KADISH, SANFORD H.

       Criminal Law and Its Processes   LB 1962

A masterly review of its subject by authors who maintain a balance between the purely legal and the wholly sociological views of crime. The cases are summarized and quoted from with a sure sense of what exposition and explanation require, and the commentaries are equally clear and judicious. See also: Supplements issued in 1964 and ff.

3255   PEARSON, EDMUND (LESTER) (1880–1937)

       Murders That Baffled the Experts   Signet 1967

A selection of ten cases from the master's works, notable for the inclusion of: Parkman, The Green Bicycle, Dougal, Wainewright, Constance Kent, and the remarkable failure of Frederick Small.

3256 Studies in Murder   ModL 1938; orig. 1924
      Biog. Note on the author
      Plans of murder sites

The eight cases collected in this volume made the author's reputation with
the general public, after he was known to librarians for his writing on their
art, and after he had caught the eye of magazine readers with his essays
on true crimes. The cases here treated are: Lizzie Borden (120 pages);
the Benjamin Nathan murder; the three murders by Mate Bram on the
Herbert Fuller; the murder of Miss Page in Weston, Mass.; the disappearance of Russell Colvin; the murder of the nearly indestructible Michael
Mallory; and two discussions—the quality of the evidence in the Haupt-
mann case (kidnapping of the Lindbergh baby), and the likelihood of
wrong executions. The so-called Appendix merely gives sources for the
several chapters.

On rereading after twenty years, Pearson does not retain the impressiveness of his first appearance. His philosophizing and his prose are not in
a class with those of Roughead, Bolitho, Lustgarten, or Wallace; and
the re-examination of the Borden case by Radin (see No. 3263) has made
a bad dent in his scholarliness. Pearson's chief merit is his curiosity,
which led him to dig up good forgotten cases. But see also No. 3167.

3257 PINKERTON, ALLAN (1819–1894)

      The Expressman and the Detective   Keen 1874

The first volume of Pinkerton reminiscences, with the merits and defects
of the period—a commonplace style and outlook, crime and detection
without much variety and imagination, and a total absence of social or
psychological insight; besides which, fact is hopelessly mixed with fiction.
Still, these very defects are indicative of a time and mood.

3258 PINKERTON. See also:

      The Bankers, Their Vaults, and the Burglars   Fergus (Chicago) 1873
      Claude Melnotte as a Detective and Other Stories   Keen 1875
      Criminal Reminiscences and Detective Sketches Carleton (N.Y.) 1879

3259 POST, MELVILLE DAVISSON

      The Man Hunters   Sears 1926
      Illus.

Large in bulk but loose in texture, this book attempted to give the layman
of the time a comparative view of criminal investigation as practiced by
the countries leading in "method." The text relies on Gross and Niceforo
and has some very good pictures illustrative of the mechanical factors
in walking, and the like. The English, German, French, Austrian, and
Italian systems each receive a chapter. The American way is declared un-
systematic, and the truth is borne out by the organization of the book.
Chapters are given to: Bloodstains, Bank Looting, Codes, and Forgeries,
and scanty anecdotes are thrown in to help moisten what it is feared will
seem dry as dust.

3260   POSTGATE, RAYMOND

      Murder, Piracy, and Treason   HM 1925
       Illus.

A collection of cases to illustrate the theme of "society gets the crime it deserves, because it generates them." The author evinces a Marxist animus, which tends to regard character and circumstance as having no reality. Some of the cases from 1380 to 1879 survive this treatment by their inherent drama, and the compiler is sufficiently interested in detail to give in an appendix the City Marshal's list of flash words current at the beginning of the 18th century. From it we learn that *pad* and *darbies* already had their present meanings.

3261   PRATT, FLETCHER (1897–1956)

      Secret and Urgent   BM 1939
      The Story of Codes and Ciphers

A clear but colloquial account of the history and methods of cryptography by an authority on naval strategy, who had firsthand information about American methods of decoding and deciphering. He was profoundly skeptical about the use of machines, at least in their early application.

3262   PUJOL, ALAIN

      Dictionnaire de l'Espion   Solar 1965

Technical and sometimes tendentious definitions of the main aspects of spywork, some familiar to readers of fiction, others quite new. The author is a well-read man who takes cognizance of the literature of spying as well as of his professional practice.

3263   RADIN, EDWARD D. (1901–1966)

      Lizzie Borden: The Untold Story   S&S 1961

The first thorough account of a case everybody thought he knew. Radin rehabilitates Lizzie, shows the incompetence of the police, the shrewdness of certain contemporary journalists, and the willful blindness of Pearson and those who have copied from him. And he points to a more likely culprit than Lizzie—though by no means all readers will agree with him.

3264   Twelve Against Crime   Col 1961

The late dean of crime reporters describes twelve men or organizations that have substantially contributed to crime detection, usually through applied science:

Dr. Thomas A. Gonzales, Chief Medical Examiner, N.Y.C.
A. Bruce Bielaski, arson investigator
Captain Adam Yulch, laundry mark identification
Professor A. O. Gettler, Chief Toxicologist, N.Y.C.
Dr. J. Paul de River, police psychiatrist

George H. Lamb, manhunter
John F. Tyrrell, examiner of questioned documents
Dr. Alexander S. Wiener, serologist, N.Y.C.
George Chenkin, parole officer
Arthur Koehler, wood technologist (cf. the Lindbergh case and its ladder)
W. H. ("Buddy") Gasque, Special Investigator for the State of Florida
John A. Dondero, fingerprint expert

In a final chapter the author discusses the cases of unsuspected murder in the U.S. (estimated then at 3,000 a year), and he excoriates the coroner system, which he deems an invitation to crime.

3265   RADZINOWICZ [SIR] LEON (b. 1907)

    A History of English Criminal Law and
    Its Administration Since 1750   4 v. Stev 1948–1968

This monumental and extremely readable work is the first grand survey since Fitzjames Stephen's (1863 and 1883). But it is not a lawyer's account of cases, precedents, and points. It is a social history, based on freshly dug materials, and told with brilliance and judgment. As such it concerns the reader of both fiction and true crime, even if the former of these is illuminated chiefly by the later portions of the history. But note that the beginnings of the modern police and, with it, of the attitude that made detective fiction possible are related to Sir Robert Peel's penal reforms, which are dealt with in Volume I of the present work.

3266   Ideology and Crime   CUP 1966

A discussion by the professor of criminology at Cambridge of the relation between modern views of crime and contemporary political opinions. The author ends by discarding both the liberal and the deterministic positions and adopts "the pragmatic position." These three lectures should be read in conjunction with Devlin, Guttmacher, Szasz, St. John-Stevas, and Bedford (qq.v.).

3267   REYNOLDS, QUENTIN

    Courtroom   Farr 1950

Another biography of Samuel Leibowitz as a defender of the oppressed or unjustly accused, much better done than *Not Guilty!* (No. 3252). The details of each case are clearly set forth, though with much sentiment, as befits a journalist who started out as a lawyer. Leibowitz ends up as a judge, the book itself as a best seller.

3268   RICHARDS, GUY

    The Hunt for the Czar   Dday 1970

Fiction or fact?—that is the difficulty with this fascinating work, which the author puts forth with obvious honesty as the product of thorough historical research into the fate of the Romanovs. His sources (as he admits) are hard to authenticate, and at many points he expresses skepticism, but he concludes that all seven of the family presumably murdered at Ekaterinburg on July 16, 1918, survived and fled. *The Hunt* is good detection and inference, and it is a kind of sequel to *Imperial Agent.*

3269   Imperial Agent   DA 1966

An excellent reporter's excellent account of what was disclosed when he wondered about the escape of the convicted traitor George Blake from an English prison.

3270   ROBERTS, C(ARL) E(RIC) BECHHOFER, ed.

    The Mr. A. Case   Jarr [1925]
    Illus.

High comedy arises from the account of a conspiracy to defraud an Indian prince by means of a sexual lure. The characters and events are beautifully depicted by the practiced editor of the Old Bailey Series (q.v.), and some of the elegantly off-color episodes are unforgettable. (See also No. 3248.)

3271   RHODES, HENRY T. F.

    The Criminals We Deserve   Meth 1937
    A Survey of Some Aspects of Crime in the Modern World
    Illus.

The author, a member of the Institute of Criminology at the University of Lyons, defends the thesis in his title by pointing to our "mass-production of crime," the rising traffic in drugs and women, the ever-higher cost of delinquencies of all kinds, and the growth of gangsterism. Good chapters on forgery and its detection and on cunning, high and low, lighten the book. But the thoughtful reader looking about him a third of a century after Mr. Rhodes' warnings can hardly think them effective.

3272   RHODES, ed.

    In the Tracks of Crime   Turns 1952
    Bibliog.

An odd compilation, which puts under one cover a Sherlock Holmes story, a sketch of Bertillon, statistics about murder and suicide, extracts from prison newspapers, discussions of flogging and the law of libel—indeed anything remotely connected with *mens rea* and *corpus delicti.* If one can stand the choppiness of the seventy-odd sections, one picks up a good number of interesting points, but it is not the easiest kind of reading.

3273   ROBINSON, HENRY MORTON (1899–1961)

    Science Versus Crime   Bell 1937

A well-documented and expertly written account of the contributions of applied science in the detection of crime and the pursuit of criminals. For a sequel by other hands to bring the history up to date, see No. 3313.

3274 ROLPH, C. H.

The Trial of *Lady Chatterley*   Peng 1961
Illus.

Instructive on the subject of evidence and on the views of intellectual
people about life and literature. The report makes one wonder how their
testimony would have been changed if more of them had been readers of
detective fiction, while one also regrets their frequent lapses into arrogance and irrelevance. On this point, see John Sparrow, *Controversial
Essays* (Chil 1966).

3275 ROUGHEAD, WILLIAM

Classic Crimes   Cass 1951
Pref. by James Bridie

Twelve retellings of great cases, culled from the more than two dozen
volumes by this recognized authority. Whatever one may think of his
bias or freedom from bias, he can tell the facts of a crime or a trial so
that no doubts and no loose ends remain. What is offered here is: Katharine Nairn, Deacon Brodie, The West Port Murders, Madeleine Smith,
Constance Kent, The Sandyford Mystery, the Balham Mystery, Dr.
Pritchard, The Arran Murder, The Ardlamont Mystery, Oscar Slater,
and The Merrett Case.

3276 "Katharine Nairn"
        In: The Pocket Mystery Reader (No. 2873)

A succinct yet well-rounded account of the enigmatic affair of 1765, in
which an attractive young married woman and her brother-in-law, the
lieutenant Patrick Ogilvie, were charged with murdering the brother-
husband with arsenic. The medical evidence was poor; the lieutenant was
executed; she escaped; and the role of the inevitable confidant, Miss Anne
Clark, was never made clear.

3277 Trial of Oscar Slater   Hodge 1910
        NST
        Illus.

A luminous account of the case that agitated the British Isles for a decade
and kept Conan Doyle writing and petitioning for even longer. The lack
of a satisfactory solution, coupled with the wrecking of lives and careers,
makes this an archetypal case.

3278 ROVERE, RICHARD

Howe and Hummel   Farr 1947
        Their True and Scandalous History
        Introd. by Judge J. G. Wallace
        Illus. by Reginald Marsh

A terse and brilliant account of a pair of mouthpieces, whose ingenuity
in defending crooks, as well as themselves, partakes of farce—not to say
of the American Tall Tale. But it is attested fact. R.R. has never surpassed

the prose or drama of this narrative in all his distinguished career as a political writer.

3279 ROWLAND, JOHN

A Century of Murder   Roy 1950

A satisfactory recital of classic cases, with a few unusual ones added: the Lightfoots, Dr. Palmer, Madeleine Smith, Franz Muller, Pritchard, Mrs. Maybrick, Louise Masset, Dickman, Crippen, Seddon, George Joseph Smith, Armstrong, Thompson and Bywaters, Rouse, Stoner and Rattenbury, Hulten and Jones. See also the author's *Poisoner in the Dock* (Arc, 1960), which contains twelve studies of less familiar murderers.

3280 SABATINI, RAFAEL (1875–1950)

The Historical Nights' Entertainment   2 vols. HM 1924;
    1st and 2d series   orig. 1917–19

Not especially perceptive retellings of historical murders and massacres, from Rizzio to Casanova and Gustavus III. The prose is quick and shallow, and in the end all the events sound alike.

Note that the second series includes three items from *The Justice of the Duke* and that "The Absolution" is entirely fictional.

3281 ST. JOHN-STEVAS, NORMAN, M. P.

Life, Death, and the Law   IUP 1961

The authoritative work on the relation of legal provisions and Christian morals in England and America. The main topics are: abortion, contraception, artificial insemination, sterilization, homosexuality, suicide, and euthanasia. The author's scholarly stance enables him to be detached, though not indifferent; so that the reader, whether committed or not, can begin to think with the aid of facts and solid reasoning.

3282 SAYERS, DOROTHY L.

"The Murder of Julia Wallace"
    In: The Anatomy of Murder (No. 3287)

Another short masterpiece by the famous author of fictional murders. The case is perhaps the supreme puzzle, made most appealing of all others by the human circumstances, and D.L.S. treats it with all her genius for intellectual and emotional understanding. (See also No. 3095.)

3283 SCOTT, SIR HAROLD (RICHARD), ed. (1887–1969)

The Concise Encyclopedia of Crime and Criminals   Hawth 1961

Forty competent contributors supply articles on criminological technique and procedure as well as on famous crimes and criminals. Topics are dealt with at greater length than persons, and the organization of the police forces of the Western world is ably described. A few errors of names are not serious enough to spoil the work.

  Illus.

The author is a thoroughly educated and experienced civil servant, who
has been involved in Home Office matters since 1911. He was commissioner of the Metropolitan Police from 1945 to 1953 and his survey is
accordingly complete and satisfying, as well as interspersed with original
details about famous cases—e.g., Setty, Haigh, Heath, and Christie. The
photographs are first-rate.

3285   SHAW, E. SPENCER

       A Companion to Murder   Knopf 1961
       Bibliog.

A dictionary of mainly British murders committed between 1900 and
1950, together with accounts of judges, counsel, et al., supplemented by a
"Note on the British Judicial System." The entries are well chosen and
well written; the Note is purely procedural, and useful for details of style,
dress, and nomenclature in the English courts. One regrets certain glaring
omissions—e.g., the Wallace case, Sydney Smith, and others.

3286   SILLITOE, [SIR] PERCY (1889–1962)

       Cloak Without Dagger   Pan n.d.; orig. 1955

The reminiscences of a chief constable who served in Rhodesia, cleaned
up Sheffield and Glasgow, and went on to head M.I.5: excellent from
every point of view.

3287   SIMPSON, HELEN, ed.

       The Anatomy of Murder   Macm 1937
       Jacket shows a realistic skull

Seven famous crimes are critically considered by as many famous authors:

The Death of Henry Kinder by Helen Simpson
Constance Kent by John Rhode
The Case of Adelaide Bartlett by Margaret Cole
An Impression of the Landru Case by E. R. Punshon
The Murder of Julia Wallace by Dorothy L. Sayers
The Rattenbury Case by Francis Iles
A New Zealand Tragedy by Freeman Wills Crofts

3288   SMITH, A. DUNCAN

       Trial of Eugène-Marie Chantrelle   Hodge 1906
       NST
       Illus.

The editor's 27-page Introduction is sober and straightforward, and the
four-day trial is full of legal and toxicological interest. Chantrelle, a teacher
of languages, had insured his wife for £1000 about ten years after their
marriage, and within less than a year had despatched her with opium. His
attempts to have her death taken as asphyxiation by gas were thwarted by
the nascent toxicology of the day and he was executed on May 31, 1878.

3289 SMITH, SIR SYDNEY

Mostly Murder   Harrap 1959
    Pref. by Lord Cameron

An admirable autobiography, detailing work as a medico-legal expert in
Egypt, India, and Scotland. The accounts of great cases (Sidney Fox,
Ruxton, Gall.) are lucid and full. There is a good chapter on Dr. Bell
and Sherlock Holmes, another on ballistics, and a most important critique
of Spilsbury's behavior in later days. Altogether a first-rate example of the
historical spirit applied to the self and coupled with the equally admirable
spirit of science.

3290 SÖDERMAN, HARRY

Policeman's Lot   F&W 1956

The author died before the book went to press. He was the son of a rural
police chief in Sweden, and as a young man secured on his own an ap-
prenticeship with Edmond Locard at Lyon. This was in the twenties,
and we get a picture of life there and then which does more than satisfy
the reader's interest in science. Indeed, the trouble with the book is that
it hovers between autobiography and a report on modern detection.
    S. returned to Sweden and opened a private agency, only to be snapped
up to head the National Institute of Criminology. Later he came to N.Y.C.
—the circumstances being left vague—and remained there several years.
His English is uneven and unedited. His personality is mixed—partly pruri-
ent and cruel, partly amiable and moral. A few of his cases are excellent,
especially his account of the protracted dispute over the archaeological
finds at Glozel.

3291 SÖDERMAN, HARRY, and O'CONNELL, JOHN J.

Modern Criminal Investigation   F&W 1945/1935
    Illus. by Charles A. Harrold as well as by photographs

The fourteen chapters of this excellent compendium set forth the best
police practice of Sweden and the U.S. a quarter century ago. Practically
every aspect of criminal investigation is discussed in detail and illustrated
with tables of data and drawings. That the book was intended as a textbook is shown by the inclusion of questions at the end of each chapter,
but it is excellent reading for the armchair detective.

3292 "SOLICITOR" (pseud. of Conway Loveridge Hodgkinson, b. 1879)

English Justice   AL 1941/Rout 1932

This anonymous attack on the English courts, principally the lower courts,
demonstrates how badly institutions work when the personnel is ordinary
and "human." The writer does a brilliant job of exposition and exposure,
and he offers good suggestions, but he does not tell us where we shall
obtain more intelligent, imaginative, and conscientious people.

SPARROW, JOHN (HANBURY ANGUS) (b. 1906)

b. New Oxley; educ. Winchester and New Coll., Oxf.; barrister 1931; officer in Coldstream Guards during second world war; on mission in Washington; then Warden of All Souls'. Noted as essayist and polemicist, scholar in East European languages, astute critic of politics and society.

3293   After the Assassination   Chil 1968

Unquestionably the best summary of the objections to the Warren Commission Report on the assassination of President Kennedy and the clearest argument for their wrongheadedness. Quite apart from the facts of the case, the reasoning about evidence and the reminder about the nature of testimony should form part of the reader's and the writer's working knowledge in matters of crime and detection. He also dispels current myths about the ease and efficiency of murder plots. The author is a lawyer as well as a literary scholar.

3294   SPARROW. See also:

        Controversial Essays   Chil 1966
        Independent Essays   Chil 1963

3295   STEAD, PHILIP JOHN

        The Police of Paris   Stap 1957

A beautifully concise and clear account of the organization since early modern times, without reference to great cases or famous detectives. Vidocq, whose life the author has written, occurs only in his capacity as chief of the Sûreté. The book corrects many misconceptions perpetuated by writers of fiction, and it is written with an excellent knowledge of the historical and political circumstances of each period.

3296   STEWART, A. W.

        "The Mystery of Chantelle"
        In: Alias J. J. Connington (No. 3038)

For those who relish unsolved crimes, this speculative account of what happened or did not happen in the little French town when the strange and promiscuous Mme Achet somehow disposed of an importunate lover will prove a delight. The enigmatic Mme A, who was tried and sentenced to twelve years' hard, is a fit companion piece for Madeleine Smith.

3297   STONE, [DR.] JAMES W.

        Report of the Trial of Prof. John W. Webster, Indicted for the
        Murder of Dr. George Parkman

            2d ed., rev.   Phil 1850
            Illus.

This is a complete "phonographic" report of this celebrated trial before the Supreme Judicial Court of Massachusetts, "holden at Boston, on Tuesday, March 19, 1850."

Professor Webster, a lecturer in chemistry at the newly established Medical College, was in debt to Dr. Parkman, and under pressure for payment knifed him in his own lecture room. He then employed a variety of ineffectual means to rid himself of the dismembered body. Suspicion was finally directed to Webster by his abnormal activities during the Thanksgiving holiday, and a thorough search revealed identifiable remains of the victim, in particular a set of "mineral" teeth which the dentist who made them for Parkman was able to swear to—perhaps a first in this branch of forensic medicine.

The rather long-winded proceedings of the trial (twelve days, under Chief Justice Lemuel Shaw) are occasionally enlivened by the sprightly comments of Oliver Wendell Holmes, who was Parkman Professor of Anatomy and Physiology in the Medical College and was called as a witness.

3298 SYMONS, JULIAN

A Pictorial History of Crime   Crown 1966
    In Eng.: Crime and Detection . . . Since 1840

Seventy-five pages bring us to 1900; two hundred more cover our age of crime par excellence. The captions and comments are adequate, but the pictures leave much to be desired. The volume as a whole suggests the adjective *popular* rather than *scholarly*.

3299 A Reasonable Doubt   Cress 1960
    Some Criminal Cases Re-examined

Thirteen cases of murder, in which there is some doubt as to the correctness of the verdict, or in which the mystery remains unsolved. Three are dealt with at considerable length: Steinie Morrison, James Camb (the "porthole murderer"), and John Bennett, the Yarmouth wife-murderer. In each of these Symons shows the inconsistencies in the evidence which raise doubt. Of the nine other cases, treated quite briefly, the Gorse Hall mystery of 1909, the Kenya society murder (Broughton-Erroll) of 1940, and the murder of Sir Harry Oakes in 1943 are the most interesting.

3300 SZASZ, THOMAS S.

Psychiatric Justice   Macm 1965

A close argument, by a physician and psychiatrist, against the abuse of expert medical testimony in criminal trials. The author is adept at showing the dangerous paradoxes in the softer forms of justice influenced by specialists in mental disease. He illustrates his points with the aid of four cases which he analyzes in detail.

3301 TAYLOR, ALFRED SWAINE (1806–1880)

The Principles and Practice of Medical Jurisprudence   Chur 1865
    Illus.

This hefty book (1186 pages) was unsurpassed in its day and still holds much interest for the student of past crime and general history. Its main headings are: Medical Evidence, The Dead Body, Poisoning, Wounds,

Spontaneous Combustion, Asphyxia, Pregnancy and Delivery, Legitimacy and Paternity, Infanticide, Rape, Insanity, and Life Insurance. The first of the many illustrations is: Dr. Parkman's Remains Restored. The case histories are superb and the exposition throughout is masterly.

N.B. Connoisseurs (and bibliographers) will forgive the mention here that the copy of this work owned by these readers is that used by R. Austin Freeman, who borrowed it from Dr. Pitcairn: Dr. P.'s stamp is on the flyleaf and title page. A very few marks in pencil may be Freeman's, whose wife has written an identification inside the front cover.

3302   THOMSON, [SIR] BASIL (1861–1939)

The Criminal   H&S n.d. [1925]

The author started the career that brought him to the top of the CID by being a prison officer. His book is part autobiography, part criminology. He argues for more detective police to permit wider investigation, and he promises in return less crime and hence less prison expense. His best account is that of the Penge murder (the Stauntons) and his best discussion is that of Lombroso's fallacy. Thomson did not live long enough to see a return to this fallacy in the form of social-psychiatric determinism.

3303   The Story of Scotland Yard   LitG 1936

Deliberate in pace and knowledgeable in tone, this account by an ex-commissioner goes back to origins and deals intelligently with important cases from the time of Sir John Fielding to his own. The mood of subdued drama is more effective here than in his fiction. (See Nos. 2050–4.)

3304   THORWALD, JÜRGEN

The Century of the Detective   HB 1965/1964
    Trans. from the German by Richard and Clara Winston
    Illus.

Less comprehensive but more up to date than Söderman (q.v.), and with more emphasis upon historical background. The four main sections deal with: Identification, Forensic Medicine, Toxicology, and Ballistics. Many classical cases are described in detail. The illustrations are well above average and the book in English is a pleasure to read: it makes one almost forgive the translators for their vulgar literary treatment of G. B. Shaw.

3305   TOZER, BASIL

Confidence Crooks and Blackmailers   Laur 1929

Designed to guard the reader against the menace, this work is lavish in obvious information and skimpy on the subtler and more interesting stratagems for selling the Tower of London to the stranger from Australia.

3306   TRAIN, ARTHUR

Courts, Criminals, and the Camorra   Scrib 1912

The book follows the three parts indicated in the title. The best is the third. Train was in Naples when the trial of the Camorra was going on, and he boned up on its earlier history, so that in a few pages he gives a good account of this organization, and the facts and legends about it.

Train was Assistant D.A. of N.Y. County for seven years and his inside views of trials, prosecutions, police collusion, and criminal practices are extensive. The chapter on Detection is worth noting, though it contains nothing to startle or instruct an experienced reader.

3307   Yankee Lawyer   Scrib 1942
         The Autobiography of Ephraim Tutt
         Illus.

A blend of fact and fiction, with pictures of the author-hero and his family. Chapter 16 deals, somewhat superficially, with "Murder and Its Defense"; Chapters 17 through 20 discuss various legal points.

3308   TRAIN. See also:

         From the District Attorney's Office   Scrib 1939
         ("a popular account of criminal justice," i.e.,
         exposition rather than anecdote)
         The Prisoner at the Bar   Scrib 1906
         (discussion of crime, advocacy, and justice)
         True Stories of Crime from the District Attorney's Office   Scrib 1908
         (Thirteen anecdotes of true crime)

3309   TRAVER, JOHN

         The Jealous Mistress   LB 1967

The retired Michigan judge John D. Voelker looks back on his years of service and passes judgment on prisons, sentencing, the cruelty of public opinion, and other matters regional and universal—a delightful and all-too-short set of reminiscences, much better written than his best seller, *Anatomy of a Murder* (No. 2060).

3310   VIDOCQ, FRANÇOIS (EUGENE) (1775–1857)

         Mémoires   Tenon (Paris) 1828–29
         Chef de la police de sûreté jusqu'en 1827
         4 vols. (1st ed.)

The English version is: *Memoirs of Vidocq, Principal Agent of the French Police* (Bohn 1859). It is doubtful whether Vidocq wrote his own memoirs; the "authors" have been guessed at and listed in various places. The main interest lies in the disclosure of an amazing career. V. was first a convict—eight years' hard labor for having helped a criminal to escape. He himself escaped twice, having learned enough about thieves to be accepted as a police spy in 1809. He retired in 1827, but was induced to resume his duties in 1832. Vidocq's amazing personality inspired Balzac to create the figure of Vautrin (see No. 96), and, what is more, it dominated both the official and the under-world during his active career. His second retirement ended in his death, poor and obscure.

3311 WAITE, FREDERICK C., M.D.

"Grave Robbing in New England"   BMLA July 1945

A circumstantial account, medical and legal, of this interesting sport, from
colonial times through the nineteenth century. (See De Quincey, No.
3126.)

3312 WALLACE, W. STEWART

Murders and Mysteries: A Canadian Series   Macm 1931

A series of sixteen little narrative gems, almost all new and gruesome.
They bring before us not only some mysterious events not generally known,
but also the atmosphere and social realities of Canada in the last and
present centuries. Note one more treatment of H. H. Holmes.

3313 WALLS, H. J.

Forensic Science   Praeg 1968
    Illus.

This is an excellent book by an English police scientist, who appears to
have been a member of the Durham County constabulary. The writing is
clear and terse, with a touch of humor here and there, and though the
book is anything but cumbersome, the scientific explanations are full and
the illustrations numerous. WHT knows of no other work that manages
to make clear to the semi-scientific reader just what the principles are
upon which modern forensic science operates: chromatography, spectro-
photometry, electrophoresis, and serology are all just as clearly presented
as the more classical areas of toxicology, ballistics, and comparison
microscopy. Sherlock Holmes, to whom several references are made,
would have rated it high.

3314 WELCOME, JOHN

Cheating at Cards   Faber 1963
    Bibliog.

This is not a book on how to do it, but a series of cases in court. The
scandals and trials leave one with a vivid and singular impression of high
life in the 1890s—if the surroundings of the future Edward VII may be
called high in any but a gamy sense.

3315 WELLMAN, FRANCIS I.

The Art of Cross-Examination   Macm 1936/1903
    4th ed., rev.
    Pref. by John W. Davis

The classic treatise on the subject, containing numerous examples taken
from important English and American cases, plus two chapters written by

680

fellow cross-examiners. The passages from the Henry Ward Beecher and Russell Sage cases supply good comedy amid more somber stuff.

3316   WERTHAM, FREDRIC (b. 1895)

Dark Legend   DS 1943

A leading student of the relation of law to psychiatric knowledge relates his analysis of the young murderer Gino. The boy lost his father and helped support his mother, who carried on with a succession of men. Gino finally killed her after dreaming that his dead father was urging him to do it. Hamlet to the life, though without poetry or philosophy—that is, on the boy's part. The recital is gripping, and a play was made out of it in 1952.

3317   The Show of Violence   Dday 1949
         Introd. to ppb. ed. dated 1967

With *The Circle of Guilt* and *Dark Legend,* this work constitutes a classic study of the motives to murder by a psychiatrist who is also an educated man and who has kept a sane judgment about life in the midst of the viewy professionalism of the day. Excellently written and comprehensive in its range of actual cases.
   The title quotes *Hamlet,* I, 1, 144.

3318   WHITAKER, BEN(JAMIN CHARLES GEORGE)

The Police   E&S 1964

The author is a barrister (educated at Eton and Oxford), who does a concise job of surveying the police problem in Britain. He discusses the need for a "national force," police corruption, the police "image," and concludes that the public gets the service it deserves.

3319   WILLIAMS, EMLYN

Beyond Belief   RH 1967
         A Chronicle of Murder and Its Detection

It is indeed beyond belief that the author has devoted 350 pages to an account of the Moors Murders (England, 1963–65) without providing a clear picture of what took place. So far from emerging from the mass of "psychology" the characters of the criminals are obscured by it, and the victims (three children aged 10 to 17) fare no better. Even the sadism, pornographic photography, and tape-recording of some of the crimes are muddled in presentation.

3320   WILLIAMS, GLANVILLE

The Proof of Guilt   2d ed., Stev 1958/1955

Short but thorough, this authoritative treatment by the Reader in English Law at Cambridge should be required reading for anyone who professes to review, in his living room or in the bus, the findings of courts and commissions of inquiry. The technicalities are made plain and are illustrated from cases whenever needful.

3321 WILLIAMS, NEVILLE

Captains Outrageous: Seven Centuries of Piracy   Macm 1962
Illus.

A compact history of ocean hijacking before the days of jet planes. Particularly valuable is the circumstantial story of Captain Kidd, whose name unfortunately connotes what he probably was not—like Dr. Crippen and Mata Hari. The other main characters are William Marsh, Edward Teach, John Avery, Bartholomew Roberts, John Killigrew, and Ching Yih.

3322 WILSON, COLIN, and PITMAN, PATRICIA, eds.

Encyclopedia of Murder   Putn 1962/1961
Introds. by the editors

Contributions to this volume by other hands than the authors are listed in the acknowledgments. The two Introductions set forth the thesis that the work is meant to illustrate. The alphabetically arranged articles together form the best of the encyclopedias in print on this subject. The writing and the judgments deserve all respect, and the degree of completeness is the highest so far attained.

The first introduction (obviously by C.W.) is a remarkable essay by one of the best social philosophers and the most interesting novelist of his generation. It takes account of the modern "morality of guilt" by which the criminal is admirable and the law-abiding citizen contemptible, but it uses and explains this conclusion without accepting it. Altogether an indispensable work.

3323 WIMSATT, WILLIAM K(URTZ), JR.

"Poe and the Mystery of Mary Rogers"   *PMLA* Mar 1941

The Yale scholar goes over the ground of fact with unprecedented care and minuteness and his conclusion about Poe's powers of reasoning and weighing evidence is not favorable. His comments relate, of course, to the facts of the case, not to the merits of the story in either its first or its revised version. For a later and longer study, see No. 3053.

3324 WINKS, ROBERT W.

The Historian as Detective   Harp 1969/1968

A discussion of Evidence in real life, apart from criminal events, followed by a score of "cases" treated by leading historians. The parallel with true crime is not forced and the selections are at once enticing and unhackneyed.

YARDLEY, [MAJOR] HERBERT O(SBORN) (b.1889)

b. Worthington, Ind.; started as telegraph operator and became leading cryptographer of the U.S. After the first world war was chosen to head the new "Black Chamber" organized to serve the War and Navy Depts. It was Yardley who cracked the Japanese code during the Washington Disarmament Conference of 1921. The Chamber was discontinued at the request of Secretary Henry L. Stimson, an act that prompted Yardley to write. His book was criticized as unpatriotic by many Washingtonians. Yardley's next task was to set up the code department for the forces of Chiang Kai-shek in China. Thereafter he took to novel writing and finally to keeping a restaurant in Washington.

3325   The American Black Chamber   Faber 1931
         Illus.

A breezy and not always fully explicit account of the achievements of M.I.8, the cryptographic division of U.S. Military Intelligence during and after the first world war. By then the author was the man in charge and the tackling of the Japanese code was, of course, his *pièce de résistance*.

3326   YOUNG, FILSON (1876–1938), was the brilliant editor of Page Four (special articles) of the *Daily Mail* under Northcliffe. His interest in social philosophy and crime led him to prepare two notable Notable Trials: *Hawley Harvey Crippen* (Hodge 1950/1920) and *The Seddons* (Hodge 1952/1914). F.Y.'s introductions are rich in analytic intelligence, knowledge of the law, and (in Crippen's case) moral sensitivity.

PART V

THE LITERATURE OF
SHERLOCK HOLMES:
STUDIES AND ANNOTATIONS
OF THE TALES,
NONFICTION PARODIES, AND
CRITICAL PASTICHES

Gems from the Literature

Though he might be more humble,
There's no p'lice like Holmes.
  —E. W. Hornung

Sherlock Holmes . . . is described somewhere as being incapable of falling in love because of his logical nature. You might as well say that he could not be expected to have much appetite for lunch because of his proficiency in mathematics.
  —G. K. Chesterton

Not a Merry Old Christmas—just the bashful British meiosis: "Compliments of the season." Wary old Watson, one of Britain's great understatesmen.
  —Christopher Morley, *A Textbook of Friendship*

Not only was there never a second Mrs. Watson; there was not even a first Mrs. Watson. Furthermore, there was no Doctor Watson.
  Please keep your chairs.
  —Rex Stout, "Watson Was a Woman"

   •

NOT WATSON, JUST DOCTORS:
  But the doctor, as my uncle said, was a bit of a bounder—or at least on the boundary line.
  —Horace Hutchinson

His medical practice had been so punctuated by scandals that he had practically abandoned the practice the better to apply himself to the scandals.
  —Thorne Smith

   •

After Holmes, the Deluge!
  —Vincent Starrett

3327 BAKER STREET JOURNAL, THE, was founded in New York in 1946, Edgar W. Smith (q.v.), editor; Ben Abramson, publisher, thirteen issues brought out, the last in Jan 1949 (Old Series *printed*).

The New Series, E. W. Smith, editor, began with the issue of Jan 1951, marked "New Series," offset typing, and 40 pages in bulk as against 132 pages in the O.S.

In 1961, after the death of E. W. Smith, Dr. Julian Wolff became editor, continuing the format, bulk, and features of the New Series.

3328 BARING-GOULD, W(ILLIAM) S(TUART), ed.

    The Annotated Sherlock
    Holmes   2v. Crown (for Clarkson Potter) 1967
        Introd., Notes, and Bibliog. by the editor
        Illus.; Endpapers of London and other Holmesian regions

The four novels and fifty-six short stories are reprinted and flanked by comment, exegesis, and illustrations reproduced from the original sources. A mine of information and reference indispensable to the S.H. scholar, though marred by many misprints, errors of fact, and errors of judgment. Nonetheless an achievement.

3329   Sherlock Holmes of Baker Street   Bram 1962
      A Life of the World's First Consulting Detective

This uneven but entertaining work owes much to earlier writers, as its author is quick to acknowledge. Much of the material used here to fill the twenty-five short chapters is freely synthetic, but tied in at many points with the "actual events" of Watson's narrative. Two appendices present "The Chronological Holmes" and "The Bibliographical Holmes." The first of these is an expansion of material, first published in *BSJ* and then privately, as a pamphlet, in 1955. The bibliography, although selective, is large and valuable.

3330   BARZUN, JACQUES, made three trifling contributions to the Sherlock Holmes literature: "Prolegomena to Watson's Ninth Marriage" (by "Giovanni Antipasto") in *BSJ*, Jan 1955/"How Holmes Came to Play the Violin" *(BSJ*, July 1951), which sets straight the genealogy and chronology of Holmes' relation to the Vernet family/ and "Holmes's Will: a Forgery" *(BSJ*, Apr 1956), which demolishes the notion that Holmes would write like a blend of Gene Stratton Porter and *Time* magazine, even if he made his will *in extremis* at the Reichenbach Falls. For the text of the will, see *London Mystery Magazine,* June 1955.

3331   "5000 Orange Pips; or, The Seeds of
        Pedantry"   *Amer Sch* Autumn 1968

A review of Baring-Gould's *Annotated Sherlock Holmes* (q.v.), containing a few important corrections of that text.

3332   BELL, H(AROLD) W(ILMERDING) (1885–1947)

Baker Street Studies   *BSI* 1955; orig. Const 1934
Foreword by Edgar W. Smith

Important essays by Dorothy Sayers, Helen Simpson, Vernon Rendall, Ronald Knox, A. G. Macdonell, S. C. Roberts, and H. W. Bell (two articles). Noteworthy feature is the contrast between the early scholarship (Knox through Rendall) and the later (S. C. Roberts onward). Experts will appreciate the nuances.

3333   Sherlock Holmes and Doctor Watson   *BSI* 1953; orig. Const 1932
A Chronology of Their Adventures
Limited ed. (350)

The distinguished archaeologist, graduate of Harvard, and member of the Princeton Expedition, who lived in England for some years before retiring to Boston, was the first to attempt dating the Holmes stories from internal evidence. He gave everybody else a chance to refute him on small points—all inconclusive—and in time he came to revise three of his datings. But his work is a landmark and a model of method.

3334   BENGIS, NATHAN L., ed.

"Baker Street Legacy: The Will of
Sherlock Holmes"   *LMM* June 1955

A document said to have been "found" by the purveyor of it to the magazine. Internal evidence showing its lack of authenticity was supplied in No. 3330, and an inadequate rebuttal offered by Mr. Bengis in No. 3327.

3335   BENGIS, NATHAN L.

Baker Street Rubaiyat   Priv. ptd., Christmas 1949
Limited ed. (100)

Attributed to Sherlock Holmes and as good as such things are—which does not necessarily mean worthy of him.

3336   BLAKENEY, T(HOMAS) S.

Sherlock Holmes, Fact or Fiction?   Murray 1932
Reprinted by BSI in 1954

A scholarly work of much charm and insight. Other scholars will certainly fault the indication—doubtless absent-minded—that Jean-Paul and Richter were two German authors read by Sherlock Holmes (p. 14). Otherwise sound work.

3337   BLEGEN, THEODORE C.

The Crowded Box-Room   Sumac 1951
Sherlock Holmes as Poet

The late Dean Blegen of Minnesota examines the great detective as a man of imagination. The striking figures of speech employed by Holmes talking are shown to be drawn from a great variety of interests, imaginatively employed. Nor is Holmes the philosopher neglected in this neat little pastiche of the New Criticism.

3338   BOOTHROYD, J(OHN) B(ASIL) (b. 1910)

"The Air-Gun, Colonel Moran"   *Punch* Feb 3, 1954

Fair fooling, by a connoisseur.

3339   BROADCASTS, ETC. The radio, later TV, and simultaneously the
comics (cf. *New York Herald Tribune* in the mid-1950s), popularized
still further the Holmes-Watson image by adaptations and imitations far
more freehanded than even the plays and movies. The late Basil Rathbone
(1892–1967) as Sherlock Holmes and the late Nigel Bruce as Dr. Watson went through hundreds of audible anecdotes close to the original canon
of sixty tales, or so farfetched as to suggest that nothing but the names
of the protagonists was known to the writers. Discs have been made
from some of the original tales (e.g., "The Speckled Band" and "The
Final Problem," read by Basil Rathbone, Caedmon TC 1172). Finally
a musical comedy was staged in New York in October 1969, in which
the strong suggestion was made that the historic pair was linked by
homosexual love. At this point, it seems better to lock up all literature
in bank vaults and let the New Imagination have free scope without
hindrance from the past.

3340   CHRIST, J. FINLEY, ed.

"Finch's Final Fling"   Cand 1963
       Limited ed. (200)

A collection of short items about the S.H. literature by Mr. Christ pretending to edit others. The titbits, which appeared in the *Chicago Tribune,*
elucidate such terms and facts as *commissionaire,* S.H. and music, Irene
Adler, and S.H. as anthropologist, lawyer, and medical scientist.

More solid, though not so readable, are the same author's *Irregular
Guide to S.H. of Baker Street: A Concordance* (PH/Argus, 1947) and
An Irregular Chronology of S.H. of Baker Street (FH), a new dating of
the tales.

3341   CORRINGTON, [DR.] JULIAN D.

"Baker Street Weather"   *SaMag* Nov 1957

The author is professor of zoology at the University of Miami. He makes
an entertaining if not profound addition to the Holmes scholarship in this
pleasant summary of atmospheric phenomena as they affected the residents of 221B Baker Street, pointing out several inconsistencies in Doyle's
treatment of the weather—elementary, my dear Watson.

3342   DOYLE, A. CONAN

The Adventure of the Blue Carbuncle   *BSI* 1948
       Introd. by Christopher Morley
       Notes by Edgar W. Smith; Illus.
       Trade and Limited ed. of 1,500 copies

Morley points out with great acumen that here is a perfect Christmas story without sentimentality, and he elucidates a few of its obscurities for the young and the non-English. At the back of the book he gives a short history of the Baker Street Irregulars, together with its Constitution and By-Laws.

Association Item
3343 "Juvenilia"   Lipp   1894
         In: My First Book, by Various Hands

The volume tells of the vicissitudes of the writers in getting their first work published or noticed. The accounts do not vary greatly, but the one by Doyle presents a curious feature in reference to Sherlock Holmes, the curious feature being that there is no reference to S.H. Doyle's "first book" turns out to be Micah Clarke, two years after A Study in Scarlet. The date of this report coinciding with the appearance of The Memoirs of S.H. (1894), it seems clear that Doyle was sick and tired of S.H. quite early in their career.

The other more important point is that the picture of Doyle waiting for the success of A Study in Scarlet to decide in favor of literature is inaccurate. He had been writing and selling stories to Chambers' Journal and other magazines for several years before he turned to S.H. and was earning thereby more than £50 a year.

3344   Association Item

FAY, CHARLES EDEY, reported his research into the fate of the brigantine Mary Celeste in a book published by the Peabody Museum of Salem, Mass., The Odyssey of an Abandoned Ship (1942). Its findings are summarized in a series of articles that appeared in Sea Breezes, the Liverpool "Ship Lover's Digest" (Aug. and Sept. 1950) and were reprinted in No. 3142. The relation of this work to the Holmes literature is explained in No. 3091.

3345   FISH, ROBERT L.

         The Incredible Schlock Homes   S&S   1966

Twelve indifferent attempts at parody, not at all "hilarious" though the blurb would have it so. To these readers the name invented as a takeoff on the famous character is a sufficient clue to the quality of these would-be imitations.

3346   GARDNER, [THE REV.] RALPH

         "Baker Street and the Bible"   Hibbert Journal Apr 1952

The Cambridge (Eng.) theologian takes up Sherlock Holmes and the historical Jesus as manifestations of the power of literature to induce the emotions of belief. Not that he doubts the existence of an historical Jesus, but that he sees historicity as unimportant in comparison with the faith generated by the written and spoken word. Holmes and Watson, known to be fictitious, arouse admiration and discussion and generate the sense of their actuality. The point is not that they once lived, but that they live now, like Christ in the believer's mind. The critic does not, however, point out the causes of the readiness to believe.

3347   GILLETTE, WILLIAM

The Painful Predicament of Sherlock Holmes   BA 1955
        A Fantasy in One Act

This trifle was written in 1905 as a curtain-raiser for Gillette's new comedy *Clarice,* then opening in London. Confronted by a loquacious young woman who forces herself upon him, Holmes sits by his fire and says not a word, but indulges in some note-scribbling, the result of which is the visitor's removal to the loony bin from which she has just escaped. More amusing is the fact that the part of Billy the page was taken at the first performances by Master Charles Chaplin.

3348   GRAZEBROOK, O. F.

Studies in Sherlock Holmes   Priv. ptd., n.d. [1950]

Seven parts apparently composed this effort. The interest varies, but the merit is steady, despite some laboring of the obvious or previously done.

3349   HAMILTON, J. R., ed.

My Life with Sherlock Holmes   Goll 1969

Conversations in Baker Street: rehash without originality or charm.

3350   HARDWICK, MICHAEL and MOLLIE

Four Sherlock Holmes Plays   JM 1964
        Foreword by the adapters
        Photograph of the room at 221B Baker Street

The authors make the excellent point that the S.H. stories naturally fall into acting scenes, and they are careful to keep as much as they can of the original dialogue, also inherently dramatic. They acquired practice in doing radio skits from the stories for the BBC, then produced these one-act affairs out of: "The Speckled Band," "Charles Augustus Milverton," "The Mazarin Stone," and "The Blue Carbuncle." The last is the best.

3351   The Man Who Was Sherlock Holmes   JM 1964

A thin and derivative account of Holmes, thirty years late. (See No. 3381.)

3352   HARRISON, MICHAEL

In the Footsteps of Sherlock Holmes   Fell 1960
        Illus.

A scholar and novelist's retracing of the paths followed by Holmes and Watson when the game was afoot. Much miscellaneous and enchanting information about London and the rest of England is supplied in good, quick, and quiet English prose: the equivalent of any *Shakespeare's Eng-*

land that you can name. (For a late and great new discovery, see M.H. in *EQMM* Feb 1971.)

3353   HAYCRAFT, HOWARD, ed.

Sherlock Holmes's Greatest Cases   FW 1967
        Introd. by the editor

This edition is in large type (18 pt.) for the use of readers with impaired sight. The volume contains: *The Hound of the Baskervilles,* "The Red-Headed League," "The Speckled Band," "A Scandal in Bohemia," "The Musgrave Ritual," "Silver Blaze," and "The Blue Carbuncle."

As for the Introduction, it tells the new reader all that he should know about Holmes, Doyle, and the rise of their tradition—and tells it charmingly.

3354   HOFFMANN, BANESH

"Sherlock, Shakespeare, and the Bomb"   *EQMM* Feb 1966

An excellent parody-pastiche that combines Holmesian mathematics with Shakespeare ciphers and—what is rarer—a nice sense of language and atmosphere in the representation of Holmes and Watson.

3355   HOLMES, H. H. (pseud. of William Anthony Parker White; also
        Anthony Boucher, q.v.)

Nine Times Nine   DS 1940

This rather long work is full of good theorizing, of references to Sherlock Holmes, and of other hors d'oeuvres not functionally related to a tale of organized crime.

3356   HOLROYD, JAMES EDWARD

Baker Street By-Ways   A&U 1959

This small collection of essays by the chairman of the S.H. Society in England is full of good pictures and it also contributes a number of interesting or amusing points about the literature.

3357   KLINEFELTER, WALTER

Sherlock Holmes in Portrait and Profile   SUP 1963
        Introd. by Vincent Starrett

This is more than a picture book, for the text fills about one-half of the available space (xii + 104 pages) and provides a complete chronological account of the various efforts at illustrating the Sherlock Holmes saga.

3358   KNOX, RONALD A.

Essays in Satire   Dutt 1930

Eleven essays on various literary topics, of which the world-famous fifth is "Studies in the Literature of Sherlock Holmes." It sparkles still after sixty years and it includes, among much else of moment, the indispensable identification of the "Sherlockismus."

3359 LYTTELTON, GEORGE

[Communication on Holmes' University]
In: James Agate, The Later Ego, ed. J. Barzun (Crown 1951), p. 514

A conclusive bit of evidence, physical and biographical, which is ignored by, or unknown to, the controversialists on the issue of which university Holmes attended. The writer's slip in giving the title of "The Three Students" does not invalidate his reasoning or the facts on which it is based.

3360 MacCARTHY, DESMOND

"Dr. Watson"   *List* Dec 11, 1929

Literary controversy at its best. One must know the Chinese intricacy of the scholarly situation at that date to enjoy the eminent critic's defense and attack.

3361 McDADE, THOMAS M.

"Sherlock Holmes and the F.B.I."   *EQMM* Feb 1957

A short article by an ex-FBI man who is also a Baker Street Irregular and gifted, moreover, with a sense of analogy. He shows how able Holmes was in his use of a variety of means to detection, all of which are still useful even if somewhat changed in form. A delightful essay.

3362 MILNE, A. A.

"The Watson Touch"
In: If I May (Dutt 1921)

A rather flimsy piece on the fact that writers of detective stories have things all their own way when they "deduce"; they choose the inference they like and neglect alternatives. Milne proves this by battering at Holmes' remarks about Watson's ride in a hansom cab: the essay is worth reading for this bit alone.

3363 MONTGOMERY, JAMES

"A Case of Identity"   Priv. ptd., Phila 1955
1955 Montgomery's Christmas Annual
Limited ed. (300)

A posthumous collection of photographs illustrating events in the S.H. stories, gathered and commented on by a recognized scholar. Earlier annuals were:

Art in the Blood & What Is This Thing Called Music?	1950
Sidelights on Sherlock	1951
Three Trifling Monographs	1952
Shots from the Canon	1953

3364   A Study in Pictures   Intnl 1954
            Illus.

The iconography of Holmes, with a long and learned Introduction, two reference tables of illustrators, and an index of names. Indispensable to the scholar and attractive to the amateur.

3365   MORLEY, CHRISTOPHER

            Introduction to "The Adventure of the
            Blue Carbuncle" by Arthur Conan Doyle   *BSI*, N.Y. 1948
               The Baker Street Limited ed. (1500)

This attractive volume of 65 pages (boxed) is the first separate edition of any of the Holmes adventures, as Edgar Smith points out in his excellent bibliographical note. Christopher Morley's Introduction, in which he pays tribute to ". . . this most kindly and unintentional of Christmas stories . . . ," is as usual informative and amusing in a Lamb-like fashion.

3366   MORLEY, ed.

            Sherlock Holmes and Dr. Watson   HB 1944
               A Textbook of Friendship
               Introd. by the editor

Contains: *A Study in Scarlet, The Sign of the Four,* "The Final Problem," "The Adventure of the Empty House," "The Adventure of the Bruce-Partington Plans," a Guide to the Complete Sherlock Holmes (thumbnail sketches of the tales), and a brief bibliography. The Introduction by the editor is a definitive essay.

3367   PORGES, ARTHUR

            "Her Last Bow"   *EQMM* Feb 1957
               An Adventure of Stately Homes

A 3-page parody of Sherlock Holmes, Dr. Fell, and Sir Henry Merrivale, sprinkled with the names of several other famous figures of fiction, and ineffectual about each and all.

3368   RANNIE, ALAN

            "Sherlock Holmes and Railways"   *Rway Mag* (Eng) May 1935

Astute comments by one who knows his lines and times. See also the letter by A. G. R. Hickes in the number following (June 1935) in which the question is raised, at what point Sir Henry Baskerville caught his first glimpse of the moor.

3369   RENDALL, VERNON (HORACE) (b. 1869)

            "Belsize as Commentator—Sherlock Holmes"
               In: The London Nights of Belsize (*Lane 1917*)

Chapter 8 makes mincemeat of the "facts" in "The Three Students" and leaves the reader wondering what would happen if the whole canon were so analyzed.

3370 ROBERTS, [SIR] SYDNEY CASTLE

"Doctor Watson"   Faber 1931
*Prolegomena to the study of a biographical problem, with a
bibliography of S.H.; Criterion Miscellany No. 28, orig. in
Life and Letters, 1930, No. 4.*

The well-known essayist, biographer of Macaulay, and Johnson scholar
tackles the vicissitudinous story of Dr. Watson, his friend, and his marriage. The entire piece is scholarly and delightful; it contains, among other
momentous discoveries, the suggestion of the identity of the names Verner
and Vernet. See also Nos. 3330, 3371, and 3373.

3371 Holmes and Watson   OUP 1953
       A Miscellany

The one-time vice-chancellor of the University of Cambridge, and fertile
producer of academic skits and parodies, has gathered in this slim volume
writings of his own on the Holmes saga that he began to publish in the
late twenties, in magazines and as fugitives. The life and loves of Watson,
the character and tastes of Holmes, the scene of 221B form the bulk of
this scholarly *Beitrag*.

    It is followed by two slight fictions, of which the second brings Holmes
to look into the theft of books from the Megatherium Club (the Athenaeum). The work is sure to have a perennial appeal, since as late as the
summer of 1970 that selfsame club was entreating its members by a posted
notice not to walk away with library books.

3372 ROBINSON, HENRY MORTON

"The Baker Street Irregulars"   *Sat Rev* Dec 4, 1943

An early description of the aims and activities of the BSI—puff, puff.

3373 SAYERS, DOROTHY L.

       Unpopular Opinions   HB 1947

Contains excellent scholarly disquisitions on:

Holmes' College Career   The Dates in the Red-Headed League
Dr. Watson's Christian Name   Aristotle on Detective Fiction
Dr. Watson, Widower

to which are appended, severally, certain notes on:

Reginald Musgrave   Watson's Handwriting
The Dates of "The Sussex Vampire" and "Lady Frances Carfax"

3374 SHAW, JOHN BENNETT

       The Whole Art of Detection   BCP n.d.
       Introd. by Vincent Starrett

A compilation of aphorisms from the Holmes stories that purports to fulfill the title. But the book is a miniature publication (2½" x 2") and the

text falls short of its aim. The Introduction adds nothing but a pleasant note of contentment with the existence of S.H.

3375   SHERLOCK HOLMES EXHIBITIONS 1951–52

Two catalogues, one each for the English and the American exhibitions that were held; the first: at Abbey House, Baker St., London, May–Sept 1951 (Illus.), 59 pp.; the second: at the Plaza Art Galleries, New York, July 2, 1952 ff. (Illus.), 52 pp.

SMITH, EDGAR WADSWORTH (1894–1960)

b. Bethel, Conn.; educ. New York Univ.; enlisted in 1917 after a short secretaryship at J. P. Morgan's. Staff work in War Dept., then for the rest of his life with General Motors, of which he became Director of International Trade. A founder of the BSI, editor of the *BSJ* (q.v.), and scholar-publisher extraordinary in Holmesian lore, E.W.S. had a light touch and the right instinct for subjects in the canon worth exploring or fantasticating about.

3376   Baker Street and Beyond,   BSI 1957
Together with Some Trifling Monographs
      Limited ed. (350)
      Illus. and Maps
      Foreword by Christopher Morley
      Introd. by Vincent Starrett

Contains E.W.'s useful Sherlockian Gazetteer, and a miscellany of entertaining essays and amusing verse, all by the editor.

3377   SMITH, ed.

The Incunabular Sherlock Holmes   BSI 1958
      Limited ed. (350)
      Illus.

The *Incunabula* of the literature consist of sketches and short essays by Arthur Bartlett Maurice, Frank Sidgwick, Arthur Chapman, Charlton Andrews, Ronald A. Knox, Edmund Pearson, A. A. Milne, and a few others of more recent fame. The chronological span of the book is 1902 to 1944, but the true "early times" end c. 1930.

3378   SMITH. See also:

A Baker Street Quartet (4 of the tales in verse)   PH 1950
Letters from Baker Street   PH 1942
The Long Road from Maiwand   PH 1940
The Napoleon of Crime: Prolegomena to a Memoir of
      Professor Moriarty   PH 1953
Profile by Gaslight   S&S 1944
      (40 contributions by experts on the private life at 221B)

3379 STANLEY, DONALD

Holmes Meets 007   BP 1967
  Limited ed. (*247*)

A 7-page pastiche by the Book Editor of the *San Francisco Examiner,*
originally published in that paper Nov 29, 1964. Holmes and Watson confront James Bond and Moriarty, with predictable results. Only mildly
entertaining and scarcely canonical.

3380 STARRETT, VINCENT

"Monologue in Baker Street"   Merm 1960

An extended Christmas card, merry and scholarly, from one of the Founding Fathers of the literature.

3381 The Private Life of Sherlock Holmes   Macm 1933
  Rev. ed.; illus.; (Univ. of Chicago Press 1960)

The first edition, though lacking the benefit of subsequent findings, is a
more solid and better written work than its revision a quarter century
later. The second edition is diffuse and over-quotatious and suffers from a
regrettable self-consciousness, as if burlesque did not depend on straight-
faced attention to the business in hand. Find, if you can, the splendid
original.

  As this *Catalogue* goes to press, a third edition (for paperback publication) is under way.

3382 "Sherlock Holmes,   *Bookman* (U.S.) Feb 1933
  Notes for a Biography"

This article is an inchoate start of *The Private Life of Sherlock Holmes.*
It winds up with a list of the writings of the Master and explanatory
comments.

3383 STARRETT, ed.

221B: Studies in Sherlock Holmes   BSI 1956; orig. Macm 1940
  Limited ed. (*350*)
  Foreword by Edgar W. Smith
  Illus.

A parody skit by Conan Doyle, a Sherlockian crossword puzzle by
F. V. Morley, a Holmes-story pastiche by V. Starrett, a repertory of
Holmes' clients and cited names by Edgar Smith, and twelve essays on
mooted points in the canon constitute this invaluable work of reference.
Useful, entertaining, imaginative, it belongs on every reader-insomniac's
bedside shelf. The principal contributors are:

A. Conan Doyle	The Field Bazaar (brief travesty)
Christopher Morley	Was Sherlock Holmes an American?
R. K. Leavitt	Nummi in Arca (the fiscal Holmes)
Elmer Davis	On the Emotional Geology of Baker Street

Jane Nightwork [Christopher Morley] ·	Dr. Watson's Secret
Earle F. Walbridge	The Care and Feeding of Sherlock Holmes
H. W. Bell	Three Identifications (places in London)
James Keddie	The Other Boarder
Harvey Officer*	Sherlock Holmes and Music
P. M. Stone	Sussex Interview
Vincent Starrett	The Adventure of the Unique Hamlet (fiction)
Richard D. Altick	Mr. Sherlock Holmes and Dr. Samuel Johnson
Frederic Dorr Steele	Sherlock Holmes in Pictures
Henry James Forman	The Creator of Holmes in the Flesh
	(Doyle, not Gillette)
Edgar W. Smith	Appointment in Baker Street
F. V. Morley	A Sherlock Holmes Cross-Word

* This able critic also produced *A Baker Street Song Book* (words and music about 221B) (PH 1943).

3384 WARRACK, GUY

Sherlock Holmes and Music   Faber 1947

A "trifling monograph" of interest to both the collectors on both counts. It is a thorough and witty examination of all the relevant points in the canon, and takes the view long held by JB about the "polyphonic motets of Lassus." Incidentally, the book is dedicated to the author's son John, who must have been a small child on the date of publication but is now a well-known music critic, member of the Berlioz Centenary Committee, as well as a good littérateur and conversationalist.

3385 WINCOR, RICHARD

Sherlock Holmes in Tibet   W&T 1968

It must be said with regret that this attractively printed little volume is an example of Sherlock Holmes "scholarship" overreaching itself. It is neither entertaining nor memorable. Purporting to present an account of the famous sojourn in Tibet (c. 1891, after the presumed death in the Reichenbach Falls), the detective himself reports upon a session he attended at which Tibet's leading metaphysician, Lama Nordup, explained "the secrets of life and death and the mysteries of existence." At the end of this farrago, Moriarty (present as a spy) is unmasked. More than half of the book is devoted to reprinting Berkeley's philosophical views verbatim.

3386 WILLIAMS, STEPHEN

"An Unsung Heroine"   *Punch* Jan 6, 1954

Mrs. Watson's life sympathetically imagined, at the expense of the over-liberated males, S.H. & W.

3387 YUHASOVA, HELENE

A Lauriston Garden of Verses   PH 1946

Six Sherlockian sonnets and a Ballade (limited to 250 copies, a compassionate thought).

PART VI

GHOST STORIES,
STUDIES AND REPORTS
OF THE SUPERNATURAL,
PSYCHICAL RESEARCH,
AND E.S.P.

Gems from the Literature

"Do I believe in ghosts?" I have seen too many to believe in them.
—Samuel Taylor Coleridge

On one occasion, when Dr. Phelps was alone, walking across the room, a key and a nail flew over his head and fell at his feet. That same evening, in the presence of the whole family, a turnip fell from the ceiling.
—Sacheverell Sitwell, *Poltergeists*

A hypochondriac at best, I fell to worrying about my health.
—Carl Jacobi, "The Unpleasantness at Carver House"

They were almost to a letter the most esoteric communications, dealing with mystical matters beyond my ken . . . belonging as these matters did to an age of superstition all but lost since the Dark Ages.
—H. P. Lovecraft, "The Horror of the Middle Span"

Man may shudder from a momentary contact with the unknown.
—Alfred Hitchcock, "The Quality of Suspense"

Dark walks home at night after dining with the uncle. Curious disturbances as they pass through the shrubberies.
—M. R. James, "Stories I Have Tried to Write"

. . . be content to cause us a mild and pleasurable discomfort.
—"Philemon" on the Ghost Story

3388   ASQUITH, [LADY] CYNTHIA (MARY EVELYN CHARTERIS), ed. (1887–1960)

A Book of Modern Ghosts   Scrib 1953
   In Eng: The Second Ghost Book

An unusual lot of good pieces by the masters and near masters, including:
Danse Macabre by L. A. G. Strong; Memoirs of a Ghost by G. W. Stonier;
The Guardian by Walter de la Mare; The Chelsea Cat by C. H. B. Kitchin;
The Amethyst Cross by Mary Fitt.
   See also: *The Ghost Book* (Scrib 1927).

3389   BIERCE, AMBROSE

In the Midst of Life   ModL n.d. [1926]; orig. 1891
   Introd. by Geo. Sterling
   Pref. by the author

This is Bierce's deservedly famous collection of brief and shocking Tales
of Soldiers and Civilians (the original title). The author tells in his six-
line Preface how the book was denied first publication in America. Its
appearance there was due to the courage and judgment of Albert and
Charles Boni in 1909, and the work is now a classic of "our" literature.
   Everybody has a favorite among these twenty-six tales. The one that
perhaps concentrates more of life, imagination, reality, unreality, mental
anguish, and horror is "An Occurrence at Owl-Creek Bridge." It may be
noted by the curious that although style is the whole secret of this sort
of literature, Bierce, who obviously is a master of the right style for it,
does not write with marked elegance or distinctiveness. Cf. Blackwood,
below.

3390   BLACKWOOD, ALGERNON (1869–1951)

Tales of the Mysterious and the Macabre   Hamlyn 1968/1966

A collection of twenty-three tales that successfully displays the facets of
his craft and thereby shows his limitations. What he conceives is usually
original and strong, but he repeats his *données,* and his facility with words
—indeed his excess of them—obscures the idea and drowns out the telling
phrases. The longest story here—The Damned—demonstrates this with
finality. The best shorter pieces are: The Wings of Horus / The Olive /
The Sea Fit / Special Delivery / The Tryst.
   Note that "First Hate" is an excellent tale of crime, with no touch of
the supernatural. The Dr. Silence story, last in the book, does not fairly
represent the series in which the Doctor appears.

3391   BLACKWOOD. See also:

The Centaur   Macm 1911
Day and Night Stories   Dutt 1917
The Empty House and Other Ghost Stories   Nash 1906
John Silence, Physician Extraordinary   Dutt 1920

3392 BROWN, FREDRIC

"Don't Look Behind You"   *MD* July 1957

An effective horror story that involves the reader as something more than a spectator. A trick, if you will, but one that justifies itself, thanks to good prose.

3393 BULWER-LYTTON, EDWARD

The Haunted and the Haunters (*in No. 3400*)   Orig. 1859
   The House and the Brain

This masterpiece of the supernatural with detection added must be read by anyone claiming familiarity with the best work. Its peculiar merit is two-fold: it creates horror by the simplest means and it combines in the explanation something vaguely "scientific" with the absolutely unnatural. This tour de force was not repeated in the author's second effort, *A Strange Story* (1862), though it is worth reading none the less.

3394 BURTON, JEAN

Heyday of a Wizard   Harrap 1948
   Pref. by Harry Price

This excellent life of the medium Daniel Dunglas Home finds a place here because of the unexplained—if not inexplicable—events for which he was responsible, repeatedly and under fairly stringent controls. Andrew Lang (q.v.) thought him sufficiently "unsolved" to number him among his *Historical Mysteries* (No. 3207).

3395 CALDECOTT, [SIR] ANDREW

Not Exactly Ghosts   LG 1947

Twelve anecdotes of the supernatural, told with just the right degree of matter-of-factness, and showing a fine perception of the quietly fearsome. The reader is left wishing for more.

3396 CALDER-MARSHALL, ARTHUR

The Scarlet Boy   Harp 1962

A well-written novel which has both a haunted house and a ghost, yet manages to make both incidental to its art, very much recalling "The Turn of the Screw."

3397 CANNING, JOHN, ed.

Fifty Great Ghost Stories   Odhams 1966
   Introd. by the editor

All the fifty (at the rate of about 10 pages each) were written "special" for this book, which continues the excellent Odhams tradition of "fifties" in mystery, detection and the like, brought up to date every decade or so. The trouble with this group is that many of the tales are nonfiction fiction and we are not told which are which. The dialogue supplied in recitals of factual events is meant to "entertain, not prove or disprove" authenticity. Yet doubt as to the character of what we are given lessens entertainment, for the reasons advanced in No. 3404.

3398   CARR, A. H. Z.

"A Sudden Dread of . . . Nothing"   *EQMM* Jan 1955

A ghost story with a new device for compassing the mysterious deaths, but perhaps too long for its substance.

3399   CARTER, BETTY

"October the Nineteenth"   *LMM* Summer 1954

A good, simple, short ghost story about love, hatred, and revenge, with a logical ending of the utmost originality.

3400   CERF, BENNETT, ed.

Famous Ghost Stories   ModL 1944
      Introd. and Critical Note by the editor

These fifteen are well chosen and their merits fully understood by the editor, who concludes with a discussion of the "current crop," meaning the anonymous anecdotes going the rounds of dinner parties in New York in 1943. They are well retold, as one might expect from this practiced raconteur.

The anthology numbers ten classics by: Bulwer-Lytton, Oliver Onions, Saki, M. R. James, Bierce, W. W. Jacobs, Kipling, Blackwood, E. F. Benson, and Brander Matthews. The other five are equally good, if one happens to like Isaak Dinesen's long-drawn-out and over-detailed Supper at Elsinore. There can be no question, though, about: The Considerate Hosts by Thorp McClusky / August Heat by W. F. Harvey / and The Return of Andrew Bentley by August Derleth and Mark Shorer. As for the brief and poignant On the Brighton Road by Richard Middleton, it is a neglected masterpiece.

3401   CHRISTIE, AGATHA

The Hound of Death   CCC 1933

Twelve short stories that deal mostly with the supernatural but also include the celebrated "Witness for the Prosecution." For other collections containing her ghost stories, see Nos. 2416 and 2425.

3402   CLARKE, IDA CLYDE

Men Who Wouldn't Stay Dead   Ack 1945
      Illus.

Twenty ghost stories based on testimony of supernatural events, from the time of John Wesley and Andrew Jackson to that of Woodrow Wilson and Houdini. The accounts are brief, refer to documents (letters, remarks), and are rather tonelessly written.

3403 DAVENPORT, BASIL, ed.

Ghostly Tales to be Told   Faber 1952
Introd. by the editor

Arranged by the author for telling (not reading) and introduced by ad-
vice on how to do so. The best are the famous Monkey's Paw by
W. W. Jacobs and Crouching at the Door by D. K. Broster. Next come
May Sinclair's Where Their Fire Is Not Quenched and Jane Rice's The
Refugee. The remaining dozen are by good authors (Dickens, M. R. James,
Algernon Blackwood, Thomas Burke, and Arthur Machen, among others)
but they are not their authors' best, by far.

3404 DE LA MARE, COLIN, ed.

They Walk Again   Dutt 1931
An Anthology of Ghost Stories
Introd. by Walter de la Mare

The highly qualified introducer makes a fundamental point about the dif-
ference between the disquiet caused by a reported or investigated "true"
ghost and the pleasurable anxiety caused by a well-wrought fictional one.
Then we read the apt selection of tales familiar and unfamiliar by: Bierce,
Dunsany, Blackwood, Edith Wharton, J. D. Beresford, R. H. Benson,
L. P. Jacks, E. F. Benson, Oliver Onions, M. R. James, W. W. Jacobs,
L. P. Hartley, Le Fanu, and several others—a treasury of good stuff.

3405 DE LA MARE, WALTER (JOHN) (1873–1956)

Collected Tales   Knopf 1950
Chosen and introduced by Edward Wagenknecht

The twenty-four tales are of all kinds; the ghost-seeker will find here
Seaton's Aunt, Missing, Strangers and Pilgrims, and All Hallows. Not all
of these contain indisputable ghosts, but horror inhabits them nonetheless.
   Seaton's Aunt is a classic of quiet horror in the country. The means
are so spare, the words so subdued, it is a miracle to find them causing
shudders and sustaining their effect long after the tale is told.

3406 DENT, JOHN CHARLES

The Gerrard Street Mystery and   Ross 1888
Other Weird Tales
Prefatory sketch about the author

The author was trained in law, was active as a journalist, and wrote extensively in the fields of Canadian biography and history. The four tales
are: The Gerrard Street Mystery, Gagtooth's Image, The Haunted House
on Duchess Street, and Savareen's Disappearance. All are laid in upper
Canada (Ontario) in the early or midnineteenth century, and the first,
set in the Toronto of 1857, is the most interesting, with its blend of the
supernatural (a ghostly uncle) and the very natural and absconding
forger.

3407 DERLETH, AUGUST, ed.

Travellers by Night   Goll 1968

Fourteen stories labeled supernatural, of which very few are tolerably
good. The moderns write badly and their imaginations seem tired and
reminiscent. The best tales are in fact by old-timers, though they also are
afflicted by latter-day breeziness and incoherence. Read H. R. Wakefield,
Death of a Bumblebee (an excellent situation disappointingly resolved)
and John Metcalfe, Not There (humor misplaced at the end). William
Hope Hodgson, The Wild Man of the Sea, is good, but not ghostly at all;
and Joseph Payn Brennan, Episode on Cain Street, is full of good touches
but poorly worked out. As for the contribution by H. P. Lovecraft, whom
many deem a master, one must confess that The Horror from the Middle
Span seems feeble in conception, long-winded, and productive of shudders
only by its diction and grammar.

3408 DICKENS, CHARLES

"The Signal Man," in *The Best Short Stories of Dickens* (Scrib
1947); orig. in *Mugby Junction* (1866)

Sometimes preceded by the phrase "Branch Line No. 1," the title of this
tale calls up a moving series of incidents whose impact is out of proportion
to the cause. Dickens had the secret of making both reality and unreality
vibrate with meaning, and here, in his most famous ghost story, he managed to link the mystery of death with the awe inseparable from railroading.

For other tales by the same master hand, see "To Be Read at Dusk" and
the ghostly interludes in *Pickwick Papers,* the *Christmas Stories,* and
other volumes of any collected edition of D.'s works.

3409 DOBREE, BONAMY

Introduction to *The Mysteries of Udolpho* by Ann Radcliffe (No.
1779)

This Introduction by the English scholar and master of Wadham College
makes the important distinction between terror and horror in literature
and between the supernatural and the superstitious. He also confirms these
readers in their admiration of Walter Scott's essay on Mrs. R. and points
out how frequently *Udolpho* has been reprinted, presumably in answer to
a steady demand for a century and three-quarters. The last previous reissue, it is interesting to note, was edited by R. Austin Freeman (q.v.).

3410 EVANS, WAINWRIGHT

"The 'Return' of Conan Doyle"   *MD* July 1957

An interview with Adrian Conan Doyle about his father's helpful message
and explanations of the why and how. Feeble on all sides. It is interesting
to recall that in an early story *Arthur C. D.* had written of "those elusive
phenomena which are grouped, with much that is foolish and much that is
fraudulent, under the common heading of spiritualism," and had deplored

that his hero's "researches, which had begun with an open mind, ended unhappily in dogma. . . . He represented in our little group the body of men who have made these singular phenomena into a religion" (*Round the Fire Stories*, 1909, pp. 126–27).

3411   FORSTER, E(DWARD) M(ORGAN) (1879–1970)

"The Other Side of the Hedge"
   In: The Collected Tales of E. M. Forster (*Knopf 1947*)

This fantasy of a supernatural return to the Garden of Eden by a 25-year-old pedestrian "on the road" has been anthologized as a ghost story. It is rather a fantasy, like the other eleven in the collected tales. All were written before 1914 and have a common theme, akin to that of the story here described. "The Story of the Siren" also mingles the supernatural with everyday life, using pagan mythology instead of Christian.

3412   GOODRICH-FREER, A. (also Miss X)

The Professional and Other Psychic Stories   Hurst 1900

The author is a psychical researcher who contributes three tales, supposedly based on fact, to this compilation in which four others have one story each. The writing is good in the manner of the nineties—brisk, satirical, and elegant. The episodes are uneven, the best being Olive Birrell's story of second sight, The History of Malcolm Mackenzie. The other contributors are: Christabel Coleridge, M. E. Bramston, and G. M. Robins.

3413   HAINING, PETER, ed.

Caligari's Black Book   WHA 1968
   An Excursion into the Macabre in 13 Acts
   Introd. by the editor

The title was chosen in the belief that the famous German film of 1920, *The Cabinet of Dr. Caligari* (star, Werner Kraus; director, Robert Weine), was the start of a new cinematic art and the inspiration of much macabre literature. The film was a good one, but it drew on past writings rather than inspired later ones. This collection proves the point by bringing together authors who antedate Caligari in chronology and in literary devices. The thirteen tales—all involving some kind of grisly performance—are:

S. L. Dennis	The Second Awakening of a Magician
Ray Bradbury	The Jar
Lady Eleanor Smith	Satan's Circus
Agatha Christie	The Last Seance
August Derleth	Mrs. Elting Plays Her Part
Anthony Gittins	The Third Performance
A. M. Burrage	The Waxwork
Robert Bloch	The Sorcerer's Apprentice
Marcel Aymé	The Dwarf
J. B. Priestley	The Demon King
Hazel Heald	The Horror in the Museum
H. R. Wakefield	Farewell Performance
Barry Pain	The End of a Show

HALIFAX, LORD (Frederick Lindley Wood, first earl) (1881–1959)

British ambassador in Washington during the second world war; took important part in his country's politics between the wars. His interest in the supernatural began in early manhood, when he started record of true and fictional events. Later published by his son, now the second earl.

3414 HALIFAX, VISCOUNT, ed.

Lord Halifax's Ghost Book   Didier 1944
    Two forewords by the editor

Sixty-seven long and short recitals of ghostly occurrences, going back to the eighteenth century and covering the experience or hearsay of numerous friends of the Halifax circle. An important conclusion after reading is that accounts of "real" ghosts do not compare with fiction for interest and horror. In this collection the best pieces are those that have been dressed up for magazine publication before reaching Lord H.'s hands and those that are frankly fiction, like Lord H.'s own contribution. These preferred pieces are: The Shrouded Watcher, Labédoyère's Doom, The Restless Dead, Colonel P's Ghost Story, The Bordeaux Diligence.

3415 HAMMETT, DASHIELL, ed.

Creeps by Night   Tudor 1931
    Also: Modern Tales of Horror
    Introd. by the editor

Twenty tales of the supernatural, marked by a preference for authors established in general literature. The selections are:

William Faulkner	A Rose for Emily
John Collier	Green Thoughts
André Maurois	The House
Peter Fleming	The Kill
Philip MacDonald	Ten O'clock
L. A. G. Strong	Breakdown
William Seabrook	The Witch's Vengeance
Conrad Aiken	Mr. Arcularis
Harold Dearden	The Strange Case of Mrs. Arkwright
Stephen Vincent Benét	The King of the Cats
W. E. Backus	The Phantom Bus

and nine others.

3416 HARPER, C. ARMITAGE

American Ghost Stories   Jarr 1929

Standard anthology pieces by: Washington Irving, Poe, Hawthorne, Fitz-James O'Brien, Mark Twain, Frank Stockton, Joel Chandler Harris, Brander Matthews, Ambrose Bierce, Edith Wharton, Mary E. Wilkins Freeman, F. M. Crawford, Ellis Parker Butler, Theodore Dreiser, and Wilbur Daniel Steele.

3417 HARRISON, MICHAEL

"At the Heart of It" *LMM* Summer 1954

Bookshops have been frequently haunted, but a book has rarely been used as a receptacle for malign survivals. In this story the mixture of historical past and present and the exhibition of supernatural effects in the course of ordinary business is adroitly done, though with rather less horror arising than one might desire.

3418 HEARD, H. F.

The Great Fog and Other Weird Tales   Van 1944

Of the eight tales in this collection, only the one in the title of the book had appeared earlier. It is a fairly usual science-fiction story, in which the giant fog produced by a proliferating fungus brings about dramatic changes in terrestrial existence—for man's good, perhaps? More straightforward, and actually the first item in the book, is The Crayfish. Here near-science is blended with detection in the story of the contrived death of a wife. The method is clever but impractical. Of the remaining six let it be said that M. R. James has done this sort of thing so well that comparisons are odious. But Wingless Victory and Dromenon at least aspire to the true style.

3419 HEARN, LAFCADIO (1850–1904)

Some Chinese Ghosts   ModL 1927; orig. 1887
Introd. by Manuel Komroff
Notes and Glossary

Six tales written by Hearn in his New Orleans days and based on much study for color and verisimilitude. They are short, strange, and moving, and the "prose poetry" of the Symbolist period here seems appropriate.

3420 HEYWOOD, ROSALIND

The Sixth Sense   C&W 1959
In U.S.: Beyond the Reach of Sense

A solid and well-written discussion of the classical topics: survival after death, mediumship, and qualitative and quantitative studies of thought transference; all this followed by four interesting attempts at explanation by physicists, biologists, psychologists, and philosophers.

3421 HILL, DEREK

"Could There?"   *LMM* Summer 1954

A good short tale of the supernatural, done in a workaday setting: new gimmicks and a fair thrill without horror—unless it be that of the sane man surrounded by the mad.

708

3422 HOFFMANN, ERNEST THEODOR WILHELM (1776–1822)

Tales   Wyn 1946
    Trans. by Christopher Lazare (?)
    Biog. sketch by the trans.

It will not do to forget one of the great creators of the modern story of
the supernatural, in which some idea or feeling—philosophical or amatory
or artistic—is conveyed by the blending of the usual and the preternatural.
Offenbach's opera has popularized the author's name but scarcely given
the public a notion of Hoffmann's range and powers. For the musical, it is
recommended that they begin with "Don Juan" and go on to "The
Doubles" and "The Legacy." Seven other tales are provided here, the
first in readable English. The well-versed reader will see how much Hoffmann influenced Hawthorne, Poe, and Stevenson.

    N.B. Hoffmann's usual initials E.T.A. embody his substitution of
Amadeus for *Wilhelm,* out of musical passion for Mozart.

3423 HOPKINS, R. THURSTON, ed.

Cavalcade of Ghosts   WW 1956
    Introd. by the editor

The two parts of this excellent collection divide the field into fact and
fiction, which the discursive but not unpleasant introduction weaves in
and out of to prepare the reader for the feast. Fourteen of the "real"
ghosts are anonymously reported; three (Frank R. Gardner, Nancy Price,
S. Baring-Gould) come from known connoisseurs of apparitions. Of the
remaining nine pieces (fiction), the two "Stoneground" stories by
E. G. Swain are the best—fully as good as M. R. James; and the three
by Michael Saltmarsh come second. For more of Swain, see No. 3466.

3424 IRVING, WASHINGTON

Selected Writings   ModL 1945
    Introd. by Saxe Commins

A convenient volume for reading Irving's tales and sketches of ghosts
and hauntings, none of them especially strong, but pleasant examples of
"the traveler's tale" of old coach-and-inn days.

3425 JAMES, HENRY

"The Turn of the Screw"   1898
    Repr. in The Complete Tales of Henry James,
      ed. L. Edel, vol. 10 (Lipp 1964)

Horror without trappings dominates in this masterpiece by the sheer
force of portrayed evil and its effect on innocence. The events are cloudy
but their invisible consequences are palpable and not to be forgotten. A
tale to read and reread without "interpretation"—unless one is compelled
to earn a Ph.D.

    Also in Thomson, *Mystery Book* (No. 2836).

3426   JAMES, H. See also:

The Ghostly Tales of Henry James, ed. Leon Edel;
Introd. by ed. (18 tales, spanning James' entire career)   RUP 1948

3427   JAMES, MONTAGUE RHODES (1862–1936)

Collected Ghost Stories of an Antiquary   Arn 1970/1931

The modern master of the genre insisted with excess modesty that he was
only following in the footsteps of Sheridan Le Fanu (q.v.), who was *the*
Master. But James added a distinctive element of "scholarship"—he was
himself a great scholar, recognized as such by Lord Acton when James
was only 30—and he used a style at once stripped and skillfully pedantic
which was all his own. Almost all his tales were superbly successful. If one
had to choose a single example of his merits, perhaps "The Mezzotint"
would strike many readers as the best. In this volume see also the final
Stories I Have Tried to Write.

For reference, here is the chronology of the volumes later collected.
The very first pair of stories dates back to 1893. They were written
for reading to a group of friends, including A. C. and E. F. Benson; so
were a few of the later ones.

Ghost Stories of an Antiquary	1904
More Ghost Stories	1911
A Thin Ghost and Others	1919
A Warning to the Curious and Other Ghost Stories	1925
"The Wailing Well: A Ghost Story"	1928
Collected Ghost Stories	1931
"The Experiment: A Ghost Story"	1931

3428   JAMES, M. R. See also:

"The Edwin Drood Syndicate"   Camb Rev 1905–6, 123; 142
"About Edwin Drood"   Camb Rev 1910–11, 346–7
Twelve Medieval Ghost Stories (from manuscript sources)   Arn 1922
The Five Jars (fantasy for children)   Arn 1922
Madam Crowl's Ghost and Other Tales by J. S. Le Fanu (ed.)   1923
Introd. to *Ghosts and Marvels* (ed. by V. H. Collins)   WldCl 1924
Introd. to *Uncle Silas,* by J. S. Le Fanu   WldCl 1926

3429   JAMES, WILLIAM

"Final Impressions of a Psychical Researcher"
     In: Memories and Studies   LG 1911

This essay for the general public sums up the conclusions James reached
after twenty-five years of attention to supernormal events and the scientific studies published about them. He declares himself baffled, no further
advanced in understanding than at the beginning, but more convinced
than at first that here is a legitimate and important subject for investigation. He proposes as a working hypothesis the idea that has come to be
known as the collective unconscious. For the technical work of direct
observation and analysis by James, see his "Report on Mrs. Piper's Hodgson Control" (*SPR* [Eng. and U.S.] 1909).

3430   JENKINS, ALAN C(HARLES), b. 1914, ed.

Thin Air   Blackie 1966

A good 500 pages of the regular stuff, no worse for being familiar, but
no extension of our trembling horizons: "The Monkey's Paw," "The
Canterville Ghost," and the like from the pens of M. R. James, A. Blackwood, Maupassant, Poe, Saki, and a very few moderns, who suffer by
comparison.

3431   JOHNSON, ROSSITER (1840–1931), ed.

Little Classics: Intellect   24th ed. HM 1912; orig. 1874

   Vol. 2 of the Little Classics

The all-embracing term Intellect covers, in this oft-reprinted collection, a
disparate set of seven pieces, beginning with Bulwer-Lytton's masterpiece,
The House and the Brain (the alternative title of The Haunted and the
Haunters). Poe's Fall of the House of Usher and Hawthorne's extraordinary Wakefield are the other two well-known tales. De Quincey's
Murder as One of the Fine Arts is a classic and contains narrative but is
not a story like the rest. Perhaps the gem of the collection is Dickens's
tale of Chops the Dwarf—amazingly modern in feeling. The remaining
pair attempt the supernatural with poor success: Harriet Prescott
Spofford's D'Outre Mort is flowery-sentimental and Rebecca Harding
Davis's Captain's Story falls back on a natural and flat explanation, but
both can claim some period interest.

3432   Little Classics: Mystery   24th ed. HM 1912; orig. 1876
           Vol. 8 of the Little Classics

Leisurely but sufficiently gripping stories of unexplained occurrences by
eight authors, among them Dickens, The Signalman, Hawthorne, The
Birthmark / Allan Cunningham, The Haunted Ships / Amelia B. Edwards,
The Four-Fifteen Express / Robert T. S. Lowell, A Raft That No Man
Made / Catherine Crowe, The Advocate's Wedding Day / William D.
O'Connor, The Ghost / and Frances O'Connor, The Invisible Princess.

3433   JONES, LOUIS C(LARK) (b. 1908)

Things That Go Bump in the Night   H&W 1963/1959

The director of the New York State Historical Association in Coopers-
town is an American folklorist who has collected popular tales of ghosts
and also written ghost stories for children. In this book he relates in a
casual style the facts and beliefs about the supernatural that he has
gathered in the course of his scholarly work. He produces some unexpected statistics. Only 13 percent of ghosts are hostile; 29 percent are
benevolent, or at least amiable; 58 percent are completely indifferent. Is
one to suppose that this majority has become alienated?

3434   KIPLING, RUDYARD (1865–1936)

Phantoms and Fantasies   Dday 1965
    Half-page introd. by anonymous ed.
    Illus.

The book is probably intended for boys, but the adult reader enjoys the tall format and good print—as well as the twenty tales. They form a good skimming of the author's output in the genre designated by the title. We are given They / The Phantom Rickshaw / The Mark of the Beast / The Man Who Would Be King / The Return of Imray / My One Time Ghost / and other lesser-known ones that embody crime or horror or both.

3435   LANDON, PERCEVAL

Raw Edges   Hein 1908
    Illus.

Thirteen imaginative short stories, several providing considerable suspense and a few giving amusing touches of the science and technology of the early twentieth century. There is much to admire, as well as much to disappoint. "Thurnley Abbey" and "The Gyroscope" are particularly memorable. These two tales and two of the others are effectively illustrated by Alberto Martini.

3436   LAWRENCE, MARGERY

No. 7 Queer St.   M&M 1969

Though these five tales provide but a mild sort of entertainment, they are unusual in their use of supernatural powers to serve the ends of detection. Dr. Miles Pennoyer, who neither smokes nor drinks, relies on getting in tune with the extrasensory in order to ascertain human relationships and the truth of misdeeds. Good London and England country settings and good writing.

3437   LOVECRAFT, H(OWARD) P(HILLIPS) (1890–1937), was born and lived in and near Providence, R.I. He was an ailing youth and never attained much health. He traveled little and bent his energies on writing and amateur printing, while also pursuing an interest in astronomy and the occult. He created mythic lands and persons and used these in his stories of the supernatural. His work is highly prized by a devoted band of readers; to those outside this circle he seems to write pretentiously and badly, and his imaginings appear to lack originality (see No. 3407). His output was large, given his handicaps, and it is to be supplemented by the publication of his Selected Letters (vol. I, 1965). See: *The Outsider and Others* (ss), *Beyond the Wall of Sleep, Marginalia, The Lurker at the Threshold* (with August Derleth), *The Survivor and Others* (with August Derleth), *Collected Poems,* and the substance of three other volumes, to be published.

3438 McNEAR, ROBERT

"The Green Gorevan" *EQMM* Dec 1969

A most unusual tale concerning the theft of Oriental rugs, one of which (as titled) has a malign power of its own.

3439 MACHEN, ARTHUR (1863–1947)

Tales of Horror and the Supernatural Knopf 1948
  Ed. by Philip Van Doren Stern
  Note on Machen by Robert Hillyer

A good selection of the work the author did in his best period, shortly after the turn of the century. The stories are not of ghosts, but of elemental evil spirits, as in Machen's masterpiece, *The Great God Pan.*

3440 MACHEN. See also:

Children of the Pool and Other Stories Hutch 1936
The Cozy Room Rich 1936
The House of Souls Knopf 1923
The Shining Pyramid Knopf 1925
The Three Impostors Knopf 1923

3441 MALDEN, R. H.

Nine Ghosts Arn 1968/1947

Written from time to time between 1909 and 1942, these stories are explicitly credited by the author to the inspiration given by M. R. James and, through him, by Sheridan Le Fanu. These small tales are worthy of their ancestry without exhibiting any great natural talent; they show what can be done by taking pains with style and detail, in support of the wish to give pleasure.

3442 MARGOLIES, JOSEPH A(ARON), ed. (b. 1889)

Strange and Fantastic Stories WH 1946
  Introd. by Christopher Morley

The book buyer of Brentano's collected fifty tales of the ghostly and macabre, including in his ambit some of the best known by Henry and M. R. James, Kipling, E. T. A. Hoffmann, F. M. Crawford, E. F. Benson, Max Beerbohm, Algernon Blackwood, Dickens, Dunsany, Hawthorne, Bierce, Le Fanu, Fitz-James O'Brien, Poe, Scott, Stevenson, May Sinclair, Maupassant, Hugh Walpole, Michael Arlen, Arthur Machen, and E. M. Forster.

His commendable additions from less usual sources include:

Balzac The Executioner (El Verdugo)
S. V. Benét Daniel Webster and the Sea Serpent
J. D. Beresford The Criminal
Wilkie Collins "Blow-Up with the Brig"
Richard Garnett The Elixir of Life
W. F. Harvey August Heat

D. H. Lawrence	The Woman Who Rode Away
W. S. Maugham	Lord Mountdrago
D. Sayers	The Cyprian Cat
James Stephens	Desire

The Beresford story just misses being a triumph of the supernatural in its effort to make us believe that the universally execrated criminal in the dock is a projection of every man's guilt: he fails to appear on a photographic plate exposed in court, and he probably is not executed, though officialdom thinks he is.

The Introduction, by the way, is but a longish excuse for not writing an introduction, and it consequently adds little to the book except biographical details about the editor. But the reprinting of Alexander Woollcott's retelling of "The Vanishing Lady" (orig. in *While Rome Burns* (1934) with comments on the ubiquity of the idea is useful for retracing its many appearances, as far back as 1889 at least. Anna Katharine Green is omitted, however, and naturally enough Crispin's *Moving Toyshop,* q.v.

3443 MASON, A. E. W.

"The House of Terror"
In: The Four Corners of the World (*H&S 1917*)

A very fair tale of jealousy, revenge, remorse, and the subtly supernatural, with a convenient quicksand to bring about the original death.

3444 THE MERCURY STORY-BOOK   LG 1929
Introd. by J. B. Priestley

This chunky anthology shows to what extent English literature of high quality is devoted to (obsessed by?) the supernatural. A good third of these tales, published in the normal course of magazine editing over a decade, can rate as stories of the supernatural; horror or simple mystery being the occasion for character-drawing or comment on the universe. Among the outstanding pieces are: Jessie K. Marsh, The Shortest Night of the Year (an historical ghost) and Stacy Aumonier, The Everlasting Club.

3445 THE SECOND MERCURY STORY BOOK   LG 1931
Introd. by Robert Lynd

The second squeezing from the *London Mercury* is even richer in noteworthy ghost tales. See especially:
Arnold Smith, The Face in the Fresco (ecclesiastical mystery and horror) / Francis Brett Young, A Message (telepathy and love triangle in wartime) / Dorothy Johnson Simcox, The Explanation / Margaret Irwin, The Book (retribution by means of preternatural events).

3446 METCALFE, JOHN has to his credit two stories, much anthologized, which are considered classic in the very special genre of "horror without adequate cause." One of these is The Double Admiral, which will be found in No. 3459 and elsewhere. The other is The Smoking Leg, in No.

3444. In the second, the sea, the East, and the vagueness of the trouble conspire to bring about the shivers.

3447   NASH, OGDEN

"The Three D's"   *EQMM* Feb 1957; orig. 1948

An extremely short tale of the supernatural, far from the humorous, but near to the witchcraft of Salem, which is the setting.

3448   NETHERWOOD, BRYAN A., ed.

Medley Macabre   Hamm 1966

A large and as it were standard collection of short ghost stories (M. R. James, H. G. Wells, J. B. Priestley, Oliver Onions), supplemented with a choice group of lesser-known writers, e.g., Noel Langley.

3449   O'BRIEN, FITZ-JAMES (1828–61)

The Poems and Stories   Osgood 1881
       With a Memoir of the Author

O'Brien was a gifted writer who succumbed in the American Civil War. Of the thirteen stories in this volume, several are worthy to rank beside those of Poe and Bierce. The masterpiece among them is certainly "What Was It?" which JB thinks better than Bierce's The Damned Thing.

N.B. This volume is difficult to come by, though not a rare book in the technical sense.

3450   OGDEN, GEORGE W.

Custodian of Ghosts   Hale 1951

A long, improbable tale of apparitions in an army post. They are scarcely scary and the hero colonel not very mili-tary. Henry McLeod does bring about a solution and a reunion of living and dead to an accompaniment of love and kisses, but it's all stuff out of books.

3451   ONIONS, OLIVER

Widdershins   C&W 1968; orig. Secker 1911

This group of nine stories has for its almost exclusive theme the life of the artist, which supplies unusual opportunities for the supernatural. The leading tale, The Beckoning Fair One, is long and generally known through anthologizing. It is better about literature than about ghosts. Io is superb and Benlian a close second, together with The Accident. Then come The Cigarette Case and Hic Jacet, both with good claims to attention. Phantas and Rooum seem poor in comparison with the rest.

N.B. The title, often used as a synonym for "counterclockwise," actually means "contrary to the course of the sun" and connotes events contrary to nature.

3452 POE, EDGAR ALLAN

Tales of Mystery and Imagination   Everyman 1966/1908
Introd. by Padraic Colum

Poe was the creator not only of the detective story, but also of the horror story as the genre is practiced today. When speaking of ghost stories, John Hampden makes the point clear by comparing the kind of interest evoked by tales addressed to religious believers with the different thrill and concern of the secular and quasi-scientific mind contemplating the supernatural. For the tales of ratiocination, See No. 2718.

3453 PRICE, HARRY (1881–1948)

Fifty Years of Psychical Research   LG 1939
Illus.

A lively, lucid, and appropriately skeptical account of activities which at a given point merge with the narrative of the author's own dedicated career. Before one can criticize either the enterprise or its promoters, one must at least read this book and weigh the adequacy and applicability of the methods used in pursuit of spirits, poltergeists, and co.

3454 The Most Haunted House in England   LG 1940
Ten Years' Investigation of Borley Rectory

The good thing about this volume is that it is nine-tenths documents. They are ably set side by side and linked by the veteran field worker of the SPR and one may be sure there is no hugger-mugger in the sources and reports. The question remains—how to account for the events, which include thermometer readings.

3455 "Q." [QUILLER-COUCH, (SIR) ARTHUR] (1863–1944)

Old Fires and Profitable Ghosts   Dent 1928; orig. 1900

Fifteen tales of persons who either in spirit or in body revisit old scenes— mostly good for mild shudders. Among the best are: "The Room of Mirrors," "The Penance of John Emmet," and the final enigma, "Which?"

3456 Q.'s Mystery Stories   Dent 1937
Pref. by the author

This collection of twenty tales from a wide range of previous publications is slightly mislabeled: all the tales are of dreamland or the supernatural. Some belong to the first class of works of this kind, but in every instance the telling is rendered precious by continual self-interruption and contorted ways of putting simple things.

3457 REEVE, ARTHUR B., ed.

The Best Ghost Stories   ModL 1925
Introd. by the editor

Eleven tales of classic cut, supplemented with a chapter on Banshees and fourteen extracts from newspapers, going back to 1884, under the heading

716

of Real American Ghosts. The introduction, though in bullet-like para-graphs and full of silly rhetorical questions, makes the good point that modern science has affected the tone of the ghost story as it has affected the contents of detective fiction.

We are also told that the choice of tales in the volume was recom-mended by J(oseph) L(ewis) French. The choice consists of: Defoe, The Apparition of Mrs. Veal / M. R. James, Canon Alberic's Scrapbook / Bulwer-Lytton, The Haunted and the Haunters / Leopold Kompert, The Silent Woman / E. F. Benson, The Man Who Went Too Far / Algernon Blackwood, The Woman's Ghost Story / Kipling, The Phantom Rick-shaw / Brander Matthews, The Rival Ghosts / Bierce, The Damned Thing / Ellis Parker Butler, Dey Ain't No Ghosts / Vincent O'Sullivan, The Interval.

3458   ROLT, L. T. C.

Sleep No More   Const 1948
    Twelve Stories of the Supernatural

All are brief—the little book totals only 162 pages—and each provides evidence of the skill which the author shares with such artists as Machen and M. R. James. Rolt knows his canals, mines, railways, and motorcars so well that he can add his supernatural ingredients so as to produce a homogeneous blend, palatable to all sensible men. Would that more engineers wrote like this!

3459   SAYERS, DOROTHY L., ed.

"Mystery and Horror"
    Section of: The Second Omnibus of Crime (No. 2779)
The contents are:

Stacy Aumonier	Miss Bracegirdle Does Her Duty
R. H. Barham	The Leech of Folkestone
Max Beerbohm	A. V. Laider
Ambrose Bierce	The Damned Thing
Algernon Blackwood	Secret Worship
Mrs. E. Bland	No. 17
A. M. Burrage	The Waxwork
Stephen Crane	The Open Boat
Clemence Dane	The King Waits
Walter de la Mare	The Tree
Ford Madox Ford	Riesenberg
Holloway Horn	The Old Man
Violet Hunt	The Prayer
W. W. Jacobs	The Well
Manuel Komroff	Ants
J. S. Le Fanu	Mr. Justice Harbottle
Edward Bulwer-Lytton	The Haunted and the Haunters
Arthur Machen	The Great Return
Frederick Marryat	The Story of the Greek Slave
John Masefield	Anty Bligh
Herman Melville	The Bell-Tower

John Metcalfe	The Double Admiral
Mrs. Oliphant	The Library Window
Barry Pain	Rose Rose
Eden Phillpotts	The Iron Pineapple
Edgar Allan Poe	Berenice
Sir A. Quiller-Couch	The Roll-Call of the Reef
Naomi Royde-Smith	Mangaroo
Saki (H. H. Munro)	Sredni Vashtar
Henry Spicer	Call to the Rescue
Hugh Walpole	The Enemy
H. G. Wells	The Inexperienced Ghost

3460 SHELLEY, MARY (WOLLSTONECRAFT GODWIN) (1797–1851)

Frankenstein   OUP 1969; orig. 1818
 Or, The Modern Prometheus
 Prefs. by P. B. and Mary Shelley
 Ed. M. K. Joseph

An early magic (or science-fiction) tale, which has given a useful word to
the language, and which shows by its concern with the soul and with ethics
how far the setting of horror has changed in 150 years—and how little
Shelley's atheism and naturalism influenced his wife as literary artist. As a
triple murderer in temperate and arctic regions, F. deserves a place among
the successful practitioners.

Note that another modern reprint in *Three Gothic Tales* (Peng. Eng.
Libr., 1968) also gives the unsigned preface that Shelley wrote for his wife
(and as if by her) in 1817. It is not important except for its reference to
Erasmus Darwin. More valuable is the general Introduction to this volume
by Mario Praz.

3461 SIMMS, WILLIAM GILMORE

"Grayling, or Murder Will Out"
 In: The Wigwam and the Cabin (*No. 3462*)

Said Poe: "the best ghost story ever written by an American."

3462 The Wigwam and the Cabin   1845–46

Thirteen stories of folklore and superstition drawn from Indian, Negro, and
other backwoods beliefs. Note especially "The Armchair of Tustenuggee,"
"The Giant Coffin," and "Grayling" (No. 3461). "The Lazy Crow" is a
humorous but affectionate treatment of voodoo and its practitioners.

3463· SINCLAIR, MAY

Uncanny Stories   Macm 1923
 Illus. by Jean de Bosschère

The title for these seven interesting tales is misleading: they are not uncanny and produce no shivers. They do raise moral and emotional issues

by bridging common life and the hereafter. Perhaps the best is *Where Their Fire Is Not Quenched*. In a different genre, with clues and comedy both, is *The Victim*, which is at once ingenious, fanciful, and plausible.

3464 SITWELL, SACHEVERELL

Poltergeists   UB 1959
        *An Introduction and Examination Followed
        by Chosen Instances
        Poem "The Drum" by Edith Sitwell
        Illus.*

The work is organized so as to present a general view of the subject, followed by a discussion of typical cases, which are then printed at full length from the original sources. The author makes no attempt to explain the facts, which he believes are well attested and must obtain credence from "all but a minority of skeptical readers." The examination of cases is excellent—lucid, rational, witty where appropriate. The ten chosen instances are:

The Epworth Phenomena (1716), by John Wesley
The Haunting of Willington Mill (1835), by John Procter
The Drummer of Tedworth (1661), by Joseph Glanvil
The Haunting of Hinton Ampner (1771), by Mrs. Ricketts
Strange Phenomena in a Calvados Castle (1875), by Camille Flammarion
The Poltergeist of the Germans (1773–1849), by Catherine Crowe
Report on the Enniscorthy, Derrygonelly and Other Poltergeist Cases
    (1909–11; 1877), by Sir William Barrett
The Great Amherst Mystery (1888), by Walter Hubbell
The Case of Mr. G—— in Sumatra (1903), by Anon. (Jal of SPR)
The Workshop and Wen Poltergeists (1883), by Frank Podmore

3465 SMITH, LADY ELEANOR (FURNEAUX)

"Mrs. Raeburn's Waxwork"
        In: The Second Mercury Story Book (*No. 3445*)

A neat tale that leaves the reader to choose between the natural and the supernatural in the precincts of past crime. (See also No. 3413.)

3466 SWAIN, E. G.

The Stoneground Ghost Tales   Heffer (Camb.) 1912; also
                                                     Simpk., London
        *Recollections of the Reverend Roland Batchel
        Dedic. to M. R. James*

This scarce volume, sampled in No. 3423, owes much to the stylistic example of M.R.J. The nine episodes (including one humorous tale that succeeds in being funny and ghostly at once) are all agreeable to read and easy to remember; for Batchel is a character and his visions *have* character. No contemporary Americans have yet matched the English School of James in the strict genre.

3467 TYRELL, G. N. M.

Science and Psychical Phenomena;
Apparitions (2 v. in 1)   UB 1961; orig. SPR 1953
Foreword by Laura Dale

Direct reports to the SPR by one of its accredited investigators, coupled with case studies and estimates of evidential value. No conclusions are forced on the reader and few are reached by the researcher. Advance, if any, is slow, despite enormous effort and attention, perhaps because the premises are wrong.

3468 VARIOUS HANDS (No ed.)

Some Good Ghost Stories   NAB 1904

Eleven "shivers" (so called in the text) by Sheridan Le Fanu, Sir Charles Young, Fitz-James O'Brien and others. On the whole a collection of good tales not met with in every anthology.

WAKEFIELD, H. RUSSELL (1890–1964)

b. Birmingham, son of the bishop of that city; educ. Marlborough and Oxf., where he took a second in history. Then secretary to Lord North-cliffe; served in both world wars; scriptwriter for BBC; author of five collections of short stories, three novels, and two recitals of true crime: *Landru* and *The Green Bicycle Case*. He is unquestionably a master in the supernatural genre, to which, in the generation following M. R. James, he imparted a new tone and twist.

3469 The Clock Strikes Twelve   Arkham 1946
        Preface: "Why I Write Ghost Stories"

Eighteen short tales of uneven merit. But some of them show great art, notably Into Outer Darkness / 'I Recognized the Voice' / and Death of a Poacher / all of which have stunning endings.

3470 "He Cometh and He Passeth By"   *RSMQ* Aug 1945

A masterpiece of plausibility and horror, made all the more impressive by the fact of conflict between occult forces, instead of the usual destruction of the innocent and powerless at the hands of the transcendent powers. It is a longish short story, but every word and every detail is in place and necessary.

3471 They Return at Evening   App 1928

A famous collection of ghost stories, a few of which keep appearing in anthologies and magazines of mystery. Though not detection in the ordinary sense, H.R.W. is so circumstantial that certain detective effects necessarily result—and his prose is topnotch.

3472 "The Voice in the Inner Ear"   *EQMM* Apr 1967; orig. 1946
        In Eng.: "I Recognised the Voice"

A superb story on the borderline of the natural and the supernatural—the reader can without straining take it either way. There are clues and there is reasoning—*plus* an odd bit of explanation for the source of the reasoning. And, curiously too, one of the two characters is called Lefanu.

3473 WAKEFIELD. See also:

Belt of Surprise	CCC 1936
Hearken to the Evidence (crime without det.)	Bles 1933
Hostess to Death	CCC 1938
Imagine a Man in a Box (fantasy and horror ss)	App 1931
Others Who Returned	CCC 1936
The Strayers from Sheol	Arkham 1961

3474 WELLS, H. G.

The Short Stories of H. G. Wells   Benn 1927; orig. 1894 ff.

For a description of the volume, see No. 2859. The stories of the supernatural are:

The Door in the Wall
In the Avu Observatory
The Temptation of Harringay
The Flowering of the Strange Orchid
The Remarkable Case of Davidson's
  Eyes
The Moth
The Plattner Story
The Story of the Late Mr. Elvesham

The Apple
Pollock and the Porroh Man
The Red Room
The Man Who Could Work Miracles
The Magic Shop
The Truth About Pyecraft
Mr. Skelmersdale in Fairyland
The Inexperienced Ghost
The Stolen Body

These tales as a group are better than Wells' crime stories. The best among the above are: The Door in the Wall / The Story of the Late Mr. Elvesham / The Red Room / and The Stolen Body. For humor gentle and macabre, The Inexperienced Ghost and The Truth About Pyecraft are notable.

3475 WEST, D(ONALD) J.

Psychical Research Today   Peng 1954
  A Pelican Book

It is interesting to compare this treatment of the subject with that of W. F. Barrett, *Psychical Research,* prepared for the Home University Library in 1911. The difference is not between earlier confusion or credulity and later lucidity and science. Both men distinguish sharply between science and superstition. In both the cultural and historical aspects of the scientific investigation begun by F. W. H. Myers and others in the nineties are dealt with as important. The only difference is that the modern movement has added mathematical data tending to support ESP.

3476 WILDE, OSCAR (FINGAL O'FLAHERTIE WILLS), 1854–1900, wrote two parody-satires of the ghost tale: "Lord Arthur Savile's Crime," which begins in cheiromancy and ends in lighthearted murder; and "The Canterville Ghost," which is a simple reversal of roles in the business of causing dismay. Wilde also wrote a shorter and more serious tale of unresolved doubt, "The Sphinx Without a Secret." All three may be read in *The Novels and Fairy Tales of O. W.* (Cosmo 1915).

Finally, Wilde's review-essay "Pen, Pencil, and Poison: a Study in Green" (repr. in *Intentions*, 1891) portrays the murderer Wainewright as a conscious and misunderstood artist and defends his memory according to the chief critical canon of the post-Victorian age: "The fact of a man being a poisoner is nothing against his prose."

INDEX

Gems from the Literature

Murder there has been, and that's a fact, but as to who done it, I know no more than the babe unborn.
—Horace Hutchinson, *Mystery of the Summer House*

The murderer may be said, not unfairly, to have lost the first fragrance of his innocence.
—G. K. Chesterton

Then if he's going to kill me, I'll make it difficult for him by taking up residence with him.
—The estranged wife in MacGregor Urquhart, *The Grey Man*

It is fortunate for the mystery monger that, whereas up to the present there is only one known way of getting born, there are endless ways of getting killed.
—Dorothy L. Sayers

Sir Harold insisted on champagne being served with every meal at which a guest was present, not counting early morning tea as a meal.
—Neil Gordon, *The Silent Murders*

The body has recently taken a small meal, consisting of tea, milk, bread, honey, butter, and cyanide.
—Edwin de Caire, *Death Among the Writers*

He pictured the assailant with his syringe ready poised. . . . Should the victim look up, explanations would have been difficult.
—John Rhode, *The Last Suspect*

I sincerely hope that sailors at sea are praying for those in peril on the shore.
—The battered hero in Paul McGuire, *7.30 Victoria*

All references are to the number of the entry, not to page numbers.

A reference given as 330/B refers the reader to the unnumbered paragraph of biographical information that immediately precedes entry No. 330.

Names of authors are in SMALL CAPITALS; titles of books in upper and lower case roman; subjects in **bold face.** Short stories, plays, and articles are distinguished by quotation marks. Pseudonyms appear as names. Persons cited are in small capitals, like authors.

Subjects, for the purposes of this Index, consist mainly of the fifty types of scene or setting (excluding the geographical) that characterize the tales in the *Catalogue*. For a list see p. xvi. A few other subjects, such as **Plays** and **Cases, Criminal,** lead to information scattered throughout the text, the references to cases being alphabetized under that entry.

Names of detectives are not indexed, except when they appear as topics of criticism (e.g., Nero Wolfe) or as pseudonyms (e.g., Sherlock Holmes). Books that list detectives are so indicated in the descriptive entries above and are also mentioned under Miscellaneous Information, p. xxix.

For the reader's convenience, all the Sherlock Holmes short stories are indexed under the substantive part of their titles, whether or not these begin with the words "The Adventure of . . ." This shortened form does not apply to works by other authors, or to parodies of S.H.

AARONS, E. S., 1
" 'A' as in 'Alibi,' " 2839
"Abbey Grange, The," 2480
ABBEY, KIERAN, 1796/B
ABBOT, ANTHONY, 2–3, 2136
ABBOTT, GEORGE, 2395
ABBOTT, W. C., 3062
ABC Murders, The, 537
"Abel Crew," 2319
Abominable Snowman, The, 200
"About Edwin Drood," 3428
"About Shockers," 2926
About the Murder of Geraldine
    Forster, 3
About the Murder of the Clergyman's
    Mistress, 2
About the Murder of the Night-Club
    Lady, 3
Above Suspicion, 1490
Abracadaver, 1613
"Abraham Lincoln's Clue," 2746
ABRAHAMSEN, D., 3063
ABRAMSON, BEN, 3327
"Absence of Mr. Glass, The," 2405
"Absent-Minded Coterie, The," 2342,
    2382, 2642, 3008
"Absolutely Elsewhere," 2776
"Absolution, The," 3280
"Academic Crime, An," 2703
Academic Question, An, 1950
Accent on Murder, 1384
Accessory After the Fact, 2048
"Accident" (Christie), 2361, 2418,
    2429
"Accident, The," (M. Kennedy), 2321
"Accident, The" (Onions), 3451
Accident by Design, 1407
"Accident of Crime, The," 2333
Accidents Do Happen, 352
Accomplice, The, 1107

According to the Evidence, 473
Accounting for Murder, 1344, 1350
Achilles Affair, The, 1577
Acquittal, 1935
ACRE, STEPHEN, 1043
ACTON, LORD, 2972, 3427
ADAM, H. L., 3064–5
ADAM, J., 3168
ADAM, J. C., 3168
ADAMS, CLEVE F., 4
ADAMS, HERBERT, 5–15, 916, 1023,
    2117
ADAMS, S. H., 2136, 2305, 2795
Addicted to Murder, 766
"Additions, etc., to Ordean Hagen's
    Who Done It?," 2963
"Adelphi Bowl, The," 2604
Adopted Daughter, The," 2724
"Adventure of Foulkes Rath, The,"
    2474
"Adventure of Johnny Waverley,
    The," 2419
"Adventure of the Abbas Ruby, The,"
    2474
"Adventure of the African Traveler,
    The," 2366, 2569
"Adventure of the Black Baronet,
    The," 2474
"Adventure of the Clapham Cook,
    The," 2779
"Adventure of the Clothes-Line,
    The," 2741
"Adventure of the Dark Angels, The,"
    2474
"Adventure of the Deptford Horror,
    The," 2474
"Adventure of the Gold Hunter,
    The," 2474
"Adventure of the Highgate Miracle,
    The," 2474

"Adventure of the Illustrious Impostor, The," 2741
"Adventure of the Lost Locomotive, The," 2470
"Adventure of the Murdered Art Editor, The," 2741
"Adventure of the Norcross Riddle, The," 2741
"Adventure of the One-Penny Black, The," 2324
"Adventure of the Pilot Engine, The," 2861
"Adventure of the Purloined Periapt, The," 2365
"Adventure of the Red Widow, The," 2474
"Adventure of the Remarkable Worm," 2741
"Adventure of the Sealed Room, The," 2474
"Adventure of the Seven Clocks, The," 2474
"Adventure of the Table Foot, The," 2741
"Adventure of the Two Collaborators, The," 2741
"Adventure of the Two Women, The," 2474
"Adventure of the Unique Hamlet, The," 2741, 3383
"Adventure of the Wax Gamblers, The," 2474
Adventures in Murder, 3164
Adventures of Caleb Williams, The, 1002
Adventures of Captain Ivan Koravitch, The, 2860
Adventures of Detective Barney, The, 2684
Adventures of Dr. Thorndyke, The, 2521
Adventures of Ellery Queen, The, 2734
Adventures of Jimmy Dale, The, 2695
Adventures of Martin Hewitt, The, 2674
Adventures of Romney Pringle, The, 2329
Adventures of Sam Spade and Other Stories, The, 2545
"Adventures of Shamrock Jolnes, The," 2741
Adventures of Sherlock Holmes, The, 2475, 2483
Adventures of Solar Pons, The, 2469

Advertising Agencies, 16, 871, 1512, 1902
"Advocate's Wedding Day, The," 3432
"A.E.P.," 2741
Affacombe Affair, The, 1365
Affair at Aliquid, The, 573
Affair at Helen's Court, The, 435
"Affair at Lahore Cantonment, The," 2461
Affair at Little Wokeham, The, 671
"Affair at Saltoner Priory, The," 2453
"Affair at the Bungalow, The," 2428
"Affair at the Novelty Theatre, The," 2689
"Affair at the Semiramis Hotel, The," 2653
"Affair of Samuel's Diamonds, The," 2673
"Affair of the Avalanche Bicycle & Tyre Co., The," 2542
"Affair of the Corridor Express, The," 2861
"Affair of the German Dispatch-Box, The," 2861
Affair of the Substitute Doctor, The, 1800
Affairs of State, 1968
African Millionaire, An, 2307
African Poison Murders, The, 1197
"After a Century, Will Anyone Care Whodunit?," 2951
After Dark, 2435
"After Death the Deluge," 2732
"After-Dinner Story," 2575, 2590
After House, The, 1864
Aftermath of Murder, 1094
Afternoon to Kill, An, 1946
After the Assassination, 3293
"After the Event," 2376
After the Fine Weather, 982
After the Funeral, 495
Against the Evidence, 782
Against the Public Interest, 920
AGATE, JAMES, 3162, 3359
Agatha Christie, Mistress of Mystery, 3009
"Age of Miracles, The," 2569, 2723
AIKEN, CONRAD, 2745, 3415
AIKEN, JOAN, 16–17
AIRD, CATHERINE, 18–21
Airplanes, 143, 508, 1243, 1305, 1604, 1630, 1884, 2243, 2248, 2616, 2680
Air That Kills, An, 1592
"Akin to Love," 2376

ALAN, A. J., 2836
Alarm, The, 1857
Alarm at Black Brake, 479
Alarum and Excursion, 1696
ALBRAND, MARTHA, 22/B–23, 2459
Album, The, 1864
"A.L.C.C.," 2306
ALDINGTON, R., 3066, 3141
ALDRICH, THOMAS BAILEY, 24
ALEXANDER, C. J., 1247
ALEXANDER, DAVID, 25, 2367
Alias Basil Willing, 1423
Alias J. J. Connington, 582/B, 3296
"Alibi, The" (Squire), 2779
Alibi (Carmichael), 428
Alibi for a Corpse, 1365
Alibi for a Judge, 473
Alibi Innings, 2290
"Alibi Problem, The," 2699
Alice in Wonderland, 1919
ALINGTON, ADRIAN, 2321
ALINGTON, C. A., 26/B–29, 2882
Alington Inheritance, The, 2207
"Alkali Dust in Your Eyes," 2976
ALLARDYCE, PAULA, 30, 194
"All at Once, No Alice," 2864
Allen, Grant, 2307/B–07, 3051
ALLEN, H. W., 31, 147/B, 149
ALLEN, RAYMUND, 2778
All Fall Down, 2006
All for Fun: Brainteasers, 2857
All for the Love of a Lady, 868
All Grass Isn't Green, 804
"All Hallows," 3405
"All in a Maze," 2391
ALLINGHAM, MARGERY, 32/B–45,
    466/B, 1132/B, 1928, 2308–13,
    2322, 2360, 2367, 2525, 2732,
    2738, 2765, 2845–6, 2853, 2874,
    3042
"All in the Night's Work," 2668, 2846
All Is Discovered, 411
All Men Are Liars, 2005
All Men Are Murderers, 196
All Souls' Night, 2395
Almighty Gold, 582/B
Alphabet Hicks, 2003
ALTICK, RICHARD D., 3067, 3383
"Aluminium Dagger, The," 2517
Always Ask a Policeman, 2078
Amateur Crime, The, 165
"Amazing Dr. Clitterhouse, The,"
    2627
Amber Eyes, The, 630
AMBERLEY, RICHARD, 46–7

AMBLER, ERIC, 48–50, 87, 492, 2341,
    2738, 2767, 2947
Ambrose Bierce, 3034
Ambrose Bierce, a Bibliography, 3034
Ambush for Anatol, 1929
American Black Chamber, The, 3325
American Detective Stories, 2854
American Ghost Stories, 3416
American Gun Mystery, The, 1776
American Mystery Stories, 2855
American Penman, An, 1104
American Tragedy, An, 1932
AMES, DELANO, 51/B–59, 165, 1152,
    1911
Amethyst Box, The, 1030
"Amethyst Cross, The," 3388
AMIS, KINGSLEY, 1525, 2883
Among Those Missing, 421
Amongst Those Missing, 421
AMOS, ALAN, 1312
Anatomy of a Murder (Traver),
    2060, 3309
"Anatomy of Body Disposal," 2650
Anatomy of Murder, The
    (V. Hands), 3280, 3287
Anatomy of Villainy, The, 3070
And Be a Villain (Cannan), 412
And Be a Villain (Stout), 1975, 1996
And Dangerous to Know, 701
And Died So?, 976
ANDERSON, FREDERICK IRVING, 2315
ANDERSON, ISAAC, 2955
And Four to Go, 2803
And on the Eighth Day, 1770
And Presumed Dead, 862
ANDRÉ, MAJOR, 3147
ANDREWS, CHARLTON, 3377
And the Moon Was Full, 1442
And Then Put Out the Light, 1407
And Then There Were None, 496
And to My Beloved Husband, 1408
Angel of Death, The, 1412
Angel of Light, The, 1443
"Angel's Eye, The," 2338
"Angel Street," 1073, 2395
ANGUS, DOUGLAS, 60
Annals of Medical Detection, 1891
Anniversary Murder, The, 1713
Annotated Sherlock Holmes, The,
    3328, 3331
Another Man's Life, 1108
Another Mystery in Suva, 72
Another's Crime, 1104
"Another Shot in the Locker," 2836
ANTHONY, PETER, 1919

"Anthropologist at Large, The," 2517
Antidote to Venom, 671
"ANTIPASTO, GIOVANNI," 3330
"Anti-tank," 2849
"Ants," 3459
"Anty Bligh," 3459
ANVIL, CHRISTOPHER, 2325–6
Anxious Conspirators, The, 2089
Any Shape or Form, 694
"Apartment Hunter, The," 2636
Apocrypha, The, 2566
"Appalling Politician, The," 2382
"Apparition of Burling Court, The," 2520
"Apparition of Mrs. Veal, The," 3457
Apparitions, 3467
"Apple, The," 3474
Apple a Day, An (Brinton), 271
"Apple a Day, An" (Irish), 2590
Appleby at Allington, 1211
"Appleby's First Case," 2458
Appleby Talks Again, 2585
"Appointment in Baker St.," 3383
Appointment in Iraq, 1497
Appointment in New Orleans, 541
Appointment with Death (Christie), 537
Appointment with Death (Frankau), 878
Araway Oath, The, 15
Archdeacons Afloat, 26/B
Archdeacons Ashore, 26/B
ARD, WILLIAM, 62–3
"Are Murders Meant?," 1765
Arena, The, 1050
"Aren't Our Police Wonderful!," 2376, 2846
ARISTOTLE, 3019
"Aristotle on Detective Fiction," 3019
ARLEN, MICHAEL, 64, 2327, 3442
Armchair Detective, The, 2886
"Armchair of Tustenuggee, The," 3462
Arm of the Law, The, 2099
ARMOUR, RICHARD, 2955
ARMSTRONG, ANTHONY, 65/B–70, 2134
ARMSTRONG, APRIL, 2
ARMSTRONG, CHARLOTTE, 71, 759, 2328, 2367, 2447, 2601
Army, incl. Home Guard, Navy, RAF, and Theaters of War, 300, 366, 370, 653, 1379, 1474, 1616, 1835, 2271, 2461, 2581
ARNOLD, BENEDICT, 3147

AROUET, FRANÇOIS-MARIE, 2141
Arrogant Alibi, 1303
"Arrow o'er the House, An," 2776
"Arrow of God, The," 2367
Arrow Pointing Nowhere, 701
Arsène Lupin, 3032
Arsène Lupin versus Holmlock Shears, 1359
"Art and the Detective," 2920
"Artful Jane," 2316
Art: Galleries, Studios, Museums, Experts, and Forgers, 34, 125, 141, 285, 436, 455, 515, 656, 819, 902, 931, 966, 989, 1219, 1224, 1227, 1274–5, 1355, 1494, 1606, 1664, 1679, 1687, 1693–4, 1740, 1748, 1782, 1812, 2518, 2529, 2588, 2655
ARTHUR, FRANK, 72/B–75, 1171
Arthur Machen: a Biography, 3011
ARTHUR, ROBERT, 2365, 2874
"Artifice, An," 2658
Artificial Man, The, 713
"Artificial Mole, The," 157, 2323, 2352, 2614
Art in the Blood & What Is This Thing Called Music?, 3363
Artist Dies, An, 1812
"Artist in Crime, An" (Mackail), 2614
Artist in Crime, An (Ottolengui), 1675
Artists in Crime (Marsh), 1555
Art of Cross-Examination, The, 3315
Art of Detection, The, 3146
"Art of Melville Davisson Post, The," 2999
Art of Simenon, The, 2989
"Art of the Detective Story, The," 905, 2765, 2944, 2955
Art of the Mystery Story, The, 2955, 3018
Arts of Cheating, Swindling and Murder, The, 3078
As a Thief in the Night, 887
Ascent of D-13, The, 946
"Ascot Tragedy, The," 2339
As for the Woman, 175, 1209
As Good as Dead, 743
A.S.F., 1856
ASHBY, R. C., 76–7
ASHDOWN, CLIFFORD, 887/B, 2329–30, 2523, 2542, 2917
ASHE, GORDON, 78, 2931
Ashenden, 1580, 2979
Ashes of Loda, The, 947

"Balcony, The," 2874
BALDERSTONE, JOHN L., 2466
BALDICK, ROBERT, 2890
BALDWIN, HANSON, 2575
BALDWIN, WILLIAM, 2340
"Ballad of Danny Deever, The," 2461
BALLARD, K. G., 1884/B, 1890
BALL, DORIS BELL COLLIER, 113/B
BALL, JOHN, 94–5
BALMER, EDWIN, 2795
BALZAC, HONORÉ DE, 96, 2013, 2877, 3022, 3181, 3310, 3442
Balzac jurisconsulte et criminaliste, 96
BALZAC-RIDEAUX, CHARLES DE, 2134
Bamboo Screen, The, 1098
BANGS, JOHN KENDRICK, 2739, 2741
Banker's Bones, The, 1912
Bankers, Their Vaults, and the Burglars, 3258
Banking on Death, 1345
BANKOFF, GEORGE ALEXIS, 251
Banks and Business Offices incl. the Stock Market, 85, 220, 249, 284, 528, 716, 873, 913, 963, 1050, 1337, 1344–50, 1395, 1458, 1741, 1843, 1976, 2001, 2032, 2076–7, 2232, 2293, 2380, 2528–9, 2637, 2656
Banner for Pegasus, A, 226
Bannerman Case, The, 2756/B
BARBETTE, JAY, 97
BARHAM, R. H., 3459
BARING-GOULD, SABINE, 3423
BARING-GOULD, WILLIAM STUART, 2891/B–91, 3328–9, 3331, 3423
BARKER, ELSA, 2360
BARLAY, BENNETT, 474
BARLOW, JAMES, 98
BARLOW, R. H., 2675
Barnaby Rudge, 3001
BARNARD, ALLAN, 2341
BARNES, RONALD GORELL, 1011
"Baronet's Finger, The," 2850
"Baron Starkheim, The," 2725
Barrakee Mystery, The, 2100/B, 2109
BARRETT, MONTE, 99
BARRETT, (SIR) WILLIAM F., 3464, 3475
BARRIE, (SIR) JAMES, 2741, 2332, 2939
BARR, ROBERT, 2642, 2741, 2778–9, 2795, 2342/B, 3008
BARR, STEPHEN, 2343, 2493
BARRY, CHARLES, 100–102
Bar Sinister (Ballard), 1890
Bar Sinister (MacTyre), 1514

BARSLEY, MICHAEL, 103
BARTON, (DR.) ROBERT, 1784, 1910, 2660, 2780
BARZUN, JACQUES, 1995, 2344, 2347, 2489, 2892–8, 2927–8, 2947, 2992, 3071, 3330–1, 3359
BASHFORD, (SIR) H. H., 104, 2345
"Bat, The," 1864, 2395
Bats Fly at Dusk, 804
Bats in the Belfry, 1400
Battlefields. See **Army**
Battle for Inspector West, A, 637
Battle of Steam, 444/B
"Battle of Wits," 2785
BAUDELAIRE, 882
BAWDEN, NINA, 105
BAX, ROGER, 106–10, 946/B
BAXTER, VALERIE, 1586/B
"Bay City Blues," 2399
BEACH, STEWART, 2346
Beast in View, The, 1592
Beast Must Die, The, 199
Beat Not the Bones, 1243
BEAUMARCHAIS, 2344, 2347, 2389, 2489, 2897
BEAUMONT, EDGAR, 2661
"Beautiful Nuzzly, The," 3246
Beauty for Inspector West, A, 637
Beauty Queen Killer, The, 637
BECCARIA, 3072
"Beckoning Fair One, The," 3451
Beckoning Lady, The, 35
BEDFORD, SYBILLE, 3073–4, 3266
Bedrooms Have Windows, 804
BEECHER, H. W., 3315
BEEDING, FRANCIS, 111–12, 2732
BEELEY, A. L., 3075
BEERBOHM, MAX, 1252, 1520, 2872, 3442, 3459
BEETHOVEN, 261, 1372/B
Before I Die (McCloy), 1424
"Before I Die" (Stout), 2812
Before Midnight, 1977
Before Scotland Yard, 2566
"Before the Act," 2851
Before the Fact, 175, 1210
"Before the Party," 2755
Beggar's Choice, 257
Beginner's Luck, 1954
Beginnings of Mr. P. J. Davenant, The, 2544
Behind Closed Doors (Green), 1030
Behind Locked Doors (Poate), 1729
"Behind the Beyond," 550/B
Behind the Fog, 104

"Betrayers, The," 2496
Better Dead (Bonett), 223
BETTERIDGE, DON, 1648
Better Off Dead (Bonett), 223, 225
Better Off Dead (McCloy), 2631
Beware of Midnight, 2196
Beware of the Bouquet, 16
"Beware of the Trains," 2448
Beware of the Trains, 645, 2363, 2448
Beware Your Neighbor, 388
BEYNON, JANE, 177, 1372/B
Beyond a Reasonable Doubt (Grafton), 1018
Beyond Belief, 3319
Beyond Reasonable Doubt (Hull), 1183
Beyond the Atlas, 2065
Beyond the Reach of Sense, 3420
"Beyond the Sea of Death," 2367
Beyond the Wall of Sleep, 3437
"Bickmore Deals with the Duchess," 2505
BIELASKI, A. B., 3264
BIERCE, AMBROSE, 2600, 2855, 3034, 3389, 3400, 3404, 3416, 3442, 3449, 3457, 3459, 3100
BIERSTADT, E. H., 3089
Big Ben Alibi, The, 1007
Big Bow Mystery, The, 2304, 2881
Big Business Murder, 573
Big Clock, The, 817, 819
Big Four, The, 498
BIGGERS, EARL DERR, 178
"Bigger the Lie, The," 2572
Bigger They Come, The, 804
Big Greed, The, 997
Big Heat, The, 1477
Big Kidnap, The, 2032-3
Big Knockover, The, 1074/B, 2547, 2961
"Big Money, The," 2365
Big Sleep, The, 480
"Billiard-Room Mystery, The," 550/B
Billion-Dollar Brain, The, 722
BILLY THE KID. See BONNEY, W. H.
Biltmore Call, The, 2130
BINGHAM, JOHN, 179/B-84
Biographies, of writers, 2901; of detectives. See Detectives
Biography for Beginners, 2921
Biography of the Blind, 2368
Bird-Cage, The, 1660
"Bird in the Cellar, The," 2337
"Bird Watcher, The," 2500, 2821

BIRKENHEAD, F. E. S., EARL OF, 3079, 3231
BIRKETT, N., 3080-1, 3221
BIRKLEY, DOLAN, 115, 1664
BIRMINGHAM, G. A., 185/B-86, 2224/B, 3082
BIRRELL, OLIVE, 3412
Birthday, The, 2259
Birthday Murder, The, 1372
"Birthmark, The," 3432
BISHOP, JIM, 3083
BISHOP, MORRIS, 1258
Bishop Murder Case, The, 2121
Bishop's Crime, The, 89, 2336
Bishop's Purse, The, 1608
BISMARCK, 3174
"Biter Bit, The," 2382, 2779
"Bit of Wire-Pulling, A," 2321
"Bitter Almonds," 2776
Bizarre Murders, The, 1776
"Black and White," 2320
Black Baroness, 2217
Black Beech and Honey Dew, 1535/B
Black Béret, 1302
BLACKBURN, JOHN, 188-93
"Black Cabinet, The," 2391
Black Cap, The, 2332
"Black Cat," 2459
Black Cross, The, 1069
Black Death, The, 15
"Black Disk, The," 2632
"Black Doctor, The," 2481
Black Dog Mystery, The, 1776
Black Door, The (Markham), 1526
Black Door, The (Wilcox), 2237
Black Dream, The, 1382
Black Dudley, 32/B
Black Envelope, The, 868
"Black Fury, The," 2835
Black Glass City, The, 1712
Black Hole and Other Essays, The, 3119
"Black Hole of Calcutta, The," 3119
Black Is the Colour of My True Love's Heart, 1705
Black Land, White Land, 90
Black Leather Murders, The, 1895
BLACK, LIONEL, 187
"Blackmail," 2643
"Blackmailer, The," 2722
Blackmailers and Co., 3139
"Blackmailers Don't Shoot," 2398, 2401
Blackmail in Blankshire, 26

Body in the Boudoir, The, 2143
Body in the Bunker, The, 5
Body in the Library, The, 500, 2428
Body in the Road, The, 690
Body in the Silo, The, 1318-9
Body Missed the Boat, The, 1202
Body's Guest, The, 1511
Body's Imperfections, The, 2006/B
"Body-Snatcher," 2755
Body to Spare, A, 1753
Body Unidentified, 1803
Body Was of No Account, The, 607
Bogue's Fortune, 2020
Bohemia, incl. Gambling and Underworld Dives, 22, 60, 80, 98, 150, 207, 253, 288, 340, 626, 879, 893, 928, 931, 945, 957, 972, 1012, 1112-3, 1249-50, 1322, 1538, 1560, 1679, 1895, 1969, 2047, 2236, 2241, 2647
BOHLE, EDWARD, 221
BOILEAU-NARCEJAC, 222, 2902
BOILEAU, PIERRE, 222, 2359, 2902
Boiled Alive, 336
BOLEYN, ANNE, 3227
BOLITHO, WILLIAM, 3088, 3193, 3257
"Bombay Duck," 2783, 2837
Bond Affair, The, 2934
BOND, NELSON, 2694
BOND, R. T., 2360-1, 2903
"Bond Strikes Camp," 2767, 2930
Bone and a Hank of Hair, A, 308
Bone Is Pointed, The, 2109
"Bone of Contention, The" (Sayers), 2569
Bones in the Brickfield, 353
Bones of Contention (Candy), 408
BONETT, EMERY, 223/B-28
BONETT, JOHN, 223/B-26, 228
BONI, A. and C., 3389
BONNAMY, FRANCIS, 2362
BONNELL, JAMES FRANCIS, 229
BONNEY, J. L., 230-2
BONNEY, W. H., 3102
Bony and the Black Virgin, 2100
"Booby Trap," 2805-6
Bookman, The: Special No., 2904
Book of Modern Ghosts, A, 3388
Book of Remarkable Criminals, A, 3191
Book of Strange Murders, A, 3145
Book of the Crime, The, 695
Book of the Dead, The, 701
Book of the Lion, The, 701

Book Publishers, 38, 202, 266, 394, 1049, 1159, 1433, 1858, 1992, 2010, 2026, 2028
Booksellers' Catalogues, 2905
Bookshops, 151, 188, 407, 809, 1035, 1619, 1645, 1678, 2006, 2305, 2503
"Book, the Bibliographer, and the Absence of Mind, The," 2892
Boomerang (Garve), 948
Boomerang Clue, The (Christie), 537
BOORE, W. H., 233-4
BOOTHBY, G., 2542
BOOTH, C. G., 235
BOOTHROYD, J. B., 3338
"Bordeaux Diligence, The," 3414
BORDEN, MARY, 236
"Borderline," 2310
Borderline Case, A (Williams), 2242
"Borderline Case, The" (Allingham), 2310-11
BORGES, J. L., 2367
BORNEMAN, J. E., 1422
"Born Killer," 2463
Born to Be Hanged, 1489
Borough Treasurer, The, 861
BORROW, GEORGE, 347, 3089
BOSSUET, 2985
BOSTON, C. K., 1043
BOSWELL, CHARLES, 3090
BOSWELL, JAMES, 724, 2977
"Bottle Party, The," 2337
BOTTOME, PHYLLIS, 2361
"Bottomless Well, The," 2407
BOTTOMLEY, HORATIO, 3187
BOUCHER, ANTHONY, 127, 237/B-41, 290, 492, 574, 1164, 1210, 1425, 1616, 2341, 2359-60, 2363-5, 2367, 2500, 2573, 2737-8, 2741, 2751, 2774, 2906, 2955, 3222, 3355
Boudoir Murder, The, 1765
Bound to Die, 2079
Bound to Kill, 188
BOURNE, PETER, 1016
BOWDEN, J. H., 2697
BOWEN ELIZABETH, 1364, 2332, 2765
BOWEN, IAN, 2931
BOWEN, MARJORIE, 2601
BOWERS, DOROTHY, 242-5
Bowery Murder, 1949
BOX, EDGAR, 246-8, 1912
Box from Japan, The, 1270
Box Hill Murder, The, 861
"Box of Coins, The," 2732
Box Office Murders, The, 665
BOYD, FRANK, 1260

BOYD, JANE, 249
BOYER, RALPH L., 1493
Boy's Book of Great Detective Stories, The, 494
BRACE, TIMOTHY, 250
BRADBURY, RAY, 2755, 3413
BRADDON, GEORGE, 251
BRADDON, M. E., 252, 3051
BRADFORD, GERSHOM, 3091
Bradmoor Murder, The, 2722
BRADY, NICHOLAS, 1184
BRAHMS, JOHANNES, 638/B
BRAMAH, ERNEST, 253/B–53, 1286, 2322–3, 2350, 2368–72, 2542, 2642, 2692, 2735, 2750, 2774, 2778, 2779, 2784, 2795, 2836, 2875, 3013
BRAMLETTE, PAULA, 2298
BRAMSTON, M. E., 3412
BRAMWELL, J. G., 394
"Branch Line No. 1." See "The Signal Man"
BRAND, CHRISTIANNA, 254–6, 2091, 2373–6, 2846, 3092
Branded Spy Murders, The, 1567
Brandon Case, The, 590
Brandon in New York, 2174
Brandon Returns, 2175
Brandon Takes Over, 2175
BRANDON, WILLIAM, 2525
BRANDT, TOM, 741/B
BRANNON, W. T., 2365
BRANSON, H. C., 257–63
BRASH, J. C., 3159
Brass Chills, The, 1695
Brass Ring, The, 1326
Brat Farrar, 2040
Bravo of London, The, 253/B–53
"Bread and Butter Case, The," 2604
"Breakdown," 3415
Break in the Circle, The, 1409
"Break-Up," 2774
BREAN, HERBERT, 264–5, 2908
BREBNER, P. J., 2377–8
BREMNER, MARJORIE, 266/B–67
Brenda Entertains, 175
BREND, W. A., 3229
BRENNAN, J. N. H., 2196/B
BRENNAN, J. P., 3407
Bressant, 1102/B
Bricklayer's Arms, 1847
Bridal Bed Murders, The, 1557/B
Bride Regrets, The, 426
Bride's Castle, 2251
Bride Wore Black, The, 2289
Bridge of San Luis Rey, The, 1738

"Bridge of Sighs, The," 1418
BRIDGES, VICTOR, 268–9
BRIDGES, YSEULT, 3093–5
BRIDIE, JAMES, 3275
"Briefbag of Felonies, A," 2893
Brief to Counsel, 3106
"Bright Facts and Pleasurable Fears," 2898
BRIGHT, JOHN, 2167/B
Brighton Murder Trial, Rex v. Rhodes, The, 1066
BRINEY, R. E., 2931
Bring Me Another Corpse, 1778
Bring the Bride a Shroud, 1665
Brink of Silence, The, 1244
BRINTON, HENRY, 270–1
British Agent, 3217
British Common People, The, 1737/B
"British or the American Story, The," 2908
Broadcasting and Film Studios, 226, 640, 691, 979, 1072, 1100, 1128, 1153, 1205, 1275, 1422, 1439, 1450, 1502, 1575, 1791, 1975, 1977, 2287, 2296, 2628, 2651
"Broadcast Murder, The," 2316
Broadcasts. See Plays, Films, and, 3339
"Broadsheet Ballad, A," 2439
"Broadway," 2395
BROCHET, J.-A., 307
BROCK, A. S. L., 306, 3097
BROCK, LYNN, 272/B–80, 566
BRODIE, J. P., 727
Broken Alibi, 1234
Broken Boy, The, 189
Broken Jigsaw, The, 1954
Broken O, The, 2204
Broken Penny, The, 983, 2021
"Broken T, The," 2746
"Broken Toad, The," 2336, 2338
Broken Vase, The, 1978
"Broker's Special," 2495–6
"Bronze Box, The," 2384
"Bronze Hand, The," 2541
"Bronze Parrot, The," 2518
Bronze Perseus, The, 1172
Brooklyn Murders, The, 560
BROOKS, CYRUS, 776
BROOKS, V. C., 1594/B
BROOKS, W. R., 494
BROOME, ADAM, 281–3
BROPHY, BRIGID, 284/B
BROPHY, JOHN, 284/B–86, 3095
BROSTER, D. K., 3403
Brother Cain (Capon), 423

Brother Cain (Raven), 1782
Brothers and Sisters Have I None, 2111
Brothers-in-Law, 473
Brothers Sackville, The, 561
BROUN, DANIEL, 287–8
BROWN, C. B., 289
BROWNE, D. G., 296/B–305, 880, 1055, 1081, 2153, 3096–8
BROWNE, GORDON, 296/B, 2307
BROWNE, HOWARD, 2458
BROWNE, K. R. G., 2614
BROWNE, NELSON, 2909
BROWNE, R. F. G. See GORE-BROWNE, R. F.
BROWNE (SIR) THOMAS, 2222
BROWN, F. K., 867/B
BROWN, FREDRIC, 290/B–94, 2365, 2379, 3392
BROWNING, ROBERT, 1414/B
BROWNING, STERRY, 1034
BROWN, MALCOLM, 3204
BROWN, M. D., 825
"Brown Paper, The," 2336–7
BROWN, ROBERT CARLETON, 2380
Brownsville Murders, The, 1273
"Brown Wallet, The," 2333
BROWN, W. C., 295
BRUCE, JEAN, 307
BRUCE, LEO, 308/B–26, 2321
BRUCE, NIGEL, 3339
"Bruce-Partington Plans, The," 2320, 2478, 3366
BRUCKNER, ANTON, 1720
BRULLS, CHRISTIAN, 1930
Brush with Death, A, 1727
BRUTON, ERIC, 327/B–29
BRYSON, CHARLES, 100
BUCHAN, JOHN, 330/B–35, 1170, 1173, 1499, 1669/B, 2381
BUCHAN, WILLIAM, 335
BUCKINGHAM, BRUCE, 336–7
BUDE, JOHN, 338–9
BUELL, JOHN, 340
Bullet for a Beast, 1933
Bullet for Rhino, A, 2260
Bullets for Brandon, 2175
BULLETT, GERALD, 341–2, 1739, 1752, 3068
BULLOCK, HUMPHREY, 3099
BULL, R. C., 2382
Bull's Eye, 1288
BULWER-LYTTON, EDWARD, 343/B–45, 2601, 3078, 3393–4, 3431, 3457, 3459

Bump in the Night, 2181
"Bunch of Violets, The," 2372
Burden, The, 2209
Burden of Proof, The (Ashford), 79
Burden of Proof, The (Barlow), 98
BURGE, M. R. K., 1288/B
BURGESS, ANTHONY, 345
BURGESS, GELETT, 346/B–46, 2642, 2694, 2854, 2856
Burglars in Bucks, 573
Burial Service, 1483
Buried Alive, 141
Buried Day, The, 208, 718
Buried for Pleasure, 638
BURKE, NOEL, 1151, 1664
BURKE, THOMAS, 347, 1623/B, 2323, 2341, 2383, 2774, 2780, 2846, 3008, 3100, 3403
BURLEY, W. J., 348–50
BURNEY, CHRISTOPHER, 3101
Burn Forever, 868
BURNHAM, DAVID, 351
Burning Court, The, 458
Burning Question, The, 442
BURNS, W. N., 3102
"Burnt Tout, The," 2447
BURRAGE, A. M., 2575, 3413, 3459
BURRARD, MAJOR, 3118
BURTON, JEAN, 3394
BURTON, MILES, 352/B–88, 1800/B, 2988
Bury Him Darkly (Blackburn), 193
Bury Him Darkly (Wade), 2145
Bury Me Deep, 1576
BUSH, CHRISTOPHER, 389–91, 2319, 2321–2, 2477
"Business Minister, The," 2875
Business of Bodies, A, 2206
Business offices. See Banks and Business Offices
Business of Loving, The, 1944/B
Busman's Honeymoon, 1898/B–98, 2782
Bus Station Murders, The, 1799
But Death Runs Faster, 1479
"Butler, The," 2441, 2642
BUTLER, E. P., 3416, 3457
BUTLER, GWENDOLINE, 392–3
But Not Forgotten, 822
But Soft—We Are Observed!, 139
Buttercup Case, The, 630
Butterfly, The, 398
But the Patient Died, 1936
"Button and the Banknote, The," 2316
Button, Button, 1884

3221–2; *Wright, Bella, 3068, 3256,*
Wright, Harry, 3202
    Yarmouth Beach. See *Bennett, H. J.*
Cases in Court, 3178
Cases of Susan Dare, The, 781
Case to Answer, A, 1418
Case with Four Clowns, The, 310
Case with Nine Solutions, The, 583,
    602
Case with No Conclusion, The, 326
Case with Ropes and Rings, The, 326
Case with Three Husbands, The, 791
Case Without a Corpse, The, 311
CASEY, R. J., 2955
Casino Murder Case, The, 2121
Cask, The, 646
"Cask of Amontillado, The," 2718,
    2755
Cas Simenon, Le, 2989
CASSITY, (DR.) J. H., 3234
CASSWELL, J. D., 2846
CASTIER, JULES, 2741
CASTLE, EGERTON, 2568
Castleford Conundrum, The, 584
Castle of Otranto, The, 2171
Castle Skull, 465
Casual Murderer, The, 2509
Cat, 977
CATALAN, HENRI, 469
Catalogues (of Crime and Detection),
    2905
Catalyst Club, The, 778
Cat Among Pigeons, 503
Cat and Mouse, 256
"Cat and the Canary, The," 2395
Cat and the Clock, The, 235
Catch as Catch Can, 1385
Catch Me if You Can, 1470
Cat Jumps, The, 354
Cat's Eye, The, 888
"Cat's Paw, The," 2496
Cats Prowl at Night, 804
Catt out of the Bag, 2262
Cauldron Bubbles, The, 2039
Cause for Alarm, 50
Cause of Death, 2099
Cautious Overshoes, The, 1912
Cavalcade of Ghosts, 3423
CAVENDISH, PETER, 1170
"Cave of Ali Baba, The," 2767, 2779,
    2798
CAVERHILL, W. M., 1582
Caves, 960, 1583, 1716, 1817, 2103,
    2256, 2331
Cease upon the Midnight, 2070

CECIL, (LORD) DAVID, 1252
CECIL, HENRY, 470–3, 1682, 2396,
    2788, 3106
CEILLIER, RENÉ, 3107
Celebrated Cases of Charlie Chan,
    The, 178
Celebrated Crimes, 2489
Celebrated Trials and Remarkable
    Cases of Criminal Jurisprudence
    . . . to 1825, 3089
Cellar at No. 5, The, 1947
CENEDELLA, ROBERT, 2397
Centaur, The, 3391
Century of Detective Stories, A, 2319
Century of Murder, A, 3279
Century of the Detective, The, 3304
CERF, BENNETT, 2395, 3400
Certain Dr. Thorndyke, A, 905
Certain Woman, A, 1435/B
CHABER, M. E., 474–6, 1612
CHADWICK, JOHN, 3108
"Challenge, The," 2367
Challenge to Murder, 2215
Challenge to the Reader, 2735
CHALMERS, STEPHEN, 477
CHAMBERS, PETER, 478
CHAMBERS, R. W., 2750
Champagne for One, 1979
CHANCE, J. N., 479
CHANCELLOR, JOHN, 2134
Chance to Kill, A, 1332
CHANDLER, F. W., 2917
CHANDLER, P. W., 3069
CHANDLER, RAYMOND, 96, 396/B,
    480/B–86, 982/B, 1126, 1449,
    1461/B, 2354, 2366, 2398–2403,
    2525, 2654, 2787, 2885, 2918–19,
    2947, 2950, 2955, 2980, 3061, 3113
CHANDOS, DANE, 336
"Changed Immutable, The," 2521
Change of Heir, A, 1214
CHAPMAN, ARTHUR, 3377
CHAPMAN, JOHN, 2395
CHAPMAN, RAYMOND, 1640
Charabanc Mystery, The, 388
Charity Begins at Home, 2182
"Charles Augustus Milverton," 2480,
    3350
CHARLES, FRANKLIN, 4
CHARLES II (of England), 3062
CHARLETON, WILLIAM, 3011
CHARNWOOD, GODFREY RATHBONE
    BENSON (LORD), 487/B–87
Charred Witness, The, 618

CLARK, A. A. G., 3027
CLARK, DOUGLAS, 539
CLARKE, ARTHUR, 2738
CLARKE, (SIR) EDWARD, 2774, 3081, 3221
CLARKE, IDA CLYDE, 3402
CLARKE, ROBERT, 540
CLARK, GEOFFREY, 3114
Clark Gifford's Body, 818
Classic Crimes, 3275
Classic Crimes in History and Fiction, 2566
Classics of Adventure and Detection, 2166, 2621
Claude Melnotte as a Detective, 3258
Claverton Affair, The, 1804, 1816
Claverton Mystery, The, 1804
Claw of a Cat, The, 1708
CLAYMORE, TOD, 541–4
CLAYTON, R. H. M., 1050/B
"Clean Kill, A," 1458, 2533
Cleansing of Personville, The, 1076
Cleek, the Man of Forty Faces, 2553
Cleek, the Master Detective, 2554
CLEEVE, BRIAN, 545/B–45
CLEMENS, SAMUEL L., 2080/B
CLEMENTS, E. H., 546–9
CLENDENING, LOGAN, 2741
Clerical Error, 1877, 2142/B
Clerihew(s), 2921
Cleveland Murders, 3171
CLEVELY, HUGH, 541
"Clever Cockatoo, The," 2351, 2361
"Cleverest Clue, The," 2324
Cleverest Murder in Fact or Fiction, The, 3050
"Clever Mr. Fall, The," 2352
"Clever Mrs. Straithwaite, The," 2369, 2774
Clew of the Forgotten Murder, The, 944
"Clew of the Single Word, The," 2561
"Clifford Ashdown: a Retrospect," 2330
CLINTON-BADDELEY, V. C., 550/B–52
Cloak and Cipher, 3241
"Cloak Without Dagger" (Beaumarchais), 2347
Cloak Without Dagger (Sillitoe) 3286
Clocks, The, 504
Clock Strikes Thirteen, The, 265
Clock Strikes Twelve, The, 3469
Clock Without Hands, 2607
Close Call, A, 1724
Closed Circuit, 1054

"Closed Doors; or, The Great Drumsheugh Case," 2774
Close His Eyes, 777
Close of Play, 1783
Close Quarters, 985
Cloth of Silver, 1659
"Cloud, The," 2796
Clouds of Witness[es], 1899
CLOUSTON, J. S., 553–4, 2836
Cloze Papers, The, 1383
"Club of One-Eyed Men, The," 2837
Clue, The, 2204
Clue for Mr. Fortune, A, 2334
"Clue from Bing Crosby, A," 2605
Clue from the Stars, A, 1715
Clue in the Air, The, 1674
Clue in the Clay, The, 1664
CLUENTIUS, 3113
Clue of the Bricklayer's Aunt, The, 1618/B
Clue of the Dead Goldfish, The, 1435
Clue of the Fourteen Keys, The, 359
"Clue of the Hungry Horse, The," 2530
Clue of the Judas Tree, The, 868
Clue of the Poor Man's Shilling, The, 1312
"Clue of the Red Wig, The," 2393
Clue of the Second Murderer, The, 2005
Clue of the Silver Brush, The, 356
Clue of the Silver Cellar, The, 384
"Clue of the Tattooed Man, The," 2365
Clue of the Twisted Candle, The, 2166
"Clues" (Rodell), 2955
"Clues" (Scott), 2316
Clues for Dr. Coffee, 2356
Clues of the Caribbees, 2816
Clues, or Leaves from a Chief Constable's Notebook, 3180
Clues to Burn, 1659
"Clue That Wasn't There, The," 2826
CLURMAN, ROBERT, 2444
Clutch of Constables, 1535
CLUTTON-BROCK, ALAN, 555
Coast of Fear, The, 1890
COBB, BELTON, 556/B–58, 2732, 3115–16
COBBETT, WILLIAM, 3079
COBB, IRVIN S., 2361
"Cocaine," 2873
"Coconut Trial, The," 2612

Danvers Jewels, The, 2415
D'Arblay Mystery, The, 889
DARDIS, MARTIN, 2460
DARE, ALAN, 1004
Darkening Glass, The, 2164
Darkest Hour, The, 1479
Dark Hollow, The, 1030
Dark Is the Tunnel, 357
Dark Journey, 650
Dark Legend, 3316–7
Darkling Death, 2139
Dark of the Moon, 2048
Dark Omnibus, The, 492
Dark Street, The, 492
DARLINGTON, W. A., 2317
Dartmoor Enigma, The, 2051
DARWIN, ERASMUS, 3460
D as in Dead, 2064
Date with Darkness, 1067/B–67, 2575
Date with Death (Blaisdell-Linington), 198, 1380
Date with Death (Ford), 868
Daughter of Dr. Fu Manchu, The, 1876
Daughter of Time, The, 2040/B, 2041
Daughter's a Daughter, A, 2209
Daughters in Law, 473
"Dauphin's Doll, The," 2447
D'AUREVILLY, BARBEY, 2877
DAVENPORT, BASIL, 3403
DAVEY, JOCELYN, 706/B–09
Davidian Report, The, 1178
DAVIDSON, AVRAM, 2367, 2461–2
Davidson Case, The, 1805, 1840
DAVIDSON, T. L., 710/B–10, 2036
DAVIES, L. P., 711–13
DAVIOT, GORDON, 2040/B, 2043
DAVIS, D. B., 2933
DAVIS, DON, 1058/B
DAVIS, D. S., 714–15, 2463–4
DAVIS, ELMER, 3383
DAVIS, GEORGE, 716–17
DAVIS, J. W., 3315
DAVIS, NORBERT, 2774
DAVIS, REBECCA HARDING, 3431
DAVIS, RICHARD HARDING, 2465, 2795
Dawson Pedigree, The, 1906
Day and Night Stories, 3391
Day He Died, The, 1326
Day in Monte Carlo, A, 22
DAY-LEWIS, CECIL, 199/B, 206, 208, 718, 2222/B, 3031
"Daylight Adventure, A," 2815
Daylight Murder, 1484
Day of the Adder, The, 842

Day of the Arrow, 1410
Day of the Ram, The, 972
Days of Danger, 637
Days of Misfortune, 1960
Day They Robbed the Bank of England, The, 284
DEACON, RICHARD, 3123
Dead Against My Principles, 1169
Dead and Dumb, 639, 644
Dead by the Light of the Moon, 2206
Dead Center, 1341
Dead Cert, 875
Dead Don't Bite, The, 297
Dead Don't Scare, The, 1528
Dead Ernest, 2035
Deadfall (Cory), 612
Deadfall (Hamilton), 1069
Dead Fall (Wilmer), 1573, 2248
Dead for a Ducat, 312
Dead Indeed, 1159
"Dead Leaves, The," 2334
Deadlier Than the Male, 1161
Deadline, 741
Deadline at Dawn, 1231
Dead Lion, 224
"Deadlock," 2747
Dead Low Tide, 1445
Deadly Climate, The, 688
Deadly Duo, 45, 2309
Deadly Nightshade, 701
Deadly Reaper, The, 1942
Deadly Truth, The, 1426
Dead Man Inside, 1958
"Dead Man in the Water," 2459
Dead Man Running, 193
Dead Man's Folly, 506
"Dead Man's Gloves," 2723
Dead Man's Knock, The, 460
"Dead Man's Mirror," 2324, 2421
Dead Man's Riddle, 1279
Dead Man's Shoes (Bruce), 326
Dead Man's Shoes (Innes), 1216, 2447
Dead Man's Watch, 562
Dead Man Twice, 390
Dead March for Penelope Blow, 138
Dead March in Three Keys, 1393
Dead Men at the Folly, 1806
Dead Men Don't Ski, 1626
Dead Men of Sestos, The, 1412
Dead Men Rise Up Never, 1334
Dead Men's Bells, 1045
Dead Men's Shoes (Chance), 479
Dead Mrs. Stratton, 162
Dead Ned, 1559

DEFOE, DANIEL, 2566, 2835, 3123, 3457
DEFORD, MIRIAM ALLEN, 2361, 2367, 2774, 3167
DEIGHTON, LEN, 722
DEKOBRA, MAURICE, 723, 1358/B
DELAFIELD, E. M., 174, 1209, 2921
DE LA MARE, COLIN, 3404
DE LA MARE, WALTER, 2872, 3404-5, 3459
DE LA TORRE, LILLIAN, 724-5, 2306, 2467-8, 2774, 3099
Delayed Payment, 1857
DEL BUONO, ORESTE, 2934
Delights of Detection, The, 2344, 2622
DELL, E. M., 2921
DELL, JEFFREY, 2395
"DELTA," 2207
DELVING, MICHAEL, 726
DE MILLE, AGNES, 3124
DE MILLE, CECIL B., 2921
Democrat Dies, A, 878
Demon in the Blood, 1528
"Demon King, The," 3413
De Mortuis, 3227
DENBIE, ROGER, 727
DENNING, LORD, 3125
DENNIS, ALLAN, 864
DENNIS, S. L., 3413
DENNISTON, ELINORE, 864
DENT, J. C., 3406
"Denton Boudoir Mystery, The," 2854
Denver Murders, 3171
Department of Dead Ends, The, 2848
Department of Queer Complaints, The, 2391, 2473
Departure of Mr. Gaudette, The, 757
D. E. Q., 1014
DE QUINCEY, 2460, 2532, 2566, 3078, 3126, 3311, 3431
DERING, JOAN, 728-9
DERLETH, AUGUST, 730/B-32, 2330, 2365, 2469-71, 2675, 2741, 3400, 3407, 3413, 3436-7
DESCARTES, 2920
Desert Lake Mystery, The, 2004
Design for Dying, 1434
Design in Diamonds, 1312
"Desire," 3442
"Desk, The," 2321
DESMOND, HUGH, 733
Desperate Moment, 23
Desperate People, The, 775
"Destroyer, The," 2324

"Detection and the Literary Art," 2992
Detection Club, The (London), 162/B, 2135, 2914, 2955
"Detection Club Oath, The," 2955
Detection Medley, 2765
Detections of Sam Johnson, The, 2468
Detection Unlimited, 1135
Detective, The (Thorp), 783, 2055
Detective (Vance), 2113
Detective Duff Unravels It, 2684
"Detective Fiction" (Carter), 2916
Detective Fiction (Carter), 2905, 2915
Detective Fiction (W. B. Stevenson), 3037
"Detective Fiction" (London Times), 3048
Detective in Fiction, The (Seaborne), 2784, 3025
"Detective in Fiction and in Fact, The" (Rhodes), 3012
Detective-Inspector Richardson, C.I.D., 2054
"Detective novel" et l'influence de la pensée scientifique, Le, 2981
"Detective Novels," 2977
"Detective Police, The," 2566, 3128
Detectives and Togas, 2255
Detective's Holiday, The, 101
Detective Short Story, The: a Bibliography, 3004
"Detective Short Story, The: The First Hundred Years," 2955
Detectives, Names and "Lives" of, 2365, 2642, 2915, 2954, 2957, 2988, 2998, 3005, 3047
Detective Stories of Today (Postgate), 2732
"Detective Story, The," 2898
"Detective Story Decalogue, A," 2955
"Detective Story in Britain, The," 3043
"Detective Story Mystery, The," 2927
"Detective Story, The—Why?," 2955
Detective Unawares, A, 1355
Detour at Night, 788
DE TRAZ, GEORGES, 2943
Detroit Murders, 3171
Dette de Sang, 1327
Development of the Detective Novel, The, 2988
Devereux Court Mystery, The, 367
Devil at Your Elbow, The, 734
Devil Drives, The, 1527

Devil in the Bush, The, 1111
"Devil's Foot, The," 2478
Devil's Own, The, 686
Devil's Pawn, The, 329
Devil's Reckoning, 388
Devil's Steps, The, 2102
Devil's Stronghold, The, 868
DEVINE, D. M., 734–40
DEVLIN, LORD, 3074, 3106, 3127, 3266
Devouring Fire, The, 1011
Dewer Rides, 2006/B
Dewey Death, 30, 194
DEWEY, GEORGE, 741/B
DEWEY, JOHN, 3250
DEWEY, MELVIL, 194
DEWEY, T. B., 741/B–43
"Dey Ain't No Ghosts," 3457
D.I., The, 81
Diagnosis: Homicide, 2357
Diamond Master, The, 2527
Diamond Pin, The, 2204
Diamonds Are Forever, 853/B
Diamonds Are Trumps, 6
Diary of a D.A., 3148
["Dickens and Mystery in the Novel"], 3001
DICKENS, CHARLES, 550/B, 576, 744, 896, 1016, 1623/B, 1690, 2435, 2472, 2566, 2797, 2888, 2941, 2962, 2964, 2988, 2993, 3036, 3128–30, 3408, 3431–2, 3442
DICKINSON, PETER, 466, 745/B–47
DICKSON, CARR, 457/B, 1919
DICKSON, CARTER, 475/B, 748–9, 1858, 2473, 2569, 2747, 2765
Dictionary of Clocks and Watches, 327/B
Dictionnaire de l'espion, 3262
"Did Bierce Die, Or—?," 3100
DIDELOT, FRANCIS, 750
Did She Fall?, 1948
Die All, Die Merrily, 320
Die, Darling, Die, 329
Died in the Red, 1022
Died in the Wool, 1542
Die Laughing, 1475
Die Like a Dog (Halliday), 1059
"Die Like a Dog" (Stout), 2810
Die Like a Man, 726
Die of a Rose, 1521
Difficult Problem, A, 1030, 2541
"Dilemma" (Sayers), 2776
"Dilemma, A" (Mitchell), 2665
Dilemma for Dax, 682
Dilemmas (Mason), 2652, 3233

DILLON, D. A., 2207/B
DILLON, EILIS, 545, 751/B–53, 3037
DILNOT, GEORGE, 754, 910, 3130–2
Dime Detective, 2950
Diminishing Returns, 2258
DINESEN, ISAAK, 3400
Dinner Party at Bardolph's, 2169
"DIPLOMAT," 755
Diplomatic Cover, 2057
Diplomatic Death, 872
Diplomat's Folly, 2147
DIPPER, ALAN, 756
"Dirt Cheap," 2776
Dirty Story, 50
'Disappearance of an Actor, The," 2387
"Disappearance of Count Collini, The," 2689
"Disappearance of Lady Francis Carfax, The," 2478
"Disappearance of Marie Severe, The," 2368
"Disappearance of Mr. Davenheim, The," 2642
"Disappearance of Mr. James Phillimore, The," 2741
"Disappearance of Philip Mansfield, The," 2432
"Disappearances," 2531
Disappearing Parson, The, 368
"Disappearing Servant Wench, The," 2365
Discord in the Air, 546
Disentanglers, The, 1340
Disgrace to the College, 573
Disguise for a Dead Gentleman, 579
DISHER, M. W., 2935
Dishonoured Bones, 2066
DISNEY, DORIS M., 757
DISNEY, DOROTHY C., 758
Disposing Mind, 1951
Disposing of Henry, 110
DISRAELI, 3174
Distant Clue, The, 1386
Diva's Emeralds, The, 1440
Dive Deep for Death, 1583
Diversions of Dawson, The, 2441
DIVINE, A. D., 2575
Divine Songs, 1919
Diving Death, 872
Division Bell Mystery, The, 2239
DNA Business, The, 405
DOBREE, BONAMY, 1779, 3409
DOBSON, AUSTIN, 3208
DOCHERTY, J. L., 489

Docken Dead, 2068
Doctor and the Corpse, The, 1638
Dr. Bentiron, Detective, 1730
Dr. Bruderstein Vanishes, 1929
Dr. Crippen, 982/B
Doctor Died at Dusk, The, 1168
Doctor Dodd's Experiment, 1915
Dr. Goodwood's Locum, 1800
"Doctor, His Wife, and the Clock, The," 1030, 2843
Dr. Jekyll and Mr. Hyde, 2138, 2797
Doctor Philligo, 2142/B
Dr. Priestley Investigates, 1841
Dr. Priestley Lays a Trap, 1816
Dr. Priestley's Quest, 1817
Doctors Also Die, 735
Dr. Sam Johnson, Detector, 2467
Doctors Are Doubtful, The, 2210
Doctor's offices. See also **Hospitals,**
114, 116, 127, 187, 251, 385, 412,
519, 641, 712, 735–6, 805, 1381,
1461, 1713, 1800, 1810, 1889, 1914,
2187, 2213, 2235, 2437, 2479, 2482,
2552, 2570, 2601, 2658, 2661
Doctor S.O.S., 2048
Dr. Sun, 1525
Dr. Tancred Begins, 566
Dr. Thorndyke Intervenes, 890
Dr. Thorndyke Omnibus, The, 2523
Dr. Thorndyke's Case Book, 2516
Dr. Thorndyke's Cases, 905, 2517, 2523
Dr. Thorndyke's Crime File, 905, 2944
Dr. Thorndyke's Discovery, 891
Doctor Was a Lady, The, 1118
"Dr. Watson" (MacCarthy), 3360
"Doctor Watson" (Roberts), 3370
"Dr. Watson Speaks Out," 2982
"Dr. Watson's Secret," 3383
Documents in the Case, The, 1910
Documents of Murder, 1234/B
Dodd Cases, The, 2350, 2624
DODGE, FRED, 3133
"Dodie and the Boogerman," 2367
"Dog in the Daytime, The," 2447
Dog It Was, The, 1094
"Dog's Life, A," 2321
Doll for the Toff, A, 637
Dolls Are Murder, 2654
Dolly and the Singing Bird, 1060
DOLMETSCH, CARL, 2936
Domestic Agency, The, 1823
"Domesticity of Detectives, The," 2923

Dominant Third, 1123
DONALDSON, NORMAN, 887/B, 2330, 2937
Don Among the Dead Men, 2143
DONAVAN, JOHN, 1618/B
DONDERO, J. A., 3264
"Don Juan," 3422
DONNEL, C. P., 2738
DONNELLY, R. C., 3071
Do Not Disturb, 1434
Do Not Murder Before Xmas, 1208
DONOVAN, F. P., 2938
"Don't Guess, Let Me Tell You," 2955
Don't Just Stand There, 2243
"Don't Look Behind You" (Brown), 3392
Don't Look Behind You! (Rogers), 1874
Doom Dealer, The, 1674
Doomsters, The, 1461
Doom Stone, The, 2289
Door, The, 1862
Doorbell Rang, The, 1982, 3039
Door Between, The, 1776
Door Fell Shut, A, 23
"Door in the Wall, The," 2456, 3474
Door Nails Never Die, 2295
Door of Death, The, 792
Doors of Sleep, The, 2180
Doors Open, The, 988
"Door to Death," 2808
Dope, a Story of Chinatown, 1876
Dorcas Dene, 2998
"Dormant Account," 2354
Dorrington Deed Box, The, 2671
Dossier no. 113, Le, 918
DOSTOEVSKY, 2797
"Double Admiral, The," 3446, 3459
Double Barrel, 880
Double-Barrelled Detective Story, A, 2080, 2741
Double Blackmail, 573
"Double Clue, The," 2416
"Double Cross," 2376
Double-Cross Purposes, 1316
Double Death, The (Chance), 479
Double Death (Crofts), 652
Double Death (Forsyte), 872
Double Death (V. Hands), 2134
Doubled in Diamonds, 419
Double Doom, 118
"Double Entry," 2501
"Double Exposure," 2321
Double Florin, The, 1818

Double for Death, 2003
Double Identities (Rhode), 1854
Double Identity (Coxe), 627
Double Image, The, 1491
Double Indemnity, 396, 398, 2911
"Double Lover," 2324
Double or Quits, 799
"Double Problem, The," 2750
"Doubles, The," 3422
"Double Sin," 2416, 2458
"Double Six Domino," The, 2732
Double Take, 307
Double Thirteen, The, 1528
Double Tragedy, 671
Double Turn, The, 442
DOUGLAS, LORD ALFRED, 3209
DOUGLASS, D. M., 759–61
"D'outre Mort," 3431
Dover Goes to Pott, 1733
Dover One, 1734
"Dover Pulls a Rabbit," 2721
Dover Three, 1736
Dover Two, 1735
DOWERS, PENN, 1234/B
Down Among the Dead Men, 1629
DOWNIE, R. A., 2934
Downland Corner, A, 2224/B
DOYLE, ADRIAN CONAN, 457/B, 2474, 2741, 3410
DOYLE, ARTHUR CONAN, 457/B, 762/B–65, 917, 918, 1185, 1358, 1493/B, 1623/B, 1689, 1732, 1894, 2304, 2320, 2322, 2350, 2360, 2437, 2456, 2458, 2461, 2475–87, 2518, 2568–9, 2642, 2665–6, 2692, 2735, 2750, 2767, 2771, 2778, 2784, 2795, 2836, 2853, 2875, 2912–3, 2928, 2939, 2955, 2975–6, 2988, 2996, 2999–3000, 3003, 3008, 3022, 3051, 3091, 3142, 3168, 3250, 3272, 3277, 3342–3, 3353, 3365, 3383, 3410
Do You Know This Voice?, 156
DRACHMAN, T. S., 766
Dracula, 1972, 2466
Dracula's Guest and Other Weird Stories, 1972
Dragon Murder Case, The, 2121
"Dragon's Head, The," 2750
"Dramatizations of the Great Literary Detectives and Criminals," 3029
Dram of Poison, A, 71
DRAWBELL, J. W., 2134
"Drawing Room B," 2856
"Drawn into Error," 2500
Dreadful Hollow, The, 216

"Dream, The," 2425, 2459
Dream Detective, The, 1876
Dream Doctor, The, 2760
"Dream-Gown of the Japanese Ambassador, The," 2656
"Dreams and Fairies," 2904
DREISER, THEODORE, 1932, 2855, 3219, 3416
Dresden Green, The, 881
DRESSER, DAVIS, 1058/B
Dressing-Room Murder, The, 861
DRESSLER, DAVID, 3134
"Dressmaker's Doll, The," 2416
Drink to Yesterday, 574
Driven to Kill, 2274
"Dromenon," 3418
Dromio Family, The, 1230
Drood Case, The, 2888
Drood Murder Case, The (Baker), 2889
Drood Murder Case, The (Walters), 3054
Drop Dead, 1646
Drop to His Death, 1858
Drowning Pool, The, 1462
Drug on the Market, 270
"Drum, The," 3464
DRUMMOND, CHARLES, 767–9
DRUMMOND, JUNE, 770–1
"Drury Lane," 2992
Drury Lane's Last Case, 1882
"Dublin Mystery, The," 2642
Dublin Nightmare, The, 1411
DuBOIS, THEODORA, 772
DUBOISGOBEY, F. H. A., 538, 773
DUBOURG, MAURICE, 2940
Duca and the Milan Murders, 1911
Ducats in Her Coffin, 2178
"Duchess and Lady Torrent, The," 2652
Duchess of Malfi, The, 1238
"Duchess of Wiltshire's Diamonds, The," 2542
"Duello," 2779, 2850
Due Process, 2242
Due to a Death, 1280
Duke of York's Steps, The, 2148
DUKES, (SIR) PAUL, 3123, 3135–6, 3217
DUKE, WINIFRED, 2732
DULAC, EDMOND, 2904
Dull Dead, The, 392–3
DULLES, ALLEN, 1669/B, 2488, 2885, 3137–8
DUMAS, ALEXANDRE, 2344, 2489

"Empty House, The" (Doyle), 2480, 3366
"Empty House, The" (Graeme), 2324
Empty House and Other Ghost Stories, The (Blackwood), 3391
Encyclopedia Brown, Detective, 494
Encyclopedia of Murder, 3322
End Is Known, The, 1057
Endless Colonnade, The, 1087
Endless Night, 509
End of a Call Girl, 974
"End of a Judge," 2732, 2774
End of an Ancient Mariner, 564
End of Andrew Harrison, The, 671
"End of a Show, The," 3413
End of Chapter, 202
End of Her Honeymoon, The, 1414
End of Mr. Garment, The, 1958
"End of Sherlock Holmes, The," 2741
End of Solomon Grundy, The, 2023
End of the Line, 1151
End of the Track, The, 952
End of Violence, The, 145
ENDORE, GUY, 788–90, 3140
End Play, 2604
Enemies of the Bride, 1597
"Enemy, The," 2367, 2447, 3459
Enemy Unseen, 653
Energies of Art, The, 2898
Engaged to Murder, 1116
ENGLAND, G. A., 2316, 2750
English Justice, 3292
"English Lesson," 2559
"Englishman, The," 2658
Englishman in Paris, An, 2114
English Murder, An, 1079
Enormous Shadow, The, 1088
Enough to Kill a Horse, 825
Enquête criminelle et les méthodes scientifiques, L', 3216
Enter a Murderer, 1543
Enter a Spy, 2215
Enter Sir John, 703
"Entertaining Episode of the Article in Question, The," 2642
Enter Three Witches, 1482
Entry of Death, An, 1476
"Envelope, The," 2836
Envious Casca, 1137
EON, CHEVALIER D', 3207
"EPHESIAN," 3248
Epic of the Gestapo, An, 3136
Epilogue, 744, 1016
"Epilogue: To Will H. Low," 3036

"Episode of the Codex' Curse, The," 2747, 2774
"Episode of the Nail and the Requiem, The," 2608, 2780
"Episode of the Sinister Inventor, The," 2609
"Episode of Torment IV, The," 2608
"Episode on Cain Street," 3407
Epitaph for a Spy, 50
E. Q. Anthologies, 2492–3, 2747
E. Q. Mystery Annuals, 2747
"Error at Daybreak," 2473
"Error in Chemistry, An," 2367
Error of the Moon, 2279
ERSKINE, JOHN, 2136
ERSKINE, MARGARET, 791
ERSKINE, THOMAS, 3081
Escale à Pago-Pago, 75
Escape, 2112
"Escape of Koravitch, The," 2860
Escape to Murder, 1914
Escape to Quebec, 1293
ESENWEIN, J. B., 3057
Essay on Circumstantial Evidence, 3118
Essay on Man, 1521
Essays in Satire, 3358
Essence of Murder, The, 1311
ESTABROOKS, G. H., 1392
Estate of the Beckoning Lady, The, 35
ESTEVEN, JOHN, 792/B–93
Esthétique du roman policier, 2990
ESTRIDGE, ROBIN, 1408
Etched in Arsenic, 3112
"Ethics of the Mystery Novel, The," 2955
ETON, ROBERT, 1586/B
Etruscan Net, The, 989
Eugene Aram, 343
Europe: A Personal and Political Survey, 26/B
Eustace Diamonds, The, 2069
EUSTACE, ROBERT, 1784, 1910, 2542, 2660, 2765, 2778, 2780
EUSTIS, HELEN, 794–5
EVANS, DAVID, 2317
EVANS, WAINWRIGHT, 3410
EVELYN, J. M., 2089/B
Evening Standard Detective Books, The, 2321
"Eve of the Wedding," 2746
Evergreen Death, The, 879
"Everlasting Club, The," 3444
EVERMAY, MARCH, 796–7

Every Man Has His Price, 2232
"Everything Under Control," 2955
Evidence of the Accused, 1248
Evidence of Things Seen, 697
Evil in Our Midst, 2071
Evil of the Day, The, 1963
Evil of Time, The, 156
Evil Shepherd, The, 1669
Evil That Men Do, The, 1695
Evil Under the Sun, 537
"EVOE," 1316/B
"Evolution of the Whodunit in . . .
  World War II," 2956
"Examination of Prisoners, The:
  Emile Gaboriau," 3174
Excellent Intentions, 1180
Ex-Detective, The, 2686
"Executioner, The," 3442
"Executions at Cape Remittance,"
  2512
"Exhibit A," 2683
Exit Charlie, 83
Exit Dying, 1662
Exit the Skeleton, 15
Expeditions, incl. Safaris, Missions,
  and Digs, 155, 222, 507, 745, 837,
  839, 898, 1198–9, 1314, 1516, 1789,
  1960, 2066
Expendable Man, The, 1177
"Expense of Justice, The," 2659
Expensive Place to Die, An, 722
"Experiment, The," 3427
Experiment in Crime (Rhode), 1836
Experiment Perilous, 443
Experiments in Crime (Frankau),
  2512
"Experts, The," 2525
"Explanation, The," 3445
"Exploit of the Adjusters, An," 2316
Exploits de Rocambole, Les, 1731
Exploits of Fidelity Dove, The, 2739
Expressman and the Detective, The,
  3257
EX-PRIVATE X. See BURRAGE, A. M.
"Eye, The," 2437
Eye in Attendance, The, 2245
Eye in the Museum, The, 588, 603
Eye of a Serpent, The, 1708
Eye of Osiris, The, 904, 905
Eyes of Max Carrados, The, 2350,
  2368
Eye-Witness, 620

FABRICANT, NOAH, 2437
Fabulous Clipjoint, The, 290/B, 294

"Face in the Fresco, The," 3445
"Face in the Target, The," 2407
"Face Is Familiar, The," 2955
Faceless Enemy, 2195
"Face of the Corpse, The," 2698,
  2875
Face on the Cutting-Room Floor,
  The, 345, 1422
Faces of Justice, The, 3073
"Fact and Fiction in Criminology,"
  3075
Factories, 24, 217, 569, 923–4, 1201,
  1282, 1315, 1635, 1696, 1737, 1943,
  2232, 2248, 2258
"Facts Concerning the Recent Carni-
  val of Crime in Connecticut, The,"
  2080/B
"Facts in the Case of the Missing
  Diplomat, The," 2562
FADIMAN, CLIFTON, 2898
"Fad of the Fisherman, The," 2407,
  2750
FAIR, A. A., 798/B–804, 932/B
Fairbairn Case, The, 150
Fair-Haired Lady, The, 1359
FAIRWAY, SIDNEY, 805
"Fairy Gold," 2607
FALKNER, J. M., 806
Falling Star, 1633
Fall of a Sparrow, 980
"Fall of the House of Usher, The,"
  3431
Fall Over Cliff, 120
"Fall River Legend," 3124
False Colors, 1748–9
False Scent, 1544
False to Any Man, 868
"False Weight," 2776
False Witness, 2091
Family Affair, A (Innes), 1219
Family Affairs (Rhode), 1857
Family, Large, The, incl. Christmas
  and Birthday Parties, 43, 107, 254,
  275, 304, 440, 505, 510, 531–2, 535,
  575, 614, 631, 650, 1132, 1137,
  1140–1, 1402, 1536, 1541, 1545,
  1632, 1886, 1974, 2106–7, 2118
Family Tomb, The, 989
Famous Bank Forgeries, Robberies,
  and Swindles, 3183
Famous Canadian Trials, 3177
Famous Criminal Cases, 3150
Famous Criminal Trials, 3245
Famous Detective Stories, 2646

762

Final Curtain, 1545
Final Deduction, The, 1984
Final Exposure, 1523
"Final Impressions of a Psychical Researcher," 3429
"Final Problem, The," 2479, 3339, 3366
Final Proof, 1675
"Finch's Final Fling," 3340
Find the Clock, 1270
"Find the Woman," 2747
FINGER, C. J., 3145
"Finger Man" (Chandler), 2403
"Finger Man, The" (Prince), 2365
"Finger of Death, The," 2758
Fingerprint, The, 2207
Fingerprints (Browne and Brock), 306, 3097
Fingerprints (Galton), 3152
FINNEY, JACK, 2747
Finsbury Mob, The, 329
Fire at Greycombe Farm, 1857
"Fire in the Galley Stove," 2575
Fire in the Thatch, 1401
Fireside Book of Suspense, The, 2575
"Fires in the Rue St. Honoré, The," 2563
First Came a Murder, 637
First Come, First Kill, 1387
First Detectives, The, 3115
"First Hate," 2355, 3390
FIRTH, ANTHONY, 831
FISCHER, BRUNO, 2654
FISHER, DOUGLAS, 834–5
FISHER, JACOB, 3146
Fisherman's End, 1044
"Fisher of Men, A," 2516
Fish or Cut Bait, 804
FISH, R. L., 832–3, 1394, 2501–2, 3345
FITT, MARY, 836–9, 2306, 2502, 2600, 2732, 3388
FITZGERALD, F. SCOTT, 2456
FITZGERALD, G. F., 1072
FITZGERALD, NIGEL, 545, 840/B–49, 1072, 3037
FITZSIMMONS, CORTLAND, 850–1
5A King's Bench Walk, 905
Five Alarm Fire, 1962
Five-Day Nightmare, The, 291
5:18 Mystery, The, 807
Five Fragments, The, 780
Five Jars, The, 3428
Five Murderers, 2398
Five Passengers from Lisbon, 781

Five Red Herrings, The, 1905
Five Roundabouts to Heaven, 184
"Five Swords, The," 2320
"5000 Orange Pips; or, The Seeds of Pedantry," 3331
FLAGG, JOHN, 852
Flame of Murder, The, 1647
"Flaming Phantom, The," 2529
FLAMMARION, CAMILLE, 3464
FLANAGAN, THOMAS, 2367
FLANNER, JANET, 2774
Flash, 1892
Flash Point, 307
Flat Tyre in Fulham, A, 121
FLAUBERT, 1274/B, 2503, 3208
Flaw in the Crystal, The, 1944
"Flaw in the Organization, A," 2652
Fleet Hall Inheritance, The, 1301
FLEMING, IAN, 307, 853/B–54, 2853, 2883, 2885, 3123
FLEMING, JOAN, 855, 2306, 3092, 3218
FLEMING, OLIVER, 1451/B
FLEMING, PETER, 3415
FLETCHER, (SIR) H. L. A., 2144/B
FLETCHER, J. S., 856/B–61, 2316, 2322–3, 2504–7, 2614, 2779, 2904, 2969, 3068
FLETCHER, LUCILLE, 862
Flight of a Witch, 1701
"Flight to the World's End," 2607
Floating Admiral, The, 2135
Floating Dutchman, The, 151–2
"Flood on the Goodwins," 2575
FLORA, FLETCHER, 2508
"Florentine Dante, The," 2739
Florentine Finish, 1150
Flowering Death, 1518
"Flowering of the Strange Orchid, The," 3474
Flowers for the Judge, 38
Flush as May, 1174
Flying Finish, 876
"Flying Hat, The," 2316
FLYNN, BRIAN, 863
"Fly Paper," 2547
F. O. B. Murder, 1151
"Fogull Murder, The," 2642
Folded Paper Mystery, The, 866
FOLEY, RAE, 864
Follow as the Night, 1472
Follow Me, 1797
Follow the Toff, 637
Fontego's Folly, 954
Fool Killer, The, 795

GADDA, C. E., 919
"Gagtooth's Image," 3406
Gaily, Gaily, 3179
GAINES, ROBERT, 920–1
GAINSBOROUGH, THOMAS, 3139
GAIR, MALCOLM, 922
Gaîté faite à Londres, 2347
GAITE, FRANCIS, 574
Galatea, 398
GALE, JOHN, 923–4
GALÍNDEZ, J. DE, 474
Gallant Affair, The, 1154
GALLICO, PAUL, 2739
GALLIE, MENNA, 925–6
Galloway Case, The, 956
Gallows' Foot, 976, 980
Gallows Garden, The, 474
GALT, JOHN, 2835
Galton Case, The, 1465
GALTON, (SIR) FRANCIS, 3110, 3152
GALWAY, R. C., 927
GALWEY, G. V., 927, 928/B–30
Gambit, 1985
Gambler, The, 1322
Gambling. See Bohemia and Sporting Events
Game for Three Losers, 1418
"Game Played in the Dark, The," 2369, 2542
Game Without Rules, 2534
Gammon and Espionage, 151/B
Gantry Episode, The, 770
GARBER, FREDERICK, 1780
Garden in Asia, The, 2722
Garden Murder Case, The, 2121
"Garden of Forking Paths, The," 2367
"Garden of Proserpine, The," 1334
Gardens and Garden Parties, 6, 694, 899, 1211, 1726, 2224, 2226, 2275
Gardens at 19, 2596
GARDINER, DOROTHY, 2918
GARDINER, STEPHEN, 931
GARDINER, WILLIAM, 2223
GARDNER, E. S., 798/B–99, 932/B–44, 2111, 2354, 2493, 2530, 2873, 2928, 2945–6, 2950, 2955, 3146, 3153–5, 3182
GARDNER, F. R., 3423
GARDNER, JOHN, 945
GARDNER, (THE REV.) RALPH, 3346
GARNETT, DAVID, 2960
GARNETT, RICHARD, 3442
GARNETT, ROGER, 1618
GARTH, WILL, 1325/B
Garthoyle Gardens, 2596

GARVE, ANDREW, 106, 183, 536, 946/B–70, 1954, 2256, 2363, 2464, 2738
GASK, ARTHUR, 971, 2324
GASKELL, ELIZABETH, 2531–2, 2566
"Gas Light," 1073
GASQUE, W. H., 3264
"Gatewood Caper, The," 2354, 2547
Gaudy Night, 1488, 1900, 2955
Gauge of Deception, The, 1890
GAULT, BILL, 972
GAULT, W. C., 972–4
Gaunt Woman, The, 193
GAVIN, CLARK, 3156
GAWSWORTH, JOHN, 2789–90
GAZE, RICHARD, 923
GEARON, JOHN, 852
G-8, 2950
Gelignite Gang, The, 632
"Gemini," 2872
"Gemminy Crickets Case, The," 2373
General Besserley's Puzzle Box, 2688
Generally Speaking, 2926
Generous Heart, The, 821
Genre(s), Studies and Comments on, Part III and: 26, 28, 162/B, 309, 463, 504, 548, 939, 944, 971, 1164, 1291, 1296–7, 1381, 1520, 2134–5, 2228, 2368, 2424, 2444, 2447, 2488, 2523, 2586, 2598, 2614, 2639, 2770, 2778, 2787, 2873
"Gentleman from Paris, The," 2367, 2393, 2447
Gently by the Shore, 1188
Gently Does It, 1188, 1193
Gently Down the Stream, 1193
Gently Dust the Corpse, 617
Gently Floating, 1189
Gently in the Sun, 1190
Gently Through the Mill, 1193
Gently Where the Roads Go, 1191
Gently with the Painters, 1193
"Genuine Tabard, The," 2351, 2765, 3008
"George Barnwell," 2306
"George H. Jay and the Lady from Moolgamboolloo," 2323
GEROULD, G. H., 975
"Gerrard Street Mystery, The," 3406
Gerrard Street Mystery and Other Weird Tales, The, 3406
"Getting Away with Murder," 2945
GETTLER, A. O., 3264
"Gettysburg Bugle, The," 2367, 2500
"Ghost, The," 3432

"Ghost at Massingham Mansions, The," 2368
Ghost Car, The, 1313
Ghost It Was, The, 1183
Ghostly Tales of Henry James, The, 3426
Ghostly Tales to Be Told, 3403
"Ghost of Dorothy Dingley, The," 2835
"Ghosts," 2658
Ghosts and Marvels, 3428
Ghost's High Noon, The, 462
Ghosts in Daylight, 1668
Ghost Stories of an Antiquary, 3427
"Giant Coffin, The," 3462
Giant's Bread, 2209
GIBBON, PERCEVAL, 2575
GIBBS, HENRY, 1097
GIDE, ANDRÉ, 3006, 3031
Gideon Omnibus, The, 1534
Gideon's Day, 1534
Gideon's Fire, 1530
Gideon's Night, 1531, 1534
Gideon's River, 1532
Gideon's Vote, 1533
"Gideon's War," 2650
Gideon's Week, 1534
"Gideon: The Hooligans," 2649
GIELGUD, JOHN, 2040/B
GIELGUD, VAL, 976–80, 2835
Gigantic Shadow, The, 2027
GILBERT, ANTHONY, 981, 2321, 2447, 2765, 2908
GILBERT, MICHAEL, 982/B–92, 1458, 2166, 2321, 2464, 2493, 2500, 2533–8, 2555, 2558, 2621, 2738, 2767, 2788, 2846, 2853, 2908, 2947–8, 3157
GILBERT, STUART, 1930
"Gilded Girls, The," 2337
"Gilded Pupil, The," 2732
GILES, KENNETH, 767, 993–7, 1476
GILES, KRIS, 1653
GILLETTE, WILLIAM, 865/B, 999, 2395, 2487, 3347
GILL, JOSEPHINE, 998
GILL, PATRICK, 2931
GILMAN, C. P., 2855
GILROY, HARRY, 2572
Gin and Murder, 418
"Gioconda Smile, The," 2583, 2755, 3008
"Giraffe Problem, The," 2699
Girl from the Mimosa Club, The, 868
Girl in Cabin 54, The, 862

Girl in the Cage, The, 851
Girl Meets Body, 1204
"Girl on the Train, The," 2418
"Girl Overboard," 1686, 2365
"Girl Who Saw Too Much, The," 2768
Girl Who Vanished, The, 1885
Girl with a Hole in Her Head, The, 1974
"Girl with the Golden Eyes, The," 96
GIRVAN, WAVENEY, 2949
GISSING, GEORGE, 1623/B
GITTINS, ANTHONY, 3413
Give a Man a Gun, 637
Give 'Em the Ax, 800
Give the Devil His Due, 1015
"Gladstone's Candlestick," 2449
GLADSTONE, W. E., 3195
GLAISTER, (DRS.) JOHN, 3158–9, 3229
GLANVIL, JOSEPH, 3464
GLASPELL, SUSAN, 2458
Glass Cage, The, 2249
Glass-Domed Clock, The, 2734
Glass Mask, The, 1659
Glass on the Stairs, 1912
Glass-Sided Ants' Nest, The, 745
Glass Spear, The, 614
Glastonbury Romance, A, 813
"Gleanings from the Wreckage," 2519
Glimpses of the Moon, The, 638/B
"Gloria Scott, The," 2479
Gloved Hand, The, 1968
GLOVER, DOROTHY, 2928, 2998
Glozel, 3290
Goblin Market, The, 1427, 1430
"The Gods, to Avenge . . .," 2610
GODWIN, JOHN, 1000–1, 3160
GODWIN, WILLIAM, 343, 1002, 3040
GOETHE, 476
Goggle Box Affair, The, 979
Gold and Gaiters, 28, 2882
Gold Brick Island, 604
"Gold Bug, The," 2319, 2718/B, 2854
Gold Bullets, 235
Gold Comes in Bricks, 804
"Gold-Digger Happening, The," 2458
"Golden Age of English Detection, The," 3042
Golden Ashes, 656
"Golden Ball, The," 2418
Golden Bough, The, 1212
Golden Deed, The, 957
GOLDEN, F. L., 2437
"Golden Pince-Nez, The," 2480
Golden Slipper, The, 1030

Golden Snail, The, 1435/B
Golden Violet, The, 1924
Goldfinger, 853/B
"Goldfish," 2398, 2401, 2403
GOLDSMITH, GENE, 1003
GOLDSMITH, H. S., 2354, 2950
GOLDSTEIN, A. S., 3161
GOLDSTEIN, JOSEPH, 3071
GOLDSTONE, L. A., 2064
Gold Was Our Grave, 2151
Golf Courses, 9, 15, 388, 520, 916, 1321, 1517, 1983, 2086, 2294, 2351
Golf House Murder, The, 9
GOLLANCZ, VICTOR, 420, 589, 1297, 2049, 2134
Go, Lovely Rose, 1745
GONCOURT, EDMOND, and LOUIS DE, 1414/B
GONZALES, (DR.) T. A., 2357, 3264
Goodbye Is Not Worthwhile, 1609
"Goodby, Miss Lizzie Borden," 2774
GOODCHILD, GEORGE, 1004, 2539, 3248
GOODIS, DAVID, 1005
GOODMAN, JONATHAN, 3162
Good-Night, Ladies, 2132
Good Night, Sheriff, 1959
GOODRICH-FREER, A., 3412
Goodwin, Archie. See **Wolfe, Nero**
GORDON, GORDON, 2540
GORDON, HORATIO, 1194
GORDON, M. N., 2540
GORDON, NEIL, 1006–7
GORDON, REX, 1172
GORDON, R. M., 2458
GORDONS, THE, 2540
GORE-BROWNE, R. F., 1008–10
GORELL, LORD, 1011–14, 2765
GOREY, EDWARD, 135
GORON, CHEF DE LA SÛRETÉ, 3165
GOULD, R. T., 3163
Government Offices. See **Embassies**
"Governor of Cap Haitien, The," 2816
GOWING, SIDNEY, 2837
Gownsman's Gallows, 815
GOYDER, MARGOT, 1646
GRAAF, PETER, 1015
Gracie Allen Murder Case, The, 2121
GRAEME, BRUCE, 744, 1016–17, 2324
GRAEME, DAVID, 1016
GRAEME, RODERIC, 1248
GRAFTON, C. W., 1018–20
"Graham Greene," 2927
GRAHAM, WHIDDEN, 1021
Grand Babylon Hotel, 142, 2348, 2437

Grand Central Murder, The, 1515
"Grandest Game in the World, The," 2912
GRANT, AMBROSE, 489
GRANT, DOUGLAS, 1673/B
GRANT, LANDON, 1034
Grass Widow's Tale, The, 1703
Grave Case of Murder, A, 107
Grave Maker's House, The, 2192
Grave Matter, A (Davies), 711
Grave Matters (Rhode), 1823
"Grave Robbing in New England," 3311
"Graves for the Living," 2680
GRAVES, ROBERT, 2745, 2951–2
Graveyard Rolls, The, 1754
GRAY, DULCIE, 1022
GRAY, JONATHAN (ADAMS), 5
GRAY, JONATHAN (TAYLOR), 1023
"Grayling or Murder Will Out," 3461–2
"Gray Man, The" (Green), 2541
GRAZEBROOK, O. F., 3348
Great American Detective Stories, 2366
"Great Auto Mystery, The," 2529
Great Bank Robbery, The, 1104
"Great Bear, The," 2316
Great Book of Thrillers, The, 2835, 3046
Great Brighton Mystery, The, 861
"Great Detective, The," 2970
Great Detectives and Their Methods, 3130, 3132
"Great Detective Stories, The," 2955
Great Detective Stories About Doctors, 2437
Greatest Sea Mystery, The, 3142, 3344
Great Fog and Other Weird Tales, The, 1115, 3418
"Great God Pan, The," 3439
Great Hotel Murder, The, 1958
"Great Impersonation, A" (Overton), 2999
Great Impersonation, The (Oppenheim), 1669/B, 1670
Great K. and A. Train Robbery, The, 269
"Great Pegram Mystery, The," 2741
Great Portrait Mystery, The, 2518
"Great Return, The," 3459
Great Southern Mystery, The, 572
Great Spy Stories from Fiction, 2488
Great Stories of Detection, Mystery, and Horror, The, 2781

Great Tales of Mystery, 2382
Great Thames Mysteries, 3246
Great Train Robberies of the West, 3085
Great True Spy Stories, 3137
Great Unsolved Crimes, 3068
"Great Wet Way, The," 2837
"Greedy Night," 2751
Greek Affair, The, 1043
Greek Coffin Mystery, The, 1776
"Greek Interpreter, The," 2479, 2767
Greek Myths, The, 2417
"Greek Play, The," 2336
Greek Tragedy, 565
Green Ace, The, 1683
GREEN, ALAN, 727
GREEN, A. K., 24, 1024/B–30, 1414/B, 2201/B, 2366, 2415, 1541–2, 2575, 2646, 2843, 2854, 2920, 3442
Green Carnation, The, 1144
"Green Check Jacket, The," 2520
GREEN, C. M., 932/B
Green Diamond, The, 1623
GREENE, GRAHAM, 883, 1031, 2542, 2928, 2998
GREENE, (SIR) HUGH, 2542
Greene Murder Case, The, 1881, 2118, 2912
Green-Eyed Monster, 1686
Green Eye of Goona, The, 1623
Green for Danger, 256
"Green Gorevan, The," 3438
Green Grow the Tresses—O!, 1201
"Green Ice" (Palmer), 2739
Green Ice (Whitfield), 2230
Green Jade Hand, The, 1270
Greenmantle, 330
Greenmask (Farjeon), 808
Greenmask! (Linington), 1381
Green Memory, 2006/B
Greensea Island, 269
"Greenshaw's Folly," 2416
"Green Thoughts," 3415
Greenwell Mystery, The, 1407
GREENWOOD, WALTER, 2774
GREGG, C. F., 1032/B–33, 2324
Grell Mystery, The, 910
Grensen Murder Case, The, 1234/B
"Greuze, The," 2323, 2453
GREW, WILLIAM, 2683
GREX, LEO, 1034
GREY, LOUIS, 1034
Grey Man, The (Urquhart), 2110
Grey Room, The, 1717
Grey Sentinels, The, 1313

Grey Shepherds, The, 1516
Grey Wig, The, 2304
GRIBBIN, LENORE S., 2953
GRIBBLE, LEONARD, 1034, 2324, 2350, 2846, 2872, 3164–6
GRIERSON, EDWARD, 1035/B–39
GRIERSON, FRANCIS, 1040
Griffith Case, The, 150
GRIFFITHS, ARTHUR, 1041–2, 2543
GRIGSON, GEOFFREY, 2306
Grim Grow the Lilacs, 1781
Grim Vengeance, 582, 589, 3219
Grindle Nightmare, The, 1686
Groom Lay Dead, The, 622
Groote Park Murder, The 657, 663
GROSS, GERALD, 3167
GROSS, HANS, 2118, 3118, 3168, 3186, 3215, 3229, 3259
Ground for Suspicion, 388
"Grounds for Divorce," 2579
GRUBER, FRANK, 1043
G-String Murders, The, 1363
"Guardian, The," 3388
Guest in the House, 1460
"Guide to the Underworld, A," 2970
"Guilty!," 2571
Guilty or Not Guilty?, 3218
"Guilty Vicarage, The," 2887
GUINNESS, K. D., 1044
Gun for Inspector West, A, 637
Gun for Sale, A, 1031
GUNN, VICTOR, 1045–7
"Guns at Cyrano's," 2398, 2400–1, 2403
GUSTAVUS III (of Sweden), 3281
"Gutting of Couffignal, The," 2547
GUTTMACHER, (DR.) M. S., 3169, 3266
GWYER, MAURICE, 982/B
Guys and Dolls, 2770
"Gypsy Moth, The," 2336
"Gyroscope, The," 3435
Gyrth Chalice Mystery, The, 39

HADDOW, DENNIS, 1048
HAGEN, O. A., 2892, 2954
HAGGARD, H. RIDER, 1049, 3051
HAGGARD, WILLIAM, 1050/B–54, 2853
Hag's Nook, 465
Ha-Ha Case, The, 590
HAINING, PETER, 3412
"Haircut," 2619
HALE, GARTH, 684
HALE, LESLIE, 3170
HALE, NATHAN, 3147

HALE, PHILIP, 3240
HALÉVY, DANIEL, 1800/B
"Half a Clue," 2740, 2746
Half Hunter, The, 1928
Half-Mast for the Deemster, 137
Half-Mast Murder, 1294
Halfway House, 1776
Half-Way to Murder, 2071
HALIFAX, (DR.) CLIFFORD, 1784, 2661
HALIFAX, 1ST EARL, 3414/B
HALIFAX, VISCOUNT, 3414
HALL, ANGUS, 1055
HALL, CYRIL, 1056
HALL, EDWARD MARSHALL, 3081, 3221, 3231
HALL, GEOFFREY, 1057
HALLIDAY, BRETT, 1058/B–59, 2365, 2635, 2654
HALLIDAY, DOROTHY, 1060
HALLIDAY, MICHAEL, 1061, 1186, 2300, 2931
Hall of Death, 2084
HAMER, A. C., 3171
HAMILTON, BRUCE, 978, 1062/B–66
HAMILTON, DONALD, 1067/B–69
HAMILTON, (LORD) ERNEST, 1070/B–70
HAMILTON, (LORD) FREDERIC, 2544
HAMILTON, IAN, 1071–2
HAMILTON, J. R., 3349
HAMILTON, PATRICK, 1073, 2395, 3172
Hamlet, 231, 312, 401, 412, 753, 789, 984, 1065, 1220, 1252, 1473, 1963, 1975, 1986, 2419, 3082, 3120, 3316–17
Hamlet, Revenge!, 600, 1211/B, 1220, 1227
"Hammerpond Park Burglary, The," 2858–9
Hammersmith Maggot, The, 1610
Hammersmith Murders, The, 868
Hammers of Fingal, 1518
HAMMETT, DASHIELL, 96, 396/B, 480, 482, 1074/B–77, 1477/B, 2354, 2366, 2545/B–51, 2694, 2735, 2750, 2787, 2856, 2919, 2927, 2950–2, 2955, 2961, 2980, 2992, 3006–7, 3018, 3061, 3173, 3415
Hammett Homicides, 2548, 3006
HAMMOND, W. A., 2552
HAMPDEN, JOHN, 3452
"Hampstead Murder, The" (Bush), 2319

Hampstead Mystery, The (Rees and Watson), 1794
"Ham Sandwich, The," 2849
Hand and Ring, 1026
Handbook for Poisoners, 2361, 2903
"Handbook of Swindling, The," 3078
Handbuch für Untersuchungsrichter, 2118
"Handkerchief Problem, The," 2699
Hand in Glove (Marsh), 1546
Hand in the Glove, The (Stout), 1994, 2003
Hand of Dr. Fu Manchu, The, 1876
"Hand on the Latch, The," 2415, 2541
Hands of Death, 575
Hands of Mr. Ottermole, The," 2323, 2341, 2780, 2846, 3008
"Hand upon the Waters," 2459
Handwriting on the Wall, The, 1674
Hanged by a Thread (Haddow), 1048
Hanged in Error, 3170
"Hangin' Crazy Benny," 2525
Hanging by a Thread (Kahn), 2601
Hanging Captain, The, 2152
Hanging Judge, The, 1063
Hanging Woman, The, 1824
Hangman's Holiday, 2775
Hangman's Moon, 1034
Hangover Square, 1073
HANLEY, CLIFFORD, 404
"Hannah Dustin," 2774
HANNAY, J. O., 185/B
HANSHEW, THOMAS W., 2553–4
HARBAGE, ALFRED, 1327
Hard-Boiled Dick, The, 3018
Hard-Boiled Omnibus, The, 2787
Hardly a Man Is Now Alive, 264
Hardway Diamonds Mystery, The, 388
HARDWICK, MICHAEL, 3350–1
HARDWICK, MOLLIE, 3350–1
HARDY, A. E. G., 3174
HARDY, THOMAS, 1713/B, 1758, 2745
HARE, CYRIL, 1078/B–86, 2321, 2500, 2555–8, 2947
Hare Sitting Up, 1221
HARLING, ROBERT, 1087–90
Harlot Killer, The, 2341
Harness of Death, The, 2016
HARPER, C. A., 3416
HARRINGTON, H., 2614
HARRINGTON, JOSEPH, 1091–2
HARRIS, J. B., 2754
HARRIS, JOEL CHANDLER, 3416
HARRISON, ERNEST, 2559

Here Comes the Copper, 2350, 2849
"Heredity," 2319
HERFORD, OLIVER, 1608
HERITAGE, MARTIN, 1170
Heritage of Cain, The, 1674
Heritage Perilous, 812
"Heritage Portrait, The," 2588
"Her Last Bow," 3366
"Hermit of ——— Street, The," 2541
HERODOTUS, 2566
Hero for Leanda, A, 957, 2575
HERSCHEL, (SIR) WILLIAM, 3110
HERVEY, A. J. (Earl of Bristol), 3239
He Should Have Died Hereafter, 1080
HEWART, LORD, 3162
He Was Found in the Road, 70
HEXT, HARRINGTON, 1128–31, 1713/B
Heyday of a Wizard, 3394
HEYER, GEORGETTE, 1132/B–43, 2574
HEYWOOD, ROSALIND, 3420
HIBBERT, E. B., 1167
HICHENS, ROBERT, 1144, 2872
HICKES, A. G. R., 3368
Hickory, Dickory, Death, 511
"Hic Jacet," 2376, 3451
"Hidden Law, The," 2366
"Hidden Witness, The," 2320
Hide and Go Seek, 959
Hideaway, 1755
Hide Her from Every Eye, 1693
Hide in the Dark, 1096
"High Court," 2616
High Jump, The, 980
High Pavement, 227
High Sheriff, The, 2154
HIGHSMITH, PATRICIA, 1145–6, 2493, 2767
High Tide, 1175
High Window, The, 482
High Wire, The, 1051
HILBERY, JUSTICE, 3114
Hilda Wade, 2307
HILL, BRIAN, 1519
HILL, DEREK, 3421
HILLERMAN, TONY, 1147
HILLYER, ROBERT, 3439
HILTON, JAMES, 1148
HILTON, J. B., 1149
Himself Again, 1725
HIRSCHBERG, CORNELIUS, 1150
"His Brother's Keeper," 2575, 2591, 2750
His Last Bow, 2478, 2483

"His Last Scrape: or, Holmes, Sweet Holmes," 2741
His Name Was Death, 294
His Own Appointed Day, 737
Hi-Spy Kick the Can, 1441
Histoire des Treize, 96
Histoire et technique du roman policier, 2943
Historian as Detective, The, 3324
Historical Mysteries, 3207, 3394
Historical Nights' Entertainment, The, 3281
History of Capital Punishment, A, 3211
History of English Criminal Law, A, 3265
History of Socialist Thought, A, 559/B
"History of Susanna, The," 2566
History of the British Secret Service, A, 3123
History of the Footguards, A, 2144/B
HITCHCOCK, ALFRED, 2218, 2346, 2575–6, 2871
HITCHENS, BERT, 1151
HITCHENS, DOLORES, 1151, 1664
Hive of Suspects, A, 1726
HOBSON, FRANCIS, 1152
HOBSON, HANK, 1153–4
HOBSON, HARRY, 1153
HOBSON, POLLY, 1155
HOCH, E. D., 2576–8
HOCKABY, STEPHEN, 1601/B
HOCKING, ANNE, 1156–7
HOCKING, MARY, 1158
HODEMART, PETER, 84
HODGE, ALAN, 2952
HODGE, WILLIAM, 3245
HODGKIN, ALAN, 1159/B
HODGKIN, M. R., 1159/B–60
HODGKINSON, C. L., 3292
HODGSON, W. H., 2542, 3407
HOFFMANN, BANESH, 2306, 3354
HOFFMANN, E. T. W., 3022, 3422, 3442
HOGARTH, CHARLES, 2931
HOGG, JAMES, 2835
Hog's Back Mystery, The, 671
HOHNEN, DAVID, 220
HOLBROOK, STEWART, 3193
HOLDEN, GENEVIEVE, 1161
HOLDING, E. S., 1162, 2694, 2525
HOLDING, JAMES, 2579
Hold Out, The, 329
"Hole in the Glass, The," 2722
Hole in the Ground, A, 960

"Hole in the Mahogany Panel, The," 2728
"Hole in the Parchment, The," 2336
"Hole in the Wall, The" (Chesterton), 2407
Hole in the Wall, The (Morrison), 1624
"Holford Will Case, The," 2670
Holiday Adventures of Mr. P. J. Davenant, The, 2544
Holiday for Murder, A (Christie), 510
Holiday with Murder (G. Carr), 449
Holladay Case, The, 1968
Hollow, The, 512
"Holloway Flat Tragedy, The," 2370, 2642
Hollow Chest, The, 2035
Hollow Needle, The, 623
Hollow Sunday, The, 1089
"Hollywoodunit," 2955
HOLMAN, C. H., 2914
"Holmes and the Dasher," 2741
Holmes and Watson, 3371
HOLMES, GORDON, 1163, 2058
"HOLMES, H. H.," 237/B, 241, 1164, 2739, 3355
Holmes Meets 007, 3379
HOLMES, O. W., 3297
HOLMES, PAUL, 3182
"HOLMES, SHERLOCK," 2962
"Holmes' Will: a Forgery," 3330
"Holmlock Shears Arrives Too Late," 2741
"Holocaust of Manor Place, The," 2485
HOLROYD, J. E., 3356
HOLT, GAVIN, 1165
HOLT, HENRY, 1166
HOLT, VICTORIA, 1167
"Holy Well, The," 2336
Home Book of Quotations, The, 1967/B
"Homecoming" (DeFord), 2774
"Homecoming" (Johns), 2367
HOME, DANIEL DUNGLAS, 3070, 3394
Home Guard. See Army
HOME, MICHAEL, 389
HOMES, GEOFFREY, 1168
"Homesick Buick, The," 2637
"Homespun Silk," 2642
Homicide House, 868
Homicide in American Fiction, 2933
Homicide Trinity, 2814

Hon. Algernon Knox, Detective, The, 2688
Honorable Peter Stirling, The, 869/B
HOOD, THOMAS, 1418
HOPE, ANTHONY, 1752
HOPE, BRIAN, 2931
Hopjoy Was Here, 2184
HOPKINS, KENNETH, 1169
HOPKINS, R. T., 3423, 3183
HOPLEY, GEORGE, 1231/B, 2289
HOPPIN, HECTOR, 2927
HOPWOOD, AVERY, 2395
"Horace Walpole," 3024
Horizon, 1490
Horizontal Man, The, 794
HORLER, SYDNEY, 1170
HORNE, GEOFFREY, 1655
"Hornets' Nest, The" (Brand), 2376
Hornets' Nest (Landon), 1335
HORN, HOLLOWAY, 3459
HORNIBROOK, F. A., 1171
HORNUNG, E. W., 2354, 2580-2, 2750, 2778, 2875
"Horror," 2855
"Horror at Staveley Grange, The," 2323
"Horror from the Middle Span, The," 3407
"Horror in the Museum, The," 3413
"Horrorotario," 2767
"Horse of the Invisible, The," 2542
Horse Under Water, 722
HOSKEN, C. J. W., 1301
Hospital, The, 821
"Hospital Nurse, The," 2332
Hospitals, incl. Nursing Homes. See also Doctors' Offices, 116, 122-3, 187, 372, 408-10, 435, 441, 615, 688, 781, 1118, 1239, 1352, 1449, 1556, 1915, 1936-7, 2041, 2165, 2208, 2210, 2332
Hotels and Restaurants, incl. Inns, Motels, Boardinghouses, and Pubs, 11, 52 65, 87, 137, 142, 167, 212, 223 225, 276, 311, 319, 322-3, 336, 339, 350, 377, 413-14, 416, 437, 439, 455, 464, 486, 497, 502, 511, 647, 751, 814, 844, 850, 884, 964, 986, 1044, 1046, 1272, 1320, 1324, 1382, 1437, 1447, 1495, 1508, 1538, 1568, 1596, 1609, 1759, 1818, 1820, 1829, 1879, 1901, 1961-2, 1964, 1973, 2131, 2184, 2189, 2263, 2300, 2349, 2367, 2496, 2537, 2542, 2549, 2575, 2601, 2653

Hot Line, 307
"Hot Money," 2473
HOTSON, J. L., 2774
"Hot Water," 2835, 2866
"HOUDINI," 3402
HOUGHAM, ARTHUR, 2614
HOUGH, S. B., 1172
HOUGHTON, HADWIN, 2201/B
"Hound of Death, The," 3401
Hound of Ireland and Other Stories, The, 2384
Hound of the Baskervilles, The, 762/B-62, 765, 2483, 2518, 3353
"Hounds of Fate, The," 2873
Hours to Kill, 688
"House, The," 3415
"House and the Brain, The." See "The Haunted and the Haunters"
House at Satan's Elbow, The, 465
"House at Shiraz, The," 2420
House by the River, The, 1128
"House Dick," 2549
HOUSEHOLD, GEOFFREY, 1173, 2459
House in Demetrius Road, The, 159
"House in Goblin Wood, The," 2393, 2569, 2747
House in Lordship Lane, The, 1563
House in the Mist, The, 1030
"House-in-Your-Hand Murder, The," 2367
House Is Falling, The, 843
House Next Door, The, 2219
House of Brass, The, 1772
House of Cards, The, 784
House of Darkness, 1499
"House of Ecstasy, The," 2575
House of Green Turf, The, 1705
House of Silence, The, 1163
House of Soldiers, The, 961
House of Souls, The, 3440
"House of Terror, The," 3443
House of the Arrow, The, 1562, 2977
House of the Sword, The, 306
House of the Whispering Pines, The, 1030
"House of Three Candles, The," 2873
House on the Beach, The, 2259
House on the Saltings, The, 268
House on Tollard Ridge, The, 1826
"House Party, The," 2496
House Party Murder, 2172
House Without a Door, The (Sterling), 1964

House Without the Door, The (Daly), 701
House with the Blue Door, The, 866
HOUTS, MARSHALL, 3184
Hovering Darkness, The, 156
"Hover Through the Fog," 2493
HOVICK, ROSE, 1363
HOWARD, RICHARD, 1615
"How Does Your Garden Grow?," 2425
"How Doth the Little Busy Bee," 1919
How Doth the Little Crocodile?, 1919
"How Holmes Came to Play the Violin," 3330
Howe and Hummel, 3278
HOWE, R. M., 3168/B, 3186, 3232
HOWES, BARBARA, 2927
HOWE, WILLIAM F., 3278
How like a God, 1986
"How Love Came to Professor Guildea," 2872
How Many Cards?, 1674
"How the Bank Was Saved," 2861
"How the Bishop Kept His Appointment," 2861
"How the Captain Tracked a German Spy," 2779, 2860
"How the Express Was Saved," 2861
"How the Modern Detective Gets His Man," 3186
How to Enjoy Detective Fiction, 3045
"How to Make It Authentic," 2908
How to Write Detective Novels, 2986
HUBBARD, P. M., 1174–6
HUBBELL, WALTER, 3464
HUBIN, A. J., 2886, 2928, 2963
Hue and Cry (Dewey), 743
Hue and Cry (Hamilton), 1066
Hugger-Mugger in the Louvre, 1687
HUGHES, COLIN, 2931
HUGHES, D. B., 1177–8
HUGHES, RUPERT, 2136
HUGO, VICTOR, 3181
HULL, HELEN, 1179
HULL, RICHARD, 1180/B–83, 2321
Human Face, The, 284/B
"Humbleby Agonistes," 2321
HUME, DAVID, 1184, 2134
HUME, FERGUS, 1185, 2739, 2998
HUMMEL, A. H., 3278
HUMPHREYS, CHRISTMAS, 3185–6
HUMPHREYS, (SIR) TRAVERS, 3185, 3187, 3189–90
Hungary and Democracy, 1800/B
Hungry Dog, The, 1043

Hungry Leopard, The, 236
"Hunt Ball Murder, The," 671, 2732
"Hunted Down," 2472
HUNTER, ALAN, 1188–93
Hunter at Large, 743
HUNTER, EVAN, 1419
Hunter Is the Hunted, The, 684
Hunterstone Outrage, The, 2078
Hunt for the Czar, The, 3268
HUNT, KYLE, 1186–7, 2931
HUNT, VIOLET, 3459
Hurry the Darkness, 1764
HUTCHINSON, HORACE, 1194–6
HUTTON, J. B., 2885
HUTTON, SARA, 2277
HUXLEY, ALDOUS, 1197/B, 1274, 2583, 2755, 2778, 3008
HUXLEY, ELSPETH, 1197/B–1200
HUXLEY, JULIAN, 1197/B
HYDE, H. M., 3188–90, 3209
HYLAND, STANLEY, 1201
Hymn-Tune Mystery, The, 185–6
HYNE, C. J. W., 2584

IAMS, JACK, 1202–8, 1912
IBSEN, HENRIK, 1493
Ice-Axe Murders, The, 456
Ice-Cold in Alex, 1339
I Could Murder Her, 1402
Identification of Firearms and Forensic Ballistics, 3118
"Identity Problem, The," 2699
Ideology and Crime, 3266
"Ides of Michael Magoon, The," 2365
If Death Ever Slept, 1987
If I May, 3362
"If Judges Wrote Detective Stories," 3052
If Wishes Were Hearses, 679
ILES, FRANCIS, 162/B, 175, 1209–10, 3287
I Like a Good Murder, 1519
I'll Be Judge, I'll Be Jury (Hely), 1123
I'll Be Judge, I'll Be Jury (Kennedy), 1298
"I'll Be Waiting," 2401–3
I'll Eat You Last, 260
Illegal Tender, 740
Ill-Met by Moonlight, 868
"Ill-Omened Groom, The," 2658
I'll Sing at Your Funeral, 1695
I'll Tell You Everything, 1752
Illustrious Prince, The, 1671

"Image in the Mirror, The," 2775
Image of Murder, 422
Imaginary Interviews, 3006
Imagine a Man, 844
Imagine a Man in a Box, 3473
I Met Murder, 1252
Immaterial Murder Case, The, 2024
Impact, 1663
Impact of Evidence, 442
Imperfect Lover, An, 1010
"Imperfect Myths," 2927
Imperial Agent, 3268–9
"Impersonation Problem, The," 2699
"Importance of Trifles, The," 2462
"Impossible Theft, The," 2493
"Impression of the Landru Case, An," 3287
In Accordance with the Evidence, 1667, 1668
In a Deadly Vein, 681
In a Glass Darkly (Caird), 399
"In a Glass Darkly" (Christie), 2425
"In a Glass Darkly" (McCloy), 2458
In a Lonely Place, 1178
"In a Telephone Cabinet," 2432, 2732
In at the Death, 868
"Incautious Burglar, The," 2390–1
Incitement to Murder, 47
Inconsistent Villains, The, 710, 2036
"Incredible Elopement of Lord Peter Wimsey, The," 2775
Incredible Schlock Homes, The, 3345
"Incredible Theft, The," 2421
Incredulity of Father Brown, The, 2405
Incunabular Sherlock Holmes, The, 3377
"Incurable Complaint, The," 2455
"Indifferent Shot, The," 2321
"Industrial Secrets and Crime," 3172
"I Never Forget a Face," 2321
"Inevitable Flaw, The," 2350
"Inexperienced Ghost, The," 3459, 3474
In Face of the Verdict, 1827
"Inference as an Art," 2970
Information Received, 1767
"Ingenious Mind of Mr. Rigby Lacksome, The," 2370
"Ingenious Mr. Spinola, The," 2368
In Homespun, 2679
Initials Only, 1030
Inland Revenue, The, 488
"In Memoriam" (Morley), 2477
INNES, HAMMOND, 1969

Killed by Scandal, 1643
Killer Dolphin, 1547
"Killer in the Rain," 2399
Killer's Choice (McBain), 1421
Killer's Choice (Miller), 1573
Killers in Paradise, 1001, 3160
Killer's Moon, 1442
Killer's Payoff, 1421
Killers Unknown, 1001, 3160
Killer's Wedge, 1421
"Killing Bottle, The," 2332
Killing Game, The, 1313
Killing in Hats, A, 706
Killing of Julia Wallace, The, 3162
Kill Me Tomorrow, 1751
"Kill Now, Pay Later," 2811
Kindest Use a Knife, The, 1799
"Kind Lady," 2395
Kind of Anger, A, 50
KINDON, THOMAS, 1302
"Kinetoscope of Time, The," 2656
King Against Anne Bickerton, The, 2291
KING, C. DALY, 1303/B–06, 2608–9, 2774, 2780
King Cholera, 1395/B
King Diamond, 329
Kingdom of Death, 37
"King in Yellow, The," 2402–3
"King of the Cats, The," 3415
"King of the Gigolos, The," 2739
King of the Rainy Country, The, 882
KING, RUFUS, 1307, 2437, 2610–11, 2750
KINGSLEY, CHARLOTTE MAY, 2553
KINGSMILL, HUGH, 2741
"Kingsmouth Spy Case, The," 2368
"King's Private Eye, The," 2489
"King Waits, The," 3459
Kink, The, 274–5, 278
KINNAIRD, CLARK, 2770
KIPLING, RUDYARD, 853, 1211/B, 2361, 2384, 2461, 2568, 2755, 3022, 3051, 3400, 3434, 3442, 3457
"Kiskadee Bird, The," 2525
Kiss Before Dying, A, 1371
Kiss Me, Deadly, 1955
"Kiss Problem, The," 2699
Kitchen, The, 885
KITCHIN, C. H. B., 1180/B, 1308/B–09, 3388
KITCHIN, F. H., 1308, 2441
"Kite, The," 2376
KLEINERT, CHARLOTTE, 2255
KLINEFELTER, WALTER, 3357

KLINGER, HENRY, 1310–11
Knife, The, 15
Knife for the Killer, A, 1618
Knife in the Dark, 573
KNIGHT, DAVID, 1750
KNIGHT, K. M., 1312
"Knight's Cross Signal Problem, The," 2369
Knight's Gambit, 2499
Knives Have Edges, 2283
Knock 3-1-2, 294
KNOPF, BLANCHE, 2919
KNOTT, G. H., 3203
KNOTT, HAROLD, 2991
KNOWLTON, DON, 2611–13
KNOX, BILL, 1313–15
KNOX, R. A., 710, 1070, 1316/B–21, 2036, 2135, 2322–3, 2350, 2614, 2780, 2845, 2872, 2923, 2925, 2955, 2967, 3049, 3056, 3332, 3358, 3377
KOEHLER, ARTHUR, 3264
KOMPERT, LEOPOLD, 3457
KOMROFF, MANUEL, 3419, 3459
KORGANOFF, ALEXANDRE, 3204
KRASNER, WILLIAM, 1322–4
KRAUS, WERNER, 3413
KRUTCH, J. W., 2955, 2968
KUBY, ERICH, 3205
KUMMER, F. A., 2837, 2741
KUNSTLER, W. M., 3206
KURNITZ, HARRY, 1678
KUTTNER, HENRY, 1325/B–26
KUYUMJIAN, DIKRAN, 64
KYD, THOMAS, 1327–9, 2615–16
KYLE, SEFTON, 2137

"Labédoyère's Doom," 3414
Laboratories and Research Stations, 82, 210, 441, 548, 608, 710, 779, 923–4, 1696, 1737, 1815, 1825, 1846, 1927, 2257, 2279, 2443, 2527
Labors of Hercules, The (Christie), 2417
"Labor of Hercules, A" (Lowndes), 2316
LACHMAN, MARVIN, 3029
LACLOS, CHODERLOS DE, 1614
Lacquer Screen, The, 2129
LACY, ED, 1330
Ladies in Boxes, 346
Ladies Won't Wait, 491
Lady Audley's Secret, 252
Lady Chatterley's Lover, 1588, 3274

"Lawyer Looks at Detective Fiction, The," 2955
Lawyer When Needed, A, 3109
Lay Her Among the Lilies, 489
Layton Court Mystery, The, 174–5
LAZARE, CHRISTOPHER, 3422
"Lazy Crow, The," 3462
LEACOCK, STEPHEN, 550/B, 2350, 2456, 2620, 2741, 2784, 2955, 2969–70
LEACROFT, ERIC, 2302
Leaden Bubble, The, 261
"Leading Lady, The," 2339
LEA, EDUARD, 3234
LEA, G. F. PERCIVALE, 1355
League of Frightened Men, The, 498, 1989, 2912
"Leak, The," 2320, 2528
"Learned Adventure of the Dragon's Head, The," 2676
LEASOR, JAMES, 1356–7
Leavenworth Case, The, 1027
"Leaves from the Editors' Notebook," 2955
Leave to Presume Death, 1056
LEAVITT, R. K., 3383
LEBLANC, MAURICE, 1251, 1358/B–59, 2316, 2322, 2621, 2735, 2741, 2843, 2917
LE CARRÉ, JOHN, 1360/B–62, 1580, 2853, 2894
Ledger Is Kept, The, 1737
"Leech of Folkstone, The," 3459
LEE, GYPSY ROSE, 1363
LEE, M. B., 1770/B, 1880
LEE, NORMAN, 611
LEES, WILLIAM, 2134
LE FANU, J. S., 1364, 2138, 2835, 2909, 3404, 3427–8, 3441–2, 3459, 3468
Left-Handed Death, 1183
"Legacy, The," 3422
Legacy Lenders, The, 1576
Legacy of Death, 372
LEGGETT, WILLIAM, 2344, 2622, 3033
LEGMAN, G., 2971/B–71
LEHMANN, R. C., 2741
LEIBOWITZ, SAMUEL, 3252, 3267
LEIGH, JOHANNA, 1898/B
"Leiningen versus the Ants," 2575
LEMARCHAND, ELIZABETH, 1365
LENEHAN, J. C., 1366
Lenient Beast, The, 292
"Lenton Croft Robberies, The," 2382, 2542, 2672

LEONARD, CHARLES L., 1116/B, 1367–8
LEON, H. C., 470
"Leopard Lady, The," 2776
LE QUEUX, WILLIAM, 1369, 2542, 2623, 2853, 3212
"Lernean Hydra, The," 2417
LEROUX, GASTON, 1370, 2912
LESLIE, SHANE, 2332
"Lesson in Anatomy," 2747
"Lesson in Crime, A," 2319, 2835
Lesson in Crime and o.s., A, 573, 2431
"Lesson in Firearms, The," 1414
L'Estrange Case, The, 150
Let Him Die, 547
Let Him Have Judgment, 1063
Let's Choose Executors, 2280
"Letter of the Law," 2321
Letters from Baker Street, 3378
Letters of E. A. Poe, The, 3002
"Letter to Philip P. Cooke," 3002
"Letter to the Reader," 3006
"Letter Writing as a Fine Art," 2460
Let the Man Die, 615
Let X Be the Murderer, 2264
"Level Crossing, The," 2382, 2453
Levin, Ira, 1371/B
LEWIS, ARTHUR, 1372/B
LEWIS, C. DAY. See DAY-LEWIS, CECIL
LEWIS, LANGE, 177, 1372/B–76
LEWIS, M. C., 254
LEWIS, M. G., 1377
LEWIS, SINCLAIR, 1394
Lewker in Norway, 450
Lewker in Tirol, 451
Lexow Report, The, 3103
Liaisons dangereuses, Les, 1614
Liberty Hall, 555
Libraries. See also **Colleges and Universities,** 28, 194, 299, 698, 1258, 2503
Library, The, 3208
Library of the World's Best Mystery and Detective Stories, 2567, 2965
"Library Window, The," 3459
Licensed for Murder, 1829
Lieutenant Pascal's Tastes in Homicides, 1695, 2708
Life and Death of a Spanish Town, The, 1687/B
Life and Death of Sir Harry Oakes, The, 3087
Life, Death, and the Law, 3282
Life Has No Price, 1666
"Life Is Weird Sometimes," 2680

Long Death, The, 779
"Long Dinner, The," 2338
Long Divorce, The, 641
"Longer View, The," 2310
Long Farewell, The, 1222
LONGFELLOW, 2745
LONG, G. M., 1924
Long Goodbye, The, 485
LONGMATE, NORMAN, 1395/B–99
Long Road from Mailwand, The, 3378
Long Shadows, 415
Long Short Cut, The, 962
Long Shot, The, 1124
"Long Still Streets of Evening, The," 2525
Long Tunnel, The, 805
Long Weekend, The, 2952
Look Alive!, 388
Look Behind You, 97
Looking-Glass Murder (A. Gilbert), 981
Looking-Glass Murders, The, (Browne), 306
Look to the Lady (Allingham), 39
Look to The Lady! (Bonney), 230–1
LOOMIS, STANLEY, 3220
LOOS, ANITA, 853/B
Loot of Cities, The, 2348
LORAC, E. C. R., 435, 1400–7, 2321
LORAINE, PHILIP, 1408–12
"Lord Arthur Savile's Crime," 3476
"Lord Chizelrigg's Missing Fortune," 2779
Lord Edgeware Dies, 537
Lord Halifax's Ghost Book, 3414
Lord Have Mercy, The, 1947
LORD, MINDRET, 2525
"Lord Mountdrago," 3442
"Lord of the Moment," 2597
Lord Peter devant le cadavre, 2984
Lord Peter Views the Body, 2777, 2779, 2798
"Lord Winton's Adventure," 2725
Loring Mystery, The, 811
Losing Game, A, 660
"Loss of Sammy Crockett, The," 2750
Loss of the Jane Vosper, The, 661
Lost Gallows, The, 465
Lost Lawyer, The, 185/B
Lost Man's Lane, 1030
Lost Naval Papers, The, 2442
"Lost Phoebe, The," 2855
Lost Sir Massingberd, 1690

"Lost Special, The," 2481
Lost Without Trace, 556
"Lot's Wife," 2739
Lotus for Miss Quon, A, 489
Loudwater Mystery, The, 1251
Louise, 729
Louse for the Hangman, A, 326
"Love Affair," 2830
"Love Affair of George Vincent Parker, The," 2485
Love and Death, 2971
"Love Comes to Miss Lucy," 2367, 2747
LOVECRAFT, H. P., 730/B, 2675, 3408, 3437
"Love Detectives, The," 2419
Love from Elizabeth, 838
Love in Amsterdam, 883
"Lovely Lady, The," 2332
Love Lies Bleeding (Crispin), 642
"Love Lies Bleeding" (MacDonald), 2367
"Lovely Voice, The," 2332
Love Nest and o.s., The, 2619
LOVESEY, PETER, 1413
Love's Lovely Counterfeit, 398
LOWELL, ROBERT T. S., 3432
LOWNDES, Mrs. BELLOC, 1414/B–17, 2316, 2322–3, 2332, 2341, 2732, 2778–9
LOW, WILL H., 3036
LOY, MYRNA, 1074/B
LUBBOCK, S. G., 2972
LUCAS, E. V., 2955
"Luck of Barnabas Mudge, The," 2518
Lucky Jane, 53
Lucky Stiff, The, 1859
Lucretia, 344
LUDLOW, GEOFFREY, 1586/B
LUGOSI, BELA, 2466
"Lukundoo," 2872
Lunatic at Large, The, 553
LUND, PAUL, 3120
Lure of the Bush, The, 2109
Lure of the Limerick, The, 2891/B
Lurker at the Threshold, The, 3437
Lust for Murder, 1310
LUSTGARTEN, EDGAR, 1418, 3095, 3162, 3166, 3221–4, 3257
Lycanthrope, 1724
LYCURGUS, SOLON, 2080/B
LYNDE, FRANCIS, 869, 2626
LYNDON, BARRÉ, 2627
LYND, ROBERT, 3445

Maigret Goes to School, 1931
Mainstream of Modern Art, The, 1107/B
MAINWARING, DANIEL, 1168
MAINWARING, MARION, 1520
Majestic Mystery, The, 1495
Major's Candlesticks, The, 185/B
Make a Killing (Masur), 1575
Make a Killing (Williams), 2241
Make Mine Murder, 537
Maker of History, A, 1672
Makropoulos Secret, The, 2388
Malcolm Sage, Detective, 2377, 2594
MALDEN, R. H., 3441
Malice Aforethought, 175
Malice Domestic (Capon), 423
Malice Domestic (Woods), 2283
Malice in Wonderland, 204
Malice Matrimonial, 855
Malle Sanglante de Millery, La, 3216
MALLESON, L. B., 981
MALLETT, RICHARD, 2741
MALLOCH, G. R., 2323
MALLOWAN, M. E. L., 495/B
Maltese Falcon, The, 1074/B, 1075, 1077, 2550
"Mamie 'n' Me," 2680
"Man Alive," 2808
Man Behind Me, The, 479
"Man Behind Sherlock Holmes, The," 2975
"Man Bites Dog," 2750
"Man Called Spade, A," 2545, 2551
Man Called Spade, A, 2545, 2551, 3007
"Mandarin's Jade," 2399
Mandarin's Pearl, The, 2517
Man Drowning, 1326
MANER, WILLIAM, 1521
Man from Nowhere, The, 855
Man from Scotland Yard, The, 868
Man from the River, The, 567
Man from the Sea, The, 1223
"Mangaroo," 3459
"Manhattan Midnight," 2842
Manhattan Murder, 2059
"Manhood of Edward Robinson, The," 2418
Man Hunters (Dilnot), 3132
Man Hunters, The (Post), 3259
Man in a Cage, 329
Man in Ambush, 1756
Man in Grey, The (Orczy), 2690
Man in Lower Ten, The, 1863

"Man in the Blue Spectacles, The," 2564
Man in the Brown Suit, The, 495/B, 537
Man in the Corner, The, 2691
Man in the Dark, The, 823
"Man in the Green Hat, The," 2774
"Man in the Inverness Cape, The," 2739
Man in the Jury Box, The, 1674
Man in the Moonlight, The, 1434
Man in the Queue, The, 2040, 2043
Man in the Red Hat, The, 1301
Man in the Tricorn Hat, The, 54, 59
Man Lay Dead, A, 1548
MANN, ABEL, 2931
"Man Named Thin, A," 2550-1
MANNING, A. F. O., 574
Manning Burke Murder, The, 2058
MANNING, E. W., 3230
MANN, J. DIXON, 3168, 3229
MANN, LEONARD, 1522
"Man of a Thousand Faces, The," 3135
Man of Last Resort, The, 2731
Man of Two Tribes, 2103
Man on All Fours, The, 732
"Man on Ben Na Garve, The," 2345
Man on the Balcony, The, 1940
Man on the Cliff, The, 968
"Man on the Ladder, The," 2604
"Manor Park," 2321
Man out of the Rain, The, 2638
Man Overboard!, 648
MANSFIELD, KATHERINE, 2648
MANSFIELD, PAUL, 1523
MANTON, PETER, 2931
Mantrap, 479
Manuel de technique policière, 3215
Manuscript Murder, The, 1378
Man Who Called Himself Poe, The, 2675
Man Who Convinced Himself, The, 1674
"Man Who Corrupted Hadleyburg, The," 2080/B
"Man Who Could Work Miracles, The" (Wells), 3474
Man Who Didn't Fly, The, 143
Man Who Disappeared, The, 221
Man Who Explained Miracles, The (Carr), 465, 2391
Man Who Had Too Much to Lose, The, 1974
Man Who Killed Fortescue, The, 2005

Man Who Killed Himself, The, 2025
Man Who Killed the King, The, 2217
Man Who Killed Too Soon, The, 2093
"Man Who Knew How, The," 2775
Man Who Knew Too Much, The, 2320, 2407
Man Who Laughed at Murder, The, 78
"Man Who Liked Dickens, The," 2873
"Man Who Liked Dogs, The," 2399
Man Who Looked Back, The, 855
"Man Who Lost, The," 2529
"Man Who Lost His Taste, The," 2358
"Man Who Made Rings, The," 2316
"Man Who Murdered in Public, The," 2751
Man Who Rang the Bell, The, 1298
Man Who Shot Birds, The, 2502
"Man Who Spoke in Rhyme, The," 2772
"Man Who Spoke Latin, The," 2305
"Man Who Understood Women, The," 2389
Man Who Was Dead, The, 2017
"Man Who Was Not Dead, The," 2741
Man Who Was There, The, 2037
Man Who Was Thursday, The, 140, 490, 2921
"Man Who Was Too Clever, The," 3193
Man Who Watched the Trains Go By, The, 1930
"Man Who Went Too Far, The," 3457
"Man Who Went to Taltavul's, The," 2367
Man Who Went Up in Smoke, The, 1940
"Man Who Would Be King, The," 3434
Man Who Wrote Detective Stories, The, 2800
Man with a Calico Face, The, 1947
"Man with Big Hands, A," 2316
"Man with Half a Face, The," 2709
Man Without a Face, The, 1867
"Man with the Green Umbrella, The," 2406
"Man with the Nailed Shoes, The," 2320, 2517
"Man with the Sack, The," 2311

Man with the Scarred Hand, The, 2193
Man with the Tattooed Face, The, 388
"Man with the Twisted Lip, The," 2475
"Man with the Watches, The" (Doyle), 2481
Man with Three Chins, The, 54
"Man with Three Eyes, The," 2608
Man with Three Jaguars, The, 55
Man with Three Passports, 54
"Man with Two Watches, The" (Kemelman), 2604
Man with Two Wives, The, 1686
Man with Yellow Shoes, The, 1120
Many a Slip, 2451
Many Brave Hearts, 759
Many Mysteries, 2688
Map of Mistrust, 1500
MARAT, 3227
Marathon Mystery, The, 1968
Marauders by Night, 971
"March of the Modern Mystery Novel, The," 1914/B
March to the Gallows, The, 1281
MARCH, WILLIAM, 2493
MARDER, IRVING, 1524
"Marginal Comment," 2994
Marginalia, 3437
"Margin of Safety," 2556
Margin of Terror (Capon), 423
Margin of Terror (McGivern), 1479
MARGOLIES, J. A., 3442
"Marihuana," 2590
MARIE-ANTOINETTE, 3079, 3207
MARJORIBANKS, EDWARD, 3231
Marked for Murder (Halliday), 1059
Marked for Murder (R. Macdonald), 1466
Marked "Personal," 1030
Markenmore Mystery, The, 861
"Market Basing Mystery, The," 2426
MARKHAM, ROBERT, 1525
MARKHAM, VIRGIL, 1526–7
"Markheim," 2797
Mark of a Buoy, The, 1706
Mark of Displeasure, A, 1125
"Mark of Maat, The," 2525
"Mark of the Beast, The," 3434
"Mark on the Window, The," 2727
MARLOWE, PIERS, 1528
Marmion, 201
MARQUAND, JOHN, 1529
MARRIAGE, ELLEN, 96
MARRIC, J. J., 1530–4, 2649–50, 2931

MARRYAT, FREDERICK, 1493, 3459
MARSDEN, ANTONY, 2319
MARSDEN, JAMES, 2931
MARSHALL, MARGARET, 2976
MARSHALL, RAYMOND, 489
MARSH, J. K., 3444
MARSH, NGAIO, 32/B, 1132/B, 1535/B-56, 2651
MARSH, REGINALD, 3278
MARTIENSEN, ANTHONY, 3232
MARTIN, A. E., 1557
Martin Hewitt, Investigator, 2672
MARTINI, ALBERTO, 3435
MARTIN, J. B., 3193
MARTIN, R. B., 176
MARTIN, RICHARD, 293
MARTIN, STUART, 1558-9
Martyrdom of Man, The, 1787
MARVEL, E. J., 2290
MARX, KARL, 1739
"Mary Burnett," 2835
Mary Celeste, 2575, 2608, 3091, 3142, 3204, 3344
Marylebone Miser, The, 1718
MARY, QUEEN OF SCOTS, 3237, 3245
"Mary Queen of Scots Jewel, The," 2741
Mary Roberts Rinehart Crime Book, The, 1864
Mary Roberts Rinehart's Mystery Book, 1864
MASARYK, THOMAS, 373
MASEFIELD, JOHN, 1435/B, 1559, 3459
"Masked Crusader, The," 2710
Mask for Danger, 1069
Mask for Dimitrios, A, 48
Mask of Glass, The, 1890
MASON, A. E. W., 1561/B-66, 2652-3, 2900, 2912, 2977, 3123, 3233, 3443
MASON, TALLY, 730/B
MASON, VAN WYCK, 1567
Massingham Affair, The, 1036
Mass Radiography Murders, The, 1915
Master Detective, The, 2378
MASTERMAN, J. C., 1568/B-70
MASTERMAN, W. S., 1571-2, 2925
Master of Mysteries, A (Meade), 2660
Master of Mysteries, The (Burgess), 345/B
Master of the Day of Judgment, The, 1699
"Master of the Murder Castle, The," 3193

Masterpieces of Crime (Vandam), 2114
Masterpieces of Murder (Pearson), 3167
Masters of Mystery, 2955, 3047
MASTERSON, WHIT, 1573, 2493
MASTERS, R. E. L., 3234
MASUR, H. O., 1574-6, 2365, 2654
MATA HARI, 3233, 3321
"Mate in Three Moves," 2316
Material Witness, 1585
MATHER, BERKELEY, 1577
MATHER, F. J., JR., 2655
Matrimony Most Murderous, 425
Matter of Accent, A, 1275
Matter of Business and o.s., A, 812
"Matter of Form, A," 2308
"Matter of Goblins, A," 2585
Matter of Iodine, A, 1276
Matter of Millions, A, 1030
"Matter of Speculation, A," 2335
"Matter of Taste, A," 2320
"Matter of Time, A," 2321
MATTHESON, RODNEY, 2931
MATTHEWS, A. E., 1698
MATTHEWS, BRANDER, 1578, 2656, 2854, 2978, 3400, 3416, 3457
MAUGHAM, LORD F. H., 3235-6
MAUGHAM, ROBIN, 1578, 2767
MAUGHAM, W. S., 1579-80, 1650, 2332, 2657, 2755, 2853, 2979-80, 3442
MAUPASSANT, GUY DE, 2658/B-59, 3430, 3442
MAURICE, A. B., 3056, 3377
MAUROIS, ANDRE, 3415
Max, 1252
Max Carrados, 2369
Max Carrados Mysteries, 2370
"Maxims on the Popular Art of Cheating," 3078
MAXWELL, (SIR) HERBERT, 3237
MAXWELL, W. B., 2332, 2837
Mayhem in B-Flat, 1688
MAYNE, SIR RICHARD, 3115
May-Week Murders, The, 296-7, 301
May You Die in Ireland, 1300
"Mazarin Stone, The," 2476, 3350
MEADE, D. C., 1581
MEADE, L. T., 1581, 1784, 2542, 2660-1, 2778
MEALAND, RICHARD, 2955
Meaning of Murder, The, 3095
"Meaning of the Act, The," 2308
Measure for Murder, 2265
Meat for Murder, 1374

"Mechanism of Crime, The," 2521
"Mechanism of Detection, The," 2521
MECHAN, PATRICIA, 3204
Medbury Fort Murder, The, 1379
Meddle with the Mafia, 1937
Medical Jurisprudence and Toxicology, 3158
Medical Murderer, The, 3151
Medico-Legal Aspects of the Ruxton Case, 3159
MEDINA, (JUDGE) HAROLD, 2838
"Meditations on the Literature of Spying," 2894
Medium for Murder, 579–80
Medley Macabre, 3448
Meet a Body, 1895
"Meet Dr. Thorndyke," 905
Meeting Place and o.s., The, 159, 2352
Meet Mr. Fortune, 2336
"Meet Sam Spade," 3007
MEGRUE, ROI C., 2395
Megstone Plot, The, 963
"Melancholy Baby," 2774
Melancholy Journey of Mr. Teal, The, 488
Melodrama: Plots That Thrilled, 2935
MELVILLE, ALAN, 1582
MELVILLE, HERMAN, 3459
MELVILLE, LEWIS, 3239
Memoir of Montague Rhodes James, A, 2972
"Memoirs of a Ghost," 3388
"Memoirs of a Mystery Critic" (verse), 2997
"Memoirs of a Private Detective, The, 2955
Memoirs of Constantine Dix, The, 2697
Memoirs of Sherlock Holmes, The, 2479, 2483, 3343
Memoirs of Solar Pons, The, 2470
Memoirs of Vidocq, Principal Agent of the French Police, 3310
Memorials of a Yorkshire Parish, 861
Memories and Adventures, 2930
Memories and Studies, 3429
Menace on the Downs, The, 373
MENCKEN, H. L., 396/B
Men Die at Cyprus Lodge, 1857
Mendip Mystery, The, 276
Men in Her Death, The, 1528
Men, Maids, and Murder, 637
"Me No Frego," 2732
Men Who Wouldn't Stay Dead, 3402

MERCER, C. W., 2297
Merchant of Venice, The, 2178
Mercury Story Book, The, 3444–6
MEREDITH, GEORGE, 589
Merely Murder, 1134
Mere Mortals, 3227
MERRILL, P. J., 1884/B, 1890
"Merry-Go-Round, The" (Brand), 2376
"Merry Go-Round" (Crispin), 2450
Merry Hippo, The, 1198
MERTON, R. K., 3134
MESSAC, RÉGIS, 2981
"Message, A," 3445
Message from Sirius, 1250
"Message from the Deep Sea, A," 2517
"Message on the Sun-Dial, The," 2323
MESSENGER, ELIZABETH, 1583–85
Metal Flask, The, 2054
METCALFE, JOHN, 3407, 3446, 3459
Methinks the Lady, 789
Method in His Murder, 2179
Methods of Sergeant Cluff, The, 1657
Methylated Murder, 1866
MEYNELL, LAURENCE, 1586/B–91, 2324
"Mezzotint, The," 3427
"Miami Papers Please Copy," 2611
Micah Clarke, 3343
Micah Faraday, 2660
"Michael Shayne," 2365
Middle Class Murder, 1062
Middle Temple Murder, The, 858, 859
MIDDLETON, RICHARD, 3400
Midnight Bell, The, 1073
"Midnight in Beauchamp Row," 2415, 2541
Midnight Mail, The, 1166
Midnight Plumber, The, 1757
Midsummer Malice (Fitzgerald), 845
Midsummer Murder (Witting), 2266
Midsummer Mystery, A (Gerould), 975
Might as Well Be Dead, 1990
Mignonette, 1924
Mildred Pierce, 398
Mile-Away Murder, 65/B
MILES, STELLA, 1591
"Milk Bottles, The," 2776
Milk-Churn Murder, The, 356
MILLAR, KENNETH, 1461/B, 1592, 2747, 2874
MILLAR, MARGARET, 1461/B, 1592
MILLAY, EDNA ST. V., 2745

MILLER, BILL, 1573
MILLER, F. A., 495/B
MILLER, HENRY, 3031
MILLER, WADE, 1573
"Million-Dollar Mystery, The," 2733
Million-Pound Day, The, 488
Mill Mystery, The, 1030
MILLS, ARTHUR, 2324
MILLS, H. T., 1593, 2062
MILLS, OSMINGTON, 1594/B–97
MILNE, A. A., 710, 1126, 1598/B–1600, 2036, 2662–4, 2765, 2982, 3362, 3377
MILTON, JOHN, 3097
Mimic a Murderer, 617
Mind of the Murderer, The, 3169
Mind Readers, The, 45
Mind's Eye, The, 284/B
Mind to Murder, A, 1239
Minister and the Choir Singer, The, 3206
"Ministering Angel, The," 2351
Minister of Injustice, 681
Minor Operation, A, 592
MINOT, G. E., 3240
Minstrel Boy, The, 2006/B
Minute for Murder, 205
"Miracle of Moon Crescent, The," 2405
"Miracle of the Fifteen Murderers," 2570
"Miracles Do Happen," 2746
Miranda Must Die, 405
MIRRIELEES, E. R., 2774
Mirror Cracked [from Side to Side], The, 537
"Mirror of the Magistrate, The," 2405
Mirror Room, The, 1336
Misadventures of Sherlock Holmes, The, 2741
Miscast for Murder, 822
Mischief in the Lane, 732
Mischief in the Offing, 2267
Miser's Money, 1724
Misguided Missile, 1597
Misinforming a Nation, 2116/B
"Misogyny at Mougins," 2323
Miss Allick, 308/B
Missa pro defunctis (Palestrina), 2608
Miss Bracegirdle and Others, 2333
"Miss Bracegirdle Does Her Duty," 2333, 2739, 3459
"Missing," 3405
"Missing Actress Sensation, The," 2368

Missing Aunt, The, 573
"Missing Baronet, The," 2432
"Missing John Hudson," 2642
Missing Link, The, 816
Missing Man, The, 2188
Missing Money-Lender, The, 2017
"Missing Mortgagee, The," 2518
"Missing Necklace, The," 2642
Missing Partner (Stephenson), 1961
Missing Partners, The (Wade), 2156
"Missing Passenger's Trunk, The," 2759, 2837
"Missing Three-Quarter, The," 2480
"Missing Undergraduate, The," 2850
"Missing Witness Sensation, The," 2370, 2371
Missing Years, The, 1475
Mission of Mercy, A, 2057
"Miss Marple Tells a Story," 2425
"Miss Mary Pask," 2456
"Miss Paisley's Cat," 2846
Miss Pinkerton, 1864
Miss Pym Disposes, 2044
Miss Seeton Draws the Line, 467
Miss Silver Comes to Stay, 2207
"Miss X," 3412
"Mistake, A," 2658
"Mr. Arcularis," 3415
Mr. Babbacombe Dies, 388
Mr. Bowling Buys a Newspaper, 1126
"Mr. Brisher's Treasure," 2859
Mr. Campion and Others, 45, 2310
Mr. Campion: Criminologist, 2311
Mr. Campion's Farthing, 466
"Mr. Campion's Lucky Day," 2312
Mr. Campion's Quarry, 466/B
"Mr. Cholmondeley Jones," 2441
Mr. Digweed and Mr. Lumb, 1724
"Mr. Eastwood's Adventure," 2418
Mr. Evans, 29
"Mr. Flexman's Boast," 2732
Mr. Fortune Here, 2337
Mr. Fortune Objects, 2338
Mr. Fortune's Practice, 2339
"Mr. Higginbotham's Catastrophe," 2320
"Mr. Holmes, They Were the Footprints of a Gigantic Hound!," 3060
Mr. Jelly's Business, 2104
Mr. Justice Avory, 3209
"Mr. Justice Harbottle," 3459
"Mr. Ledbetter's Vacation," 2859
"Mr. Leggatt Leaves His Card," 2614
"Mr. Lepel and the Housekeeper," 2435

MORRISON, ARTHUR, 1493/B, 1623/B–
  24, 2542, 2642, 2670–4, 2735,
  2750, 2765, 2795, 2875, 2920
MORRIS, R. A. V., 1622
MORRISSEY, J. L., 1625
Mort écarlate, La, 750
MORTON, ANTHONY, 2931
MORLEY, F. V., 1620, 3383
Moscow Murder (Newman), 1648
MOSKOWITZ, SAM, 2675
Moss Rose, 1824
Most Contagious Game, A, 19
Most Haunted House in England, The,
  3454
Mostly Murder (Brown), 2379
Mostly Murder (Smith), 3289
Most Private Intrigue, A, 1883
"Most Reliable Witness, A," 2321
"Most Wanted Man in the World,
  The," 2394
Moth, The (Cain), 398
"Moth, The," (Wells), 3474
Mother Finds a Body, 1363
Mother Hunt, The, 1991
Moth-Watch Murder, The, 388
"Motive, The," 2350, 2872
"Motive for Murder," 2459
"Motive Shows the Man, The," 2453
"Motive v. Opportunity," 2428
Motor Coach Mystery, The, 2088
Motoring, 67, 104, 367, 424, 773, 947,
  1191, 1313, 1349, 1369, 1448, 1485,
  1816, 1832, 1847, 1865, 2096,
  2196/B, 2199, 2278, 2529
MOTTE, PETER, 1093
Mountains, 413, 444/B–56, 922, 946,
  1051, 1272, 1626, 1981, 2012, 2479
Mouse in Eternity, 2085
"Mousetrap, The," 2419, 2430
Mousetrap, The, 495/B, 537
Moving Finger, The, 537
Moving Target, The, 1467
Moving Toyshop, The, 643, 3442
MOYES, PATRICIA, 1626–33
MOZART, 792, 1702, 3422
"MS. in a Safe," 2827
Much Ado About Nothing, 1229
MUDGETT, HERMAN W., 237/B
Mugby Junction, 3408
Mugger, The, 1421
"Mugs' Game, The," 2750
MUIR, AUGUSTUS, 1634
MUIR, DEXTER, 1034
MULHOLLAND, JOHN, 851
MULLER, R. C. P., 3205

"Mum Is the Word," 2746
Mummy Case, The, 1621
Mummy Case Mystery, The, 1621
MUNDELL, E. H., JR., 2987
"Munera Pulveris" (Freeman), 2521
MUNKITTRICK, R. K., 2741
MUNRO, H. H., 2872–3, 3400, 3430,
  3459
MUNRO, HUGH, 1635
MÜNSTER, SEBASTIAN, 2676
MURCH, A. E., 2988
Murder Against the Grain, 1348, 1350
Murder à la Mode (Moyes), 1631
Murder à la Mode (Sellars), 1917
Murder Amid Proofs, 266
Murder Among Friends, 1376
Murder Among Members, 439
"Murder Among the Lovebirds," 2774
Murder, a Mystery, and a Marriage,
  A, 2081
Murder and Blueberry Pie, 1388
Murder and Its Motives, 3196
Murder and the Trial, The, 3222
Murder Arranged, A, 2053
Murder at Belle Camille, 99
Murder at Bratton Grange, 1805
Murder at Cambridge, 1685
Murder at Crome House, 568
Murder at Derivale, 1815, 1830
"Murder at Eleven," 2664
"Murder at Elstree, 347
Murder at Exbridge, 2225
"Murder at Fernhurst, The," 2837
Murder at Fleet, The, 2302
Murder at Geneva, 755
Murder at Government House, 1200
Murder at Hazelmoor, 513
Murder at High Noon, 1484
Murder at High Tide, 235
Murder at H. Q., 1106
Murder at Larinum, 3113
Murder at Lilac Cottage, 1831
Murder at Manor House, 1014
Murder at Mavering, 1014
Murder at Midnight, 190
Murder at Radio City, 1618
Murder at School, 1148
Murder at Sea, 581
Murder at "The Angel," 1443
"Murder at the Automat," 2680
Murder at the College, 2225
Murder at the Flea Club, 1112
Murder at the Inn, 276, 277
"Murder at the Magnificent," 2512
Murder at the Moorings, 375

"Nebuchadnezzar," 2776
Nebuly Coat, The, 806
Necessary Corpse, The, 2285
Necessary End, A, 978
"Necessity of His Condition, The," 2367
Neck and Neck, 326
"Necklace of Pearls, The," 2775
Need for Criminology, The, 3266
"Needle's Eye, The," 2742
NEFF, EMILY, 2874
NELSON, H. L., 1645
NELSON, JAMES, 899, 2403
Nemesis at Raynham Parva, 589
Nero Wolfe of West Thirty-Fifth Street, 2891
Nerve, 874
NESBIT, E., 2678–9
Nest of Vipers, 542
NETHERWOOD, B. A., 3448
NEUGROSCHEL, JOACHIM, 2621
Neurotica, 2971/B
"Nevada Gas," 2398, 2400, 2403
Never Bet Your Life, 627
Never by Chance, 2034
"Never Come Mourning," 2365
Never Fight a Lady, 2077
Never Let Me Go, 109
"Never Trust a Murderer," 2764
"Never Trust the Obvious," 2365
Never Turn Your Back, 1912
NEVILLE, B. A., 408
NEVILLE, MARGOT, 1646–7
NEVINS, F. M., JR., 2680, 2940, 2991–2
"New Administration, The," 2725
New Adventures of Ellery Queen, The, 2734
New Arabian Nights [Entertainment, The], 490, 2465, 2685, 2798
New Era, 2681, 3244
Newgate Calendar, The, 3080
New Graves at Great Norne, 2159
"New Investigation, A," 2589
"New Invisible Man, The," 2473
"New Jersey Sphinx, The," 2516, 2875
New Lease of Death, A, 1798
NEWMAN, BERNARD, 1648
NEWMAN, COLEY, 2774
"New Murders for Old," 2473
New Orleans Murders, 3171
New Paths in Book-Collecting, 2916
New Scotland Yard, 3132
New Shoe, The, 2105
"News in English, The," 2575

New Sonia Wayward, The, 1230
Newspapers and Magazines (as scene of crime), 46, 327, 403, 739, 817, 929, 949, 993, 1089, 1203, 1262, 1484, 1488, 1524, 1741, 2028, 2240
NEWTON, DOUGLAS, 2317
New Year's Eve in Lan-Fang, 2844
"New Zealand Tragedy, A," 671, 3287
"Next Witness, The," 2810
NEY, MARSHAL, 1568/B
Nice Derangement of Epitaphs, A, 1704
NICEFORO, ALFREDO, 3259
Nice Friendly Town, A, 405
Nice Place to Die, A, 681
Nicholas Goade, Detective, 2687
NICHOLAS, ROBERT, 1649
NICHOLAS II (of Russia), 3268–9
NICHOLS, BEVERLEY, 1650–2
"Nick Carter and the Professor," 2444
Nick Carter, Detective, 2444
"Nick Carter's Beautiful Decoy," 2444
"Nick Carter's Enemy," 2444
"Nick Carter's Mysterious Case," 2444
"Nick Grimes, Deck-hand," 2441
"Nicobar Bullion Case, The," 2670
NICOLAS, F. R. E., 880
NICOLL, W. ROBERTSON, 2993
NICOLSON, HAROLD, 2994
NICOLSON, MARJORIE, 2955, 2995
NIELSEN, HELEN, 1653
NIETZSCHE, 792
Night and Morning, 344
Night at the Vulcan, 1549
"Night Call, The," 2732
"Night in the Old House, A," 2458
Night Exercise, 1835
Night Extra, 1479
Nightmare (Blaisdell-Linington), 198
Nightmare (Woolrick), 2289
Nightmare at Dawn, 1711
Nightmare in Dublin, 1411
Nightmare in Pink, 1449
"Night Must Fall," 2395
Night of Errors, A, 1225
Night of Fear, The, 692
"Night of the Garter, The," 2614
Night of the Kill, 1235
Night of the Rape, The, 2221
Night of the Storm, 689
"Night Reveals, The," 2590
Night's Black Agent, 183
Night's Cloak, 1768
"Nightshade," 2630

Night Squad, 1005
Night Visitors and o.s., The, 2349
Night Walk, 698
Night Walker, The, 1069
NIGHTWORK, JANE, 3383
Nine and Death Makes Ten, 748
Nine Coaches Waiting, 1971
Nine Dark Hours, The, 1659
Nine Days' Murder, 1501
Nine Ghosts, 3441
"Nine-Mile Walk, The," 1284/B, 2188, 2447, 2747
Nine-Mile Walk, The, 2604
"Nine of Diamonds, The," 2321
Nine Tailors, The, 1903, 2908, 2912
19th Hole Mystery, The, 15
Nineteen Twenties, The, 3055
Ninth Earl, The, 812
Nine Times Nine, 1164, 3355
Nine Wrong Answers, The, 463
No Bail for the Judge, 470
"Noble Bachelor, The," 2475
Nobody Wore Black, 57
No Bouquets for Brandon, 2175
No Case for the Police, 551
"No Crime in the Mountains," 2366, 2399
No Escape, 123
No Evil Angel, 198
No Friendly Drop, 2152, 2160
No Future for Luana, 731
No Grave for a Lady, 223, 228
No Known Grave, 154
NOLAN, JEANNETTE, 1654
NOLAN, W. F., 2963
No Love Lost, 45
No Man's Hand, 232
No Mask for Murder, 954
No Match for the Law, 1597
No More a-Roving, 2075
No Mourning for the Matador, 59
"No Murders at Andermatt?," 2942
None Shall Sleep Tonight, 1444
Nonsense Novels, 2620, 2784, 2970
No Orchids for Miss Blandish, 489
Noose, The, 1454
No Other Tiger, 1564
"No Parking," 2742-3, 2746
No Past Is Dead, 596
"No Place to Live," 2746
No Proud Chivalry, 1764
No Question of Murder, 687
Nordenholt's Million, 582/B, 597
NORDON, PIERRE, 2996
NORTHCLIFFE, LORD, 3326, 3469/B

NORTH, GIL, 1655-7, 2682
Northing Tramp, The, 2166
North of Welfare, 1323
Norwich Victims, The, 112
"Norwood Builder, The," 2480, 2665
Nose on My Face, The, 1691
Notable British Trials, 3245
Not a Leg to Stand On, 380
Notched Hairpin, The, 1115
No Tears for Hilda, 964, 966
"Not Easy to Kill," 2876
"Note on the Inadequacy of Poe as a Proofreader, etc., A," 2895
Notes on Primitive Modes of Detection, 2927
"Notes on Production," 2466
Not Exactly Ghosts, 3395
"Not for a Chorus Girl," 2667
Not Guilty!, 3252, 3267
Not Guilty and Other Trials, 3177
"Not Herbert," 2880
Nothing but the Truth, 1836
Nothing Can Rescue Me, 699
Nothing Like Blood, 321, 323
No Time for Death, 423
Not in the Script, 226
Not Proven, 728
Not Quite Dead Enough, 2806
"Not So Deep as a Well," 2321
"Not There," 3407
Notting Hill Mystery, The, 61, 2138
Not to Be Taken, 169
"Not 'Whodunit' but 'How'?," 2898
Novel in Motley, The, 3026
"Novelist and the Critic, The," 2397
"Novel of the Black Seal, The," 2647
Novels and Fairy Tales of Oscar Wilde, The, 3476
Novels of Mystery from the Victorian Age, 61, 2138, 3014
"November Night," 2849
No Wind of Blame, 1139
Now Seek My Bones, 617
Now Will You Try for Murder?, 1663
NOYES, ALFRED, 2360, 2904
Number 87, 1131
No. 7 Queer St., 3436
"No. 17" (Bland), 3459
Number Seventeen (Tracy), 2058
"Number's Up, The," 2680
No. 3, The Square, 2920
Number Two, North Steps, 729
"Nummi in Arca," 3383
Nursemaid Who Disappeared, The, 1457

Nursing Home Murder, The, 1556
Nursing Homes. See **Hospitals**
NYDORF, SEYMOUR, 2751

O as in Omen, 2064
OATES, TITUS, 3070
Obelists at Sea, 1304
Obelists en Route, 1306
Obelists Fly High, 1305
"Object Lesson," 2746
"Oblong Box, The," 2718
O'BRIEN, FITZ-JAMES, 2855, 3416, 3442, 3449, 3468
Obsequies at Oxford, 644
"Obsequies of Mr. Williams, The," 2774
Obsession, 2220
Obstinate Murderer, The, 1162
"Occurrence at Owl-Creek Bridge, An," 2855, 3389
"Occurrence up a Side Street, An," 2361
O'CONNELL, J. J., 3291
O'CONNOR, FRANCES, 3432
O'CONNOR, W. D., 3432
"October the Nineteenth," 3399
Oddities, 3163
Odd Man In, 2822
Odds Against, 877
Odds on Death, The, 769
Oddways, 11
O'DONNELL, BERNARD, 3248
O'DONNELL, DONAT, 2927
O'DONNELL, ELLIOTT, 3246-7
Odor of Violets, The, 1286
O'FARRELL, WILLIAM, 2683
OFFENBACH, 2422
OFFICER, HARVEY, 3383
OFFORD, L. G., 1658/B-59, 2997, 3194
Off with Her Head (Cole), 570
Off with His Head (Morrissey), 1625
Of Missing Persons, 1005
Of Unsound Mind, 431
OGDEN, G. W., 3450
OGNALL, L. H., 428
O'HARA, KENNETH, 1660-1
O'HARA, KEVIN, 682/B
"Oh, England! Full of Sin," 2955
O. HENRY, 2360, 2738, 2741, 2749
O'HIGGINS, HARVEY, 2360, 2642, 2684
Old Age of Lecoq, the Detective, The, 773
Old Bailey and Its Trials, The, 3248

Old Bailey Trial Series, 3245, 3248, 3270
Old Ebbie, Detective Up-to-Date, 2852
OLDE, N., 2320
Old English Peepshow, The, 466, 746
"Old-Fashioned Apache, The," 2351
Old Fires and Profitable Ghosts, 3455
Old Hall, New Hall, 1226
Old Jew Mystery, The, 15
"Old Lag, The," 2521
"Old Man, The," 3459
Old Man in the Corner, The, 2689/B-89, 2691
"Old Man in the Window, The," 2310-11, 2525
Old Mill, The, 2252
Old Mrs. Camelot, 227
Old Sinners Never Die, 715
"Oleander, The," 2361
OLESKER, HARRY, 1662-3
OLIPHANT, MRS., 3459
OLIVER, GEORGE, 1667/B
OLIVER, ROLAND, 3162
OLSEN, D. B., 1151, 1664-5, 2365
OMAN, (SIR) CHARLES, 3249
"Omit Flowers," 2808
Omnibus Fleming Stone, The, 2202
Omnibus Mystery, An, 773
Omnibus of Crime, The, 2778, 2955
"Once a Murderer . . . ," 2663
Once upon a Crime, 1612
"Once upon a Train," 2766
On Christmas Day in the Morning, 45
On Crimes and Punishments, 3072
"On Detective Novels," 2926
"On Duty with Inspector Field," 3128
One Alone, 2132
"One and a Half Murders," 2680
"One Best Bet, The," 2305
One by One They Disappeared, 693
"One Chance in a Million," 2525
One Cried Murder, 617
One Down, 219
"One Drop of Blood," 2868
"One Good Turn," 2849
"One Hundred in the Dark," 2599
101 Years' Entertainment, 2744, 2955
"$106,000 Blood Money," 2547
One Kind and Another, 2698
One More Unfortunate, 1418
"One Morning They'll Hang Him," 2313
"One Night in Barcelona," 2680
O'NEILL, DESMOND, 1666

O'NEILL, EGAN, 197, 1380
O'NEILL, KERRY, 1493/B
One-Man Show, 1227
"One of the Dead," 2459
"One on the House," 2510
"One-Penny Black, The," 2743, 2750
"One Real Horror, The," 2392
One That Got Away, The, 1429
One to Play, 15
"On Green Paper," 2698, 2875
On Her Majesty's Secret Service, 854
ONIONS, OLIVER, 1667/B-68, 2332, 3400, 3404, 3448, 3451
"Only a Detective Story," 2955, 2968
Only a Matter of Time, 552
"Only on Rainy Nights," 2367
On Moral Courage, 2975
"On the Brighton Road," 3400
"On the Emotional Geology of Baker St.," 3383
"On the Night of the 18th . . . ," 1587
On the Shady Side, 2015
"On Trial," 2395
"Open Boat, The," 3459
Opening Night, 1549
Open Verdict, 1837
"Open Window, The," 2872
Operation Doctors, 1889
Operation Pax, 1230
Operation Piracy, 1954
OPPENHEIM, E. P., 492, 1669/B-72, 2316, 2322, 2350, 2423, 2614, 2685-8, 2835, 2999
Opperman Case, The, 150
OPPIANICUS, 3113
"Oracle of the Dog, The," 3008
Orange-Yellow Diamond, The, 859
Or Be He Dead (Byrom), 394
. . . Or Be He Dead (Carmichael), 432
Orchids to Murder, 865
Orcival Crime, The, 2920, 3174
ORCZY, BARONESS, 2354, 2542, 2614, 2642, 2689/B-93, 2735, 2739, 2765, 2779, 2784, 2795, 2950
Ordeal by Innocence, 524
Ordeal of Mrs. Snow, The, 2753
Ordeal of Richard Feverel, The, 589
"Order and License," 2927
"Orderly World of Mr. Appleby, The," 2496
"Ordinary Hairpins, The," 2351, 2779
Oriental Crime, 3064
Oriental Tales, 2965

Orient Express, 103
"ORIGINEE, AB," 2080/B
"Orphan Diamond, The," 2694
ORSINI, 3196
OSBORN, A. S., 3118, 3250-1
OSBORNE, ERIC, 2998
OSBOURNE, LLOYD, 1969, 3036
Osiris Died in Autumn, 1342
OSTRANDER, ISABEL, 1673/B-74
OSTROM, JOHN WARD, 3002
Othello's Occupation, 2007
"Other Boarder, The," 3383
"Other Hangman, The," 2473
Other House, The, 1237
Other Island, The, 548
"Other Side of the Curtain, The," 2367
"Other Side of the Hedge, The," 3411
Others Who Returned, 3473
Other Worlds, 2802
OTTOLENGUI, RODRIGUES, 1675
Où est le garlic?, 722
Our Jubilee Is Death, 324
"Our Mr. Smith," 2741
OURSLER, FULTON, 2, 2136
Outbreak, 187
OUTERSON, WILLIAM, 2575
Out for the Kill, 981
Outline of History, 1787
Outline of Scientific Criminology, An, 1617/B, 3242
Outline of Sexual Criminology, An, 1617/B
Out of Control, 1287
Outsider, The (Wilson), 2249
Outsider and Others, The (Lovecraft), 3437
Outsiders, The (Martin), 557/B
Out Went the Taper, 77
Overdose of Death, An, 525
Overdrive, 992
Over My Dead Body, 2003
OVERTON, GRANT, 2999
Overture to Death, 1550
"Overwhelming Evidence," 2692
OWEN, FRANK, 2525, 2694
OWEN, ROBERT, 2112
Owl in the Cellar, The, 1912
Owls Don't Blink, 801
Oxford Murders, The, 283
"Oxford Mystery, The," 2432
Oxfordshire, 411/B
Oxford Tragedy, An, 1568-70
"Oyster Catcher, The," 2500, 2536
OZAKI, MILTON K., 1676/B-77

PACKARD, FRANK L., 2695
Packed for Murder, 193
"Packet-Boat Murder, The," 2321
Paddington Mystery, The, 1838
PADGETT, LEWIS, 1325/B–26
PAGE, MARCO, 1678–81
Pages from the Goncourt Journal, 2890
PAIN, BARRY, 1682, 2332, 2696, 2700, 2875, 3413, 3459
Painful Predicament of Sherlock Holmes, The, 3347
Painted for the Kill, 610
Pale Horse, The, 526
Paliser Case, The, 1896
PALMER, J. L., 111
PALMER, STUART, 1683, 2365, 2525, 2701, 2739, 2741, 2750
"PAN," 160/B
"Pandora's Box," 2519
PANGBORN, EDGAR, 2367
Panic, 1430
Panic Party, 164
Paper Bag, The, 1839
Paper Chase, The, 2020
Paper Dolls, The, 713
Paper Palace, The, 1090
Parachute Murder, The, 1604
Paradine Case, The, 1144
Paradise Court, 861
Paradise Formula, The, 756
Paradoxes of Mr. Pond, The, 2408
"Parcel, The," 2453, 2774
Parcels for Inspector West, 637
PARGETER, EDITH, 1700, 2702/B–02
Paris Bit, The, 1524
Parker Pyne Investigates, 2420
Parliament, incl. Political Figures, 163, 246, 267, 750, 878, 921, 975, 1010, 1087–9, 1152, 1398, 1474, 1533, 1788, 1934, 2191, 2201, 2239, 2441, 2465, 2650
PARR, ERIC, 2767
"Parrot's Beak, The," 2324
PARRY, H. T., 2703–4
Part for a Poisoner, 1407
"Partner in Crime (Neff), 2874
Partners in Crime (Christie), 537, 2424
PARTRIDGE, ANTHONY, 1669, 2685
Party of Twenty, 2898
PARY, JULIETTE, 530
PASLEY, F. D., 3252
"Passage to Benares, A," 2366, 2816
Passenger from Calais, The, 1042

Passing of Mr. Quin, The, 2422
Passionate Victims, The, 1375
Passport to Oblivion, 1356
Past Praying For, 2281
"Pathologist to the Rescue, The," 2519
"Patient at Peacock's Hall, The," 45
Patient in Room 18, The, 781
Paton Street Case, The, 179
Patrick Butler for the Defense, 464
PATRICK, Q., 1684–6, 1777, 2365, 2367, 2705, 2747, 2874
Patriotic Murders, The, 525
Pattern of Murder, 2031
PAUL, ELLIOT, 1687/B–88
PAUL, LOUIS, 2525
Paul's Apartment, 2132
PAULSEN, M. G., 3134, 3253–4
Paulton Plot, The, 15
"Pavilion on the Links, The," 2568
"PAX," 2415
Payment Deferred, 870–1
"Payment Deferred" (play), 2395, 2801
PAYNE, LAURENCE, 1691–2
PAYNE, WILL, 2525
PAYN, JAMES, 1689–90, 3051
"Pay-Off, 2746
"Peacock House," 2717, 2835
Peacock House and Other Mysteries, 1724, 2717
"Pearl Among Women, A," 2832
"Pearls Are a Nuisance," 2402–3
Pearls Before Swine, 42
PEARSON, EDMUND, 1415, 3124, 3167, 3193, 3213, 3256, 3263, 3377
PEARSON, HESKETH, 3000
PECHEY, A. T., 2316
Peculiar Service, A, 3147
PEEL, (SIR) ROBERT, 3265
Pelham, 344
PEMBERTON, (SIR) MAX, 2542, 2706
"Pen, Pencil, and Poison," 3476
"Penance of John Emmet, The," 3455
PENDER, LEX, 1234/B
PENDERS, MARILYN, 1234/B
PENDOWER, JACQUES, 1234/B
Penhallow, 1140
Penknife in My Heart, A, 207
PENN, ANNE, 1234/B
"Penny-a-Worder, The," 2680
Pennycross Murders, The, 1758
Penrose Mystery, The, 898
PENTECOST, HUGH, 1693/B–95, 1711/B–7, 2367, 2493, 2694, 2707–12

People Ask Death, The, 780
People Will Talk, 1406
"Percival Bland's Proxy," 2518
PERDUE, VIRGINIA, 1696/B–97
PERELMAN, S. J., 3103
Perfect Alibi, The, 2664
"Perfect Butler, The," 2310
"Perfect Crime, The," 2756, 2837
Perfectionist, The, 1264
"Perfect Model, The," 2786
Perfect Murder, The, 1266
"Pefect Secretary, The," 2365
Perfume of the Lady in Black, The, 1371/B
Perhaps a Little Danger, 549
Peril at Cranbury Hall, 1840
Peril at End House, 527
PEROWNE, BARRY, 2582, 2713
Persecutor, The, 1072
"Personal Adventures in the Spirit World," 2970
"Persons or Things Unknown" (C. Dickson), 2473
Persons Unknown (P. MacDonald), 1460
Perturbing Spirit, 401
PERTWEE, ROLAND, 1698
PERUTZ, LEO, 1699
Perverse Crimes in History, 3234
"Peter Crane's Cigars," 2861
PETERS, ELLIS, 1700–5
PETERS, GEOFFREY, 1706–8
"Petit-Jean," 2323
PETRIE, RHONA, 1709–10, 2714
Petrovka 38, 1918
PETTIWARD, DANIEL, 2306, 2715
"Phantas," 3451
"Phantom Bus, The," 3415
Phantom Lady, 1232
Phantom of the Opera, The, 1371/B
"Phantom of the Subway, The," 2525
Phantom of the Temple, The, 2128
"Phantom Rickshaw, The," 3434, 3457
Phantoms and Fantasies, 3434
"Phantom Woman, The," 2722
PHELPS, W. L., 2872
Philadelphia Murder Story, The, 868
"Philanthropy of Fritz Haarman, The," 3193
PHILIPS, J. P., 1693/B, 1711/B–12
PHILLIPS, D. T. A., 478
PHILLIPS, JOHN, 1529
PHILLIPS, STEPHEN, 2316
"Phillpotts' Detective Fiction," 3017

PHILLPOTTS, EDEN, 527, 577, 1129, 1713/B–24, 2320, 2350, 2716, 2717, 2778, 2835, 2843, 2872, 3017, 3459
PHILMORE, R., 2955
"Philomel Cottage," 2323, 2418, 2429
Philo Vance Omnibus, The, 3049
"Phyllis Annesley's Peril," 2520
Physician Heal Thyself, 1713
Piccadilly Murder, 167
PICKERING, HARRY, 1725
"Pick-up on Noon Street," 2400, 2403
Pick-up on Noon Street, 2400
Pick Up Sticks, 1350
Pickwick Papers, 809/B, 3409
Pick Your Victim, 1470, 1474
Pictorial History of Crime, A, 2018/B, 3298
Picture Miss Seeton, 468
Picture of Guilt, 1230
Picture of Millie, 1176
"Piece of String, A," 2658
"Pierre Chambrun and the Black Days," 2712
"Pigeon on the Sill, The," 2837
"Pig-Keeper's Problem, The," 2699
"Pig's Feet," 2837
Pig-Tail Murder, The, 775
Pilgrim's Rest, 2207
"Pillar of Fire, The," 2779
"Pimlico Mystery, The," 2774
PIM, SHEILA, 1726/B–7
Pinehurst, 1841
"Ping-Pong," 2316, 2750
PINKERTON, ALLAN, 3130, 3173, 3257–8
"Pink Murder Case, The," 2955
PINTER, HAROLD, 2600
Pin to See the Peepshow, A, 1253
Pipe Dream, The, 2027
PIPER, H. B., 1728
PIPER, MRS., 3429
Piper on the Mountain, The, 1705
Pistols for Two, 2574
PITCAIRN, (DR.) J. J., 887/B, 2329, 2330, 3301
PITMAN, PATRICIA, 3322
Pit-Prop Syndicate, The, 663
Place for a Poisoner, 1407
Place for Murder, A, 1351
"Place of Sacrifice, A," 2704
Plain Man, The, 2028
Plain Murder, 871
Planned Departures, 2500
Plan XVI, 302
Platinum Cat, The, 388

"Problem of Thor Bridge, The," 3168
"Problem Solver and the Burned Letter, The," 2325
"Problem Solver and the Hostage, The," 2326
Pro Cluentio, 3113
PROCTER, JOHN, 3464
PROCTER, MAURICE, 1753/B–64, 2458, 2733, 2846, 2947
Professional and Other Psychic Stories, The, 3412
"Professional Debut," 2573
"Professor and the Detective, The," 2955, 2995
Professor Boynton Rereads History," 2774
"Professor's Manuscript, The," 2776
Professor's Poison, The, 1007
Profile by Gaslight, 3378
PROFUMO, (SIR) JOHN, 3125
Progress of a Crime, The, 2029
"Prolegomena to Watson's Ninth Marriage," 3330
Prologue to the Gallows, 1489
Proof of Guilt, The, 3320
PROPPER, MILTON, 1765
Provenance of Death, A, 997
"Proverbial Murder, The," 2393
Prudence and the Pill, 1593
Psychiatric Justice, 3300
"Psychiatrist Looks at Television Violence, A," 3214
Psychical Research Today, 3475
Psychology of Consciousness, The, 1303/B
Psychology of Crime, The, 3063
Pub Crawler, The, 1759
"Public Benefactor, The," 2351
"Publicity," 2310
Public School Murder, The, 2286
Publishers. See Book Publishers and Newspapers and Magazines
"Puff of Smoke, A," 2849
PUJOL, ALAIN, 3262
PUNNETT, IVAR, 1933
PUNNETT, MARGARET, 1933
PUNSHON, E. R., 1766/B–69, 2321, 2732, 2765, 3287
PURCHASE, W. B., 3098
"Purloined Letter, The," 2319, 2382, 2569, 2718/B, 2718, 2875, 2895, 2920, 3008
"Purple Cow, The," 346/B
"Purple Emperor, The," 2750
"Purple Jewel, The," 2316

Purple Noon, 1145
Purple Sickle Murders, The, 665
Pursuit, The, 1505
Pusher, The, 1421
PUSHKIN, 2600
Put Out the Light, 2078
Puzzle for Fiends, A, 1686, 1777
Puzzle for Fools, A, 1686, 1777
Puzzle for Pilgrims, A, 1777
Puzzle for Players, A, 1777
Puzzle for Puppets, A, 1686, 1777
Puzzle for Wantons, A, 1686, 1777
Puzzle in Poison, A, 169
"Puzzle Lock, The," 2520, 2642
Puzzle Lock, The, 2520, 2523
Pyx, The, 340

"Q." See QUILLER-COUCH, SIR ARTHUR
Q. E. D., 276–7, 2746
"Q-Loan Problem, The," 2699
Q's Mystery Stories, 3455
"Quality of Mercy, The," 2367
"Quality of Suspense, The," 2575
Qualtrough, 1055
QUEEN, ELLERY, 783/B, 1770/B–76, 1880, 2308 2324, 2365–7, 2444, 2447, 2458, 2493, 2496, 2500, 2540, 2548, 2569, 2654, 2675, 2694, 2734–51, 2790, 2848, 2874, 2902, 2906, 2908, 2912, 2955, 2959, 2994, 3004–8. See also under E.Q.
QUEEN, ELLERY, JR., 1770/B
Queen of Hearts, The, 2436
Queen's Awards, The, 2747
QUEENSBERRY, MARQUESS OF, 3189
Queen's Bureau of Investigation, 2748
"Queen's Experiments in Detection," 2746
Queen's Gate Mystery, The, 12
Queen's Hall Murder, The, 283
"Queen's Square, The," 2775
"Queer Feet, The," 2323, 2382, 2405, 2642
QUENTIN, PATRICK, 1684, 1686, 1777, 2738, 2752–3, 2927
Quer Pasticciaccio brutto di via Merulana, 919
Quest for Corvo, The, 2018/B
Questioned Documents, 3251
"Question Mark, The," 2310
Question of Murder, A, 981
Question of Proof, A, 209
"Quick One, The," 2361
Quick Red Fox, The, 1450
Quiet Horror, 2496

"Quietly . . . Comfortably," 2732
QUILLER-COUCH, SIR ARTHUR, 3051, 3455, 3459
Quintessance of Queen, The, 2367
QUIRKE, A. J., 3118
QUIRK, LESLIE, 2254

RABE, PETER, 1778
"Race of Orven, The," 2789
Race Tracks. See Sporting Events
RACHMANINOFF, 1550
RADCLIFFE, ANN, 1779–80, 2013, 3024, 3409
RADIN, E. D., 1415, 2908, 3095, 3124, 3166–7, 3213, 3257, 3263–4
RADZINOWICZ, SIR LEON, 3161, 3265–6
Raffles, 2581, 2697
Raffles and the Key Man, 2582
"Raft That No Man Made, A," 3432
Railways, 103, 136, 176, 278, 304, 306, 356–7, 384, 430, 478, 516, 523, 536, 603, 634, 651–2, 657, 668, 723, 727, 773, 806, 869, 892, 947, 950, 999, 1041–2, 1151, 1194, 1213, 1216, 1241, 1366, 1515, 1608, 1616, 1672, 1752, 1765, 1796, 1813, 1852, 1863, 1875, 1880, 1905, 2134, 2218, 2293, 2340, 2363–4, 2369, 2418, 2447, 2451, 2453, 2470, 2478, 2481, 2495–6, 2517, 2540, 2543, 2575, 2626, 2641, 2705, 2716, 2792, 2728, 2766, 2856, 2860–1, 2938, 3085–6, 3133, 3139, 3218, 3408, 3432, 3458
Railway Tragedy, A, 773
"Rainbow Murders, The," 2862
"Raincoat," The," 2453
RAIS, GILLE[S] DE, 3234
"Rajah's Emerald, The," 2418
"Ralston Bank Burglary, The," 2529
RAMPO, EDOGAWA, 2754/B–54
RAMSAY, ALLAN, 2741
RAMSEY, G. C., 3009
RANDOLPH, G. A., 1859
RANDOLPH, MARION, 1781
Randolph Mason, Corrector of Destinies, 2731
RANGER, KEN, 2931
RANNIE, ALAN, 3368
"Ransom," 2744
Ranson's Folly, 2465
Rape of the Lock, The, 643
RAPHAEL, CHAIM, 706/B
"Rappaccini's Daughter," 2361
Rasp, The, 1451/B, 1456, 1458
RASPUTIN, 3070

Rat Began to Gnaw the Rope, The, 1019
RATHBONE, BASIL, 3339
"R. Austin Freeman," 2937
RAVEN, SIMON, 1782–3
Raw Edges, 3435
RAWLINS, E., 1784
RAWSON, CLAYTON, 1785/B–86, 2365, 2367, 3010
RAY, CYRIL, 2755
RAY, GEORGES, 421/B
"Raymond Chandler," 2898
Raymond Chandler Speaking, 2918
RAYMOND, RENÉ, 489
Rayner-Slade Amalgamation, The, 861
Reader's Digest of Books, The, 538
"Readers' Guide to Crime, A," 2955, 3018
READE, WINWOOD, 1787
"Reading and Writing Detective Stories," 3041
Readings in Criminology and Penology, 3134
"Real-Life Policeman, The," 2908
"Real Thing, The," 2850
"Rear Window," 2590
Reasonable Doubt, A, 3299
Rebecca's Pride, 759–60
Recent Advances [in Physical Chemistry, etc.], 582/B
Recipe for Homicide (Blochman), 217
Recipe for Murder (Starrett), 1958
Reclining Figure, 1679
"Reconciliation, The," 2859
Red Box, The, 1993
Red Carnation, The, 1968
"Red Circle, The," 2478
Red Coats Galloping, 2196/B
Red Dusk and the Morrow, 3135
Red Escape, 110
"Red Hand, The," 2647
Red Harvest, 1074/B, 1076
Red-Headed League, The," 2475–6, 2569, 2875, 3008, 3353
Red House Mystery, The, 1599, 2662, 2664
Red Lamp, The, 1864
REDMAN, BEN RAY, 2351, 2756/B–57, 2837
"Red Orchestra, The," 3137
Red Pavilion, The, 2129
Red Redmaynes, The, 1721
"Red Room, The," 2835, 3474
"Red Signal, The," 2429
Red Threads, 1994

Richardson's Second Case, 2052
Richardson Solves a Dartmoor Mystery, 2051
RICHTER, JEAN-PAUL, 3336
Richter und sein Henker, Der, 776/B
RICKETTS, MRS., 3464
RIDDELL, JOHN, 1861
Riddle of Samson, The, 968
"Riddle of the Blueblood Murder, The," 2525
Riddle of the Frozen Flames, The, 2554
Riddle of the Mysterious Light, The, 2554
Riddle of the Sands, The, 493, 1670
"Riddle of the Tired Bullet, The," 2365
"Riesenberg," 3459
"Rifle, The," 2622, 3033
Rigging the Evidence, 442
Right Honorable Corpse, The, 1637
Right to Die, A, 1995
RILEY, TEX, 2931
RINEHART, M. R., 1862/B–64, 2395
RING, DOUGLAS, 1750
Ringer, The, 2166, 2801
Ring Fence, The, 1724
Ringnecker, The, 617
Ring of Roses, A, 191
Riot, The, 1256/B
"Ripening Rubies, The," 2542
Ripper, The, 1760
Rise of Scotland Yard, The, 3096
Rising Storm, The, 2217
Ritual in the Dark, 2249
"Rival Ghosts, The," 2656, 3457
"Rival Sleuth-Hound," 2521
Rivals of Sherlock Holmes, The, 2542
RIVER, J. P. DE, 3264
River Mystery, The, 1793
RIVETT, E. C., 435, 1400
RIZZIO, DAVID, 3280
"RMS Titanic," 2575
Road Block, 2190
Road to Buenos Ayres, The, 589, 3219
Road to Murder, The, 1047
Road to Rhuine, The, 2071
Roag's Syndicate, 717
"Robbery at Bowden, The," 2432
Robbery at Rudwick House, The, 2227
"Robbery at the Castle," 2512
Robbery with Violence, 1843
ROBBINS, CLIFTON, 1865–7
ROBBINS, GRENVILLE, 2316
Robert Elsmere, 582/B

ROBERTS, BECHHOFER, 1004, 2778, 3248, 3270
ROBERTS, D. K., 2955
ROBERTS, MARY-CARTER, 1868
ROBERTSON, HELEN, 1869–70
ROBERTS, R. ELLIS, 2732, 2904
ROBERTS, S. C., 2486, 2741, 3015, 3332, 3370–1
ROBESPIERRE, 3070
ROBINS, G. M., 3412
ROBINSON, E. ARNOT, 421
ROBINSON, GOVERNOR, 3224
ROBINSON, H. M., 3273, 3372
ROBINSON, L. G., 1378
ROBINSON, ROBERT, 1870–1
ROBINSON, TIMOTHY, 1872
ROBSART, AMY, 386
Robthorne Mystery, The, 1844
ROCHE, A. S., 2837, 2856
Rocket to the Morgue, 240, 1164
RODDA, CHARLES, 1165
RODELL, MARIE, 1781, 2955, 3016, 3171
Roger Bennion's Double, 15
ROGERS, F. R., 2082
Roger Sheringham and the Vane Mystery, 175
ROGERS, MARY CECILIA, 3053. See also Cases, Criminal
ROGERS, MICHAEL, 2321
ROGERS, SAMUEL, 1873–4
Rogue Cop, 1479
Rogue Male, 1173
Rogue Running, 1761
Rogues Fall Out, 15
Rogue's Gallery, 2749
Rogues in Clover, 2238, 2779
ROHDE, ROBERT H., 1875
ROHDE, W. L., 1875
ROHMER, SAX, 1876/B–76, 2525
"Roll-Call of the Reef, The," 3459
Rolling Road, The, 2006/B
ROLLS, ANTHONY, 1877–8, 2142/B
ROLPH, C. H., 3274
ROLT, L. T. C., 3458
Romance of Poisons, The, 2454
Romances of Roguery: Spain, 2917
Roman Hat Mystery, 1771, 1774–5
Roman policier, Le, 2902, 2910
Rome Express, The, 1041
Romeo and Juliet, 2160
ROMER, R. C., 1579
RONNS, EDWARD, 1
ROOF, K. M., 1879
Room at the Hotel Ambre, A, 65

Shadow of the Wolf, The, 905
Shadow on the Cliff, The, 370
Shadow on the Downs, The, 2288
Shadow on the Left, The, 1634
Shadow on the Wall, The, 693
Shadows Before, 244
Shadowy Third, The, 1679–80
SHAFFER, ANTHONY, 1919
SHAFFER, PETER, 1919
SHAKESPEARE, 243, 446, 455, 642, 1211/B, 1327, 1373, 2035, 2041, 2047, 2140, 2160, 2165, 2178, 2277, 2280, 2699, 2934, 2952, 3126, 3149
Shakespearean Ciphers Examined, The, 3149
"Shakespearean Problem, The," 2699
Shakespeare Murders, The, 1007
Shake-Up, The, 1236
Shall Perish by the Sword, 1039
"Shall We Join the Ladies?," 2332
SHANE, SUSANNAH, 76
SHANNON, DELL, 197, 782, 1380, 1920
"Shape of Crime to Come, The," 2992
Shape of Fear, The, 1695
SHARMAN, MIRIAM, 2785
SHARP, DAVID, 1921–3
SHARP, LUKE, 2342/B
SHARP, MARGERY, 2738, 2786
SHAW, E. S., 3285
SHAW, G. B., 1435/B, 3013, 3304
SHAW, HERBERT, 69
SHAW, J. B., 3374
SHAW, J. T., 2787
SHAW, LEMUEL, 3297
SHEARING, JOSEPH, 1924
Shed a Bitter Tear, 1617
She Died a Lady, 749
She Fell Among Thieves, 2297
SHELLABARGER, SAMUEL, 792/B
SHELLEY, MARY, 3460
SHELLEY, P. B., 3460
She Married Raffles, 2582
SHEPHERD, ERIC, 1925–6
SHEPHERD, NEAL, 1618, 1927
SHEPPERSON, A. B., 3026
Sheridan le Fanu, 2909
Sherlock Holmes. See Part V and: 230, 457/B, 463, 640, 1114, 1164, 1359, 1602, 1620, 1623/B, 2296, 2341, 2487, 2609, 2944, 3038, 3289, 3313
"Sherlock Holmes" (Roberts), 3015
Sherlock Holmes (Heritage ed.), 2483
Sherlock Holmes (broadcast stories), 2296

Sherlock Holmes (play), 865/B, 2395, 2487
Sherlock Holmes and Dr. Watson: A Chronology, 3333
Sherlock Holmes and Dr. Watson: A Textbook, 3366
"Sherlock Holmes and Music" (Officer), 3383
Sherlock Holmes and Music (Warrack), 3384
"Sherlock Holmes and Railways," 3368
"Sherlock Holmes and the F.B.I., 3361
"Sherlock Holmes Cross-Word, A," 3383
Sherlock Holmes, Fact or Fiction?, 3336
"Sherlock Holmes in Pictures," 3383
Sherlock Holmes in Portrait and Profile, 3357
Sherlock Holmes in Tibet, 3385
"Sherlock Holmes, Notes for a Biography," 3382
Sherlock Holmes of Baker Street, 3329
Sherlock Holmes: Selected Short Stories, 2486
Sherlock Holmes's Greatest Cases, 2486, 3353
Sherlock Holmes versus Arsène Lupin, 1359
"Sherlock, Shakespeare, and the Bomb," 3354
SHERWOOD, JOHN, 1928/B–29
She Shall Have Murder, 58
She Should Have Cried on Monday, 1893
She Stands Accused, 3225
She Walks Alone, 1434
She Wouldn't Say Who, 59
SHIBATA, TETSUO, 2788
SHIBUK, CHARLES, 3027–9
SHIEL, M. P., 1163, 2058, 2789–90
Shilling for Candles, A, 2045
Shining Pyramid, The, 3440
"Ship of the Desert, The," 2521
Ships and Cruises. See also **Boating**, 214, 376, 534, 565, 648, 655, 661, 670, 748, 759–60, 860, 978, 1065, 1304, 1475, 1552, 1559, 1578, 1642, 1704, 1706, 1716, 1830, 1883, 1889, 1957, 1969, 2157, 2301, 2321, 2365, 2441–2, 2575, 2584, 2652, 2689, 2855

SHIRLEY, DOUGLASS, 2675
Shivering Mountain, The, 1954
Shock Tactics, 307
Shoot if You Must, 1749
Shoplifter, The, 1952
Short Circuits, 2970
Short Course in the Secret War, A, 3144
"Shortest Night of the Year, The," 3444
Short Reaction, The, 923
Short Stories of H. G. Wells, The, 2859, 3474
"Short Trip Home, The," 2456
Short Wave, 307
"Shoscombe Old Place," 2476
Shot at Dawn, 1857
"Shot at Goal, A," 2776
"Shot in Question, The," 2538
Shot of Murder, A, 1206
Shot on the Downs, 2228
Shots from the Canon, 3363
Shot Towers, 1493/B
Show of Violence, The, 3317
Shrieking Pit, The, 1790
"Shrouded Watcher, The," 3414
Shroud for Unlac, A, 617
Shrunken Head, The, 833
SHULMAN, MAX, 2791
"Shylock Holmes: His Posthumous Memoirs," 2741
Siamese Twin Mystery, The, 1776
Sic Transit Gloria, 1297
Sidelights on Sherlock, 3363,
SIDGWICK, FRANK, 3056, 3377
SIEGEL, DORIS, 2205
"SIEUR LOUIS DE CONTE," 2080/B
Signal for Death, 1857
"Signal Man, The," 3408, 3432
Signal Thirty-Two, 1261
Sign for Cain, A, 3317
Sign of Fear, The, 732
Sign of Four, The. See Sign of the Four
Sign of the Four, The, 761, 763, 1787, 2304, 2483, 3366
"Sign of the '400,' The," 2741
Silence After Dinner, 2270
Silence for the Murderer, 667
Silence Observed, 1228
Silence of Herondale, The, 17
Silent Are the Dead, 626
Silent Bullet, The, 2761
"Silent Informer, The," 2633
Silent Liars, The, 2097

Silent Murders, The, 1006
Silent Pool, The, 2207
Silent Siren, The, 1965
Silent Speaker, The, 1997
Silent Witness, The (Desmond), 733
Silent Witness, The [A], (Freeman), 900
"Silent Witness, The" (play), 2801
Silent Witness, The (Post), 2727
"Silent Woman, The," 3457
Silk Road, 1097
Silk-Stocking Murders, The, 171
SILLITOE, (SIR) PERCY, 3286
"Silver Age, The," 3048
"Silver Blaze," 2479, 2642, 2750, 3353
"Silver Curtain, The," 2473
"Silver Mask," 2395
Silver Street, 1256
SIMCOX, D. J., 3445
SIMENON, GEORGES, 883, 1191, 1930–1, 2654, 2738, 2792–3, 2885, 2940, 2951, 2989, 2994, 3030–2
SIM, GEORGES, 1930
SIMMS, W. G., 1932, 3040, 3461–2
Simon Lash, Private Detective, 1043
SIMON LORD, 3190
SIMONS, ROGER, 1933
Simon Wheeler, Detective, 2082
"Simple Art of Murder, The," 2403, 2525, 2918–9, 2955
Simple Art of Murder, The, 2400, 2402, 2403, 2919
Simple Case of Ill-Will, A, 156
SIMPSON, HELEN, 703, 1934–5, 2133, 3287, 3332
SIMS, G. R., 2998
SINCLAIR, FIONA, 1936–8
SINCLAIR, MAY, 3403, 3442, 3463
Sinful Stones, The, 747
"Sing a Song of Sixpence," 2418
SINGER, HEDWIG, 1699
Singing Bone, The, 887/B, 2521, 2523, 2900
Singing Clock, The, 1697
"Singing Diamonds, The," 2500
Singing Diamonds and o.s., The, 2634
Singing in the Shrouds, 1552
Singing Masons, The, 2140
Singing Sands, The, 2046
"Singing Stick, The," 2367
Single Hair, A, 15
Sinister Errand, 492
Sinister House, 235
Sinister Stones, 2106
Sinners Go Secretly, 2293/B

"Spy Who Came out of the Night, The," 2577
Spy Who Spoke Porpoise, The, 2292
"Spy Who Took the Long Route, The," 2578
"Squeeze Play," 2751
SQUIRE, J. C., 2779
Squire's Story, The, 2532, 2566
"Sredni Vashtar," 3459
S.S., The, 2744, 2789
Stab in the Back, The, 15
STACPOOLE, H. DE VERE, 2316, 2317, 2323, 2837, 2904
STAGGE, JONATHAN, 1684
Stag Party, 1324
"Staircase at the Heart's Delight, The," 2541
Stalemate, 156
"Stalking Horse, The," 2519
STANDISH, ROBERT, 2459
STANGE, G. R., 2927
STANLEY, BENNETT, 1172
STANLEY, DONALD, 3379
STANNERS, H. H., 1956
STANSFELD, ANTHONY, 336
"Stanway Cameo Mystery, The," 2672, 2875
STARRETT, VINCENT, 744, 1957/B–58, 2469, 2482–3, 2521, 2525, 2675, 2694, 2739, 2741, 2794–5, 2837, 2955, 3033–4, 3357, 3374, 3376, 3380–3
Stars Are Dark, The, 492
"Start from Scratch," 2365
Starvel Hollow Tragedy, The, 658
Stately Home Murder, The, 21
State of Siege, 49
States of Human Consciousness, 1303/B
"Stay of Execution," 2536
STEAD, P. J., 3295
Stealthy Terror, 824
"STEAM COAL," 2849
STEEGER, HENRY, SR., 2354, 2950
STEEGMÜLLER, FRANCIS, 1274/B–76
STEEL, BYRON, 1274/B
STEELE, FREDERIC DORR, 2741, 3383
STEELE, WILBUR DANIEL, 2367, 2874, 3416
Steel Mirror, The, 1068
STEEVENS, H., 2320
STEEVES, H. R., 1096, 1959, 2955, 3035
STEIN, A. M., 87/B, 1960, 1973
STENDHAL, 3181

STEPHEN, (SIR) JAMES FITZJAMES, 3112, 3238, 3265
STEPHENS, JAMES, 3442
STEPHENSON, CARL, 2575
STEPHENSON, H. M., 1961
Step on the Stair, The, 1030
STERLING, GEORGE, 3100, 3389
STERLING, STEWART, 719, 1962, 2253, 2365
STERLING, THOMAS, 1963–6
STERN, G. B., 2872
STERN, JAMES, 2796
STERN, P. V. D., 2955, 3439
STERN, RICHARD, 2459
STEVENSON, B. E., 1967/B–68
STEVENSON, R. L., 490, 1499, 1752, 1969–70, 2138, 2465, 2522, 2568, 2685, 2755, 2763, 2771, 2797–9, 2836, 2877, 3014, 3036, 3051, 3422, 3442
STEVENSON, W. B., 3037
STEWART, A. W., 582/B, 597, 3038, 3296
STEWART, J. I. M., 1211/B
STEWART, K. L., 1383
STEWART, MARY, 1971
Stiffsons and O.S., The, 2595
Still Dead, 1319
Stillwater Tragedy, The, 24
STIMSON, H. L., 3325
Sting of Death, The, 2208
"Sting of the Wasp, The," 2837
STINNETT, CASKIE, 3039
STIRLING, EDWARD, 69, 2801
Stitch in Time, A, 1352
Stoat, The, 280
"Stock-Broker's Clerk, The," 2479
STOCKTON, FRANK, 3416
STODDARD, R. H., 3001
STOKER, BRAM, 1972, 2466
Stoke Silver Case, The, 279
"Stolen Bacillus, The," 2859
Stolen Bacillus and Other Incidents, The, 2858
Stolen Boat Train, The, 306
"Stolen Body, The," 3474
"Stolen Cigar Case, The," 2741, 2854
"Stolen Ingots, The," 2516
"Stolen Letter, The," 2435
"Stolen Necklace, The," 2861
"Stolen Rubens, The," 2366
Stolen Squadron, The, 1368
"Stolen Treasure, The," 2722
Stolen White Elephant, etc., The, 2841
STOLPER, B. J. R., 2367

816

Stone Cold Dead in the Market, 1337
STONE, EDWARD, 3040
Stoneground Ghost Tales, The, 3466
STONE, G. Z., 2112
STONE, HAMPTON, 87/B, 1960, 1973–74
STONE, (DR.) J. W., 3297
STONE, P. M., 905, 3383
"Stone of the Edmundsbury Monks, The," 2789
Stoneware Monkey, The, 901–2
STONG, PHIL, 2802
STONIER, G. W., 3388
Stop at Nothing, 2199
Stories from the Diary of a Doctor, 2661
"Stories I Have Tried to Write," 3427
Stories of American Life, 2622
Story of a Criminal, The, 1932
Story of Crime, The, 3064
Story of Louie, The, 1668
"Story of O Toyo, The," 2837
Story of Ragged Robyn, The, 1667/B
Story of Scotland Yard, The, 3132, 3303
Story of ST 25, The, 3135
"Story of the Greek Slave, The," 3459
"Story of the Late Mr. Elvesham, The," 3474
"Story of the Siren, The," 3411
Story of the World's Police, The, 3175
STOUT, REX, 498, 759, 1975/B–2003, 2447, 2493, 2569, 2654, 2738, 2803–14, 2891, 2912, 2955, 3041
STRACHEY, JOHN, 3042
STRAHAN, KAY, 2004
"Strange Affair in a Hotel," 2349
Strange and Fantastic Stories, 3442
Strange Bedfellow, The, 155
Strange Blue Yawl, The, 862
"Strange Case of Cyril Bycourt, The," 2370
Strange Case of Dr. Earle, The, 649, 671
Strange Case of Harriet Hall, The, 693
"Strange Case of Joan Winterbourne, The," 2652
Strange Case of Mr. Henry Marchmont, The, 861
Strange Case of Mr. Pelham, The, 70
"Strange Case of Mrs. Arkwright, The," 3415
Strange Disappearance, A (Green), 1028

Strange Disappearances (O'Donnell), 3247
"Strange Jest," 2419
STRANGE, J. S., 2005
Strange Murder of Hatton, K. C., The, 13
Strangers and Afraid, 1966
"Strangers and Pilgrims," 3405
Strangers at the Wedding, 688
"Stranger's Latchkey, The," 2517
Strangers on a Train, 1146
"Stranger Unravels a Mystery, The," 2741
Stranger with My Face, 1475
Strange Schemes of Randolph Mason, The, 2729, 2998
Strange Story, A, 3394
Strange Studies from Life, 2485
Strangled Witness, The, 868
Strangler Who Couldn't Let Go, The, 1974
STRAUS, RALPH, 2575
"Straw Man, The" (Kemelman), 2604
"Straw Man, The" (Post), 2843
Strawstack, 758
Streamlined Murder, 1515
STREET, C. J. C., 352/B, 373, 1800/B
Stretton Darknesse Mystery, The, 693
STRIBLING, T. S., 2366, 2735, 2642, 2747, 2751, 2815–20
"Strictly Diplomatic," 2391
Strike for a Kingdom, 926
Strike Out Where Not Applicable, 884
"Strikers, The," 2861
Strip Death Naked, 1397
Strip for Murder, 1750
"Stripper, The," 2751
Strip Tease Murders, The, 1363
"Stroke of Thirteen, The," 3099
STRONG, L. A. G., 1702, 1870, 2006/B–11, 2500, 2821–6, 2947, 3068
Strong Poison, 1904, 3209
STUART, JAY, 1683
Student Body (Hodgkin), 1160
Student Body, The (Fitzgerald), 847
Studies in Murder, 3257
Studies in Sherlock Holmes, 3348
"Studies in the Literature of Sherlock Holmes," 3358
Studies of French Criminals of the Nineteenth Century, 3192
Study in Pictures, A, 3364
Study in Scarlet, A, 24, 762/B, 763, 764, 1689, 1852, 2483, 2939, 2976, 3343, 3366

Tales of Eccentric Life, 2552
Tales of Fantasy and Fact, 2656
Tales of Horror and the Supernatural, 3439
Tales of Mean Streets, 1623/B
Tales of Mystery and Imagination, 2718, 3452
Tales of the Longbow, 2410
Tales of the Mysterious and the Macabre, 3390
"Talking Eyes, The," 2867
Tall, Balding, Thirty-Five, 831
"Tall Story," 2367
Taming of Red Butte Western, The, 869
"Tangible Illusion, The," 2608
Tangled Web, A (Blake), 201
Tangled Web, A (Moffatt), 1605
"Tape-Measure Murder," 2419
Tapping on the Wall, A, 1179
Target for Terror, 1234/B
"Tarn, The," 2332, 2835
TARO, HIRAI, 2754/B
"Tasmanian Jim's Specialty," 2652
Taste for Honey, A, 1114
Taste for Murder, A (Heard), 1114
Taste of Murder, The (Cannan), 416
Taste of Power, A, 348
Taste of Proof, The, 1315
TATE, SYLVIA, 2034
Tau Cross Mystery, The, 599
TAYLOR, (DR.) A. S., 3168/B, 3229, 3301
TAYLOR, F. S., 2955
TAYLOR, H. B., 2186/B
TAYLOR, ISABELLE, 2955
TAYLOR, JACK, 1023
TAYLOR, P. A., 2035
TAYLOR, R. L., 3044
"Tea and Sympathy," 1278
Tea at the Abbey, 2142
"Tea Leaf, The," 2780
"Tea Shop Assassin," 2537
Tea-Tray Murders, The, 390, 391
"Technicalese," 2908
Technique for Treachery, 2078
Technique of the Mystery Story, The, 3057
Teleman Touch, The, 1054
Telephone Call, The, 1848
"Telephone Fisherman, The," 2820
"Telling," 2332
TEMPLE-ELLIS, N. A., 1866, 2036/B–39

"Temple of Silence, The," 2407
TEMPLE, PAUL, 775
Templeton Case, The, 2229
TEMPLETON, JESSE, 1004
"Temptation of Harringay, The," 3474
Tenant for Death, 1082
Ten Days' Wonder, 1776
Tender Killer, The (Hough), 1172
Tender Poisoner, The (Bingham), 184
"Ten-Franc Counter, The," 2316
Ten Little Indians, 496
Ten-Minute Alibi, The, 65/B–65, 69, 2801, 3219
"Ten O'clock," 2324, 3415
Ten-O'clock Scholar, The, 2604
Ten Rillington Place, 3201
10:30 from Marseilles, The, 1241
TERHUNE, A. P., 2575
"Terribly Strange Bed, A," 2435, 2767
Terriford Mystery, The, 1417
"Terror in a Penthouse," 2742
"Terror Racket, The," 2540
TESSIER, E. M., 723
"Testimony of Dr. Farnsworth, The," 2437
Tether's End, 45
TEY, JOSEPHINE, 2040/B–47
THAILING, WILLIAM, 2991
That Affair Next Door, 1030
That Awful Mess on Via Merulana, 919
That Dinner at Bardolph's, 2169
That's the Spirit, 1119
That Yew Tree's Shade, 1083
THAYER, LEE, 2048
"The Air-Gun, Colonel Moran," 3338
Theaters (for Opera, see Musical Events), 33, 83, 113, 287, 389, 422, 560, 611, 644, 731, 1121, 1328, 1363, 1373, 1376, 1425, 1451, 1473, 1495, 1543–4, 1547, 1549, 1643, 1658, 1662, 1726, 1774, 1886, 2007, 2043, 2233, 2265, 2473, 2589, 2689
"Theft of the Royal Ruby, The," 2416
"Their Masterpiece," 2774
Theme Is Murder, The, 1165
Then There Were Three, 1168
There Came Both Mist and Snow, 1229
There Is a Tide, 532
There Sits Death, 1489
"There's Murder in the Air," 2955
"There's Still Tomorrow," 2445
There's Trouble Brewing, 212

There Was a Crooked Man, 2272
"There Was No Mystery in What the
   Crime Editor Was After," 2906
These Are Strange Tales, 3
"These Artists!," 2849
These Hurrying Years, 1114/B
"They," 3433
They Came to Baghdad, 534
"They Can Only Hang You Once,"
   2545
They Can't All Be Guilty, 1117
They Died in the Spring, 416
"They Don't Read De Quincey in
   Philly or Cincy," 2677
They Found Him Dead, 1141
"They Never Get Caught," 2310
They Never Looked Inside, 992
They Rang Up the Police, 417
They Return at Evening, 3471
They Talked of Poison, 796
They Walk Again, 3404
They Were Seven, 1722
They Wouldn't Be Chessmen, 1566
Thief, 308/B, 3121
Thin Air, 3430
Thing at Their Heels, The, 1129
Thin Ghost and Others, A, 3427
"Thing on the Hearth, A," 2728
Things That Go Bump in the Night,
   3433
Thing That Happens to You, A, 156
"Thinking Machine, The" (Conning-
   ton), 2324
"Thinking Machine, The" (Futrelle),
   917, 2529
Thinking Machine on the Case, The,
   917
Think of a Number, 220
Think of Death, 1390
Thin Man, The, 1074/B, 1077
"Third Bullet, The," 2393
Third Bullet and o.s., The, 2393
Third Encounter, The, 2282
"Third-Floor Flat, The," 2419, 2569
Third Girl, The, 533
"Third Ladder, The," 2525
Third Mystery Book, The, 2524
Third Mystery Companion, The, 2525
Third Omnibus of Crime, The, 2781
Third-Party Risk (N. Bentley), 152
Third-Party Risk (Cullingford), 679
"Third Performance, The," 3413
Third Skin, The, 179/B
Thirteen, The (Balzac), 96

Thirteen (Loraine), 1410
Thirteen at Dinner, 537
Thirteen for Luck, 2426
Thirteen Guests, 808
Thirteen Problems, The, 2428
"Thirteenth Card, The," 2323
Thirteenth Chair, The, 2395, 2801
Thirty-first of February, The, 2021,
   2030
Thirty Manhattan East, 2189
Thirty-Nine Steps, The, 330, 332, 786
31 New Inn, 2944
This Crooked World, 559/B
This Death Was Murder, 797
This Friendless Lady, 3243
This Is Murder, 944
This Is Murder, Mr. Jones, 916
This Is What Happened, 544
"This King Business," 2547
This Necessary Murder, 2194
This Path Is Dangerous, 2215
This Side Murder, 225
This Undesirable Residence, 358
This Week's Stories of Mystery and
   Suspense, 2346
This Won't Hurt You, 849
"This Won't Kill You," 2809
THOMAS, ALAN, 2049, 2321
THOMAS, DYLAN, 2745
THOMAS, GILBERT, 3045
Thomas Masaryk, 1800/B
THOMPSON, LEONARD, 2751
THOMPSON, LEWIS, 3090
THOMSON, (SIR) BASIL, 2050/B–54,
   2322, 2778, 2834, 3123, 3302–3
THOMSON, H. DOUGLAS, 1561, 2835–6,
   2955, 2957, 3046–7, 3425
"Thor Bridge," 2476
THOREAU, 730/B, 2774
THORNDIKE, RUSSELL, 2845
THORP, RODERICK, 783, 2055
THORWALD, JÜRGEN, 3304
Those Days, 147/B, 2899
"Thou Art the Man," 2366
"Thousand Pounds, The," 2732
Thou Shell of Death, 213
"Thrawn Janet," 2797
Three-Act Tragedy, 537
Three at the Angel, 1764
Three at Wolfe's Door, 2814
Three Bad Nights, 337
"Three Bears, The," 2338
"Three Blind Mice," 2430
Three Blind Mice and o.s., 537, 2419

Umgasi Diamonds, The, 721
Uncanny Stories, 3463
"UNC Detective Collection, The," 2914
Uncle Abner, Master of Mysteries, 2730
Uncle Paul, 908
Uncle Silas, 1364, 3428
Uncommercial Traveller, The, 3129
Uncommon Danger, 50
Unconscious Witness, The, 902
Uncounted Hour, The, 31
Under a Cloud, 2132
"Under Cover," 2395
Under Cover for Wells Fargo, 3133
Under Dog, The, 2426
"Underground," 2783
Undertow, 612–13
Under Western Eyes, 606
UNDERWOOD, MICHAEL, 2089/B–99
Underworld. See Bohemia
Undetective, The, 1017
Undiplomatic Exit, 1929
Undoubted Deed, The, 706/B, 709
Unexpected Guest, The, 495/B
Unexpected Night, 700
Unfinished Clue, The, 1142
Unfinished Crime, The, 1434
"Unfinished Game, The," 2696
Unfortunate Murderer, The, 1183
Unhallowed Murder, 1644
Unhappy Rendezvous, 1639
"Unique Guinea, The," 2343
"Unique Hamlet, The," 2741
United in Crime, 3190
Universities. See Colleges and Universities
Unknown Assailant, 1073
"Unknown Murderer, The," 2339, 2642
"Unknown Peer, The," 2351
Unlawful Occasions, 472
"Unloaded Gun, The," 2525
"Unlocked Window, An," 2324
"Unluckiest Murderer, The," 2558
Unlucky Break, 1597
Unnatural Causes (Hawton), 1106
Unnatural Causes (James), 1240
Unnatural Death, 1906
Unneutral Murder, 866
"UNOFFICIAL OBSERVER," 755
Unpleasantness at the Bellona Club, The, 1907
Unpopular Opinions, 1898/B, 3019, 3373

Unprofessional Spy, The, 2098
"Unpunctual Painting, The," 2837
Unquenchable Flame, The, 1792, 2758
Unquiet Sleep, The, 1053
Unravelled Knots, 2693
"Unrecorded Instance, An," 1417, 2332, 2779
Unseen Enemy, 1338
Unseen Hands, 1674
"Unsung Heroine, An," 3386
Unsuspected, The, 71
UNTERMEYER, LOUIS, 1210
Untimely Death (Hare), 1080
Untimely Ripped (McShane), 1513
Untimely Slain (Gray), 1023
Unwanted Corpse, 388
Unwilling Adventurer, The, 905
UPFIELD, ARTHUR, 1147, 2100/B–09
Up for Grabs, 804
"Upper Berth, The," 2855
Upstairs and Downstairs, 441
Up the Garden Path (Burton), 388
"Up the Garden Path" (Perowne), 2713
Up the Garden Path (Rhode), 1857
Urn Burial, 2222
URQUHART, MACGREGOR, 2110
Uses of Diversity, The, 2923
USHER, JACK, 2111
Uttermost Farthing, The (Freeman), 903
Uttermost Farthing, The (Lowndes), 1417
UZZELL, T. H., 2842

Vacancy with Corpse, 365
VACHELL, H. A., 2323
Vagrant Mood, The, 2980
"VALENTINE." See PECHEY, A. T.
Valentine Estate, The, 786
VALENTINE, JO, 71
Valley and the Shadow, The, 234
Valley of Fear, The (Creasey), 637
Valley of Fear, The (Doyle), 762/B, 765, 2483, 2912
"Vampire of the Village, The," 2412
VANCE, ETHEL, 2112
VANCE, JACK, 1325/B
VANCE, LOUIS JOSEPH, 2113
VANDAM, A. D., 2114
VANDERCOOK, J. W., 2115, 2367
"Van der Valk and the Four Mice," 2514

"Van der Valk: the High School Riot," 2515
VAN DEWATER, F. F., 2837
VAN DINE, S. S., 2, 92, 150, 829, 1881, 2116/B–21, 2136, 2304, 2843, 2889, 2912, 2936, 2955, 3049
VAN DOREN, MARK, 2367, 2745
VAN GULIK, ROBERT, 507, 2122/B–30, 2844
Vanished, 427
"Vanished Man, The" (Post), 2727
"Vanishing Diamond, The," 2324
Vanishing Diary, The, 1855
"Vanishing Harp, The," 2608
"Vanishing Lady, The," 3442
"Vanishing Lawyer, The," 2351
Vanishing Man, The (Freeman), 904
"Vanishing of Mrs. Fraser, The," 2779
"Vanishing of Vaudrey, The," 2405
"Vanishing Prince, The," 2407
VAN SILLER, HILDA, 2130–2
Vasiliko Affair, The, 680
VATSEK, JOAN, 2874
VAUBAN, 1800/B
VEDDER, J. K., 1043
"VEENDAM, S. S.," 2955
Vegetable Duck, 1850
"Veiled Lodger, The," 2476
"Veiled Prophetess, The," 2762
VEILLER, BAYARD, 2395
Venetian Blind, 1054
"Vengeance of the Statue, The," 2407
Venner Crime, The, 1857
VENNING, MICHAEL, 1859
Venom House, 2109
VENTRIS, MICHAEL, 3108
Verdacht, Der, 776/B
Verdict in Dispute, 3224
Verdict of Twelve, 1739
Verdict of You All, The, 2163
Versprechen, Das, 776/B
"Vertical Line, The," 2694
Very Cold for May, 1478
VÉRY, PIERRE, 2955
Very Quiet Place, A, 970
Vesper Service Murders, The, 1567
VETTER, MARJORIE, 2458
Veuve Lerouge, La, 918
Viaduct Murder, The, 1321
Vicar's Experiments, The, 1877, 2142/B
Vicious Pattern, 1119
VICKERS, ROY, 2137, 2324, 2367, 2447, 2500, 2739, 2751, 2846–8, 2902

Vicky Van, 2202–3
Vicomte de Bragelonne, Le, 2489
"Victim, The," 2658, 3463
Victim Must Be Found, A, 1157
Victorian Detective Fiction, 2998
Victorian Scandal, 3195
Victorian Studies in Scarlet, 3067
VIDAL, GORE, 246
VIDOCQ, 96, 2013, 3295, 3310
Village Afraid, A, 383
"Village Murder," 2739
Villages. See also: Farms, 6, 15, 30, 37, 84, 129–30, 169, 195, 213, 233–4, 242, 264, 296, 300, 352, 354, 381, 383, 427, 468, 499, 517–9, 539, 546, 551, 588, 591, 601, 638, 642, 678, 686, 690, 711, 720, 730, 741, 753, 828, 879, 890, 924–6, 930, 976, 1028, 1083, 1155, 1174, 1296, 1333, 1480, 1506, 1508–9, 1550, 1588, 1595, 1641, 1655–7, 1684, 1714, 1747, 1758, 1760, 1790, 1808, 1837, 1869, 1877, 1906, 1954, 2008, 2010, 2047, 2071, 2086, 2158–9, 2178, 2182, 2186, 2222–3, 2250–2, 2261–4, 2266–9, 2272, 2280, 2284, 2504, 2739
Villainous Saltpetre, 2273
VILLIERS, GÉRARD DE, 75
VINCENT, (SIR) HOWARD, 3118
Vintage Murder, 1555
Violence, 2289
Violent Brothers, The, 329
Violent End, 1263
"Violet Farm, The," 2323
"Virginiola Fraud, The," 2386
Virgin Kills, The, 2231
Virgin Luck, 1590
VIVIAN, E. C., 2324
VIVIAN, FRANCIS, 2139–40
VOELKER, JOHN, 2060, 3309
Voice from the Dark, A, 1723
"Voice in the Inner Ear, The," 3472
Voice Like Velvet, A, 1127
Voice of Air, The, 156
Voice of the Corpse, The, 1638
Volpone, 1963
VOLTAIRE, 2141, 2171, 2347, 2489, 2566, 2897, 3190
Voodoo, 793
Vote Against Poison, 1929
Vote for Death, 1398
VULLIAMY, C. E., 1877, 2142/B–43

WHITE, LIONEL, 2219–21
WHITE, L. T., 2525
White Menace, The, 67, 1856
White Night, The, 638/B
"White Patch, The, " 2727
WHITE, R. J., 1250, 2222/B–23
White Shroud, The, 1649
WHITE, W. A. P., 237/B, 3355
WHITFIELD, RAOUL, 2230–1, 2787, 2861
WHITMAN, WALT, 2745
WHITNEY, ALEC, 2232
Who Calls the Tune, 105
"Who Cares Who Killed Roger Ackroyd?," 2955, 3060
"Who'd Do It?," 2927
Who Dies for Me?, 617
Who Done It, 2892, 2954
"Who Do You Think Did It?," 2456
Who Goes Hang?, 1201
Who Is the Next?, 2193
Who Killed Aunt Maggie?, 827
"Who Killed Barker?," 2447
"Who Killed Castelvetro?," 2511, 2513
"Who Killed Charlie Wimpole?," 2779
Who Killed Chloe?, 33
Who Killed Cock Robin?, 1130
Who Killed Diana?, 1130
Who Killed Netta Maull?, 75
Who Killed Pretty Becky Low?, 685
Who Killed Stella Pomeroy?, 2054
Who Killed the Doctor?, 385
"Who Killed the Mermaid?," 2705
Who Killed the Mermaid?, 1686
Whole Art of Detection, The, 3374
Who Lies Here, 1704
Whom God Hath Sundered, 1667–8
Who's Calling?, 1434
Whose Body?, 1898/B, 1908
Who Shall Hang?, 1519
"Who Stole the Black Diamonds?," 2689
Who's Whodunit, 2953
Who Told Clutha?, 1635
Who Was Claire Jallu?, 222
Who Was Old Willy?, 1298
Why Didn't They Ask Evans?, 537
"Why Do People Read Detective Stories?," 3060
Why Do Women?, 611
"Why I Write Ghost Stories," 3469
Why Shoot a Butler?, 1143
WHYTE-MELVILLE, G. J., 2233
Wicked as the Devil, 1187

Wicked Saint, 328
Wicked Women, 2874
WICKWARE, F. S., 2234
Widdershins, 3451
Wide Awake Pleasure Book, 2318
Widening Stain, The, 1258
Widower, The, 2132
"Widow in Waiting," 2365
Widow Lerouge, The, 3174
Widow's Cruise, The, 214
Widow's Plight, 822
Widow's Walk, The (Bramlette), 2298
"Widow's Walk, The" (Finney), 2747
WIEGAND, WILLIAM, 2235
WIENER, (DR.) A. S., 218, 3264
WIGMORE, J. H., 3250–1
Wigwam and the Cabin, The, 3461–2
Wilberforce Legacy, The, 128
WILCOX, COLLIN, 2236–7
WILDE, JIMMY, 2931
WILDE, OSCAR, 2877, 3189, 3476
WILDE, PERCIVAL, 2238, 2778–9, 2862
Wilder's Walk Away, 265
WILD, JONATHAN, 3080
Wild Justice, 186
"Wild Man of the Sea, The," 3407
Wilful and Premeditated, 671
WILKES, JOHN, 1737/B
"Wilkie Collins' Moonstone," 3021
WILKINSON, E. C., 2239
Will and the Deed, The, 1705
WILLARD, JOHN, 2395
WILLIAMS, BEN AMES, 2240, 2837, 2856
WILLIAMS, BRAD, 2241–2
WILLIAMS, CHARLES (1886–1945), 2244
WILLIAMS, CHARLES, 2243–4
WILLIAMS, E. A., 720
WILLIAMS, EMLYN, 2395, 3319
WILLIAMS, GRANVILLE, 3320
WILLIAMS, H. S., 2837
WILLIAMS, I. A., 2774
WILLIAMS, M. W., 791
WILLIAMS, NEVILLE, 3321
WILLIAMS, STEPHEN, 3386
WILLIAMS, VALENTINE, 2134, 2245, 3058–9
WILLIAMS, VINNIE, 2367
"William Wilson's Racket," 2391
Will in the Way, A, 386
WILLIS, G. A. A., 65/B
WILLOCK, COLIN, 2246–7
Will of the Tribe, The, 2107

A Tentative Taxonomy

I. Genus "Detection"

   A. Species
1. Short (1845)
2. Very long (1860)
3. Long (1912)
4. Medium long (1940)
5. Short short (1925)

B. Varieties
1. Normal
2. Inverted
3. Police routine
4. Autobiographical
5. Aeroidal

C. Habitat
1. Interior
2. Limited (train, ship, room, etc.)
3. Village
4. Big city
5. Open country (moor preferred)
6. Exotic (Nile, Suva)
7. Underworld (Los Angeles)
8. Institutional (school, hospital, nunnery, etc.)

D. Temper
1. Omniscient
2. Humorous (farcical)
3. Historical (real crime reconstructed)
4. Amateur (boy-and-girl team, et al.)
5. Ineffectual (drunk, fool, boor detective)
6. Private eye (decent, deplorable)
7. Official (and a Yard wide)